SOUTH EAST ASIA

THE TRAVELLER'S GUIDE

3rd edition

BY STEFAN LOOSE & RENATE RAMB

TRANSLATED BY DAVID CRAWFORD & PETER CONOLLY-SMITH

SPRINGFIELD BOOKS LIMITED

SOUTH EAST ASIA

The Traveller's Guide

Published by

SPRINGFIELD BOOKS LIMITED

NORMAN ROAD, DENBY DALE, HUDDERSFIELD HD8 8TH
WEST YORKSHIRE, ENGLAND

Third edition 1988

TRANSLATED FROM THE 6TH GERMAN EDITION BY
David Crawford & Peter Conolly-Smith

WRITTEN IN COOPERATION WITH
Werner Mlyneck (Indonesia),
Richard Doring & Ursula Spraul-Doring (Thailand)

PRINTED AND BOUND
in Hong Kong by Colorcraft Limited

MAPS AND LAYOUT BY
Klaus Schindler

PHOTOGRAPHY BY
South East Asia Picture Archives Renate Loose

British Library Cataloguing in Publication data

Loose, Stefan
South East Asia, the traveller's guide.
Rev. and updated ed.
1. South East Asia - Visitors' guides
I. Title II. Ramb, Renate III. Sudostasien handbuch.
English
915.9'0453

ISBN 0-947655-38-7

TABLE OF CONTENTS

PREFACE

"Sounds great, but..." Every traveller needs some rough answers to the *how much, what if, when,* and *where* questions that follow "but" in such a statement. Planning a trip to a distant part of the world requires a bit of thought. In today's world where nothing seems to stand still, old makes way for the new, roads are built, accommodation and establishments change, and prices rise. And sometimes sadly enough, South East Asia is no exception. We want to give you practical tips and useful information about the everchanging as well as the timeless in South East Asia.

In South East Asia it is possible to live more cheaply than in the "West". Many travellers are seduced by the low travel costs: cheap hotels, food, and local transportation, as well as budget flights. Travelling cheaply for as long as possible sometimes becomes an aim in and of itself. Among backpack travellers you'll seldom find the character who lets loose and blows his savings on luxuries. In every South East Asian country it's possible to have your dinner bill quickly exceed the monthly income of your waiter. Try to keep in mind the relationship between the income of the local population and your own expenses. And because price information is quickly outdated, we have given the inflation rate at the beginning of each country's section.

Anyone on the road for a year hardly needs a travel guide. A constant flow of people, choking with enthusiasm for the best place they've ever visited and tips on how to get there, provides the most current information available. Few travellers, however, are actually able to take off from school and job for months or even years. If your boss is unsympathetic to your pleas for travel time, despite slide shows and curry dinners, or if it's your imagination rather than your wallet that is unlimited, then prepare for your trip carefully.

It is possible to gain some understanding of a foreign culture in as little as six weeks, but only if you restrict the extent of your travel. If you plan to "do" Bangkok, Pattaya, Penang, Singapore, Jakarta, and Bali in three weeks, then you won't find this book very helpful. Such tours will show you the recent advancements in tourist services, but the scrambled-egg culture is Hilton-Hyatt rather than Thai or Malaysian. Living in a tourist ghetto, package-deal tourists seldom meet any locals not engaged in the tourist industry. Consider yourself a traveller. Those who take to the road on their own will find themselves immersed in the local cultures of ordinary South East Asian people. Not only will the traveller learn more about the country being visited, but a sensitivity for the traditions and habits of the local hosts may also develop.

In many parts of South East Asia you see the negative impact of tourism. Those who speak badly of Pattaya being marketed as a "bachelor's paradise" should take a closer look at the "traveller's paradise" at Kuta Beach on Bali. In both places tourism has greatly disturbed the local culture, if not destroyed it. You won't be able to prevent the relentless onslaught of *western civilization* into the depths of the tropical rainforest. It's already happened! You can, though, through your actions, help keep the disturbances to a minimum. The farther your travels take you from the Bangkok - Bali path, the more sensitivity you should show for the local people and their culture. Inform yourself by checking out some of the suggested reading in each country's section. Newspapers and magazines are also another important source of information on each country. Two regional magazines - the *Far Eastern Economic Review* and *Asiaweek,* report weekly on the political, economic, and cultural situation in Asia.

If you first find South East Asia quite western oriented, with further exposure you'll discover more and more discrepancies between western and Asian cultures and thought. You'll find even greater differences when comparing Buddhist Thailand with Muslim Malaysia or Hindu Bali. The constant exposure to this kaleidoscope of cultures makes South East Asia fascinating for travellers.

Everywhere you go you'll be confronted with the problems of the Third World. Countries here used to be called developing nations because the western world assumed they would want to follow the path to industrialization. For centuries Europeans were noted in the Third World for their preachy, self-righteous attitude. With the end of colonial imperialism, it would be a shame to see the rise of cultural chauvinism through tourist colonies. Much has been written about Third World tourism. The problems are apparent to everyone who travels with open eyes. At the same time, however, such journeys permit evaluation of one's own values and an understanding of the lifestyles of other people. On the beach in Ko Samui or in a hut with the Akkha hilltribes, this topic is sure to stir up many different opinions from the other travellers you encounter.

We hope you travel with an open mind and a desire to understand. Give some thought to the role you will play in the Third World and prepare for your journey carefully. And of course have a great time in South East Asia too!

CLIMATE & TRAVEL SEASONS

A sandy tropical beach bathed in sunshine or a Buddhist temple whose golden stupa towers in the deep blue sky. We all know these pictures from travel brochures, but for much of the year you might not find the sun shining. This disaster befalls distraught travellers whose August beach trip to Phuket literally fell in the water, or who've slid through the slime of the North Thailand mountains from Akkha village to Akkha village without being able to shoot a roll of film because there were no tropical blue skies.

Nobody would plan to go swimming off Iceland in December, but travellers forget to take the South East Asian wet and dry seasons into account.

Temperatures range in the course of the day between 22° C and 32° C (72° F and 90° F). During the dry season it's a little warmer and after a cooling rain shower the temperatures drop a bit. The closer to the equator, the smaller the temperature range. Even in the continental climates of Burma and Northern Thailand the temperature rises just before the rainy season to 36° C (97° F) bringing the best laid plans to a halt.

Rain is more difficult to predict. Many islands have their own wind systems, and rainy seasons can change from coast to coast. Those who know their way around can avoid rain or find it every day of the year. And when it rains, it pours: more rain in a day than ever seen in a dreary European month. You'll see stormy winds on the sea, unpaved roads turned to impassable mud, and whole parts of towns flooded. The rainy season is only pleasant for freaks. Their Magic Mushrooms thrive in the moisture. On such trips who'd care if the roof flies off.

Wind brings rain if it's off-shore, whereas it's dry when overland. From May to September, the Southwest Monsoon sheds tremendous rainfall on the west coast of Sumatra, Northwest-Malaysia, Thailand and Burma. From November to March the Northeast Monsoon brings rain to the Indonesian islands and the east coast of West Malaysia. South of the equator, the winds change directions and during the time of the Southwest Monsoon predominate from the southeast and during the Northeast Monsoon from the west.

GENERALLY THERE ARE THREE CLIMATIC REGIONS IN SOUTH EAST ASIA:

The continental monsoon determined region - during the northern summer expect heavy rain, while from October to May is the dry season. Visit at the beginning of the dry season:
BURMA (Nov.-Feb.), **CENTRAL THAILAND** (Nov.-Feb.), **SOUTHERN THAILAND** (Dec.-March).

The inner-equatorial region - rising air due to the direct sunshine causes showers every afternoon all year round. There are no real dry seasons. During the northern summer it rains less in the following areas:

CLIMATE AND TRAVEL SEASONS IN SOUTH EAST ASIA AND NEIGHBOURING COUNTRIES

LOCATIONS	MONTH	Jan	Feb	Mar	Apr	May	June	July	Aug	Sept	Oct	Nov	Dec
BURMA	Rangoon				(31^0)	//////////////////////582////////////////////							
	Mandalay				(32^0)		//145//						
THAILAND	Bangkok				(30^0)		///////////////////////////////////344//////////////						
	Chiang Mai	(21^0)			(30^0)			////////////////////////249/////					
	Phuket					//370////////////////////							
	Ko Samui	/////				(29^0)					//////////////////////554		
	Chanthaburi					/////////////////////////////////620//////////////							
	Udon					/////////////260//////////////////////////////////							
MALAYSIA	Kuala Lumpur			/////////279//////////////							275////////////////////////		
	Penang			(28^0)	////////////////////				/////////////////////428////////////				
	Cameron Highlands		(17^0)		//////////297//////					//////////340//////////////////////			
	Temerloh	//////									/////////240////////////		
	Kota Bharu	//////								//////////////673////////////			
	Kuala Trengganu	//////								//////////////610////////////			
	Mersing	//////////////										///////////500	
	Kuching	610//////////////////////////////////////					(28^0)				//////////////////////////		
	Kota Kinabalu						(27^0)		////////////////////////////////353///////////				
	Labuan					(28^0)///465///////////							
	Sandakan	483//////////////									////////////////////////////		

LOCATIONS	MONTH	Jan	Feb	Mar	Apr	May	June	July	Aug	Sept	Oct	Nov	Dec
BRUNEI						////////////////			////////////513////				
SINGAPORE		////////////										//////////265	
INDONESIA	Jakarta	300////////////////											/////
	Medan					(27^0)				/////////259/////////////////////			
	Padang			////////////////////////////////					///////////////////////////////581////////////				
	Palembang	/////////		//////////////////////								//////////315	
	Bandung			230////////////////							(23^0)/////////////////////		
	Surabaya	308//////////////											/////
	Ujung Pandang	686///////////////////////////(27^0)											/////
	Pontianak	/////////			//////////////////						////////389/////////////		
	Ambon		(30^0)			////////////////638////////////////////////							
	Kupang	389////////////									(30^0)		
INDIA	Bombay					(29^0)//							
NEPAL	Kathmandu						/////////373///////////						
SRI LANKA	Colombo				//////////394/////////////						/////////////////////		
PHILIPPINES	Manila				///////////////////////////////437///////////								
TAIWAN	Taipei		(15^0)				322////////////////////////						
HONG KONG			(15^0)			///////////479/////////////////////////////////////							

////// months of high precipitation /254/ highest monthly precipitation in mm (28^0) temperature of the warmest / coldest month

EAST COAST OF THE MALAY PENINSULA (Apr.-Sep.), **SARAWAK** (May-June), **SOUTH KALIMANTAN** (June-Aug.), **SULAWESI** (Apr.-Aug.), **SUMATRA** (June-Aug.), **NORTH**- and **WEST-SUMATRA** (Jan.-Feb. as well), **TERNATE** (July-Sep.). During the northern winter it rains less in the following areas: **SABAH** and **BRUNEI** (Jan.-March), **CENTRAL MOLUCCAS** (Nov.-March).

The monsoon determined island region - with a southeast wind during the northern summer and a northwest wind during the northern winter, you'll find ideal travel weather south of the equator from April to September:

JAVA, BALI, LOMBOK, SUMBAWA, FLORES, SUMBA, TIMOR, IRIAN JAYA.

VISAS

In some parts of the world most travellers don't have to worry about visas. This is not the case in South East Asia. For Malaysia, Singapore and Thailand an entry visa can be obtained at the border. Thailand, however, only allows a stay of 15 days if you get your visa at the border. Extensions are not possible. If you get your visa in advance, you may stay two months with a 1 month extension sometimes possible.

WHERE TO GET YOUR VISA AT HOME:

BURMA:

AUSTRALIA: 85 Mugga Way, CANBERRA, A.C.T. 2600, tel 950045.
CANADA: 116 Albert Street. OTTAWA, tel 2369613.
HONG KONG: A.I.A. Bldg., 1 Stubbs Rd., HONG KONG, tel 5729241.
GREAT BRITAIN: 19A Charles Street, LONDON W1, tel 6299531.
UNITED STATES: 2000S St. N.W., WASHINGTON, DC. 20008, tel 3029044.

THAILAND:

AUSTRALIA: 15 Mugga Way, CANBERRA, A.C.T.2603. tel 731149.
CANADA: 85 Range Road, Suite 704, OTTAWA 2, tel 2371517.
GREAT BRITAIN: 20-30 Queen's Gate, LONDON SW7 5 JB, tel 5892834.
NEW ZEALAND: 2 Burnell Avenue 1, WELLINGTON, tel 41094.
UNITED STATES: 2300 Kalorama Rd. N.W., WASHINGTON, DC. 20008, tel 6671446.

INDONESIA:

AUSTRALIA: 8 Darwin Av., CANBERRA, ACT 2600, tel 733222.
CANADA: 287 Haclaren Street, OTTAWA, tel 2367403.
GREAT BRITAIN: 38 Grosvenor Square, LONDON W1X 9AD, tel 4997661.
HONG KONG: 127-129 Leighton Road, Causeway Bay, tel 7904421.
NEW ZEALAND: 11 Fitzherbert Terrace, WELLINGTON, tel 736669.
UNITED STATES: 2020 Massachusetts Av., WASHINGTON, DC. 20036, tel 2931745.

Details and tips about visas for the individual countries can be found in the respective chapters. If planning a long trip, it's best to get a visa in advance before entering a neighbouring country. We have never been asked to show proof of finances or employers when applying for a visa.

INFORMATION

Get information about the countries you want to visit before your trip. It's better to ask for detailed info; for example don't just ask about *Thailand* but request *Phuket, Chiang Mai* or just bus connections. Those people are there to help you!

INDONESIA (Indonesian Tourist Promotion Offices)

USA: 323 Geary Street, Suite 305, SAN FRANCISCO, CA 94102, tel 981 3585.
EUROPE: Wiesenhüttenplatz 26, D 6000 FRANKFURT 1, tel 233677.
JAPAN: c/o Asia Trans Co., 2nd Floor Sankaido Building, 1-9-13 Akasaka, Minato-ku, TOKYO, tel 5853588.
AUSTRALIA: c/o Garuda, 4 Bligh St., SYDNEY NSW 2000, tel 2326044.

MALAYSIA (Tourist Development Corporation - TDC)

USA: Transamerica Pyramid Building, 600 Montgomery Street, SAN FRANCISCO, CA 94111, tel 7883344.
AUSTRALIA: R & W House, 92 Pitt Street, SYDNEY NSW 2000, tel 2323751.
UK: 17 Curzon Street, LONDON WIY 8DR, tel 4997388.

SINGAPORE (Singapore Tourist Promotion Board)

USA: Suite 1008, 342 Madison Avenue, NEW YORK, NY 10173, tel 6870385; 251 Post Street, SAN FRANCISCO, CA 94108, tel 3918476.
AUSTRALIA: 8/F Goldfields House, 1 Alfred Street, Circular Quay, SYDNEY, NSW 2000, tel 2413771.
UK: 33 Heddon Street, LONDON W1R 7LB, tel 4370033.

THAILAND (Tourism Authority of Thailand)

USA: 5 World Trade Center, Suite 2449, NEW YORK, NY 10048, tel 4320433; 3440 Wilshire Boulevard, Suite 1101, LOS ANGELES, CA 90010, tel 3822353.
AUSTRALIA: Royal Exchange Building, Bridge Street, SYDNEY, NSW 2000, tel 277549.
UK: 9 Stafford Street, LONDON WIX 3FE, tel 4997679.

PLANE TICKETS

Novices may find myriad of prices and classes offered to the international air traveller confusing. No wonder, it's intended that way. IATA (International Air Traffic Association) is a cartel of airlines which sets artificially high prices for all airline services including plane tickets. This is their theory: no matter which airline you fly, you should be overcharged by the same amount.

In practice, fortunately, it's possible to find cheaper flights. Officially a one way ticket London-Bangkok costs $710. Buy your ticket in Bangkok, and you'll only have to pay $300. Even in Europe it's possible to find tickets on the *Grey Market*. Check the travel agencies. They often have cheaper rates they're not permitted to advertise, even on airlines belonging to IATA.

In general we recommend:

If you have a set itinerary: Buy a return ticket (round trip) at home to Bangkok or Singapore. Any tickets that you need within South East Asia should be bought there. Check the cheap travel agencies for worthwhile offers. They can organize an itinerary to fit your wishes.

If you have no set plans: A one way ticket is best (except to Burma and Indonesia which require a ticket out for your entry visa). No matter where you end up, you can always get the tickets you need in Bangkok, Penang, Singapore or Jakarta.

If you are long on the road: Normally a plane ticket is good for one year. Check for "valid for one year" on your ticket. Many cheap flights offer limited services including restricted validity. Most student tickets are only good for six months as well as being "non refundable" and "non endorsable". You're stuck with the ticket even if you can't use it. Sometimes you can still get some money back if you agree to pay a cancellation fee.

If you're a student or have an International Student Identification Card (ISIC), you can get cheaper plane tickets. Your card is usually honoured by Thai Airways International, Cathay Pacific and Malaysian Airlines for a 25 % discount.

Normally people get an ISIC card because they are genuine students somewhere, no matter what their age. There are certain places in South East Asia where non-students can buy the cards. In Bangkok the hotels Atlanta and Malaysia are market places for forged ISICs. Watch out for bad forgeries!. Experts, such as the people in travel agencies, recognize them immediately. If you want to buy a fake card, have a good look at a real one beforehand. Otherwise, bye-bye 300 Baht.

STUDENT TRAVEL AGENCIES IN ASIA:

JAKARTA: Indo Shangrila Travel, Jl.Gajah Mada 219 G, tel 6392831, 6392376.
BALI: STA, Kuta Beach Club, Kuta Beach, tel 5051 ext.80.
BANGKOK: STA Travel, Thai Hotel, 78 Prajathipatai Road, tel 2815314-5.
KUALA LUMPUR: MSL Travel, South East Asia Hotel, 69 Jl.Haji Hussein, tel 984132.
PENANG: MSL Travel, 340 Chulia Street and Ming Court Hotel, Macalister Road, tel 616112, 616154.
SINGAPORE: Holiday Tours & Travel, 12 Mezzanine Fl., Ming Court Hotel, tel 7347091.
NEW DELHI: STIC Travels, Hotel Imperial, Janpath, tel 344789.
HONG KONG: KKFS-STB, 8/Fl., 130-132 Des Voeux Rd., Central Hong Kong, tel 5-414841.
MANILA: YSTAPHIL, Room 104, Marietta Apartments, 1200 Jorge Bocabo Street, Ermita, tel 5210361.

HEALTH

Most important for travel in South East Asia is good physical health. To reduce the effects on your body of the sharp climatic changes and jet lag, take it easy just before and after flying. If you work overtime up to the last day and get little food or rest, don't be surprised if you spend your first week of vacation in bed with a cold or fever. Be especially careful when going to the steaming tropics with only a plane ride for preparation. Try to sleep a lot for the first couple of days until your body has adjusted to the new environment.

Two or three months before you travel, you should start getting inoculations. Check with a doctor who knows something about tropical medicine. Even better, go to a national inoculation centre or an institute for tropical medicine at a university hospital where advice is given on tropical diseases. Besides your shots, get prescriptions for any medication you want to take with you, and ask about the latest inoculation requirements.

Each immunization must be registered in your International Certificate of Vaccination, which details place, date, signature of the doctor, and an official seal from the local health office.

SMALLPOX: This scourge has been officially eradicated according to WHO.

CHOLERA: Officially you only need a cholera vaccine to visit Niger. The reality is, however, that cholera still thrives and is endemic in rural regions during the rainy season. There is some question as to the effectiveness of the inoculation. Bad reactions are common. If you are careful about hygiene and your health is good, there isn't much danger. Discuss with your doctor whether you need the shots. An immunization involving two shots within 14 days is good for six months. Thereafter your should get a booster.

HEPATITIS: There is now an expensive vaccine against the dangerous liver ailment Hepatitis B. Three shots of H-B-VAX (or HEPATVAX) must be taken at one to five-month intervals. You will require revaccination after five years. You can continue to take GAMMAGLOBULIN shots (US$35) against Hepatitis A, which are of questionable value, but do seem to increase your general resistance to infections. You can check whether you need the inoculations at all with an antibody test (US$20).

TETANUS: There is always the possibility of being injured yourself somewhere on the road. For this reason get two inoculations four weeks apart, then one booster shot a year later. You should then be safe for seven to ten years.

POLIO: If you haven't had the Salk oral vaccine in the last ten years, then check with your doctor. Allow several weeks!

TYPHOID / PARATYPHOID: The oral vaccination TYPHORAL L or a new Swiss product VIVOTIF (about US$20) is now offered. It's taken over a period of six days and lasts for two years. If you have to take the oral vaccination against Polio as well, you must take it three days after typhoid. Allow three weeks if you do it the other way round.

MALARIA: According to WHO, malaria is making a come-back. All of South East Asia is a malaria region - especially the tropical jungles and swamps. Maintaining a high level chloroquine in your blood can help prevent infection, but it's no guarantee. Most people take RESOCHIN (or CHLOROQUINE, NIVAQUINE, ARALEN), twice a week. In some areas the plasmodia (malaria carriers) are immune to RESOCHIN (East and West Malaysia, Burma, Thailand, especially Kanchanaburi and Chanthaburi, Kalimantan, Sulawesi, Sumatra and Moluccas). In these areas combine the RESOCHIN with one DARAPRIM tablet per week (the Sunday pill). Use FANSIDAR only for treatment of malaria and not as prophylactic. However, this shouldn't be taken by pregnant women. Start your medication one week before visiting these areas and continue for four weeks after your trip home (incubation period!).

If you have unusual spells of fever and aching joints even after your return home, go to a hospital immediately. Tell your doctor that you were in a malaria region. Symptoms are aches in your head, back and joints and high periodical fever. Many doctors will diagnose these symptoms as simple flu and give the wrong treatment. This has led to several deaths in Europe.

The malaria carrying mosquito, Anopheles, usually bites between sunset and sunrise. A mosquito net or coil can help reduce your risk. Coils are green spirals which burn like incense, scenting the air. It is better to get used to the smell rather than to spend sleepless nights chasing mosquitos. The insect repellent AUTAN can be put on your skin, but it doesn't last very long. Be sure your mosquito net doesn't contain a mosquito before you get inside it. Even a lone mosquito can disturb your sleep. Check it for holes and use tape to make sure it's secure.

DIARRHOEA: Every Asian traveller can expect to experience the runs, especially in the beginning. Diarrhoea, so much a part of Third World life that it's been christened imaginatively: Bali-belly, Rangoon-runs, Hong Kong-dog, Ho-Chi-Minhs, Tokyo-trots, not to forget Mexico's Montezuma's revenge.

If you're afflicted, you'll usually find that a coal-sulfamide compound (FORMO CIBAZOL or FORBINA) will give you some relief. If necessary, you can try combining it with IMODIUM (but only in small doses), in order to relax your bowel functions. There are also the alternative 'Globetrotter tips' such as egg yolk mixed with nutmeg, or having a rice and tea day. Don't take stronger medications if the above doesn't work - see a doctor! You could have a bacteriological or amoebic dysentery.

Simple diarrhoea can be caused by spoiled food, unpeeled fruits, and ice-cream. Micro-organisms in water are also a major cause. You will have to decide how much of a risk you want to take by drinking the water. Mineral water is not to be found everywhere, and it's not always possible to have the water boiled, filtered, or purified through the use of purification tablets such as MICROPUR. You should even think twice about that ice cube in your coke! Outside Singapore, never drink tap water! Drink tea. You don't have to use tea to brush your teeth though.

Even more common than the runs is constipation. This is easily taken care of by eating a few peeled fruits. Pineapple helps!

WORM INFESTATIONS: It's possible to pick up large and small varieties on any part of your body. Usually they are found weeks after returning home. Most are quite harmless and eliminated with a simple treatment. Others are dangerous such as the infamous Hookworm which bores its way through the soles of your feet. Therefore always wear sandals when walking on damp ground! After travel in outlying areas, try to have your bowel movement checked for worms in an institute for tropical medicine. This is a must if a slight discomfort continues over a longer period of time.

SORES: Even scratched mosquito bites, if left untreated, can develop into dangerous infections under unhygienic conditions . Keep your wounds clean, perhaps using a plastic spray dressing along with a vitamin ointment.

SKIN DISEASES: Just by sweating you can pick up an itchy fungus in the tropics. The warmer and damper the environment, the higher the parasite to host ratio. A hot and sweaty body is sure to attract fleas, lice, mites, and bedbugs. The best protection is two baths a day and frequent changes of clothing. To protect against skin fungus wear cotton clothes. Tiny guests can be eliminated by smearing yourself with JACUTIN. The best bet against head lice is the American shampoo QUELLADA.

SNAKE AND SCORPION BITES: Here there is no real danger. There are few poisonous snakes in South East Asia, and those found, only attack when they feel threatened. The scorpions here are not deadly.

VENEREAL DISEASES: Gonorrhea and the even more serious syphilis are ever present diseases in South East Asia, especially among prostitutes. The Bangkok and Manila varieties of gonorrhea are no joke; they are resistant to penicillin. Go to a good hospital where they have the equipment to test which drugs are effective against your variety of VD. Only then should you let them pump you up with medication. If they give you the wrong stuff, they risk making the VD almost immune to all drugs. It is irresponsible to let yourself be a carrier - see a doctor.

Women are especially liable to fungus infections. Talk to your gynaecologist before you leave and get a prescription for some medication in advance. Cream is better than a suppository.

For further information, check Richard Dawood's ***TRAVELLERS' HEALTH,*** *Oxford University Press 1986.*

If your insurance company back home won't pay for some of these health supplies, remember that they and inoculations are often cheaper in South East Asia.

SUGGESTED FIRST AID KIT: (for more developed regions)

FIRST AID: Bandages (elastic bandage, adhesive tape, spray on plaster) disinfectant (Savlon cream).

PAINS & FEVER: thermometer - aspirin - Buprenorphine (Temgesic) - Nystatin (Nystan) against fungal infections - antibiotics (Bactrim or similar against bacterial infections)

MOTION SICKNESS: Transderm - Dramamine - Marzine.

DIARRHOEA: Imodium - Lomotil - use powders such as Dioralyte, Infalyte or Sodium Chloride.against dehydration.

MALARIA: Paludrine - Nivaquine - Aralen - Resochin - Fansidar only for treatment.

OTHER: vitamin pills - insect spray or repellent (Off, Baygon, Autan) - chlorination or iodination tablets (Micropur) for water disinfection - suntan lotion (SPF 12 - 15) - calamine lotion - Indocin for strong sunburn.

HEALTH CARE IN SOUTH EAST ASIA

MALAYSIA AND SINGAPORE: The quality of the doctors and the hospitals in both countries is good. Even in the smaller towns of Sarawak, such as Kapit, there are hospitals with competent doctors. Due to the excellent infrastructure in West Malaysia, it's always possible to reach the next larger town quickly. Treatment in Malaysian public hospitals is free. It's not worth trying to find a private doctor: those in the hospitals are just as good. In Singapore you will have to pay for your treatment, but the fees at a super modern private clinic are much cheaper than in the west.

THAILAND: In many hospitals you'll find the typical Asian indifference. At the same time Bangkok and other larger cities have well equipped hospitals with doctors who speak English. You'll have to pay for your treatment, but the costs are minimal.

BURMA: In case of sickness don't go to a private doctor; seek the free treatment in a hospital (also important if you need to extend your visa!). Medication is difficult to find outside the public clinics.

INDONESIA: Provincial hospitals can be a catastrophe. If you are seriously ill or need an operation, fly to Singapore if possible.

There are many reports of negligent and indifferent care by doctors in the larger hospitals in Denpasar. Patients who arrive in critical condition lie on stretchers in the corridor for hours. Sometimes ambulances never arrive when called. We don't have accident statistics, but any inexperienced motorbike rider should see the photo exhibition at the Traffic Police Station in Denpasar before setting out on a journey. Hospital treatment is free aside from a small admission fee. You'll have to pay for the (for Indonesia) overpriced medication, however. It's frequently worthwhile to resort to a private doctor.

OUTFITTING YOURSELF

In most cases a tour of South East Asia requires more than a toothbrush and a checkbook. On the other hand the days of the hundredweight trunk belong to the last century. Avoid the extremes:

Many of your provisions are more cheaply purchased in South East Asia itself. In Bangkok, Penang, or Singapore you will find the goods listed below with * cheaper than in the west. Caution! Large sizes of shoes and clothes may be hard to find. Maximum sizes follow; jeans length and waist 32, or shoe size 8 (British), 42 (German), or 9 (American). In department stores you may have better luck, but the prices are higher.

CLOTHES

- ❑ ***SHOES:*** SHOES, SANDALS, BATHING SLIPPERS* (rubber sandals for wear in bathhouses and toilets are a must. The staple footwear in Asia, they can be found in all sizes)
- ❑ ***PANTS / SHIRTS:*** JEANS*, LONG COTTON PANTS (good for long bus rides if not too tight fitting), SHORTS (women should not wear them away from the beach and men are always discouraged from their wear).
- ❑ ***JACKET*** (cotton) / ***SWEATER*** (for those cool evenings) / ***SHIRT* / BLOUSE**** / ***T-SHIRTS**** (you'll have fun choosing the prints - definitely buy in Asia).
- ❑ ***SUN WEAR:*** HAT / SUN-GLASSES* / SUNTAN LOTION (in unbreakable container)
- ❑ ***RAIN WEAR:*** PONCHO* (can also be used as a tarp when your pack is on the roof of a bus) / UMBRELLA*.
- ❑ ***UNDERWEAR:*** UNDERPANTS / 2 Pairs of SOCKS.
- ❑ ***BATHING SUIT / BIKINI:*** In conservative areas a one-piece suit is best - for example in Brunei bikinis are illegal. In back areas it is best for men and women to bath in a sarong.
- ❑ ***SARONG**** the local wrap-around dress from one piece of cloth. In our opinion, this is the most important piece of clothing you'll be carrying. Besides for bathing, you can wear it as a dress or cover up. It is best not to wear this or any other peasant clothes in the cities. Not only will you be branded as the lowest social level, you'll also be the laughing stock in the western oriented metropolises.

OTHER NEEDS

- ❑ ***TOWELS:*** one small and one large for bathing.
- ❑ ***WASH KIT:*** SOAP in a break-proof holder / TOOTHBRUSH / TOOTH-PASTE / SHAMPOO / NAIL SCISSORS / WET RAZOR (better than finding a fitting plug) / TAMPONS (impossible to get up-country; in Burma and Indonesia only to be found in expensive international hotels and supermarkets - much better than sanitary napkins in the tropical heat).
- ❑ ***SEWING KIT:*** strong thread, needles, safety-pins, and string.
- ❑ ***FLASHLIGHT / POCKET-KNIFE / PLASTIC BAGS*** (trash bags best, to keep your dirty laundry, protect camera equipment and bags during boat

rides) / ***WATER BOTTLE / TOILET PAPER*** (replaces handkerchiefs and hard to find in Burma and parts of Indonesia) / ***PLASTIC BRUSH*** (for doing laundry, detergent*) / ***ALARM CLOCK*** (best is a watch with a built in alarm) / ***AIR PILLOW*** (to sit on during long bus rides and on hard wood benches on trains; only necessary in Burma and Indonesia) / ***PADLOCK / MOSQUITO NET*** (for those who want to be as safe as possible - usually COILS* are enough - see HEALTH) / ***FIRST AID KIT*** (see HEALTH) / ***NOTEBOOK / BALL POINT PEN / PRESENTS.***

- ***DOCUMENTS AND MONEY***: PASSPORT / INTERNATIONAL CERTIFICATE OF VACCINATION / ISIC (International Student Identity Card) / INTERNATIONAL DRIVER'S LICENCE / COPIES OF ALL OF THESE DOCUMENTS / CASH / TRAVELLER'S CHECKS / RECEIPT FOR CHECKS BOUGHT / PLANE TICKETS / MONEY BELT*.
- ***INFORMATION:*** TRAVEL GUIDE BOOK / MAPS / READING MATERIAL OF LOCAL FLAVOUR.

If you are planning to do some mountain climbing or jungle trips, the above list wouldn't be enough. In damp lowland jungles, proper shoes are a must. Jungle boots from Malaysian or Singaporean army surplus have proved their worth. They can be found in both countries. Whether you need to carry the extra weight of a tent or a sleeping bag depends on your destinations. Unless you are going to visit mountain areas, a light sleeping bag or a sheet is enough.

Those with electric appliances in their travel kit should keep in mind the variety of electric plugs and voltages used in Asia. See each country's chapter for additional advice. The best appliances are those which take both 220 V and 110 V as well as run on batteries. The right plug should be bought in Asia.

Photography buffs should check the photo section of this book.

When deciding on the clothes to take, remember that there are times when you want to dress comfortably relaxed, while at other times you need to dress up a bit. In South-East Asia people are judged by their dress much more than in the west. A sloppy appearance is not easily understood by people who, with very little money, go to great pains to dress properly. Almost everywhere you can get your clothes washed and ironed cheaply within 24 hours. At the beach and in traveller hotels you can save some money by doing your own laundry.

WHERE TO PUT THE STUFF?

BACKPACK: This is the most manoeuvrable means of transport for your things. But how much walking do you plan to do with your full outfit?

TRAVEL BAG: For shorter trips or for people with fewer things a bag with a wide (and strong!) shoulder strap may be a good idea. The advantage: you won't be saddled with the negative image often associated with backpack tourists. They are also easier to stow away on public transport than the oversized backpacks.

VALUABLES

Who at home carries all of their possessions around with them? Because you are forced to do so when travelling, you face a higher risk of theft.

Any traveller can tell you stories of thefts, hold-ups and other unpleasant incidents. With millions of vacationers passing through South East Asia with fat wallets, it isn't surprising. Even only $400 (and who hasn't that much at the beginning of a trip), is for many of the people you meet a year's income. Here are some representative letters from our readers on the subject:

MALAYSIA: In Telok Bahang you have to be careful about theft. One person had a bag with all of her important papers stolen from the house one evening. She had to go to the embassy in Kuala Lumpur. Even Georgetown has a bad reputation - there they often grab women's handbags.

THAILAND: Now I have to discuss the ugliness spreading in Thailand. There have never been so many hold-ups of tourists. During tours to the hilltribes, on the river from Thadon to Chiang Rai, street crime in Chiang Mai, on ac-busses from Bangkok to Chiang Mai or Phuket - and even in Phuket, all the tourists in a restaurant on Patong Beach were held up one evening around 11:00 pm. Another example: It is very dark on the street between Je t'aime Guesthouse in Chiang Mai and the first main road. Four guests were robbed in one week within 50 yards of the house. I was robbed on a boat trip from Thadon to Chiang Rai. I was lucky and only lost some clothes and money. Others less fortunate came back from a trip to the mountains with only their underpants. The police do nothing about it. Our boatman on the trip to Chiang Rai was put in jail. The next morning he was gone.

INDONESIA: Legian (Bali) is by now the same as Kuta Beach - with fewer people it is therefore more dangerous after dark. Lately some pretty bad things have been happening on Bali. Supposedly forty Javanese have come over to ruin the Bali reputation (from me, Renate: If something happens on Bali, it is always the Javanese!). The truth is that an Australian was stabbed during the day on the beach, and a Swiss or Frenchman was stabbed at night. Someone knocked, he opened, and he was stabbed. They both are still alive according to the newspapers. Patrols (Balinese) carrying night-sticks walk the streets at night.

Change the names and places and the stories would be just as representative. As far as we know none of these incidents, however, took place off the tourist trail. No wonder, where there are few tourists, there is no organized crime. On our last three trips to Thailand, in 1980 for two months including six weeks in Bangkok, in 1981 seven weeks between Mae Sai and Haad Yai, and in 1985 another seven weeks we had no problems. We heard some bad stories from other travellers though. In English language newspapers such as the Bangkok Post, there is always extensive reporting on crime against foreign tourists.

Only a prophet can tell which bus will be hit next. There are some things you can do however:

❑ CARRY AS FEW VALUABLES WITH YOU AS POSSIBLE!

Cash is much more sought after than checks; so cash only as many traveller's checks as you need to at one time. Expensive jewelry belongs at home. When staying at a hotel or especially when you're staying in a hut on the beach, stow your valuables in the hotel safe or give it for safe-keeping in exchange for a receipt.

❑ SECURE YOUR ROOM AGAINST PROWLERS!

A strong padlock is a must in your luggage. Sometimes hotel doors can be opened with simple tools so you need extra protection. Many hotel rooms can only be secured by a padlock. While you will usually get a lock, you never know who has the second key. In dormitories always secure your pack with a lock. Not every traveller is an honest bed-mate!

❑ KEEP VALUABLES UNDER YOUR CLOTHES!

Some people say your passport, traveller's checks and cash should be hung around your neck, bound to your body, or sewn into your clothes. We suggest a moneybelt large enough to hold all your essentials. As long as you are wearing pants it can always be hidden underneath. You can sew a wide cloth belt yourself. Use cotton (it soaks sweat best) and make several pockets one of which must be large enough for your passport. Don't make it too tight, and protect your important papers including money and plane tickets from destructive sweat by keeping them in plastic. No money should be carried in handbags or wallets. A few bank notes and some change should be kept in a deep pants pocket. Cameras must be carried in a bag, but it shouldn't look as if it contains something expensive. The bag should be of durable material (slit open!) and you should be able to lock it.

❑ SECURE YOUR BAGS IN BUS AND TRAIN!

When travelling it isn't always possible to keep an eye on things - especially on a train, bus or boat. So don't leave any valuables in your pack, and be sure to lock it with your padlock. Keep your handbag with you at all times. Seek out friendly seat mates; elderly local women are usually the friendliest and safest. If your pack is on the roof for a long bus ride use a chain to prevent it from falling off or being stolen.

❑ FRIENDS AND TRAVEL PARTNERS ARE IMPORTANT!

If you travel with a partner or friends you can take turns looking after your things. When you arrive in a new town one can find the best place to stay while the other keeps watch. Be careful when choosing travel companions, especially the "I want to practise my English"-types. Many 'nice' people have disappeared with all of their friend's belongings.

Taking a walk at night on the beach is often dangerous. Don't walk around with a camera and a tripod for night photography! Go in pairs or small groups.

❑ WHAT TO DO IF SOMETHING HAPPENS?

Hotel room break-in: Call the police. If you're insured you can only collect if you present a police report. If it isn't in English, then get it translated and notarized in Asia. Singapore has many inexpensive translation offices.

When traveller's cheques are stolen:
You must always keep your cheque receipts separate from the cheques themselves. Only when you can show the receipt, will the checks be replaced. American Express is the only company that offers immediate replacement.

If you lose your passport:
All of your important papers should be photocopied - copies should be kept separate, of course! It is then much easier to prove your identity at your nearest consulate.

If you are down to your underpants:
If your luck is really bad, you will be dependent on your fellow travellers at first. Go to the nearest police station and from there to the nearest consulate or embassy. Your consulate may loan you money for the trip home and a new passport.

Remember that thieves are only interested in your money and valuables. Don't struggle unless you know that you can get away. We know of some travellers who are now dead for this reason.

MONEY

"How do I carry my travel money?" There is no simple answer to this question. If you're planning to travel in remote areas without spending much time in the larger towns, then you'll need to carry a good amount of US Dollars in cash. Even in a city, a few dollar bills can be helpful - for a quick taxi from the airport, perhaps. Carrying large amounts of cash is risky: if you lose it, it's gone.

Your safest bet is traveller's cheques. You can buy them at any bank for a one percent fee. AMEXCO (American Express) traveller's cheques can be bought in several different currencies, but US dollars are best known in remoter areas. If lost or stolen, they will be replaced at the nearest American Express office.

A good alternative for people with a high income is the American Express Card. Credit card privileges cost around US$60 initially plus US$60 per year. With the credit card you can buy things such as plane tickets without cash. Perhaps more important, every three weeks you can cash a personal check for up to US$650 at your local American Express office. The money is paid partly in local currency and partly in AE $-traveller's cheques. Get more info at any AE office.

MONEY TRANSFER

If you are planning to travel for several months, don't carry all of your resources with you. Open an account at a major bank and have the money transferred to you when you need it. The major banks have offices (or at least correspondent banks) in the Asian metropolises to which the money can be transferred. Here's how it works:

You go to the bank where you want to receive the money. If you want the money fast, they'll send a telex (before you leave home, note your bank's telex number along with your account number). Otherwise it's possible by mail. A specific amount of money from your account will be ordered transferred. It can be even faster if you telephone and have the money telegraphed. Your money will take two days to reach Singapore from Europe. If you have a friend at home with access to your money, then he or she can simply telegraph the money. Money transfers are recommended in Singapore, Bangkok, Kuala Lumpur or Penang. We've heard from people in Indonesia that, no surprise, it's a long wait.

FREE MARKET

To get the latest quotes on the official and unofficial exchange rates for South East Asian currencies check the latest edition of Far Eastern Economic Review or Asiaweek. They contain the 'free market' rates from Hong Kong. There as in Singapore, the prices are set by supply and demand. Weaker currencies such as the Burmese Kyat or the Indonesian Rupiah are always much cheaper than the official rate given in the country itself. Newsweek carries the official rates but no longer lists the unofficial ones. Of the countries in this handbook only Burma has a real Black Market rate. All the other currencies are basically stable.

MAKING MONEY

During your travels you will meet many people who have been on the road for years drifting between Tokyo and Sydney. These are the two places where jobs can be found. It is possible to work teaching foreign languages in South East Asia, but don't count on it. Remember South East Asia is poor, and it is hard to save travel money in impoverished surroundings.

MONEY FROM THE CONSULATE

In many cases, such as if you are robbed, you may be forced to get money from your consulate to keep you afloat until you can get a flight home. That is what the consulates are there for: to protect and support their citizens overseas. However this service has been greatly abused by travellers in recent years. Consulates or embassies are no longer as friendly as they used to be. An example:

A cheap flight is cancelled, and the money gone. P. goes to his consulate where they give him seven dollars to last for three days. A stamp is placed in P.'s passport with a brief handwritten explanation. When departing there is a hassle because the immigration authorities can't read the writing and think that the passport is void. At each stop en route home the same hassles. Finally home, the stamp is never removed.

MAIL

There are many ways to receive mail from home while you are travelling. The simplest method, and the one we generally use, is to give your friends a rough idea of your itinerary. They can then send your mail to be picked up (poste restante, general delivery) at the post office you name. In your letters home give the name of the next major town or city you plan to visit and let your mail pile up there until you arrive. That has always functioned well. Air mail to Singapore or Bangkok from Europe only takes three days but to Indonesia one can expect it to take one or two weeks. The larger the city and the better the air communications the faster the mail. Quite often letters get lost somewhere. This is especially true of letters with stamps worth collecting.

Your mail should be addressed as follows:

> FIRST NAME LAST NAME
> CITY COUNTRY
> GENERAL POST OFFICE
> POSTE RESTANTE

Upon presentation of your passport you can pick up your mail at the poste restante counter. In smaller towns make sure that the teller checks for mail listed under your first name; the same goes for double names. Usually letters are kept for three months and sent back to the return address. Telegrams, however, are generally returned after four weeks. In addition in some post offices (such as Bangkok) telegrams must be picked up at a separate counter, or as in Singapore, they may only be listed in a special book.

If you are expecting mail, there is always the possibility of having it sent on to a forwarding address by filling out a form. The chances of success are only middling, however. The mail either stays put or follows your journey in eight week intervals. An alternative is to have your mail addressed to your respective embassy in the country you are visiting. Addresses can be found in the section for each country. In this case it is important that your letters be addressed: C/O EMBASSY OF.....

Anyone carrying an American Express Card, or at least using American Express Traveller's Checks can use the AE-offices as a mailing address. Be sure such letters contain: C/O AMERICAN EXPRESS.

When sending mail home, aerograms are the cheapest. Important letters should always be sent by registered mail.

During long trips you'll begin to collect a lot of things which you've bought along the way and which clutter up and weigh down your backpack. Send these things on home in a package. Remember that seamail will take several weeks, but it's much cheaper. Only valuable and light items such as slides are worth sending by airmail. Be sure to send your packages off from a city where the mail system functions well. The safest bets in our opinion are Singapore, Kuala Lumpur, Penang, Bangkok and Hong Kong. Singapore offers the best postal rates by far. The maximum weight for a package is 10 kg (22 lb).

If you have bought something a bit larger, you will have to engage a shipping firm (expensive!), unless the seller is willing to make the arrangements (in which case you should demand an exact receipt). The shipping costs are determined by the rate for shipping by sea to your nearest harbour plus the land rate to your home town from there. Expect the land rate to be higher.

If you are over your luggage limit for the flight home, it is cheapest to have part of your baggage go by sea. An alternative is to send your overweight case as 'unaccompanied luggage' on the same airline with which you are flying. Your bag will arrive on the first flight with space available.

Everything that you send through customs must have a Customs Declaration Form attached. It will have to state worth, weight and other facts. The forms are in the local language and in French.

TELEPHONING

In South East Asia a long distance telephone call isn't easy to make. Often the connections are bad, or the call you have been waiting hours to go through may just be forgotten somewhere. Here are some tips:

Don't telephone from Burma! Even in International Hotels you will have to wait a whole day. In other countries try to make your calls from the capital city. There the telephone exchange (usually in the main post office) is open 24 hours a day. Check the individual chapters for detailed info. In Indonesia, besides Jakarta, only Denpasar has good overseas telephone connections. Collect calls to certain countries are possible only from Thailand.

You pay for a minimum of three minutes for long distance calls. The following rates to Europe are in effect at the moment (spring 1988):

THAILAND: 210 Baht (station/station), 320 Baht (person/person)
INDONESIA:13,710 Rp (station/station); 22,850 Rp (person) in Jakarta
MALAYSIA: 27.- Malaysia $
SINGAPORE: 13.50 Singapore $

Keep the time differences in mind when making phone calls. Your telephone partner may have trouble understanding everything within three minutes if you call at 4:am.

TIME DIFFERENCES TO G.M.T. (Greenwich Mean Time):

+ 6 1/2 hours:	**BURMA**
+ 7 hours:	**THAILAND, INDONESIA** (Sumatra, Java, Bali)
+ 8 hours:	**MALAYSIA, SINGAPORE, BRUNEI, INDONESIA** (Kalimantan, Nusa Tenggara, Sulawesi)
+ 9 hours:	**INDONESIA** (Moluccas, Irian Jaya)

The American Continent is 13 - 16 hours behind the times of South East Asia (with the same differences within the region). Australia lies in the same time zones as South East Asia. New Zealand is 3 to 5 1/2 hours ahead.

PHOTOGRAPHY

There are many arguments for and against taking pictures when travelling. Just because of your camera, you will be looked on as a typical tourist.

When you see a Japanese on vacation in South East Asia, you'll notice that they are always in a hurry (because they only have a few days off) and that they have a camera hanging from their neck. Once in a while they'll have a movie camera as well. Incredibly, they only use all this equipment to take the usual group pictures: laughing stiffly in front of the Merdeka Memorial in Jakarta, at the Snake Temple in Penang, or the Wat Pho in Bangkok.

Perhaps they'll take a short excursion to the 'tourist' Meo village near Chiang Mai where, because the Meo aren't dumb, they'll have to pay a few Baht for each picture taken. The phenomena being observed here is pure tourism - if you see it, leave quickly. Really interesting images, which you can find on every street corner, don't exist for the partially blind photographer. Europeans, of course, are not any better: on that fat belly you'll find not only a single reflex camera, but over the shoulder there is sure to be a leather gadget bag marking the carrier for all thieves as a worthwhile target.

We do think that it's worthwhile to take pictures, but leave your 25 lb. gadget bag at home. 'I was there' snapshots in front of monuments are equally to be avoided. Look around for the landscapes, people and incidents which you will enjoy reliving through your photos.

If you do decide to take pictures, then do it properly and leave the instamatic at home. Your camera should have variable exposure setting whether manual or automatic - sunny and cloudy are not enough. A camera with TTL (through the lens metering) is also helpful considering the sharp tropical contrasts of light and shadow.

Due to the variety of subjects, you might want to have several lenses. You can then get the whole temple in the picture and still be able to get some detail in other shots. Beginners should start with an inexpensive model from one of the major camera makers. Later when you move up to a better camera, you can still use your old lenses.

Should your ***CAMERA*** have automatic shutter speed control, aperture automatic or be fully automatic? You will have to decide this yourself depending on your interests. For landscapes and temple shots automatic shutter speed is best because you can set the aperture to ensure good depth of field. If you are more interested in moving targets such as people then you would want automatic aperture so that you can set the shutter speed to a fast level and get sharp pictures despite subject movement.

If you are planning to do some macro-photography, then you should look into a camera with an adjustable flash so that it is possible to down stop the lens.

Another point of controversy concerns the ***LENSES.*** Your basic lens should be a fast 50-55 mm so that you can do good available light photography when you use a fast film. For a telephoto you can use a zoom but be warned that zooms aren't very fast (f 3.5-4 at best). You will lose many pictures in the tropical shadows unless you get a faster lens. A 135 mm/2.8 or even a 200 mm/2.8 would be much better. For the wide angle area a zoom (28-70 mm or 28-50 mm) is ideal. Because the buildings aren't going to walk away you can use longer exposure times to get the pictures you want even in poor light.

SLIDES are your best bet for capturing the motley colours of the tropics. You can always have prints made of your best shots. Besides your standard 64 or 100 ASA film you should also take some of the faster 200 ASA along. It is also a good idea to have a couple rolls of 400 ASA for poor light conditions. If need be, you can push the 400 ASA film to 800 or even 1600 ASA and forget your flash. Don't keep your film in a refrigerator! You will have trouble finding one and when you remove the film it will be spoiled due to condensation - watch out for air conditioners as well. Pack film in the middle of your pack. Be careful about X-ray searches at the airports. Keep your camera and lenses in your hand luggage and try to protect them from dust and water in addition to bumps.

You can have your KODAK and AGFA films developed cheaper in Bangkok, Singapore or Hong Kong than at home. The price of film seems to be about the same everywhere so you can bring some from home. If you need more, then try to get it in Singapore.

Remember how you feel when someone aims a camera at you. Keep yourself in the background and don't be pushy just to get a good picture. It is their country and we are only guests. These are people who eat, sleep, pray and die. Let them live in peace without selling their souls for your picture album or slide show at home.

FEMALE BACKPACKERS

The weight you carry isn't just your pack; it's the patriarchal world in which you travel. South East Asia is remote from the western world, not so much in air travel time as in the mentality of its people. Western moral standards are something South East Asians learn to a certain extent from contact with tourists, but even more so through Hollywood. Cheap films and television depict a world of violence, and murder; sex and hatred, where women throw themselves at the feet of the hero.

Think about the effect such films must have in Malaysia or Indonesia where some women are still veiled, male-female contact in public is taboo, and a bra is a must. Even the Gogo-Girls in Bangkok can be seen leaving the bars and clubs after midnight in conservative dress including a bra. Correct appearance is especially important in Thailand. Emancipation hasn't had much success in this part of the world.

'White is beautiful' at least for South East Asian men. Whereas during colonial times the white 'memsahib' was unapproachable, today sexually free western tourists are within grabbing distance. Considering the reputation western women get from Hollywood, there are sure to be problems. There is no surefire repellent such as for mosquitos or leeches to protect women from forward men. So no matter what you wear (bra, a long dress or a sweaty blouse) it won't protect you from the Indonesian men who stare at you, speak rudely, and try to grab.

It's easy to avoid such people. All you have to do is to stay in the big, international hotels. The more tourists, the more expensive and exclusive the atmosphere, the fewer contacts you will have with local men other than liftboys, waiters or chauffeurs. But not everyone will let themselves be imprisoned in the western enclaves. Outside of these protected areas, life is more complicated for everyone. But for women, especially those who travel alone, life can be difficult.

Few women actually travel alone in South East Asia. Sometimes women will travel in pairs, but usually women travel with a male partner. In the tourist areas you will find quite a few female travellers, but the outlying areas are mostly male territory. The single women found here are very independent. Those who don't like to travel alone find it unbearable.

For unusual trips it's best to find a partner. It'd be a shame to have your trip spoiled because of a few rude men. You might even be attacked in which case it's always best not to be alone. In rural areas particularly, check out the attitude of local men toward foreign women. It is not nice being treated as if you don't exist: No invitations to tea or difficulties in finding a guide.

Don't let this dissuade you from discovering Asia, even without male escort. Many women who travel find that, while there are some problems, on the whole travelling alone can also be enjoyable and rewarding.

How you should act when confronted by aggressive males depends on the situation. It's important to maintain your self-confidence and sense of humour. If you look as if you want something, they'll come running; if you give the masher a fictional description of the husband for whom you are waiting then he'll lose interest quickly. Of course it isn't always that simple - often you don't even speak the same language.

It is just the opposite in Thailand. Here male travellers are constantly directed to prostitutes. It can be a problem when you need a taxi to the train station but keep being delivered to some whorehouse. Women on the other hand don't have too many problems in Thailand.

What you want to make of your trip to South East Asia is up to you. There, half of the people are women too. Though they are less likely than men to speak your language (less education), they are often happy to make you feel welcome. There are many fewer social pressures in the women's world, and it shouldn't be difficult for you to make friends and to learn something about the hidden world of Asian women.

BOOKS AND MAPS

Before and during your travels, you should make a real effort to learn about your host country. Here is some suggested reading about Asia. In the various chapters you will find suggestions for the specific countries. This is only a short list of our favourites - not a complete list.

MAPS

These are listed in the chapters. The only good map of the whole area is the ***BARTHOLOMEW SOUTHEAST ASIA.***

TRAVEL GUIDES

ALL ASIA GUIDE (new edition biannually, Far Eastern Economic Review, Hong Kong). Stands out in an average field but written for the moneyed traveller. Made by people who think of Asia as their home.

SOUTH-EAST ASIA ON THE SHOESTRING (Wheeler, Tony; Australia 1985). Up-dated every two years, this book is helpful for travellers who stick to the beaten path. Many money saving tips but little background info. The Australian favourite.

GENERAL READING

A HISTORY OF SOUTH EAST ASIA (Hall, D.G.E.; London 1964). Wide ranging standard text, for everyone who wants to understand the region better an absolute must.

ASIAN DRAMA - AN INQUIRY INTO THE POVERTY OF NATIONS (Myrdal, Gunnar; New York 1972). Those who want to understand the problems of economic underdevelopment in Asia should read Myrdal. Abridged edition of the tremendous three part work.

ASIA AWAKES (Wilson, Dick; Harmondsworth 1985 - Penguin).The best simple introduction into the problems of today's Asia. Good reading!

AN EYE FOR THE DRAGON (Bloodworth, Dennis; Harmondsworth 1988 - Penguin). An easy to read book by a journalist who has spent 20 years working in Asia. New edition 1988.

THE LAND AND WILDLIFE OF TROPICAL ASIA (Time-Life Books, New York 1975). A wide ranging book for nature lovers with many photos and pictures.

THE MALAY ARCHIPELAGO (Wallace, A.R.; reprint New York 1972). This 1869 classic of the English nature researcher profits from Wallace's years of travel on the islands and mainland Malaya - emphasis on fauna and flora.

LIGHT READING

LORD JIM (Conrad, Joseph). Conrad uses South East Asia, especially the islands, as a background for many of his works. Though Conrad may not be to everyone's taste, Lord Jim is a classic. Other books by Conrad: ***TALES OF UNREST, VICTORY, AN OUTCAST OF THE ISLANDS, and ALMAYER'S FOLLY.***

COLLECTED SHORT STORIES (Maugham, W. Somerset; Pan Books 1976). South East Asia in the 1920s and 30s, Maugham shows the colonial character and life before the break-up of the European empires. A must for South East Asia freaks!

PASSAGE OF ARMS (Ambler, Eric; London 1977). An exciting story of the weapons trade during the uprising in Sumatra 1958-59.

SERPENTINE (Thompson, Thomas; Jade Books 1980). The life story of a robber murderer who met his victims in the traveller milieu between India and Bangkok. Partially based on a true story.

FURTHER READING (based less on South East Asia and more on Indochina, China and Japan)

THE QUIET AMERICAN (Greene, Graham; 1956). The life of a journalist in the French Vietnam of the 1950s. You'll see political intrigue and American naivete are to be found not just in Vietnam.

TAIPAN (Clavell, James; Del Books 1976). The story of the founding of Hong Kong and the Opium Wars.

NOBLE HOUSE (Clavell, James; Coronet Paperbacks 1982). Dramatic, 1415 page long story of Big Business in the Hong Kong of the 1970s. Many references to 'TAIPAN'.

SHOGUN (Clavell, James; Coronet Paperbacks 1976). British adventurer in medieval Japan. One of the best historical novels ever, it gives a good picture of the traditional Japanese mentality.

DYNASTY (Elegant, Robert; New York 1980). The story of a remarkable family told from the standpoint of an English woman. Takes place this century.

THE WORLD OF SUZIE WONG (Mason, Richard; New York 1957). A classic of some kind - a love story about a Chinese prostitute and an English artist in Hong Kong.
Other European-Asiatic love stories by the same author: ***THE WIND CANNOT READ*** (1960), ***THE FEVER TREE*** (1962).

Of course there are many other novels worth reading, such as those by Hougron, all of which are set in the old French colonies of Laos, Vietnam and Cambodia. You can find them at the library.

In Asia itself you will always find people willing to trade books. Make good use of this informal institution and don't carry a book around for months that you've already read three times. Our book list consists mostly of paperbacks which you can both afford and carry easily.

BRUNEI

Welcome to a real Islamic sultanate that's still as British as in colonial times. Brunei offers the contradictions of an impassable jungle and a car choked capital.

This relatively obscure country of 5765 km² on the north coast of Kalimantan (Borneo) was a British protectorate until 1971; since 1984 it is independent of Great Britain even in its defence and foreign policy. The standard of living in Brunei is high compared to the rest of South East Asia due to its oil exports. The prices reflect this affluence.

75% of Brunei is covered with tropical rain forests. The country is divided into two parts by a sliver of Sarawak land. A paved road runs parallel to the coast from the border of Sarawak to Bandar Seri Begawan. There is not much of interest to tourists in the sultanate; it is mainly a way station for people on the road from Sarawak to Sabah.

VISA

Most western visitors won't need a visa. Check with a Brunei Embassy or a British consulate for details. Addresses:

SINGAPORE, 7a Tanglin Hill (tel 4743393)
KUALA LUMPUR, 112 Jl.U Thant, (tel 4562635)
BANGKOK, 14th Floor, Orakarn Bldg., Chidlom Road (tel 2501483)
JAKARTA, Central Plaza, 9th Floor, Jl.Jend.Sudirman 48 (tel 510576).
UK consulates in:
KUCHING, Chartered Bank, Jl. Tuanku Abdul Rahman (tel 52233)
KOTA KINABALU, Hong Kong & Shanghai Banking Corp. (tel 56722)

CLIMATE & TRAVEL SEASONS

Like Sabah, the rainy season is from September till November while it's driest in January to April. The daily temperature range throughout the whole year is between 24°C and 31°C.

FESTIVALS & HOLIDAYS

National holidays include January 1, May 31 for the founding of the Royal Brunei Malay Regiment, June 3 Queen Elizabeth's official birthday, July 15 the Sultan's birthday, September 29 Constitution Day, and Christmas. In addition all Islamic holidays are honored - check the Malaysian and Indonesian chapters for a list.

GETTING AROUND

Public buses and rather expensive taxis are the means of transport in Brunei. River and coastal boats can take you to Sarawak or Sabah.

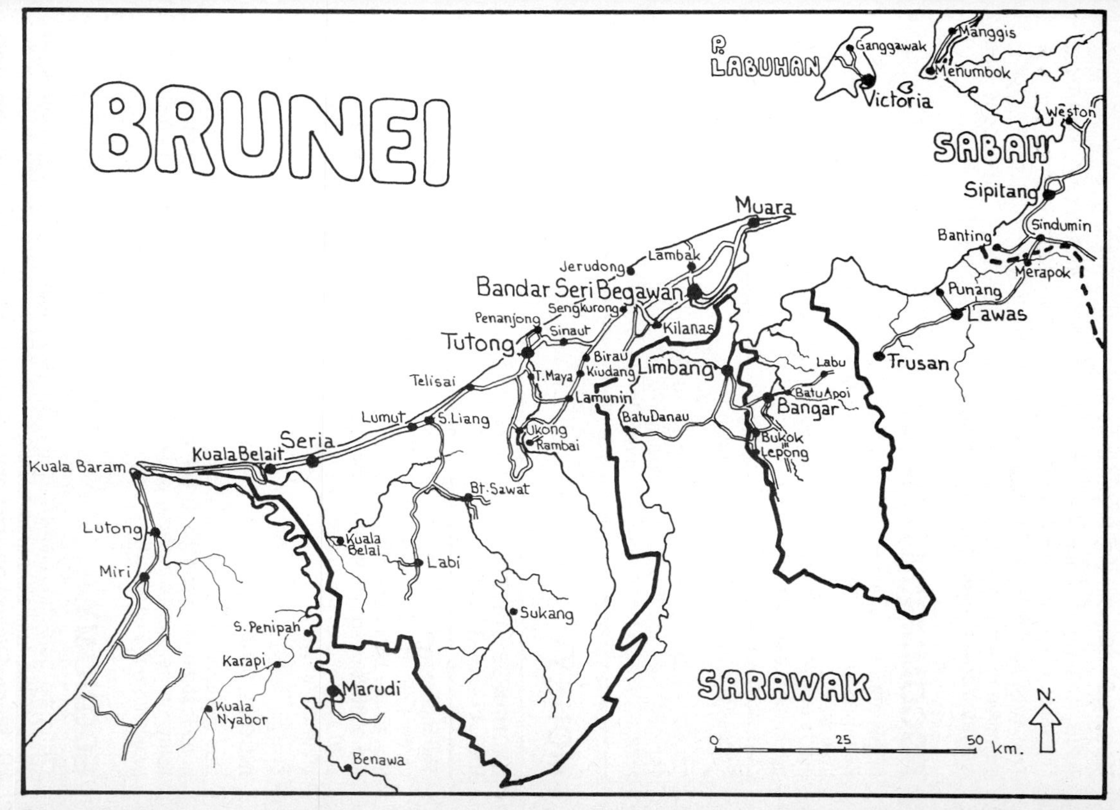
BRUNEI
P. LABUHAN
Ganggawak
Victoria
Manggis
Menumbok
Weston
SABAH
Sipitang
Sindumin
Banting
Merapok
Punang
Lawas
Trusan
Muara
Lambak
Jerudong
Bandar Seri Begawan
Sengkurong
Penanjong
Sinaut
Kilanas
Tutong
Birau
Kiudang
Limbang
Labu
T. Maya
Telisai
Lamunin
Batu Apoi
Bangar
Lumut
S. Liang
Batu Danau
Ukong
Rambai
Bukok
Lepong
Seria
Kuala Belait
Kuala Baram
Bt. Sawat
Lutong
Kuala Belai
Labi
Miri
Sukang
S. Penipah
Karapi
Marudi
Kuala Nyabor
Benawa
SARAWAK
N.
0
25
50 km.

Rent a car in Bandar Seri Begawan from:

AVIS, 108 1st Fl. Bangunan Gadong tel 24921, ***SHARIKAT YURAN,*** Jl. Chevalier 144. Both have also offices.at the airport.

The AVIS self-drive rate is cheapest - 59 B$ per day or 354 B$ per week for unlimited mileage in a Daihatsu. You can get a Jeep for 140 B$ per day. Special rates are charged for cars crossing over to Miri (Sarawak).

ACCOMMODATION

In this area Brunei proves just how expensive it really is. Hotels in Bandar Seri Begawan (BSB), along with Seria and Kuala Belait won't be found cheaper than 50 B$ a night. There aren't any cheap Chinese hotels. The only alternative is the YOUTH CENTRE (Pusat Belia). With luck and persuasion you might get in there and find BSB worth visiting for a couple days.

Prices for a room with double occupancy:

*	**up to 20 B$**
**	**up to 40 B$**
***	**up to 70 B$**
****	**over 70 B$**

MONEY

EXCHANGE RATE	**1US$ = 2.02 B$**
INFLATION RATE:	**3 %**

The monetary unit is the Brunei-Dollar with 100 cents. Notes in circulation include 1, 5, 10, 50,100 and 1000 B$. Coins include: 5, 10, 20, and 50 cents. Due to the oil wealth, the Brunei Dollar is very stable and about the same as the 1988 Singapore Dollar. Exchange rates: 1 US$ = 2.02 B$ = 2.01 S$ = 2.48 M$. There are no restrictions on the import or export of the B$ or any other currency.

INCOME AND COST OF LIVING

Due to the oil wealth, Brunei is one of the wealthiest states in the region. There is no income tax, yet schools and hospitals are free. We have no reliable statistics on per capita income, but it seems that the majority of the population profits from the oil wealth.

ECONOMY

Oil is the dominant element in the Brunei economy; oil and gas make up 99 % of the nation's export earnings. 130 000 barrels a day are shipped by the Brunei Shell Petroleum Company making Brunei 30th in the ranks of oil exporting nations. In 1984 the state earned 6.6 billion B$ but was only able to spend 2.1 billion B$. This small sultanate is said to have nearly 18 billion B$ in currency reserves.

According to the fourth Five Year Development Plan, ***agriculture*** and ***forestry*** are to be furthered and the infrastructure to be improved. An expressway parallel to the coast is under construction. The country's interior has no roads at all. Neither is there a direct connection between the two parts of the country whereas even the most distant longhouses are connected with Brunei's telephone system via ultra short wave.

80 % of all food is imported. Agriculture is largely restricted to farmers producing for their own needs. Only a few large farms are of importance economically. In the interior, slashing and burning is used to create fields. The loss of woodcover is so great that scientists have been warning of the negative effects - especially the feared loss of the entire coastal jungle in the near future.

The state is supporting the setting up of new industries: without much success up to now. The largest natural gas liquification facility in the world was built in Lumut in 1973 to serve Japan's needs.

NATIONALITIES & RELIGIONS

Of the 250 000 people in Brunei, 54 % are of ***Malay*** origin and 26 % ***Chinese*** (who are spread all over South East Asia controlling much trade and small business). 16 % are proto-Malayan consisting of the major tribes ***Iban, Kadazan, Murut***, and ***Kedayan.*** Brunei is an Islamic country - especially in the coastal areas where the the Malay populations are settled. The remaining 4 % of the population consists of European, American, and Australian specialists who work in the oil industry.

HISTORY

Old Chinese writings between 518 AD and 616 AD mention a place with the name Puni or Poli geographically located between China and Java. Today we assume that this must be Brunei. The 15th century marriage of the princess of Johore / Riau with the local ruler caused him to take up the Islamic faith. With this first Sultan, Mohammed, Islam began to spread on the north coast of Borneo.

The Sultanate of Brunei developed over the centuries into a power dominating large parts of Kalimantan, the Sulu Archipelago and Mindanao. The locally made cannon are well known in the whole region. Despite two attempts by the Spanish fleet to capture the Sultanate's capital, Spain was only able to occupy the city for a short time in 1578.

The Sultanate lost power over the next two hundred years. This was due to the spreading power of England and Holland, and to increasing local piracy. At the same time the White Rajahs of Sarawak were able to capture more and more territory until in 1904 Brunei had shrunk to the mini-state size we find it today. Protectorate status established in 1888 gave Britain political control.

Brunei decided not to join the Federation of Malaysia when it was founded by the British in 1963. Sultan Sir Omar Ali Saifuddin wasn't going to share Brunei's oil with Malaysia. In 1967 Sir Omar abdicated the Sultanate in favour of his son Hassanal Bolkiah Muizuddin Waddaulah, the 29th ruler in the dynasty. After final independence in 1984, the country became the 6th member of ASEAN.

LANGUAGE

The national language is Malay. Because of the many Shell employees, English is understood practically everywhere.

SUGGESTED READING

Because of the close historical ties of Brunei with Sarawak and Sabah, the history and culture are similar. Check the suggested reading section in the chapter East Malaysia.

BANDAR SERI BEGAWAN

The capital of Brunei is a quiet and comfortable place to stay if you have the money or are able to get a bed in Pusat Belia. One of the most imposing mosques in South East Asia,

MESJID SULTAN OMAR ALI SAIFUDDIN, was built in 1958. Except at prayer time (Friday). you can take a lift to the top of the minaret 44 m high. Here you have a good view of the city and the
KAMPONG AYER. Between the pile houses of the 'water village' (Malay: kampong = village; ayer = water) you can take a walk on concrete footbridges. Unlike its poorer counterparts in the rest of South East Asia, the water village here has both running water and electricity. The big street in front of the village is packed with cars. Something new to check out near Kampong Ayer is the
ARTS AND HANDICRAFT CENTRE where traditional handwork is made and sold. You can find traditional handwork in silver, brass, bronze, along with beautiful sarong, plaited mats and baskets. A river tour can be quite worthwhile.
The
CHURCHILL MUSEUM (Churchill Memorial Gallery) is a kind reminder in South East Asia of Brunei's English influences - open daily except Tuesdays. Next door the
SULTAN HASSANAL BOLKIAH AQUARIUM with a good collection of tropical fish is open daily except Mondays - admission: 30 cents. Official work of the capital takes place in the
LAPAU (Royal Ceremonial Hall) and in the
DEWAN MAJLIS (Legislative Assembly).
BRUNEI MUSEUM (open daily except Mon 09:30-17:00 h, closed Fri 11:30-14:30 h) - good ethnographic and natural history exhibits. Don't miss the history of oil exploration. Nearby is the

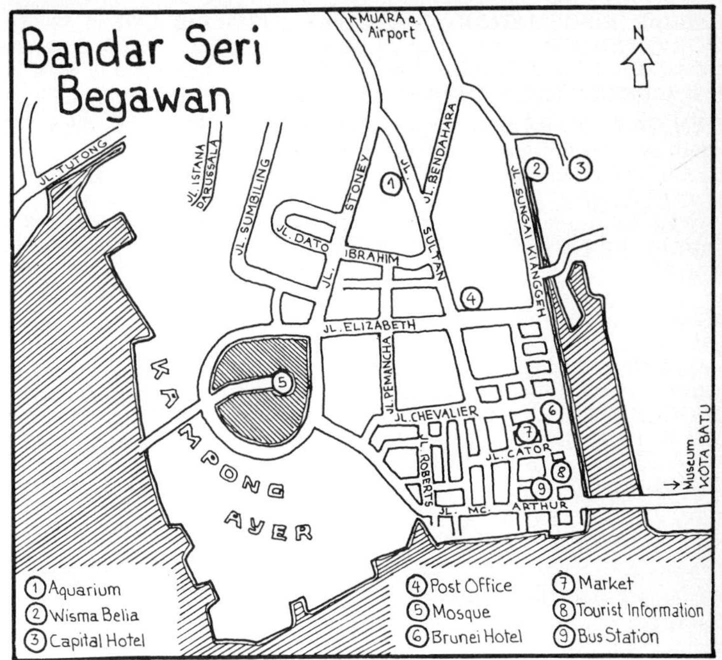

MAUSOLEUM of the famous Sultan Bolkiah, the fifth sultan of the dynasty. Also worth a look is the new *SULTAN'S PALACE* which is said to have cost 350-600 million US$.

HOTELS

Try to get into *PUSAT BELIA,* a youth centre set up by the government. The complex includes: a dormitory, gym, swimming pool, library, and a restaurant. Normally you are asked to show an ISIC or an International Youth Hostel Card but they aren't absolutely necessary! The first three nights cost 10 B$, thereafter 7.50 B$. Everything else is expensive: *CAPITAL HOSTEL*****, Jl.Berangan right behind Pusat Belia. Or try *ANG'S HOTEL*****, Jl.Tasek (tel 23553) or *BRUNEI HOTEL*****, 95 Jl.Chevalier (tel 22372). There are also the International hotels such as *SHERATON UTAMA*****, Jl.Bendahara, tel 27273.

FOOD

In BSB as in the rest of the Sultanate there are lots of Chinese, Malay, and Indian restaurants and food stalls. Try *MOHAMMED'S COFFEE SHOP* on Jl.Sultan for Malay-Indian fare. Good but expensive Chinese food can be found at *HOOVER*, Jl.Sungei Kianggeh. Alcohol is only available in Chinese restaurants.

GENERAL INFORMATION

INFORMATION - Tourist Information Centres at the Airport and on Jl.Mc Arthur, Customs Wharf (near bridge).

AMERICAN EXPRESS - represented by Travel Centre (Borneo) Ltd., G6 Tek Guan Place, 56-60 Jl. Sultan, tel 29601.

LEAVING BSB

BY AIR

The following airlines serve BSB: MAS, British Airways, Qantas, Cathay Pacific, Singapore Airlines, and Royal Brunei Airlines. A taxi to the airport (5 km) costs 15 B$. SAMPLE PRICES: HONG KONG 596 B$, KOTA KINABALU 65 B$, MANILA 444 B$, JAKARTA 531 B$, KUCHING 192 B$, SINGAPORE 320 B$.

OVERLAND TO SARAWAK

First bus to SERIA for 4 B$. From Seria to KUALA BELAIT in 30 minutes for 1.20 B$. At 7:00, 9:00 and 14:00 h catch a thru bus to MIRI for 9.50 B$.

OVERLAND AND BY SEA TO SABAH

For this route you have several possibilities. The simplest is to take a boat to LABUAN leaving at 8:00 and 13:00 h costing 13 B$. You can find more info on the route Labuan - Kota Kinabalu in the Sabah chapter.

Another possibility is the boat to LAWAS for 15 B$. WARNING: The boat only goes as far as PUNANG where you switch to a bus or taxi (cost included in the 15 B$ fare). From Lawas you can take a bus to MERAPOK - costs 3.50 M$ and leaves at 14:00 h. Check the Sabah chapter for more information.

DAY TRIPS AROUND BSB

Only to be considered if you should fly into BSB and want to have a look around. Otherwise make a stopover on the land route between Sabah and Sarawak.

TUTONG / KUALA BELAIT / SERIA

These are the centres of the Brunei oil industry. However, Tutong and Lumut do have nice beaches. Two hotels in Kuala Belait, SENTOSA**** and SEAVIEW**** are on Jl.Seria. Buses run regularly to TUTONG (1.80 B$), SERIA (4.50 B$) and from Seria to KUALA BELAIT (1.20 B$).

TEMBURONG

This is the smaller part of Brunei surrounded by Sarawak. A boat trip from BSB takes 45 minutes and costs 6.50 B$. There you will see lots of the Iban longhouses, but not as good as the ones in Sarawak.

LIMBANG

In Sarawak, a boat trip costs from BSB 6 B$. A good idea for people who want to save themselves the high cost of staying in a Brunei hotel. Several relatively cheap hotels include: SOUTH EAST ASIA**, 27 Market Street, tel 21013; AUSTRALIA**, 63 Bank Street, tel 21860 and NAK** on the same street.

From LIMBANG you can take the 7:00 h express boat to LAWAS. MAS flies to LAWAS for 25 M$ and MIRI for 45 M$.

BURMA

Since independence, and especially since 1962, Burma has cut itself off from foreign influences. Forget about finding Coca Cola, Unilever, and Sony products here except perhaps on the black market. Since 1980, however, Burma has opened up a little. Western investment is now permitted, even if western consumer goods are still hard to find. We'll have to wait to see how things develop in the coming years.

Due to the lack of western influence, Burma is fundamentally different from its neighbours, though you may not think so when you experience the bureaucratic barriers at the airport. You'll like this land of wonderfully hospitable people - a Buddhist country that will enchant anyone interested in experiencing Asia unspoiled. You won't be able to see much of the country for two reasons: First, you are only able to get a seven day visa, and second many parts of the country are unsafe due to separatist struggles by ethnic minorities against the central government.

In Rangoon you'll still find some tell-tales of colonial days - mossed over to be sure - but the past presence of the British Raj cannot be denied. Paddle steamers from the days of Kipling ply

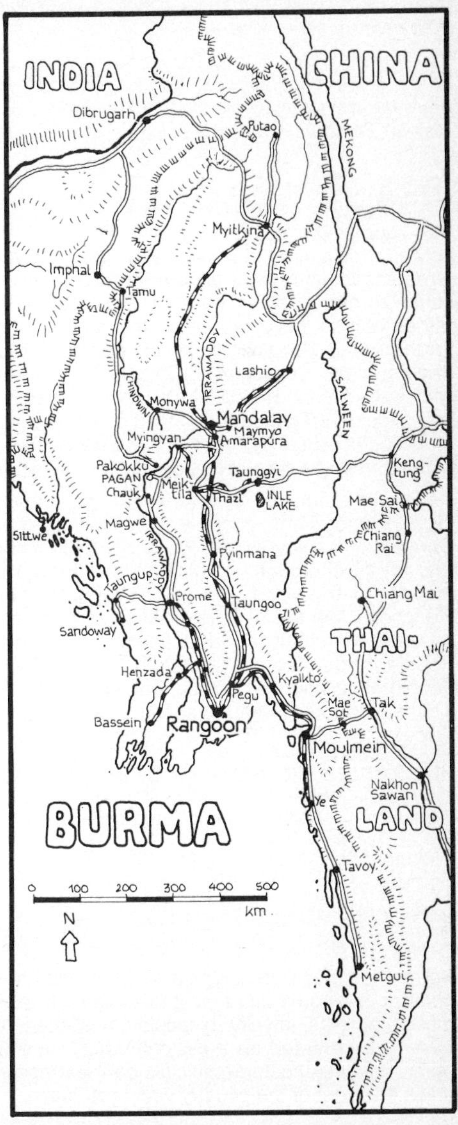

the Irrawaddy. In towns like Maymyo you'll think time has stood still and the 20th century never was.

The trouble with a Burma trip is the short visa. You'll just have enough time to do the quick run: Rangoon, Mandalay, Pagan, Rangoon. By the way, the seven day visa is only available since 1971. From 1961 - 1971, you were only able to stay for 24 hours on a transit visa.

VISA

Get your seven day visa at one of the Burmese embassies or consulates abroad. You'll need to present your passport, a ticket in and out of the country, three application forms along with three passport pictures. You get the application forms at the embassies. Theoretically it is possible to arrive by ship rather than air, but we've never met anyone who has done this. You can apply for the visa in Bangkok, Colombo, Jakarta, Delhi, Kuala Lumpur, or Singapore. The Burmese Consulate in Calcutta no longer issues visas. In Asia the visa will cost you about US$5 (100 Baht in Bangkok).If you get up early enough you might even get your stamped passport back on the same day in Bangkok. In Europe, it usually takes 1 - 2 weeks. The visa is valid for three months starting from the date of issue.

There are a number of wild rumours concerning the possibilities of extending visas. Forget them - there is no way you can spend more than seven days in Burma, unless you should fall seriously ill. There is no point in faking, though; you will be thoroughly examined by a Burmese doctor who will confirm your inability to travel. Should this happen, immediately contact the officials. In Rangoon: Ministry of Foreign Affairs (Immigration Department, Phayre Street, between Merchant- and Mahabandoola Street).You will find yourself in deep trouble if you stay in the country without the necessary stamp. A couple of people have had little choice, however, because their flight was over-booked. These unfortunates had to spend their last days scurrying in and out of various offices.

EMBASSIES IN NEIGHBOURING COUNTRIES

INDIA, 3/50F Shantipath, New Delhi, tel 70251.
THAILAND, 132 North Sathon Rd., Bangkok, tel 2332237.
NEPAL, Thapathali Road, Kathmandu, tel 13146.
BANGLADESH, Plot 38, Rd. no. 11, Banani Town, Dhaka, tel 301915.
MALAYSIA, 7 Jl.Taman U Thant, Kuala Lumpur, tel 423863.
INDONESIA, Jl.Agus Salim 109, tel 320440.
SINGAPORE, 15 St.Martin Drive, tel 2358704

CUSTOMS

Burma has thorough customs officials, and on arrival you will have to fill out a number of lengthy and time-consuming forms. All valuables (cameras, lenses, movie cameras, jewelry, binoculars, walkmen, transistor radios, wrist-watches) have to be entered on a customs form, sometimes even with the serial numbers. This way customs officials can rest assured that you will take the valuables back out of the country when you leave.

The import of 200 cigarettes and one bottle of alcohol is duty free. The happy days during which one could pay for one's whole week in Burma by selling a carton of 555 (Triple Five) and a bottle of Red Label Whisky have unfortunately passed. However, one can still get up to 500 Kyat (about US$60) for them in Rangoon (top prices!). The price depends on the supply and demand as well as your adeptness at driving a bargain. It can therefore fluctuate. The price for these items in Bangkok Airport's duty-free shop is about US$13. Whether or not you should become involved is your own decision.

There is also a great demand for other "western wares", i.e. t-shirts, jeans, cassette tapes, cosmetics, watches, pens, pocket calculators, medicine, etc. (Only sell items that you have not declared!) On the other hand, you shouldn't have too many Kyat left over, either, since many expenses (hotels and transportation) will be documented on your Money Declaration Form and you will be checked when you leave. Take care!

EMBASSIES IN RANGOON

AUSTRALIA, 88 Strand Road, tel 15711.
UNITED KINGDOM, 80 Strand Road, tel 15700.
UNITED STATES, 581 Merchant Street, tel 18055.

CLIMATE & TRAVEL SEASONS

Burma has three different seasons which vary according to region, time and intensity. The warmest period is from February till May when the temperatures range from 24°C to 36°C. In central Burma expect temperatures to be 4°C higher, and in Mandalay the mercury can go up to 45°C. April and May are hot times to visit.

At the end of May the monsoon season begins, first on the coast and then farther northward. The greatest rainfall comes in July and August (Rangoon 582 mm, Mandalay 422 mm). You'll notice some cooling as the temperatures sink below 30°C, but the rising humidity keeps the discomfort high. The southwest monsoon from the Gulf of Bengal gives the Irrawaddy delta most rainfall during the rainy season. Sometimes, such as in 1975, central Burma hardly gets any rain from the monsoons. The heaviest rains fall during the afternoon and evening.

The best time to visit Burma is between November and February. The temperature could then fall to around 16°C. But in 1986, for example, it rained so hard between the 14th and 21st November that all our plans were drowned in Pagan and Taunggyi. We can only give you a general picture; each year the weather is a bit different.

FESTIVALS & HOLIDAYS

The Burmese traditionally use a ***lunar calendar;*** the first day of every full moon is the first day of the month. The ***western calendar***, however, is used officially for scheduling holidays.

STATE HOLIDAYS

January 4 is *INDEPENDENCE DAY.* You'll see pageants and demonstrations everywhere, all of Rangoon is lit up, and on Royal Lake boat races are held. February 12 is *UNION DAY* in honour of the founding of the Union of Burma in 1947. High points are dancing by members of the different nationalities and celebrations on Royal Lake as well as at the former race course (Kyaikkasan). March 2 is *FARMERS' DAY* with exhibitions and a carnival at Kyaikkasan. March 27 , *RESISTANCE DAY,* is celebrated with big military parades in Rangoon. *MAY DAY* also brings parades and pageants followed by an evening of classical Burmese theatre. *MARTYRS' DAY* on July 19, is celebrated in remembrance of the murder of Aung San and his comrades. Government and party leaders gather at the mausoleum (near Shwedagon Pagoda) for ceremonies. Christmas Day is also a work holiday.

RELIGIOUS HOLIDAYS

PWE - this is the Burmese term for holidays and parties. Expect to see all night presentations of traditional, dramatic dance, singers and some not so serious clowns to entertain the audience. In March the *FULL MOON OF TABAUNG* is celebrated in the Shwedagon-Pagoda. In March/April you can see the famous *FIRE WALKERS* among the Hindu community in Rangoon. Firm believers walk a considerable distance in a state of trance across glowing hot coals spread out. The *BURMESE NEW YEAR* is celebrated in about the middle of April. As in Buddhist Thailand, people spray themselves with water. In May the *FULL MOON OF KASON* is honoured in the Shwedagon. In remembrance of Buddha's enlightenment under a Bodhi Tree, the trees are watered along the Shwedagon by young girls. In the middle of July the Buddhist time of fasting begins and new monks are taken into the monasteries. The end of the fasting season comes in October when all towns are lit up. Theatre presentations and shorter amusements are again allowed - this is *THADINYUT.*
The exact dates of the various festivities can be found at Tourist Burma.

GETTING AROUND

The statistics aren't bad. In a country of 676,522 km^2, there are 4272 km of railroad, 22,317 km of roads (highways by official definition), and 9201 km of navigable rivers. The figures may be correct, but the infrastructure is very old and not up to western standards. This causes many economic problems, which is why a major overhaul is being planned. Since 1979, 664 km of road are being improved from Rangoon to Mandalay. At the same time new Krupp diesel locomotives from Germany and heavy Toyota trucks from Japan have been procured. New passenger trains are coming into service, but because the track was laid so long ago, it still takes 14 hours to ride from Rangoon to Mandalay.

TRAINS - still the most important means of transport. Tourists will be interested only in the route Rangoon - Mandalay and in the Thazi junction, where two smaller lines run to Shwenyaung (Taunggyi) and Myingyan. No other lines are for tourist use. Tickets can only be purchased directly from Tourist Burma. Get them a day ahead of time.

BUSES - JEEPS - PICK-UPS - useful only for short trips such as from Rangoon to Pegu, Pagan to Thazi, or from Mandalay to Pagan or Taunggyi (and that will take a good while!).

RIVERBOATS - these go the entire length of the Irrawaddy and the delta. The river trip from Rangoon to Mandalay would certainly be interesting, but it'd take weeks. The only boat ride to consider is the trip from Mandalay to Pagan. For the 200 km, you'll need between 14 and 24 hours in one of the old fashioned paddle-wheel steamers if you don't get hung up on a sandbank.

PLANES - flying is much more expensive than the overland travel alternatives, but you save a lot of time if you can get a flight! You'll have trouble booking with BAC (Burma Airways Corporation). Bookings are made through Tourist Burma. BAC uses Fokker F28, F27, and Twin Otter planes.

It is important to have a general itinerary worked out before your arrival in Rangoon. Think in terms of alternatives if the train or plane you want is booked up. The usual tour taken by 80% of the visitors is:

1st day: *Arrival in Rangoon, buy train tickets, sightseeing.*
2nd day: *Train to Mandalay.*
3rd day: *Sightseeing in Mandalay or an excursion.*
4th day: *Bus or boat ride to Pagan.*
5th day: *Sightseeing in Pagan.*
6th day: *Return trip to Rangoon or 2nd day in Pagan.*
7th day: *Return to Rangoon or Rangoon sightseeing.*
8th day: *Departure from Rangoon.*

Whole groups of people will be following this route which means that you will be constantly seeing the same faces on buses, trains, and boats. Why not break the monotony?

You save lots of time if you fly some of the routes. Even if your departure from Rangoon is set for the late afternoon of the eighth day, you should try to be there well in advance, possibly a full day. Delays of several hours are common in Burma, and if you miss your flight back to Thailand, you'll find yourself in a lot of trouble.

Instead of the quick tour, why don't you visit just one place for a while. In 1980 we stayed four days in Mandalay and vicinity, in 1981 we spent four days in Taunggyi and at Lake Inle , and in 1985 we only went to Pagan. You'd have time to spend a night in Kalaw or Maymyo, something few people do.

ACCOMMODATION

Most of the hotels have to be booked through Tourist Burma, or the expense for accommodations must be listed on your money declaration form. With some delicacy you can find out which hotels or guest houses will let you pay without that form. If you don't use the form, you can spend money acquired through means other than the official exchange rate. Where you get these excess Kyat is your business.

Luxury hotels on an international standard are only in Rangoon and to a certain extent in Mandalay.

We decided on the following price table for Burma - all prices are for double rooms:

*	**up to 30 Kyat**
**	**up to 50 Kyat**
***	**up to 100 Kyat**
****	**over 100 Kyat**

FOOD & DRINK

If you've just come from India, you won't have to adjust to new food. The staple diet is rice with different curries. ***Sybian*** is typical, though it isn't as hot here as in India. A soup is almost always served with it, such as ***Hincha*** with vegetables and fish. You'll find a bowl of ***Ngapi*** or fish sauce with chillies any place serving food. On the side are served fresh vegetables such as cucumber, cabbage and salad. You'll also see ***Balauchaung*** made of chilli, dried crab, onions, lots of garlic, and shrimp sauce. Often you'll get bamboo sprouts as a side dish. ***Mohinga*** is a soup of noodles, fish, eggs, onions, and fresh coriander.

Small cafes, serving tea (unsugared) without charge and offering small sweets, are everywhere. Typical is the Shwe Pa Laung on Mahabandoola Road.

There are several kinds of soft drinks: mostly carbonated, very sweet and luke warm. If you've ever seen the way ice is made and chopped into smaller pieces in Burma, then you'll never use it again to cool a soft drink. Western drinks (Coca Cola) are only found in the Inya Lake Hotel. Expensive but good is Mandalay beer, made at the People's Brewery & Distillery. Local beverages are palm wine and rice liquor.

Besides Indian and Chinese food, you can also find European style food in the Strand Hotel in Rangoon. Outside the capital, such foods are only found in Mandalay.

In general be careful about eating and drinking in Burma. The sanitation and hygiene aren't the best, and dysentery is very unpleasant.

MONEY

EXCHANGE RATE	**1US$ = 6.13 Kyat**
INFLATION RATE:	**5%**

The Burmese monetary unit is the Kyat (say: Chut) with 100 pyas. The following banknotes are in circulation: 1, 5 and 10 Kyat. In September 1987, all 25, 35, and 75 Kyat bills were declared invalid overnight. The planned distri-

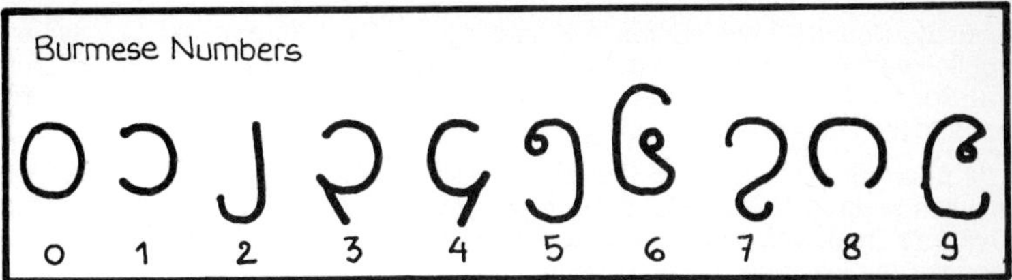

bution of new 45 and 90 Kyat bills was announced. In 1985, all 20, 50, and 100 Kyat bills had already been declared invalid.There are also coins of 1, 5, 10, 20, 50 pyas as well as 1 Kyat. Coins are marked with Burmese numerals; bills have both the Burmese and Arabic version. Watch out when exchanging money - you may be offered old, invalid bills.

You can bring as much foreign currency with you as you please, both in cash and traveller's cheques, but you have to declare everything on your ***Money Declaration Form***. The importation of Kyat or undeclared money is illegal.

The figures on your money declaration form have to be reconcilable with the amount of money that you have with you. Every time you change money, book hotels, planes, or trains, the transaction must be noted on your form. Then they can check when you leave whether you actually changed enough money at the official rate to account for your expenses. You won't be able to buy plane tickets unless you can prove with your declaration form that you've changed enough money officially to afford it. It's important that all the numbers add up when you leave.

On the free money markets in Singapore or Hong Kong, the exchange rate for the Kyat is 60 to US$1. In Burma itself you will be offered 20 to 30 to a dollar on the shadowy black market. Watch out for money changers who actually work for the police! Often you'll be offered old, invalidated banknotes - it's not worth the hassle!

You can sell things, though, that are hard to find in Burma such as jeans, t-shirts, western cigarettes, whisky, cosmetics, medicines, watches, etc. Don't sell anything registered on your customs declaration form! Cameras are always registered! The duty free bottle of red label whisky and carton of 555 cigarettes can be sold for about 500 Kyat - as mentioned above - not a bad deal!

Another trick is the Diplomatic Store in Rangoon. Imported goods are available to those with dollars. There are two sets of prices, one for tourists and a cheaper set for diplomats. You can buy cigarettes here and sell them to Burmese for Kyat. This will give you an effective exchange rate of 20 - 30 Kyat to a dollar. It is illegal to export Kyat. Unused Kyat can be re-exchanged if you can prove that they were bought officially.

INCOME AND COST OF LIVING

According to the ASIA YEARBOOK 1986, the average yearly income in Burma is US$181 a year. Monthly wages exceeding 200 Kyat are rare. If employed in industry, workers make approx. 1 Kyat per hour. Even here, in this socialist republic, women earn about 20% less than men. The statistics only cover Central Burma, but one can safely assume that people living in more secluded parts of the country earn even less.

The price for basic foods in the state-run shops are reasonably low. Sudden inflation of up to 100% is not unheard of, however, and people of a low income level are frequently heavily burdened. Most wares are sold at free markets, though, and who knows who controls them.

If you live cheaply, you'll be able to get by on about 40 Kyat a day in Burma. This makes the country cheap to travel around in, even if you exchange money at the official rate. **By the end of the trip you have to have officially exchanged US$100, otherwise you will end up having trouble.** This means a total of 650 Kyat or approx. 80 Kyat a day.Your trip will be more expensive if you plan to fly, of course. Diethelm Travel offers a Burma package deal for a staggering US$400!

According to Tourist Burma, approx. 30,000 tourists visit the country every year. Even though each one is only allowed to stay a week, the average visitor manages to spend the yearly income of a Burmese inhabitant per visit!

ECONOMY

65% of the gainfully employed are engaged in agriculture, making it the most important branch of Burma's economy. Only 45% of the gross national product, however, is achieved in ***agriculture*** (tillage, forestry, and fish processing industry). In contrast, the 9.5% employed by ***industry,*** construction, and mining produce 12.7% of the gross national product.

During the period of British colonialism, Burma was the most important rice-exporting country of the South East Asian region. Rice is grown all over the country, especially in the Irrawaddy delta area. Almost two thirds of the entire areas suitable for cultivation in Burma are planted with rice. During World War II production sank drastically, however, as it has continued doing ever since. In the last few years there has been a slight rise. This can be noticed when taking a look at the export figures of the country: 1975, US$74 million; 1977, US$117 million; 1983, US$437 million. The entire mountain areas of Burma (approx. 2/3 of the total national territory) are of lesser importance for agriculture. Burning mountain forests in order to gain new areas suitable for cultivation is a common custom here. The population mainly produces rice for its own use. Fine woods are the second most important product that the country exports. I t has been estimated that Burma has the largest teak forest of the world.

According to the 1974 constitution, the state owns all the land in Burma. Land can only be used for agriculture with the state's approval and permission. Local councils can revoke this permission if farmers do not comply with the state's general rules that their products be sold to state-run organizations at set prices, etc. These days, many farmers have become organized in co-operative associations. During the last few years the contributions farmers have to make to the state have been reduced. For this reason a much larger variety of agricultural products can be found on the free markets than seven or eight years ago.

In 1985 ***industrial production*** increased by nearly 11%. It still lies beneath the goal of the country's economic plan, though. The oil industry has grown considerably during the last couple of years. This is in part due to foreign investment, a symptom of the gradual economic reforms that are being introduced to the country. All in all, there are only 500-600 state-run industrial businesses that employ more than 50 people. They were mainly founded as a means of reducing imports, and since the market for which they produce is reasonably closed, they are in no position to compete with either the quality or the price of foreign products.

After General Ne Win came to power in 1962, Burma's entire economy was nationalized rather rashly. This upset production in all branches of the economy. One of the results of this policy has been the development of a flourishing black market where products - especially from India, Thailand, and China - can be bought for high prices. Experts estimate that US$1/2 million worth of goods are smuggled in daily from Thailand alone.

NATIONALITIES & RELIGIONS

As you can tell by the country's name, Socialist Republic of the Union of Burma, the country is a federation of states. These include:

State/District	area in sq km	Population in millions 1986	Population density per sq km
Arakan	36900	2,227	60,3
Chin	36100	0,421	11,7
Kachin	89100	0,957	10,7
Karen	30500	1,115	36,5
Kayah	11900	0,164	13,8
Mon	12400	0,934	75,3
Shan	155900	4,136	26,5
Irrawaddy	35200	5,405	153,5
Magwe	44900	3,426	76,3
Mandalay	37100	4,766	128,5
Pegu	39500	4,132	104,6
Rangoon	10300	4,148	402,7
Sagaing	94800	4,055	42,8
Tenasserim	43500	1,709	39,3
Burma-Total	678100	37,595	55,4

Ethnic Burmese make up 67 % of the population. Other nationalities include: Shan 11%, Karen 5%, Chin 1.2%, Kachin 2.5%, Indian 2%, Chinese 2%, Arakanese 6% , and Mon 3%.

You won't meet any non-Burmese minorities because you aren't allowed to visit most of Burma. Some of the minority populations have been engaged in open rebellion against the central government for as long as 20 years. The Shan, Karen, and Kachin have guerilla armies which control certain parts of their states. In addition there are groups of the BCP (Burmese Communist Party) which operate in northeast Burma along the Chinese border.

Opium is big business, especially in Shan State. Bandits often attack the mule caravans which carry raw opium worth millions to the Thai border and into Thailand. The diverse rebel armies (who as often as not hate each other) hire heavily armed guards for the caravans. For a price of course! Modern weapons are easy to acquire due to the large amounts of money generated by the opium trade and the availability of American weapons in the region since the Vietnam war. Cooperation between the different groups and rebel armies has not been successful up to now, in spite of several attempts to get together. Even the Burmese army, despite receiving one third of the national budget, is not able to control the entire country. Many regions are just inaccessible.

Guerilla actions rarely make the international press unless whites are somehow involved. In 1978, for example, a BAC plane on an inland flight was shot down, most probably by guerillas. Several Europeans who were aboard died. Trains travelling from Mandalay to Rangoon were bombed in 1985 and again in January 1988. For an outsider, the whole problem seems very difficult to understand - tourists hardly ever experience violence in Burma. To you, Burma will seem a peaceful country with inhabitants who are even more peaceful.

The constitution guarantees freedom of religion, but Buddhism is practically a state religion. The Burmese road to socialism, as it is called by state ideology, finds no contradictions with Buddhism. About 85% of the total population is Hinayana-Buddhists (Burmese, Shan, Mon). There are also Hindus and Muslims (Arakanese) and especially among the Karen there are many Christians.

HISTORY

Visit Pagan for a meaningful impression of the long and checkered Burmese history. From 1044 to 1287, ***Pagan*** was the capital of a great kingdom. King Anawratha brought Pagan to blossom, ruling a land nearly geographically identical to the Burma of today. Buddhism was declared the state religion, and a type of writing, derived from Sanskrit and borrowed from the Mon, was further developed and unified in form.

The decline of the Pagan kingdom began in the 13th century with repeated Mongol attacks and pressure from invasions of Thai people (Shan) in the north-east. In 1287, Pagan was almost completely destroyed by the Mongols.

Not until the ***Toungoo Dynasty*** (1531 - 1752) could part of the old kingdom be re-established. The arch-enemy Thailand was annihilated in 1767 when its capital Ayutthaya was razed to the ground.

Already in 1519, ***Portugal*** was able to secure trade concessions for itself from Burma. The colonial power that would leave a lasting impression, however, was ***Britain.*** In the course of three wars (1824/26, 1852, and 1887) Burma was assimilated piecemeal into the British Empire. The rivalries between the Burmese on the one hand, and the Mon, Karen, or Shan on the other, were used expediently. British merchants were interested in trade with China, and the land route to the north through Chinese Yunnan province seemed especially profitable.

During the 1920s and 30s, the British administration began to import large numbers of Indian workers who were employed in the Rangoon harbour and on the railroads. Before World War II, Rangoon was almost purely Indian. In 1930 the Indian dockers striked. In response Burmese dock-workers were employed, though they lacked the skills of their Indian colleagues. There was trouble between the two nationalities. The same year saw the beginning of a large peasant rebellion led by ***Saya San*** in the Tharrawaddy region north of Rangoon. It took two years to put down the rebellion; 10,000 supporters of Saya San were killed, 9,000 taken prisoner and 128, including Saya San, were hanged.

From the 1930s many political student groups and clubs were formed. The politicians ***U Nu, U Thant,*** and ***Ne Win*** at one time were active in these circles. One important political group of nationalist students was called Thakin. It wanted to achieve the independence of Burma with the aid of Japan. Many Thakin went to Japan, including Ne Win and ***Aung San,*** where they received military training on the occupied island of Hainan. In early 1942 Burma was invaded not just by Japanese troops but by members of the Burmese Independence Army under the leadership of Aung San. The British troops retreated quickly to India.

In 1943 Japan was induced by the clever political leadership of Burma to grant the country its independence. Relations between the Japanese and Burmese armies at the time were very tense. 1944 saw the formation of AFPFL (Anti-Fascist People's Freedom League). Units of the Burmese National Army prepared to rise up against the Japanese occupation. In April 1945 units of the BNA occupied Rangoon - one day later they were followed by the British army.

After long and difficult negotiations with the old colonial power, elections were held in April 1947 to choose delegates to a constitutional convention. The AFPFL achieved an overwhelming victory. In July 1947 Aung San and six of his political comrades were assassinated. So it was U Nu who declared the Republic of Burma on January 4, 1948.

In March 1962 the army under General Ne Win overthrew the government of U Nu and set up a military dictatorship based on socialist ideology. Until 1982 Ne Win was the President of the Socialist Republic of the Union of Burma. Ne Win gave as his reason for the 1962 coup his concern about a dissolution of the union. It's true that differences among the nationalities at the time almost led to a state of war. On the other hand, there are rebel groups now as then, despite a general amnesty offered by Ne Win in 1980.

A statement by a Burma explorer is still worth repeating: The Burmese are a charming, tolerant, and generous folk with cunning minds full of irony.

LANGUAGE

During the census of 1931, 136 different languages were registered. No differentiation was made, however, between a language and dialect.

The main and national language is ***Burman (or Burmese)*** which belongs to the Tibeto-Burman language family. Important regional languages are Arakanese, Shan, Karen, Chin, and Kachin.

English is still an acknowledged language of trade, though not as widely spoken as during the colonial period. Other European languages are practically unknown.

Like Thai and Chinese, Burmese is a one-syllable ***tonal language*** in which four different tones differentiate the meanings of the words. It is very difficult for Europeans on a seven day tour to learn a basic vocabulary. At the YMCA in Rangoon, you can get a mimeographed tiny language guide which gives you the important words, expressions and numbers.

Burmese writing was developed from the Mon script. It is written from left to right without any spaces between the words. The alphabet has 11 vowels and 32 consonants. In order to read street and bus numbers you should at least learn Burmese numbers.

SUGGESTED READING

There are several recommended travel guides dealing with Burma:

BURMA (Klein, Wilhelm; APA Productions, Singapore 1981).Like all APA travel guides, with lots of colour pictures and detailed route descriptions. Too heavy to take with you however!

BURMA - a travel survival kit (Wheeler, Tony; Australia 1979). Practical tips in shoestring style.

HISTORICAL SITES IN BURMA (Aung Thaw; Rangoon 1978). Recommended even if the quality of the pictures is lacking. Only found in the Diplomatic Store.

PICTORIAL GUIDE TO PAGAN (Rangoon 1975). Wide ranging guide to Pagan with a large map of the region. Only in Diplomatic Store.

THAILAND-BURMA TRAVELLERS' HANDBOOK (by us; Huddersfield 1988). A new guide with more information about the country.

Books with more general information:

A HISTORY OF MODERN BURMA (Cady, J.F.; Ithaca 1958).The standard introduction to the country's history.

A NARRATIVE OF THE MISSION TO THE COURT OF AVA IN 1855 (Yule, Henry; reprint by Oxford University Press, Kuala Lumpur 1968).Detailed description, beautiful print reproduction with colour plates.

BURMESE DAYS (Orwell, George; Penguin 1975).The best novel about 20th century Burma.

RANGOON

Rangoon has only been the capital of Burma since 1885. It was built by the British colonial power as an administrative city and harbour. Before this there was only a small village, Dagon, known largely due to the nearby Shwedagon Pagoda. The city of moss-covered, colonial style buildings is sure to leave you with a lasting impression. The streets run in straight lines on a checker board joining to form perfect right angles. It is impossible to get lost because the streets are numbered consecutively. First Street runs in a north-south direction in the west.

Rangoon, during British colonial rule, was almost an Indian city. Today it is dominated by Burmese influences with a sprinkling of Indians and Chinese. North of the train tracks, Rangoon spreads out. You'll find lots of green, many lakes, and the houses of the more affluent. Today about four million people live in the Burmese capital.

The city's landmark is the *SHWEDAGON PAGODA*, the most impressive pagoda in South East Asia. You should put aside lots of time for your visit. It is nicest in the late afternoon at sunset.

According to ancient legend, a pagoda was first built here in 585 BC. In 1446 it was expanded and enlarged. At the end of the 18th century it had achieved its present height of 107 m. The temple itself sits on a hill of 60 m, making the golden stupa easy to see from the air when you fly into Rangoon. Stairs lead to the top from all directions. It's important to remove your shoes before starting up - take them up with you.

The circumference of the golden pagoda is about 500 m. On a platform surrounding the shrine are a large number of smaller pagodas. Here the Burmese perform religious ceremonies. The Shwedagon is gold plated; its roof is made of many parasols raised one above the other and ornamented with diamonds, sapphires and rubies. Above these is a weather vane containing 2500 jewels. The crown is a ball of about 25 cm in diameter which is inlaid with over 4000 diamonds and other jewels.

If you have time to go through the temple in a relaxed manner, you'll enjoy yourself immensely. There are not many tourists, although every once in a while a group hurries by from one stupa to another. Few tourists try the long climb up from the west side. Walk from Prome Road directly towards the Shwedagon. Otherwise you can take bus 10 from the YMCA (Theinbyu Road).

Not far from the Shwedagon is the *MARTYRS' MAUSOLEUM* where Aung San and seven other national heroes are buried.

Two other pagodas worth seeing in the city are *SULE PAGODA* right in the city centre and *BOTATAUNG PAGODA* along the Rangoon River on Strand Road.

A beautiful reclining Buddha can be found in the *KYAUK HTAT GYI PAGODA* (Shwegondine Road, northeast of the Shwedagon). It is 71 m long making it longer than the reclining Buddha in Pegu.

Be sure to visit the *NATIONAL MUSEUM,* Phayre Street (Pansodan Street) right behind the Strand. Hotel. Open Sun to Thurs, 10:00 to 15:00 h and Sat 12:00 to 15:00 h. Here you can see the famous Lion's Throne of King Thibaw. At the end of the third Anglo-Burmese War the throne and many other valuable objects were robbed and taken to Britain. Not until the visit of Ne Win to London in 1964 were the treasures returned.

Check with Tourist Burma for dates of performances in the *STATE SCHOOL OF MUSIC AND DRAMA.* Public performances take place during the rainy season on weekends. You may also attend rehearsals during the week. The dance performances organized by Tourist Burma in the Inya Lake Hotel are very expensive.

HOTELS

The backpackers' meeting place is still the *YMCA,* 263 Mahabandoola Street, tel 72110. Double room* and triple**. You can pick up a lot of info plus the cafeteria isn't bad. You can also try the *GARDEN GUEST HOUSE* on Sule Pagoda Road, tel 71516. A good location right next to Tourist Burma and Thai Airways. Dormitory*, other rooms** - clean, but rooms are only sleeping cabinets with paperthin walls. Women can check out the *YWCA,* 119 Brooking Street, tel 72108, dormitory*, rooms**. More expensive is *DAGON**-***,* 256 Sule Pagoda Road, tel 71140. It used to be called Orient, is clean, and has some atmosphere.

The *THAMMADA***,* Signal Pagoda Road, tel 71499, is north of the train tracks. If you are in this price bracket, however, you belong in the *STRAND****,* 92 Strand Road, tel 77635. Absolutely recommended, both the Viceroy of India, Lord Curzon, and Somerset Maugham, have stayed here. Tourist groups are usually housed in the Soviet built *INYA LAKE HOTEL****.* Rooms are expensive even by international standards. In the former English Boat Club, Lake Rd., is the *KANDAWGYI HOTEL****,* tel 80412.

FOOD

Begin the day right with a good breakfast of pastry and tea (as much as you can drink!) in the *SHWE PA LAUNG CAFE* on Mahabandoola Street diagonally across from Tourist Burma. The *GOLDEN COIN* on the other side of the street is also good. Milkshakes and yoghurts at *NILAR WIN'S,* 377 Mahabandoola Street (between 37th and 38th St.). You can get Burmese 'mohinga' in Botataung Pagoda Road. Real Burmese atmosphere can be found in *RED DRAGON* on the small street right behind the Dagon Hotel. There are a number of Chinese restaurants. On Latha Street are: *SHANGHAI* (no. 159) or *MWEE KOON.* Others are on Sule Pagoda Rd. *(CHUNG WAH,* no. 162) and on 37th St. (*PALACE RESTAURANT,* no. 84). There's cheap Indian food in *YANNAN* on the corner of Sule Pagoda and Anawratha. Not far from there is *DAGON* - cool Mandalay Beer is available for 18 Kyat on the first floor at noon and in the evenings until 21:00 h. Good, though rather expensive Indian food is also served. An experience that is certain to be worth its price is a meal in the *STRAND* with its cold and inexpensive beer. The lobster is top quality - the perfect place to spend the last Kyat before flying out of the country.

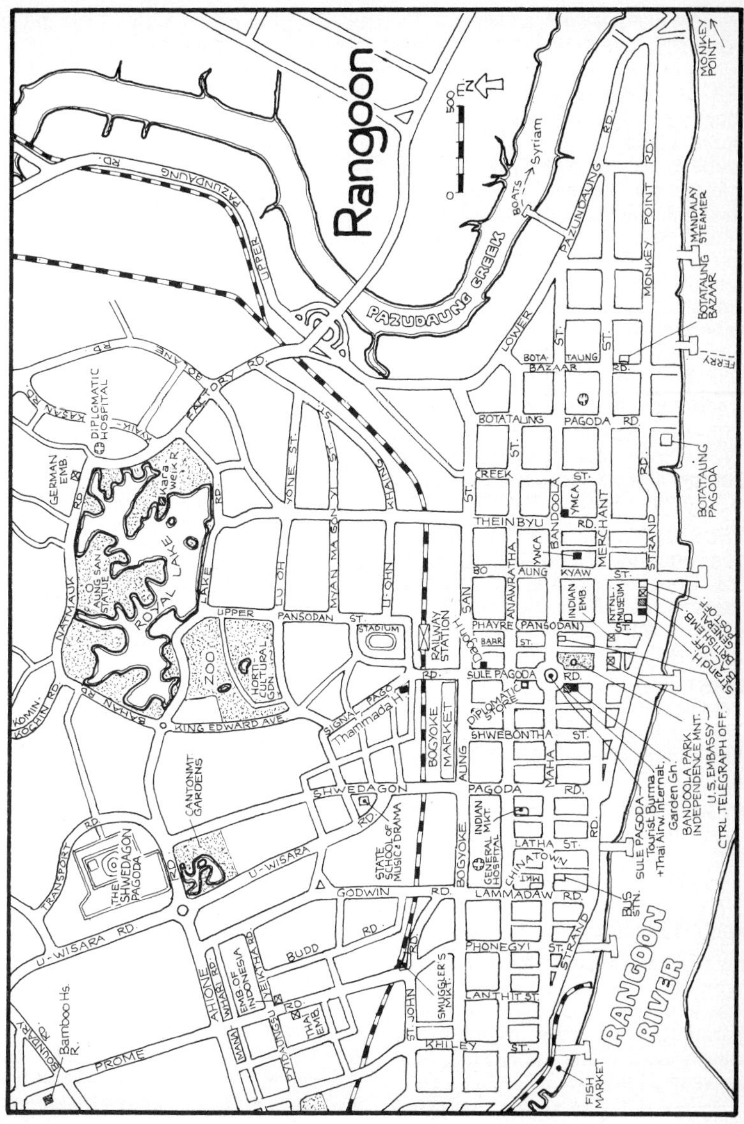

GENERAL INFORMATION

TOURIST INFORMATION - Tourist Burma, 77-79 Sule Pagoda Road, tel 78376, 75328, and 80321 is the country's state-run tourist office. This is the place to go for information, coupons, tickets, and Kyat (for US$). You can pay in cash, with traveller's cheques, and an American Express Card. Tourist Burma may well remind you of the all-encompassing Intourist in the USSR, but the people here are friendlier! The newest hotel and transportation prices are listed on a large board on the wall. Open Mon-Fri 9:30-20:00 h, Sat until 12:00 h.

GENERAL POST OFFICE - on the corner of Strand Road and Aung Kyaw Street. Also handles General Delivery (Poste restante). Open Mon to Fri 9:30 to 16:00 h, Sat till 12:30 h.

TELEPHONING - only in emergencies! From the Central Telegraph Office, Pansodan, corner of Mahabandoola Street. Daily from 8:00 h to 21:00 h. International calls cost approximately 70 Kyat for three minutes.

FIRST AID - foreigners should go to the Diplomatic Hospital near Royal Lake, tel 50149. The doctors can also take care of any visa problems if necessary.

NEWSPAPERS - there are two English language dailies in Rangoon: THE WORKING PEOPLE'S DAILY (circulation 20,000) and THE GUARDIAN (circulation 17,500). They are worth looking at.

ENTERTAINMENT - there is no real night life. The many films shown in the evenings (both Western and Burmese) are very popular and quickly sold out. Restaurants close between 21:00 and 22:00 h.

GETTING AROUND - ancient buses and small Mazdas that are not quite as old cost 1 Kyat. They drive certain routes regularly. A 2 km ride in a trishaw will cost you approx. 5 Kyat. If you wish to charter a small Mazda for a ride around town you will have to pay about 5 Kyat.

SHOPPING

There isn't a lot to buy in Burma, but perhaps that is a good reason for visiting some of the very charming markets in the city. The biggest market hall is the ***BOGYOKE MARKET*** on Bogyoke Aung San Street. Shan shoulder bags, jewelry, some antiques, lacquerware and longyis, the traditional wrap around dresses, can be found. Not far away on the corner of Prome Road and St.John St. is the ***SMUGGLER'S MARKET*** where you can find things smuggled across the unprotected border from Thailand. It's also interesting to take a tour through Rangoon's ***CHINATOWN,*** today mostly along Lanmadaw Street. A Chinese temple is on the corner of Strand Rd. More Chinese market life can be found in Lanmadaw St. between Mahabandoola and Anawrahta Street. Check out the ***INDIAN MARKET*** on 26th St. Today it's mostly a fruit and vegetable market with mountains of chillies and all kinds of spices. Like the other markets, it is best to go early.

There are some ***BOOKSTORES*** in Maung Talay Street where you can get rid of your old paperbacks (no. 35 Theingy Maw Bookstall). A tip for bookworms is Pagan Bookshop, no. 100, 37th Street.

LEAVING RANGOON

BY AIR

You can get to Mingaladon Airport by taxi: costs 60 Kyat. Or take bus 9 but you have to walk the last 1 km. In the city you can usually find a taxi in front of Tourist Burma. Because you have to show a ticket out of the country when applying for your visa you won't have to book an international flight. But it's important to confirm your departure flight on arrival in Rangoon. Addresses:

AIR FRANCE, 69 Sule Pagoda Road, tel 70736.
AEROFLOT, 18 Prome Road.
BANGLADESH BIMAN, 106/108 Phayre Road, tel 75882.
BURMA AIRWAYS CORPORATION (BAC), 104 Strand Road, tel 74566.
CAAC, 67 Prome Road.
INDIAN AIRLINES, 533 Merchant Street, tel 72410.
THAI AIRWAYS INTERNATIONAL, 441-45 Mahabandoola Street, tel 75936.

Domestic flights have to be booked with Tourist Burma. You can only buy one way tickets which means that you'll have to book your return flight to Rangoon at the place you are visiting. Remember that BAC planes often leave ahead of schedule! The airport tax in Rangoon is two dollars (15 Kyat). Prices: MANDALAY 545.-, HEHO 460.-, PAGAN 495.- Kyat.

BY TRAIN

Tickets again only through Tourist Burma to MANDALAY, THAZI and SHWENYAUNG! Get your tickets on the day of your arrival because the few tickets available for tourists are quickly sold out. To Mandalay costs 44 Kyat 2nd class, 110 Kyat 1st class, 138 Kyat upper class sleeper; Thazi 36 Kyat, 99 Kyat, 132 Kyat. Second

SHWEDAGON PAGODA , RANGOON

class passengers sit on reserved wooden benches. Upper class is well worth the money - especially on the night train. Two trains leave daily at 6:00 and 21:00 h to Mandalay. The ride takes about 14 hours. Food and drink can be found at train stations. If you have a water bottle, have it filled!

BY BUS

All buses must be booked through Tourist Burma. Hardly any leave from Rangoon at all these days. Should you be lucky enough to get a ticket for one of the extremely rare rides, you'll have to pay 121 Kyat to get to TAUNGGYI, 88 Kyat to MANDALAY.

DAYTRIPS AROUND RANGOON

The average visitor to Burma doesn't even think about using their valuable time to have a look outside Rangoon proper. If this isn't your first visit, it can be rewarding to check out lesser known but not far off places of interest.

PEGU

The old capital of the Mon Kingdom was founded in the 8th century. For almost a millenium Mon and Burmese were close rivals. Originally from the Red River Delta area (today Vietnam), they settled in the western part of Thailand and southern Burma. Their culture has been greatly influenced by India - Mon brought Buddhism to the Burmese. After a long military struggle, in which they were finally defeated in 1752, the Mon have lost practically their entire national identity.

From the river bridge you can see the 114 m high stupa of the SHWEMAW-DAW PAGODA. The main entrance is guarded by two giant red stone lions. To get to the pagodas on the other side of the river, it's best to take a taxi because of the distance and bad roads. KALYANI SIMA is an ordination hall built in the 15th century where young monks are still ordained. In any case, have a look at the huge reclining Buddha in the SHWETHALYAUNG PAGODA along with other pagodas.

Several trains a day leave for Pegu from Rangoon Station (costs 4 Kyat). Or if you take the night train from Mandalay to Rangoon, just get off in Pegu - you can carry on to Rangoon in the evening. Buses cost 5 Kyat and leave from 18th Street. The last bus returns at 16:30 h. You can also hire a taxi for an entire day in Rangoon (approx. 120 - 150 Kyat) and let it take you to Pegu. This way you will not have to organize any further transportation once there.

SYRIAM

The town is, like many villages in the Irrawaddy Delta, still largely populated by Indians, though many were deported following independence and in 1962. Since the 16th century, when Portugal built a fort here, Syriam had been a trading post for export goods. In 1756 the town was destroyed and later Rangoon took over its role. Only a few ruins are left. It's nice to take a bus from here (3 Kyat) to the KYAUK TAN PAGODA which is situated on a small island in the middle of the river. A boat to the island costs 1 Kyat. Take a ferry across the Pazundaung River to Syriam for 1 Kyat. It leaves hourly from the pier at the end of Mahabandoola Street.

TAUNGGYI

One of the most beautiful tours of the countryside is the ride up to Taunggyi, the capital of Shan State, lying at 1550 m in altitude on the edge of a plateau in the mountains. The city in the "Mountains (= Taung) the Great (= gyi)" has a population of about 150,000 people. You can still see something of the old colonial atmosphere north of the arrow-straight Main Street.

Still remaining is the *CATHEDRAL* next to the sports field and the houses along the slope. On hilltops all around are pagodas. Especially beautiful is the view you get from the (wish granting) *PAGODA* south of the city. You can see the town, the surrounding countryside, and, if the weather is right, on down to Lake Inle. Everything else worth seeing involves a good walk from the Main Street. Even if you aren't staying there, you should visit the park surrounding the *TAUNGGYI HOTEL* in the east of the city. Not far is the *MUSEUM* (often closed) with its ethnic and natural sciences exhibits of Burmese origin. The main attraction, however, is the *CENTRAL MARKET* where many tribal people - some from remote areas - sell their wares daily. The main market is every five days.

HOTELS

The old colonial hotel, *TAUNGGYI HOTEL***(*)* (formerly Strand Hotel) has huge rooms and hot water. In the lobby is the Tourist Burma office with friendly staff. All the other hotels, as far as they deserve the name, are constantly full. Try *SAN PYA*** (the best bet), *MAY KYU*** or *THI THANT GUESTHOUSE***. Good breakfast on the Main Street in the *SHWE TAIK CAFE,* good food in the *SHANGHAI.*

HOW TO GET THERE

The easiest way is the daily flight from Rangoon (460 Kyat) or Mandalay (205 Kyat), though they are generally booked up. The airport at HEHO is about 40 km away. For 15 Kyat you can take a Tourist Burma bus.

SHWENYAUNG is the end of the train line. A taxi-jeep the rest of the way costs 7 Kyat. Even faster, get off the train in THAZI (from Rangoon 10 hrs. and 55 Kyat) and take a completely overloaded pick-up up the mountains to Taunggyi (over 6 hours, 55 Kyat).

There are buses to and from PAGAN (120 Kyat) and MANDALAY (12 hrs., 143 Kyat). You'll drive through KALAW, an interesting town. Spend the night in KALAW HOTEL***.

DAYTRIPS AROUND TAUNGGYI

LAKE INLE

For 7 Kyat in a taxi-jeep (or with a chartered taxi for 110 Kyat) you can visit the 27 km distant Lake Inle. The famous lake (measuring 15 km in length and from 2 - 5 km in width) is in the middle of a huge, swampy area. It is rather difficult to find out what its actual size is, since the lake merges with large, reedy areas on all sides. About 80,000 Intha actually live on the lake. They grow tomatoes and other vegetables on floating islands made of reeds and live in stilt houses. In order to have their hands free to get through the reeds, they row their boats with their feet. More and more, however, the traditional 'leg-rowing' is being replaced by the sound of outboard motors.

YAWNGHWE on the northern end of the lake is the end station for taxis from Taunggyi. From here for 20 Kyat you can take a boat to the 'floating' town of YWAMA - they leave at 7:00 and 8:00 h. It's very expensive to charter a boat (about 300 Kyat). Spend the night in Yawnghwe at the INLE INN** or BAMBOO GUEST HOUSE*. Both outside of the village, but nice for those who like country living. Every year at the end of the rainy season there is a big rowing festival on the lake.

PAGAN

Burmese chronicles tell of the founding of this city in the 2nd century. It wasn't until 1044 under King Anawrahta that Pagan began to rise over the next 200 years into one of the greatest metropolises of the world at the time. King Narathihpati's diplomatic mistakes led to the destruction of the city by the forces of Kublai Khan in 1287.

Today in an area of about 30 km^2, there are about 5000 ruins, some of them restored. Pagan, the largest archaeological site in South East Asia, was unfortunately greatly damaged by an earthquake in 1975. The huge temple city is quite an experience - especially from the Thatbyinnyu at sunset. When you look out over the endless sea of pagodas, the red stone takes on a ruby red colouring from the setting sun, while the white ruins shine like silver.

IMPORTANT: Even if the temples are ruins, they are still holy for the Buddhists, and you have to take your shoes off!

At the very least try to check out the following sites which are all near the village:

ANANDA TEMPLE - This, the most highly venerated temple of Pagan, is also the best known. It was built around 1091. The central part of the temple has a perfectly square floor-plan, with each of the walls measuring 60 metres in length. All four walls have adjoining, gable-shaped entrances, giving the temple a perfect cross structure when seen from above. Six terraces, each one smaller than the preceding one, rise from the central structure. The square shikara on top of these merges with a Burmese stupa further up. The peak is made up of a gilded, umbrella-like structure. The building reaches a total height of 60 metres. There are four 10 metre statues in the interior, each depicting different incarnations of Buddha.

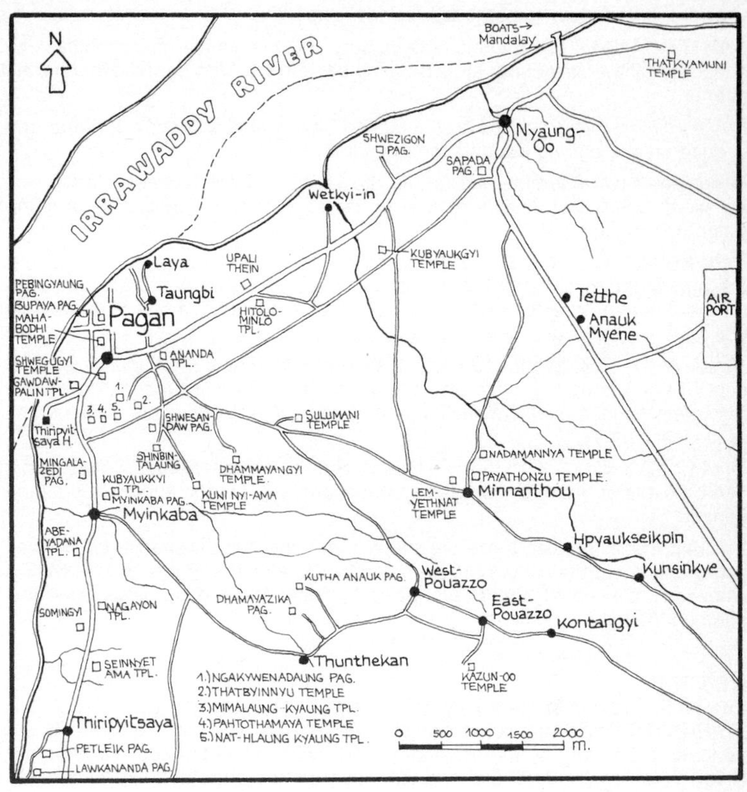

THATBYINNYU - This temple stands within the old town fortification and is the highest in all of Pagan (64 metres). It symbolizes the endless wisdom of Buddha. There is a Buddha statue gazing to the east in the upper part of the temple. The construction of the Thatbyinnyu began in the middle of the 12th century and marked the advent of the Burmese style of temple architecture, which is characterized by two cubes set on top of each other. The two cubes are frequently separated by three terraces, as is the case with the Thatbyinnyu. You will have a wonderful view from the uppermost terrace in the evenings.

GAWDAWPALIN - This temple was erected between 1174 and 1178. The temple grounds were almost entirely destroyed in the 1975 earthquake. It was modeled after the Ananda temple more than any other building in Pagan. The view of the Irrawaddy from the top terrace is beautiful.

PAHTOTHANAYA - Built in the 10th century, this temple was still strongly influenced by Mon architecture. Murals dating back to the Mon period decorate the interior.

MAHABODHI - This pagoda was modeled after an Indian temple in Bihar and is quite unique among Pagan's temple ruins.

There are several temple grounds in the south and southeast of Pagan that are worth a visit, but you'd be better off travelling to these by bicycle or some other form of transport.

SHWESANDAW - The cylindrical stupa and the five terraces leading up to it are a most impressive sight. A hair of Buddha's, seized by King Anawratha after the defeat of the Mon in 1057, is said to be embedded in one of the temple walls.

SULAMANI - The layout and general style of this temple are vaguely reminiscent of the Thatbyinnyu. The many murals are much more recent, however - they were painted over the original temple murals by monks during the course of the last century.

DHAMMAYANGYI - Only the vestibules and the outer terraces of this temple can be explored - the interior was probably bricked up soon after the construction.

Besides these temples there are many other sites all around Pagan. A welcome change to the culture program can be found in the village of MYINKABA where you can watch women producing lacquerware. A good place is the first shop on the right (U Tin Aye).

HOTELS

The ac-bungalows of the luxury hotel *THIRIPYITSAYA***** are set in a quiet, peaceful area, right by the Irrawaddy River. If you can't afford to spend the night here, you can at least come and enjoy a cool Mandalay Beer in the evenings. You can exchange money here, too. All other hotels can be found on the main road of new Pagan: The *COOPERATIVE INN**, diagonally across from the new museum, has a good restaurant and serves Mandalay Beer in the evenings. The *ZARNEE REST HOUSE** is at the road branching off to the new paved road. Along the main road you'll find the *MOE MOE HOTEL*, AUNG THA HAYA GUEST HOUSE*, MIN CHAN MYEI GUEST HOUSE*, BURMA REST HOUSE**, and the *MYA THI DA HOTEL** - all of the above charge the same rates and have similar furnishings. The *IRRA IN*** is on the road leading to the Irrawaddy - peaceful, clean, friendly people.

FOOD

Travellers like hanging out at the *NATION RESTAURANT*, at the entrance of town, opposite Tourist Burma. Meals cost between 5 and 15 Kyat, good yoghurts are available. The vegetarian *MARIE MAN* restaurant is next door. The Burmese and Chinese dishes served at the *MAY YADANA* across the road are better, though. The place is owned by a friendly woman. The food served at the *CO-OPERATIVE INN* is also quite good. Excellent Burmese and Chinese food, reasonably priced and served by friendly people, is available at the *AYE YAKETHAR YAR* near the Irra Inn. If you've got a couple of Kyat to spare, why not treat yourself to a multi-course lunch at the *THIRIPYIT-SAYA*.

GENERAL INFORMATION

TOURIST BURMA - by the entrance of town, open daily from 8:00-20:00 h. You can also exchange money here.

NEW MUSEUM - well worth a visit, open 9:00-16:30 h except Mon & Fri.

ART GUIDE - you should definitely buy the *Pictorial Guide to Pagan* for 40 Kyat (30 Kyat if you bargain well).

GETTING AROUND - 4-5 people can get together and rent a horse-drawn carriage, a charming way to see more in the little time available. The cost is 10-20 Kyat an hour or about 60 Kyat for the entire day. Bicycles cost 10-15 Kyat a day, jeeps approx. 30 Kyat per hour. A ride to Nyaung Oo in a carriage or a trishaw will cost you 15 Kyat.

LACQUERWARE SCHOOL - diagonally across from the Irra Inn. Open until 16:30 h daily. You can buy nice pieces of lacquerware opposite the Ananda temple.

LEAVING PAGAN

BY PLANE

The small Pagan airfield lies by the road leading to Kyaukpadaung from Nyaung Oo. Every now and then BAC sends down a small mini-bus free of charge. Taxis cost 10 Kyat. There is a daily flight to MANDALAY (30 minutes, 152 Kyat) and RANGOON (1 hour, 445 Kyat). You will have to fly via Mandalay if you wish to get to HEHO (304 Kyat).

BY BUS / TAXI-JEEP / PICK-UP

All buses have to be booked through Tourist Burma. The fares have to be entered on your Money Declaration Form. Buses to TAUNGGYI cost 110 Kyat, to MANDALAY 66 Kyat. Departure at 3:30 h in the morning and 11:00 h, arrival (with a little luck) at 14:00 and 21:30 h.

In order to catch the train from Mandalay to Rangoon in THAZI, you'll have to get one of the Thazi-bound pick-ups that stand in front of Tourist Burma and leave at around 2:00 h in the morning and 13:30 h. The ride will cost you 55 Kyat per person. At least 10 people have to come along, and the drivers usually even manage to squeeze 20 people or more into one car. There is no other way you can possibly be in Thazi on time for the morning train.

If you're forced to take public transport to Thazi or Mandalay because the morning pick-up is booked up weeks in advance, here's the way to do it (we have been told that this method is now illegal!?): Catch one of the ancient, heavily loaded trucks to NYAUNG OO at 6:00 h (1 Kyat). From here catch a similar truck to KYAUK-PADAUNG (5 Kyat) at 7:00 h. From here you can catch a pick-up to THAZI or MANDALAY (25 Kyat).

The last Mandalay-bound pick-up leaves around 16:00 h. The trip will take you 10-12 hours. Be prepared for 30 - 40 fellow travellers.

MANDALAY

650 km north of Rangoon, a good day's ride by train, is one of the old capitals of Burma. The country was ruled from here in the years 1857 - 1885. King Mindon fulfilled an ancient prophecy: When Buddha and his disciple Ananda visited the present day Mandalay Hill, the enlightened predicted that in the year 2400 of his religion (1857) a great city would be founded at the foot of the holy hill. The city has maintained even today its own fascinating character. Horse carts, jeeps, old buses, and trishaws make up public transport. Life on the Irrawaddy goes on as it did in the days of Kipling. Women and girls do laundry in the river as children dive into the mud-brown water to cool off. Paddle-wheel riverboats steam by majestically. In 1984 a huge fire destroyed almost all of the buildings right in the city.

It's worth while to spend several days in Mandalay. There is a lot to see in the surrounding area, the mountain town Maymyo is a wonderful place to spend the night.

On your first evening take a walk up *MANDALAY HILL* - it's best not to try during the heat of the day. There are two ways to get up. The easiest is to take bus no 5 from Mandalay Hotel direct to the main stairway. The second takes you past the Mandalay Palace through a small village to the west side of the hill. You won't be able to miss the covered stairs. From the top you have a tremendous view of the Shan State mountains in the east and the setting sun across the Irrawaddy to the west.

When climbing Mandalay Hill, visit the *KUTHODAW PAGODA* next to the southern stairs. In the 729 small pagodas spread around the larger pagoda are marble plates on which the teachings of Buddha are engraved. Nearby are several other temples.

MANDALAY PALACE was completely destroyed in 1945 just before the end of the war. King Mindon had it built of wood - only the thick surrounding walls were of stone. All together it formed a square 1600 m (about one mile) on each side. A part of it is used by the army today, and you can view the remains of the palace only when accompanied by members of the military. In the middle is a wooden model of the way it used to look.

In the southern part of the city, on the road to Ava, stands the second holiest Pagoda in Burma (after the Shwedagon) - the *ARAKAN PAGODA,* sometimes also known as Maha Muni. A four metre high Buddha is covered with repeated layers of gold plating. In the courtyard there is a gong weighing five tons.

The huge covered *ZEGYO MARKET* in the centre of the city doesn't have a large selection of goods, but the atmosphere makes it worth a long visit. The rubies and sapphires for sale are usually third class, though Burma is one of the most important jewel producers in the world. The best stones are exported or sold in the Diplomatic Store in Rangoon for dollars. Starting at 18:00 h near the Man Sandawin (80th Street / 31st Road) is the *NIGHT MARKET,* one of the few places in the world where potential customers are asked what they have for sale.

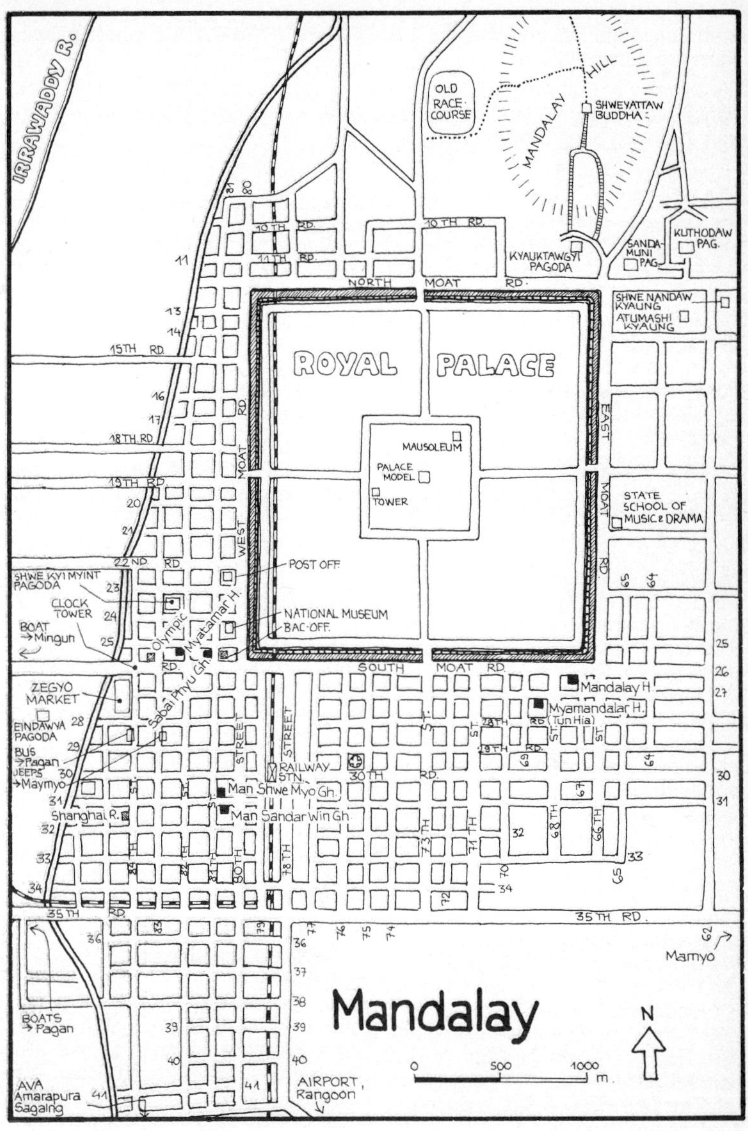
IRRAWADDY R.
OLD RACE COURSE
MANDALAY HILL
SHWEYATTAW BUDDHA
10TH RD.
11TH RD.
KYAUKTAWGYI PAGODA
SANDAMUNI PAG.
KUTHODAW PAG.
NORTH MOAT RD.
SHWE NANDAW KYAUNG
ATUMASHI KYAUNG
15TH RD.
ROYAL PALACE
18TH RD.
19TH RD.
22ND RD.
MAUSOLEUM
PALACE MODEL
TOWER
WEST MOAT RD.
EAST MOAT RD.
STATE SCHOOL OF MUSIC & DRAMA
POST OFF.
NATIONAL MUSEUM
BAC OFF.
SHWE KYI MYINT PAGODA
CLOCK TOWER
BOAT → Mingun
Olympic
Myatamar H.
Sabai Phyu Gh.
SOUTH MOAT RD.
Mandalay H.
Myamandalar H. (Tun Hia)
ZEGYO MARKET
EINDAWYA PAGODA
BUS → Pagan
JEEPS → Maymyo
RAILWAY STN.
30TH RD.
28TH RD.
29TH RD.
Man Shwe Myo Gh.
Man Sandar Win Gh.
Shanghai R.
35TH RD.
Mamyo
BOATS → Pagan
AVA Amarapura Sagaing
AIRPORT, Rangoon
Mandalay
0 500 1000 m
N

From Zegyo Market, take bus no. 2 down to the *IRRAWADDY* where evening walks are especially nice.

The Ministry of Culture in Mandalay has set up an *ACADEMY OF FINE ARTS* (dance presentations) east of the palace wall and the old *MUSEUM* with its library has also been moved here.

HOTELS

The *MANDALAY*****, on the corner of 26th Road / 3rd Street, is the top hotel in town. Clean, quiet, and next to the palace, ac-rooms cost around US$ 20. Here you will also find the Tourist Burma office, the only place in town where you can legally exchange money and buy tickets. You'll get better value at the *MYA MANDALAR**** (formerly the Tun Hla), just around the corner. Rooms of various standards are offered, most of them are frequently booked, however. The *SABAI PHYU RESTHOUSE**** is on 81st Street, between 25th and 26th Road. You will have a good view of the entire city from the upper-floor rooms and the penthouse of the large, concrete building. You will find a number of cheaper hotels in town, all of them **: *MAN SANDAR WIN,* no. 149, 31st Road, between 80th and 81st Streets - friendly people; *MAN SHWEMYO,* no. 142, is opposite, rather tacky, no mosquito nets; the *AUNG TI YI GUESTHOUSE* is on 31st Road, near 80th Street. We would not recommend the *SHWE GONE* on 35th Rd., between 82nd and 83rd Streets.

FOOD

Ignore the shabby exterior of the *SHANGHAI,* no. 172, 84th Street - good Chinese food is served here. The same can be said of the *SHWE WAH,* 80th Street, between 32nd and 33rd Road. You will find the *MANN RESTAURANT* near the Zegyo Market. The *OLYMPIC CAFE* is opposite. Tea, cakes, and filled pastries are served. Fruit juices, ice cream and milkshakes are available at the *NYLON ICE CREAM BAR* right next door. You will find the *MIN MIN RESTAURANT,* good Chinese food, just a couple of houses further on, between 26th and 27th Roads. The Chinese food served at the *KAINKYI* on 29th Rd., between 83rd and 84th Streets, is also good.

GENERAL INFORMATION

TOURIST BURMA - the office is in the luxurious Mandalay Hotel. Information and coupons are available from 8:00-20:00 h daily, tickets are only sold until 14:00 h.

GETTING AROUND - public buses cost between 20 Pyas and 1 Kyat. No. 1 goes to the Maha Muni Pagoda; no. 2 to the landing-place for Mingun; no. 4 and 5 to Mandalay Hill. A short ride through town in a trishaw may cost up to 5 Kyat, longer rides cost up to 15 Kyat. A complete city-tour will cost you around 40 Kyat. Horse-drawn carriages (tongas) may cost up to 20 Kyat, depending on the distance. A city tour to all the important sights will cost you approx. 40 Kyat. A day-tour to Sagaing / Amarapura in a taxi costs 200 Kyat.

LEAVING MANDALAY

BY AIR

You will find the BAC office on the corner of 25th Road / 80th Street. Free BAC buses travel to and from the airport from here. You can also catch the bus 11 for 50 Pyas. On arrival in Mandalay, immediately book the ticket for your next destination

(PAGAN 195, HEHO 205, RANGOON 545 Kyat).

BY TRAIN

Again, tickets have to be bought at Tourist Burma. Trains to RANGOON leave at 7:00 and 18:15 h (650 km, 1st class 110 Kyat, 2nd class 44 Kyat, Upper Class Sleeper 138 Kyat). We would suggest taking a bus if you're headed to TAUNGGYI or PAGAN.

BY BUS / TAXI-JEEP / PICK-UP

Buses and pick-ups leave for PAGAN at 4:00 h in the morning (66 Kyat). Leave early enough - some rickshaw drivers are slow on purpose. The first bus to TAUNGGYI leaves at 4:30 h (143 Kyat). Toyota pick-ups need approx. 8 hours and leave Mandalay at 5:30, 8:00, and 10:00 hours. For information go to the Taunggyi Booking Office next to the Olympic Cafe.

BY RIVERBOAT

A Tourist Burma steamboat leaves the 35th Street landing place at 5:00 h in the morning every Thur and Sun. It is meant to arrive in NYAUNG OO by 17:30 h (!!) - deck ticket 120 Kyat, cabin 150 Kyat including transfer, breakfast, and lunch. You will be separated from the local passengers, but it is a pleasant trip nevertheless. There is also a daily steamboat, but tourists are allegedly (?!) not allowed to travel on it anymore - check up on this! Women selling fruit, eggs, and drinks come on board whenever the boat drops anchor along the way. 'White' tourists will find themselves besieged by women with coloured blankets, who are out to trade. The Irrawaddy's water-level sinks dramatically during the weeks prior to the monsoon. It takes hours and sometimes even days for the trip to continue once the ship has run aground on a sandbank, something which happens quite frequently. We would not recommend doing the trip between February and June if you do not have much time to spare.

DAY TRIPS AROUND MANDALAY

AMARAPURA

Bus 8 leaves from the market to Amarapura and Ava. Amarapura is about 12 km south of Mandalay and was capital of Burma from 1782 to 1857. Several pagodas, remains of walls and some ruins can be seen today, though badly damaged by earthquakes. The wooden U BEIN BRIDGE to the south is 1200 m and spans the TAUNGTHAMAN LAKE which can hardly be seen just before monsoon season. The village elder U Bein had the bridge built two hundred years ago with the wood from the old palace in Ava. On the other side is the KYAUKTAWGYI PAGODA erected in 1847 on a model of the Ananda Pagoda in Pagan. Villages nearby are famous today for their weaving and the village of KYI TUN KHAT for its production of bronze Buddha statues.

AVA

Ava became Burma's Royal city after the destruction of Pagan. Amarapura took over this role in 1782. Ava was also the name given to Burma by the Europeans until well into the last century. It is located on the river-bank, near the point at which the MYITNGE RIVER merges with the Irrawaddy. Take bus no. 8 from the market in Mandalay to the Ava-bridge (20 km), then walk down to the Myitnge river ferry. Horse-drawn carriages await you on the opposite bank. Ever since the 1930s, this has been the only bridge to cross the Irrawaddy river. Two of its 16 arches were destroyed by British troops during World War II, and it was almost 10 years before the bridge could be re-opened to traffic and the general public in 1954. The MAHA AUNGMYE BONZAN MONASTERY with its old tamarind trees and the northern part of the former CITY WALL is definitely worth a visit. You will find the so-called 'leaning tower of Ava', the NANMYIN TOWER, at the NORTHERN ENTRANCE. The upper parts of the tower once collapsed and the foundation subsequently sank due to an earthquake.

SAGAING

lies on the west side of the Irrawaddy where the only road bridge from Ava across the river ends. For 50 years (1315 - 1356) Sagaing had its turn as the capital of Burma. The hills are blanketed with small pagodas. About a kilometre to the west in the village of YWATAUNG you can watch silversmiths at work. Ten kilometres further west is the KAUNG MU DAW PAGODA.

MINGUN

is about 12 km north of Mandalay. Get a boat for 2.50 Kyat at the end of 26th St., takes an hour upstream. The last boat returns at 15:00 h. Check out the MINGUN PAGODA. At one time it was supposed to be made into the biggest temple complex in the world as you can see from the model 600 m to the south. The 90 ton bell is the second largest in the world. Also see the HSINBIUME PAGODA, 150 m north of the landing place. Tourist Burma occasionally organizes excursion boat-rides, costs 25 Kyat per person.

MAYMYO

This hill station built by the British, with its sleepy colonial atmosphere, lies 900 m above Mandalay. The clock tower on the main road still tolls out the hour with the sound of Big Ben. Another attraction is the MORNING MARKET. Besides the Shan, Lahu, Lisu, people from other hilltribes come to sell their products. At the lower end of the market you can find good strawberry milkshakes during harvest time (Jan to March). In the cool mountain climate all kinds of vegetables flourish. Check out the 175 hectare BOTANICAL GARDENS and the many WATERFALLS to be found up to 24 km from the city.

Use a horsecart for 15 Kyat an hour to get around the town. From Mandalay (29th St.) take a jeep for 22 Kyat (2 hrs.). The train ride is more romantic and costs half as much, but, due to the zigzagging, takes twice as long; leaves at 5:00 h. Be at the station before 4:00 h in order to be sure of a ticket.

Try a night in the MAYMYO RESTHOUSE** (formerly Candacraig). Good food, you sit around evenings in front of a nice fireplace. NAN MYAING HOTEL*** is quite new. Food is good and cheap in SHANGHAI.

Beyond Maymyo (which gets its name from Colonel May of the 5th Bengal Infantry Regiment) begins the area controlled by the rebels or insurgents as they are known officially. Only 300 km away is LASHIO, the most important town in the northern Shan States, unfortunately off limits for tourists. If you go by rail, the train will be full of smuggled goods en route to and from Lashio. It is a good opportunity to meet Burmese and other nationalities.

INDONESIA

13,677 islands spread over both sides of the equator are just waiting to be discovered. More than half are unpopulated, while islands with impassable jungles such as Sumatra, Kalimantan, and Irian Jaya have many ethnic groups.

On the world's second biggest island live stone age people today. Formerly called New Guinea, the western half belongs to Indonesia. The high civilizations of Java and Bali give evidence of the Hindu and Buddhist influences which reached the islands in the first millenium AD through trade with India.

A country full of contrasts! Take Java, the most heavily populated island in the world. With one village pressing against another, no fertile soil can be allowed to go untended. Elsewhere are unpopulated forests and swamps that are only occasionally crossed by hunters and gatherers. Distances are tremendous. The east to west span from the Asian continent to Australia (Sabang - Merauke) covers 5,120 km.

The tourist industry is not as developed as in Thailand or Malaysia. There are no good roads and there are few international hotels offering the comforts and amenities that tourists have come to expect. Exceptions are Java, Bali, and to a certain extent the tourist centres of North Sumatra, West Sumatra and South Sulawesi. Those who travel elsewhere should have lots of time and some knowledge of the national language, Bahasa Indonesia.

The language, which evolved from High Malay, is taught in all the schools. There are 250 different local languages and several hundred different dialects. The central government hopes that the use of a national language will help unite a culturally and geographically divided population.

You'll notice Indonesia's diversity even when travelling through a small area. If you want to get to know one of the larger islands, you'll need a month or more. Visiting Indonesia in three weeks is like doing Europe in seven days.

VISA

To visit Indonesia all nationalities (except people from ASEAN countries) need a ***PASSPORT*** that won't expire within a half year and a ***DEPARTURE TICKET*** by air or sea.

On a Tourist Pass, which is stamped into your passport upon arrival, you can stay up to two months, if you meet the following criteria:

you are American, Australian, British, Canadian, New Zealander, Austrian, Belgian, Danish, Dutch, Finnish, French, German, Greek, Icelandic, Italian, Japanese, Luxemburger, Norwegian, South Korean, Spanish, Swedish, Swiss, or the citizen of an ASEAN country.

Additionally, you must arrive or depart at one of the following points: Medan Harbour or Airport, Pakanbaru Airport, Padang Airport (Sumatra), Batu Besar Airport or Batu Ambar Harbour (Batam), Cengkareng Airport and Tanjung

Priok Harbour (Jakarta), Surabaya Harbour, Denpasar Airport and Benoa Harbour or Padang Bai Harbour (Bali), Manado Airport and Harbour (North Sulawesi), Ambon Airport and Harbour (the Moluccas), Biak Airport (Irian Jaya), Pontianak Airport, Kupang Airport.

TOURIST VISA

If you want to enter or exit at another point, you will have to apply in advance for a visa at an Indonesian consulate. The visa is valid for 30 days and can be extended once for two weeks. There is no charge for West Germans. An extension costs 1150 Rp.

VISITOR'S VISA, WORKING VISA, EDUCATION VISA

These are given out only in special cases. You must have an influential host or a special reason for travel (i.e. research project, family reasons, etc.). You have to apply in advance in your home country for these visas which you can extend up to six months once you're in Indonesia.

VISA EXTENSIONS

You might get an extension of your Visitor's Visa at all immigration offices (kantor imigrasi), but it takes two days to a week so apply early. There are no extensions on the 60-day Tourist Visa. As in other countries, treat the authorities with care (be polite and neatly dressed) so that they don't get an urge to prove their authority. Cost is US$25, Germans no charge.

The extension of a Visitor's, Working, or Education Visa for more than three months costs a minimum of 30,000 Rp per extension. A stay for more than six months is even more expensive; then foreigners, like Indonesians, are obliged to pay an exit tax of 250,000 Rp per person (also applies to children).

If your visa expires, don't overstay more than three days. Otherwise you'll have trouble when departing and face a fine set by a border official. Usually they will ignore an overstay of up to three days, especially if you leave by ship. If you can prove your plane is overbooked, then you can get a few days' extension from the immigration office.

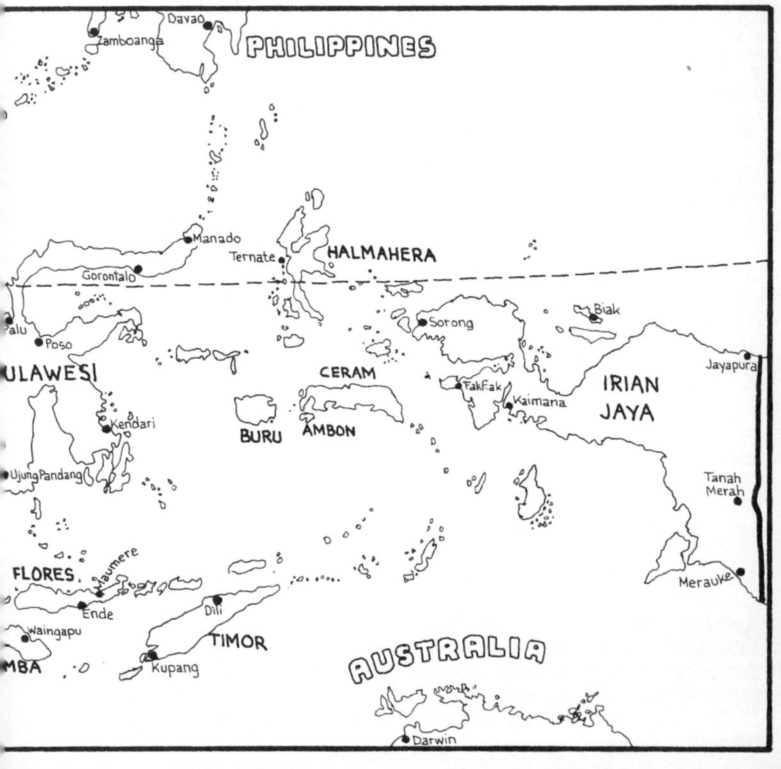

INDONESIAN EMBASSIES IN NEIGHBOURING COUNTRIES

SINGAPORE, 7 Chatsworth Road, tel 7377422.
MALAYSIA, 233 Jl.Tun Razak, Kuala Lumpur, tel 2421011; Penang, 467 Jl.Burmah, tel 25162. Other consulates in: Kuching, Kota Kinabalu and Tawau.
THAILAND, 600 Petchburi Rd. Bangkok, tel 2523135/40.
PHILIPPINES, Salcedo Street, Manila, tel 855061/68.
AUSTRALIA, 8 Darwin Avenue, Yarralumla, Canberra, tel 733222. Other consulates in: Darwin, Melbourne and Sydney.
PAPUA NEW GUINEA, Sir John Guisa Drive 6, Sec 410 Lot 182, Baroko, Port Moresby, tel 253116/18.

EMBASSIES AND CONSULATES IN INDONESIA

AUSTRALIA, 15 Jl.Thamrin, Jakarta, tel 350511, 323109.
CANADA, 4th Floor, Wisma Metropolitan, Jl.Jend.Sudirman, tel 584039.
UK, 75 Jl.Thamrin, Jakarta, tel 330904. Consulate: MEDAN.
NEW ZEALAND, 41 Jl.Diponegoro, Menteng, Jakarta, tel 357924/5.
UNITED STATES, 5 Jl.Medan Merdeka Selatan, Jakarta, tel 360360. Consulates in: SURABAYA and MEDAN.

EMBASSIES OF NEIGHBOURING COUNTRIES IN INDONESIA

BURMA, Jl.Agus Salim 109, tel 320440.
MALAYSIA, Jl.Iman Bonjol 17, tel 332846. Consulate in MEDAN.
PAPUA NEW GUINEA, , Jl.Jend.Sudirman, Panin Bank Centre, tel 711218.
PHILIPPINES, Jl.Iman Bonjol 6-8, Jakarta, tel 348917. Consulates in MANADO, TARAKAN and SURABAYA.
SINGAPORE, Jl.Proklamasi 23, tel 348761. Consulate in MEDAN.
THAILAND, Jl.Iman Bonjol 74, tel 343762.

IF YOUR VISA HAS EXPIRED, BUT YOU STILL WANT TO TRAVEL IN INDONESIA, then take the cheapest route to a neighbouring country, and apply for a new visa there, or return via a visa free port. Up to now there have been no problems and in three days you'll be able to return. Here are the most important routes out:

MEDAN - PENANG *(by air or by ship): Visafree entry-exit point.*
PAKANBARU - MALACCA *(by air): Visafree entry-exit point.*
PAKANBARU - SINGAPORE *(by air): Visafree entry-exit point.*
DUMAI - MALACCA *(by ship): Visa needed (Singapore / KL)*
PAKANBARU - TANJUNG PINANG - BATAM - SINGAPORE *(by ship): When entering or leaving via Batam no visa needed.*
DENPASAR / JAKARTA - SINGAPORE *(by air): Visafree entry-exit point.*
PONTIANAK - KUCHING *(by air): Visa needed (Singapore / KL / Kuching)*
PONTIANAK - SINGAPORE *(by air): Visafree entry-exit point.*
TARAKAN - TAWAU *(by air)* ***- KOTA KINABALU*** *(overland): Visa needed. Consulate in KK: Coastal Road, Karamunsing, tel 54245, 54459 and in Tawau, Wisma Indonesia.*
TARAKAN - ZAMBOANGA - DAVAO *(by air): Visa needed. Consulate in Elolend Subdivision Matina, Davao, tel 78480/86.*
MANADO - GUAM *(by air): Visafree entry- exit point.*
JAYAPURA - WEWAK - PORT MORESBY *(by air): Visa needed. Consulate in Port Moresby (address see above)*
BIAK - HONOLULU *(by air): Visafree entry-exit point.*
DENPASAR - DARWIN *(by air): Visafree entry-exit point.*
KUPANG - DARWIN *(by air): Visafree entry-exit point.*

CLIMATE & TRAVEL SEASONS

Due to its geographical location on both sides of the equator and to its many islands, Indonesia has a pronounced tropical climate. The monsoon winds bring dry air to almost all land areas from June to September and rain from December to March. The heaviest rainfall and highest humidity is encountered in December and January.

Temperatures range in the lowlands from 22°C to 34°C though it's often hotter in the early afternoon. More comfortable are the highlands where midday temperatures rarely exceed 30°C. In the evening the mercury can fall quickly, quite often below 5°C on the Bromo or Dieng Plateau. Snow, however is only found on the highest mountains of Irian Jaya. Keep in mind that every island has its own specific weather system and climate; here's a quick look:

SUMATRA: Governed by the Southwest Monsoon which brings lots of rain to the southwestern coast and mountains. Most rain falls in the south of the island making many roads impassable especially in November and December. The further north you go, the earlier the rainy season begins - Palembang 404 mm in December, Padang 518 mm in November, Medan 259 mm in October. Between Medan and Padang you'll find another (not as intensive) rainy season in April and May. In the lowlands the temperature ranges between 22°C and 31°C. On Lake Toba expect 16°C to 26°C.

JAVA: From November to March the west and northwest winds bring heavy rainfall to the entire island - Jakarta 300 mm in January and February, Bandung 230 mm in March and April, Surabaya 310 mm in January. Except in the southwest, there is hardly any rain during the northern summer - the farther east you go, the more pronounced the dry season. The temperature range year round varies little: in Jakarta 24°C at 13:00 h. On volcanoes over 1500 m high you'll see some frost at night. Keep this in mind when hiking on the Dieng and Ijen Plateau.

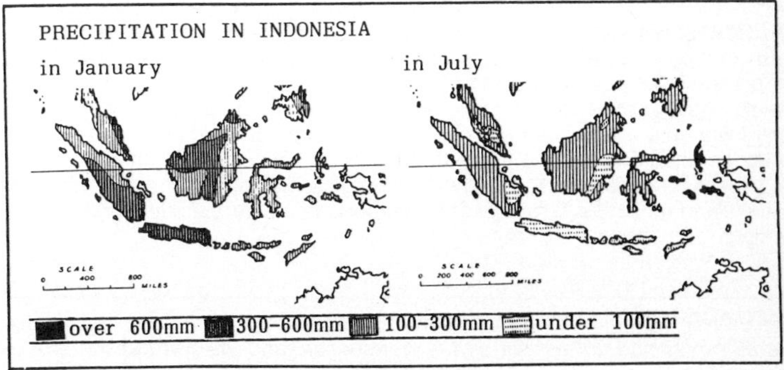

BALI: The dry season is from April to October. During this period expect less than six days of rain per month. December and January have the most rain but you won't stay dry in February and March. You'll see a bit of the sun, however. It's not English weather!

NUSA TENGGARA: The dry season from July till October is much more pronounced on these islands than in the rest of Indonesia. In Timor the average monthly rainfall in August and September is only 3 mm - in Central Europe it's 45 mm. It really gets hot at the end of the dry season - in Kupang 23°C at night and 33°C at midday, though it will also go up to 38°C in the shade at times. Tropical cyclones hit the furthest southeasterly island of Timor three to five times a year. All the other islands are closer to the equator leaving them out of the usual range of cyclones.

MOLUCCAS: There is heavy rain on the Central and Southeast Moluccas between May and August. In Ambon you can expect as much rain in 24 hours as experienced in several months in northern temperate climates. The Northern Moluccas conversely experience the heaviest rains during the northern winter. The temperature ranges year round between 24°C and 31°C. During the rainy season many scheduled flights are cancelled and ships are hindered from moving about the islands.

SULAWESI: Due to its unusual shape and position on the equator, Sulawesi is influenced by several different wind currents. The rainy season changes depending on coastal position, predominant winds, and protective mountains. In northern and southern areas, the most rain falls during the northern winter. Ujung Pandang has a distinct dry season during the northern summer but extremely heavy rainfall from December to March: January 686 mm. Parts of the central region have several rainy seasons per year. The temperatures in the centre are somewhat higher than on the coast where they range from 23°C to 30°C.

KALIMANTAN: While the northern part of the island is influenced by the winds of the northern hemisphere, the regions south of the equator experience the predominant southeast winds of summer and the northwest winds during winter. There are no fixed rainy seasons. The whole year round it's hot and humid with lots of rain. Get out your rain things about midday when the rising hot air has had a chance to mix with the cool air above. Over 3000 mm of rain per year is quite common - Central Europe gets 700 mm. In the southern part of the island more rain falls between October and March than during the rest of the year.

***SEASONS**: The only difference between the seasons is that the hot season is a bit hotter and not as wet as the wet season, and the wet season is a bit wetter and not as hot as the hot season.*

FESTIVALS AND HOLIDAYS

In this diverse island country containing so many cultures, there are many, many holidays. It's impossible to list all the regional, religious, and familial holidays. Popular are the temple festivals on Bali or the wayang performances in Java where the ancient story of the epic poem Ramayana is brought to life with puppets, shadow figures, or masked characters.

At the bull races on Madura, cock fights on Bali, and bull fights on Sumatra, sporting competition and fun often take second place to the large sums of money being gambled. Often these competitions are connected to religious festivals.

Indonesians honour many gods. Offerings are made from cliffs to the Goddess of the Sea and from the craters of active volcanoes to the Gods of Fire. The birthdays of Mohammed and Christ are also celebrated. Hundreds of supernatural beings dominate life in the jungles, villages, and cities.

A good source of information is the annual ***CALENDAR OF EVENTS*** published by the General Director for Tourism in the Ministry of Transport, Communication and Tourism. You can pick it up before your trip at the tourist office in your home country (Sydney, Singapore, Tokyo, San Francisco, Frankfurt). Or if you are lucky, you might find it in Indonesia at one of the regional tourist offices. A complete list of Balinese festivals and holidays can be found at the tourist office there. You can get more info about the bull races on Madura at the office in Surabaya and about the Ramayana productions in Yogyakarta. The dates change from year to year, so check at a tourist office for exact dates.

Our ***western calendar*** with 365 days governs the official and economic year, but most holidays are determined by the Islamic ***lunar calendar*** which contains somewhat fewer days. In addition the Batak on Sumatra and the Balinese both have their own individual calendars. In Bali one year has only 210 days, so temple festivals are often celebrated twice in one of our years.

We list the regional festivals in the appropriate chapters. Here are the major national holidays:

STATE HOLIDAYS

On January 1, ***NEW YEAR*** is celebrated with firework displays in Jakarta, processions and dances in North Sulawesi, and mainly with eating and drinking in Christian regions.

On August 17, ***INDEPENDENCE DAY***, the liberation of Indonesia from the Dutch, is observed. In Banjarmasin (Kalimantan), Palembang (Sumatra) and in other towns of West Sumatra boat races take place. Every village organizes sporting events, colourful processions, puppet and other traditional performances - *dari Irian Jaya ke Sumatra, dari Timor ke Sulawesi.*

On December 25, ***CHRISTMAS*** is celebrated - mainly in the centres of tourism and Christian regions (Minahasa, Toraja, Batak, Flores).

KARTINI DAY is a kind of Indonesian Mother's Day which is primarily celebrated on Java. Raden Kartini was the first woman who openly demanded women's rights. Because of her good education, received as a princess, she was able to call attention to the centuries old problems and sufferings of women. In many published letters, she reported to friends in Holland about growing up in a traditional Javanese household. In the end she submitted to the pressure of her parents, was married and died of childbed fever at the age of 24. Big celebrations are held in Rembang (Central Java) where she is buried.

ISLAMIC HOLIDAYS

During ***RAMADAN***, the month of fasting, you'll become starkly aware that you are in an Islamic country. As long as the sun is in the sky, the restaurants are closed. If you can't find any Indians or Chinese, you'll have to go hungry. This is most true in *ACEH, SUMBAWA, SOUTH SULAWESI,* and *BANJARMASIN.* Just before sunrise everyone is busy cooking and eating. At the end of a long day, when the signal is sounded from the mosque, everyone rushes for the warung and restaurants. During Ramadan, strict Muslims give up not just food and drink but smoking as well.

At the end of Ramadan, ***IDUL FITRI*** *(or HARI RAYA PUASA)* is celebrated. People thank Allah that they were able to make the fast. For two whole days people try to make up for all they missed during Ramadan. Early in the morning people gather in the mosques and town squares to sing Koran verse. Neighbours and friends are visited, presents exchanged and mistakes of the past year are forgiven.

On ***IDUL ADAH,*** the Islamic day of sacrifice, it's time for the Haj. Those who can afford the state subsidized flights, visit Mecca to fulfil a major Islamic commandment. Others gather at their mosque for prayer.

MUHARAM is the Islamic New Year's Day.

MAULI NABI MUHAMMAD, the prophet's birthday, is celebrated splendidly in the Surabaya region with nightly costume parties, pageants and folk dances spread over an entire week. It begins twelve days after Muharam.

MI'RAJ NABI MUHAMMAD is the Ascension Day of the Prophet.

CHINESE AND BUDDHIST HOLIDAYS

The Chinese celebrate their ***NEW YEAR*** in January or February as in the rest of South East Asia with family reunions and temple visits. Check out Glodok, the Chinese section of Jakarta, where greeting cards and tasty treats are sold days ahead of time. Pageants and fireworks are banned from the streets.

WAICAK Festival, the holiest Buddhist holiday, is celebrated in remembrance of the birth, enlightenment and entrance of Buddha into Nirvana. Especially impressive at Borobudur.

GETTING AROUND

The only way to travel between the many Indonesian islands is by ship or plane. Conditions vary on land. Even if from a map it seems that Indonesia has a good road system, reality is quite different. Don't trust any map - not even those provided by the government or this book! People have had to walk for three days through the jungle because they made that mistake. On the smaller islands few roads are paved, and public transport runs at best irregularly. If you do travel around, you'll have to put some mileage on your hiking boots. Otherwise you'll be dependent on trucks, boats or horse and ox carts.

SUMATRA: South Sumatra has a railroad system, though parts of it are only for goods transport. The same for the route Medan - Rantauprapat. Long distances are usually served by the famous overland buses (even offering video) run by various private companies. During the rainy season it's best to stay away from the southern part of the island because many bridges are washed out and it's hard to tell where the roads used to be. Between Medan and Lake Toba there are good roads along which even the big tourist buses rip. The part from Solok to Lubuklinggau is the best road in the whole of Sumatra. Other sections of the Trans-Sumatra Highway that are connecting the north and the south (and which is economically vital for the exploitation of the island's raw materials) are in poorer condition. Especially bad is the route south of Lubuklinggau. Expect a north-south journey (Banda Aceh - Panjang) to take at least three days of driving under the best conditions.

JAVA: The most populated island has the best (but also the most overloaded) transport system. Between Jakarta and Bogor, a resort area 60 km from the capital used by rich residents including the President, is a good strip of super highway. Another super highway runs from Jakarta to Merak. The overland buses can go pretty fast along the east-west road Jakarta - Bandung - Cirebon (parts are flooded during the rainy season) - Semarang - Solo - Surabaya - Malang. Excursions to the volcano region of Central Java are difficult as are those on the southern coast. If you want to get away from the beaten path, try taking an overfilled bemo or colt for a slow ride through the countryside. The available transport usually only runs until early afternoon, so think ahead about where you want to spend the night. An alternative to the cramped but cheap buses is the express bus (more expensive). You'll find trains of every quality, from the luxury Bima Express to jam packed third class compartments with wooden seats on local trains.

BALI: On the smaller islands you can cover everything in one day. If there isn't any public transport for some routes, you can still take an interesting walk. The most common means of transport are the colts and buses. The faster colts go to practically every part of the island. On the roads with some traffic you can also hitchhike. The coastal road circling the island is not paved in the east despite some maps. If you want your own set of wheels, you have the choice of a

Yank Tank complete with chauffeur, a chartered bemo, a rental car, a motorcycle, or a bicycle.

SULAWESI: Despite years of planning, there still isn't any good road connection between Manado in the north and Ujung Pandang in the south. The only convenient way to get from one side of this island to the other is by ship or plane. Those who want to tackle Sulawesi by land will have lots of problems. The connections by water are a matter of luck or of money (charter!). An acceptable road system on which buses and bemos can drive is only found around Manado, Palu, Ujung Pandang and up to Tanah Toraja. The Trans Sulawesi Highway allows you to do the overland trip but it takes time. Off the main roads, you'll find only unpaved and unmaintained trails which can only be used by jeeps or trucks.

KALIMANTAN: The road system around Pontianak, Banjarmasin and Balikpapan/Samarinda vanishes quickly into unpaved paths and trails. You are again dependent mostly on boats and planes. The major rivers are navigable quite far inland. Even large ships are able to come up the Kapuas to Putussibau, the Bario up to Muara Tewe, or the Mahakam up to Long Iram. If you're taking a local boat you'll need lots of time.

TRANSPORT ON THE ISLANDS

TRAINS: Only good on Java. Recommended for long trips. If you don't have a reserved seat or are so bold as to get on a train that is already filled, then you may end up having to stand packed in the aisle at the mercy of hordes of hawkers. Every train has its own price class and level of luxury. Student rates are usually only available in 3rd class - always try anyway! No luck, however, on the more expensive express trains. You need to buy tickets far enough in advance. If you don't want to wait for hours at a train station ticket window, you can get your ticket right away from a travel agency for a fee.

BUSES: Generally the cheapest way to get around. Express lines cross western Indonesia in eight days from Aceh to Bima (Sumbawa), though you usually have to change buses. The Mercedes buses are smaller than the ones used in Europe, but still carry many more passengers. Ac-buses, much more expensive, offer more luxury (service, comfortable seat), but you can easily catch a nasty cold too.

If your luggage is put on the roof, be sure that it is properly secured. It's best to lock your luggage with a chain to the roof rack. Valuables should be in your handbag. You can use your bag as a pillow at night. If you are picked up by an overland bus somewhere along the way, expect to sit on a piece of luggage in the aisle. Anyone who has travelled on one of the infamous Sumatra buses can testify to the number of curiosities being transported. You are in trouble with long legs; hardly anyone fits into the small seats. If you have some choice, then choose a seat with some leg room. Usually it's the seat behind the driver.

Therefore buy tickets for express buses several days in advance. If you're confused, ask other passengers about the right price. Due to the rising cost of energy (even in the OPEC country Indonesia), the cost of tickets is sky-rocketing. Try to get a student discount - it works sometimes.

If you are travelling long distance, keep an eye on the driver. Some drive 12 hours or longer without a break or are drunk. If so, get off, and take the next bus; it's cheaper than the hospital.

On the road from Padang to Pakanbaru our driver's eyes kept closing at regular intervals. At the next police station on a mountain-route we got off. As our bags were being unloaded the driver fell completely asleep, but it didn't bother the other passengers or the police. One of the next buses took us the rest of the way. One of our new fellow passengers was surprised that in this no man's land 'orang putih' should be wandering about. When we told him our story, we learned that only two days before a bus had fallen into the gorge.

OPLETS, COLTS, MINIBUSES, BEMOS: As public transport these vehicles have certain regular stops (stasion, terminal), but they are allowed to pick up passengers anywhere they find them. Sometimes they will make detours to let you off at the place you wish to go. Ask local people in advance what the correct fare should be. Additional detours can be very expensive because the driver just assumes you have chartered his vehicle (except in east Nusa Tenggara and parts of Sulawesi).

With several variations, each of the islands has a system of small buses which handles the lion's share of local transport. Sometimes you'll find comfortable minibuses carrying the names Datsun or Colt (Mitsubishi trade name). With less luck you'll hunch on the low wooden benches of a Bemo which are only fastened on to the storage part of a small transporter. There are no regular schedules. Often the Bemo only leaves when the driver figures that nobody else will fit in. Expect skin contact on market days! Sometimes the driver adds atmosphere by playing his only music cassette full blast for hours on end. Prices vary from region to region, but are usually higher on poor roads and less frequented routes. Where roads are poor or lightly travelled, you'll be forced to use the relatively expensive motorcycle taxis. Be sure to check the price in advance and bargain.

BECAKS: Bicycle rickshaws are the best form of transport in many towns. Prices are bargained individually. Some vehicles are artfully decorated or painted. The becaks are usually rented by the drivers so that one third of the fares goes to the owner of the becak. Don't be too angry, if as a white person, you have to pay a little bit more. Particularly in mountainous regions, the somewhat cheaper horse carts or coaches (dokar, bendi, delman, cidomo) are available.

TAXIS, RENT A CAR, MOTORBIKES: Outside of Jakarta there are hardly any taxis with a meter. You have to bargain a price ahead of time! Profitable routes, such as between cities and airports, are hardly ever served by public transport giving taxi drivers an assured source of income. For this reason you should share a taxi with other guests. Rented cars are mostly only to be had with a chauffeur, in which case, they are more expensive than a taxi. Motorbikes are widely rented on Bali. Petrol (premium) costs 385 Rp at Pertamina stations and 500 Rp in rural areas.

LONGER DISTANCE TRANSPORT

BY SHIP:

Your best way between the islands. Since 1983 six modern made-in-Germany passenger ships steam between the major harbours from Banda Aceh to Jayapura at 20 knots (14 knots for the latter and smaller two): KM. Kambuna, KM. Rinjani, KM. Kerinci, KM. Umsini, KM. Kelimutu, and KM. Lawit. The entire route takes 14 days.

PELNI TIMETABLE

KM.KERINCI Route: Tanjung Priok (Tue) - Surabaya (Wed) - Ujung Pandang (Thu) - Balikpapan (Fr) - Palu (Sat) - Toli Toli (Sat) - Tarakan (Sun) - Toli Toli (Mon) - Palu (Mon) - Balikpapan (Tue) - Ujung Pandang (Wed) - Surabaya (Thu) - Tanjung Priok (Fr) - Padang (Sat) - Sibolga (Sun) - Padang (Sun) - Tanjung Priok (Tue) - etc.

KM.KAMBUNA Route: Tanjung Priok (Wed) - Surabaya (Thu) - Ujung Pandang (Fr) - Balikpapan (Sat) - Palu (Sun) - Bitung (Mon) - Palu (Tue) - Balikpapan (Wed) - Ujung Pandang (Thu) - Surabaya (Fr) - Tanjung Priok (Sat) - Belawan (Mon) - Tanjung Priok (Wed) - etc.

KM.RINJANI Route: Tanjung Priok (Wed) - Surabaya (Thu) - Ujung Pandang (Fr) - Bau Bau (Sat) - Ambon (Sun) - Sorong (Mon) - Ambon (Tue) - Bau Bau (Wed) - Ujung Pandang (Thu) - Surabaya (Fr) - Tanjung Priok (Sat) - Belawan (Mon) - Tanjung Priok (Wed) - etc.

KM.UMSINI Route: Tanjung Priok (Thu) - Surabaya (Fr) - Ujung Pandang (Sat) - Bitung (Mon) - Ternate (Tue) - Sorong (Wed) - Jayapura (Thu) - Sorong (Sat) - Ternate (Sun) - Bitung (Sun) - Ujung Pandang (Tue) - Surabaya (Wed) - Tanjung Priok (Thu) - etc.

KM.KELIMUTU Route: Semarang (Sun) - Banjarmasin (Mon) - Surabaya (Tue) - Padang Bai (Wed) - Lembar (Wed) - Ujung Pandang (Thu) - Bima (Fr) - Waingapu (Sat) - Ende (Sat) - Kupang (Sun) - Ende (Mon) - Waingapu (Mon) - Bima (Tue) - Ujung Pandang (Wed) - Lembar (Thu) - Padang Bai (Thu) - Surabaya (Fr) - Banjarmasin (Sat) - Semarang (Sun) - etc.

KM.LAWIT Route: Tanjung Priok (Wed) - Muntok (Thu) - Dumai (Fr) - Belawan (Sat) - Lhokseumawe (Sun) - Malahayati (Sun) - Lhokseumawe (Mon) - Belawan (Mon) - Dumai (Wed) - Muntok (Thu) - Tanjung Priok (Fr) - Ketapang (Sun) - Pontianak (Mon) - Ketapang (Tue) - Tanjung Priok (Wed) - etc.

SAMPLE PRICES FOR ALL CLASSES FROM TANJUNG PRIOK

BELAWAN	110,700	80,900	61,700	48,500	35,700 Rp
SIBOLGA	89,000	68,300	52,400	41,600	34,300 Rp
PADANG	63,300	48,200	36,800	28,900	23,600 Rp
SURABAYA	44,400	33,900	23,100	20,500	16,800 Rp
UJUNG PANDANG	108,700	79,600	61,100	48,500	36,200 Rp
TOLI[2]	145,900	106,700	81,700	64,600	50,600 Rp
BALIKPAPAN	118,900	87,500	67,800	54,700	43,800 Rp
BITUNG	203,900	149,200	113,700	87,500	66,700 Rp
PALU	135,900	98,700	74,900	58,500	45,000 Rp
TARAKAN	153,500	112,300	86,600	69,000	54,100 Rp
BAU[2]	123,700	90,300	69,200	55,100	43,500 Rp
AMBON	169,700	123,800	94,700	74,400	58,300 Rp
SORONG	216,400	150,800	121,800	96,800	76,200 Rp
TERNATE	210,800	155,000	118,900	95,000	71,400 Rp
JAYAPURA	283,000	207,100	158,600	125,600	98,600 Rp
MUNTOK	46,500	36,600	-	-	19,400 Rp
DUMAI	88,000	64,900	-	-	29,900 Rp
LHOKSEUMAWE	138,000	101,700	-	-	48,300 Rp
MALAHAYATI	153,700	120,100	-	-	58,300 Rp
KETAPANG	56,500	45,200	-	-	23,600 Rp
PONTIANAK	69,900	55,100	-	-	28,300 Rp

Listed prices are per person for 1st class (2-bed cabins), 2nd class (4-bed cabins), 3rd class (6-bed cabins), 4th class (8-bed cabins), Economy Class (dormitories). The two smaller ships (KM. Lawit and KM. Kelimutu) don't offer 3rd or 4th class.

There is room for 1596 to 1729 passengers on the roomy, well-kept ships. One-third travels economy class (AC dormitory with individually numbered beds, bring your own food to supplement the rice & fish menu). Another 40 - 100 passengers enjoy 1st class (AC double cabins, showers, TV, music programs, restaurant - food included, bar, disco). Others make home in 2nd class (4-bed cabins), 3rd class (6-bed), and 4th class (8-bed). All rooms are air conditioned. There are plenty of wash rooms with hot and cold water. Recorded music, colour video, and live music in the disco provide entertainment. Practicing Muslims have the services of a Musholla. If you've travelled on Indonesian ships in the past, you'll feel like you're on a luxury liner, but how long will it last? The two smaller ships, KM. Lawit and KM. Kelimutu, can only carry 920 passengers, but the amenities are the same.

Several travellers have had problems getting a ticket for these "booked solid" ships, but then the ship would depart half empty. To avoid hours in a queue and tumultuous conditions before the ticket window, just go through the back door and ask to speak to an English-speaking employee. Tourists usually receive preferential treatment.

Most Indonesian ships look quite different. They are usually so overloaded that a dry spot to sleep is difficult to find. The sanitary conditions are awful. Better

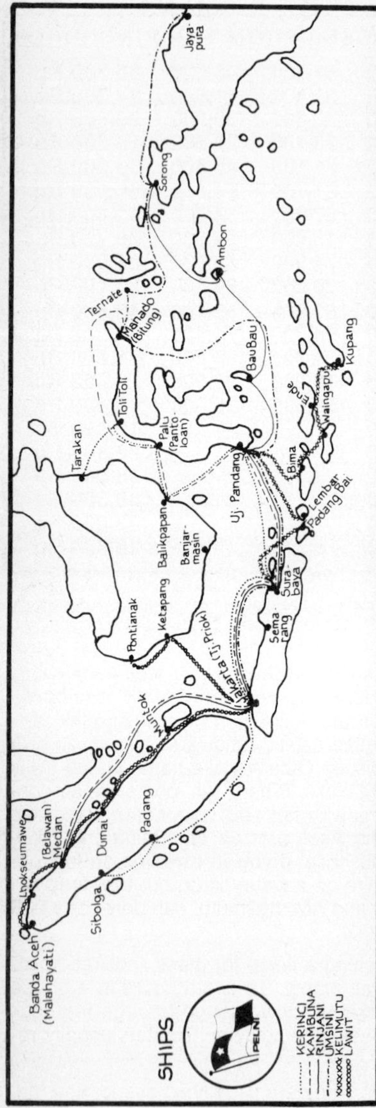

just bring your own food. Only the larger companies run regular schedules. The outer islands are visited by ships only sporadically and without a schedule. The best source of information about ships is the harbourmaster (syahbandar). For a real adventure, take a trip in one of the traditional sailing ships - only recommended for male travellers.

There are ***regular passenger ferries*** between:
Medan / Sumatra-Penang / Malaysia
Dumai / Sumatra-Malacca / Malaysia
Pakanbaru / Sumatra-Tanjung Pinang / Riau
Pulau Batam-Singapore
Bakauheni / Sumatra-Merak / Java
Surabaya / Java-Kamal / Madura
Panarukan / Java-Kalianget / Madura
Banyuwangi / Java-Gilimanuk / Bali
Padang Bai / Bali-Lembar / Lombok
Labuhan Lombok / Lombok-Alas / Sumbawa
Sape / Sumbawa-Komodo-Labuanbajo / Flores
Bone / South Sulawesi-Kolaka / Southeast Sulawesi

On ***Kalimantan*** ships or aircraft are the only means of penetrating the interior. Riverboats run frequently along the Kapuas from Pontianak to Putussibau (870 km), on the Barito from Banjarmasin to Muara Tewe (470 km), and on the Mahakam from Samarinda to Long Iram (400 km). Riverboats also ply the streams of southeastern Sumatra: from Palembang on the Musi to Muara Kelingi (350 km) and on the Lalang to Bayung Lincir (300 km); on the Tebo from Jambi to Muara Bungo (310 km); or along the coast to Kuala Enok (385 km). Additional coastal ships run from Tembilahan and Pakanbaru.

KAPAL LAUT: seaworthy, large ship
KAPAL MOTOR: small, motorized coastal ship
KAPAL LAYAR: big sailing boat, Bugis schooner
PRAHU: small, wooden outrigger
KLOTOK: riverboat in Kalimantan with outboard motor, often canopied
SPETBOT: fast river boat (speed-boat)
LONGBOT: fast river boat, sometimes with several outboard motors
SAMPAN: small rowboat.

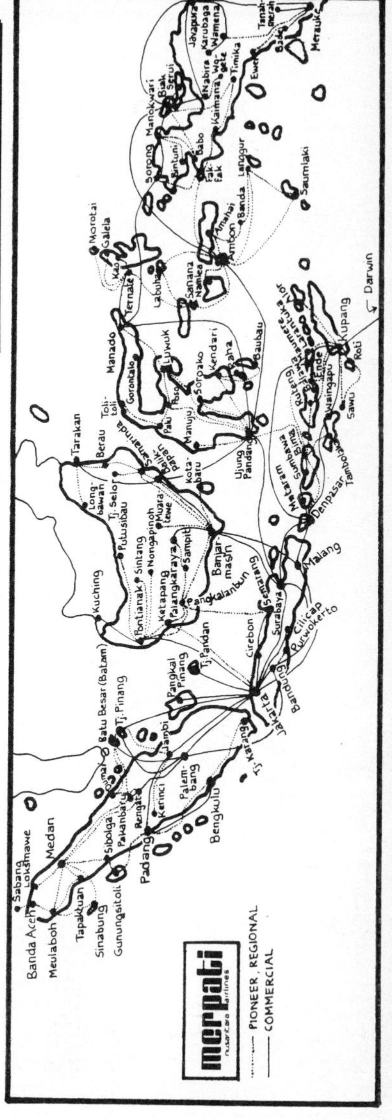

BY AIR:

This is the quickest but most expensive way to island hop. GARUDA is a large state-run company which also provides most international flights.

Within Indonesia the other airlines average about 25 % cheaper. *MERPATI*, also the most reliable, flies to all parts of the country. *BOURAQ* handles Kalimantan, Sulawesi, the North Moluccas, and NTT. *MANDALA* does flights between Java and Sumatra, Sulawesi, and Ambon. *SEMPATI* flies between Southern Sumatra, Jakarta, and Singapore. *SMAC* (Sabang Merauke Air Charter) flies over Sumatra. *DAS* (Dirgantara Air Services) flies only over Kalimantan. If you take one of the smaller planes or pioneer flights (perintis) by Merpati, SMAC, or DAS, your weight limit is 10 kg (22 lb.) of luggage. *PELITA*, the airline of the national oil company PERTAMINA, flies from the oil fields on Sumatra and Kalimantan. Supposedly it takes some private passengers. We didn't have any luck, however, or should we have raised our bribe?

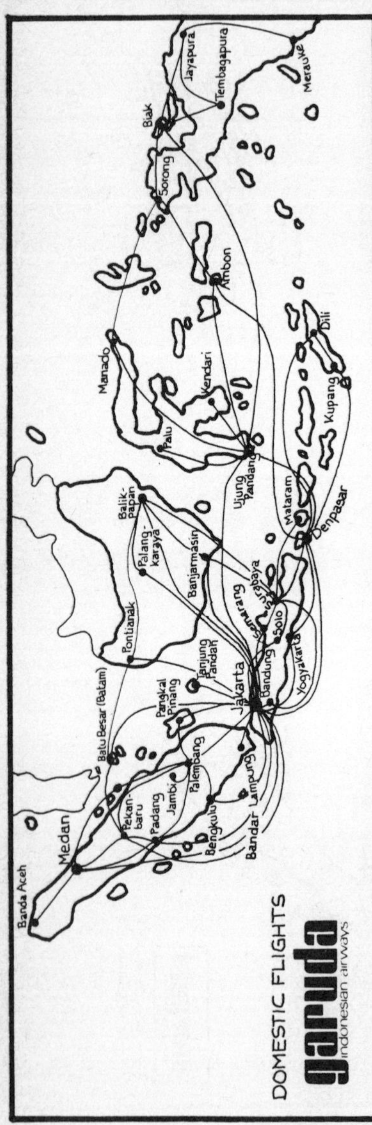

Garuda offers an ***AIRPASS*** on its domestic routes which for US$300, US$400, or US$500 allows passengers meeting certain criteria to make 5, 10, or 35 flights within a 10, 20, or 60-day time period. It is required that you begin your flights in Jakarta, Medan, Denpasar, Pakanbaru, Pontianak, Manado, or Biak. The Airpass may only be purchased in Europe, Japan, Australia, New Zealand, or North America. Perhaps the most important requirement is a bit of planning: 35 flights in 60 days allows no time (a city every two days) to see Indonesia beyond the departure lounges. You must specify your travel route in advance, although they will issue open-date tickets. Plan at least 4-5 days per destination. To get the most from your Airpass, choose the most isolated destinations such as Northern Sumatra or Irian Jaya. The majority of Garuda's destinations are not tourist attractions; you are frequently forced to take connecting flights on Merpati or another airline. Any visitor to Ujung Pandang will want to make a sidetrip to Tanah Toraja, and Jayapura is hardly worth a stopover unless you go on to Wamena. There are several conditions detailed by Garuda in writing, but not always strictly enforced. For example, you are only permitted one stopover at any location, and you can only fly any route once. Garuda counts any stay of more than four hours as a stopover.

The ***AIRPORT TAX*** in Jakarta and Denpasar is 9000 Rp for international flights and 2000 Rp for domestic flights. Other airports charge 500 - 2000 Rp. In Indonesia, the airport tax is usually included in the cost of your ticket.

ACCOMMODATION

In the larger cities you'll find lodgings of all price classes and categories. Those of you who aren't planning to stay in an international hotel should inspect your rooms before checking in. See if anything else is living in your mattress, whether the toilet and washroom are clean, and if it is possible to lock your room securely. Ask the hotel owner if it is possible to deposit your valuables and get a receipt!

HOTELS - The most expensive category and the most variable class. Expect a range from the most luxurious hotel to the biggest fleabags (charging incredibly high prices). If you have any complaint, at least try to get them to lower the price.

WISMA - These small family businesses are comparable to the European pensions. Breakfast is usually included and brought to your room. The price can vary widely according to the standards - expect 6000 Rp and up. In the higher price classes you'll have your own bath and many comforts, the cheaper places aren't much different from the losmen.

LOSMEN - Family businesses but cheaper in price. Found in almost every town, price range from 2000 Rp in Java and Bali and up to 10,000 Rp in the Moluccas and North Sulawesi. The bathroom usually has a ***Mandi*** (a big container of cold water which you ladle to clean yourself with) instead of a shower . In the container the water stays nice and cool. Leave the mandi clean for the next person! Never wash your hands or do the laundry in the mandi! For reasons of hygiene, always wear rubber sandals in the washroom. Never expect to find toilet paper available; Indonesians use water and their left hand. If you aren't willing to follow suit then buy your own in advance. In remote areas toilet paper, if you can find it, is prohibitively expensive. Many Losmen offer guests tea free of charge. Sometimes breakfast is also included in the price. Another name for Losmen (often seen on Bali) is HOMESTAY.

PENGINAPAN - In many parts of Indonesia this is the cheapest category of lodging. They are usually (but not always!) cheaper than Losmen. In the cheap price area there isn't all that much difference between a hotel, losmen, wisma, or penginapan. You'll even find losmen which are better and more expensive than some hotels.

PRIVATE ACCOMMODATION - If you are in a village where there is no place to stay and you've to spend the night somewhere, then ask the ***kepala desa*** (village leader or chief). He'll usually let you stay at his house because hospitality still means something in rural areas.

If you can't stay at the village chief's then ask someone of social or governmental position such as a policeman or storekeeper and offer money. Sometimes there is a fee you have to pay to be registered with the police (if there is any police) similar to the registration papers in the hotels.

ADJUST TO LOCAL LIFESTYLE WHEN STAYING PRIVATELY! Don't make any special requests, just accept what they offer. Don't embarrass your host by asking for beer or meat dishes.

Especially in more remote areas, your arrival is a special situation. There will be lots of talks - and in non-Muslim areas - lots of drink from local liquors whose strength is impossible to judge. If you drink as usual, you may end up in a state of unusual drunkenness - it complicates everything. If many people live in one room, you have to be considerate of each other. If one person goes to sleep the others are then quieter or go home.

When among animists, respect their rituals and gods. Try to find someone before you enter a village who can fill you in on the local culture. A local person who has some dealings with westerners, such as a boatsman, teacher or local official would be good.

The local hygiene won't be up to your standards. There aren't any toilets and you bathe in the river - so don't forget your sarong.

Take some presents with you, but not colonial style junk jewelry. Food is often a much better gift than consumer goods, though cigarettes and small amounts of money are fine in some situations. If they ask you for some kind of medication from aspirin to antibiotics, malaria or stomach pills, then leave them as much as you can. But try to make sure people will take them for their benefit and not misuse them.

We decided on the following price table for Indonesia - all prices are for double rooms:

*	**up to**	**5000 Rp**
**	**up to**	**10,000 Rp**
***	**up to**	**20,000 Rp**
****	**over**	**20,000 Rp**

FOOD & DRINK

As in the rest of South East Asia rice is the staple food here . Indonesian food is famous for its use of many different kinds of spices. The struggle between the European powers for control of the spice monopoly (Moluccas = 'spice islands'), shows the importance of spice cultivation in the archipelago.

The most important ***spices*** are:

LOMBOK: chilli - ***MERICA:*** pepper - ***CENGKEH:*** cloves - ***JAHE:*** ginger ***SERAI:*** lemongrass - ***KETUMBAR:*** coriander - ***GARAM:*** salt - ***BAWANG PUTIH:*** garlic.

Several other tasty basic parts of Indonesian cooking include:

AIR KELAPA: coconut milk - ***KRUPUK:*** a fish cracker baked in oil - ***KECAP:*** soysauce - ***SAMBAL:*** chillipaste.

REGIONALLY, YOU'LL FIND THE FOLLOWING STYLES OF COOKING:

PADANG: Lots of spicy-hot foods, served cold in separate bowls, and rice. You pay only for what you eat. Tea is a help for those used to milder fare. Speciality: Rendang (beef).

BATAK / TORAJA: Mostly vegetarian. Solid food is mainly fatty pork (to the horror of Muslims); the Toraja also eat beef.

SUNDANESE: Light, mild and sweet dishes. Speciality: Goldfish.

MADURESE: Speciality is thick soup (soto madura) and chicken on skewers (soto ayam madura).

BALINESE: Dishes with duck and pork, lots of sweet foods made of rice. In the tourist centres, international cooking.

BUGIS: Many fish and shell fish dishes.

EASTERN ISLANDS: Instead of rice people here eat 'manioc', the root of the 'cassava' plant (lots of protein but little starch) and 'sago', the granulated pulp of the sago palm (prepared often as bread).

TYPICAL INDONESIAN DISHES:

NASI CAMPUR can be found at every foodstall. Along with rice are served different vegetables, roasted peanuts, shredded coconut, beef, chicken, fish, or egg. A thick sauce covers everything. Costs 300 to 600 Rp depending on region and ingredients for a filling meal.

NASI RAMES and ***NASI RAWON*** (with peanut sauce) are prepared like Nasi Campur.

NASI GORENG is fried rice with vegetables and a bit of meat or crab, sometimes with egg (nasi goreng istimewa).

MEE GORENG is the same with noodles (mee = noodles).

SOTO is a thick soup or stew including thickened coconut milk, vegetables, meat, and rice. Other soups are known as ***SOP.***

CAP CAI, derived from Chinese 'chop suey', is a dish of cut up meats and vegetables, sometimes with a fried egg.

LONTONG, sticky rice wrapped in banana leaves.

PISANG GORENG, baked banana, like Lontong a small snack.

BEVERAGES

Even in the smallest village you can get something to drink if only boiled water ***(AIR MASAK)*** or tea. There are several kinds of alcoholic beverages found mostly in non-Muslim areas.

SOFT DRINKS

TEH	tea	served	***PAHIT***	black
KOPI	coffee		***MANIS***	with sugar
COKLAT	chocolate milk		***SUSU***	with milk

You'll rarely see fresh milk. Tea often costs twice as much with sugar and three times as much with milk.

PANAS (warm drink): teh manis panas (hot sugared tea)
ES (with ice): teh manis es (ice sugared tea)

ALCOHOLIC BEVERAGES

TUAK: palm wine

BREM: rice wine, both hit the head quickly though they vary regionally

BINTANG BIR - beer brewed under license from Heineken/Holland, costs up to 2000 Rp a bottle.

Besides soft drinks which come in incredible colours (though served in bottles from the major international soft drinks producers), there are many different fruit juices (air...). They are a real speciality everywhere which you simply must sample! Here's a list of the most common:

FRUITS

BLIMBING - a small, yellow or green fruit, very juicy but sour - best during the dry season when it's a bit sweeter.

DELIMA - pomegranate, a round fruit whose refreshing pulp is divided into several sections, yellow with a spotty brown skin.

DURIAN - a green fruit with thorns the size of a watermelon containing a sticky yellow pulp around big kernels. Its strong musty odour (as fitting the 'queen of fruits') makes it less popular among westerners. At harvest time the whole of Indonesia revels in Durian frenzy. Your body won't like durian together with alcohol.

JERUK - a huge orange that tastes like a mixture of grapefruit and orange. Also a general term for all citrus fruit.

KELAPA - coconut. Refreshing is its cool milk from young fruits ***(KELAPA MUDA).***

MANGO - a fruit of green or reddish colouring with a nutty taste that's sweet or sour depending on its ripeness.

MANGOSTEEN -the size of an apple and deep purple with sweet sour segments. The skin juices stain! Never sweeten with sugar!

NENAS - pineapple, cheap to buy on markets, especially sweet in Pakanbaru.

NANGKA - Jackfruit, an oval green fruit which can weigh up to 20 kg (44 lb.) with sweet yellow fruit pulp in sections.

PAPAYA - a melon like yellow green fruit with an orange red interior and commonly served as desert.

PISANG - the general term for bananas, of which there are several varieties for grilling, cooking, or eating as a fruit as we eat them. Especially tasty are the small bananas which you never see in Europe.

RAMBUTAN - hair (=rambut), the name is appropriate for this red-yellow fruit the size of a tennis ball under whose soft skin you'll find sweet white pulp.

SALAK - a small brown fruit with a hard skin (like snake skin) and an apple-like taste.

SAWO - Manila fruit, brown, shaped like a potato with a taste like a ripe pear.

SEMANGKA - watermelon.

If you're hungry you won't have any difficulties finding something to eat at any time of day. The cheapest dishes are sold on the streets and markets. Food-stalls offer Satay, Krupuk, Lontong, Pisang Goreng or other dishes.

WARUNG: foodstalls, which you'll find at central locations or in the evening on the streets, serving the usual nasi campur, sate, soto or other foods prepared before your eyes inexpensively. Drinks are equally cheap, though often there isn't any ice or it costs extra. Better yet, drink tea! Be sure that the meat is well cooked.

RUMAH MAKAN: (= food house) are cheap restaurants where the food can taste quite good. During the heat of the day you can sit more coolly and comfortably here than in a warung. In a rumah makan the meals served are displayed in bowls and on plates in a show-case by the entrance. You just pick out the dish you want. The food is usually served cold, but due to the large quantities of chillies, it doesn't spoil very quickly even in the tropical heat. In the centres of 'alternative tourism' there are lots of cheap places that serve European style 'hippie food'. There are pancakes, porridge, or muesli for breakfast, nasi goreng, omelets and milder forms of the national dishes for main meals along with fruit salad and fried bananas. At all meeting points for young people in South East Asia (whether in Chiang Mai, Phuket, Ko Samui, Bukittinggi, Lake Toba, Malacca or Kuta), when the western munchies are served, the traveller's heart beats faster.

RESTORAN: Restaurants are determined by their menus, air conditioning, and especially their prices. While you can eat in a rumah makan for 800 to 1600 Rp, you'll have to dig deeper into your pockets at a restoran!

MONEY

EXCHANGE RATE	**1US$ = 1650 Rp**
INFLATION RATE:	**4%**

The Indonesian monetary unit is the Indonesian Rupiah (Rp). Notes in circulation include denominations of 10,000, 5000, 1000, 500, and 100 Rp. The 100s are often so used and dirty that they appear to be little more than filthy red scraps of paper. Coin denominations: 5, 10, 25, 50, and 100 Rp.

For all practical purposes there isn't a black market rate for the Indonesian Rupiah. Even the money changers in Penang or Singapore give about the same rate as the major banks in Jakarta. In general you get the best exchange rate when you sell US dollars - with a few exceptions. In all tourist centres and most provincial capitals, banks do generally accept DM, A$, Sfr, ¥ and £. In smaller towns and on the outer islands the value of all foreign currency falls greatly, less so with the US dollar. You can get the best exchange rates on all Sumatra in Medan and Bukittinggi, on Bali in Denpasar, Sanur and Kuta. When criticized about the exchange rate an employee of a small bank in Tanjung Pinang said: "We're only a small bank!"

Traveller's checks don't always get the best exchange rate; some banks pay more for cash. Always have a few dollars in cash for emergencies. If you want to fly out of Denpasar, you can buy your ticket using US$ and save the cost of exchange. You can import or export up to 50,000 Rp. Save your currency exchange receipts, so that if you have changed too much, you can change back.

INCOME AND COST OF LIVING

In the developed parts of Indonesia the average monthly income of an industrial worker is about US$90 a month. The majority of the population working in agriculture earns much less. Women working in textile and canning factories receive between 500 and 1000 Rp per day. The World Bank estimates that more than 50% of the population lives at or below the poverty level. The monthly income of a hotel employee at many big hotels is less than the cost of a room for one night.

Rice, the staple food, costs about 350 Rp per kilo. More nourishing foods are much more expensive. 1 kg tomatoes costs 600 Rp, 1 kg fish 1400 Rp, 1 kg beef 5000 Rp, one egg 80 Rp. Food prices are highly inflationary; costs have quadrupled in the last ten years. The result has been increased vitamin deficiencies and other illnesses in children.

Travellers, who are looking to live cheaply, should expect to pay about 3000 Rp for lodging per night (double occupancy). Meals at a warung or cheap restaurant cost 800 to 1200 Rp. Getting around on buses and trains is relatively cheap, but the distances are huge. If you want to travel outside of Sumatra, Java, and Bali, you should allow for the extra cost of plane tickets. All transportation costs were raised three times since 1980 (each time by one third). A flight from Jakarta to Ujung Pandang cost 42,000 Rp in 1979, but 156,000 Rp in 1987.

ECONOMY

Indonesia is one of the richest countries in the world as far as natural resources go and one of the poorer in standard of living. The positive side of the economy can be seen in the following statistics: ***Oil*** produces four fifths of the country's export earnings. In times of energy shortages, this adds meat to the financial reserves. Bauxite, copper, nickel, and tin are other important raw materials for export. Many deposits have yet to be exploited; other raw materials lay hidden under the thick rain forests forming a basis for future affluence. The ***forests*** provide a tremendous wood supply; the large islands contain coverages of 70% on Irian Barat, on Sumatra 40%, and Kalimantan 60%.

The volcanic soil on Java allows intensive agricultural techniques. The ***rice*** crop is increased through the use of artificial fertilizers and irrigation; population growth is even greater, though. Foreign reserves must be tapped to import food. Overpopulation is having a noticeable effect on Java with almost 100 million people. The farm sizes have declined from generation to generation until the point where they are too small to support a family. The children move to the overpopulated cities where they fill the ranks of the unemployed because they have no skills, some are forced to perform unskilled labour for wages below subsistence level.

Even so, 55% of the population is still on the farms, 90% of the farms have less than 2 ha, in Central Java some families are often forced to live off less than one hectare. Many peasants are in debt. Private money lenders, who sometimes charge 20% per month, often own the entire crop before it is harvested. It's next to impossible for illiterate sharecroppers to get bank loans. Besides sharecropping, the bane of landless peasants, traditional but expensive family celebrations ensure that the debt burden persists. Money is becoming ever more important to the farmer who is looking to use technology to increase output. The ancient system of 'gotong royong' or trading labour is being replaced by a wage system.

Overpopulation is affecting the environment through leaching of the soil. Climate fluctuations are becoming more extreme due to destruction of rainforests by logging which has practically removed the last forest areas from Java.

Similar problems can be seen on other islands due to the increasing wood exports. Reforestation programs don't create the quick profits sought by the US and Japanese wood companies.

Only 12% of the employable population is employed by ***industry.*** Most are employed by small firms in the textile and food packaging industries. Java is the most industrialized region, including Jakarta with its many large firms. Other major industrial areas are Surabaya, Bandung, Semarang, Cirebon and outside of Java Ujung Pandang, Manado, Medan, and Palembang.

NATIONALITIES & RELIGIONS

More than 170 million people live in Indonesia. Every year you can add another 3 million. The population increases at a rate of 2.1% per year so that almost 41% of the population is under 15 years of age. About two thirds of the people live on the central island of Java where the economic and political power is concentrated. Using the motto 'Unity by Diversity', the national government holds together a country whose population speaks 250 different languages and contains over 300 cultural groups. Even today, some of the Negrito people on Sumatra and Kalimantan live from hunting and gathering. They and the Melanesides in Nusa Tenggara and in the Moluccas are among the most ancient inhabitants of the archipelago.

Proto- and deutero-Malays migrated in several waves from southern China to the islands. The first Malayan (proto-Malays) have remained peasant farmers until today with their own culture in the interior of the islands. The tribes include on Sumatra the *Batak* and *Minangkabau*, on Kalimantan the *Dayak,* and on Sulawesi the *Toraja.*

Under Buddhist and Hindu influences the deutero-Malays developed an impressive high culture. You can see examples today in the temple architecture on Java. Islam has been superimposed on this culture since its arrival in the 12th century by way of Aceh. Only on Bali and on parts of Lombok has the Hindu religion held its own. The population of Java, (Sundanese, Javanese and Madurese) are Muslim, as is 90% of the total population. The really true believers, however, are only a minority living on the coasts of a few outer islands - South Sulawesi, Sumbawa, Aceh, and South Kalimantan. Otherwise Islam has mixed with other religions such as Buddhism and Hinduism as well as mysticism.

Chinese traders have been on the islands for centuries, though most of the present day Chinese came in the 19th and the beginning of this century to work as wage labourers. From the beginning they were refused the right to own land, so they settled in the cities where they could engage in trade. Many problems surround the 4 million ethnic Chinese. Only 1.6 million have been able to buy Indonesian citizenship, 1 million are stateless and the rest are citizens of China. Just as in other countries of South East Asia, the ethnic Chinese control a percentage of the local trade and industry far out of proportion to their population size. Many confrontations, some bloody (the last in December 80) with the 'pribumis' (ethnic Malay-Indonesian) have occurred over the years. In the riots of 1965 thousands of Chinese were killed. Since then rich Chinese have turned their houses into fortresses. Many Chinese are Buddhists, though some are 'paper' Christians, so that they won't be accused of being communist.

Official government policy is to assimilate the Chinese. Even at the traditional temple festivals in Cirebon or Semarang, the young people can be heard speaking Bahasa Indonesia. Chinese characters are rarely seen and used anymore, even among the older generations of Chinese.

Beside the Chinese there are ***Arab, Indian,*** and ***Eurasian*** minorities in this multinational country. For an outsider it's interesting how Indonesians strive for their own identity "dari Sabang ke Merauke" (5120 km as the crow flies - Sabang is a small island at the northernmost top of Sumatra - Merauke a small town on the southern coast of Irian Barat next to the border of PNG). More and more young people regard themselves first as Indonesians and second as Batak, Sundanese, Bugis, Chinese or Moluccan. Fascinating people in the most fascinating country of South East Asia.

INDONESIAN ISLANDS: PROVINCIAL CAPITALS, POPULATION, AREA

Island / Provincial capitals	Population	Area
JAVA/MADURA	104,7 Mill.	132 187 km^2
Jakarta, Bandung, Semarang, Surabaya, Yogya		
SUMATRA	33,0 Mill.	473 606 km^2
Palembang, Bengkulu, Jambi, Telukbetung, Pakanbaru, Banda Aceh, Medan, Padang		
SULAWESI	11,7 Mill.	189 216 km^2
Manado, Palu, Kendari, Ujung Pandang		
KALIMANTAN	8,0 Mill.	39 460 km^2
Pontianak, Banjarmasin, Samarinda, Palangkaraya		
NUSA TENGGARA	8,5 Mill.	88 488 km^2
Mataram, Kupang, Dili		
BALI	2,7 Mill.	5 561 km^2
Denpasar		
IRIAN JAYA	1,4 Mill.	421 981 km^2
Jayapura		
MALUKU	1,6 Mill.	74 505 km^2
Ambon		

FAMILY PLANING IN INDONESIA

HISTORY

Indonesia dates back to the beginning of humanity. In 1891 a skeleton was discovered in Central Java which anthropologists call *pithecantropus erectus* or ***Java Man***. More than half a million years ago, when parts of the archipelago were still connected to the Eurasian continent, these people were walking on Java.

Since then several waves of immigrants have hit the islands. 30,000 years ago came the ***Negrito,*** a curly haired, dark skinned people whose descendants today have been forced back into the inaccessible jungles of east Sumatra and the Lesser Sunda Islands. They were pushed back 10,000 years ago by another group of immigrants of whom we can find traces in Wajak in East Java. The ***proto*** and ***deutero-Malays***, who came later, brought with them the art of working bronze and iron. Since 3000 to 2500 BC, wet rice has been planted and the fields plowed by water buffalos.

About 2000 years ago the first Indian traders began to visit the coast their countrymen had known of for some 600 years. In the centuries to come Buddhist and Hindu kingdoms were established, mostly on Java and Sumatra. Their sphere of influence encompassed almost all of South East Asia. At the centre of the important trade route between China and India, the ***Sri Vijaya*** empire achieved a position of dominance in the 7th century AD. For many centuries it was more than a first rate political power; it personified (for Chinese, Indians, Arabs, Persians, and South East Asia) both wealth and a blossoming culture. Trade, both of its own products and as a middle man, was the source of its wealth. All ships were forced to stop at the Sri Vijaya harbours to pay duty. A mighty fleet threatened those who would try to avoid tribute, and kept vassals in line. Sri Vijaya wasn't a centralized kingdom, rather a city state which subjugated other principalities and forced them to pay tribute. It is assumed today that the capital was located near Palembang.

At the end of the 13th century the east Javanese ***Majapahit*** became the leading power in the archipelago. The old Javanese poem ***Nagarakertagama*** (dating from 1365) tells the story of Majapahit's rise to power. The most important statesman of this period was ***Gajah Mada.*** He conducted an active foreign policy to spread the power and influence of Majapahit. Unlike Sri Vijaya, he used governors and tribute-paying princes to rule his provinces. Through the fusion of Indian influences to Javanese traditions, the first real Indonesian culture began to develop.

Along the trade routes between China, India and Arabia, Islam began to spread during the 13th and 14th century. Followers of the new religion at first were mostly traders and merchants with Muslim foreign partners. The process of Islamization spread out beyond the circle of traders to reach all classes and social groupings.

Starting in 1515, the ***Portuguese*** were able to influence the islands for almost a hundred years, using their superior weaponry to seize control of trade. Campaigns against the weak princes were carried out under the sign of the cross, bringing murder, plunder and slave trade to the islands. The unfortunate victims living on the islands weren't considered to be human beings - only heathen. Competition for the lucrative spice trade came from Europe: first the Spaniards, then the English and Dutch. All the Europeans used the same methods against the indigenous population.

In 1596 ***Dutch*** ships landed at Banten, West Java and returned home shortly thereafter richly loaded with spices. It was the beginning of 350 years of Dutch domination. The ***East India Company*** was founded in 1602 and continued to exploit the islands until 1795. Profit was the only motive for the development of huge plantations which grew coffee, pepper, cotton, rubber, tea and other colonial goods on Java and Sumatra. Labour was cheap and punitive expeditions always provided more. Blinded by their sense of European superiority, there was no concern for the centuries-old indigenous culture. Both the 'Belanda' or Europeans and the subjugated natives came to believe that all that was good and true came from Amsterdam, Rotterdam, or The Hague.

A typical example is a situation in Batavia described in a travel book, that was put together by a traveller on Captain Cook's global expedition in 1771:

The judges are accused of being improperly partial. They are overly severe with the natives; while with the Dutch their leniency in judgement borders on impropriety. A Christian guilty of the most heinous crime always has the right to a fair trial; the poor Indians on the other hand are hanged, broken alive on the wheel, or even burned at the stake."

It is no wonder that throughout the 19th century there were uprisings on every island. The Dutch weren't able to move into new areas without a fight.

Timetable of the annexations: Batavia, Ambon - 1619, parts of West Sumatra, South Sulawesi and the Moluccas by 1684, all of Java under control 1830, parts of Kalimantan, Sumatra, Bali and Lombok by 1900. Around Aceh in North Sumatra a thirty-year-long war raged until 1904 when the Dutch were able to bribe the leader of the Acenese and gain control of the north of the island.

The most famous freedom fighter was the son of a Javanese Sultan, ***Diponegoro,*** who led a guerilla war from 1825 - 30 until captured by the Dutch after he had been promised free passage in order to conduct peace negotiations. He was then exiled to Makassar.

At the beginning of the 20th century, many Indonesian young people went to study in Holland. When they returned, they formed the hard core of the independence movement. The original intention of the colonial power to develop a submissive local elite backfired. ***Budi Utomo*** (Great Endeavour), a nationalist group, was formed in 1908; other nationalist groups, political parties and trade unions soon followed. A free Railroad Workers Trade Union was formed on Java in 1908. ***Sarekat Dagang Islam,*** the first nationalist mass organization, pressed for an Islamic government in 1911; the first communist party in Asia followed suit: ***Perserikatan Kommunist di India (PKI)*** in 1924, and the ***Partai Nasional Indonesia*** established by an engineer named ***Sukarno*** 1927.

When the ***Japanese Army*** invaded Indonesia in 1942, it was greeted as an Asian liberator from European oppression. The nationalists Sukarno and Hatta worked with them closely. Feelings for Japan changed quickly, however, when people realized that they only traded one oppressor for another.

On August 17, 1945, Sukarno declared the ***independence*** of the United States of Indonesia.

After the fall of Japan, Holland tried in a three year long war to redominate Indonesia. With help from the United Nations, the new Republic was able to achieve her own sovereignty on December 27, 1949. Many problems faced Indonesia. The war had caused great damage, the economy suffered as the foreign managers were gone, and on many islands, separatist movements began to make themselves known.

President Sukarno declared in 1957 a 'Guided Democracy' which he would lead to end the party squabbles. Foreign policy became increasingly neutralist in keeping with the Non-aligned Movement. Separatist activities on several islands received support from the United States Government. In February 1958 troops rebelled on Sumatra and Sulawesi. It took loyal troops several months to put down the rebellion.

Another foreign policy problem was the creation of the Federation of Malaysia by the British which Sukarno actively fought against ***(KONFRONTASI)*** as a product of neo-colonialism.

The deteriorating economy, struggles between the political parties and the military, the growing influence of the PKI led to a domestic political crisis in 1965. Left wing elements in the military tried to pull a coup, but were put down by right wing army units. Hundreds of thousands died in the ensuing communist witch hunt.

A new government was formed under General ***Suharto***, while Sukarno remained the official head of state. This government has managed to stay in power until today. Through controlled foreign investment the economy is moving. Many problems of the infrastructure have been alleviated.

In April 1987, ***GOLKAR*** (functional groups), the government party won the elections (73%) against the ***PPP*** (Islamic party with 16%) and the ***PDI*** (PARTAI DEMOKRASI INDONESIA with 11%).

For an impression of the changing course of Indonesian history consider the miniature scenes set up in the basement of the Merdeka Memorial in Jakarta.

Shieldbearer of the Indonesian Coat of Arms is the Garuda which has 17 wing and 8 tail feathers. This symbolizes the Indonesian Day of Independence: 17/8/1945.

The five basic principles of Indonesia are represented in the escutcheon itself:

PANCA SILA. The star symbolizes the belief in God no matter whether the Christian, Islamic, Buddha or Shiva. The buffalo head represents Indonesian Nationalism and that all Indonesian ethnic groups must become unified. The Banyan tree represents democracy which is based on village tradition. The rice and cotton plants symbolize the fairness of society in which there is enough food and clothing for everyone. The chain symbolizes the humanitarian nature of society.

THE INDONESIAN COAT OF ARMS

BHINNEKA TUNGGAL IKA

SUMATRA

Sumatra is an island almost as big as France (473,000 km²). From north to south it measures 1800 km; at its widest 400 km. About one third of the island, including the whole east coast between Medan and Palembang, is swamp and tropical rain forest. Great plantations were established here by Europeans around the turn of the century. A mountain chain, Bukit Barisan, rises along the west coast. Among the mountains are 50 volcanoes nine of which are still active. Many mountains are over 3000 m; the highest, Gunung Kerinci, is 3805 m.

Between the swamp areas in the east and the mountains in the west there is almost untouched tropical rain forest though this may change soon. The Trans-Sumatra-Highway is now paved along almost its entire length with all the southern bridges completed, allowing travel from Bukittinggi to Jakarta in just two days. Other unpaved roads turn to mud pits in the rainy season, especially south of Lubuklinggau where bridges wash out and landslides block traffic.

In the mountains and jungles of Sumatra live 2000-2500 elephants, 100-170 rhinos, tigers, leopards, tapir and other endangered species. As in any jungle, you rarely get a chance to see the larger wild animals.

One is acutely aware of the lack of people on Sumatra - especially if one comes directly from overpopulated Java. There are only 33 million people (1985) here. You can travel 40 km without seeing a settlement sometimes, even though most people obviously live near the roads. Sumatra has an interesting ethnic composition: in Aceh you find the firmest believers of Islam, in North Sumatra the partly Christian Batak, in West Sumatra the matriarchal society of the Minangkabau. On the island Nias and the Mentawai islands are completely different ethnic populations. In the south there are many people from Java.

There are only two real tourist areas: Lake Toba and the Bukittinggi region. Everywhere else is basically undiscovered territory for tourists. Two weeks isn't enough time to do justice to Sumatra, but due to the closeness of Singapore and Malaysia it is possible to get cheap tickets in and out.

TRAVEL ALTERNATIVES TO MALAYSIA AND SINGAPORE

MEDAN - PENANG daily MAS flights and twice weekly ferry.
MEDAN - SINGAPORE daily flights by SIA and GARUDA
PAKANBARU - SINGAPORE daily flights by GARUDA
PAKANBARU - MALACCA fly Friday with MALAYSIA AIR CHARTER
PAKANBARU - TANJUNG PINANG daily MERPATI / SEMPATI flights*
PAKANBARU - TANJUNG PINANG daily boats.*
* TANJUNG PINANG - BATAM - SINGAPORE daily boats.
* TANJUNG PINANG - SINGAPORE fly once weekly with SEMPATI
DUMAI MALACCA one boat a week
PALEMBANG - SINGAPORE daily flights by GARUDA

Check for details the appropriate chapters.The cheapest and quickest way is by ferry from DUMAI to MALACCA (no visafree entry-exit point).

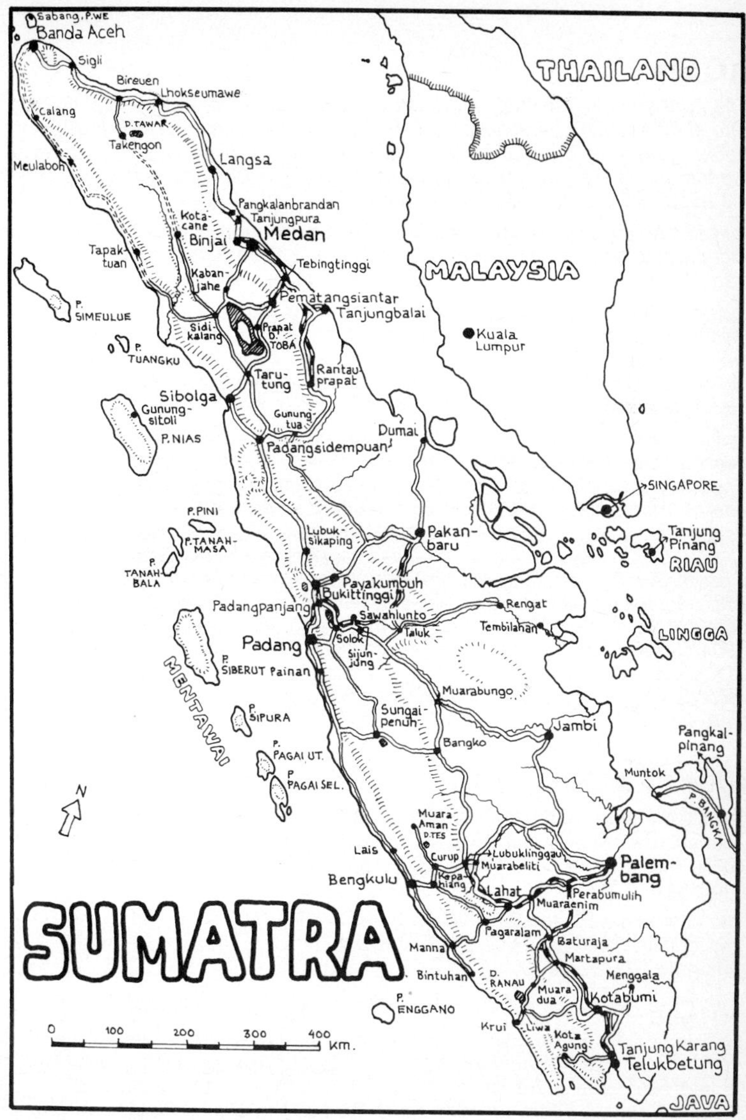
SUMATRA
THAILAND
MALAYSIA
Kuala Lumpur
SINGAPORE
RIAU
LINGGA
JAVA
Sabang, P.WE
Banda Aceh
Sigli
Bireuen
Lhokseumawe
Calang
D. TAWAR
Takengon
Meulaboh
Langsa
Pangkalanbrandan
Tanjungpura
Medan
Kota-cane
Binjai
Tapak-tuan
Tebingtinggi
Kaban-jahe
Pematangsiantar
Tanjungbalai
P. SIMEULUE
Sidi-kalang
Prapat
D. TOBA
P. TUANGKU
Rantau-prapat
Taru-tung
Sibolga
Gunung-sitoli
P. NIAS
Gunung-tua
Dumai
Padangsidempuan
P. PINI
P. TANAH-MASA
P. TANAH-BALA
Lubuk-sikaping
Pakan-baru
Tanjung Pinang
Payakumbuh
Bukittinggi
Padangpanjang
Rengat
Sawahlunto
Tembilahan
Taluk
Padang
Solok
Sijun-jung
P. SIBERUT
Painan
MENTAWAI
Muarabungo
P. SIPURA
Sungai-penuh
Jambi
P. PAGAI UT.
Bangko
P. PAGAI SEL.
Pangkal-pinang
Muntok
P. BANGKA
N
Muara Aman
D. TES
Lais
Curup
Lubuklinggau
Muarabeliti
Palem-bang
Bengkulu
Kepa-hiang
Lahat
Perabumulih
Muaraenim
Pagaralam
Baturaja
Manna
Martapura
Bintuhan
D. RANAU
Menggala
Muara-dua
Kotabumi
P. ENGGANO
Krui
Liwa
Kota Agung
Tanjung Karang
Telukbetung
0 100 200 300 400 km.

ACEH

The northernmost province of Sumatra is a 'Daerah Istimewa' (special district). The strict Muslim character of the local population is reflected in the statute books governed by Islamic law. Ramadan is taken seriously here which means during the day nothing to eat or drink (try a Chinese restaurant; often the doors are only closed but not locked!)

In 1292 Marco Polo stopped in Aceh on his way from China to Persia. He thought that he had discovered one of Europe's fabled unicorns in the Sumatran jungles. It was a one-horned Sumatra rhino!

In the 16th century Aceh had become the most dangerous rival of Malacca. Residing in Banda Aceh were traders and merchants from China, India, Persia, Syria, and Arabia. Relations with the outside world were so extensive, that in 1560 the Turkish sultan sent soldiers to Aceh to aid Sultan Alauddin against the Portuguese.

Holland was only able to bring Aceh under its control by the beginning of this century. Up until 1872 the Sultanate was de jure independent. It lay in the English and Dutch spheres of interest. In 1871 the two great powers agreed to one of the typical trades of the colonial period which might resemble a real estate deal today. England gave Holland its trading rights with Aceh in exchange for the Dutch giving up its African possession on the Gold Coast (today Ghana). A thirty year long war broke out when Holland learned that the Sultan was negotiating with Turkey, Italy, and the USA for aid. The Dutch were only able to control the coastal areas - the mountains belonged to the Acehnese. In 1904 General van Daalen made the first deep penetration into the hinterlands of the Gayo and Alas. It was sadistic and gruesome. Van Daalen kept exact records of his murders. Whole villages were crushed - then victory photos were taken.

BANDA ACEH

Check out the *ACEH MUSEUM (RUMAH ACEH)* - admission 100 Rp. Tourists are still a rare species in Banda Aceh! Near the river is the *GUNUNGAN*, the 'moving palace' which was built by a sultan of Aceh for a Malay princess.

You can take a trip to *SABANG* on Pulau We for 2500 Rp from Krueng Raya. Two hotels: *SABANG HILL GUEST HOUSE*** on Jl.Sabang Hill and on Jl.Diponegoro *HOTEL SABANG****.

HOTELS

Traditional colonial atmosphere in the *ACEH**(*)* on Jl.Mohammed Jam 1. Or less expensive is the *MEDAN*** on Jl.Jen.A.Yani 10. There are also several cheaper losmen in this area.

HOW TO GET THERE

Fly with GARUDA from JAKARTA (185,000 Rp) via Medan. Daily flights from MEDAN to Banda Aceh cost 55,600 Rp. Blang Bintang Airport is about 15 km east of the city. Daily overland Mercedes buses leave MEDAN for BANDA ACEH. ALS or Kurnia are the most comfortable - costs 7500 Rp. Other companies charge 1000 Rp less.

TAKENGON

This quiet lovely place on the banks of Danau Tawar, surrounded by steep mountains and fragrant coniferous forest, is situated in the centre of the cool Gayo Highlands. The Gayo are ethnically related to the Batak but were converted to Islam more than 300 years ago. In spite of strict police checks, cannabis is still being widely grown - there are several tourists in Takengon jail for smoking grass. Best to stay at *LOSMEN BUNTUL KUBU*** on a hill at the lake, near the market. Several more hotels are in the area.

HOW TO GET THERE

From MEDAN there are direct buses to TAKENGON (13 hrs., 6500 Rp) or go via BANDA ACEH, change at BIREUEN. Regular buses from Banda Aceh.

From Takengon also a direct route to LAKE TOBA. Jeeps are said to run to Blangkejeren (8000 Rp) every 2 or 3 days. Otherwise you'll have to hike for at least 2-3 days. Catch a bus to UWAQ (5 hrs. cost 2500 Rp), from here 7 hrs. hike uphill - stay the night in one of the huts on the way through the jungle - many tracks of tigers. It's best to hike only between 9.00 h and 15.00 h. The next afternoon you reach RIKIBGAIB. From there bus for 1000 Rp to BLANGKEJEREN, known for its colourful jackets and materials. Stay at *HOTEL JULIE**. Bus to KUTACANE for 2500 Rp, takes 4-5 hrs. Another 5-6 hrs. for 2500 Rp will get you to KABANJAHE.

NORTH SUMATRA

This 70,787 km² is one of the richest provinces in Indonesia. According to their own statistics, 30 % of the Indonesian GDP is produced in the province (60% of the country's GDP is from the whole of Sumatra).

Along a 250 km strip of coast are a string of plantations totaling 1000 km². While many of these plantations today are nationally owned, others belong to transnational corporations such as Goodyear, Uni-Royal, or Harrison & Crossfield. Rubber plantations take up 40% of the area; palm oil trees occupy an equal share of soil. Tea, tobacco, and cocoa make up the rest of the agricultural economy. The first plantations appeared about one hundred years ago - the same time as in Malaya. This development is typical of the Dutch colonial policy.

"Deli today is one of the most blossoming colonies on earth. When a visitor first steps foot on land at Belawan and rides the iron horse past the thriving plantations on the way to Medan, how could he know how many human corpses fertilized the soil in order that it should bear such fruit." This was written by a German doctor and ethnologist at the beginning of this century.

The long fertile plain on the east coast of Sumatra has been created by river silt deposits over thousands of years. The area used to be dense jungle - the agriculture being based on slash and burn cultivation. Every couple of years the fields are allowed to lie fallow in order to regenerate and be usable again. This fallow field economy gave the Dutch a means of completely changing the traditional land rights of the area. All land lying fallow or uncultivated became state owned. The Sultan of Deli and the colonial government leased the land to plantation owners. This generated tremendous profits. The Maimoon Palace in Medan was built with the proceeds. Workers usually had to be imported from Java or Southern China. It is impossible to imagine the suffering of the coolies, who despite their recruitment, were little more than slaves. Many died in a short period of time. In the 1880s an epidemic of beri beri killed almost 80% of the plantation workers - the disease is caused by vitamin B deficiency. Because dead coolies are unprofitable, the living standards of the coolies began to improve slowly. Even so it was common for workers to run away and hide in the mountains. Draconian laws were instituted by the colonial government in Batavia which allowed the plantation owners to be laws unto themselves. Whippings were a daily occurrence.

In 1926 the yearly wages of a man was 163.20 guilders and for women 145.20 guilders. The 'subsistence wage' as it was known would suffice only for the most basic necessities and food. Business must have been good because, just in the year 1930, the plantations of North Sumatra earned 200 million guilders profit. After independence the plantations were either nationalized or divided among smallholders (in 1979 about 11% of the total area under cultivation). Production began to fall due to lack of financial resources by the central government in Jakarta, but also due to mismanagement and corruption. After 1965 foreign investment was again allowed.

MEDAN

The capital of North Sumatra has a population of about 1,400,000 people. Back in 1860 there were only a few houses of a Malay kampong here along the Deli River. The city was founded in 1864 by the Sultan of Deli.

Travellers usually avoid Medan because of the noise, exhaust and heat on the congested streets.

Worth a look is the *MAIMOON PALACE* built in 1888 from resources mentioned above. The *MESJID RAYA* (Great Mosque) is partially built from the stones of ancient Buddhist and Hindu temples. In the city you'll also find examples of colonial Dutch architecture, particularly along Jl.Jen.A.Yani and its extension Jl.Balai Kota. The Bank Indonesia building was constructed in 1907 as the *JAVASCHE BANK*. Dating from the same period are the *TOWN HALL (BALAI KOTA)* and the *CENTRAL POST OFFICE*. Sniff the colonial atmosphere in the old wing of *HOTEL DHARMA DELI* which was known in 1898 as Hotel De Boer.
Worth seeing is the *HISTORY & ETHNOLOGY MUSEUM*, Jl.Palang Merah. On *JL.PANDU* you'll find the oldest Chinese temple in the city.

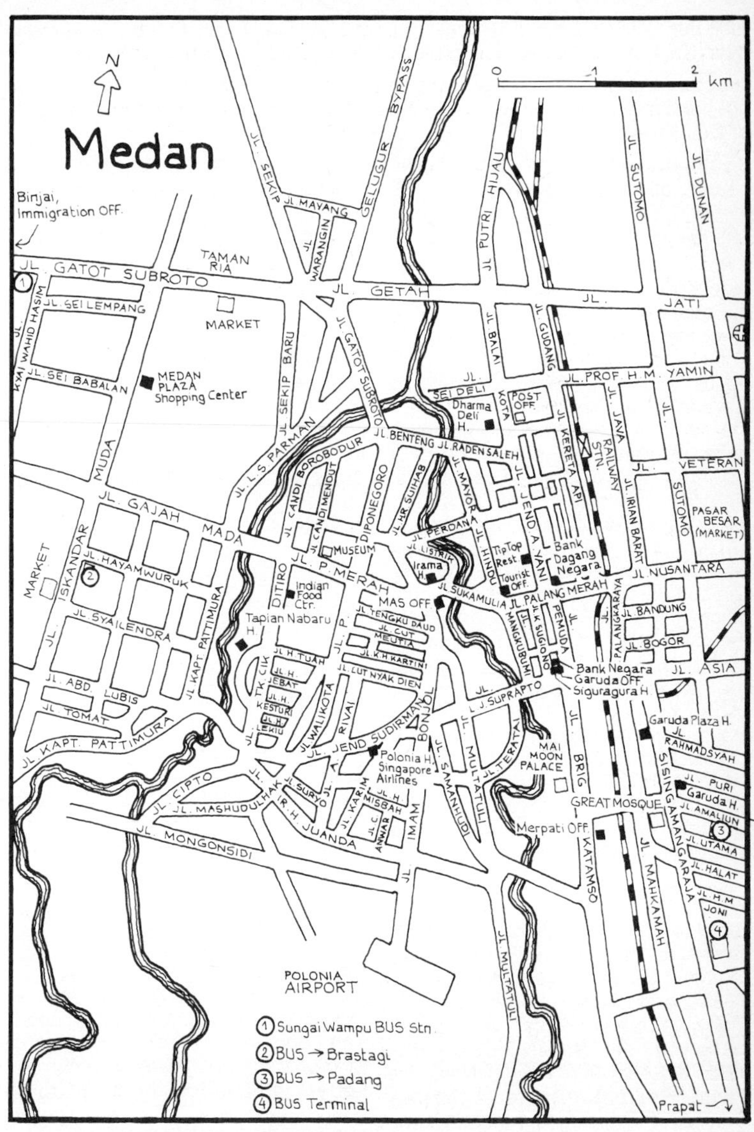
Medan
N
0 1 2 km
Binjai, Immigration OFF.
JL. GATOT SUBROTO
TAMAN RIA
JL. GETAH
JL. JATI
MARKET
MEDAN PLAZA Shopping Center
JL. SEKIP
JL. GELUGUR BYPASS
JL. MAYANG
JL. WARANGIN
JL. PUTRI HIJAU
JL. SUTOMO
JL. DUNAN
JL. SEI LEMPANG
JL. KYAI WAHID HASIM
JL. SEI BABALAN
JL. SEKIP BARU
JL. GATOT SUBROTO
JL. BALAI KOTA
JL. GUDANG
JL. PROF. H.M. YAMIN
JL. SEI DELI
Dharma Deli H.
POST OFF.
JL. BENTENG
JL. RADEN SALEH
JL. L.S. PARMAN
JL. CANDI BOROBODUR
JL. CANDI MENDUT
JL. DIPONEGORO
JL. HR. SUJHAB
JL. MAYOR
JL. KERETA API
RAILWAY STN.
JL. JAVA
JL. VETERAN
JL. MUDA
JL. GAJAH MADA
JL. JEND. A. YANI
JL. IRIAN BARAT
JL. SUTOMO
PASAR BESAR (MARKET)
JL. PERDANA
JL. LISTRIK
MUSEUM
JL. HINDU
TipTop Rest.
Tourist OFF.
Bank Dagang Negara
JL. ISKANDAR
MARKET
JL. HAYAMWURUK
JL. P. MERAH
Irama H.
JL. DITIRO
Indian Food Ctr.
JL. SUKAMULIA
MAS OFF.
JL. PALANG MERAH
JL. NUSANTARA
JL. PALANGKARAYA
JL. BANDUNG
JL. SYAILENDRA
Tapian Nabaru H.
JL. TENGKU DAUD
JL. CUT MEUTIA
JL. MANGKUBUMI
JL. K. SUGIONO
JL. PEMUDA
JL. BOGOR
JL. KAPT. PATTIMURA
JL. H. TUAH
JL. K.H. KARTINI
JL. CUT NYAK DIEN
Bank Negara
Garuda OFF.
Siguragura H.
JL. ASIA
JL. ABD. LUBIS
JL. TOMAT
TK. CIK
JL. H. JEBAT
JL. H. KESTURI
JL. H. LEKIU
JL. WALIKOTA
JL. RIVAI
JL. BONJOL
JL. SUPRAPTO
Garuda Plaza H.
JL. RAHMADSYAH
JL. KAPT. PATTIMURA
JL. JEND. SUDIRMAN
Polonia H.
Singapore Airlines
JL. SAMANHUDI
JL. MULTATULI
JL. TERATAI
MAI MOON PALACE
JL. BRIG. KATAMSO
JL. PURI
Garuda H.
JL. CIPTO
JL. SURYO
JL. KARIM
JL. H. MISBAH
JL. C. ANWAR
GREAT MOSQUE
JL. AMALIUN
JL. MASHUDULHAK
JL. IR. H. JUANDA
JL. IMAM
Merpati Off.
JL. SISINGAMANGARAJA
JL. UTAMA
JL. MONGONSIDI
JL. HALAT
JL. MAHKAMAH
JL. H.M. JONI
JL. MULTATULI
POLONIA AIRPORT
① Sungai Wampu BUS Stn.
② BUS → Brastagi
③ BUS → Padang
④ BUS Terminal
Prapat

Visit the *CROCODILE FARM,* 8 km from Medan in Asam Kumbang, home to over 1000 of the reptiles. Open 9:00-17:00 h, feeding time is 16:30 h.

A good road (buses 300 Rp) leads to *BELAWAN,* Medan's harbour. You are not permitted to photograph within the port. In town you'll find a large selection of Chinese porcelain.

If you'll be in Medan for a while, make an excursion to *PANTAI CERMIN* (mirror beach), 50 km southeast of the city. Colts depart from Jl.Sisingamangaraja.

HOTELS

Two hotels are the backpackers' meeting places in the city: *IRAMA***, Jl.Palang Merah 112, (dorm*) quiet, clean, and safe (near Hotel Danau Toba) and *SIGURAGURA**, (dorm*), on Jl.Let.Jen.Suprapto 2/K, next to Garuda office, run down, loud. About the same is *SIAR** on Jl.Sutomo. A better alternative is *TAPIAN NABARU HOTEL**(*), Jl.Hang Tuah 6, tel 512155, centrally located, clean, breakfast included, the owner studied in Germany. The old Dutch Hotel de Boer is today called *DHARMA DELI****, Jl.Balai Kota 2, tel 327011 - the place is 100 years old and looks it. At the *GARUDA***** on Jl.Sisingamangaraja 27, tel 22775, the disco on the roof keeps you awake till 5 a.m. Many rooms don't have a window. Diagonally across at no. 18 is the *GARUDA PLAZA HOTEL*****. Better try *NEW POLONIA HOTEL*****. Quieter is *TIARA*****, Jl.Cut Mutia, tel 516000. The last four hotels have swimming pools.

FOOD

Good is *TIPTOP* at Jl.Jen.A.Yani 92. Opens at 10:00 h. On Friday & Saturday nights enjoy live music dateline 1920s and '30s. Service is great. Enjoy vegetarian Indian and homemade yogurt in *INDIAN FOOD CENTRE,* Jl.Kediri 96. Several *Nasi Padang Restaurants* are at the beginning of Jl.Sisingamangaraja near Jl.Pandu.

Foodstalls are set up on Jl.Selat Panjang at about 18:00 h. Till 1:00 in the morning you can eat here good and cheap - not far from Siguragura or ask any becak driver for 'Selat Panjang'. Foodstalls are also set up at the Amusement Park *(TAMAN RIA)* on Jl.Jen.Gatot Subroto. Lots of restaurants in the new shopping centres, try the 4th floor of Medan Plaza Shopping Centre, Jl.Iskandar Muda, for the *HOUSTON* and the *PLAZA INTERNATIONAL.*

SHOPPING

On Jl.Jen.A.Yani there are lots of souvenir and antique shops. Prices have jumped in recent years though. It's still a good place for the last few rupiah. Look in at TOKO ASLI, no. 62 or TOKO SENI, no. 2.

Tremendous shopping centres have opened in the last three years (GOLDEN SHOPPING CENTRE, MEDAN PLAZA, DELI PLAZA) with a selection of wares to compete with Penang or Kuala Lumpur. For your daily needs, head for CENTRAL OLYMPIA, south of the big market.

GENERAL INFORMATION

TOURIST INFORMATION - at Jl.Palang Merah 66 and at the airport. They don't have much info (maps of Medan and Lake Toba). You can get better information from a travel agency such as NITOUR at Jl.Prof.H. M.Yamin 21 E. (tel 516906).

PPA OFFICE - Jl.Sisingamangaraja KM 5.5 a new building complex on the west side of the street, open Mon-Thurs 08:00-14:45 h, Fri 08:00-11:30 h, Sat-Sun 08:00-14:00 h.

BANKS - for the best exchange rate try Bank Negara Indonesia 1946, Jl. Pemuda 12, (also at the airport), Bali Bank, Jl.Balai Kota 10, or in Bank Dagang Negara Jl.Jen.A.Yani 109.

AMERICAN EXPRESS - Pacto Ltd., Jl.Palang Merah 26F, tel 513669.

IMMIGRATION - Office is on Jl.Binjai. Beside Medan, the only place in North Sumatra where you can extend your visa is Pematang Siantar.

CONSULATES - in Medan there are 13 foreign consulates: Great Britain, Jl.Jen.A.Yani 2 (tel 325735); Malaysia, Jl.Diponegoro 11 (tel 323261); Holland, Jl.Abdullah Lubis 7a (tel 526034); Singapore, Jl.Teuku Daud 3 (tel 327978); USA, Jl.Iman Bonjol 13 (tel 322200).

GETTING AROUND IN MEDAN - for short and middle distances fly by 'becak dayung' (bicycle rickshaw), costs 300-500 Rp. For longer distances a 'becak mesin' (motorcycle rickshaw) for 500-1000 Rp. Becak dayung are not permitted to drive on main roads.

LEAVING MEDAN

BY AIR

Polonia airport is only 1-2 km from town. You don't need to take a taxi; just outside the airport you'll find becaks waiting that only charge 500 Rp. At the coupon taxi stand expect to pay 4000 Rp into town. The airport tax is 6000 Rp on international flights and 2000 Rp for domestic. MAS flies daily to and from Penang. Merpati, Garuda, Mandala, and SMAC offer domestic flights. Addresses:

MAS, Jl.Iman Bonjol 17 (Danau Toba International), tel 519333 - GARUDA, Jl.Let.Jen. Suprapto 2D, tel 511927 - MERPATI, Jl.Katamso 41J, tel 514057 - SIA (New Polonia Hotel), Jl.Sudirman 14, tel 325300 - MANDALA, Jl.Katamso 37E, tel 513309. SMAC, Jl.Iman Bonjol 59, tel 515934 (near the airport).

SAMPLE PRICES: PENANG 60,000 Rp (only MAS), PALEMBANG 120,000 Rp (GA), SINGAPORE 113,000 Rp (SIA / GA), BANDA ACEH 61,900 Rp (GA), PADANG 73,000 Rp (GA), PAKANBARU 65,800 Rp (GA), JAKARTA 136,000 Rp (MZ / Mandala), 160,000 Rp (GA), DUMAI 54,700 Rp (MZ), BATAM 87,000 Rp (MZ). SMAC flies daily (7:30 h) to GUNUNGSITOLI (Nias); one way 62,900 Rp.

BY BUS / TRAIN

There are two bus stations in town. Buses to Brastagi, Kabanjahe leave from Jl.Iskandar Muda(1 1/2 hrs., 750 / 850 Rp). Buses to Pematang Siantar and Prapat leave from Jl.Sisingamangaraja.

SAMPLE PRICES: BANDA ACEH 6500 Rp, TAKENGON 6500 Rp, PRAPAT 2000 Rp, SIBOLGA 5000 Rp, BUKITTINGGI 9500 Rp, PADANG 10,000 Rp, TANJUNG KARANG 25,000 Rp, PAKANBARU 11,000 Rp.

Long distance is best with ANS (Office: Jl.Sisingamangaraja 16) or with ALS (Jl.Amaliun 2A). They are the two biggest companies and have the most comfortable vehicles. Long distance buses south or north depart from the companies' offices in Jl.Sisingamangaraja and side roads. Trains to RANTAU PRAPAT cost

2200 Rp, TANJUNG BALAI 1700 Rp and PEMATANG SIANTAR 1800 Rp.

BY TAXI

Overland taxis depart from the airport or from several taxi offices to PRAPAT (25,000 Rp) or to SIBOLGA (38,000 Rp); there is room for five passengers.

BY SHIP

Belawan, 26 km from town, is Medan's harbour. Buses cost 300 Rp from the Pelni Office on Jl.Kol. Sugiono/Cakrawati 5-7, tel 25100, 25190. Two ships, KM.Kambuna (1596 passengers) and KM.Rinjani (1729 passengers) depart alternately from Belawan every Monday at 12:00. The KM.Kambuna sails via Jakarta, Surabaya, and Ujung Pandang to Balikpapan, Palu, and Manado. The MV.Rinjani continues from Ujung Pandang to Bau-Bau, Ambon, and Sorong. Both ships are German built, in keeping with European standards: 2-bed cabins in 1st class (AC, TV, showers, and WC). In 2nd class you've 4-bed cabins, in 3rd class 6-bed, in 4th class 8-bed; economy class offers a dorm with individual spaces to sleep. The ship is quite new and clean.

SAMPLE PRICES (economy class; triple the price for 1st class):

JAKARTA 35,700 Rp (1 1/2 days), SURABAYA 50,500 Rp (3 days), UJUNG PANDANG 64,200 Rp (4 days, 5 hrs.), BAU-BAU 72,600 Rp (5 days), AMBON 86,700 Rp (6 days), SORONG 99,300 Rp (6 days, 22 hrs.), BALIKPAPAN 71,000 Rp (5 days), PALU 75,200 Rp (6 days), MANADO 95,700 Rp (6 days, 16 hrs.).

The KM.Lawit steams out of Belawan every second Saturday via LHOKSEUMAWE (8000 Rp) to BANDA ACEH (16,400 Rp). The return trip every Tuesday sails via DUMAI (15,400 Rp), MUNTOK (32,800 Rp), to JAKARTA and on to KETAPANG and PONTIANAK.

The GADIS LANGKASUKA departs Belawan on Tues & Thurs at 20:00 h, and arrives in PENANG the next morning, costs: deck 40,600 Rp, reclining seat 66,000 Rp, cabin or 78,600 Rp. The harbour tax adds 2500 Rp. The agent in Medan is P.T. Ekasukma Wisata Tour & Travel, Jl. Katamso, tel 515562.

BOHOROK

Bohorok Orang Utan Rehabilitation Centre was opened in 1973 to prepare orangutan for their new life in the jungles. At one time, young 'mawas' as the animals are known in Indonesian, were captured and sold to pet shops and zoos after the mother orangutan had been shot. The emotional stress of seeing their mothers shot often leaves the animals psychologically deranged. Now that the orangutan is an endangered species, they are trying to take the animals raised as house pets and return them to their native habitat.

Get your permit first in Medan or in Bukit Lawang at Dinas Perlindungan dan Pengawetan Alam (PPA). Feeding time is daily at 8:00 and 15:00 h. It is also a good place to take jungle walks or go swimming.

The village is at the eastern edge of the tremendous Leuser National Park (8500 km^2, of which two-thirds are in Aceh province). It is practically impossible to get from here into the park interior, but you can get a good impression of the wilderness on leisurely day hikes. Around the centre is an excellent network of well-marked footpaths. If you don't have confidence in your sense of orientation, or plan a trek of several days, hire a guide (3000-5000 Rp per day).

Spend the night in the Resthouse or Ranger House (2500 Rp) in Bukit Lawang across the narrow river bridge. There are warung and shops in the village to buy food.

HOW TO GET THERE
Buses leave from Jl.Sungei Wampu corner of Jl.Binjai. Bus to Bukit Lawang (1200 Rp) at midday - otherwise take the bus to BINJAI (300 Rp) and from there change to BOHOROK (800 Rp - 3-5 hrs.). Last bus back at around 14:00 h.

The Bohorok administration building is right by the bus stop. From Bukit Lawang it is a 30 minute walk along a footpath through the banana and rubber plantations to the ferry.

The last sampan departs at 15:30 h. Across the river in the jungle by a loop in the river is the rehabilitation centre. From here it is 500 m steep uphill to the reservation where you can observe the animals.

THE BATAK HIGHLANDS

With Lake Toba at its centre, the highlands of Bukit Barisan is home to several Batak tribes. Pressed by deutero-Malay immigrants, the Batak took refuge in the secluded mountains where they were able to maintain their culture in almost complete isolation until the end of the 19th century. Tales of cannibalism among warlike Batak tribesmen did much to dissuade white men from penetrating the highlands. First the missionaries, then the Dutch, today tourism has conquered Lake Toba, spelling doom for an ancient culture. Traditional houses are now used as tourist accommodations. Wood carving is mass produced for the tourist trade. Part of the problem are travellers, out for cheap thrills (skinny dipping, drugs), without thought for the people of Lake Toba.

BRASTAGI

The drive from Medan to Brastagi which lies at 1320 m in the mountains is quite an experience. The steep, endlessly winding road leads to a plateau - wide rolling country framed by the volcanoes of Sibayak and Sinabong. Since the twenties this has been a resort for white managers, a retreat from their plantations in the malaria-infested swamps.

On the hills west of the main road, many houses have been built by people with money. Find them on the way to *GUNDALING HILL* (admission 200 Rp on Sundays). After walking about half an hour, you get a wonderful view of the highlands and the volcanoes. There is a *MARKET* in the centre of Brastagi, along the main road, where Batak sell fruit and vegetables.

THE BATAK

There are 1.3 million Batak living in North Sumatra, two-thirds of whom are Christian while the remainder are mostly Muslim. They are smaller and more thickset than other Malay people, forming several ethnic groups each with individual languages and dialects. The Toba, who are considered the original Batak, settled upon Samosir Island and along the coast of the lake which bears their name. About 180,000 Karo live in over 200 villages in the highlands of Brastagi and Kabanjahe where they are engaged in intensive agriculture and planting of wet rice. In the east is the homeland of the Simalungun with its capital at Pematang Siantar. The Pakpak (also called Dairi) are settled northwest of the lake around Sidikalang. In the south are the Angkola and Mandailing. By accepting Islam, the Mandailing Batak have lost their former culture. The Toba and Karo Batak are Christian, mostly Protestant with a few Catholics, but they have maintained much of their traditional culture. They form the largest Christian culture in Indonesia. Attend a funeral or high mass in one of the many churches; you'll see the great role religion plays in this society.

There is no written history of the Batak, leaving much in doubt. Scientists have established that humans have been cutting the forests around Lake Toba for 6000 years. However, the Batak are said to have migrated into this region 2500 to 3000 years ago from present-day southern China, northern Thailand, and Burma. They first landed on the west coast of Sumatra between Barus and Sibolga. As a mountain people, they settled again in the mountainous region around Mount Pusuk Buhit where they founded their kingdoms in isolation from the Malay coastal inhabitants.

The ancient villages, particularly around Lake Toba, were surrounded by high earthen walls with only a narrow gate for admission. The homes of wealthy families were built of wood, set on stilts, one or two metres above ground. The over-sized roofs, which vary greatly according to region, are covered with palm leaves. A steep stair provides access to the dark, roomy, interior. The kitchen is in the back with an open fire. No walls divide the living space shared by several families. The homes, assembly halls, and rice barns surround a central square, the Alaman.

The Batak reputation as cannibals should be viewed within their own traditional framework. The harmony of the Middle World (Sumatra was the Middle World with Lake Toba at its centre) was disturbed by murderers, adulterers, traitors,and spies (which included all non-Bataks who entered the region uninvited). The universal penalty was cannibalization, because only a sacrificial meal could restore harmony.

The Batak story of creation is quite interesting. There are three phases. In the beginning the god Mula Jadi stood in the upper world. He had three sons, one of whom was very bad. Muda Jadi then created a tree in which a hen lived and laid three giant eggs. Out of each of the eggs hatched a girl who would later marry one of Muda Jadi's sons. They were all god-like in nature. In the second phase the earth was created. One girl was supposed to marry the delinquent son. To avoid this fate, she spun a long thread with which she was able to lower herself to the middle world. But there was only water. Mula Jadi had sympathy for her plight, so he sent her some earth which she was able to spread out on the water. In the water, however, lived the dragon of the underworld on to whose head the earth fell. The dragon tried to throw it off and writhed in the water. The princess pinned him in place with her sword. Once in a while the dragon still squirms resulting in an earthquake.

Then in the third phase people were created. The princess married the wayward son who had changed his appearance. Many children were born including two twins. A great festival was celebrated at which Mula Jadi announced that the twins would have to remain on the earth. The gods then returned to the upper world and the great thread was cut. After many generations descendants of the twins gave birth to a son, Si Raja Batak. He was the first Batak.

The direct descendants of Si Raja Batak were god-kings, the last of whom died fighting the Dutch in 1907. According to their lineage and closeness to the gods, ranged the royal nobility, peasants and slaves. Priests were important members of society because only they had the power of prophecy and the ability to set the dates of important holidays.

The Batak typically live in large families whereby many families of the father's relations live together. Up to ten such families will live together in one village (huta). Several 'huta' make up a 'marga' that traces its history from a single ancestor. The whole 'marga' is invited to funerals and other important festivities. In spite of Christianity, this tradition continues today, and those who have taken part in a Batak festival know how big a 'marga' can be.

Due to their Christian education, many Batak are better accustomed to western ideas, culture, and technology than their Muslim counterparts. Additionally, poor soil, high birth rates, and a lack of jobs, forced many Batak to leave home. They are well represented in the Indonesian government, military, and music scene, testimony to the Batak love of music. A guitar or cassette recorder is always around, on walks, in a bus, or at an evening get together. Powered by liberal doses of toddy (palm wine), young men sing melodic Batak tunes and rhythmic western songs. The women demonstrate their musical talents primarily at Sunday church services.

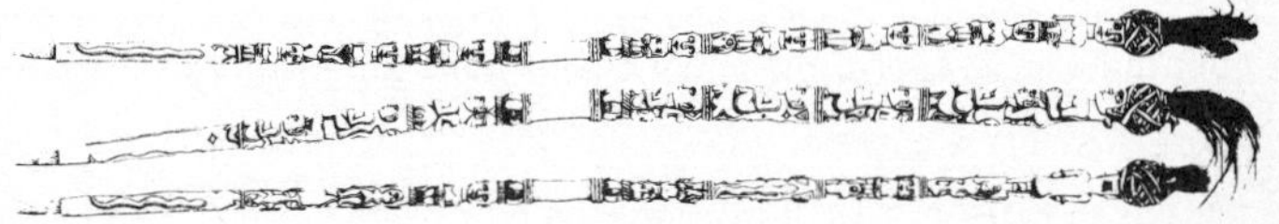

At the memorial there are four souvenir antique shops which offer some interesting objects. In the Modesty Souvenir Shop (very expensive) you can get a photocopied map for climbing Sibayak mountain. The most reasonably priced shop is Tannta, Jl.Petran 76.

HOTELS

One of the best maintained colonial style hotels is the *BUKIT KUBU INTERNATIONAL* on the road to Medan. Rooms cost up to 30,000 Rp a night. Just opposite is the new *HOTEL RUDANG***** where you can get fresh and cool marquisa juice. At the other end of the main road are nice rooms in *WISMA DIENG***. Right across the way is *GUESTHOUSE SIBAYAK*** (also dorm*). Cheap is *LOSMEN GUNUNG* * on Jl.Veteran 98. Right at the memorial are *GINSATA HOTEL*** and *TIMUR HOTEL***. Helpful staff in the *BUKIT TONGGING HOTEL***, Jl.Veteran 48.

FOOD

ASIA RESTAURANT, Jl.Veteran (across from the post office) is the most expensive place in town with its Chinese cooking. You get lots of atmosphere and cheap prices at *BUDI AMAN KEDAI NASI ISLAM* in No 92. Not far is *RUMAH MAKAN MINANG* with good Nasi Padang. Try Nasi Campur for 500 Rp. On Jl.Veteran you'll find two places that sell 'babi panggang'. The traditional Karo Batak meal is made of pork, blood gravy and rice. On the main street in the evening you can listen to guitar music and have a great time drinking lots of 'tuak', maybe at *ORA ET LABORA.* Tuak is quite potent so people who don't drink a lot should be careful. There are coffee and cakes for breakfast at *KEDAI KOPI OSAKA,* opposite Losmen Gunung. Be sure to try the marquisa fruit sold in the market.

HOW TO GET THERE

Minibuses leave regularly from MEDAN for 800 Rp. The direct bus PRAPAT - BRASTAGI costs 2200 Rp. An alternative: Take the daily boat from SIMANINDO (Samosir) to HARANGGOAL (1000 Rp), TUKTUK - SIMANINDO costs 500 Rp. Get from here the bus via SERIBUDOLOK (350 Rp) to KABANJAHE (300 Rp). Or: PANGURURAN bus to SIDIKALANG and KABANJAHE.

DAY TRIPS AROUND BRASTAGI

GUNUNG SIBAYAK

The 2300 m high volcano can be climbed on a day's outing. Take the first bus (100 Rp) toward Medan, and after 8 km you're at the outset of your hike. After 500 m you'll reach the first sulphur springs. A further 4 km get you to the village of RADJA BERNE = SEMANGAT GUNUNG. The path begins at the village's last warung. You go past the hot sulphur springs and rice fields into the mountain jungle. The path is very steep and quite slippery. Wear good shoes! Takes two to three hours. On the way back to Brastagi you can take a direct path from the village over a mountain chain. Don't get caught in the dark - takes about 1 1/2 hours.

LINGGA

Take the bus to KABANJAHE (150 Rp) - the only place in Batak Land where you can change money. Bank Indonesia 1946 offers a worse rate than in

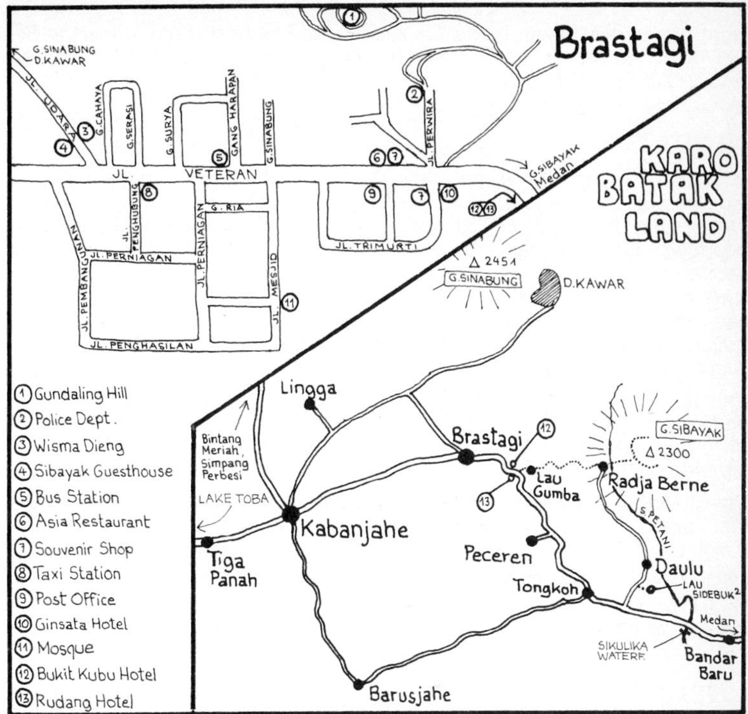

Medan. Then take a bus to LINGGA for 150 Rp (you can also do the 5 km on foot). LINGGA is a quite well preserved Karo-Batak village - 200 Rp admission.

BARUSJAHE

Bus from KABANJAHE (300 Rp) to the village 15 km away. Here too you'll see well preserved, traditional houses. Rattim Barus, the friendly village chief, will show you around. You can also spend the night.

PEMATANG SIANTAR

The 130 km long bus ride from Medan to the city of Pematang Siantar leads through an endless line of plantations. You'd really only come here for a visa extension. This is the only place in North-Sumatra besides Medan where it's possible.

The *SIMALUNGUN MUSEUM* is worth a visit (open daily except Sun 8:00-12:00 h and 14:00-17:00 h).

There are several cheap hotels on Jl.Merdeka. The best place in town is *SIANTAR HOTEL***** on Jl.W.R. Supratman 3. It's in a park. Buses to Brastagi for 1500 Rp, to Prapat for 600 Rp.

PRAPAT

As soon as you get along the Trans-Sumatra-Highway at Pematang Siantar and head up into the mountains, you leave the plantations behind you. Pine forests cover the steep, barren slopes; water buffaloes graze on the volcanic meadows. Coconut, tapioca, peanuts, fruit, vegetables, and increasing amounts of cloves are the staples of agriculture. The highland specialties include the marquisa, passion fruit, and avocados. There is a similarity to the lake region of northern Italy. The mild climate, particularly in the morning, is reminiscent of a hot summer day in central Europe. In the afternoon, dark clouds appear around the mountain tops, and heavy rains fall.

The tourist centres around Lake Toba are Prapat and Tuk Tuk on Samosir Island. There are many comfortable hotels in Prapat, the lake's most important town. Bus loads of package tourists spend the night here, and make daytrips into the surrounding area.

Have a look at the *MARKET* held every Saturday on Tiga Raja Square, by the boat landing. From the surrounding villages, women arrive by boat and minibus to sell fruit, vegetables, fish and rice. While they carry their heavy loads through the bustling market, the men enjoy fresh toddy.

On Jl.Haranggaol, leading down to the market, there are a number of antique and souvenir shops.

HOTELS

If you arrive late in the evening in Prapat or you have to take an early bus to Sibolga / Bukittinggi / Padang, then spend the night in town. Otherwise find cheaper lodgings on Samosir. Cheap is *DAVID GURNING'S RESTHOUSE**, Jl.Sisingamangaraja, by the lake. Next door at *ANDILO TRAVEL SERVICE**, no. 41, you can stay in simple rooms on the ground floor by the lake. There are other lodgings along the road. If you want to spend a bit more money, try *PAGO PAGO INN***, Jl.Haranggaol, toward the market. The higher-priced hotels generally offer a view from the slopes overlooking the large bay. In the upper category are the three-star *PRAPAT*****, Jl.Marihat 1, tel 410121; *DANAU TOBA HOTEL*****, Jl.Samosir 17, tel 41583; next door *BUDI MULYA*****, tel 41216; the two *TARABUNGA***** hotels, Jl.Samosir 20, tel 41700 or Jl.Sibingo, and *WISMA DANAU TOBA*****, tel 41302. The other hotels on this street are somewhat cheaper or at least offer some cheaper rooms.

FOOD

Be adventurous, try exotic Batak food in the warung around the market. Like in nasi Padang restaurants, you can choose from pots of hot food. Try SANG SANG (dog curry) or be less brave with NANIARSIK (fish in a hot, spicy sauce). We have not been impressed by the usual Chinese or nasi

Padang restaurants. Most restaurants are located on Jl.Sisingamangaraja *(MINANG, ASIA, SUDIMAMPIR, BRASTAGI)*. East of the Government Office is *ANDILO* with traveller food. On Jl.Haranggaol is the Padang restaurant *KUALA LUMPUR*, the Chinese *HONGKONG*, and the Indonesian *BALI*. In Prapat, as in Brastagi, you've excellent marquisa, passion fruit, and mangos at street stands and in the market.

GENERAL INFORMATION

TOURIST OFFICE - by the big Horas archway, at the upper Jl.Samosir, few tips, open weekdays 8:00-19:00h.

BOATS - further along the street you can rent pedalboats and excursion boats, see the posted price list.

BANK - There isn't one in town, yet. So bring enough rupiahs, or if you must, change in hotels or by Andilo (who will change cash or US$ travellers cheques at a fairly reasonable exchange rate).

LAKE TOBA FESTIVAL - the annual Horas Festival (since 1980) is celebrated around the lake, featuring traditional dances, folklore, boatraces in Prapat and Muara (southern bank), and horseraces in Siborongborong (south of Muara). The festival is usually held during the summer.

LEAVING PRAPAT

BUSES

All long distance and local buses stop in front of the travel agencies on Jl.Sisingamangaraja. Nancy S. and Aladin of ANDILO TRAVEL SERVICE are reliable. Find them at No. 41, tel 41548. Januari Lamagu and David Yunan of GORAHA RAJA TOUR, No. 87, tel 41246 speak good English too and also rent rooms. You can book passage aboard the ship GADIS LANGKASUKA to Penang or air tickets in Prapat. As communications with Medan don't always work, it is better to organize it yourself in Medan.

You don't have to buy tickets in advance for the local Oplets and minibuses. From Samosir take the first boat to Prapat, go up the street to the main road and stop the first bus. PEMATANG SIANTAR 600 Rp, BALIGE 750 Rp, BRASTAGI 2000 Rp. Departures 7:00-12:00 h. For 3000 Rp you can go all the way to SIBOLGA, takes 6 - 8 hrs., for the 220 km. After SIBORONGBORONG the road winds snake-like through the mountains.

You might take your time enroute to Bukittinggi on a three-day tour: From PRAPAT to BALIGE (traditional houses; 750 Rp), and on to TARUTUNG (650 Rp) - PADANGSIDEMPUAN (1300 Rp) - KOTANOPAN (1100 Rp) - PANTI; a chance to visit the Rimba Panti Nature Reserve, (800 Rp) - BUKITTINGGI (1200 Rp). Where and how you spend the night along this route will depend upon the bus departure and arrival times.

You can book overland buses by Andilo or Goraha Raja Tour (see above). Long-distance buses to Jakarta depart from Medan and are already full when they leave there. They usually run via Tarutung / Sipirok / Padangsidempuan and not via Sibolga. Careful if you want to go to Nias! ALS has the best express buses with wide reclining seats and air conditioning.

SAMPLE PRICES (the highest price and shortest time are for the ALS buses whose departure times are listed): MEDAN 2000 Rp; SIBOLGA 3000-3500 Rp, 5 1/2 - 6 hrs., departs

11:00, 12:00, and 13:30 h; BUKITTINGGI 6000-7000 Rp (15-20 hrs.), departs 13:00 h; PADANG 6500-7500 Rp; JAKARTA with ALS in 47 hrs. for 35,000 Rp, departs 14:00 h.

TAXIS

From Medan to Prapat you might share a taxi or a privately offered car for the two hour ride to Lake Toba. With bargaining you can pay 4-5000 Rp per person with five passengers.

BOATS

Boats to various jetties on Samosir Island depart from 7:00 h to sundown from the landing by the market or from Andilo Travel Service or David Gurning. The regular price is 500 Rp. On Saturdays the ride with the market boats (departing at 10:00 h and returning at 16:00 h) costs just 250 Rp. Most boats stop at Tomok. If you want to go to Tuktuk, ask first where the boat is landing. Usually they will drop you off where you want or at the nearest convenient location. Big boats make the trip in 30 - 45 min., to Ambarita 15 min. longer, but the same price! The first boat from Samosir leaves at 7:30 h. Sometimes the boats are cancelled at midday due to storms.

There is a new ferry at least five times daily between Tomok and Ajabata, 700 m south of Prapat. The ride costs 300 Rp per person. Departure times are posted.

DAY TRIPS FROM PRAPAT

BALIGE

Buses for 750 Rp. There's a nice market where you can get Batak scarves. On Sungei Asahan, one of the rivers draining Lake Toba, an aluminium plant and the largest hydro-electric plant in Sumatra (pictured on 100 rupiah notes) have been built recently with Japanese cooperation. The two tremendous industrial projects are held responsible for the alarming fall of Lake Toba's water level (see below). Here too is SIGURA WATERFALL.

PORSEA

East of Porsea the PPA has established the Dolok Surungan Animal Reserve (22,800 ha). The flatland and mountain forests between 200 m and 2200 m altitude are populated with deer, tapir, wild boar, and several species of ape in addition to the rich flora. Between Porsea and Prapat are three Toba-Batak villages, still in good condition and surrounded by bamboo hedges. LUMBAN GARAGA is about 1 km from the main road. The other two villages are NANGGAR and PITOLUAN.

LAKE TOBA

The geologically unique scenery is the result of an explosion. In one of the greatest volcanic eruptions 75,000 years ago, 2000 km^3 of ash was propelled under tremendous pressure into the atmosphere. It was deposited over much of South-East Asia, all the way to Sri Lanka. Due to the large magma loss, the volcano collapsed within itself. Within the huge crater lake, after thousands of years, more volcanic eruptions and increasing pressure below, two ancient craters reappeared upon the surface: the island of Samosir and the mountain chain between Prapat and Porsea.

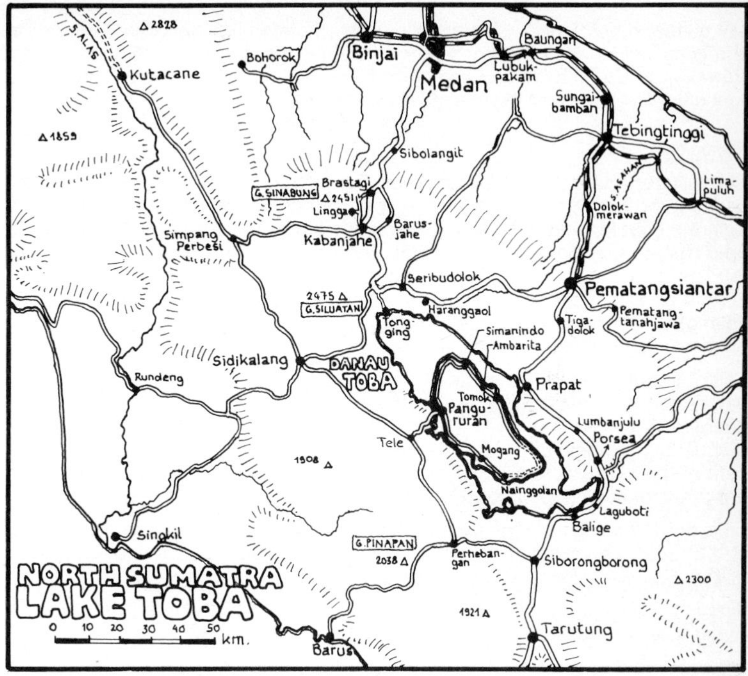

The present-day lake, at 900 m altitude, covers 1146 km^2 with depths of over 450 m, making it by far the largest lake on Sumatra. In the middle of the 80 km long and up to 26 km wide lake is the island Samosir (627 km^2). The east coast of the island rises steeply from the water (up to 500 m). Then the island falls off slowly to the western water line. Both banks of the lake are quite steep. Four volcanoes, each over 2000 m, surround the lake. The unstable tectonic equilibrium may have been disturbed by the sinking water level. Notice how high the boat landings are above the water. The shallow bays at Tuktuk are sanding; the losmen are no longer right by the water. Blame for the water loss has been variously laid upon deforestation of the jungle (causing reduced precipitation), or the huge aluminium plant and hydro-electric dam. Due to reduced water pressure, there are indications of a renewed breakup in the underground volcano.

SAMOSIR ISLAND

For ten years the island has been the traveller meeting place on Sumatra, particularly during the European summer. You can rent simple, cheap lodgings right by the water, where hotels have also begun to sprout. The food is still cheap, if not varied. On foot or by rented motorbike, you can explore the changing scenery and villages along the island's narrow, traffic-free roads. However, tourism has put an end to traditional Batak life in Tuktuk, Tomok, and Ambarita. Every type of tourism leaves its residue!

Tomok

The village is the main destination on the island. Loads of package tourists cruise over from Prapat to view the royal tombs. A line of sales stands runs from the boat landing up to King Sidabutar's tomb. The stands sell a mix of old (and real) to new (imitation) Batak art. Don't buy anything when a boat load of tourists is going through. 'Ulos', the traditional Batak scarves, cost up to 20,000 Rp depending on the quality. Also available are bone-carvings, Batak calendars, wood carvings, magic staffs, musical instruments (mandolins, xylophones), magic books, textiles, and more.

Left of the path, a stone stair leads from the main road up to a less frequented, empty square. Here you'll find a stone table and chairs next to a royal tomb, guarded by two elephants. The stone tomb, the front of which is decorated with a squatting human figure, crowned with a mask-like, horned head, is reminiscent of the much more famous tomb further up in the hills. In the background are a row of figures, probably depicting former rulers.

Follow the souvenir stands up past four lovely Batak houses. Occasionally SI GALE GALE performances are held here featuring dancing, wooden puppets.

A 'Museum' in an old Batak house, reputedly a former royal residence, offers a look in the living room at various household objects, pictures, etc., including a Si Gale Gale puppet. The family expects a donation.

SI GALE GALE

The life-size puppets were traditionally used in funeral rituals to aid those who died childless on the road to eternity. The eyes, shoulders, arms, and legs can be manipulated by strings providing a human appearance.

The souvenir stands end at the entrance to the tomb of King Sidabutar, his son and grandchild. Hariar trees were planted next to the graves 200 years ago.

Follow the path up the hill from the tombs for an hour and a half to a village on the ridge. If the weather is good, you've a lovely view of the island and the lake. Outside Tomok you pass several houses, at the last of which reasonably-priced coffee is served. The narrow path widens and is shaded when you reach the forest.

Tuktuk

Once just a quiet village on the peninsula facing Prapat, ten years ago it became the traveller hangout on Sumatra, particularly during the northern summer. Along the bank of the peninsula are simple lodgings in imitation or even original Batak houses. You can swim in the lake, and the small restaurants serve reasonable meals, prepared by the woman of the house. Some travellers have settled here. Marriages between local people and Westerners are not uncommon, adding a few western dishes to the menu.

Because most Bataks in Tuktuk live from tourism, many speak English. If you want to experience real Indonesia, move on. In addition to the simple losmen, there are several comfortable lodgings.

You can circle the peninsula in a comfortable half-day tour. Walk from Little Tuktuk across the field path past the Catholic church where on Sundays the religious teacher Antonius preaches impressively - in the Batak language. When you reach the northern bay, you can either make a sidetrip to Ambarita (see below), or follow the steep road to the right. You've a great view of the bay from the restaurant in Losmen Kuridin. The entire northern tip of the peninsula is occupied by the most luxurious hotel on the island, the Toledo Inn, with its bungalows and employee living quarters. The road now runs inland. Past a travel agency, a book rental shop (500 Rp per book), and various losmen, you arrive in the actual village. Besides the losmen, this is the location of the island's only petrol station, numerous souvenir shops, and a billiard hall where local youths hang around. By the police-station, a road leads off to the bungalows of Carolina, some of which are decorated with lovely Batak carving.

BATAK CARVING
The motifs of traditional carving include geometric patterns and stylistic depictions of people and animals - accentuated with white, rust-brown, and black paint. The colours symbolize the division of the world into its three parts: the universe, middle earth, and underworld.

Follow the winding road back to Little Tuktuk, past the ugly new hotel, and the sporadically occupied losmen. Enjoy the view of the southern bay. By Horas in Little Tuktuk you can buy used books - don't expect anything special. You are best off bringing your own literature from home or Singapore. You have lots of time to read as evenings are quiet.

If you want to explore the island, you can rent motorbikes at several losmen (Carolina, Abady, and in the village) for 10,000 Rp per day plus petrol.

In the south of the island the roads are poor and not for beginners. It is not possible to cross the island over the mountains by motorbike. Minibuses to Tomok or Ambarita cost 150 Rp. If you want to continue on, walk to the main road where minibuses are more frequent. The best way to get around is on the water. You can rent a canoe for 5-6000 Rp per day.

Ambarita

En route from Tuktuk to Ambarita you pass several peaceful losmen. Half way is the traditional village Siallagan where you can visit a large, stone royal tomb, crowned by three nearly life-size figures of the Siallagan rulers buried here. Further along toward the lake, chairs, benches and tables have been hewn from stone where the king once met with village representatives to palaver. The discussion often gave way to legal judgements, and hard punishment. Executions were performed off to the side where the victim was required to lay his head upon a stone for the axe. The island's only clinic and high school (SMP) is in Ambarita. Watch the fishermen in the harbour and take a break in a warung.

Simanindo

Heading north along the lakeside you pass through hilly, ever-changing scenery, cross wooden covered bridges, and pass tiny villages for 16 km to Simanindo. Just beyond the entrance to town, a path leads off to the right to Buta Bolon, an ancient settlement of King Sidauruk which has been preserved as a museum in its original form, admission 300 Rp. Right behind the ticket stand, under a protecting roof, is a traditional dug-out canoe.

You enter the open-air museum through a narrow gate in the wall. Around the large, empty square are various buildings, including a row of old houses whose roofs are covered with corrugated iron rather than traditional sugarcane leaves. King Sidauruk's former residence is decorated with carvings and sculpture to repel evil spirits. You enter via steep stairs for a look at the wood carvings, weapons, kitchen utensils, brass containers, and other examples of Batak handicrafts. Eventually you will be invited, for a donation, to visit the interior of some of the other, still inhabited houses. Every morning at 10:00 h Batak dances are performed on the square - admission 1800 Rp.

Spend the night in a losmen* across from the Museum (1500 Rp per person), nice family, or in the losmen* 500 m before the Museum. Nice view of the lake.

Off Simanindo is the tiny island ***TAO*** - a beach facing north and a hotel with salted prices invite you to relax.

About 13:00 h, there is a bus to Pangururan (ask the Losmen owner), costs 500 Rp, or walk to ***SANGKAL***. By the road, women sit in a long, cool cave, weaving mats.

Pangururan

Through several villages, some with lovely, old Batak houses, you come to Pangururan which is connected with the mainland by a bridge (due to the sinking water level it's really connected). The island market, which moves daily from village to village, is held 1 km outside town each Wednesday. To the right, behind the bridge, a road leads up 3 km to hot *SULPHUR SPRINGS,* bubbling from the rocks.

You can spend a night in small losmen by the spring or in town. *WISATA SAMOSIR***, Jl.Kejaksaan 42, tel 50 is managed by the helpful Brasilian John Randolph. Very simple lodgings in *BARAT LOSMEN & GUESTHOUSE**.

From PANGURURAN, there is a bus via TELE, SIDIKALANG (1200 Rp) to MEREK (4 hrs., 1500 Rp). From there you have connections to BRASTAGI / KABANJAHE.

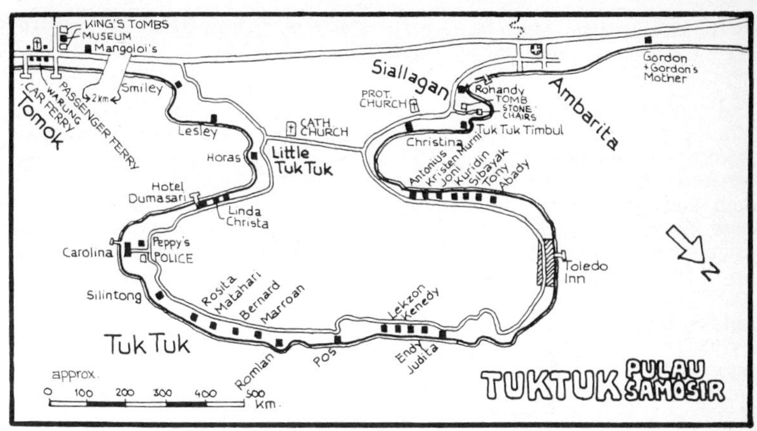

From Sidikalang you've buses to KUTACANE. During the ride over the high plateau, you've a tremendous view of the lake.

Hiking across the Island

An alternative to pick-up trucks or renting a motorbike is the somewhat dangerous hike across the island to PANGURURAN. Several paths lead across the island; some used for hunting wild boar. The paths are not marked and frequently overgrown. During the rainy season they become mudholes. There is a steep path from Tomok and Ambarita. Even better, take the Sunday 9 o'clock boat to Pangururan (4000 Rp) and begin there to avoid the steep climb. Otherwise you could try the 40 km hike around the north part of the island. Or take a minibus from Tomok for 1200 Rp per person.

Start your trek at sunrise; it gets extremely hot about midday. Only head out during good weather. Frequently there are heavy rains in the afternoon. Calculate 5-6 hrs. to ROONGURNI HUTA. Spend the night at Mr. Siboro's house. Half way, you can swim in a small lake. Then it is another 2-3 hrs. to PARTUNGKAN where you can spend the night in the village. Then it is a 90 minute descent to Ambarita. The opposite direction takes 3 hrs. This shortest route, however, is overgrown and very difficult to follow. It is better to take the broader, but very nice, path to PARMONANGAN, south of Tomok (5 hrs.), and then continue 7 km to Tomok.

HOTELS

You have the largest selection of lodgings in Tuktuk. The universal price for a night in an old Batak house is 2000 Rp, with several exceptions. Be sure the rooms are safe from thieves and use your own padlock. In recent years, most houses have hooked into the electric system. However, the falling water level has created a new problem. Many losmen do not have their own water, leaving you high and dry.

The shallow bay off Little Tuktuk has already been partially sanded shut. Additionally the new and ugly *DUMASARI HOTEL***** pollutes the lake with sewage making the lodgings here *(CHRISTA, LINDA, HORAS)* not to be recommended. At the southeast tip of the peninsula is *CAROLINA COTTAGE**(*)*, tel 41920. The comfortable Batak houses are surrounded by luscious flowers and trees. Each house has its own toilet and shower, well worth the price. Houses No. 5 & 6 are lovely, on the slope. You have a view of the bay from the restaurant and most houses along the bay.

Don't expect peace and quiet in the village at *ROSITA,* next to the billiard hall. *MATAHARI* and *BERNARD* have a nice restaurant. *MARROAN* is a friendly and good lodging. Watch out for your belongings in the Batak houses of *ROMLAN* on the tiny peninsula, where a Dutch woman cooks. A bit off to themselves are the following losmen: *POS, KENEDY, ENDY, JUDITA.* Good lodgings and food at *LEKZON.*

The bungalows of luxurious *TOLEDO INN*****, tel 22785, are on the steep northwest bank of the peninsula. Beyond, on the side streets, are several losmen (imitation Batak houses) right by the lake where it is deeper and still invites a swim. *ABADY* is recommended, as is *TONY'S,* with a friendly owner. More luxurious is *KURIDIN.* The owner of *ANTONIUS* is a teacher of religion, good tips. Outside town are the more peaceful losmen: toward Ambarita is *CHRISTINA,* a Batak house with a restaurant by the shallow bay. *ROHANDY* offers rooms in Batak houses by the jetty. Lovely is *TUKTUK TIMBUL* on a headland with its own landing.

2 km beyond Ambarita, 200 m off the road, are the losmen *GORDON 2* and *GORDON'S MOTHER* with their own beach set in the greenery. However you are quite isolated and dependent upon the losmen restaurant. Additionally, we have heard disturbing reports ranging from theft, to salted bills, and the day-long absence of the losmen owner.

Toward Tomok, the losmen *LESLEY* and *SMILEY* are a bit run-down. In Tomok your best bet is *MANGOLOI'S,* nice people, good tips. Additional lodgings in Simanindo, Tao, and Pangururan.

FOOD

Almost every losmen has a small restaurant. The losmen owners are pleased to feed you occasionally as their income from renting rooms is meagre. On the other hand, it is not good if you stay in an isolated losmen where you have explored the menu three times.

A favourite among the mostly vegetarian fare is avocado salad, guacamole. A particularly nice variety with peanuts is served at *KURIDIN.* Besides avocados, salads, and fruit salads, try the mixed drinks and sandwiches. Toast in all its varieties dominates the menu. There are toasts with butter, banana, honey, avocado, jam, garlic, tomato, and eggs as you like them. For a big appetite, try omelettes, tacos, potato chips, fried fish, and nasi goreng (fried rice). Another favourite is fruit salad featuring banana, papaya, pineapple, avocado, sprinkled coconut, and peanuts. Meat dishes are rare; there is no intensive breeding of livestock. Don't be surprised if a chicken costs ten times the price in Medan from where they are delivered. Suckling pigs are sometimes slaughtered on special occasions and served immediately. As refrigerators are still rare, it is difficult to store meat. Some restaurants offer suckling pig - we advise abstinence - it is very fat. Even fish, which should be plentiful in the lake, is rare. Just look at the fishermen and the meagre catch they take with their dug-out canoes.

The variety of drinks is extensive, unlike the food. Hot or cold tea, with milk or sugar (which can double or triple the price), coffee and mixed drinks are available almost everywhere. Popular is marquisa juice, hot or with ice, as a milkshake, or as served by *ANTONIUS* - spiced with local brandy. All bottled drinks are expensive since they have to be shipped to the island in twelve-packs.

One institution is *PEPY'S*. She now lives in France, but her sister has taken over the restaurant. For 2500 Rp per person you can enjoy smörgasbord - a mixture of various items on the menu.

Good sate and steaks in *CAROLINA*, where the bread is baked daily. More good food in *BERNARD'S*, *LEKZON*, *ROHANDY*, *TONY*, and *ANTONIUS*.

MOVING ON

Between Tomok and Pangururan, infrequent, sometimes overloaded minibuses charge 1200 Rp. Tuktuk - Simanindo (500 Rp). On Monday and Thursday afternoons at 15:00 h, from Ambarita and Simanindo, there are boats for 1000 Rp and 750 Rp to the market at HARANGGOAL, nice trip. From here you can go via SERIBUDOLOK (350 Rp), KABANJAHE (300 Rp), to BRASTAGI (150 Rp). On Sunday there is a tourist boat from Tomok via Ambarita and Simanindo to 4000 Rp to Pangururan. Tickets for long-distance buses are available for a 500 Rp surcharge in Tuktuk.

THE WEST COAST OF NORTH SUMATRA

Except the off-shore island of Nias with its megalith culture, the villages along the west coast are signposts for tourists en route to West Sumatra. The land of the Mandailing Batak has few tourist attractions.

SIBOLGA

A boring place on the west coast of Sumatra. If you have to wait for several days for a ship to Nias, go to the beaches of ***PANDAN*** (8 km) or ***KALANGAN*** (14 km) on the road to Padangsidempuan. Beautiful sunsets - the road from Prapat winds down the coast and you get the best view of a colourful sundown from the top.

HOTELS

The cheapest can be found around the mosque, *SUDIMAMPIR*** at Jl. Mesjid 98 with small rooms and radio music all night! Next door is *RODAMINANG***. Not far from the harbour in Jl.Suprapto *LOSMEN ANWAR**. Go for the cheaper and less noisy rooms on the first floor. At the corner of Jl. Diponegoro is *HOTEL SUBUR**. Better than most of the fleabags around the mosque is *INDAH SARI**** on Jl. Jen.A.Yani 29. A bunch of warung are across from the movie theatre. There are also some restaurants around the mosque. Only the Chinese places serve Bintang beer!

GENERAL INFORMATION

BANK - change money in BANK DAGANG NEGARA, Jl.Yani / Jl.Katamso. Ask for small bills (1000 Rp) if you plan to visit Nias.

SHOPPING - buy a mosquito net if you don't carry one already and are Nias-bound. The island is plagued with malaria. A large net costs about 5000 Rp.

LEAVING SIBOLGA

BY BOAT

Sibolga has a 'small harbour' (pelabuhan kecil) and a 'big harbour' (pelabuhan besar). From the small harbour, 3 km south of town, freighters depart every second day to TELUKDALAM on southern Nias. Several shipping agents have their offices along the road to Mole. Try DAMAI, whose Restu Jaya sometimes ships to Telukdalam, costs 6000 Rp, takes 13 hrs.

To GUNUNGSITOLI on northern Nias the cruise takes 10 hrs., costs 6200 Rp, cabins 3000 Rp extra, no food on board. Ships leave daily out of the big harbour; most depart at 21:00 h and arrive at 6:00 h. Get aboard several hours early, everything is full by 19:00 h. The modern passenger ship M.V.KERINCI (see introduction) puts in every second Sunday (arrives 6:00 h, departs at 9:00 h). SAMPLE PRICES (1st class / economy class) PADANG (27,000 / 11,000 Rp), JAKARTA (88,000 / 33,000 Rp), SURABAYA (130,000 / 49,000 Rp), UJUNG PANDANG (195,000 / 67,000 Rp). The ship continues via Balikpapan, Palu, Toli Toli, to Tarakan.

The M.V.BARUNA ARTHA puts in twice each month along the route Sibolga - Gunungsitoli - Telukdalam - Pulau Telo (Batu Islands) - Padang and return. Tickets from PELNI: e.g. Telukdalam - Padang (2 days & nights) 5000 Rp, cabins 7500 Rp extra, including simple board. You've a night stopover in Pulau Telo where you can eat at the Rumah Makan by the harbour or a Chinese restoran (near the Chinese temple).

BY BUS

Express bus companies have their offices at the new bus terminal (becak 200 Rp) on Jl.Sisingamangaraja. To PRAPAT 3000 Rp, to BUKITTINGGI 6000 Rp, to PADANG 6000 Rp (15 - 20 hrs.). There is no exact schedule, as buses from Medan or Padang only stopover in Sibolga. An exception is PO.TERANG whose buses are based in Sibolga, i.e. you'll get a proper seat instead of a stool in the corridor of a crowded bus! Local buses to BALIGE, BARUS or PADANGSIDEMPUAN (800 Rp) leave from the bus station .

PULAU NIAS

The 4800 km^2 island is about 125 km southeast of Sibolga. Major city is Gunungsitoli, whose airstrip is serviced by SMAC with daily flights from Medan (62,900 Rp). More than 200,000 people live on Nias. Besides the native Niah, there are many Batak, Chinese, Acehnese, and Minangkabau.

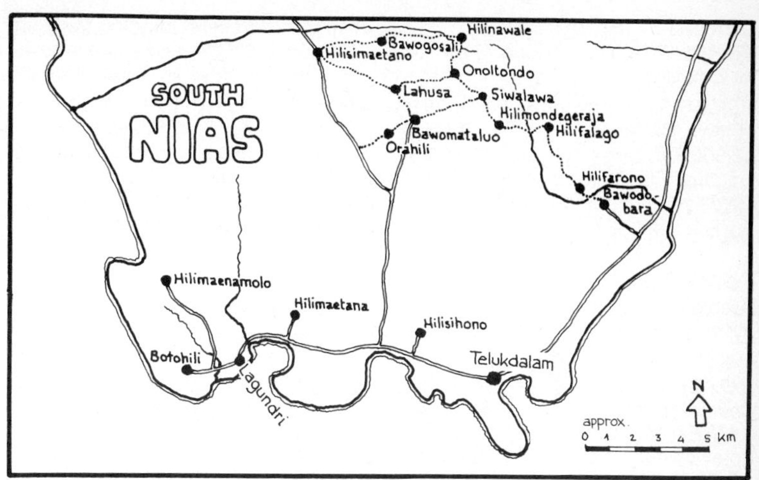

Gunungsitoli

If you land here, why not check out the north of the island where tourists are seldom seen. This town is the best place to shop on the island.

Between 8:00-10:00 h, buses, converted from trucks, drive for about 3000 Rp a new route through the island interior to Telukdalam (via Miga, Lalowi, Dola, Moi, Ambucha, Soliga, and Aksimastani) instead of along the old overgrown coastal road. A suspension bridge is closed to buses and trucks. The road is paved in parts with only rough stone, and is in poor condition. The demanding 125 km journey takes 5-8 hrs. or longer.

From Gunungsitoli you head first southeast on a good, winding road up into the mountains. Past rice fields, coffee, cocoa, and clove plantations, you'll see after 15 km the first traditional Nias houses: round wooden structures on stakes, roofed with palm leaves. Your compensation for the deteriorating road is a phantastic panorama of the coast and the tropical jungle with its tree ferns and orchids. After 30 km, on a banana plantation, is a stone statue of a man which a son erected for his deceased father. In a village further south is another monolith depicting a chief upon his throne.

HOTELS

The best hotel in Gunungsitoli is *SOLIGA***, lovely, on the main road 4.5 km from town, good food. *WISMA LAGUNDRI***, 2.5 km from town on Jl. Diponegoro 356, tel 211230, nice people. *WISATA***, a bit out of town, Chinese food. The most expensive, but not the best hotel on the island is *GOMO***, the only hotel with ac, loud. Good Chinese food in the restaurant *ASIAN*, Jl.Sirao.

GENERAL INFORMATION
SMAC OFFICE - Jl.Gomo 4, tel 154, Mr.Edward.

FLIGHTS - the airport is 24 km west of town. To Medan in a 21-seat Casa, 62,900 Rp, takes 1 h, just 10 kg free luggage! Flights to Padang only when seven passengers are willing.

BANK - money exchange, just US$ cash or travellers checks (only in emergency as the exchange rate is poor!) in Toko Sinar by Tapak Wong.

AROUND GUNUNGSITOLI
Traditional houses in Sifalaete and in Bawodasalo, 13 km south. There is a lovely beach 3 km further in Foe. Talubaliku, 15 km north of Gunungsitoli, is situated in a picturesque bay.

Telukdalam

A small, harbour town set on a lovely bay, which even has electricity until morning. The tourist office is usually closed.

HOTELS
Several losmen in town: *JAMBURAI**, *AMPERA***, simple and clean, the hotel owner's parents prepare food, *FRIENDLY** etc.

Ask for Andreas Duha who owns a little toddy shop opposite the cinema if you want information about *TREKKING TOURS.* He speaks English, knows Nias and its culture, and can be hired as a guide.

GENERAL INFORMATION
Until recently there was a boat that left twice monthly for Padang. Check out whether it still sails, price about 5000 Rp. Boats to Siberut only leave from Padang.

CHANGING MONEY can be a problem. Try James Wong of the Canon Photo Copy shop or Kosasih Long, Photo Copy. Both offer bad rates, however.

Lagundri / Jamburai

The two villages are a surfer's and diver's paradise - beautiful reefs. Apart from the surf and the reefs, you'll find sandy beaches that stretch for miles. Collect the colourful shells!

HOTELS
There are some simple losmen e.g. *AMAN** or *MAGDALENA**, without electricity. All losmen charge the same. Food mainly consists of noodles, fruit salad, rice and potato chips as most goods have to be shipped over from the mainland. But you do get fresh fish and other seafood.

HOW TO GET THERE
If your bus comes from GUNUNGSITOLI, ask your driver to bring you right to Lagundri. Costs some Rupiahs more. Buses only run on market days (Sat) to and from TELUKDALAM (6 km) for 500 Rp, trucks want 300 Rp, motorcycles 1500 Rp. Rent your own motorcycle for 10,000 Rp a day!

Bawomataluo

Take a trip from Telukdalam or Lagundri to BAWOMATALUO about 14 km from TD. Bus to ORAHILI and then climb the 480 ancient stone steps. Here

you find traditional pile houses, roofed with palm leaves, surrounding the stone plates of the village square. The biggest house on the square is the 'omo namada laowa' or the chief's house. Its floor is stepped at several levels on which the chief's followers are seated according to rank. The uppermost level is reserved for the chief alone. On the village square are a stone throne and benches used for traditional ceremonies. You'll also find a 180 cm high 'jumping stone'. If you pay well, the local youths will perform stone jumping and war dances. A photo permit from the chief costs 500 Rp. Many local people will offer handicrafts and other souvenirs.
Equally interesting are the villages ***BOTAHILI*** west of Lagundri (less pushy people, nice stone masonry) and ***HILISIMAETANO*** 16 km north of Telukdalam (lovely stonework at the start of the stairs).

Gomo

In the district of Gomo, where according to legend, the original ancestors descended from heaven, you can find a large number of stone carvings and megaliths which have now been covered by jungle. Gomo is about halfway between Gunungsitoli and TD.
PPA has made a 50,000 ha animal reserve in the island's last forest area around ***GUNUNG LELEMATSYUA*** (886 m), the tallest mountain on Nias, just north of Gomo.

THE PEOPLE OF NIAS

Mention of the island can be found in old Arab and Persian writings - the merchant Soleiman wrote in 851 AD of the headhunters on Nyang (Nias). At the end of the 17th century the Dutch East India Company set up a base and later added it to its colonial empire.
The ethnic origin of the Nias people is uncertain. They speak their own language and call the island tano niha which means land of the people. The Dutch got the name Nias from 'niha'. The social structure contains three different classes each with its own position and function. The si ulu are the nobility. The si ila consist of the village leaders and elders. The rest of the people are the sato. Women have a special position of respect on Nias. If a man and a woman meet on a small path, the man will move to the side. Only men do heavy field work.
Signs of a megalith culture can be found especially in the south of the island. Everywhere you'll find stone pyramids, menhir and dolmen, some of which are ornately inlaid, as well as large stone benches called daro daro. Even village streets are paved with stones. Long stone stairs lead up to the villages. At one time stones were used as tools, jewelry and even for money. In southern Nias a game of stone jumping is played in which stone pyramids (sometimes pedestals) up to 2 m high are attempted. Young unmarried men spring over the obstacle from a 40 cm high rock placed about 70 cm away. It's especially impressive when they jump with swords drawn. At one time this sport was used to train for the storming of palisades and walls of enemy villages. Today it's only performed on special occasions or for tourists.

WEST SUMATRA

About 3.1 million people live in 'Tanah Minang', the land of the Minangkabau. Two thirds of the land is still covered with forest and only 15 % of it is used for agriculture. Important exports are wood, rotang, resin, and gambir (dye). West Sumatra today is self sufficient in rice which it exports to the neighbouring provinces of Jambi and Riau.

Development organizations have been active in the area for some time. These "experts" maintain that agricultural production has increased since their arrival. Artificial fertilizers and insecticides have been introduced along with general mechanization. At the same time conflicts have appeared with the traditions of the Minangkabau who don't recognize individual ownership of land, rather group ownership. All owners must get together and decide what to do with the land - a time consuming process. This gets in the way of some development projects. Attempts are being made to end group ownership and to establish a single (usually male) family member as legal owner of the land. Development aid is often a product of what outsiders, who consider themselves experts, choose to institute and not what the people need. An old Minang saying existed before the development people came: "Put a stick into our earth and it will grow." The soil was always fertile here.

PADANG

The capital of the province has a population of 300,000 but has avoided a sticky or unfriendly big-city character. It has twice been acclaimed the cleanest city in Indonesia. Padang is the most important harbour on the west coast with regular services to Java, the Mentawai Islands and the northern west coast of Sumatra.

The new *MUSEUM ADITYAWARMAN* on Jl.Diponegoro is worth checking out. It is a copy of a traditional Minangkabau house (Rumah Gadang). Two rice barns are in front. Lovely carvings! The textile exhibits are particularly interesting.

Directly across is the *CULTURAL CENTRE* (Taman Budaya) with regular dance and music performances, readings, exhibits, etc., open daily 08:00-14:00 h, costs 150 Rp.

Padang's intact *CHINATOWN* (Kampong Cina) is worth a visit. Find it between Jl.Dobi, Jl.Cokroaminoto and Jl.Pondok.

West of town is the ocean, in the south is Sungai Harau. From here you board the small ships across to the Mentawai Islands. It is a nice walk along the Sungai Harau where the harbour road is dotted with *DUTCH STOREHOUSES* and office buildings. Get a sampan (50 Rp) across the river and climb up to the *CHINESE CEMETERY*.

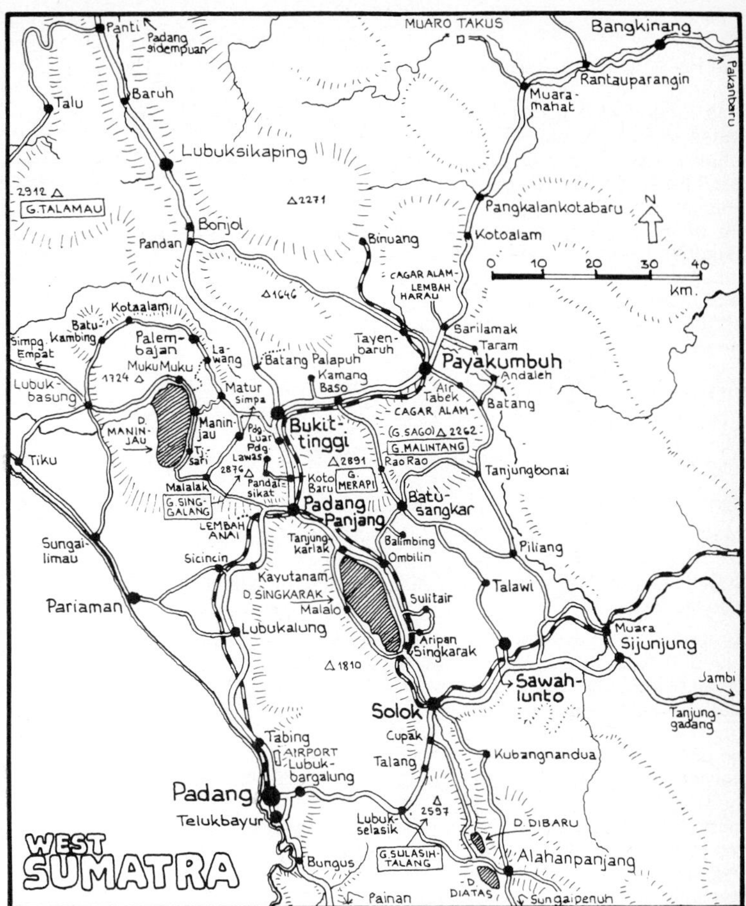

HOTELS

Expensive town to stay. The *TIGA TIGA*** Jl.Pemuda 31 (tel 22633) is right at the bus station, loud, musty. Similar is *CENDRAWASIH*** at No 27 (tel 22894). Cleaner, quieter, and hardly more expensive is *SRIWIJAYA***, Jl.Alang Lawas 15, tel 23577. Also ok are the economy rooms in *GARUDA*** at Jl.Pasar Raya 4 (tel 22176). Middle class: *HANG TUAH* ***, Jl.Pemuda 1, tel 26556, get a room in the back. Of the expensive hotels, *NATOUR MUARA HOTEL*****, Jl.Gereja 34, tel 25600, is worth the price. Ask for a room in the new wing facing the museum. *MARIANI INTERNATIONAL*****, Jl.Bundo Kandung 35, tel 25466. Despite the name, Madame Mariani only has 30 rooms.

FOOD

Nasi Padang, as you'd expect, is from the area. They'll serve you a whole table loaded with bowls of different dishes. You only pay for what you actually eat. Nasi Padang is very spicy! Be sure to try Rendang. Here's a recipe to perk your appetite before you go or to bring back those old memories later: 1 lb. beef cooked together with 1 litre coconut sauce (sold as Santen), and many spices such as 4 garlic cloves, 1 big onion, 1 teaspoon laos, 1 teaspoon turmeric, lemon grass, bay leaves, ginger, and 2 tablespoons of sambal olek. Bring to boil and thicken with flour. Bon appétit! You can find Nasi Padang in the following restaurants: *BOPET IRAMA,* Jl.Prof.M.Yamin 114; *SERBA NIKMAT,* Jl.Agus Salim 20; *SIMPANG RAYA,* Jl.Pasar Baru 34. *TANPA NAMA,* Jl.Rohana Kudus 87 and *RODA BARU,* Jl.Pasar Raya 6. Each claims to be the best.

European and Chinese dishes are served in *NATOUR'S HOTEL MUARA,* Jl.Gereja 34. There are several good Chinese restaurants in Kampong Cina (Chinatown). Expensive and good is *PHOENIX,* Jl.Niaga 136; likewise *KING'S,* Jl.Pondok 85B. There is live music in *CHAN'S,* Jl. Pondok 94. We recommend the seafood in *APOLLO MANDARIN,* Jl. Cokroaminoto 36A. In the evening, foodstalls are set up on Jl.Samudra, right by the sea, offering shrimp omelette, sate, and es jendur.

GENERAL INFORMATION

TOURIST OFFICE - for West Sumatra / Riau, at Jl.Khatib Sulaeman, Padang Baru, tel 23231. Good tips about Mentawai, open 7:30-14:00 h, Fri till 11:30 h, Sat till 13:00 h. City Tourist Office (Cabang Dinas Padang) is in Jl.Samudra 1. Very helpful is the travel agency Pacto, Jl. Pemuda 1, next to Hang Tuah Hotel.

PPA - Jl.Raden Saleh 8A.

IMMIGRATION OFFICE - at Jl. Pahlawan (toward the airport); nice people!

POST OFFICE - Jl.Bagindo Aziz Chan 7, open Mon-Thurs 8:00-16:00 h, Fri 8:00-12:00 h, Sat until 13:00 h. Telephone from the Telecommunications Office on the same street.

BANKS - Bank Dagang Negara, Jl.Bagindo Aziz Chan 21; Bank Negara Indonesia 1946, Jl.Dobi 1. If you have cash, try the money changer Eka Yasa Utama on Jl.Niaga.

SHOPPING - The shopping street is Jl.Iman Bonjol with several department stores, e.g. Ramanda and Matahari. At no. 47 and no. 5 are souvenir and antique shops.

GETTING AROUND - local 'bis kota' cost 100 Rp within town, 150 Rp to Tabing Airport. Depart from the Oplet Terminal. Bendis cost 500 Rp for about 2 km, becaks up to 1000 Rp. Taxis from Taxi Plaza, Jl.Mohammed Yamin near the pasar. Cost for a day 40,000-60,000 Rp. To Bukittinggi 30,000 Rp.

FESTIVALS - several times a year, on special holidays, Batang Harau becomes the site of exciting boat races, e.g. 17 August (Independence Day) and the end of Ramadan (Idul Fitri). Similar celebrations are held in the coastal villages Painan (south of Padang) and Pariaman (to the north).

About three months after Idul Fitri an exotic ceremony is held in Padang and Pariaman in memory of the martyrdom of Hasan and Husain in the Karbala War. The souls of Prophet Mohammed's two grandchildren,

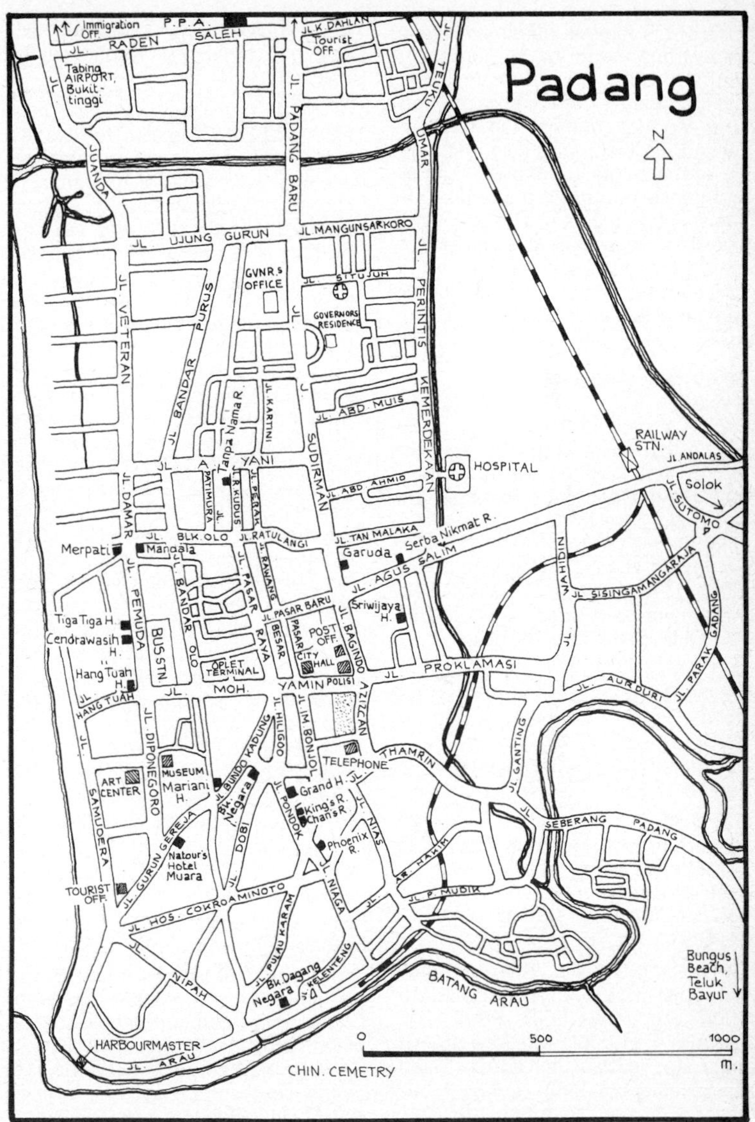
Padang
N
Immigration OFF.
P.P.A.
JL. RADEN SALEH
Tabing AIRPORT, Bukit-tinggi
JL. K. DAHLAN
Tourist OFF.
JL. PADANG BARU
TEUKU UMAR
JL. JUANDA
JL. UJUNG GURUN
JL. MANGUNSARKORO
JL. VETERAN
JL. BANDAR PURUS
GVNR.S OFFICE
JL. SITUJUH
GOVERNORS RESIDENCE
JL. PERINTIS KEMERDEKAAN
JL. KARTINI
Tanpa Nama R.
JL. ABD. MUIS
JL. SUDIRMAN
RAILWAY STN.
JL. ANDALAS
JL. A. YANI
HOSPITAL
JL. DAMAR
PATIMURA
JL. R. KUDUS
JL. PERAK
JL. ABD AHMID
Solok
JL. SUTOMO
JL. BLK. OLO
JL. RATULANGI
JL. TAN MALAKA
Serba Nikmat R.
Merpati
Mandala
Garuda
JL. AGUS SALIM
JL. WAHIDIN
JL. SISINGAMANGARAJA
JL. PEMUDA
JL. BANDAR OLO
JL. PASAR RAYA
JL. RAWANG
JL. PASAR BARU
Sriwijaya H.
JL. PARAK GADANG
Tiga Tiga H.
Cendrawasih H.
BUS STN.
BESAR
PASAR
POST OFF.
CITY HALL
JL. BAGINDO AZIZCAN
OPLET TERMINAL
Hang Tuah H.
JL. MOH. YAMIN
POLISI
JL. PROKLAMASI
JL. AUR DURI
JL. HANG TUAH
JL. DIPONEGORO
JL. HILIGOO
JL. IM. BONJOL
JL. GANTING
TELEPHONE
JL. THAMRIN
ART CENTER
MUSEUM
Mariani H.
JL. BUNDO KADUNG
Bk. Negara
Grand H.
King's R.
Chan's R.
JL. PONDOK
JL. NIAS
JL. SAMUDERA
JL. GURUN GEREJA
Natour's Hotel Muara
JL. DOBI
Phoenix R.
JL. SEBERANG PADANG
JL. AR. HAKIM
TOURIST OFF.
JL. HOS. COKROAMINOTO
JL. NIAGA
JL. P. MUDIK
JL. PULAU KARAM
JL. NIPAH
Bk. Dagang Negara
KELENTENG
BATANG ARAU
Bungus Beach, Teluk Bayur
HARBOURMASTER
JL. ARAU
0
500
1000
m.
CHIN. CEMETRY

sons of his famous daughter Fatima, were transported by a Bouraq (a winged horse with a female head) into paradise. The celebration features wooden frames (tabut) representing the biers, and colourful models of the horse carried with music and dance through the streets, then thrown into the ocean. The spectators dive into the waves to catch part of the decorations as souvenirs. The Indonesian Muslims are Sunni, but this ceremony is clearly Shiite.

LEAVING PADANG

BY AIR

Tabing Airport is 9 km north of the city. A taxi costs 4000 Rp, from the airport taxi-counter to Bukittinggi 30,000 Rp. GARUDA office at Jl. Jen. Sudirman 2 (tel 23431); MERPATI at Jl.Pemuda 51B (tel 21303); MANDALA next to Hotel Tiga Tiga, at Jl. Pemuda 29A (tel 21979). Since 1987 there have been direct flights to SINGAPORE. SAMPLE PRICES:

MEDAN 73,100 Rp (GA), DUMAI 50,300 Rp (MZ), PAKANBARU 28,900 Rp (GA), PALEMBANG 65,200 Rp (GA), JAKARTA 97,700 Rp (MZ / Mandala), ROKOT (Pulau Sipora, every Fri) 17,300 Rp (MZ).

BY BUS

As in the rest of Sumatra ALS, ANS, and Bunga Setangkai lines are the best and most reliable. All have offices at the bus station. SAMPLE PRICES:

MEDAN 10,000 Rp, PRAPAT 8000 Rp, BUKITTINGGI 1000 Rp, DUMAI 6000 Rp, SIBOLGA 6000 Rp, JAKARTA 21,000 Rp, PAKANBARU 3600 Rp, LUBUKLINGGAU 10,000 Rp (takes about 24 hrs. during the dry season, better fly during the rainy season), SUNGAIPENUH 3500 Rp, TANJUNG KARANG 17,500 Rp. Take Bengkulu Indah for 15,000 Rp to BENGKULU.

BY SHIP

The KM.KERINCI leaves for Jakarta (Tanjung Priok), Surabaya, Ujung Pandang, and via Balikpapan and Toli Toli to Tarakan, every second Sunday at 23:00 h. Every second Saturday she arrives from Tanjung Priok in Teluk Bayur and departs at 19:00 h for Sibolga. Cheapest category with numbered cots in the dorm (500 people) costs 23,500 Rp including restaurant meals to JAKARTA (UJUNG PANDANG 54,000 Rp). Better and slightly more expensive the 8-berth cabin with lockers for 28,500 (UP 69,800 Rp). For the taste of luxury try a 2-bed cabin in 1st class, 62,900 Rp (UP 161,800 Rp). The night trip to SIBOLGA costs 10,200 Rp (ekonomi) and 26,300 Rp (1st class). As the bus ride is very demanding, taking the boat can be a convenient alternative. Book well in advance, as tickets are hard to get, although there may still be room on the boat. At the agencies in town, tickets are 2500 Rp more expensive. Try directly at Teluk Bayur harbour's Pelni-Office, Jl.Tanjung Priok 32, tel 21408 and 22109.

MV Baruna Artha (Pelni) runs twice monthly the route PADANG - P.TELO (Batu Islands) - TELUKDALAM (Nias) - GUNUNGSITOLI - SIBOLGA and back - but it is said to run no longer, check!

Other ships besides Pelni's go up and down the west coast of Sumatra. Check at the harbour MUARA at the mouth of Sungai Arau or at TELUK BAYUR, the harbour for larger ships, to the south of the city. A help is PACTO at Jl.Pemuda 1 (tel 23022).

DAY TRIPS FROM PADANG

There are lots of nice beaches north and south of town - some still to be discovered.

PANTAI NIRWANA

8 km from Padang, is the favourite and quite full on weekends.

AIR MANIS (=sweet water)

A fishing village, about 3 km south of town. Quiet, idyllic, and right by the beach you can stay at Papa Cili Cili*, a friendly man who might take you out night fishing, and whose kitchen serves tremendous portions of tasty food. The two off-shore islands are Pulau Pisang Besar (=big banana) and Pulau Pisang Kecil (=little banana). When the tide is out you can walk to the small island. More complicated is the route from Padang to Air Manis: oplet (100 Rp) to the small harbour Muara, then a sampan (50 Rp) across the river, and an hour walk through the lovely coastal scenery heading south. Or one hour's walk north of Teluk Bayur. There is no road to the village!

BUNGUS BAY

25 km south, stay the night in one of the many homestays or in Carolina Indah**. Rent a boat to visit the nearby islands.

BUKITTINGGI

At 920 m altitude 'high hill' (literally translated) is one of the most beautiful and pleasant places in Sumatra with lots of excursion possibilities.

Under the Dutch, Bukittinggi was called Fort de Kock, after a Dutch general who in the Padri Wars of 1821-1838 had an important fort built here. At the time the colonial power united 'adat' adhering Minangkabau rulers to fight the puritanical reformers who sought to bring Islam to West Sumatra.

Be sure to take an evening walk up to the *FORT DE KOCK.* There isn't much left there to see other than the wonderful view and the terrific sunsets. On the hill across the road (Jl.Yani traverses the valley between the hills) you'll find the *BUNDO KANDUNG MUSEUM* (admission 200 Rp) and a small run-down *ZOO* (350 Rp). The museum, in a rebuilt Minangkabau house, is the oldest museum in West Sumatra. The interesting exhibits include traditional garments, antique jewelry, household and kitchen utensils, and several models of Minangkabau buildings. But don't miss the curiosities: stuffed two-headed calves. Some of the signs are in English. The zoo, though poorly maintained like most zoos in South East Asia, does offer a good survey of Sumatra's fauna. The *AQUARIUM* charges an additional 200 Rp admission. On Wednesday and Saturday 13:00 and 15:00 h, plus Sunday at 9:00-14:00 h, Minangkabau dances are performed in front of the Museum.

From the square around the *JAM GADANG* (clock tower), you can see both of the volcanoes south of the city. The Merapi in the east (still active) reaches 2891 m while the Singgalang is 2877 m. Right near the clock tower is the new building of the *PASAR ATAS,* the new market containing many shops and stalls. Every Wednesday and Saturday there is a big market on the steps leading down from here. It is visited by village people from the surrounding area. At *PASAR BAWAR*, the lower market, fruit, vegetables, spices, and fish are sold at stands daily. In the lower market's two buildings you'll find many shops. Handicrafts (Minangkabau jewelry, baskets) are sold in the southern building.

The *ARMY MUSEUM* (open till 16:00 h) is on Jl.Panorama (formerly Jl.Iman Bonjol). In addition to many weapons, see picture documentation about the trial of the leader of the PKI of West Sumatra. A diorama depicts an ambush by Dutch troops of Republican soldiers.

From a small park across the street from the Army Museum, you can look down into the *NGARAI CANYON* or even take the small path down in. You can visit ammunition stores of the Japanese occupation forces. The caves and tunnels (LOBANG JEPANG) are deep underground by the road to the canyon, admission 250 Rp.

HOTELS

There are many cheap hotels on Jl.Jen.A.Yani. If you come by bus from the north (Sibolga, Medan), then have them drop you off at Jl.Jen.A.Yani / Jl.Veteran. Only Wisma Tiga Balai is open at night however. Many travellers stay in the *GRAND***, no. 99 (tel 21133), which was completely renovated and rebuilt in 1987. Next door to the Grand is the *YANI* with its high prices and unfriendly staff. On the corner of Jl.Kesehatan is *MURNI** (no. 115), a small clean family hotel. At no. 113 is *NIRWANA*(*)*, diagonally across at no. 130 is *SINGGALANG**, at no. 70 is the slightly run-down *GANGGA***. Further down is *WISMA BALAI TIGA**, good, nice atmosphere. *MOUNTAIN VIEW***** at Jl.Yos Sudarso 3 (tel 21621) is on the western hill; four people could share two separate bedrooms and a bath - frequently booked. Next door is *WISMA BUKITTINGGI*(*)*. On Jl.Benteng is a cheap guesthouse, *SUWARNI**, clean and quiet; Madame Suwarni is a great cook. If you want to spend more money, enjoy 1930s atmosphere in *HOTEL BENTENG*****, tel 21115, right next door, rooms with TV and a lovely view of town. Similar prices in *MINANG***** at Jl.Panorama 20 (tel 21120). The house is in a beautiful garden. Expensive is *DENAI*****, tel 21460, Jl.Rivai 26, bungalows up to 50,000 Rp, and *LIMA'S***(*)*, Jl.Kesehatan 34, tel 22641. Cheaper rooms* without a mandi are overpriced compared to Jl.Yani. Package tourists are packed into the most expensive hotel, *DYMEN'S*****, Jl.Nawawi, tel 21015.

FOOD

Here you'll find the usual 'hippie-food' scene but also the best nasi Padang for miles. Across from the Singgalang Hotel the *COFFEE HOUSE* is a traveller institution. You can enjoy tacos, milkshakes and good music. Day tours are organized (7000 Rp) to the interesting sights; ask for Bujang, a good guide. The same quality and prices in *THREE TABLE COFFEE HOUSE*. In front of the Singgalang are good soto and sate warung. A slightly expensive Chinese restaurant is *MONALISA*,

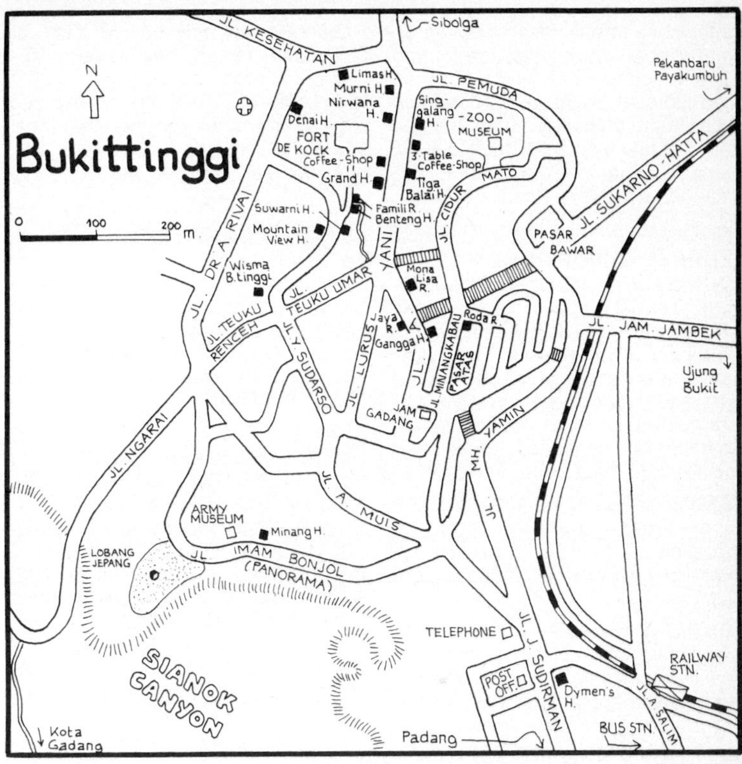

Jl.Yani 58, tasty tourist specialties. Try nasi Padang in many other restaurants and rumah makan. We think *FAMILY* at Jl.Benteng 1 near Fort de Kock is great. There are several good Padang food places near the market. *SIMPANG RAYA* is across from Gloria cinema above the drug store (Jl.Minangkabau). Try 'belud', small, bound eels which have been smoked and dried. Behind the market is *RODA BARU* with similarly good food. As mentioned before, in all places serving nasi Padang you get a great number of dishes placed before you, but you only pay for what you actually eat. Usually there are price schedules prominently displayed. If not, ask what each bowl costs (sauces are free!). Don't be put off by looks or location.

SHOPPING

There are lots of antique and souvenir shops in Bukittinggi. It's questionable, though, whether you should buy wayang golek puppets here - they are much cheaper on Java. At Jl.Yani 2 and 14, you'll find two somewhat expensive shops. On Jl. Minangkabau are several fascinating shops which sell everything from old water pots to gongs and household items. At the market, you can buy fine ground coffee by the lot. Fresh cloves, nutmeg, cinnamon, cardamom, and coriander are sold at Pasar Bawar.

GENERAL INFORMATION

TOURIST INFORMATION - Bukittinggi Tourist Office is diagonally across from the Three Table Coffee House on Jl.Jen.A.Yani. The manager organizes reasonably priced tours and occasionally comes along as a guide. The office plans to move! More tips in the coffee house and from Parindo, next to Grand Hotel.

BANKS - try Bank Indonesia 1946 in Pasar Atas, open 8:00-11:00 h. Sometimes they want to see the receipt from where you bought your TCs.

BENDIS & BEMOS - you can reach everywhere around town by foot. The local transport within town are bendis, two-wheeled horsecarts. They wait at Pasar Bawar and on Jl. Yani at Jl.Tengku Umar. The drivers frequently charge tourist prices, within town think 500-1000 Rp. To the bus station or further out use the local bemos, which stop everywhere. Bemos also wait at Pasar Bawar.

LEAVING BUKITTINGGI

BY BUS

Most hotels organize long distance buses which stop right in front of your hotel. The big bus companies, ANS, ALS, or ENGGANO, have offices at the new bus station at Jl.Agus Salim. SAMPLE PRICES:

PRAPAT 7500 Rp, SIBOLGA 6000 Rp, MEDAN 9500 Rp, PADANG 1100 Rp, PAKANBARU 3000 Rp, DUMAI 6000 Rp, JAKARTA 23,000 Rp, LUBUKLINGGAU 11,000 Rp, BENGKULU 14,000 Rp, TANJUNG KARANG (about 35 hrs.) 17,000 Rp, PALEMBANG 13,000 Rp. Local minibus prices: PADANG PANJANG 300 Rp, PAYAKUMBUH 500 Rp, SOLOK 800 Rp, BATUSANGKAR 750 Rp, MANINJAU 650 Rp, PANTI 900 Rp.

DAY TRIPS AROUND BUKITTINGGI

KOTA GADANG / NGARAI CANYON

From Jl.Panorama take a small footpath down into the 100 m deep canyon. At the end of Jl.Panorama is a small paved road into it as well. Go along the left bank upstream until you get to a bridge. On the other side are some steep steps back up to KOTA GADANG. In the houses, lace is made and worked with silver from Palembang into lovely filigree. A souvenir shop, which also sells silver wares, is on the main road to SIANOK. It's called 'Kerajinan Amai Setai'.

From here it's not far to the next village (SIANOK) where there is another path down into the narrow western canyon for the walk to Bukittinggi. Kota Gadang is the birthplace of many public figures in Indonesia. Today many of the buildings are empty as wealthy families have moved to Padang or Jakarta.

KOTA BARU

Get a bus toward Padang Panjang to KOTA BARU. Just before the turn-off to Pandai Sikat is a lovely mosque, mirrored in a small pond. In the background is Gunung Singgalang. The village is your departure point for climbing Merapi.

Because this tour is longer and more difficult, don't head out without a guide. The tiny villages west of Kota Baru on the slopes of Gunung Singgalang are great for hiking. Since the paths aren't marked, you have to keep asking the way ("Dimana jalan ke ...?").

PANDAI SIKAT

A village of wood carvers and weavers. In several buildings artistic frames, furniture and small objects are carved and painted. Right by the road is a lovely, new house, whose outer walls and interior are completely decorated with carvings. It belongs to a weaver family engaged in the production of traditional Minangkabau 'kain songket'.

BULL FIGHTS

Every Tuesday except during Ramadan, bull fights are held in PASAR REBO, KOTO LAWAS, or PINCURAN TUJUH. Ask for 'adu kerbau'. The atmosphere is tense with two bulls fighting against each other until one takes flight. The ring is formed only by men standing in a loose circle. Other sporting activities favoured by Minang men include horse racing in the major towns (Padang, Payakumbuh, Batusangkar, Bukittinggi, Padang Panjang), and on Sundays, hunting wild boar (which frequently destroy crops).

CLIMBING GUNUNG MERAPI

If you want to do the tour without staying overnight, best take the first bus at 5:00 h to KOTA BARU. Register your trip with the police (200 m after the turn-off to Pandai Sikat). Since there aren't any markers, check the route in advance, perhaps in your hotel, or take a guide. After 1 hour's hike you'll get to the derelict forestry house and bamboo shelters (Saturdays' 'weekly warung' and a place to stay the night, if need be). Hike a further 2 hours through the jungle. At the edge of the forest, behind the trench, take the zig-zag path leading further up left through lava rubble. After another hour you'll reach the peak (2891 m), which will be covered in clouds after 10:00 or 11:00 h.

DANAU MANINJAU

Probably the most beautiful lake on Sumatra! Especially impressive is the view of the lake and the surrounding mountains from PUNCAK BUKIT. Take the early bus to LAWANG (400 Rp). From here it's 45 minutes by foot to PUNCAK BUKIT, 400 m above lake level. A footpath leads through the jungle down to BAYUR. Logging is increasing here, unfortunately, to clear ground for cinnamon. In the woods left of the path are many macaques; if you don't see them, you're sure to hear them. The descent takes two hours - from BAYUR it's 3 km to the village of MANINJAU. There is a bath house with warm water left of the road 300 m before Maninjau. The best seafood restaurant far and wide is MUKO MUKO at the northern end of the lake.

It is worth spending a night in Maninjau; you can swim in the lake and enjoy the scenery. Rooms of varied quality in MANINJAU INDAH***(*), right by the lake with an expensive but poor restaurant and boat rentals. It is cheaper not far away in the PASANGRAHAN*. The last bus back to Bukittinggi leaves at 17:00 h (600 Rp). The paved road makes 45 hairpin turns going back up. A great view when the bus isn't overfilled.

THE MINANGKABAU

'Minang' (sometimes 'menang') means victory; 'kabau' (today usually 'kerbau') means buffalo. An old legend tells how the 3 million Minangkabau acquired their name. A Javanese army wanted to conquer the land. There were so many soldiers that whole rocks disappeared when they sharpened their swords. The king of the Minangkabau made an agreement with his Javanese counterpart. Two buffalos should fight to settle the matter without a war. The Minangkabau let a young calf hunger for a long time and fastened a spear-head on its nose. The thirsty calf jumped to milk its opponent thereby slitting its stomach open. The Javanese buffalo died.

It is interesting to observe the mixing of two such contradictory cultures as Islam, which emphasizes the male role in society, and the traditional Minangkabau culture with its matrilineal social structure. Matrilineal doesn't necessarily mean matriarchate or the domination of women, rather a female line of ancestral descent. The paddy fields and houses are owned by the Minangkabau women.

The unwritten laws and traditions called 'adat' determine one's entire life. For a young boy the most important male relative is not the father but the mother's eldest brother. Until marriage he remains in his mother's home where he is raised by his mother's relatives. After marriage he moves in with his wife and mother in law.

The Minangkabau civil and social system is quite complex. Four clans (suku) are considered today to be the oldest population groups: the bodi, caniago, koto, and piliang. They are distributed throughout the entire region. The next highest civil unit is the village with its fields (nagari). A 'nagari' is only complete when it contains people from all four 'suku'.

The inheritance system, both materially and spiritually (passing down of names etc.), goes from mother to daughter. Men according to 'adat' are there to defend the system. At his wife's home the man is a guest. He must divide his work responsibilities between that for his mother and that for his wife. He is only entitled to a part of his mother's proceeds as determined by 'adat'. The fruits of the work he provides for his wife are for her and the children alone. The eldest son manages the estate of the mother.

Decisions are first discussed separately in the family council which includes both sexes. Everyone has the right to speak. The eldest family member (whether male or female) then announces the decisions of the council.

According to 'adat' there is no suppression of the males. The monopoly of decision making and ownership found in a patriarchy has been withdrawn.

***RUMAH ADAT**: The traditional 'big house', characteristically found with a pointed tapered roof. The number of horns represent the number of sons in law of the wife or mother.*

***RANGKIANG**: A supply house often found near a 'rumah adat' and possessing a similar roof.*

***BALAI RUNG SARI**: Meeting house, a 300 year old one is in TABEK LIMA KAUM not far from BATUSANGKAR.*

***PENCAK SILAT**: Traditional self-defence.*

***BAJU KRUNG**: An inherited piece of women's clothing. A sort of long dress reaching about the knees. Underneath a sarong is worn.*

***PACU ITIK**: In the tiny village of LIMBUKAN not far from PAYAKUMBUH, you'll find one of the strangest races in the world: duck races. The first duck to fly over the finish line wins.*

BATANG PALUPUH

12 km north of Bukittinggi on the Trans-Sumatra-Highway, the rafflesia, the largest flower in the world blooms during the summer months. Batang Palupuh is just a small 'cagar alam' (nature reserve) of 3.4 ha, but it borders a large forest reserve where tapir, wild boar, and other animals find a habitat. Ask first in Bukittinggi whether the flower is actually in bloom; phone the PPA office in Bukittinggi at tel 22621, but even there the info is not always accurate. Take a bus going north and get off at BATANG PALUPUH. From here you have to hike about half an hour through a narrow valley, at the end of which is the nature reserve. You can pick up a guide at the village for 500 Rp per person, who will show you the hidden spots where the flower blooms. He will want a tip if he is successful.

NGALAU KAMANG

Via a poor road which rarely sees public transport, it is 15 km from Bukittinggi to the village of Kamang. There you will have to accept several of the local youths as guides. For a substantial price (try to bargain!) they will lead you over an unpaved road to the entrance of the Kamang Caves, open the entrance, and light your way through a 2 km labyrinth of stalactite caverns. During the Padri wars (1821-1837) Tuanku nan Renceh and his warriors, supporting Iman Bonjol, hid here from the Dutch. In remembrance, a number of stone statues have been placed in the cavern, creating a spooky atmosphere. On the way to Kamang it is very easy to see how the flooded rice fields are also used as fish ponds.

BASO

Get a bus toward Payakumbuh / Pakanbaru and get off 17 km out of Bukittinggi. Walk one km north to SUNGAI JANIAH. The large fish in the lake are considered sacred and quite tame. A narrow road leads across the railway south via TABATPATAH (lovely scenery, cinnamon plantations) and RAO RAO (lovely mosque) to Batusangkar (see next page).

PAYAKUMBUH

Get a bus from Bukittinggi toward PAKANBARU and get off at Payakumbuh (1000 Rp). Along the road beyond Baso, you pass several 'krupuk factories', which you can visit. The red and white pieces drying in the sun, point the way. A few kilometres before the village a road leads off to the left to a CAVE. You have to walk 2 km up a steep path - refreshment stands at the top. There you will find guides with petroleum lamps. The view way down into the valley is really more fascinating than the stalactite caves themselves. The less than stimulating town of PAYAKUMBUH has a big market every Saturday. In the new buildings around the central square are a number of Padang restaurants. Some rent rooms. You can rest better and quieter in a small WISMA** on the road toward AIR TABIT. Beyond Air Tabit in BATANG you can bathe to the right of the road in a natural swimming pool. Parallel to this road, running north, is the lovely scenery of TARAM VALLEY. It is accessible either from the main road to Pakanbaru or via the road before Harau branching east. Or beyond Batang take the side-road to ANDALEH. For kilometres along the road, you pass villages decorated with flowers. In the background rice fields reach to the mountain slopes. South of Payakumbuh, on the slopes of GUNUNG SAGO (G.Malintang, 2762 m), is a forest reserve (5500 ha), where you can find the rafflesia too.

LEMBAH HARAU NATURE RESERVE

15 km northeast of PAYAKUMBUH is a wonderful valley surrounded by steep rock walls. Of the 300 ha reserve, 10 % has been set aside for recreation with hiking trails, rest areas, and observation platforms. The reserve is due to be expanded to take in over 23,500 ha of mountain forest in the east (toward Riau), where tiger, forest goat, and other endangered species find habitats. Take the bus to PAYAKUMBUH, then another 10 km by minibus to SARILAMAK at the valley's entrance. It is straight on, by foot 1 1/2 hrs. to the Information Office. On market day, Saturdays, buses bring you out for 250 Rp. From here head right about 2 km to a beautiful, 150 m high waterfall. Another one is 1 km away.

RIMBO PANTI NATURE RESERVE

About 100 km north of Bukittinggi is this nature reserve, 3400 ha in size covering both sides of the road. About 570 ha are set aside for recreation, including hot springs. RIMBA PANTI is a good place to get a first glance of the Sumatran jungle. If necessary, you can get a park guide through the Tourist Office in Bukittinggi. Buses from Bukittinggi (1200 Rp). In the reserve, as in the forest to the south between Bonjol and Lubuksikaping, and on the slopes of Gunung Talamau (=Mt.Ophir, 2912 m), Sumatra establishes a second floristic record with the tallest flower in the world, amorphophallus titanum - the name says it all.

BONJOL

On the way to Rimba Panti you pass the equator at a point not far from BONJOL. It's marked by a globe next to the road.

In almost every Indonesian town there is a Jalan Iman Bonjol. Tuanku Iman Bonjol was the religious and military leader of the Muslims during the Padri Wars (1821-38). He had his headquarters in Bonjol. His house of prayer and some old Dutch cannon can still be seen today. In 1837 Iman Bonjol was captured by Dutch troops and exiled first to Ambon and then to Manado. New Indonesian history books describe him as one of the first national heroes to fight against colonial rule.

BATUSANGKAR

60 km southeast is the centre of Minangkabau culture, Batusangkar. Have a look at the new 'balai adat'! Get a minibus from Bukittinggi (750 Rp). There is a losmen and a good nasi Padang in Simpang Raya, Jl.Yani 18.

About 30 minutes walk will take you to PAGARUYUNG. In the village, right by the road, is as 1.5 m tall stone with Sanskrit and Kawi inscriptions dating from the days of King Adityawarman (14th century).

Other 'batu tulis' (=inscribed stones) can be found in the nearby villages BENDANG, SARUASO, and LIMAKAUM. In Saruaso are royal tombs with stone phalluses. About 2.5 km further is an exactly rebuilt istana. The interior of the tremendous royal palace is covered with chloride cloth. Several kings' tombs are still cared for by their descendants.

Ancient meeting houses can be seen in LIMAKAUM and PARIANGAN.

DANAU SINGKARAK

Not as nicely situated as Lake Maninjau, the Bukittinggi - Solok main road goes along the lake's eastern bank. In OMBILIN, the downstream river crossing, you can rent a boat.

Stay the night in OMBILIN (great nasi Padang, better and cheaper than in Bukittinggi), between the main road and the lake in BATU TEBAL at MINANG HOTEL**(*) or in SINGKARAK at HOTEL JAYAKARTA***, tel 21279. You can swim right in the lake; the water is cool and clear.

Idul Fitri, the end of Ramadan, is celebrated in the villages with folklore presentations and boat races.

From Singkarak take at midday the last bus to SULITAIR. Here you'll find one of the best preserved Minangkabau houses, about 70 m long. Twenty families live in it. The last bus back to the main road leaves Sulitair around 15:00 h. Otherwise you have to walk 14 km. The bus from Singkarak to PADANG PANJANG costs 400 Rp. From there it's 250 Rp to Bukittinggi.

PADANG PANJANG

The town stretches endlessly along the steeply climbing main road. It rains every afternoon, which has given the town the nickname 'Kota Hujan'. Among the luscious green and wealth of flowers are a row of old Minangkabau houses belonging to some of the 30,000 tradition conscious residents.

Get a bendi from the bus station at the central crossroad via Jl.Puti to ASKI, Jl.Bungsu 35, the Minangkabau Academy for Dance and Music. Weekdays, except during school holidays, music is played everywhere until 14:00 h, including dancing, sometimes in traditional costumes. The school principal doesn't mind if you drop by and listen to a class, but dress properly.

You can stay 50 m above the post office in WISMA SINGGALANG***, Jl. Pancasila 134, tel 213.

LEMBAH ANAI NATURE RESERVE

Only a few kilometres beyond PADANG PANJANG on the road to PADANG. There's thick rain forest and a 40 m high waterfall. The 221 ha reservation borders 96,000 ha of forest reserve, creating a spectacular country of tigers and siamangs.

Further south toward Alahanpanjang are 6000 ha of forest reserve on the slopes of Gunung Sulasihtalang (2597 m) with its small, but lovely lakes, Danau Diatas and Danau Dibaru. Nearby is the northern section of tremendous Kerinci Seblat National park (see Jambi). An unusual biotope are the Lunang peat swamps and forests along the coast at the southern tip of the province (Tg.Batu) - accessible from Tapan, where the road branches off to Sungaipenuh, Danau Kerinci.

MUARO TAKUS

The candi of Muaro Takus, Buddhist stupas, date back to the same age as the temples of Padanglawas (northern Sumatra). You get here from Muara Mahat, half way between Payakumbuh and Pakanbaru. Stay in the losmen ARGA SONJA.

RIAU

The province of Riau, with over 2.5 million inhabitants, consists largely of the east coast of Sumatra and the island archipelagos of Riau and Lingga. The islands of Anambas and Bunguran, found between Kalimantan and West-Malaysia, are also part of the province.

North of the capital city Pakanbaru are oil wells connected by pipeline to the refineries in Dumai, bringing the province wealth. South of Pakanbaru are further oil fields in Lirik and Pudu.

Most of Riau is covered by swamp and jungle. Here one can still find the Sumatra rhinoceros, though estimates are that only 100-170 remain. The smallest of non-extinct Asian rhinos is only 1.5 to 3 m long, and its armour is quite hairy. You can even find a few tigers and elephants. But because the swampland and forest is being steadily threatened by new roads and logging, one can expect these species to die off soon. An example is the Java rhino, of which only 20-25 are still living in the Ujong Kulon Nature Reserve.

As mentioned Riau is being polluted by ever more roads and pipelines. All-weather roads have been laid from Bukittinggi to Pakanbaru and on to Dumai. Another road goes from Pakanbaru to Rengat and then connects up with the Trans-Sumatra-Highway. The broad rivers also serve as major transport arteries as even large ships are able to steam far upstream.

PAKANBARU

This is a city with lots of administrative and bank buildings, giving an idea of the oil wealth. Prices are accordingly high. Otherwise you'll find the best pineapple in Sumatra here for 100 Rp a piece. The harbour, kampong air, and the house boats on Sungai Siak are worth a stroll off the main road. Or you could take an excursion out to the multinational Caltex oil facilities to have a look.

HOTELS

The cheap places are really dirty and run-down. Go for *LOSMEN MUSLIM*** on Jl.Sudirman (Jl.Agus Salim 21) across from the bemo station). About the same are the losmen near the harbour (Sungai Siak) such as *NIRMALA***, Jl.Moh.Yamin) About the best is *DHARMA UTAMA**** on Jl.Sudirman. In general Pakanbaru is expensive.

LEAVING PAKANBARU

BY AIR

Simpang Tiga Airport is about 10 km out of town on the road to Bukittinggi. Travel agencies and airlines offer a minibus service for 1000 Rp. Otherwise take a bus towards Bukittinggi and get off at Lapangan Terbang. Garuda office at Jl.Sudirman 207 (tel 21026); Merpati at Jl.Cokroaminoto 18 (tel 23558). Sempati flights should be booked through P.T.Cendrawasih Kencana Tours & Travel, Jl.Iman Bonjol 32 (side street off Jl.Sudirman just a bit beyond the market). Very helpful people! They also sell tickets for the Friday PMAC (Pan Malaysia Air Carrier) flights to MALACCA for 65,000 Rp. SAMPLE PRICES: TANJUNG PINANG 53,700 Rp (MZ), RENGAT 31,700 Rp (MZ), DUMAI 36,200 Rp (MZ), BATAM 46,800 Rp (GA), MEDAN 65,800 Rp (GA), PADANG 32,300 Rp (GA), JAKARTA 116,800 Rp (GA), SINGAPORE about 120,000 Rp (daily with Garuda), PALEMBANG 72,200 Rp (GA).International airport tax 3000 Rp, national 1400 Rp.

BY BUS

The long distance bus station is just out of town on the road to Bukittinggi. All the major companies such as Aldilla, Kurnia, Bunga Setangkai have offices there. Bemos within the city limits cost 200 Rp. This applies to the route between bus station and harbour too, even if you're asked to pay 1000 Rp at first. SAMPLE PRICES: BUKITTINGGI 3000 Rp (6 hrs.), PADANG 3600 Rp, MEDAN 12,000 Rp, DUMAI 3000 Rp, TANJUNG KARANG 22,000 Rp, RENGAT 3000 Rp (12 hrs.).

Local oplets, bemos, and minibuses all leave from the market (Jl.Sudirman). To RUMBAI (Caltex) go first by Oplet, and then change into a minibus.

BY BOAT

At least one ship a day goes down the Sungai Siak to TANJUNG PINANG. They leave between 16:00 and 18:00 h. Price just rose, costs 12,500 Rp for deck (not to be recommended) and 17,500 Rp for a bed!!! The trip takes 40 hours. The boats are generally overcrowded and deck passengers can hardly find a seat. You'll have to bring your own food. Keep an eye on your luggage, especially at night! Stops at SELATPANJANG (Pulau Tebingtinggi), TANJUNG BATU (Pulau Kundur), and MORO (Pulau Sugibawah). The countryside is beautiful but otherwise only for people who can stand the strain. On the second day you arrive in Tanjung Pinang at about 10:00 h.

DUMAI

This place is only interesting for people who want to catch the ferry over to Malacca (Peninsular Malaysia). Get there by bus from BUKITTINGGI (6000 Rp, 12 hrs.) or PAKANBARU (3000 Rp).

HOTELS

Small but clean rooms in *PENGINAPAN ANDYS NUR***, Jl.Jen.Sudirman 147.

Not so good is *TIP TOP HOTEL*** in the same street.

Best place in town is *TASIA HOTEL***** on a little side street off Jl.Sudirman. The guy behind the desk seems to be the only person in Dumai able to speak English.

LEAVING DUMAI

Every Friday a ferry leaves for MALACCA. Departure is at 10:00 h. The trip takes only 2 1/2 hrs. Prices: 40,000 Rp and 1250 Rp harbour tax in Dumai. Buy your tickets in the green building near the harbour. A trishaw from the hotel area to the harbour costs 500 Rp. You're only allowed to enter or leave Indonesia via Dumai if you're in possession of a 30-day Tourist Visa.

TANJUNG PINANG

The most important city in the Riau Archipelago is only 80 km by air or a four hour boat ride from Singapore. Due to their geographical proximity, the islands to the south of Singapore are lucrative bases for smugglers. The majority of the population is ethnic Chinese. They sit every evening in front of their TVs and watch programmes from the 'Lion City' or Malaysia.

Most travellers only spend a couple of hours in Tanjung Pinang before hastening on to a ferry. Too bad, because the town is a place from which to visit the neighbouring islands. And such trips are worth it!

Tanjung Pinang itself doesn't have much to offer. Half the town is built on stilts over the sea - modern stilts today are concrete columns. In the evening take a walk on the *BUKIT* to see the sunset. 2 km out of town on the road to Kijang is a small museum, *KANDIL RIAU.* Raja Razak, the founder and owner is seldom around, however, so the museum stays closed.

Several beautiful lonely beaches can be found on the eastern part of the island of Bintan. *PANTAI BERAKIT* is in the northeast and can be reached by bus. *PANTAI TRIKORA* is one of the nicest beaches you'll ever see. It can now be reached by a new road - you could rent a motorbike privately in TP for about 8000 Rp a day. Take the road to *KIJANG.* At batu (milestone) 10 take the left fork after the mosque and follow the road 18 km to KAWAL. In the village go right, and it's another 9 km to the beach. Pantai Trikora consists of several beaches one after the other. On the way back at batu 12 and 16, you pass through the infamous 'villages of joy'.

To climb *GUNUNG BINTAN,* which at 348 m is the highest mountain on the island, take a prahu to KG.SEKUNING - stay the night with the 'kepala desa'. Next morning do the 2 to 3 hour climb. Ask Ahmady in TP for more info!

PULAU PENYENGAT is a small island right off TP. Only Malays live here and speak the purest Malay. There are no cars or motorbikes on the island. To get there costs 300 Rp in a sampan. Look for Raja Ibrahim Sulaiman to show you the island and the ruins of the old palaces.

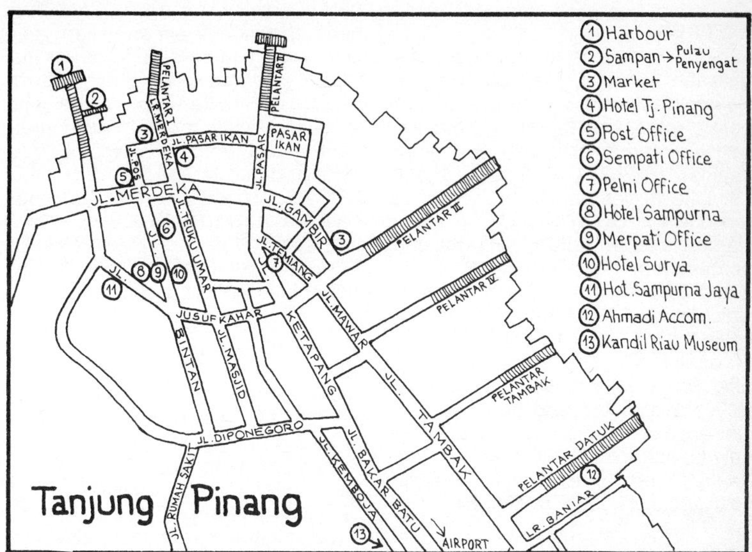

Raja Ibrahim Sulaiman is an actual descendant of the Johore-Riau dynasty. In the 18th century Pulau Penyengat was the most important city of the sultanate, which at the height of its power ruled the entire Riau-Lingga archipelago and a large part of Sumatra, as well as the present day Malaysian states of Johore and Pahang. Up until 1819 there was only one Sultan of Johore-Riau, but then the British (in the person of Stamford Raffles) made the famous agreement concerning the island of Singapore with Sultan Hussein, the rightful heir to the throne. His brother Abdul Rahman had usurped the throne and was dealing with the Dutch openly. In 1824 an agreement was signed between Holland and Great Britain which clarified the situation. Hussein became Sultan in Johore, Abdul Rahman in Riau. The great power spheres of influence were defined and the Sultanate of Johore-Riau was divided. The ruins and graves of the former sultans can be found on the island of Penyengat, which has returned to its old village lifestyle.

On the island of Bintan, across from Tanjung Pinang, is KG.SENGGARANG. Sampans cost 200 Rp and leave from the landing place near Hotel Tanjung Pinang. There are 80% Chinese in the water village (kampong air). Turn left and you come to three Chinese temples. On the way back is a school where Khalid, a teacher, speaks pretty good English.

HOTELS

Tanjung Pinang is an important link between Sumatra, Riau and Lingga, Kalimantan, and especially Singapore. Hotels are therefore both expensive and over-booked. A good deal is *AHMADY**, Jl.Pelantar Datuk 10. Like a sleeping hall! Somewhat run down is *SONDANG***, Jl.Yusuf Kamar. On Jl.Bintan next to and across from the Merpati office are *SAMPURNA INN**** and *SURYA**** which at least has a nice garden. You could try *HOTEL TANJUNG PINANG* *** on Jl.Pasar Ikan. Many people will offer you a place to stay upon arrival in TP. Watch out and don't go with just anyone - too many thieves! The new luxury hotel is the *SAMPURNA JAYA***** on Jl.Yusuf Kamar. Rooms cost about 30,000 Rp. Good food at the Chinese night market.

LEAVING TANJUNG PINANG

BY AIR

Kijang Airport is about 12 km out of town. Share taxis - old American yank tanks known to break down from time to time, will take you out - from the taxi stop on Jl.Gambir 5000 Rp a cab. On a motorcycle you pay only 2000 Rp. When leaving the airport, they'll demand horrendous prices. Keep your nerve, wait, and bargain! When all the passengers have left, the waiting drivers will soften up. There are occasional buses for 700 Rp. Merpati and Sempati (both on Jl.Bintan) fly to several different places. SAMPLE PRICES: JAKARTA 104,000 Rp, PANGKAL PINANG 60,000 Rp (Sempati each Friday), PAKANBARU 53,700 Rp, PALEMBANG 53,800 Rp. Unfortunately there's still no regular flight to Kalimantan.

BY SHIP

PELNI office at Jl.Temiang 190. The different ships are announced on the blackboard. If you're lucky, you can go to SINGKAWANG (north of Pontianak) for about 20,000 Rp. There are regular ships to PAKANBARU (17,500 Rp and 12,000 Rp) and at 11:00 h each day ride to BATAM (SEKUPANG) for 5000 Rp with the slow boat. Two daily express boats at 9:00 and 14:00 h for 15,000 Rp. Another slow boat leaves daily at 11:00 h for Pulau Batam's second harbour, BATU AMPAR, for 5000 Rp. Express boats Mon, Wed, and Fri for 7500 Rp. From here daily ferries to SINGAPORE. No visa is needed for entering Indonesia via Batam. For further details see Batam.

PULAU BATAM

Batam is short for Batu Ampar. Because imigrasi at Tg.Pinang won't let you in or out without a proper visa, this island is a through station for all Tourist Pass holders coming from Singapore. There are big plans to develop Pulau Batam into a little Singapore, or at least to offer the Lion City a little competition (duty-free shopping, industrial estates, etc.). Broad streets, unusual in Indonesia, have already been laid out but not much more. Nobody even knows what will eventually be the main town. At the moment, Nagoya is the town with the most hotels and losmen***-****. Nagoya is accessible by bus for 500 Rp (there aren't any colts, bemos, etc.) from Sekupang harbour. Boats are so frequent that you can usually leave within hours. Or does anyone know a good reason to stay longer?

LEAVING PULAU BATAM

BY AIR

Only taxis serve the airport (12,000 Rp to Sekupang). The Garuda office is in the Persero Building, 2nd floor, Batu Ampar. Direct connections to MEDAN 102,200 Rp, JAKARTA 108,900 Rp, PAKANBARU 46,800 Rp, PONTIANAK 79,100 Rp, or to PALEMBANG 64,900 Rp.

SHIPS FROM SEKUPANG

SINGAPORE: 8 times daily from 8:30-17:00 h, 30 minutes, 11,500 Rp; you can pay in Singapore dollars (S$20); ticket sales and imigrasi in the harbour at the ferry jetty. One of the boats, the AUTO BATAM I, is a Hovercraft built in England; only flying is nicer! Departs at 8:30, 13:00, and 16:30 h. All ferries offer total luxury (comfortable seats, ac, etc.). Remember, Singapore time is one hour ahead of Western Indonesian Time. You arrive in Singapore at Finger Pier, Prince Edward Road; the closest money changers are a 20 minute walk at Clifford Pier. TANJUNG PINANG: two luxury express boats daily, 11:00 and 15:00 h, takes 2 h, 15,000 Rp; or the slow boat, 10:00 h, 5 h, 5000 Rp. Tanjung Balai (Pulau Karimum): daily 13:00 h, 15,000 Rp.

SHIPS FROM BATU AMPAR

SINGAPORE: twice daily, 10:00 and 16:00 h, 30 minutes, 11,500 Rp. TANJUNG PINANG: a fast boat Tues, Thurs, and Sat about 10:00 h, 2. 1/2 - 3 hrs., 7500 Rp; a slow boat daily at 11:00 h, 5 hrs., 5000 Rp. There is a bus for 1000 Rp between the two harbours Sekupang and Batu Ampar. From Kabil at the southeastern tip of Batam island, there is a ferry every half hour to Tanjung Uban, Pulau Bintan. Since Batam represents a major development project, things are going to change quickly. Let us know what you see. Write to us!

SOUTH SUMATRA

The following provinces are in the south of Sumatra: Jambi (1.6 million), Bengkulu (980,000), South Sumatra (5.6 million) and Lampung (6.5 million). There are two ways from West Sumatra to Panjang or Bakauheni io get the ferry to Java. Firstly go to Jambi and from there to Palembang or secondly via Muarabungo and Bangko to Lubuklinggau and from there by train to Palembang. Southern Sumatra is swamp, jungle, oil-fields and bad roads.

JAMBI

A most uninteresting city, lying on Sumatra's longest river, the Batang Hari. In the last few years the Indonesian Observer has carried a number of stories of people being attacked by tigers in the area.

HOTELS

On Jl.Sultan Agung are 2 hotels: *MUTIARA***, no. 21 (tel 23595) and *MUSTIKA****, no. 31 (tel 24672). More expensive is *MAKMUR****, Jl. Taman Bahagia 14 (tel 23226). Or try the most expensive place: *TELANAIPURA ***(*)*, Jl.Jen.Sudirman 126, tel 23827.

LEAVING JAMBI

BY AIR

Garuda office on Jl.Dr.Wahidin (tel 22303); Merpati at Jl.Damar 83 (tel 22184). SAMPLE PRICES: JAKARTA 81,700 Rp, PALEMBANG 33,600 Rp. Other flights by SMAC (P.T.Sabang Merauke Air Charter) - they supposedly fly to Singapore. Also check Pertamina Airline Pelita.

BY BUS

ANS and ENGGANO go to Bukittinggi or Padang - costs 8000 Rp. To get to Palembang it's best to take a bemo to BAYUNGLENCIR for 2200 Rp and from there go by riverboat for 7500 Rp to PALEMBANG. Daily buses to SUNGEIPENUH for 5500 Rp, takes about 24 hrs.

SUNGEIPENUH

This is the main village in the wide Tanah Kerinci high valley with Sumatra's highest volcano (3800 m) in the north and Lake Kerinci in the south east. You can take a trip by minibus round the lake. The volcano can be climbed from KAYUARO in 2-3 days; you'll need a guide though.

HOW TO GET THERE

Several direct buses a day for 5000 Rp (24 hrs.) to JAMBI. Or go by boat to MUARABUNGO and from there by bus to BANGKO. The bus from Bangko to SUNGEIPENUH takes 6 hrs. and costs 3000 Rp. Buses from PADANG (dept. 9:00 h, 15:00 h) via TAPAN take 14 hours and cost 3500 Rp.

BENGKULU

This tiny place on the west coast of Sumatra was, until the 1970s, one of the most isolated places in Indonesia. In 1933, Sukarno was exiled by the Dutch to Bengkulu for nine years. He certainly kept himself busy here because in 1945 the resistance movement against the returning Dutch was concentrated in Bengkulu.

As can be read in Marsden's History of Sumatra, on June 25, 1685, an agreement was signed between the representatives of the British East India Company and the local Raja. The English received exclusive rights to purchase the pepper crop plus a place to build a fort. The East India Company tried with this and other settlements to take a share of the lucrative pepper trade from the Dutch. Other British settlements were at Indrapura, Natal and Manjuta. For 150 years the British remained in 'BENCOOLEN' but never achieved economic success. In 1824 the area was traded for Dutch Malacca.

Visit the British *FORT MALIOBORO (BENTENG),* named by Stamford Raffles after the Duke of Marlborough. From the fortress you have a good view of the city and harbour. Nearby are lots of old British gravestones. The benteng is open daily except on Mon / holidays from 8:00 to 14:00 h, Fri until 11:00 h, Sat until 12:00 h.

Not far from town are nice beaches such as *PANTAI PANJANG.*

HOTELS

Bengkulu is not marked on Indonesian tourist maps. There aren't too many hotels. Try *SAMUDRA** on Jl. Benteng in the old town. The best for your money is probably *WISMA BALAI BUNTAR*****, Jl.Khadijah 122, not far from the fort in a quiet sidestreet. Large rooms with ac and friendly people.

LEAVING BENGKULU

BY AIR

Garuda in Hotel Asia, Jl.Jend.A.Yani 922; daily 9:00 h to PALEMBANG for 42,200 Rp; daily 14:45 h to JAKARTA for 76,400 Rp. No other connections! Airport Padang Kemiling is 14 km south of the city. Take Microlet from taxi terminal Pasar Minggu for 250 Rp - charter 2500 Rp.

BY BUS

Terminal Bis Panorama is 5 km out of town, take Microlet from here to Pasar Minggu (100 Rp). Buses leave regularly to LUBUKLINGGAU via CURUP (stay the night in Wisma Sarina - nice place) for 2500 Rp. There are direct buses to BUKITTINGGI and PADANG doing the 50 hour ride for 12,500 Rp. From Lubuklinggau there is a daily train to Palembang (5000 / 3500 Rp).

PALEMBANG

South Sumatra's capital has around 800,000 inhabitants. All roads and both rail lines lead to Palembang. Nearby is a big oil refinery. In the 7th century the Sri Vijaya Empire came into existence in South Sumatra, and it is thought that its capital was somewhere near Palembang. The city was probably built of wood, which accounts for the lack of ruins.

In the 11th century Sri Vijaya was at the height of its power. Merchants from all over the world lived in the city. In the great libraries and universities, Buddhism and Sanskrit were studied. Chinese men of learning came here to translate ancient writings. At the beginning of the 14th century, Sri Vijaya split up into many small principalities, and Malacca became the most important centre of trade in the orient.

The *SRI VIJAYA MUSEUM*, Jl.Rumah Bari, is worth a look. In the front building are the ethnological and archaeological exhibits while in the back is the zoological. The different markets are also worth checking out. *PASAR ILIR* is the old China Town. Today there's one shop after another. The batik and songket selection is quite large. Here and there you'll find traditional jewelry of gold and silver. Many interesting shops are on Jl.Guru. Not bad is Kud Mawar Melati, 30 Ilir, Jl.Tl.Kerangga 276 with its old textiles and paintings. The Dutch fort *(BENTENG)*, built in 1780, is still there. It's occupied by the army.

HOTELS

One of the most expensive is *SANJAYA*****, Jl.Kap.Rivai 6193. You eat well here. Some restaurants on Jl.Jen.Sudirman are also good. You can find a cheap bed in *AMAN*(*)*, Jl.Lematang 453. Several rooms have their own bath. Similar prices at *LEMBANG***, Jl.Kol.Atmo 16. At Pasar Ilir are several cheap losmen and hotels: *SEGARAN***, Jl.Segaran 15 (a bit musty) or *SENTOSA**, Jl.Depaten Baru 52-58.

LEAVING PALEMBANG

BY AIR

Talangbetutu airport is about 15 km north of the city. Garuda at Jl.Kap. Rivai 35 (tel 22029) - Merpati at Jl. Kap.Rivai 6193 (tel 21604). SAMPLE PRICES: BENGKULU 42,200 Rp (GA), JAKARTA 53,300 Rp (MZ), JAMBI 33,600 Rp (GA), MEDAN 120,800 Rp (GA), PADANG 73,300 Rp (GA), PANGKALPINANG 30,400 Rp (GA), PAKANBARU 72,200 Rp (GA), TANJUNG PANDAN 53,100 Rp (MZ), BATAM 64,900 Rp (MZ / GA), RENGAT 59,100 Rp (MZ), SINGAPORE (via Pakanbaru) 151,000 Rp (GA).

BY BUS

All the major bus companies go to Palembang. Both bus terminals are close to the new Japanese-built bridge across Sungai Musi. SAMPLE PRICES: JAKARTA 9500 Rp, TANJUNG KARANG 6500 Rp, BUKITTINGGI / PADANG 14,800 Rp, LUBUKLINGGAU 5600 Rp.

BY RAIL

KERTAPATI station is on the southern bank of the Musi. 200 Rp by bemo. Two trains daily to PANJANG (7500 Rp, 2nd class; 3900 Rp, 3rd class). LUBUKLINGGAU is 5000 / 3500 Rp. Reductions with your ISIC.

BY SHIP

Daily connection to KAYURANG (Pulau Bangka) for 5200 Rp, 15 hrs. You can also steam to MUNTOK and go from there by minibus to PANGKALPINANG (stay in Hotel Ranggi***) and then fly with Sempati for 60,000 Rp to Tanjung Pinang. Another regular boat connection: Palembang - BAYUNGLENCIR for 6200 Rp, then go by bemo to JAMBI (1800 Rp).

FERRIES TO JAVA

PANJANG is the old harbour for ships to Java. There are two ferries daily at 10.00 h and 23.00 h to MERAK. Costs: 1st cl. 3700 Rp, 2nd cl. 2600 Rp, 3rd cl. 1300 Rp. Merak - JAKARTA depending on train, between 1100 Rp and 1800 Rp. Today more ships for MERAK leave from BAKAUHENI. The bus from Bandar Lampung to the ferry station costs 1000 Rp and takes two hours. Every 75 minutes round the clock a ferry leaves for Java. Prices: 3rd cl. 850 Rp, 2nd cl. 1400 Rp, 1st cl. 1750 Rp. If you come by train you can buy a ticket straight from Jakarta or Palembang which includes the cost of the ferry from Panjang.

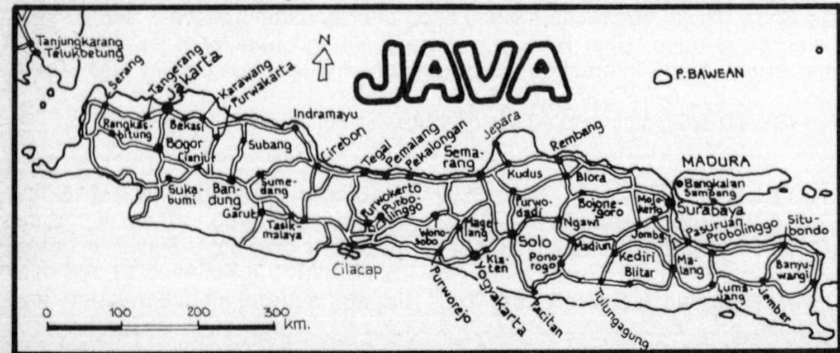

JAVA

When one speaks of Indonesia, one usually means Java. The majority of the Indonesian people live here and it is where the major political and economic decisions are made. Hundreds of years ago powerful kingdoms existed on this island and developed a high cultural identity. Today we see the population growing at one of the fastest rates in the world with power and beauty along-side sickness and poverty. Traditional social structures are disappearing on this fast developing island. But where will the changes take Java?

Sir Stamford Raffles, the founder of Singapore, wrote during his time as governor of British Java from 1811-1819 the most scholarly and comprehensive work about his beloved island - The History of Java.

"The soil is in general extremely fertile and can be brought to yield its produce with little labour. Many of the best spots still remain uncultivated, and several districts are almost desert and neglected, which might be the seats of a crowded and happy peasantry...The term of life is not much shorter than in the best climates of Europe...As the Javans are a quite domestic people, little given to adventure, disinclined to foreign enterprize, not easily roused to violence or bloodshed, and little disposed to irregularities of any kind, there are but few families left destitute, in consequence of hazards incurred or crimes committed by their natural protectors."

See for yourself if it has changed in the 170 years since this was written: experience the modernities and the ancient temples as well as the volcanoes, rice terraces, beaches, villages and people of this island south of the equator.

The island has a good transport system - you can get just about everywhere, but not necessarily comfortably. No matter where you plan your route, you'll still run into people - 690 per square kilometre. The largest population groups are the Sundanese in the west and the Javanese and Madurese in the east. Jakarta is the melting pot of all Indonesia. Most of you will begin your tour of Java here before going on to Bali. Try to get off the beaten path a bit or make at least a couple of excursions out to the villages.

It is fairly simple to climb volcanoes here - a range of them runs the length of the island. Few people are aware of the beautiful beaches - it doesn't always have to be Bali!

JAKARTA

Indonesia's metropolis has an estimated 8 million residents (Greater Jakarta 10 million). There is an extreme contrast between rich and poor - many people are living in slums right next to the fancy administrative palaces. Half of the population increase is due to migration from the countryside. The hope is to find a job. The lights of the city attract young people away from the monotony of the 'desa' (Indonesian for 'village')

Some facts on Jakarta's history: In all probability the estuary of the Ciliwung River has been settled for more than thousand years. At the end of the 15th century the main port of the Pajajaran Kingdom, Sunda Kelapa, was situated here. The Dutch took possession of the area in 1619 and for the following 330 years it was called Batavia.

"I do not expect you'll want to hear any more about it.." So began a description by one of Captain Cook's passengers of Dutch Batavia around 1770. "There are few streets in the city through which a fairly large canal hasn't been laid; while at least five or six rivers pass through her. The streets are universally wide and the houses big; for both of these reasons, the city in relation to the number of buildings is much larger than any comparable city in Europe...The canals are filled mostly with stagnant and polluted water which evaporates during the hot season creating an unbearable odour. Many trees prevent a breeze which might clear the air of the unhealthy contaminants. During the wet season...the dirty water rises to overflow the banks of the canals and floods the ground floors of houses in the low lying areas. Afterwards one finds incredible amounts of slime and mud...Of every hundred soldiers sent here from Europe only fifty remain alive at the end of one year...In all of Batavia we have yet to find one person giving the impression of health and exuberance."

Begin your tour of colonial Jakarta north of the main train station at the end of Jl.Pintu Besar Utara. Around the old town square several colonial buildings were restored with aid from UNESCO, among them the *JAKARTA MUSEUM* (Fatahillah Museum). Built in 1626, it is one of the oldest buildings in Jakarta and served as 'stadthuys' (townhall) during the Dutch administration before becoming a military headquarter after independence and a historical museum in 1974. Those who like old maps, war history, and other relics of Dutch influence in Batavia should have a look. Open: Tues-Thurs 9:00 to 14:00 h, Fri 9:00 to 11:00 h, Sat until 13:00 h, Sun until 15:00 h.

The *WAYANG MUSEUM* is on the west side of the square. It contains an exhibit of South East Asian traditional puppet theatre. Besides the puppets you can see the instruments and other things used for a performance. The building itself is an old protestant church. Open: Tues-Thurs and Sun 9:00 to 14:00 h, Fri 9:00 to 11:00 h, Sat 9:00 to 13:00 h. Sun 10:00 h performances of wayang kulit or wayang golek,admission 200 Rp.

(1) Jayakarta Tower Hotel	(12) University	(23) Hilton
(2) Kalideres Bus Stn.	(13) St Carolus Hospital	(24) Ratu Plaza Shopping Ctr.
(3) Grogol Bus Stn.	(14) Botschaft Singapore	(25) Panin Ctr. / Botschaft PNG
(4) JL BATUCEPER	(15) Sasmita Loka Museum	(26) Embassy of the Netherlds.
(5) Bouraq Off.	(16) Gedung Perintis Kemerdekaan	(27) Museum Abri
(6) Merpati Off.	(17) Pasar Burung	(28) Pertamina Hospital
(7) Pelni Off.	(18) Artha Loka Building	(29) Kebayoran Baru Bus Stn.
(8) Duta Merlin Shopping Ctr.	(19) Sahid Jaya Hotel	(30) Block M
(9) Pasar Baru Shopping Ctr.	(20) Canadian Embassy	(31) Pasar Minggu Bus Terminal
(10) Pulo Gadung Bus Stn.	(21) Wisma Metropolitan	(32) Taman Mini
(11) Textile Museum	(22) Indonesian Bazar	(33) Cililitan Bus Stn.

Jakarta
Tanjung Priok
Ancol
DETAILED MAP OLD CITY
DETAILED MAP CITY
KOTA STN
ANGKE STN
TANAH ABANG STN
GAMBIR STN
SENEN ST.
MANGGARAI STN
JATINEGARA STN
ARSIP NATIONAL
MESJID KEBON JERUK
KLENTENG ANCOL
DUNIA FANTASI
SW POOL
OCEANARIUM
RACE COURSE
Kebayoran Baru
ZOO
Bogor, Ciawi
km

Those who are more deeply interested in Indonesian arts should check out the *BALAI SENI RUPA & MUSEUM KERAMIK* (museum for art and painting & museum for ceramics) on the east side of the square. In the offices of the West Jakarta administration you'll find paintings instead of files. The ceramic section is interesting. Open: Tues-Thurs 9:00 to 14:00, Fri 9:00 to 11:00, Sat 9:00 to 13:00, Sun 9:00 to 15:00 h. Even those who don't like museums should go to get a feel of the atmosphere in the traditional administrative buildings of Batavia. By the way, the cannon *(SI JAGUR)* across from the townhall on the north side of the square is an old fertility symbol to which many women, even today, pray to for children.

Walk from Fatahillah Square along Jl.Kali Besar Timur V to *KALI BESAR* canal. Everywhere you'll see trading houses, businesses and warehouses from the Dutch era. Dating from the early 18th century are two buildings on the west side of the canal (Jl.Kali Besar Barat), the Chartered Bank on the corner, and 'Toko Merah', today PT Satya Niaga at no. 11. Keep walking north along the canal to the latest restoration, a draw-bridge over 200-years-old, *HOENDERPASARBRUG* ('chicken market bridge').

Continue north and cross the bustling Jl.Pakin. At the mouth of the canal is a *WATCH TOWER,* built in 1839, from which the harbourmaster could keep track of arriving ships. It is built on the walls of a fortress, *BASTION CULEMBORG,* constructed in 1645. From the tower you have a good view of the canal and the red-tiled roofs of the old buildings.

Past waiting rickshaws and merchants, heading north, cross busy Jl.Pasar Ikan to the entrance of *MUSEUM BAHARI,* a small nautical museum, in a former warehouse of the East India Company. More interesting than the exhibits (small boats and model ships, maps, tools) is the building, constructed in 1652 with tremendous walls, where the company stored spices, coffee and tea. The high wall facing the street is part of the old town wall. Open Tues-Thurs, 9:00-14:00 h, Fri 9:00-11:00 h, Sat 9:00-13:00 h, and Sun until 15:00 h.

Via a pedestrian bridge you reach the old fish market, *PASAR IKAN,* where the lively trade begins just after sunrise. The big fish market is 3 km to the west at Muara Amke. Here you can see fishing boats unloaded and the different fish and shell fish brought for sale into two giant halls. Walk back to Jl.Pakin and cross the big bridge.

To the left, make your way up to the quay - 100 Rp admission. Be sure to take a walk along the pier to the sailing ship harbour *KALI BARU* and the tall-masted Bugis schooners. Wild-eyed figures unload wood from Kalimantan and peddlers sell perfume and souvenirs to the sailors. You can get a boat to row you through the harbour - find one on the way back from the pier, the price goes down automatically.

TAMAN IMPIAN JAYA ANCOL - a large recreation and amusement park right by the sea. Since there is always a cool breeze, it isn't as hot as in the city. Because it isn't far, Ancol is a good spot to relax in the afternoon after a strenuous day of sightseeing. Get a taxi (about 2500 Rp from the city) or bus 64, 65 from Kota Station (Arion Bus 60 from Lapangan Banteng) toward Tanjung Priok. Don't come out on weekends when it is crowded and everything is more expensive. Admission is 400-600 Rp, plus charges for all facilities, shows, etc. Past the golf-course and the bowling alley is Fantasy World - 'Dunia Fantasi', which opened in 1985. Admission 600 - 1100 Rp depending upon the day; open Mon-Fri 14:00-21:00 h, Sat 14:00-22:00 h, Sun 10:00-21:00 h. An Indonesian mixture of Disneyland and carnival, with shops and stands in styles from every era, country and continent, plus a Ferris wheel (great view!), lots of merry-go-rounds, and the Kodak Puppet World for the enchantment of children.

Further on toward the beach is the marina. From here you can get a boat to Pulau Seribu (see *Around Jakarta*). There are a number of seafood restaurants on the peninsula. Right by the sea are a luxury hotel, bungalows, and a lagoon with boat rentals. To the south you pass through the jaws of an oversized whale to a large swimming pool (admission 1000 Rp, open daily, 4:00-21:00 h) with a tremendous slide, wave machine, etc.

A short walk south of Fatahillah Square is the old Chinese quarter *GLODOK*. The typical Chinese atmosphere is slowly being lost with the rise of sterile new buildings in the place of the open shops, restaurants, and workshops. Instead we see modern shopping centres (Glodok Shopping Centre - corner of Jl.Pancoran and Jl.Gajah Mada), banks and apartment buildings all done with the same monotonous concrete. Only in the evening does the old Chinese atmosphere reappear as the foodstalls move into the streets.

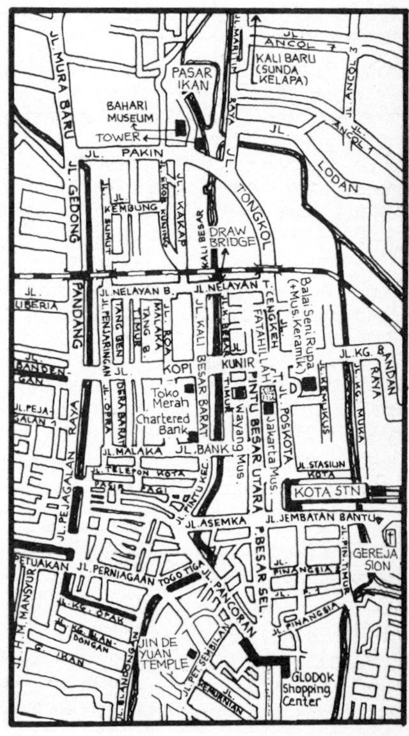

Jl.GAJAH MADA runs south along both sides of the canal. A stink rises from the water, just as in the days of Captain Cook. Today it is mixed with the exhaust from the traffic jams. For this reason be sure to take a bus for the 3 km (but not S.M.S Bus 70 which is plagued by thieves!) or other transport. If you drive south, then stop at *ARSIP NATIONAL* at Jl.Gajah Mada 111. The last colonial country house, constructed by Governor-General Reiner de Klerk in 1760 remains set in its nice garden much as it was in the 18th century. Today the National Archive is housed in the building.

In the centre of *MERDEKA SQUARE* (Independence Square) rises an impressive 132 m high piece of 'Sukarno memorial architecture', the *NATIONAL MONUMENT (MONAS)* with a flame containing 35 kg of gold plating. For 1500 Rp (students 500 Rp) you can take the lift up to the observation platform (115 m) for a good view of Jakarta. The admission price includes a visit to the historical museum in the basement - diorama illustrate important events in Indonesian history - and the Independence Hall, a carved marble tribute to the greatness of the nation, where the voice of Sukarno can be heard making the original declaration of independence. Open daily 8:00-17:00 h.

West of the square you'll find the *NATIONAL MUSEUM* or Gedung Gajah (elephant building), so called because of the bronze elephant - a gift from the King of Thailand. Give yourself plenty of time because this is one of the biggest and best museums in South East Asia. Open: Tues-Thurs 8:30-14:00 h, Fri 8:30-11:00 h, Sat 8:30-13:00 h, and Sun 8:30-15:00 h. Each Sunday from 9:30-10:30 h you can listen to traditional Sundanese music. Admission (as for almost all museums) 200 Rp.

Plan to spend at least a morning in the museum if you want to have a look at everything. If you're just starting your trip to Indonesia, you can learn something here about the volcanoes and islands, people and their customs, and traditional arts and crafts of all the islands. Here you'll find an important porcelain collection with pieces from the Han, Tang, Sung, and Ming dynasties. Beyond the porcelain collection is an exhibit of the remains of the prehistoric Java Man (pithecantropus erectus). The library, containing over 700,000 titles, is the largest in Indonesia.

South of the square is the *JAKARTA FAIR GROUND.* On its southwestern side (corner of Jl.Merdeka Barat and Selatan) is the amusement park *TAMAN RIA.* Open after 17:00 h, Sun at 9:00 h, with merry-go-rounds for children and on Sundays Indonesian pop music in the evening. *GAMBIR STATION* dominates the east of the square. Set back from the road across from the station is *IMANUEL CHURCH,* a round building with a dome and an entrance gate reminiscent of a doric temple. Built in 1839 as the 'Willemskerk' in honour of King Willem I, it was the first united church of Lutherans and Reformists.

Walk up Jl.Pejambon beyond the bridge to *GEDUNG PANCASILA,* the Independence Building, constructed in classical style in 1830 as a residence for

(34) Garuda OFF.	(42) Immigration OFF.	(51) British Embassy
(35) Mandala Airlines	(43) Taman Ismail Marzuki	(52) Thai Embassy
(36) Lapangan Banteng Bus Stn	(44) Australian Embassy	(53) Indonesia Hotel
(37) Borobudur Hotel	(45) Burmese Embassy	(54) Embassy of Malaysia
(38) Pasar Senen Shopping Ctr. + Bharata Theatre	(46) Art & Curio Restaurant	(55) Embassy of the Philippines
	(47) Oasis Restaurant	(56) Embassy of New Zealand
(39) U.S.Embassy	(48) Wisma Nusantara	(57) Souvenir Stalls
(40) Wisma Ise	(49) Wisata International Hotel	
(41) Sarinah Department Store	(50) Mandarin Hotel	

JL. IR. H. JUANDA
JL. POS
CENTRAL POST OFFICE
MAKAMAH AGUNG
JL. G.S. 3
JL. G. SAHARI 2
JL. SURYOPRANOTO
JL. MAJAPAHIT
JL. VETERAN
JL. VETERAN 4
JL. VETERAN 3
JL. VETERAN 2
JL. VETERAN 1
ISTANA MERDEKA
ISTIQLAL MOSQUE
CATHEDRAL
DEPT. OF FINANCE
JL. GUNUNG SAHARI
JL. STASIUN SENEN
JL. DR. WAHIDIN
JL. PERWIRA
JL. M. MERDEKA UTARA
JL. TANAH ABANG 1
JL. ABD. MUIS
TAMAN PRASATI
NATIONAL MUSEUM
NATIONAL MONUMENT
MONAS
GAMBIR STN.
JL. MEDAN MERDEKA TIMUR
JL. TAMAN PEJAMBON
GEDUNG PANCASILA
JL. ABD. RAHMAN SALEH
JL. KWINI 2
JL. SENEN RAYA
SENEN STN.
JL. PASAR SENEN
IMANUEL CHURCH
JL. PEJAMBON
JL. M. MERDEKA BARAT
JL. B. KEMULIAAN 2
FAIR GROUND
JL. PEKAN RAYA
TAMAN RIA
JL. BATU
JL. PRATAPAN
JL. KWITANG
JL. KRAMAT RAYA
JL. BUDI KEMULIAAN
JL. M. MERDEKA SELATAN
TELECOM
DETAILED MAP
JL. M. IKH. MENTENG RAYA
JL. KRAMAT
JL. KRAMAT 3
JL. KEBON SIRIH
JL. THAMRIN
JL. K.H. WAHID HASYIM
JL. HAJI AGUS SALIM
JL. JAKSA
JL. TAMAN CUT MUTIA
JL. PENGARENGAN
JL. JOHAR
JL. SUNDA
JL. SUMATRA
JL. SUMBAWA
JL. KEMIRI
JL. CEMARA
JL. DR. S. RATULANGI
JL. GEREJA THERESIA
JL. LOMBOK
JL. MALUKU
JL. IRIAN
JL. YUS. ADIWINATA
JL. MOH. HUSNI THAMRIN
JL. COKROAMINOTO
JL. TANJUNG
JL. CENDANA
JL. TEUKU UMAR
JL. JAMBU
JL. CUT NYAK DIEN
JL. GONDANGDIA LAMA
JL. CIKINI RAYA
JL. RADEN SALEH RAYA
JL. SUWIRYO
JL. SULTAN SYAHRIR
JL. PROF. M. YAMIN S.H.
KEB. KACANG R.
JL. INDRAMAYU
JL. BLITAR
JL. KEDIRI
JL. IMAM BONJOL
JL. M.H. THAMRIN
JL. HOS. COKROAMINOTO
JL. BESUKI
JL. SYAM SURIZAL
JL. PURWAKARTA
JL. TEUKU CIK DITIRO
JL. CILACAP
JL. SURABAYA
JL. PEGANSAAN TI.
JL. CILOSARI
JL. PASURUAN
JL. DIPONEGORO
JL. DR. S.H. KUSUMA ATMAJA
JL. SUMENEP
JL. SUNDA KELAPA
JL. MADIUN
JL. CIMAHI
JL. CIANJUR
JL. LEMBANG
JL. MANGUN SARKORO
0 250 500 m.

the military commander. The People's Council began meeting here in 1918. Membership of the council was controlled by white colonials and it exercised little real power. In 1945 a constitutional convention, established by the Japanese, began work here under the leadership of Sukarno. On 1 June 1945, he proclaimed from here Pancasila, the national philosophy. *HOTEL BOROBUDUR,* an oasis of Western luxury, is at the end of the street. A room costs over US$120 a night, much more than the monthly pay of the average Indonesian.

In the east the *MINISTRY OF FINANCE* is housed in a building whose construction began in 1809 under Governor General Herman Daendels (1807-1811). He attempted to restructure Batavia with a firm hand and tried to end corruption throughout the colony. He had many old buildings torn down, new canals and fortresses were built, and the colonial administration was moved to new Batavia.

North of the ministry is *MAHKAMAH AGUNG,* a neo-classical building where the supreme court has met since 1848. In the west, the *CATHOLIC CATHEDRAL,* built in 1900 in neo-gothic style, shows some Indonesian influence. The 77 m tall towers were constructed of teak; the stone towers of the previous 1833 cathedral collapsed under their own weight in 1880.

The new *ISTIQLAL MOSQUE,* a monumental building of the Islamic state, is the largest in South East Asia. There is a separate entrance for women and visitors during prayers. Men may also visit the main hall. From the upper galleries, you can observe the faithful at prayer. The tremendous, modern, domed building is between Medan Merdeka and Lapangan Banteng.

Walk west down Jl.Merdeka Utara to the well-guarded *PRESIDENTIAL PALACE* (Istana Merdeka) where President Suharto resides. It was constructed in 1879 as the official residence of the Dutch governor, who preferred, however, the cooler climate of Buitenzorg (Bogor).

HOTELS

The traveller scene gets together at the cheap lodgings on Jl.Jaksa. On this street are many but often full losmen. The best time to find a room is in the morning - in the late evening forget it. Best known is *WISMA DELIMA* at no. 5, with a dorm* or single room **, double**. People are constantly coming and going - reservations don't always work out. At no. 17 *LOSMEN JAKSA***, breakfast included, new but small rooms in a garden. A nice, family place is *BLOEMSTEEN HOSTEL*** on the side street Jl.Kebon Sirih Timur Dalam, Gang 1, no. 173. Across at no. 175, *KRESNA HOUSE* ** is less pleasant. On Jl.Jaksa is *HOSTEL NOORDWIJK*** at no. 27, and *DJODY HOSTEL*** (dorm*), and at no. 35 *DJODY HOTEL**-****, tel 346600. Both are newly renovated, pleasant, and clean with showers, western toilets, fan or AC. Several more expensive rooms are furnished with antique Chinese beds, in addition to the 4-bed family room. Airport service. In a side street (Jl.Kebon Sirih Barat Dalam 35, tel 320095) is the *BORNEO HOSTEL***, (dormitory*). Prices are too high for what is offered! Also here *WIM'S HOMESTAY***; no. 1, friendly people, and *WHITE HOUSE* **. *KARYA HOTEL***-*****, Jl.Jaksa 32-

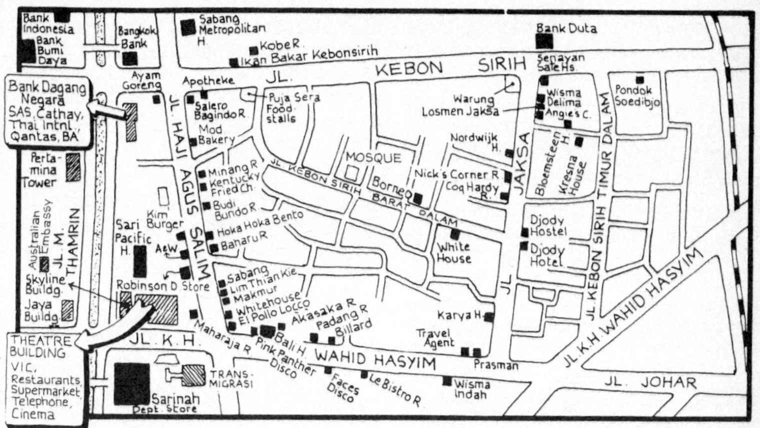

34, tel 320484 has rooms with fan or AC, higher prices with bath and TV. Even with a student discount the *BALI INTERNATIONAL* **** (tel 353748) isn't worth the money. Point out the deficiencies and the price will go down - the people are happy when anyone is willing to stay in their ghostly ruin and dream about what would happen if... Check it out at Jl.K. H.Wahid Hasjim 116. On the other side of the same street across Jl. Thamrin at no. 168 is *WISMA ISE**** (tel 333463) on the second and third floor with a big terrace. Friendly atmosphere, breakfast for 600 Rp. At Jl. Kebon Sirih 23, behind the travel office, is *PONDOK SOEDIBJO*** with a cool and quiet courtyard, though rooms are unfortunately always full.

Most sightseeing is within walking distance of *HOTEL SRI VIJAYA***** (Jl.Veteran 1, tel 370409) which offers big clean rooms with a fan or ac for those who can pay over 15,000 Rp. North of Merdeka Square is *SURYA ***(*)* at Jl.Batuceper 44-46 (tel 378108). Near the immigration office and university is *MATRUH***** at Jl. Raden Saleh 12 (tel 341319). *MUTIARA**** has a quiet location at Jl.Kramat Pulo 17-21 (tel 341992). Both *MENTENG HOTELS***** have a swimming pool and are located near Taman Ismail Marzuki cultural centre, doubles cost US$30.-; find no. I in Jl. Gondangdia Lama 28, tel 325208 and no. II in Jl.Cikini Raya 105, tel 326311.

FOOD

For all of you staying on Jl.Jaksa and not wanting to spend much money, it is worth trying one of the neighbourhood warung. Nothing special - nasi goreng is served with kecup, and for lukewarm beer there's ice - but it's cheap. Good Nasi Campur in *NICK'S CORNER RESTAURANT;* you can breakfast here or in *ANGIE'S CAFE.* Lots of foodstalls in the new *PUJA SERA* on Jl.Kebon Sirih, but they have this clean, almost Singapore-sterile, foodstall atmosphere. Stay away from the satay-sellers - the meat lies in the sun all day long, and on the slowburning charcoal fire everything collected during the day doesn't necessarily die off. Several people have had some painful stomach problems as a result.

If you want to be careful and can afford to spend more, don't miss the wonderful satay in *SENAYAN SATE HOUSE,* Jl.Kebon Sirih at Jl.Jaksa.

A large selection of food specialities is around Jl.Agus Salim. Chinese *(MAKMUR, LIM THIAM KIE),* Padang *(SALERO BAGINDO, MINANG, NATRABU, BUDI BUNDO),* and those not especially cheap fast-food restaurants *(KENTUCKY, KIM BURGER, A&W, HOKA HOKA BENTO, WHITE HOUSE, PIZZA HUT)* - all 'halal' in keeping with Muslim dictates. There is also Indonesian food in *BAHARU,* Indian in *MAHARAJA,* chicken specialities in *EL POLLO LOCCO* or cheaper in *AYAM GORENG JAKARTA,* Mexican in *GREEN PUB,* Jakarta Theatre Bldg., French in *LE BISTRO,* and cheaper in *COQ HARDI.* An Indonesian speciality is 'ikan bakar', grilled fish, served in *IKAN BAKAR KEBON SIRIH.* There are also two Japanese restaurants, *KOBE* in Dewan Press Bldg., and *AKASAKA* behind Bali Hotel. Cakes and pies in all colours and sizes, with snacks and ice cream in *MODERN BAKERY, SABANG RESTAURANT & BAKERY,* and in *SARINAH DEPARTMENT STORE.*

FOODSTALLS are set up evenings in many parts of the town. Try Jl.Pecenongan (side street off Jl.Juanda not far from the mosque), Glodok in Jl. Mangga Besar (off Jl.Hayam Wuruk - lots of Chinese, Indian, and Nasi Padang), or Blok M in Kebayoran Baru, the new town in the southwest. After dark, foodstalls open on the Sarinah Department Store parking lot on Jl. Thamrin. On the ground floor of Sarinah Jaya department store at Blok M in Kebayoran Baru, you can try countless foodstall specialities from all over Indonesia and Europe - you pay with coupons. Here in the centre of the new town on Jl.Melawai are many Indonesian and Chinese restaurants.

ART & CURIO, Jl.Kebon Binatang III 8a, tel 322879, next to the rail lines, is a European restaurant in Dutch colonial style, a 1950s atmosphere with music and large servings. Noticeably more expensive, with old colonial atmosphere, *OASIS,* Jl.Raden Saleh 47, tel 326397. Worth recommending is the 'Rijstafel' - young waitresses are constantly on the move, bringing new bowls to your table. Batak music begins at 21:00 h. Try typical West Java food in *SARI KURING* at Jl.Batuceper 55, tel 341542. At no. 69 on the northern end of the same street try good seafood in *JUN NYAN,* meals begin at 4000 Rp. Besides other cheap restaurants in Glodok, the best Chinese place for those with money to spend is *CAHAYA KOTA,* Jl.Wahid Hasyim 9, tel 353015. Well-spiced north Indian food is served in *OMAR KHAYAM,* Jl.Antara 5 (opposite the GPO). *RAGUSA GELATERIA* has been making Italian ice cream for generations; large servings for 300 Rp in Duta Merlin Shopping Arcade, in Hayam Wuruk Plaza and at Jl.Veteran 1/10.

SHOPPING

In Jakarta you'll find a rich selection of art and craft work from all over Indonesia: Batak calendars from Sumatra, batik and wayang puppets or masks from Java, ikat blankets from Sumba and Flores, wood carvings from Irian Barat, woven bags and baskets from Kalimantan and much more. You could take a souvenir tour through the whole archipelago, though if you want to travel rather than just spend money, you'd be better off buying on location where everything is much cheaper.

Don't let yourself be seduced into buying more than you can carry. If your visa is still valid, trust your take-home memories to the post office in Singapore or Malaysia where you can be certain that they will get home some day.

There is a large ***ARTS & CRAFTS DEPARTMENT*** and a Batik department in Sarinah Department Store, Blok M and also on Jl.Thamrin, open daily 9:00-18:00 h. This is the place for people who don't like to bargain; otherwise everything is cheaper at the street merchants and small shops.

In Ancol amusement park, at the large ***HANDICRAFTS MARKET***, Pasar Seni Ancol, carvings, paintings, baskets, and hand-woven cloth are both sold and produced. There is an art exhibit in the adjoining two-storey building.

INDONESIAN BAZAAR, a large arts & crafts exhibition, opens daily for sales, 10:00-18:00 h. It is on Jl.Gatot Subroto, near the major intersection with Jl.Sudirman, north of the Hilton Hotel.

Dutch or Chinese ***ANTIQUES*** can be found in shops along Jl.Majapahit and Jl.Kebon Sirih Dalam Timor.

On the northern end of ***JL.SURABAYA*** you can buy souvenirs and antiques. Many shops have much the same things to offer. If you are good at bargaining, you can get a good price. Take your time! By the way, buying an inexpensive, giant Kalimantan carving doesn't guarantee that you will get it home in one piece. Rare woods are heavy and require special care or they will dry out, split or rot. Be sure that it is packed properly before sending anything by seamail.

ATTENTION: Cultural objects are only plundered, endangered species are only hunted, and old heirlooms are only sold when a buyer can be found. By your actions you determine whether Indonesia is plundered within a short time of its natural and cultural treasures!

MARKETS aren't only interesting if you are planning to buy something. Besides the fish market Kali Baru, check out the Bird Market south of Jl. Pramuka at the beginning of the city highway.

From food to luxury items, you can buy anything in the ***SHOPPING CENTRES*** Pasar Baru, Glodok, Hayam Wuruk and Gajah Mada Plaza on Jl.Jen.Sudirman and Blok M in Kebayoran Baru.

A ***SUPERMARKET*** with a large selection of western groceries is GOLDEN TRULY. The centrally located branch in the Jakarta Theatre Building has, to the amusement of the local customers, speaking cash registers.

There are only a few ***BOOKSHOPS*** that sell English books. Gunung Agung Bookstore at Jl.Kwitang 6 is a state run shop - also sells maps (mostly Pembina). The best bookstore is Gramedia at Jl.Gajah Mada 109 and Jl.Pintu Air 72. There is also a good book department in Sarinah Department Store, Jl.Thamrin. You might find English books too at the souvenir stand in the National Museum. Jakarta doesn't have the best selection of English books. If you are passing through Singapore, stock up there.

When buying ***FILM***, make sure that it was stored properly - that means only buying in stores with ac. Prices are higher than in Singapore but less than in Malaysia. Often the duty free shops are closed or have run out of films. Though there's a Kodak lab in Jakarta, you are better off getting your rolls developed in Singapore.

GENERAL INFORMATION

INFORMATION - The Visitor's Information Centre (VIC) in the Theatre Building, Jl.Thamrin 9, is open Mon-Thurs 8:00 to 15:00 h, Fri till 11:00 h, Sat till 13:00 h (tel 354094). The office at Halim Airport is also open on Sun 8:00 to 20:00 h. Dinas Pariwisata Jakarta in Jl.Gatot Subroto, tel 586053, 586045.

IMMIGRATION - extensions of visitor's, tourist, education, and working visas at Jl.Teuku Umar 1, tel 349811 and 349812. Open Mon-Thurs till 15:00 h, Fri till 11:00 h, Sat till 13:00 h. Since the introduction of visa-free entry, many fewer foreigners are processed here; still there are a number of forms (100 Rp) to fill out, and the wait is at least two days.

POST - GPO on Jl.Pos Utara 2, tel 350004. Open Mon-Thurs 8:00-13:00 h, Fri until 11:00 h, Sat until 13:00 h.

TELEPHONING - not only do the phone numbers in Jakarta change frequently, but it can take hours to get a connection. TELECOMMUNICATION OFFICES can be found at Jl. Merdeka Selatan 12 (open 24 hours a day), in the Jayakarta Tower Hotel at Jl.Hayam Wuruk 126, and in the Skyline Bldg., Jl.Thamrin. From here you can place calls anywhere in the world - works quite well via Singapore. Three minutes, self-dialled to Europe cost 13,710 Rp (4570 per minute). Operator-assisted, and person to person calls are more expensive (3 minutes 22,850 Rp). Collect calls are only possible to Australia, Canada, the Netherlands, New Zealand, United Kingdom, and the United States. Public telephones cost 25 Rp (rarely work) or 100 Rp (chances are better).

BANKS - Bad exchange rates at the airport. Try to change at Bank Dagang Negara, Jl.Thamrin 5, corner of Jl.Kebon Sirih, tel 321707.

AMERICAN EXPRESS - Arthaloka Bldg., Jl.Jen.Sudirman (towards Kebayoran Baru), tel 587401. Amexco mail service is at P.T.Golden Pacto Jaya, Jl.Sukarjo Wiryopranoto 9, tel 652706. It is hard to find, ask for Lippo House or Bank Perniagaan Indonesia. Pacto is the representative for all of Indonesia, and one of the largest travel agencies with branch offices in Sanur (Bali), Surabaya, Bandung, Ujung Pandang, Medan, Padang, and Yogyakarta.

PPA - For a visit to Kepulauan Seribu National Park (1000 islands, see below), info and permits at Jl.Salemba Raya 16 (near the university).

MEDICAL ATTENTION - try one of the following hospitals: St.Carolus Hospital, Jl.Salemba Raya, tel 882401; or Pertamina Hospital, Jl. Kyai Maja 43 in Kebayoran Baru, tel 707211.

NEWSPAPERS - foreign newspapers and magazines can be bought at the international hotels such as BOROBUDUR. Stories about Indonesia, along with naked women, have usually been blacked over or ripped out. The Indonesian English language papers are INDONESIA TIMES, JA-

KARTA POST and INDONESIA OBSERVER.

CITY MAPS - in VIC you'll find quite a useful city map. The best is the Falk Map of Jakarta. Something for people who plan to spend a lot of time in the city - costs 9000 Rp.

NIGHTLIFE - gets going on Jl.Gajah Mada, Jl.Hayam Wuruk, Jl.Thamrin, and in Blok M in Kebayoran Baru. Movie theatres, discos, pubs and other common male oriented entertainment. Nightclubs and discos can be found in almost all the major hotels, but are expensive.

CRIME - in town a number of tourists have been robbed, some with knives. It is particularly dangerous at night around Gambir Station and on Jl. Agus Salim. But there have also been thefts in crowded buses and in Bajaj, while they are stopped at street lights. Pickpockets are infamous on Bus 70.

CULTURE

The cultural centre ***TAMAN ISMAIL MARZUKI*** is at Jl.Cikini Raya 73 (tel 337357). Offers a wide spectrum of activities - every day there's something on: music, theatre, readings by local or foreign authors, films, and exhibitions. The monthly program can be had at the VIC.

Other cultural events are held in ***TAMAN MINI INDONESIA INDAH*** and ***PASAR SENI ANCOL.*** Events are announced in the press and in monthly program magazines.

Regular performances of ***GAMELAN MUSIC***: Sundays 9:30-10:30 h in the National Museum and Sunday noon in Taman Mini.

WAYANG KULIT performances: Sundays 10:00-12:00 h in the Wayang Museum, each 2nd and 4th Saturday of the month in the National Museum, and once a month in Ancol. There is a Wayang Workshop, Jl. Agus Salim 80, tel 368231, Thursdays 20:00-22:00 h. Wayang Golek is performed in Dinas Kesenian, Jl.Salemba Raya 18, Sundays 20:00-22:00 h.

FOLK DANCE from various Indonesian provinces is performed on Sunday afternoons in Taman Mini Indonesia and Tues-Sun 19:00-20:00 h in Balinese Theatre, Indonesian Bazaar (see shopping); Friday afternoons in Hotel Borobudur and Saturday evenings or Sunday mornings in Ancol Art Market.

TRADITIONAL THEATRE - 'Sirmulat' with humorous insertions and merry songs in a relaxed atmosphere can be seen at 20:00-23:00 h in Ria Loka, Taman Ria Remaja Senayan. 'Ketoprak', traditional Javanese theatre, takes its themes from epics and fairytales, Mondays and Thursdays at 20:15 h in Bharata Theatre, Jl.Kalilio. On other weekdays at 20:15 h 'Wayang Orang' performances, based upon the Ramayana and Mahabharata epics, are presented here.

GETTING AROUND

TAXIS

The most comfortable way to get around is also easy to find. Some drivers insist upon bargaining a fixed (excessive) price. All have taximeters, which can be to your disadvantage when it ticks during a detour. If you don't know the proper price, insist that the taximeter be switched on. If necessary, sit next to the driver and follow the route on a map. The initial charge is 600 Rp (ac) or 500 Rp (non-ac) plus 300 Rp (ac) or 250 Rp (non-ac) for each additional kilometre. The Bluebird taxis (tel 325607) are the most reliable and can be ordered by phone in advance. You can also rent a taxi by the hour. Calculate 4000 Rp for a ride from Cililitan Terminal to Jl.Jaksa. For 6000 Rp you can cross the entire city. For 12,000 Rp you can get to the airport using the meter.

BECAKS

The familiar, but now disappearing, bicycle rickshaws cost about 300 Rp for a short ride. Bargain the price in advance! Since 1986 they have been banned completely from the city. Many were sunk in Jakarta Bay, only to be pulled back out by fishermen and resold to the original owners.

BAJAJ

Your cheapest transport are the small red motor scooters with room for two people behind the driver. For 500 Rp to 1000 Rp you can cover the entire town. Always bargain the price in advance!

BUSES

For 200 Rp, you can travel by bus from one end of Jakarta to the other. Some major routes are served by new, comfortable buses - on others, rat traps. 'Patas' line buses cost 300 Rp, but are considered safer and faster than other buses, due to fewer stops. Beware of thieves in packed buses, particularly bus 70 between Kota Station and Blok M!

LEAVING JAKARTA

INTERNATIONAL FLIGHTS

All international and domestic flights depart from Soekarno-Hatta Airport in CENGKARENG, 23 km west of Jakarta. It is accessible from the city via a highway. Damri bus company provides Mercedes buses (white with blue strips) to the airport for 2000 Rp. Departs from Blok M, Gambir Station, Kemayoran Airport, Rawamangun Bus Terminal, Pasar Minggu Bus Terminal, and Halim Terminal every 30 minutes. They stop at most of the major hotels on Jl.Sudirman, Jl.Merdeka Barat, Jl.Veteran, and Jl.Gajah Mada. Damri claims to operate from early morning to late evening, 3:00-22:30 h, but don't rely upon it. Buses don't always run after 21:30 h. The drive takes 45 minutes to 2 hrs. during rush hour. Taxis from downtown charge 12,000-15,000 Rp. Wisma Delima, Jl.Jaksa provides a minibus service, carrying 1-8 passengers with advance reservations to Cengkareng for 12,000 Rp. There are also many private taxis with whom you must bargain a price. The Bluebird taxis utilize the fastest route by highway upon which they receive a discount rate. By local bus, calculate at least 2 1/2 hours, get bus 913 to Kalideres, then change to bus 214 to the airport.

There are three terminals at Soekarno-Hatta:

A) international flights
B) Garuda domestic flights
C) other domestic flights

Airport Tax: domestic flights 2000 Rp, international flights 9000 Rp.

Sample prices to neighbouring countries, in parenthesis ISIC prices (all in US$):BANGKOK 381.-(180.-), BOMBAY 649.-, COLOMBO 601.-, DARWIN 480.-(160.-), HONG KONG 538.-, KUALA LUMPUR 190.-(80.-), KUCHING (Merpati via Pontianak) 130,000 Rp, MELBOURNE 755.-(277.-), OSAKA 753.-, PENANG 215.-PERTH 609.-(160.-), SEOUL 789.-, SINGAPORE 156.-(86.-, UTA twice weekly 98.- or 136.- return, often booked up), TAIPEI 627.-, TOKYO 753 US$.

ISIC tickets can be bought at Indo Shangrila Travel, Jl.Gajah Mada 219

(Chinatown), tel 6392831 / 6392376. The regular ticket prices mentioned above can often be had cheaper. Flights to Europe with ISIC cost about US$400. Here is a list of the important international airlines which serve Jakarta:

AIR INDIA, Hotel Sari Pacific, Jl. Thamrin, tel 325470.

BRITISH AIRWAYS, Wisma Metropolitan, Jl.Sudirman, tel 5782460.

CATHAY PACIFIC, Hotel Borobudur International, tel 3806664.

CZECHOSLOVAK AIRLINES, Wisata International Hotel, Jl.Thamrin, tel 320408.

CHINA AIRLINES, Duta Merlin, Jl. Gajah Mada 25, tel 354448.

JAPAN AIRLINES, Wisma Nusantara, Jl.Thamrin, tel 322207.

KLM, Hotel Indonesia, Jl.Thamrin, tel 320708.

LUFTHANSA, Panin Centre Bldg., Jl.Jend.Sudirman, tel 710247.

MAS, Hotel Indonesia, Jl.Thamrin, tel 320909.

PHILIPPINES AIRLINES, Hotel Borobudur, tel 370108.

QUANTAS, BDN Building, Jl.Thamrin 5, tel 327707.

SINGAPORE AIRLINES, Sahid Jaya Hotel, Jl.Sudirman 86, tel 584021 / 854041.

SWISSAIR, Hotel Borobudur, Jl.Lapangan Banteng Selatan, tel 373608.

THAI AIRWAYS INTERNATIONAL, BDN Bldg., Jl.Thamrin 5, tel 320607.

UTA, Jaya Bldg., Jl.Thamrin 12, tel 323609.

DOMESTIC FLIGHTS

Domestic flights also depart from Soekarno-Hatta Airport. Unlike other South-East Asian countries, domestic flights are essential in Indonesia if you want to go anywhere outside of Sumatra, Java, or Bali. If you plan several longer flights offered by Garuda within Indonesia, check whether the ***Indonesia Air Pass*** will save you money. See *Getting Around.*

GARUDA, Jl.Juanda 15, tel 370709; Jl.Angkasa, tel 417808; Wisma Nusantara, Jl.Thamrin, tel 333408.

MERPATI, Jl.Angkasa 2, tel 417404.

MANDALA, Jl.Veteran 1, tel 368107.

BOURAQ, Jl.Angkasa 1, tel 655150.

SEMPATI, P.T.Espede, Jl.Sawah Besar 8.

Garuda is the most expensive; the others are all about 15% cheaper. SAMPLE PRICES:AMBON 189,500 Rp (MZ), BANDA ACEH 209,900 Rp (GA), BALIKPAPAN 125,300 Rp (MZ), BANDUNG 30,500 Rp (GA), BENGKULU 76,400 Rp (GA), BANJARMASIN 97,800 Rp (MZ via Surabaya - direct GA 115,000 Rp), BATAM 64,900 Rp (MZ via Palembang, direct GA 96,500 Rp), BIAK 270,400 Rp (MZ via Surabaya, UP, Ambon - direct GA 318,100 Rp), CILACAP 53,000 Rp (MZ), CIREBON 33,100 Rp (MZ), DENPASAR 88,600 Rp (MZ via Surabaya, direct GA 104,200 Rp), JAMBI 72,700 Rp (MZ), JAYAPURA 325,300 Rp (GA), KUPANG 177,900 Rp (MZ via Surabaya, Denpasar, Maumere - direct GA 193,100 Rp), MEDAN 136,100 Rp (MZ), MALANG 85,800 Rp (MZ), MANADO 233,300 Rp (GA), MAUMERE 185,700 Rp (MZ), PALEMBANG 53,300 Rp (MZ), PANGKALPINANG 54,700 Rp (MZ), PADANG 97,800 Rp (MZ), PONTIANAK 79,600 Rp (MZ), SEMARANG 45,000 Rp (MZ), SURABAYA 73,000 Rp (MZ, GA 88,500 Rp), TANJUNG PANDAN 48,500 Rp (MZ), TANJUNG PINANG 104,200 Rp (MZ), UJUNG PANDANG 133,200 Rp (MZ via Surabaya, direct by GA 156,700 Rp), WAINGAPU 173,700 Rp (MZ), YOGYAKARTA 60,100 Rp (GA).

BY RAIL

From Jakarta you have train connections to Central and East Java as well as South Sumatra. The departure times change as with everything else, so check beforehand at the Kota or Gambir stations.

Student rates, mostly available on the cheap day trains, are often only allowed after permission is granted by the station manager. Allow for the time! You can also get tickets at Jl. Menteng Raya 24 (near Jl.Jaksa).

JAKARTA - PALEMBANG (via MERAK): trains from Tanah Abang 3 times daily to Merak 1800 Rp. Ferry 1300/2600/3700 Rp, daily. Two trains to Palembang for 3900 / 6300 Rp.

JAKARTA - BANDUNG: trains from Kota 5 times daily, from Gambir 6 times daily, from Manggarai once daily for 6000 / 4500 / 1800 Rp (1st, 2nd, 3rd cl.).

JAKARTA - CIREBON: trains from Kota 6 times daily (Bima), from Priok twice daily, from Gambir 9 times daily, from Senen 5 times daily, between 2200 Rp and 7000 Rp depending on train and class; Bima: 20,200 Rp (sleeper) or 13,200 Rp (1st. cl.).

JAKARTA - SEMARANG: trains from Priok once daily, from Kota once daily, and from Senen twice daily depending on train and class; 3700 Rp to 7800 Rp; Mutiara Utara 1st cl. 17,500 Rp.

JAKARTA - SURABAYA: trains from Gambir once daily, Kota twice daily and from Senen once daily for 15,300 / 28,200 Rp Bima, 6800 Rp 3rd cl., GBM Selatan; Mutiara Utara 1st cl. 22,000 Rp.

JAKARTA - YOGYAKARTA: trains from Priok once daily, from Gambir 7 times daily and from Kota once daily (Bima) between 3900 Rp and 9200 Rp; Bima 20,200 Rp (sleeper) or 13,200 Rp (1st cl.).

BY BUS

All local buses going south and east leave from CILILITAN BUS STATION south of the city. They are usually packed. At times of much travel, such as holidays, the buses are literally stormed. The prices vary according to route, company and bus age! Take bus 401 / 409 from Gambir. Sample prices: BANDUNG 2400 / 3600 Rp, BOGOR 650 Rp, 1 h, SUKABUMI 1200 / 1900 Rp, CIBADAG 1200 Rp, SEMARANG 5100 / 7300 Rp, SURABAYA 12,500 / 16,500 Rp, YOGYAKARTA 6400 / 9100 Rp.

For longer trips take an ac bus. They leave daily from the offices of the express bus companies to all the larger cities. Most of the offices can be found on Jl.Kebon Sirih.

Buses east such as to KRAWANG (700 Rp) or CIREBON (2700 / 3800 Rp) leave from the PULO GADUNG BUS STATION, east of town. Here you also find ac buses going in this direction.

Buses to Sumatra (MERAK 1300 Rp, BUKITTINGGI 21,700 / 28,600 Rp, PALEMBANG 9700 / 13,200 Rp, BANDA ACEH 39,300 / 52,200 Rp) leave from KALIDERES BUS STATION to the west.Take bus 913.

BY SHIP

PELNI, the state shipping company, has its main offices on Jl.Angkasa 18, tel. 416262, 415428, 358398; Jl.Pintu Air 1, tel 358398 and in Tanjung Priok, Jl.Palmas 1, tel. 491034, 491035.

Prices and departures / arrivals see under *Getting Around.*

KALI BESAR, JAKARTA

DAYTRIPS AROUND JAKARTA

TAMAN MINI

About 20 km out of Jakarta on the road to Bogor. Get a bus to Cililitan bus station, e.g. P.P.D Bus 401 from Gambir and then Metro Minibus T55. Open daily 09:00-17:00 h, admission 500 Rp. The museums are only open until 15:00 h; the larger cost 200 Rp admission. All of Indonesia is reproduced on a 160 ha format, providing visitors with a look at the country's diversity. From a cable car you can look down on Kalimantan, Sulawesi, and the other islands, or just ride by in a boat. Around the lake, reproductions of traditional regional houses are used to exhibit industrial products, arts and crafts, and agricultural goods. The following buildings are worth looking inside: *Java* and *Sumatra provinces, Bali, Irian Jaya, Nusa Tenggara Timur, Kalimantan Timur and Timor Timur,* and of course the provinces you plan to travel in. In some, regional museums have been established, displaying costumes, tools, musical instruments, and photos of the province. Frequently there is somebody from the region available to answer questions. In some province houses, informational material is available, or you can buy regional souvenirs. Additionally, every world religion has its own building. Religious events are held in the mosque, temples, and churches.

MUSEUM INDONESIA, built in Bali style, offers extensive exhibits of handicrafts, garments, and daily utensils from all over Indonesia. Inside the tremendous Komodo dragon is MUSEUM KOMODO - a zoological exhibition. Stuffed animals from the archipelago are exhibited over two floors. Philatelists can view a large stamp collection in MUSEUM PRANGKO. Quite a few steam locomotives are exhibited in the southeastern part of the grounds.

There is an orchid garden, a large children's playground, and a bird park. The snail-shaped TEATER KEONG EMAS IMAX shows several films about Indonesia daily 11:00-17:00 h (later on weekends), admission 2000 Rp per film. You've an impressive view of volcanoes and people on an oversized screen (the largest screen in the world according to the Guinness Book of Records). Many Indonesian visitors flock here on Sundays. You can get together with the Moluccans or Timorese in 'their' houses, hear bands from north Sumatra play Batak music, and see folk dancers from Bali or Borneo. Picnic on the tremendous lawns. There is plenty to eat and drink in the warung and restaurants. If you come on Sunday, you'll experience a full day of events in Taman Mini.

RAGUNAN ZOO

16 km from town, get a bus to Blok M, then change to the green Bus 108 or Metro Mini S77 to the zoo. Bus 87 departs directly from Jl.Cikini Raya, Jl.Rasuna Said. Open 9:00-18:00 h, on weekends it's packed, admission 500 Rp. The 185 ha zoo is good for getting out of hectic Jakarta! There are 3600 species of animal including the almost extinct Java tiger, along with Komodo dragons, anoa, and banteng.

PULAU PULAU SERIBU

A thousand islands - actually only 110 - in Jakarta Bay about 60 km from the city. White beaches, coral islands, perfect for diving. The cheapest way to get out to the islands is by regular boat from Tanjung Priok. The boat runs via PULAU BIDADARI (very touristic) - nearby are Pulau Kelor, Pulau Kahyangan, Pulau Onrust, Pulau Cipir all with tourist facilities - and PULAU UNTUNG JAVA (Sunday market) to PULAU PANGGANG. Information and bookings at P.T.PULAU SERIBU PARADISE, Jakarta Theatre Bldg., Jl.Thamrin. The most expensive islands are PULAU PUTRI (25 bungalows on the beach), PULAU PETUNDANG, PULAU MELINTANG, PULAU PELANGI and PULAU MATAHARI.

Much cheaper (10 - 20 US$ p.P. and day) are the bungalows on PULAU PAPA THEO and PULAU SEPAK. Bring your own food. Diving equipment can be rented for 20,000 Rp a day. Daily the M.V.Pelangi Express leaves Ancol Marina Pier around 8:00 h to Pelangi, Putri and Papa Theo. Information and bookings at P.T.VAYATOUR, Jl.Batutulis 38, tel 365008.

WEST JAVA

The province of West Java, covering the region between Merak and Cirebon, is a diverse land of paddies, beaches and volcanoes. The Sundanese population here has its own language and culture. In addition you can find Badui, who were once the original inhabitants of Java but are now only found in the remote mountains south of Rangkasbitung.

If you want to experience typical Sundanese folk art, then check out a wayang golek performance. In this theatre wooden stick puppets are used to play parts of the ancient epic Ramayana accompanied by the sound of a traditional bamboo instrument, the 'angklung'.

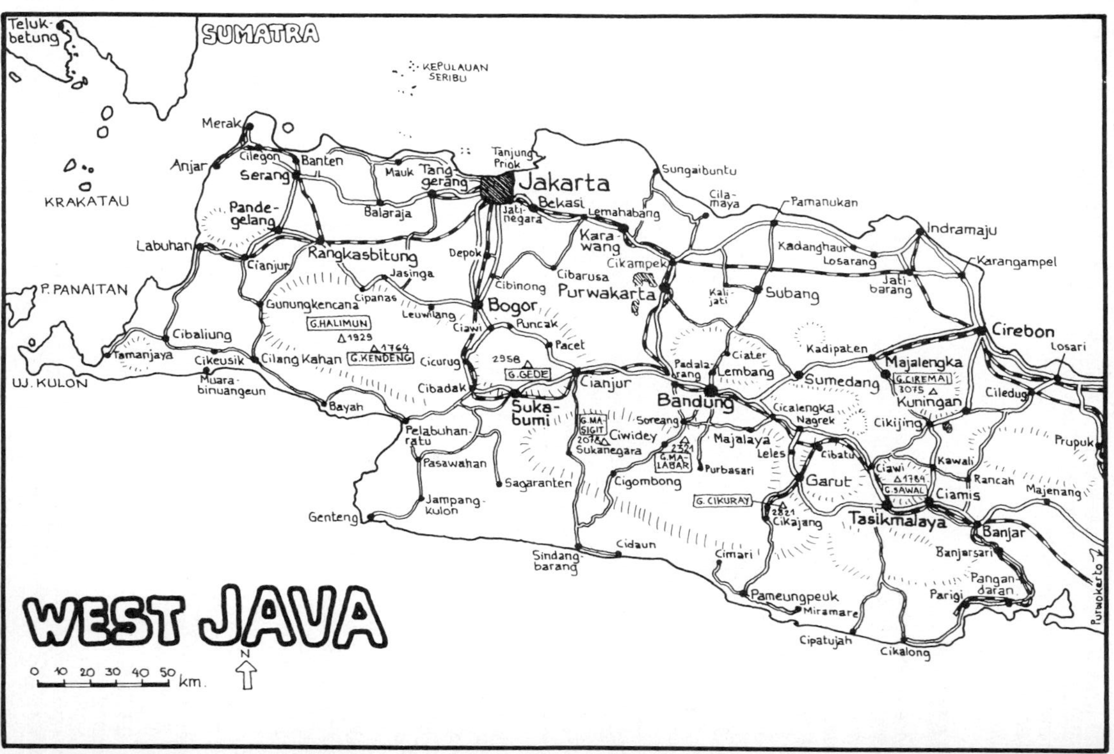
Teluk-betung
SUMATRA
KEPULAUAN SERIBU
KRAKATAU
Merak
Anjar
Cilegon
Banten
Serang
Pandegelang
Labuhan
Cianjur
Rangkasbitung
Mauk
Tangerang
Balaraja
Tanjung Priok
Jakarta
Jatinegara
Bekasi
Lemahabang
Sungaibuntu
Cilamaya
Pamanukan
Indramaju
Karangampel
Kadanghaur
Losarang
Jatibarang
Karawang
Cikampek
Depok
Cibinong
Cibarusa
Purwakarta
Kalijati
Subang
Jasinga
Cipanas
Gunungkencana
Leuwilang
Bogor
P. PANAITAN
G.HALIMUN
1929
1764
G.KENDENG
Ciawi
Puncak
Pacet
Cibaliung
Tamanjaya
Cikeusik
Cilang Kahan
Cicurug
2958
G.GEDE
UJ. KULON
Muara-binuangeun
Cibadak
Bayah
Pelabuhanratu
Pasawahan
Sagaranten
Jampang-kulon
Genteng
Sukabumi
Cianjur
G.MASIGIT
2078
Ciwidey
Sukanegara
Soreang
Bandung
Padalarang
Ciater
Lembang
Kadipaten
Sumedang
Cirebon
Losari
Majalengka
G.CIREMAI
3075
Kuningan
Ciledug
Cicalengka
Nagrek
Cikijing
Prupuk
Majalaya
2321
G.MALABAR
Purbasari
Leles
Cibatu
Garut
Ciawi
1764
G.SAWAL
Kawali
Rancah
Ciamis
Majenang
Cigombong
G. CIKURAY
2821
Cikajang
Tasikmalaya
Banjar
Banjarsari
Purwokerto
Pangandaran
Parigi
Sindangbarang
Cidaun
Cimari
Pameungpeuk
Miramare
Cipatujah
Cikalong
WEST JAVA
0 10 20 30 40 50 km.
N

The capital of West Java and its cultural centre is Bandung - a refreshing mountain town and comfortable place to stay while exploring the enchanting surrounding countryside. But west of Jakarta there are also interesting, hardly ever visited places. The beaten track leads, however, from Jakarta straight to Yogya.

BANTEN

Once a powerful and affluent kingdom, ruled by strict orthodox sultans, in the 15th and 16th centuries it was one of the most important trade centres between the spice islands and India. In 1684, Holland completed its final conquest of the Sultanate of Banten. Not much remains today of its former glory except ruins.

Just out of Banten on the tiny road to *SERANG* is the great mosque, *MESJID AGUNG.* Commissioned by Sultan Maulana Yusuf, it was built under the direction of a Dutch Muslim in front of the Sultan's palace. Graves of the royal family can be found in a neighbouring building.

On Muslim graves, which are always pointed towards Mecca, you can tell the sex of the deceased by the gravestone - a round phallic symbol for the males and a flat, swirled gravestone for women.

Interesting remains of past centuries can be viewed in the small *HISTORICAL MUSEUM.* Of the nearby *PALACE,* which covered 4.5 ha of land and which was enclosed by thick walls, only a few ruins remain. After a centuries long struggle with the Dutch, it was destroyed in 1809.

North of the mosque, standing almost in the ocean, was *FORT SPEELWIJK.* Only ruins remain of this Dutch fort maintained from 1685 until the beginning of the 19th century. Nearby is the old *CHINESE TEMPLE,* the gift of a Muslim sultan to his large Chinese community. It is said that it was given in thanks for the supply of medicine during a malaria epidemic. However, a large source of the kingdom's wealth was based on trade undertaken by the Chinese. Behind the eastern gate of the fort, surrounded by sand and mud, is an old *EUROPEAN CEMETERY.* On an old gravestone you can read: "Here lyeth the body of Capt. Roger Benitt, commander of the Bombay merchant, deceased on 30 of January 1677."

HOTELS

Spend the night in Serang at *WISMA KASIHSAYANG**, Jl.Tirtayasa, in *SERANG HOTEL****, Jl.Jen.A.Yani 5, tel 81641 or in *HOTEL ABADI**** , 200 m south of the bus station.

HOW TO GET THERE

It's 95 km from Jakarta to SERANG, the largest town. There are regular buses from Jakarta for 1400 Rp, or take the train - leaves less often but is cheaper.

MERAK

On the way to Merak, you pass through CILEGON. The Krakatau Steelworks, one of the largest industrial projects in Indonesia, was built here in 1960 with Soviet aid. Now it belongs to Pertamina, the state owned oil company.

Despite the industry, there are a number of nice beaches in the area. PANTAI FLORIDA is 5 km north of town. The former resort area with cheap foodstalls and lodgings has slowly been taken over by industry.

HOTELS

Several hotels / losmen are within 500 m of the ferry: *HOTEL ANDA****, Jl.Florida 4, with private mandi. Next door is *HOTEL ROBINSON****; and further along *LOSMEN KURNIA***, *PENGINAPAN BAHARI*** and *PENGINAPAN VIOLETA***. One kilometre from the ferry toward Jakarta is *HOTEL SULAWESI II****. More expensive is *MERAK BEACH HOTEL* (some call it Ramayana), between the road and the beach, booked up on weekends by people from Jakarta. The offshore islands offer water sports.

HOW TO GET THERE

Buses to SERANG 360 Rp, 30 km; JAKARTA 1300 Rp, 125 km; CILEGON 200 Rp. Car ferries to BAKAUHENI, Sumatra - every 75 minutes, around the clock, takes 2 hrs.; 1st class 1750 Rp, 2nd class 1400 Rp, 3rd class 850 Rp.

Rail and car ferries to SRENGSEM / PANJANG, 1st class 3700 Rp, 2nd class 2600 Rp, 3rd class 1300 Rp, motorcycle 3500 Rp, jeep 25,000 Rp. Three trains daily to JAKARTA (just 3rd class) for 1100 Rp or 1800 Rp.

LABUAN

A coastal town and ferry port, departure point for visits to the volcanic island Krakatau, which you can see from the beach, and Ujung Kulon National Park.

It is much nicer along the Sunda Straits between Labuan and Merak, than in Merak itself. Wealthy visitors from Jakarta flock here on weekends. It is particularly nice on the stretch of beach south of *ANYAR* lighthouse, around Anyar Beach Hotel, and in *KARANGBOLONG,* 7 km further south. If you are looking for a white, sandy beach in a sheltered bay, surrounded by coconut palms, *CARITA* is 9 km south of Labuan, bemos (250 Rp, 15 minutes).

HOTELS

In Labuan *CITRA AYU HOTEL**** with breakfast. *CARITA KRAKATAU BEACH HOTEL***** (also called Beach Club) is an entire bungalow village founded by a German development aid volunteer. High society gathers here on weekends, when rooms cost US$45 (weekdays US$ 22.50). Information at Hotel Menteng in Jakarta, tel 325208. Hotels and clubs have a few expensive restaurants, otherwise there are just a couple of cheap warung nearby. The Beach Club has a small *HOSTEL***, across from the main entrance. Hotel guests have free admission to the club grounds (otherwise 400 Rp).

Umbrellas, beach chairs, swimming rings, etc., are rented for a substantial fee. Worth a look (no charge) is the collection of Indonesian maps and info brochures about Krakatau, Ujung Kulon, and the Badui. The sea is dotted with 'kelong', large fish traps with platforms supporting small huts in which the fishermen can live for weeks while catching fish at night.

HOW TO GET THERE

There is a lovely mountain route from SERANG (700 Rp, 64 km). From CILEGON / SIMPANG TIGA get a minibus along the coast for 1000 Rp. Direct from JAKARTA (155 km, 4 1/2 hrs. - longer on weekends, 1800 Rp with ac, 1500 Rp non-ac).

KRAKATAU

A volcanic island in the Sunda Straits which in 1883 was the scene of the world's biggest volcanic eruption. 18 km^3 of stone and ash was hurled into the atmosphere (the eruption of Mount St. Helens in May 1980 was only 1 km^3!). The sky over many parts of the earth darkened. Some of the smaller neighbouring islands were formed by the masses of discharged rock. The island has now taken on a friendly tropical green appearance, though inside the volcano it's still boiling. The water surrounding the island is heated and steaming clouds of sulphur can be seen rising.

Tours to Krakatau, lasting two days and nights, cost 250,000 Rp, if organized by Yayu Wahyuddin, Jl.Raya Caringin 55 in Labuan. In Labuan, or better at the Beach Club (see before), you can charter boats for a Krakatau day trip (50,000-150,000 per boat) or for a 2-3 day tour of Ujung Kulon National Park (80,000-200,000 Rp per boat). In the club there are often a number of people looking to form a group. During the rainy season (November-March) and the strong southeast wind (July-August), a cruise through the Sunda Straits is little fun - the cheaper and smaller the vessels, the less seaworthy they are.

UJONG KULON NATURE RESERVE

You can reach the 60,000 ha national park on the southwestern tip of Java from Labuan. The park was originally planned as a reserve to prevent the extinction of the Java rhinoceros. In addition several other endangered species have been saved. From a hide, you can patiently try for a glimpse of the rare white rhino. Or take a boat trip to Peucang island. There you'll find a few simple shelters; you have to bring your own food.

Just to get into the park you need to have permission in advance from the PPA (Dinas Perlindungan dan Pengawetan Alam), the Nature Conservation Service in Bogor, Jl.Juanda. With some luck they will also assign you a place to stay on Peucang, Pulau Handeuleum, or in Tamanjaya (Park Headquarters) for 3000 - 5000 Rp. Organize a boat from Labuan for the twelve hour ride to Peucang Island. A trip of several days should cost about 150,000 Rp Simpler, but very expensive, are the trips organized by Jakarta travel agencies. They provide for the permit, a guide, and a day of relaxation afterwards on the beach.

RANGKASBITUNG

South east of town 39 villages, populated by between 2000 and 4000 Badui, surround the volcano KENDENG . They're divided into two groups: the 'inner' and the 'outer' Badui. The former consist of about 400 people living in three villages which are cut off from the rest of the world by the 'outer'. Civilization hasn't been able to penetrate the 'inner' villages; everything from the outside world is taboo and is rejected. It is thought that the Badui, who are original Javanese, withdrew to the mountains during the Islamization in the 15th and 16th centuries. The little that is known of their religion indicates that it contains some Buddhist and animistic elements.

While you should respect the privacy of the 'inner' Badui, you can visit the 'outer' Badui, who are responsible for external contacts, trade etc. You need written permission from the district office (Kantor Bupati) in Rangkasbitung to visit the villages. It is easiest to visit the village of KADUKETING, 40 km south of town. Bemos leave Rangkasbitung daily around 9:00 h to CIBOLEGER (1500 Rp). From here it is 1 km on foot.

BOGOR

After steamy Jakarta, this town with its cool climate (even though it is only 290 m above sea level) is pleasurably refreshing. Even in the days of the Dutch, the colonial administrators liked to retire from the dank, malaria infested capital to the mountains. In 1744 Governor General van Imhoff had a residence built in Buitenzorg (Dutch: "Free of Care"). *ISTANA BOGOR,* residence of the Dutch governors, is now a favourite of President Suharto.

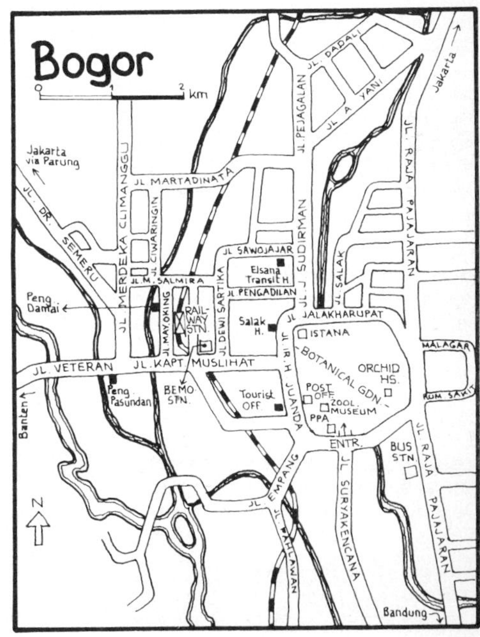

In the centre of town is the 111 ha *BOTANICAL GARDEN* with its impressive collection of jungle trees, delicate orchids, and palms from all over the world. Enjoyable even for non-botanists! You'll need at least one morning just for the garden. Do something different in the afternoon since it usually rains and the orchid house is closed.

Just inside the southern main entrance (admission 800 Rp) is the memorial built in 1814 by Sir Stamford Raffles for his dead wife. In the western part of the garden is the orchid house in which 3000 different orchids are cultivated. You'll find Indonesians in the park making themselves available as conversational partners and guides. Some of them really know their stuff but negotiate a price in advance or there'll be problems at the end of the walk around.

Have a look at the *ZOOLOGICAL MUSEUM* (100 Rp) just to the left of the entrance.

In addition there is the *HERBARIUM* in town and one of the best botanical *LIBRARIES,* both of which are part of the university and are in a building next to the tourist office.

HOTELS

Two cheap losmen west of the train tracks: *PENGINAPAN DAMAI**,* Jl. Mayor Oking 29 (rooms with or without bath). Or stay at *WISMA TELADAN***;* Jl.Sawojajar 3A. Friendly staff, nice garden! The centrally located, but noisy, *HOTEL SALAK***** has just been renovated. *ELSANA TRANSIT HOTEL****,* Jl.Sawojajar, tel 22552 - quiet with a courtyard, and rooms with private shower and toilet.

FOOD

Across from the main entrance to the Botanical Garden is the shopping centre and a market with cheap restaurants. North of Bogor is the famous restaurant *LEBAK WANGI* in the middle of a lake; they serve typical Sundanese cooking. Good sate in *BARU RESTORAN* across from the movie house at the north end of Jl. Suryakencana. Lots of warung on Jl. Dewi Sartika and Jl.Kapt.Muslihat.

GENERAL INFORMATION

INFORMATION - Jl.Juanda 39 - open Mon-Thurs 8:00-14:00, Fri 8:00-11:00, 14:00-18:00, Sat 8:00-13:00 h.

PPA - If you are planning to visit a national park, you need a permit from the nature preservation authority which has its central office in Bogor. Address: PPA (Direktorat Perlindungan dan Pengawetan Alam), Jl.Juanda 9, left of the entrance to the Botanical Garden.

HOW TO GET THERE

Buses from Jakarta (Cililitan) cost 650 Rp. The more expensive buses use the fast Jagorawi Highway. SAMPLE PRICES: YOGYA 6250 Rp (Express), BANDUNG 1500 Rp (3 hrs., non ac), CIPANAS / PUNCAK bus 500 Rp, Colt 700 Rp. The bus station is south of town. For this reason it is better to get off at the Botanical Garden when arriving in town. Otherwise a ride into town with a bemo costs 150 Rp. Due to the large park in the middle, the town is very spread out. The wide sidewalks with lots of trees and the cool climate make long walks a pleasure. From the train station in the centre, a train to Jakarta Kota costs 500 Rp (3rd cl.).

PELABUHAN RATU

This is a favourite weekend retreat for wealthy Jakartans who fly into this village, 90 km south of Bogor, with Pelita airlines. Unlike the beaches to the west, swimming here can be dangerous. 'One' lodges in the SAMUDRA BEACH HOTEL 6 km out of town - a six storey modern building, whose rooms cost US$30-90. There are cheaper places: LOSMEN SINDANG**, a bit noisy but rooms have a balcony overlooking the ocean, BAYU AMARTA*** with good seafood and WISMA PUTRA** in the centre.

At the beginning of April the people of Pelabuhan Ratu celebrate a great festival in honour of ***Nyai Roro Kidul,*** *the goddess of the south seas who controls the oceans and decides the success and fate of fishermen. In order to placate her and win favour, a colourful ceremony takes place in which flowers and a bull's head are sacrificed by being sailed out to sea on splendidly decorated sailing boats. According to an old legend, a beautiful daughter was born to a wise ruler, causing great jealousy among the concubines. Banned to the uninhabited jungles and bewitched by the black magic of the women, she managed to reach the coast. A mysterious voice invited her to throw herself into the waves in order to recover her lost fortune. Since then the ocean has never given up its prize. To this day, the princess, living in the ocean, protects the fishermen.*

HOW TO GET THERE

There is a good road via Bogor, Cibedak - a bit more difficult is the connection via Labuan. During the rainy season the poor road via Cilangkahan and Bayah is impassable. Buses and bemos only run parts of the route or go from CIANJUR (Puncak) to SUKABUMI (bus 350 Rp); from here buses for 700 Rp to Pelabuhan Ratu.

CIANJUR

The main road from BOGOR to CIANJUR runs via PUNCAK PASS From the valley the road climbs up in countless bends to 1200 m. Tea plantations cover the mountain slopes. In CIPANAS, lots of hotels, restaurants, and visitors from Jakarta. On weekends it's packed! Fairly good is HOTEL SIMPANG*** (restaurant) on the main road. Towards Bandung, in a huge park, is the *ISTANA CIPANAS,* a governor's palace dating from 1750.

Take a short trip to CIBODAS (colt 300 Rp) and its *BOTANICAL GARDEN* (admission 700 Rp, Sun 300 Rp) planted on the slopes of the GEDE and PANGRANGO volcanoes at an altitude of 1300 m. Since 1862, 80 ha of plants enjoy the highland climate. A beautiful place to take a walk!

Try climbing the volcanoes. You'll need 6-7 hours to reach the burst crater of the still active *GUNUNG GEDE,* 7-8 hours up to the perfect cone of *GUNUNG PANGRANGO.* As the area is a nature reserve, register and get your info beforehand in Cibodas at the administration office behind the parking lot of the botanical garden.

BANDUNG

A city which north of the train tracks leaves the impression that the Dutch have only just left or the time of colonial rule has not quite ended. Bandung, however, is also the city where the new nation states of Africa and Asia met in 1955 for the first non-aligned nations conference. In the university many important new personalities in Indonesian history received their education. Behind the clean facades, excesses against the Chinese minority took place in the 1960s.

Bandung is split by the railroad tracks: to the north the more European influenced areas, to the south it's more Indonesian, a hectic city full of exhaust fumes and, due to the university, packed with many intellectuals and young people. Soon the city will have 1.7 million inhabitants, making it the third largest city of Indonesia.

JALAN ASIA-AFRIKA, one of the largest streets in the city, is a reminder of the Bandung Conference of 1955. On the corner of Jl.Braga is the *GEDUNG MERDEKA,* a 100 year old Dutch colonial building where the conference was held.

Representatives from 29 different Asian and African countries met here, among them *Chou En Lai* from China, *Nehru* from India, and *Nasser* of Egypt. Many of these nations had only recently achieved independence. With the exception of Japan, all were developing countries which declared themselves independent according to the ten principles of non-alignment for peaceful coexistence. It was the first conference with an obvious anti-colonial character.

The *BANDUNG INSTITUTE OF TECHNOLOGY* is certainly the most important university in the country with high scientific standards and many politically active students. Sukarno himself, who still carries the local nick-name 'Bung Karno', was a graduate. The institute was founded during colonial times; the buildings are partly traditional and partly modern. In 1920 the Dutch administration founded the Technical College.

In the university it is easy to meet students keen to show you around. Let them show you the arts department. You'll find information on sculpture, weaving, textiles, sketching, etc. If you want, you can combine your visit to the institute with a look at the *ZOO,* though unfortunately it's a bit run down.

Connoisseurs of local cooking shouldn't miss the chance to visit the Sundanese restaurant *BABAKAN SILIWANGI* - great atmosphere! Order a goldfish dish (the specialty!). The fish is taken from the water before your eyes. Those with smaller budgets - 1 kg fish costs 4000 Rp - can try a 'bajigur' (coconut milk, coffee, brown sugar, and 'kulang kaling') or 'bandrek' (ginger milk, coconut and brown sugar).

The *GEOLOGICAL MUSEUM* is not just a grouping of old stones: it's an interesting collection of fossils, thematic maps, models of volcanoes (and pictures of eruptions), pieces of bones from extinct species, and the topper - the skull of a Java Man. Open: Mon-Thurs 9:00-14:00 h, Fri till 11:00 h and Sat till 13:00 h. Admission is free. Find it at Jl.Diponegoro 57.

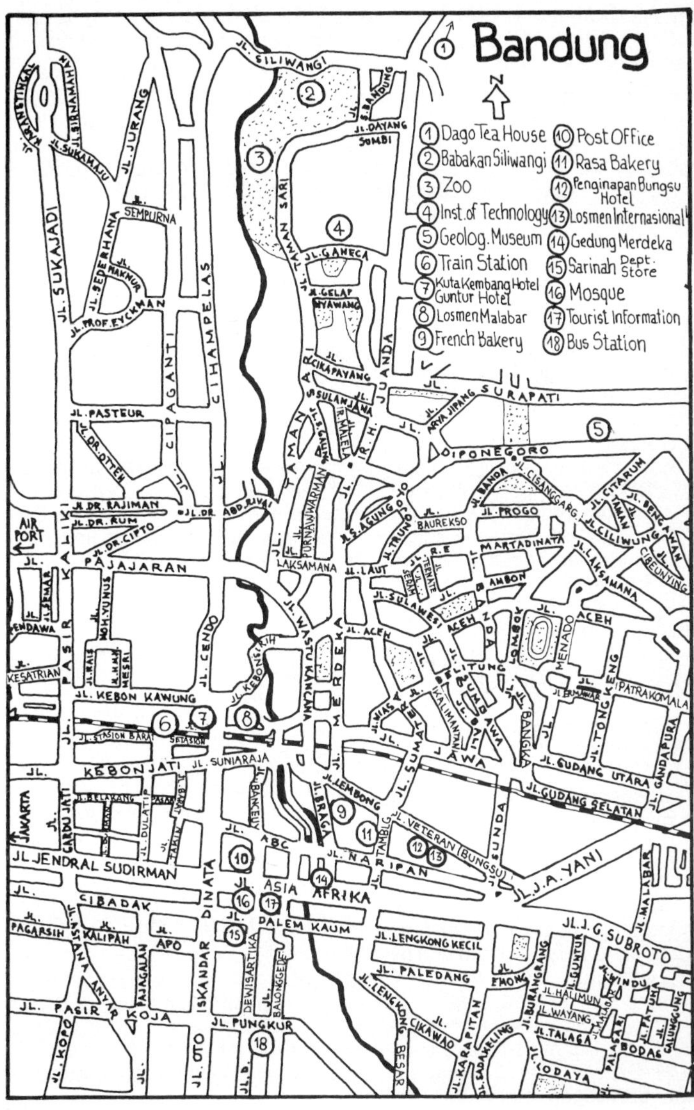
Bandung
N
1 Dago Tea House
2 Babakan Siliwangi
3 Zoo
4 Inst. of Technology
5 Geolog. Museum
6 Train Station
7 Kuta Kembang Hotel Guntur Hotel
8 Losmen Malabar
9 French Bakery
10 Post Office
11 Rasa Bakery
12 Penginapan Bungsu Hotel
13 Losmen Internasional
14 Gedung Merdeka
15 Sarinah Dept. Store
16 Mosque
17 Tourist Information
18 Bus Station

An army museum, the *MUSEUM MANDALA WANGSIT SILIWANGI,* is near Istana Hotel on Jl.Lembong displaying arms and other things from the time of the independence struggle. Opening times as above.

A nice excursion in the surrounding area might be the *DAGO TEA HOUSE.* Open until 22:00 h. Stop a 'Dago' bemo (200 Rp) on Jl.Asia Afrika near Hotel Grand Preanger heading north; you'll be dropped off about 3 km out of town. The last bit of the "climb" uphill you'll have to do on foot. You get a beautiful view of the city. A steep path leads to the waterfall *CURUG DAGO.*

HOTELS

On Jl.Veteran (formerly Jl.Bungsu) are four cheap losmen: *INTERNASIONAL**, BUNGSU**, GANIA PLAZA*** and *EMPONG**,* no. 9 - all furnished about the same. Near the train station is *LOSMEN MALABAR**,* Jl. Kebon Jukut 3 (with courtyard). Right around the corner on Jl.Oto Iskandardinata 3 are more expensive hotels: *HOTEL JAYA***,* no. 22, rooms with private WC and mandi; *HOTEL GUNTUR****,* no. 20, with bath and courtyard balconies, across the way is *HOTEL SAHARA***,* no. 3, not so good. *HOTEL BRAGA* is certainly not worth the price they charge - or has it improved in the meantime? More comfortable are *HOTELS MELATI I* and *II****,* Jl.Kebonjati 24 and 27, tel 56409/56228, as well as *MUTIARA ***(*),* Jl.Kebon Kawung 60, tel 36356 and *CATELLYA****,* Jl.Dr. Rum 12. These hotels all are in the price category up to 30,000 Rp.

FOOD

A real treat for people long on the road is the large number of bakeries serving good pastry and tarts. The selection is huge at *RASA BAKERY,* Jl.Tamblong 15 - great place to breakfast, but prices have gone up recently. Good, but more hectic, is the *FRENCH BAKERY* at Jl.Braga 18. You can get cheap but good nasi rames (we hope still) at the tiny warung next to the Sarinah Department Store on Jl.Braga. If you eat cheaply here for a couple of days, maybe your travel resources can afford a meal at *BABAKAN SILIWANGI* (see above). In the evening you'll find lots of food stalls set up around Alun Alun Square, especially on Jl.Cikapundung and on Jl.Dalem Kaum west of the square. In the area you'll also find lots of cheap restaurants which become packed when the movie theatres close. A lot happens here and on the side streets. Try Chinese food at *QUEEN*.

GENERAL INFORMATION

INFORMATION - In the northeast on ALUN ALUN SQUARE, across from the mosque is the TOURIST INFORMATION OFFICE. You can pick up a map and a number of tips. If you have special questions, check with the central office of West Java, less conveniently located on Jl.K.Penghulu Hasan Mustafa, tel 72355.

PPA - Jl.Jend.A.Yani 276.

IMMIGRATION - Office at Jl.Diponegoro 34.

BANKS - if you have to change money, compare the rates at BANK NEGARA INDONESIA, Jl.Asia Afrika 119; BANK DAGANG NEGARA, Jl. Asia Afrika 51 and the other banks in this street.

WAYANG GOLEK AND TOPENG PRODUCTION IN BANDUNG

HOSPITALS - 'Rumah Sakit' in Bahasa Indonesia - there are quite a few in Bandung such as: BOROMEUS HOSPITAL, Jl.Juanda 80, tel 81011; SANTO YUSUF, Jl.Cikutra 9, tel 71108.

WAYANG GOLEK PERFORMANCES - normally held every Saturday night from 21:00 h till early in the morning at YAYASAN PUSAT KEBUDAYAAN, Jl.Naripan 7, admission 500 Rp - you'll see the Ramayana or another West Javanese fairytale.

KETUK TILU DANCE - a traditional dance, popular on holidays. There is a difference between performances and free dance where the audience, directed by signals, can participate. You can see this dance in PURWA SETRA, Gang Tegallegan, Jl.Oto Iskandardinata, from 21:00 to 1:00 h. Entrance fee 2000 Rp.

MOVIES - this town has lots of theatres, especially on Jl.Alun Alun Timur, Jl.Jen.Sudirman and on Jl. Merdeka. Lots of American films, but also local products which you should be sure to check out.

PUBLIC TRANSPORT - bemos drive all over town - one way will cost you 200 Rp. City buses go either north-south or east-west. There are two bus stations, Kebun Kelapa for traffic west and Cicaheum on Jl.Jend. A.Yani for buses heading east. Accessible via local bus 1. The two bus terminals are connected by minibus no. 2. Take note if you arrive from Bogor and want to continue right on to Garut.

LEAVING BANDUNG

BY AIR

The airport is only 4 km from the city centre. BOURAQ, Jl.Cihampelas 27, tel 437896; MERPATI, Jl.Lembong 5, tel 57474; GARUDA, Jl.Asia Afrika 73, tel 56986. SAMPLE PRICES: JAKARTA 25,900 Rp / 30,500 Rp (BO / GA), SEMARANG 47,600 Rp (MZ), SURABAYA 58,700 Rp (MZ, BO), YOGYA 43,400 Rp (BO). Only for the jetset!

BY RAIL

At least six trains leave daily for Jakarta - takes three to four hours, costs between 6000 Rp 1st cl. and 1800 Rp 3rd cl. Two trains daily to Surabaya (via Yogya, Madiun and Solo), one train daily to Yogya only (9 -10 hrs.). Costs to Surabaya: 14,500 Rp 1st cl. or 10,100 Rp 2nd cl. with the Mutiara Selatan. Other trains 7300 Rp 2nd cl. and 5500 Rp 3rd cl. Yogya costs 11,000 Rp or 8100 Rp with the Mutiara Selatan, and between 3200 Rp and 4700 Rp with other trains.

BY BUS

One bus station is on Jl.Kebon Kelapa in the south part of town for buses going west. The other in Cicaheum on the continuation of Jl.Jen.A. Yani.

Buses leave throughout the day for Jakarta - takes five to seven hours and costs 2400 Rp to 3600 Rp depending on bus. SAMPLE PRICES: BOGOR 1500 Rp, CIREBON 1400 Rp, (3 1/2 hrs., 120 km), GARUT 750 Rp, MERAK 3200 Rp, SEMARANG 3850 Rp, SOLO 5600 Rp, TEGAL 2200 Rp, TASIKMALAYA 1400 Rp, YOGYAKARTA 5400 Rp (night express 6300 Rp), SUMEDANG 550 Rp, CIPANAS 1200 Rp, SUKABUMI 1150 Rp, PURWAKARTA 850 Rp, PURWOKERTO 3000 Rp, BANJAR 1800 Rp, 146 km, 4 1/2 hrs.

Only from KEBON KELAPA TERMINAL: MAJALAYA 400 Rp, 34 km (by Colt further to GARUT) and CIWIDEY bus 350 Rp, Colt 400 Rp, 30 km.

Important bus companies in Bandung: BANDUNG EXPRESS, Jl.Martadinata 7, tel 58131; APOLLO EXPRESS, Jl.Lengkong Besar; YOGYA EXPRESS, Jl.Sunda 56, tel 52507; MAJU MAKMUR, Jl.Martadinata, tel 58854; DAMRI, Jl.Merdeka

DAY TRIPS AROUND BANDUNG

LEMBANG

16 km from Bandung - take a colt (350 Rp) from the train station - this mountain town is famous for its fruit market and cool air. Vegetable gardens rise up the mountain slopes. In town you'll find the GRAND HOTEL**** which was well loved by the Dutch.

TANGKUBAN PARAHU CRATER

North of LEMBANG, take a bus towards SUBANG another 12 km and get off at the mountain road to walk the last 4 km to the top. If you're unlucky, the buses that go racing up will have been rented by Neckermann's Highland Tour or Dutch organizations. On the other hand, an Indonesian school class might come chugging along in a truck and give you a ride. 250 Rp admission per person, for vehicles 1500 Rp at the start of the road. A guide to the hot springs is unnecessary (awful prices!). Do the tour in the early morning. If you have a bad day, everything will be fogged in by 9:00 h.

At one time the volcano was conical, until a tremendous explosion blew the top of the mountain away and the masses of earth descended around Bandung. You can still see the hills today. The river backed up creating a giant lake up to 75 m deep. The original Bandung, 40 km to the south, even received a name that normally would only go to a coastal town. But with time the river dug itself an underground bed (creating the many caves in the area) and the water flowed into the sea. Since then the mountain looks like a tipped over ship - and so its name 'tangkuban parahu'. The volcano is by no means extinct. Four times this century there have been eruptions and one of the ten craters still spews steam.

HOT SPRINGS

As a result of the volcanic activity, most of the hot springs in the Bandung area are pretty touristic. The easiest to reach is MARIBAYA HOT SPRINGS (150 Rp admission), ten minutes from Lembang. You can catch a colt for 150 Rp, or foot it via the DAGO TEA HOUSE and a tunnel - takes you two hours. In Maribaya you will find sleeping accommodation, restaurants and bath-halls. Even more touristy is CIATER HOT SPRINGS, located 35 km north of Bandung, 15 minutes by colt from CIATER. Lots of white people and Japanese.

SUMEDANG

is located 45 km northeast of Bandung in the mountains. It was one of the best known Dutch resort areas. In YAYASAN PANGERAN SUMEDANG MUSEUM, a small historical museum, you can view old gamelan instruments, weapons, and jewelry. With some luck you might see some ram-fighting in the area. Better known, however, are the 'kuda renggong', the horse dances where horses move their hooves in time to a monotonous rhythm.

GARUT

Located 65 km from Bandung, halfway down the road to TASIKMALAYA. Around 13 km from town you'll find one of the first Hindu temples ever built on Java, CANDI CANGKUANG. Take bus to LELES (200 Rp) and walk the last 2 1/2 km through paddies, rivers, and bamboo forests.

PANGANDARAN

A fishing village on the south coast with long white beaches and gentle waters. It is a stopover for travellers en route from Jakarta to Yogya. The eastern edge is well built up; here too are the fishing boats. In the west it is more spread out, flat, planted with trees and shrubs. There is only one hotel by the water. Several times each year the hotels are packed, e.g. on Mohammed's birthday, Idul Fitri, Christmas, and Hajat Laut, a sacrificial feast made by fishermen to honour the Goddess of the Sea, Nyi Loro Kidul.

The bus stand in Pangandaran is 2 km from the losmen in PANUNJUNG, but that is no problem; becak drivers will look out for you. You must pay 300 Rp admission at the beginning of the street. The becak drivers receive a high commission from the losmen owners, making the drive to the lodgings cheaper, but drivers refuse to take more than one passenger, milking the hotel commission for all it is worth. Calculate 500 Rp for the return trip with two passengers aboard the becak. About half way along the route, a long row of hotels begins. Because an isthmus stretches south, you can choose between beaches facing east or west, at the narrowest point just 300 m apart. Take your time looking for a hotel. The becak driver shouldn't mind. He will get his commission no matter where you decide. If you move after the first night, the hotel owner will take a big loss. By the way, Indonesians pay five times the regular hotel rate on major holidays.

The biggest problem, according to numerous reports we've received, is the number of young Indonesians who are specialized at exploiting the purses of single female travellers. This is especially true among the ranks of 'jungle guides'. Before a woman begins an affair, she should take into consideration the cost of food, drink, motorbike rentals, etc.

Despite tourism, fishing remains the primary source of income. The villagers are very conscious of their local tradition.

HOTELS

Good are *PENGINAPAN MINI I*(*)*, very clean, balconies; and *LOSMEN LAUT BIRU*(*)*, also dorm*, tea and coffee are free. Popular among travellers are *LOSMEN HAMBALI** and *ADEM AYEM*(*)*, *LOSMEN ADEMIYEN**, *TRAVELLER'S HOMESTAY SAMUDRA**, *PONDOK WISATA OMAN ROCHMANA***, Jl.Kalen Buaya, Pantai Barat, or *LOSMEN BAHTERA JAYA***. Here you should be careful when ordering rail tickets. Extreme over-charges have been reported. If you have the cash, there are a number of comfortable hotels. Try *PANGANDARAN BEACH HOTEL*** (*)* or *BUMI PANANJUNG***** on the eastern beach.

FOOD

Popular, with good, cheap traveller food, are the simple warung around Pananjung's only crossroads, e.g. *WARUNG NASI AMPERA* across from Losmen Laut Biru. Enjoy fruit pies with chocolate sauce in *SYMPATHY COFFEE SHOP* diagonally across from Losmen Mini I. Visit the fish market in the early morning. Shark, ray, and occasionally a 3 - 4 m long marlin are auctioned to the highest bidder. On many beaches you can purchase your own specialty; then arrange to have a warung prepare it for you. Prices per kilo vary with supply and demand: shrimp (udang) 2500-3500 Rp, octopus 2000-3000 Rp, shark 500 Rp.

LEAVING PANGANDARAN

Heading West: Everything goes via BANJAR, two trains daily; minibuses are faster 1100 Rp, 65 km, 1 h; or head right on to TASIKMALAYA 1400 Rp, 107 km, 3 hrs.

Heading East: Also possible via BANJAR, but the boat ride to CILACAP is a lot more fun. Get the early bus toward BANJAR only to KALIPUCANG 450 Rp, 16 km, 30 minutes. Then walk 200 m to the dock of the small motor-vessel. Departures at 7:30, 8:30, 10:30, 12:30 h - the last boat is certainly too late to get a connection out of CILACAP. For 1200 Rp, enjoy a 3 hrs. cruise down the Sungai Citanduy through mangroves between Java and Nusakambangan. Stops in small kampongs and stilt houses. You'll see artistic fish traps in the large open lagoons, fishermen in dug-out canoes, lots of water fowl, and the funny mud-jumpers, small fish with elongated eyes which live on land. (CILACAP, see *Central Java*).

AROUND PANGANDARAN

NATIONAL PARK

Just a couple of hundred metres from your door, whether via the backway along the beach, or through one of the two entrances (admission 300 Rp), is a National Park of over 500 ha. In a small section of the park, you can follow wide paths to the cemeteries, caves, Japanese bunkers and tiny beaches. Particularly pretty is PASIR PUTIH in the west. Over 90% of the peninsula is in a wilderness state of primary or secondary jungle, and open pastures with herds of banteng.

THE WEST COAST

This is more than just a never-ending beach. The tour by minibus is a waste of time because you constantly have to walk 1 or 2 km from the road; try renting a motorbike. At CIKALONG (km 9) or CIBENDA (km 12), turn off to the lagoon MUARA KARANGTIRTA where three rivers are blocked by a sand dune before they flow into the sea. Despite a steady ocean breeze, you've a wide expanse of still water, great for wind-surfing. Just 1 km further BATU HIU (=shark rock) rises above the surf. Pay 100 Rp admission. There are lots of warungs and three penginapan. When the coast bends to the southwest you'll discover a large lagoon MUARA BOJONG SALAWE, turn off just beyond PARIGI (km 19). CIJULANG (km 23) is the last stop for buses and trains from BANJAR, but you can continue on by minibus. Just beyond the village is a turn-off to PANTAI BATU KARAS (about 5 km) with waves for surfing. There are two losmen*. The road is paved for another 50 km, ending at TASIK. At kilometre marker 69 is PANTAI PONCOL, also known as SIXTY-NINE BEACH. Several beaches west of PANGANDARAN are visited regularly by sea turtles to bury their eggs in the sand.

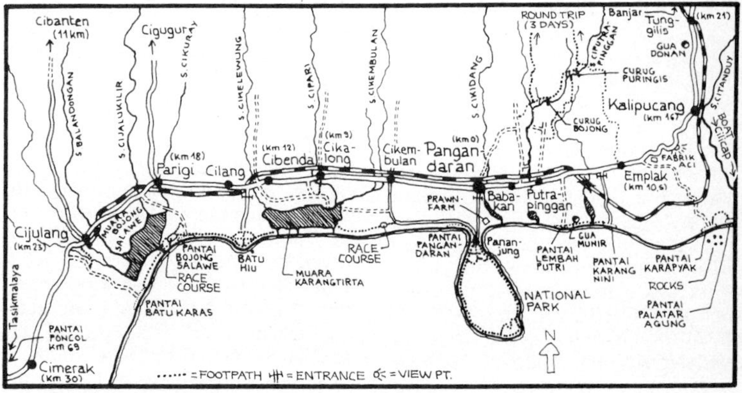

THE ROAD EAST

There is more to see on the road to Banjar. The villages PUTRAPINGGAN (km 5) and EMPLAK (km 10.5) are departure points for treks of up to three days. Ask in LOSMEN LAUT BIRU. At km 6 is a turn-off to PANTAI LEMBAH PUTRI, the "beach in the valley of the princess". Another 1 km along the beach is GUA MUNIR, a meditation cave where a certain Munir is said to have become aware of the lottery number which made him a millionaire. At km 7 you can walk across a 160 m-long railway bridge and enjoy a tremendous view of the sea. After 2 km the road branches off to PANTAI KARANG NINI, the "grandmother's coral beach" (100 Rp admission).

CIREBON

Capital of an old Javanese sultanate and an important harbour on the north coast of the island, the city is also known as 'Kota Udang' - crab town, because krupuk and other shellfish dishes are the local speciality. Hindu and Muslim rulers fought for control of this city on the border between the Javanese and Sundanese spheres of influence in the 15th century. Even at this early date, there was a sizeable Chinese community.

Dating from the year 1658 is one of the oldest and most beautiful Chinese temples in Indonesia. The *THIAW KAK SIE,* with its lovely wall paintings, is on Jl.Kantor near the harbour. You can find two sultan's palaces in the south of town. The *KRATON KASEPUHAN,* across from the mosque, was built in 1529. The walls are decorated with countless Delft tiles, as well as Chinese porcelain of the Ming Dynasty. Tip a guide to show you the tiny museum where you'll find weapons, wood carvings, and other curiosities as well as a splendid coach used by the Sultan during Mohammed's birthday pageant. The pageant still continues today though without the sultan who has been deposed. Behind the market is a smaller palace, the *KRATON KANOMAN,* which is a bit run down. It has a museum as well which charges admission!

HOTELS

The losmen, as the town itself, are all very clean. Not bad is *HOTEL ASIA**(*),* quiet with a courtyard; find it on Jl.Kalibaru Selatan 33, tel 2183. Cheaper but not as good are the losmen at the train station (Jl.Stasiun Kereta Api) or the *HOTEL FAMILI** on Jl.Siliwangi 66, tel 2324, or *HOTEL ISLAM** at no. 125. On the same street are a few better (***) hotels, such as *CORDOVA,* no. 75-77, tel 4677, *SIDODADI,* no. 74, tel 2305, *PRIANGAN,* no. 108, tel 2929, or *SLAMET,* no. 183, tel 3296. The absolute luxury hotel is the *GRAND****,* no. 98.

FOOD

In the evenings you'll find many warung with good food behind the market hall in the centre of town (Pasar Pagi). Sundanese dishes are served in *KENCANA,* Jl.Karang Kencana. Better Sundanese food, however, is served a bit out of town on Jl. Bay Pass in *LEMBUR KURING.* Or try *RESTAURANT BAHAGIA,* south of Hotel Asia at Jl.Bahagia 45.

LEAVING CIREBON

BY AIR

Daily at 8:30 h and 16:20 h Merpati flies with a CASA to JAKARTA. Costs 33,100 Rp.

BY RAIL

There are several connections daily by train to JAKARTA for 2900 Rp 3rd cl. up to 13,200 Rp (Bima). Going east, there is a line along the north coast to SEMARANG (usually flooded during the rainy season) and another line inland to YOGYAKARTA. Ten trains daily to YOGYA, three trains daily to SEMARANG.

BY BUS

The bus station is 5 km out of town - take taxi kota G9 or G7 for 150 Rp. SAMPLE PRICES: BANDUNG 1400 Rp, 130 km, 3 1/2 hrs.; PEKALONGAN 1350 Rp; CIAMIS 1200 Rp, 106 km; JAKARTA 2700 Rp, 250 km; SEMARANG 2700 Rp, 240 km; TASIKMALAYA 1300 Rp, 124 km, 3 1/2 hrs.; YOGYA 3200 Rp and SURABAYA 5050 Rp.

DAY TRIPS AROUND CIREBON

Go by bemo on the following tours, costs 150 Rp in town and 200 Rp outside.

GUA SUNYARAGI

On the ring road (Jl.Bay Pass), about 4 km from town (taxi kota G8) is the old palace which was built in one night as a country seat by Sunan Gunung Jati for himself and his Chinese wife according to legend. The Chinese community tells another story of Chinese settlers who arrived with the princess and built the castle in her honour. You can still be mystified by the strange architecture; clearly discernible in the ruins are caves, secret chambers, stairs and tunnels which lead to nowhere. On the way north in taxi kota G6, you can visit the TOMB of this ruler.

SURA NANGGALA LOR

Also interesting is this village, 12 km away on the road to Indramayu, where topeng carvers work. You can see how the carefully cut and painted masks take on their expressive character for use in the wayang topeng dances.

TRUSMI

In the Cirebon area there are many batik villages where the colourful cloths are woven. Easy to reach is Trusmi, only 9 km with bemo taxi kota G4. From the main road you have to walk another km up the narrow village street to the batik workshops.

CENTRAL JAVA

In the middle of Java you can still find evidence today of the Hindu and Buddhist high cultures - check out the temple complexes at Prambanan and Borobudur or the ruins on the Dieng Plateau.

After the fall of the Majapahit kingdom due to the spread of Islam in the 16th century, a Muslim sultanate arose in Central Java - the New Mataram Kingdom - with its centre in the area of Demak and Kudus. Through the intrigues of western merchants fighting for control of the spice trade monopoly, the kingdom fell after only four sultans.

Much remains today of the royal high culture especially in the Sultanate of Yogyakarta, where wayang performances and splendid theatre, hardly seen elsewhere, are presented and schools still teach and develop the traditional dances and gamelan music. At the same time, Central Java - in particular Solo, Pekalongan and Yogyakarta - is an important centre of the batik industry.

With 30 million inhabitants, this is one of the most densely populated provinces of Indonesia - problems of over-population (division of family rice fields down to the size of towels) are seen here all too clearly.

CILACAP

The only harbour on Java's 1000 km long southern coast suitable for large ocean-going vessels. At the same time the city is an important industrial centre. Interesting for you is the boat connection to Pangandaran. If you have to stay overnight try LOSMEN LIMA**, about 600 m from the dock in a quiet side-street. More expensive is GRAND HOTEL***(*) on Jl.Wahidin 5.

LEAVING CILACAP

A daily Merpati flight connects the city with JAKARTA (53,000 Rp). The ferry to KALIPUCANG leaves at 7:00, 8:00, 12:00. and 13:00 h. The trip takes about 3 hrs. and costs 1200 Rp. The minibus to PANGANDARAN costs from there 450 Rp. If you arrive with the first ferry from Kalipucang you can easily make it to YOGYA or DIENG on the same day. Direct bus to Yogya 2100 Rp, 196 km, about 5 hrs. Or go to PURWOKERTO, 800 Rp, 2 hrs., continue from there to WONOSOBO for 1100 Rp in 2 1/2 hrs., and take a minibus to DIENG for 800 Rp.

DIENG PLATEAU

On a swampy high plateau (2093 m) in the middle of Java's mountain world are eight simple, unassuming temples which once formed a temple village or monastery. By the early 9th century this was a centre of Shiva worship and a place of pilgrimage, home to priests and monks, but also remarkable architects. Archeologists have discovered the foundations of a large building complex, including another 32 temples.

The plateau, 'di hyang' (Refuge of the Gods), is the crater of a long extinct volcano, just the right place to honour Shiva, God of cosmic destruction. Although considered extinct, there is still life in the volcano. Steam drifts over the warm waters of the lake, lending a strange aura of green-blue to the smell of sulphur and pools of bubbling mud before the afternoon fog settles in.

Wander along slippery mountain paths, through picturesque scenery. Giant heads of cabbage grow on terraced vegetable fields Through the forest, a world unto itself, you pass steep rocks covered with ferns, discovering mountain lakes and villages.

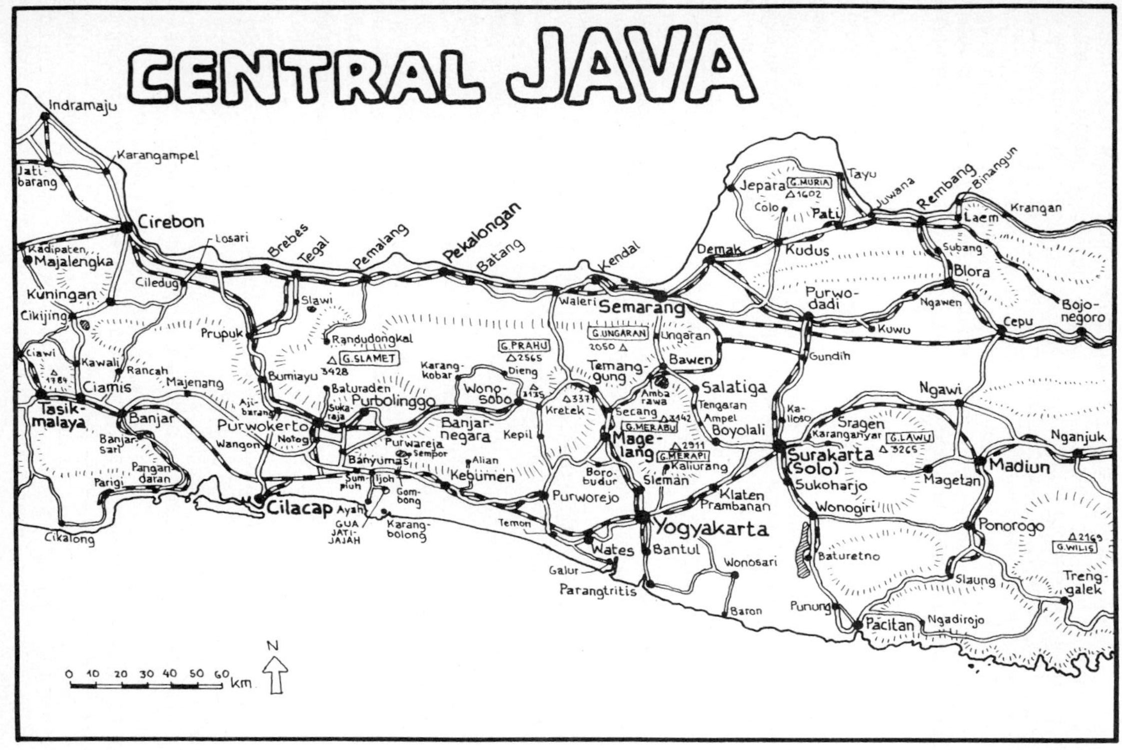
CENTRAL JAVA
Indramaju
Karangampel
Jatibarang
Cirebon
Losari
Brebes
Tegal
Pemalang
Pekalongan
Batang
Kendal
Demak
Jepara
G.MURIA
Δ1602
Colo
Tayu
Pati
Juwana
Rembang
Binangun
Laem
Krangan
Kudus
Subang
Blora
Bojonegoro
Kadipaten
Majalengka
Ciledug
Kuningan
Cikijing
Slawi
Prupuk
Randudongkal
G.SLAMET
3428
Waleri
Semarang
G.UNGARAN
2050
Ungaran
Purwodadi
Ngawen
Kuwu
Cepu
Ciawi
1784
Kawali
Rancah
Ciamis
Majenang
Bumiayu
Baturaden
Purbolinggo
G.PRAHU
Δ2565
Karangkobar
Dieng
Wonosobo
3135
Δ3371
Temanggung
Bawen
Salatiga
Gundih
Ngawi
Tasikmalaya
Banjar
Ajibarang
Purwokerto
Sukaraja
Banjarnegara
Kretek
Ambarawa
Secang
3142
Tengaran
Ampel
Boyolali
Kalioso
Sragen
Karanganyar
G.LAWU
Δ3265
Nganjuk
Banjarsari
Wangon
Notog
Purwareja
Sempor
Kepil
G.MERABU
Magelang
Δ2911
G.MERAPI
Kaliurang
Surakarta (Solo)
Madiun
Pangandaran
Parigi
Banyumas
Alian
Kebumen
Borobudur
Sleman
Sukoharjo
Magetan
Sumpiuh
Ijoh
Gombong
Purworejo
Klaten
Prambanan
Cilacap
Ayah
GUA JATIJAJAH
Karangbolong
Temon
Yogyakarta
Wonogiri
Ponorogo
Δ2169
G.WILIS
Cikalong
Wates
Bantul
Wonosari
Baturetno
Galur
Parangtritis
Slaung
Trenggalek
Baron
Punung
Pacitan
Ngadirojo
N
0 10 20 30 40 50 60 km

On clear days from one of the look-out hills you can see, especially at early morning, six or seven nearby volcanoes, most notably the twins GUNUNG SUNDORO (3151 m) and GUNUNG SUMBING (3371 m) in the southeast, as well as all the way to the coastlines north and south. Way off in the distance, volcanic cones break the misty plains in the east (GUNUNG MERBABU / MERAPI) and in the west (GUNUNG SLAMET).

In years past, there have been a number of gas explosions on the western end of the plateau costing several hundred lives. The area is now marked, and the road detours the danger.

A confusing network of footpaths criss-crosses the area, recently supplemented by roads. As Pertamina seeks to harness the powers of creation, using geothermal power to generate electricity, the unreal and and ghostly atmosphere is disrupted.

Eight small candis, named in recent past for heroes of the Mahabharata epic, can be visited in the course of an easy walk. West of the village of Dieng, a path branches off to the most frequented temple ruins, the *ARJUNA COMPLEX,* in a swamp. The path leads from the parking lot along the foundations of a former palace. Just a few metres further is the first and largest temple, *CANDI ARJUNA,* across from a small flat building called *CANDI SEMAR.* It might have once served as living quarters. The wall reliefs, depicting Vishnu, are particularly nice in the next temple, *CANDI SRIKANDI.* Beyond are the smaller temples *CANDI PUNTA DEWA* and *CANDI SEMBADRA.* Further south is *CANDI GATUTKACA,* across from a small MUSEUM featuring excavations finds.

Very unusual is *CANDI BIMA* on a small hill at the southwestern end of the plain. A row of faces stare at you from window recesses. Along the northern path from Dieng to Candi Bima, you pass *TELAGA WARNA,* truly a 'lake of many colours', whose surface shimmers, depending upon the light, in many shades of turquoise.

South of Candi Bima, clouds of sulphur fumes point the way to several bubbling mud holes where boiling-hot, sulphur-rich water gushes from porous rock. The path to *SIKIDANG CRATER* runs over Pertamina property and is closed.

Across the mountains, south of Goa Semar, the highest village on Java, *SEMBUNGAN* (2100 m) is said to be nestled on the *TELAGA CEBONG.*

HOTELS

There are many simple losmen in the village of Dieng such as *ASRI** and *BU JONO**. In Bu Jono is a restaurant; Mr. Sulistio offers info and tips, and he will rent you a colt, 15,000 Rp without a driver or 17,500 chauffeured. Bring warm clothes and, if possible, a sleeping bag - temperatures drop at night to near freezing. There are also clean losmen and restaurants in Wonosobo. By the minibus terminal are two unpretentious losmen, *RAHAYU** and *PENDAWA LIMA**. Plus there is *LOSMEN SURYA***. Good is *ASIA***. At Jl.Jend.A. Yani 45 is *LOSMEN JAWA TENGGAH***, lovely, nice family, tea is on the house. *NIRWANA****, Jl.Tanggung 13 and *ARJUNA GUESTHOUSE***. Outside of town at Jl.Dieng 20 is *LOSMEN SURABAYA***, right by the road, barrack style. *RESTAURANT DIENG* in Wonosobo is a self-service restaurant with a large selection of tasty dishes and drinks. The owner, J. Tjugianto, is a good source of information; the food is excellent, lots of groups. In Kalianget, by the hot springs is the luxurious *WISATA KALIANGET**** with a tennis court.

HOW TO GET THERE

Several hotels in Yogya offer daytrips (including Borobudur) by minibus for 8500 Rp. From YOGYA buses to MAGELANG are 600 Rp, 1 h; then continue by minibus to WONOSOBO 1000 Rp, 2 1/2 hrs.

Beyond TEMANGGUNG, centre of tobacco growing, the road climbs up the 1500 m KLEDUNG PASS between the volcanoes GUNUNG SUMBING (3371 m) in the southeast and GUNUNG SUNDORO (3135 m) in the northwest. From Wonosobo Bus Terminal: Dokar 300 Rp, 2 km to the Colt Terminal and via a serpentine road climbing dizzily in 1 1/2 hrs., from 780 m to Dieng (2093 m), over 28 km, 800 Rp.

WONOSOBO is also accessible via AMBARAWA (1000 Rp) and PURWOKERTO (1100 Rp). Coming from the west (Cilacap, Purwokerto), take the sidetrip BANJARNEGARA - KARANGKOBAR - BATUR - DIENG, in three stages by colt each for 600 Rp over 55 km.

An alternative to the return trip is a 3 hrs. hike to BAWANG. The path starts by the police-station in Dieng heading north, continuing downhill through a ravine. From BAWANG you've colts to PEKALONGAN, or BANYUPUTIH, then on by bus to SEMARANG.

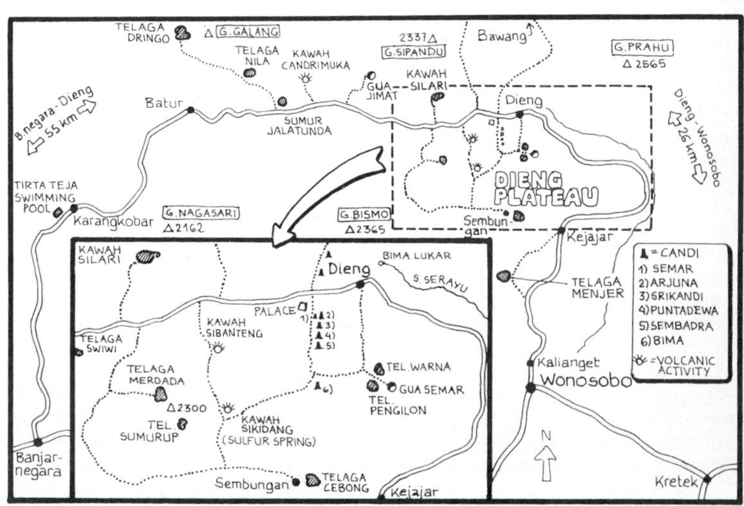

SEMARANG

The capital of the province with just about 1.2 million people and a busy harbour, the city has an interesting history. In the 17th century the harbours of the flourishing neighbouring cities of Demak, Jepara, and Pati began to silt up with sand. As a result the tiny fishing village began to take on a new importance in the area.

Only a few of the Chinese and Dutch trading houses remain today; you can find a bit of colonial atmosphere on *JALAN SUPRAPTO.* On the same street is *GEREJA BLENDUK,* the second oldest church on Java built in 1753. Especially worth a look is the old *CHINATOWN*, northwest of the big bus station. Take a walk in the evening along Jl.Pekojan. In front of the bridge take a right on Gang Lombok. There are lots of Chinese restaurants here and a small square with one of the most beautiful Chinese temples, built in 1772 *(KINTENG TEMPLE).* Inside you'll find 18 fierce looking Buddhas sitting surrounded by the smoke of burning joss money and incense.

Be sure to check out another temple which can be found a bit out of town. *SAM PO KONG TEMPLE* is one of the oldest Chinese temples on Java. Originally it was only a cave to pray in - therefore the name *GEDUNG BATU* - until an ambassador of the Ming Dynasty visited it. Take a bemo to *PASAR KARANG AYU* (200 Rp), and then another bemo direct to the temple.

HOTELS

Most hotels in the city centre are on Jl.Pemuda or Jl.Iman Bonjol. Among them are many flea-bags such as *ISLAM**,* Jl.Pemuda 8. A bit better is *OEWA ASIA**,* Jl.Iman Bonjol 1, though it has seen better days. Other lodgings on the street include *PONCOL*,* no. 60, *ARJUNA**,* no. 51, and *RAHAYU***,* no. 35-37. Cheaper is *MARTANOVA*,* Jl.Gendingan (the street runs between Jl.Iman Bonjol and Jl.Pemuda), or *JAYA**,* Jl.Haryono 85, tel 23604. The *PUTRA JASA HOTEL***** is the best hotel in town with a swimming pool, tennis courts, and other forms of recreation, all rooms with TV and AC, hot water, and other luxuries, US$50 for a double, on Jl.Sisingamangaraja, Candi Baru, tel 314441, near the golf course, on a hill 5 km from town. If you don't want to spend that much, but still need your comfort, try the mid-class hotel *CANDI BARU***,* Jl.Rinjani 21, tel 315272, about 3 km south of town near Sam Po Kong. On the corner of Jl.Pemuda and Jl.Imam Bonjol is the old *DIBYA PURI***** with a somewhat faded atmosphere. Also centrally located is *SURYA***,* Jl.Iman Bonjol 28, tel 24250, with clean rooms and a big courtyard.

FOOD

Nasi Padang at Jl.Pemuda 50 and in *SIMPANG RAYA,* Jl.Gajah Mada at Jl.Pemuda. Many cheap warung can be found on Jl.Depok (between Jl. Gajah Mada and Jl.Pemuda). Enjoy European, Chinese or Indonesian food in colonial atmosphere, served by old, shuffling waiters in *OEN,* Jl.

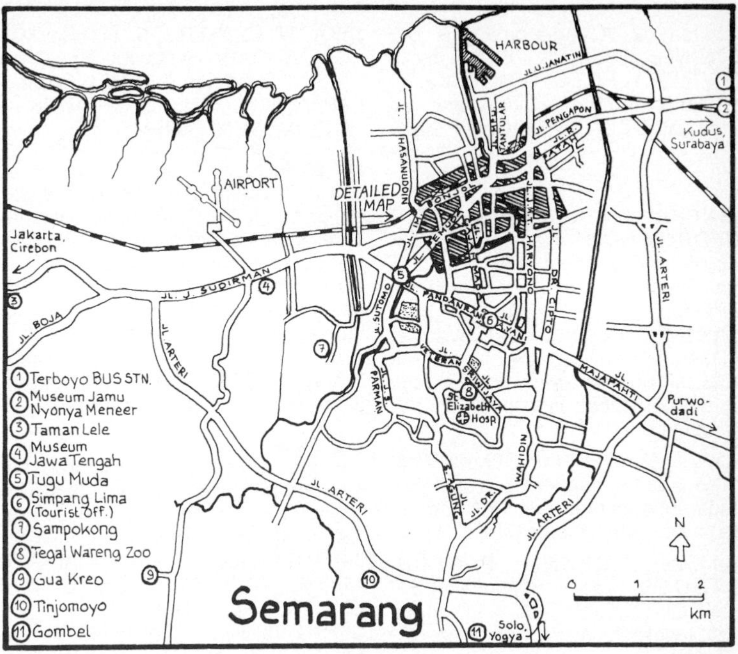

HARBOUR
AIRPORT
DETAILED MAP
Jakarta, Cirebon
Kudus, Surabaya
Purwodadi
Solo, Yogya
JL. U. JANATIN
JL. PENGAPON
JL. HASANUDDIN
JL. TANTULAR
JL. J. SUDIRMAN
JL. BOJA
JL. ARTERI
JL. SUTOMO
JL. PANDANARAN
JL. VETERAN
JL. S. PARMAN
JL. SRIWIJAYA
JL. MAJAPAHIT
JL. M. T. HARYONO
JL. DR. CIPTO
JL. WAHIDIN
St. Elizabeth Hosp.
N
0 1 2 km

1. Terboyo BUS STN.
2. Museum Jamu Nyonya Meneer
3. Taman Lele
4. Museum Jawa Tengah
5. Tugu Muda
6. Simpang Lima (Tourist Off.)
7. Sampokong
8. Tegal Wareng Zoo
9. Gua Kreo
10. Tinjomoyo
11. Gombel

Semarang

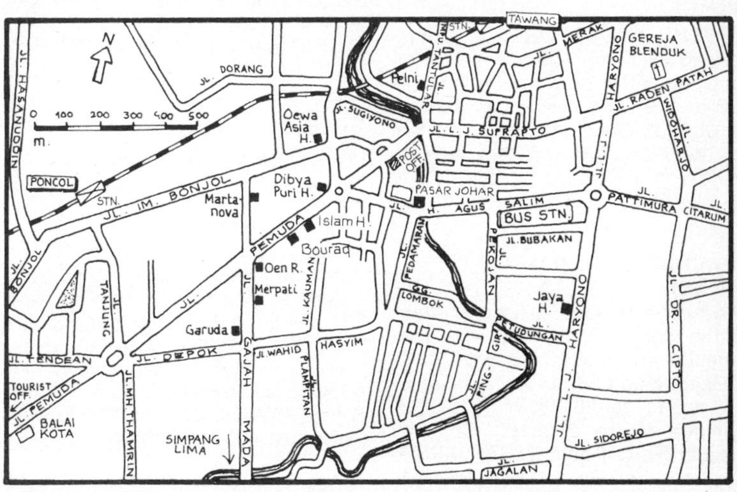

Pemuda 52. A good bakery is *DE KONING,* Jl.Pemuda 78. Nearby is *KENTUCKY FRIED CHICKEN* at Jl. Pandanaran 78. Try steak and ice cream at *BOUNDY,* Jl.Gajah Mada 125.

GENERAL INFORMATION

INFORMATION - maps and the latest information about Central Java is available at Diparda Jawa Tengah at Jl.Pemuda 171, tel 24146. The Depparpostel Office for Central Java is at Jl.Dahlan 2, tel 311169. There is a local information office in Simpang Lima. All offices are open in the mornings only.

POST OFFICE - the General Post Office is at the northern end of Jl. Pemuda. International calls from the Telecom Office behind the GPO.

WAYANG ORANG PERFORMANCES - daily in the NGESTI PANDOWO THEATRE (Jl.Pemuda 116) - worth a visit but they are expensive.

PUBLIC TRANSPORT - local buses and Daihatsu minibuses provide transport within and around town for 125 to 150 Rp from the bus terminal on Jl.Agus Salim. In town you can ride by becak, although they are prohibited on Jl.Pemuda, costs 300-500 Rp for a short ride.

LEAVING SEMARANG

BY AIR

The airport is about 8 km from town on the road to Cirebon. BOURAQ, Jl. Pemuda 40A, tel 23779; MERPATI, Jl.Gajah Mada 58, tel 23027; GARUDA, no. 11, tel 20178; MANDALA Jl. Pemuda 40, tel 285319. Consider the BOURAQ flights to BANJARMASIN for 81,700 Rp. SAMPLE PRICES: JAKARTA 45,100 Rp / 55,500 Rp (MZ / GA), SURABAYA 33,400 Rp (GA), BANDUNG 47,600 Rp (MZ), BALIKPAPAN 111,900 Rp (GA), PANGKALANBUN 76,600 Rp (MZ).

BY RAIL

The train station is in the north eastern part of town (Semarang Tawang). Three trains every night to SURABAYA (2300 Rp, 3rd. cl.; 17,500 Rp Mutiara Utara). Two trains daily via PEKALONGAN to CIREBON (2200 Rp, 3rd cl.) or JAKARTA (3700 Rp 3rd cl.; 7800 Rp 2nd cl.; 17,500 Rp Mutiara Utara). To SOLO daily 12:40 h by a 3rd cl. train 900 Rp. Arrival 16:17 h.

BY BUS

The bus terminal is 4 km from town on the road to Kudus. Get local bus 1 to Jl.Pemuda (200 Rp), other buses to Jl.Iman Bonjol. SAMPLE PRICES: JAKARTA 5100 / 7300 Rp, MALANG 4400 Rp, SURABAYA 4000 Rp, YOGYA 1300 Rp, DEMAK 300 Rp, MADIUN 2200 Rp, SALATIGA 550 Rp, SOLO 1100 Rp (100 km), PEKALONGAN 1150 Rp, JEPARA 775 Rp, KUDUS 600 Rp, AMBARAWA 500 Rp, CIREBON 2700 Rp, REMBANG 1200 Rp.

BY SHIP

Pelni Office at Jl.Mpu.Tantular 25, tel 20917. Every two weeks on Sundays the KM. Kelimutu docks in Semarang. She sails on the following route: Semarang (Sun) - Banjarmasin (Mon) - Surabaya (Tues) - Padang Bai (Wed) - Lembar (Wed) - Ujung Pandang (Thurs) - Bima (Fri) - Waingapu (Sat) - Ende (Sat) - Kupang (Sun) and back. SAMPLE PRICES: (1st cl. / ekonomi): BANJARMASIN 61,600 / 26,500 Rp, SURABAYA 68,400 / 29,800 Rp, KUPANG 161,800 / 85,200 Rp.

DAY TRIPS AROUND SEMARANG

PEKALONGAN

Those driving along the north coast should be sure to stop here. Batik fans will feel at home! The most beautiful Javanese batik comes from Pekalongan. Hand-drawn, stamped and machine printed batik in soft red and blue colours are sold in many shops. Here they are much cheaper than in Semarang or Jakarta. The most (and also the most expensive) batik comes from the village of KEDUNGWUNI, 8 km away.

You are best off spending the night at the clean and quiet SURYA**, Jl.K.H.M.Mansyur 43. Many of the other cheap hotels are either flea-bags or brothels (Gajah Mada, Damai, Ramayana). On the main street Jl.Hayam Wuruk 31 is the PURIMAS BAKERY with tasty treats.

GEDUNG SONGO

This temple complex in the mountains (up to 1800 m), south of Semarang, is easy to visit as a rest stop on the way to YOGYA. Take the bus to BAWEN (250 Rp) or straight to AMBARAWA. From here get a bemo to BANDUNGAN. From there it's 6 km on foot. You'll see beautiful countryside at the slopes of GUNUNG UNGARAN (2050 m)! The nine Hindu temples, dedicated to Shiva, have been standing for more than 1000 years, each on its own hill. After 11:00 h the mountains become covered in fog; sudden storms cause the landscape to disappear - a ghostly atmosphere. It takes about three hours to walk to all the temples. Those wanting to spend some time here can stay in BANDUNGAN. There are many hotels and losmen such as: DARUKI**, MURIA***, PARAHITA*** or TIGA DARA**. In addition there are several comfortable and more expensive hotels.

According to legend, King Damasuka was buried alive here. The people up in the mountains often hear the crying of a man near death coming from underground. They believe that this is the lost king. By the way, don't take any alcohol into the region or the ghost of King Damasuka will haunt you!

DEMAK

This former port - today land-locked - is easy to reach by bus (250 Rp) only 25 km to the east. Under Sultan Gunung Jati, who had a country seat built for his Chinese wife in Cirebon, the influence of the sultanate reached from Demak to West Java. The MOSQUE on the great square, despite its unpretentious appearance, is an important holy place. Next to it are the graves of the sultans.

KUDUS

It's worthwhile to continue on 50 km to Kudus - bus from Semarang for 600 Rp. Today the town is famous as a place where kretek cigarettes are made. Have a look at a factory; the largest is on Jl.Jen.A.Yani.

At the same time the town, partly due to its exciting history, shows a lot of atmosphere. Take a walk through the old town, KAUMAN, west of the present day centre. The minaret of the MOSQUE in Jl.Menara, dating from the 16th century, shows both Islamic and Hindu elements. Looking closely enough, you'll even find some Chinese traces. An especially splendid sultan's tomb is in the cemetery behind the mosque. Sultan Kudus is still honoured by the present day population.

YOGYAKARTA

All roads lead to Yogya - at least for travellers and tourists on Java. Here you'll meet the old hands back for the umpteenth time to check out the Prambanan area or some yet undiscovered ruins or those who've missed the fourth evening of the Ramayana performance. The fast trotting backpackers on the road between Jakarta and Bali take a well deserved pit stop here. There are more old temples, cultural opportunities, batik factories, and souvenir shops than almost anywhere else in Indonesia. From Yogya you can go diving in the ocean or climb a volcano. Last but not least, you'll find the tourist infrastructure to meet every wallet. For people who like the idea and aren't bothered by the presence of the 'alternative' or the 'normal' tourists and the effects of mass tourism, Yogya is the perfect place to visit.

This city of 443,000 was founded in 1755 when the Mataram Kingdom was divided at Dutch insistence. Yogya became the sultan's seat. In 1812, during the British administration of Java, Stamford Raffles had the Kraton stormed by European troops and the reigning sultan deposed. The library and many of the artistic treasures were plundered; they can be viewed today at the British Museum in London.

In 1946 Yogya became the provisional capital of the Republic of Indonesia. Two years later the returning Dutch tried to conquer the last republican bastions including Yogya and arrest the entire ruling elite of Indonesia. Hamengkubuwono IX, sultan at the time, agreed only to participate in short negotiations with the Dutch concerning the immediate withdrawal of Dutch troops! Today Yogya is the only relatively autonomous sultanate in the republic.

There is a city within the city - the *KRATON*. The buildings for representative purposes and the residence of the sultan and his family are within the Kraton walls to the north. To the left and right are the living quarters and workshops for his employees and their dependents. Adjoining the Kraton to the west and east are the generously planned upper class (bureaucracy, officials) residential neighbourhoods. In the south are many workshops which serve the sultan's court, but can't find room within the walls (e.g. batik workshops). The western side of Alun-Alun, facing Mecca, is reserved for the mosque. Near the central square are the major offices of the former Dutch colonial government.

1. ASTI
2. Diponegoro Monumt. Warung Soto Pak Sholeh
3. BUS-STOP → North
4. Bank Niaga/Merpati
5. BUS-STOP → Solo, Kaliurang
6. Angkatan Darat Museum
7. Affandi Museum Ambarrukmo Palace H, Ayam Goreng, Nyonya Suharti, Sapto Hoedjo Gallery,
8. Malioboro Restaurant
9. Garuda
10. Bank Bumi Daya
11. Yogya Craft Center, Immigration Off., → Airport
12. Rama Restaurant
13. Arjuna Plaza H.
14. Telephone Off.
15. Institute of Fine Art Amri Yahya Gallery
16. Nitour
17. Chines Temple
18. Museum Biologi
19. Jend. Sudirman Memorial House
20. Batik Research Ctr.
21. Zoo
22. Kusuma
23. Astuti
24. THR
25. Mulyosuhardjo
26. Birds' Market
27. Taman Sari
28. Oriental Restaurant
29. Dalem Pujokusuman
30. BUS-STATION
31. BUS-STOP → Parangtritis
32. Swasthigita
33. Agastya
34. Soemihardjo
35. Kota Gede

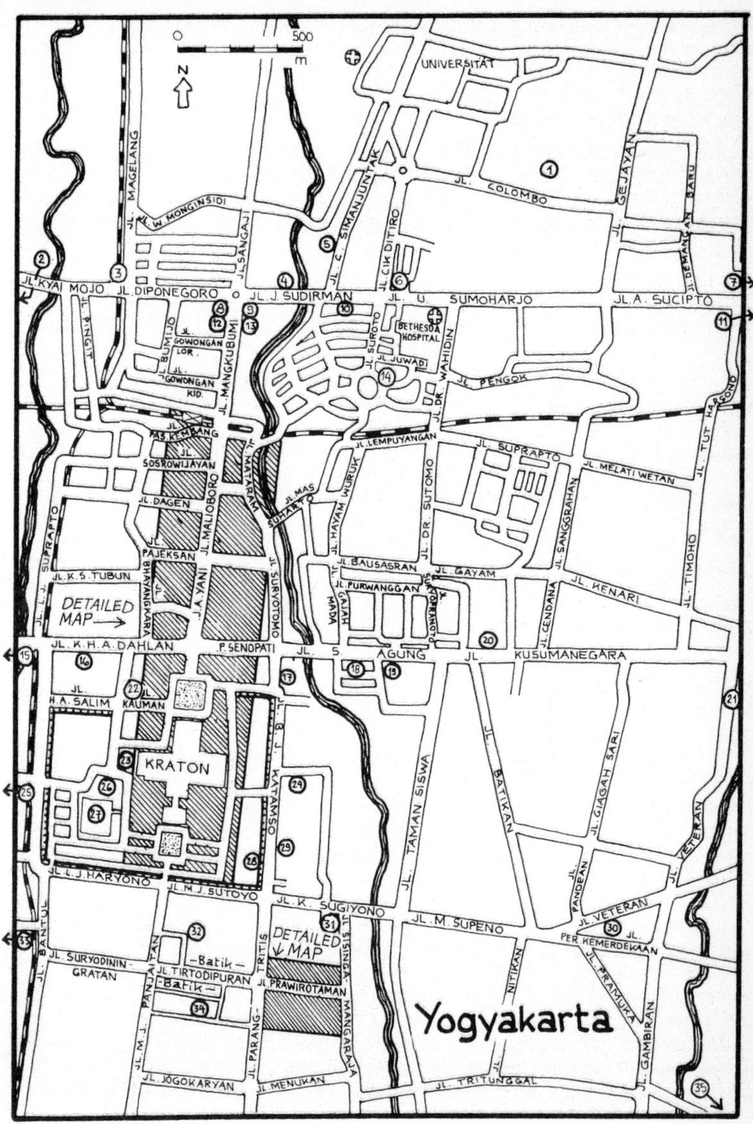
Yogyakarta
0 500 m
N
UNIVERSITAT
JL. COLOMBO
JL. GEJAYAN
JL. DEMANGAN BARU
JL. C. SIMANJUNTAK
JL. CIK DITIRO
JL. MAGELANG
JL. W. MONGINSIDI
JL. SANGAJI
JL. KYAI MOJO
JL. DIPONEGORO
JL. J. SUDIRMAN
JL. U. SUMOHARJO
JL. A. SUCIPTO
JL. PINGIT
JL. BUMIJO
JL. GOWONGAN LOR
JL. GOWONGAN KID.
JL. MANGKUBUMI
JL. SUROTO
BETHESDA HOSPITAL
JL. JUWADI
JL. DR. WAHIDIN
JL. PENGOK
JL. TUT HARSONO
JL. PAS. KEMBANG
JL. SOSROWIJAYAN
JL. MATARAM
JL. LEMPUYANGAN
JL. SUPRAPTO
JL. MELATI WETAN
JL. MAS SUHARTO
JL. DAGEN
JL. MALIOBORO
JL. HAYAM WURUK
JL. DR. SUTOMO
JL. SANGGRAHAN
JL. TIMOHO
JL. PAJEKSAN
JL. BAUSASRAN
JL. GAYAM
JL. K. S. TUBUN
JL. BHAYANGKARA
JL. A. YANI
JL. SURYOTOMO
JL. PURWANGGAN
JL. GAJAH MADA
JL. SUPADMOKOTO
JL. CENDANA
JL. KENARI
JL. L. J. SUPRAPTO
DETAILED MAP
JL. K.H.A. DAHLAN
P. SENOPATI
JL. S. AGUNG
JL. KUSUMANEGARA
JL. H.A. SALIM
JL. KAUMAN
KRATON
JL. B. J. KATAMSO
JL. TAMAN SISWA
JL. BATIKAN
JL. GIAGAH SARI
JL. VETERAN
JL. PANDEAN
JL. L. J. HARYONO
JL. M. J. SUTOYO
JL. K. SUGIYONO
JL. M. SUPENO
PER. KEMERDEKAAN
JL. PRAMUKA
JL. BANTUL
JL. SURYODININGRATAN
JL. PANJAITAN
-Batik-
JL. TIRTODIPURAN
JL. PRAWIROTAMAN
JL. TRITIS
DETAILED MAP
JL. SISINGAMANGARAJA
JL. NITIKAN
JL. GAMBIRAN
JL. M. J. PANJAITAN
JL. PARANGTRITIS
JL. JOGOKARYAN
JL. MENUKAN
JL. TRITUNGGAL
1
2
3
4
5
6
7
8
9
10
11
12
13
14
15
16
17
18
19
20
21
22
23
24
25
26
27
28
29
30
31
32
33
34
35

White walls, 4 m high and just as thick, form a square one kilometre per side, surrounding the complex. Once it was defended by a water moat and accessible only through five gates. Sultan Hamengkubuwono I had the palace built in 1755. Between the walls and the actual palace is a densely-built up residential quarter with narrow streets.

To the north and south these open onto two tremendous rectangular squares, *ALUN ALUN LOR* (in the north) and *ALUN ALUN KIDUL* (in the south). Coming from the north, you'll see the *PAGELARAN,* which is normally closed, at the southern end of the square. Once upon a time the pavilion was used for official receptions.

Walk past to the west and just a few metres from the main entrance, the Rotowijayan building houses a small *COACH MUSEUM.* The admission price of 100 Rp includes an English-speaking guide. You can admire 18 coaches (some are splendid) dating from 1761 to 1927. Made in Indonesia, Holland and Germany, all were owned by the sultans.

Hawkers with souvenirs mark the way to the first inner court of the Kraton, *KEMANDUNGAN* (Keben). Through the *REGOL* (= gate) *SRIMANGANTI* is a second court with the *SRIMANGANTI* (right) and *TRAJUMAS* (left) *PAVILIONS.* Pay 300 Rp admission. The admission price includes a guide who can speak English, German, French and other languages. Open daily 8:30 to 13:00 h, Fri and Sat until 11:30 h. Take your time, even if your guide tries to hurry you, in order to appreciate the many interesting details of the plain, wooden palace. Don't expect anything fantastic!

The instruments of the oldest *GAMELAN ORCHESTRA,* dating from the 16th century and once belonging to the Sultan of Demak, are still played once a year on Mohammed's birthday (Seketan) in the great mosque. It is housed in the *PURWARETNA BUILDING* to the right of the next gate.

Through this *DANAPRATAPA GATE,* which is guarded by two demonic figures (Gupala), you arrive in the *INNER KRATON.* The sultan still lives here with his large family and court in the western section behind *GEDUNG KUNING,* which is closed to the public.

In the west of the square *PLATERAN KEDATON,* the Sultan's Secretariat, boasts marble, chandeliers and mirrors - a unique mixture of 18th-century Javanese architecture and Victorian art. Beyond is the central *BANGSAL KENCONO,* the Golden Pavilion. Adjoining to the west is *BANGSAL PROBOYAKSO* in which the sultan's family resides. To the south is *BANGSAL MANIS,* the Sweet Pavilion. This is where state banquets were held, with musicians performing in the three smaller pavilions across the way. Past these you arrive in the eastern *KESATRIAN* section of the Kraton. This is where a number of objects belonging to the Sultan's court are kept, including wayang figures and the instruments of a gamelan orchestra which are played regularly at dance performances. In the last section of the Kraton is a *MUSEUM* with an ancestral gallery containing the sultan's family tree. In the *GEDUNG KOPO PALACE MUSEUM,* gifts of the second to seventh sultan families are displayed together with the sultan's throne.

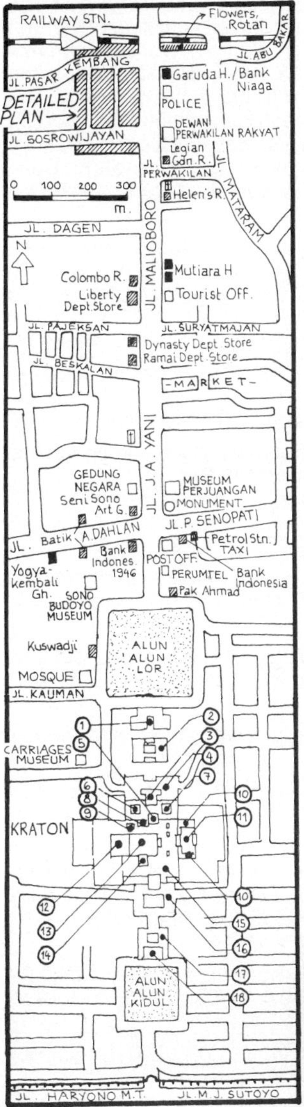

1 Pagelaran	7 Trajumas Pavillon	13 Bangsal Kencono
2 Siti Hinggil	8 Purwaretna-Building	14 Bangsal Manis
3 Srimanganti-Gate	9 Gedung Kuning	15 Plateran Kedaton
4 Kemandungan (Keben)	10 Museum	16 Kemandungan
5 Danaprapata-Gate	11 Kesatrian	17 Kemandungan Kidul
6 Srimanganti-Pavillon	12 Bangsal Proboyahso	18 Siti Hinggil Kidul

Have a look at *TAMAN SARI*, the Water Palace, southwest of the Kraton. A Portuguese architect laid the flower garden with its cool courtyard in 1765. Much was destroyed during the British occupation; little has been restored. Most of the buildings in the complex are reduced to ruins, leaving little indication of their former splendour. Among the ruins, within the 10 ha grounds, a number of one-storey tile-roofed homes dot the grounds. In the labyrinth of tiny streets you'll find many batik galleries and studios.

The northern section of the complex, the former *SEGARAN POOL*, is accessible without charge from the Bird Market. In the middle of this artificial lake were three buildings accessible by boat or through underground tunnels. The superstructure of these tunnels, which has been restored, uses shafts to provide air and light. The large *KENONGO BUILDING* was used for show. The smaller *GEDUNG CEMETI* to the south was probably used as a dining hall. The interesting round building, *SUMUR GEMULING*, was probably a mosque.

The entrance to the restored *UMBUL BINANGUN*, the fountain of youth, is in the southeast, 200 Rp admission. The decorative stone masonry can still be seen, particularly in the *GEDUNG GAPURA AGUNG* building behind the three bathing pools. The adjoining southern district, with the sultan's chambers is mostly destroyed.

Near the water palace is the *BIRD MARKET*. The narrow pathways are crowded with cages hanging from trees and houses. Inside are tropical birds for sale.

In the *SONOBUNDOYO MUSEUM,* Jl.Trikora 2, located in the north west part of the great square, you can get a good idea of Javanese culture. The first rooms are devoted to ancient times - stone statues from Wonosari, bronze drums, and metal weapons from Nusa Tenggara Timur. Islamic art, from the Majapahit Empire to more recent calligraphy, is exhibited in the next room. The strength of the exhibition is a collection of wayang kulit (shadow-play figures), wayang golek (carved wooden stick puppets) and wayang topeng (masks). There are also exhibits of batik, central Javanese and Balinese art. Open Tues-Thurs 8:00-13:30 h, Fri till 10:30 h, Sat & Sun till 11:30 h, admission 200 Rp.

Continue walking north, cross the big street towards Jl.Malioboro. On the right, behind the war memorial, is *MUSEUM PERJUANGAN* in the former Benteng (= fort) Vredeburg. Open Sat & Sun 9:00-14:00 h, admission 200 Rp. The small museum, in which the story of Yogyakarta is depicted in 30 diorama, is situated in a Dutch colonial building, once used as a military headquarters.

In the army museum, *MUSEUM ANGKATAN DARAT,* Jl.Sudirman corner of Jl.Cikditiro, Bintaran Wetan, the history of the revolution is told. There are exhibits from the days of resistance against the Dutch from 1945-1949.

Plants and stuffed animals from every part of the archipelago can be seen in *MUSEUM BIOLOGI,* Jl.Sultan Agung 22 (admission 100 Rp).

ART & CULTURE

WAYANG KULIT

The traditional shadow play using figures made of perforated leather can be seen performed in many places in Yogyakarta - along with the manufacturing of the puppets. Performances are held:

AGASTYA ART INSTITUTE, Jl.Gedong Kiwo Md.3 / 221 daily except Sat from 15:00 to 17:00 h, admission 1600 Rp. Men are also trained here as *'dalang',* masters of wayang kulit.

AMBAR BUDAYA (in the craft centre), Jl.Adisucipto; Mon, Wed, and Sat from 21:30 to 22:30 h, admission 1600 Rp.

ARJUNA PLAZA HOTEL, Jl.Mangkubumi 43; Tues 19.00 to 21.00 h. Admission 2000 Rp.

SITI HINGGIL KIDUL (southern Alun Alun) is held every second Saturday of the month from 21:00 h until early morning. The real wayang kulit - unlike that performed for tourists - always takes about 9 hours or all night. The huge epics are performed without a break. Admission 500 Rp, 750 Rp, and 1000 Rp.

WAYANG GOLEK

Though more typical of West Java, those who haven't seen it yet can take the opportunity at AGASTYA ART INSTITUTE, Jl.Gedong Kiwo Md.3 / 221, every Sat from 15:00 till 17:00 h, admission 1600 Rp.

NITOUR, Jl.Ahmad Dahlan 71, daily except Sun from 11:00-13:00 h (1600 Rp). Buy good but expensive puppets here.

ARJUNA PLAZA HOTEL; Jl.Mangkubumi 43; Sat 19.00-21.00 h, 2000 Rp.

GAMELAN MUSIC

Performed every Mon and Wed from 10:30 to 12:00 in the Kraton, admission 300 Rp. The music is an inseparable part of dance and theatre performances. The seemingly monotonous tone of the gongs, drums, and xylophones, accompanied sometimes by a stringed instrument, sounds very unusual to European ears.

CLASSICAL DANCE

Every Sunday from 10:30 till 12:00 (300 Rp admission) rehearsals of the classical Kraton dance school are performed in the Kraton. Observe the training as the children learn the artistically slow movements. At one time the court dances weren't allowed to be performed outside of the palace walls. Today there are schools outside, such as BAGONG KUSSUDIARJO on Jl.Wates, where to some extent, modern variations of the classical dances are taught. Also every Mon, Wed, or Fri from 20:00 to 22:00 h DALEM PUJOKUSUMAN, Jl.Brigjen.Katamso, admission 3000 Rp.

THE SHADOW PLAY

The wayang kulit performances are an important part of Javanese culture. Even during the pre-Hindu, animistic period, the forerunners of today's shadow figures were popular. After the death of important leaders one was able to stay in touch with him through a medium, the 'dalang'. Through the puppets, he was able to communicate the messages of the ghosts to the living. When Hinduism reached Java, the shadow play lost some of its magical functions but took on a new function by giving performances of the Ramayana and Mahabharata epics to the unanimous pleasure of audiences. Even today, however, especially in times of difficulties, wayang kulit is used as a means of communicating with the great beyond. The Hindu elements have survived Islamization. The 'dalang', at the same time story-teller, performer, and conductor of the accompanying orchestra, is held in high esteem socially. During the performance, he sits behind a white screen with a lamp above him to make the shadows on the back of the screen. The figures themselves are stuck onto banana stalks or thick bamboo, on one side the good and on the other side the evil figures. Before the performance a 'gunungan' (a triangular figure shaped like a pointed mountaintop) is placed in the middle of the stage; during the performance two such 'gunungan' are used to demarcate the edge of the action. The 'dalang' sits with his legs crossed behind the screen and for hours on end tells the story. He uses different voices for the heroes and the beautiful women to keep the audience in suspense, moves the puppets on the stage and shakes a rattle with his feet to underline certain action packed scenes. Dialogue between the different characters is always separated by the hollow thump of a wooden hammer. The story is accompanied by a gamelan orchestra sitting behind the 'dalang'. At traditional performances the audience is seated according to sex. Only the women sit in front of the screen and can see the shadows; the men watch from the other side where they can see the 'dalang' and the orchestra at the same time. For them the puppets are colourfully painted.

RAMAYANA BALLET

From May to October, on the weekend (Fri-Mon) following full moon, performances of the Ramayana epic are held in front of the temple ruins of Prambanan (Roro Jonggrang Open Air Theatre) from 19:00 till 21:00 h. Some of the most worthwhile theatre you'll ever see! The Tourist Office organizes a minibus there, return fare 2000 Rp. Admission: 1st evening 5000 Rp, 2nd evening 4000 Rp, and 2500 Rp for the last two evenings.

1st evening: The Abduction of Queen Shinta; 2nd evening: The Battles with Hanuman; 3rd evening: The Death of Kombokarno; 4th evening: The Purification of Queen Shinta.

Further performances are held daily from 20:00 to 22:00 h in the Sasanasuka Bldg.; THR - (Taman Hiburan Rakyat), 2500 Rp.

RAMAYANA

THE STORY OF THE ABDUCTION AND RETURN OF PRINCESS SHINTA

Dasarata, King of Kosala, had four sons by different women of his harem. When he grew old, he designated his eldest son, Rama, to be his heir. But the mother of Barata, a younger son, wanted to see her own child on the throne of Kosala, and she reminded the king of a long forgotten, though no less binding, promise. In this way Barata became king against his own will, and his brother Rama was sent into exile for 14 years. Together with his beautiful wife Shinta and his brother Lesmana, he lived in the woods of Dandaka - until Rawana, the demon king, discovered their hiding place; blinded by Shinta's beauty, he decided to kidnap her. He lured the two brothers away from the hut by changing himself into a beautiful golden deer. Shinta, who remained behind, was now defenceless against the demon who, changed into a giant bird, picked her up in his claws and carried her across mountains and oceans to his kingdom of Alengka. From the king of the birds the two brothers learned of Shinta's fate and decided to rescue her. Along the way they met the monkey general Hanuman whom they helped to recover his kingdom. By way of thanks, Hanuman decided to help Rama free his wife from the demon. He went to scout out Alengka and faced many dangers before he managed to discover Shinta in Rawana's palace. Due to the presence of the monkey general, a wave of fear went through Rawana's capital. Hanuman was taken captive but was able to free himself; he left behind a city in flames. Rama was happy to learn that Shinta was still alive. The opposing armies prepared for war. The first battles were won by Rama. Rawana, however, had been made immortal by magic. In the final decisive battle, Hanuman was able to break this spell and Rawana fell mortally wounded to the ground after being hit by Rama's arrow. Rama and Shinta then returned to their kingdom where they were happily accepted as regents after 14 years in exile.

SHOPPING

If you want a quick look at everything offered for sale in Yogya, all you have to do is take a walk up Jl.Malioboro. Street hawkers are ready to sell everything in the less expensive price range: leather sandals and bags, lampshades and wayang kulit figures made of stamped goat skin or cheap batik sarongs, shirts and other textiles, bamboo flutes, wood-carvings and, and, and. Spend a week or more here and you'll soon know many of the hawkers. Take the necessary time to bargain! Wares of better quality are to be found in the various shops. Late in the afternoon the batik women make their rounds through the losmen. You really have to bargain with them as they start with ridiculously high prices. They come almost every evening and sell printed and stamped batik along with other clothes, mostly from Solo. Lately they have been known to be charging rip-off prices.

WAYANG KULIT

Those who want to see how the figures are made should check out a wayang kulit workshop. You can observe the slow process of stamping out the leather, the fine painting and colouring, and the fastening of the leather to the horn sticks. New figures can be quite expensive; depending on size and the finesse of the work up to 50,000 Rp. Sometimes you get a good price on used wayang kulit figures - but not in the antique shops - rather in the wayang kulit schools such as:

SWASTHIGITA - studio and workshop, south of the Kraton in a small alley, left at the beginning of Jl.Panjaitan, Jl.Ngadinegaran MJ 7 / 50, very expensive.

AGASTYA, Jl.Gedong Kiwo MD III / 221.

MULYO SUHARDJO also produces huge leather screens in the same way as the figures but for prices to make a millionaire jump. Located west of the Winongo River on Jl.Tamansari 37 B.

LEATHER

Here you'll find bags of thick, light coloured leather (quite durable), shoes, and other leather goods which would cost at least twice as much in Jakarta. The leather factory KUSUMA is on Jl.Kauman, BUDI MURNI on Jl.Kusuma Negara. The various shops on Jl.Malioboro and Jl.Pasar Kembang are cheaper, however.

SILVER

The village of KOTA GEDE, 3 km southeast of town, is famous for its silverwork (bus no. 1 and 4, horse drawn carriage or becak 750 Rp). Tourist buses often visit Tom Silversmith. He is the most expensive shop in the village, charging on average 20% more than other shops. This village is especially worth visiting for those who want to see the people working - the filigree work is quite painstaking. Jewelry isn't sold by weight, making it rather expensive. In general, silver is more expensive on Java than in Thailand. A good place to shop for arts and crafts is the CRAFT CENTRE, Jl.Adisucipto (near Ambarrukmo Sheraton Hotel).

BRASS-WARE

is made and sold at PRAPTO WIHARDJO, Jl.Laksama Martadinata 29.

BATIK

Especially south of the Kraton, you can find lots of batik factories which will let you have a look at how they work.

BATIK

The white cotton cloth is first covered in certain places with hot wax so that during the dyeing process it will retain its original colour (in the beginning white). This waxing can be done by use of a stamp (for stamp batik), a paint brush or a fine wax container - 'canting' for hand drawn batik. Then the cloth is placed in a tub of dye for colouring. Next the wax is removed in hot water. Now new wax is placed over the already dyed portion of the cloth along with any parts which aren't to be coloured with the second colour. This process can continue until up to eight different colours have been applied according to quality. The fine hand batik is quite artistic and takes a long time to produce. The average daily wage of a batik worker in a factory is about 1000 Rp! The factory owners seem to be better off, as you can see from their modern houses.

In addition to cloth batik which is used for clothing and sheets, more and more batik artists are specializing in making batik pictures. Besides many modern motifs, themes are often taken from the Ramayana epic. The work of some Yogya batik artists is prohibitively expensive. Often they don't even do the work themselves, designing only the motif. The painstakingly fine handwork is done by women - especially the delicate work with the 'canting'. You yourself can take classes in several schools. Those who really want to learn something shouldn't just go to any young person for two or three days of the basics - find an experienced teacher.

BATIK LESSONS, not exactly cheap but quite good, are offered by the BATIK RESEARCH CENTRE, Jl.Kusumanegara 2. A three month course costs about 150,000 Rp (1987). They also have an outstanding exhibition which is open Mon - Thur 7:30-13:30 h, Fri until 11:00 h, Sat until 12:00 h. Intensive and informative batik classes are offered near the main entrance to the Water Palace (TAMAN SARI) by HADJIR DIGDODARMODJO, Taman Kraton KPIII / 177. Cost for six afternoons including materials is 23,000 Rp; three days, 11,500 Rp (1987).

BATIK FACTORIES: Check them out before you buy anything. You will learn something about the process of waxing and colouring and so have a better idea as to the quality of a batik. All the factories sell batik, but the prices are cheaper at the stores in town.

RORO JONGGRANG, Jl.Tirtodipuran 6a - hand drawn and stamped. BATIK PLENTONG, no. 28 and BATIK WINOTOSASTRO, no. 34 are the biggest factories on this street. Several other somewhat smaller factories are in the area. SURYAKENCANA, Jl.Ngadinegaran (in the same alley as SWASTHIGITA) is also one of the largest factories with a good selection in its salesroom.

BATIK PAINTINGS - can be found everywhere. Cheapest are the small shops south of the train station, though the best known artists charge more than 400 US$ per picture:

AMRI GALLERY, Jl.Gampinga 67 (behind ASRI academy of arts); Amri Jahya, one of the best known artists, prefers abstract motifs. Very expensive!

TULUS WARSITO, Jl.Nyai Dahlan 74 (mostly abstract painting though some landscapes and people).

KUSWADJI, Jl.Alun Alun Utara, Pojok Barat Daya. The pioneer of batik painting died in 1986. His children and some students continue his work and paint in the most diverse styles.

SHOPPING STREET

is Jl.Malioboro. In countless shops you can find antiques, batik, jewelry, rarities and junk - be sure to bargain! At the southern end is PASAR BERINGHARJO, a huge market where you can find food, cheap cloth, cookware, tobacco, herbs and many other things. On Jl.Dahlan are two shops selling quality batik often cheaper than at the factories: KEMBALI and RAMAYANA.

DON'T USE A GUIDE WHEN SHOPPING! *- Especially the ostensible art students will patiently show you the sights of town and, of course, bring you to the batik factories and galleries. There you'll automatically be charged a 20% surcharge which will later go to your guide - it is the same with the becak drivers. So don't let yourself be dropped off in front of a shop; get out somewhere nearby. Only go to shops when the drivers are out of sight. You'll get a much better price! People have also had bad experiences after being invited to eat some mushrooms - they are supposed to be magic but can be unpleasant!*

HOTELS

No other town in Indonesia has so many cheap losmen. Often the walls of the cheapest places are no more than plaited bamboo, the water has to be carried by hand from a well and every comfort is at a minimum. Many of these losmen can be found south of the train station on Gang I. *BU BURWO** with tea served free of charge day and night, family atmosphere. *LUCY'S** has rooms for the same price. *BETA** has the cheapest rooms without windows. *HOME SWEET HOME** is by no means more comfortable. Almost twice as expensive are *RAMA*** and *YOGYA***, but you get nothing for the extra expense. The same with the hotel *KARTIKA*** on Jl.Sosrowijayan. *HOTEL AZIATIC* ** at no. 6 has large rooms and huge beds and is safe. Also good is *HOTEL INDONESIA*** at no. 7. There are lots of hotels in this price range south of the train station - most on Jl.Pasar Kembang seem a bit overpriced. *HOTEL ASIA-AFRIKA*** at no. 25 has big rooms, with private mandi***. *PENGINAPAN 21*** at no. 21 has some very dark rooms so take one in the back. *HOTEL RATNA***, no. 17a is set back a bit from the street with quiet courtyard. East of Gang 1 are *MULIA KENCANA****, no. 15, has a courtyard and single rooms which are cheaper though the huge beds easily sleep two people. *ASIA AFRIKA GUESTHOUSE****, no. 11, and *CANDI***, no. 5. On Gang II *BAGUS HOTEL*** 'bagus' and clean; *LOSMEN SETIA*** and *LOSMEN GANDHI*** with nice courtyard.

South of the Kraton on Jl.Prawirotaman are several good wisma and guesthouses. Almost every room has a shower, bath, or mandi, plus a fan or ac. Breakfast is frequently included in the price. *KIRANA****, no.30, tel 3200, with ac****, simple, sunny rooms, includes breakfast, lots of antiques in the entrance hall. *PARI KESIT****, no. 24b, tel 3902, includes breakfast. *PERWITA SARI****, no. 23, tel 5592, its 'French Grill' restaurant promises more than it delivers. *ROSE GUESTHOUSE***(*)*, no. 22, rooms vary, some with hot water and ac. The rooms surround a quiet garden with a restaurant and swimming pool. *DUTA GUESTHOUSE***-*****, no. 20, tel 5219, a real Javanese house with lots of nooks and crannies, a restaurant surrounds two cool courtyards with a goldfish pond and swimming pool; upper price rooms are nicely furnished. At no. 18a is *SUMARYO****, tel 2852 and in no. 12 *WISMA INDAH****, tel 88021, friendly manager and nice personnel, fans, shower or bath, includes breakfast. At *SRIWIJAYA****, no. 7, tel 2387, mostly Indonesian clientele, includes breakfast. Two of the cheapest, but not the nicest, in the area are *PUTRA JAYA****, no. 4a, tel 5185 and *BOROBUDUR****, no. 5, tel 3977. *AIRLANGGA*****, no. 4, tel 3344 is a new, lovely hotel with lots of Sapto Hoedoyo art and a swimming pool, includes breakfast. *WISMA GAJAH***-*****, no. 2a, tel 2479 has rooms with ac, a swimming pool and a restaurant. The quieter parallel street to the south has more hotels including *PALUPI****, no. MG VII / 56, tel 3823, with a restaurant and small garden. *AGUNG****, no. 68YK, tel 2715, rooms with hot water, includes breakfast. There's a small pool in the garden behind the restaurant. In the two houses of *METRO****, tel 3982, across the way, you've rooms with bath, hot water, and a great breakfast. Nice people, motorbike rentals, laundry, taxi service, a safe. You can eat in the small garden under a mango tree. The opposite house has a large, clean swimming pool. Be careful: in some of the more expensive hotels, tax and service charges are added on to the hotel price.

On Jl.Malioboro 72 is the oldest establishment, opened in 1911, *HOTEL GARUDA*****, tel 88196, formerly the 'Grand Hotel de Djokja'. The stylish, completely renovated hotel charges US$50 and more per room. On the same street are the old and new wings of the *MUTIARA HOTEL*****, tel 3272, with similar prices and comfort. The new wing has a swimming pool. On the road to Solo is the best hotel in the upper price class, *AMBARRUKMO PALACE HOTEL*****, tel 88488.

FOOD

Lots of traveller restaurants in the cheap hotel district south of the railway station. Get your banana pancakes and omelettes at *SUPERMAN* on Gang I. Also not bad for other dishes - the place is usually packed. *MAMA'S* at Jl.Pasar Kembang 76 doesn't have quite as much selection and isn't as cheap as it once was - good avocado salads and sandwiches in season. The usual fare including steaks in *FRENCH GRILL*, and next door in *STEAK BURGER CORNER* on Gang I. Two old get-together spots, *HELEN'S* - now a fast-food place - and *COLOMBO* - large selection of Chinese and Indonesian food - on Jl.Malioboro, are now more expensive, but they still have some good dishes. There are good steaks and fish, but expensive, in *LEGIAN*

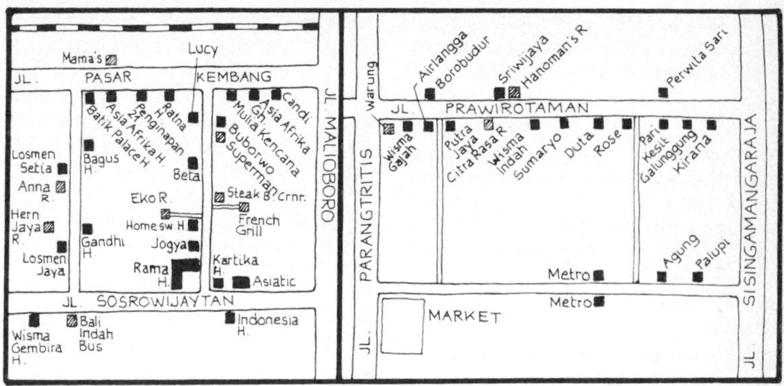

GARDEN RESTAURANT. You sit in the half-open 2nd floor of a corner house, Jl.Perwakilan 9, tel 87985, open 10:00-14:00 h and 17:00-22:00 h. A good Chinese restaurant at Jl. Brigjen Katamso 110 is *ORIENTAL* - great dishes for 2000 Rp. Famous even beyond the environs of Yogyakarta is the broiled chicken of *AYAM GORENG NYONYA SUHARTI* on the road to Solo, 3 km from town. The American variety of ayam goreng can be sampled in front of the Ambarrukmo Palace Hotel, on the same street, upstairs, in a supermarket: *KENTUCKY FRIED CHICKEN.* In the area of Jl.Prawirotaman, south of the Kraton, you'll find a number of hotel restaurants with limited menus. Plus there are *CINTRA RASA* and *HANOMAN'S FOREST PUB* where you can sit in the garden and enjoy a variety of entertainment every evening. These restaurant have compromised so completely with western tastes, that fans of real Indonesian food are sure to be disappointed. A cheap alternative are the warung at the corner of Jl. Parangtritis and Jl.Prawirotaman. There are lots of murtabak stands on Jl.Jen.A.Yani. Try cheap nasi rames in the warung and rumah makan around the People's Park - this is where the Indonesians eat! More food stalls can be sampled at the northern Alun Alun. The sate kambing and murtabak in *PAK AHMAD* are excellent. In front of the Arjuna Plaza Hotel and around the Bird Market, you can find cheap rumah makan - dishes for 500 Rp. The best soto ayam (chicken stew) is served in the warung along Jl.Laksmana, better known among the locals as 'Katipira'. For fantastic and cheap beef soup, even worth the long way, try *WARUNG SOTO PAK SHOLEH* in Tegalredjo, just beyond the turn-off for the road to Diponegoro Monument.

GENERAL INFORMATION

TOURIST INFORMATION CENTRE - Jl.Malioboro 16 (tel 2812 ext 30). Very competent people will give you town and regional maps free of charge, info on cultural events, and current tips on hotels and transportation, including a list of local bus routes and connections to Parangtritis and Bromo. Open daily except Sun, 8:00-21:00 h.

IMMIGRATION OFFICE - on Jl. Adisucipto, by km 10, way out of town on the road to Solo and the airport, tel 4948.

CENTRAL POST OFFICE - an old white colonial building on Jl.Senopati near the extended Jl.Malioboro (Jl. Jen.A.Yani). You can send a telegram or telex from the PERUMTEL Office behind the GPO on the road to Alun Alun. Open Mon-Thurs and Sat 7:30-20:00, Fri 11:00-13:30 h, Sun 8:00-12:00 h.

TELEPHONE OFFICE - for overseas calls is north of the rail-lines in Kota Baru, Jl.Suroto, get bus 2.

BANKS - near the Central Post Office is the BANK NEGARA INDONESIA 1946. Changes money Mon-Fri 7:45-12:00, Sat till 10:30 h. At Jl.Sudirman 67 behind the bridge is BANK DAGANG NEGARA and at no. 42 BANK BUMI DAYA, open except Sun 7:30-11:45 h, Sat till 10:30 h. Good exchange rates also in BANK NIAGA, Jl.Sudirman and in Hotel Garuda (open weekdays 8:00-14:00 h, Sat till 13:00 h). A money changer is open 8:00-22:00 h, next to Hotel Asia Afrika.

GETTING AROUND YOGYA

BECAKS

Bicycles dominate the streets making becaks the best way to get around. Tourists, of course, are charged much higher prices, so be sure to bargain before starting off! Remember, though, that the becak driver has to live too and pay rent on his vehicle - the usual price is (1987) 250 Rp per km. You can rent a becak for 500 Rp per hour.

HORSE DRAWN CARRIAGES

Sometimes you'll see them all, one after another in a long procession through the city, and you know that some travel agency has hired every carriage in town again to take two busloads of tourists for a quick spin. Mostly, though, you find them standing around on the road to KOTA GEDE (buses and bemos going to PRAMBANAN pass by the town to the north, right past Tom Silversmith - though many bemos refuse to let you off there). You pay 150 Rp per km for the horse and driver and you can fit three people in a carriage. The round trip costs about 4000 Rp per coach.

BICYCLES

A real alternative to public transport. Yogya is perfect bike country. Get one for 1000 Rp per day from the Aziatic or Kartika near Gang I. Remember that you aren't insured - not even against theft.

MOTORCYCLES

They can be rented across from the Asia-Afrika Hotel on Jl.Pasar Kembang for 6000 - 8500 Rp per day. You buy the gas. In the south you can rent them also at Metro Hotel, Jl.Prawirotaman.

BEMOS & COLTS

Only a few bemos service the town but usually not in the city centre (Kraton / Jl.Malioboro). Within city limits, bemos and buses cost 150 Rp, slightly more to the outer areas. Buses only operate till sunset. No. 2 runs between the train station and bus station, no. 1 and no. 4 from Jl.Malioboro to the bus station. Colt terminal at the shopping centre in Jl.Suryotomo.

TAXIS

A complete luxury in Yogya and totally unnecessary. You can find them on Jl.Senopati behind the central post office and in front of the big hotels. Airport into town costs 6000 Rp.

FESTIVALS AND HOLIDAYS IN YOGYA

The exact dates of the festivals change from year to year according to the Javanese or Muslim calendar. Ask for a *CALENDAR OF EVENTS* or *WELCOME TO YOGYA* at the Tourist Office.

SIRAMAN - The cleaning ceremony takes place during the first month of the Javanese year. During this holy month the sultan's heirlooms are cleaned and with great ceremony all the old coaches are washed. The cleaning of the weapons ceremony inside the Kraton is not open to the public. The water used for cleaning is said to have magical power.

GAREBEG SYAWAL - The end of Ramadan is celebrated famously in Yogyakarta. Things get started the evening before on Leparan Day. "Allah-u-akbar" resounds from buses, on the street, and from the mosques. Children parade through the streets with large, home-made paper lanterns. The next morning thousands of people assemble before the great mosque on the northern Alun Alun for prayer. Afterwards the sultan's splendidly-dressed troops parade from the Kraton in full colour via Pakelarang to Alun Alun for the Garebeg ceremony. A tall tower of groceries, the 'Gunungan', is carried to the mosque at the end of the parade for distribution to the waiting people.

SEKATEN - A week of festivities. At the beginning the entire gamelan leaves the Kraton in a procession to the Great Mosque where it will play during the week. At the end it returns to the Kraton just as splendidly with a ceremony in the palace. The palace guard, dressed in traditional uniforms and weapons, accompanies the procession. 'Gunungan', rice, vegetables, and flowers piled up in mountains as a symbol of affluence, are distributed among the population. The festivities in honour of Mohammed's birthday include a night bazaar.

WAICAK - The most important Buddhist holiday, in remembrance of the birth, enlightenment, and entrance of Buddha into Nirvana. During the full moon night, usually in May, practising Buddhists make a pilgrimage to Borobudur to celebrate the event with prayer and processions.

LABUHAN - The birthday of Sultan Hamengkubuwono IX is celebrated during April / May in different parts of the Yogya region. Quite splendid is Parangtritis where the Goddess of the Sea, Raden Loro Kidul, receives offerings.

LEAVING YOGYA

BY AIR

GARUDA, MERPATI and BOURAQ serve the airport 10 km east of town on the road to Solo. Offices: Garuda, Jl.P.Mangkubumi 56, tel 4400, 5184; Merpati, Jl.Sudirman 9-11, tel 4272; Bouraq, Jl.Sudirman 37, tel 86664. To the airport, take the bus to Solo, it's only 200-300 m from the main road. A taxi costs 6000 Rp. Airport tax 1400 Rp. SAMPLE PRICES: JAKARTA 60,100 Rp (GA only), BANDUNG 43,400 Rp (BO / MZ), DENPASAR 56,200 Rp (GA only), SURABAYA 29,300 Rp (MZ only), BANJARMASIN 89,400 Rp (BO).

BY TRAIN

The train station is downtown on the corner of Jl.Pasar Kembang and Jl. Malioboro. Tickets for the more expensive rides have to be bought a day in advance. Otherwise get to the station early - the waiting queues, especially at the third class window, are incredible.

BANDUNG: 3 times daily between 3600 Rp (3rd cl.) and 11,000 Rp (1st cl.). *JAKARTA*: 10 times daily between 4500 Rp (3rd. cl.) and 20,200 Rp (BIMA). Only two day trains (to be recommended is Fajar Utama Yogya) leave the city at 7.40 h (9200 / 6200 Rp, 1st / 2nd.cl.), all other trains leave Yogya between 17.00 and 23.30 h. *SURABAYA:* 6 times daily between 2900 Rp (3rd cl.; PURBAYA) and 20,200 Rp (BIMA). *JEMBER:* daily 6.35 h only 3rd cl. (ARGOPURO) for 2500 Rp.

BY BUS

The bus station, for short and long distance buses, as well as for local buses, is situated 3 km outside Yogya, near Kota Gede (Jl.Menteri Supeno / Jl.Veteran). Bus no. 2 goes to the train station, no. 1 or no. 4 to Jl.Malioboro. Take an express bus for longer distances. They leave Yogya from the various offices between 15:00 and 19:00 h and travel through the night. Buses north (Borobudur / Magelang) also from Jl.Magelang / Jl.Kyai Mojo. Colts to Kaliurang / Solo also from station Terban (Jl.Simanjuntak). - SAMPLE PRICES: MAGELANG 500 Rp, 1 h; SEMARANG 1300 Rp, 3 hrs.; SOLO 900 Rp, 65 km; AMBARAWA 775 Rp, PURWOKERTO 2000 Rp; CILACAP 2100 Rp, 4 1/2 hrs., 196 km.

There are several offices that sell tickets for express buses on Jl.Sosrowijayan and near Hotel Aziatic. SAMPLE PRICES: DENPASAR: 13,000 Rp, ac 19,000 Rp (Bali Ekspres, Bali Indah, Bali Cakrawala, Puspasari, Surya Indah). JAKARTA: 8500 Rp, ac 11,000 Rp (Limex, Muncul, Garuda and Yogya Express). BANDUNG: 6750 Rp (Bandung Express). BOGOR: 7500 Rp (Bogor Jaya). MALANG: 9000 Rp (Agung, Pemudi). SURABAYA: 9000 Rp (Agung, Kembang), local day bus 5250 Rp. Count on 14-16 hrs. to JAKARTA or DENPASAR.

DAYTRIPS AROUND YOGYA

BOROBUDUR

42 km northwest of town is the largest Buddhist temple complex in South East Asia. Take a bus to MUNTILAN for 400 Rp, then get a connecting bus to BOROBUDUR for 250 Rp. Admission: 300 Rp. Try to get there between 7:00 and 10:00 h because the masses of tourists won't have arrived, and you can enjoy the view of the misty landscape and the temple in the morning sun. Or even better, stay overnight - we recommend BOROBUDUR**.

The temple complex was built around 800 AD during the Sailendra Dynasty. It is thought that it took about 10,000 workers 100 years to complete this giant square construction with sides 117 m long. Whether it was built as a pilgrimage point or as a monument to Mahayana Buddhism is still under discussion. The Sailendra kingdom was destroyed in 856 by Hindu princes, and the majestic temple was buried by devastating eruptions of the Merapi for the next 1000 years. Borobudur lived on in the legends of the people, though, until excavation work began in 1814. In 1973 a mammoth project was begun with the aid of UNESCO to save Borobudur from decay. It took ten years to restore frescoes and to repair the foundations stone by stone - all in all about 25 million dollars were spent. A huge area surrounding Borobudur was declared a

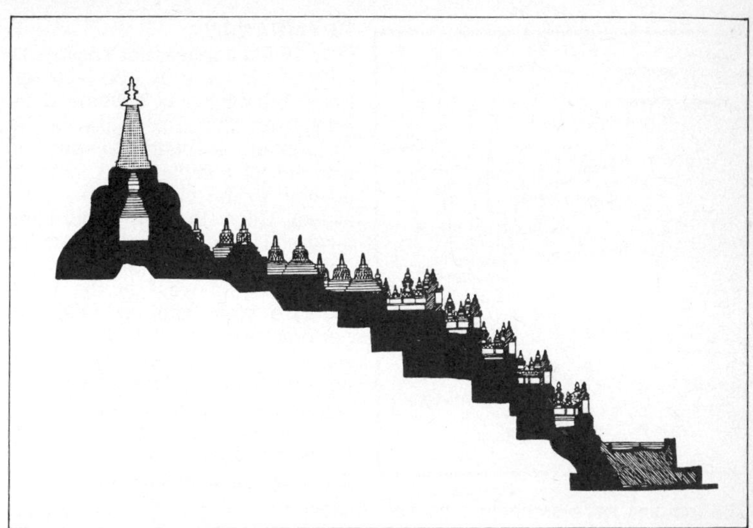

'Historical Park', and for that reason, whole villages had to be resettled. In January 1985 a bomb attack destroyed several stupas and it is thought that angry villagers were responsible for this.

Borobudur is a Buddhist giant stupa which on three levels represents the three parts of the Mahayana temporal existence: *Khamadhatu* is the lowest level of daily existence; the middle level, *Rupadhatu,* is the spiritual form; and *Arupadhatu* is the complete abstraction and separation from this world. During the climb one consummates the spiritual experience. At each level one finds almost three-dimensional reliefs showing many different scenes of Buddhist life on the various abstract levels. On the upper level one has reached Nirvana - the view across the rice fields and palm groves seems otherworldly, as do the countless Buddha statues, some sitting in small stupas, protected from the erosive tropical climate.

2 km down the way to Muntilan (before the bridge turn right for about 300 m) is the small PAWON TEMPLE which was first uncovered in 1903. It was probably an entrance temple for Borobudur.

Only 1 km further, just beyond the river, you'll find MENDUT TEMPLE, the temple in the bamboo forest. The outer structure is also from the days of Borobudur. In the dark inner rooms you'll find the nearly three metre high statues of *Buddha* (middle), *Lokeswara* (left) and *Vairapani* (right) - impressive monuments of Mahayana Buddhism. Next to the Mendut is one of the few Buddhist temples left on Java today. Admission to Mendut: 100 Rp. From here you can catch a bemo (250 Rp) back to Muntilan.

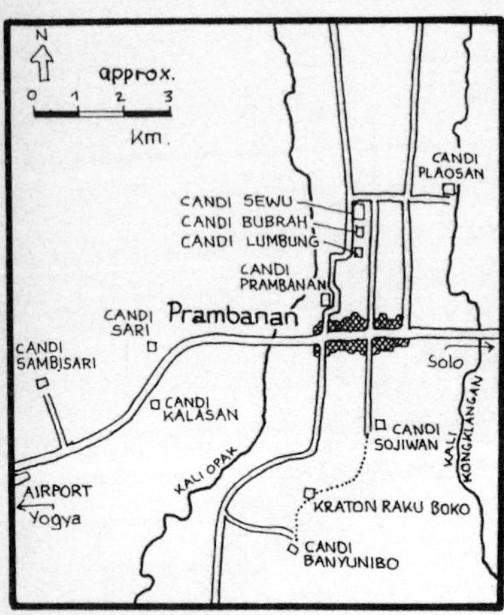

PRAMBANAN

Only 16 km northeast of Yogya - it's easy to get there by bus (400 Rp) from Jl.Simanjuntak towards Solo. Admission 200 Rp. Here, as at Borobudur, a historical park is planned for completion in 1992. In addition to the main temple, it will include Candi Bubrah, Candi Lumbung and Candi Sewu, further to the north. The grounds will include a museum, and west of the Opak River, a large open-air stage for performances of the Ramayana. During the months of May to October, mammoth performances of the Ramayana are held here. Under batteries of searchlights and supported by Japanese PA systems, up to 450 actors take part.

The temples were probably constructed at the beginning of the 10th century during the Hindu domination of Central Java. Through the last century the square stones were used for road building. In 1937 reconstruction was begun of the 47 m high Shiva temple. The complex consists of a total of eight temples and a number of smaller candi. The largest central temple is dedicated to Shiva. The Vishnu and Brahma temples are to the left and right. Opposite them are three smaller but well preserved structures called Candi Vahana because the middle temple is dedicated to Shiva's steeds.

Besides the main temples there are countless ruins of other temples - in all about 180 structures in the area surrounding Prambanan.

If you go bike riding or hiking in the area, children will often show you the way. Nearby are ruins north of Prambanan (CANDI KULON, CANDI SEWU, CANDI PLAOSAN). Or take the road south and climb the mountain to RATU BAKA, a former palace with a fantastic view.

North of Prambanan are the ruins of the tiny Buddhist temples LUMBUNG and BUBRAH. The Buddha statues are missing their heads. The buildings, which were largely destroyed, have been restored.

CANDI SEWU

This large temple complex is 2 km north of Prambanan. In the centre is a 28.5 m tall main temple with numerous niches and round arches, surrounded by 240 small shrines of the same construction. Two large stone Raksasa guards, armed with clubs, keep watch over the facility. Several shrines are being restored, although work is not yet complete.

CANDI PLAOSAN

1.5 km northeast of the Sewu Temple is this Buddhist holy place. It was probably constructed in 835 AD. The westward-looking entrances to both of the two-storey, 22 m tall main temples are guarded by demonic Raksasa statues. Originally, the central room contained a Buddha statue, while the two side rooms each contained a Bodhissattva. The two stone Bodhissattvas still remain but the Buddha statue is missing. The main temples are extravagantly decorated with reliefs inside and out. 126 stupas and 58 shrines are in three concentric circles around the main temples.

KALIURANG

In good weather, when to the north of Yogya you can clearly see the cone of the volcano MERAPI in the early morning, take a daytrip to Kaliurang, situated 900 m up on the slope of the Merapi. Take a colt (600 Rp) from Jl.Simanjuntak, about 25 km.

You can do some hiking around Kaliurang - on weekends the Indonesians stream up here, while during the week many school classes visit the waterfalls and swimming pools. From the playground (250 Rp admission) a steep path leads up to an OBSERVATION STATION, it takes one to one and a half hours.

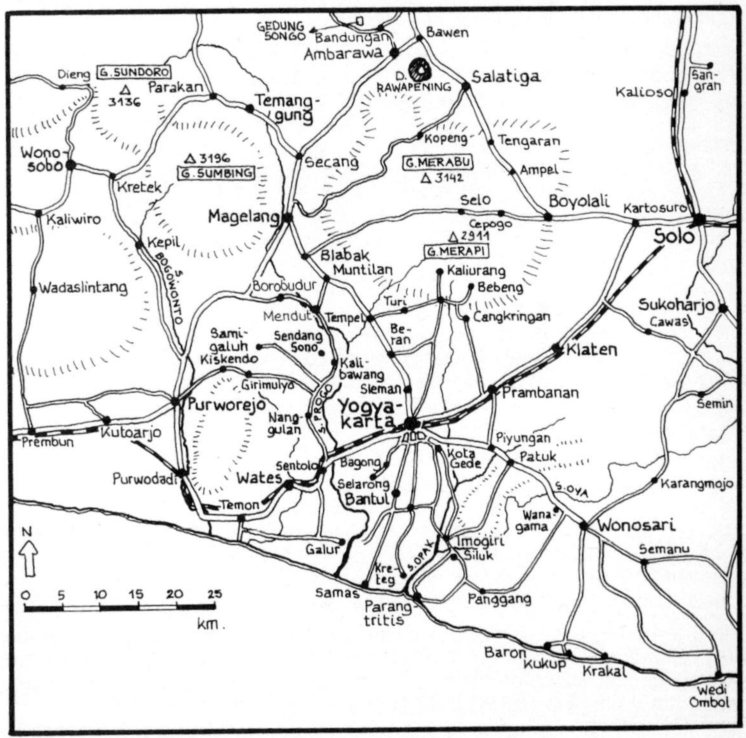

In clear weather you get a wonderful view all the way to the volcanoes of the Dieng Plateau.

In town there are several hotels such as SEDERHANA** - only two rooms, but huge beds; KALIURANG**, an old hotel on a hill with a good view of the valley though pretty run down; MERAPI**, slightly set back from the road in a garden; VOGELS* (they have a good map and info about the Merapi climb); GARUDA*, nicely furnished, people less nice, and BERLIAN***, 3 room flat with bathroom and balcony, lovely garden, good view, friendly people - situated next to the wide gorge.

GUNUNG MERAPI

The Merapi - fire mountain - does regular justice to its name. Every 5 or 6 years it erupts and there is almost always a white trail of smoke rising above its crater. Check out the pictures at the Observation Station of the last major eruption in 1954. Streams of lava burned their way through the valley - one of the largest eruptions shook Borobudur 50 km away! Many people die each year in Indonesia due to volcano eruptions; no wonder they are treated with great respect by the neighbouring inhabitants.

There are many possibilities for those who want to climb the Merapi. Here is a pretty good route. Get a bus to KARTOSURO (towards SOLO, 1 1/2 hours for 800 Rp). From there about 1 hour to BOYOLALI (300 Rp), then minibus to SELO (400 Rp). Spend the night in AGUNG MERAPI*** with hot water and a restaurant. You can hire a guide for the Merapi climb here, costs at least 5000 Rp, in groups calculate 2500 Rp per person. You are advised to carry a flashlight. Leave at about 1:00 h in the morning so that you make it to the top for the sunrise - an incredible experience. Be sure to take along food, water and warm clothes. From Selo, follow the sign 'Ke Merapi'. After 1 km on a passable road, a path branches off to the left leading steeply uphill. After 3 hours you reach PASAR PURBAR and in an additional 1 - 2 hours you reach the top. Via the route from KALIURANG (not via the Observation Station - Plawangan), on the opposite side of Merapi, you will need at least 7 hours. Procure a map for this route at Vogels (see Kaliurang). Since you must set out in the dark, it is advisable to walk up to the path the day before, so you can find the way more easily.

PARANGTRITIS

This is a beach on the southern coast of Java, 28 km from Yogya, notable for its grey sand-dunes (most of Java's beaches have dark volcanic sand). There are many dangerous currents, as on other south coast beaches. Take a direct bus from Yogya bus station (500 Rp). Head back early if you don't want to sleep in PARANGTRITIS; the last bus back to Yogya leaves at 18:00 h. Otherwise you can stay at one of the many losmen. There are lots of freaks here - especially during the mushroom (rainy) season.

There are other undiscovered beaches. ***SAMAS*** is a less frequented beach west of Parangtritis (30 km), easy to reach with a bemo for 400 Rp. There are simple lodgings. However, the beach is completely unprotected and very dangerous for swimming. ***BARON BEACH*** is 65 km to the southeast. Get a bus through lovely countryside to WONOSARI (40 km, 500 Rp) and then another

25 km along poor roads to BARON. There are two losmen by the bay, sheltered by limestone rocks. Sometimes the water is very cloudy due to an underground river flowing into the sea here. ***KUKUP BEACH,*** a small beach with light sand, is 1 km further east, accessible from Baron via a footpath. Because there are strong undertows, DON'T, swim here! ***KRAKAL BEACH,*** 75 km southeast of Yogya, is also accessible via Wonosari. Take the road toward Baron and before the beach, take the road off to the east, 7 km. There are plans to develop tourism along the kilometre of light sandy beach, surrounded by rocks.

SOLO

Those who can't take the tourist carnival in Yogyakarta any longer, who are willing to be fascinated by Javanese culture despite the lack of banana pancakes, should move on another 64 km to the east. Solo, or Surakarta, as it is officially known, is similar to Yogya but without the tourists. Both cities have been home to reigning sultans. Under Paku Buwono II, Solo became the administrative centre of the Surakarta Hadiningkrat Kingdom. While the neighbouring city of Yogya supported the independence movement of Sukarno and Hatta, the Sultan of Solo backed the Dutch. After the end of the war he lost all political power, unlike his colleague in Yogya who held the post of foreign minister in many post war cabinets.

KRATON HADININGKRAT (Sunan Palace) in the southeast part of town was built by the first ruler in 1745. At one time soldiers of the palace guard were trained on the huge Alun Alun Square in front of the palace. In 1985 the palace was badly damaged in a fire. You can still visit the museum. Admission is 400 Rp plus 200 Rp for a guide which you're required to hire.

Only part of the palace is open to the public because the sultan is still in residence here along with his six wives and 38 children, not to mention the 200 servants. In order to pay proper respect, one may not wear sandals in certain parts of the palace - either shoes or you go barefoot. Don't let your guide lead you right back outside after your tour. The cool and shady courtyard is a good place to relax. Next to the main building, which is decorated with carvings, is a tower where the sultan would meet the Goddess of the Sea, Nyai Loro Kidul, tête-à-tête. In another part of the building is a *MUSEUM* containing bronze artefacts, wayang puppets and several old sultan' carriages.

The museum is open Sat - Thurs 9:00-12:30 h.

You can get a good buy on batik at *PASAR KLEWER,* by the west gate of Alun^2 Square from 8:00 to 16:00 h. Countless stalls sell all kinds of textiles!

Batik women from Yogya come to Solo to buy batik because the biggest *BATIK FACTORIES* are here. *BATIK KERIS,* famous throughout Indonesia, has a factory on the road to Yogya as well as a shop at Jl.Yos Sudarso 37. Other batik makers can be found on the map.

Be sure to visit *PASAR TRIVINDU* on Jl.Diponegoro. Among the junk, arts and crafts, antiques, wood-carvings, brass and iron work, you'll find Chinese porcelain, old Dutch lamps and other things which, after some long bargaining, are cheaper than in Yogya or Jakarta.

Via Jl.Diponegoro you come to *MANGKUNEGARAN PALACE* which was built in 1757 during the second dynasty. Open Mon-Thurs and Sat 9:00-12:30 h, Fri till 11:30 h, admission 500 Rp. There is a daily tour from 10:00-12:00 h.

You enter the traditional Javanese-style (teakwood) palace via the southern entrance. In the centre of the large yard is a 200-year-old reception hall, the 'Pendopo', whose roof is still covered with traditional wooden tiles. In the southwest section of the palace are the instruments of a 17th century gamelan orchestra, which you can hear every Wednesday between 9:00 and 12:00 h accompanying Javanese dance. Adjoining the building to the north are the 'Dalem Ageng' rooms, used primarily for weddings and funerals. Official guests are received on the veranda 'Pringgitan', between the two buildings. Wayang Kulit performances are also held here. In the Dalem, show-cases display archeological finds from the ages of the Majapahit and Mataram empires. You can also see exhibits of weapons, masks, wayang figures, wayang beber scrolls, and other objects from the Sultan's collection. Prince Mangkunegoro and his family still reside in parts of the palace.

SRIWEDARI - the amusement park can be found west of town on Jl.Brigjen.Slamet Ryadi. No town of any size on Java can get along without this mixture of zoo, carnival, theatre and market. Wayang performances are just as much a part of it as music and dance groups. It's also a cheap place to eat in the evening.

The *RADYAPUSTAKA MUSEUM,* next to the amusement park, is open daily except Mon from 8:00-12:00 h, Fri until 11:00 h. There are weapons, wayang puppets, and a nice collection of old Javanese books and writings.

HOTELS

In the Jl.A.Dahlan and Jl.Iman Bonjol neighbourhood, you'll find several reasonable losmen and hotels. OK is *HOTEL CENTRAL**, Jl.A.Dahlan 32. Similar is *KEPRABON**, no. 14; or *LOSMEN KOTA***, Jl.Jen.Slamet Riyadi 113. There are lots of losmen near the train station such as *LOSMEN SAPTA**, Jl.Gajah Mada 182. South of the Kraton you can stay in an old Javanese house with a large quiet garden, old mango trees and many birds. Laura from Italy and her Javanese husband Hendra own *JOYOKUSUMAN GUESTHOUSE**, Gajahan RT9 / I. Or try *THE WESTERNER'S**, Kemlayan Kidul 11 (alley between Jl.Yos Sudarso and Jl.Gatot Subroto) clean place, friendly, helpful people.

FOOD

You can get good noodle dishes and mixed drinks in the restaurant *BHAKSO TAMAN SARI,* Jl.Gatot Subroto 42c. Good satay warung and restaurants at Jl.Yos Sudarso south of Jl. Slamet Riyadi. Ice cream is served at *AMERICAN BAKERY,* Jl.Slamet Riyadi, near Jl.Diponegoro. In *HOLLAND RESTAURANT,* on the same street near the market, there are good

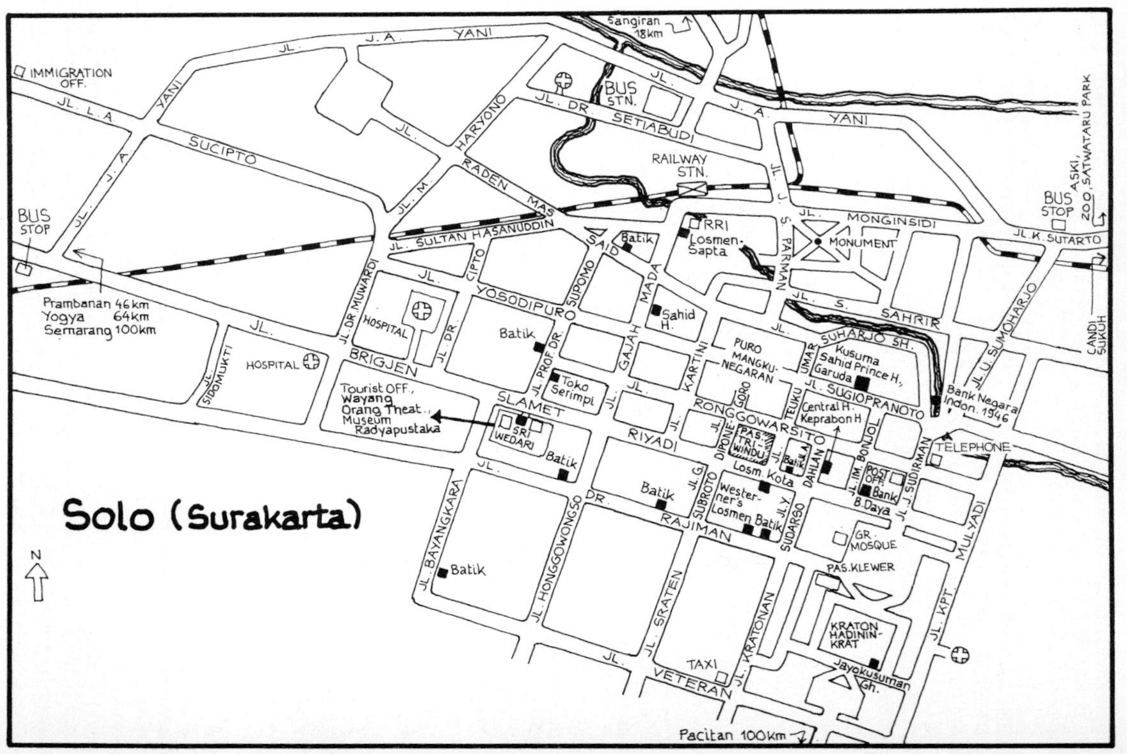
Solo (Surakarta)
N
Sangiran 18km
JL. J. A. YANI
IMMIGRATION OFF.
JL. L. A. YANI
JL. J. A.
BUS STOP
SUCIPTO
JL. HARYONO
JL. M.
RADEN MAS
JL. SULTAN HASANUDDIN
Prambanan 46km
Yogya 64km
Semarang 100km
BUS STN.
JL. DR. SETIABUDI
RAILWAY STN.
JL. J. A. YANI
JL. J. S. PARMAN
JL. MONGINSIDI
MONUMENT
BUS STOP
ASKI, ZOO, SATWATARU PARK
JL. K. SUTARTO
CANDI SUKUH
RRI
Losmen Sapta
Batik
SAID
JL. CIPTO
YOSODIPURO
SUPOMO
MADA
GAJAH
Sahid H.
JL. S. SAHRIR
JL. U. SUMOHARJO
JL. DR. MUWARDI
HOSPITAL
JL. DR.
Batik
JL. PROF. DR.
Toko Serimpi
JL. SIDOMUKTI
HOSPITAL
BRIGJEN
Tourist OFF., Wayang Orang Theat., Museum Radyapustaka
SLAMET
SRI WEDARI
Batik
KARTINI
PURO MANGKU-NEGARAN
SUHARJO SH.
Kusuma Sahid Prince H., Garuda
UMAR
TEUKU
JL. SUGIOPRANOTO
Bank Negara Indon. 1946
RONGGOWARSITO
GORO
RIYADI
JL. DIPONE
PAS. TRI-WINDU
Central H.
Keprabon H
Batik
K.H.A. DAHLAN
JL. IM. BONJOL
TELEPHONE
Losm. Kota
Wester-ner's
Losmen Batik
POST OFF.
Bank
B. Daya
JL. J. SUDIRMAN
JL. G. SUBROTO
JL. Y. SUDARSO
Batik
DR. RAJIMAN
GR. MOSQUE
PAS. KLEWER
MULYADI
JL. KPT.
JL. BAYANGKARA
Batik
JL. HONGGOWONGSO
JL. SRATEN
JL. KRATONAN
KRATON HADININ-KRAT
Jayokusuman Gh.
TAXI
JL. VETERAN
Pacitan 100km

bread, pastries, and other dishes, but not cheap. Enjoy a sate dinner in *RAMAYANA*, Jl.Ronggowarsito 2.

GENERAL INFORMATION

TOURIST INFORMATION at Jl. Jen.Slamet Riyadi 235, next to *SRIWEDARI*, tel 6508 - competent staff. Ask about cultural events. Open Mon-Sat 8:00-14:00 h.

CENTRAL POST OFFICE - on Jl. Sudirman. Find the telephone office some metres further north on the other side of the road.

DANCE PROPS - found in *TOKO SERIMPI*, Jl.Supomo, corner of Jl. Ronggowarsito.

WAYANG BEBER - the story is painted on a scroll or roll of cloth. During the show the scroll is unrolled by a 'dalang' as he reads or tells the story. Today this, the oldest form of wayang, has almost died out. In *KRATON HANDININGKRAT* (Jl.Baluwerti 80) you can visit an old master still at work today.

WAYANG KULIT - the traditional shadow play is performed every third Saturday of the month at the RRI (the local radio-station).

LEAVING SOLO

BY AIR

The airport is 9 km west of town. Airport tax 1400 Rp. Up to now only Garuda flies to JAKARTA (60,100 Rp), SURABAYA (26,700 Rp) and via Surabaya a flight to DENPASAR (69,100 Rp). Office in Kusuma Sahid Prince Hotel, Jl.Sugiopranoto, near Jl.Iman Bonjol.

BY RAIL

The train station is in the north of town - an extension of Jl.Gajah Mada. All trains to JAKARTA go via YOGYA. JAKARTA costs between 4700 Rp (Cepat 3rd cl.) and 17,000 Rp (Bima). Two trains leave daily for SEMARANG (900 Rp), two daily to BANDUNG (9700 Rp, 2nd cl. Mutiara Selatan), and four to SURABAYA (2500 Rp, Purbaya; 17,000 Rp Bima).

BY BUS

Bus station on Jl.Setiabudi. SAMPLE PRICES: YOGYA 900 Rp, 64 km; PACITAN 1200 Rp, MAGELANG 1200 Rp, MADIUN 1000 Rp, KEDIRI 1900 Rp, 4 1/2 hrs., SURABAYA 3000 Rp, 276 km, 7 hrs., JAKARTA 5200 / 7400 Rp, SEMARANG 950 Rp, 100 km, 2 1/2 hrs., PURWODADI 550 Rp, TAWANGMANGU 450 Rp, MOJOKERTO 2000 Rp.

To YOGYA: To save the expense of a becak to the bus station, take a city-bus (double decker) for 125 Rp from Jl.Jen.Slamet Riyadi to Kartosuro in the west of town. All buses to Yogya stop here.

DAY TRIPS AROUND SOLO

SANGIRAN

Near this village 18 km north of SOLO along the Solo River, remains of the so-called Java Man (pithecanthropus erectus) were found during excavation by archaeologists in 1891. This is thought to have been one of the earliest human beings. Some of the finds are displayed in a small museum. Take a colt, direction PURWODADI (250 Rp) until 2 km after KALIOSO, and walk the rest of the way (3 1/2 km) to SANGIRAN.

CANDI SUKUH

The temple at the foot of the volcano Lawu (3265 m) is located in the middle of a beautiful mountain landscape. It is dedicated to fertility. Due to its clear-cut reliefs showing intimate activity and phallic sculptures, sex education for the visitor is assured. First take a colt for 300 Rp to KARANGPANDAN, then a minibus for 250 Rp toward KEMUNING. Candi Sukuh is about 1 1/2 km from the main road. Admission at the branch-off 150 Rp and at the candi 100 Rp. Leave Solo in the morning for this trip. A two hours' hike (ask the way) gets you from Candi Sukuh to Tawangmangu.

TAWANGMANGU

40 km east of SOLO is the small village on the slope of Lawu. For people tired of the city, there is a recreation area with bungalows, swimming pools, and mini golf, all at an altitude of 1000 m. You can hike to a waterfall 65 m high. Staying the night is expensive - try PONDOK INDAH***.

Direct minibuses from Solo to TAWANGMANGU cost 600 Rp. If you want to carry on to East Java, go via CEMARA SEWU, SARANGAN (nice mountain town) to MADIUN.

EAST JAVA

East Java is the least touristy part of Java. Up until now, neither the city of Malang, with its colonial townscape and enchanting surroundings, nor Surabaya, with one of the most original sailing-ship harbours and duty free shops, have become meccas of tourism. In East Java you have isolated beaches, countless volcanoes to climb (such as Semeru which at 3680 m is the highest mountain on Java) and two national parks. One park, Meru Betiri Nature Reserve on the most southeasterly tip, is probably the last habitat of the Java tiger.

Unless you run into a group tour, you'll hardly see any Westerners, even in the "tourist centres". Madura, famous for its bull races, is only visited by a few foreign curiosity seekers during the championships. During the early local and regional play-offs, there are hardly any outside visitors. And imagine off-season...

"In the Pengantenan area we wanted to see a rounders game. When we arrived, the game was immediately broken off and about 200 people gathered around to have a look at the two foreigners. When we later said goodbye, there was clapping, shouting and waving from the whole group." (From a reader's letter.)

History enthusiasts will also be happy here. As the central Javanese Mataram Kingdom began to lose its influence, Kediri and Singosari gained both reputation and respect. During the 10th century, trade flourished with the neighbouring islands, and East Javanese artists developed their own cultural style - the first buds of the Indonesian cultural flower. The great Hindu epics were altered to fit in with Javanese culture. Many structures and temples were built - though later than those in Central Java. You can find relics and ruins in many parts of East Java.

SURABAYA

The Surabaya region is the most important industrial centre outside Jakarta, and 3 million of the 32 million inhabitants of the province live here. Indonesia's second largest city lives off industry and its harbour. Huge factories, producing steel, refining sugar and turning out more and more consumer goods, dominate the outskirts of the city. The city itself, with a few relics of the past Dutch presence, consists almost entirely of modern buildings. Following World War II the famous battle of Surabaya took place here as British troops, fighting the young Indonesian Republic, bombed the city to rubble and ashes with air and artillery attacks. Today, modern shopping centres, à la Singapore, luxury hotels and show-case administrative buildings, have taken hold. Even if Surabaya isn't a great place to relax, it is still an important junction through which many travellers pass. Certainly it is worth a one or two day stay. And it is a good base for excursions into the surrounding countryside.

Even the shortest visit should include a look at *TANJUNG PERAK HARBOUR*. On Jl.Basuki Rahmat you can get city bus no. 1 from in front of Bank Bumi Daya to the harbour for 150 Rp. The big harbour west of the lighthouse isn't open to the public. Best bet is to take the bus to the last stop and walk to the nearby ferry to Madura. Every half hour a ship leaves from here to Kamal (400 Rp). On the long street by the river you can see the interesting part of the harbour. Behind the warehouses, huge Macassar schooners are loaded and unloaded. It is fascinating to watch the activities on and off ship. Unlike the sailing ship harbour in Jakarta, there are hardly any tourists. If you want to take pictures, you need permission from the harbourmaster because every Indonesian port is a military installation. Normally, though, nobody bothers to ask. As in Jakarta, you can talk to a ship's captain about passage to Kalimantan or elsewhere. Only something for hardy male souls, and officially prohibited since the founding of the new Pelni Line! That is why schooner captains pick up their passengers under cover of darkness at some obscure coastal village. Substantial sums of money have to change hands if a police patrol boat appears.

Across from the modern building which houses the provincial government is the *HEROES MEMORIAL*, a tall, white obelisk, in remembrance of the battle of Surabaya in October 1945. Only by use of superior weapons and battle hardened troops were the British able to defeat the Indonesian forces. Because there weren't any Dutch troops in the Far East after the Japanese capitulation, the British wanted to disarm the remaining Japanese soldiers. The commanding Japanese admiral did surrender his army to the allied forces, but, as he sympathized with the Indonesian revolution, he surrendered the weapons to the Indonesians. It was an explosive situation when the British landed their troops. Soon fighting broke out.

From here, head north to the former 'European Quarter' stretching to Jl.Indrapura. On Jl.Pahlawan and its extension to Jembatan Merah Bridge, a number of prestigious colonial buildings are being restored. Even if you don't plan to send or pick up mail, take a peek inside the General Post Office - lovely inte-

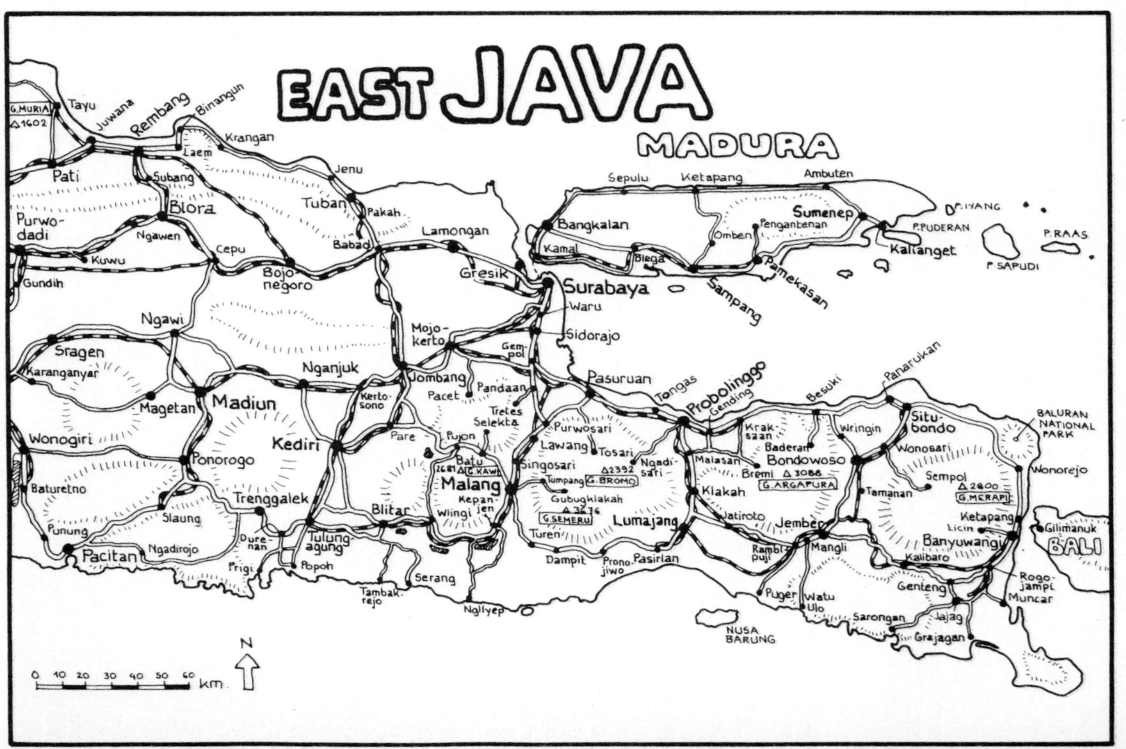
EAST JAVA
MADURA
G. MURIA
Δ1602
Tayu
Juwana
Rembang
Binangun
Krangan
Laem
Pati
Subang
Blora
Jenu
Tuban
Pakah
Purwo-
dadi
Ngawen
Kuwu
Cepu
Gundih
Bojo-
negoro
Babad
Lamongan
Gresik
Surabaya
Waru
Sidorajo
Sepulu
Ketapang
Ambuten
Bangkalan
Kamal
Blega
Omben
Pengantenan
Sumenep
Sampang
Pamekasan
Kalianget
P. PUDERAN
P. IYANG
P. SAPUDI
P. RAAS
Ngawi
Sragen
Karanganyar
Magetan
Madiun
Nganjuk
Mojo-
kerto
Jombang
Kerto-
sono
Gem-
pol
Pacet
Pandaan
Tretes
Selekta
Pasuruan
Tongas
Probolinggo
Gending
Besuki
Panarukan
Wonogiri
Ponorogo
Kediri
Pare
Pujon
Batu
2681 Δ G. KAWI
Malang
Kepan-
jen
Wlingi
Purwosari
Lawang
Tosari
Singosari
Δ2392
Ngadi-
sari
Tumpang
G. BROMO
Gubugklakah
Δ3676
G. SEMERU
Turen
Lumajang
Dampit
Prono-
jiwo
Pasirian
Baturetno
Slaung
Trenggalek
Punung
Pacitan
Ngadirojo
Dure-
nan
Prigi
Tulung-
agung
Popoh
Blitar
Tambak-
rejo
Serang
Ngliyep
Krak-
saan
Malasan
Baderan
Bremi
Bondowoso
Δ3088
G. ARGAPURA
Klakah
Jatiroto
Rambi-
puji
Jember
Mangli
Puger
Watu
Ulo
NUSA
BARUNG
Wringin
Situ-
bondo
Wonosari
Sempol
Tamanan
Δ2800
G. MERAPI
BALURAN
NATIONAL
PARK
Wonorejo
Ketapang
Licin
Banyuwangi
Kalibaro
Genteng
Sarongan
Jajag
Grajagan
Rogo-
jampi
Muncar
Gilimanuk
BALI
N
0 10 20 30 40 50 60 km.

rior. East of *JEMBATAN MERAH BRIDGE,* where the great battle for independence was fought, lay the bustling Chinatown, *KEMBANG JEPUN.*

Get a becak through the tiny streets to Sasak and the *AMPEL MOSQUE.* The last few metres through narrow Ampel Suci you'll have to do by foot. This is the old Arab quarter stretching all the way to Jl.Nyamplungan. People crowd past the wares on display. There are perfumes and dates, prayer rugs and wooden shoes, silk sarongs, scarves, veils, and other religious articles, standard in any oriental bazaar. The streets end at Ampel Mosque, which was built by Sunan Ampel, one of the nine holy wali. He died in 1481 and is buried in the cemetery behind the mosque on the left. Many devout Muslims make a pilgrimage to gather at his grave for prayer. The mosque is open daily until just before sunset.

It is worth spending an evening in *TAMAN HIBUNAN RAKYAT (THR),* Surabaya's people's park. The weekends are really most interesting. In front of the park on Jl.Kusuma Bangsa are some good warung which serve excellent murtabak. There are two entrances to the park - the smaller and cheaper entrance only offers admission to part of the park. If you want admission to the fairgrounds, you have to pay the difference. Go early because around 22:00 h everything starts to close. Many performances begin at 20:00 h. Have a look at the typical Surabaya *'ludruk'* theatre, where men play all the roles. It's fun for the whole family, and so noisy that even with a bit of talent in Javanese language, you won't understand a word in the last row. Tickets cost between 200 Rp and 500 Rp. Besides theatre, there are dance shows and live music from sentimental easy listening to hard rock. You'll find shops and stalls including a super cassette shop with stacks of tapes - and much more...

On Jl.Pemuda the Indonesian flag now flies in front of the former Dutch *GOVERNOR'S PALACE.* The colonial-style building with white columns still houses the office of the Governor of East Java. Across the way in tiny Apsari Park, next to the post office, walk past the memorial to the first governor of East Java to a much older statue at the back. Meditating here, without regard for the city bustle, is *JOKO DOLOG,* the Buddhist *'guardian of the new teak forest'.* The stone statue was first erected in 1326 for the last King of Singosari. The Dutch brought it to Surabaya over 300 years ago from its original site near Malang.

Unlike many other South East Asian cities, Surabaya really does have a nice *ZOO.* Check out the up to three metre long Komodo dragon, the babirusa (pig deer) from Sulawesi, the anoa (dwarf buffalo), and the proboscis monkey. The zoo (kebun binatang) is open daily till 18:00 h, admission 500 Rp, students 100 Rp. Situated in the southern part of town, get there with a bemo for 200 Rp or a bus for 150 Rp.

Just a few metres from the zoo, where the main road forks, is the *MPU TANTULAR MUSEUM,* an ethnographic historical museum. It features exhibits from the early Majapahit era, east Javanese wayang figures and batik, pictures from early Surabaya, and ceramics from China and Vietnam. There is also a technology department with Dutch ship models, German motorcycles, typewriters and sewing machines.

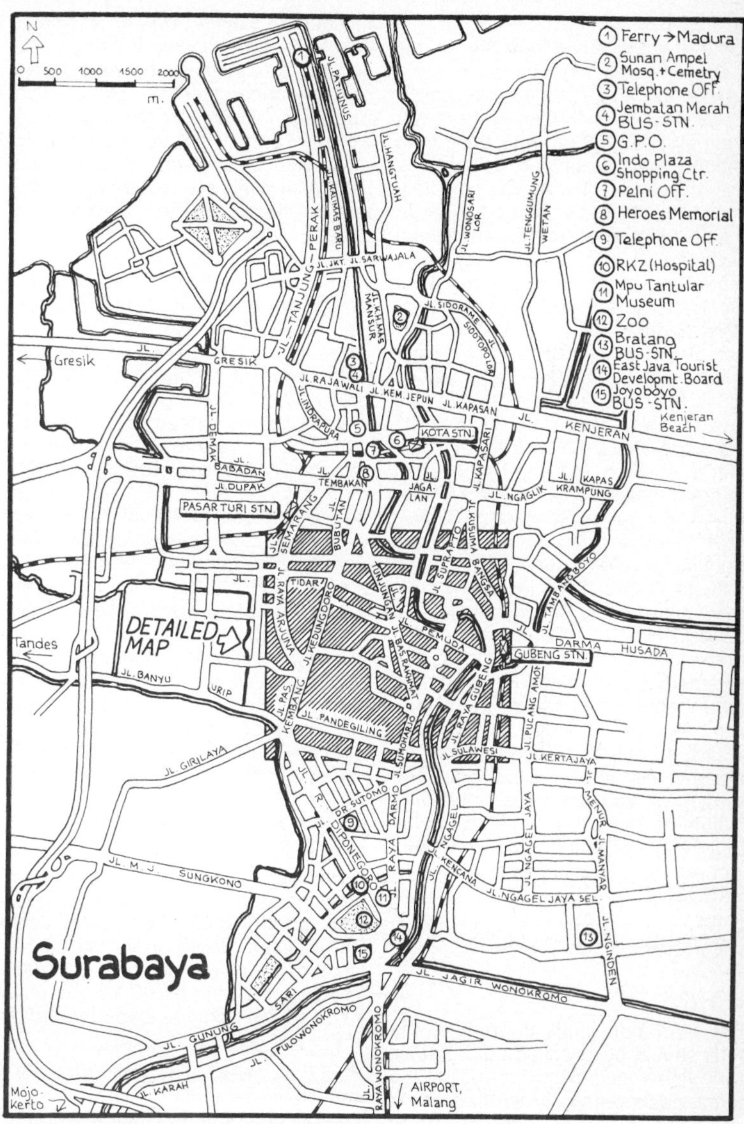

Surabaya
N
0 500 1000 1500 2000 m.
1 Ferry → Madura
2 Sunan Ampel Mosq. + Cemetry
3 Telephone OFF.
4 Jembatan Merah BUS-STN.
5 G.P.O.
6 Indo Plaza Shopping Ctr.
7 Pelni OFF.
8 Heroes Memorial
9 Telephone OFF.
10 RKZ (Hospital)
11 Mpu Tantular Museum
12 Zoo
13 Bratang BUS-STN.
14 East Java Tourist Developmt. Board
15 Joyoboyo BUS-STN.
Gresik
Kenjeran Beach
Tandes
Mojo-Kerto
AIRPORT, Malang
DETAILED MAP
KOTA STN.
PASAR TURI STN.
GUBENG STN.
JL. PATIUNUS
JL. HANGTUAH
JL. KALIMAS BARU
JL. TANJUNG-PERAK
JL. WONOSARI LOR
JL. TENGGUMUNG WETAN
JL. JKT. JL. SARWAJALA
JL. K.H. MAS MANSUR
JL. SIDORAME
JL. SIDOTOPO LOR
JL. GRESIK
JL. RAJAWALI
JL. KEM. JEPUN
JL. KAPASAN
JL. KENJERAN
JL. INDRAPURA
JL. DEMAK
JL. BABADAN
JL. DUPAK
JL. TEMBAKAN
JL. JAGALAN
JL. KAPASARI
JL. NGAGLIK
JL. KAPAS KRAMPUNG
JL. SEMARANG
JL. BUBUTAN
JL. KUSUMA BANGSA
JL. SUPRAPTO
JL. TAMBANGBOYO
JL. TIDAR
JL. RAYA ARJUNA
JL. KEDUNGDORO
JL. TUNJUNGAN
JL. PEMUDA
JL. BASRAHMAT
DARMA HUSADA
JL. BANYU URIP
JL. PASAR KEMBANG
JL. PANDEGILING
JL. RAYA GUBENG
JL. PUCANG AMOR
JL. SUMOHARJO
JL. SULAWESI
JL. KERTAJAYA
JL. GIRILAYA
JL. DR SUTOMO
JL. R. DIPONEGORO
JL. RAYA DARMO
JL. NGAGEL
JL. NGAGEL JAYA
JL. MENUR
JL. MANYAR
JL. M. J. SUNGKONO
JL. KENCANA
JL. NGAGEL JAYA SEL.
JL. NGINDEN
JL. JAGIR WONOKROMO
JL. GUNUNG SARI
JL. PULOWONOKROMO
JL. RAYA WONOKROMO
JL. KARAH

HOTELS

Some of your friends from the 'scene' in Yogya or Bali might be found in the *BAMBOE DEN** (sometimes called *TRANSITO INN),* Jl.Pemuda 19. If you come by train, get off at Gubeng train station - then it's only 15 minutes by foot. If you feel like it, you can help teach English. The front rooms vibrate with the sound of young Indonesian students at the Webb Language School which is always looking for new instructors. Another centrally located hotel is *PAVILYUN***, Jl.Genteng Besar 94, faded colonial atmosphere. North of the main train station on Jl.Stasiun, there are several cheap hotels, try *HOTEL STASIUN***. There are also a few places on Jl.Sumatera south of Gubeng Station. Not so great was *HOTEL GUBENG*** at no. 18. Far more pleasant is *GANESHA***, further down the street. Every room has a terrace. It is difficult to find because there isn't a big sign. A long, interesting history surrounds *HOTEL MAJAPAHIT*****, Jl.Tunjungan 65, tel 43351. The Dutch 'Oranje Hotel' was renamed the 'Yamato Hotel' during the Japanese occupation. In November 1945 the Indonesian flag was raised in front of the hotel, precipitating the Battle of Surabaya (see above). If you prefer a hotel with swimming pool, try *GARDEN HOTEL***** at Jl.Pemuda 21, tel 470001 (not to be confused with the new *GARDEN PALACE HOTEL*****, Jl.Yos Sudarso 11, around the corner). A double, however, costs 60,000 Rp.

FOOD

The murtabak stalls in front of the THR should be checked out before a park visit - inside the food is all the same, nasi goreng. Or try the warung in Kampong Sasak, near the great mosque, in Kayun Park, or in Taman Surya. In the shopping centres you'll find more foodstalls and restaurants of every price class. For example, in Tunjungan Plaza you've expensive Korean and Chinese restaurants along with Indonesian foodstalls and ice cream parlours - mostly on the 4th and 5th floors. Chinese food addicts should migrate to *PHOENIX* at Jl. Genteng Kali 15. More Chinese restaurants are near Jl.Pasar Besar. Diagonally across from the Bamboe Den is a bakery which sells croissants and pizza. The ice-cream is pretty good at a shop on Jl.Yos Sudarso. Cross Jl.Panglima Sudirman, several metres further south is a grocery store serving small simple dishes. Try broiled chicken in *AYAM GORENG JALAN PEMUDA.* Next door is seafood which you can select by the entrance, meals for 3000 Rp. For 8000 Rp (plus tax) the *GARDEN PALACE HOTEL* offers all you can eat in the buffet, twice a week. They serve great yoghurt on Jl.Panglima Sudirman, about 150 m south of Den. Another good ice cream parlour is *SWENSEN'S ICE CREAM* on Jl.Basuki Rahmat. Diagonally across, the American fastfood chain *KENTUCKY FRIED CHICKEN* has set up shop.

GENERAL INFORMATION

TOURIST INFORMATION - the local tourist office is at Jl.Pemuda 118 between Bamboe Den and Gubeng station, tel 472503. East Java Tourist Development Board, Jl.Darmokali 35, tel 65448/9. Open Mon-Thurs 7:00-14:00 h, Fri until 11:00 h, Sat until 13:00 h. They can give you the dates of the bull races in Madura.

POST OFFICE - The GPO on Jl.Kebon Rojo near Jl.Jembatan Merah Veteran is a sight in itself. If you are

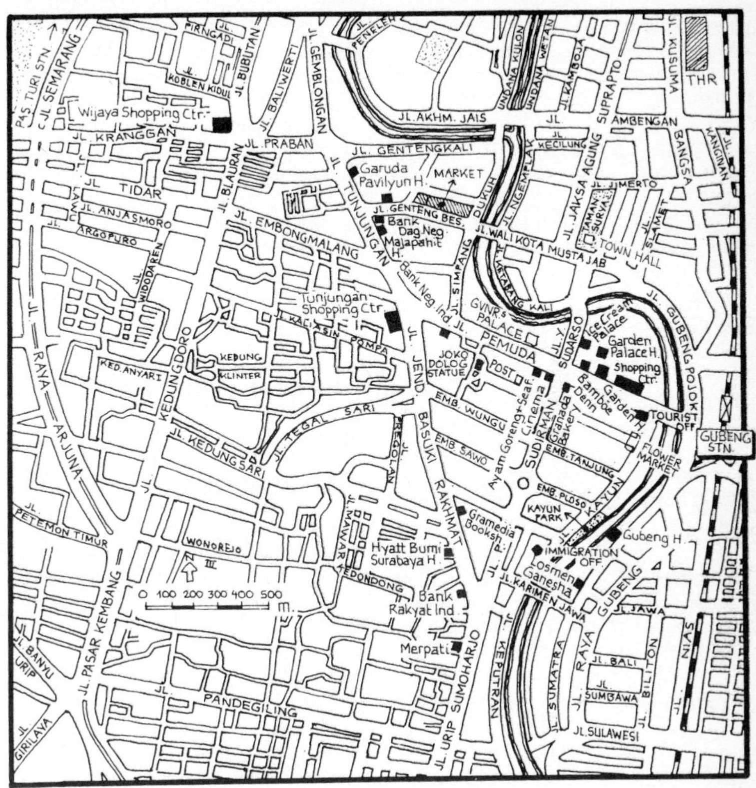

staying around Jl.Pemuda, then get a bus. Otherwise, there is a post office hidden by Taman Apsari on Jl.Pemuda. International phone calls from the Telephone Office, Jl.Garuda 4. Telegrams and telex at Jl.Veteran 1.

IMMIGRATION - south of Gubeng Station on Jl.Kayun 50, tel 40707.

HOSPITAL - the Catholic Hospital RKZ (Rumah Sakit V.A.Paulo) at Jl. Diponegoro 51, tel 67562 is modern.

PPA - Jl.Kutisari Selatan 13 / 39.

SHOPPING - best on Jl.Basuki Rahmat and Jl.Tunjungan where the big shopping centres (Tunjungan Plaza, Tunjungan Shopping Centre, etc.) give you a taste of Singapore. Within the marble and glass consumer palaces, Chinese enjoy their favourite pastimes - shopping and eating. Besides Indonesian firms, the big international fashion designers, electronics and car companies are represented. The supermarket chains Siola and Gelael offer a large selection of fresh and canned groceries, including western products. There are several book stores on both streets, but with a limited selection of English books.

GETTING AROUND IN SURABAYA

BEMOS - (Angkutan Kota) within the city limits cost 200 Rp, they run on 40 lines, but don't seem to have regular bemo stops. Just flag them down!

BECAK - cost about 400 Rp per km. Let them ride you through the residential quarters - good way to explore.

BAJAJS - loud, clattering, roofed three-wheelers, are the cheapest and fastest form of individual transport over medium distances. After bargaining, you should agree to a price of 500 to 1000 Rp depending upon distance.

CITY BUSES - they run on the main roads only. There are two kinds: Patas buses charge 200 Rp and are a bit faster than the double-deckers (150 Rp).

TAXIS - wait around the big hotels, they charge about 4000 Rp for an hour.

LEAVING SURABAYA

BY AIR

The airport is about 16 km south of town. There is a taxi service between the airport and city - taxi desk at the airport - costs 7500 Rp. If you walk more than 1 km to the main road, you can get a bemo.

Airline addresses: GARUDA, Jl.Tunjungan 29 (tel 44082); MERPATI, Jl. Urip Sumohardjo 68 (tel 40773); BOURAQ, Jl.Panglima Sudirman 70 (tel 42383); MANDALA, Jl.Raya Darmo 109 (tel 66861); CATHAY PACIFIC and BRITISH AIRWAYS, Jl.Yos Sudarso 11, tel 45052; THAI INTERNATIONAL, Jl.Basuki Rahmat 124-128, tel 40861.

SAMPLE PRICES: UJUNG PANDANG 98,700 Rp/83,900 Rp (GA/MZ-Mandala), BALIKPAPAN 103,000 Rp/92,700 Rp (GA/BO), BANJARMASIN 68,800 Rp/58,500 Rp (GA/MZ-BO), DENPASAR 42,400 Rp/36,000 Rp (GA/MZ-BO), MATARAM 54,900 Rp/46,700 Rp (GA/MZ), MAUMERE 124,000 Rp (MZ/BO via DPS), WAINGAPU 102,400 Rp (MZ/BO via DPS), KUPANG 142,600 Rp/128,300 Rp (GA/MZ-BO), AMBON 193,000 Rp/163,800 Rp (GA/Mandala), BIAK 285,500 Rp (GA), MZ every Sat via UP and Ambon 242,900 Rp, JAKARTA 88,500 Rp/73,000 Rp (GA/MZ-BO-Mandala), MANADO 196,500 Rp/167,000 Rp (GA/MZ-BO), BANDUNG 69,000 Rp/58,700 Rp (GA/MZ-BO), SEMARANG 33,400 Rp (GA), SOLO 26,700 Rp (GA), YOGYAKARTA 29,300 Rp (MZ).

BY SHIP

Surabaya is the most convenient place to get a ship to eastern Indonesia. PELNI, Jl.Pahlawan 20, tel 21041 - 21043. Tickets for tourists are also available behind the ticket window, so you can avoid the queue. Passage aboard the new Pelni ships is a pleasant experience; they are (still?) clean and well equipped. (See By Ship in the Jakarta section and Getting Around in General Information.) Every second Thurs the K.M.KAMBUNA sails via UJUNG PANDANG, BALIKPAPAN, PALU to BITUNG. On the trip back it departs Fri to TANJUNG PRIOK and MEDAN. The K.M. RINJANI leaves every other Thurs via UJUNG PANDANG (UP), BAU BAU, AMBON to SORONG. On the trip back it departs the following Fri to TAN-

JUNG PRIOK and MEDAN. The K.M. KERINCI leaves every second Wed and sails via UP, BALIKPAPAN, PALU, TOLI TOLI to TARAKAN returning one week later to continue via JAKARTA, PADANG to SIBOLGA. The K.M.UMSINI leaves every second Fri to UP, MANADO, TERNATE, SORONG and JAYAPURA, returning the Wed after next. The K.M.KELIMUTU leaves every second Tues to PADANG BAI, LEMBAR, UP, BIMA, WAINGAPU, ENDE, and KUPANG. Eight times a month you'll have therefore a straight connection to UP.

SAMPLE PRICES (Ekonomi/ 1st class; shortest route including docking): MEDAN 50,500/146,500 Rp (about 70 hrs.), JAKARTA 16,400/ 44,000 Rp (approx. 20 hrs.), UJUNG PANDANG 21,600/64,000 Rp (about. 24 hrs.), AMBON 42,600/129,900 Rp (approx. 67 hrs.), MANADO 55,400/ 165,600 Rp (approx. 50 hrs.), BALIKPAPAN 27,900/78,400 Rp (approx. 45 hrs.), JAYAPURA 84,600/257,300 Rp (approx. 130 hrs.), BANJARMASIN 23,700/56,900 Rp (approx. 19 hrs.), PADANG BAI 15,000/35,500 Rp (approx. 18 hrs.), KUPANG 55,400/ 136,300 Rp (approx. 110 hrs.).

BY RAIL

There are three railway station in town, KOTA, GUBENG (tel 40080) and PASAR TURI (tel 45014). Trains to Semarang - Cirebon - Jakarta depart from Pasar Turi. Trains to Solo - Yogyakarta - Jakarta from Gubeng (sometimes Kota) and trains to Banyuwangi or Malang from Kota via Gubeng. SAMPLE PRICES: BANDUNG: twice daily between 5500 Rp (3rd.cl.) and 14,500 Rp (1st.cl.); BANYUWANGI: twice daily 3200 Rp (2nd cl. Mutiara Timur); BLITAR: 5 times daily 1200 Rp only 3rd. cl.; JAKARTA: twice daily via Yogya and twice daily via Semarang between 6800 Rp (GBM Selatan or GBM Utara) and 28,200 Rp (1st cl. - BIMA); MALANG: six times daily between 1900 Rp and 800 Rp; SEMARANG: 3 times daily between 2300 Rp (Cepat 3rd cl.) and 17,500 Rp (Bima).

BY BUS

Most buses leave from JOYOBOYO TERMINAL near the zoo. Other buses going west leave from Jl.Rajawali. Express buses depart from in front of their offices. Kembang Express, Jl. Tidar 58, tel 42279 (accessible via the double-decker bus 9 or 10 from Jl. Basuki Rahmat / Jl.Tunjungan). Many companies have offices around the bus station. SAMPLE PRICES: SEMARANG 4000 Rp, YOGYA 5250 / 9000 Rp (Express), MAGELANG 4100 Rp, DENPASAR 7500 / 10,500 Rp (Express), SINGARAJA 9000 Rp, JAKARTA 12,500 / 16,500 Rp, SOLO 3000 Rp, 7 hrs., BANYUWANGI 3500 Rp, 6 1/2 hrs., PROBOLINGGO 1000 Rp, 2 hrs., PANDAAN 550 Rp, JEMBER 2100 Rp, MADIUN 1750 Rp, 3 hrs. and MALANG 1000 / 1350 Rp, 2 hrs. Direct buses run to LOMBOK (12,000 / 17,000 Rp) and SUMBAWA (31,500 Rp).

DAY TRIPS AROUND SURABAYA

PANDAAN

You can recover from the hot and humid coastal climate about 40 km south of Surabaya in several of the mountain villages dotting the slopes of the volcanoes Welirang, Anjasmoro, and Arjuno. Pandaan offers admirers of traditional dance a special attraction. On the full moon nights from May to October, Candra Wilwatikta, a great open air theatre holding 2000 spectators, has dance performances. Get a minibus from Surabaya or Malang for 550 Rp.

TRETES / PRIGEN / PACET

Just a few kilometres away from Pandaan is one of Java's typical mountain resort areas where wealthy residents of the major cities can be found on weekends. During the week you can bargain with the hotel owners. TRETES RAYA***, Jl.Malabar 166 has a swimming pool. Much cheaper is PRIGEN, just 4 km away. HOTEL SEMERU*** has complete 3-room apartments with bathroom and terrace from which you can enjoy the beautiful view. PACET is the neighbouring village to the west; it is a bit off the beaten path and not as well known. Located at 1000 m in the middle of paddy fields - wonderful view!

TROWULAN

The road to Trowulan is via MOJOKERTO. Take bus no. 550. A place for people interested in old Javanese culture. From MOJOKERTO, take the road to JOMBANG about 11 km to JATIPASAR. Outside the village you'll find Candi Wringin Lawang from the Majapahit period. In TROWULAN there's a museum containing objects from several excavations. It is thought that this must have been the centre of the Majapahit kingdom (11th to 14th centuries). Get a becak and enjoy a 3 hour ride to the temples, temple gates, bathing pools, and other excavation sites spread throughout the area.

MADURA

This 4470 km^2 island is famous for the bull races which take place yearly from August to October. The exact dates can be found at the Surabaya Tourist Office. At the end of harvest time, the elimination events take place at several locations. This process leads from district level competition to the finals in Pamekasan. But the island is worth visiting even for those who don't like to gamble.

Since the chalky soil on Madura isn't much good for rice, wide areas are covered with grass, making it good for cattle. The races on Madura aren't just for local entertainment; rather they play an important role in the breeding of the animals - only strong and healthy bulls are successful in competition. The festival begins early in the morning. Colourfully decorated and accompanied by enthusiastic supporters, each animal arrives at the course. After the spectators have been brought to the right level of enthusiasm with music, the races begin. Two bulls are hitched up to a wooden sled on which a 'jockey' stands or sits, trying to drive his charges across the 110-130 m long course. The first over the finish-line is the winner and is engulfed in the celebration of the excited bet winners.

Six kilometres from PAMEKASAN is the "eternal flame" (api abadi). Stick a stick in the ground and little flames will appear. The Madurese roast corn on the cob on this natural grill.

In SUMENEP you should check out the *KRATON* and the *MUSEUM* across the road. The great morning market is also worth a visit (near the mosque). The owner of the restaurant *17 AUGUSTUS,* Eddy Setiawan, has an interesting collection of old wayang topeng masks, Madura batik and other art objects.

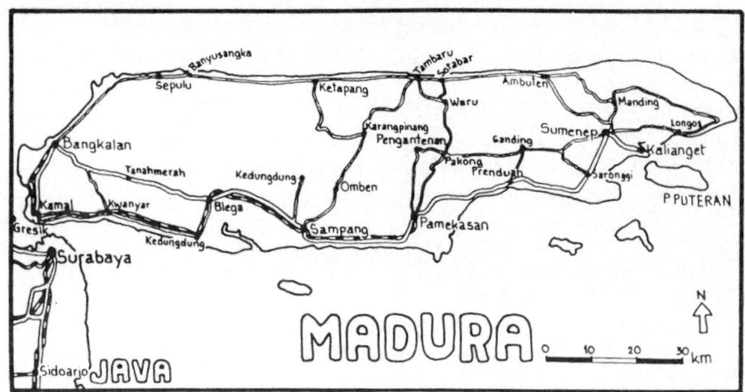

For a couple hundred Rupiahs - maybe even for free - a fisherman will take you in his prahu (artistically decorated with wood carvings) out into the ocean. Try one of the fishermen in SLOPENG, 21 km from SUMENEP, 500 Rp by bemo. A bad road runs to DUNGKE on the east end of the island. It takes 30 min. in one of the irregularly scheduled bemos along a beautiful coastal road. Lots of sandy beaches, for diving you need to go out in a boat, though.

HOTELS

In Pamekasan itself there are several cheap losmen. In the city centre is *HOTEL GARUDA* (formerly MERDEKA)** or *HOTEL RAMAYANA***, even cheaper is *LOSMEN BAHAGIA**.

In Sumenep, *LOSMEN WIJAYA****, Jl. Trunojoyo 45-47, near the bus station, the people are helpful, ask for Leong.

On Jl.Jen.Sudirman are *BAMAT**, *DAMAI**, and the old *LOSMEN MATAHARI**.

HOW TO GET THERE

Ferry and bus directly from SURABAYA to PAMEKASAN cost 1750 Rp. Every half hour there are ferries to KAMAL (225 Rp, approx. 30 min.). Buses Kamal Surabaya 600 Rp. Bemos take about two hours to Pamekasan and cost 1400 Rp. For those arriving from the east (Bali): ferry for 2500 Rp from PANARUKAN (near SITUBONDO) to KALIANGET on Madura. From here you can cross the island to KAMAL. Direct buses including ferry also from JEMBER 3850 Rp.

MALANG

Even though the Dutch left a long time ago, a lot of colonial atmosphere remains. At the *PASAR BESAR* a lot is going on in the early morning when different types of tobacco and all kinds of cigarettes are sold. This is a major tobacco growing area. Not far away is an old Chinese temple, *EN AN KIONG*. *MUSEUM BRAWIJAYA* at the end of Jl.Ijen Besar is also interesting - military history of the Brawijaya Division! Malang is a perfect base for taking excursions into the volcano dominated countryside.

HOTELS

A relative of Bamboe Den in Surabaya is in Malang: *WEBB**. Jl. Semeru 35, near Jl.Arjuno. Only dormitories. From Pattimura Bus Station get a bemo here for 150 Rp toward Dinoyo. Small but clean rooms in *LOSMEN SIMPANG TIGA***, Jl.Arif Margono 56, 1/2 km from the centre. There are several hotels near Pattimura Bus Terminal. 100 m up Jl.Kahuripan, try *HOTEL HOLIOS*** and at no. 9 *HOTEL MONTANA***, a simple Javanese house with a courtyard, family atmosphere, rooms with mandi and wc. The largest hotel in town opened under the Dutch, *PELANGI****, at the southern, central square, Jl.Merdeka Selatan 3, tel 27456.

FOOD

Many warung at the night market near the cathedral. Or try *TOKO OEN* on Jl.Basuki Rahmat which serves 'wiener schnitzel'. On the same street is also a nasi padang place. Opposite the big church - *CAFETERIA ANEKA RASA*. Chinese food in *DEPOT MUNCAL*, Jl.Basuki Rahmat 50.

GENERAL INFORMATION

TOURIST INFORMATION - Tourist Information (Pariwisata), Jl.Basuki Rahmat 11, tel 27411. The Local Tourist Office is at Jl.Tugu 1.

POST OFFICE - the GPO is at the southern central square, Merdeka Selatan. The Telephone Office is on Jl.Basuki Rahmat.

HOW TO GET THERE

From SURABAYA there are regular minibuses driving the 90 km route up to MALANG (1000 Rp). Or take a train for 800 Rp. Buses leave JEMBER (2200 Rp, 195 km) via PROBOLINGGO (1000 Rp, 90 km) or LUMAJANG (1200 Rp, 120 km). The last part of the route is through the enchanting countryside around Gunung Semeru. Further buses from BLITAR, 900 Rp and PANDAAN, 550 Rp. From the bemo station on Jl.J.Usman and at Pasar Besar, minibuses and bemos leave for the surrounding area. There is a regular Merpati flight JAKARTA-MALANG-DENPASAR and back again.

DAY TRIPS FROM MALANG

WENDIT

Get a bemo from Malang to BLIMBING, from there take a minibus to Wendit (300 Rp). It's a great place for walks. Near the village is a swimming pool with fairly tame monkeys.

TUMPANG / KIDAL

Take minibus from Wendit to Tumpang for 200 Rp. Before you reach the market there's a turn-off to the left that leads to Candi Jago. From Tumpang to Kidal you can either go by minibus for 300 Rp or horse cart. Both temples in Tumpang, Candi Jago and Candi Kidal were built in the 13th century. The numerous reliefs show traces of both Javanese and Hindu influence.

SINGOSARI

Just 12 km north of Malang is this town named for its temple, Candi Singosari. The temple, dedicated to Shiva, was built about 1300 AD. Two huge temple guardians are in two small parks west of the temple. Northwest of these two statues, on a clearing, rises a Buddhist stupa, Candi Sumberawa.

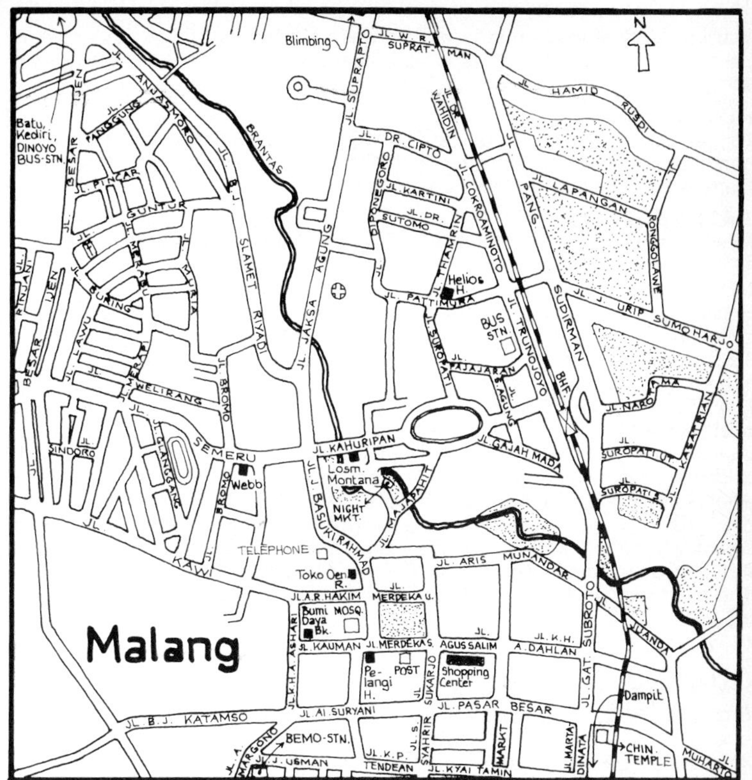

CANDI BADUT

Take a becak from Jl.Ijen or Pasar Orodowo to the tiny village of SUMBER-SARI west of Malang. From there iot is a 30 minutes walk to the temple.

BLITAR

81 km west of Malang - 900 Rp by bus. Stay the night at HOTEL SRI LESTARI****, Jl.Merdeka 173, or in PENGINAPAN AMAN**, no. 128. Be sure to pay homage to the tomb of the first President of the Republic, Sukarno. Since 1978, a marble bust adorns the grave of 'Bung Karno' who fell from power in 1965. Ask for MAKAM PROKLAMATOR.

A large and beautiful temple complex, CANDI PANATARAN, is just 9 km further on. It is one of the oldest Hindu temples on Java. Scenes from the Ramayana are portrayed on many reliefs. The complex is a bit difficult to reach. Take a colt from Blitar for 500 Rp, but they only run occasionally. Otherwise go by motor bike taxi for 1500 Rp return.

You'll pass many lakes on the way between Malang and Blitar. Karangkates Lake, which plays an important role in the water supply and irrigation of the surrounding villages and fields, is a good place to take a break.

KEBUN RAYA

25 km north of Malang, just before PURWOSARI (bus 400 Rp), is a 85 ha large beautiful botanical garden near PURWODADI you should visit. It features many kinds of palm trees (admission 100 Rp).

BATU / SELECTA

Minibuses leave Malang for the 1200 m high mountain village of Batu (450 Rp, 17 km). There are many hotels including MUSTIKA***, Jl.Budiono 2 or LOSMEN KAWI**, Jl.Jen.Sudirman 19. There are other night accommodations in Selecta, 7 km further up from Batu (colt 200 Rp, from Malang 500 Rp). Many sometimes fairly cheap losmen are on the road in the villages of PUNTEN and TULUNGREJO. These are cool, refreshing villages which offer a perfect atmosphere for taking walks in the tropical mountains on the slope of Gunung Arjuna (3340 m). Visit the park in Selecta with its rock garden and swimming pool filled with clear, cold water (admission 750 Rp). Take a minibus to the hot springs in SONGGORITO or walk (3 1/2 hrs). Hotels here often have a swimming pool and hot water mandi. From Batu take the main road further up. After 6 km in the village of PANDESARI (SEBALO) you'll come to a funny memorial: two black and white cows and a man milking them. Here a wide signposted path (2 km) turns off to a large animal park, and you'll face the 65 m high Coban Rondo Waterfall at the foot of Gunung Panderman (3037 m). The main road winds its way through varied countryside further via PARE to KEDIRI.

GUNUNG BROMO

Bromo (2392 m) is the most visited of all East Java volcanoes. The matchless beauty of the "sea of sand", the cone of the volcano, and the surrounding mountainscape with vegetables gardens on the steep slopes are all easy to reach without a lot of climbing.

The Tengger live in this isolated mountain world. When the Hindu rulers of East Java fled to Bali to escape the advancing Islam, the common people took refuge in the mountains where they were able to preserve much of their own Hindu tradition. During the 12th month of the Tengger calendar, the great Kasodo festival is held on Bromo. The fire god living in the still active volcano (last eruption 1980) holds the power of blessing and calamity. To honour and placate him, rice, fruit and flowers (along with chicken and live bulls) are thrown into the crater in a colourful ceremony.

In February the *KARO CEREMONY* is performed in Tengger villages to celebrate the creation of humanity by Sang Hyang Widi. Priests visit families in their homes where a ceremonial banquet is held. The festival begins with all the village men dressed in traditional costumes to dance the Tari Sodor. Finally, honoured heirlooms (pusaka) are blessed.

The landscape around Bromo is fascinating at sunrise when the cone of the volcano and the gray sea of sand are bathed in red light.

Remember that it gets quite cold up here, especially early in the morning. They do have thick blankets in the losmen, but you need a warm sweater or jacket for your early morning walks. A flashlight is also a big help, as you can then get around without a guide. Besides, you'll be able to hear the sound of the small Tengger horses as they carry the wealthier tourists up to the crater. On the way from NGADISARI to the crater you can bargain with the horse owners; the higher up you get, the cheaper the horses. If you go by foot you'll need

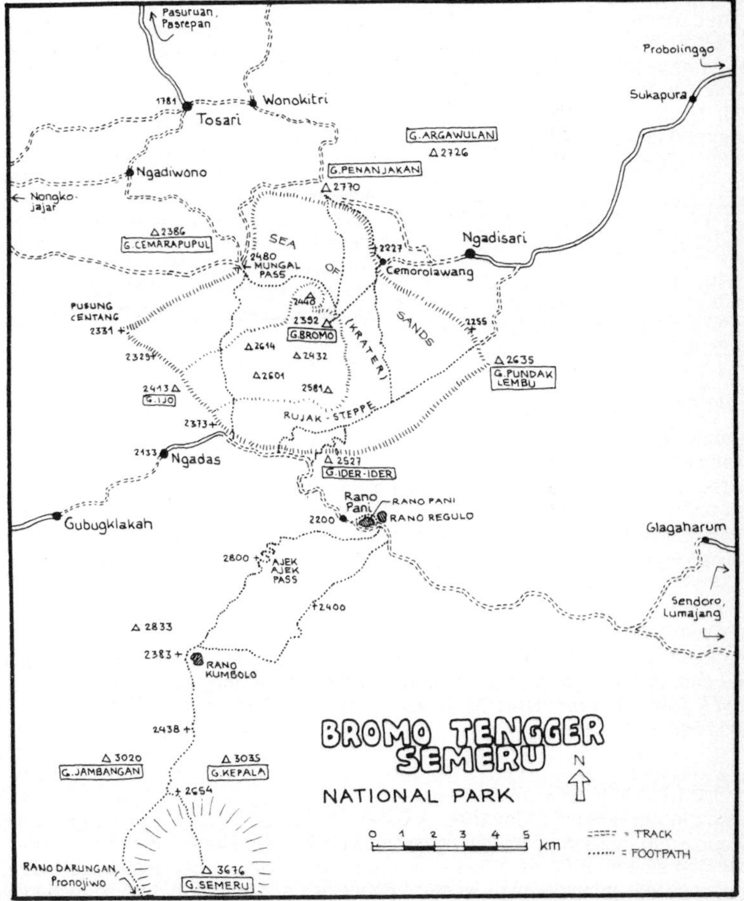

about 45 minutes (3 km) to the edge of the sea of sand, from there it's another 30 minutes to the cone. Leave about 3:00 h and you'll make it in time. Those who like the view can take other hikes through the sea of sand, such as to TOSARI (5-7 hours) where you can catch a ride back to MALANG.

HOTELS

If you have to spend the night in Probolinggo - the town doesn't have much to offer - try *VICTORIA****, Jl. Suroyo 1. Dormitory* and rooms of varied price categories in *HOTEL BROMO PERMAI II**-*****, Jl.Panglima Sudirman 237. Try to arrange your schedule so that you get to NGADISARI by evening. Many private accommodations can be found there, 2000 - 2500 Rp depending on the mood of the owner. If you want something better, go up to CEMORO LAWANG and try *HOTEL BROMO PERMAI***** right on the edge of the sea of sand. Normally group tours are housed here but if you hit it when it's empty you can often get in for a reasonable price. Cheap dorms* too.

HOW TO GET THERE

Take a bus or train to PROBOLINGGO. Buses from MALANG 1000 Rp, SURABAYA 1000 Rp and BESUKI 700 Rp.

It is 3 km from the train station to the bus station with a becak. Bemos to NGADISARI cost 1250 Rp. Sometimes the small vehicles are completely overloaded - 20 or more people with luggage is not unusual. Some sit on the roof, and it always seems like a miracle when everyone arrives safely. You can spend the night here or go on up the steep road to CEMORO LAWANG on the edge of the sea of sand. Don't take your luggage! Ponies cost 5000 Rp going uphill.

PASIR PUTIH

A relaxing place to rest up on the way to Bali is the beach at Pasir Putih. Few orang putih end up here, most visitors or vacationers are from Malang or Surabaya. You can go out to sea with a fisherman in his prahu, or just stretch out on the sand and watch Javanese beach life - much different than Kuta! In the evening, freshly caught fish are grilled by the sea. Don't come on a weekend when it's packed! Where souvenir stalls and restaurants crowd round a big parking lot, you'll have to pay 150 Rp admission - but the beach is long.

HOW TO GET THERE

Bemos and buses from PROBOLINGGO cost 900 Rp. Direct from SURABAYA 1900 Rp. From BANYUWANGI 1350 Rp.

If you arrive from Probolinggo, you'll pass several hotels situated between the road and the beach. There aren't any real cheap hotels; the least expensive is SIDO MUNCUL***.

BANYUWANGI

According to legend, a Javanese prince, who suspected his Balinese wife of treason and murderous intentions, drowned her in the stream of a river flowing from the slopes of Gunung Ijen to the east coast. Before her death, the Gods promised the princess they would present her angry and stubborn husband with a sign of her innocence. As her body was washed down the stream, a strong pleasant fragrance was released - a sign from the Gods! Since then, these waters have been known as Banyuwangi, "fragrant waters". The same name was also given to the town established at its mouth.

You can get a ferry to Bali at KETAPANG, north of town. The city doesn't offer much to those wanting to stay. If you have to kill time here, have a look at the mosque. Bemos to Ketapang 125 Rp.

HOTELS

Try to get to Bali without having to spend the night. *HOTEL SURI RAYA***, on the main street, loud; *MANYAR****, 1 km south of the ferry, poor but expensive. *SELAMAT***, Jl.Wahid Hasyim, tel 41359, diagonally across from the railway station, renovated, clean; or *BANYUWANGI****, Jl.Wahidin 17. Good is *BHAKTI***, Jl.Jend. Sudirman, tel 21129; and *BERLIAN BARAT***, Jl.Pattimura, tel 21323, near the railway station.

HOW TO GET THERE

By train from SURABAYA via JEMBER for 1800 Rp (3rd cl.) or 2400 Rp (2nd cl.) - the trains pass through PROBOLINGGO via KETAPANG.

Banyuwangi has a new bus terminal just for destinations in southeast Java and a city terminal for buses on the northern routes. To travel between them, you can get bemo line 1 for 125 Rp. From PROBOLINGGO via SITUBONDO (northern route) 2400 Rp, 190 km, 4 1/2 hrs. From PASIR PUTIH there are buses for 1350 Rp, from SURABAYA 3500 Rp, 290 km, 6 1/2 hrs. You can get off right at the ferry. From DENPASAR direct buses for 1200 Rp.

FERRIES TO BALI

Deck 300 Rp, Ekonomi 500 Rp, 1st cl. 800 Rp, motorbike 700 Rp, jeep 3700 Rp, car 5750 Rp. Ferries leave up to 16 times a day at 1-3 hour intervals.

JAVANESE WOMEN SELLING VEGETABLES

BALI

"Today almost everyone has heard of Bali. To some it means a smart place to go, one of the many ports in a round-the-world cruise; to others it brings mental images of brown girls with beautiful breasts, palm trees, rolling waves, and all the romantic notions that go to make a South Sea island paradise." This quote isn't from a glossy new travel ad or brochure, rather it was written over 50 years ago by Covarrubias.

At that time the island, discovered by sun worshipping white people, saw the beginning of a second colonization. Bali had already been conquered and plundered by the Dutch, but the systematic destruction of local culture began when the tourists came. At first there were just a few - there were only two hotels in Denpasar. Several painters settled in Ubud and, under the influence of local artists, developed their own style. Then, all of a sudden, came the age of mass tourism, bringing whole plane loads of people out to enjoy themselves in the exotic far-off tropics.

Now art is for the tourists instead of for the temples - cremation ceremonies for money instead of for the dead. People came to Bali to save their Hindu culture from the influx of Islam. But they were only able to hold out a few hundred years. What began with the Dutch will continue until the island is nothing more than a national museum for earning foreign exchange.

Most restaurants in Sanur charge the equivalent of a month's local wages - for a meal. Kuta Beach has been captured by the budget travellers. Here you'll find a carnival atmosphere which is slowly spreading north to the neighbouring Legian Beach. New beaches are constantly being opened to tourism: Nusa Dua for affluent hotel tourists, Lovina Beach near Singaraja for the freaks.

Only the island's interior has been spared. When the day trippers return to their hotels in the evening, you can find real Balinese life going on in the villages.

After a few days you'll know the men on the streets tending their fighting cocks with loving care. You'll be invited to cock-fights and tuak; join their parties and temple festivals. You'll get used to the village noises: the constant barking of dogs, the soft thump of the alarm drum, the strange rhythm of the gamelan orchestra, and the loud laughing of the children.

Discover Bali this way and you'll learn to love the island and its people.

DENPASAR

The largest city (about 300,000 people) and capital of the island since independence has practically everything that you'll want to avoid on the island: the constant noise of the unmuffled Suzukis, Hondas and bemos running up and down the one-way labyrinth of streets in town, the hectic bustle, and the stink of exhaust.

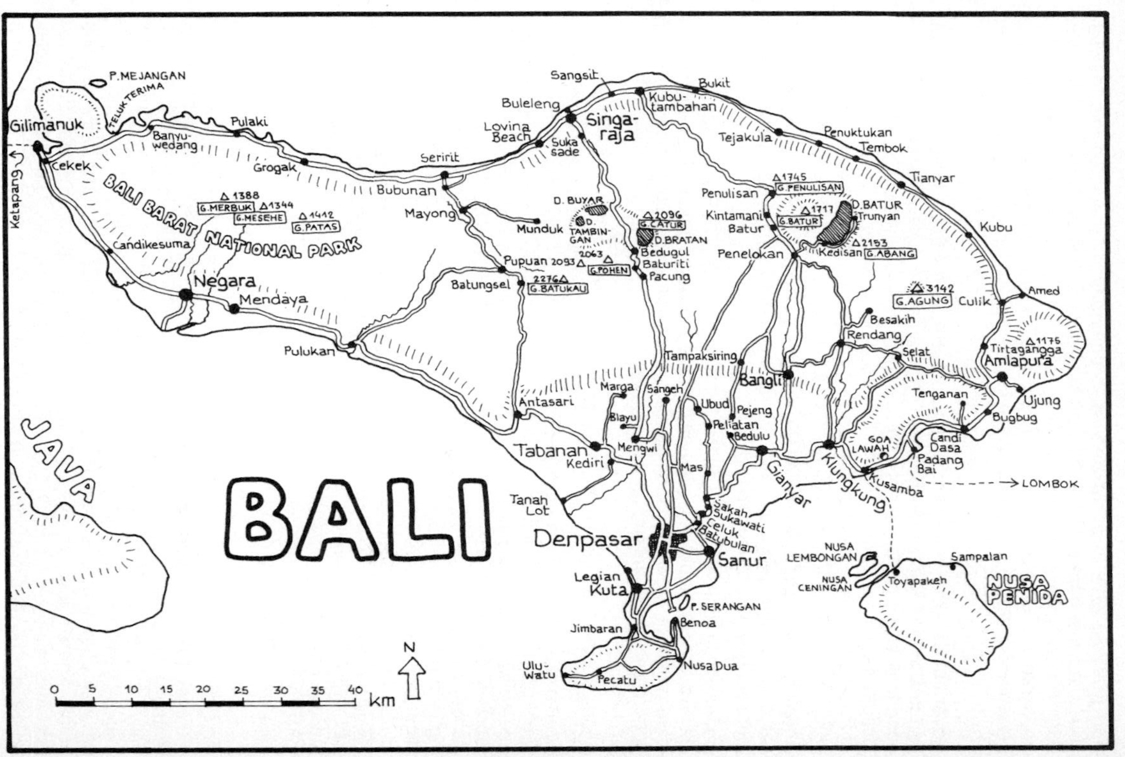
BALI
JAVA
NUSA PENIDA
BALI BARAT NATIONAL PARK
LOMBOK
Gilimanuk
Ketapang
Cekek
P. MEJANGAN
TELUK TERIMA
Banyuwedang
Pulaki
Grogak
Candikesuma
Negara
Mendaya
Pulukan
G.MERBUK 1388
G.MESEHE 1344
G.PATAS 1412
Bubunan
Seririt
Mayong
Lovina Beach
Buleleng
Sangsit
Singaraja
Suka sade
Munduk
D. BUYAR
D. TAMBINGAN
Pupuan 2093
G.BATUKAU 2276
Batungsel
G.POHEN 2063
G.CATUR 2096
D.BRATAN
Bedugul
Baturiti
Pacung
Kubutambahan
Bukit
Tejakula
Penulisan
G.PENULISAN 1745
Kintamani
Batur
G.BATUR 1717
D.BATUR
Trunyan
Kedisan
G.ABANG 2153
Penelokan
Penuktukan
Tembok
Tianyar
Kubu
Amed
G.AGUNG 3142
Culik
Tirtagangga 1175
Amlapura
Ujung
Bugbug
Besakih
Rendang
Selat
Tenganan
Candi Dasa
Padang Bai
GOA LAWAH
Kusamba
Klungkung
Gianyar
Bangli
Tampaksiring
Pejeng
Bedulu
Peliatan
Ubud
Mas
Sakah
Sukawati
Celuk
Batubulan
Sanur
P. SERANGAN
Benoa
Nusa Dua
Denpasar
Sangeh
Mengwi
Blayu
Marga
Kediri
Tabanan
Antasari
Tanah Lot
Legian
Kuta
Jimbaran
Pecatu
Uluwatu
NUSA LEMBONGAN
NUSA CENINGAN
Toyapakeh
Sampalan
N
0 5 10 15 20 25 30 35 40 km

You won't be able to avoid Denpasar, unfortunately, because this is where you'll find the banks, the airline offices, stores, bus stations, and the less sought after necessities such as hospitals and the police. Unless you have a good reason for staying in town, get one of the cheaper and much more pleasant losmen on the beach. You'll still be able to get downtown for 350 Rp.

Nevertheless, don't miss checking out the *BALI MUSEUM.* It was built in 1932 by the Dutch in the typical Balinese temple-palace style. The exhibits offer a good look at the development of art from prehistoric times until today. The collection of dance masks is especially nice. The museum is on the eastern part of Puputan Square (named after a rebel prince who fought against the Dutch). Open: Tues-Sun 8:00 to 14:00 h, Fri till 11:00 h.

A new temple, *PURA JAGANATHA,* stands next to the Bali Museum. It is dedicated to the highest Hindu God, *Ida Batara Sang Hyang Widi Wasa,* of whom there's a golden statue in the temple.

Spend some time at the *WERDI BUDAYA ART CENTER* at Jl.Bayusuta (off Jl.Raya Sanur), about 1 1/2 km east of the museum. Beautiful grounds with a lot of greenery, small lakes, exhibition areas, and a large stage used for dance performances and the annual arts festival.

HOTELS

On the road to Kuta are several relatively quiet hotels. A perfect place for people who are willing to spend a bit more is *DARMA WISATA**(*),* tel 22186, Jl.Iman Bonjol 83. The building is in the traditional Balinese style. Right in the city are several hotels on Jl.Hasanuddin, though quite loud: *HOTEL PENDAWA**(*),* no. 4; or *HOTEL MERTASARI**,* no. 24. Cheap, but not particularly clean is *WISMA TARUNA INN*(*),* Jl.Gadung 31, a few minutes from Kereneng Stasion.

FOOD

All over town are little warung and restaurants where you can fill your belly for less than 1000 Rp. In the big market building (Pasar Badung) are several cheap restaurants (doughnuts!). There's also an evening market. Another evening market can be found at the sport stadium in the north, Jl.Supratman corner of Jl.Melati. If you want to eat really well, check out Jl.Gajah Mada. In *RUMAH MAKAN PADANG II* you can get Padang food, in *PURI SELERA,* no. 16 and *HONGKONG,* no. 99 they serve Chinese food, and in *RESTAURANT MADURA* try Indonesian food.

GENERAL INFORMATION

TOURIST INFORMATION - Bali Government Tourist Office at Jl.Raya Puputan in the new administration centre, tel 22387, open Mon - Thurs 7:30 - 14:30 h, Fri and Sat till 11:30 h. Get a map of the island and the latest tips. Be sure to ask for a *Calendar of Events* which lists all the festivities. Also stop by the Badung Government Tourist Office, Jl.Surapati 2, tel 23399, for further info.

POST OFFICE - the old main post office on Puputan Square, Jl.Surapati has been moved. The telegram, telex, and telephone office is now at Jl.Veteran 66E. Open 24 hours. There are bemos going to the new post office on Jl.Puputan Raya (not far from the Tourist Office). Open: Mon-Thurs 8:00 to 14:00 h, Fri till 11:00 h, Sat till 13:00 h. Have your mail sent to another post office (Sanur: Jl.Segara; Kuta: Jl.Airport; Singaraja: Jl.Iman Bonjol 2).

IMMIGRATION OFFICE - Kantor Imigrasi, Jl.D.I.Panjaitan Niti Mandala Renon (right beside the new post office). Open: Mon-Thurs 7:00-14:00 h, Fri till 11:00 h and Sat till 12:00 h. If you stay in Kuta, the office at the airport is much nearer.

POLICE - if you want a motorcycle licence, apply at the Traffic Police (Komdak Lalu Lintas) on Jl.Supratman. New regulations require a guide. Usually it will be a losmen owner or a renter of motorcycles. The actual test costs 11,000 Rp. Calculate 20,000 Rp for the test, guide, passport photos, a day's rent for the bike and insurance. The test itself is a joke. Everyone knows the answers. Open Mon-Sat 8:00-12:00 h. For general traffic problems, go to the office on Jl. Gajah Mada. Before you rent a motorbike, check out the pictures of accident prone tourists - just about every day there's another. For other problems (theft etc.) go to the nearest police station, open in Kuta round the clock.

AMERICAN EXPRESS - for lost traveller's cheques and other needs, visit PACTO in the Bali Beach Hotel in Sanur.

HOSPITALS - are a horror for everyone who has had anything to do with them. Few of the doctors speak English. Critically injured people remain on stretchers in the hallways or don't receive adequate care. Swimming and motorbike accidents are the normal business. In case of emergency, try to fly out to Singapore where they have excellent hospitals. If you witness an accident, make sure that someone accompanies the injured person to the hospital. You can use a private practice rather than a hospital in some cases. It costs more, but the care is better. Addresses of public hospitals (rumah sakit umum): R.S.U.P. Sanglah, Jl. Nias, tel 27911. R.S. Wangaya, Jl. Kartini, tel 22141.

BANKS - exchange rates at the banks are not necessarily better than those given by money changers. Be sure to compare, and take commission and other charges into account. You can get relatively good exchange rates from the money changer Mamaja, Jl.Airport in Kuta.
Banks: BANK NEGARA INDONESIA 1946, Jl.Gajah Mada 20 (corner of Jl. Veteran); next door is BANK BUMI DAYA, Jl.Veteran 2 and BANK DAGANG NEGARA, Jl.Gajah Mada 2. BANK INDONESIA, Jl.Supratman / Jl. Trijata and BANK RAKYAT INDONESIA, Jl.Gajah Mada 3. BANK EKSPOR IMPOR, Jl.Udayana 11, cashes Thomas Cook traveller's cheques. Open: Mon-Fri 8:00-14:00 h, Sat to 12:00 h.

SHOPPING

On the beaches and in the losmen in Kuta and Legian you'll be constantly pestered by hawkers. Many of the things they offer at a 'special price' can be much cheaper in Denpasar. Check out the shops on Jl.Gajah Mada and Jl.Thamrin. You'll find textiles, woodcarvings, and other useful (useless) souvenirs. On Jl.Sulawesi are Balinese jewelry, leather goods and tailors; on Jl.Kresna and Jl.Karna behind the Bali Hotel are arts and crafts and antiques. Have a look around the market, Pasar Badung, for inexpensive odds and ends.

Always compare the prices with those in the villages. You can get cheap clothes in KUTA, woodcarvings in MAS, pictures in UBUD, leather in BEDULU, stonework in BATUBULAN, silver in CELUK, antiques, lontar and ikat in KLUNGKUNG. Details can be found in the regional sections.

Never let yourself be pressured by the words *fixed price.* Most people are willing to bargain; if they aren't buy somewhere else. The prices in the tourist centres are much too high because many people don't bother to bargain and pay any price.

GETTING AROUND IN DENPASAR AND ON BALI

Bemos and colts are the normal means of transport. Up until 18:00 h they leave for just about every part of the island. At later hours (except for Denpasar - Kuta or Legian), you'll have to hitch hike or walk. The island is so small that from Denpasar you can get just about everywhere in one day. Only Gilimanuk is more than 100 km away. Bemo drivers often seem to be training for the next road race while buses put-put contentedly through the countryside. Many are quite old and (as you'd expect) break down a lot, causing delays - that's why they are cheaper.

PUBLIC TRANSPORT

All rides within Denpasar cost 200 Rp. Bemos drive around until 21:00 h. Often you end up making an unwanted tour of the city with the bemos. This is due to the confusing one-way street system and the established routes of the bemos. End stations are at the hospital, the market, the other bemo stations and on Jl. Kartini near Jl.Gajah Mada. Sometimes you have to take two bemos, or even pay for more - e.g. from Kereneng Bus Station or Tegal to Ubung (250 Rp). Chartering within town costs about 2000 Rp.

To travel overland by bemo you have to bargain. Usually a short distance, up to 3 km, costs 100 Rp. Up to 10 km is 200 Rp, etc. Expect to pay more on mountainous routes and unpaved roads. A good map of the major bemo routes is available in the Ubud Tourist Office, Bina Wisata. In Denpasar the bemos, buses and minibuses leave from several different stations. Here are some rough sample prices:

KERENENG (going north and east): UBUD 500 Rp, KLUNGKUNG 800 Rp, BANGLI 800 Rp, GIANYAR 500 Rp, AMLAPURA 1200 Rp, SANUR 300 Rp.

UBUNG (going north and west): TABANAN 450 Rp, MENGWI 300 Rp, KEDIRI 400 Rp, SINGARAJA 1500 Rp.

SUCI (going south): BENOA 400 Rp.

KARTINI: SANGEH 500 Rp.

TEGAL: KUTA 350 Rp, LEGIAN 400 Rp, ULUWATU 700 Rp, AIRPORT 500 Rp.

MOTORBIKES

Actually a great way to get to know the island (if the things weren't so loud and so polluting). You can get everywhere as long as you watch out for wild village dogs, pot-holes, and slippery streets. However, you should have some experience with two wheeled vehicles before trying your hand in the Denpasar street system and on Bali roads.

If you don't have an international motorcycle licence you'll have to get

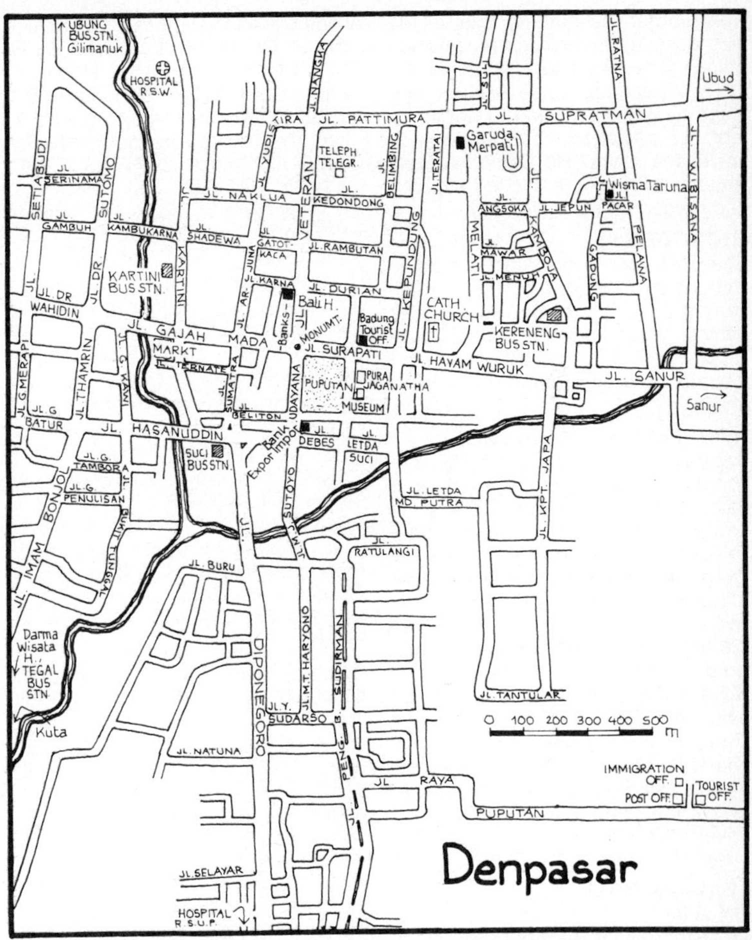

a Bali licence (see above). Full comprehensive insurance (often proves its worth in gold) costs another 10,000 Rp for three days.

Bikes in the 100-125 cc class can be rented all over Denpasar (try Jl.Gajah Mada) or Kuta and cost about 5000 Rp per day (bargain intensely). Petrol costs 385 Rp per litre. Be sure to keep a full tank because there aren't many petrol stations in the island's interior. Before taking out any machine, go for a test ride. For your own protection wear a helmet, gloves and glasses.

Don't forget the burning rays of the sun, despite the cooling breeze when riding. When visiting villages, spare the villagers the noise of your machine by getting off and exploring on foot. It's easier to meet people, and you'll see more. Be careful around Batur; motorbikes are often stopped and robbed on the main road.

BICYCLES

The best way to get around outside Denpasar. Difficult mountain routes can be done in a bemo with the bike on top. Check out the book *Bali by Bicycle* by Hunt Kooiker. Ask in your losmen - it'll cost about 1000 Rp a day.

HORSELESS CARRIAGES

Besides the US$60 yank tanks with chauffeur, there are some cheaper cars or jeeps for rent. Drivers, of course, require an International Driver's Licence. Reckon on the following average daily prices (cheaper if rented by the week): VW Safari Jeeps (20,000 Rp), large Suzuki Jeep (28,000 Rp). **Check:** brakes, lights, windshield wipers, and horn. It is worth it if you are in a group. If you have about ten happy-go-luckies who know where they want to go, why not charter a bemo? A good idea for evening village festivals. The driver, of course, needs an international driver's licence.

LEAVING BALI

BY AIR

The airport, 3 km west of Kuta, can be reached from Denpasar, Sanur, and Kuta for between 100 and 500 Rp. Bemos to the airport leave from the main street. Get your taxi from the coupon booth: Kuta 3250 Rp, Legian 4000 Rp. Airport tax: 9000 Rp for international, 2000 Rp for domestic flights.

Airline offices in Denpasar: GARUDA, Jl.Melati 61, tel 22028 / 27825; MERPATI, Jl.Melati 57 (next to Garuda), tel 22864; BOURAQ, Jl.Sudirman 19A, tel 22252. The following airlines all have their offices in the Hotel Bali Beach in Sanur: QANTAS, THAI, CATHAY PACIFIC, SIA, MAS, and SAS. Be sure to book and confirm your flights early because they are often overbooked - especially to Ujung Pandang (just Garuda) and to Australia. SAMPLE PRICES IN US$ (in brackets with ISIC which you can get at STA, Kuta Beach Club, tel 5051 ext 80, telex 35138):

MELBOURNE/SYDNEY 686 (360), PERTH 542 (205), DARWIN 254 (205), AMSTERDAM / FRANKFURT / PARIS 1471 (580), ATHENS 1289 (490), SINGAPORE 120 (RT 225), HONG KONG 537 (368), BOMBAY 711, BANGKOK (350). You rarely have to pay the full IATA tariffs. Travel agencies in Kuta usually charge slightly more than the ISIC prices for non-ISIC tickets.

DOMESTIC FLIGHTS: UJUNG PANDANG 73,100 Rp (GA only), JAKARTA 104,200 Rp / 88,600 Rp (GA/MZ via Surabaya , AMBON 155,400 Rp (GA), AMPENAN 17,800 Rp (MZ), SUMBAWA 44,200 Rp (MZ), BIMA 66,900 Rp (MZ), SURABAYA 42,400 Rp / 36,000 Rp (GA/MZ-BO), RUTENG 99,400 Rp (MZ), KUPANG 106,500 Rp / 95,800 Rp (GA/BO-MZ), ENDE 105,100 Rp (MZ), LABUHANBAJO 101,100 Rp (MZ Wed, Thur, Sun via Ampenan and Bima), MAUMERE 92,200 Rp (BO/MZ), YOGYAKARTA 56,300 Rp / 47,800 Rp (GA/MZ), WAINGAPU 85,800 Rp (BO / MZ).

BY SHIP

Ferries to Java leave from GILIMANUK (1800 Rp by bus from Denpasar). Costs 500 Rp (Ekonomi) p.p.

Ferries to Lombok leave from PADANG BAI (1500 Rp by minibus from Denpasar - or take a bus / bemo towards Amlapura and walk 2 km from the turnoff in the main road. Three ships leave daily at 8:00 h, 13:30 h and at 14:30 h. Travel time: 4 hrs.; prices: 3750 Rp (Ekonomi) or 5250 Rp (1st cl.), car 25,000 Rp, motorbike 4600 Rp. The main Bali harbour is BENOA, south of Denpasar, but ships also leave irregularly from BULELENG (Singaraja) for Nusa Tenggara. Check at the Pelni office in Benoa - you might also find a yacht owner who needs a hand.

Pelni's K.M.Kelimutu lays anchor off Padang Bai every second Wednesday, then continues on to LEMBAR (11,300 / 5000 Rp), UJUNG PANDANG (56,300 / 22,700 Rp), BIMA (62,600 / 24,700 Rp), WAINGAPU (84,800 / 32,600 Rp), ENDE (91,000 / 36,000 Rp) to KUPANG (117,800 / 41,300 Rp) and returns. It arrives back in Bali on Thursday of the following week before continuing via SURABAYA (35,500 / 15,000 Rp) and BANJARMASIN (91,300 / 32,800 Rp) to SEMARANG (72,500 / 31,500 Rp). More info on this modern passenger ship in the *Getting Around* chapter.

BY BUS

Several bus companies have daily buses from Denpasar to Java, often even non-stop to Jakarta. Less exhausting is to go by bus just to Surabaya, and on from there by train. Try BALI CEPAT or BALI INDAH - offices on Jl.Hasanuddin (leaves between 15:00 and 19:00 h), costs 11,000 Rp ac to SURABAYA. Sometimes even cheaper bus / train combination tickets are offered. You have the bus to Gilimanuk, the ferry to Ketapang and the train to different towns on Java included in the price of one ticket. Ask at PJKA, Jl.Diponegoro 172 or in Kuta at Perama Tourist Service. SAMPLE PRICES: BANDUNG 25,500 Rp, JAKARTA 29,500 Rp, BOGOR 30,500 Rp, SEMARANG 16,500 Rp, CIREBON 21,000 Rp, MALANG 10,500 Rp and YOGYAKARTA 19,600 Rp. Non ac buses are much cheaper though. Delays are such a way of life that exactly calculated connections are a sure road to grief. You can find other bus companies on Jl.Diponegoro and on Jl.Hasanuddin.

SOUTH BALI

The lure of tropical beaches fills losmen south of Denpasar. Here, where Bali has changed the most, are the beach towns of Sanur, Nusa Dua, Kuta and Legian, plus the international airport. This is the fulfilment of every tourist dream: cheap or luxury hotels, swimming pools, souvenir shops, restaurants, entertainment. But don't expect an unspoiled sandy beach. The western shore features steep cliffs washed by heavy surf. Impenetrable mangrove swamps cover the eastern shore. Except for the waterless Bukit peninsula, where the new Nusa Dua tourist resort has been established, the fertile plains of the south are heavily settled. It is a picture of tiny villages surrounded by groves of coconut palms and fields of rice. Welcome to the Bali marketed by the tourist industry.

When you drive along the coastal road to Gilimanuk, where the ferry to Java puts in, the scenery changes. West of Pulukan, there are no more roads heading north across the island. Here you can discover a very different Bali: mountain forests press closer to the coast; villages are less frequent. Even the temples, richly ornamented elsewhere, seem more simplistic. The coastal road around the island to Singaraja circles a 77,000 ha national park in which some of Bali's rarest creatures find a habitat.

KUTA / LEGIAN

For your average Australian, Bali is Kuta. Here among themselves, they swim and surf, live and eat cheaply, shop at all hours, ride motorbikes, and return at the end of the day to beer and disco music. Here you find not so much the globetrotters as the quick vacationers who spend a lot of money in two weeks while getting a good tan.

The romantic fishing village, with kilometres of lonely, sandy beach, is gone. Tourists discovered this spot over 20 years ago. At first there were just a few hippies housed in cheap lodgings; then more and more travellers were attracted. Travel agents and major hotels caught the scent, bringing in package tourists. Each year sees an increase in the number of bungalows, swimming pools, air conditioned restaurants and stylish boutiques. Fishermen have long since disappeared, replaced by business-minded hawkers in the streets, as sun-crazed tourists throng the beach. Only the sunsets remain spectacular.

In Kuta you can really see how an area is destroyed by tourism. In the morning the losmen are stormed by hawkers with their batik, woodcarvings and silver jewelry. Even on the beach you have no trouble getting cold drinks, flashy bikinis, shells, carved chess sets and chop sticks, massages...and quite often sex and drugs. The crime rate is well known in official circles, but they are afraid to do anything about it for fear of scaring off the tourists. It is the same with nude bathing, which is strictly forbidden and goes against every Indonesian concept of morality (many Javanese come to Bali just to peep at the naked white women!).

An omelette laced with so called 'magic mushrooms' is sure to send you flying, and while the police seem to turn a blind eye, be a bit careful. They have effects similar to LSD and shouldn't be underestimated. Never go swimming under the influence of drugs or alcohol! The strong current and undertow make it dangerous at full capacity. Lifeguards or not, swimming accidents are frequent, even near the beach.

Kuta, with its kilometres of sandy beach, has spread so far north that the once quiet Legian is now sharing Kuta's turbulence. Legian Street has been built up with kilometres of shops and restaurants. Through the narrow one-way street, an endless stream of motorbikes, minibuses, bemos and cars head north. The return route is further inland - along a quieter stretch of road, not yet lost to tourism. Since most losmen are on narrow alleys (= Gang), motorbikes and cars press through, forcing pedestrians literally against the wall. Early in the morning, motorbikes begin revving for a charge to the beach. There they fly recklessly at full speed through the sand and water.

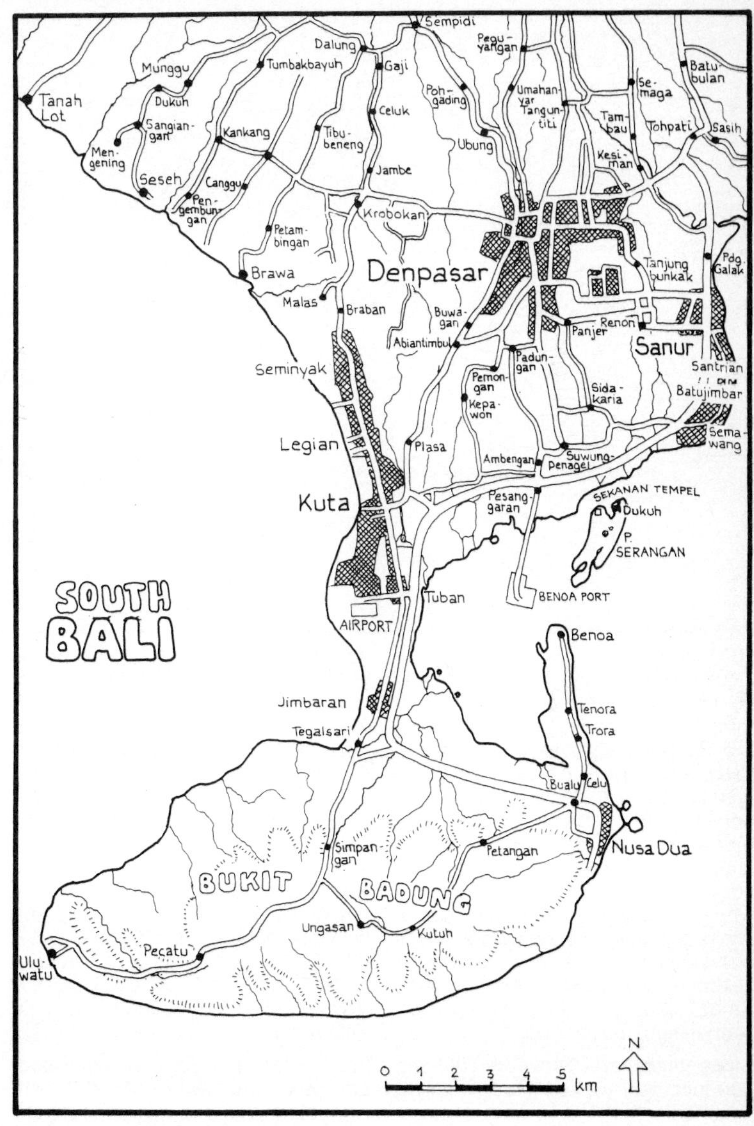
Sempidi
Pegu-yangan
Dalung
Gaji
Munggu
Tumbakbayuh
Batu-bulan
Tanah Lot
Dukuh
Poh-gading
Umahan-yar
Se-maga
Celuk
Tangun-titi
Sangian-gan
Tam-bau
Tohpati
Sasih
Kankang
Tibu-beneng
Ubung
Men-gening
Kesi-man
Jambe
Seseh
Canggu
Pen-gembun-gan
Krobokan
Petam-bingan
Pdg. Galak
Tanjung bunkak
Brawa
Denpasar
Malas
Braban
Buwa-gan
Renon
Panjer
Sanur
Abiantimbul
Padun-gan
Seminyak
Pemon-gan
Santrian
Batujimbar
Sida-karia
Kepa-won
Sema-wang
Legian
Plasa
Ambengan
Suwung-Penagel
SEKANAN TEMPEL
Pesang-garan
Kuta
Dukuh
P. SERANGAN
SOUTH BALI
Tuban
BENOA PORT
AIRPORT
Benoa
Jimbaran
Tenora
Tegalsari
Trora
Bualu
Celu
Nusa Dua
Simpan-gan
Petangan
BUKIT BADUNG
Ungasan
Kutuh
Pecatu
Ulu-watu
N
0 1 2 3 4 5 km

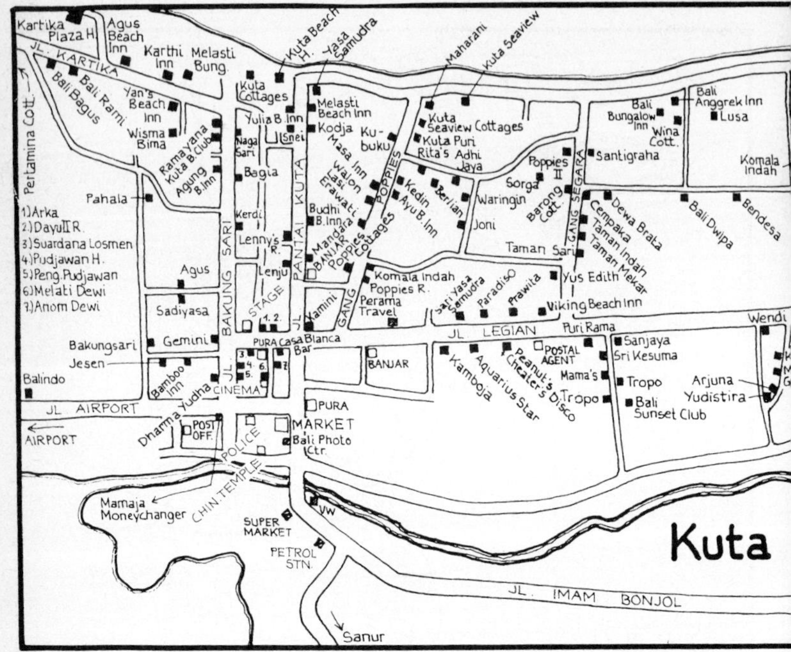

HOTELS

You're sure to find a place here in your category of price and comfort - there are so many. Most are built in the Balinese style with quiet courtyards and lots of green. The cheap losmen are a real alternative to expensive hotel facilities. For very little money you get breakfast and even a shower. To avoid theft, make sure that your room is always locked - even when you're in bed for a quick nap. If you're planning to stay a while, check out a couple of losmen. During high season (i.e. Australian vacation time, Xmas, and the European summer) everything is booked up.

Since there are between 200 and 300 lodgings, we can present only a small selection (going from south to north): The only four-star hotel is *PERTAMINA COTTAGES*****, near the airport, with every luxury. *KARTIKA PLAZA*****, all rooms with ac, pool, restaurant. *KARTHI INN***, tel 51708. *DAYU***, with separate bath - *BALINDO****, Jl.Airport, tel 51050, pool, 30 bungalows, very comfortable - *DHARMA YUDHA***, tel 51685, very loud - *ANOM DEWI*-***, simple. Near the beach on Jl.Bakung Sari is *RAMAYANA*****, 30 rooms with fan, ac, pool. Next door, *KUTA BEACH CLUB *****, across the way is *NAGA SARI****, tel 51057 - *AGUNG BEACH INN*****, tel 51263, 70 rooms with and without ac.

Lots of losmen along Beach Road, but very loud. *MANDARA*** with separate mandi and a quiet courtyard

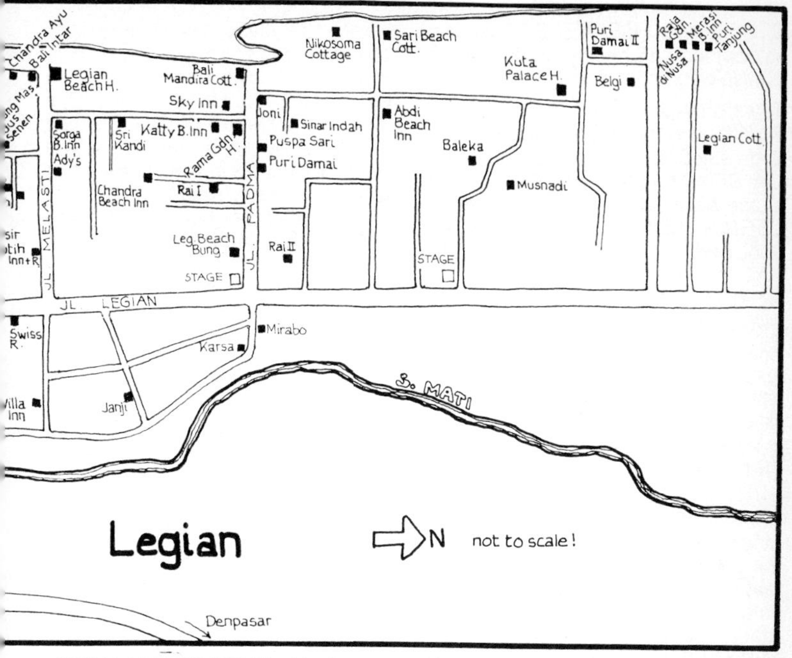

- *YULIA BEACH INN**** with pop music at breakfast - *KODJA BEACH INN***, tel 51754 - *MELASTI BEACH INN****, tel 51860 - *YASA SAMUDRA****, tel 51305, partly ac. In Gang Poppies are the traditional Bali-style bungalows of *POPPIES I ***-*****, lovely garden with a nice pool, clean, good service. Much simpler losmen include *KOMALA INDAH *** - *ERAWATI*** with restaurant - *WALON*** - *MASA INN*** - quieter: *KEDIN** - *KUBUKU*** with a large garden at the end of the street. *KUTA SEAVIEW COTTAGES*****, tel 51691, with pool, tennis, luxurious and turbulent. A simple beach hotel is *MAHARANI***, tel 51563. Pleasant losmen on the side streets include *RITA'S***, simple - *BERLIAN**** with a tropical garden - *WARINGIN*** very quiet.

If you want to stay on Jl.Legian, look for one of the rare quiet rooms: *SARI YASA SAMUDRA***, tel 51305, *PARADISO****, *PURI RAMA*****, tel 23057.

The losmen east of the road are quieter, but further from the beach. *MAMA'S***, family atmosphere, quiet, lovely garden. In *TROPO**-****, next door, you sleep in a four-poster canopy bed, quiet, clean, fan, showers, ac. The other *TROPO***** is very peaceful, bungalows with ac, lovely garden, tennis, pool, but lacking in atmosphere.

On Gang Segara *SANTHI GRAHA*** - *CEMPAKA***, a bit rural - *TAMAN SARI*** - *TAMAN INDAH**** - *TAMAN MEKAR***, with breakfast, simple, a bit too expensive, and other losmen.

Plus there is *POPPIES II*****, similar to Poppies I. Further along the beach is *ANGGREK****, tel 51265, ac.

Toward Legian on Jl.Melasti - *PASIR PUTIH INN****, the restaurant has a large selection of meat dishes - *SORGA BEACH INN****, tel 51897. Right by the beach at the end of the street is *LEGIAN BEACH HOTEL*****, with a pool and every luxury. *CHANDRA AYU****, near the beach - *BRUNA BEACH INN***, tel 51564 - *CAMPLUNG MAS****-****, tel 51580

Toward Jl.Padma are two losmen, *SKY***, not very clean, small rooms with bath and wc - *KETTY BEACH INN****, large, clean, quiet rooms. On Jl.Padma and the side streets *LEGIAN BEACH BUNGALOW****, tel 51087 and *PURI DAMAI COTTAGE* ***, tel 51965, across the way, comfortable, some rooms with ac - *PUSPA SARI I***** and *II***, with mandi, fan, mosquito nets - *JONI****, very quiet, clean, showers, with fan, large rooms, pool. By the beach is *BALI MANDIRA*****, large, luxurious, completely air conditioned tourist hotel, very comfortable. Across from Swiss Restaurant, *LOY* ***-****, if you are staying in the cheap rooms, you can use the pool at the adjoining bungalow hotel, lovely, peaceful, tropical garden.

Right by the sea is *NIKSOMA COTTAGE****, with ac****, the garden is more like a park, pool, good service, clean. A bit further from the beach, therefore quiet: *MIRABO**, between bamboo and coconut palms at the end of a path through a field - *VILLA INN** - *JANJI** with breakfast, nice people - *KARSA INN**, with bath.

FOOD

You find restaurants on Beach Street, Legian Street and Bakung Sari Street. The favourites change from season to season, like the menus. You can get bratwurst with rosti in *SWISS RESTAURANT* (have a chat with Jon the owner) or Mexican food in *TJ'S*. You don't have to worry about missing your muesli, bread or cakes. Stay away from the sea turtle steaks. Turtles are being killed off so fast that they already have to be imported from other islands (Irian Jaya) in order to meet the high demand. Have a normal steak, and don't contribute to the extermination of a species. Seafood is big though not cheap at *LENNY'S*. Chinese food at *GEMINI*, Padang food at *SARI MINANG* in Beach Road. In *DEPOT VIVA* try fresh fish off the grill. The Indian restaurant *GOA* with a bar is north of Swiss Restaurant.

Steaks and other western foods are much more expensive than the Indonesian dishes in the warung. There are so many nice drinks (wonderful milkshakes) that you'll probably not be quenching your thirst on cheap tea. This can make a meal quite expensive in the end. You can kill those hunger pangs in one of the warung between Kuta and Legian for only 600 Rp. On a tiny side street near *POPPIES* they serve tuak, rice wine in bamboo mugs, in the afternoon and early evening. Balinese men happily welcome tourists at their tables. You can get a bottle of tuak to take home, too.

GENERAL INFORMATION

TOURIST INFORMATION - a Government Tourist Information Office and the Central Java Tourist Office are on Jl.Bakung Sari near Jl.Airport in Kuta, tel 35276 . The same building houses a postal agent, telegraph office, bank, and restaurant.

POST OFFICE - in *Kuta,* Jl.Raya Kuta, open Mon-Thurs 8:00-14:00 h, Fri 8:00-11:00 h, Sat 8:00-12:30 h, (mailing address: GPO Kuta Bali 80361, INDONESIA). In *Legian,* Legian Street, open Mon-Sat 8:00-16:00 h, holidays 8:00-13:00 h, closed Sun. Both post offices provide poste restante. In Kuta on Jl.Legian is a Telecommunications Centre. Here you can make and receive international calls. It also offers telegraph and telex services. Notice of incoming messages is posted. Open Mon-Fri 8:00-18:00 h, Sat 8:00-11:00 h. There is another telephone office at the airport.

MONEY EXCHANGE - There is a branch office of Bank Negara Indonesia on Legian Street, 100 m before Swiss Restaurant. This is a good place to receive money transferred from home.
Money Changers on the corner of Beach Street / Legian Street and on Bakung Sari Street, daily 08:00-20:00 h. Be sure to compare exchange rates. Good rates at Mamaja, Jl.Airport, diagonally across from the Tourist Office. Here you can also rent a safe-deposit box. Always count your money after making an exchange!

DANCE - Performances of Kecak and Ramayana dance on several stages and at the major tourist hotels in Kuta. Tickets are sold in Kuta for performances in other villages. The price includes transport because no bemos run these routes at night. If you have your own wheels, then drive yourself to the venues where tickets are much cheaper:

Kecak Dance: Ayodya Pura in Denpasar, Jl.Raya Sanur 130 and in the Art Center, daily 18:00-19:00 h. Sun at 18:00 h in Padang Tegal, Ubud, 3000 Rp.
Legong Dance: Sat 18:00 h in Puri Agung, Peliatan (very large room, but still highly recommended!), 2000 Rp.
Barong and Kris Dance: daily at 09:00 h in Batubulan, 2500 Rp, lots of tourist buses.
Trance Dance, Fire Dance and Kecak: thrice weekly at the village temple in Bona, 2000 Rp.
In Ubud, there are additional events every day on a smaller scale.

DISCO - There are two large discos on Jl.Legian, *PEANUT'S* and *CHEATER'S.* More along the southern extension of Jl.Legian. By the way, you can pick up the latest hits in the numerous music cassette shops. You may have trouble getting them home through customs because most are bootleg copies.

DIVING - Gloria Mas (Bali Scuba Diving Service, PO Box 136, Denpasar), offers courses for US$50 per day; board, lodging, transport and equipment are included. Two dives a day usually set out from the north of the island. You can also do some diving at SANUR, NUSA DUA, TULAMBEN (shipwreck diving), SINGARAJA (Lovina, just snorkeling), PULAU MENJANGAN, PULAU LEMBONGAN (undersea grottos), NUSA PENIDA, off PADANG BAI and around PULAU KAMBING.

SURFING - on Jl.Legian, as in some of the losmen, you can rent a surfboard. Costs about 2000 Rp per day or 10,000 Rp a week. Other surfing beaches around Bali: ULUWATU (Suluban Beach), NUSA DUA (Jimbaran Beach), NUSA LEMBONGAN.

MASSAGE - on the beach and in the losmen, massage women offer their services. For 1000 Rp they'll oil your body and give you a more or less thorough rub-down from head to toe. Most of them have no training, but the Balinese tradition does call for massage against the bloodstream. Watch the women handle another 'victim' to choose a good one.

BOOKS - on Beach Street there are book stores in which you can buy used paperbacks in English, sometimes fairly expensive. They'll buy back your old books for half the price. Hawkers are also willing to sell and trade books - bargain!

SUPERMARKET - complete with bakery and Kentucky Fried Chicken for those whose tastes still look homeward. Can't be missed, you'll find everything at the entrance to town next to the petrol station.

SHOPPING - The selection is tremendous but quality isn't. Don't be tempted to buy spontaneously. Take your time, and bargain.

PLANE TICKETS - Garuda has an office at the Kuta Beach Hotel. Good prices and info at PERAMA Tourist Service on Jl.Legian, a travel agency and restaurant, tel 5155. They've their own poste restante and money exchange.

CRIME - With all the money changing hands in Kuta, expect a few less-than-honest people in search of opportunity: rooms are burglarized, in a bemo pockets can be neatly picked, or on the beach under cover of darkness bags can be lightened of a camera. Report theft and losses to the police in Kuta where they speak English and will make a report. Stay away from drugs - even magic mushrooms and marijuana - or a quick vacation can become a long prison sentence. There is a law against skinny dipping. If you are caught nude, or in a swim-suit away from the beach, the penalty is 32 months in jail.

GETTING AROUND - The closer you get to Jl.Pantai at Jl.Legian, the more emphatic the calls 'transport, transport' - usually at extravagant charter prices, but if necessary then for the standard fare. To Denpasar this is 350 Rp, to the airport (local price 100 Rp) 200 Rp and to Legian 100 Rp. In the evening, however, you'll often have difficulty finding a bemo from Kuta to Legian for the normal price. Coming from Denpasar, you will usually be dropped off at the market on Jl.Airport. Here, too, you can get a bemo or minibus for the proper price.

ADMISSION - starting in October 1987, the beaches at Kuta / Legian charge 100 Rp adult admission and 50 Rp for children.

SANUR

Sanur Beach, 9 km east of Denpasar, can be seen for miles thanks to the ten storey Bali Beach Intercontinental, a concrete testimony to tourism. The highest building on the island is (despite Balinese tradition) taller than a palm tree, a sure sign that you're in a western enclave. People stretch out under the palms by the pool next to the ocean. On the beach, except in high season, there is nobody to be seen. The occupants of the 605 sterile Bali Beach rooms are off at the golf course, playing tennis, at conferences, and willing to pay dearly for the privilege. Few Balinese could afford to have a drink or meal here. There are more than 20 other luxury hotels here as well as a few more reasonable accommodations. Just off the beach is a big coral reef. In general the beach isn't as nice as in Kuta, but it's safer to swim here. Everything is much more peaceful here than in Kuta. If you aren't staying at one of the beach hotels, you will have to use the public beach by the bemo stop north of the Bali Beach Hotel. You might rent one of the colourful out-rigger boats (jukung) for a cruise out to the coral reef, the port at Benoa, or the offshore islands Nusa Penida and Lembongan.

HOTELS

Most tourists who stay in Sanur come on package tours. For the single traveller, the prices demanded are simply too high (between US$30 and 150 per night.). Next to each other and fairly good are the hotels *TAMAN SARI**** and *SANUR INDAH**** at Jl. Segara Sanur, west of the southern cross-roads towards the post office, but far from the beach. Here too are other reasonably-priced losmen. Right by the beach is *ALIT*****, tel 8567, about US$30. A smaller facility with similar prices is *DIWANGKARA*****, tel 8577. Cheaper, but on the opposite side of the street is *RAMAYANA*****, tel 51864. The *BALI HYATT***** has no rooms under US$80.

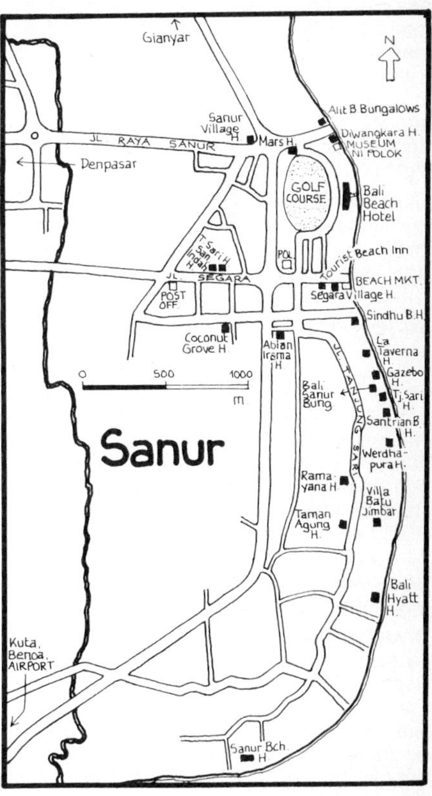

FOOD

In the hotels, but also outside, you can enjoy western food - pizzerias, piano bars, plus seafood and grill restaurants. The food tastes good at *WHITE SANDS* on the main road in southern Sanur.

HOW TO GET THERE

A four-lane highway runs east of Denpasar, passing through Sanur after 6 km. Heading south is the best (but not the busiest) road on Bali to the airport and Nusa Dua. When package tourists land on Bali they are quickly dispatched in air conditioned buses to the major hotels. If that isn't you, bemos run from Denpasar to Kereneng (300 Rp) until 20:00 h. Very few bemos run the southern route to Kuta.

SERANGAN

During high tide you can take a small boat (charter 1000 Rp and more) from *BENOA* over to 'sea turtle island' - at low tide you can walk. The best boat connections are from *KAMPUNG MESIGIT,* just a few kilometres south of Sanur, where a narrow path leads from the highway through shrimp farms to the sea. Sea turtles are brought here for fattening up (mostly from Irian Jaya) before they end up on tourist plates. The Balinese traditionally eat turtle meat on festive occasions, but the increasing demands of tourism threaten the species with extinction. The business must be profitable because whole ship loads are imported. Many turtles die on board. Many types of sea turtle are on the most endangered species list - so eat something else! Since 1981, turtle eggs have been brought from west Java for burial in the sand, so tourists can enjoy the sight of hatching baby turtles.

One of the holiest temples on Bali can be found in the village, *SAKENAN,* on the island, where centuries ago Bugis from Sulawesi settled. Hundreds of Balinese (as well as tourists and pickpockets) come to the island to celebrate Kuningan Festival.

NUSA DUA

A savanna type landscape with cactus and tiny villages, on the Bukit Peninsula, far from any village, where an increasing number of luxury hotels have been built. With the aid of the World Bank and the cooperation of the United Nations, a new concept is being developed. It has been recognized that the constant stream of tourists increasingly destroys the local culture. For this reason limits have been set to the expansion of Kuta and Legian. Only in Nusa Dua will further development be permitted. In the first phase, 310 ha along the 3 km beach will be set aside for large hotel facilities. Water and electricity supplies have been secured, a four-lane highway, sparsely used, links the future resort with the airport (10 minutes drive). Shops, travel agencies and parks are planned.

If you choose to stay here, however, be prepared to accept the 'instant Bali', marketed in tourist brochures. You will live completely isolated from the Balinese. Transport to Bali's sights is slow and very expensive. Evening events in the villages are only possible with your own wheels or on an organized tour. But if all you want is the beach, then this is the place... Still, why did you come all the way to Bali? Take a lovely walk up into the mountains looking down on the bay and *SERANGAN* island. In the background is *GUNUNG AGUNG.*

HOTELS

Luxury hotels predominate, including the architecturally interesting *NUSA DUA BEACH HOTEL*****, the top hotel on Bali with rooms starting at US$75. To the north are the facilities of *CLUB MEDITERRANEE*****. Further south are *BALI SOL HOTEL***** - *NUSA DUA***** - and *BUALU*****, in bungalow style surrounded by a large tropical garden.

ULUWATU

One of the holiest temples on Bali is situated on the southern tip of the peninsula - on a cliff, 100 m above the pounding sea. Niaratha is said to have received part of his enlightenment here. No public transport though. Only on holidays are you sure to get a bemo out. A good place to visit on a motorbike! Cycling is not such a good idea, however, since the peninsula is both hot and hilly.

Around the temple are lots of great beaches for surfing - e.g. Suluban Beach (international surfing competitions are held here), Bingin Beach, Labuansaid Beach or Nyangnyang Beach.

WEST BALI

MENGWI

16 km north of Denpasar - up until 1891, the seat of an important king. In the east, on a hill, lies *TAMAN AYUN,* the second largest temple complex on Bali. King I Gusti Agung Anom of Mengwi ordered the construction in 1634 on four levels. A bridge leads across a water moat to the first level where events are held on holidays. Through a double gate you climb stairs to the second level with a small shrine and spring of water. On the third level is a richly decorated *bale pengubengan.* The main gate to the last level is only opened on major festive occasions. In this most sacred temple district are 29 shrines of various sizes topped by up to 11 roofs, one above the other. The entrance gates (chiselled from stone) and the carved doors are excellent examples of Balinese handicrafts.

Just 10 km from Mengwi in *MARGA* is a memorial to the death of a unit of young Indonesians in the fight against the Dutch. In 1946 these soldiers, under the command of Ngurah Rai, refused Dutch surrender demands. The hundreds of little stone stupas are in remembrance of the lost fighters.

HOW TO GET THERE

Bemos or minibuses from Ubung (DENPASAR) to MENGWI (16 km, 300 Rp). With your own car, take the main road to TABANAN to the Mengwi turn-off. The temples are east of the main road, turn off by the market. Follow this road to SANGEH, or further east take the unpaved path through the fields to UBUD.

SANGEH

In the middle of a thick, dark forest of nutmeg trees, north of the village of Sangeh, west of the main road, is a moss-covered temple built in the 17th century, *PURA BUKIT SARI* (= elixir of the mountains). It is used for meditation on nights when the moon is full. All around you on the branches of the nutmeg trees and on the moss-covered temple are hundreds of partly tame monkeys who eagerly wait for you to buy a package of peanuts. Even before you're ready to feed them, they'll have ripped the nuts from your hands or out of your pockets. If you wear glasses, beware! A number of travellers have discovered that some monkeys are trained to steal glasses and to return them only in exchange for an expensive bag of peanuts. There is a lot of activity on the way to the temple. A 'donation' is expected at the temple entrance.

HOW TO GET THERE

This frequently visited temple is 20 km north of Denpasar, bemos from Jl. Kartini (350 Rp). Turn off the main road in Mengwi and head north along a side road. Along the way, notice the women with buckets carrying sand from the river up the steep embankment to the road. Beyond Sangeh, the road climbs continuously - as the rice fields give way to bamboo forest, nutmeg plantations, and vegetables. Minibuses drive to PELAGA.

TANAH LOT

From Ubung for 350 Rp, go first to KEDIRI (there's a big cattle market twice a week). Or you can get there from Mengwi by bemo. At the crossroads to Tanah Lot are many bemos which charge special tourist charter prices. Go down the road and stop the first bemo which comes along. Don't pay more than 300 Rp. Tanah Lot is by far the most beautiful temple situated by the sea. During high tide the rocks are covered by heavy waves, at low tide you can walk over. Many tourists and traders, but beautiful sunsets and fantastic scenery. If you're on your bike, head for the less crowded beaches further west!

GUNUNG BATUKAU (BATUKARU)

High on the southern slope of this 2276 m volcano, 'shell mountain', is a seldom disturbed mountain sanctuary. *PURA LUHUR* is in a clearing in virgin jungle, with the extinct crater as background. Just a few metres east of the temple buildings is a water sanctuary - steps lead past moss-covered statues and gargoyles, down to a peaceful pool with a tiny island in the middle. Luscious, primaeval vegetation grows right up to the water's edge, mirrored in the dark pond. Don't hurry; it takes time to sense the other-worldliness of this sacred spot.

On the way here, visit another holy spot, the *PENTATAHAN HOT SPRINGS.* Coming from the south, take a right just before the entrance to town. Before the end of the road, an offering is made in a small temple. The hot springs can be found with a bit of searching a few metres in front of the temple, right down by the river bank - otherwise, ask in the warung by the temple.

HOW TO GET THERE

First head for TABANAN, just a few kilometres north of KEDIRI, bemo / minibus from Ubung (350 Rp). If you have your own car, take the small road from WANGAYEGEDE through lovely rice terraces, away from all the main roads via Jatiluih to Pacung.

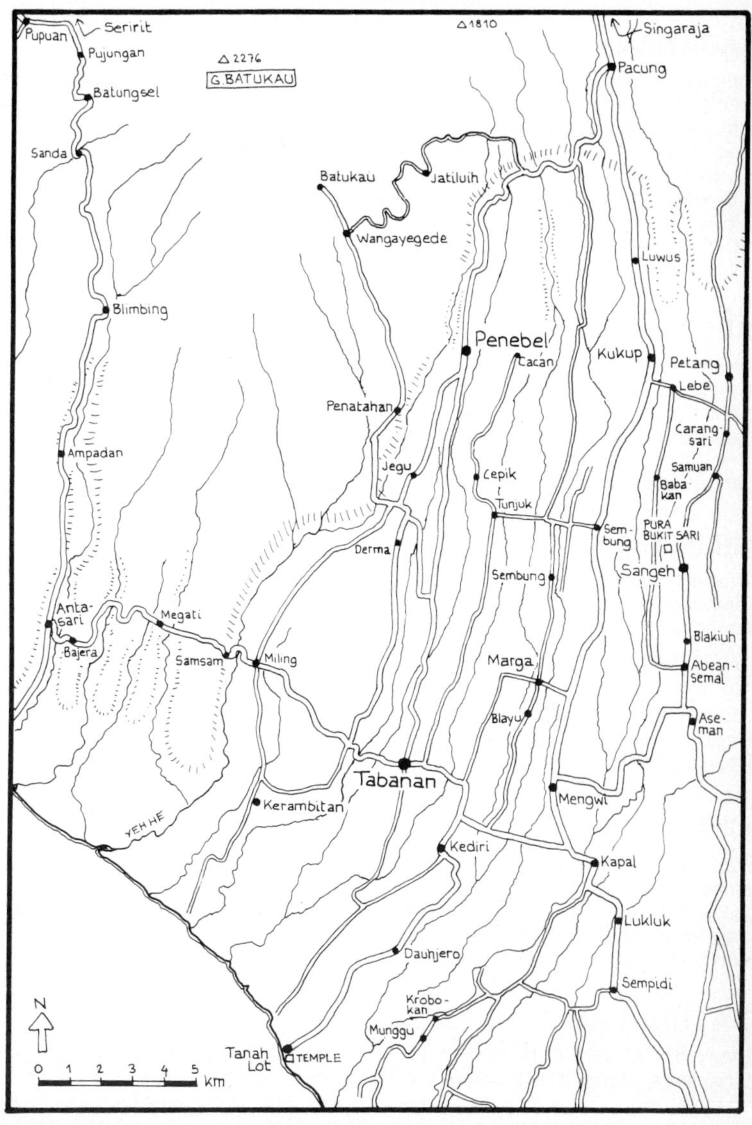

Pupuan
Seririt
Pujungan
△2276
G.BATUKAU
Batungsel
△1810
Singaraja
Pacung
Sanda
Batukau
Jatiluih
Wangayegede
Luwus
Blimbing
Penebel
Cacan
Kukup
Petang
Lebe
Penatahan
Carang-sari
Ampadan
Jegu
Cepik
Samuan
Baba-kan
Tunjuk
Sem-bung
PURA BUKIT SARI
Derma
Sembung
Sangeh
Anta-sari
Megati
Bajera
Samsam
Miling
Marga
Blakiuh
Abean-semal
Blayu
Ase-man
Tabanan
Kerambitan
Mengwi
YEH HE
Kediri
Kapal
Lukluk
Dauhjero
Sempidi
N
Krobo-kan
Munggu
Tanah Lot
TEMPLE
0 1 2 3 4 5 km

TABANAN

Although a raja once held court here, the town has since lost its charm. But many paths lead down to the sea and lovely sandy beaches. Take a walk through the paddy fields and villages! Pura Luhur is accessible by a steep road from TABANAN via WANGAYA. Lodging in Tabanan: HOTEL SEDERHANA**, Jl.Pahlawan TT, diagonally across from the police, if you aren't picky. The virgin rainforest covering Batukau is the only wilderness region on the thickly settled island other than the national park in western Bali. Here, in a nature reserve encompassing several square kilometres, ornithologists equipped with binoculars and patience will find much of interest.

NEGARA

74 km west of Tabanan (1400 Rp from Ubung or 1100 Rp from Tabanan) on the road to GILIMANUK. The town is famous for its bull races - ask at the Denpasar Tourist Office for the exact date! Two kilometres of road are turned into a race track. A small wagon and its jockey are pulled at high speed by two bulls. The Balinese use the races to ask for blessing from the gods for the coming harvest . As with all such events, the betting is heavy.

GILIMANUK

The ferry harbour from Bali to Java is 128 km from Denpasar or 88 km from Singaraja. If you don't suffer a breakdown and no bridges are out due to earthquakes, you can get there in two hours for 1200 Rp from Denpasar or 1000 Rp from Singaraja.

FERRIES TO JAVA

Deck 300 Rp, Ekonomi 500 Rp, 1st cl. 800 Rp, motorbike 700 Rp, jeep 3700 Rp, car 5750 Rp. Ferries leave up to 16 times a day at 1-3 hour intervals.

CENTRAL BALI

North of Denpasar, typical Balinese rice terraces stretch all the way to volcanic slopes. The region is too pretty to enjoy just on a tourist bus daytrip. Hike through the fields from village to village; it is a fascinating world inviting you to stay as long as possible. It is easy to understand why so many European artists have settled in Ubud since the 1930s.

BATUBULAN

Every day at 9:00 h, Barong and Kris dances (2500 Rp) are performed on three large stages. This is where the big tourist company buses make their first shopping stop. Judging by the splendid houses here, trade must be good. This village is the centre for stone masons who produce artistic statues and reliefs

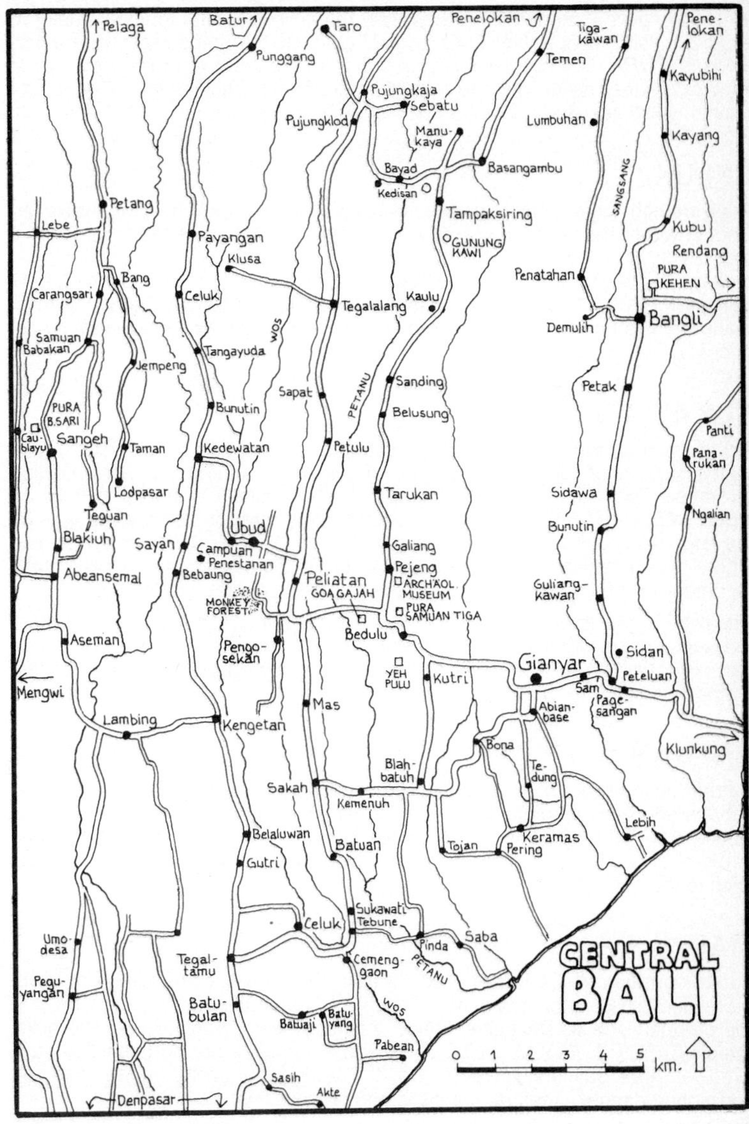
CENTRAL BALI
Pelaga
Batur
Taro
Penelokan
Tiga-kawan
Pene-lokan
Punggang
Temen
Kayubihi
Pujungkaja
Sebatu
Pujungklod
Manu-kaya
Lumbuhan
Kayang
Bayad
Kedisan
Basangambu
SANGSANG
Tampaksiring
Petang
Lebe
Payangan
Klusa
GUNUNG KAWI
Kubu
Rendang
Bang
Penatahan
PURA KEHEN
Carangsari
Celuk
Tegalalang
Kaulu
Bangli
Demulih
Samuan Babakan
WOS
Tangayuda
Jempeng
PETANU
Sanding
Petak
Sapat
Belusung
PURA B.SARI
Bunutin
Panti
Cau-blayu
Sangeh
Taman
Kedewatan
Petulu
Pana-rukan
Lodpasar
Tarukan
Sidawa
Teguan
Ngalian
Ubud
Bunutin
Blakiuh
Sayan
Campuan
Galiang
Penestanan
Pejeng
Abeansemal
Bebaung
Peliatan
ARCHAOL. MUSEUM
Guliang-kawan
GOA GAJAH
MONKEY FOREST
PURA SAMUAN TIGA
Bedulu
Aseman
Pengo-sekan
Sidan
YEH PULU
Gianyar
Kutri
Sam
Peteluan
Mengwi
Mas
Abian-base
Page-sangan
Lambing
Kengetan
Bona
Klunkung
Blah-batuh
Te-dung
Sakah
Kemenuh
Lebih
Belaluwan
Keramas
Batuan
Tojan
Pering
Gutri
Sukawati
Tebune
Celuk
Saba
Umo-desa
Pinda
Tegal-tamu
Cemeng-gaon
PETANU
Pegu-yangan
Batu-bulan
WOS
Batu-yang
Batuaji
Pabean
0 1 2 3 4 5 km.
Sasih
Akte
Denpasar

for the temples. One of the few Balinese arts difficult for the tourist industry to exploit, it still retains much of its original character. A stone mason's masterpiece is *PURA PUSEH BATUBULAN* east of the main road (turn off by the shop of a kulkul maker) next to the sahadewa stage. Besides tremendous elephants, you'll see Buddha statues in the meditating position.

CELUK

A silversmith village which produces mostly filigree work. They will, however, work to order. Balinese silver blackens easily - it's a different alloy - although if real it's 90 % pure. On the other hand the fine, painstaking work certainly makes the rings and necklaces worth their price. Don't try to buy anything here between 10:00-11:30 h, when tourist buses stop (after the barong performances in Batubulan), and it is difficult to bargain down the extravagant tourist prices.

SUKAWATI

Along the road in the neighbouring village, lots of handicrafts are sold, particularly colourfully painted wood carvings, woven bamboo baskets, musical pinwheels from bamboo (pindakan) and temple umbrellas. There's a *FRUIT & VEGETABLE MARKET* in the town centre every morning. Across the way on the large square is a modern two-storey building, *PASAR SENI,* an art market, where reasonably-priced carvings and other handicrafts are sold - particularly in the early morning when the merchants from Kuta come here to buy.

Sukawati is the home of many 'Dalang' - puppeteers and masters who bring the ancient epics to life with their 'wayang kulit' puppets. In some shops you can purchase cheap imitations of the shadow-play puppets made of buffalo leather.

BATUAN

Batuan is famous for its excellent legong dancers. A number of the wood carvers and painters developed their own school here in the 1930s. Countless workshops in the village produce wood carvings - even large pieces, such as doors and furniture. Beyond the village in SAKAH, the road forks. The next town to the north is Mas.

MAS

20 km northeast of Denpasar (250 Rp from Kereneng) is this village of Brahmans, the Hindu priest caste. Many people in Mas trace their ancestry back to the progenitor of all Balinese Hindus, *Padanda Sakti Bahu Rauh.* The great temple of *PURA TAMAN PULE* stands on the spot where he is said to have lived. A three day festival is held in the temple during Kuningan featuring cockfights, dancing, theatre, carnivals and processions.

Many of the village men work as wood carvers. They learn as small children. In the shops you can admire the artistic perfection of the master craftsmen - the prices are out of bounds. It's easy to see the village's affluence.

UBUD

Surrounded by rice terraces and lots of tiny villages (each worth a day's hike), Ubud is probably the cultural centre of Bali. Besides the things we can list here, there is much to discover on your own! The indescribable beauty of the setting sun over the rice fields, a painter mixing his colours, a farmer driving his ducks home down a dusty village lane, children swimming in the river - little wonder that on this fertile soil almost every Balinese is an artist. You'll find painters, dancers, gamelan musicians and wood carvers out in the paddy fields planting rice. Of course, even here the dusty paths through the fields are being paved over to accommodate the scream of motorcycles, and soon electricity will have penetrated the last house. On the Monkey Forest Road you are sure to meet more tourists than natives, and the shops price their wares for the better-paying foreign customers. Nevertheless, those who want to experience Balinese village life should spend a few days out here in the country. A day trip isn't an alternative! You'd just be one of many tourists sticking close to the main road where, in one studio after another, you'd be offered naive pictures from the 'young artists' at greatly inflated prices. The best that you could hope for would be a visit to the museum!

Before buying any paintings, check out the Ubud art museum, *PURI LUKISAN,* to sharpen your eye for the different stylistic variations. The building is in a garden and built in the traditional Balinese style. You'll find a collection of modern Balinese paintings which draw their motifs from daily life. European artists have lived here since the 1930s, creating a two way exchange of ideas and influence. Walter Spiess and Rudolf Bonnet spent most of their lives painting and studying in Ubud. Even today a few Europeans work here. If you want to visit the studios of Antonio Blanco or Han Snel, you'll have to pay admission.

Also of interest is *MUSEUM NEKA,* founded by Suteja Neka, on the road 2 km north of Campuan. In addition to pictures of Balinese painters (I Gusti Nyoman Lempad, Ida Bagus Made, Anak Agung Gde Sobrat) there are exhibits about other Indonesian artists (Affandi, Widayat, etc.) and European artists who have lived, worked, or are still working in Bali (Theo Meier, Covarrubias, Snel, Blanco, Donald Fried).

Dance performances are held on several evenings. Because the dates are constantly changing, check in advance for dates fitting your itinerary. During an afternoon walk through Ubud you will certainly be offered tickets.

LEGONG DANCE, Fri 18:00-19:00 h, Puri Kaleran, Peliatan; classical legong (recommended) Sat 18:30-19:45, Pura Dalem, Peliatan, 3000 Rp.
KECAK DANCE, Sun 18:00-19:00 h, Banjar, Pandangtegal, 3000 Rp.
GABOR & MASK DANCE, Thurs 19:30-20:30, Bale Banjar, Monkey Forest Road, 3000 Rp.

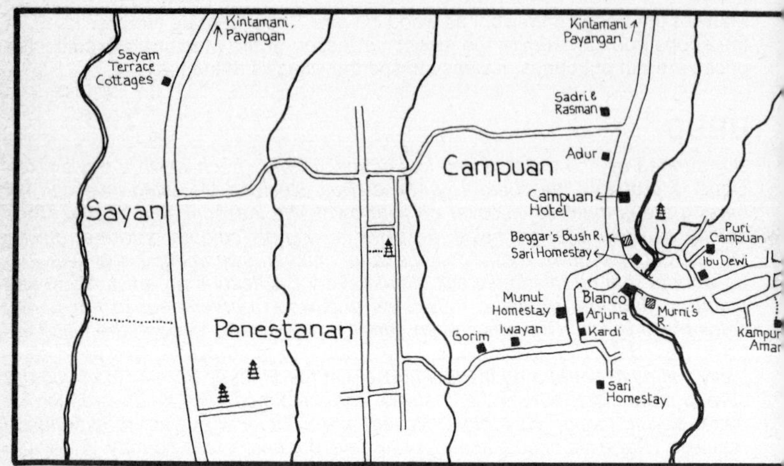

PARWA RAMAYANA BALLET, Wed 19:30-20:30 h, Hotel Menara, Ubud, 3000 Rp.
MAHABHARATA EPIC, Tues 18:30-20:00 h, Br. Teges, Peliatan, 3500 Rp.
WAYANG KULIT, Wed 19:00-20:30 h, Oka Kartini, 3000 Rp.
RAJAPALA DANCE, Tues 20:00-21:00 h, Hotel Menara, Ubud, 3000 Rp.
CALON ARANG DRAMA, Fri 19:00-20:00 h, Hotel Menara, Ubud, 3000 Rp.

Good information in *BINA WISATA,* a private tourist office, diagonally across from the museum. Here you'll find the best map of Bali with lots of additional tips, plus tickets to dance performances, newspapers, and books.

HOTELS

Not the appropriate word to describe the losmen and homestays in the Ubud region. Often you'll be staying in a typical Balinese house with a nice green courtyard and a house temple. If you're lucky, you'll be treated like a member of the family after a while. Often meals are served in the homestays. Some Balinese might even be willing to teach you the basics of dancing or painting.

Losmen in Ubud: *NIRWANA**** with breakfast at a painter's and nice rooms; *AGUNG'S** with mandi; *YOGA** - all three are a bit out of town and quiet. Similar are *RAMASITA** and *SUARTHA**. Right at the entrance to the village are *OKA KARTINI***, *ADI'S** and *IBU MASIH*,* mother Masih is an English and dance teacher. Many losmen have sprung up on the road to the monkey forest in recent years. Travellers get together at *TJANDERI'S*,* but compared with other losmen, it's a dorm. Behind: *PURI MUWA*** a traditional house with restaurant; *BANDRA*, IGNA*, IBU RAI*.* You've a lovely view over the rice terraces from *WARJI*** and *IGNA 2***. On the tiny side street are *SARI NADI***, and *OKA WATI****. Oka Wati's losmen is lovely, with every comfort. Across the rice fields you

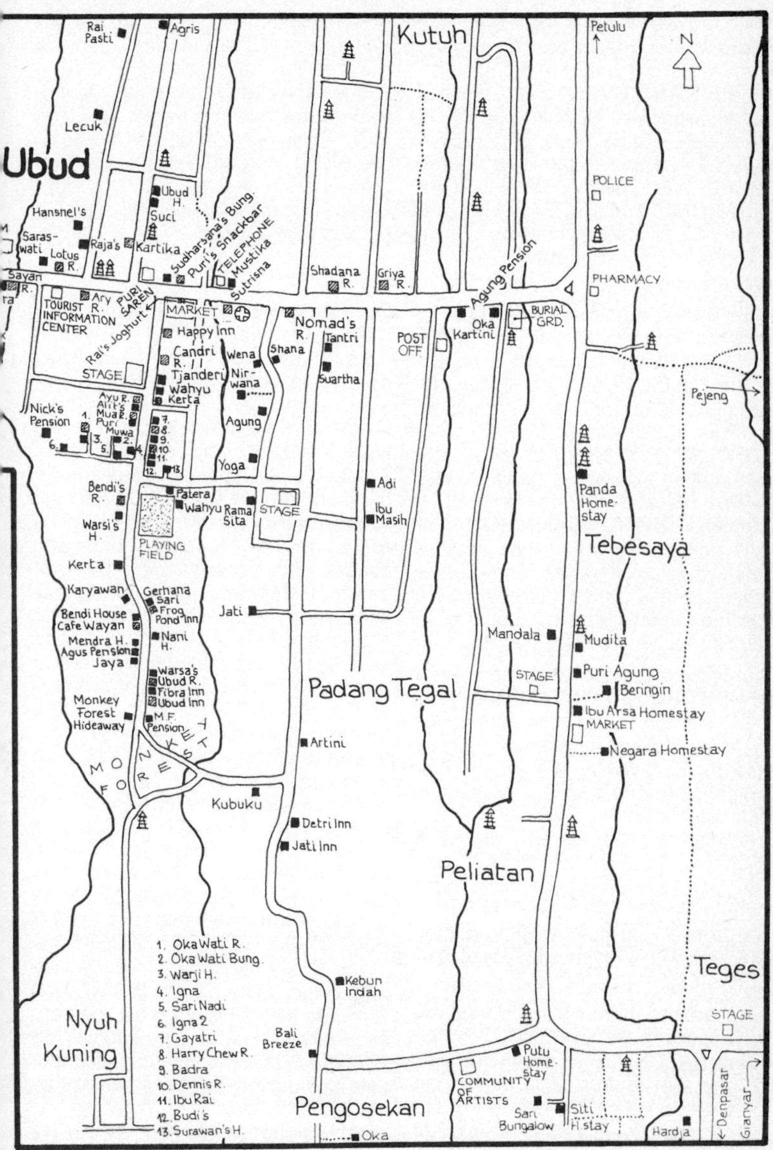

Ubud
Kutuh
Petulu
N
Rai Pasti
Agris
Lecuk
Ubud H.
Suci
Hansnel's
Saraswati
Lotus R.
Raja's
Kartika
Sudharsana's Bung.
Puri's Snackbar
TELEPHONE
Mustika
Sutrisna
Sayan
Ary R.
PURI SAREN
TOURIST INFORMATION CENTER
Rai's Joghurt
MARKET
Happy Inn
Candri R.
Tjanderi
Wahyu
Kerta
Wena
Nirwana
Agung
Yoga
Nomad's R.
Tantri
Shana
Suartha
Shadana R.
Griya R.
POST OFF.
Agung Pension
Oka Kartini
BURIAL GRD.
POLICE
PHARMACY
STAGE
Nick's Pension
Ayu R.
Alit's
Mua R.
Puri Muwa
Bendi's R.
Warsi's H.
Patera
Wahyu
Rama Sita
STAGE
PLAYING FIELD
Adi
Ibu Masih
Kerta
Karyawan
Gerhana Sari
Frog Pond Inn
Jati
Bendi House
Cafe Wayan
Mendra H.
Agus Pension
Jaya
Nani H.
Warsa's Ubud R.
Fibra Inn
Ubud Inn
Monkey Forest Hideaway
M.F. Pension
MONKEY FOREST
Padang Tegal
Artini
Kubuku
Detri Inn
Jati Inn
Pejeng
Panda Home-stay
Tebesaya
Mandala
Mudita
STAGE
Puri Agung
Beringin
Ibu Arsa Homestay
MARKET
Negara Homestay
Peliatan
1. Oka Wati R.
2. Oka Wati Bung.
3. Warji H.
4. Igna
5. Sari Nadi
6. Igna 2
7. Gayatri
8. Harry Chew R.
9. Badra
10. Dennis R.
11. Ibu Rai
12. Budi's
13. Surawan's H.
Nyuh Kuning
Kebun Indah
Bali Breeze
Teges
STAGE
Putu Home-stay
COMMUNITY OF ARTISTS
Sari Bungalow
Siti H.stay
Hardja
Pengosekan
Oka
Denpasar
Gianyar

come to *NICK'S***. Behind the athletic field is *WAHYU** with lots of greenery. Further along toward the monkey forest are *KARYAWAN** with bath and beautiful garden; *BENDI HOUSE** in the middle of rice fields; and *FIBRA HOUSE*** almost in the forest as are *UBUD INN***, *MONKEY FOREST PENSION*** and *HIDEAWAY***. Almost all the losmen have their own mandi and serve a more or less decent breakfast.

Right on the main road is *MUSTIKA**, and the antique-furnished *HOTEL PURI SAREN*****, formerly a palace of the Ubud princes. Behind the museum is *RAJAS**, and the lovely facilities of Han Snel's *SITI BUNGALOWS*****. *PONDOK INDAH** is right on the rice fields with a mandi. *MADE SADIA HOMESTAY*** is managed by a painter. *HOTEL CAMPUAN***** is built in the traditional style and located in a small valley. The painter Walter Spiess used to live here. He had the beautifully situated pool built: you can bathe there for 2000 Rp.

Surrounded by nature on the way to PENESTANAN, out of the way in a lovely setting is the small losmen *REKA** with two small rooms offering no comfort. South of the village are other lodgings in peaceful environs, surrounded by fields of rice: *MUNUT***, *ARJUNA***, managed by Blanco's daughter, *KARDI***, *I.WAYAN SADIA***, *GORIM*** and more. Most of the losmen beyond Campuan to the north are pretty expensive. Another losmen in Sayan with a lovely view is *SAYAN TERRACES****.

If it's a bit too turbulent in Ubud, you can always retreat to PENGOSEKAN. There *BALI BREEZE BUNGALOWS**** and *DEWA MADE OKA*** at the edge of the village have views of the rice terraces. Near Padang Tegal are *DETRI*** and *JATI INN***; here too is a restaurant. Other losmen can be found on the main road in PELIATAN. Though they aren't so quiet, they're easy to reach with a bemo: *MUDITA INN*** with big rooms; *MANDALA** and *PURI AGUNG**. In the south of town is *SITI HOMESTAY***, bungalows with bath, managed by a teacher, plus *SARI*** and *PUTU**.

FOOD

During the last few years, lots of new restaurants which offer everything from steaks to sandwiches have opened to exploit the tourist trade. Most losmen and homestays serve breakfast. If you're not afraid of a long walk, the best yoghurt is served in *MURNI'S WARUNG*. The prices on the menu are a bit higher, but you get what you pay for. At *OKA WATI'S* restaurant the food is good and cheap. With an advance order you can get Balinese duck and other specialities. Other cheap restaurants on the main road are *ARY*, cheap and slow (good coconut cakes); rumah makan *KARTIKA*, *KRISHNA* food & drinks, and *NOMAD'S* which offers the largest selection of alcoholic beverages and cocktails in Ubud, plus good steaks and other treats. Somewhat more expensive is *GRIYA* (grill specialities), *LOTUS* (a changing menu combines Indian and Italian specialities, closed Mondays) and *MENARA* in the library building across from the museum. *HAN SNEL'S GARDEN RESTAURANT* is in the luxury category, set a little out of the way, owned by the painter, Han Snel. On the Monkey Forest road are several restaurants including *UBUD RESTAURANT* with good coconut sate and salads. For simple tastes try *HARRY CHEW* or *BENDI'S* which has a nasi campur all its own.

SHOPPING

Take your time when shopping for paintings (or at least look that way). Usually you'll get the best prices from the painters themselves. The prices have sky-rocketed enormously in recent years, and the quality has suffered from mass production. It is noteworthy that most shops list the prices in US$. Is it any wonder? Many tourist buses stop here each day on their rounds. After a visit to the museum, the souvenirs have to be bought in only a few minutes - even if the art carries a $500 price tag. There is no time to bargain; the bus is leaving. If you have someone with you when shopping, you're sure to be charged commission.

Besides paintings, the shops on the main street offer the same kind of souvenirs you will find in Denpasar or Kuta.

Every third morning is market day in Ubud. Even in the early hours they serve tuak.

LEAVING UBUD

Bicycles at Tantri's cost 1000 Rp a day. Bemos heading south from Ubud to Denpasar charge 500 Rp. If you want to go north or east, go to BATUAN (just beyond MAS) for 150 Rp and get a ride from there. It costs 250 Rp to GIANYAR and 350 Rp to KLUNGKUNG. From Gianyar you can go on to TAMPAKSIRING, BANGLI, PENELOKAN and SINGARAJA; from Klungkung to BESAKIH, CANDI DASA and AMLAPURA.

If you have your own transportation you can take the short cut via BEDULU. The roads are pretty bad, but you can get through, except in the rainy season, from UBUD via CAMPUAN, SAYAN, KENGETAN to SANGEH (no bemos!). The roads to the north are not in the best state either. From the turnoff in PELIATAN you can go via GOA GAJAH to BEDULU (only a few bemos). From there it's all uphill through PENJENG, TAMPAKSIRING to PENELOKAN, 1480 m above sea level.

DAY TRIPS FROM UBUD

MONKEY FOREST

Take a walk from Ubud 2 km south (follow the signs); you'll come to the small MONKEY FOREST inhabited by quite tame apes (donation). Be careful when feeding the monkeys as they can become quite aggressive. By the cashier, stairs lead steeply down to the right to a peaceful spring. From the entrance cross the large empty square to the right, and walk just a few metres to the temple DALEM AGUNG PADANG TEGAL on a small hill.

PENESTANAN

Those interested in pictures by the 'young artists' can take the main road a bit further west, across the new bridge, over a deep gorge to CAMPUAN. To the left a footpath leads to the villa of the American painter Blanco. Take the next path which joins the road to Penestanan, providing a lovely walk through the rice fields to the village. Another path to Penestanan begins a bit above the main road to Campuan. There, steep steps lead uphill. After some sales galleries, you come to a footpath. They'll be waiting here to show you paintings. The prices, though, are the same as in Ubud! Perhaps they'll go down a bit if they get to know you better. There are losmen both in and outside town.

PENGOSEKAN

Painters can be found everywhere in Ubud and the surrounding villages. Take a walk through the Monkey Forest or from Tegal to Pengosekan where the artists still utilize the traditional style. During festivities the local dance troupe performs under the banyan tree in front of the temple. For lodgings, see Ubud.

PELIATAN

Famous for its excellent dancers, located between Ubud and Mas, accessible by foot from Pengosekan. Watch the girls learning legong! At 4-5 years of age, they begin to practise the graceful movements. Only young girls up to the age of puberty are permitted to perform legong dance. Some of the instructors will also take on European pupils. But even for experienced dancers, it's difficult to learn the prescribed movements. Wood carvers and painters offer their wares in a number of shops. If you want to stay away from the Ubud bustle, there are several losmen here.

GOA GAJAH

About 3 km up the road from Peliatan to BEDULU (100 Rp by bemo, but also a nice walk), you come to GOA GAJAH, the elephant cave. Admission 100 Rp, temple scarf required! The entrance to the cave is decorated with unusual sculptures chiseled into the cliffs. A demon with a huge mouth seems to swallow everyone going in. The sculptures in the cool interior suggest that the cave was occupied by a hermit. In front is a pool with nymphs which was only discovered in the 1950s. Go deeper into the gorge and you'll find other ruins. It's a wonderful place when a busload of tourists doesn't happen to be there. Souvenirs are sold up on the road - especially leather bags.

GIANYAR

27 km east of Denpasar is the centre of Balinese weaving (500 Rp by bemo). At the beginning of town you can buy cloth in air conditioned shops for prices often more expensive than in Denpasar. In the centre of town is *GIANYAR PURI,* a traditional palace. During the second half of the 19th century, there was bitter fighting between the southern Bali principalities. In 1880 the whole royal family of Gianyar was taken captive in Klungkung and the realm divided. When two sons escaped, they placed their reconquered kingdom under Dutch protection. Gianyar was therefore spared when the colonial power used force of arms to conquer the southern Balinese principalities. At that time the area developed as a centre of arts.

TAMPAKSIRING

Get here for 350 Rp by bemo from Gianyar or for 700 Rp from Denpasar. Two losmen near the big Banyan tree: TAMPAKSIRING HOMESTAY** and GUSTI**. North of the bemo stop is a path to the hot springs. The Balinese have bathed in these waters for a thousand years in search of the reported healing powers. Even the governor had a palace built here which was later used by President Sukarno. The shrine is dedicated to the god Indra who is said to have created the springs. Respect this holy place, and be sure to wear a temple scarf.

GUNUNG KAWI

South of here, left of the road, is Gunung Kawi, surrounded by steep rice terraces. Hewn from two facing walls are nine monuments taking the form of an east Javanese candi. Heavily weathered inscriptions show that this is the 11th century burial temple of King Udayana and his family. Coming from the road, you descend steps hewn into the rock to five monuments dedicated respectively to King Udayana, Queen Gunaptiya, the King's favourite concubine, and his two sons Marakata and Anak Wungsu.

The four candi on the opposite bank of the river are dedicated to four concubines of Anak Wungsu. In the south of the valley, not far from the tombs, you'll discover groups of caves hewn into the rock at some of the most idyllic spots, where hermits and ascetics led meditative existences. It is said that Anak Wungsu abandoned his throne to live a hermit life, seeking salvation through meditation and privation.

The candi of Gunung Kawi clearly show Javanese influence. Stone memorials are rare on Bali, where sacred objects are almost invariably made of perishable materials. In this respect we again mention Goa Gajah, a counterpart of the east Javanese hermit caves, dating, as does Gunung Kawi, from the 11th century. Balinese have a myth explaining the creation of these two holy sites: the giant, Kbo Iwo, scratched them from the rock with his fingernails in a single night.

BALINESE PAINTING

PEJENG

In Pejeng, on the way to Tampaksiring, you can view the largest bronze drum in the world in *PURA PENATARAN SASIH* - 'Moon of Bali' - (donation). The wonderfully crafted kettle drum is richly ornamented. It is suspended at the top of a tower and is rather difficult to see. Additionally, you can see ancient stone statues in several open buildings - a Brahma and a Shiva statue, a stone with Kawi inscriptions, and other statues dating from the 14th century, discovered in excavations on the temple grounds. The new temple buildings are of little interest.

Although this jewel of bronze casting shows typical elements of Indonesian style, its origin has never been explained. The drum dates from the 3rd century BC. It is seen as important evidence of the expansion of Dong-Son culture. Because of the unusual number and variety of finds near the North Vietnamese village, Dong-Son, it is assumed to be the cradle of South-East Asia's bronze culture. Similar, but much smaller and less ancient bronze kettle drums are used as a dowry on the island of Alor (near Timor). From Roti (another island in the region) and Lake Sentani (Irian Barat) originate some of the loveliest bronze axes, with similar workmanship and decorative motifs.

For the Balinese, the 'Moon of Bali' is very sacred; sacrificial offerings are frequently brought here. The name is explained by a legend: originally there were thirteen moons each year, but one fell to earth and was caught in the branches of a tree. His lightness disturbed the thieves at their nightly activities; so one of the bravest was determined to extinguish the light with his urine. As a result, the moon exploded, killing the transgressor, and fell to the earth as a drum. The fall also explains the damage.

BEDULU

On the way to Bedulu a small archaeological museum *(GEDONG ARCA)*, open only in the morning, displays finds from prehistoric times. Just south is a crossroads: heading west you pass the Goa Gajah caves en route to Ubud; heading east is a footpath to the interesting temple *PURA SAMUAN TIGA;* to the south is the main road. Walk along the road until it makes a turn to the east, then take the path here heading south. Past a losmen and a bathing spot, you come to the rock relief, *YEH PULU.*

BANGLI

With a bemo for 600 Rp from Denpasar (41 km), 500 Rp from Kintamani (26 km) and 250 Rp from Gianyar (13 km). Here you should stay a few days for excursions into the surrounding area. Right opposite the bemo station is ARTHA SASTRA INN**, a losmen in an old palace. Agung Artha Sastra knows the region and can give you tips. The main road makes it loud, though. A bit further north on the same street is DAMAPUTRA*. Every third day is market day here.

Go 2 km north and then left to *PURA KEHEN.* This temple is built into a hill on three levels. Wide steps lead to the top. Chinese porcelain plates have been placed in the walls. Children will try to sell you Chinese coins as souvenirs.

3 km along a road which leads west from the post office to TAMPAKSIRING (no bemos!) is the mountain *DEMULIH.* A nice walk even if it isn't the best view in the world. On the way is a hard to find path leading to a waterfall (considered holy).

EAST BALI

Traces of the last Gunung Agung eruption are still visible in the east, the poorest region on the island. From the heights of the volcano, barren lava fields stretch to black beaches along the coast. In recent years, the coastal road to Singaraja was completed, but several bridges are still missing - the rivers have yet to dig new river beds. On the southern slope of Gunung Agung is Besakih, the Mother Temple of the Balinese.

KLUNGKUNG

When the east Javanese royal court settled on Bali in the 16th century, the political centre for all princes (or raja) was located south of town in GELGEL. The Royal Court of Justice sat in Klungkung until the power of the rajas was overthrown by the Dutch. The painted ceilings of the *COURTHOUSE (KERTA GOSA)* vividly depict the penalties facing the convicted. These paintings, reminiscent of a Christian Hell made of wayang puppets, are still produced in KAMASAN. Scenes from the Ramayana are often featured. The village is 2 km to the south on the way to Gelgel. Next to the courthouse is another building surrounded by a man-made pond. Across the way is the new Handicraft Promotion Centre.

You can find relatively inexpensive lontar, antiques and other souvenirs in the different shops along the main street. Don't let yourself be influenced by the shop keepers' wishful thinking displayed on the price tags. They are intended for the bus tourists who don't have time to bargain. There is a nice night market. Just before sunset, hundreds of Balinese head down to the river to bathe and gather water.

HOTELS

The hotels are very loud.

Try *LOSMEN WISHNU*(*),* by the bus stand on Jl.Gunung Rinjani, simple, but okay.

Noticeably more expensive is *RAMAYANA PALACE HOTEL****.

HOW TO GET THERE

Bemos from Denpasar (40 km, 800 Rp). Buses and colts heading east (CANDI DASA 500 Rp, AMLAPURA 700-800 Rp) depart from the main road in the eastern town centre. The station for bemos to BESAKIH (500 Rp) is just beyond the road branching north. To PENELOKAN (1200 Rp).

BESAKIH

The mother temple Besakih is situated 20 km north of Klungkung on the slopes of the holy mountain *GUNUNG AGUNG.* On holidays you can get a colt direct from Klungkung to the temple for 500 Rp. Otherwise take a bemo to MENANGA (400 Rp). From here it's a steep road climbing up for 6 km. A bemo up this bit costs 250 Rp. Along the way, down in the valley, is the restaurant and homestay ARCA VALLEY***, plus a losmen** about 100 m from the temple entrance. In good weather you can see over the rice terraces to the sea. It's worth getting here early because by noon the temple and mountain are usually locked in the clouds.

The 3140 m high Gunung Agung is the centre of the Balinese world and the residence of the gods. At 900 m it's the largest and holiest temple on the island. The mother temple is built on the ruins of a shrine at least 1000 years old. This spot has always been considered holy. Every caste, every village, and every region has its own temple; yet Besakih is a temple for all Balinese, and every caste is represented by a building here. Thousands of pilgrims journey to the temple festivals. Non-believers and tourists, however, aren't allowed to visit the inner temples during the ceremonies. The biggest festival, Eka Dasa Rudra, takes place every hundred years; the last was in 1963. On the last day of celebration the volcano erupted after hundreds of years of peace, costing thousands of lives. The streams of lava coursed over the eastern part of the island but, like a miracle, the mother temple was spared.

It is a lovely tour (no bemos) through the villages along the southern slope of Agung. Head directly from Bangli towards Rendang. From there a narrow paved road goes on to SELAT - lovely rice terraces. Then you can continue on either via ISEH, where the painter Walter Spies used to live, back to Klungkung, or across country still recovering from the latest eruption via SIBETAN to Amlapura.

In PUTUNG, west of BEBANDEM, is PUTUNG BUNGALOWS**(*) with a fantastic view over the steep rice terraces on Padang Bai and Nusa Penida. The cottages with balconies are right on the steep slope; the adjoining restaurant is relatively expensive, but good. In the village of SIDEMEN is another homestay**.

NUSA PENIDA

Between Klungkung and Amlapura the beaches seem devoid of humanity. A few hidden bays are used illegally by nudists. Volcanic rock has given the sandy beaches at KUSAMBA their black colour. At Pasar Ikan, a side road runs down to the sea from the main road. Colourful prahus are everywhere. They will take you to Nusa Penida, a former prison island with sparse vegetation.

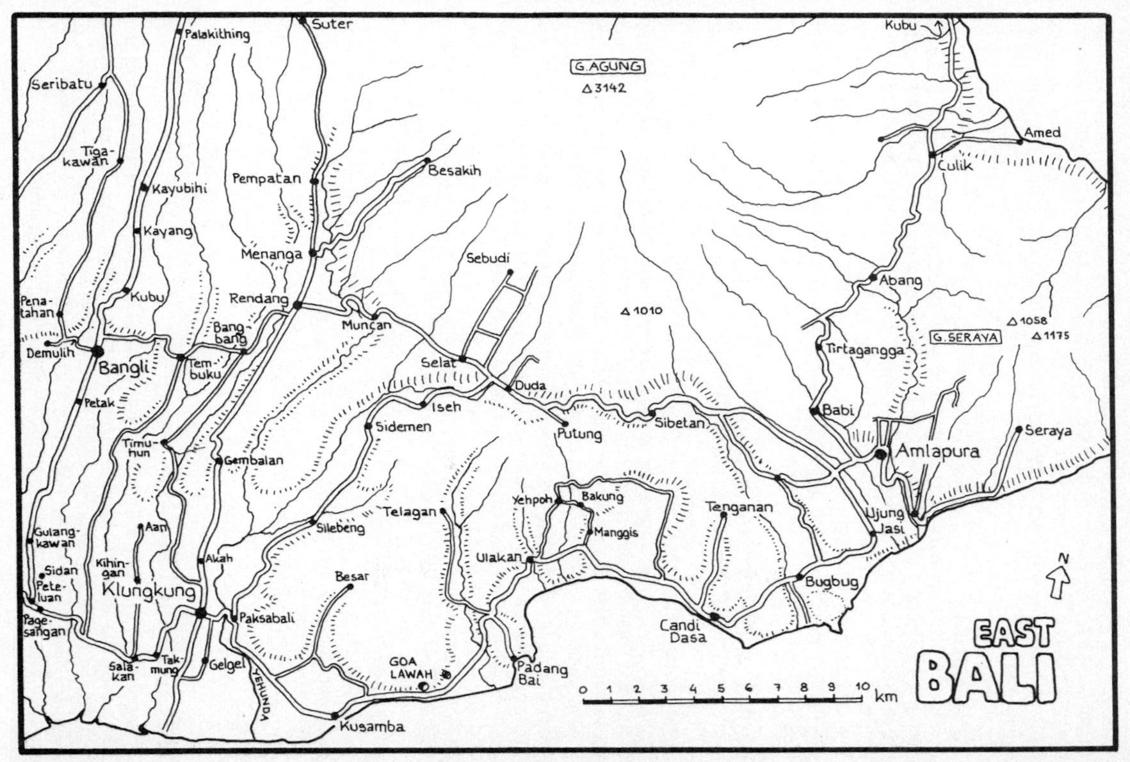
EAST
BALI
N
0 1 2 3 4 5 6 7 8 9 10 km
G. AGUNG
Δ 3142
Δ 1010
G. SERAYA
Δ 1058
Δ 1175
Kubu
Amed
Culik
Abang
Tirtagangga
Babi
Amlapura
Seraya
Ujung
Jasi
Bugbug
Tenganan
Candi Dasa
Manggis
Bakung
Yehpoh
Ulakan
Padang Bai
Putung
Sibetan
Duda
Selat
Sebudi
Besakih
Iseh
Sidemen
Telagan
GOA LAWAH
Kusamba
Besar
Silebeng
Muncan
Rendang
Suter
Pempatan
Menanga
Palakithing
Kayubihi
Kayang
Kubu
Bang-bang
Tem-buku
Gembalan
Akah
Paksabali
YEHUNDA
Gelgel
Klungkung
Tak-mung
Sala-kan
Aan
Kihin-gan
Timu-hun
Bangli
Petak
Seribatu
Tiga-kawan
Pena-tahan
Demulih
Gulang-kawan
Sidan
Pete-luan
Page-sangan

You can get a regular midday boat (2 h, 2500 Rp) to TOYAPAKEH on NUSA PENIDA. A charter costs 20,000 Rp. Typical Balinese prahus are small outriggers, powered by outboard motor. Pack everything in plastic and guard against waves, which frequently wash over the boat. If the sea is rough, you'll arrive soaked.

TOYAPAKEH

At TOYAPAKEH a lovely beach will lure you, despite the presence of some unfriendly people. Losmen* and lots of warung can be found in SAMPALAN, the largest village on the island. Unlike Bali, there is hardly a rice field on the entire island. The main crops are corn, vegetables, mangos, and coconuts. The standard of living seems much below that of Bali. In some villages, people are friendly and helpful, in others objectionable. The villages are rarely visited by strangers.

HIKING AROUND THE ISLAND

Walk south from TOYAPAKEH to SEBUNIBUS, where the road forks. The road to the right runs to SAKTI and then parallels the coast. The road to the left leads inland. The road ends at SAKTI; thereafter there's a narrow footpath through a dry, barren region. Follow the path for about two hours over the top of the hill. Then the path descends steeply into a valley thick with palms. There you'll find a small village and a nice beach. You can buy groceries from villagers, if you haven't brought your own, and perhaps stay at the beach.

From the valley it is 3 km up a steep hill to SUMPANG, an unspoiled village. The next villages are PENANGKIDAN and SEBULUH, each about 3 km apart. From SEBULUH there is another unpaved road to BATUMADEG, where you'll find several shops and bemo connections. By the path, just before BATUMADEG, is a beautiful little Hindu temple. After the village, the path forks to SAKTI / SAMPALAN and PENGAKSA. From BATUKANDIK the path leads gently uphill along a barren mountain ridge from which you can can see the northern and southern coasts at times.

In TANGLAD is a losmen* and several warungs. Two roads branch down to the steep shore. From TANGLAD it is 9 km to SUWANA, a small fishing village. There you'll find warung in which you might be able to spend the night. 3 1/2 km beyond SUWANA is KARANGSARI where you can explore a cave. Ask the people to show you the cave entrance, and take a flashlight. From TOYAPAKEH you can get a bemo.

NUSA LEMBONGAN

This tiny island is northwest of Nusa Penida. The peaceful atmosphere is unspoiled by the drone of motor-cycles and cars, which have yet to invade the island. The main village is LEMBONGAN. There are lots of losmen in JUNGUTBATU. The island has good surfing, white sandy beaches, and crystal-clear water. Snorkeling along the off-shore reef is excellent.

HOTELS

To date there are about a dozen losmen or bungalow facilities, e.g. *LEMBONGAN BEACH COTTAGES*** with private mandi. Or it is cheaper at *JOHNNY'S**. Bungalows are available at *MAINSKI INN TREEHOUSE***, the newest facility on the island. Here you can rent either the upper or lower floors. *LEMBONGAN BUNGALOWS** rents entire houses and has the largest restaurant on the island. All lodgings are right by the water.

HOW TO GET THERE

It is a 2-3 hour trip from SANUR to Lembongan. Outrigger boats depart every morning charging 6000 Rp. Boats from KUSAMBA are faster and somewhat cheaper. They depart between 6:00 and 10:00 h.

PADANG BAI

The harbour is in a beautiful bay 2 km off the main road. The Pelni office is right on the pier. From here you can get a ferry to Lombok or the K.M.Kelimutu (see LEAVING BALI). Stay in Padang Bai for a day or two of hiking and walks. A climbing expedition to the hills behind the bay is rewarded with a tremendous view. Along the coast, white, sandy beaches lie hidden, awaiting discovery. Behind Kusamba, to the left of the road, is GOA LAWAH, the bat caves, with lots of tourist bustle. At the branch off to Tenganan is a lovely, sandy beach.

HOTELS

If you've missed the ferry, stay in *HOTEL MADYA*** by the harbour - the rooms facing front are noisy and not very clean, but new rooms have been built on at the back. For the same price you can stay in the bungalows of *PADANG BAI BEACH INN*** on the beach about 500 m to the east; due to the cost of new bungalow construction, the owner seems to lack the funds to build a fence as protection against thieves. Bring in your laundry and everything else at night, and lock your doors and windows when departing; cameras and money have been lost. Two adjoining bungalow facilities are *RAI BEACH INN*** and *KERTI BEACH INN***.

FOOD

KENDEDES is a good rumah makan with friendly service. Try 'Made's Special' (the owner's name is Made), a sleeping potion: tea, lemon, a shot of coke, and a hefty portion of arak, 400 Rp a glass.

HOW TO GET THERE

If you can't get a lift direct to Padang Bai, get off at the junction on the main road and walk 2 km. Bemos charge 1500 Rp to DENPASAR, 300 - 400 Rp to CANDI DASA.

CANDI DASA

Those who flee Kuta / Legian and are disappointed by Lovina Beach but still want to enjoy beach life, usually land on the beach at Candi Dasa. The little settlement has a school and temple set on a cliff. The narrow, sandy beach

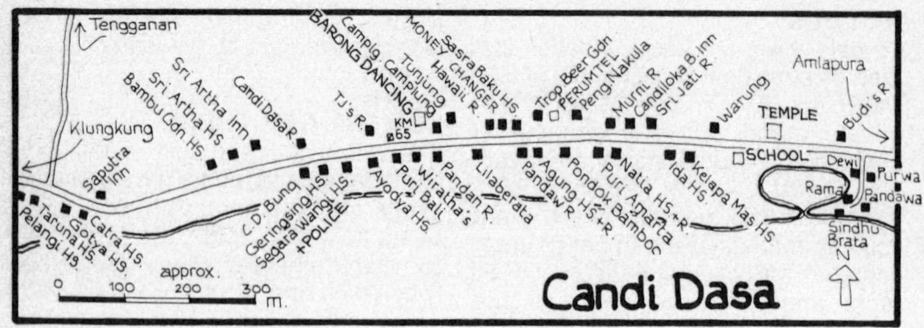

only merits the title at low tide; when the tide comes in, waves wash up to the palms. Divers can explore the coral reef and off-shore islands. Otherwise, there is little to do - so it's a great place to just relax.

A 2 km band of losmen, bungalows and restaurants has already developed along the narrow strip between the beach and the road. Other than the road, this is a very peaceful spot unspoiled by souvenir bustle.

HOTELS

There are ever more lodgings, providing a spot for every pocketbook. For example: *HOMESTAY LILA BERATA**, simple cottages, just 10 m from the beach; *HOMESTAY AYODYA*(*)* and *SRI ARTHA INN**, the latter with a restaurant. Popular and therefore full is *HOMESTAY NATIA ***. LOSMEN PANDAN***(*)* lures with its almost luxurious furnishings. In a lovely garden is *CANDI DASA BEACH BUNGALOWS****, the food is too expensive. Breakfast is included everywhere.

HOW TO GET THERE

Colts from PADANG BAI (300-400 Rp) toward Amlapura. From DENPASAR 1500 Rp.

TENGANAN

A small road leads the 3 km into the village from the main road. Since only a few bemos do this route, take a motorbike taxi from the main road into town for 300 Rp.

The people here call themselves 'Bali Aga' (= original Balinese) because they were settled here before the east Javanese royal court arrived. Today they live cut off from other Balinese in a mountain world under their own traditional laws. Covarrubias gives an excellent description of them. The village consists of two parallel streets. On the outer side of each is a row of houses. This creates a fortress-like wall to the outside world. You can only get in through one of four gates. You'll find lontar books and double ikat at deluxe prices. The lontar, while new, are made in the village using traditional methods.

AMLAPURA

The district capital is still known under its old name Karangasem. After the catastrophic volcano eruption in 1963, the town was renamed to dispel the evil spirits which buried the town and the surrounding area under a mass of lava. The former royal palace, *PURI KANGIANAN,* shows signs of European and Chinese as well as Balinese influences. The raja, whose picture hangs at the palace entrance, loved water palaces. As might be expected, you can find several of these unusual structures in the area.

About 3 km south of Amlapura (bemo 200 Rp), in UJUNG, you can see the much damaged remains of a water palace. Another is in TIRTAGANGGA. Take a bemo for 150 Rp from the turnoff heading north just before the town. It is wonderfully located on a mountain slope (admission). You can even stay right next to the palace in DHANGIN TAMAN INN** and swim in the pool. Big rooms with double beds and private mandi. TAMAN SARI** and KESUMA JAYA*** are on the hill.

HOW TO GET THERE

From Amlapura there's a road to SINGARAJA (92 km by bus for 1200 Rp). The road leads through a hot steppe-like countryside. Ticket to DENPASAR 1500 Rp by minibus.

NORTH BALI

PENELOKAN

means 'vantage point': you get a fascinating view out over Batur volcano and the surrounding mountains. On a clear day you can even see the sea. The tremendous view attracts its share of tourists, who draw the usual souvenir vendors; the atmosphere is relatively aggressive. Catch a bemo from Gianyar (900 Rp) or Singaraja (1000 Rp) to Penelokan. Some travellers have told us bad stories about bands of young people who stop motorbikes and rip off parts of the bike (if not the rider). Be especially careful on the road from Tampaksiring to Penelokan! If you want to spend the night: LAKEVIEW HOMESTAY* or LOSMEN GUNAWAN*.

AROUND PENELOKAN

TRUNYAN

First get a bemo down the steep hill 3 km to KEDISAN. There is no need to charter, however many people tell you otherwise. At the boat landing are three losmen, with another further up by the fork. Boat-rides for a tour of the lake (Trunyan, Bali Aga Cemetery, Toya Bungkah) cost 2000 Rp per person, or at least 20,000 to charter. You can reach TRUNYAN via a difficult footpath along the lake. The village, like Tenganan, is inhabited by Bali Aga, who have an unusual funeral tradition. The deceased are not cremated, as in the rest of Bali, but wrapped in white cloth and laid out in the open.

BATUR VOLCANO

From Penelokan, Kintamani, Pura Jati or TOYA BUNGKAH (TIRTA), you can climb the Batur volcano on a day's expedition - preferably with a guide. Wear sturdy shoes and take a thick sweater. From Pura Jati, just follow the white markers. From Toya Bungkah the climb and descent takes 3 hours; from Kintamani calculate 6 hours. The climb up unbelievable lava formations is quite interesting. Only go in good weather! Many losmen organize tours for 1500-2000 Rp per person. After the climb you can refresh yourself at Toya Bungkah on the bank of the lake in a pool filled by a hot spring. Near the spring are several losmen and restaurants, e.g. TIRTA YASA* by the lake at the entrance to the town on the right. In WARUNG NYOMAN PANGUS, try the excellent fish.

The road runs from Toya Bungkah via SONGAN around Batur to KOLOMBO. In Songan you can take a right to a small temple at the end of the road.

KINTAMANI

Just 8 km from Penelokan, this is a market town in the mountains. The market takes place every other day; it's especially interesting early in the morning. Stay the night at: HOTEL MIRANDA*, HOMESTAY KINTAMANI*, LOSMEN LINGGA GIRI* (nice view of Gunung Agung), WISMA ARNDT* and BATUR SARI* - here they have good food, try 'black rice'. Bemos to SINGARAJA cost 900 Rp, to BANGLI 600 Rp, and via KUBUTAMBAHAN to AMLAPURA.

BEDUGUL

A small village in the mountains at Lake Bratan right on the main road from Denpasar (48 km) to Singaraja (30 km). Stay the night in HOTEL BEDUGUL**(*) on the lake (rent boats for about 1200 Rp per person) or in HADIRAHARJO* right in the village. Take a walk along the street, north to *CANDI KUNING.* There is a market there for orchids and other jungle plants. Another market is in *BUKIT MUNGSU.* There's the *ULON DANAU BERATAN* temple for the Goddess of Water on the lakeside.

One of Bali's most interesting roads heads west about 8 km above Bedugul at the hairpin turn. It follows the ridge through villages with fantastic views (if unspoiled by clouds) of the two lakes, Buyan and Tamblingan, and north to the sea. Then it runs steeply downhill to MUNDUK. You pass through woods and clove plantations. The road is completely paved, although bemos are very infrequent. From Munduk you can continue on to MAYONG and SERIRIT (to the north) or TABANAN and DENPASAR (to the south).

You can hike on the footpaths around the lakes. Take the first path off to the left outside town before the road starts climbing uphill. The overgrown field path leads straight along the southern bank of Lake Buyan, ending at a footpath. This leads further south through tropical mountain forest to the bank of Lake Tamblingan. Continue past a temple on a hill to Tamblingan. Here it is another 2 km to Munduk where you can get a bemo.

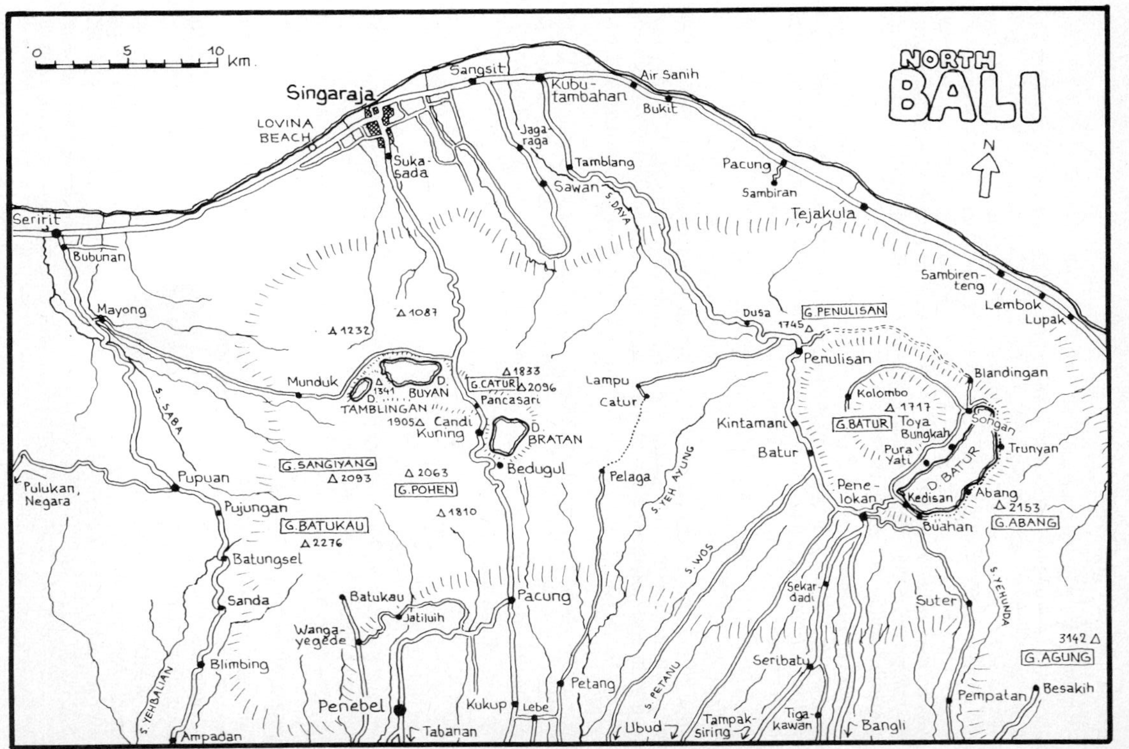
NORTH BALI
N
0
5
10 km.
Singaraja
LOVINA BEACH
Sangsit
Kubu-tambahan
Air Sanih
Bukit
Suka-sada
Jaga-raga
Tamblang
Sawan
S. DAYA
Pacung
Sambiran
Tejakula
Seririt
Bubunan
Sambiren-teng
Lembok
Lupak
Mayong
Δ 1087
Δ 1232
Dusa
G. PENULISAN
1745Δ
Penulisan
Blandingan
Munduk
Δ 1341
D. TAMBLINGAN
D. BUYAN
Δ 1833
G. CATUR
Δ 2096
Pancasari
Lampu
Catur
Kolombo
Δ 1717
G. BATUR
Toya Bungkah
Songan
Trunyan
Pura Yati
D. BATUR
S. SABA
1905Δ Candi Kuning
D. BRATAN
Kintamani
Batur
G. SANGIYANG
Δ 2093
Δ 2063
G. POHEN
Bedugul
Pelaga
S. YEH AYUNG
Pene-lokan
Kedisan
Abang
Δ 2153
Buahan
G. ABANG
Pupuan
Pulukan, Negara
Pujungan
G. BATUKAU
Δ 2276
Δ 1810
Batungsel
S. WOS
Sanda
Batukau
Jatiluih
Pacung
Sekar-dadi
Suter
S. YEHUNDA
Wanga-yegede
3142 Δ
G. AGUNG
Blimbing
S. YEHBALIAN
Seribatu
Petang
S. PETANU
Pempatan
Besakih
Penebel
Kukup
Lebe
Tabanan
Ubud
Tampak-siring
Tiga-kawan
Bangli
Ampadan

SINGARAJA

Once upon a time the Dutch lived in this north Balinese town. Everywhere else to the south were 'native provinces'. Read about it in the book by Ktut Tantri 'Revolt in Paradise'. This was the capital of the province of Nusa Tenggara and up until 1953 the administrative centre of the island - and the signs still remain. The big wide streets and houses don't look at all Balinese. The caste system died off here much earlier under Dutch influence. In addition there's the influence of the Chinese and Javanese, especially in the harbour area where the agricultural products are shipped.

The *HISTORICAL LIBRARY* on Jl.Veteran has a good collection of lontar scripts. About 3500 examples are on file, including the most ancient writings in existence from Bali. The Tourist Information Office is next door. You can change money and travellers cheques near the harbour at Bank Bumi Daya.

HOTELS

Better to stay out at Lovina beach. If you want to stay in town, there are several cheap hotels on Jl.Jen.A.Yani, *CENDRAWASIH**, no. 21, *SENTRAL**, no. 48, *DUTA KARYA***, no. 59, *GELAR SARI***, no. 87 and *SAKA BINDU***, no. 104.

The *HOTEL SINGARAJA** at Jl.Veteran 1 was once the residence of the Dutch governor.

HOW TO GET THERE

Buses leave direct from SURABAYA for 9000 Rp to SINGARAJA (Banyusari bus station west of town). Here are also buses and bemos to DENPASAR (1500 Rp) and GILIMANUK (1300 Rp). From Kampong Tinggi (bemos leave from Banyusari for 150 Rp) to KINTAMANI (900 Rp), AMLAPURA (1200 Rp) and KLUNGKUNG (1300 Rp).

LOVINA BEACH / HAPPY BEACH

LOVINA BEACH (10 km) and HAPPY BEACH (6 km) west of town (by bemo 300 Rp - be sure to bargain!) are still for people who want to get away from all the hoop-la in Kuta. Since the dark beach isn't anywhere as nice as beaches in the south and the still waters don't attract surfers, you can be sure that it will remain this way even if the sunsets are nice.

If you want to snorkel in the coral reef, you'll have to get a boat to take you out. The price for a boat with six people should be around 2000 Rp per person - be sure the use of masks, fins, and snorkel is included in the price. Out there, the sea is clear as glass, so you are really able to enjoy the underwater world.

4 km west of Lovina, near Labuhan Haji, is the *SING SING WATERFALL* (= air terjun). About 2 km above the village of BANJAR TEGA (bemos to the village, 300 Rp, 14 km, then walk) is a small Buddhist monastery, nestled in peaceful isolation on a hill. Enjoy the tremendous view all the way to the coast, or relax in one of the quiet courtyards where you can meditate among the sculptures and flowers. Ask in Banjar or at the monastery for the way to the hot springs (= air panas), a lovely spot with a natural swimming pool, losmen and restaurant.

HOTELS

The losmen and restaurants are spread out along several kilometres of the road. At Happy Beach between 6 and 8 km among others *BARUNA BEACH INN****, *SUCI JATI REEF***, *HOMESTAY AGUNG***, *SIMON'S SEASIDE COTTAGES*** and *LILA CITA**-**** Near the radio station is *KALIBUKBUK BEACH INN** - rather simple, and *BANYUALIT BUNGALOWS*** - friendly people.

Most losmen are in Kalibukbuk. Two side streets lead to the widest section of beach, the nicest spot for a swim. There are, however, lots of sea urchins and beach vendors. Here you'll find *NIRWANA LOSMEN**-**** and *RESTAURANT*. The bungalows are right next to the beach. Near the beach is *PERMATA**, bungalows with private shower** and a nice garden. *MANGGALA** is on the beach with a restaurant opposite. To be recommended is *TASIK MADU***. On the wall in the restaurant are reassuring Christian sayings. Clean, good, and nice people at *ADITYA***.

FOOD

Additional warungs and restaurants along the street. The meeting place in Lovina remains *BADAI RESTAURANT*. The wooden benches aren't the greatest, but the food is good and the blackboard contains the latest info. *MARTA'S MINI RESTAURANT* is cheap with great milkshakes. Also good is *KIKI RESTAURANT* on the main road.

THE BALINESE PEOPLE

The ancestors of most Balinese came to the island as refugees when the Majapahit kingdom fell in 1520. The whole upper class, from the nobility and their retinue, artists and priests to the rich merchants, sought refuge on the island from the spread of Islam. They were able, in fact, to maintain their own Hindu culture. In the 17th century, the kingdom broke up into several independent principalities. The Dutch took clever advantage of this political disunity in the attempt to add Bali to their East India colonies. In 1846 the conquest of north Bali began, but it took almost 40 years for the Dutch to consolidate their position. While this was going on in the north, the rulers in the south were fighting among themselves, and the weak Gianyar was voluntarily collaborating with the Dutch. The bitter resistance of the kings of Tabanan and Badung ended in a 'puputan' or fight to the last man.

The royal houses are powerless today. The art and culture, which at one time were reserved for the pleasure of the upper class and the gods, have now spread down to be enjoyed by the common people, so their preservation is ensured. Even today, however, there are descendants of the princes and kings. They are addressed in a respectful 'high language' while they answer in the 'low language' of the marketplace. A teacher once had a lot of trouble with one of his pupils. The pupil's forefather was a prince and so had to be addressed in the 'high language'. If the teacher wanted to scold the boy, he could only use the national language, Bahasa Indonesia, and not Balinese. Besides those two languages there is a 'middle language' which one uses when speaking to strangers whose caste one doesn't know.

Most people are casteless (sudras) today. The three upper castes are Brahmans (priests and teachers), Weisyas (warriors and administrators), and Ksatrias (princes). In the 'banjar', the village meetings, everyone has the same vote, however. Problems facing the village are handled by the married men. All decisions must be unanimous. This requires large discussions, where everyone assembles in the big meeting house (bale banjar) in the village - so you meet the men more often here than in the paddy fields. The beating of the 'kulkul' (wooden drum) in the evenings calls the men to the meeting. It is also sounded to announce a death or danger. Some men even prefer the 'banjar' to their own beds and spend the night there.

A banyan tree belongs to the centre of a village as much as the village temple - 'pura desa'. Two other temples can be found north and south of the town. One 'gunung agung' faces the holy mountain and symbolizes good, while the other temple faces the sea, symbolizing evil. This is also where the dead are cremated. The temples thereby represent the course of life: birth (pura puseh - north), life (pura desa), and death (pura dalem - south).

According to Balinese-Hindu beliefs, a soul will continue to be reborn until it is released to the kingdom of the gods. The release from their present condition is mixed with feelings of hope for a better existence. For this reason the colourful cremation is the most important part of people's lives because only through the expensive ceremony is the soul able to travel into the other world. Huge towers of bamboo and paper go up in flames along with the corpse of the deceased. Afterwards the ashes are spread on the sea or in a river.

Children are very important to the Balinese. A man only takes on full status in the 'banjar' when he has fathered a child. The souls of the ancestors are said to be reborn in the children. Until they can walk, children are carried because walking upright is what separates people from animals. The teeth of young Balinese are filed for the same reason.

The grouping and association of large families are of great importance to the Balinese. All occupations - including the artistic - are performed by groups. The clan lives together in one house surrounded by a high wall. You get inside through a main entrance into the courtyard. Plants and trees make this a pleasant place during the heat of the day. Rooms for living and the kitchen form a circle around the courtyard. The house temple, dedicated to the guardian god of the family, is also there. It receives new offerings every morning.

SOME RULES OF BEHAVIOUR

- ❑ Wear a piece of cloth (scarf) wrapped around your waist when you visit a temple.
- ❑ Try to keep out of the limelight at religious ceremonies.
- ❑ Ask permission before you take pictures.
- ❑ Wear the right clothes at the right place. It is considered rude to wear beach clothes off the beach and especially to visit the beach without beach wear.

- Don't bathe nude, even if everyone else does. Balinese houses usually don't have baths which is why people wash themselves (men and women separately) twice a day in the rivers. At all times they keep their private parts covered and they don't enjoy being spied upon by nosey tourists.

FESTIVALS

Balinese seem to spend about a third of their lives preparing and taking part in festivals. Every single temple has its own special festival which is celebrated for three days each year after an even longer period of preparation. Since the Balinese year has only 210 days, and every village has its own temple, there are more than 20,000 festivals on Bali. It is easy to calculate the probability that you will run into one of these festivals (odalan). Processions of women bring offerings to the temple. Dance, theatre, carnivals, and cockfights are major parts of the programme.

No family celebration or temple festival can take place without the colourful dances and sounds of the gamelan orchestra. The dancers (both male and female) perform their harmonic movements wonderfully. Besides you wouldn't want to miss the beautifully decorated costumes.

BARIS *- the war dance, performed only by men.*
BARONG *- two dancers are dressed as gigantic puppets and walk on stilts. They drive away evil and can be seen on the streets especially during the Galungan holidays.*
KECAK *- the monkey dance. A large male chorus, representing Hanuman's army of monkeys, chants and moves rhythmically while scenes from the Ramayana are portrayed.*
LEGONG *- the dance of the heavenly nymphs is performed by three young girls and portrays the resistance of a kidnapped girl.*
JAUK *- the dance of a good, but bizarrely-costumed demon.*

It is impossible to list all of the Bali festivals, so here is a short and incomplete list:

GALUNGAN *- 10 days long, the creation of the world and the victory of good over evil is celebrated. Streets and houses are decorated, often with 'janur', the artful weaving of palm-leaves.*
KUNINGAN *- at the end of Galungan the forefathers and saints are remembered for having lived according to religious scriptures - a type of Balinese 'All Saints' Day'.*
NYEPI *- New year, nobody is allowed to work, leave the house, or light an open fire. On the day before, the evil demons are driven away. All of Bali is quiet!*
There are also special holidays for plants, metal (including cars!), books, wayang kulit, rice, etc.

NUSA TENGGARA

The Indonesian name Nusa Tenggara means 'southeastern islands' and describes the Lesser Sunda Islands east of Bali. They are administratively divided into three provinces. Nusa Tenggara Barat (west) with the main islands of Lombok and Sumbawa, has 3.1 million inhabitants spread out over about 20,000 km^2. Nusa Tenggara Timur (east) consists of the islands of Komodo, Sumba, Flores and West-Timor. About 3.3 million people live here on about 40,000 km^2. The population density decreases drastically from west to east. A province of its own, East Timor is the former Portuguese territory (19,000 km^2, 550,000 inhabitants). The provincial capitals are Mataram, Kupang and Dili.

Between Sumbawa and Timor you are stepping into virgin tourist territory. Mass tourism is unheard of. Before the Indonesian solution to the Timor problem in 1976, when the eastern part of the island, until then Portuguese, was annexed by Indonesia, the overland trail from Australia to Europe crossed the islands. The cheapest air connection was Darwin-Dili, from there on island-hopping. Today the route is largely forgotten since the 'cheapest' flight is now Denpasar to Darwin for US$254. But since 1986 it has been possible to fly Darwin - Kupang for US$170, which does bring more tourists into the area.

The Wallace Line runs between Bali and Lombok. East of this line you find only sporadic examples of Asian flora and fauna. Large mammals such as elephant, tiger, leopard, tapir etc. aren't found any more. On the other hand you will find the typical Australian-Melanese fauna and flora. Instead of tropical rainforests there's mostly savanna landscape. East of Bali you'll discover a new Indonesia.

The further east you go, the more predominant the Melanese-Australian population becomes. While you often find Malayan settlements along the coasts, in the interior, for instance on Flores or Timor, Papua tribes (usually Christian) are settled. On Sumbawa and the eastern part of Lombok there are some quite orthodox Muslims and in the west of Lombok some Hindu Balinese.

The infrastructure east of Lombok is middling to poor, but progressing. Regular boat and ferry connections at the moment go as far as Flores. On Lombok and Sumbawa you'll find passable road connections going east-west, and on Timor, Sumba and Flores roads are being built or even paved. But everything takes time in Nusa Tenggara.

LOMBOK

At the beginning of the 18th century, the island was conquered by the Balinese who established four principalities. Unwanted and rebellious people from Bali were often banished here. Balinese temples and palaces are an integral part of the landscape in the western part of Lombok. The native population, the Sasak, were either forced to settle on the eastern part of the island or enslaved. This has had lasting effects, even today, on relations between the Hindu Balinese and the Islamic Sasak.

In 1843 the Balinese Raja of Mataram signed a protectorate treaty with the Dutch colonial government in Batavia. In 1894 the island was administratively added to the Dutch East Indies. Here again one can see the Dutch political skill at playing one ethnic group against the other. The Sasak princes allied themselves with the Dutch; colonial troops landed on Lombok and demanded that the Raja of Mataram pay 1 million guilders in 'reparations'. The younger princes resisted and drove the Dutch soldiers from the island. But then a punitive expedition was landed and Lombok's fate was sealed. The Raja was sent into exile and the rebellious crown prince murdered.

The number of foreign visitors to the island has risen steadily: in 1979, 1600 were counted; in 1986, almost 14,000.

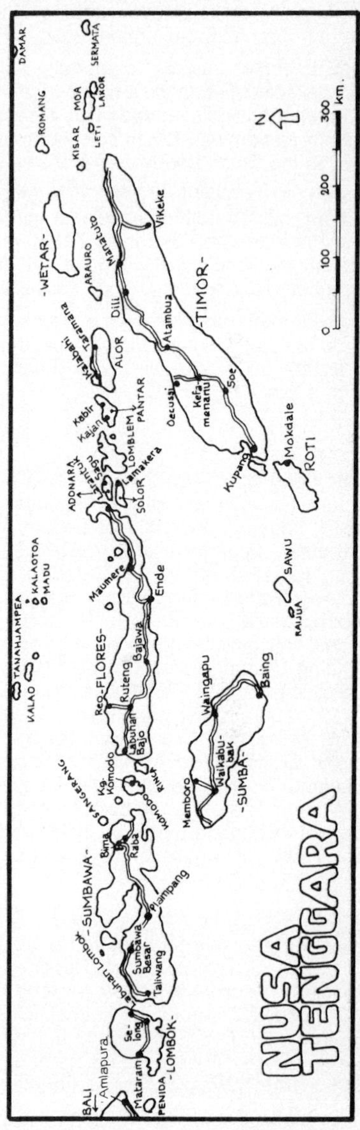

MATARAM / AMPENAN / CAKRANEGARA

The administrative capital of Mataram has grown together with its two neighbouring towns, the former port of Ampenan and the largely Chinese Cakranegara.

Lombok's largest temple, *PURA MERU,* is in Cakranegara. It was constructed in 1720 at the command of the Balinese prince Anak Agung Made Karang. Compared to the complexes on Bali, however, it seems neglected and a bit disappointing. The temple has three separate courtyards. In the outer court are kept the wooden drums with which the faithful are called to temple. The middle court has two banked platforms upon which sacrifices can be laid. In the inner court are one large and 30 smaller shrines. The three meru are symbolized by the number of roofs on the shrine: Shiva has 11, Vishnu 9 and Brahma 7.

East of Jl.Hasanuddin, diagonally across from Pura Meru, you'll find the *TAMAN MAYURA.* Once it was part of the Balinese royal court. In the middle of a man-made lake is an open hall, accessible via a footbridge. This is the site of a confrontation with Dutch colonial troops in 1894. The Balinese were able to drive all the Dutch troops from the island, but only for a few months.

There is a *CHINESE TEMPLE* in Ampenan, Jl.Pabean, not far from the old harbour, but it's nothing special. If you've a couple hours to fill, the *MUSEUM* is worth a look, on Jl.Banjar T.Negara. The relatively new building contains extensive collections of weapons, textiles, household utensils, models of traditional houses, and more. Open daily 8:00-14:00 h, Fri only till noon.

At the northern edge of town in Ampenan, by the beach, is *PURA SEGARA,* a Hindu temple, which is usually locked. Behind it is a Chinese cemetery, and a bit further on is a Muslim counterpart. The many colourful fishing-boats are worth a look.

HOTELS

Quite good is *HOTEL ZAHIR *(*),* Jl. Koperasi 9 - rooms with or without mandi, shady courtyard, nice people. Two other cheap losmen are *HORAS *(*),* Jl.Koperasi 65, tel 22049 (clean) and *KAMBOJA*,* Jl.Kamboja corner Jl.Supratman, tel 22211. In both places you get info and tips e.g. on climbing Gunung Rinjani. A bit more luxurious is *HOTEL CEMPAKA ***,* tel 23222, rates include breakfast. *LOSMEN MERPATI**,* Jl.Sultan Hasanuddin 17. *WISMA PARADISO **(*),* Jl.Lemuru Gomong (at Jl.Arif Rahmat) in Mataram is a pleasant, quiet spot. If you want to spend more, try *WISMA MELATI*****,* Jl.Langko 80, tel 23780.

FOOD

Ampenan has several restaurants on Jl.Pabean (Jl.Yos Sudarso). Recommendable Chinese and western food in *TJIREBON* across from Losmen Pabean. *SETIA* is cheaper, but it seems dingy. There's good, cheap food in *BAHAGIA,* Jl.Koperasi, across from Hotel Zahir. For Indonesia, it is relatively expensive, but the Indonesian, Chinese and European food is good in *GARDEN HOUSE & ICE CREAM PALACE* on Jl.Pejanggik, across from General Hospital in Mataram. The speciality: durian ice cream and milkshakes for 500-1400 Rp. On Jl.Hasanuddin, Cakranegara, enjoy good, cheap food in *MADYA.* Several rumah makan are also on Jl. Selaparang.

GENERAL INFORMATION

TOURIST INFORMATION - Tourist Office, Jl.Langko 70, tel 21866, across from Ampenan Post Office, 400 m from the bemo stand.

IMMIGRATION - (West Nusa Tenggara), Jl.Udayana towards the airport.

BANKS - Bank Umum Nasional, Jl. Pabean 47, Ampenan offers relatively good exchange rates, but only changes US$ traveller's cheques. For other currencies try Bank Negara Indonesia 1946, Jl.Langko.

MOTORCYCLES - In Pasar Pas in Cakranegara you can rent motorbikes for about 5000 Rp per day.

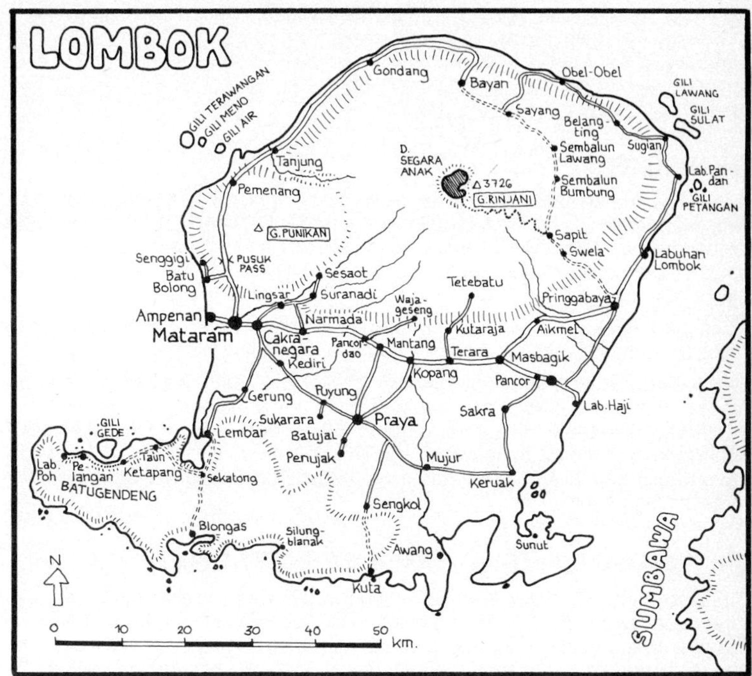

SHOPPING - Antiques and ethnographica at MUSDAH on a side street, 200 m from Zahir Hotel. For a much larger selection, check at SUDIRMAN, Jl.Yos Sudarso 88.

PPA - Office of the Nature Reserve authority PPA, Jl.Pejanggik 42 in Mataram.

LEAVING LOMBOK

BY AIR

Merpati and Garuda (offices on Jl. Langko) fly into Selaparang Airport, 2 km north of town. Bemos for 150 Rp. SAMPLE PRICES: SURABAYA 54,900 Rp (GA), DENPASAR 17,800 Rp (MZ), BIMA 46,800 Rp (MZ), SUMBAWA BESAR 28,400 Rp (MZ).

BY SHIP / FERRY

Three ferries run daily between Bali (PADANG BAI) and Lombok (LEMBAR), leaving Lembar at 9:00 h, 11:00 h, and 14:00 h. Bemos from Stasiun Sweta for 1100 Rp. Ferry prices: 5250 Rp 1st cl., 3750 Rp Ekonomi, motorcycle 4600 Rp, takes 4 hours. Ferries to Sumbawa (ALAS) taking 3 hours leave daily at 9:00 h, 10:00 h, and 12:00 h from LABUHAN LOMBOK, costs 2200 Rp.

BY BUS & BEMO

The central bus/bemo station is Stasiun Sweta, 1 km east of Cakranegara. Bemos to Ampenan or Mataram cost 150 Rp. Colts to LEMBAR cost 1100 Rp, to LABUHAN LOMBOK 1800 Rp (2 1/2 hrs.). Express buses to BIMA cost 13,000 Rp, DENPASAR 7800 / 8500 Rp incl. ferry, SURABAYA in two days, incl. food and ferries 17,000 / 21,000 Rp. Check Damai Indah, Jl.Hasanuddin 17 and Bali Cepat, no. 22.

SENGGIGI

About 10 km north of Ampenan, set on a small bay. Walk along the beach from Ampenan, after 5 km you reach SASAKA BEACH COTTAGES****. A kilometre further on is BATU LAYUR, a large Islamic Wetu Telu sanctuary, consisting of a small house containing the tomb of a famous saint. A Muslim cemetery is behind it .

Continue 2 km to BATU BOLONG, a Hindu temple set on a cliff. Here you can enjoy the sunset over Gunung Agung on Bali, just a few kilometres away.

Besides bungalow losmen** and hotels ***(*), SENGGIGI has little more to offer than sun and a long beach, beginning just a few metres from the road. Try PONDOK SENGGIGI**(*) in a garden, 50 m from the beach. The latest achievement is the 52 bungalows of SENGGIGI BEACH HOTEL****, but you'll have to pay 80,000 Rp. Several tour organizers have already added the hotel to their programme.

GILI AIR /GILI MENO / GILI TERAWANGAN

The drive north via PUSUK PASS is worthwhile. Everywhere, lovely beaches offer good surfing. It takes 45 minutes through a bamboo forest full of monkeys. There are three, thinly settled islands with white, lonely beaches but little shade. There are lovely coral reefs for diving. Until recently an open secret, increasing numbers of Lombok visitors make the stop. The first nude bathers have already been sighted. You can get an outrigger with outboard motor to the islands from the beach at Bangsal. On all three islands you'll look in vain for restaurants, but all the losmen include three meals and drinks in the lodging price!

GILI AIR

The nearest island with the most losmen**-****; a large hotel with a swimming pool is planned. The people from Zahir Hotel, Ampenan will drive you in a hotel minibus and boat for the same price as the public transport to Gili Air, dropping you off at LOSMEN GILI INDAH***. Many travellers consider this the nicest bungalow facility on the island. The 6000 Rp price includes three meals. If there is sufficient interest, the owner will organize diving expeditions for 1000 Rp per person. The lovely reef is just off the beach. LOSMEN NUSA TIGA*** is similar.

GILI MENO

The smallest island has just one losmen** and few visitors up to now. Take the Terawangan boat and explain in good time that you want to disembark at Meno.

GILI TERAWANGAN

You can circle the largest island in a 2-3 hour beach stroll. Go at low tide and wear sturdy shoes for walking over the reef. There is even a small hill to climb, a rarity in the flat Gilis. Two cannons, dating from Japan's WWII fortifications, can still be seen. Terawangan has two losmen. PAK MAJID** in the centre of the island surrounded by cotton fields is recommended by many travellers, youth hostel atmosphere. Pak Majid's wife Suparmi provides three good and plentiful meals daily. If enough people are interested, a day trip will be organized to the other islands. HOMESTAY MAKMUR is also recommended, right by the beach with a view of Lombok. Right off shore is a tremendous reef. Walk a bit along the beach, let yourself be carried by the current over the great underwater world, then return to the beach by the homestay.

HOW TO GET THERE

Bemos from Sweta 500 Rp to PEMENANG (28 km), or head right to BANGSAL for 600 Rp. Otherwise by dokar (on Lombok the small horse-carts are called 'cidomo') in 25 minutes for 200 Rp to the boat landing. Outrigger boats with outboard motors cruise to the islands, calculate 500 Rp to Gili Air, 900 Rp to Gili Meno and 1300 Rp to Terawangan. Try to get there early because in the afternoon most sampans are only available for charter. Besides, the beach is a pleasant spot to wait! Tourist prices are higher than those for local people.

LINGSAR

From the cinema in Cakranegara, bemos charge 150 Rp for a ride to the temple complex 7 km northwest of Narmada. The northern half of the complex serves the Hindu faith while the remainder is dedicated to the Islamic Wetu Telu religion. The temple complex was constructed in the early 18th century and completely restored in 1878. According to legend, a new spring began to flow when the first Hindus from Bali arrived at a spring called Aik Mual, about 200 m east of Pura Lingsar today. The Balinese named this Aik Engsar, from which the name 'Lingsar' is derived.

The northern Hindu temple, at a higher altitude, has four shrines, of which the one on the left, called Hyang Tunggal, faces Gunung Agung on Bali. The temple on the right faces Gunung Rinjani, Lombok's sacred mountain.

A pool, dedicated to the god Vishnu and containing sacred eels, is in the Wetu Telu section of the temple. A rewarding excursion!

NARMADA

11 km from Cakra with a Balinese palace dating from 1801, surrounded by a terraced garden, swimming pools (admission 100 Rp) and a lake. This is a spot where many people come to get away for the weekend, warungs available. Bring a bathing suit; women should also wear a t-shirt. Bemos from Sweta 175 Rp.

SURANADI

The oldest Hindu temple on Lombok, with a spring containing sacred eels, is located in Suranadi at the foot of the Rinjani. Lovely mountain scenery; a good departure point for walks. Get a bemo from Sweta first to Narmada and then on to Suranadi, 15 km, 175 Rp plus 125 Rp. Use of the hotel pool, next to the temple, costs 400 Rp. You can spend a night in SURANADI HOTEL****, whose older section served as a resort for Dutch colonial officials in the 1930s.

PANTAI KUTA

You'll find nothing in common with its infamous namesake on Bali apart from a beach. There are two simple losmen* and warungs by the bemo stop. Two bungalow losmen** are 500 m to the east. Lots of seaweed at the beach. Several bays are easy to reach a few kilometres to the east, each prettier than the other. The beaches are blinding white, devoid of people, and the water is crystal clear. The road from Sengkol to Kuta runs past two traditional Sasak villages, REMBITAN and SADE. The houses are constructed using traditional Sasak methods without use of corrugated iron.

HOW TO GET THERE

Get a colt to PRAYA (600 Rp), then a bemo to SENGKOL (300 Rp) and finally a bemo to Kuta (300 Rp). The bemos return to PRAYA until late afternoon, and from there you can get an evening colt to SWETA.

TETEBATU

Situated at the pleasant altitude of 600 m on the southern slope of Gunung Rinjani. You can lodge at the recommendable WISMA DR.R.SOEDJONO above the village, rooms** or nice little bungalows***(*), Sasak style, very clean, some with private mandi. There are more losmen in Kotaraja, situated under tall trees in a park-like garden between rice fields, rushing streams and fish ponds. The wisma has a restaurant, swimming pool, and two vehicles, which can be chartered for excursions. By the way, the owner, Mrs Surdini Soeweno, like her mother-in-law before her, holds the office of Kepala Desa (village chief) in Tetebatu. Just a few kilometres above the wisma the jungle begins - through it you can hike on the narrow paths. It is not possible to climb Rinjani from here.

HOW TO GET THERE

From SWETA get a colt or bus to PAOKMOTONG 600 Rp, bemo to KOTARAJA 250 Rp, horsecart to TETEBATU 400 Rp or on the back of a motorbike 1200 Rp.

GUNUNG RINJANI

Can be climbed despite its 3726 m height. Get info on the climb at either Losmen Horas or Kamboja. You can also rent sleeping-bags and tents (both for 8000 Rp). A warm blanket is actually enough for spending the night. Even though Rinjani is higher than Bromo, it isn't as cold. First get a bus at Sweta to BAYAN for 1200 Rp. Then take a bemo or catch a ride with a truck to SENARO. Stay the night in the school (about 1000 Rp including a meal). You don't really need a guide (costs 5000 Rp); the path's easy to follow. Start your climb about 6:00 h. After about an hour take the turnoff to the right. After another hour you come to a rest area. You'll arrive in the 'basecamp' another 4-5 hours later. Stay the night. The climb up to the crater takes about two hours and the descent into the crater another two hours - be sure to wear shoes with some traction. Take food and drinking water with you. On the way you can get more at the basecamp and about 100 m below the edge of the crater. The climb from the lake to the peak is undoubtedly much more difficult.

SUMBAWA

This 15,600 km^2 island has about 800,000 inhabitants. The Dodongo and Kolo, living in the mountains, are the original inhabitants. The Sumbawa in the western part of the island, as well as the Bima living in the east, are strict Muslims.

The history of Sumbawa can be traced back to very early times because its sandalwood was such an important export item. Today the best horses in Indonesia are bred on the island. The Islamic sultan of South Sulawesi always considered the island to be under his sphere of influence because many of the sultanates on the north coast of Sumbawa were either founded by him or were at least his dependencies. The island experienced a great catastrophe in 1815 when the volcano Tambora erupted. About 50,000 people died. The height of the volcano was reduced from 4300 m to a mere 2800 m.

The only road runs west to east from Taliwang via Alas, Sumbawa Besar, Plampang, Dompu, Bima / Raba to Sape. The south coast of the island is very difficult to reach. Lunjuk has an airstrip where occasionally a small Merpati Twin Otter lands. A trail leads over the mountains to Sumbawa Besar.

ALAS

Is the ferry harbour to Lombok. Ships leave daily at 8:00 h, 9:00 h and 10:00 h for Labuhan Lombok (2200 Rp). You can get from the harbour into town in a small horse cart for 200 Rp. The connection to Sumbawa Besar is quite good. A minibus picks you up and takes its time to cover the 65 km - costs 1400 Rp; a direct bus to BIMA (8 hrs.) costs 5000 / 6000 Rp including food.

SUMBAWA BESAR

The most important town in West Sumbawa, is a nice place to visit. About the only thing to see is the *SULTAN'S PALACE (DALAM LOKA)* built in 1932, which was restored some years ago.

HOTELS

On Jl.Hasanuddin are four losmen pretty close to each other: at no. 57 is *SUCI*** with private mandi, next door is *TUNAS***, and across the street are *SAUDARA*** and *DEWI***. Many warung can be found near the sultan's palace. You can get Chinese food at *ANEK RASA JAYA,* still better and cheaper is *RUMAH MAKAN GEMBIRA.*

LEAVING SUMBAWA BESAR

Merpati flies from here to DENPASAR for 44,200 Rp and to AMPENAN for 28,400 Rp. Office with its helpful staff is on Jl.Hasanuddin 94.

The road to Bima is mostly paved and except for the middle part, nice to travel. SAMPLE PRICES: ALAS 1400 Rp, BIMA 4600 / 5200 Rp, TALIWANG 2000 Rp. Dokars in town cost 100 - 200 Rp.

BIMA

An islamic town - a strictly orthodox bastion. You'll feel this especially during the month of Ramadan. The countryside is much more dry and less fertile than in the island's west - lots of cactus.

HOTELS

Multiple-bedrooms with mandi in *KOMODO***; a bit more expensive but extremely clean is *WISMA ARRIANY***. Jl.Kartini 5. In addition there's *LOSMEN KARTINA***. Since every tourist who appears in Bima wants to get to Komodo, tickets are offered in the losmen - don't fall for the trick!

LEAVING BIMA

BY AIR

The airport is a good distance out of town. A Merpati plane leaves daily for DENPASAR for 59,000 Rp. There are other flights to AMPENAN 46,800 Rp, BAJAWA 45,700 Rp, ENDE 45,700 Rp, KUPANG 105,100 Rp, RUTENG 49,000 Rp, LABUANBAJO 34,200 Rp, TAMBULAKA 33,700 Rp, UJUNG PANDANG 77,000 Rp and WAINGAPU (via Tambulaka) 48,800 Rp.

BY BUS

You need two hours by bus to the harbour SAPE, leaves hourly for 750 Rp. Express buses (e.g. Damai Indah) go to DENPASAR in 24 hrs for 20,000 Rp.

SAPE

The departure point for visiting Komodo if you're coming from the west. There are several places to stay like LOSMEN GIVE*. Buy your provisions for your trip to Komodo in advance and take along bait for the Komodo dragons. For a goat you pay the reasonable sum of 15,000 Rp here, while in Komodo it costs up to 30,000 Rp.

LEAVING SAPE

Get a dokar to the harbour for 300 Rp. Motorboats sail three times a week to KOMODO or on to LABUHANBAJO on Flores for 8100 Rp Ekonomi, 6400 Rp deck. Sat 8:00 h via Komodo to Labuhanbajo. Return Sun at 8:00 h via Komodo - takes about 10 hrs. Directly to Labuhanbajo (7-8 hrs.) on Mon and Wed at 9:00 h, back on Tues and Thurs at 9:00 h.

In addition there are Bugis ships which usually take the direct route to Flores. Unless you charter them, the smaller boats should charge about the same price; otherwise expect to pay about 120,000 Rp for a three day charter. They are expensive because there are only a few motor-boats and the trip with an outrigger is quite dangerous (costs about 120,000 Rp for charter).

KOMODO

At 300 km², Pulau Komodo is the largest island of the small archipelago between Sumbawa and Flores. Thousands of tourists come here each year to see the great attraction, the Komodo dragon, the largest lizard still living on earth. On the other hand, hardly anyone visits the neighbouring islands of Rinca and Padar. There as well, the ancient lizard was able to survive because the islands were isolated from Sumbawa and Flores by the strong ocean currents (caused by tidal movements between the Indian Ocean to the south and the Flores Sea to the north). In 1980 the area was declared a national park. The plan is to encourage tourism.

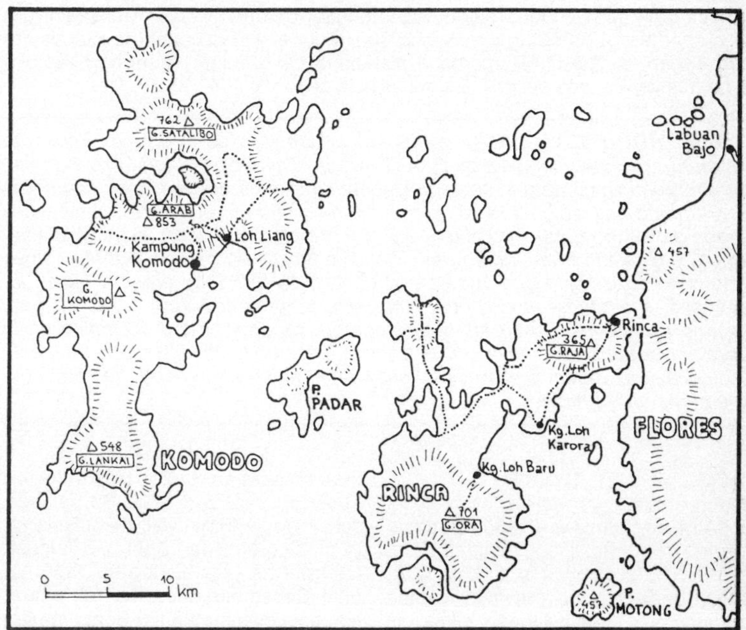

KAMPONG KOMODO

The main village on the island is KAMPONG KOMODO with about 600 inhabitants. Here you'll find a Wisma Parawisata (tourist guest house). Spend the night in the PPA rest-house, half way between the village and the 'dragon' feeding spot. The grounds are well-kept; only the mosquitos annoy. Sometimes rats and snakes seek shade in the buildings. Costs 3000 Rp per person; up to ten people can share a house. There are also more expensive 2-bed bungalows.

Food is simple and consists mostly of nasi telur or supermie. Buy canned goods or other food in advance at Sape or Labuhanbajo. Refrigerators (beer) are also available. The 20 park rangers are friendly, but don't speak English. Don't let yourself be ripped off with any overpriced dragon bait as some people charge up to 40,000 Rp. A small goat for 25,000 Rp, a dead dog or a fish is enough. North of the village in the PORENG VALLEY and along the river Liang are the best places to watch the dragons. The goat is brought to the observation point alive and slaughtered there. For photos, don't forget your telephoto lens.

If you want to climb Gunung Arab or otherwise make your way into the interior to get a better look at the dragons or other wildlife, you have to take along a PPA guide. That costs 2500 Rp per day.

A nice day trip (without a guide) is the offshore island of LASA, for swimming and snorkeling. An outrigger costs 2500 Rp per day. Typical of the islands are the 'bagan', a type of catamaran. A platform up to 5 m long is set between two long, thin boats, and a small, flat hut is built on top of it.

*The **KOMODO DRAGON** (Varanus komodoensis) was first made known to western zoologists in 1912 by P. A. Ouwens. The world's biggest lizards can be found on Komodo and some neighbouring islands nearby. They can be up to 3 m long and weigh 135 kg. Some reach an age of 100 years. Usually they creep slowly from place to place, but hey are also able to do several kilometres a day, climb trees, and swim. They live mostly on carrion, but have been known to attack wild deer, goats and horses. Even if they aren't a match for humans, their fearsome appearance, with large fangs and forked tongue, seems threatening. Their tail is a dangerous weapon; it can be rolled up to give powerful blows. They lay their eggs in holes up to several metres deep. In April/May the young, measuring about 45 cm, hatch and spend their first couple of months in trees.*

HOW TO GET THERE

Upon arrival, you register at the local PPA office. Admission 1000 Rp, photo permit 1000 Rp. Regular boats from SAPE (Saturdays) and LABUANBAJO (Sundays), see previous section for prices. Captain Nurdin takes his market boat to LABUHANBAJO on Tuesday, charging 5000 Rp per person. If you want to visit the island, try to make it between April and August. Later in the year it's too hot, and not until December does the rainy season cool things off a bit. Boat trips are dangerous during the great storms in February and March.

If your time is short, get a flight to LABUHANBAJO (Wed, Thurs, Sun) from DENPASAR via AMPENAN and BIMA for 101,100 Rp, or with the improved roads on Sumbawa, you can get to AMPENAN from LABUHANBAJO in 1 1/2 days (boat, night bus Bima - Alas) .

Several travel agencies in Kuta, Legian, or Sanur offer 3-day tours to Komodo. The flight, ferry, meals, and lodgings are included. Prices vary according to the number of participants; calculate US$300 to US$500.

SUMBA

This is one of the most isolated islands in Indonesia - 11,080 km^2 with only about 380,000 inhabitants. Most of the island is covered by savanna. The small, strong horses from Sumba are famous; they can be seen today pulling dokars on Java and Sulawesi. Once they were even exported to China in exchange for porcelain. The traditional villages have cone-shaped houses with megaliths in front - the home of their ancestors.

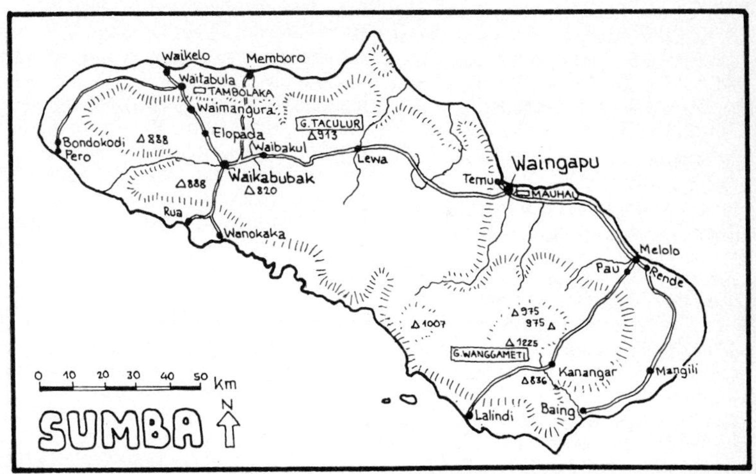

WAINGAPU

is the administrative centre and the main town on the island. Be sure to reconfirm your return flight early!

HOTELS

Several hotels and losmen in town: *HOTEL LIMA SAUDARA***, Jl. Wanggameti 2, is the cheapest possibility - family atmosphere. Somewhat more expensive *HOTEL SURABAYA***, Jl.

El Tari 2, and *HOTEL ELIM***(*)*, Jl. Jen.A.Yani 55 Most expensive place is *HOTEL SANDALWOOD*****, Jl.Metawai.

LEAVING WAINGAPU

BY AIR

Bemos to the airport 150 Rp. The Bouraq agent is P.T.Andrew Jonathan at Pasar Lama, Colt Terminal, Jl. Yos Sudarso 49, tel 36. The airline flies 3x weekly from SURABAYA and DENPASAR via WAINGAPU to KUPANG and return. The Merpati office is in Hotel Elim, Jl.Jen.A.Yani 55, across from the Pertamina petrol station, tel 32. Direct flights Wed, Fri and Sun to DENPASAR and return. Additional flights Tues and Thurs to DENPASAR via TAMBULAKA, Tues and Fri via BIMA, daily to KUPANG. SAMPLE PRICES: BIMA 48,800 Rp, DENPASAR 85,800 Rp, KUPANG 62,300 Rp, SURABAYA 102,400 Rp, JAKARTA 174,300 Rp.

BY SHIP

About every 10 days two Perintis ships, KM. BARUNA FAJAR and KM. NIAGA IX (Agent: Pelni office right in the harbour) do the cruise KUPANG - SAWU - (sometimes ROTI) - ENDE - WAINGAPU and return. Costs 10,300 Rp to KUPANG, takes 2 days and three nights. Since 1986, KM. KELIMUTU also puts in, arriving every second Saturday at 7:00 h from BIMA, before cruising on three hours later for arrival at 17:00 h in ENDE. Sunday morning she arrives at KUPANG. For the return trip on Monday morning she is in Waingapu, then continues on to BIMA, UJUNG PANDANG, LEMBAR, etc. SAMPLE PRICES (1st class / Ekonomi): BIMA 33,400 / 14,200 Rp, ENDE 22,800 / 10,500 Rp, KUPANG 44,800 / 18,200 Rp.

BY BUS

Buses only run along the 137 km road from WAINGAPU to WAIKABUBAK, the main town in west Sumba. All the side routes are served by minibuses or trucks. There are 5-6 buses daily to WAIKABUBAK and two returning; calculate 3000 Rp for the 6-hour drive, departs at 8:00 h. Tickets are available from Lotus, Toko Mawar and Toko Sinatra. Buy your tickets a day in advance and leave an address where you want to be picked up.

DAYTRIPS FROM WAINGAPU

A 2 hour drive by minibus (1200 Rp) takes you 62 km to MELOLO, your departure point for additional excursions. In the village itself you'll find many antique Ikat blankets and the last 'rumah makan' (by the market) before you set out in the wilds. There are lovely beaches along this stretch of coast! Only occasional trucks traverse the southern coastal road via PAU, KANANGGAR, MAUMARU and MAHU (traditional villages) to LALINDI.

Trucks are more plentiful along the 62 km to BAING. After 7 km you reach RENDE, a very old village on a hill in a lovely river valley. Wednesday is market day in Rende, attracting even more trucks - you can spend the night at the Kepala Desa. Sign the guest book, and pay the required sum.

WAIKABUBAK

The main town in west Sumba, the most interesting part of the island. You'll find megalith tombs on almost every road.

HOTELS
Simple but clean is *LOSMEN PELITA*(*)*, Jl.Jen.A.Yani, where you can also eat. Your own mandi and toilet and tremendous rooms in *HOTEL RAKUTA****, Jl.Veteran. Meals are included in the price. The newest losmen with a restaurant is *MONALISA**(*)*, Jl.Gajah Mada.

LEAVING WAIKABUBAK
Bus tickets to WAINGAPU are sold for 3000 Rp in several toko along the main road. Tambolaka Airport is near WAITABULA (Weetobula), 36 km northwest of Waikabubak. Minibuses cost 1000 Rp, take 1 1/2 hrs. Merpati has its own bus which will pick you up at your hotel, costs 1800 Rp. Merpati (office on Jl.Wairabula) flies Tues via BIMA (33,700 Rp) to DENPASAR (66,900 Rp). Plus every Sat to Bima, and every Thurs direct to Denpasar. To KUPANG (87,600 Rp) each Tues, Thurs, and Sat via WAINGAPU (62,300 Rp).

DAY TRIPS FROM WAIKABUBAK
DESA TARUNG
IA large, traditional village with many megalith tombs, without corrugated iron roofs, on a steep hill just 1 km from town.

WAIKELO
11 km from WAITABULA on the coast is the tiny harbour village Waikelo with a lovely beach and a waterfall for swimming. Minibuses (500 Rp) are infrequent. Occasionally there are ships from Waikelo to Bali.

FLORES

In 1544 a Portuguese trading ship sighted the eastern cape of the island, and it was named 'Cabo des Flores' (the cape of flowers). Since then the island has had its European name; even in Malay it is known as 'Pulau Bunga' (= flower island). The Portuguese influence is still felt today. About three quarters of the inhabitants are Catholic - the rest are Muslim with a few animists. Christian missionaries are found all over the island and are a good source of info. Ethnic Malays are the majority in coastal areas, while in the interior Melanese stock is predominant.

LABUHANBAJO

A small village on the outer west end of the island. It's situated on a protective bay occasionally visited by a couple of ships. You have a beautiful view from the surrounding mountains. You'll never forget the flight to Bima - the small Twin Otter passes over innumerable islands and turquoise coloured coral reefs in the deep blue sea.

HOTELS
There are a few losmen: *MUTIARA**, *KOMODO JAYA**, *BAJO BEACH INN** and *KOMODO MAKMUR**. Check out the new *WAECICU BEACH NATURE PARK*, 15 minutes away by boat.

LEAVING LABUHANBAJO

On Wed, Thur, and Sun, Merpati flies to DENPASAR (101,100 Rp), BIMA (34,200 Rp), ENDE (62,500 Rp) and RUTENG (27,400 Rp). Airport tax 700 Rp.

During the dry season, trucks or buses run between Labuhanbajo and RUTENG (12 hrs., 3500 / 4800 Rp). The road was being improved in 1986-87.

Motor and sailing boats to REO take 8-12 hours. They leave only irregularly and charge 5000 Rp per person. Three times a week (Sun, Tues, Thur), a ferry shuttles between SAPE (8100 Rp / 6400 Rp) and LABUHANBAJO - only stopping on Komodo (2250 Rp / 1800 Rp) on Sundays. Pay the same price for a private PLM (prahu lajar motor) unless you charter one.

REO

With its harbour 2 km away, used to be the end of the road. Spend the night in losmen TELUK BAYUR**. Sometimes a coastal ship will take you on to MAUMERE for about 7000 Rp. Several buses a day will take you to RUTENG for 1400 Rp. It can take up to 5 hours.

RUTENG

Lies at over 1000 m altitude and has an academy training lay catechists. Cheap losmen are KARYA** and ANYMOR**. WISMA AGUNG*** at the edge of town is very good. Buses to ENDE cost about 8000 Rp (16 hrs.), to BAJAWA 4200 Rp (9 hrs.). Merpati Twin Otters serve Ruteng: DENPASAR 99,400 Rp, BIMA 49,000 Rp, ENDE 35,100 Rp, KUPANG 65,900 Rp.

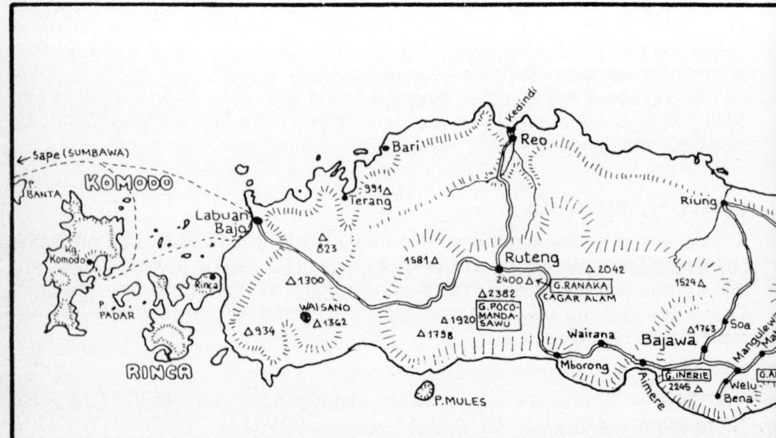

WAIRANA / BAJAWA

Wairana is a beautifully-situated little village with a big mission (no hotel!!). It is a good starting point for hikes to the surrounding villages. Around noon there's a bus going to BAJAWA (1800 Rp). Here you'll find WISMA JOHNY**, Jl.Jen.A.Yani; WISMA MAWAR*** and WISMA KEMBANG***. Bus to ENDE (a nice trip) costs about 4000 Rp.

ENDE

The most important town on Flores. It has an interesting morning market. Here you can get ikat sarong made on the eastern part of the island.

HOTELS

There are lots of cheap losmen and hotels. Try *LOSMEN KARYA*(*),* Jl. Pelabuhan (almost at the harbour). If Karya is full, go to *HOTEL MERLIN***, Jl.Onekore 2 (next to the church) with a private mandi. Or take a room on the top floor in the front building at *HAMANSYUR***, Jl.Sembonga 11. *WISMA FLORES***, Jl.Jen.Sudirman 18, has been renovated. Lights used to burn all night. Eat at the warung at the market. Or try *RUMAH MAKAN ANUGRAH* near the mosque on Jl. Gang Aembonga.

LEAVING ENDE

BY AIR

Merpati Office: Jl.Nangka (P.T.Kelimutu Permai). Bemo to the airport Ipi costs 125 Rp. SAMPLE PRICES: BAJAWA (Tues, Fri, Sun) 27,500 Rp, KUPANG (daily) 54,100 Rp, RUTENG (Sat) 35,100 Rp, LABUHANBAJO (Wed) 62,500 Rp, BIMA (daily.) 45,700 Rp, DENPASAR 105,100 Rp.

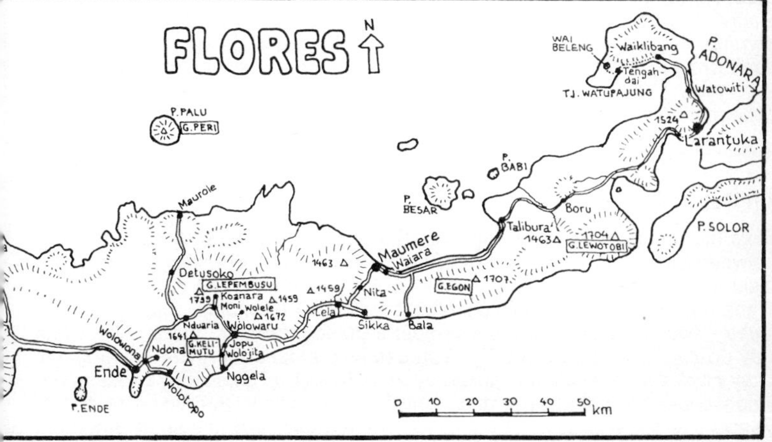

BY SHIP

Two Perintis steamers take turns (about every 10 days) shuttling from Kupang via Ende to Waingapu and back - cost is about 7000 Rp in both directions. The boats are too large to tie up at the pier, but rowing boats will take you out for 500 Rp.Since 1986 KM. KELIMUTU docks every second Sat at 17.00 h. She arrives from UJUNG PANDANG (78,200 / 32,200 Rp), BIMA (37,100 / 17,300 Rp) and WAINGAPU (22,800 / 10,500 Rp). Then she sails to KUPANG (30,400 / 12,900 Rp). On the return trip she is once again in Ende on the following Monday.

BY BEMO / BUS / TRUCK

Several buses to MAUMERE at 7:00 h for 4500 Rp (7 hrs., 148 km), MONI costs 1500 Rp. Trucks and buses to RUTENG 8000 Rp (16 hrs., 258 km), BAJAWA 4000 Rp (6 hrs., 125 km).

IKAT

Sumba is well known for its ikat work. People and animals are depicted, unlike other ikat motifs in Nusa Tenggara which mostly consist of geometric patterns. Ikat is an ancient method of weaving and colouring which is also used by other ethnic groups in Indonesia. The rectangular blankets, used to wrap the dead, take months of intensive work. The method involves preparing the individual threads for the blanket with the necessary pattern and colours, so that the motif is completed during the weaving process. The threads are bundled and wrapped in fibre, so that they retain their original colour in certain places during the dying process. In single ikat weaving only the warp (the vertical threads) are dyed to form the motif. In double ikat weaving (certainly the more complicated), both the warp and the woof (the horizontal threads) are dyed in advance to form the motif.

The traditional colours used on Sumba are blue, white, red, and brown. Natural colours are still often used today (indigo plants for blue, 'mengkudu' roots for brown-red).

Genuine ikat blankets on Sumba cost between 20,000 Rp and 200,000 Rp according to quality and motif, since a different amount of work is invested in each product. In Bali the blankets are 4 to 5 times as expensive - in Jakarta even more. You'll find the largest selection in Waingapu, but the blankets are cheapest in the villages.

MONI / GUNUNG KELIMUTU

Take the bus from Ende for 1500 Rp. Stay the night in WISMA KELIMUTU*** between the church and priest's quarters. Nice people! Breakfast and evening meal are included in the price. About 1.5 km before Moni, a road branches off to the right to *GUNUNG KELIMUTU*. It is about 14 km uphill, but not all that steep - you can make it on foot without a guide in about 3 hours. About half way up you have to pay 200 Rp. You can hike around the three crater lakes. They have different colours caused by the different minerals they contain. The moonscape-like craters are, according to local beliefs, the hiding places of spirits. The souls of boys and girls live in the green lake, the souls of the old people reside in the blue, and in the red lake the spirits of sinners are waiting until night to rise up and fly with the wind, in order to destroy every living intruder.

You can take an interesting shortcut on the way up to Kelimutu, about half way between Moni and the turnoff. From the road near the huge root is the beginning of a path through a small gorge, past two small villages and on to another village which is already on the way to Kelimutu. From there it's about 1 1/2 hours to the crater.

MAUMERE

Harbour town on the north coast of Flores. We only found one shop on the *BIG MARKET* selling ikat sarong!! Visit the *CATHOLIC CATHEDRAL*.

HOTELS

Stay at losmen *BENG GOAN** at the market, FLORA*** or BOGOR*** not far from the harbour - not very clean and too expensive. Recommended for a longer stay: *WISMA GARDENA***, Jl.T.Haryono, including good breakfast, family atmosphere. Large rooms in *LOSMEN MAIWALI**(*)*, Jl. Jen.A.Yani. Most expensive is *HOTEL MAUMERE INDAH****, Jl.Kom.A.R. Saleh 73. If you feel like spending more money, stay at *SEA WORLD CLUB***** about 12 km east of Maumere at Waiara, and go snorkeling in the coral reef or have a European meal. Even more expensive is the *SAO WISATA RESORT***** at the same location. Here they charge US$50 per person including meals and diving. The two facilities, however, are the only spots on Flores where you can get your air tanks refilled. Divers will appreciate that.

LEAVING MAUMERE

BY AIR

The airstrip is 3 km east of Maumere. Taxis from town 3000 Rp, bemos charge 1000 Rp per person. Merpati office is on Jl.Pasar Baru Timur. Hawker Siddeley 748s and Fokker Friendships fly to UJUNG PANDANG (67,000 Rp). Other connections: KUPANG (daily at least one plane) 36,300 Rp (MZ / BO), DENPASAR (daily MZ / BO) 92,200 Rp and to SURABAYA 124,000 Rp (MZ / BO).

BY BUS

Buses to ENDE 4500 Rp, 7 hrs., (148 km); LARANTUKA 4000 Rp, 6 hrs., (137 km); WOLOWARU 2000 Rp, 3 1/2 hrs., (83 km). Beginning at 7:00 h passengers are picked up, and about 2 hrs. later the bus leaves.

LARANTUKA

The town at the easternmost tip of the island serves as an important harbour for the islands of the Solor and Alor Archipelagos. There are three losmen in town: HOTEL RULIES**, WISMA KARTIKA* and HOTEL TRESNA***. Wed, Fri, and Sun Merpati flies to KUPANG (48,800 Rp). About every 10 days a Perintis ship leaves for KUPANG (about 10,000 Rp; 2-3 days) via WAIWERANG (Adonara), LEWOLEBA (Lomblem) and KALABAHI (Alor). Another daily ship via WAIWERANG (2 1/2 hrs.; 1000 Rp) to LEWOLEBA (4-5 hrs.; 2500 Rp).

TIMOR

'Nusa Cendana' or sandalwood island is how Timor is known in the Indonesian Archipelago. Sandalwood is still exported, but beef has become a much more important export thanks to the ideal pasture land in the wide open savannas. The major export harbour for cattle is Atapupu on the northern coast. 1.2 million people live on Timor, including the Atoni, the ethnic Melanese population. Timor hit the international headlines in the 1970s. The eastern part of the island, which had been a Portuguese colony for centuries, declared its independence. In the middle of July 1976, East Timor was annexed as the 27th province in the Indonesian republic. The former Portuguese part of Timor is still completely closed to foreigners.

KUPANG

with its 100,000 inhabitants is becoming the most important communications centre for East Nusa Tenggara. This is the only airport where jets can land, and in 1987 Merpati started Wednesday and Saturday F28 flights to and from Darwin, Australia. This could return Nusa Tenggara to its high, pre-1975 level of tourism. Captain Bligh, infamous captain of the 'Bounty', landed here after the mutiny. From Tahiti, where his crew must have felt more comfortable, he had sailed 6000 km.

Kupang is a fast growing town, with new sections expanding south from the older quarter along the sea. Regular bemos run down Jl.Sudirman joining the two halves. *PASAR BESAR*, east of Jl.Suharto, in the new town, is worth a look. Farmers from the villages come to Kupang to sell agricultural produce. During the dry season there's little choice. Many wear traditional red-striped ikat sarong. Take a walk through the old town centre around Jl.Siliwangi and Jl.Sukarno. In BAKUNASE, a village 3 km away, you can visit a *SANDALWOOD OIL FACTORY.*

HOTELS

There are numerous hotels, wisma and losmen in town; some, however, are far from the centre. The most expensive hotel is *SASANDO*****, charging US$36 for a double, swimming pool, on the road to the airport. Lasiana Beach (10 km from Kupang) is nearby. Between Sasando and the beach, you can stay at *TAMAM RIA INN****, right on the beach, Jl.Tim Tim 69. More expensive are the two Flobamor hotels, *FLOBAMOR I*****, Jl. Kemuning 1 (on Jl.Basuki Rahmat), a relatively new, single-storey building, water doesn't always run and air conditioning can't always be adjusted. The new *FLOBAMOR II*****, Jl. Sudirman (next to Kantor Merpati) is booked primarily by business travellers. Not bad is *LAGUNA INN****, Jl. Kelimutu 7A (at Jl.Urip Sumohardjo). Free airport service is provided by *KUPANG INDAH INN**(*)*, nearby at no. 2A. Traditional dance is performed every Saturday evening. Some losmen can be found on Jl.Sumatera. Try *MALIANA***(*)*, no. 39, and next door *SUSI**(*)*. Further toward the airport at the beginning of Jl.Tim Tim (at Jl.Sumba) is *LOSMEN NUSANTARA*** with cheap prices. Get a bemo into town.

FOOD

Many hotels and losmen offer full room and board (includes 2 - 3 meals). Otherwise try *PANTAI LAUT,* Jl. Ikan Paus, not far from the bemo station. For good seafood and a view of the sea, try *KARANG MAS* at the beginning of Jl. Siliwangi. Besides Pantai Laut, the newest Aussie success is *TEDDYS PLACE* (coldest beer in town). On Saturday and Sunday evenings, BBQs are organized on Lasiana Beach. There is disco on Wednesday and Saturday night. Two restaurants in the new town are *ROTTERDAM,* Jl. Harimau, and *KUPANG INDAH,* Jl. Suharto.

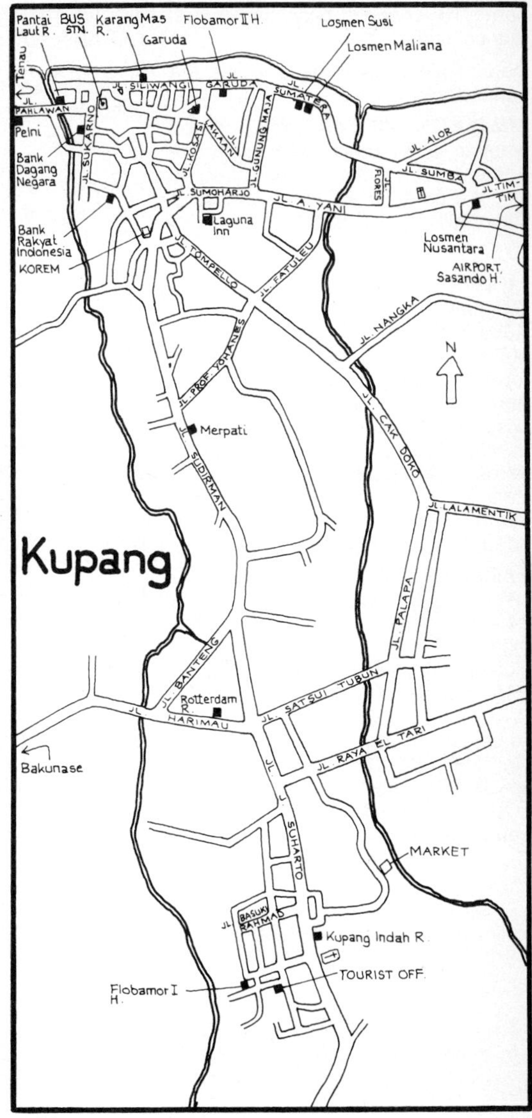

GENERAL INFORMATION

TOURIST INFORMATION - at Kantor Parawisata, Jl.Jen. Basuki Rahmat 1 in Kantor Gubernor.

PPA - office on Jl. Perintia Kemerdekaan.

BANKS - Bank Dagang Negara, Jl.Sukarno 10, changes cash and travellers cheques.

Bank Rakyat Indonesia is on the same street.

MILITARY CLEARANCE - if you want to enter the region along the border to Tim Tim or Timor Timur, try to get a permit at KOREM (Komando Resor Militer), Jl.Sukarno.

LEAVING KUPANG

BY AIR

Kupang is a visa-free entry and exit point. El Tari Airport is 15 km from town. Get a colt from the terminal in the centre toward Penfui / Baumata, costs 250 Rp, and walk the last 200 m. A taxi costs 6000 Rp. The airport tax is 1400 Rp. BOURAQ (Jl.Jen.A. Yani 21, tel 21392), Merpati (Jl.Sukarno 23, tel 21961) and Garuda (Jl. Kosasi, tel 22088) fly in and out.

SAMPLE PRICES: DARWIN US$170 (Wed and Sat with MZ F28), ENDE 54,100 Rp (daily, at least one MZ flight), BIMA 105,100 Rp (via Ende, Ruteng, MZ), DENPASAR 106,500 Rp (GA direct), 90,500 Rp (MZ/BO), WAINGAPU 62,300 Rp (BO/MZ), ALOR 46,800 Rp (MZ), ROTI 23,800 Rp (MZ), SAWU 42,200 Rp (MZ), MAUMERE daily 36,300 Rp (MZ/BO), UJUNG PANDANG 88,100 Rp (MZ connection via MAUMERE), JAKARTA 209,300 Rp (GA via Denpasar), LARANTUKA 48,800 Rp (MZ; Wed, Fri, Sun), LEWOLEBA 47,400 Rp (MZ). The MZ flights to AMBON were cancelled after a brief trial in 1987.

BY SHIP

On Tues and Thurs, the KMP.GURITA KUPANG weighs anchor for a 12 hour voyage to LARANTUKA, costs 8200 Rp. Several Pelni ships ply the route to SAWU (sometimes also ROTI), ENDE and WAINGAPU. The Pelni office is at Jl.Pahlawan 5. Tenau, the port of Kupang, is 6 km from the bemo terminal, costs 250 Rp. Ask at Kantor Syarbandar in Tenau for the best ship connections. Pelni's KM.KELIMUTU puts into Tenau every second Sunday. Sunday evening she departs for ENDE (30,400 / 12,900 Rp), WAINGAPU (44,800 / 15,000 Rp), BIMA (72,600 / 31,400 Rp), UJUNG PANDANG (85,800/34,700 Rp) where she arrives on Wednesday morning before continuing on to Lombok and Java.

BY BUS

The Central Bus / Bemo Terminal at Jl.Siliwangi and Jl.Sukarno. Sample prices: SOE 2000 Rp, 3 hrs., 110 km, departs half hourly 7:00-09:00 h, and every 90 minutes 9:00-16:00 h. KEFAMENANU 3500 Rp, 5 1/2 hrs., 197 km; ATAMBUA 6000 Rp, 8 hrs., 287 km; NIKI NIKI 2500 Rp.

MOLUCCAS

The province 'Maluku' consists of 999 islands bordering Sulawesi in the west, Irian Barat to the east, Timor to the south, and the Sangihe Islands to the north. Administratively it is divided into three 'Kabupaten' (districts): North (Ternate), Central (Masohi) and Southeastern (Tual). About 1.5 million people live here.

The fauna and flora are more markedly Australio-Melanese than on the other Indonesian islands to the west. Besides the bird of paradise (otherwise only found in New Guinea), many types of parrots make their home on Halmahera and Morotai. On the Aru and Kai Islands you can even find a kind of tree kangaroo.

The Moluccas are also known as the 'Spice Islands', because cloves, nutmeg and pepper have been cultivated here for hundreds of years. Don't forget that the European powers originally sought out the Spice Islands in order to exploit the huge profits from the spice trade. Arabian and Indian merchants monopolized the trade until the 16th century. In 1511 the first Portuguese ships landed on Ambon and Banda; the Spaniards followed in 1521, the Dutch in 1599, and the English finally made it in 1605. Using intrigue, brutal violence, and military force, the Dutch established domination over the Moluccas. Although the Portuguese only controlled the islands for less than 100 years, their cultural influence was very strong. You can hear this today in the folklore, in the names of things, and in the Moluccan vocabulary. An Indonesian language scientist was able to determine that about 250 colloquial words are Portuguese in origin. In addition, some of the older people on Ambon still speak Dutch among themselves.

During the colonial domination the whole economy was uniquely structured to maximize profit. In order to keep the world price of spices artificially high, a systematic program was begun to destroy farmland or otherwise reduce acreage. For example, in the 17th century people on Ambon were only permitted to plant 125 clove trees per person. Not until 1863 were these restrictions lifted.

Today Molucca's most important export articles are cloves, nutmeg, copra, wood and several resins. Fishing and related industries are also being expanded.

Getting around between the islands, except for a few air connections, is difficult due to the lack of an infrastructure. Merpati serves the following towns: Ternate, Ambon, Namlea (Buru), Galela, Kao (Halmahera), Sanana, Amahai (Ceram), Langgur (Kai), Labuha (Bacan), Bandaneira (Banda), Saumlaki (Tanimbar), Morotai and Mangole. Everywhere else has to be reached by ship. In line with Indonesia's PELITA development plans, rapid advances are being made in communications and infrastructure.

Tourism is as good as non-existent on the Moluccas. At most a few nostalgic, older Dutch might visit Ambon. Despite the high cost of getting there, the islands are worth a visit. Just to visit the central and northern Moluccas you'll need all the time your visa allows.

AMBON

The provincial capital (pop. 120,000) is located on the island of the same name. At one time Pulau Ambon was two separate islands (Leihitu and Leitimur) which have grown into one big island due to sand formation. Arriving by plane, you'll land at Laha Airport, 48 km from Kota Ambon. It's a beautiful drive around the bay!

Today the political atmosphere on Ambon is much more relaxed than in the 1950s, when the Republic of the South Moluccas declared its independence from Indonesia. Troops, sent by the central government in Jakarta, put a quick end to this Dutch-inspired plan. The rebels took to the mountains of Ceram from which they engaged in guerilla operations. With time the movement lost energy. Many Moluccans either surrendered or fled to Holland where 100,000 live today. They made headlines with their hostage-taking on trains in Holland. In 1963 the leader of the secessionists, Dr. Soumokil, declared the fight to be officially over.

The walls of old *FORT VICTORIA,* erected in 1575, are still standing - the fort is used by the army, which is here in force. Be sure to have a look at the new *SIWA LIMA MUSEUM* (bemo towards AMAHUSU, 250 Rp). It has interesting collections dealing with ethnology, ceramics, arts and crafts, and natural sciences. A bilingual guide book is published by the museum administration, closed Mon & Fri, open Tues-Thurs 8:00-14:00 h, Sun 10:00-14:00 h.

BATU CAPEO is on the beach below the museum. It's an unusually shaped coral rock (capeo is Portuguese for 'head'), a popular getaway spot for the Ambonese. Along the jagged coastline are a number of caves which were fortified by the Japanese during WWII. You can still see drinking water cisterns and gun mounts. There is a small Balinese temple just above the museum.

In the evening take a walk up to Karangpanjang to the *MEMORIAL* of *Martha Christina Tiahahu.* From here you have the best view of the Bay of Ambon.

Most of the people on Ambon are Christian (the city is a bishop's seat). Participation in a service at one of the town's many churches will offer you some real insight into life here. Muslims mostly live in the southwest of town around the *GREAT MOSQUE.*

HOTELS

Like everywhere on the Moluccas, carry a heavy wallet. You won't find a double room for less than 10,000 Rp. We found *HOTEL SELA***,* Jl.Anthony Rebhok (across from Merpati) to be the nicest. Also on the same street (no. 30) is *ELEONOOR***(*),* but too expensive for what it offers. Comfortable and clean is *PENGINAPAN BETA**** opposite the Kantor Gubernor. The manager speaks English and Dutch - nice atmosphere. Right next door is *HOTEL TRANSIT REZFANNY**** with similar prices. Or try *HOTEL SILALOU***(*),* Jl.Sedap Malam 41. Breakfast is included in the price. Ask here or in Sela if they will prepare 'colo colo', the Moluccan national dish. Centrally located and relatively cheap for Ambon is *HOTEL AMBOINA****,* Jl.Kapitan Ulupaha. Around the corner on Jl.Pattimura is the more expensive *MUTIARA****,*

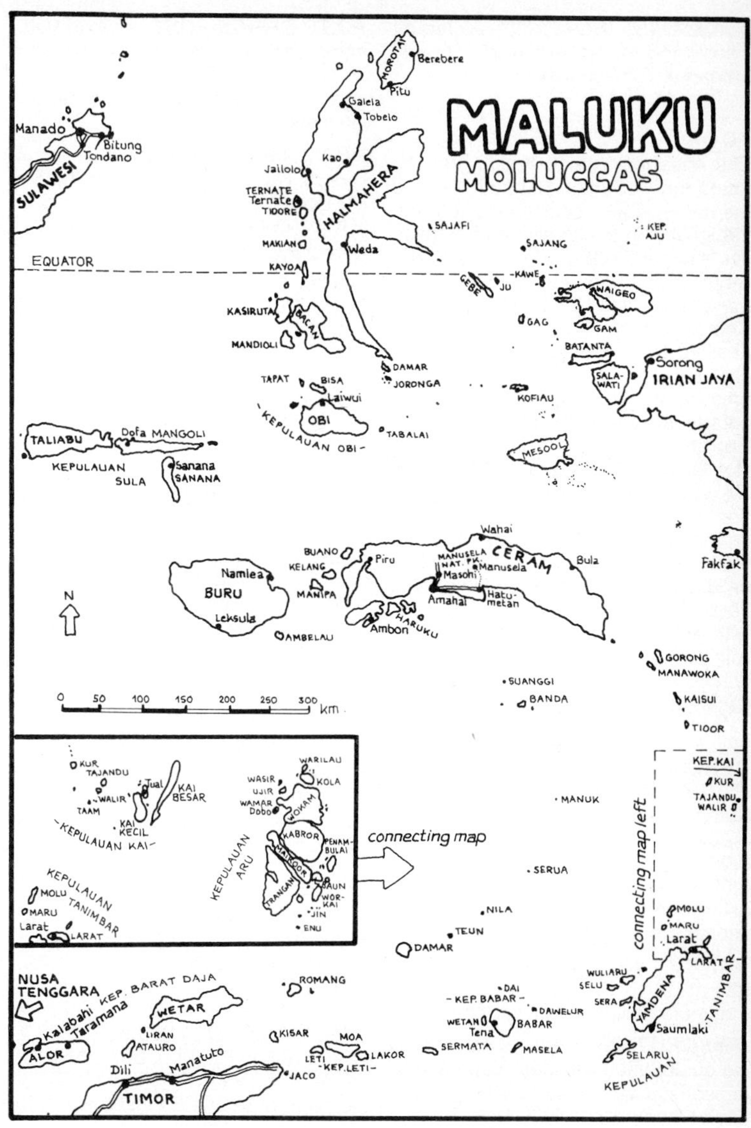
MALUKU
MOLUCCAS
Berebere
MOROTAI
Pitu
Galela
Tobelo
Manado
Bitung
Tondano
SULAWESI
Kao
Jailolo
HALMAHERA
TERNATE
Ternate
TIDORE
MAKIAN
Weda
SAJAFI
SAJANG
KEP. AJU
EQUATOR
KAYOA
GEBE
JU
KAWE
WAIGEO
KASIRUTA
BACAN
MANDIOLI
GAG
GAM
BATANTA
DAMAR
JORONGA
Sorong
IRIAN JAYA
SALAWATI
TAPAT
BISA
Laiwui
OBI
KOFIAU
KEPULAUAN OBI
TABALAI
TALIABU
Dofa MANGOLI
KEPULAUAN SULA
Sanana
SANANA
MESOOL
Wahai
BUANO
KELANG
Piru
MANUSELA NAT. PK.
Manusela
Masohi
CERAM
Bula
Fakfak
Namlea
BURU
MANIPA
Amahai
Hatumetan
Leksula
Ambon
HARUKU
AMBELAU
N
GORONG
MANAWOKA
SUANGGI
BANDA
KAISUI
TIOOR
0 50 100 150 200 250 300 km
KUR
TAJANDU
Jual
KAI BESAR
WALIR
TAAM
KAI KECIL
KEPULAUAN KAI
WARILAU
KOLA
WASIR
UJIR
WAMAR
Dobo
WOKAM
KABROR
MAIKOOR
TRANGAN
KEPULAUAN ARU
PENAMBULAI
BAUN
WORKAI
JIN
ENU
connecting map
KEPULAUAN TANIMBAR
MOLU
MARU
Larat
LARAT
KEP. KAI
MANUK
connecting map left
SERUA
NILA
TEUN
DAMAR
NUSA TENGGARA
KEP. BARAT DAJA
Kalabahi
Taramana
WETAR
ROMANG
DAI
KEP. BABAR
DAWELUR
WULIARU
SELU
SERA
YAMDENA
TANIMBAR
LIRAN
ATAURO
ALOR
KISAR
MOA
WETAN
Tena
BABAR
Saumlaki
LETI
LAKOR
SERMATA
MASELA
SELARU
KEPULAUAN
KEP. LETI
JACO
Dili
Manatuto
TIMOR

plus *MANISE HOTEL*****, Jl.Ceram. You'll find other expensive hotels around Jl.Tulukabessy.

FOOD

The cheapest rumah makan can be found on Jl.Sultan Babulah around the corner from Abdulalie Hotel. Even though it is in the Muslim part of town, you can get Bintang beer for 1200 Rp. Several nasi padang places are at the bus station *(MINANG JAYA,* Jl. Kemakmuran). Two somewhat expensive restaurants can be found on Jl.Sultan Hairun. In *HALIM* you can enjoy good Chinese food. Try a tremendous serving of udang for 4000 Rp; other dishes cost just 2000 Rp. Not far from Halim are *TIPTOP* and *SAKURA,* which despite its Japanese-sounding name does not serve Japanese food. Traditional Maluku food is served at noon in *CASANOVA* on Jl.Dana Kopra next to Hotel Mutiara. Try ikan bakar (roasted fish) with colo colo, a sweet-sour sauce with onions, tomatoes, garlic, chillies, lemon, peanut oil, soya sauce, and sugar, served with sago bread.

GENERAL INFORMATION

TOURIST INFORMATION - in Kantor Gubernor at the BAPPARDA MALUKU. Good tips! Open Mon-Thur 8:00-13:00 h, Fri 8:00-11:30 h, Sat 8:00-13:00 h. If you want to go skin diving and don't have a mask or snorkel, you can rent one from here.

BANKS - you get a good exchange rate at BANK DAGANG NEGARA, Jl. Pattimura next to the post office.

IMMIGRATION - in a modern building on Jl.Sultan Babulah. You have to register on arrival and before departure at the airport only.

POST OFFICE - GPO is on Jl.Pattimura, poste restante in the back yard in the sorting office. Open just mornings. The telephone office is across the street.

PPA - the provincial office is on Jl. Passo. The administration of the Pulau Pombo / Manusela Reserve is on Jl.Kapaha Tantui Pandan Kasturi.

BECAKS - Kota Ambon has a very unusual becak system. They come in three colours (red, white and yellow), but only on Sundays do all three colours take to the roads. On other days only one colour of becaks may drive, charging 250-600 Rp within the city limits.

LEAVING AMBON

BY AIR

Laha airport is 48 km out of town. Minibuses cost 750 Rp including bags - taxis want 12,000 Rp. Often Merpati buses go for free from/to their city office. Airport tax: 1400 Rp. Watch out - on Merpati 'perintis' flights (CASA), you are only allowed to take 10 kg of luggage! Airline offices: MERPATI, Jl. Anthony Rebhok; GARUDA, Jl.Jen. A. Yani; MANDALA, Jl.A.J.Patty.

SAMPLE PRICES: SURABAYA 193,000 Rp (GA); 163,800 Rp (Mandala daily); JAKARTA 222,900 Rp (GA); 189,300 Rp (Mandala daily); UJUNG PANDANG 107,000 Rp (GA); 90,800 Rp (daily Mandala); SORONG 60,700 Rp (GA); BIAK 107,600 Rp (GA); 91,500 Rp (MZ once weekly), JAYAPURA 163,300 Rp (GA); NAMLEA 35,700 Rp (MZ); TERNATE 73,100 Rp (MZ); AMAHAI 32,100 Rp (MZ); LANGGUR 97,900 Rp (MZ); LABUHA 70,500 Rp (MZ); BANDANEIRA 42,700 Rp (MZ); SAUMLAKI 87,100 Rp (MZ); MANGOLE 70,200 Rp (MZ); MANADO 118,000 Rp (MZ).

BY SHIP

During monsoon season, May to August, all shipping is greatly restricted. Pelni has an office on Jl.Pelabuhan 1. The manager speaks English and is very helpful. The KM.RINJANI runs the route MEDAN-JAKARTA-SURABAYA-UJUNG PANDANG-BAU BAU-AMBON(every second Sunday)-SORONG-AMBON (the following Tuesday) and return. Costs in Ekonomi / 1st class: MEDAN 86,700 / 263,900 Rp, JAKARTA 57,900 / 169,300 Rp, SURABAYA 42,600 / 129,900 Rp, UJUNG PANDANG 26,400 / 81,500 Rp, BAU BAU 19,500 / 58,400 Rp, SORONG 17,400 / 44,600 Rp. Pelni has several Perintis ships running various routes within the Moluccas. To BANDANEIRA is an overnight trip. There is a fairly regular three week cruise AMBON - NAMLEA -ARABUAYA - SANANA - BOBONG -DOFA - LAIWUI - LABUHA - TERNATE and return. It takes ten days to cruise from Ambon to Ternate. The hygiene standards aboard ship are not to everyone's taste. Another ship makes a

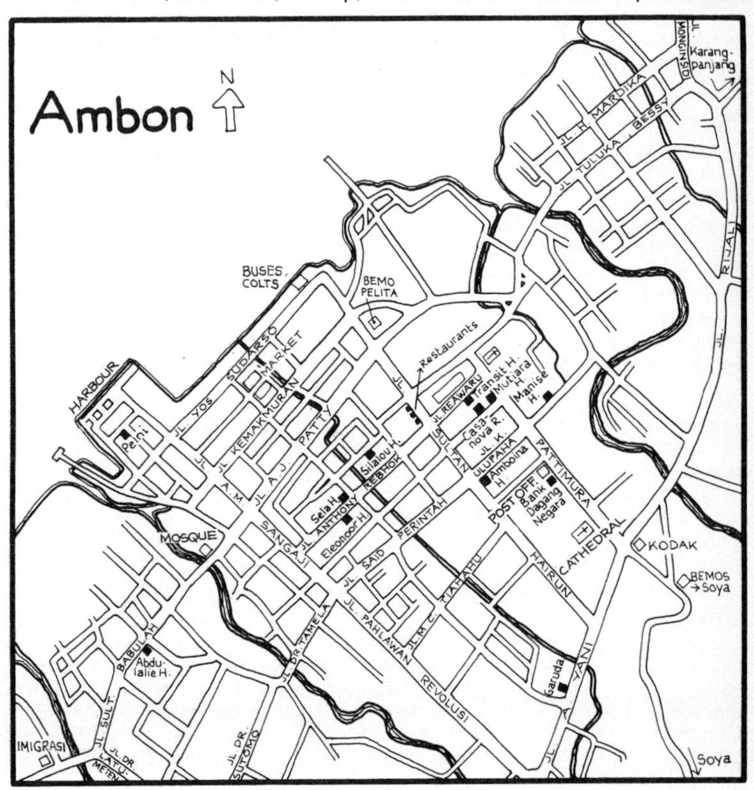

round trip through the southern Moluccas. Ports of call are BANDANEIRA, TUAL, SAUMLAKI and the island WETAR. From Wetar, PML cruises to KALABAHI on the island of Alor. Here you have connections to Nusa Tenggara.

BY BUS & BEMO

They leave either from Jl.Kemakmuran or from the bus station (Jl.Yos Sudarso). There is only about 150 km of road - mostly in poor condition.

Minibuses leave for the southwest to LATULAHAT 300 Rp or AMAHUSU 250 Rp, to the north to HILA 800 Rp, and the northeast to TULEHU 500 Rp, WAAI 600 Rp, and LIANG 750 Rp.

DAY TRIPS AROUND KOTA AMBON

SOYA

The tiny village on the top of Gunung Serimau is about two hours on foot. With a bemo (200 Rp) it's much faster! In the village is an old Portuguese church. Only 15 minutes away is the 'sacred urn' (tempayang keramat). It keeps refilling itself with water as if by magic. You can also hike over the mountain and through the jungle to EMA and from there on down the coast to LEHARI or HUKURILLA. If you do, you'll have to spend the night in a village along the way.

LATUHALAT

Get a bemo for 300 Rp to this secluded beach. Not far out is a coral reef.

LIANG / WAAI / TULEHU / NATSEPA

LIANG is situated about 34 km away on the island's north coast. Just off the coast is Pulau Pombo with one of the most interesting underwater gardens in the Moluccas. Unfortunately the fishermen in Liang and Waai charge horrendous prices to take you over. WAAI is a Christian village with friendly people. It is famous for its fishponds containing huge eels which are fed with eggs by the children. TULEHU is a small harbour for ships to Ceram. Discover the Ambonese beach life in NATSEPA - packed at weekends!

HILA

is on the north coast of the island and can be reached by minibus for 800 Rp. It's an interesting drive past sago, clove and nutmeg trees as well as eucalyptus trees. Hila harbours one of the oldest mosques on the island (1646) as well as the oldest church (1780). Christians and Muslims each make up half of the village population, and (we were told) there hasn't been any intermarriage for many years. You should check out the Dutch fort *NIEUW AMSTERDAM* or at least what's left of it. Right next door is the village school; when an *orang turis* visits, the children get the day off.

CERAM

is the largest island in the Central Moluccas with mountains up to 3000 m. The only roads are around AMAHAI and MASOHI. Another road is being built to the northern coast of the island. A small road leads along the southern coast from Amahai to SEPA. Stay overnight in Amahai at the PENGINAPAN** (the hotels in Masohi are very expensive). Take a minibus to Sepa (750 Rp) and walk back at least part of the way. You'll pass through a village of Melanesian aborigines (Naulu).

HOW TO GET THERE

Besides the weekly Merpati flight for 31,100 Rp, there is a daily ship from TULEHU (jetty in Momoking 2 km north) to Amahai for 5000 Rp.

TERNATE

In the 15th and 16th centuries, Ternate was the most important and powerful centre in the North Moluccas. Practically the entire world's production of cloves was harvested in the sultanates of Tidore, Jailolo, Bacan and Ternate. This was why the European powers intervened in the 16th century. The ruins of their fortresses can be found all over the islands.

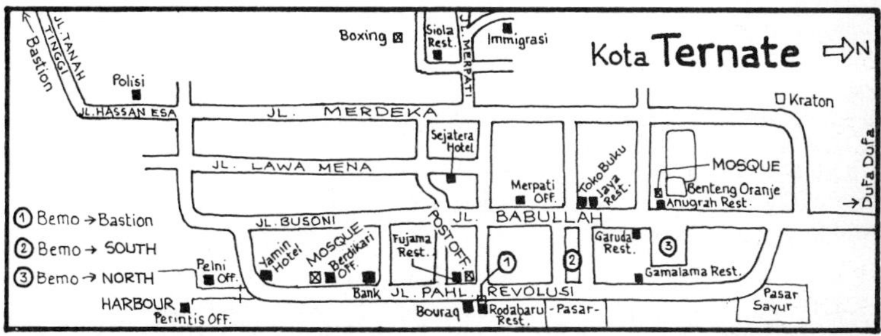

The administrative centre of the island is the town, also called Ternate. The island is only 9 km in diameter and 45 km in circumference. Towering over everything is the volcano *GAMALAMA* (1715 m). In August 1983 it erupted. Two thirds of the inhabitants fled to the neighbouring island of Tidore. Earthquakes are daily occurrences here. The volcano can be climbed (ask Udin in the Sejatera for info).

Right in town you can still see the walls and fortress facilities of the Dutch *FORT ORANJE*, built in 1607. Today a 'mobile' unit of the army is stationed here and the soldiers will take you around. The *KRATON* is now a museum. Since the death of the last sultan in 1979, the building has been restored and opened to the public. The 350-year-old *AFU CLOVE TREE* is in *MARIKURUBU* (3 km away). A similar example can be seen on the road from Ternate to Kayu Merah. Remember that the tree was only planted about 60 years after the visit of Sir Francis Drake in 1570.

An interesting day trip would be a tour around the island using public transportation. First take a bemo (100 Rp) to the fishing village DUFA DUFA and visit *FORT TOLOKO,* erected in 1512 under the Portuguese Admiral d'Albuquerque. A bit farther north you come to *BATU ANGUS,* where a stream of lava poured into the sea in 1737. Then take a bemo for 250 Rp to SULAMADAHA, a tiny village with a black beach, across from the island of Hiri. Only a few bemos go the next 4 km to *DANAU TOLIRE,* a lake in a steeply sloping crater inhabited, according to legend, by a white crocodile. Two villages on the west coast of the island are LOTO (drink tea in the toko!) and TADUMA. In CASTELA, you'll find the ruins of *FORT SANTO PAOLO,* and a couple of kilometres further on is DANAU LAGUNA. In KALUMATA on the southern tip of the island the remains of an English fort, KAYU MERAH, can be seen.

HOTELS

Despite the small rooms *SEJATERA**** Jl.Lawa Mena is quite comfortable. Udin speaks English and knows the island. Nice homey atmosphere and good food at *HOTEL HARMONIS****, Jl.Pala. Right at the harbour is *WISMA YAMIN****, Jl.Pahlawan Revolusi. All the other hotels are extremely expensive when they are not booked up. Try *MERDEKA****, Jl.Merdeka, built by the Dutch, or *NIRWANA*****, Jl.Pahlawan Revolusi - probably the best in the upper price category.

FOOD

Good Chinese food in *GARUDA,* Jl. Babullah across from the cinema. Right next door to Bioskop Benteng you get nasi padang in the *JAYA.* Or try *RODA BARU* on Jl.Pahlawan Revolusi. On the same street next to the post office is the most expensive restaurant in town, *EL SHINTA.* Drink tea in *GAMALAMA.*

GENERAL INFORMATION

BANKS - TCs in US $ are cashed by BANK EKSPOR IMPOR and BANK INDONESIA 1946. Both are on Jl. Pahlawan Revolusi. Open until 11:00 h only.

POST OFFICE - Jl.Pahlawan Revolusi next to Hotel El Shinta.

LEAVING TERNATE

BY AIR

Only MERPATI (Jl.Busori 80) and BOURAQ (Jl.Pahlawan Revolusi) fly into Babulah Airport, a couple of kilometres north of town. Up to now only with DC3s and the small CASAs. Bemos direct from the airport charge awful prices; go out through the gate onto the main road, and get a bemo there for 150 Rp.

SAMPLE PRICES: AMBON 73,100 Rp, MANADO 44,900 Rp (BO/MZ), GALELA 35,900 Rp, LABUHA 34,400 Rp, KAO 26,500 Rp, MOROTAI 41,500 Rp, SANANA 60,100 Rp, MANGOLE 71,000 Rp.

BY SHIP

The PELNI office is right at the harbour entrance. Every second Tuesday the KM.UMSINI calls at Ternate after stops at SURABAYA, UJUNG PANDANG and BITUNG. She continues via SORONG to JAYAPURA, returning to Ternate the following Sunday. Sample Prices (1st class / Ekonomi): BITUNG (Manado) 35,900 / 12,000 Rp, UJUNG PANDANG 109,600 / 37,400 Rp, JAYAPURA 115,600 / 43,700 Rp, SURABAYA 177,500 / 57,400 Rp, TANJUNG PRIOK (Jakarta) 210,400 / 71,000 Rp.

Kantor Perintis is in the harbour (opposite Pelni) and they will take you to AMBON for 9000 Rp. At least twice a week a ship leaves for TOBELO, costs 2000 Rp. To JAILOLO Mon, Wed, and Fri for 2500 Rp.

Several ships leave from BASTION, the beach south of Ternate, to PULAU MAKIAN (Kg.Ngofakiaha) 3000 Rp, PULAU TIDORE (Rum) 600 Rp, PULAU KAYOA (Kg.Guruaping) 3600 Rp, PULAU BACAN (Labuha) 7200 Rp. Ships often visit an island on market day. Ask in the harbour!

TRIPS TO THE NEIGHBOURING ISLANDS

TIDORE

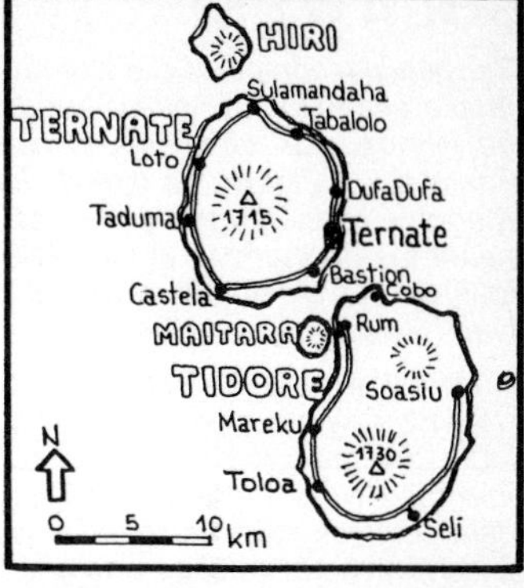

Ternate's sister island can be reached from BASTION, Pasar Impres, with a small ship for 600 Rp. The port of call is RUM. From here take a minibus to SOASIU for 650 Rp. Friday is market day, attracting many people from Halmahera. Stay the night in LOSMEN ITO GEBURA****. The *BENTENG* is worth a visit, and on the way you'll pass the crumbling remains of the *KRATON.*

HALMAHERA

At 18,000 km^2 this island is even bigger than the Falkland Islands. Up to now only a small part between TOBELO and GALELA is easily accessible. During WWII the Japanese had their headquarters for the Southwest Pacific here. The wrecks of many ships and landing craft still litter Kao Bay.

Malayan fishermen and peasants live mostly along the coast; the interior is populated by Melanesian aborigines. There are many Christian missionaries, particularly in the north, who are good sources of information.

The following round trip excursion would take a minimum of 5-6 days : a ship leaves daily from Bastion to DODINGA on the narrowest part of Halmahera (3000 Rp). From here get a bus to BOBANEIGO at Kao Bay for 1500 Rp. Then take a ship to KAO (3600 Rp). Stay the night in the only losmen - costs 5000 Rp. There is a daily 'kapal motor' to TOBELO. Two losmen: MEGARIA*** and LANTAI BARU***. Get a bus or truck to GALELA (2800 Rp). There are several losmen in the village. Return to Ternate with the Merpati Casa (35,900 Rp) or by ship for 4000 Rp. At Tobelo or Galela, you can visit villages of the 'orang primitif' as the Melanesian aborigines are called by Indonesians.

SULAWESI

The peculiar shape of the island Sulawesi is reminiscent of an orchid; some people even claim to see a huge octopus. The European name was given by the Portuguese when they circumnavigated the island in the 16th century. 'Ponto dos Celebres' is loosely translated 'Point of the Infamous', possibly a reference to the large number of pirates. Another explanation assumes they meant the northern tip of the island where many ships have been grounded or sunk by the monsoons. For this reason, until Indonesian independence the island was known as 'Celebes'.

Sulawesi is 189,216 km^2 and contains 11.7 million people, living in four provinces (Utara, Tengah, Selatan and Tenggara). The Bugis, living in the south, are famous for being the best boatmen in the archipelago. Once upon a time they were the notorious pirates. In the interior the Toraja are a proto-Malay ethnic group which today is largely Christian. The northern tip has been settled by the Minahasa, who are 90% Protestant.

Sulawesi, together with the Lesser Sunda Islands, functions as a kind of flora and fauna borderland between the Indian and Australian regions. The large mammals on Borneo and Sumatra never made it here; the marsupials, cassowaries and birds of paradise, typical of the Australian region, can't be found here either. Instead, there are several types of animals only found on Sulawesi, such as the pig deer (babirusa) and the dwarf buffalo (anoa) which is only about 2 m long and achieves a shoulder height of 1 m.

A connecting road system from Ujung Pandang in the south to Manado exists and it is possible to do the overland trip. But some segments of this road are in very bad condition and only passable with a 4WD vehicle.

Tourism, except in Ujung Pandang and Tana Toraja, is still in its infancy. North and Central Sulawesi get hardly any visitors, while Southeast Sulawesi gets none at all. Hardly any village is more than 40 km from the ocean - you'll discover beautiful, sandy beaches, coral reefs, and steep mountains. Some mountains in the interior are up to 3500 m high. Most of the island is covered by jungle.

SOUTH SULAWESI

'Sulawesi Selatan' is, next to Central Sulawesi, the second-largest province on the island with 6.87 million inhabitants spread over 64,000 km^2. The largest ethnic groups are the Makassari around Ujung Pandang, the Bugis, who are settled as seafarers along the coast, and the Toraja in the mountainous northern province, who are famous for their proto-Malayan tribal culture and extravagant burials. 'Tator' (= Tana Toraja = Land of the Toraja) has developed into a major tourist centre. The provincial capital is Ujung Pandang.

Until the Dutch conquest in the 17th century, the powerful Kings of Gowa ruled here. Their sphere of influence ranged from Sumbawa and Lombok in the

SULAWESI
0 50 100 150 km
KALIMANTAN
TELUK TOMINI
TELUK TOLO
TELUK BONE
KEPULAUAN BANGGAI
KEP. SULA
KEPULAUAN TOGIAN
KEPULAUAN TUKANG BESI
KEP. SANGIHE
KEP. SALABANGKA
P. SANGI
P. SIAU
P. TALUHAN-DANG
P. BIARO
P. BANGKA
P. LEMBEH
P. PELENG
P. BANGGAI
P. MANUI
P. WOWONI
P. MUNA
P. BUTON
P. KABAENA
P. SELAYAR
TALIABU
MANGOLI
D. TONDANO
D. MOOAT
D. LIMBOTO
D. LINDU
D. POSO
D. MATANO
D. TOWUTI
TOMORI
Manado
Bitung
Tondano
Amurang
Poigar
Mae-lang
Belang
Kotamo-bagu
Molibagu
Kwandang
Limboto
Gorontalo
Sumalata
Paleleh
Leok
Tolitoli
Tj. Binar
Ogdua
Bang-kit
Thabogan
Ongka
Moutong
Marisa
Palasa
Tinombo
Sabang
Tompe
Toboli
Pantoloan
Donggala
Parigi
Satumana
Palu
Sausu
Ampana
Marowo
Poso
Wuasa
Gimpu
Uekuli
Tentena
Pagimana
Bunta
Siuna
Luwuk
Batui
Baturube
Banggai
Dolong
Kolono-dale
Pendolo
Sampaga
Masamba
Wotu
Soroako
Bungku
Malili
Mamuju
Sa-bang
Palopo
Rantepao
Makale
Polewali
Majene
Larom-pong
Pin-rang
Enrekang
Siwa
Pangka-jene
Pare Pare
Sengkang
Sumpang-binangae
Watang-Soppeng
Watangpone
Segeri
Mare
Pangkajene
Ujung Pandang
Maros
Sinjai
Pattalasang
Bulukumba
Banta Eng
Bontosunggu
Benteng
Kendari
Wawo-tobi
Kolaka
Pomalaa
Toro-bulu
Raha
Ereke
Bau Bau
Δ2304
Δ2356
Δ3096
Δ2835
2350 Δ
Δ 3074
Δ3440
Δ2871
N

south, across the Moluccas in the east, to Kalimantan. The VOC (Vereenigde Oost-Indische Compagnie) was only able to conquer the Kingdom of Gowa militarily after years of struggle from 1615 to 1666 and, thereby, end its political power by means of support from the Bugis under the leadership of the legendary Arung Palakka. His military campaigns didn't end, though, with victory over Gowa: indeed rather many small principalities were conquered, bringing fear and suffering to the people of South Sulawesi. Many Bugis and Makassaris fled in their ships to look for new homes in Sumbawa, Lombok, Kalimantan, Java, Sumatra, the Malayan Peninsula, and even all the way to Thailand. Until well into the 19th century, these wild warriors and pirates were the scourge of the archipelago.

UJUNG PANDANG

For centuries the largest and most important city on Sulawesi was called 'Makassar'. About 700,000 people live here today. Not until the 1950s was Makassar again called Ujung Pandang, the name of the King of Gowa's fortress until 1669.

Right on the sea is the impressive *FORT ROTTERDAM.* The whole complex has recently been restored. There are two *MUSEUMS* in the grounds, 200 Rp admission, open Tues-Thur 8:00-13:30 h, Fri 8:00-10:30 h, Sat-Sun 8:00-12:30 h. On Jl.Diponegoro, you can find the grave of the national hero *DIPONEGORO.*

Prince Diponegoro was the leader on Java of a strong resistance movement against the colonial power. As an early guerilla warfare strategist, he was able to keep the Dutch and their allied native princes on the defensive from 1825 to 1830. In 1830 there were negotiations during which Diponegoro was arrested. He was banished to Makassar where he died in 1855. Even today his grave is decorated with flowers and wreaths. There isn't any town in Indonesia without the obligatory Jalan Diponegoro.

Check out the *SHELL COLLECTION* of Clara Bundt and the *ORCHID GARDEN* of Carl Ludwig Bundt at Jl.Mochtar Luthfi 15, free admission.

Ujung Pandang has three sailing ship harbours. Busiest is *PAOTERE HARBOUR* in the north. The largest Bugis schooners (pinisi) are docked near Jl.Martadinata between Jl.Sukarno and Jl.Hatta. Around sundown, take a walk by the sea (Jl.Penghibur). Young people like to get together here and enjoy the beautiful sunsets.

Ujung Pandang has a large Chinese minority residing mostly around Jl.Martadinata, Jl.Jen.A.Yani and Jl.Irian. There are four *TEMPLES,* three of which are on Jl.Sulawesi. The largest and most important temple for the Chinese minority is the *TIAN HOU GONG* at the corner of Jl.Seram.

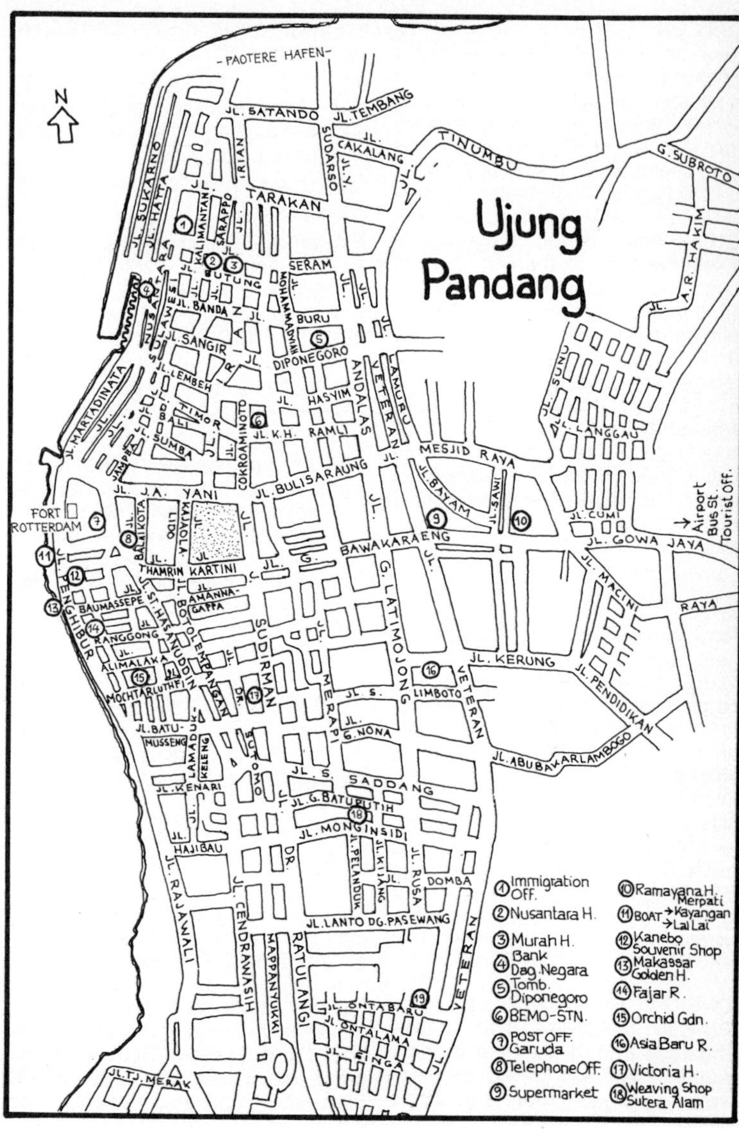
Ujung Pandang
N
PAOTERE HAFEN
JL. SATANDO
JL. TEMBANG
JL. CAKALANG
TINUMBU
G. SUBROTO
JL. SUKARNO
JL. HATTA
JL. TARAKAN
JL. SARAPPO
IRIAN
SUDARSO
JL. KALIMANTAN
JL. A. R. HAKIM
SERAM
BUTUNG
JL. BANDA
JL. BURU
MOHAMMADIYAH
JL. SANGIR
JL. DIPONEGORO
JL. MARTADINATA
JL. LEMBEH
JL. HASYIM
ANDALAS
VETERAN
LAMURU
TIMOR
BALI
SUMBA
JL. K.H. RAMLI
COKROAMINOTO
JL. SUNU
JL. LANGGAU
MESJID RAYA
JL. BULISARAUNG
JL. J.A. YANI
JL. BAYAM
JL. SAWI
FORT ROTTERDAM
BALAIKOTA
LIDO
KAJAOLA
JL. CUMI
BAWAKARAENG
JL. GOWA JAYA
Airport Bus St. Tourist Off.
THAMRIN
KARTINI
JL. MACINI
RAYA
BAUMASSEPE
AMANNA-GAPPA
HASANUDDIN
BOTOLEMPANGAN
SUDIRMAN
G. LATIMOJONG
RANGGONG
ALIMALAKA
MOCHTAR LUTHFI
PENGHIBUR
JL. KERUNG
JL. PENDIDIKAN
JL. S. LIMBOTO
MERAPI
JL. BATU-
MUSSENG
LAMADUKELLENG
KELENG
SUTOMO
JL. G. NONA
JL. ABUBAKAR LAMBOGO
JL. S. SADDANG
JL. KENARI
JL. G. BATUPUTIH
JL. MONGINSIDI
JL. HAJIBAU
JL. PELANDUK
JL. KIJANG
JL. RUSA
DOMBA
JL. RAJAWALI
JL. CENDRAWASIH
MAPPANYUKKI
RATULANGI
JL. LANTO DG. PASEWANG
JL. ONTA BARU
JL. ONTA LAMA
JL. SINGA
JL. TJ. MERAK
① Immigration Off.
② Nusantara H.
③ Murah H.
④ Bank Dag. Negara
⑤ Tomb. Diponegoro
⑥ BEMO-STN.
⑦ POST OFF. Garuda
⑧ Telephone Off.
⑨ Supermarket
⑩ Ramayana H.
⑪ BOAT → Merpati → Kayangan → Lai Lai
⑫ Kanebo Souvenir Shop
⑬ Makassar Golden H.
⑭ Fajar R.
⑮ Orchid Gdn.
⑯ Asia Baru R.
⑰ Victoria H.
⑱ Weaving Shop Sutera Alam

HOTELS

Hotels in Ujung Pandang are pretty expensive. Two cheap hotels are on Jl.Sarappo: at no. 4 is *NUSANTARA*** and at no. 103, diagonally across, is *MURAH**. Their only asset is the cheap price. The *ORIENTAL***, Jl.H.Monginsidi 38, is better. *RAMAYANA**(**)*, Jl.Bawakaraeng 121 (tel 22165), has several categories of rooms; the ones on the first floor are good. The management is proud to run a moral establishment. Diagonally opposite is *MARLIN*****, in the same building as Liman Express. Centrally located at Jl.Sudirman 24 is *HOTEL VICTORIA*****, tel 21428. At *MAKASSAR GOLDEN HOTEL*****, Jl. Pasar Ikan 52, tel 22208, a double costs US$50 to $60. The luxury hotel has all facilities including swimming pool, disco, and a choice of restaurants, etc.

FOOD

Many seafood dishes, though not cheap, can be found in UP. Try *ASIA BARU,* Jl.Salahutu (Jl.Latimojong); you pick out your own fish, costs begin at 2000 Rp. Chinese and European food in *RESTORAN HILMAN,* Jl. Jampea 2. Try 'steak babi', two pork chops with gravy and vegetables, costs 2500 Rp. Chinese and seafood in *RUMAH MAKAN SETIA,* Jl.Bacan 1a. Many warung are open evenings on Jl.Penghibur. Try 'ikan bakar' (a big piece of fish with rice, cucumber and peanut sauce).

GENERAL INFORMATION

TOURIST INFORMATION - Jl.Andi Pangerang Petta Rani - get a bemo for 200 Rp and ask for 'Kantor Parawisata', open Mon-Thurs 7:00-14:00 h, Fri 7:00-11:00 h, Sat 7:00-13:00 h, very helpful staff.

POST OFFICE - GPO is on Jl.Slamet Riyadi at Jl.Supratman. International telephone calls can be made on Jl.Balai Kota.

IMMIGRATION - at Jl.Seram 2, friendly people!

BANKS - most banks are on Jl.Nusantara (BANK BUMI DAYA, no. 72; BANK DAGANG NEGARA, no. 149) or on Jl.Slamet Riyadi (BANK NEGARA INDONESIA 1946). Latunrung money changer at Jl.Monginsidi 38 near the Oriental Hotel.

SHOPPING - the biggest souvenir shop is KANEBO, Jl.Pattimura. A lot of other antique / souvenir shops can be found on Jl.Somba Opu, parallel to the seafront promenade. CITY, a supermarket stocking western food, is on Jl.Bawakaraeng corner of Jl.Veteran. Another supermarket is JAMESON'S, Jl.Irian 147. Bugis sarongs are still woven at SUTERA ALAM, Jl. Onta 408. Work stops at 15:00 h. Silk from Soppeng is brought here for weaving and colouring.

BOOKS - the only place in UP is BHAKTI BARU on Jl.Jen.A.Yani. But few English language books are offered.

HOSPITAL - we recommend the military hospital, PELAMONIA at Jl. Sudirman 27.

GETTING AROUND UP - City bemos charge 150-200 Rp. The bemo station is on Jl.Cokroaminoto. From here you can get a double-decker bus, no. 302 or no. 303 via Hotel Ramayana to Jl.Andi Pangerang Petta Rani (Tourist Office). Becaks service the entire city. Calculate 500-700 Rp from Ramayana to Jl.Penghibur by the sea.

LEAVING UJUNG PANDANG

BY AIR

Hasanuddin Airport is 22 km north of town. Bemos cost 500 Rp. Taxis charge 9000 Rp. Airport tax 1800 Rp. All airlines fly into UP: GARUDA, Jl. Slamet Riyadi 6, tel 22705; MERPATI, Jl.Bawakaraeng 109, tel 4114; BOURAQ, Jl. Cokroaminoto 7C, tel 28057; MANDALA, Jl.Irian 2F, tel 21289.

SAMPLE PRICES: JAKARTA 156,700 Rp (GA); 133,100 Rp (MZ / Mandala with stop in Surabaya); SURABAYA 98,700 Rp (GA); 83,800 Rp (MZ / Mandala); MANADO 114,500 Rp (GA); 97,300 Rp (MZ); AMBON 107,000 Rp (GA); 90,800 Rp (MZ / Mandala); MAUMERE 67,000 Rp (MZ); BALIKPAPAN 96,900 Rp (MZ / BO); BIAK 193,200 Rp (GA); 164,200 Rp (MZ via Ambon); KUPANG 88,100 Rp (MZ via Maumere); PALU 66,600 Rp (GA); 56,600 Rp (BO); TATOR 40,300 Rp (MZ Tues, Thurs, Sat); LUWUK 121,900 Rp (MZ); POSO 73,600 Rp (MZ); KENDARI 51,900 Rp (GA); BAU BAU 78,500 Rp (MZ); SOROAKO 53,000 Rp (MZ). Only GARUDA flies for 73,100 Rp to DENPASAR.

BY BUS & BEMO

The central bemo station is on Pasar Besar (Jl.Ramli). Overland buses leave from the new bus station on Jl. Gowa Jaya (towards the airport). Many bus companies offer direct rides to Rantepao for 5000 Rp (day bus) or 6000 Rp (night bus). LIMAN EXPRESS, Jl.Laya 25, is to be recommended.

SAMPLE PRICES: PARE PARE 2500 Rp (155 km, 5 1/2 hrs.), BONE 2500 Rp (174 km, 5 hrs.), POLEWALI 4500 Rp, SENGKANG 3600 Rp, BULUKUMBA 2500 Rp, MALILI 8500 Rp, PALOPO 6000 Rp (376 km, 8 1/2 hrs., night bus: 5000 Rp).

If there are three or more of you, consider renting a minibus for a period of time. Costs are 50,000 Rp per day after bargaining or cheaper if you keep it for five days or longer. You can determine your own route, but don't try to reach Tator in one day. For info check at various travel agencies or at the Tourist Office, tel 7128 during office hours or tel 21142 evenings.

BY SHIP

The Pelni office is at Jl.Martadinata 38. Except for the KM.LAWIT all other ships land in UP. Every second Thurs the KM.KERINCI docks in UP and sails via BALIKPAPAN, PALU, TOLI TOLI to TARAKAN and back again via UP (following Wed) to SURABAYA, TANJUNG PRIOK, PADANG and SIBOLGA. Every second Fri the KM. KAMBUNA docks and sails via BALIKPAPAN and PALU to MANADO. On the following Thurs she is back in UP and goes on via SURABAYA, TANJUNG PRIOK to BELAWAN. The KM.RINJANI is in UP every second Fri, and continues via BAU BAU and AMBON to SORONG. Every following Thurs she is back in UP, to go on to SURABAYA, TANJUNG PRIOK and BELAWAN. The KM.UMSINI docks every second Sat in UP and travels via BITUNG, TERNATE and SORONG to JAYAPURA. On the Tues after next she is back in UP and sails to SURABAYA and TANJUNG PRIOK. The KM.KELIMUTU is in UP every second Thurs, and continues her trip via BIMA, WAINGAPU and ENDE to KUPANG. Every following Wed she is back in UP and sails via LOMBOK, PADANG BAI, SURABAYA and BANJARMASIN to SEMARANG.

SAMPLE PRICES (1st cl./ Ekonomi): MEDAN 185,300 / 64,200 Rp, JAKARTA 108,300 / 35,800 Rp, SURA-

BAYA 64,000 / 21,600 Rp, AMBON 81,500 / 26,400 Rp, BALIKPAPAN 55,000 / 18,700 Rp, BITUNG 102,100 / 35,800 Rp, PALU 58,900 / 22,700 Rp, JAYAPURA 182,900 / 71,000 Rp, BIMA 37,800 / 15,000 Rp, LOMBOK 41,400 / 17,100 Rp, PADANG BAI 56,300 / 22,700 Rp.

DAY TRIPS FROM UJUNG PANDANG

PULAU KAYANGAN

West and southwest of UP are several islands, some still largely untouched. Motorboats cost 900 Rp to KAYANGAN. On weekends a stage there is used for pop concerts, and transport costs soar to 1800 Rp. Also one losmen, warung, and restaurants.

BANTIMURUNG

Situated about 40 km to the northeast - bemos cost 600 Rp to MAROS, where you change and get to Bantimurung for another 200 Rp. Visitors are attracted by the waterfall, stalactite caves and, particularly, the many butterflies (admission 500 Rp). Stay the night in LOSMEN BANTIMURUNG, two-bed bungalows with toilet and bath for 6000 Rp.

MALINO

A minibus to the 850 m high Malino costs 1400 Rp. It is situated about 70 km to the southeast, on the slopes of Gunung Lompobatang. With several losmen, it's a good place for hikers.

BIRA

Located on the southwestern tip of Sulawesi, this is one of the few places today where traditional Bugis schooners (pinisi) are still being built. First take a bus to BULUKUMBA, and then a bemo to Bira. Beautiful beaches, but up to now no sleeping accommodation. From Bira you can get the Mon to Sat ship to BENTENG (PULAU SALAYAR) for 2250 Rp. Stay the night in Benteng in LOSMEN HERMINTA*.

FROM UJUNG PANDANG TO TANA TORAJA

There are several ways to get to Tator. Simplest is the direct bus getting you to Rantepao in 10-12 hours. The other alternatives are hardly ever used by travellers.

Get a bus to ***WATAMPONE*** for 2500 Rp. Sometimes you see the town referred to as Watangpone or just Bone. The harbour is busy - there's a tiny museum in town. Lots of losmen: centrally located, loud, but clean is PENGINAPAN NIRWANA**(*), Jl.Makmur 41, expensive rooms with private mandi. WISMA MERDEKA**(*), Jl.Merdeka 4, quiet, well kept; just like next door (no. 6) WISMA BOLA RIDIE**-**** with a lovely courtyard and rooms in various categories, including breakfast.

Then get a minibus for 5000 Rp to ***PALOPO.*** Worth recommending is PENGINAPAN LIMA*, Jl.Kartini, right next to HOTEL RIO RITA. Although centrally located, it is quiet and clean. The extra expense is not worth it at HOTEL PALOPO***, Jl.Kelapa 11, with ac, by the bus terminal, or at HOTEL ADIFATI***(*), Jl.Pattimura.

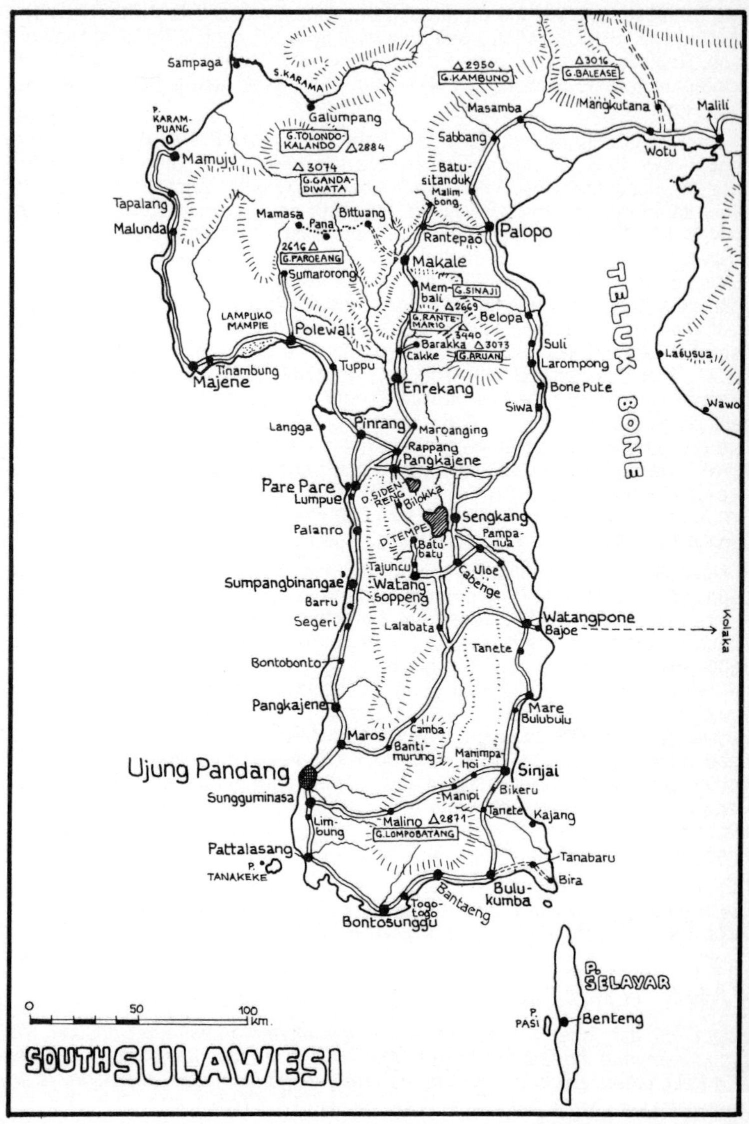
SOUTH SULAWESI
Sampaga
S. KARAMA
Galumpang
G. TOLONDO-KALANDO
2884
P. KARAM-PUANG
Mamuju
3074
G. GANDA-DIWATA
Tapalang
Malunda
Mamasa
Pana
Bittuang
2616
G. PAROEANG
Sumarorong
LAMPUKO MAMPIE
Polewali
Tinambung
Majene
Tuppu
2950
G. KAMBUNO
3016
G. BALEASE
Masamba
Mangkutana
Malili
Sabbang
Wotu
Batu-sitanduk
Malim-bong
Palopo
Rantepao
Makale
Mem-bali
G. SINAJI
2669
G. RANTE-MARIO
3440
Belopa
Barakka
3073
Cakke
G. ARUAN
Enrekang
Suli
Larompong
Bone Pute
Siwa
TELUK BONE
Lasusua
Wawo
Langga
Pinrang
Maroanging
Rappang
Pangkajene
Pare Pare
Lumpue
D. SIDENRENG
Bilokka
Sengkang
Palanro
D. TEMPE
Pampa-nua
Batu-batu
Tajuncu
Uloe
Cabenge
Sumpangbinangae
Watang-soppeng
Barru
Segeri
Lalabata
Watangpone
Bajoe
Kolaka
Tanete
Bontobonto
Pangkajene
Mare
Bulubulu
Maros
Camba
Banti-murung
Manimpa-hei
Ujung Pandang
Sinjai
Sungguminasa
Manipi
Bikeru
Tanete
Kajang
Lim-bung
Malino
2871
G. LOMPOBATANG
Pattalasang
P. TANAKEKE
Tanabaru
Bira
Bulu-kumba
Bantaeng
Togo-togo
Bontosunggu
P. SELAYAR
P. PASI
Benteng
0
50
100
km.

An alternative to this is the trip around the southern coast (BONTOSUNGGU, BANTAENG, BULUKUMBA - see *Day trips from UP* - and SINJAI) to Watampone. Regular minibuses leave Palopo, going over the mountains and through stone-pine forests to ***RANTEPAO*** (Merdeka buses take 2 hours and cost 2000 Rp).

Another possibility is this: get a bus from UP to ***PARE PARE,*** the second largest town in Sulsel (you guessed, the Indonesian nickname for Sulawesi Selatan), costs 2500 Rp. You've an astonishingly good selection of hotels in every category: the cheapest, clean, but loud, on a major road is PENGINAPAN MURNI**, Jl.Bau Massepe 173. Just a bit more expensive is HOTEL SISWA**, Jl.Baso Daeng Patompo 30, an old building in need of renovation. In the same price range is WISMA RIO**, Jl.Pinggir Laut 10, small rooms in a quiet area. Diagonally across we recommend HOTEL YUSIDA***, (no. 3), right by the water, with balconies above the water and a large, airy lounge. From here it is just a few steps to Kantor Pos and the bus terminal. HOTEL KARTIKA****, Jl.Gunung Lompobatang 110, and HOTEL PARE INDAH****, next door, are not far from the bus terminal. There are several good, but not cheap, seafood restaurants in town. The warung around the night market are cheaper. The offices of the shipping companies are on Jl.Usahawan and Jl.A.Cammi. Try P.T.Harapanku, Jl.Usahawan 38, which frequently sends small freighters to east Kalimantan. TARAKAN / NUNUKAN 45,000 Rp; SAMARINDA 25,000 Rp, 35 hrs.; BALIKPAPAN 22,000 / 25,000 Rp. The bus and colt terminal is between Jl.Veteran and Jl.Lompobatang. RANTEPAO 2600 Rp, 173 km, 5 hrs.

For people wanting to hike across the mountains, the following route is recommended. From Pare Pare get a minibus to ***POLEWALI*** (1800 Rp). Stay the night in WISMA ANDA** across from the police station. Get a 'surat jalan' for Mamasa from them. A minibus goes daily up the mountain to ***MAMASA,*** costs 3500 Rp. The 'road' is very bad but is being improved. Don't even try during the rainy season! Often you can only get as far as ***SUMARORONG.*** There you can rent horses for about 4000 Rp per day, or you can walk the rest of the way to Mamasa. Stay the night in WISMA MAMASA*. Here you can also get a hand drawn map of the area with rough kilometre estimates. Very helpful! You've got a 64 km hike ahead of you, leading through the following villages: Rantebuta (3 km) - Pakassasan (8 km) - Lombonan (5 km) - Timbaan (14 km) - Mawai (4 km) - Tabang (7 km) - Ponding (3 km) - Belau (5 km) - Paku (4 km) - Pasangtau (5 km) - Pali (4 km) - Bituang (2 km).

During the rainy season think in terms of 6 days. Sometimes the way will seem like a mud bath; watch out for landslides! Spend the night in villages. From ***BITUANG*** you can get a jeep to ***MAKALE*** for 2500 Rp.

TANA TORAJA

About 750,000 Toraja live on Sulawesi today. More than half are Christian, 5% are Muslim, and the rest are animist. Many live in the mountains between Tator and Palu; others are to the west in the area around Mamasa.'Tator' today is an administrative district, but it doesn't include all of the Toraja.

Tator is the most important region for tourism in southern Sulawesi. The Toraja people live harmoniously in the mountainous region cut by fertile river valleys. Easy mountain hikes or adventurous trekking tours are inviting in the relatively cool mountains, averaging 700 m in altitude. New hotels have sprung up, particularly in the Rantepao region. A Merpati CASA lands 3x weekly on the grass airstrip at Rentetaya, 12 km west of Makale. Comfortable buses from Ujung Pandang require 8-10 hrs. Most visitors arrive between August and October, attracted by the tremendous funeral ceremonies held after the harvest. At other times of the year you receive a discount in many hotels, unless a cruise ship has put into Pare Pare or a large tourist bus has unloaded hundreds of tourists for a day or two. The rainy season is December to March. But even during the rest of the year, expect afternoon rains.

RANTEPAO

This town is the most important in Tator except for Makale, the county seat. It is a good base for trips into the surrounding countryside!

Every six days a *MARKET* is held. Farmers from up to 15 km away bring produce to sell. Frequently you'll see Toraja with long, freshly-cut bamboo poles walking to market. These contain 'balok', the local tuak. Balok is a palm wine, made from sugar palms. Often livestock are sold at a special *BUFFALO AND PIG MARKET* (Pasar Hewan). Mature pigs sell for 175,000 Rp, a year-old cow brings 375,000 Rp, and a white buffalo brings up to 4 million rupiahs. Ask when market days are held in the other five Tator villages! Other markets are held in Sangalla, Mengkendek, Rembon, Sadan and Buntao. These more isolated markets still have more of their traditional atmosphere than Makale or Rantepao.

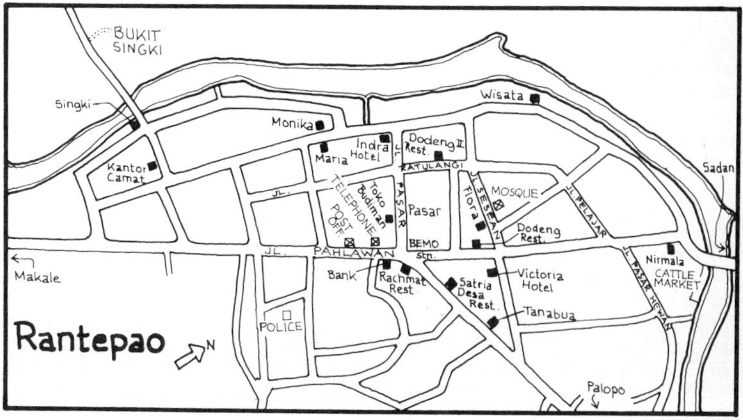

You can find *SOUVENIR SHOPS* on the main street between pasar and the mosque. In general, very expensive! On the other side of the river you can climb the small mountain *SINGKI*, and get a good look at Rantepao and its vicinity.

HOTELS

*LOSMEN FLORA** (across from the mosque) used to be the place where the backpackers got together. Since then lots of other wisma and losmen have opened which are better recommended. *WISMA MONIKA***, for example, or *WISMA NIRMALA*** just before the bridge to the north. Good value at *WISMA MARIA I**(*)*, Jl.Sam Ratulangi. Family atmosphere at Sismay Tulungallo's *WISMA MARTINI*** on the same road. At the end of the road to Palopo is *WISMA TANABUA**(*)* and be sure to bargain, as well as in *HOTEL INDRA**** - outside of high season you can get a discount. Good - *LOSMEN IRAMA**** about 200 m east of the buffalo market. *TORAJA COTTAGE***** on the road to Palopo has a swimming pool and costs 50,000 Rp for a double. Similar prices at *MISILIANA HOTEL***** on the road to Makale. The disadvantage of the two hotels is the 3 km distance from Rantepao. The same at *MARIA II*****. All three hotels cater mostly for tourist groups.If you want to stay longer, ask around the 30 or so wisma and get yourself the best price.

FOOD

RACHMAT across from Pasar Besar isn't to be recommended anymore - loaded prices! You're better off trying *DODENG I* on the main street by the mosque. Newly established is *DODENG II* (the former cook of no. I is having a go on his own) on the street behind the pasar. Besides them, on the street behind the mosque try *MURNI*, and on the road to Palopo *RUMAH MAKAN SATRIA DESA*. Muslim food only. 'Balok' is sold every morning in long bamboo tubes (500 Rp) - it's enough to do in three people.

GENERAL INFORMATION

TOURIST INFORMATION - a new Tourist Office has opened on the road to Makale. When we visited, there was nobody available who spoke English. Officially a 5000 Rp per person *Tourist Tax* is charged, meaning at some point somebody will appear at your hotel to try to collect the money. During several visits over the last six years we never met the tax man.

BANKS - BANK RAKYAT INDONESIA changes traveller's cheques and cash, but at a worse exchange rate than in UP. Open Mon-Fri 8:00-12:00 h, Sat till 11:00 h. Compare the rates at the bank with the money changer next door. Good exchange rates also from the money changer next to the Indra Hotel.

POST OFFICE - across from the bank, open Mon-Thurs 8:00-14:00, Fri till 11:00, Sat till 12:30 h.

TREKKING TOURS - there are several possibilities for longer treks, but you should be well prepared and have a guide. Ask in Wisma Martini for Sismay Tulungallo, who organizes trips of up to 14 days to the northern Toraja. Count on 50,000 Rp p.p. for such an unusual tour, and add another 3000 to 5000 Rp for food and accommodation in the villages. However, most of the time you'll sleep in a tent in the jungle. Bring a tarp, good shoes (jungle boots), sleeping bag, flashlight, pullover, some medicine, and a water bottle. If you intend to make such a trip write well in advance to Sismay.

LEAVING RANTEPAO

BY AIR

Merpati flies a CASA three times weekly to UJUNG PANDANG (40,300 Rp). The flight is worthwhile if you have a connecting flight the same day out of UP. The Merpati agent is on the road to Makale. Ask in the office for Yussuf, who knows Tator well. You are only permitted 10 kg free luggage, although enforcement is lax as the planes are usually not booked up.

BY BUS

Most bus companies have their offices on the main road, Jl.Pahlawan; e.g. Liman in Hotel Marlin charges 5000 or 6000 Rp for the night bus to UJUNG PANDANG. The bus will pick you up at your hotel. Arrange a pick up time as late as possible, so that you do not have to enjoy a free two-hour sightseeing tour of Rantepao. You won't lose your reserved seat. Sample bus prices: PARE PARE 2600 Rp, PALOPO 2000 Rp, BONE 7500 Rp, MALILI 5000 Rp, SOROAKO 7500 Rp. Several companies also offer tickets to central Sulawesi. The drive to Palu often takes 40 hours, costs 24,000 Rp. To POSO 15,000 Rp. Minibuses and bemos for short hauls wait in the pasar. Sample prices: MAKALE 500 Rp, LONDA 150 Rp, SIGUNTU 150 Rp, TILANGA 200 Rp, LEMO 200 Rp, MARANTE 150 Rp, NANGGALA 300 Rp, PALAWA 350 Rp, SADAN 400 Rp, BATUTUMONGA 2000 Rp, LOKOMATA 2500 Rp, KETE KESU 200 Rp, BUNTAO 500 Rp.

THE TORAJA

The ancestors of the Toraja came to Sulawesi from Indo-China between 2500 and 1500 BC. Like the Batak and Dayak, they are members of the proto-Malayan population. According to legend, they landed on a mountain near Kotu called ***Bamba Puang,*** *the god's gate. Bamba Puang has a shape similar to a female vagina (every bus up from UP makes a stop here). The traditional shape of houses looks like the stern of a ship. This could have something to do with the migration of the Toraja which must, of course, have taken place by ship.*

The traditional Toraja village consists of two rows of houses facing each other, running east to west. On one side are the living quarters ***(tongkonan),*** *while the rice is stored in the barns across the way* ***(alang).*** *They can hold many bundles of rice, weighing in all about 20,000 kg. The alang are built on rounded, wooden posts, while the tongkonan are built on rectangular posts. All the living quarters are roofed with layers of bamboo with the* ***longa*** *or tip of the roof taking the shape of a buffalo horn. The horns of sacrificed buffalos are hung on the roof's supporting beam; the number of horns depends on the house-owner's social standing in the community. The outer walls are carved and decorated with geometric ornaments of red, black, white, and yellow colours. Nails are never used in the traditional building method.*

*The word Toraja stems from the words **to ri aja,** roughly meaning 'those who came from above'. By this, they probably meant the north. Even if many Toraja today are Christian, the old traditions are still respected and followed. This is reflected in the respect for ancestors as well as in the elaborate burials.*

*According to Toraja beliefs, this life is only a phase, and only the next existence is of real importance. For this reason, funeral rituals last for weeks. A burial is never officially announced until all the blood relatives have gathered together. Gifts are brought. These could be buffalos, pigs or balok (palm wine, otherwise known in Indonesia as tuak) or something else. The deceased lies in state until the burial. The body is bathed and wrapped in cloth, the quantity and quality of which again give an indication of the social status. The liquids secreted from the body **(koropi)** are collected in a bamboo tube and spread on the earth. Then a **lambak tree** is planted on top.*

*The ritual follows carefully prescribed guidelines. First, while the deceased is lying in state at home, the embalming, wrapping in cloth, and carving of the wooden figure of the late loved one **(tao tao),** takes place. Then the reception of guests begins, and the buffalo sacrifice **(sibemba)** takes place. It isn't at all sad, rather they celebrate extravagantly with eating and drinking, dancing, and buffalo and cock-fights.*

A funeral ritual in which only one buffalo is sacrificed can end after one day and one night. For the nobility several hundred buffalos might be sacrificed. Afterwards, meaning after the actual burial, the period of mourning begins. On the third day the clothes are blackened and, after a week, laid on the grave. The period of mourning lasts for ten days. During the whole period of mourning, none of the friends or relatives of the deceased is allowed to eat rice. Then the ceremony of joy and suffering follows, for only now has the deceased become a heavenly spirit.

*The higher the social status of the dead, the longer the duration of the burial festivities because more buffalos are killed traditionally - with a lance **(merok)** causing slow death. Today the animals are usually killed with a **patinggoro,** a type of sword. The meat is then distributed according to established guidelines in which social status is again the main consideration.*

The Toraja bury their dead in cliff graves, like those in Lemo. The tao tao dressed in the clothes of the deceased stand in front of each individual wall niche of the 100 m high cliffs. At one time the dead were simply placed in wooden coffins and laid to rest on special burial rocks like those in Londa. Often things of value were buried with them, but the arrival of the Dutch brought thievery. For this reason new burial customs were developed, and can be seen in Lemo.

*Other important ceremonies are the **rambu tuka** and the **rambu solo.** The latter is a festival of homage to the souls. Rambu tuka is a festival of the gods where the gods are asked to bless the village with a good harvest and protect it from mischance and sickness. At all ceremonies and festivals there's lots to drink and eat - the balok really starts flowing.*

DAY TRIPS AROUND RANTEPAO

You're best off on foot, hiking through the surrounding villages. Motorbikes can be rented for between 10,000 and 15,000 Rp per day (try from TOKO BUKU IMANUEL). If you're a group, it could be worthwhile renting a minibus for around 30,000 Rp a day. On many roads and paths, though, you can get a ride in a minibus, bemo or truck. A minibus will take you between Rantepao and Makale at any time of day for 600 Rp. You can also ride part of the way and then just get out and walk on through the villages. Or you could plan a round trip.

The Toraja villages are still relatively intact communities even if hordes of children fall all over you and scream 'kasih gula gula' which basically means 'give me some sweets'. On the longer hikes, keep asking the way to the next village. The younger people in the village will usually speak this much Bahasa Indonesia ('dimana jalan ke...?').

HEADING SOUTH

To reach these frequently visited villages, get one of the many bemos toward Makale, then walk the last couple of kilometres into the village.

SIGUNTU

7 km, bemo 150 Rp, 2 km west of the road. An old king's village sitting on a hilltop with three well preserved tongkonan, across from an impressive row of alang. A good roundtrip is the path from SINGKI to Siguntu and over the river to the main road.

LONDA

6 km, bemos just along the main road, you walk the last 2 km. This valley has the most famous cliff graves. Only those for whom a *dirapai* has been arranged are buried here. It's best to take pictures of the cliff walls in the afternoon. Unfortunately, the tao tao have also been removed to prevent theft as experienced in Lemo. Village children with oil-lamps will bring you into the caves and show you the funeral rocks (they ask 1000 Rp). There are two caves at Londa. In the largest, the coffins are stacked along the walls. If you enjoy the macabre, you might peek into some of the open coffins deeper inside. The smaller coffins contain children; Christians rest in the black coffins.

TILANGA

9 km, bemo 200 Rp, walk the last 2 km from the main road. The natural swimming pool is no longer functional. A lovely lake is in the forest.

LEMO

12 km, bemos (200 Rp) along the main road, then walk 2 km. Behind the village so many graves are set in a 40 m high cliff wall that the whole cliff seems hollow. Just a few years ago, over 60 tao tao were standing in front. Most have been stolen.

HEADING EAST

There are hourly bemos toward Palopo. Expect to walk back if you stay until the late afternoon. The villages are all near the road.

MARANTE

7 km, bemo 150 Rp. Traditional village on the road, similar to the neighbouring village TONDON.

NANGGALA

16 km, minibuses from Rantepao 300 Rp. Lots of 'alang' (rice storehouses) with lovely decorations along the bottom. There is one especially well preserved 'tongkonan' (family home). From here, there is a footpath 8 km over the mountain to PANIKI, lovely view.

HEADING NORTH

These villages can be visited in a single day. Minibuses to Sadan and Palawa.

PALAWA

9 km, minibuses from Rantepao, 300 Rp. Walk uphill to the entrance to this traditional village. About half way you'll see two megalithic circles south of the road. In the village itself are a number of tongkonan in a row, facing a straight row of rice storehouses. The completely preserved traditional village is frequented by tourist buses. Souvenirs are sold in every house!

SADAN

12 km, minibuses from Rantepao 400 Rp. Walk to MALIMBONG from here. The path leads off to the left just before the bridge, 400 m to the village. Colourful cloth with traditional patterns is made on simple looms in two houses. Lace, ikat and batik from other regions of Indonesia is also sold. There is a beautiful 'tongkonan' with 91 horns.

HEADING NORTHWEST

You need an entire day to visit these two villages, accessible only via extremely poor roads. The scenery, however, is fascinating and well worth the difficult drive. Since only a few minibuses and trucks pass this way, check when the last ride back is leaving, unless you want to return by foot. Walking back is also recommended. A shorter alternative is the hike from Deri.

DERI

Get a minibus to Deri (1000 Rp). Lovely traditional houses. The walk down to BORI takes 30-45 minutes. Right by the main road is a cliff grave, and in the village itself is a *rante* (special field for funeral ceremonies).The infrequent bemos to Rantepao charge 400 Rp. Otherwise walk 1 km to PARINDING with its well preserved tongkonan and alang.

BATUTUMONGA

30 km, 2000 Rp by a rebuilt truck. Depart early in the morning on the long, interesting drive, and enjoy every jolt. The village is up in the mountains with a nice view over the plains and the adjoining valley to the north. Behind the village toward Lokomata, there is a footpath via PANA and TIKALA to Rantepao. You descend through bamboo forest and rice terraces, takes 3 hours.

LOKOMATA

6 km beyond Batutumonga, 2500 Rp from Rantepao. Lots of graves in the big cliffs. The village is on the slopes of Gunung Sesean.

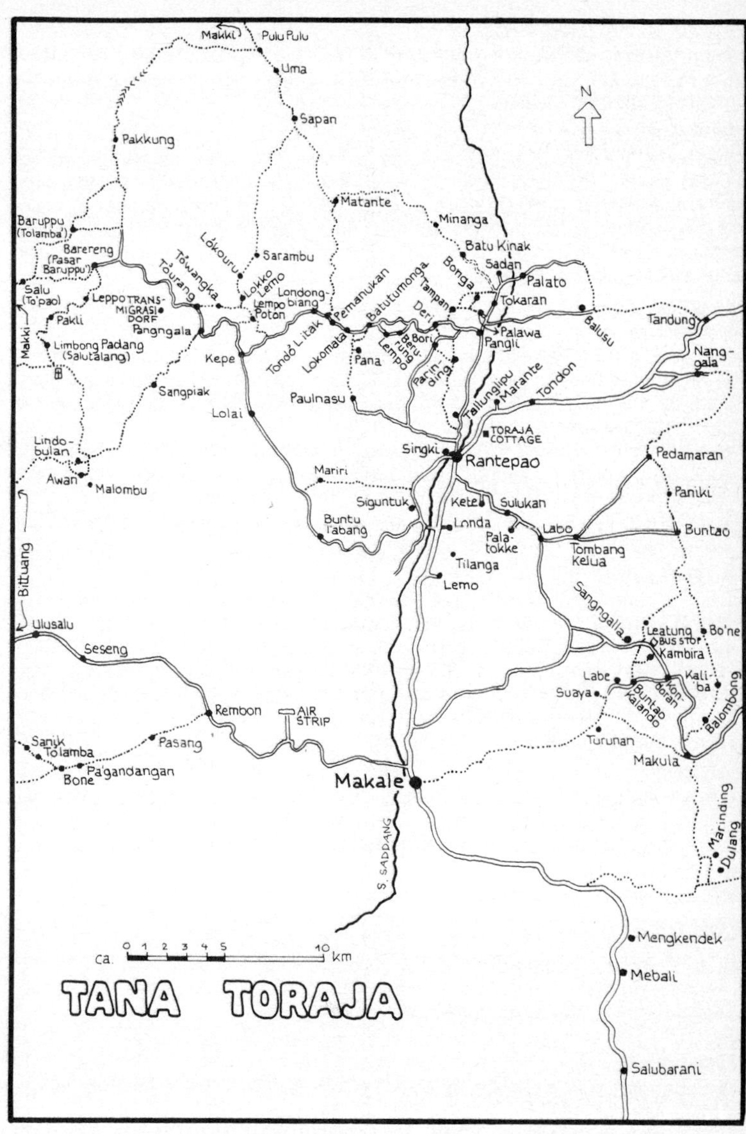
TANA TORAJA
Rantepao
Makale
Makki
Pulu Pulu
Uma
Sapan
Pakkung
Matante
Minanga
Baruppu (Tolamba')
Barereng (Pasar Baruppu')
Salu (To'pao)
Leppo
TRANSMIGRASI DORF
Pakli
Pangngala
Limbong Padang (Salutalang)
Kepe
Sangpiak
Lolai
Sarambu
Lokouru
Towangka
Tourang
Lokko Lemo
Londong-biang
Lempo Poton
Pemanukan
Batutumonga
Bonga
Tampan
Deri
Batu Kinak
Sadan
Palato
Tokaran
Palawa
Pangli
Balusu
Tandung
Nanggala
Tondo Litak
Lokomata
Pana
Beru-rung
Lempo
Bori
Parinding
Paulnasu
Tallunglipu
Marante
Tondon
TORAJA COTTAGE
Singki
Pedamaran
Paniki
Buntao
Lindo-bulan
Awan
Malombu
Mariri
Siguntuk
Buntu Tabang
Kete
Sulukan
Londa
Palatokke
Labo
Tombang Kelua
Tilanga
Lemo
Bittuang
Ulusalu
Seseng
Sangngalla
Leatung
Bo'ne
BUS STOP
Kambira
Labe
Suaya
Buntao Kalando
Kondorah
Kaliba
Balombong
Turunan
Makula
Rembon
AIR STRIP
Sanik
Tolamba
Pasang
Bone
Pa'gandangan
S. SADDANG
Marinding
Dulang
Mengkendek
Mebali
Salubarani
N
ca. 0 1 2 3 4 5 10 km

HEADING SOUTHEAST

Bemos traverse the narrow road to BUNTAO (400-500 Rp) and SANGALLA (from Makale 350 Rp). The villages KALANDO, SUAYA and MAKULA are 13, 14, and 16 km from Makale.

KETE KESU

4 km, bemo 200 Rp. The tourist village in Tator. The buildings are placed like exhibits among the flowers, and joined. atypically, by souvenir stands. Just behind the village, accessible via a paved path, you'll find a number of disintegrating coffins, a few hanging tombs, and a modern tao tao. This depicts a former minister who, in January 1987, was laid to rest in a tremendous stone tomb in Tator's biggest funeral.

PALATOKKE

9 km from Rantepao. Get here via KETE KESU and SULLUKANG. Bemos to LABO cost 300 Rp. A tiny path leads through rice fields (30 minutes) to the village and its famous hanging graves (ERONG). The path to Palatokke is difficult to find, off the main road, to the right at Posko KKN UNHAS. Look for the red sign. There are few tourists and no admission charge. Be sure, however, to compensate the villagers who show you the way up to the 700-800 year old tombs, set on a free hanging scaffold built into the rock. Several skulls have been placed as ornamentation at the foot of the cliff. In Labo the road forks. To the left are BUNTAO and PANIKI (see above). To the right is SANGALLA. Public transport, however, is infrequent.

SANGALLA

Easiest to reach from Makale (350 Rp). Get a bus or bemo on the route to TUMANETE. Walk from here along the main road, past a school, to the children's tombs in a tree at KAMBIRA. Walk on along a path to BUNTU KALANDO. A small museum has been founded in a former king's house. In SUAYA there are royal tombs and lots of tao tao. Continue uphill to MAKALE. Stop briefly just before Makale in TONDON for a look at the royal tombs and tao tao in a cliff wall next to the path.

MAKULA

3 km beyond the fork to Suaya, the HOT SPRINGS are on your right. You can swim in the pool, or splash out on a bath in the bath house. An old royal palace stands on a hill behind the bath house. After being destroyed in a fire, it was rebuilt.

MAKALE

The administrative centre of Tana Toraja was built by the Dutch in the 20s. Not as many tourists as in Rantepao! A beautiful market once a week. Rantepao, however, is by far the nicer place to stay.

HOTELS

The cheapest is *PENGINAPAN MAKALE**. Not far away is *LOSMEN MERRY***. On the road to Rantepao is *LOSMEN MARTHA***. Much more expensive are *WISMA BARANA***** and *WISMA HASANUDDIN*****.

LEAVING MAKALE

Minibus connections: SANGALLA 350 Rp, BITUANG 2000 Rp, RANTEPAO 500 Rp, PARE PARE 2500 Rp, 155 km, 4 1/2 hrs. Buses to UP cost 4500 Rp (night buses 5500 Rp). Minibuses to PALOPO 2200 Rp. Buses to BONE for 4200 Rp, MALILI 5000 Rp, SOROAKO 7000 Rp.

FROM MANGKUTANA TO PENDOLO / SULAWESI TENGAH

To get from Tator to Central Sulawesi, you have to go via Palopo. The route is really only recommended during the dry season - between December and March it will take a long time.

First, take the bus from Palopo to WOTU or MANGKUTANA (2200 Rp). Several losmen. The next bit to PENDOLO, on the southern end of Lake Poso, can take more than 12 hours. During the dry season you can get a ride with a Toyota Land Cruiser for 13,500 Rp per person. Sometimes there are motorbikes - you have to sit on the back with all your gear. They are cheaper, but much more dangerous since you often have to cross bridges made only of logs. In Pendolo stay at the only losmen (PENGINAPAN DANAU POSO* or PENGINAPAN MASAMBA*) and recuperate a bit on the nicest lake on Sulawesi. Boats will take you across the lake to TENTENA for 1500 Rp. HOTEL DUSELEMBA*(*) is near the landing-place. A minibus to POSO takes 2 hours, costs 2000 Rp.

CENTRAL SULAWESI

Thanks to the fairly new road between Wotu and Poso, a few travellers occasionally stray into this part of Sulawesi, almost untouched by tourism. Palu, the provincial capital, is of interest as a place to get flights to Kalimantan or North Sulawesi.

PALU

This town is situated on a very pretty bay. Get info at Jl.Cik Ditiro 32. Take a side trip to DONGGALA (minibus for 1100 Rp) with its beautiful beaches! Stay in WISMA RAME**. Hotels in Palu: KITA*, Jl.Cut Nyak Dien 18 or GARUDA*, Jl.Hasanuddin 33.

LEAVING PALU

BY AIR

BOURAQ office is at Jl.Mawar 5 (tel 21195); MERPATI is in Hotel Garuda, Jl.Hasanuddin 33, tel 21295; GARUDA tickets are available from PT.Rajawali Ashab, Jl.S.I.S.Aldjufri 2B. SAMPLE PRICES: UJUNG PANDANG 56,600 Rp (MZ/BO), BALIKPAPAN 52,900 Rp, BANJARMASIN 98,000 Rp (via Balik with BO) SAMARINDA 79,700 Rp (via Balik with BO), TARAKAN 124,900 Rp (via Balik with BO), GORONTALO 50,000 Rp (BO), TOLI TOLI 54,600 Rp (MZ), LUWUK 68,000 Rp (MZ), POSO 34,300

Rp (MZ), MANADO (via Luwuk with Merpati or via Gorontalo with Bouraq) 93,000 Rp.

BY SHIP

Pelni tickets: Jl.Gajah Mada 86 in Palu. Every second Sun Pelni's modern KM.KAMBUNA sails from Palu's harbour Pantoloan to BITUNG (Manado), returns the following Tues, and continues via BALIK, UJUNG PANDANG, SURABAYA, TANJUNG PRIOK to BELAWAN. The KM.KERINCI docks every second Sat in Pantaloan, and sails via TOLI TOLI to TARAKAN. On every following Mon she is back in Palu, and continues via BALIK, UJUNG PANDANG, SURABAYA, TANJUNG PRIOK to West Sumatra.

SAMPLE PRICES (1st cl./Ekonomi): TANJUNG PRIOK 135,500 / 44,600 Rp, SURABAYA 93,500 / 32,100 Rp, BALIKPAPAN 33,900 / 14,800 Rp, UJUNG PANDANG 58,900 / 22,700 Rp, TOLI TOLI 30,300 / 11,000 Rp, MANADO 62,500 / 24,800 Rp.

BY BUS

Bemos in town charge 150 - 300 Rp depending on distance. To DONGGALA (1100 Rp, 34 km, 1 h) from Jl. Imam Bonjol. To the harbour Pantoloan (600 Rp, 22 km, 1/2 h) from Jl.Dr.Wahidin, Stasion Besusu. To PARIGI (3100 Rp, 84 km, 2 1/2 - 3 hrs.) from Jl.S.Lewara.

Book long distance minibuses one or two days ahead in one of the companies' offices.They'll pick you up right at your hotel. To POSO with P.O.Sahabat Baru and A.L.S., Jl.Dr.Sam Ratulangi 73 for 5000 Rp. Heading towards GORONTALO / MANADO (22,000 / 33,000 Rp), PALOPO / UJUNG PANDANG and AMPANA / LUWUK (15,000 / 33,000 Rp).

It takes 30 - 40 hrs. or more to reach Gorontalo. Most of the time roads are unpaved, and during the rainy season you can only hope and pray that you see plenty of trucks and jeeps that can pull you out of the mud.

NORTH SULAWESI

Sulawesi Utara is the smallest of the island's four provinces with 25,786 km^2 and 2.4 million inhabitants. Sulawesi's northernmost peninsula is only 50 km across but 500 km long. To the northeast it finds its continuation in the Sangihe and Talaud island groups.

The first contact of the Minahasa population with Europeans came in the 16th century, when first the Portuguese and then the Spaniards landed. At the beginning of the 18th century the Dutch followed, and 100 years later most of the inhabitants had been converted to Christianity. Today North Sulawesi is the Indonesian province with the highest per capita income and standard of living. It is probably the region of the country most open to western ideas. During Dutch rule, the Minahasa made a name for themselves by collaborating with the colonial power. Many served in the Dutch army, and when the 1958 uprisings against the central government took place on Sumatra and Sulawesi, the Minahasa also took part. At that time Manado was bombed.

The main agricultural products are copra, cloves, nutmeg and other spices. Unlike on Java, the villagers here are quite well off - one can make a good living off cloves in Indonesia today!

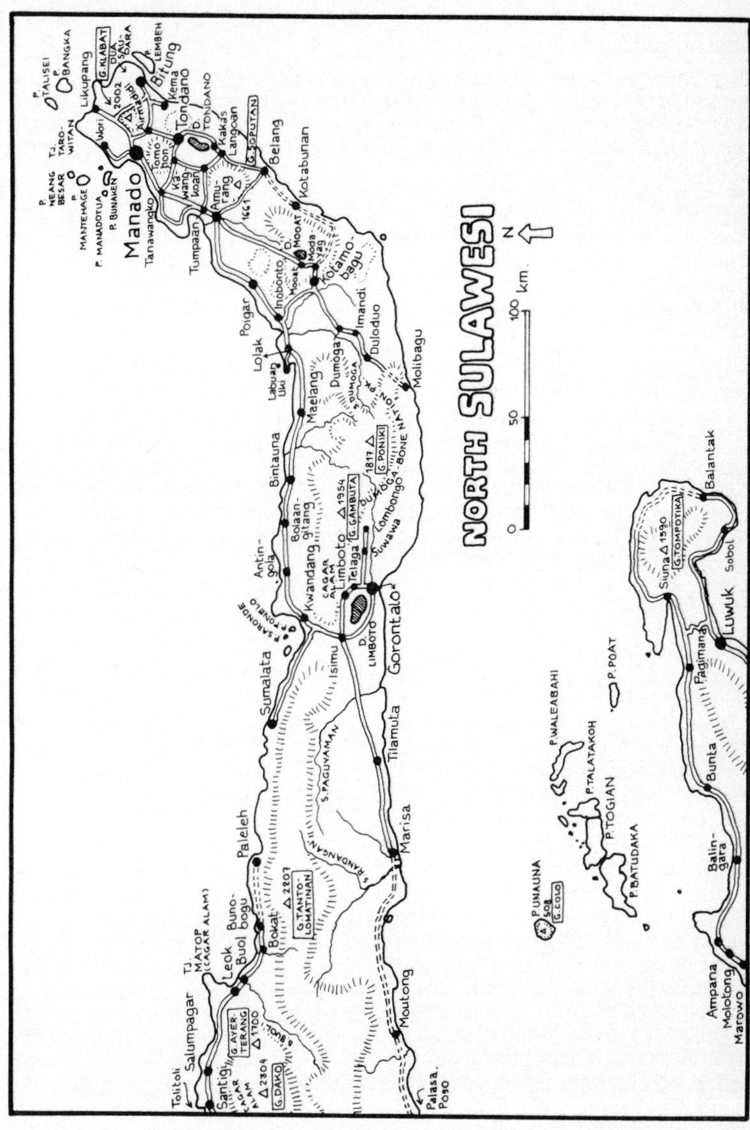
NORTH SULAWESI
0
50
100
km.
N
Manado
Tanawangko
Tumpaan
Amurang
Kawangkoan
Tomohon
Tondano
D. TONDANO
Kakas
Langoan
G. SOPUTAN
Belang
Kotabunan
Airmadidi
2002
G. KLABAT
Likupang
Wori
Kema
Bitung
P. LEMBEH
DUA SAUDARA
P. BANGKA
P. TALISEI
TJ. TAROWITAN
P. NEANG BESAR
P. MANTEHAGE
P. MANADOTUA
P. BUNAKEN
1661
D. MOOAT
Mooat
Modayag
Kotamobagu
Inobonto
Poigar
Lolak
Labuan Uki
Imandi
Duloduo
Dumoga
S. DUMOGA
Molibagu
Maelang
Bintauna
Bolaangitang
Antingola
1954
G. GAMBUTA
1817
G. PONIKI
DUMOGA BONE NAT. PK.
Lombongo
Suwawa
Telaga
Limboto
CAGAR ALAM
Kwandang
P. PONELO
P. SARONDE
D. LIMBOTO
Gorontalo
Isimu
Sumalata
Tilamuta
S. PAGUYAMAN
Marisa
S. RANDANGAN
2207
G. TANTOLOMATINAN
Paleleh
Buol
Bunobogu
Bokat
Leok
TJ. MATOP (CAGAR ALAM)
Salumpagar
Tolitoli
Santigi
CAGAR ALAM
2304
G. DAKO
1700
G. AYER-TERANG
Moutong
Palasa
Poso
P. UNAUNA
508
G. COLO
P. BATUDAKA
P. TOGIAN
P. TALATAKOH
P. WALEABAHI
P. POAT
Siuna
1590
G. TOMPOTIKA
Balantak
Sobol
Luwuk
Pagimana
Bunta
Balingara
Ampana
Molotong
Marowo

MANADO

The capital of the province has about a quarter of a million inhabitants, most of whom are Christian. Right away you'll notice the large middle class. Poverty and class differences are much less pronounced. The city pulsates, people promenade in the evening, and for the girls the sarong is taboo; they prefer skirts and blouses.

The most important festival of the Chinese community, *TOA PEH KONG,* is in February, two weeks after Chinese New Year. A large parade of Chinese passes through town. The oldest temple is *KWAN IM TONG* on Jl.Sisingamangaraja.

HOTELS

PENGINAPAN KELUARGA,* Jl.Tengku Umar 20 (right behind the bridge) is the cheapest place to stay and looks like it. Right round the corner *LOSMEN KOTAMOBAGU*** has similar standards and is often fully booked. *HOTEL ANGKASA RAYA***,* Jl.Soegiono 12a - more centrally located. Disco on the 4th floor. In the medium price range you find *HOTEL KAWANUA***,* Jl.Yos Sudarso 40 - known as Kawanua Kecil. The friendly staff often give you a discount. Everything else costs much more than 15,000 Rp, e.g. the small new *MANADO INN****,* a bit out in Teling, Jl. Pebruari 14. Similar prices at *MINAHASA***(*),* Jl.Sam Ratulangi 199/200 or in the largest hotel *KAWANUA CITY****,* Jl.Sam Ratulangi 1, tel 52222.

FOOD

Good Chinese food in *FIESTA*, Jl. Babe Balar. On the same road seafood in *MENTARA*. There's Minahasa food at *TINOOR JAYA*. Nasi padang in *SINGGALANG*, Jl.Sam Ratulangi 127. A cheap rumah makan can be found across from the hospital Gunung Wenang on Jl.Yos Sudarso.

GENERAL INFORMATION

TOURIST INFORMATION - Kanwil Depparpostel at Jl.Diponegoro 111. Diparda Sulawesi Utara at Jl.Edi Gagola (near Jl.17.Augustus, not far from Kantor Imigrasi). Ask about the different festivals, especially those at clove harvesting time (June to October).

IMIGRASI - Jl.Supratman. Friendly people but it takes at least half a day to get a visa extension.

BANKS - best rates for US$-TCs in BANK DAGANG NEGARA, Jl.Dotulolong Lasut. 15. Or try BANK EKSPOR IMPOR, Jl.Yos Sudarso 29.

LEAVING MANADO

BY AIR

Sam Ratulangi Airport is situated about 18 km northeast of town. Bemos leave from Jl.Sisingamangaraja for 400 Rp. Taxis cost 6000 Rp. Airline Offices: GARUDA, Jl.Diponegoro 15 (tel 52154); MERPATI, Jl.Sam Ratulangi 138 (tel 4027); BOURAQ, Jl.Sarapung 27 (tel 2757); MANDALA, Jl.Sarapung 17 (tel 52086). Since Autumn '86, Garuda flies every Sat from Jakarta via Denpasar and Manado to GUAM. Manado airport is

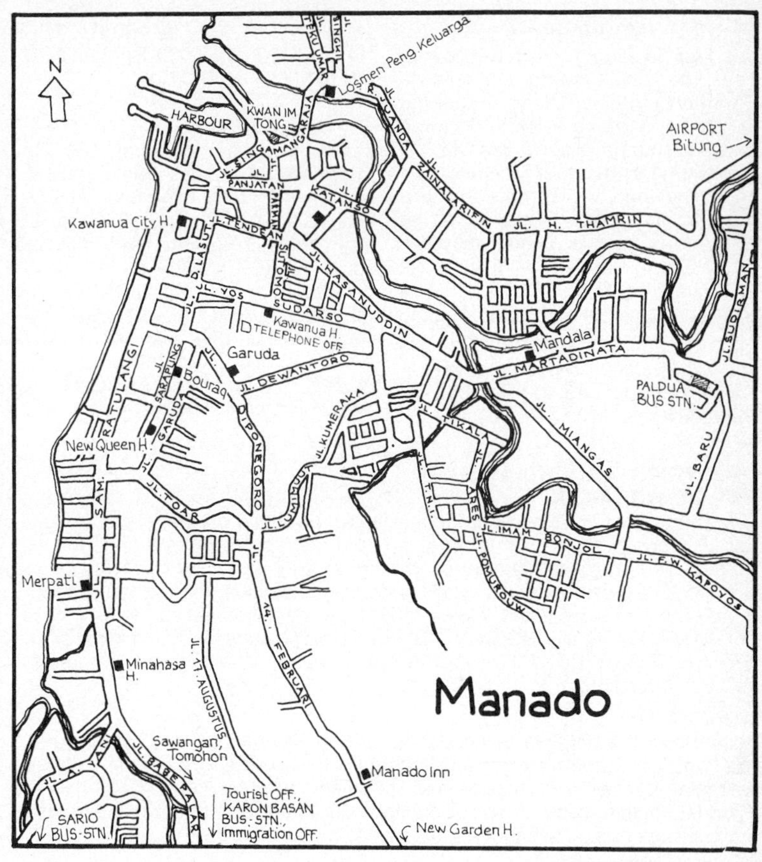

a visa-free entry / exit point. SAMPLE PRICES: JAYAPURA 194,100 Rp (GA), BIAK 165,900 Rp (GA), PALU 93,000 Rp (BO direct, MZ via Luwuk), SURABAYA 167,000 Rp (BO), UJUNG PANDANG 97,300 Rp (BO / MZ), TERNATE 44,900 Rp (BO / MZ), BALIKPAPAN 132,400 Rp (BO direct), GORONTALO 42,800 Rp (BO / MZ), JAKARTA 259,400 Rp (GA, BO via Balik 220,500 Rp), AMBON 118,000 Rp (MZ), LUWUK 58,500 Rp (MZ), POSO 102,100 Rp (MZ), NAHA 52,700 Rp (MZ, Tahuna, Pulau Sangir), MELANGUANE 66,200 Rp (MZ, Pulau Talaud).

BY SHIP

Bitung is Manado's big harbour and all the larger ships tie up here. Get here by bemo or bus for 1000 Rp. Pelni Office in Manado on Jl.Sam Ratulangi.

The KM.KAMBUNA docks every second Mon in Bitung. On the following Tues she leaves Bitung and sails via Pantoloan, Balik, Ujung Pandang, Surabaya, Tanjung Priok to Belawan and back again. Pelni's KM.UMSINI is in Bitung every other Mon and continues her tour via Ternate and Sorong to Jayapura. Every following Sun she is back in Bitung and sails on via Ujung Pandang and Surabaya to Tanjung Priok.

SAMPLE PRICES (1st cl. / Ekonomi): MEDAN 284,500 / 95,700 Rp, JAKARTA 203,500 / 66,300 Rp, SURABAYA 165,600 / 55,400 Rp, UJUNG PANDANG 102,100 / 35,800 Rp, BA LIKPAPAN 81,400 / 32,100 Rp, TERNATE 35,900 / 12,000 Rp, JAYAPURA 131,600 / 51,000 Rp.

BY BUS / BEMO

Inside town bemos cost 150 Rp. There are three bus / bemo stations: PAL DUA for East Minahasa (AIRMADIDI 600 Rp, BITUNG 1000 Rp, LIKUPANG 800 Rp, PANTAI KEMA 550 Rp) - KARONBASAN for the south (TOMOHON 500 Rp, LANGOWAN 800 Rp) - SARIO for the west (KOTAMOBAGU 3600 Rp, AMURANG 1800 Rp, POIGAR 2800 Rp, INOBONTO 4500 Rp, GORONTALO 11,000 Rp, up to 36 hrs.).

DAY TRIPS AROUND MANADO

PULAU BUNAKEN

One of the best coral reefs in Indonesia can be found off the island of Bunaken. It drops straight down several hundred metres. Visibility is good for 10 - 15 m. This is a great place for snorkeling, as well as for scuba diving. There are two diving centres where you'll find accommodation, food, and scuba diving on the reef twice a day. Costs: US$65 per day. Addresses (both in Manado): NUSANTARA DIVING CENTRE, Malalayang I, Jaga V, P.O.Box 15. TIRTA SATWA DIVING CENTRE (400 m further east), Malalayang I, Lingkat IV, P.O.Box 82, tel 3822.

AIRMADIDI

Leave from the Pal Dua bemo station for 600 Rp. About 3 km from the main road you'll find a fine example of *waruga.* These are special stone coffins in which the deceased is placed to rest in a sitting position surrounded by lots of material objects, such as gold, porcelain etc. There are many friendly people in the village, happy to show you the way to the two cemeteries.

DANAU TONDANO

First take a bemo to TOMOHON (500 Rp). Stop if possible in TINOOR with its many restaurants. Minahasa food, which includes dog, mouse, and bat, is served for your delight. Go by bemo from here to Tondano. Take a walk down the main street extension to the lake (2 - 3 km). The 50 km^2 Lake Tondano lies about 600 m above sea level and is surrounded by hills and mountains. In the middle of the lake is the tiny island LIKRI.

DUA SAUDARA NATIONAL PARK

PPA with an office on Jl.Supratman 68 has established a 8867 ha nature reserve around the two mountains of Dua Saudara (1351 m) and Tangkoko (1109 m). Get a permit ahead of time from the PPA office. Then take a minibus toward Bitung up to GIRIAN. From here get a taxi via TANAO WUDU (get your permit confirmed in the Camat) to KAMPONG BATUPUTIH (takes almost an hour to do the 20 km). There is simple accommodation near here. Lookouts have been erected in several places to watch the animals. You'll see many monkeys as well as hornbills, cockatoos, and the maleo bird.

GORONTALO

The second largest town in North Sulawesi is located on a plateau surrounded by mountains. In the centre is Danau Limboto.The town has developed into a very important traffic centre between the provinces of Sulut and Sulteng. You can reach Central Sulawesi by plane, by ship and even overland.

HOTELS

Cheap is *HOTEL MELATI***, Jl.Wolter Monginsidi 33, an old villa with a large veranda, typical Gorontalo architecture; the owner speaks Dutch and English. Two villas in the same style are *HOTEL ASIA****, Jl.J.S.Parman 10 and *PENGINAPAN TELUK KAU****, Jl.Jend.S.Parman 42, cool, airy rooms. Diagonally opposite is *PENGINAPAN SHINTA****, no. 35.

1 1/2 km from the city centre is *HOTEL DANAU TOBA**-*****, Jl.Cendrawasih 56. If you want to spend more, stay at *HOTEL MINI SARONDE*****, Jl.Walanda Maramis 17, with free airport taxi. Similar are *CITY HOTEL*****, Jl.Jen.A.Yani 20 or *HOTEL WISATA ******, Jl.23 Januari 19, not far from the post office.

LEAVING GORONTALO

BY AIR

Airport Jalaludin is 32 km northwest near Isimu. Taxis cost 2500 Rp; direct minibuses cost 1200 Rp; only to Isimu costs 550 Rp and the last bit by bendi for 300 Rp. MERPATI, Jl.Jen.S.Parman 5; BOURAQ, Jl.Jen.A.Yani 34. SAMPLE PRICES: MANADO 42,800 Rp (MZ / BO), PALU 50,000 Rp (BO).

BY SHIP

Take a bemo (Angkutan Kota) to the harbour at the mouth of Sungei Bone for 175 Rp or a bendi for 300 Rp. Irregularly and not too often there are freighters to Manado / Bitung, Ujung Pandang or Surabaya. Every week there are small ships to MOLIBAGU (3000 Rp, 8-12 hrs.) and via Tomini Bay to Central Sulawesi: seldom directly to Poso (25-30 hrs.), most times with stopovers in PAGIMANA 10,000 Rp (10-12 hrs.), DOLONG 14,500 Rp, WAKAI 16,000 Rp, BUNTA 15,000 Rp, AMPANA 19,500 Rp, POSO 21,000 Rp.

BY BUS

The terminal is 1 1/2 km from the centre. SAMPLE PRICES: BATUDAA 350 Rp, 17 km; LIMBOTO 350 Rp, 17 km; KOTAMOBAGU 9000 Rp, 275 km, 15 hrs.; MANADO 12,000 Rp, 400 km, 20 hrs.; PALU (22,000 Rp, 607 km) count on 35-40 hrs. (or more).

KALIMANTAN

The third largest island in the world is still often referred to as 'Borneo'. Actually this is the name of the northern Sultanate of 'Berunai' (Brunei) which the English language turned into Borneo and used for the whole island. The Dutch colonial masters kept the name, and not until Indonesian independence did the island get the name 'Kalimantan'. Most of Kalimantan today belongs to Indonesia and is divided into four provinces: West, Central, South and East. The northern part of the island, Sarawak and Sabah, belonged to the British empire and became federated to Malaysia in 1963. The tiny Sultanate of Brunei has been independent since 1984. Not until the 1920s was the interior of the island explored. Today there are still inaccessible, undeveloped areas. Rivers are the main arteries of transportation. A road system exists only in a limited area around Pontianak and between Banjarmasin and Samarinda. The Trans-Kalimantan Highway project is still hardly beyond the planning stages. As might be expected, airplanes make a significant contribution.

On the 539,500 km^2 island (= 28% of total Indonesian national territory) there are only 8 million people (= 4.5% of the population) mainly concentrated in coastal towns. The population density is only 15 inhabitants per km^2 - in Central and East Kalimantan only 6 per km^2. West Kalimantan and the coast are settled mostly by ethnic Malay people and Chinese. In the interior, on the other hand, you find two to three million Dayak. These consist of 150 to 200 different tribes settled within artificial borders set by the Dutch and British. Information about the most important Dayak tribes can be found in the Sarawak chapter.

Wood and oil form the foundation of Kalimantan's economic wealth. It is estimated that 60% of the island is covered by tropical rain forest. Foreign licencees, mainly from America and Japan, have bought up huge areas and are undertaking a terrible denuding strategy. Reforesting programmes are hardly instituted even though the wood exports increase yearly. The resulting topsoil erosion is now being fought by government action, such as restrictions on the export of unprocessed timber. Oil and small amounts of natural gas can be found on Kalimantan's east coast. Important areas of exploitation lie around Tarakan, Bontang, Balikpapan, and Tanjung. A pipeline operates between Bontang and Tanjung; there's a refinery in Balikpapan. All the provinces of Kalimantan have yet to see the influx of tourism. Several travel agencies offer tours, but they are restricted.

Anyone who wants to get to know Kalimantan first needs lots of time. River tours up the Mahakam or Barito are not to be recommended for fast-paced backpackers. In addition, crossing the island through the borders between Indonesia and Sarawak, closed to foreigners (see Sarawak chapter), is practically impossible. On the other hand, the borders between Sabah and East Kalimantan are open. There are travellers who make it from the source region of the Mahakam to the Kapuas - but it's not something for beginners. Keep in mind the possibility of flying out of Tarakan or Pontianak when planning your trip to Kalimantan. Since 1987 Pontianak has been a visa-free exit entry point and can be reached by plane from Kuching or Singapore.

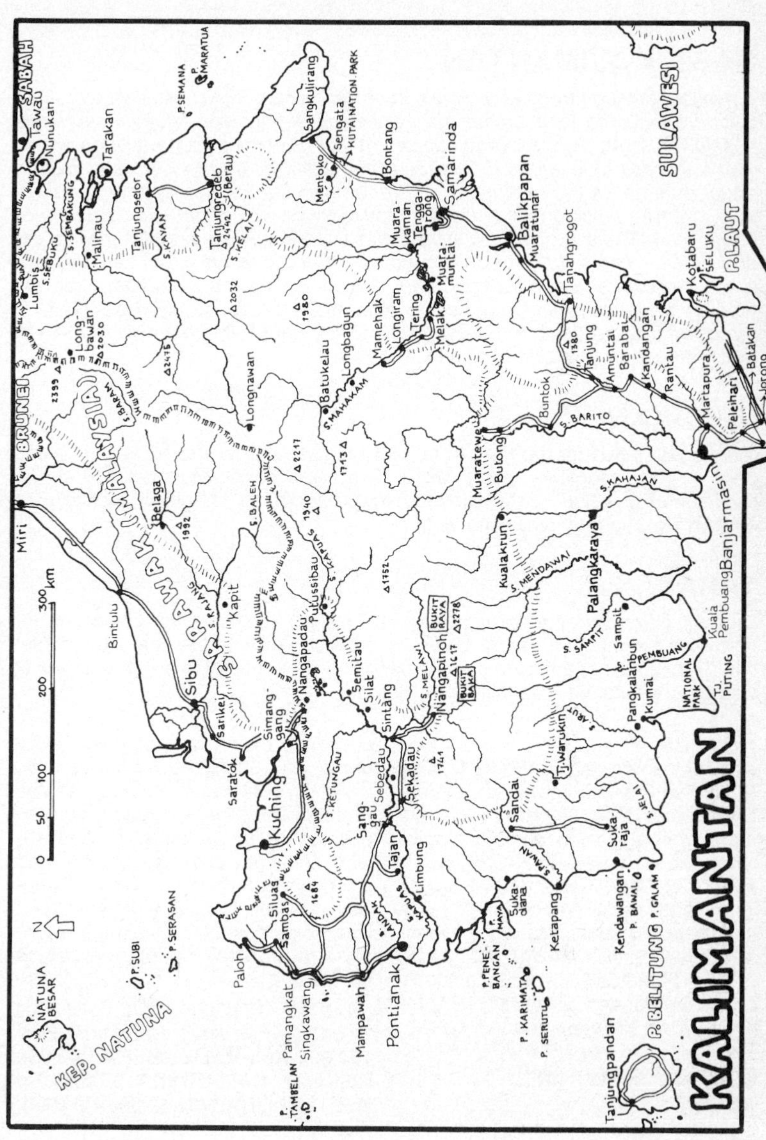
KALIMANTAN
SARAWAK (MALAYSIA)
SABAH
BRUNEI
SULAWESI
P. LAUT
P. BELITUNG
KEP. NATUNA
0 50 100 200 300 km
Miri
Bintulu
Sibu
Sarikei
Saratok
Kuching
Kapit
Belaga
Simanggang
Nangapadau
Putussibau
Semitau
Silat
Sintang
Sebedau
Sekadau
Sanggau
Tajan
Limbung
Pontianak
Mampawah
Singkawang
Pamangkat
Sambas
Siluas
Paloh
Ketapang
Sukadana
Sandai
Sukaraja
Kendawangan
Pangkalanbun
Kumai
Sampit
Palangkaraya
Kualakurun
Kuala Pembuang
Banjarmasin
Martapura
Pelaihari
Rantau
Kandangan
Barabai
Amuntai
Tanjung
Buntok
Muaratewe
Butong
Tanahgrogot
Balikpapan
Muaratunan
Samarinda
Tenggarong
Muarakaman
Muaramuntai
Melak
Tering
Longiram
Mamehak
Longbagun
Batukelau
Longnawan
Bontang
Sengata
Mentoko
Sangkulirang
Tanjungredeb (Berau)
Tanjungselor
Malinau
Lumbis
Longbawan
Tarakan
Nunukan
Tawau
Kotabaru
Batakan
Jorong
Tanjungpandan
Nangapinoh
BUKIT RAYA
BUKIT BAKA
S. MAHAKAM
S. BARITO
S. KAHAJAN
S. MENDAWAI
S. SAMPIT
S. PEMBUANG
S. KAPUAS
S. MELAWI
S. KETUNGAU
S. BALEH
S. RAJANG
S. KAYAN
S. KELAI
S. SEBUKU
S. SEMBAKUNG
S. BARAM
S. JELAI
S. PAWAN
S. ARUT
KUTAI NATION. PARK
NATIONAL PARK
TJ. PUTING
P. NATUNA BESAR
P. SUBI
P. SERASAN
P. TAMBELAN
P. KARIMATA
P. SERUTU
P. PENEBANGAN
P. MAYA
P. BAWAL
P. GALAM
P. SEMANA
P. MARATUA
P. SELUKU

EAST KALIMANTAN

Travellers driving through the province of Kalimantan Timur usually come from Sabah, since the long detour via Jakarta is expensive. Another unreliable possibility is the flight to Zamboanga in the Philippines. Huge swamp areas, with hundreds of lakes, in the deltas of the great rivers are just as difficult to travel through as the rainforests where, among the 800 different types of orchid, the rare black orchid blooms. If you're lucky, you might even spot a wild orang utan. There are rehabilitation centres for these rare animals in Bontang and Sebelu. The oil town of Balikpapan is a traffic junction - from here you can reach the capital Samarinda by land. A river trip up the Mahakam, past the floating markets and long houses, is something nobody should miss. While in the coastal areas you'll run into a few tourists; further upstream you'll have to depend on your own organizational talent.

NUNUKAN

is the end station for the ferry from TAWAU (Sabah). It crosses several times daily in both directions, costs M$12. There are several losmen and cheap hotels. Buy a ticket in the Nunukan Express Office for about 9000 Rp to TARAKAN. The ferry takes one night.

TARAKAN

lives on oil and the landscape shows it. It is an important traffic junction for northeast Kalimantan. Part of the town is built on stilts in the sea. Don't forget that Tarakan is not a visa-free entry exit point, so you have to apply for a tourist visa before entering Indonesia from Sabah.

HOTELS

A lot of losmen, e.g. *JAKARTA LOSMEN** with small rooms on Jl.Jen. Sudirman 112. In this area there are more cheap losmen and the somewhat expensive *HOTEL ORCHID**** at no. 171. A bit further down the road you'll reach *WISATA HOTEL**(*)* with comfortable rooms. The most expensive hotel in town *TARAKAN PLAZA* **** (tel 502) is on Jl.Yos Sudarso. To be recommended is *WISMA RAMAYANA**** on the same road.

LEAVING TARAKAN

BY AIR

Bemos right from the airport ask 2500 Rp for the 3 km to town centre. Walk out to the main road and catch a city bemo for 150 Rp. Both Merpati (Jl. Sudirman 34) and Bouraq (Jl.Yos Sudarso 9B) fly into Tarakan. As travellers weren't permitted in 1987 to take the night ship to Nunukan and the connecting ferry to Tawau, there was only the Bouraq flight. Swift Air flies irregularly from Tarakan to Zamboanga in the Philippines, costs US$160.

SAMPLE PRICES: BALIKPAPAN 72,000 Rp (BO/MZ), BANJARMASIN 107,500 Rp (BO/MZ), BERAU 40,000 Rp (MZ), SAMARINDA 67,600 Rp (MZ), LONGBAWAN 47,600 Rp (MZ), SEMARANG 183,900 Rp (BO), JA-

KARTA 181,000 Rp (BO / MZ via Balik), PALU 124,900 Rp (BO), TANJUNG SELOR 24,600 Rp (MZ), UJUNG PANDANG 174,600 Rp (MZ).

BY SHIP

Ferry to NUNUKAN leaves daily at 7:30 h for 9000 Rp. Takes 12 hours. Every five days there's a river boat to MALINAU for 8000 Rp. Fairly regularly boats sail to Sulawesi (PARE PARE and PALU / DONGGALA). Expect to pay up to 45,000 Rp. Almost daily there's a coastal ship to TANJUNG SELOR, costs about 5000 Rp. The town is the starting point for river trips up the Sungei Kayan. In Tanjung Selor there is the possibility of getting a ship to TANJUNG REDEB (Berau). Several boats a week leave from Berau to SAMARINDA. If you have time, endurance, and enthusiasm, you can even travel down the whole east coast. Pelni has an office on Jl.Yos Sudarso. Every other Sun the KM. KERINCI sails via TOLI TOLI (13,900 / 34,100 Rp), PALU (18,300 / 50,800 Rp), BALIKPAPAN (21,600 / 53,800 Rp), UJUNG PANDANG (35,100 / 105,100 Rp) to SURABAYA 40,000 / 103,100 Rp and further on to TANJUNG PRIOK and SUMATRA. Prices Ekonomi / 1st cl.

SAMARINDA

About 210,000 people live in this provincial capital. Even large ships are able to navigate the 4 km wide Sungei Mahakam. Tree trunks float on the river, bound together as rafts. Along the banks are the saw mills of the major timber companies. If you arrive by ship, you'll first see the *GREAT MOSQUE.* Make an excursion to *SEBERANG* on the other bank of the river; the ferry costs 200 Rp. Here you can get one of the famous Samarinda sarong, costs up to 40,000 Rp.

HOTELS

Not a cheap place to spend the night! Try *LOSMEN AIDA***, Jl.Temenggung, clean and centrally located or *LOSMEN HIDAYA*** right near by. Good are *HOTEL HAYANI***(*),* Jl. Pirus 17, *HOTEL DIANA MAS****,* Jl. Veteran and *HOTEL RAHAYU****,* Jl. K.H. Abdul Hasan 17, family atmosphere. Most expensive places are *HOLIDAY INN*****,* Jl.Pelabuhan 29 and *HOTEL SUKARNI*****,* Jl.Panglima Batur 154.

FOOD

The warung and rumah makan around the jetties and along Jl.Niaga Selatan are good and cheap. On the same road is the night market. Or try MODERN BAKERY, Jl.Jen.Sudirman corner of Jl.Veteran diagonally across from Bank Ekspor Impor.

LEAVING SAMARINDA

BY AIR

Taxis to the airport Temindung charge 2000 Rp, bemos cost 200 Rp. Bouraq (Jl.Mulawarman 12) and Merpati (Hotel Jakarta, Jl.Sudirman) serve the town. Smaller airlines often fly charters into the interior. Garuda agent is P.T. Perisah, Jl.Diponegoro. SAMPLE PRICES: BERAU 62,600 Rp (MZ), BALIKPAPAN 31,500 Rp (MZ / BO), TARAKAN 67,600 Rp (MZ).

BY SHIP

Several shipping companies have their offices by the river on Jl.Yos Sudarso. River buses / river taxis navigate up the Mahakam to LONG BAGUN (523 km, 7800 Rp), LONGIRAM (409 km, 6500 Rp), MELAK (325 km, 5000 Rp), MUARA PAHU (269 km, 4400 Rp), MUARA MUNTAI (201 km,

3500 Rp), or TENGGARONG (45 km, 1200 Rp). There's also a new road to Tenggarong.

BY BUS / TAXI / BEMO

Bemos in town cost 200 Rp. Quite a few new roads have been built in the Samarinda area. From SEBERANG on the other side of the river you can go by minibus to TENGGARONG for 1000 Rp (SEBERANG - LOA JANAN - LOA KULU - TENGGARONG 45 km, 2 hrs.). Or you can take the through road (135 km) from Seberang to BALIKPAPAN. By bus it costs 1800 Rp.

SUNGEI MAHAKAM

The source of Borneo's second largest river is on the border with Sarawak. If you intend to do a trip to 'ulu', as the up-river area here is called, your most important requirement will be the necessary amount of time. The further 'ulu' you go, the more irregular the boat connections. Remember that on Kalimantan the only 'Kantor Imigrasi' where you can get your tourist visa extensions are in Balikpapan, Banjarmasin, Tarakan and Pontianak. If you are in the middle of nowhere, you run the risk that your visa will expire before you can reach one of the offices. In such cases you'd have to go to the next police station and give an excuse: sickness, boats wouldn't go due to high water, etc. The land border to Sarawak is closed, which means it is unclear what would happen if you crossed over. See Sarawak section for more information.

TENGGARONG is the first stop on the trip. The town is over 200 years old and was the seat of an important Raja. His palace was built by a Dutchman in the 1930s - today it contains the MUZIUM TENGGARONG, open daily 9:00-14:00 h, Fri till 11:00 h, and Sun till 17:00 h. Stay the night in one of the two PENGINAPAN ANDA** with breakfast. About noon the boats from Samarinda arrive. Three hours upstream from Tenggarong is an orang utan rehabilitation centre in **SEBULU** (1500 Rp).

After Tenggarong the boat connections become more irregular. To **MUARA MUNTAI** it can take up to 20 hours. Depending on the boat it costs between 2200 Rp and 3800 Rp. You can be on the river up to 35 hours getting to Melak (6000 Rp). Take a boat from Muara Muntai via **JANTUR** to **TANJUNG ISUI,** takes 1 1/2 hours. Stay the night in the longhouse (LAMIN**). Groups of tourists are occasionally brought up this far. Several Dayak villages such as **MANCONG** (8 km away) can be reached from here.

There are now several losmen in **MELAK**. Make an excursion to the KRESIK LUWAI nature reserve area near **BARONG TONGKOK.** Here, about 18 km south west of Melak, you'll find about 5000 ha of orchid forest. In the orchid house right next to the administration building, several types of the famous black orchid are being raised. They bloom between September and December. Nearby you'll find many waterfalls and even a losmen in the village. From here there is a passable road to **TERING**. Motorbike taxis go between Melak, Barong Tongkok, and Tering. Of course, you can also follow the river further upstream.

LONGIRAM can be reached directly from Tenggarong twice a week - takes up to two days. Three losmen here, all under 5000 Rp. Tering and Longiram lie only 9 km apart, connected by a road. In the village all three losmen are under 3000 Rp. The next stop is **LONG BAGUN**. Boats cost up to 5000 Rp and leave irregularly. On the way are several rapids and waterfalls where the boat has to be portaged. This can take hours. During the rainy season nothing works any more. Between **LONG PAHANGHAI** and **LONG APARI** the river becomes a bit calmer. There is supposedly an 'imigrasi' post here since the border to Sarawak isn't far away. From here you can visit some of the nearby Bahau villages - orang utan still live in the forests. From the upper reaches of the Mahakam, you can cross by foot over the Müller Mountains to the source of the Kapuas River.

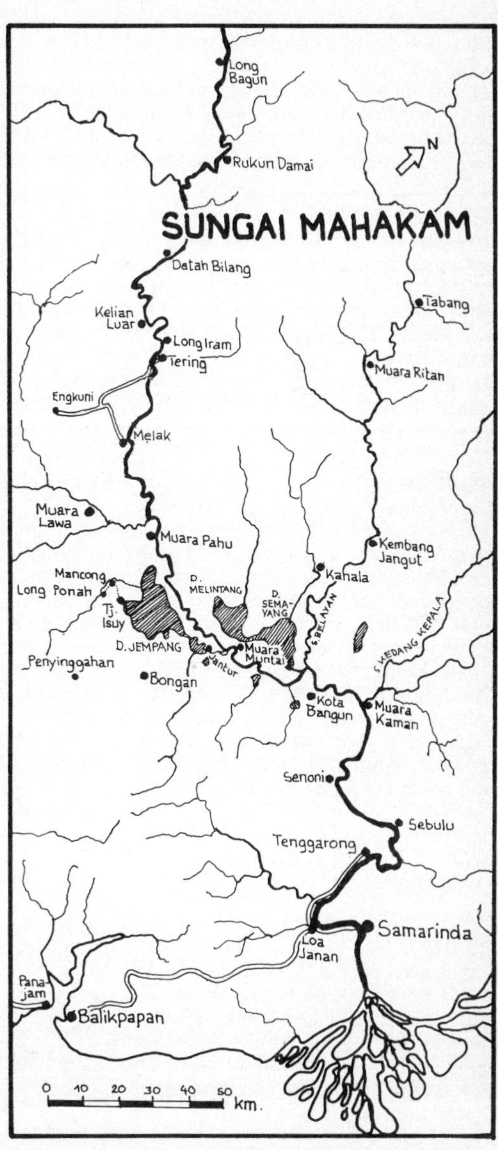

BALIKPAPAN

One of the most important oil towns in Indonesia, many Europeans, Americans, and Australians live and work here. The oil business has brought out a strange contrast between two cultures. On the one side, there are the white expatriates living in fully air-conditioned settlements and being well paid in dollars. And on the other side there are the masses of Indonesians who dream of getting some benefit from the oil. There are extreme differences between the neo-colonial residential areas and the kampongs of the unskilled Indonesian workers. Balik, after the 1976 census, had 150,000 inhabitants; today there are more than 250,000.

BLOWPIPES

You can still find blowpipes, even if they are sometimes a bit dusty. These weapons, simple as they may seem, require great skill in the making. They are made from a straight piece of hard wood, which has been dried before the work begins. With the aid of an iron rod it is then drilled - a process taking several weeks. The pipes, about 2 m long, are then rubbed smooth on the outside with a 'parang' and sand. The diameter is about 1 cm. At the upper end you'll usually find a lance-tip. The tiny darts are painted with a poison which is supposed to be more powerful than the South American curare.

HOTELS

Many hotels and losmen are cat houses - watch out! One of the most expensive hotels in Indonesia is the *REGENT OF BENAKUTAI*, Jl.Antasari 4. Normal double rooms cost well over US$100. Many hotels and reasonably priced losmen are around Pasar Kampong Baru (Jl.Panjaitan). Clean is *HOTEL AIDA**(*)*, no. 50, with private mandi and breakfast. Right next door is *SINAR LUMAYAN****, Jl.Agus Salim 24, *MURNI*** and *MAMA***. A bit more expensive is *KALTIM****, Jl.Kg.Baru Tengah, at the northern edge of town. At the *BLUESKY HOTEL*****, Jl. Suprapto, rooms include bathroom, TV and ac.

FOOD

Expatriates often eat in the *RAINBOW COFFEE SHOP* (Blue Sky Hotel), Jl. Suprapto 1. But it is extremely expensive. Or try the similarly priced *BAHTERA*, Jl.Gajah Mada I/47. On the same street are several nasi padang places.

LEAVING BALIKPAPAN

BY AIR

Sepinggan Airport is about 8 km northeast of town, taxis cost 5000 Rp from Pasar Baru, ojek cost 2000 Rp. Garuda (Jl.Antasari 19, tel 22300); Merpati (Jl.Antasari 2, tel 22380) and Bouraq (Hotel Benakutai, tel 21107) fly into Balik. Garuda flies 3x weekly via PONTIANAK to SINGAPORE. SAMPLE PRICES: BANJARMASIN 53,100 Rp (GA); 45,100 Rp (MZ / BO); SURABAYA 103,000 Rp; 92,700 Rp (BO); SEMARANG 111,900 Rp (BO via Banjar); PONTIANAK 107,800 Rp (GA); SAMARINDA 31,500 Rp (MZ / BO); PALANGKARAYA 58,700 Rp (GA); JAKARTA 125,300 Rp (BO direct); 147,400 Rp (GA); TARAKAN 72,000 Rp (BO / MZ); UJUNG PANDANG 96,900 Rp (MZ / BO); PALU 52,900 Rp (BO).

BY SHIP

All the major Indonesian shipping companies sail into the Balik harbour: Pelni (Jl.Pelabuhan 1, tel 22187), Jakarta Lloyd, Samudra and Sri Vijaya Lines. The KM.KAMBUNA and KM.

KERINCI dock here on their regular bi-weekly schedule. SAMPLE PRICES (Ekonomi): MEDAN 71,000 Rp, JAKARTA 43,400 Rp, SURABAYA 27,900 Rp, UJUNG PANDANG 18,700 Rp, PALU 14,800 Rp, MANADO (Bitung) 32,100 Rp, TOLI TOLI 18,400 Rp, TARAKAN 21,600 Rp. To Sulawesi (PARE PARE, DONGGALA / PALU) you often get smaller ships for 20,000 / 25,000 Rp.

BY BUS / BEMO / TAXI
Buses from Rapak Terminal to SEBERANG (Samarinda) cost 1800 Rp, 114 km, 2 hrs. Buses to BARABAI 7500 Rp, 12 hrs., and to BANJARMASIN 9200 Rp leave from Panajam on the southern shore of the bay. Cross the bay by ferry, klotok (500 Rp) or speedboat (1000 Rp). Depending on road conditions the ride to Banjarmasin can take up to 26 hrs. Very often the road south is completely impassable - especially the section between Muara Koman and Kuaro.

SOUTH KALIMANTAN

A large part of South Kalimantan is covered by swamp. Even Banjarmasin was founded in a swampy area on the east bank of the Barito. The Banjarese are strict Muslims and take Ramadan seriously - every evening the sirens sound announcing the end of the day's fasting. From the beginning of Dutch influence the VOC had a factory in Banjarmasin. But, until the middle of the last century, the Sultan of Banjarmasin was the undisputed ruler. In 1857 the colonial power tried to enthrone the unpopular son of the former ruler along with his Chinese wife. In 1859 an uprising began under the leadership of Prince Pangeran Antasari, who joined up with a peasant leader. With heavy losses by the Dutch, the rebellion was crushed. Only at the beginning of this century, however, was the province completely pacified.

BANJARMASIN

The provincial capital is criss-crossed by many canals and has a beautiful floating market that can easily match Bangkok's. Charter a klotok for half a day, which will cost about 10,000-15,000 Rp. Best to get boats underneath the bridge on Jl.Samudera. The *KUIN FLOATING MARKET* is the first stop early in the morning. From here you can cross in 15 minutes to an island in the Barito *(PULAU KEMBANG)* on which you'll find both an old Chinese temple and partly tame monkeys. By the way, the orang Banjar believe that it brings luck to be surrounded by a lot of monkeys.

PULAU KAGET, another island about 5 km away, is today a nature reserve where you can find proboscis monkeys (nasalis larvatus; Indonesian: bakantan) which exist only on Borneo. Banjar is an ideal place to shop. Many diamonds and precious jewels are found in the province, and there are the antique objects from old Dayak longhouses which are brought to Banjar for sale. Lots of shops on Jl.Sudimampir.

HOTELS

Cheap and quiet is *LOSMEN SINAR AMANDIT**, Jl.Ujung Murnung, with restaurant. Also good is *LOSMEN ABANG AMAT**, Gg.Penato 17, in a narrow alley, with courtyard. Nice owners in *HOTEL KURIPAN***, Jl.Yani 126. Three hotels are very close to each other on Jl.Haryono: *BEAUTY***, *KALIMANTAN*** and *MESTIKA***. *HOTEL PERDANA***(*)*, Jl.Katamso 3, tel 3276 is a comfortable and centrally located place with a nice courtyard. Other similar hotels are found on Jl.Jen.A.Yani, e.g. *FEBIOLA***** and *RAHMAT****.

FOOD

Good *BAKERY* at the corner of Jl.Samudera and Jl.Pasar Baru. Watch the life on the river from the terrace of *RUMAH MAKAN TAMAN SARI* on the other side of Jl.Pasar Baru. This is one of the few places in town where you can get beer. You get good but not cheap Chinese food in *BLUE OCEAN*, Jl.Hasanuddin or *PHOENIX*, Jl.Jen.A.Yani right beside the hospital. Another recommendable restaurant is next to Hotel Perdana.

GENERAL INFORMATION

TOURIST INFORMATION - Dinas Pariwisata on Jl.Pancaitan 31. Kanwil Depparpostel, Jl.Kantor Telegraf.

BANKS - two banks on Jl.Lambung Mangkurat: Bank Ekspor Impor has good rates. Otherwise try changing TCs or cash at the travel agent PT. Adi Angkasa, Jl.Hasanuddin.

POST OFFICE - Jl.Lambung Mangkurat, corner of Jl.Katamso.

GETTING AROUND BANJAR - three-wheel red motor scooters (bajaj) and motorcycle taxis (ojek) are the means of transport in town. Both charge about 200 Rp / km. The yellow 'Angkutan Kota'-Bemo cost 150 Rp. The bemo terminal is located at the end of Jl.Samudra, in front of the bridge. Bus terminal 'km 6' (Kilometre enam) is out of town on the road to Banjar Baru. Becaks charge about 300-500 Rp depending on distance.

LEAVING BANJAR

BY AIR

Near Banjar Baru is Syamsuddin Noor Airport (26 km). Get there by minibus for 500 Rp right to the turnoff and walk 1 km, or pay 1000 Rp straight to the airport. Taxis cost 6000 Rp and wait along Jl.Bank Rakyat. Offices of the airlines: GARUDA, Jl. Hasanuddin 11A; MERPATI, Jl. Suprapto 5A; BOURAQ, Jl.Lambung Mangkurat 40D, tel 2445, DAS (Dirgantara Air Service), Jl.Hasanuddin. DAS is a small company founded by former air force pilots. It's certainly an experience to fly with one of these small DAS planes from an airstrip in West or South Kalimantan. SAMPLE PRICES: BALIKPAPAN 53,100 Rp (GA); 45,100 Rp (BO/MZ); JAKARTA 115,000 Rp (GA); 97,800 Rp (BO direct); PALU 98,000 Rp (BO); SEMARANG 81,700 Rp (BO); SURABAYA 68,800 Rp, (GA); 58,500 Rp (MZ/BO); PALANGKARAYA 36,300 Rp (MZ, DAS); PANGKALANBUN 59,100 Rp (DAS); MUARA TEWE 54,100 Rp (DAS); SAMPIT 49,700 Rp (DAS); KOTABARU 44,300 Rp (DAS)

BY SHIP

Banjar has two harbours. Pelabuhan Lama is on Sungei Martapura near Jl. Pasar Baru / Jl.Lambung Mangkurat. Smaller freighters and pinisi schooners sail from here to SURABAYA. Takes about 40 hrs. and costs 15,000 Rp. Larger ships like the KM.KELIMUTU dock at Trisakti harbour. Pelni

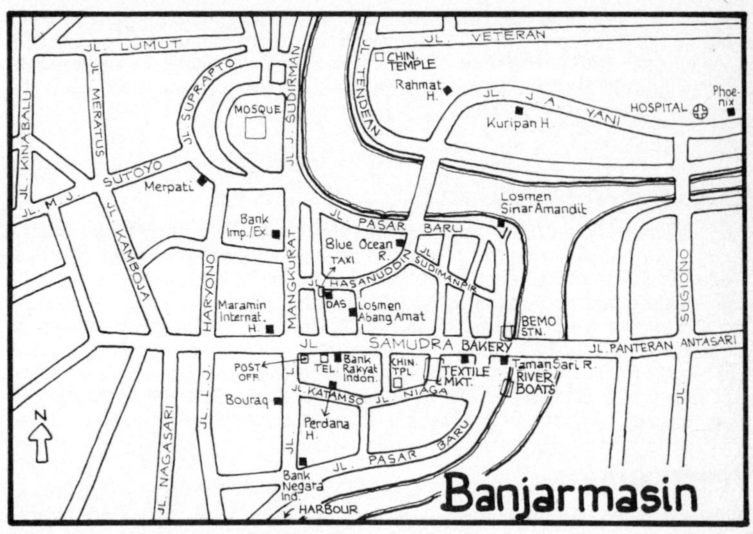

office at Jl.Martadinata 192. To reach Trisakti, take a bemo for 200 Rp, ojek 500 Rp. Every other Mon the KM.KELIMUTU docks in Trisakti arriving from Semarang, and sails on via Surabaya, Padang Bai, Lembar, Ujung Pandang, Bima, Waingapu, Ende to Kupang. On the way back she'll be in Trisakti again every other following Saturday. SAMPLE PRICES: SEMARANG 26,100 / 61,200 Rp, SURABAYA 29,400 / 56,900 Rp, PADANG BAI 31,500 / 72,500 Rp, UJUNG PANDANG 40,200 / 113,300 Rp.

River boats (river bus / speedboat): KUALA KAPUAS 42 km, 700 Rp, 6 - 7 hrs. / 3300 Rp, 3 hrs; PALANGKARAYA 245 km, 4500 Rp, 18 - 20 hrs. / 19,000 Rp, 7 hrs.; AMUNTAI 189 km, 3200 / 16,000 Rp; MUARA TEWE 470 km, 7500 Rp, 42 hrs. / 33,000 Rp, two days.

BY BUS

There are about five buses daily to PANAJAM (BALIKPAPAN; 9200 Rp, 15-16 hrs. with average road conditions). Better to take a minibus to all other places on this road. SAMPLE PRICES: KANDANGAN 2000 Rp, 135 km, 3 hrs.; BARABAI 2500 Rp, 165 km, 3 1/2 hrs.; AMUNTAI 3500 Rp, 190 km, 4 1/2 hrs.; TANJUNG 4000 Rp, 230 km, 5 1/2 hrs.

DAYTRIPS AROUND BANJARMASIN

Take a colt (600 Rp) to BANJAR BARU, the new town about 1/2 hour southeast of Banjar. Besides the many administrative buildings, you'll find the new NEGERI LAMBUNG MANGKURAT MUZIUM. Open except Mon and Fri from 8:30 - 14:00 h. There's lots of information about 450-year-old Banjarmasin. In

Banjar Baru, the centre of the rattan industry, beautiful mats and furniture are made. 6 km away is CEMPAKA, where diamonds are panned using very simple methods. MARTAPURA is the centre of diamond cutting. Everywhere on the new artificial lake of RIAM KANAN, people are trying to find their luck in the shape of a large, glittering rock.

WEST KALIMANTAN

2.85 million people (1986) live in Kalimantan Barat. The percentage of Chinese in the population is much higher than in any other Indonesian province. Since the Sultan of Sambas needed many workers for the mining of ore in the 18th century, many Chinese settled here. Today the province is the second most important rubber producer after North Sumatra. Planting can mostly be found north of Pontianak, as well as along the banks of the Kapuas, which at 1156 km is the longest river in Indonesia. Large ships can sail upstream as far as Putussibau. Such a trip can take up to 15 days since the ships stop all along the way. The border to Malaysia is closed at least for foreigners.

PONTIANAK

With about 300,000 inhabitants, including many Chinese, this is the largest and most important city in the province. Situated right on the equator, the town spreads out on both sides of the Sungei Landak. This is the smaller mouth of the big river Kapuas, which is up to 2 km wide here. Worth checking out are the *SULTAN'S PALACE* and the 250-year-old *MOSQUE*.

HOTELS

On Jl.Tanjung Pura, you'll find *ORIENT HOTEL****. *WIJAYA KUSUMAH**(*)* has a nice view over the river. Expensive is *FATIMAH****, Jl. Fatimah 5.

LEAVING PONTIANAK

BY AIR

Sungei Durian Airport is about 18 km south east of town. Taxi 6000 Rp. GARUDA, Jl.Rohadi Usman 8A, tel 4222; MERPATI, Jl.Juanda 50A, tel 2332; BOURAQ, Jl.Gajah Mada 57, tel 2683, DAS, Jl.Gajah Mada. SAMPLE PRICES: JAKARTA 93,600 Rp (GA); 79,600 Rp (MZ / BO); KUCHING 60,000 Rp (MZ every Fri); SINGAPORE three times weekly with GA; BALIKPAPAN 107,800 Rp (GA). DAS flights: KETAPANG 35,000 Rp, SINTANG 51,600 Rp, PUTUSSIBAU 77,500 Rp, NANGAPINOH 60,800 Rp.

BY SHIP

Pelni's (Jl.Pelabuhan 1) KM.LAWIT docks every second Mon in Pontianak and sails via KETAPANG (10,700 / 27,100 Rp) and JAKARTA (27,900 / 69,500 Rp) to Sumatra.

BY BUS

A good paved road runs via SINGKAWANG to SAMBAS, costs about 4000 Rp and takes about 8 hours. Another road runs parallel to the Kapuas River via SANGGAU to SINTANG.

LANGUAGE

With 250 regional languages in one country, there's a real need for a common tongue. You can be understood using ***Bahasa Indonesia*** in just about the whole archipelago since it is taught in every school in the republic and widely understood. 'One nation - One country - One language'. The slogan of the Indonesian nationalists in the 1920s makes clear the political importance of a universal language. Since 1945, the national language has been one developed from classical Malay. Many words have also been taken from foreign languages - from Indonesian regional tongues as well as Arabic, Chinese, Dutch, and recently English.

Relatively new word creations can be found which you'll have little trouble understanding without a translator: An ***INTELEKTUAL INGGERIS*** *with lots of* ***EMOSI*** *is on the* ***TALIPON*** *in a* ***RESTORAN,*** *trying to get from* ***IMIGRASI*** *(sh..****BIROKRASI****) at long last his* ***PAS*** *and* ***PERMISI*** *to* ***IMPOR*** *a* ***MOBIL.*** *But the* ***AGEN POLISI*** *has an* ***INFEKSI*** *and has gone by* ***TAKSI*** *to the* ***DOKTER*** *and to an* ***APOTIK.***

Unfortunately, it isn't always so easy to understand, so here are a few hints:

SPELLING: Since the spelling reform of 1972, basic rules have been established for speaking and writing the Malay languages (Bahasa Malaysia and Bahasa Indonesia). (dj) has changed to (j) - Djakarta to Jakarta, (j) to (y) - Jogja to Yogya, (tj) to (c) - Tjirebon to Cirebon, just to give a few of the more important examples. Be sure to check in dictionaries for the correct spelling. Once in a while, especially on old maps, you'll even find relics from the days of the Dutch, such as Bandoeng instead of Bandung.

PRONUNCIATION: Generally the words are pronounced the way they are written with a few exceptions:

(a)	*sama - identical*	as in father
(e)	*meja - table*	spoken quickly like dead
(i)	*manis - sweet*	as in seize
(o)	*kotor - dirty*	as in bought
(u)	*minum - drink*	as in pool
(ai)	*sungei - river*	separately pronounced as in fine
(au)	*pulau - island*	as in now
(c)	*candi - temple*	as in chair
(j)	*juta - million*	as in judge
(kh)	*khabar - news*	like German Achtung
(ng)	*bunga - flower*	as in singer but never as in finger
(r)	*roti - bread*	rolled like rrrrroom
(y)	*yang - which*	as in you

LITERATURE: If you want to become more involved with Bahasa Indonesia or Malay, you can get a dictionary or book of instruction in Singapore, Jakarta or in Malaysia.

PRACTICAL INDONESIAN , BAKER, JOHN. (Bagus!) - for all travellers who want a quick guide to practical phrases when travelling.

HOW TO MASTER THE INDONESIAN LANGUAGE, ALMATSIER, A.M. Jakarta 1967 - to learn for yourself.

BAHASA INDONESIA. JOHNS, JOHANNI . Canberra 1977 - good!

TEACH YOURSELF INDONESIAN. KWEE, London 1968

SPEAK MALAY. KING, EDWARD S. Singapore 1986.

A small dictionary - there are many different ones available - is always useful. Remember that in Indonesian, a word can be completely changed by its prefix or suffix. In order to find a word, you first have to figure out the root, which can sometimes involve real detective work!

A SMALL DICTIONARY AND PHRASE GUIDE

During your travels you'll constantly be asked the same questions - *and here are a few suggested answers:*

APA KHABAR? - How are you? ***KHABAR BAIK.*** *- I'm fine*

SIAPA NAMAMU? - What's your name? ***NAMA SAYA.*** *- I'm...*

DARIMANA? - Where are you from? ***DARI BULAN.*** *- The moon. or* ***DARI AMERIKA, DARI AUSTRALIA, DARI SELANDIA BARU.***

(PERGI / MAU) KEMANA? - Where're you going? ***KE PANTAI.*** *- To the beach. Or* ***JALAN-JALAN*** *and* ***MAKAN ANGIN*** *(eat some wind) - take a walk.*

TINGGAL DIMANA? - Where are you staying? ***DI LOSMEN.*** *- In a losmen.*

BERAPA LAMA DI INDONESIA? - How long have you been in Indonesia? ***SUDAH LAMA.*** *- Pretty long. Or* ***SATU HARI SAJA.*** *- Just a day or* ***SATU MINGGU.*** *- One week.*

BISA BICARA BAHASA INDONESIA? - Do you speak Indonesian? ***SEDIKIT*** *- A bit. or* ***SAYA (TIDAK) MENGGERTI BAHASA INDONESIA.*** *- I can (can't) understand Indonesian.*

UMUR BERAPA? - How old are you? ***SATU TAHUN.*** *- One year.*

SUDAH KAWIN? - Are you married? *And if yes then the inevitable question:*

BERAPA ANAK-ANAK? - How many children? *3, 10 but never none!*
...and don't forget that old English phrase: I want to practise my English. *So that the conversation isn't completely one-sided.*

GREETINGS:

Always put the word ***SELAMAT*** in front, such as:

SELAMAT PAGI! - Good morning! **SELAMAT MINUM**! - Cheers! **SELAMAT TIDUR!** -Sleep well! **SELAMAT DATANG!** - Welcome!

QUESTIONS:

APA	what	**Apa ini?** (What's this?)
SIAPA	who	**Siapa nama mu?** (What's your name?)
BERAPA	how much/ how many	**Berapa lama?** (how long?) **Berapa jauh?** (how far?)
KAPAN	when	**Kapan bis datang?** (When is the bus coming?)

PERSONAL PRONOUNS:

SAYA / AKU	I	Nama saya... (My name is...)
KAMU / ANDA	you	more polite: **SAUDARA**
DIA / IA	he, she, it	
KITA / KAMI*	we	*without the person addressed
MEREKA	they	plural

FORMS OF ADDRESS:

SAUDARA	Mr / Mrs (formal)
TUAN / NYONYA / NONA	Mr / Mrs / Miss (traditional)
BAPAK (PAK) /IBU (BU)	father / mother / elder brother (to an older person - informal)

TIME:

PAGI / SIANG / SORE / MALAM		morning (till 11:00 h) / noon / afternoon. (till sunset) / evening	
HARI INI / BESOK / KEMARIN		today (this day) / tomorrow / yesterday.	
SEKARANG	now	**SEBANTAR**	soon
NANTI	later	**BELUM**	not yet
SUDAH	already	**YANG LALU**	...ago
JAM / PUKUL BERAPA?		What time is it?	
JAM KARET		rubber-time (typical Indonesian time)	
MENIT	minute	**JAM**	hour
HARI	day	**MINGGU**	week
BULAN	month	**TAHUN**	year

NUMBERS:

(1) **SATU**	(6) **ENAM**	(11)**SEBELAS**, (12)**DUA BELAS**
(2) **DUA**	(7) **TUJUH**	(20)**DUA PULUH,** (30)**TIGA PULUH**
(3) **TIGA**	(8) **DELAPAN**	(45)**EMPAT PULUH LIMA**
(4) **EMPAT**	(9) **SEMBILAN**	(100)**SERATUS,** (200)**DUA RATUS**
(5) **LIMA**	(10) **SEPULUH**	(1000)**SERIBU,** (2000)**DUA RIBU**

SETENGAH	half	**SEPEREMPAT**	quarter
BANYAK	much, many	**SEDIKIT**	few, little
KURANG	less (-)	**TAMBAH**	more (+)

SHOPPING:

(MEM)BELI	buy	**(MEN)JUAL**	sell
BERAPA HARGA?	How much is it?	(literal: how much price?)	
MAHAL	expensive	**MURAH**	cheap
HARGA PASTI	set price	**HARGA BIASA**	real price

ACCOMMODATION:

DIMANA ADA LOSMEN / HOTEL?	Where is a losmen/hotel?
SAUDARA ADA KAMAR KOSONG?	Do you have a free room?
UNTUK 2/3 ORANG (MALAM)	for 2/3 people (nights)
KAMAR(MANDI)	room(bath)
KOSONG/PENUH	empty / full
KUNCI	key
NYAMUK	mosquito

FOOD & DRINK:

MAKAN	eat (food)	**MINUM**	drink
MAKAN PAGI	breakfast	**MAKAN SIANG**	lunch
SAYA MAU MAKAN...		I want to eat...	
TEH / KOPI	tea, coffee		
AIR (MASAK)	water (boiled)		
ES	ice	**ES JERUK**	lemon juice
PANAS	hot	**DINGIN**	cold
PAHIT	bitter		
TEH PAHIT	tea without milk and sugar		
MANIS	sweet (=with sugar) -		
TEH MANIS ES	sweet ice tea		
SUSU	milk (usually sweet, canned milk)		

NASI PUTIH	boiled rice	**MIE**	noodles
ROTI	bread	**KUE**	cake
DAGING	meat		
SAPI	beef	**KERBAU**	buffalo
BABI	pork	**AYAM**	chicken
KAMBING	goat	**BEBEK**	duck
HATI	liver	**JANTUNG**	heart
IKAN	fish		
UDANG	crab (shrimp)	**UDANG KARANG**	lobster
SAYUR	vegetables		
KENTENG	potato	**KETIMUN**	cucumber
BAYAM	spinach	**TERONG**	eggplant
BAWANG MERAH	onion	**BAWANG PREI**	leeks
APOKAT	avocado	**TOMAT**	tomato
BUAH	fruit		
NENAS	pineapple	**KELAPA**	coconut
MANGGA	mango	**SEMANGKA**	watermelon
NANGKA	jackfruit	**PISANG**	banana

TRAVEL:

KEMANA	where to
(PERGI KEMANA?)	Where are you going?
DARI MANA	where from
(DARI MANA DIA DATANG?)	Where is he coming from?
DIMANA	where
(DIMANA ADA?)	Where is?
KE / DI / DARI	to / in / from
SAYA PERGI KE...	I'm going to...
SAYA DATANG DARI...	I come from...
SAYA TINGGAL DI...	I live in

TERUS	straight	**KIRI /KANAN**	left / right
UTARA/SELATAN	north /south	**TIMUR / BARAT**	east / west

SURROUNDINGS:

KOTA	city	**KAMPONG**	village
PULAU	island	**GUNUNG**	mount
BUKIT	hill	**HUTAN**	forest
MATA AIR	well	**AIR TERJUN**	waterfall
DANAU	lake	**SUNGEI**	river
LAUT	sea/ocean	**PANTAI**	beach

TRANSPORTATION:

BIS	bus	(**BIS MALAM** - nightbus **SETASIUN BIS**- bus station)
KAPAL TERBANG	plane	**(LAPANGANTERBANG** or **PELA BUHAN UDARA** - airport)
KAPAL LAUT	ship	**(PELABUHAN** - harbour)
KERETA API	train	**(SETASIUN KERETA API** train station)
TAKSI	taxi	**(TEMPAT TAKSI / STANPLATZ)**

KARCIS	ticket	**LOKET**	ticket window
KELAS	class	**KORTING**	discount
TEMPAT DUDUK	seat	**CEPAT / PELAN**	fast / slow

HEALTH:

SAKIT	sick	**SEHAT**	healthy
JATUH SAKIT	getting sick	**RUMAH SAKIT**	hospital
OBAT	medicine	**DOKTER**	doctor
APOTIK	pharmacy	**DEMAM**	fever
BERAK-BERAK	diarrhoea	**INFEKSI**	infection
(KAKI) PATAH	(leg) broken		

PARTS OF THE BODY:

KEPALA	head	**LEHER**	throat
MATA	eye	**HIDUNG**	nose
PERUT	stomach	**LENGAN**	arm
TANGAN	finger	**KAKI**	leg

CONVERSATION:

SAYA SUKA / MAU / BISA /HARUS	I like / want / can / must
TERIMA KASIH! SAMA-SAMA!	Thanks a lot (you're welcome!)
TOLONGLAH! / SILAHKAN!	Please! (asking / offering)
PERMISI! / MAAF!	Excuse me! / I'm sorry!
YA / TIDAK (BUKAN)	Yes / no (with a noun)
SELAMAT DATANG!	Welcome!
SELAMAT TINGGAL!	Goodbye! (to those staying)
SELAMAT JALAN!	Goodbye! (to those going)
BAIK / KABAR BAIK	good / I'm fine!
BAGUS / LOSMEN INI BAGUS	good (OK) / This losmen is good.
ENAK / MAKANAN ENAK	tastes good / This food...
CANTIK / INDAH	good-looking (people) / pretty (things)
LELAH / LAPAR / HAUS	tired / hungry / thirsty
KOTOR / JELEK	dirty / ugly
JAUH / DEKAT / BESAR / KECIL	far / near / large / small

LEARNING:

SAYA BELAJAR BAHASA INDONESIA	I'm learning Indonesian.
APAKAH SAUDARA BISA BAHASA... INGGERIS / JERMAN?	Do you speak English / German?
TOLONGLAH BICARA PELAN-PELAN!	Please speak slowly!
SAYA TIDAK MENGGERTI.	I don't understand!
APA INI? / APA ITU?	What's this / that?
APA NAMANYA DI BAHASA I..?	What's this in Indonesian?
BOLEH MEMOTRET / FOTO?	May I take pictures?

SUGGESTED READING

Indonesia is just too big and varied to be handled in all aspects by this type of travel guide. If you want to intensify your relationship with the country, you'll find a couple of tips here. Some are books you can read before (or after) your trip in order to get more in-depth knowledge of certain subjects. Also included are books to take with you. Some novels are best read at the scene of the crime, so to speak. English language books can be found in Indonesia, though the selection is much greater in Singapore or Malaysia.

GENERAL READING:

TWENTIETH CENTURY INDONESIA (Neill, Wilfried T.; New York 1973). General guide to the modern history.

NUSANTARA: A HISTORY OF MODERN INDONESIA (Vlekke, B.; Brussels 1959). A standard historical work which ends with the Japanese occupation in 1942.

THE DUTCH SEABORNE EMPIRE 1600 - 1800 (Boxer, C.R.; Harmondsworth 1973). The history of Dutch conquests with lots of pictures and maps.

A HISTORY OF MODERN INDONESIA (Ricklefs, M.C.; London 1981). A wide ranging text about the history from 1300 until today - good and understandable.

THE INDONESIAN TRAGEDY (May, Brian; Singapore 1978). A social history of the post-war period under Sukarno and Suharto with background information about the 1965 uprising.

THE MALAY ARCHIPELAGO: THE LAND OF THE ORANG UTAN AND THE BIRD OF PARADISE (Wallace, A.R.; reprint New York 1962). This book was written in 1869 by the great English naturalist who spent many years on the islands - emphasis on flora and fauna.

ART OF INDONESIA (Bodrogi, Tibor; London 1973). A good art guide to prepare you for your visit.

THE WORLD OF INDONESIAN TEXTILES (Warming/Gaworski; London 1981). A large and informative work especially about ikat and batik.

BOOKS WITH REGIONAL EMPHASIS:

SUMATRA - ITS HISTORY AND PEOPLE (Loeb, E.M.; reprint Kuala Lumpur 1972). Social history of the different ethnic groups and religions of this island.

TROPIC FEVER (Szekely, Ladisla; Kuala Lumpur 1979). The experiences of a European planter at the beginning of this century in North Sumatra - funny and exciting.

HISTORY OF SUMATRA (Marsden, William; Kuala Lumpur 1975). Reprint of a work first published in 1783, with a wide ranging description of the island at that time. Try to find it in a good library; it's worth it!

HISTORY OF JAVA (Raffles, Sir Stamford; Kuala Lumpur 1978). Another reprint by Oxford University Press. A wide ranging, two volume work by the (for a brief time) governor of the island. First published in 1817.

LIFE IN THE FORESTS OF THE FAR EAST (Spenser, St. John; reprint Kuala Lumpur 1974). A two volume description from 1862 of North and West Borneo.

ISLAND OF BALI (Covarrubias, Miguel; New York 1972). The best and most comprehensive book about Bali. Much of it is still fascinatingly current although it first appeared in 1937.

BORNEO (Time Life; New York 1974). A picture book to get you in the right mood for your trip.

TRAVEL BOOKS - NOVELS:

REVOLT IN PARADISE (Tantri, K'tut; London 1960). A young American goes to Bali in the thirties. She becomes a member of a Balinese family and takes part in the struggle for independence. A fascinating historical account.

PASSAGE OF ARMS (Ambler, Eric; London 1959). A novel about the smuggling of arms to Sumatra during the rebellion in 1958.

LETTERS OF A JAVANESE PRINCESS (Kartini, Raden; New York 1964). Selected letters of the Indonesian national and women's movement heroine to her Dutch friends - very moving.

THIS EARTH FOR MANKIND (Toer, Pramoedya Ananta; Harmondsworth 1980). The best novel of this great author.

TWILIGHT IN JAKARTA (Lubis, Mochtar; London 1963). The heroes are from the lower classes, and the descriptions are of corruption in the early days of the republic. The book's worth can be measured by the number of times Lubis has been imprisoned.

ATHESIS (Miharja, Achidist; London 1956). The problem of cultural differences between east and west provides the background for this novel set in the 1940s.

FROM SURABAYA TO ARMAGEDDON (edited by Aveling, H.; Singapore 1976). An excellent collection of short stories by Indonesian authors.

THE FUGITIVE (Toer, Pramoedya Ananta; Singapore 1975). The English translation of a story dating from the end of the Japanese occupation. The Javanese author is one of the best known writers held prisoner on Buru because of his political beliefs.

THE EASTERN SEAS (Earl, G.W.; Kuala Lumpur 1971). A reprint of a travel book taking you through the Indies during the years 1832-34.

THE FLAMING EARTH - POEMS FROM INDONESIA (edited by Ali, A., Karachi 1949). A lyrical anthology of the important national poets.

CONTEMPORARY INDONESIAN POETRY (edited by Aveling, H.; Brisbane 1975). A newer lyrical collection.

TRAVEL GUIDES:

INDONESIA HANDBOOK (Dalton, Bill; Franklin Village, USA 1977). Wide ranging and almost too detailed. Hopefully a more up to date edition will appear soon.

BALI (APA Photo Guide; Singapore 1973)

JAVA (APA Photo Guides; Singapore 1976). Lots of background information as well as practical tips in these beautifully illustrated books.

BALI BY BICYCLE (Kooiker, Hunt; Singapore 1977). Recommended for those planning a tour of Bali - even for pedestrians and motorbike riders.

MALAYSIA

More than half of Malaysia is still covered by jungle. Most people live on the west coast of the Malay peninsula, where the ethnic Chinese are dominant. Kuala Lumpur, colloquially referred to as KL, Malacca, Ipoh, Taiping and Penang are all almost completely Chinese cities with a sprinkling of Indian and Malay. At the same time signs of the British colonial inheritance can still be found. The old administrative buildings have received Malay lettering, and the splendid estates now have Malaysian occupants, but the typical colonial architecture still retains some of the atmosphere of the past. Tin mines, palm oil and rubber plantations stretch from Perlis in the far north down to Johore Bharu. The east coast is completely different. The Malay, Islamic influence is dominant - especially in the conservative states of Trengganu and Kelantan. Here you can see the lifestyles of fishermen and peasants in a kampong by the sea. Along the beach, almost 500 km long and one of the most beautiful in Asia, everything is much more relaxed than on the west coast. The beach stretches from Kota Bahru in the north, where the Japanese invaders landed during the second world war, down to the island of Singapore. Unfortunately the results of industrialization have left their marks on a few stretches, especially in Trengganu and northern Pahang. Off the coast are countless inhabited and uninhabited islands with wonderfully coloured coral reefs. Between these two quite different halves of the country lie the constantly green tropical rain forests. A train line and a new road cross this area from north to south.

One of the largest national parks in South East Asia, the Taman Negara, is easy to reach. You'll never forget a night in the jungle with its strange sounds. The forest is home to the Orang Asli, the Malay peninsula aborigines. Sarawak and Sabah on the north coast of Borneo belong politically to the Federation of Malaysia, but they differ greatly both geographically and ethnically from the mainland. Only by boat or plane is it possible to reach the interior, which is almost completely covered by jungle. Here, settled in long houses on the banks of the rivers, are different Dayak tribes.

VISAS

People from most countries which have agreements with Malaysia (Western Europe, Commonwealth, Scandinavia, USA) can stay for a maximum of three months without applying for a visa in advance. In general you'll usually get a three month stamp in your passport on entry. The only difficulties occur if you have too little money or your appearance is unkempt. Large groups of travellers are also frowned upon. In Sarawak and Sabah they'll give you one of their own visas. If you only get a two week visa, you'll have to apply at an immigration office at the end of this period for an extension. You'll find these offices in the state capitals as well as in Kuala Lumpur. Be sure that you use a registered hotel as your address when filling in the forms.

EMBASSIES OF MALAYSIA IN NEIGHBOURING COUNTRIES

AUSTRALIA, 71 State Circle, Yarralumla, Canberra, ACT 2600.
BURMA, 65 Windsor Road, Rangoon.
HONG KONG, Lap Heng House 47-5, Gloucester Road.
INDIA, 50-M Satya Marg Chanakyapuri, New Delhi 110021.
INDONESIA, Jl.Iman Bonjol 17, Jakarta, tel 332846. Consulate: Jl.Diponegoro 11, Medan.
PHILIPPINES, Republic Glass Bldg., Galarda St., Makati, Metro Manila.
SINGAPORE, 301 Jervois Road, Singapore 1024, tel 2350111.
THAILAND, 35 Sathon Tai Road, Bangkok, tel 2861390-2. Consulate: 4 Sukum Road, Songhkla.

EMBASSIES AND CONSULATES IN MALAYSIA

AUSTRALIA, 6 Jl.Yap Kwan Seng, KL, tel 423122.
CANADA, AIA Building, Jl.Ampang, KL, tel 89722.
NEW ZEALAND, 193 Jl.Tun Razak, KL, tel 486422.
UNITED KINGDOM, Wisma Damansara, 5 Jl.Semantan, KL, tel 941533. Consulates: Birch House, 73 Jl.Datuk Keramat, Penang, tel 63702; Hong Kong & Shanghai Banking Corp., Kota Kinabalu, tel 56722; Chartered Bank, Jl.Tuanku Abdul Rahman, Kuching, tel 52233.
UNITED STATES, 376 Jl.Tun Razak, KL, tel 26321/9.

EMBASSIES OF NEIGHBOURING COUNTRIES IN MALAYSIA

BURMA, 7 Jl.Taman U Thant, KL, tel 423863.
INDONESIA, 233 Jl.Tun Razak, KL, tel 2421011. Consulates: 467 Jl.Burmah, Penang, tel 25162/3; Wing On Life Building, 1 Jl.Sagunting, Kota Kinabalu tel 54100; Wisma Indonesia, 19 Jl.Deshon, Kuching, tel 20551; another consulate is in Tawau.
PHILIPPINES, 1 Cangkat Kia Peng, KL, tel 484233.
THAILAND, 206 Jl.Ampang, KL, tel 488222. Consulates: 1 Air Rajah Rd., Penang, tel 63377; 4426 Jl.Pengkalan Chepa, Kota Bharu, tel 22545.

CLIMATE & TRAVEL SEASONS

As in the other South East Asian countries, the climate on the Malay peninsula is determined by the monsoons. These bring the rainy and dry seasons, while the temperatures year round remain about the same. Deviations from the average of 27°C are only found in the hill stations (Cameron Highlands, Fraser's Hill) where it is much cooler. Here the maximum mean daily temperature is only around 22°C (in KL 32°C) and the minimum mean temperature is 13°C (KL 23°C). Remember to take a jacket or sweater with you because after a couple of weeks in the tropics you'll freeze just as much as an Asian. A trip along the east coast or through the jungles of Malaysia shouldn't be attempted between October and February when everything is submerged in a deluge. The other parts can be visited year-round since the rainy season isn't as heavy. The eternally blue sky in this tropical country (as in all others) is only found in the travel ads.

Geographically, four different climate areas can be identified for Peninsular Malaysia:

A) ***NORTHWEST*** (Alor Setar): Two periods of heavy rains (April / May; September / October) and at least two months each year of little rain (January / February).

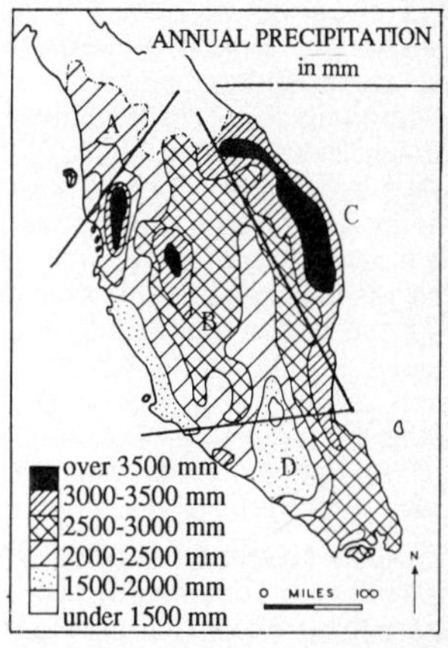

B) ***WEST*** (KL): Two short periods of heavy rains (April and October), but no real dry season.

C) ***EAST COAST*** (Kota Bharu): One heavy rainy season (October to January) - minimal rains from June to August.

D) ***SOUTH*** (Johore Bharu): Rains pretty much evenly distributed over the whole year.

You can find three Malaysian seasons determined simply by the amount of rain:

NORTHEAST MONSOON: November to March. During this period the whole east coast receives heavy rains. In December and January the Taman Negara is also closed since the rivers are too high.

SOUTHWEST MONSOON: June to August. Except in Penang and some areas in Northwest Malaysia, there is relatively little rain because the peninsula is situated in the rain shadow of the mountains on Sumatra (clouds, forced up over the mountains, lose their moisture there leaving only dry air on the other side).

INTER-MONSOON: April to May and September to October. Normally months of quite heavy rains which, however, aren't caused by monsoons, but rather by hot air masses rising up to cooler heights.

FESTIVALS & HOLIDAYS

Many local festivals are mentioned in the regional sections. Here is a list of those festivities which are celebrated all over Malaysia:

The great Hindu festival, ***THAIPUSAM,*** is celebrated at the end of January / beginning of February at all temples in the country. The main festivities take place in Penang and in the Batu Caves near Kuala Lumpur, where Subramaniam, the youngest son of Shiva, is especially revered.

Before sunrise, thousands of believers collect at the foot of the mountain. Some have pierced their skin with steel needles from which they've hung tiny bells or peacock feathers. Long silver needles are stuck through the tongue or cheek without (it seems) causing any pain. Others carry heavy wooden bows, the kavadi, above their heads, held only by hooks digging into their flesh as they climb the steep steps. While the priests strike up religious songs, many Hindus fall into trance and dance through the crowd. In other places, people walk on glowing coals.

Every year between the 21st of January and the 20th of February the Chinese celebrate the ***NEW YEAR.*** The exact date is determined by the lunar calendar and is set on the first full moon. In a 12 year cycle, each year is named after an animal. So 1988 is the year of the Dragon, then follow the years of the Snake, Horse, Goat, Monkey, Rooster, Dog, Pig, Rat, Buffalo, Tiger, and Cat. Days before, the rush of shoppers begins. A week before the new year apartments and houses are cleaned, since the god of the kitchen will make a report to heaven about every family. An especially sweet and sticky pastry made of molasses is baked so that the god has something sweet on his lips. Others say that the pastry makes his mouth so sticky that he can't say anything. On the evening of the last day of the year the whole family gets together for a huge meal. The children receive tiny red envelopes with money *(ang pao).* Considering the large size of many Chinese families, the new year's partying can be quite expensive - the one, two or three months extra pay which workers receive at this time of year comes in very handy.

Muslims celebrate ***MANDI SAFAR,*** originally a Hindu festival, marking the first full moon of the rainy season, in the middle of April. Quotes from the Koran are written on pieces of paper which then are carried off by the waves and waters of the rivers, the lakes or the ocean. Afterwards, people bathe symbolically in the water to wash away bad luck or *malang.* A good place to see this is in Tanjung Keling near Malacca. At the beginning or middle of June the ***DRAGON BOAT FESTIVAL*** is celebrated in many Chinese communities. Try to see it in Penang, where boat races are held. The most important festival in Malaysia is ***HARI RAYA PUASA,*** the end of *Ramadan.* For four long weeks, people fast between sunrise and sunset, and in the conservative Muslim states of Kelantan and Trengganu this is strictly adhered to. After days of preparation the festivities can only begin when at least three different villages have spotted the moon. On the 31st of August, the Malaysian ***NATIONAL DAY,*** *Hari Kebangsaan Malaysia,* is celebrated in remembrance of the founding of Malaysia in 1957. The second most important Hindu festival is ***DEEPAVALI*** which is celebrated in October or November. Literally translated it means *deepa* (lamp) and *vali* (row) referring to the light which drives away darkness. On this day flaming wreaths are hung in all Hindu regions.

Two popular legends tell of the creation of Deepavali. The first goes back to the Ramayana and tells of the triumphant return of Rama to Ayutthaya after 14 years of banishment in the jungle. The inhabitants greeted the returning hero with countless lanterns and torches to celebrate his victory over the evil Ravana. The second legend tells of the victory of the god Krishna over the king Narakasura. He, it is said, had a harem of over 16,000 girls, and even the daughters of the gods weren't safe from him. While dying, he pleaded with Krishna to create a holiday for the people to honour him each year.

In the multi-racial country of Malaysia, state holidays and official events take place according to the western Gregorian calendar. The Islamic calendar, on the other hand, begins with the flight of Mohammed from Mecca on the 16th of

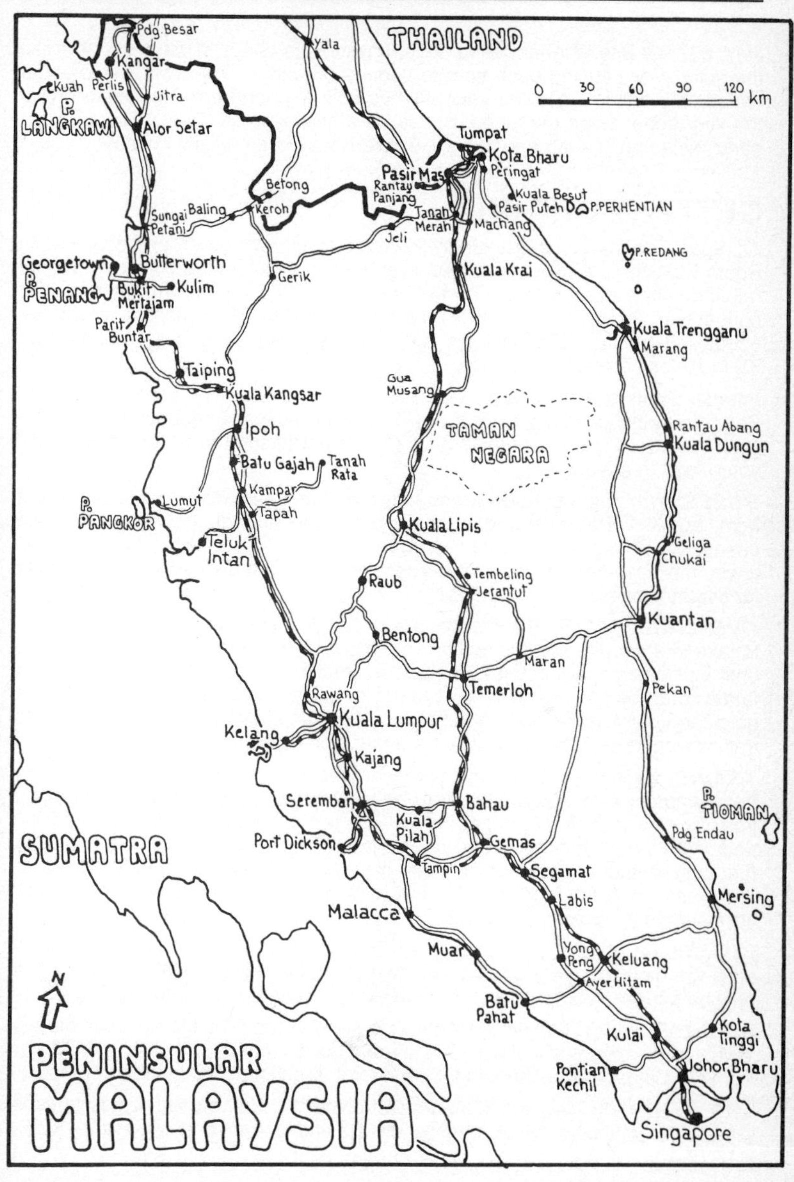
THAILAND
0 30 60 90 120 km
Pdg. Besar
Yala
Kangar
Kuah
Perlis
Jitra
P. LANGKAWI
Alor Setar
Tumpat
Kota Bharu
Peringat
Pasir Mas
Rantau Panjang
Betong
Kuala Besut
Pasir Puteh
P. PERHENTIAN
Sungai Petani
Baling
Keroh
Tanah Merah
Machang
Jeli
P. REDANG
Georgetown
P. PENANG
Butterworth
Bukit Mertajam
Kulim
Gerik
Kuala Krai
Parit Buntar
Kuala Trengganu
Marang
Taiping
Kuala Kangsar
Gua Musang
TAMAN NEGARA
Ipoh
Batu Gajah
Tanah Rata
Kampar
Tapah
Lumut
P. PANGKOR
Rantau Abang
Kuala Dungun
Teluk Intan
Kuala Lipis
Geliga
Chukai
Raub
Tembeling
Jerantut
Kuantan
Bentong
Maran
Temerloh
Pekan
Rawang
Kuala Lumpur
Kelang
Kajang
Seremban
Kuala Pilah
Bahau
P. TIOMAN
Port Dickson
Gemas
Pdg Endau
SUMATRA
Tampin
Segamat
Labis
Mersing
Malacca
Muar
Yong Peng
Keluang
Ayer Hitam
Batu Pahat
Kulai
Kota Tinggi
N
PENINSULAR MALAYSIA
Pontian Kechil
Johor Bharu
Singapore

July, 622 AD and is lunar based. This, however, is about 11 days shorter than the solar year causing each year to begin a bit earlier. The Chinese calendar varies only a little since the year still has 365 days and only the beginning of the year depends on the moon. Sunday is a holiday in all states except Trengganu, Kelantan, Kedah and Johore, where Friday is an official holiday.

GETTING AROUND

As regards its infrastructure, Malaysia is one of the best developed countries in South East Asia. An excellent road system is complemented by a north-south rail line with a branch to the north east. Since 1985 a four-lane expressway, connecting Johore Bharu and Padang Besar on the Thai border, has been under construction. The sections from Padang Besar to Ipoh as well as from KL to Melaka are already in use.

Internal flights are relatively cheap and of great importance for Sarawak and Sabah. During school vacation and important holidays (especially Chinese New Year, Hari Raya, Christmas), all means of transport are packed. So book your place in advance.

BUSES: With the local buses you can reach any kampong on the peninsula fairly quickly. The overland buses are reliable and quite cheap. Express buses, which are air-conditioned, travel between the major cities. In most towns the bus stations are centrally located and often also serve as terminals for overland taxis.

OVERLAND TAXIS: The fast taxis with the yellow roofs are allowed by law to take four people. For this reason you frequently have to wait at the taxi stand until four passengers going in the same direction are found. If you rent a taxi for two or three people, you'll have to pay for the empty seats. The price for this quick and comfortable way to get around lies just above the rate for 2nd class train travel, though the local buses are much cheaper.

TRAINS: Except for a few short branch lines, only the main north-south line from Singapore to KL, Butterworth, and Thailand, along with the connection from Tumpat via Kuala Krai and Kuala Lipis to Gemas are of interest. The Ekspres Rakyat and Ekspres Sinaran on the main line stop only in a few places (i.e. they're faster) and offer only two classes. On the express trains a bed in 2nd class (between M$6 and 8) is worth it on long rides. You can book your tickets up to 60 days in advance.

For M$85 (or M$175) you can buy a *RAILPASS* with which you can ride for 10 days (30 days) in every class on every train of the Malayan Railway. They can only be bought in Singapore, KL, Butterworth, Penang, and Padang Besar.

FLIGHTS: MAS (Malaysian Airline System - 'mas' in Malay also means 'gold') is the national carrier. The airport tax for national flights is M$3, for flights to Singapore or Brunei M$5, and for international flights M$15.

CAR RENTALS: Malaysia is the perfect place to drive yourself. Large firms in Singapore rent cars which can be driven and returned in Malaysia. AVIS, HERTZ, and SINTAT all have different rates so compare right away. Watch out for the special tariffs. There are special day or weekend rates with limited mileage, or excursion rates with unlimited mileage. If you rent a car for a longer period of time, a smaller one without ac may cost you as little as M$1300 for a month - provided you bargain hard enough. It is up to you which firm you choose. Only the international companies guarantee you a good car. If you want to leave from Singapore, you should check the prices at the various offices in Johore Bahru (Malaysia) if possible. They are often cheaper, making it worth taking a bus across the causeway and renting the car there.

HERTZ: SINGAPORE, Tanglin Shopping Centre., tel 7344646 - KL, 52 Jl. Ampang, tel 2329125 - PENANG, 38 Farquar St., tel 375914 - KUANTAN, 22 Jl.Telok Sisek, tel 212015.

AVIS: SINGAPORE, Singapura Forum Hotel, tel 7377870 - KL, 40 Jl.Sultan Ismail, tel 2743057 - PENANG, 38/6 Leboh Farquhar, tel 361685 - JOHORE BHARU, Tropical Inn, 15 Jl.Gereja, tel 221157 - KUANTAN, Loo Bros Bldg., 59 Jl.Haji Abdul Aziz, tel 23659 - KUALA TRENGGANU, Hotel Warisan, tel 27654.

SINTAT: SINGAPORE, 50 Collyer Quay, tel 2244155 - KL, Holiday Inn, tel 2743028 - PENANG, Lone Pine Hotel, Batu Ferringhi, tel 811101 - KUANTAN, Hotel Merlin, tel 24716.

Other local rent-a-car companies can be found in KL, Penang, or Singapore (see Singapore chapter). With them, however, you have to turn in the car where you rented it, which isn't always convenient.

MAYFLOWER ACME TOURS, Angkasa Raya Building, 123 Jl.Ampang,KL, tel 2486739.
NATIONAL RENT A CAR, 78 Jl.Ampang, KL, tel 2489188.
EXPRESS RENT A CAR, G02 Wisma Stephens, Jl.Raja Chulan, KL, 2423682.
TOYOTA RENT A CAR, Lot 5, Federal Hotel, Jl.Bukit Bintang, KL, tel 4388387.
SMAS RENT A CAR, Pernas Bldg., Jl.Rajah Laut, KL, tel 2936233.
BUDGET RENT A CAR, Wisma MCA, 163 Jl.Ampang, KL, tel 2621122.

In Singapore and Malaysia a national driver's licence is enough to rent a car. It's worth M$7-10 daily to get some extra insurance (collision damage waiver) which removes your liability for damages of up to M$1000 to the car. Petrol in Malaysia costs about 1.10 M$ per litre (1987). Get yourself one of the good roadmaps provided at just about every petrol station by the major oil companies.

When planning your route, remember that rented cars aren't Landrovers and can't necessarily be used on every road shown on the map. Except for the sections of the north-south line already mentioned , there are no super highways. In addition, you'll find completely different traffic conditions on Asian roads; so don't expect to cover any great distances in one day. While at home you may find a forest of signs warning of every possible road situation; in Asia be ready for surprises around every corner, whether it's a pot-hole or buffalo. During the rainy season, many roads are under water. These are specially marked on the Mobil maps. Expect completely different behaviour from other drivers and pedestrians. Pedestrians always assume that they have enough time to make it across the street in front of your car, and drivers in the other direction who want to pass always assume that you'll brake.

ACCOMMODATION

You'll find accommodation in all price classes and categories in West Malaysia. Many of the cheaper places are managed by Chinese. Some are slightly run down, but in general pretty clean. Always expect small bedmates in the cheap places, however; check your mattress in advance for bugs and take a couple of coils or a mosquito net with you.

We decided on the following price table for Peninsular Malaysia - all prices are for double rooms:

*	**up to**	**12 M$**
**	**up to**	**25 M$**
***	**up to**	**50 M$**
****	**over**	**50 M$**

In Chinese hotels the huge beds in single rooms are usually big enough for two people, or a double room for three people. So be sure to have a look before you check in. During the high season, and especially during Malaysian school holidays, telephone ahead to book your room - important if you're planning to arrive in the late afternoon or evening. Keep this in mind in KL, Penang, and along the east coast during turtle season. Government rest houses are nice old relics from the past (in Malay: *Rumah Persinggahan Kerajaan)* and are often found in out of the way places.

An English *resident* or colonial official during the days of Somerset Maugham used to look forward to the evening in the rest house. After a hard day on the road, it was wonderful to sit on the veranda sipping a gin or scotch while being fanned by the *pukah boy* sitting quietly in the corner.

FOOD & DRINK

Malaysia has a lot to offer in this area. As you'd expect, considering the multiracial population, there's no trouble finding Indian, Malay, Chinese and European food. Sometimes they have influenced each other, such as the Nonya food prepared here by local Chinese. The way it's prepared is Chinese, the spices are hot like in Malay food, and it's not eaten with chopsticks, but with fork and spoon. While in Malay restaurants you always eat with a fork and spoon; in the rural areas you always eat with your hand - like the Indians using only the right hand. The left hand is considered unclean and should never be used to touch food. Many tiny foodstalls offer the thrifty traveller things to munch on for friendly prices. Since the sea is never far away, you'll find fantastic fish and other seafood everywhere.

INDIAN: Curries, the typical basic spice, are varyingly hot. A good curry should be made of at least 20 different spices - it isn't to be compared with the yellow powder commercially available in western shops. The hottest curries are *CURRY MADRAS* and *CURRY CEYLON* - too hot for some Europeans. You can reduce the strength of any curry somewhat by mixing it with yoghurt or sugar. Beginners with Indian cooking should order a *KOOMA* (sometimes written 'kormah') which is a mildly spiced curry dish. Traditional curries are always made with vegetables, but you can also get lamb, chicken, crab, and beef (of course not from Hindus). It is served either with rice or bread. *CHAPATHIS* are breads made of wheat flour and water which are baked dry. *PARATHAS* are similar but baked with butter. *NAN* is the simplest kind of bread. Be sure to try *MURTABAK,* a kind of pancake with a spicy filling of onions, vegetables, egg, and sometimes meat.

MALAY: All over the country you'll find stalls selling *SATAY* - tiny pieces of meat coated in sugar and spices and grilled over charcoal. They are served with a spicy-sweet peanut sauce. The following meats *(DAGING)* are used: beef *(LEMBU),* mutton or goat *(KAMBING),* and less often chicken *(AYAM).* What the Muslims hate and the Chinese love is pork *(BABI). GADO GADO* is a cold vegetable salad served with a peanut sauce dressing. If you have any suspicions as to the hygienic conditions, then forgo on the peanut sauce. *ROTI* is a general term for bread. The best known dish is *NASI GORENG* - fried rice mixed with white boiled rice *(NASI PUTIH)* and the following ingredients: egg *(TELUR),* different vegetables *(SAYUR-SAYURAN)* and sometimes meat or shrimps *(UDANG). NASI BERIANI* is an Indian variation of this dish served with hot curries. Besides fried rice, there's also fried noodles *(MIE GORENG),* fried vegetables *(SAYUR GORENG),* and of course for breakfast your fried egg *(TELUR GORENG). LAKSA* is a typical Malaysian noodle dish. A speciality is *PENANG LAKSA,* a noodle soup spiced with fish paste.

In KL and the Cameron Highlands you should get a group of people together to go out and eat *STEAMBOAT,* a kind of fondue, in which different kinds of meat and vegetables are cooked in a pot of boiling stock on the table. In the end you have a rich soup into which eggs are beaten.

Look at the *Singapore Food & Drink* chapter for details about Chinese cuisine.

For drinks you can try *AIR* (water), *TEH* (tea), *TEH OH* (tea with sugar), *SUSU* (milk, usually canned), *KOPI* (coffee), and *BIR* (beer). Liquors are very expensive and hard to find. The fruit juices offered everywhere are fantastic. Be sure to try sugar-cane juice. The fruit juices are always made with ice, *AIR BATU* (means 'water stones'). The cheapest places to eat are the *WARUNG* or food stalls. *KEDAI KOPI* (coffee shops) have friendly prices unlike the *RESTORAN* or restaurants. Really like your food? Then say: Makananmu enak sekali!

MONEY

EXCHANGE RATE	**1US$ = 2.49 M$**
INFLATION RATE:	**0.6%**

The monetary unit is the Malaysian dollar with 100 cents. The term *Ringgit* is becoming ever more popular as a name for the dollar. Bank notes are in the following denominations: 1, 5, 10, 50, 100 and 1000. The coins of 1, 5, 10, 20 and 50 cents (in Malay: sen). The Malaysian dollar is one of the stable currencies in Asia so there isn't a black market. The exchange rate to the Brunei and Singapore dollars just a couple of years ago was 1:1:1. Today the Singapore dollar is worth a bit more, but the Singapore coins are still used interchangeably in Malaysia. When entering the country you can bring up to M$10,000 with you. It is illegal to import more than 3000 Indonesian Rupiahs or 270 Indian Rupees. All other currencies may be imported in any amounts you choose. The export of M$ is limited to M$5000.

Besides the US$, traveller's cheques in European currencies (DM, £, sfr) or in Australian $ get the best exchange rates; only money changers are willing to take bank notes. Compare the often greatly varying exchange rates and don't forget the often expensive *stamp duty* and *commission* charges.

INCOME AND COST OF LIVING

The average monthly per capita income is about M$450 - 500. As with every statistic, you have to remember that a few earn much more and that many earn much less. The income of many people living by agriculture is far below the minimum subsistence of M$385 per person. For example the monthly pay of an employee on a palm oil plantation in 1983 was about M$300; the foremen earn a bit more. The weed-pickers, however, have only about half this amount as take home pay. The average worker in the textile industry, one of the most important export industries, earned only about M$280 per month in 1984. The female workers in the tiny batik factories in Kelantan, of course, receive much less. The official wage for unskilled workers is set at M$16 per day.

The average traveller, wanting to travel cheaply, will have to think in terms of M$14 per night for a double room. Meals at a foodstand or cheap restaurant run to about M$3. If you want to save, drink tea. In comparison to Indonesia, the cost of travelling by bus and train is also a bit higher. You don't have such long distances to go, though, and everything is much more efficient. Local buses are the cheapest. Hitch-hiking is possible but is not recommended after dark. All prices on the peninsula are below those in Sarawak and Sabah.

ECONOMY

Malaysia has a population of 15.7 million (1985). Almost 37% of the employed are in ***agriculture*** (including fishing and forestry). This, however, produces only 20% of the GDP. Typically Asian small farms are mostly found in the north (Kelantan, Trengganu, Perlis, Kedah). Tourists, though, will take home memories of the plantations, especially ***rubber*** and ***palmoil.*** Today these are no longer wholly owned by the multi-nationals (Dunlop, Sime Darby, Guthrie, Harrisons). During the last few years they have mostly been taken over by Malaysian holdings. Malaysia produces 33% of the world's natural rubber. Demand for this raw material is sinking, however, due to increasing use of synthetics and a general fall in world demand. The government is therefore supporting the planting of oil palms and other products. At the same time the important rubber producers have joined together to form the ANRPC (Association of Natural Rubber Producing Countries) in order to stabilize prices by cutting production. The most important Malaysian export products today are ***oil and petro-chemicals*** (25% of all exports in 1986). Vast reserves are suspected in huge offshore fields off Sarawak and Trengganu. Malaysia is also the leader in ***tin*** production, turning out 20% of world output. In the export balance, however, this metal is only in fifth place at 9%. Tin is mostly used for tin cans and by the electrical industry.

Western style ***industry*** only began developing in the 1960s as measures were taken for export production. Manufacturing now produces almost 30% of the GDP. Foreign investment is generously encouraged but also planned and controlled by the Federal Industrial Development Authority. Expansion is sought in those industries which will reduce imports and expand exports.

Malaysia's balance of trade showed red figures in 1981 for the first time in many years. Sinking demand and falling world market prices for tin, oil, rubber, and wood were major reasons. Trade, industry, banks, and insurance companies are still disproportionately controlled by Chinese. Through state support for the *bumiputra* (sons of the earth = Malay), an attempt is being made to enlarge the percentage holdings of the Malays. This policy has made it just about impossible for Chinese to get a licence to run a hotel or taxi. Many wealthy Chinese get around this problem by using Malays as sleeping partners.

NATIONALITIES & RELIGIONS

The pot-pourri of nons and adjectives, *Malaysia* and *Malaya, Malay* and *Malaysian,* can be pretty confusing. Malaysia is the name of the state which was founded in 1962 and whose Malaysian population includes 45% ethnic Malays, 36% ethnic Chinese, 9% ethnic Indians, and 8% ethnic proto-Malayan tribes. These figures are for the entire country including Sarawak and Sabah. On the mainland peninsula the ethnic ***Malays*** make up a majority, with 54%. Malaya, the old colonial name, is still used in English for the Malay Peninsula. The Malays, today, are basically the national population, even though they are a numerical minority. *Bahasa Malaysia* is the official national language and is taught in all preparatory schools, including the Chinese and Indian.

The great migrations of ***Chinese*** and ***Indians*** began last century when the British colonial masters were desperately seeking workers for the plantations and tin mines. The Chinese came mostly from the southern provinces of middle kingdom to try their luck in South East Asia. China at the time was suffering from starvation, and civil war was raging in many parts of the country. The goal of the immigrants was to make their fortune so that they could return home in prosperity. Only a few actually made it. The Chinese were good workers and businessmen, and were very different from the quiet, less materialistic Malays.

Over many generations the immigrants have achieved a position of economic dominance, controlling most of the businesses. In the eyes of the Malays, they are usurious moneylenders and cutthroats. There are similar problems in just about all South East Asian countries with Chinese minorities.

The most diverse religions come together in the multi-ethnic country of Malaysia. Besides *Taoism, Buddhism* and *Christianity* with largely Chinese membership, there is also a *Hindu* minority of Indians. Malays and small numbers of Indians are *Muslim.* As in other predominantly Muslim areas, there has been great unrest among the Islamic fundamentalists. In 1978 Muslim extremists stormed a Hindu temple near KL. Four of the attackers were killed by Indian temple guards. In 1980 a group of Muslim fanatics attacked a police station in Batu Pahat (Johore). Several people died. On the other hand, the theocratic Islamic parties weren't able to achieve a breakthrough at the polls in 1986. Only in the east coast states of Kelantan and Trengganu did they have notable success. At the same time, Islamic extremists are up in arms against the other nationalities. Maintaining balance between the Muslim Malays, Hindu Indians, and Taoist or Buddhist Chinese is one of the major tasks of every government.

Another word about Islam. Many Malays carry the title *Haji* in their name. That means that the person has made the obligatory pilgrimage to Mecca. The *Haj* is one of the five keystones of Islam. The second is participation in the fast during the month of *Ramadan.* Another is the prescribed payments to the poor *(zakat).* Every believer is required to give a part of his income to the sick and needy. The fourth is *praying* as dictated by the Koran, five times a day. The general *profession of belief* is the most important: 'There is only one God, Allah, and Mohammed is his prophet.'

You'll come across Islam more often in the conservative states such as Kelantan and Trengganu. In both states Friday is the weekly holiday. Shoes have to be removed every time you visit a mosque (masjid), and your clothes shouldn't be provocative. We recommend women to ask first whether they are permitted to enter the mosque. Be sure to take these rules seriously and to act in accordance with local tradition.

It isn't possible here to go more deeply into the basic principles of Islam or the Indian and Chinese religions. Religion plays a much larger role for Malaysians than for Europeans, making it well worthwhile to read up on the subject.

HISTORY

About 5000 years ago the Malay Peninsula served as a land bridge over which the ***proto-Malays*** made their migration from continental Asia to the East Indies and Polynesia. They pushed the former inhabitants of the peninsula (whose descendants are the Senoi and Semang) into the remote jungle areas. For about 2000 years trade between China and India involved several harbours in Kedah and Johore. During the first century AD, Malaya was dominated by the Funan Kingdom, the most important Hindu realm in the region.

Langkasuka, situated in what is now northern Malaysia, was a Malay Hindu centre of power for almost 1000 years. In the 7th and 8th centuries, the Indies, as well as large portions of the mainland, were ruled over by ***Sri Vijaya.*** Langkasuka, Kelantan, Pahang and Trengganu were forced to pay tribute. Chinese travellers wrote of the powerful trading and seafaring state. Buddhism was the state religion and ancient Malay, written in Sanskrit, the major language. The oldest writings discovered in the region date from that period. In the second half of the 13th century, the Central Javanese power, ***Majapahit,*** became a determining force in South East Asia. For about 100 years the Malay peninsula was a permanent place of confrontation between Majapahit and the Thai Kingdom Ayutthaya. In 1349, Temasik (today Singapore) was conquered by the Thais. The rise of Malacca from a small fishing village to a world class metropolis will be described in detail later on.

The beginnings of ***Islam*** in Malaya are difficult to date. Arabian traders in the 13th century first brought the Buddhist and Hindu-influenced population into contact with the teachings of Mohammed. The kingdoms of North Sumatra were the first to establish Islam as the official religion. On the mainland the *Trengganu Stone,* dating from the year 1303, is seen as the first positive evidence of Islam in Malaya. It is important to remember that long before the arrival of Europeans, high cultures existed in South East Asia. For hundreds of years, active contacts were maintained with the two most important political and cultural civilizations in the world at the time - India and China. The relations were disturbed if not destroyed by the arrival of the Europeans on the Asian stage.

Between 1511 and 1641, ***Portugal*** was the major power in South East Asia - later replaced by ***Holland.*** But neither the Portuguese nor the Dutch ever considered that they had the whole of Malaya under their control. After the conquest of Malacca by the Dutch, the city never regained its former beauty and influence. International trade increasingly moved via the Sultanate of Aceh on the northern coast of Sumatra and through the capital of the ever more powerful Johore Kingdom. Even the Dutch traders used Batu Sewar (situated near Kota Tinggi on the Johore River).

Not until 1786 did ***England*** make inroads on Malaya. Sir Francis Light made a treaty with the Sultan of Kedah, ceding the island of Penang. The East India Company needed a base on the Straits of Malacca for their lucrative trade with China (opium to China; tea, silk, and porcelain to India and the homeland). In 1824 another deal was made: the British received Malacca, the Dutch got Bencoolen (today Bengkulu on the west coast of Sumatra). In 1826 the colonies of Penang, Malacca, Dindings (Pangkor) and Singapore were consolidated into the Straits Settlement.

In Malaya there were several quite powerful sultanates, some of which were controlled by the Thai Kingdom (Perlis, Kedah, Kelantan, Trengganu). On the other hand, due to the Industrial Revolution, Britain had new economic interests: the region offered *colonial goods* and a market for England. The colonies took on importance as suppliers of raw materials for industrial production. Between 1874 and 1896, the sultanates of Perak, Selangor, Pahang, and Negri Sembilan came under British control by way of treaty. The sultans were only permitted to make political decisions with the concurrence of the *British Resident.* Only questions of Malay customs and religion were left to the respective sultans. In 1896 the ***Federation of Malayan States*** was created, comprising the sultanates mentioned above. In 1909 Thailand signed over all her rights in the northern sultanates (Kedah, Perlis, Kelantan, and Trengganu) to the British. Johore joined the federation in 1914.

Through a complicated system of treaties, Britain managed to bring the whole of Malaya under its political control. Somerset Maugham's short story descriptions of Malaya in the 1920s and '30s offer worthy illustrations of this period. Tin and rubber became the most important exports. Huge plantations, mostly owned by a British monopoly, ranged over the land.

In December 1942 ***Japanese troops*** landed at Songkhla, Patani and Kota Bharu. Two months later Singapore fell. Until the 12th of September 1945, Malaya was ruled by the Japanese military. The Japanese secret police (Kempetai) set up a brutal system of repression under which the Chinese in particular suffered. The army plundered the country and so did Japanese companies (Mitsui and Mitsubishi profited greatly at that time!). Japanese was taught in all the schools and the different nationalities were played against each other. Resistance in the population mounted. Under the leadership of the Malayan Communist Party (MCP), a guerilla war was waged against the occupiers. Parallels can be found in Burma, Indochina, and the Philippines. The armed struggle of the MCP continued after the war. In 1948, a state of emergency was declared which was only lifted in 1960. On August 31, 1957, the Federation of Malaya achieved its independence with Tunku Abdul Rahman as premier. He is considered to be the architect of independence (Merdeka). In 1963, the ***Federation of Malaysia*** was founded including Malaya, Singapore, Sarawak, and Sabah. Just two years later, Singapore decided to leave the federation. The reasons were economic, political and racial. Even today political and racial problems exist in the country. But the ***National Front government,*** which comprises the important parties of the Malays, Chinese, and Indians, has been successful in all elections and seems to be the only power that can minimize tensions between the nationalities.

THE STATES OF MALAYSIA: AREA AND POPULATION

KEDAH	Alor Setar	9,516 km^2	1,116,000
PERLIS	Kangar	806 km^2	148,000
KELANTAN	Kota Bharu	14,960 km^2	900,000
PERAK	Ipoh	20,748 km^2	1,850,000
PAHANG	Kuantan	35,932 km^2	799,000
PENANG	Georgetown	1,014 km^2	960,000
SELANGOR	Shah Alam	8,216 km^2	1,560,000
NEGRI SEMBILAN	Seremban	6,708 km^2	570,000
MALACCA	Malacca	1,664 km^2	470,000
TRENGGANU	Kuala Trengganu	13,130 km^2	542,000
JOHORE	Johore Bharu	19,958 km^2	1,650,000
SABAH	Kota Kinabalu	76,409 km^2	1,002,000
SARAWAK	Kuching	125,450 km^2	1,320,000
FEDERAL DISTRICT	Kuala Lumpur	244 km^2	950,000

LANGUAGE

Malaysia's official language is Bahasa Malaysia. Chinese and Indian languages are also spoken. All schools in the country teach Bahasa Malaysia. Estimates are, that about half of the population uses English to converse with people of other nationalities. Those who want to#learn some Bahasa Malaysia, should pick up a copy of 'SPEAK MALAY, Edward S.King, Kuala Lumpur.

SUGGESTED READING

A PORTRAIT OF MALAYSIA AND SINGAPORE (Tan Ding Eing; Kuala Lumpur 1980 - Oxford Progressive History). An history book ranging from the Malacca Empire until today. Economic and social problems are well handled.

ORANG ASLI - The Aboriginal Tribes of Peninsular Malaysia (Carey, Iskandar; Kuala Lumpur 1976). An important work about the aboriginies of West Malaysia by a former commissioner for Orang Asli Affairs.

THE MALAY ARCHIPELAGO - The Land of the Orang Utan and the Bird of Paradise (Wallace, Alfred Russel; 1st published 1869, Reprint 1962, New York). A classic by the great English natural scientist, who spent years on the mainland and islands of Malaysia. Emphasis on flora and fauna.

MALAYSIA'S GREEN AND TIMELESS WORLD - An Account of the Flora, Fauna and Indigenous Peoples of the Forests of Malaysia (Shuttleworth, Charles; Kuala Lumpur 1981). The wide-ranging report of a nature lover featuring lots of black and white and color photos.

THE SINKING ARK - Environmental Problems in Malaysia & Southeast Asia (Lee, David; Kuala Lumpur 1980). A recommendable look at Malaysia's various ecological problems and their effects.

THE GOLDEN CHERSONESE - Travels in Malaya in 1879 (Bird, Isabella L.; Reprint Kuala Lumpur 1980). The adventure packed trip of Mrs.Bird through Selangor, Negri Sembilan, Sungei Ujong and Malacca, recommended.

CULTURE SHOCK! What not to do in Malaysia and Singapore, How and Why not to do it (Craig, JoAnn; Singapore 1980). A well recommended paperback, written for expatriats, but which fits nicely in the hands of every tourist.

THE MALAYS - A CULTURAL HISTORY (Winstedt, Richard; Singapore 1981, 1st published 1947). A classic by a great Malaya expert. The new edition features an excellent appendix by Tham Seong Chee on new developments.

MALAY MYTHS AND LEGENDS (Knappert, Jan; KL 1980). An easy to read introduction to the ancient Malay myths.

SEJARAH MELAYU Malay Annals (Ed. and translated by Brown, C.C.; Kuala Lumpur 1970). The best translation of the classic of Malay literature.

MALAYAN TRILOGY (Burgess, Anthony; Harmondsworth 1981). Three autobiographical novels situated in post-war Malaya.

ALMAYER'S FOLLY (Conrad, Joseph; London 1859). A Conrad novel about the life of a European during the colonial era. There are other Conrad novels.

KUALA LUMPUR

The history of the city began in 1857 when a couple of adventurous miners paddled up the Klang River looking for tin. At the confluence of the Gombak and the Klang rivers, they built their huts. The first campsite must have been on pretty swampy ground: Kuala Lumpur means 'muddy estuary'. Despite malaria, fire, and floods, the prosperous tin mines were soon so sought after that battles broke out between the Chinese and Malays. In 1896 KL (pronounced 'K' 'L') became the capital of the Federation of Malayan States.

Today the Malaysian capital has become a big modern city which includes everything from highways and shopping centres to concrete and glass structures. In between, however, are lots of green areas and some relics of British colonial architecture with impressive facades, such as one of the most beautiful train stations in the world (it looks more like a mosque). There are also the old Chinese business establishments which are becoming fewer and fewer each year. As in Singapore, the traditional living and business quarters are being torn down to make room for 21st century architecture. On the other hand, there are attempts to create a new Malaysian architecture, such as the new mosque and the National Museum. Unlike Penang, the nation's capital isn't a tourist mecca, even though there's enough here to make a two or three day stopover worthwhile. It's rewarding to wander around in the tiny shops and markets in Chinatown and the Indian quarter near Jl.Tuanku Abdul Rahman.

Begin your tour right at the river junction of Sungei Klang and Sungei Gombak. Here you'll find a red and yellow structure in oriental style. The *JAME MOSQUE* was at one time the national mosque. On Jl.Raja and Jl.Tun Perak, the Malayan colonial past returns to life. The old administrative buildings, which unlike their modern counterparts are worth expending film on, have been renovated as has the *SELANGOR CLUB*, a real piece of England in Malaysia. You'll enjoy a walk through *JALAN TUANKU ABDUL RAHMAN* - check it out if you aren't staying there (see *SHOPPING*).

East of the river, between Jl.Sultan, Jl.Petaling, Jl.Cecil and Jl.Sultan Mohamed is the old *CHINATOWN* or what's left of it. On Jl.Bandar you'll find a beautiful old *HINDU TEMPLE*. Life really pulsates in this quarter during the late afternoon and evening - stands are set up everywhere, and the restaurants do great business. On the streets you can buy anything from cheap T-shirts to live pythons and Chinese medicines. When a paper airplane is burned on Jl.Petaling, it goes over into the great beyond where it is of use to a deceased person as a means of quick transport. The *CENTRAL MARKET* on Jl.Hang Kasturi was completely renovated and ever since has been a tourist attraction with shops, foodstalls, restaurants, and cultural shows.

At religious festivals and when visiting temples remember to keep out of the limelight and behave within the bounds of tradition! On a hill to the south is the *NATIONAL MOSQUE*. The minaret sits proudly 75 m above a pool of water. The main dome with 18 pointed stars symbolizes the 13 states of Malaysia and the five basic principles of Islam. The 48 smaller domes emulate the great mosque in Mecca.

Not far from here is the *RAILWAY STATION,* built in 1910 in a Moorish style. Facing it and complementing the colonial motif is the Malayan Railways Building. Visit the new *NATIONAL ART GALLERY* that has been opened in the former Majestic Hotel, an old traditional building. There are 17,000 pieces of art on display in its permanent collection. Open daily except Sun and public holidays from 10:00 to 18:00 h.

Another must is the *NATIONAL MUSEUM* (Muzium Negara), only 10 minutes walk from here.

On the outer wall of this modern Malaysian building you can see two paintings showing the high and low points in Malaysian history and the production of arts and crafts. On the ground floor, you'll find an ethnological exhibit with information about the different ethnic groups as well as the history of the Malaysian states. Quite interesting are the handwork and arts and crafts exhibits, such as the wayang kulit puppets from different regions, presenting a comparison from all over the world. Just as informative is the exhibit on the Orang Asli. There is, however, hardly anything representative of Sabah and Sarawak (go there yourself and check out the museum in Kuching). Upstairs are fauna and flora, industry, and transportation. Open: daily 9:00-18:00 h; Fri closed from 12:15 - 14:45 h; during Ramadan open only till 17:00 h. Admission free.

You can recover from your museum visit in the nearby *LAKE GARDEN.* In the northernmost part of the park is the *NATIONAL MONUMENT,* built in memory of the state of emergency before 1960. Seven larger than life statues represent members of the Malaysian security forces in their fight with communist guerillas. Even though the state of emergency was lifted in 1960, members of the illegal MCP were still active enough in 1975 to cause great damage to the memorial with a bomb attack.

HOTELS

Since many houses - among them many cheap hotels - on Jl.Tuanku Abdul Rahman have been razed, you may find it necessary to look for lodgings elsewhere. Despite this, here is a list of hotels still standing: *COLISEUM***, no. 98, tel 2926270, an old hotel from the 1920s with huge rooms. *REX***, no. 132, tel 2983895, get a room on the first floor (the ground floor is too loud). Right next door is *NEW TIVOLI***, tel 2924108. Besides that there's the *PARAMOUNT***, no. 154, tel 2927274, *KOWLOON****, no. 142, tel 2926455, *HAN MING***, no. 149, tel 2985034. Parallel to Jl.Tuanku Abdul Rahman, on Jl.Rajah Laut, there are several cheaper hotels such as *BEE SENG***, no. 60, tel 2929584, *ALISAN****, no. 132B, tel 2986905. Many of the cheaper places are paid for by the hour or are actually brothels. More expensive and respectable are *SENTOSA*****, no. 316, tel 2925644 or the *NEW CYLINMEN****, no. 110, tel 2982088.

You can be centrally located if you settle down in Chinatown near the night market. *LEE MUN***, 11 Jl.Sul-

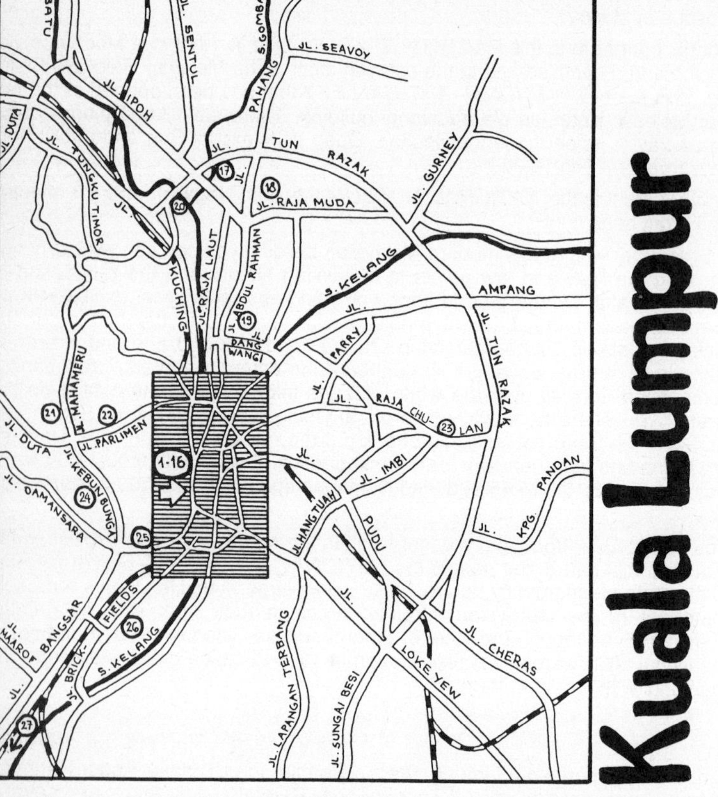

1. A.I.A. Building QANTAS Canadian Emb.
2. City Hall
3. Bukit Nanas
4. Telegraph Office
5. Selangor Club
6. Sultan Abd. Samad Buildg.
7. Jame Mosque
8. Post Office
9. Pudu Raya Bus & Taxi Station
10. Central Market
11. Hindu-Temple
12. Chinatown (Hotels)
13. Stadium Negara
14. National Mosque
15. Railway Stn.
16. U.M.B.C. Building
17. Pahang Bus Station
18. General Hospital
19. Wisma Loke
20. Tourist Off.
21. Parliament
22. National Monument
23. Karya Neka Handicraft Ctr.
24. Lake Garden
25. National Museum
26. Y.M.C.A.
27. Immigration Dept.

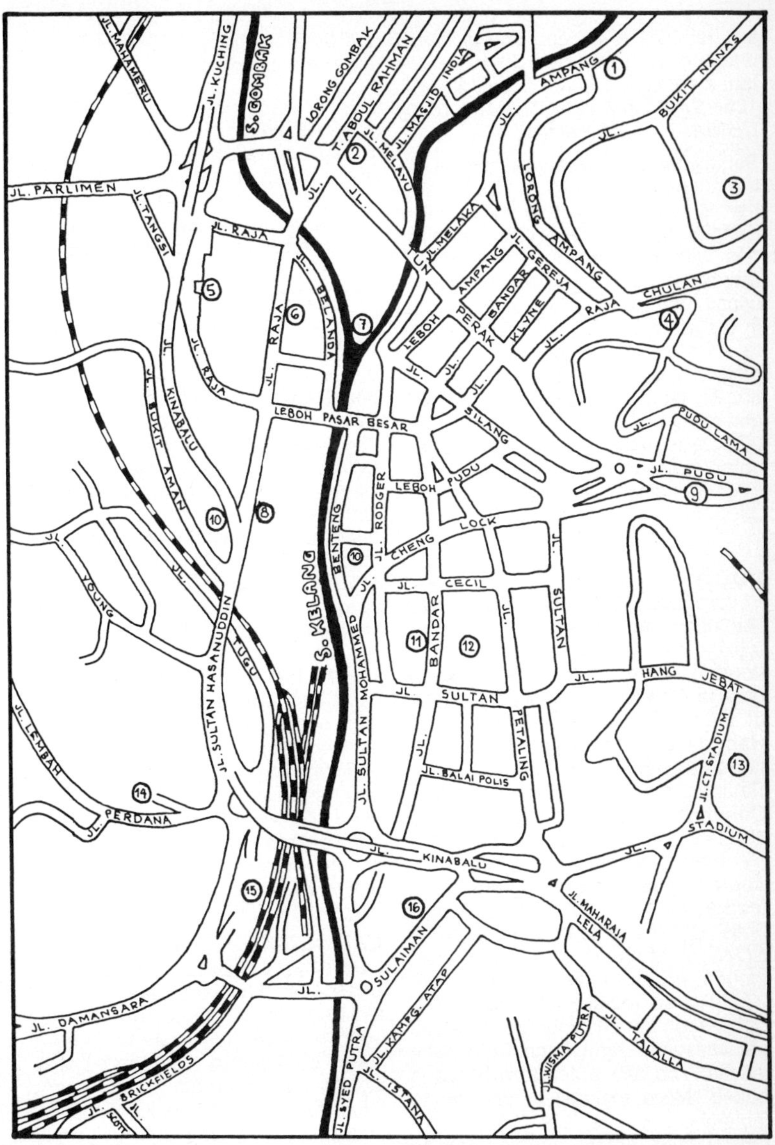

tan, tel 2382981, clean and pleasant but loud. *COLONIAL*** 39-45 Jl.Sultan, a creaky old hotel. *LENG NAM***, 165-167 Jl.Bandar, tel 2301489, or try *DUNIA****, 142 Jl.Petaling.

Somewhat out of the way, but an alternative, is the *YMCA*, Jl.Kandang Kerbau, corner of Jl.Brickfields (Jl.Tun Sambanthan), tel 2741439. Dormitories with 6 beds*, single rooms*** with ac. If the Y is full, which isn't unusual, then try one of the many hotels in the area. Look on a parallel street to Jl.Brickfields behind the Lido Cinema, Jl.Thambadillai: *WING HENG***, no. 24, tel 2741650, with fan, shower and toilet, or *PENG AUN***, no. 20, tel 2741263. Renovations have been completed at the *STATION HOTEL*****, right in the railway station, tel 2302250.

FOOD

In the *COLISEUM,* Jl.Tuanku Abdul Rahman, you can still get good and inexpensive steaks served with a flourish. Chinese food is naturally best in Chinatown. Good steamboat at the foodstalls on Jl.Sultan or Jl. Hang Lekir. Another steamboat restaurant is *THE PINES* on 297 Jl.Tun Sambanthan (Jl.Brickfields). Back in Chinatown is *ENGLISH HOT BREADS,* Jl.Sultan 60. Besides pastry, they serve pizza and spaghetti. There's good Chinese vegetarian food at *FATT YOW YUEN,* Jl.Balai Polis. Get hot Indian curries in *CEYLON,* Jl.Melayu. Much cheaper, though, are the Indian shops: *DEVI*, 27 Jl.Travers (off Jl.Brickfields) or *TAJ MAHAL* on Leboh Ampang. Here you eat with your right hand from palm leaves. You can watch how bread is baked. More expensive, with white table-cloths and ac, is *AKBAR,* Jl.Medan Tuanku. Across the way next to the MARA building is *SHIRAZ,* serving Pakistani food.

SHOPPING

KL isn't a duty-free shopping centre like Singapore or Hong Kong, but you'll still be able to whet your palate with a large selection of arts and crafts and other typical Malaysian goods. The following list should help you in your search for souvenirs:

JALAN TUANKU ABDUL RAHMAN - especially on the northern part of the street, between Jl.Raja Muda and Jl.Raja Bot, there are many Chinese shops offering cheap textiles, wood-carvings, and things made of rattan. The morning market on Jl. Chow Kit is quite good. Here you'll find homemade goods such as peasant hats and bamboo shopping baskets. You'll find arts and crafts in the MARA Building (corner of Jl.Semarang) and near Jl.Campbell is the Pertama Shopping Complex offering just about everything you can imagine. At the lower end of the street you'll find several bookstores and Indian shops offering everything from saris to religious literature (similar to comics) from the subcontinent. A good selection of travel guides is offered in MINERVA BOOKSHOP under the Kowloon Hotel. Other good bookshops, notably MPH and BERITA BOOK CENTRE, are in Bukit Bintang Plaza, Jl.Bukit Bintang.

KARYANEKA HANDICRAFT CENTRE (JALAN RAJA CHULAN) - On Jl.Imbi fourteen traditional Malay wooden houses have been built representing the 14 federal states of Malaysia. You can buy Malaysian arts and crafts here - everything from batik to woodcarvings. It's only interesting for people with little time to scout around Malaysia for themselves - moderate prices! Open daily 9:30-18:00 h. On Jl.Raja Chulan across from Wisma MPI is a supermarket (Fairtrade) for those who miss cheese, bread, and wine. Find another supermarket in Yow Chuan Plaza (Jaya) on Jl.Tun Razak/Jl.Ampang.

MARKETS - NIGHT MARKET are in Chinatown at the corner of Jl.Cecil/ Jl. Sultan. Music cassettes are reasonably priced (make them play it before you buy!) and textiles ranging from cheap T-shirts to brand name jeans sell for about M$35. Many street vendors sell antiques or things easily mistaken for such - be careful! Every Saturday night the so-called Sunday Market is held until very late in Kampong Baharu (Jl.Raja Muda Musa / Jl. Alang). You can combine eating and shopping, though it isn't all that great.

GENERAL INFORMATION

TOURIST INFORMATION - TDC (Tourist Development Corporation) has its information centre in Putra World Trade Centre, 24th/27th floor, Jl.Tun Ismail, tel 2935188, open Mon to Fri 8:30-16:45 h, Sat 8:30-13:00 h. It has info on other Malaysian states including Sarawak and Sabah. Other information offices are at Subang Airport, tel 7755707, open daily 9:00-23:30 h and diagonally across from the railway station, tel 2301369, open Mon to Fri 8:30-16:45 h, Sat 8:30-13:00 h. Pick up *Kuala Lumpur - Map and Guide* free of charge - it offers current info and practical tips.

IMMIGRATION - there's usually no problem getting visa extensions. The window for Commonwealth citizens is always busy since many Indians don't have Malaysian passports. Address: Immigration Headquarters, Jl.Pantai Bharu, tel 7578155.

POST OFFICE - the new General Post Office is on Jl.Hishamuddin, open from 8:00-19:00 h except Sun. The charges are generally reasonable, though parcels can be sent more cheaply from Singapore. If you are expecting mail, have them check at the poste restante window under both your first name and last name.

TELEPHONE - calls within town cost 10 c. For international calls go to the Central Telegraph Office on Bukit Mahkamah (Jl.Raja Chulan), open round the clock. At the airport you can make international calls from 7:30-23:30 h. Connections are fairly quick. Some European countries, the United States, and Australia can be dialled directly. For international information call 108 (0). You can call everywhere in Malaysia without difficulty. It's cheaper between 18:00 and 7:00 h. Area codes for long distance calls: Singapore (02), Kuala Lumpur (03), Penang (04), Ipoh (05), Malacca (06), Taiping (044), Seremban (067), Kuantan (075), Kuala Trengganu (076), Kota Bharu (077).

BRITISH COUNCIL - has a good library, Jl.Hishamuddin/Jl.Bukit Aman.

BANKS - KL banks are open Mon to Fri 10:00-15:00 h; Sat 9:30-11:30 h. Most banks can be found in the administrative centre around Masjid Jame.

AMERICAN EXPRESS - main office in Jl.Raja Chulan in the Plaza See Hoy Chan Bldg. (tel 289911) - see them about credit cards, loss, etc. Representatives in Malaysia are Mayflower Acme Tours, 18 Jl.Segambut Pusat (tel 6267011). Buy Amexco checks at the Chase Manhattan Bank, 88 Jl.Raja Chulan (Wisma Stephens), tel 2482011.

CITY MAPS - the free city map is quite good and useful - found as a supplement to the *Kuala Lumpur - Map and Guide.* The satellite city of Petaling Jaya is missing, however. For those who need a more detailed map, the *Street Atlas & Index A-Z Kuala Lumpur / Petaling Jaya / Subang Jaya* for M$9.50 is recommended.

MEDICAL HELP - the General Hospital is north of town between Jl. Tun Razak and Jl.Pahang. It is new with modern equipment, English-speaking doctors, efficient labs and its own dispensary. Treatment is free of charge. In case of emergency call 999. Also to be recommended is the University Hospital (Jl.Universiti) near the freeway to Petaling Jaya. The treatment is rather expensive in Pantai Hospital, Jl.Bukit Pantai.

NEWSPAPERS - the most important English language newspaper is the *NEW STRAITS TIMES.* Though critical reports about the country are usually missing, it's quite informative. Foreign language papers, magazines, and books can be found in all the big hotels, as well as the bookstores mentioned above.

DRUGS - even if things are a bit more relaxed in Thailand, watch out here! The jails are already filled with tourists who were caught with small amounts, and death-penalty quantities are within every tourist's budget.

GETTING AROUND

The old days of the rickshaws are gone - in KL today you use a taxi, minibus (bas mini), and big buses.

TAXIS

The drivers usually speak some English. Be sure that the meter is turned on. The charges for ac taxis are M$1 for the first mile (non ac 70 c) and 30 c for each additional half mile. It costs 10 c for every third or fourth passenger. Between 0:00 and 6:00 h there's a 50% surcharge for night travel. Renting by the hour costs M$12 per hour (ac).

MINIBUSES

All routes within town cost 50 c. Bas Mini 11 runs an important route from Jl.Petaling via Leboh Pudu, Jl.Hang Kasturi, Jl.Raja Laut and Jl.Ipoh to the Batu Caves. No. 12 runs from Jl.Tuanku Abdul Rahman via Jl.Bandar, Jl. Sultan, Jl.Brickfields (Jl.Tun Sambanthan) to Jl.Universiti in Petaling Jaya. No. 13 runs from Jl.Tuanku Abdul Rahman via Jl.Ampang, Jl.Gereja to Jl.Pudu. Bas Mini 17 starts at Jl. Cheng Lock and runs via Jl.Ampang right to the zoo. No. 22 runs right from Jl.Tuanku Abdul Rahman to Petaling Jaya.

BUSES

Several large private companies run routes in KL. Here too, only the important lines: buses no. 170 and 177 (big bus) go to the National Zoo and the Aquarium from Leboh Ampang, across from the AIA Building. Len bus no. 70 leaves from Leboh Pudu to the Batu Caves. Len buses no. 66, 78, 83 and 81 leave from Puduraya bus station to Templer Park.

LEAVING KL

BY AIR - INTERNATIONAL

Subang International Airport is served by many airlines. Like Singapore, Bangkok, and Penang, it is an important stop for cheap flights. The drive to Subang by taxi costs about M$15. From Jl.Sultan Mohamed, across

RAILWAY STATION, KUALA LUMPUR

from the Toshiba Building, bus 47 leaves hourly for the airport for M$1. When you land in Subang and want to take a taxi into town, get a coupon at the *Taxi Coupon Booth* first. You don't have to pay the driver anything else. The airport tax for international flights is M$15, for domestic flights M$3, and for flights to Brunei and Singapore M$5. The addresses of the most important airlines serving KL:

AEROFLOT, Yayasan Selangor Bldg., Jl.Bukit Bintang, tel 2423231.
AIR INDIA, Bangunan Angkasa Raya, 123 Jl.Ampang, tel 2420166.
ALIA, Kompleks Dayabumi, level 3, tel 27493060.
BIMAN, Bangunan Angkasa Raya, 123 Jl.Ampang, tel 2483765.
CATHAY PACIFIC AIRWAYS, MUI Plaza, Jl.P.Ramlee, tel 2433755.
CHINA AIRLINES, 64 Jl.Bukit Bintang, tel 2427344.
CSA, Czechoslovak Airlines, 68 Bangunan GGI, Jl.Ampang, tel 2380176.
GARUDA, Bangunan Angkasa Raya, 123 Jl.Ampang, tel 2420481.
KOREAN AIRLINES, Wisma MPI, Jl. Raja Chulan, tel 2428311.
MAS, UMBC-Building, Jl.Sulaiman, tel 7747000.
PAKISTAN INTERNATIONAL, Bangunan Angkasa Raya, tel 2425444.
PHILIPPINE AIRLINES, Jl.Raja Chulan, Wisma Stephens, tel 2429040.
QANTAS, AIA Building, Jalan Ampang, tel 2389133.
SINGAPORE AIRLINES, 2 Jl.Dang Wangi, tel 2923122.
THAI INTERNATIONAL, 84 Jl.Ampang, tel 2937100.

Student tickets can be booked at: MSL Travel, 1st Floor, South East

Asia Hotel, 69 Jl.Haji Hussein, tel 2984132. Here are SAMPLE PRICES in M$ to neighbouring countries, in parenthesis the ISIC prices: BANDAR SERI BEGAWAN 294.-, BANGKOK 403.-(198.-), HAT YAI 169.-, HONG KONG 821.-(454.-), JAKARTA 426.-(251.-), MADRAS 843.-(567.-), MANILA 699.-(507.-), SINGAPORE 130.-(night flight: 113.-), TAIPEI 1105.-(631.-), TOKYO 1459.-(798.-).

BY AIR - DOMESTIC

MAS (Malaysian Airline System) is the national carrier. The main office is located at the UMBC-Building, Jl.Sulaiman, not far from the railway station. From KL you can fly into just about every airport in West and East Malaysia. SAMPLE PRICES in M$, in parenthesis the price for night flights: ALOR SETAR 94.-, JOHORE BHARU 77.-(58.-), KOTA BHARU 86.-(61.-), KOTA KINABALU 380.-(266.-), KUALA TRENGGANU 80.-, KUANTAN 61.-, KUCHING 231.-(162.-), MALACCA 39.-,PENANG 86.-(61.-).

OVERLAND TAXIS

are used in Malaysia for the overland routes. Most leave from the new bus / taxi terminal at Jl.Pudu / Jl.Cheng Lock. Search for the right taxi on the first floor of the huge complex. Information at the following telephone numbers: 2320821 and 2325082. SAMPLE PRICES in M$: MALACCA 16.-, JOHORE BHARU 31.-, IPOH 15.- BUTTERWORTH 30.-, KOTA BHARU 45.-, KUALA TRENGGANU 35.-, TEMERLOH 10.-, KUANTAN 23.-, TANAH RATA 21.-.

OVERLAND BUSES

Most long distance buses leave from the bus/taxi terminal Puduraya. Some buses for Pahang leave in the morning from Pahang Bus Station, Jl.Tun Razak (tel 631473). SAMPLE PRICES in M$: SINGAPORE 17.-(Night express, ac, 19.50, best to book several days in advance) MALACCA 6.50, BUTTERWORTH 12.70 (15.50 ac), KUANTAN 12.10, KOTA BHARU 19.-(25.- ac), KUALA TRENGGANU 17.-(20.- ac), TAPAH 6.- (7.20 ac), PORT DICKSON 3.30, TANAH RATA 7.75, JOHORE BHARU 15.50, ALOR STAR 19.50(20.- ac), KUALA KANGSAR 8.-, IPOH 7.20 (8.20 ac), GERIK 11.50 (14.- ac). Locations are served by several companies. Usually the prices are the same. The important companies have their offices in the terminal: MARA EXPRESS, the largest company, serves most places in Malaysia, tel 2386990; KUALA LUMPUR - SINGAPORE EXPRESS and KUALA LUMPUR - MALACCA EXPRESS, tel 2327553.

BY RAIL

The architecture of the railway station is clearly one of a kind - or should we call it *railway mosque?* Latch on to a copy of the timetable there (Malay: Jadual Waktu) for the Malayan Railway (Keretapi Tanah Melayu). KL is situated on the main line from Singapore in the south and Butterworth (Penang) in the north. Some trains go on through to Bangkok (change at Butterworth, takes about 1 1/2 days). If you want to go along the east coast (Kota Bharu), you have to go via the railroad junction, Gemas, south of KL. It'd be quicker, though, to take a taxi or bus to Kuala Lipis or Temerloh (the train station Mentakab is about 10 km to the west on the big east-west road), and then switch to the train.

For long trips, get your ticket in advance. For 1st and 2nd class you can book a month in advance. For night trains reserving a bed is recommended. Costs in 2nd class M$6 for the upper bed and M$8 for the bottom in International Express trains: M$ 6.40 and M$9.10. SAMPLE PRICES (in M$ for one-way in 2nd cl. (3rd cl.):

SINGAPORE 21.90 (13.50), BUTTERWORTH 21.40 (13.20), HAT YAI 31.50, BANGKOK 59.-, JOHORE BHARU 20.30 (12.50), IPOH 11.50 (7.10), ALOR SETAR 25.80 (15.80), PADANG BESAR 29.60 (18.20), TAPAH 8.50 (5.30).

SAMPLE PRICES (express trains - in parenthesis ac-compartments in M$): SINGAPORE 17.-(28.-), BUTTERWORTH 17.-(28.-), JOHORE BHARU 16.-(24.-), TAPAH 9.-(15.-), KUALA KANGSAR 13.-(21.-).

DAY TRIPS AROUND KL

BATU CAVES

Twelve kilometres north of KL, spread over a square mile, steep limestone cliffs dominate the landscape. At the foot of the cliff, a batik factory and many refreshment stands await the tourist buses. 245 steps lead up to the big caves. Occasionally you'll meet partially tame monkeys on the stairs, begging for peanuts.

The longest and largest cave is the DARK CAVE (almost always closed) - about 400 m long and 120 m high. It was first discovered by Europeans in 1879 even though the Orang Asli traditionally collected bat guano here - they weren't averse to the flesh either. Via another 42 steps you come up to the LIGHT CAVE, sometimes called the MAIN CAVE. It is about 120 m long and a central place of worship for Malaysian Hindus. A shrine to the Hindu god *Murugan* was built here in 1892. Every year in January / February it plays a central role in the *THAIPUSAM FESTIVAL,* the largest Hindu festival outside India, where 70,000 people gather in front of the Batu Caves. For 20 c you can visit a cave museum exhibiting colourful Hindu sculptures.

TEMPLER PARK

On about 1600 ha of land, just 22 km north of KL, is this well-preserved bit of the jungle, set up with walking paths. Towering limestone cliffs, 305 m high, complete the view. If you're not planning to trek through the Taman Negara, then use this opportunity to visit a tropical forest in comfort. The path up to the waterfall is very pretty. On weekends many people come here from the city, though most of them only picnic near the parking lot.

In 1954 the National Park was opened and named for the last British High Commissioner of Malaya, Sir Gerald Templer. Thus a tiny piece of natural jungle was saved from the land-eating tin mines and rubber plantations, as well as the constantly expanding city. Many types of butterflies, flying lizards, and other small wildlife have had a bit of their habitat preserved.

NATIONAL ZOO / AQUARIUM

From Jl.Ampang take bus 170 or 177 to the zoo, located 13 km out of town. The drive passes through rubber plantations; you can see how the trees are tapped. In the zoo there are 200 kinds of animal and many types of Malaysian plant. Those who weren't able to see any large animals in the Taman Negara can make up for it here. Open daily from 9:00-17:00 h; admission for the aquarium and zoo: adults M$3, children M$1.

PETALING JAYA

About 10 km south of town on the highway to Port Kelang is this town, originally planned as a residential community. Independent of KL today, PJ is a city of its own with shopping and administrative centres, a university, and lots of industry. Working, living, and shopping all go hand-in-hand here. The whole town, with its streets running in half circles and lots of greenery, was designed on a drawing board, yet is not half as sterile as many of our suburban communities. It's also the preferred residential area for Europeans and rich Malaysians.

KELANG

The sultan's seat in the state of Selangor is Kelang. 8 km away is the most important national harbour, Port Kelang, although most of Malaysia's foreign trade passes through Singapore. Check out the Istana and the Royal Mosque in the new capital of Selangor, Alam Shah.

BETWEEN KL AND PENANG

If you have enough time on the way from KL to Penang or Thailand, you'll be able to find lots of places to hike, swim, and sightsee. Most tourists rush right from KL to Penang. A few might make a side trip to the Cameron Highlands. Not many stray off to Fraser's Hill or Pangkor Island. Hardly anybody visits the almost completely Chinese towns of Ipoh, Kuala Kangsar and Taiping.

FRASER'S HILL

Louis James Fraser was an English adventurer who was doing a thriving trade in opium around the turn of the century. It's said he ran an opium den almost 1524 m above sea level! In 1916 Fraser disappeared suddenly, never to be seen again. Back then only a small path ran up the 7 km from the Gap. Today there's a narrow road which is open for upward-bound traffic on the odd hours, and downward-bound traffic on the even hours.

Across from the Lodging House is the information centre where they have maps of Fraser's Hill. In the cool of the mountains you can take enjoyable walks; try the 5 km to JERIAU WATERFALL. The view of the Malayan mountains, covered by impassable forest, is by itself worth a drive. However, more and more luxury bungalows are being built here all the time. Fraser's Hill is a vacation area for rich local tourists who like to play golf and tennis in the cool mountain air.

HOTELS

Right on the road at the Gap is the peaceful *GOVERNMENT REST-HOUSE***, room reservation tel 071 / 382227. At the top you've the new *MERLIN HOTEL*****, tel 09 / 382279. There's no really cheap place to stay. A bit more reasonable are *FRASER'S HILL BUNGALOWS*****, tel 09 / 382201, and *THE LODGING HOUSE* ****. Be sure to phone in advance!

HOW TO GET THERE

With your own car take the route KL -

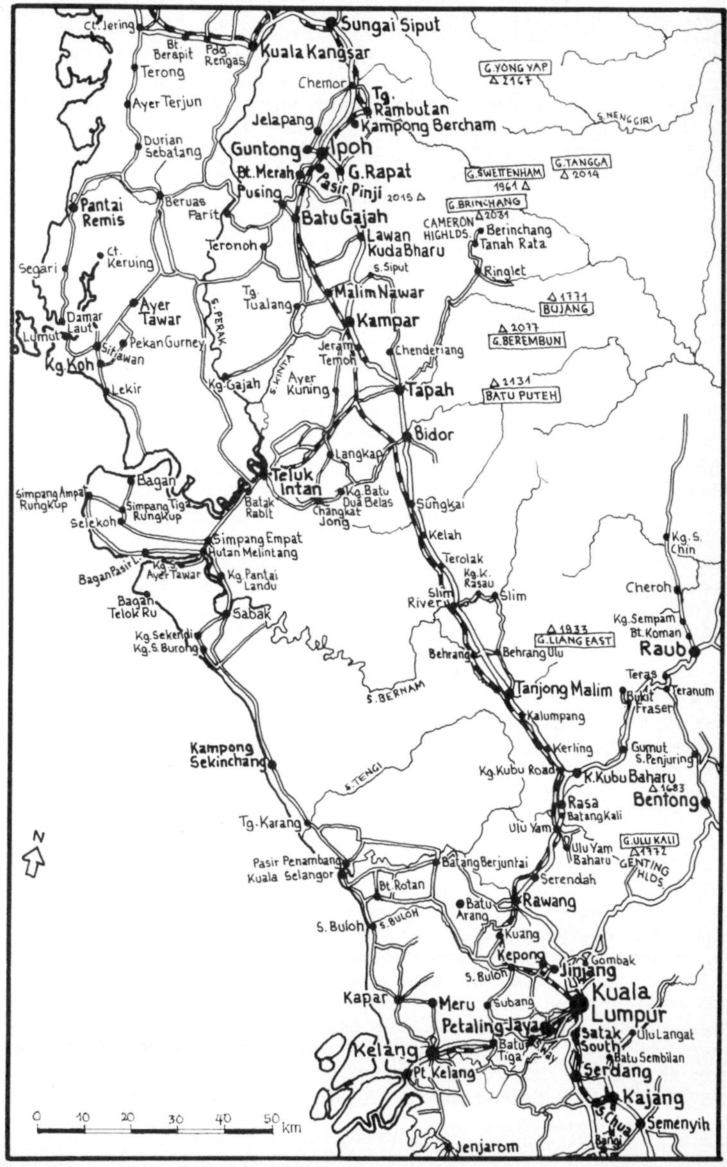
Ct. Jering
Sungai Siput
Bt. Berapit
Pdg. Rengas
Kuala Kangsar
Terong
Chemor
G. YONG YAP
2167
Ayer Terjun
Tg. Rambutan
Jelapang
Kampong Bercham
S. NENGGIRI
Durian Sebatang
Guntong
Ipoh
Bt. Merah
G. Rapat
G. SWETTENHAM
1961
G. TANGGA
2014
Pasir Pinji
Pusing
2015
G. BRINCHANG
2031
Pantai Remis
Beruas
Parit
Batu Gajah
CAMERON HIGHLDS.
Berinchang
Tanah Rata
Lawan Kuda Bharu
Teronoh
Ct. Keruing
Segari
S. Siput
Ringlet
Tg. Tualang
Malim Nawar
1771
BUJANG
Ayer Tawar
S. PERAK
Damar Laut
Lumut
Kampar
2077
G. BEREMBUN
Pekan Gurney
Sitiawan
Jeram
Temoh
Chenderiang
Kg. Koh
S. KINTA
Ayer Kuning
1131
BATU PUTEH
Lekir
Kg. Gajah
Tapah
Bidor
Langkap
Bagan
Teluk Intan
Simpang Ampat Rungkup
Simpang Tiga Rungkup
Batak Rabit
Kg. Batu Dua Belas
Changkat Jong
Sungkai
Selekoh
Simpang Empat Hutan Melintang
Kelah
Kg. S. Chin
Bagan Pasir L.
Kg. S. Ayer Tawar
Kg. Pantai Landu
Terolak
Kg. K. Rasau
Cheroh
Bagan Telok Ru
Sabak
Slim River
Slim
Kg. Sekendi
Kg. S. Burong
1933
G. LIANG EAST
Kg. Sempam
Bt. Koman
Raub
Behrang
Behrang Ulu
Teras
Tanjong Malim
Bukit Fraser
Teranum
S. BERNAM
Kalumpang
Kampong Sekinchang
Kerling
Gumut
S. Penjuring
Kg. Kubu Road
K. Kubu Baharu
S. TENGI
1683
Rasa
Batang Kali
Bentong
Tg. Karang
Ulu Yam
N
G. ULU KALI
Ulu Yam Baharu
1772
GENTING HLDS.
Pasir Penambang
Kuala Selangor
Batang Berjuntai
Serendah
Bt. Rotan
Batu Arang
Rawang
S. Buloh
S. BULOH
Kuang
Kepong
Gombak
S. Buloh
Jinjang
Kuala Lumpur
Kapar
Meru
Subang
Petaling Jaya
Sg. Way
Satak South
Ulu Langat
Kelang
Batu Tiga
Batu Sembilan
Pt. Kelang
Serdang
Kajang
0 10 20 30 40 50 km
S. Chua
Semenyih
Bangi
Jenjarom

KUALA KUBU BHARU for about an hour, then it's another hour on the road to RAUB. Buses leave KL regularly for Kuala Kubu Bharu on the great North-South Road. From there buses leave daily at 8:00 and 12:00 h directly to Fraser's Hill. Going back they leave at 10:00 and 14:00 h. For M$4 you can take an overland taxi from Kuala Kubu Bharu; from KL the whole taxi would be about M$60. 25-seater ac coaches leave on Tues, Wed, Thurs, Fri, and Sun from the KL Merlin Hotel at 15:00 h for M$16.50, on Sat they leave at 11:00 h and 17:00 h.

CAMERON HIGHLANDS

The Cameron Highlands in the State of Pahang offer a beautiful contrast to beach, palms, and ocean. In 1885, William Cameron, a surveyor, was travelling under contract to the colonial authorities and discovered 'a fine plateau with gentle slopes shut in by lofty mountains'. Tea planters and vegetables farmers were quick to appreciate the climatic advantages of a plateau up to 2000 m high. Later a road was built, and the area became a favourite vacation place for the English suffering under the hot sun.

At first you pass through rubber plantations and rice fields, then the road becomes smaller and winds with countless bends up the mountains. The vegetation changes as well - huge ferns and other mountain plants are typical of the evergreen tropical montane forests. Occasionally you'll see scattered Orang Asli villages. The Cameron Highlands is a good place to relax. Spend a week hiking in the fresh mountain climate, especially after a spell in the tropics. The evenings and nights can get quite cool. The coldest temperature ever recorded in the Highlands was 2°C, one January night.

ORANG ASLI

About 50,000 people fit into the ethnic category called 'Orang Asli' (literally translated: 'native, original people'). They are jungle and coastal dwellers whose forefathers were here before the Malays. The term 'Orang Asli' is used to describe many very different ethnic groups including about 1800 Negritos, the oldest population, who are mostly settled in the northern jungle areas or the proto-Malayan, which include about 1800 Orang Laut, the sea people. The largest group are the 30,000 Senoi, some of whose villages can be found in the forests of the Cameron Highlands. Many tribes such as the Temiar, Semai, Mah Meri, and the Semok Beri are sub-groups of the Senoi. They are said, like the Negritos, to have migrated into the region 6000-8000 years ago. Their skin, however, is lighter and unlike the nomadic Negritos they live by slash and burn agriculture. They have been pushed back by the Malays into hard-to-reach jungle regions. Some still live there today, completely cut off from civilization. Others, especially those living near the major cities and along the main transportation links, have largely taken on the lifestyle of their former enemies. Many Senoi have opened themselves up to the influences of modern times. Some of their children go to school, and small groups of Senoi work on the Highland tea plantations.

Their social structure is set up to avoid any kind of controversy or conflict. The traditional settlement is a long house which holds about 50 people, usually a clan with an old man as chief - the founder of the house or one of his sons. Decisions are made in collective discussions, with the chief taking the role of mediator. Visiting back and forth is a regular pastime, so you'll always find a number of guests.

Besides a blowpipe or a rifle and a few durian trees, the individual has no private property. Every clan has its own carefully defined fishing grounds and a section of jungle which it works. The forest is usually cleared in a two year cycle for the planting of mountain rice and tapioca. Only males are permitted to cut down trees, while harvesting and gathering of fruit and vegetables is women's work. Hunting and fishing is a privilege of adult men. The take is then divided among all members of the community. The traditional weapon, a blowpipe with poisoned darts over 2 meter long, is still used. During the 'emergency' from 1948 to 1960, the Orang Asli were courted by both the MCP and the British. They were the only people who knew their way around in the jungle. There is still a Senoi Pra'ak Regiment in the Field Force Police which is used against the MCP - even though 'war' and 'fight' are new concepts for the Senoi who traditionally seek compromise.

Three small villages form the centre of the Cameron Highlands: **RINGLET** (disappointing, leave quickly!), **TANAH RATA** (the nicest place) and **BRINCHANG.** An information office is on the road into Tanah Rata, though they only offer an old hotel directory and a map for 80 c.

Here are some tips for your tours and hikes:

If you've got a car, be sure to drive up to *GUNUNG BRINCHANG* (over 2000 m). If you're in a small group, you can rent a taxi - about M$50-60 to the top. To the foot of the mountain you'll only have to pay about M$7, but then you face a 1 3/4 hours hike (beautiful countryside!). From Tanah Rata the road leads to Brinchang, and from there you go left, steeply up (about 20 km from Tanah Rata). You'll pass through seemingly endless tea plantations and then through mountain jungles up to the highest point in Malaysia accessible by car. On the top is a TV and radio station - the view in good weather is fantastic! To the west you can see down to the ocean, to the east, the jungle-covered mountains of Malaysia spread out before you.

On the way back stop a bit at *PALLAS TEA ESTATE* (closed Mon) and have a talk with the Indian tea pickers. You can also watch the tea leaves being processed. The factory is about a kilometre from the road. Daily at 11:30, 13:30 and 16:10 h a bus leaves from Tanah Rata to the plantation entrance. On the main road, just beyond the fork, a *FRUIT AND VEGETABLE MARKET* is held every day where produce grown further up the valley is sold. Tourists seem to be willing to pay any price asked here, at least the prices fit this pattern - so bargain hard! On the street, butterflies and other insects are sold in glass containers. You'll help preserve the local wildlife, if you reduce the demand for the Rajah Brookes and other butterflies - so find another souvenir!

Jungle hikes and walks are much more comfortable in this climate than in the humid heat of the lowland forests. You won't miss the battalions of leeches either! (joy!) On longer trips, however, you should still be sure to wear sturdy shoes. For getting started, try a walk along the paved path to *ROBINSON WATERFALL,* only 15 minutes from Tanah Rata. Afterwards, try path 8 to *GUNUNG BEREMBAN.*

In just 1 1/2 hours you can climb the 1855 m high *GUNUNG JASAR* - take path 10 from Tanah Rata. The path is a bit steep and partially overgrown.

Only a kilometre away on a Brinchang side street is *SAM POH TEMPLE,* a beautiful Chinese temple with huge, shiny, gold temple guardians.

Path 2 heading south is quite difficult because it's so steep. Expect a five hour hike from Tanah Rata via the waterfall to *ROBINSON FALLS POWER STATION* and via *HABU POWER STATION* back to the main road. From there you can go by bus or hitchhike to the *BHARAT TEA ESTATE* and then back to Tanah Rata. This tea plantation is situated near the road to Ringlet, about 5 km south of Tanah Rata. *EMAS TEA ESTATE* is another tea plantation a bit further south, 3 km off the main road - closed Fridays and after 16:00 h. Here you can follow the whole process of tea production from picking to packing. You can buy cheap tea to send home - remember customs duties at home!

Tea has been grown in the Cameron Highlands since 1926. The English started the first plantations with tea plants from Assam. The workers were mostly brought from southern India. They were considered to be the best plantation workers because they were more willing than the Chinese to obey the orders of white owners and because they were used to working in a hot tropical climate. Until 1938, when the emigration of unskilled labour to Malaysia was prohibited by the Indian government, hundreds of thousands of immigrants (especially Tamils) came in this way. They form the majority of the plantation population. All over the palm-oil, rubber and tea plantations you can still see the barrack settlements of the Indian workers, complete with tiny Hindu temples.

HOTELS

Reasonably priced is *WONG VILLA**, 113 Main Road, on the road out of Brinchang, tel 941145. Simple rooms with a basin, like losmen in Indonesia - a room holds up to four people. Next to the Hindu temple on the road to the Sam Poh Temple is the *JOLLY VILLA** offering about the same. Find *BALA'S CHALETS** about 1.5 km up from Tanah Rata, small rooms, food is served. Otherwise Tanah Rata is a better place to stay. *HIGHLAND'S LODGE** is right at the end of town.

On the main road are lots of middle priced hotels, usually with a private bath and warm water: *SEAH MENG* ***, no. 39, tel 941618; *HOLLYWOOD* ***, no. 38, tel 941633; *TOWN HOUSE***, no. 41, tel 941666 and others. Not bad is the *RESTHOUSE* ***, Jl.Tepi Sungei to the right off the main street. Those who want to spend more should try the bungalows at the *GARDEN HOTEL*****, tel 941911. Absolutely luxurious is *YE OLDE SMOKE HOUSE* near the golf course with rooms up to M$250.

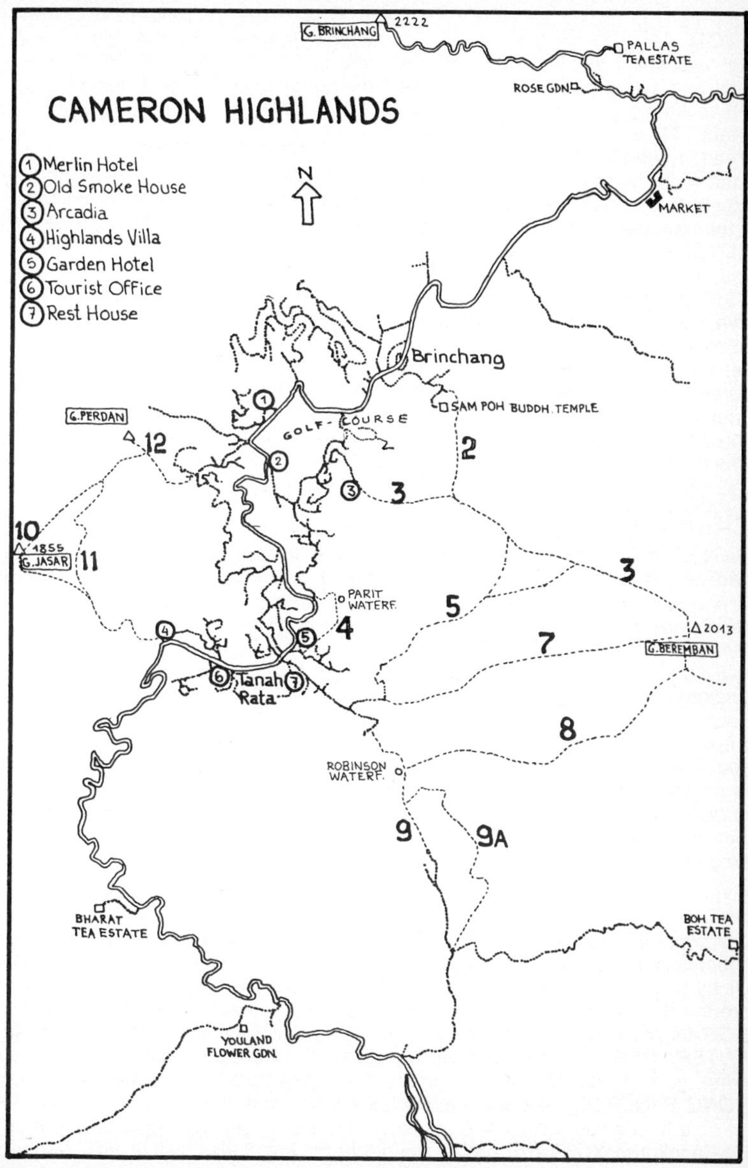
CAMERON HIGHLANDS
1 Merlin Hotel
2 Old Smoke House
3 Arcadia
4 Highlands Villa
5 Garden Hotel
6 Tourist Office
7 Rest House
N
G. BRINCHANG
2222
PALLAS TEA ESTATE
ROSE GDN.
MARKET
Brinchang
SAM POH BUDDH. TEMPLE
GOLF-COURSE
G.PERDAN
12
2
3
3
10
1855
G.JASAR
11
PARIT WATERF.
5
4
2013
7
G.BEREMBAN
Tanah Rata
8
ROBINSON WATERF.
9
9A
BHARAT TEA ESTATE
BOH TEA ESTATE
YOULAND FLOWER GDN.

FOOD

Get a cheap breakfast of local milk teas and sweet pastry at one of the Indian shops on Tanah Rata's main street. They also offer curries and bread. *KUMAR RESTORAN* serves good food. More expensive, but with excellent Chinese and western food is the restaurant in the *HOLLYWOOD HOTEL*. If there are three or four of you, try a steamboat, costs about M$10 per person. Good, but expensive, are the strawberries from the surrounding fields. Find long-forgotten colonial atmosphere with English porcelain and silverware, antique furniture and a plushness (which of course you pay for!) in *YE OLDE SMOKEHOUSE INN*, about 3 km towards Brinchang by the golf course and in *FOSTER'S LAKEHOUSE* on the bridge between the 2 reservoirs.

HOW TO GET THERE

From TAPAH on the big North-South Road, buses leave 7 times a day until 16:00 h for the two hour drive to TANAH RATA (M$3). From KL there's a direct Ekspress Nasional bus at 8:30 for M$8. Taxis cost M$21 per person. From Tapah you have regular connections to IPOH, BUTTERWORTH and to the south. If you come by train, get off at Tapah Road, and then go either by taxi up into the mountains, or first by bus to Tapah and then as explained above.

PULAU PANGKOR

Unlike the east coast, the west coast isn't blessed with countless sandy beaches, islands, and coral reefs. 12 km long and 4 km wide, Pangkor Island is one of the few exceptions, challenging the east coast. All around the main island are smaller isles, easy to reach by fishing boat. The inhabitants live mostly from fishing. Besides Malays, many Chinese and Indians live here making this one of the few places in Malaysia where you can find Malabari (Indian) fishing villages. The island features in an ancient legend: many, many years ago a young warrior from Sumatra fell in eternal love with a princess whose hand he hoped to win. To prove himself in battle, he sailed over the sea. The princess waited many months for his return before she finally decided to go and seek him. And so she landed on Pulau Pangkor, where she learned of his death. When the villagers showed her his grave, she flung herself from a cliff in complete despair. Even today the beach still carries the name of the beautiful princess, Pantai Puteri Dewi.

If you're a group of 10-12 people, it's worthwhile to rent a fishing boat to visit other beaches e.g. on *PULAU PANGKOR LAUT*. The latest establishment on this small island is the PULAU PANGKOR LAUT COUNTRY RESORT. The snorkeling is especially good at *EMERALD BAY* on the west side of the island. Or try to get the regular boat from the beach near the Seaview Hotel. A walk around the Pangkor Island takes about 5 hours - leave early! From *PASIR BOGAK* you'll come upon two nice beaches about 3 km to the north, *PANTAI PUTERI DEWI*. Then go across the island. On the east coast further to the north, go to *GOLDEN SANDS*, where the ferries from Lumut dock. To *KAMPONG PANGKOR*, hike south through the jungle where, with some luck, you'll be able to see some birds and monkeys. Another good walk might be south of Kg.Pangkor to *KOTA BELANDA*, the old Dutch fort. It was built in 1680 to pro-

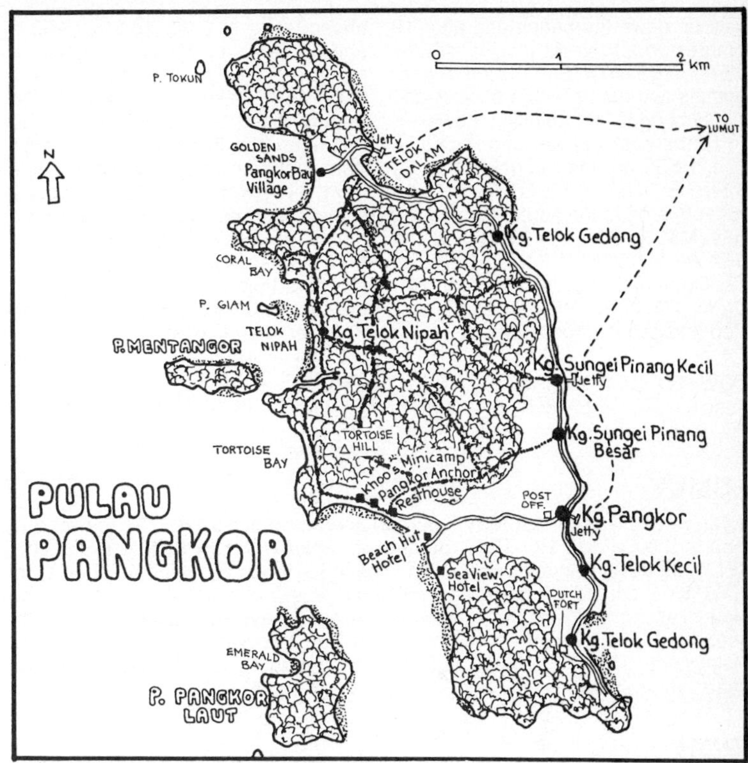

tect Dutch tin traders from attack by Malay pirates. It was heavily fortified and its cannon could cover the whole Strait of Dinding. But by 1690 the Dutch were forced to leave the fort after an attack by the Malays. The Dutch reoccupied the fort from 1745-1748.

HOTELS

Most accommodation is in Pasir Bogak, facing the open sea and can be reached from Kg.Pangkor by taxi for M$4. One of the first cheap places was *KHOO'S MINICAMP*. Mini is by now maxi. The business-minded Mr. Khoo has built an assortment of different sized huts priced about M$10 per night. During school vacations, whole school classes sometimes terrorize his camp; grab your ear muffs! A pleasant alternative is the camp *PANGKOR ANCHOR***, run by Agnes Wong, who offers the same prices despite being much cleaner. Take a walk on down the beach and after 10 minutes you arrive at the *GOVERNMENT RESTHOUSE***. Each bungalow has two rooms with a shower and fan. First rights of habitation, however, go to the cockroaches and bedbugs. Over M$50 are the bungalows at the *BEACH HUTS HOTEL*****, tel 951159, a bit to the south. Rooms are only M$35. Similarly priced is the *SEAVIEW HOTEL*****, tel 951605. On the Golden Sands is the *PAN PACIFIC RESORT*****, peacefully situated and serving good seafood.

HOW TO GET THERE
Buses leave from Ipoh for LUMUT, the ferry port for Pangkor. Direct buses leave at 8:00, 10:30, 13:00 h and 16:00 h for M$4. If they've already left, take a bus for 3.50 M$ to SITIAWAN (takes 45 minutes) and then for M$1 take the 15 minute ride to Lumut. Taxis charge about M$6 from Ipoh. An alternative is the bus from Butterworth for M$8. If you're coming from KL, go to Ipoh first. The ferry to KAMPONG PANGKOR costs M$1 and leaves every half hour. The first boat from Lumut is at 6:45 h and the last at 19:30 h. From Kampong Pangkor the first boat is at 6:45 h and the last at 18:30 h. Other ferries to GOLDEN SANDS BEACH for M$1.20 from Lumut at 8:30, 10:30, 13:30 and 16:15 h.

LUMUT

If you've missed the last ferry, you can spend the night here. On the road to Ipoh is the LUMUT HOTEL**. Somewhat better is the PHIN LIM HOOI HOTEL**, 93 Jl.Titi Panjang, tel 935641. The RESTHOUSE can be reached at tel 935938. A couple of years ago the town was made a major base for the Malaysian navy. From the ferry you can see quays, wet docks, and warehouses. A few kilometres south of town are the beaches used mostly by Malaysians: TELUK RUBIAH, TELUK MURUK and TELUK BATIK. On the last beach you can rent simple bungalows.

IPOH

The profitability of tin can be seen in the town of Ipoh. Sometimes this place is called millionaire city, since many of the one-time tin prospectors are now wealthy mine owners. You can meet them on weekends at the race track. Hardly any other town in West Malaysia has so much greenery - with money you can do everything. The town of Ipoh's original name was Paloh - 'Pool of Stagnant Water'. Fishermen dammed water on the Kinta River. The first wooden huts of the tin miners were built here. Everything else was jungle.

The town's last Ipoh tree, from which the city got its name, is in the biggest park, *TAMAN DR.SEENIVASAGAM.* Today the Ipoh tree (Antiaris toxicaria), once widely distributed, is found only in the jungle areas of Malaysia. At first glance it looks like any of the rubber trees on the plantations. The Orang Asli get a poison from the white latex which they use for their blow pipe darts. Fibre cloth is made from the bark.

The Kinta River separates the old and new parts of town. In the old town, which hasn't changed much in the last 60 years, you'll find the obligatory *CLOCK-*

TOWER and an incredible *RAILWAY STATION* built in 1917. Be sure to take a tour 6 km north of town (near the main road) to *PERAK TONG* - one of the largest Chinese temples in Malaysia. In a 120 m high limestone cliff are different Buddhist and Chinese deities in caves. Some steps lead to the top where you have a good view. More cave temples lie to the south of town *(SAM PO TONG, NAM THIAN TONG).*

HOTELS
Many of the hotels in this town (famous for its nightlife) are red light establishments. Colonial atmosphere (too expensive to stay here!) at *STATION HOTEL**** in the train station, tel 512588. Many hotels are on Chamberlain Road. Relatively expensive are the big *CITY HOTEL*****, no. 79, tel 512911 and the *HOLLYWOOD HOTEL*****, no. 72-76, tel 515322. Cheaper are *CATHAY HOTEL****, no. 88-94, tel 513322 and *EMBASSY HOTEL****, no. 35. In the still cheaper

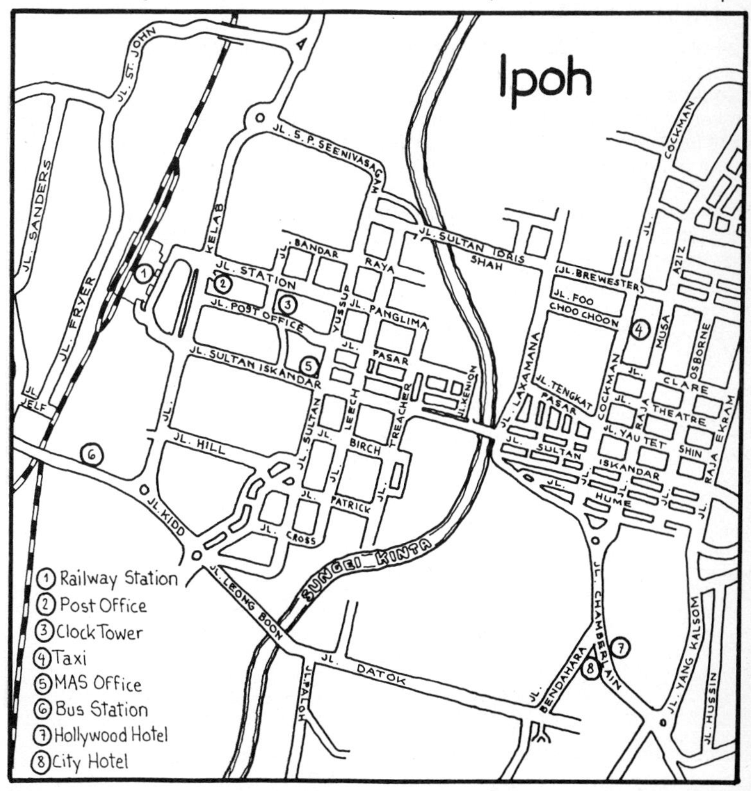

category are the smaller Chinese hotels: *IPOH HOTEL***, 163 Jl.Sultan Idris Shah, *KUO MIN HOTEL***, 48 Jl.Cockman, tel 512087, *CONTINENTAL HOTEL***, 62 Cowan Street or *CHEW NANYANG HOTEL****, 22-24 Jl.Yang Kalsom. Many foodstalls in the evenings on Jl.Osborne.

LEAVING IPOH

Quick flights which are seldom of interest: KOTA BHARU M$113, KL M$55, PENANG M$41. Buses leave from Jl.Tun Abdul Razak: KL M$7.20, MALACCA M$11, (ac: M$13) SINGAPORE M$20 (ac:M$25), JOHORE BHARU M$16 (ac:M$20), KAMPAR M$1.55, LUMUT M$4 (last bus leaves at 16:00 h), KUALA KANGSAR M$2.50, takes 1 1/2 hours stopping in every village.

Overland taxis cost M$13.50 to BUTTERWORTH and M$15 to KL. Six trains leave daily for KL (3rd cl. M$7.10) or BUTTERWORTH (3rd cl. M$6.30). Information in the train station at tel 540481.

KUALA KANGSAR

The old sultan's seat in Perak is situated about half way between Ipoh and Taiping. Check out the famous *UBUDIAH MOSQUE,* one of the most beautiful mosques in Malaysia with golden cupolas and thin minarets. Next to it are the graves of the royal family. You can get to the mosque by walking along the river from the town. After going through the big gate, it's another kilometre. About 500 m further on is the majestic *SULTAN'S PALACE,* the Istana, sitting on a hill. Be sure to check out the wood-carvings on the light coloured house a bit off to the side. About half way between the mosque and the main road is the RESTHOUSE which has a great view of the Perak River. Just behind it is an old Chinese cemetery.

HOTELS
Besides the not so clean *REST-HOUSE***, tel 851699, there are several other hotels in town. Near the bus station and movie theatre on the road out of town is the *DOUBLE LION HOTEL***, 74 Jl.Kangsar, tel 851010, somewhat more expensive is the *TIN HEONG HOTEL*** on Jl.Raja Chulan, tel 851255.

TAIPING

In English Taiping means 'the city of everlasting peace'. One of the most ancient towns in the country was given this name in 1874 when the bloody feud between two Chinese clans, the Hai San and Ghee Hin, found a peaceful settlement here. As just about everywhere else in Perak, the trouble (lasting 25 years) was over tin. Taiping is located in the oldest tin mining area in Malaysia.

As early as 1890, a beautiful park - *LAKE GARDEN* - was set up on the site of an abandoned tin mine. The *PERAK MUSEUM* is the oldest in Malaysia. The exhibits include Malayan weapons, many different types of kris, jewelery, tools of the Orang Asli, and archaeological finds collected since the turn of the century. There are two temples to check out. Near the museum, a bit further out of town, is the *LING NAM TEMPLE* - the oldest Chinese temple in Perak. A hundred years ago many statues, urns and antique weapons were brought here from China - since then they have been gold plated. On the other side of the train tracks, on Station Street, is a *HINDU SHRINE* - the deities seem like a pyramid between the coconut palms.

Ten kilometres inland, at a height of about 1000 m, is the oldest *hill station* in Malaysia, *MAXWELL HILL.* Today called Bukit Larut, it's situated on the slopes of Gunung Hijau (green mountain). From the highest point, The Cottage, you can see along the whole coastline from Pulau Pangkor up to Penang on clear days. Those wanting to relax in a cool climate can find fairly reasonably priced bungalows. The road, built by Japanese prisoners after WWII, is paved but is still so bad that only Landrovers spaced an hour apart, between 8:00 and 18:00 h, are allowed up. The ten kilometres take more than 40 minutes. They leave from the end of the Lake Garden; it costs M$3 up the twisting road to the Cottage.

HOTELS IN TAIPING AND ON MAXWELL HILL
The *RESTHOUSE***** is beautifully located, tel 822044, right on the slope with a view of the Lake Garden. On foot you'll need about 45 minutes, by taxi it's M$2 per person. On Jl.Iskandar are two cheap hotels: the *CHEONG ONN HOTEL**, no. 24, tel 822815 and at no. 32 the *PEACE HOTEL***, tel 823397. Quite reasonable hotels can also be found near the market hall, such as on Jl.Kota, *WAH BEE HOTEL**, no. 62-64, tel 822065, and *TOWN HOTEL***, no. 220, tel 821166. The best hotel in town is *MIRAMAR*****, 30 Jl.Peng Loong, tel 821077. All bookings for Maxwell Hill should be made by phone with the superintendent, tel 886241. There are only bungalows for M$100 or smaller rooms for M$15.

PENANG

The tourist centre of Malaysia is Pulau Pinang - the 'island of the betel palms'. This is where the package tour vacationers relax in air-conditioned, luxury hotels for a few days on the beach at Batu Ferringhi, and where the experienced travellers get together in the numerous Chinese hotels to exchange stories on the way between India and Indonesia. Here you can stretch out on a tropical beach (even if the beaches sag under the weight of mass tourism) or enjoy the bustle of a Chinese city (with some sprinklings of Malay and Indian). See the remains of British colonial atmosphere, magnificently coloured temples, restaurants from all over the world (offering everything from curry to steak), and hundreds of tiny shops with a wide selection of wares. The staid modern banks and insurance companies keep a low profile - the town still has character and atmosphere. Pulau Pinang, as the island is called in Malay, gained its importance when the Portuguese moved into Malacca in 1511. Penang, one of the largest islands in the Strait of Malacca, became a hideaway for many pirates. Originally the island belonged to the Sultan of Kedah, but he restricted his activities to the mainland. The island was covered by jungle and practically uninhabited when Francis Light of the East India Company was looking for a suitable base, east of the Bay of Bengal. At the time company ships , damaged by monsoons had to sail all the way around the southern tip of India to Bombay for repairs. A typical colonial treaty was signed with the Sultan of Kedah: Pulau Pinang would be given over to the English and the British Empire offered military protection in exchange. On August 11, 1786, the Union Jack was raised, and work soon began on a wooden fortress. The sky-threatening cannon on the walls of Fort Cornwallis date from that time. By 1804, Georgetown had become one of the most cosmopolitan cities of South East Asia. The governor at the time, Sir George Leith, wrote: 'There is not, probably, any part of the world, where in so small a space, so many different people are assembled together, or so great a variety of languages spoken.' It's best to check out downtown on foot. You'll find lots of interest on the ever-busy streets. The colourful street markets are still here, fortune tellers read palms under the arcades of the old houses, rickshaw drivers offer their services, the food stalls simmer. Indian and Chinese families are forced by lack of space on to the streets just like the wares from the small shops; there's hardly any room anywhere.

Start your walk at the *CLOCKTOWER*, an area where the colonial character of the city is best preserved. *FORT CORNWALLIS* now stands on the side of Sir Francis Light's old wooden fortress. Prisoners built the stone walls and buildings at the beginning of the 19th century. The huge cannon is revered by women as a fertility symbol. On Leboh Light, corner of Leboh Pantai (Beach Street), many old *ADMINISTRATION BUILDINGS* stand behind Victorian columns. Here you'll find the immigration and registry offices. Across the road near the sea is the *TOWN HALL*, built in traditional colonial style. The inscription on the Town Hall has by now been translated into Malay. At sundown the square in front bustles with activity. Other British-built buildings are on Jl.Farquhar, such as the *SUPREME COURT,* the *MARINER'S CLUB,* and *ST.GEORGE'S CATHEDRAL,* which in 1817 was the first Anglican church in South East Asia. A statue of Francis Light stands in front of the *MUSEUM* next door. It's the place for people interested in the history of the British Empire in South East Asia. The building was the first English language public school east of Suez, established in 1816.

Down Leboh Pitt, you'll find the *GODDESS OF MERCY TEMPLE,* built in 1880, whose carved roof features a fire breathing dragon. The best time to see Chinese temple life is during the big holidays. Life in an Indian temple is very different. Visit *SRI MARIAMMAN TEMPLE* just before Chulia Street. Just a few steps further down the same street is one of the largest mosques in Malaysia, the *KAPITAN KLING MOSQUE.* Work was begun at the beginning of the last century, financed by a merchant from southern India. Turn left just before Leboh Aceh into a small side street. There you'll see one of the most beautiful buildings in South East Asia, the *KHOO KONGSI.* It was built in 1906 and completely renovated in 1955 - just to see the roof with its countless splendidly coloured porcelain figures is worth a visit.

***KONGSIS** are clan houses, built by Chinese families sharing the same name and origin, if they have the money. The Khoos are one of the most prosperous families, as can be seen by looking at the plaques of their ancestors. The deceased have all studied at the greatest universities in the world. Other 'kongsi', by no means so impressive, can be found on Leboh Armenian (Yap Kongsi) and on Jl.Burma (Khaw Kongsi, Lee Kongsi) as well on the corner of Leboh Codrington (the kongsi of Chuah, Sin and Quah).*

Those who enjoy temples can visit other holy places of the city's different religions. Take bus no. 4 from Leboh Victoria to Anson Road. The stop is across from the *PENANG BUDDHIST ASSOCIATION* which you can visit. Inside the old villa you'll find Italian marble and Bohemian chandeliers. One of the world's largest reclining Buddhas can be found in the Thai temple, *WAT CHAIYAMANGALARAM.* Two huge temple guardians keep watch over the 35 m long Buddha. Across from it is the only *BURMESE TEMPLE* on the island. You might combine trips to these temples with a visit to Batu Ferringhi or the Botanical Garden. Take a blue bus from Jl.Maxwell and get off at the Pulau Tikus police station. The temples are on Burmah Lane, near Jl.Kelawai.

HOTELS

Hardly any other Asian city has so many hotels in every price class. According to statistics, there are 62 hotels for budget travellers and 21 for other tourists. Most of the budget hotels are centrally located and a bit set back from the road so that they aren't too noisy. Some even have small gardens. On Leboh Chulia is *SWISS HOTEL*** at no. 431, tel 370133 or the old backpackers' hangout, *TYE ANN HOTEL**,* no. 282, though it's said to have run down a bit. *ENG AUN HOTEL**,* no. 380, tel 612333 is good. About the same is the *NOBLE HO-*

*TEL**, 36 Market Lane, tel 22372, behind the Tye Ann. Another backpacker's pitstop is the *NEW CHINA HOTEL**, 22 Leith Street, tel 218522. Other cheap Chinese hotels are on Love Lane such as *WAN HAI***, no. 35, tel 627876; *TEONG WAH***, no. 23, tel 62057; and the less good *PIN SENG HOTEL****, no. 82, tel 379004.

There are many hotels on Penang Road (Jl.Pinang - don't confuse with Leboh Pinang = Penang Street), though they are pretty noisy, being on a main road: *NAM KOK**, no. 481B, tel 65363, *WHITE HOUSE***, no. 72, tel 60142, etc. Those who want to spend more money can try *CATHAY HOTEL****, 15 Leith Street, tel 26271, with large rooms and quite an atmosphere at affordable prices. Much has changed since the days of Somerset Maugham though the colonial atmosphere remains, with servants in livery and dinner reminiscent of old-time England. The *EASTERN & ORIENTAL HOTEL *****, Farquhar Street, tel 375322. Rooms with a view of the sea cost about M$100. Next to the E&O is the *YOUTH HOSTEL* where you pay M$4.50 for the first night and M$3 thereafter.

FOOD

Penang is probably the biggest food trip in Asia. You can eat Chinese one evening, Indian the next, and Malay, Western, or even Nonya food. From the cheap foodstalls on the street to the luxury restaurants, there's something for every budget. First the Indian for hot curry lovers: Excellent is the *HAMEEDIYAH,* 164A Leboh Campbell. We recommend the mild mutton kurma or the famous curry kapitan. On the corner of Jl. Pinang / Leboh Chulia is the *TAJ MAHAL,* a good and inexpensive establishment. A bit more expensive, though not quite as exclusive as its facade might make you think, is the *DAWOOD,* 63 Queen Street. Everyone has his favourite among the countless Chinese restaurants. Vegetarians should check out *EE HOE CHAI,* 450 Dato Kramat Road. The *HSIANG YANG CHAP* is a good Kedai Kopi, below the Honpin Hotel on Chulia Street. Between Leboh Chulia and Campbell on Leboh Cintra are numerous Chinese restaurants and foodstalls. Good dishes for M$3-13 at *CHUEN HEONG,* Kg.Malabar. A fantastic mixture of Malay and Chinese food has been developed by the Nonyas or the South East Asian Chinese. Be sure to give it a try, even if it isn't cheap, in *DRAGON KING,* 99 Leboh Bishop. Reasonably priced seafood in *ORIENTAL CAFE* across from Wisma Macalister, Macalister Road. The typical Malay dish, Satay, can be found in many restaurants on Penang Road as well as from food stands at the *NIGHT MARKETS.* These are constantly changing their locations. During the day, many foodstalls can be found on Leboh Union by the post office as well as on Leboh Light between Penang Street and King Street. In the evening try the Esplanade, today Jl.Tun Syed Sheikh Barakbah and on the square in front of the Town Hall. A typical Penang speciality is Laksa, a clear noodle soup with a fish base and lots of fresh ingredients. Have them press you a fresh fruit juice to go with it. Those who want to rough it with sailors and Australian RAAF men will find lots of pubs in this town, such as the *HONGKONG BAR,* 371 Leboh Chulia or the *BOSTON PUB,* 477 Penang Road.

TOWN HALL, PENANG

SHOPPING

Penang is no longer the duty free shopping paradise of days gone by. Even so you'll find a huge selection of goods, and it's worthwhile looking around for typically Asian things. Handicrafts and other local products are much more expensive in Penang than where they are made. On the other hand you'll find everything here in one place, and the selection is much larger than anywhere else in Malaysia.

On ***JALAN PINANG*** the Chinese shops are lined up one next to the other, offering everything of possible interest to tourists from antiques to tin products from Selangor. Mixed in you'll find Indian tailors ready to take your measurements for a suit of Malay batik or Chinese silk. There are western style department stores as well as market halls for local foodstuffs (Chowrasta Food Market), and almost next door, on the corner of Jl. Maxwell, is a Chinese emporium offering lots of goods from China. Next to it, street dealers offer cheap cassette recordings (make them play it first) and colourful, printed T-shirts. This is one place where you really have to bargain.

At the end of Penang Road is a modern shopping centre á la Singapore. In Kompleks Tun Abdul Razak, or ***KOMTAR*** for short, there are modern boutiques, electronic and western goods shops, as well as many services. Another department store where you'll find a western food department is ***GAMA*** at the roundabout, 1 Jl.Dato Kramat.

The scene in the ***INDIAN QUARTER*** is completely different, Here you'll find fewer things offered, but they're no less interesting. You'll find crazy shops on Leboh Gereja, Leboh Pinang and Leboh Bishop. Also have a look at Leboh Light, Leboh Kimberley and Rope Walk.

Tourists can, under certain conditions, make duty free purchases. You must, however, leave Malaysia within two weeks, and only open the sealed packages outside the country. There are about 40 shops in Penang calling themselves ***DUTY-FREE SHOPS,*** mostly offering electronic goods in addition to liquors and cigarettes.

Photographers can buy rolls of colour slide ***FILM*** for about M$9.50 plus M$7 for developing.

Apart from the ***BOOKSHOP*** in the E&O, the English literature scene is pretty dreary. However, there are a bunch of small bookshops on Leboh Chulia near the Swiss Hotel and on Jl.Macalister which mostly deal in second hand books.

GENERAL INFORMATION

TOURIST INFORMATION - at the Tourist Office, 10 Jl.Tun Syed Sheikh Barakbah, tel 616663. There are lots of shiny brochures as well as the monthly publication *Penang Tourist Tips* and *Penang for the Visitor.* For people on a budget, they offer little useful info. Open Mon to Thurs 8:30-12:45 h, and 14:00-16:30 h; Fri 8:30-12:30 h, and 14:45-16:30 h; Sat 8:30-13:00 h. There's another information centre at the airport.

IMMIGRATION - not as busy as in KL, nice people. Office on Leboh Pantai, corner of Union Street, tel 365122.

POST OFFICE - General Post Office on Leboh Downing, tel 366461, open Mon to Sat from 8:00 to 18:00 h. Pickpockets in the city have a nice trait: if your valuables have been stolen, there's a good chance that your passport will end up in one of the city mail boxes. Check in the GPO!

TELEPHONE - within Malaysia see KL. Overseas calls from the Telegraph Office (Pejabat Taligerap), tel 23492, on Leboh Downing next to the GPO and open round the clock.

BANKS - most banks are in the old administrative quarter around the GPO. Don't just compare the exchange rate: check the charges. Some banks charge up to M$6 per cheque! Open Mon to Fri 10:00-15:00 h, Sat 9:30-11:30 h. Often you'll get a better rate at the money changers.

MONEY CHANGER - usually Indian, they're found mostly in the banking quarter and on Leboh Pitt. Unlike the banks, they're almost always open, and they change cash. You can bargain for the exchange rate, especially for large notes and amounts. Be sure to check the rates in advance in the newspaper and at the banks. The purchase of so-called weak currencies, mainly the Indian Rupee or Burmese Kyat might be of interest. Both countries have import restrictions on their own currencies so watch out!

AMERICAN EXPRESS - office at 8 Green Hall, Unit 2, off Leboh Light behind the Town Hall.

DRUGS - if you're offered hard or soft drugs on the street, never let yourself be tempted here. Many a rickshaw driver seems to have everything from grass to skag for sale, even in kilo quantities if you want - they can be informants! Since the drug laws in Malaysia were hardened, the death penalty has become quite frequent. So stay away from the stuff here - jail is always a bad trip!

FIRST AID - for police, ambulance or fire department call 999. In case of emergency, you'll be brought to the General Hospital on Western Road (near the polo grounds). Otherwise there are a number of private clinics such as: Medical Centre, 1 Jl.Pangkor, tel 20731 - Adventist Hospital, 465 Jl.Burmah, tel 24134 or Mt. Miramar Hospital, Jl.Bulan, tel 366201.

CONSULATES - most important is the Thai consulate, which you have to visit for a visa. The Thais want 3 passport pictures and M$15. *ROYAL THAI CONSULATE,* 1 Ayer Rajah Road, tel 63377 (bus 7), open Mon - Fri from 9:00-12:00 h and from 14:00-16:00 h. *INDONESIAN CONSULATE,* 467 Jl.Burmah, tel 25162/3 (blue bus), open Mon-Fri from 9:00-12:00 and from 14:00-15:00 h.

GETTING AROUND

Most of the time you'll be in the city centre where you can get everywhere on foot. Some places do lie a bit out of the way so you'll need to use public transportation.

TRISHAWS - the bicycle rickshaws are the perfect way to get around downtown - you sit in front of the driver and have a perfect view of the road including all its dangers. Bargain for the price in advance because the first one offered is always too high! Foreigners seem to do worst here. A ride should cost about M$ 1.50 per kilometre.

TAXIS - though most vehicles have a meter installed, it's almost always said to be broken. The first mile costs 70 c, each additional half mile is 30 c. Waiting is set at 20 c per 8 minutes. If you rent a taxi, the rate is M$4 for the first half hour and M$1 for each additional 15 minutes. For a trip to the airport expect to pay about M$10-12.

BUSES - five different bus companies serve the city and island. The MPPP buses all leave from Leboh Victoria except buses 8, 12, and 13. Take bus 7 to the Botanical Garden, bus 8 to Penang Hill, and bus 11 to the south. An exact listing of the bus routes can be found in *Penang for the Visitor*. Prices vary according to distance from 30 c and 60 c. Green, blue and yellow buses leave from Jl. Maxwell. You can catch the blue to Batu Ferringhi and Telok Bahang. The yellow goes south to the airport, Snake Temple, etc.

FERRIES - although the impressive bridge to the mainland is complete, ferries scurry between Penang and Butterworth round the clock. During the day they come and go every 7 - 10 minutes, at night between 24:00 and 7:00 h they leave less frequently. The ferry from Penang to Butterworth is free. Going back you pay 50 c, cars cost M$4-6 according to size. The dock is at Pengkalan Weld. Long distance buses and trains leave right from the dock in Butterworth.

LEAVING PENANG

BY AIR - INTERNATIONAL

Bayan Lepas Airport is about 18 km south of town. Yellow buses leave from Jl.Maxwell for 85 c; a coupon-taxi costs M$13.50. The airport tax is M$15 for international flights, M$5 to Singapore and Brunei, and M$3 for domestic flights. SAMPLE PRICES for flights to neighbouring countries in M$:

THAILAND: (MAS or Thai Airways) HAT YAI 83.-, PHUKET 112.-, BANGKOK 220.-M$

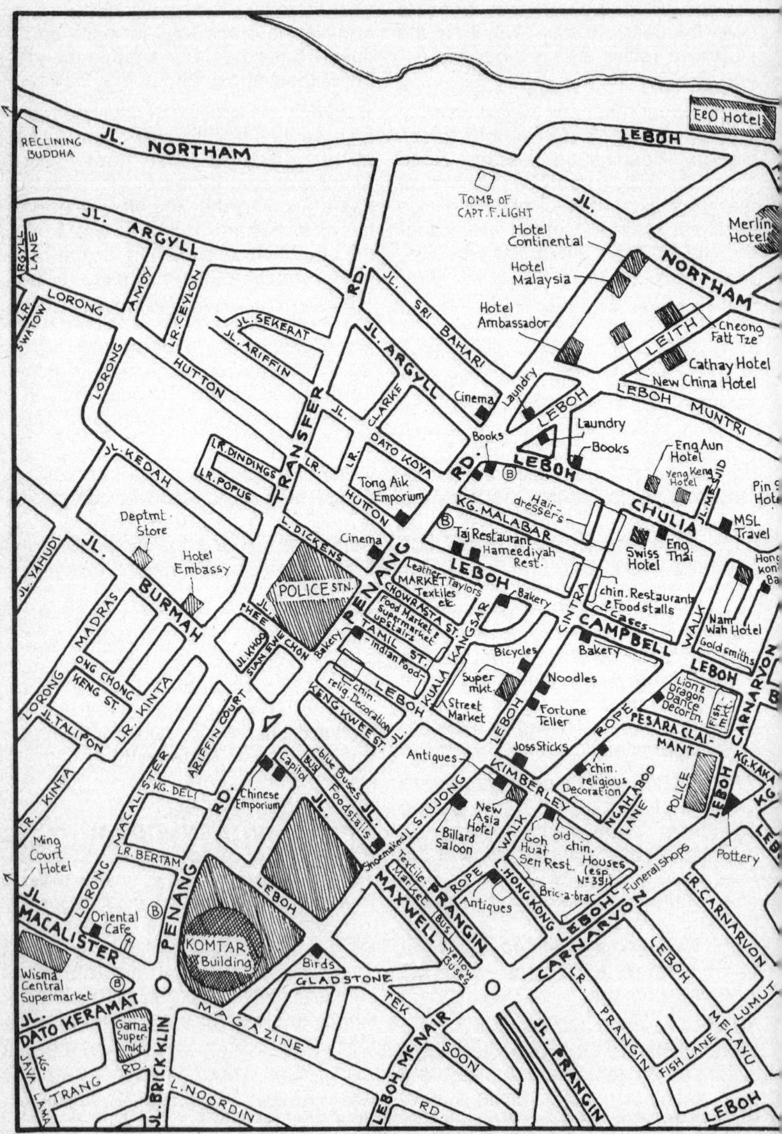

JL. NORTHAM
RECLINING BUDDHA
E&O Hotel
LEBOH
TOMB OF CAPT. F. LIGHT
Hotel Continental
Hotel Malaysia
Hotel Ambassador
Merlin Hotel
NORTHAM
LEITH
Cheong Fatt Tze
Cathay Hotel
New China Hotel
LEBOH MUNTRI
JL. ARGYLL
ARGYLL LANE
LR. SWATOW
LORONG
AMOY
LR. CEYLON
JL. SEKERAT
JL. ARIFFIN
RD.
JL. SRI BAHARI
JL. ARGYLL
Cinema
Laundry
LEBOH
Laundry
Books
Books
LEBOH
HUTTON
LORONG
TRANSFER
JL. CLARKE
LR.
DATO KOYA
LR. DINDINGS
LR. POPUS
Tong Aik Emporium
HUTTON
RD.
Hair-dressers
KG. MALABAR
Eng Aun Hotel
Yeng Keng Hotel
JL. MESJID
CHULIA
MSL Travel
JL. KEDAH
Deptmt. Store
Hotel Embassy
JL. BURMAH
L. DICKENS
Cinema
POLICE STN.
Taj Restaurant
Hameediyah Rest.
LEBOH
Leather
MARKET Taylors
Textiles etc.
CHOWRASTA ST.
Food Market & Supermarket upstairs
TAMIL ST.
Indian Food
PENANG
Swiss Hotel
Eng Thai
chin. Restaurants & Food stalls
Cases
CINTRA
CAMPBELL
Bakery
WALK
Nam Wah Hotel
Goldsmiths
LEBOH
CARNARVON
JL. YAHUDI
MADRAS
ONG CHONG
KENG ST.
LR. KINTA
LORONG
JL. TALIPON
JL. PHEE CHOON
JL. KHOO
SIAN EWE
Bakery
chin. relig. Decoration
LEBOH
KENG KWEE ST.
KUALA KANGSAR
Bakery
Bicycles
Super mkt.
Street Market
LEBOH
Noodles
Fortune Teller
Lion & Dragon Dance Decor'n.
Fish mkt.
PESARA CLAI-
MANT
ROPE
Joss Sticks
chin. religious Decoration
ARIFFIN COURT
JL.
Antiques
KIMBERLEY
POLICE
LEBOH
KG. KAKA
LR. KINTA
MACALISTER
KG. DELI
Capitol
BUS
blue Buses
Foodstalls
Chinese Emporium
RD.
JL.
JL. S. UJONG
New Asia Hotel
Billard Saloon
WALK
NGAH ABOD LANE
Pottery
Ming Court Hotel
LR. BERTAM
LORONG
PENANG
Shoemaker
Textile Market
MAXWELL
PRANGIN
BUS
ROPE
Goh Huat Seng Rest.
old chin. Houses (esp. No 391)
L. HONG KONG
Bric-a-brac
Funeral Shops
Antiques
LEBOH
CARNARVON
LR. CARNARVON
JL. MACALISTER
Oriental Cafe
LEBOH
KOMTAR Building
Birds
Yellow Buses
Wisma Central Supermarket
GLADSTONE
TEK
SOON
JL. PRANGIN
LR. PRANGIN
LEBOH
FISH LANE
MELAYU
LUMUT
JL. DATO KERAMAT
Gama Super-mkt.
KG. JAVA LAMA
TRANG RD.
JL. BRICK KLIN
MAGAZINE
L. NOORDIN
LEBOH McNAIR
RD.
LEBOH

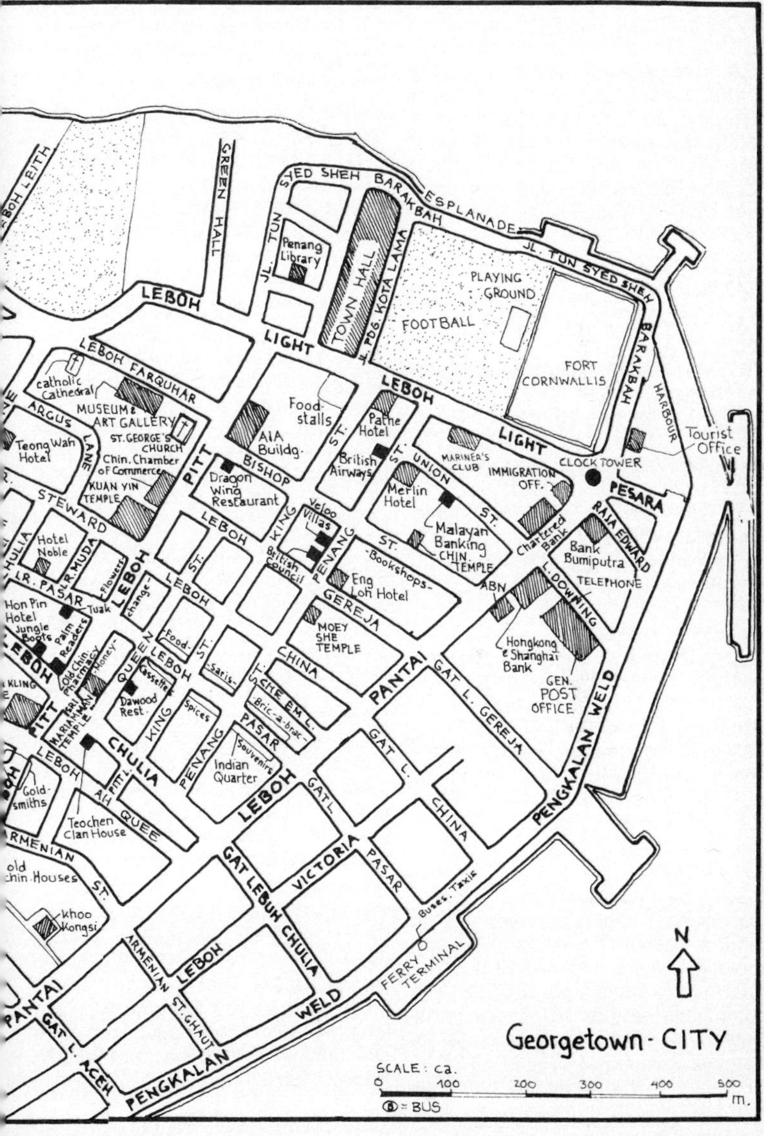

Georgetown - CITY
LEBOH LEITH
GREEN HALL
JL. TUN SYED SHEH BARAKBAH
ESPLANADE
Penang Library
TOWN HALL
L. PDG. KOTA LAMA
PLAYING GROUND
FOOTBALL
JL. TUN SYED SHEH BARAKBAH
FORT CORNWALLIS
HARBOUR
Tourist Office
LEBOH LIGHT
LEBOH FARQUHAR
catholic Cathedral
MUSEUM & ART GALLERY
ST. GEORGE'S CHURCH
Chin. Chamber of Commerce
KUAN YIN TEMPLE
ARGUS LANE
Teong Wah Hotel
STEWARD
Food stalls
AIA Buildg.
Pathe Hotel
British Airways
PITT
BISHOP
Dragon Wing Restaurant
MARINER'S CLUB
IMMIGRATION OFF.
CLOCK TOWER
PESARA
RAJA EDWARD
UNION ST.
Merlin Hotel
Malayan Banking
CHIN. TEMPLE
Chartered Bank
Bank Bumiputra
TELEPHONE
L. DOWNING
ABN
Hongkong & Shanghai Bank
GEN. POST OFFICE
Veloo Villas
British Council
KING
PENANG
ST.
-Bookshops-
Eng Loh Hotel
GEREJA
MOEY SHE TEMPLE
CHINA
PANTAI
GAT L. GEREJA
Hotel Noble
L.R. MUDA
LR. PASAR
Hon Pin Hotel
Jungle Boots
Palm Readers
Tuak
Flowers
change
LEBOH
Food
Saris
Old Chin. Pharmacy
Honey
QUEEN
Cassette
Dawood Rest.
SRI MARIAMMAN TEMPLE
KLING
PITT
CHULIA
Spices
LEBOH CHE EM L.
Bric-a-brac
PASAR
Souvenirs
Indian Quarter
LEBOH
GAT L.
GAT L. CHINA
Gold-smiths
PITT L.
AH QUEE
Teochen Clan House
ARMENIAN ST.
old Chin. Houses
khoo Kongsi
GAT LEBUH CHULIA
VICTORIA
PASAR
Buses, Taxis
FERRY TERMINAL
PENGKALAN WELD
ARMENIAN
LEBOH
ST. GHAUT
PANTAI
GAT L. ACEH
PENGKALAN
WELD
N
SCALE: ca.
0 100 200 300 400 500 m.
Ⓑ = BUS

INDONESIA: (MAS) MEDAN tickets for the half-hour long flight cost about M$100. Flights from Penang to Europe and Australia are relatively cheap. Check in the cheap travel agencies; be sure to ask about student discounts and compare prices! If you have an International Student Identity Card (ISIC), you can save even more at MSL-Travel, Macalister Arcade, Macalister Road.

Here's a list of the most important airline offices:

MAS, Komtar Bldg., Jl.Pinang, tel 620011.
CATHAY PACIFIC, AIA Building, 88 Leboh Bishop, tel 620411.
GARUDA, Wisma Chocolate Products, Aboo Sitee Lane, tel 365257.
THAI AIRWAYS INTER, Wisma Central, Macalister Rd., tel 64848/9.
THAI AIRWAYS CO.LTD., 9 Pengkalan Weld, tel 626622.
SIA, Wisma Penang Garden, 42 Jl. Sultan Achmad Shah, tel 363201.

BY AIR - DOMESTIC

Only of interest to East Malaysia and for those in a real hurry: IPOH 41.-, KOTA BHARU 72.-, KL 86.- (61.-), SINGAPORE 150.-, KUALA TRENGGANU 80.- (3 times a week), LANGKAWI 65.-M$. All flights with MAS; MACAIR flies to LANGKAWI 65.-, ALOR SETAR 39.-, and KL 74.-M$.

BY TRAIN

Trains leave from Butterworth Railway Station. You can get tickets in Penang at the ferry terminal (Railway Booking Station - tel 610290) or at Butterworth Station, tel 347962. Six trains leave daily for KL. To the north there's an international express to Bangkok that leaves daily at 13:35 h. Next morning at 8:00 h you'll arrive. In addition there's a regular train at 6:45 h to Padang Besar (arrival 10:40 h).

Sample one-way prices in M$, second class (third class):

TAIPING 5.30 (3.30), IPOH 10.20 (6.30), KL 21.40 (13.20), JOHORE BHARU 41.60 (25.60), SINGAPORE 43.30 (26.60), KUALA LIPIS 43.30 (26.60), HAT YAI 11.20, BANGKOK 38.70 (83.30 1st cl.). Ekspres Rakyat / Ekspres Sinaran (dept.7:45 h and 14:15 h) cost to KL 17.- / 28.- ac.

BY BUS / OVERLAND TAXI

They all leave from Butterworth bus station where the ferry docks. You can get your tickets for KL or Singapore in advance at a travel agency or a hotel in Penang. The local buses leave quite often making advance bookings unnecessary. SAMPLE PRICES in M$ for buses and (overland taxis):

KL 12.70, ac 14.70 (30.-), SINGAPORE 30.-, JOHORE BHARU 29.- (60.-), ALOR STAR 3.25 (7.80), TAIPING 3.50 (7.25), IPOH 5.50 (13.50), MALACCA 17.50, ac 21.40, KUALA KANGSAR 4.- (9.40), KUALA PERLIS 6.- (12.-), LUMUT 8.- (15.25), PADANG BESAR (14.50), KOTA BHARU (daily 9:30 and 10:00 h with MARA) 18.- (36.-). Several times a week there are direct buses via HAT YAI (20.-) to KO SAMUI (34.-) and PHUKET (36.-). Get your ticket in one of the backpacker hotels.

BY SHIP

The GADIS LANGKASUKA leaves on Fri at 23:00 h, Swettenham Pier in Georgetown for PULAU LANGKAWI. Prices: M$35 per person, M$10 motorbike, M$100 for a car up to a length of 5 m. Every Mon and Wed she leaves at 20:00 h for MEDAN. Prices: M$55.

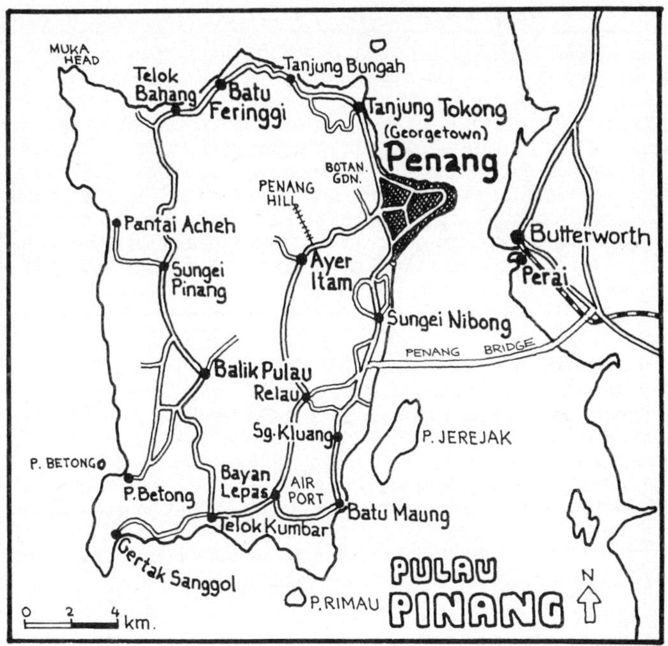

DAY TRIPS AROUND GEORGETOWN

PENANG HILL / KEK LOK SI TEMPLE / MOSQUE

Take MPPP bus 1 for 55 c to the end station AYER ITAM. On the way at the corner of Jl.Ayer Itam and Green Lane you pass the *MOSQUE* of the State of Penang, newly-constructed in a modern style. You have a good view from the top of its 57 m high minaret. From Ayer Itam, take bus 8 (20 c) to the funicular railway station (Lower Station). Every half hour the car leaves on the 24 min. trip almost 710 m up. A return ticket costs M$3. From *PENANG HILL* you have a beautiful view of Georgetown, the island of Penang and in good weather even the mountains of Kedah and Pahang. Twice a week the funicular railway runs late into the night. It's worth it to stay and check out the night-time panorama. On top you'll find a restaurant and hotel. It is 6°C cooler than in the city - the wonderfully coloured vegetation reflects this. Behind the post office a well-marked path starts down to the Botanical Garden - takes about 1 hour.

From the Lower Station, you can go on foot to *KEK LOK SI TEMPLE.* The pagoda of the ten thousand Buddhas dominates the village of Ayer Itam. Most of these Buddhas, however, are only pictures on the wall tiles. A donation is often expected at the temple.

The temple complex is one of the most important Buddhist monasteries in Malaysia. The abbot of the Goddess of Mercy Temple on Leboh Pitt came from China in 1885; the Ayer Itam landscape reminded him of his homeland. He began collecting money from rich Chinese merchants and the huge terraced temple was built. On the way up you pass a turtle pond. Hundreds of turtles stick out their long necks and wait for 'kangkong' - a green vegetable, sold by dealers nearby. For the Chinese, the turtle is a symbol of long life. The pagoda is built in three different styles: the lower follows a Chinese design, the middle section is Thai-Buddhist, and the upper level's spiral shape is Burmese. In the upper section, which is closed to visitors, there is real treasure including a Buddha relic, a statue made of pure gold, diamonds and silver coins.

BOTANICAL GARDEN / NATTUKOTTAI CHETTIAR TEMPLE

Take bus 7, leaves every 30 minutes from Leboh Victoria. On the way there you pass through the colonial villa quarter. The *BOTANICAL GARDEN* is a favourite excursion and the crowds at weekeends reflect this. It is situated in a valley surrounded by jungle-covered hills. Right at the entrance, a huge pack of monkeys waits for you to buy a packet of peanuts which they'll quickly rid you of. Have a nice walk through the small, natural jungle section! In addition, there is a tiny zoo with sun bears, and deer. Near Waterfall Road is the *NATTUKOTTAI CHETTIAR TEMPLE,* one of the most famous Hindu temples on the island. The Thaipusam festival in February is celebrated here.

ROUND TRIP OF THE ISLAND

For just M$5 you can cover the whole 74 km route around Pulau Pinang. First take a blue bus to BATU FERRINGHI and then switch to another blue bus to TELOK BAHANG. From here there are relatively few buses to BALIK PULAU. If none is running, you could try hitchhiking. From here, there are also yellow buses no. 65C and 66 back to Georgetown. Unless you make a long stop, the round trip should take about 4 - 5 hours.

If there's a group of you, you could rent a car and split the expenses. Ask about and compare the single day rates and special tariffs. Here is a list of companies:

AVIS, E&O Hotel, Leboh Farquhar, tel 361685.
HERTZ, 38/7 Leboh Farquar, tel 375914.
ISLAND TAXI & TOUR AGENCY, 40 Leboh Ah Quee, tel 372481.
SINTAT, Airport, tel 830958.
NATIONAL, 24 Jl.Sultan Achmad Shah, tel 374152.

Here's the trip around Pulau Pinang again, this time clockwise, with some of the sights along the way.

Start on the yellow bus 66, 78 or 65C to the *SNAKE TEMPLE,* easily recognized by the souvenir stands. The snake temple was built in 1850. Snakes were said to be the disciples of the god Chor Soo Kong, to whom the temple is dedicated. Very poisonous Wagler pit vipers, dazed by the incense, laze around sleepily in the temple - don't touch! Just for the tourists, a few of the snakes have had their fangs pulled and are placed out for you to photograph.

At the BAYAN LEPAS AIRPORT a road cuts off left to the fishing village of BATU MAUNG where you can enjoy excellent seafood. Otherwise there's a footprint of the famous Chinese admiral Cheng Ho who is said to have landed here and to whom a small shrine is dedicated. The yellow buses serve this village as well.

In TELOK KUMBAR, take the fork road to GERTAK SANGGOL, bus 78 and 80. There are beaches here; they are packed on weekends and dirty, though. Back to Telok Kumbar - the road winds up into the mountains where there's terrific landscape and wonderful views. On the slopes, cloves and nutmeg are planted. Across the way are rubber plantations.

BALIK PULAU is the stop for the yellow bus. Only four or five times a day, the last at 16:00 h, bus 76 goes up to Telok Bahang. Another sidestreet goes down to PANTAI ACHEH (bus 75), a small fishing village. A few kilometres beyond the fork, you can bathe under the *TITI KRAWAN WATERFALL* - but don't expect anything overwhelming!

TELOK BAHANG is a village where mainly Malabar fishermen live. Just beyond the crossroads to Balik Pulau on the right is a Malay kampong where batik is made and sold at inflated prices to tourists. Across the way is an orchid nursery (admission). You can walk along the beach to MUKAH HEAD, the northwestern tip of the island. From Telok Bahang go on with the blue bus. There are places to stay here, but we don't recommend Telok Bahang as it permanently stinks of fish, has a dirty beach, and doesn't have much to offer. Nearby is a forest reserve of 100 ha with quite an interesting museum *(MUZIUM PERHUTANAN)*. A few trails lead to several pools.

BATU FERRINGHI, meaning *Portuguese rock,* is the tourist centre of Penang today. High-rise hotels hide the soil and can be seen in every travel brochure. Reflected in the prices! At least the beach is several kilometres long. Between Holiday Inn and Casuarina Hotel you find reasonably priced foodstalls and restaurants. The last village before Georgetown is TANJONG BUNGAH. We can't recommend the beach, but there are a few cheap hotels and good seafood restaurants.

BETWEEN PENANG AND PADANG BESAR

The two northernmost states in Malaysia, Kedah and Perlis, are usually just pitstops for travellers on the road from Haad Yai to Penang and back again. Together these states are the rice basket of the country. Archaeological finds made here confirm the existence of a Buddhist-Indian empire between the 2nd and 10th centuries. Langkasuka stretched right across the Malay Peninsula. Within its sphere of influence lay one of the earliest trade routes between the Bay of Bengal and the Gulf of Thailand.

BUTTERWORTH

A really uninteresting town with lots of industry and a big port. It contains a Royal Australian Airforce base, which under the terms of the Five Powers Defence Pact (Singapore, Malaysia, Australia, New Zealand, UK) is home to two squadrons of Mirage fighters. For this reason you meet a lot of Australians, especially in the bars and pubs of Georgetown.

GUNUNG JERAI

A few miles north of Sungei Patani, the 1330 m high Gunung Jerai towers over the flatlands. On the slopes of this sandstone mountain some archeological finds have been made. The best known site is Candi Bukit Batu Pahat, about 2 1/2 km north of KG.MERBOK (bus M$1.30 from Sungei Patani). There's a new museum somewhat below the candi. You'll get to the peak of the Jerai from the northeast via a road (11 km) a few km north of GURUN which lies on the main road Sungei Patani - Alor Setar.

KEROH

36 km to the north, in SUNGEI PATANI, an important road branches off to Yala and Patani in Thailand. KEROH is the checkpoint. The whole border region to Thailand is an area of MCP (Malayan Communist Party) guerilla activity. Fighting on the Thai side of the border are Muslim separatists as well as units of the Communist Party of Thailand. In times of need they can always slip across the border into the other country. Under a treaty signed in 1975, the security forces of both countries are permitted to cross the border. You must check the situation regarding travel into the interior for yourself - it changes all the time. The road from YALA to BETONG in Thailand and on to Keroh is open during the day and used by taxis. You'll probably have to spend the night in Keroh if you want to take this unusual route into Thailand. Stay the night at KONG AUN HOTEL* or CHEUNG FONG* or at one of the other cheap hotels. Taxi to the border M$1.50, bus 80 c.

GERIK

Another road, also within the MCP activity range, runs from Keroh on down to the big North-South Road just before Kuala Kangsar. Gerik, about 50 km south of Keroh, is the most important town on the route. In the area are several Orang Asli villages which you may not visit on your own. The main headquarters of the MCP remnants is said to be somewhere around Gerik. North of town the East-West Highway branches off to Kota Bharu, a route which was finally finished after many years of construction. Altogether 10 years were spent building this road. Construction equipment was frequently blown up, and guerilla attacks on work teams weren't uncommon. The costs ran up to 360 million M$. Its importance for the infrastructure of the country is enormous. Before completion, in order to get from Penang to Kota Bharu one had to make a tremendous detour via KL and Kuantan - altogether more than 1000 km.

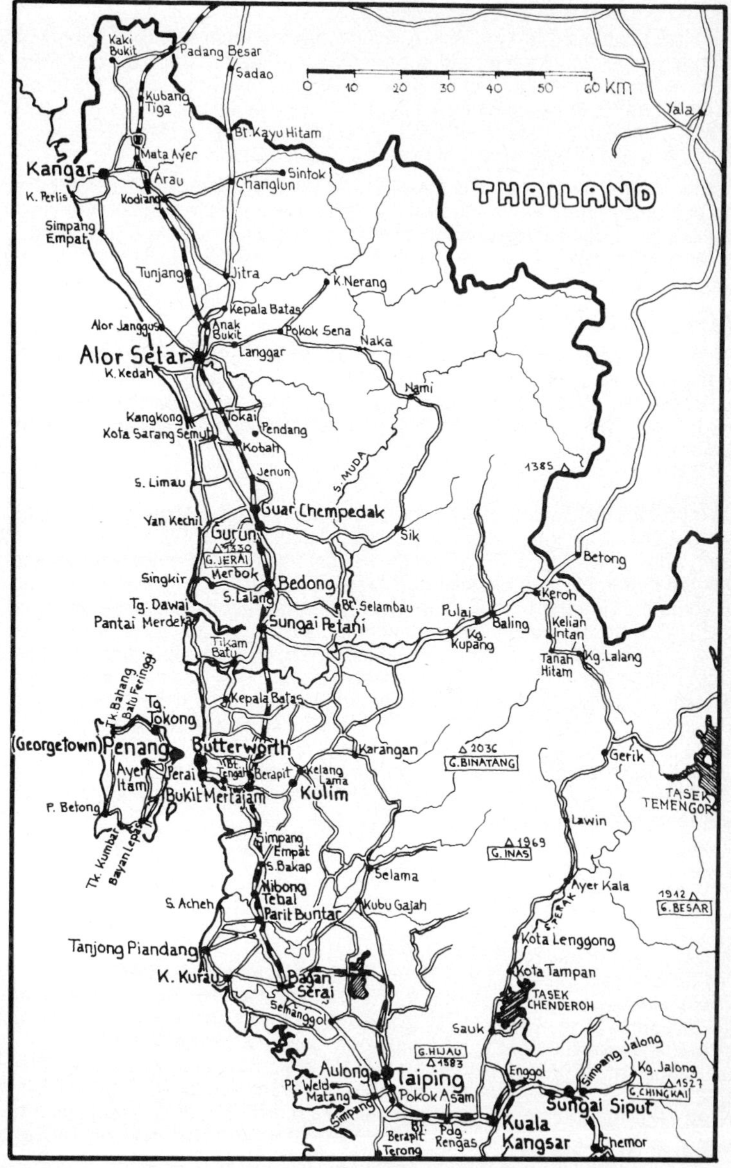

THAILAND
0 10 20 30 40 50 60 KM
Kaki Bukit
Padang Besar
Sadao
Kubang Tiga
Bt. Kayu Hitam
Yala
Mata Ayer
Kangar
Arau
Sintok
Changlun
K. Perlis
Kodiang
Simpang Empat
Tunjang
Jitra
K. Nerang
Kepala Batas
Alor Janggus
Anak Bukit
Pokok Sena
Naka
Alor Setar
Langgar
K. Kedah
Nami
Kangkong
Tokai
Pendang
Kota Sarang Semut
Kobah
S. MUDA
1385
Jenun
S. Limau
Guar Chempedak
Yan Kechil
Gurun
Sik
1330
G. JERAI
Betong
Merbok
Singkir
Bedong
S. Lalang
Keroh
Tg. Dawai
Bt. Selambau
Pulai
Baling
Kelian Intan
Pantai Merdeka
Sungai Petani
Kg. Kupang
Tikam Batu
Tanah Hitam
Kg. Lalang
Tk. Bahang
Batu Feringgi
Tg. Tokong
Kepala Batas
(Georgetown) Penang
Butterworth
Karangan
2036
G. BINATANG
Gerik
Ayer Itam
Perai
Bt. Tengah
Berapit
Kelang Lama
Kulim
TASEK TEMENGOR
P. Betong
Bukit Mertajam
Tk. Kumbar
Bayan Lepas
Lawin
Simpang Empat
1969
G. INAS
S. Bakap
Selama
Nibong Tebal
Ayer Kala
S. Acheh
Kubu Gajah
1912
G. BESAR
Parit Buntar
S. PERAK
Kota Lenggong
Tanjong Piandang
K. Kurau
Kota Tampan
Bagan Serai
TASEK CHENDEROH
Semanggol
Sauk
G. HIJAU
1583
Simpang Jalong
Kg. Jalong
1527
G. CHINGKAI
Aulong
Taiping
Enggol
Pt. Weld
Matang
Pokok Asam
Sungai Siput
Simpang
Kuala Kangsar
Bt. Berapit
Pdg. Rengas
Terong
Chemor

Now it has been cut down to 365 km. Even today the route isn't completely free of danger, which is why the road is closed after 16:00 h. 10 km beyond Gerik you have to pass through a checkpoint. A taxi to Kota Bharu costs M$16 per person. The bus to KL costs M$13.60. For those wanting to spend the night, ROME**, 1 Jl.Tan Saban, tel 885242 is the most expensive place. Everything else is*, such as DRAGON and others on Jl.Takong Datoh.

Heading south, there's a road through the jungle to TASEK CHENDEROH (one bus daily). The lake is filled by the Perak River. In the background you'll see the high, jungle covered mountains. Once in a while there's a fishing boat - fantastic landscape.

ALOR SETAR

This sultan's seat and capital of Kedah has developed in the last few years into the business and trading centre of northwest Malaysia. Like the rest of the west coast, the ethnic Chinese can be seen at a glance to form the majority of the city's population. Even so, you'll see more Malays on the streets here than in other towns.

The important buildings surround the main square. The *ZAHIR MOSQUE* is, next to Kuala Kangsar, probably the most beautiful oriental mosque in the country. The *BALAI BESAR,* meaning 'the great hall', is the place where even today the sultan holds audiences on special occasions. The *BALAI NOBAT* is 400 years old and the home of the royal orchestra. Its instruments consist of drums, kettle drums, gongs and a trumpet. Be sure to check out the small *MUSEUM* on the main road to the north (2 1/2 km out of town, closed on Fri afternoons) built in the same style as the Balai Besar. The exhibits include a large collection of archaeological finds from around Kedah. If you have the time, you might make an excursion to KUALA KEDAH. Buses and taxis leave regularly. The town at the mouth of the Kedah River was already an important port for the trade with India a thousand years ago. The ruins of an old fort, built between 1771 and 1780, can be seen. Kuala Kedah is well known for its many seafood restaurants, which are reasonably priced.

HOTELS

On the side streets between the taxi stand and the bus station are many cheap Chinese hotels: *STATION HOTEL***, Jl.Langgar, tel 723855 or *LIM KUNG**, 36A Jl.Langgar, or *KUAN SIANG*(*),* no. 73, tel 733563. On Jl. Kancut there are two more expensive establishments: *FEDERAL HOTEL****,* no. 429 and the *SAMILA HOTEL*****,* no. 27, tel 722344. You can eat cheaply in the Indian shops on Jl. Langgar and at the foodstalls behind the bus station.

LEAVING ALOR SETAR

From the Central Bus station you have connections in all directions: bus to PENANG for 3.25(ac 7.80) - 1 1/2 hrs., KL 19.50 (ac 20.-), SINGAPORE 34.-(ac 40.-), KUALA PERLIS 2.20, IPOH 10.-M$. The taxis are faster and more comfortable. Costs:

PENANG 7.80, KL 32.-, KUALA PERLIS 3.50, KOTA BHARU via Gerik 26.- M$. The train station is on Jl.Setesen, corner of Jl.Langgar, tel 731798. The express train from Bangkok to Butterworth stops here as well. In addition, there are two daily trains to Padang Besar. Also stopping in Padang Besar, the international train leaves at 14:53 h (fare to Padang Besar: 2nd/3rd cl. - M$5.10 or 3.20). In the opposite direction to Butterworth the train departs at 10:51 h. From the airport 11 km away you can get flights to KOTA BHARU 59.-, KL 94.-and PENANG 39 M$.

PULAU LANGKAWI

This island group in the northwest of Malaysia consists of 99 tiny islands. The largest is Pulau Langkawi, twice as large as Penang, with the main town, Kuah. On the island there are many rubber plantations, tropical forests, fishing villages, and sandy beaches - in short, a miniature Malaysia. Some of the islands are really just coral reefs; others with limestone cliffs are covered by jungle. Most have beautiful sandy beaches and are unpopulated. Langkawi is a good place to lie back and relax. This idea has found favour with the overworked Malaysians, so during school vacations it's hard to find an empty room. Outside the high season, there's no problem.

The island figures in many tales and legends. On being condemned to death Princess Mahsuri cursed it: "For seven generations this island shall not prosper!" Seven generations have long since passed, but not even the building of the Langkawi Country Club (now Langkawi Beach Resort) has brought prosperity. Government plans to create a gigantic tourist centre have left their marks on Pantai Rhu where half-finished bungalows rot away. Roads have been enlarged and 747s will soon land at the airfield .

HOTELS

Not far from the ferry is the *LANGKAWI BEACH RESORT*****, tel 749209. Rooms, however, cost M$90 and up. The prices seem to reflect the comfort offered. The village of Kuah has three hotels: *LANGKAWI HOTEL**** (tel 749248), *HOTEL ASIA*** (tel 749216) and *FAIRWINDS HOTEL****, all of which have about the same standards. At the end of town there is one inexpensive shop that also rents rooms. It is, however, 3 km from the ferry, so you'll have to take the bus for 40 c. *MOTEL MALAYSIA** is on the right side. Nice family atmosphere with the family of Mr Velu. During your round trip of the island you might also ask in the villages about accommodation offered there. Several bungalow villages are on Pantai Cenang / Pantai Tengah and even more were being built in 1987. Try *SANDY BEACH MOTEL***, or *SSS CHALET*** right beside it. More expensive is *SEMARAK RESORT*****. A taxi from the jetty to Pantai Tengah costs M$15. Rather expensive is *MUTIARA***** on Pantai Rhu. They built 48 chalets and even more were planned but are not yet finished. The whole beach looks like an abandoned construction site. Cheap beachhuts are found on Pulau Bumbun *(WAN JAMIL*)*. Reach the island by sampan for M$3 per person.

FOOD

Mr Velu, in the restaurant of *MOTEL MALAYSIA*, serves excellent Indian food. The hotels in Kuah serve Chinese food. At *WENG FUNG*, across from the hospital, they have excellent seafood. Malay foodstalls are in the hawker centre *TAMAN SELERA*.

GETTING AROUND LANGKAWI

BY BUS - quite irregular and undependable. About once an hour, one of the island's buses leaves from Kuah to Tanjung Rhu and Pantai Tengah. To get to the beach itself, you'll have to walk another two kilometres.

BY TAXI - about 50 taxis drive on the 100 km of paved road. They charge M$10 per hour or M$40 per day. If there are four of you, it's a good deal.

BY MOTORBIKE - the perfect way to get around. The roads are well paved and there's hardly any traffic. Watch out that you don't run over one of the huge monitor lizards which sprawl out on the road sunning themselves. Motorbikes (small Honda 75s or 90s) can be rented for about M$20 per day at several shops and in the hotels.

BY BICYCLE - costs M$3.50 - 4 per day. Pick it up the night before, so that you can head out early, since you should rest during the heat of the day. You can cover the all-paved roads by bike in 4 or 5 days. Although the highest mountain, Gunung Raya, is almost 1000 m high, there are hardly any really steep stretches on the island.

BY BOAT - to snoop around the other islands you can rent a boat at the village dock for the whole day (10:00 to 18:00 h). After a lot of bargaining, expect to pay about M$100. Up to 20 people can fit into a boat, so try to get all the travellers to go in with you. At the Langkawi Beach Resort, horrendous prices are charged for boat trips.

LEAVING LANGKAWI

To reach the ferry in Kuah, you'll either have to take an expensive taxi or walk two km. Several ferries leave daily from Kuah to Kuala Perlis, more often during high season. Price depend on the kind of boat, M$8-10. From Kuala Perlis, take a bus or a taxi to Alor Setar or Kangar. A taxi to Padang Besar (the border) costs M$4. Malaysia Air Charter flies from KL (112.-) and PENANG (42.-M$).

Since April 1984 the GADIS LANGKASUKA sails between Penang and Langkawi. Leaves Teluk Ewa every Sun at 9:00 h and arrives in Penang at 16:00 h. Price: M$35 adult.

A ROUND TRIP OF THE ISLAND

To get to know Pulau Langkawi, you shouldn't just hang around Kuah, which is always pretty much the same. Here are some ideas for excursions:

A round trip of the island can be done in one day on a Honda. By bicycle, of course, it takes longer. Take the road west to the golf course and the right fork, and ride to *MAHSURI TOMB (MAKAM MAHSURI)*.

Princess Mahsuri was condemned to death for alleged adultery. Her husband was often away on trips, and the beautiful princess became friends with a

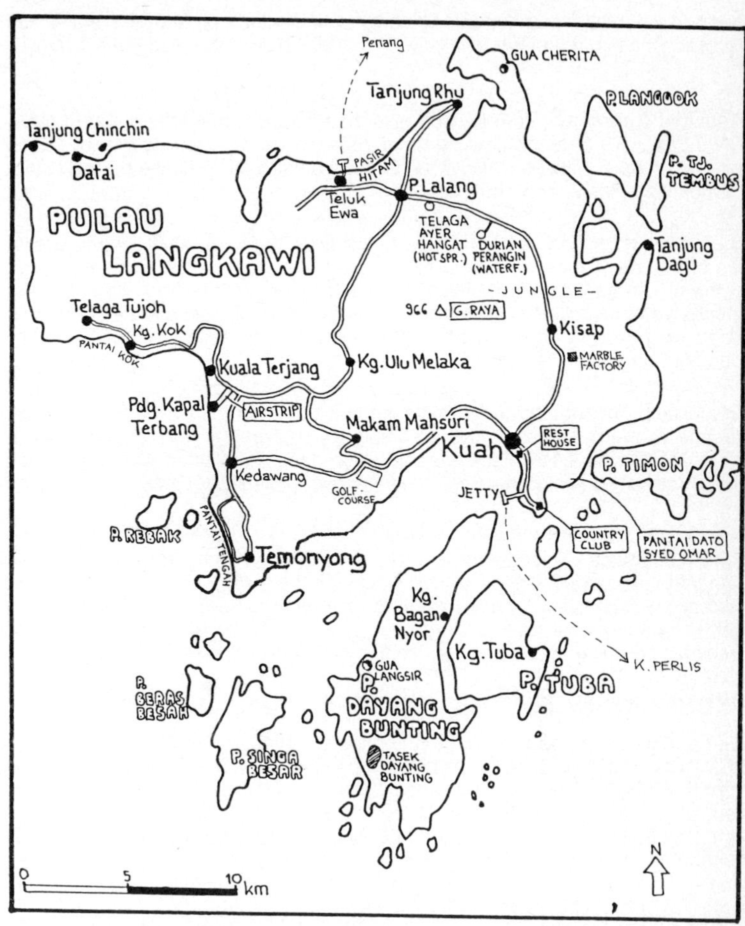

young poet. For this reason her mother-in-law had her charged with adultery. Though she always protested her innocence, she was sentenced to death. On January 22, 1355, she was executed, as you can read on her tombstone. Her curse, that the island would suffer seven generations of poverty, soon became reality. The Thais attacked the island, killing, plundering, and burning. They burned Matsirat and razed the village to the ground. On Padang Matsirat, where the main village of the island was located at the time, burned rice is still found in excavations, since the inhabitants at the time buried their entire rice harvest. Check out the *PADANG BERAS TERBAKAR* - the place of the burned rice.

From Mahsuri's tomb, go back and take the left fork at the golf course to *PANTAI TENGAH* - a beautiful white sandy beach with an offshore island, 18 km away from Kuah. Buses to TEMONYONG, a small fishing village on the southernmost tip of the island, cost 95 c.

Then ride up to KUALA TERIANG, 22 km from Kuah, a small fishing village, site of the island's new airport. From Kuala Teriang, you can take a new road to the seven springs *(TELAGA TUJUH).* They are 8 km away. To reach the springs you must climb for the last 15 minutes. A small river splatters into seven pools lying one after the other. New water piping has been laid. Walk up the creek right into the jungle!

From Kuala Teriang, head right across the island, north, past the 'burned rice', through jungle landscape. At the completely unexpected roundabout, take a left to *PANTAI HITAM* (black beach), which has little to offer other than black sand. The new dock for the *Gadis Langkasuka* is in TELUK EWA.

The road to the north from the roundabout leads to TANJUNG RHU. When the tide's out, you can walk over to the island - remember to head back in time! At high tide in the evening they get big waves on the beach. If you were to take a right at the roundabout, you'd pass through rubber plantations and past Indian workers' settlements on your way back to Kuah. At the 9th milestone a path branches off to the right leading to *DURIAN PERANGIN WATERFALL.*

EXCURSIONS TO THE NEIGHBOURING ISLANDS

With a rented boat, you can get to the second largest island, PULAU DAYANG BUNTING - the 'Island of the Pregnant Girl'. There's a fresh water lake not far from the beach; it's said a girl who'd long remained childless became pregnant after bathing in its waters. There are coral reefs between the islands of PULAU SINGA BESAR and PULAU BERAS BESAH. The beaches are second to none and unspoiled - right behind them it's jungle.

PADANG BESAR

This is the border town for Thailand, reachable by bus, taxi, or train. You can change money in the train station building or in the coffee shop at the bus station. But they don't give a very good exchange rate. Overland taxis leave from the train station. The cheapest way into Thailand is to walk up the street to the Malaysian checkpoint, get the necessary stamp in your passport, and then go up the bit of no-man's-land along the road to the Thai border station. An alternative is to go across by motorbike. On the Thai side there are buses for 15 Baht to Haad Yai.

BETWEEN KL AND JOHORE BHARU

Here, too, it's worth taking some time mapping out your travel route. Of course you can always go right on from KL to Malacca or even Singapore, but places like Seremban or Kuala Pilah are hardly ever visited by tourists and are certainly worth at least a stopover.

Like the area north of KL, the towns and smaller villages here are mostly Chinese, while the kampongs belong to the Malays. For mile after mile on the way south you pass through seemingly endless rubber and palm oil plantations, which at one time were owned by large English companies.

SEREMBAN

The most important town in the state of Negri Sembilan, which carries the name 'nine countries'. Before the creation of this state by the British there were nine different kingdoms here.

Not far from the bus station, southeast of town, is the *LAKE GARDEN* (Taman Bunga). The modern *NEW MOSQUE* is mirrored in the lake. It stands on nine pillars representing the nine countries, Negri Sembilan. Today a *MUSEUM* is in an old Minangkabau palace where a prince used to live. The 19th century structure once stood in Ampang Tinggi. It was built of wood without the use of a single metal nail. However, during the rebuilding in Seremban they weren't able to follow the original plans completely. It's on Jl.Sungei Ujong (feeder road to KL Highway) about 3 km out of town. The Minangkabau, literally 'buffalo horns', is a Malay tribe which today is mainly settled in West Sumatra (see *West Sumatra* in the Indonesian section). Between the 15th and 17th centuries many Minangkabau moved to Negri Sembilan. Their typical architecture is marked by pointed roofs reminiscent of buffalo horns.

HOTELS

The *ORIENTAL HOTEL***, 11 Jl.Lemon, tel 713069, is cheap. Several hotels can be found on the parallel street, Jl.Birch, such as *TONG FONG***, no. 104, tel 713022 and *WAH SONG CHAN**, no. 111, tel 714334. Otherwise there are cheap Chinese places on the side streets, Jl. Cameron and Jl. Tuan Sheikh. Somewhat better is the *CARLTON**** at no. 47 Jl.Tuan Sheikh, tel 725336.

HOW TO GET THERE

Bus and taxi station in Jl.Labu / Jl. Lemon. By bus from KL for 2.40, taxis M$5. From MALACCA for 2.85 (taxi M$5), PORT DICKSON bus M$3.20 and BAHAU 1.90 (taxi M$5). There are six trains daily to KL (2nd/3rd class) M$4.10/2.50, Ekspres Rakyat/ Sinarang M$5.40/10.

KUALA PILAH

is about 37 km east of Seremban. Taxis cost M$3. On Jl.Lister, near the bus station, is a very old Chinese temple. Take a bus from here to SERI MENANTI, takes 45 minutes and costs 50 c. Seri Menanti is the royal seat. Check out the *ISTANA LAMA*, built in 1908 and a good example of traditional Minangkabau architecture. The Istana is located at the end of the street, through the big archway. The *ROYAL MOSQUE* is to your left. From Kuala Pilah you have a connection to Bahau - buses leave every 20 minutes. From there you can go on to Tasek Bera or up to Temerloh.

MALACCA

For more than 100 years, Malacca was the most important trading centre in South East Asia. The accepted date of its founding is 1398; by 1450 the city had 40,000 inhabitants. Back then, Malacca was probably the most cosmopolitan city of the world. Arabs, Chinese, Indians, Javanese and Thais, as well as Bugis, Persians, Gujaratis, Klings and Acehnese lived here. Malacca lies on the dividing line between the Northeast and Southwest monsoons. Trading ships from the west and east could pick a strategic wind system when sailing to and from its harbour. A Portuguese captain described the city this way in a letter to Lisbon: "Malacca is the richest seaport in the world - with the most merchants and full of trading goods."

Parameswara, a Malay prince from Palembang (Sumatra), was forced to leave the capital of the Sri Vijaya Kingdom after a failed coup attempt. He fled first to Temasek, today Singapore, but was driven away by the warlike Thais. He finally made it to a small fishing village on the west coast of the Malay peninsula whose population lived by fishing and piracy. This was, as mentioned, 1398. Only 80 years later, Malacca controlled the Malay peninsula up to Songkhla, the Riau and Lingga Archipelagos, and most of Sumatra.

In 1511 Alfonso d'Albuquerque was able to conquer the city with a force of only 800 Portuguese and 300 Malabar Indians. Internal weaknesses became ever more apparent under the last sultan. The non-Malay merchants were too heavily taxed - causing them to intrigue with the Portuguese. Corruption and intrigue became the rule among the Malay leadership. During the next 130 years the Portuguese made Malacca into the most important fortress of their colonial empire in Asia. Trade flourished, and Portuguese policy was much more farsighted than that of the Dutch later on. In 1641, after a six months' siege of the city by the Dutch and troops of the Sultanate of Johore, the last Portuguese governor surrendered. This marked the final decline of Malacca, since the VOC (Vereeinigde Oostindische Compagnie) now controlled the entire spice trade and Batavia (today Jakarta) became the important trading centre. In 1824, the Dutch traded their unprofitable colony to the British for Bencoolen (Bengkulu) on Sumatra's west coast. Except for three years of Japanese occupation during World War II, the Union Jack flew over Malacca until independence in 1957.

Malacca is no longer a metropolis; its former grandeur has disappeared. But each of the nations involved with its past has left traces. You'll find the mixture of western and oriental traditions very interesting.

Meru
S.Buloh
Kepong
GENTING HLDS.
Kelang
Pt. Kelang
Subang
Petaling Jaya
Jinjang
S.Tua
Gombak
Batu Tiga
Kuala Lumpur
Ampang
Satak South
S. Besi
Serdang
Batu Sembilan
Jenjarom
S.Manggis
S.Chua
Kajang
Morib
Banting
Kanchg. Laut
Kg.Dingkil
Bangi
Semenyih
Beroga
Batu Laut
Kg. Jangging
Tanjong Sepat
Salak
Beranang
Kg. Pajam
Kg.Tembok
Labu
Mantin
S. Pelek
Tirol
Tanah Merah
Seremban
Chuah
Rasah
Mambau
Rahang
Pt. Dickson
Kg. Lukut
Kg. Bagan Pinang
Rantau
Pedas
Seri Menanti
Kg. Tk. Kemang
Kuala Pilah
Rembau
Pasir Panjang
Johol
Kg. K Linggi
Lubok China
Kota
Dangi
Kg. S. Baru
Tampin
Peng Balak
Ayer Gajah
Machap Baharu
Tg. Keling
Kelebang Besar
Malacca
Selandar
Nyalas
Josin
Ayer Molek
Simpang Bekoh
P. BESAR
Tk. Mas
Umbai
Tangkak
Sagil
Merlimau
Bt. Kangkar
S. Rambai
Kesang
Pt. Bungah
S.MUAR
Gerisek
Muar
Bt. Pasir
Panchor
Lenga
Simpang Jeram
Pagoh
Bakri
Paya Bakri
Pt. Jawa
Parit Sulong
Semerah
Yong Peng
Tongkang Pechah
Batu Pahat
Seri Gading
Ayer Hitam
Keluang
Karak
S.KELAU
Kerdau
A.1462
G.BESAR HANTU
Telemong
Mentakab
Temerloh
S.PAHANG
Kg. Manchis
Kg. Jawi
Mengkarak
Durian Tipus
Simpang Durian
Terlang
Kg. Meng-karak
Kuala Kelawang
Peradong
Kg. Kerayong
Kemayan
Pertang
Simpang Pertang
S. SERING
Ayer Hitam
TASEK BERA
Fort Skandar
Bahau
Ldg. Geddes
Rompin
Kg. S. Dua
Londah Pth.
Ayer Kuning S.
Gemas
Batu Enam
Kg. Bt. Tunggai
Pekan Jabi
Kg. Tengah
Jementah
Segamat
Bt. Siput
S.MUAR
Bt. Kepong
Pekan Ayer Panas
Labis
Kg. Batang Merbau
Chaah
Bekok
Beradin
Paloh
Chamek
Nyior
N
0 10 20 30 40 50 60 km.

Begin your tour of Malacca's (Malay: Melaka) history at the Sungei Melaka. This is the 'Red Square' of the city. The *STADTHUYS* (town hall) is the oldest remaining Dutch building in Asia. It was built between 1641 and 1660 and today contains the *MELAKA MUZIUM.* It has an excellent exhibition on the history of the city, mostly in old engravings and pictures, as well as objects from the life of the people (Malay and Chinese) and their conquerors. Admission is free. Right next to it is the massive *CHRIST CHURCH* dating from 1753. Even bricks and roof tiles were brought from Holland. By the way, you can take the best photos from the terrace of the tourist office.

On Jl.Kota, which runs in a great curve around *ST.PAUL'S HILL,* you'll find the only remains of the greatest Portuguese fortress in Asia, *PORTA DE SANTIAGO.* Behind it is a path leading uphill to the ruins of the Portuguese *ST.PAUL'S CHURCH.* The gravestones set in the ruin are of great historical interest. Keep in mind the situation of the Dutch or Portuguese in the 17th and 18th centuries. Their journey to the east lasted many months, and then they were completely cut off from their homelands. They were forced to survive in the unfamiliar tropical climate and frequently faced deadly diseases. Adventure, profit and power were sought by many! In front of the church ruins is a memorial to *ST.FRANCIS XAVIER.* In 1541, he left Lisbon and spent the next 11 years on missionary trips. He clocked up 38,000 miles before dying in 1552 on a tiny island off the coast of China. In 1553 his remains were brought back to Malacca and buried in St.Paul's Church. However, after just three months, he was again exhumed for transport to Goa.

Back on Jl.Kota, when circling the hill, you'll come to the wooden replica of the *SULTANATE'S PALACE.* The architectural design is based on the description in the *Sejarah Melayu* (Malaya Annals), the masterpiece of traditional Malay literature. The palace today houses the *MELAKA CULTURAL MUSEUM.* A bit further along on Jl.Kota you come to an old *DUTCH CEMETERY,* now returning to the wild!

Probably the most beautiful, well-preserved old Chinese buildings in Asia today still stand on Jl.Tun Tan Cheng Lock and Jl.Temple. The *BABA NONYA HERITAGE MUSEUM* has been established in one of the buildings on Jl.Tun Tan Cheng Lock. *CHEN HOON TENG TEMPLE* was built as far back as 1644, making it the oldest Chinese temple in Malaysia.

Try to visit *ST.PETER'S CHURCH* (Jl.Tun Sri Lanang) on Good Friday! It is the centre of the Catholic Church in Malaysia. The Easter processions, here in the middle of Asia, are a once in a lifetime experience, more reminiscent of Spain or Portugal than Malaya. The church was built in 1710 when the Dutch reinstituted religious freedom. The architecture is similar to that of churches in Goa and Macau.

BUKIT CHINA is the largest Chinese cemetery outside the Middle Kingdom. It has an interesting history. In the 15th century a tribute-paying delegation of the then Sultan Mansur Shah returned from the Ming Royal Court. As a "gift" it brought back the Princess Hang Li Po. She was accompanied by 500 "girls of great beauty" as one can read in the old annals. The princess and her royal household were given the hill (bukit = hill) as a residence. There's nothing left of the buildings today. At the foot of the hill, near the *SAM PO KONG TEMPLE*, you'll find the Asian version of the Fontana di Trevi, the *SULTAN'S WELL*.

An excursion along the coast to the south will bring you to the *PORTUGUESE SETTLEMENT* on Jl.Albuquerque. About 2000 people, most of them fishermen, live here and speak Portuguese. The newly constructed *MEDAN PORTUGIS* resembles a fortified town. Besides Portuguese restaurants you can visit local cultural shows every Saturday night. Admission M$2.

A Portuguese community has managed to survive here for 450 years. It speaks its own dialect, similar to the language spoken in Portugal several hundred years ago. One reason for the existence of this linguistic and cultural island is the population policy of the former colonial power. Unlike the Dutch or British, ther Portuguese allowed intermarriage. Marriages between Portuguese men and Malay women or even between Malay men and Portuguese women were common practice. So you can still find Portuguese-speaking Eurasians on Jl.Albuquerque. All strict Catholics, of course! By the way, should you ever be in Malacca in June, be sure to take part in the Festa de San Pedro (a festival in honour of St. Peter, the patron saint of fishermen).

TOWN HALL, MALACCA

A bit further south in KG.UMBAI (about 10 km towards Muar), get a boat ride over to PULAU BESAR for M$4. This is a beautiful island with bungalows** and the well preserved buildings of a German development aid project gone bad. Due to lack of water, livestock production died along with the animals. The inhabitants are quite superstitious and avoid the property. On Sat/Sun there's a boat for M$8 return from Quayside Malacca.

On your way back to Malacca, make a stop at *ST.JOHN'S HILL.* Originally a Portuguese chapel stood on the hill. Later the Dutch built a fort; you can still see the remains.

Worth checking out is an interesting example of Malay architecture on Jl.Tranquerah. The *TRANQUERAH MOSQUE* is about 150 years old. Sumatra visitors will find many parallels; the minaret and the ornamentation on the roof show Chinese influence. Here, too, is the grave of Hussein Shah, Sultan of Johore, who in 1819 was party to the famous treaty with Stamford Raffles, signing over the island of Singapore.

HOTELS

In TANJUNG KELING on Pantai Kundur, about 10 km north of town, cheap accommodation in a backpacker's atmosphere. There's a regular connection with bus 51 from the bus station (Jl.Kilang). Even if the beach is nothing compared to the east coast - nearby is an oil refinery -, everyone gets together here. Right on the beach are the huts of *SHM'S** (Slow Harmonic Motion). If you sleep in the old huts, expect to get wet if it rains. Still, it's a friendly place! Next door are the huts of *RASA SAYANG**, *SUNSET** and a bit further north the *HAWAI**, and *BEACH BUNGALOWS* *. At SHM'S, Nora is an excellent cook, but have a little patience; the kitchen's small and there are lots of travellers. Those who want to stay more comfortably can try *MOTEL TANJUNG KELING*** (tel 511256), right on the beach with a palm garden and restaurant.

In the city itself there are hotels of every category, size, and shape. Try Jl. Bunga Raya: *NG FOOK***, no. 154; *CHIN NAM***, no. 49 or *CATHAY***, no. 100-104. Lots of atmosphere in *MAJESTIC***, no. 188 (tel 222455). On Jl.Kee Ann, a side street off Bunga Raya: *NEW LONDON HOTEL***, no. 54 (though somewhat loud in the morning because of the market!) or *TONG AH**, no. 16. Quieter are the *EASTERN**, 85 Jl.Bendahara, tel 223483, *CHONG HOE***, Jl.Tukang Emas (clean). More upmarket is *PALACE HOTEL*****, 201 Jl.Munshi Abdullah, tel 225115.

Two travellers' guesthouses are in town: *KANE'S PLACE***, (dorm*) 136A Jl.Laksamana Cheng Ho, tel 235124. Frankee has a lot of info and he manages the Atlas Travel Agency. The other place is *TRILOGY HOMESTAY**, 218A Jl.Parameswara. Take bus 17 and get out at the Chinese temple.

FOOD

A whole row of different restaurants can be found on Jl.Taman / Jl.Melaka Jaya. Often there's no menu, so ask about the prices before you order! Try one of the two Nonya food restaurants: *OLE SAYANG* and *NONYA MAKKO.* Still around is *UE TEA*

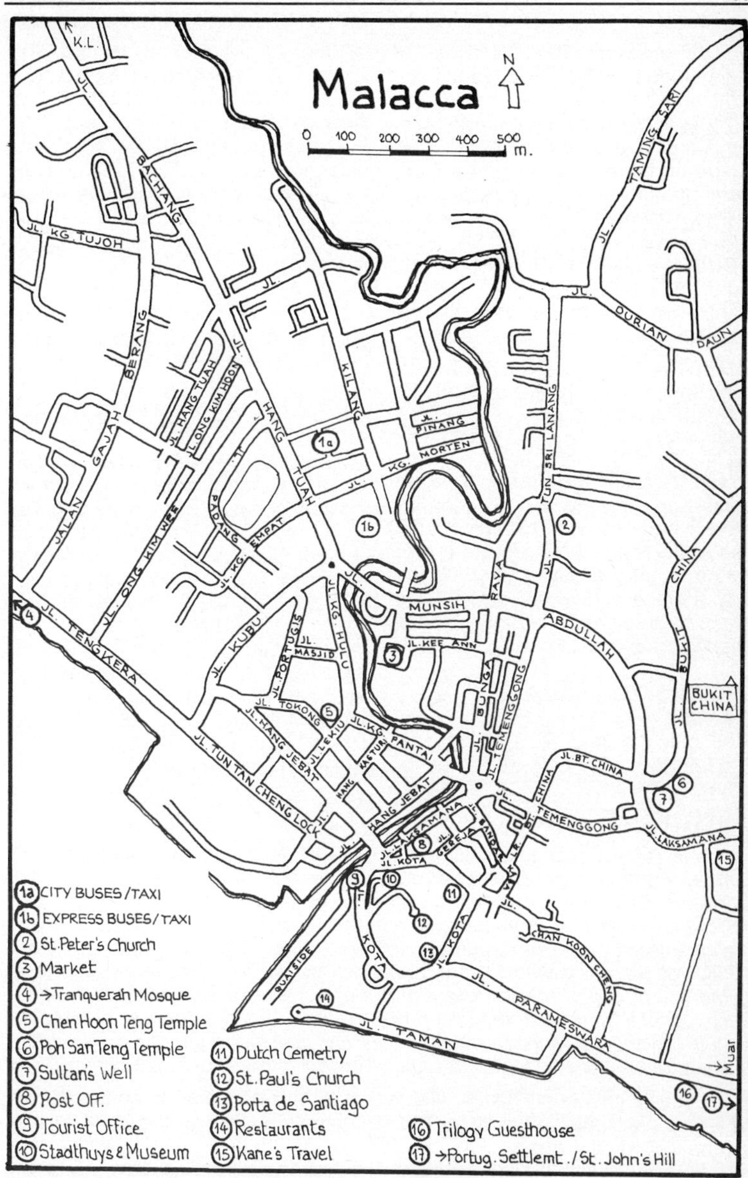
Malacca
N
0 100 200 300 400 500 m.
K.L.
JL. BACHANG
JL. KG. TUJOH
JALAN GAJAH BERANG
JL. HANG TUAH
JL. ONG KIM HOON
JL. HANG TUAH
JL. KILANG
JL. PINANG
JL. KG. MORTEN
PADANG EMPAT
JL. KG.
JL. ONG KIM WEE
JL. TENGKERA
JL. KUBU
JL. PORTUGIS
JL. MASJID
JL. KG. HULU
JL. MUNSIH
JL. KEE ANN
JL. TUN SRI LANANG
JL. DURIAN DAUN
JL. TAMING SARI
RAYA
ABDULLAH
JL. BUNGA
JL. TEMENGGONG
JL. BUKIT CHINA
BUKIT CHINA
JL. BT. CHINA
JL. TOKONG
JL. HANG JEBAT
JL. LEKIU
JL. KG. PANTAI
KASTURI
HANG JEBAT
JL. TUN TAN CHENG LOCK
JL. LAKSAMANA
TEMENGGONG
JL. LAKSAMANA
JL. KOTA
GEREJA
BANDA HILIR
JL. KOTA
JL. CHAN KOON CHENG
JL. PARAMESWARA
QUAYSIDE
JL. TAMAN
Muar
1a CITY BUSES/TAXI
1b EXPRESS BUSES/TAXI
2 St. Peter's Church
3 Market
4 →Tranquerah Mosque
5 Chen Hoon Teng Temple
6 Poh San Teng Temple
7 Sultan's Well
8 Post Off.
9 Tourist Office
10 Stadthuys & Museum
11 Dutch Cemetry
12 St. Paul's Church
13 Porta de Santiago
14 Restaurants
15 Kane's Travel
16 Trilogy Guesthouse
17 →Portug. Settlemt. / St. John's Hill

HOUSE at Lorong Bukit China 20. Try Indian food in *MAJEEDIE,* 96 Jl.Bendahara. Good Malay food in *ANDA,* 8 Jl.Hang Tuah. They serve nasi campur. Chinese in *LIM TIAN PUAN,* 251 Jl.Tun Sri Lanang. Beneath the Paris Hotel on Jl.Kee Ann, there's a baker selling hot bread.

GENERAL INFORMATION

TOURIST INFORMATION - Tourist Centre on Jl.Kota, tel 225895 - a good source.

IMMIGRATION - in the big new administration building on the corner of Jl.Kubu / Jl.Hang Tuah.

POST OFFICE - Jl.Laksamana.

SHOPPING - the many antique shops on Jl.Hang Jebat (Jonker Street) have become too expensive due to the tourist trade. At the end of Jl.Kee Ann is the local market. On the way there are different stands. On Temple Street you'll find many shops offering temple articles.

LEAVING MALACCA

BY AIR

MAS office is on Jl.Melaka Jaya, tel 315722. Daily flights to KL for M$40. Of interest are the (up to now) Fri flights with Pan Malaysia Air Carriers to PAKANBARU, costs M$140. This is the most reasonable way to get to Sumatra (Bukittinggi) by air. From Singapore it costs M$172. Book at: Atlas Travel Service, 5 Jl.Hang Jebat, tel 220777. Airport tax: M$15.

BY SHIP

Since September 1983 a ferry ship has run every Tues, Wed, Fri, and Sun between MALACCA and DUMAI (Sumatra). Price: M$80. Takes about 4 hrs. Bookings at Jahe Shah Shipping (across from the clock-tower).

OVERLAND BUSES AND TAXIS

All long distance buses depart from the central bus station on Jl.Hang Tuah / Jl.Kilang. Taxis next to the bus station. SAMPLE PRICES (taxis in brackets): SINGAPORE 8.50 ac 11.-, KL 6.50(13.-), KOTA BHARU 25.- ac 29,-, BUTTERWORTH ac 21.40, PORT DICKSON 3.20(5.-), SEREMBAN 2.85(6.60), TAMPIN (connection to the North-South Rail line) 1.60, MUAR 1.80, JOHORE BHARU 8.- ac 10.-(17.50), LUMUT 18.50 ac, TEMERLOH 6.30 ac 7.80 M$.

JOHORE BHARU

Not until 1866 did this town become the seat of the Sultan of Johore. The sultanate, however, was established as early as 1564, when the son of the last Sultan of Malacca retreated to the Johore River. By the end of the 17th century, Johore was the heir to Malacca. Except for a small area around the city of Malacca which was Dutch, Johore controlled most of the old kingdom. Before 1866, Johore was called 'Ujung Tanah', which means 'land's end', since this is the actual end of the Eurasian land mass. Today a dam (causeway) connects Johore Bharu with the island of Singapore. Foreign tourists hardly ever stop in JB, though Singapore's sister city has developed into the major industrial centre of southern Malaysia while still keeping much of its old charm.

The Sultan's private residence, featuring a 33 m high tower, is on the *BUKIT SERENE,* well outside the town. The *ISTANA BESAR* and the palace garden can be visited daily (except Fri) from 9:00 to 12:00 h. You must, however, register in advance with the tourist office. The architecture shows strong Victorian

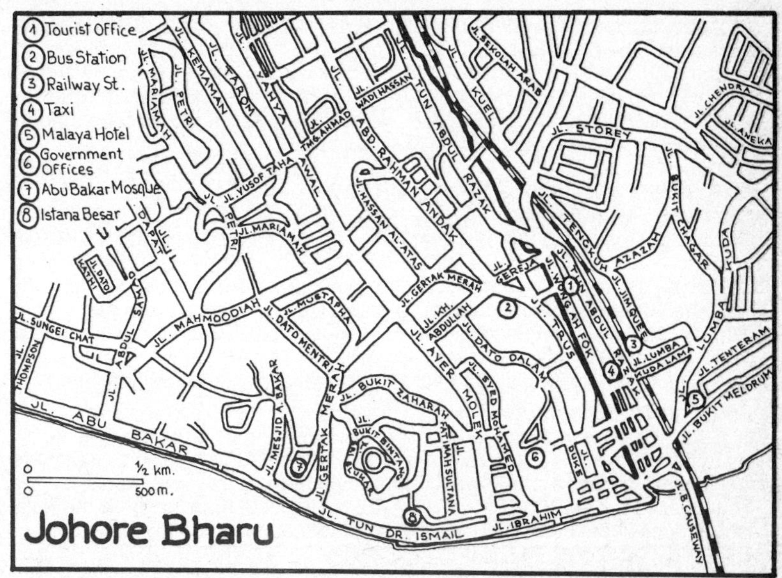

influence. Sultan Abu Bakar had it built in 1866. In the Istana, you'll find the crown jewels and royal insignia as well as other works of art. Not far away is the *ABU BAKAR MOSQUE,* large enough to hold 2500 of the faithful.

HOTELS

You'll find the cheapest hotels on Jl.Ah Fook and Jl.Meldrum. *TONG FONG***, 5 Jl.Ah Fook or on Jl. Meldrum: *TONG HONG***, no. 37-39 or *FOOK LOY***, no. 5A. Middle priced: *MALAYA HOTEL****, 20 Jl.Bukit Meldrum; *FIRST HOTEL****, Jl.Station or *HONGKONG****, 31A Jl.Meldrum.

LEAVING JOHORE BHARU

MAS office can be found in the Orchid Plaza Building on Jl.Wong Ah Fook (tel 220888). It is certainly worthwhile for Singapore visitors to check out the flights to Kuching and Kota Kinabalu. Flights from Senai Airport (20 km north of JB) are considered domestic and are therefore cheaper. The Malaysian government has plans to make the airport competitive with Singapore. SAMPLE PRICES (all in M$): KOTA KINABALU 301.- (night flight 256.-; from SGP 346.-), KUCHING 147.- (night flight 125.-; from SGP 170.-), KL 77.- (from SGP 130.-). Taxi to Senai costs M$15. MAS buses also run from Singapore City Terminal, Singapore Shopping Centre, 190 Clemenceau Avenue, tel 3366777.

Buses and taxis leave from Jl.Terus. SAMPLE PRICES (taxi prices in brackets): MALACCA 8.- ac 10.- (17.50), KL 15.50(31.-), SINGAPORE 80 c, MERSING 5.- (10.-), KUANTAN 9.50 (25.-), KOTA TINGGI 2.- (3.-) M$.

The train station is on Jl.Campbell, not far from the Causeway. For information call 224727. Singapore M$1, 3rd cl., 30 min. SAMPLE PRICES (M$) KUALA LUMPUR 20.30 (12.50), BUTTERWORTH 41.70 (25.60), SEREMBAN 16.50 (10.10), IPOH 31.80 (19.50). All prices 2nd class, in brackets 3rd class. If you want to transfer to the jungle railroad in GEMAS, take the 20:25 h train north out of JB.

DAY TRIPS AROUND JOHORE BHARU

GUNUNG MUNTAHAK

On the way from JB to the east coast of Malaysia, try a stop in KOTA TINGGI. Buses from JB for M$2, taxis M$3. From here you can get a bus to Gunung Muntahak, 15 km to the north, for 90 c. Several waterfalls have cut the cliffs smooth and formed natural swimming pools. Up to five people can rent a bungalow - costs M$30 with a kitchenette, refrigerator, etc. Good for jungle walks! Up to now there's only one restaurant (which is priced that way!). Bring your own food from Kota Tinggi. On weekends the place is packed with people.

KOTA JOHORE LAMA

In Kota Tinggi you can rent a boat and sail down the Johore River. About 15 km to the south are the restored ruins of KOTA JOHORE LAMA, the sultanate's first capital between 1547 and 1587. Later the fortress was razed by the Portuguese. In KAMPONG MAKAM, 1 1/2 km south of Kota Tinggi, is the royal mausoleum where most of the sultans of Johore are buried in 15 graves.

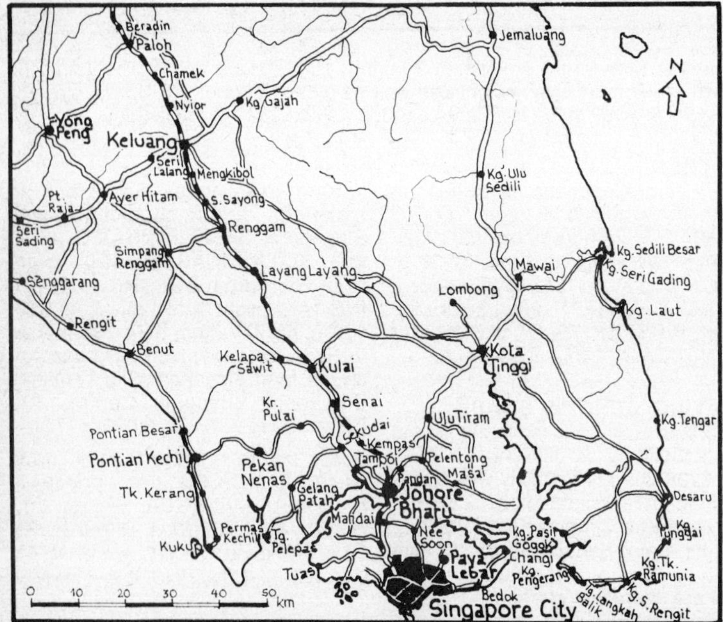

BETWEEN JOHORE BHARU AND KUANTAN

The southern part of the Malaysian east coast is much less touristy than the section between Kuantan and the Thai border. This is where the stress-suffering Singaporeans come to spend their hard-earned vacations. During the months from November to January, however, the sea is quite rough, making it dangerous for swimming and diving.

Off the coast is an archipelago of about 60 inhabited and uninhabited volcanic islands, some of which are surrounded by coral reefs. Beyond the coast road, the tremendous tropical forests and mangrove swamps are everywhere. If you have the organizational talent and the endurance, you can get a ride up the huge rivers. However, it may be difficult to find a suitable boat.

DESARU

This is the new holiday resort south of Kota Tinggi. At the moment several large hotels are finished; others are being built. A holiday centre for rich Singaporeans with some lower price accommodation on the side is planned. The facilities are located in the middle of jungle on a long, white, sandy beach. The next village is several kilometres away. Several years ago the whole peninsula was covered by jungle. The forest has now given way to huge, 300,000 ha plantations.

HOTELS

Worth recommending is the *DESARU HOLIDAY RESORT* (tel 838211). There are 35 chalets (M$60 - 75/4 people), two dormitories (M$10) and several huts (dangkau) for M$28. An additional M$2 is charged for a mattress. Try to get a discount with your ISIC if you're planning to stay a while! The restaurant, which you can't really avoid, is pretty expensive. The *DESARU VIEW HOTEL*****, tel 838221 and *DESARU MERLIN INN *****, tel 838101, both charge much more than M$100 for a double room per night.

HOW TO GET THERE

Take bus 41 or taxi from Johore Bharu to KOTA TINGGI and then a taxi for M$5 per person or a bus for M$3.30 to Desaru. There are daily buses at 12:30 h and 15:00 h to KG. RAMUNIA. You can also come directly from SINGAPORE. Take a ferry from Changi Point to KG.PENGGERANG (S$5), and then a taxi for M$30 to Desaru. New 42 seat ferries will cut the travel time to just 50 minutes. From the landing point it takes another 50 minutes to reach Desaru.

MERSING

This port town is only really important as a departure point for trips to the various islands. Often you'll be forced to spend a day here. Take a walk up to the *MOSQUE* or go out to a beach. Take a right, 9 km to the north (towards Endau) where you see the sign *Pantai*. This branch road leads through several coconut forests and small kampongs, and over two ancient wooden bridges. You can see *PULAU SETINDAN* from the long white beach. By the way, when the tide's out you can walk over to the island. A quicker way to the water is by taking the Mersing-Endau road before the fork.

HOTELS

Beautifully situated on a hill, but unfortunately a bit too expensive, is the *RESTHOUSE***** (tel 791101), 490 Jl.Ismail. The small hotels in town are much more reasonable; try *MERSING**, 1 Jl.Dato Timor (tel 791004). The manager also arranges cheap trips to the islands. The restaurant is good as well. Near the bus station and taxi stand, at 53 Jl.Abu Bakar, you'll find the cheapest double room in Mersing in *TONG AH LODGING HOUSE**. Other cheap hotels: *MANDARIN**, 12 Jl.Sulaiman (tel 791231); *GOLDEN CITY***, 23 Jl.Abu Bakar; *EMBASSY***, 2 Jl.Ismail (tel 791302).

LEAVING MERSING

Taxis and buses leave from the bus stop: JOHORE BHARU 5.-(10.-), KELUANG 5.-(8.20), ENDAU 2.-(3.-), KOTA TINGGI 3.50(7.40), KUANTAN 11.-(15.-)M$. If you want to go on your own to some of the islands, find a fishing boat. PULAU RAWA always has to be booked in advance, and you're expected to use the Rawa boat. After arrival you'll be continually approached by touts offering boats. People in the Tioman Office, 5 Jl.Abu Bakar, tel 791772 almost always have a boat. BABI BESAR costs M$16 one-way, there's a daily boat at 11:00 h, bungalows** available. TIOMAN costs M$30 by speedboat (leaves at 13:30 h) otherwise M$15 (leaves at 12:00 h). Check out Wonderland Tour (near the bus station), tel 791229.

PULAU RAWA

Book at Rawa Safari well in advance, tel 791204. The office is near the river, almost at the mouth. Small bungalows cost M$48 for two people, larger ones with a shower for M$53. For the hour-long ride over you pay M$14 (round trip). The island is privately owned by a nephew of the Sultan of Johore. The youthful Tengku Mohammed Archibald Ibni Temenggong Achmad is quite a businessman, and his small bungalow village on the otherwise unpopulated island is usually booked up. The only place to eat is in the restaurant, which isn't the cheapest in the world. But to compensate, you can jump from your hut, over the sandy beach, and right into a coral reef full of fish. You can rent a snorkel and mask for M$10 per day (for that price you can buy both in Singapore).

PULAU TIOMAN

This is the largest island in the archipelago - about 39 km long and 19 km wide. Depending on the boat, the ride over takes 2 1/2 to 5 hours (slow fishing boat). Of the eleven tiny kampongs on the island, TEKEK, JUARA and NIPAH are of interest. The island is mountainous with lots of jungle. Gunung Kajang is over 1000 m high. There's lots of coral reef surrounding Pulau Tioman - or go

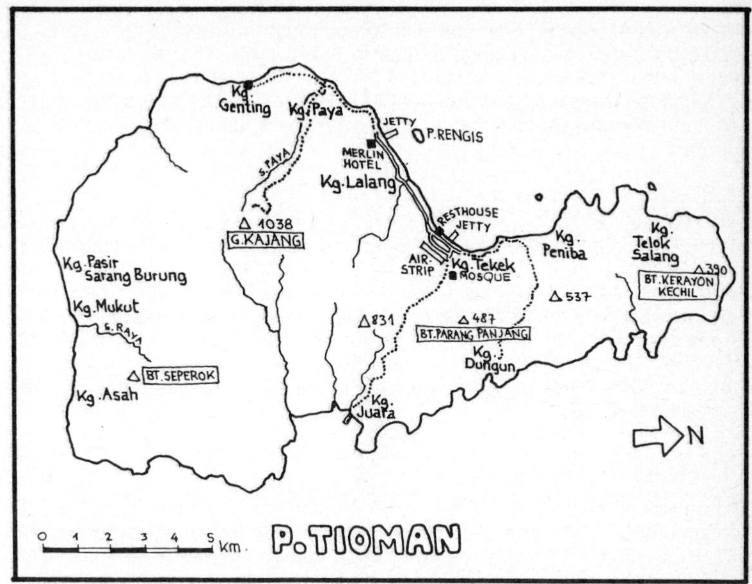

out deep-sea diving (equipment at Tioman Island Resort for approximately M$45, boats M$150). In addition there are many possibilities for long walks!

Arab and Chinese seafarers were aware of the island 2000 years ago. It offered a good anchorage and, more important, fresh water. About 1960 years later, Tioman was selected as the location for the Rodgers & Hammerstein musical *South Pacific.*

Tourism doesn't get out of hand because there's only one luxury hotel, the Tioman Island Resort. Prices range from M$90-180. Book rooms in advance at tel 791772. Their boat leaves daily at 12:00 h and charges M$30 one-way. People with little time and a lot of money can fly with Malaysia Air Charter from KL or Singapore. Freaks mostly seem to crash in KG.TEKEK, costs M$4 - 8 per night. A nice place is NASRI's camp on a sandy beach, 45 minutes from the village. Expect to shell out M$15 including meals. Bring your own fruit and cookies from Mersing; on the island there's just bananas and coconuts. Up to 12 persons can rent a boat for M$80 a day and visit beautiful coral reefs. About 500 m north of Nasri you'll find TIOMAN HOUSE* and ABC HUTS*.

ENDAU - KUALA ROMPIN - NENASI

The only place to spend the night at the moment is in KUALA ROMPIN (RESTHOUSE**, tel 095 65245, good food!). Buses run several times a day between the towns (Endau - KR M$1.60; KR - Nenasi M$2). For a princely sum (about

M$120 plus expenses), you can rent a motorboat in Endau to take up to 10 people on a trip up the Sungei Endau to KG.PUNAN. The trip lasts up to 8 hours - another 38 km upstream is KG.PATAH. After that there are only Orang Asli villages. There's a new road from KG.LEBAN CHONDONG a few kilometres north of Kuala Rompin that leads to highway 12, connecting Segamat and Kuantan.

PEKAN

Just 47 km south of Kuantan, you'll find the sultan's seat in Pahang. Worth checking out is the modern *ISTANA ABU BAKAR.* Near Sungei Pahang are *ABDULLAH MOSQUE* (masjid lama) and the new *ABU BAKAR MOSQUE.* Visit the *ABU BAKAR MUSEUM* (open daily except Fri from 9:30 to 17:00 h). On the road to Kuantan, right at Sungei Pahang, is *PAHANG SILK WEAVING CENTRE.* Wonderful sarongs are made here. Ask the bus driver in Malay for *Tenunan Sutra Pahang.* Spend the night in the RESTHOUSE** (tel 421240), or in PEKAN HOTEL*.

KUANTAN

The capital of the state of Pahang is developing more and more into the economic centre of the whole east coast. Tourism, too, has really increased. On *TELOK CHEMPEDAK* beach are two huge hotels - the Merlin and the Hyatt. You'll have to see for yourself whether the city is really as interesting as everyone says. It is important, however, as a traffic junction and as a base for excursions into the surrounding countryside.

HOTELS

You'll find lots of cheap hotels on Jl. Telok Sisek and Jl.Besar. Try *EMBASSY***, 60 Jl.Telok Sisek; *SAMUDRA****, no. 50 (has a good restaurant); *PLANET***, no. 32. The *MENG HENG HOTEL** on 22 Jl.Mahkota is a bit cheaper.

LEAVING KUANTAN

BY AIR

MAS office is at Wisma Persatuan Bolasepak Pahang, Jl.Gambut (tel 512218). SAMPLE PRICES: JB 77.-, KL 61.-, SINGAPORE 120.-M$. The airport is about 16 km to the west on the road to Temerloh.

BY BUS / OVERLAND TAXI

The bus station is by the market on Jl.Besar. Taxis depart from Jl.Mahkota (next to the Rex Cinema). SAMPLE PRICES (bus / taxi): KL 12.10 (23.-), KUALA TRENGGANU 7.-(15.-), KOTA BHARU 13.-(22.-), SINGAPORE 17.-ac 22.-, MERSING 11.-(15.-), KUALA DUNGUN (9.50), ENDAU 7.-(12.-), KG. LUBOK PAKU 4.50, MELAKA 13.-, PEKAN 2.20(3.50), JERANTUT 6.40 (14.-), TEMERLOH 4.30(8.50) M$.

BY SHIP

Since 1986 a new car-passenger ferry, the CRUISE MUHIBAH, follows this route: Kuantan (Sat) - Kuching (Sun) - Kota Kinabalu (Tues) - Kuantan (Thurs) - Singapore (Fri) - Kuantan (Sat). Tariffs from Kuantan are: KUCHING 160.- (Standard cabin);

235.- (De luxe cabin); 350.-M$ (suite). KOTA KINABALU 265.- (Standard cabin); 380.- (De luxe cabin); 550.-M$ (suite).
SINGAPORE 99.- (Standard cabin); 140.- (De luxe cabin); 210.- M$(suite). Get your tickets at the Feri Malaysia Office, Menara Utama UMBC, Jl.Sultan Sulaiman, KL, tel 2388899, or right in Kuantan at Wisma Bolasepak, Jl.Gambut, tel 526800. In Peninsular Malaysia, Feri Malaysia is also represented by Reliance Shipping & Travel Agencies Sdn. Bhd. They have offices in Penang, Malacca, Ipoh, and Johore Bharu.

DAY TRIPS AROUND KUANTAN

You can get good info about Pahang as well as about excursions in the Kuantan area from the TOURIST OFFICE on Jl.Haji A. Aziz.
Try a visit to SUNGEI LEMBING, 43 km to the northwest. Buses cost M$1.60. Here you'll find one of the largest tin mines in Malaysia, more than 1000 m deep. On the way back stop in PANCING - right in the middle of a rubber plantation is a limestone cliff. In the huge CHARAH CAVE, a Buddhist monk from Thailand has erected a 10 m long reclining Buddha. To climb the cliff you have to use the slippery stairs. Take bus 39 for 50 c to PANTAI TELOK CHEMPEDAK; the last bus leaves at 16:00 h and the first back to Kuantan is at 7:00 h. To the right, behind the row of restaurants and nightclubs, smart Chinese businessmen rent rooms in single family homes - costs between M$6 and M$15. A four-bed room will run to about M$20. Also good are the KUANTAN HOTEL**** (tel 24755) and the ASRAMA BENDAHARA*.

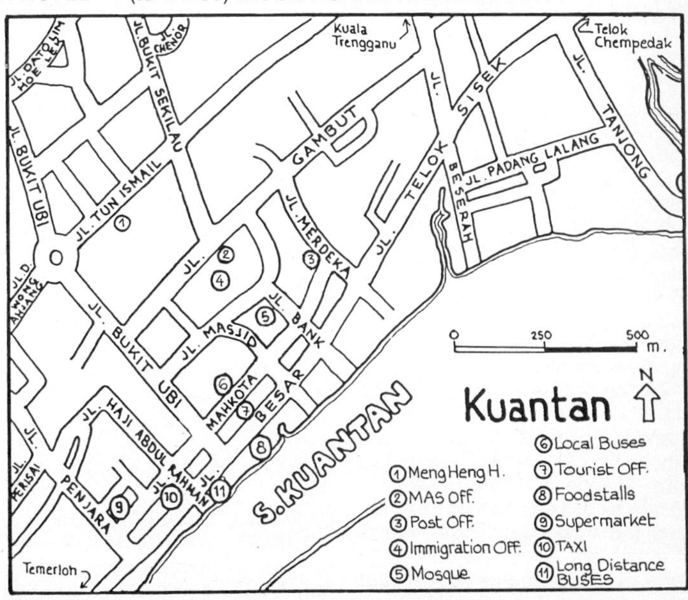

BETWEEN KOTA BHARU AND KUANTAN

This is the part of the east coast most visited by tourists. It's 380 km of long sandy beach. The states of Kelantan and Trengganu are orthodox Muslim; Friday is an official holiday here. During Ramadan you'll get food in the cities only from Chinese; everyone fasts in the kampongs. The quiet village life on the east coast is a nice change from the bustling (Chinese) west coast. This is a good place to try and adjust to the Islamic lifestyle. Don't walk through the village in your bathing suit. Women should never lie around topless on the beach. That's only accepted in the closed-off Club Mediterranee. Malays are wonderful people and hosts, but some kinds of 'openness' are just beyond their comprehension. Don't accuse us of being moralistic; instead, try to understand Islam. Thank you!

KOTA BHARU

The capital of Kelantan is only a few miles from the Thai border. On Merdeka Square is the *MOSQUE* and the *ISTANA BALAI BESAR* - the 'palace with the huge hall of audience'. It was built in 1844 for Sultan Mohammed II. Right next to it is the *ISTANA JAHAR* with the Kelantan State Museum. Open daily except Wed from 10:30-18:00 h. Admission free. In the centre of town is *PASAR BESAR*, a big market located in a relatively new building. You can get fresh seasonal fruit from the market women.

HOTELS

Quite a few guesthouses have sprung up during the last few years in Kota Bharu. The cheapest roof in town is *RAINBOW INN**, 4423 Jl.Pengkalan Chepa, next to the Thai consulate. Take bus 4 about 1 1/2 km towards the airport. Opposite is *MUMMY'S HITEC HOSTEL** (no. 4398). On Jl. Padang Garong 5504A (behind the MAS office) is *IDEAL TRAVELLERS' HOUSE** . Also dorm*. To be recommended is *REBANA HOSTEL** on a kampong-style side alley of Jl.Sultanah Zainab, across from the Istana Lama. It's a nice house set in a garden and the owner Pok Jak knows a lot about Malay culture. Other hotels in town include *TOKYO HOTEL****, 3945 Jl.Tok Hakim, tel 22466, right behind the bus station. The hotel's best rooms are upstairs off the huge terrace. On the same street but cheaper are the *NORTH MALAYA HOTEL***, no. 3856, tel 22171 and the smaller *NEW BALI HOTEL***, no. 3655, tel 22686.

FOOD

There are lots of foodstalls near the bus station. Good food at the *MEE CHIN HOTEL*. Chinese businessmen amuse themselves in *HOTEL MURNI*, where a nightclub offers hostess service. Many foodstalls are on the eastern side of the Merdeka Square and at Jl. Mahmud corner of Jl.Bayam. Thai and Malay food is available at *SHAFFIE RESTAURANT* not far from Rebana. Get good Chinese food at *LOK KAU HOCK*, Jl.Kebun Sultan.

GENERAL INFORMATION

TOURIST INFORMATION - Jl.Sultan Ibrahim (next to Majlis Perbandaran). Very eager to help. Open Sun to

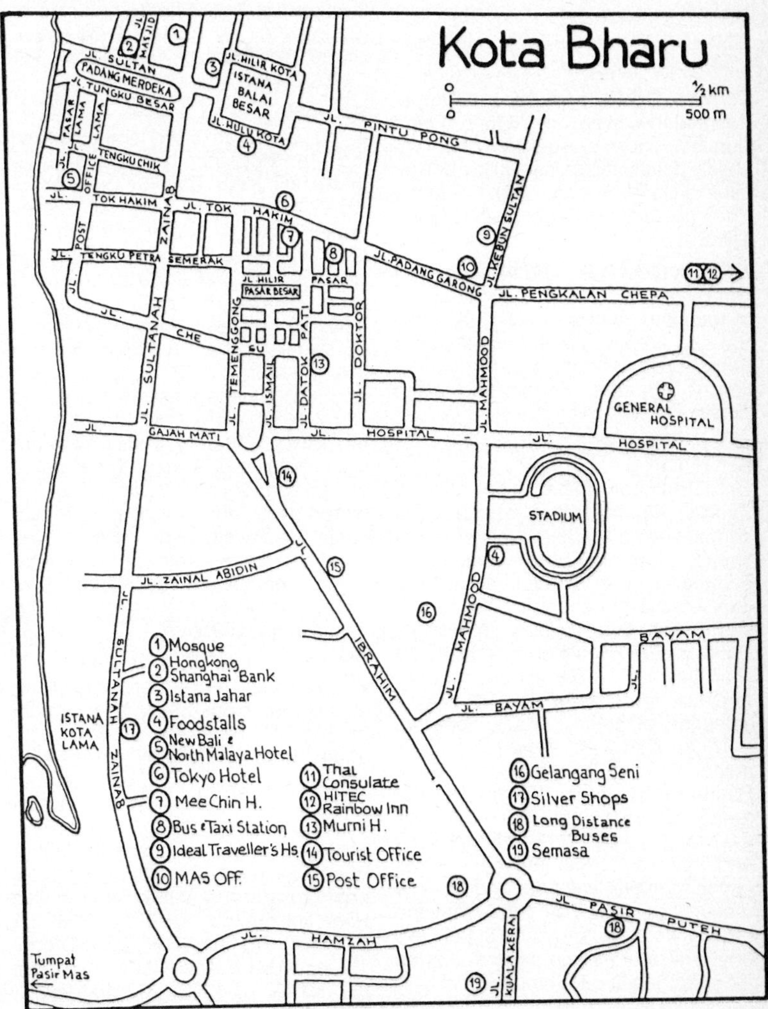
Kota Bharu
0 ½ km
0 500 m
1 Mosque
2 Hongkong Shanghai Bank
3 Istana Jahar
4 Foodstalls
5 New Bali & North Malaya Hotel
6 Tokyo Hotel
7 Mee Chin H.
8 Bus & Taxi Station
9 Ideal Traveller's Hs.
10 MAS OFF.
11 Thai Consulate
12 HITEC Rainbow Inn
13 Murni H.
14 Tourist Office
15 Post Office
16 Gelangang Seni
17 Silver Shops
18 Long Distance Buses
19 Semasa
JL. SULTAN
JL. MASJID
PADANG MERDEKA
JL. TUNGKU BESAR
JL. HILIR KOTA
ISTANA BALAI BESAR
JL. HULU KOTA
JL. PINTU PONG
PASAR LAMA
JL. TENGKU CHIK
JL. POST OFFICE
JL. TOK HAKIM
JL. TOK HAKIM
JL. KEBUN SULTAN
JL. TENGKU PETRA SEMERAK
JL. PADANG GARONG
JL. PENGKALAN CHEPA
JL. HILIR PASAR BESAR
PASAR
JL. CHE SU
JL. TEMENGGONG
JL. ISMAIL
JL. DATOK PATI
JL. DOKTOR
JL. SULTANAH ZAINAB
JL. MAHMOOD
GENERAL HOSPITAL
JL. GAJAH MATI
JL. HOSPITAL
JL. HOSPITAL
STADIUM
JL. ZAINAL ABIDIN
JL. IBRAHIM
JL. MAHMOOD
BAYAM
JL. BAYAM
ISTANA KOTA LAMA
JL. SULTANAH ZAINAB
JL. PASIR PUTEH
JL. HAMZAH
JL. KUALA KERAI
Tumpat Pasir Mas

Wed 8:30-16:30 h, Thurs/Sat 8:30-13:15 h.

IMMIGRATION OFFICE - Jl.Dusun Muda near Jl.Bayam.

THAI CONSULATE - 4426 Jl. Pengkalan Chepa, tel 782545. Open Sun to Thurs 9:00-16:00 h. Two check points for crossing the border into Thailand: Sungei Golok - Rantau Panjang and Kg.Pengkalan Kubor - Tak Bai.

GELENGGANG SENI - cultural centre off Jl.Mahmud; performances of traditional dances and plays every Sat and Wed during the months from February to October with the exception of Ramadan. Further info at the Tourist Office.

SHOPPING

On Jl.Sultanah Zainab, right after Jl. Zaimal Abidin, there are several shops selling Kelantan silver - not cheap, though! If you're looking for batik and other souvenirs, have a look around the shops in Wisma Iktisad, the modern building on Jl.Maju. South of town, on the road to Kuala Krai (beyond Jl.Kg.Putih and just before Lee Motors), you'll find a large selection of batik at Batik Samasa. You can also watch how the batik is made. Another place to shop is on Jl. Pantai Cinta Berahi, the road to the 'Beach of Passionate Love'. Get off the bus in KAMPONG PENAMBANG and have a look at the batik workshops, songket weavers and the kite makers' houses. You can watch the people working, but you can't always buy. There are some small shops on the road heading to the beach.

LEAVING KOTA BHARU

BY AIR

Sultan Ismail Detra Airport is 10 km out of town. MAS office on Jl.Padang Garong (tel 743144). Daily flights to KL 86.- (61.-), PENANG 72.-, JOHORE BHARU 163.- and ALOR SETAR 59.- M$.

BY RAIL

If you want to take the jungle railroad to KL or Singapore, you'll have to go to PASIR MAS (bus 6) or WAKAF BHARU (bus 19, 27). A train leaves Wakaf Bharu daily at 10:58 h to GEMAS where you have to change for SINGAPORE. Takes about 20 hours, price M$89.90 1st, M$40.50 2nd, and M$24.90 3rd class. If you only want to go as far as KUALA LIPIS, you can take the train at 6:42 h; allow 9 hours. Another whistle-stopper leaves at 13:57 h for KUALA KRAI and GUA MUSANG. Offering only 2nd / 3rd class, it costs M$3 from Wakaf Bharu and takes more than 2 hours. Bus 5 is faster over the 70 km stretch and costs the same. From Kuala Krai there's another train at 5:00 h to Kuala Lipis. There are a number of cheap Chinese hotels* right by the train station in Krai.

BY BUS / OVERLAND TAXI

Those crossing the border to Thailand can take bus 29 for M$1.80 right to RANTAU PANJANG. A taxi costs about M$3. A bridge leads right across the river to a border post, but it's only open until 18:30 h. Local buses and taxis depart from Jl.Pendek. Long distance buses to Johore Bharu, Singapore and ac buses to KL from Langgar bus station, other buses from Jl.Hamzah. SAMPLE PRICES (bus/taxi): KUALA TRENGGANU 6.80 (12.-), KUALA DUNGUN 11.-(17.-), KUANTAN 13.-(22.-), KL 19.- ac 25.-(45.-), JOHORE BHARU 22.-(50.-), GERIK (via East-West Highway) by taxi 16.-, BUTTERWORTH 18.-(36.-) M$.

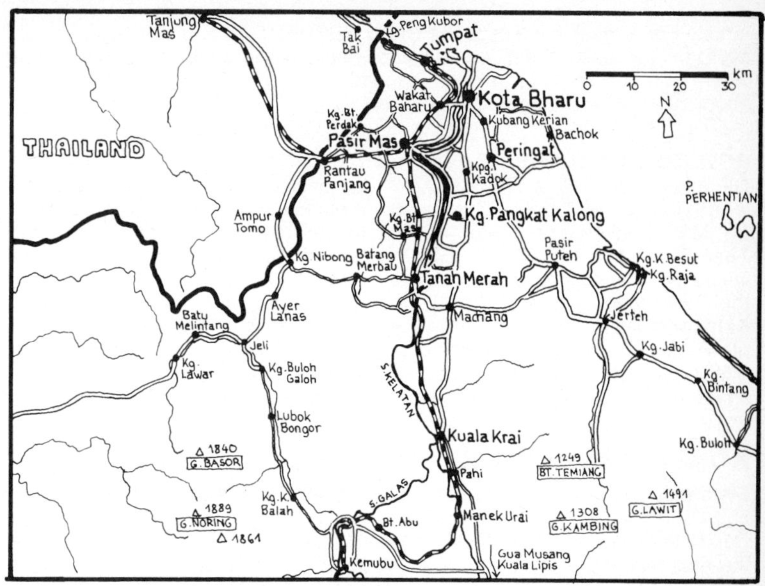

DAY TRIPS AROUND KOTA BHARU

PANTAI CINTA BERAHI

The Beach of Passionate Love is definitely not one of the most picturesque beaches on the east coast, but it does have a nice name and an interesting history. Here and further to the north, Japanese troops landed in December 1941. They pushed their way south on bicycles. Two months later, Singapore surrendered. There are several hotels right on the beach: SRI DESA RESORT offers rooms*** or bungalows****. Much more expensive is RESORT CINTA BERAHI (tel 097 21307). More reasonably priced is LONG BEACH MOTEL (tel 097 740090) Double rooms cost between M$30 and 50, in the dorm you pay only M$7. Take bus 10 from Kota Bahru.

PANTAI DASAR SABAK

Another beach is PANTAI DASAR (Sabak). Take bus 8, 8A or 9 for 70 c and watch the fishermen returning in their boats.

PULAU PERHENTIAN

The two islands are 2 hours from KUALA BESUT. On PULAU PERHENTIAN BESAR (= big), there's a resthouse with several bungalows, costs about M$10 - 15 for two people. Or move into one of the huts of Pak Dahan or Ibu Ciki. On a lonely beach with lots of coral, you can go diving and see the sharks and sea turtles. For a meal, head over to PULAU PERHENTIAN KECHIL (= small) and eat in the kampong. Right beside the resthouse a new coffee shop has opened where you can stock up on rice, canned food, tea, etc. In 1988 there were about 10 - 15 bungalows and huts to rent.

HOW TO GET THERE

Get a taxi from KUALA TRENGGANU to JERTEH for M$7 or bus 3 from KB for M$4 (leaves every half hour). Then get a bus to KUALA BESUT, where you have to book and pay for the Resthouse on the island at the Kampong Raja Resthouse (on the other side of the river). Boats cost M$10 per person if other people share the ride. Otherwise, it's more expensive! As there are only a few rooms for rent on the island, it's better to call (09 976328) first: don't risk making the laborious trip to Kuala Besut in vain. You can spend the night in Kg.Raja Resthouse. It isn't worth a long stay, though - the beach doesn't have any trees, and the river water's dirty. There is a bridge between Kuala Besut and Kg.Raja.

KUALA TRENGGANU

Even though it's the sultan's seat of Trengganu, this is a pretty sleepy town. Even a couple of modern 20th century buildings haven't changed things much. Due to the large offshore oilfields, however, Trengganu is sure to develop over the next few years into a real bustling city. One walk that you should take is along *JALAN BANDAR* (formerly Jl.Kampong Cina). Many houses are more than 100 years old. At the end of the street, *PASAR BESAR,* the big market, is now located in a modern building, but it still manages to have atmosphere. On the ground floor and in the courtyard you'll find the staples of Malay village life; upstairs there are more "sophisticated" goods such as expensive batik. Go early in the morning when the fishermen are bringing in their catch! *ISTANA MAZIAH,* right around the corner, is fairly modest looking at first glance. On closer examination, you'll see that the window frames of this completely wooden structure are covered with Arabic quotes from the Koran. Take a trip to *PULAU DUYUNG,* the largest of the 13 islands lying at the mouth of the Sungei Trengganu. Boats leave regularly for 50 c from the jetty near the taxi station (Jl.Bandar / Jl.Sultan Ismail). Malay prahus are still built here today. Ask for Awee and Rohenny; the latter is a French woman who married a Malay. They'll put you up for M$15 per day, including meals. About 4 km to the south on the road to Kuantan is the new *ISTANA BADARIAH* - diagonally across from part of the old istana which was dismantled and moved here. In CHENERING, several km south of town, you'll find the *HANDICRAFT CENTRE* (Kraftangan Malaysia). Various Malay crafts are practised here. Look in the exhibition room. Open 9:00 - 17:00 h.

HOTELS

*IBI'S GUESTHOUSE**, Jl.Haji Busu on Pantai Batu Burok, is south of town. There are several reasonable hotels on Jl.Masjid Abidin: *REX* **, no. 112 (tel 621384), *SEAVIEW***, no. 18A (tel 621911). On Jl.Banggol: *MALI***, no. 78 (tel 623278) - pretty loud downstairs but OK on the upper floors - *CITY***, no. 97-99 (tel 621481), *BUNGA RAYA***, no. 105-11 (tel 621166) or *GOLDEN CITY***, no. 101-103 (tel 621777). A few other hotels can be found on Jl.Sultan Ismail (formerly Jl.Paya Bunga) such as *LIDO*** at no. 62 or *SRI TRENGGANU****.at no. 20. For those looking for more comfort: *PANTAI PRIMULA HOTEL*****, Jl.Persinggahan, tel 622100, rooms cost M$90 and up.

LEAVING KUALA TRENGGANU
There are daily flights to KL M$86, PENANG M$80.- and JOHORE BHARU M$163. MAS office: Wisma Maju, Jl.Sultan Ismail (tel 62260). Telega Batin Airport is situated about 14 km north of town on the road to Merang. A taxi costs M$12.

Some taxis leave from the taxistop on the river (Jl.Bandar / Jl.Sultan Ismail); others leave from the bus station Jl. Masjid/Jl.Banggol. SAMPLE PRICES for buses and taxis: KUALA DUNGUN 3.60(6.-), KOTA BHARU 6.80(12.-), KUANTAN 7.-(15.-), KL 17.-, ac 20.-(35.-), RANTAU ABANG 3.50 M$.

DAY TRIPS AROUND KUALA TRENGGANU
KUALA BERANG
Go by bus for M$1.90. The village boasts a hotel and a resthouse. Across a new bridge an access road runs to Ulu Trengganu. We were told, however, that boat trips to 'Ulu' are better made from Dungun. The famous Trengganu stone with Arabic-Malay inscriptions dating from 1303 was discovered near

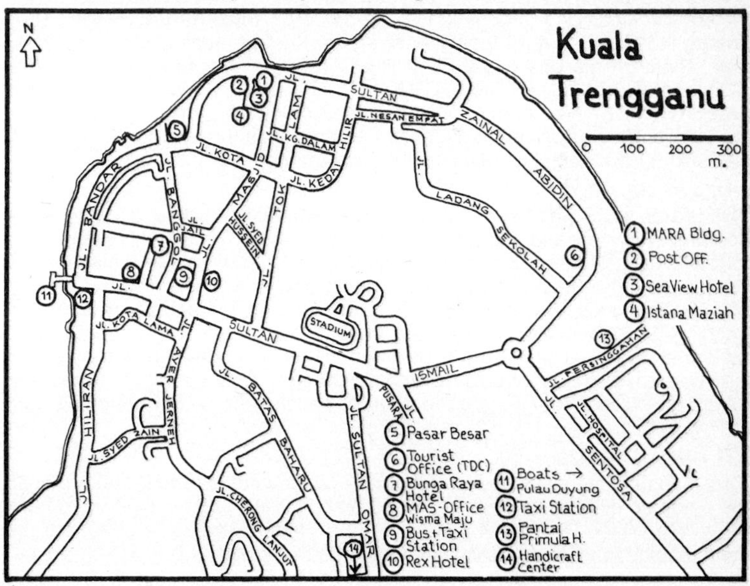

Kuala Berang. It is considered to be the oldest evidence of Islamic presence in Malaysia. The stone can be seen today in the Muzium Negara in KL. You can get a bus from Kuala Berang to SEKAYU. There are many waterfalls to visit - great place to hike! At the bottom of a cascade-like waterfall are bungalows (M$35) and dormitories. The last bus back to KT leaves at about 17:00 h.

BATU RAKIT

30 km north of KT, on a beach in the middle of a kampong, is a Resthouse asking M$20 for one of its three rooms. Other than the manager's daughter, there's nobody around who speaks any English. In October 1988 she married, however, and if she moves out conversation will be very limited. If you order in advance, you can get a huge serving of nasi goreng. The sunrises on this part of the coast are particularly nice. On the beach you'll find many fishing boats and some wrecks left by Vietnamese 'boat people'. Just off the coast, you can see PULAU BIDONG. Up to 40,000 Vietnamese made do there during the high point of boat people activity in 1979. If you're travelling by car, take the road up to KG.PENAREK. Take the ferry from KT to KG.SEBERANG TAKIR and then a bus for M$1.50 (or taxi M$2.50).

MARANG

Situated south of KT, you might stop off on the way in KG.RUSILA where they've made a name for themselves weaving mats, hats, baskets, and handbags out of palm leaves. From Marang, you can cross over to PULAU KAPAS, a small island with a nice coral reef. Four bungalows have already been completed. Bookings and information at the office of Pulau Kapas Resort. They charge M$15 for a return trip. Stay at one of the four guesthouses in the village. Right on the beach are BEACH HOUSE**(*) with friendly owner Haji Sulaiman, next to it MARE NOSTRUM*-***, nearer to the main road ZAKARIA GUESTHOUSE* nice rooms and good food or KAMAL* on the other side of the village. Zakaria will organize boat trips up Sungei Marang for M$15 p.p. If you're lucky, you might see crocodiles, monitor lizards, or monkeys.

PULAU REDANG

This island, which has been declared a marine national park, is situated about 40 km off the mainland and has beautiful coral reefs. The normal way is to go to KUALA BESUT, register at the Pejabat Daerah, and reserve a place in the Resthouse (costs about M$20). Chartering a boat, however, will run you up to M$100. The cheapest time is on Thursday or Friday when lots of boats are heading back to the island from the market. Those who can speak a bit of Malay might try talking to the fishermen in the kampongs between BATU RAKIT and PENAREK. Maybe they'd be cheaper! Stay the night in the kampongs on Pulau Redang - a good idea for people who want to improve their Malay.

KG.PULAU RUSA

This is about three miles upstream from KT on the road to Kota Bharu. You can get a ride up by boat for M$3 to 5 or go by bus. Batik and songket workshops are in the village. Two batik factories can be found set back a little from the main road; a songket workshop is right on the main road.

RANTAU ABANG

The road between Kuala Trengganu and Kuala Dungun runs partly through infertile swamps. There's a second road parallel to the coastal road. Forests have disappeared, monotonous palmoil plantations stretch to the horizon or alang[2] grass grows in abundance. Very desolate.

56 km south of Trengganu and a couple of kilometres north of Dungun is probably the best known place on the east coast of Malaysia. The Department of Fisheries in KL has set up a breeding ground in Rantau Abang to save the leatherback turtle from extinction. In a fenced area on the beach the eggs are buried to protect them from those who consider turtle eggs a delicacy. The tiny newborns are then taken out to sea by boat for release.

HOTELS

You can stay the night right on the beach next to the breeding station. Simple bungalows with prices between M$8 and 20 are rented by *AWANG*, *SANY*, or *ISMAIL*. During the turtle season prices soar. Trips by boat out to PULAU TENGGOL are also organized from here. Charges are M$18 p.p. Not far away is the *RANTAU ABANG VISITOR'S CENTRE*****,

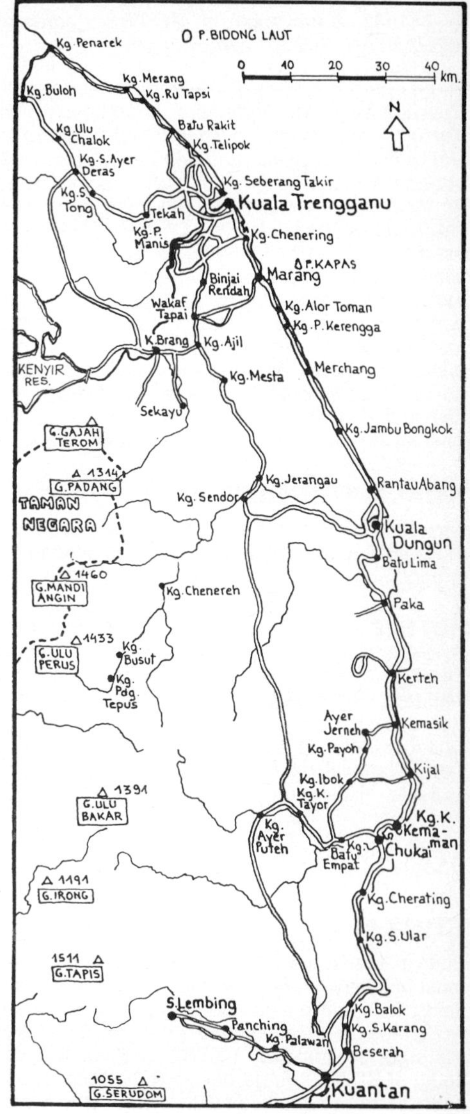

tel 841533. 3 km south is *MOTEL MERANTAN INN* ***. Unfortunately there's no shade on the beach.

Between May and September, and especially in August, huge ***Leatherback Turtles*** *(Dermochelys coriacea) come ashore to bury their eggs in the sand. Unlike the other types of turtles known to us, they lack a hard shield-like shell but have an almost smooth leathery skin. Leatherback turtles also lack claws on their feet; instead they have real fins. The turtles drag their tremendous weight up the beach looking for the right place to bury their eggs. The fins are used to dig a sort of nest in the sand where up to 100 eggs are laid. All the while they sob and sigh; sometimes you can see real tears running from their eyes. Afterwards, sand is pushed over the eggs, and the turtle disappears back into the ocean. Particularly in Rantau Abang, the animals are used as a tourist attraction. Whole swarms of visitors come armed with flashlights and cameras. People must realize that this disturbs the creatures. Don't pay any so-called 'turtle-guide' - they're only there to hinder the turtles' return to the sea so that even the last fancy tourist gets his snapshot!*

KUALA DUNGUN

was once important for the shipping of iron ore mined at Batu Besi. Today that's all over and the town is again dependent on fishing. The morning market is good.

HOTELS

*KASANYA***, 225-227 Jl.Tambun (tel 841704) offers reasonable rooms with fans. *SIN CHEW***, 10K Jl.Besar (tel 841412) is about the same. Cheaper is the *SEAVIEW**, 222 Jl.Lim Teck Wan, tel 841891 or *MEDO***, 146-147 Jl.Tambun (tel 841246). A few kilometres north is the most expensive hotel, *TANJONG JARA BEACH HOTEL*****, tel 841801.

HOW TO GET THERE

Taxis leave from the stop behind the market on the harbour (KUANTAN 9.50, KUALA TRENGGANU 6.-M$).

Long distance buses from KT-Kuantan Highway, local buses from the main road.

Last bus to Rantau Abang leaves at 18:00 h.

CHUKAI

Four or five years ago, the beaches south of Kuala Dungun used to be the most beautiful on the east coast. Ever since the discovery of huge offshore oilfields, industrialization has started in southern Trengganu. Gigantic electrical works and an oil refinery have been built in PAKA. KERTEH is now the seat of the state oil company PETRONAS' administrative centre; a few kilometres south of KIJAL, a large deep-sea harbour, steel works and a huge LNG plant have been constructed. Only KEMASIK, a small fishing village with lovely beaches, has been spared.

Chukai is the business centre of Kemaman. From here you can make excursions to the different beaches. Be sure to eat at TONG YUAN in Jl.Sulaiman. Try stuffed crab for M$9.50 or some other seafood. You can stay the night here, too. If the Tong Yuan is full, go over to the RESTHOUSE** across the road.

KAMPONG CHERATING

is another village where you can spend a couple of quick days. It's about 45 kilometres north of Kuantan. You can stay the night with some of the village people such as MAK DE SEMAH (3 meals and a bed for M$12) or at the MAK LONG TEH GUESTHOUSE - good seafood, COCONUT INN**, or the more expensive CHERATING HOLIDAY VILLA**** with pool. Cherating was where the freaks met on the east coast but times change and expensive profit-oriented establishments have grown. A mile north of town is CHENDOR MOTEL (tel 095 591369) - doubles without ac run about M$40. Here, too, you can see the turtles laying their eggs. Right next door, by the way, is the first Club Mediterranee in Asia! The beach isn't closed off and you can walk for miles.

KAMPONG SUNGEI ULAR

North of the village you might try the TITIK INN****, no restaurant. In the village fine pandan mats, fans, and baskets are produced. BESERAH is located just 5 miles north of Kuantan. Here you can spend the night in the kampong at YAFFAR'S HOUSE*. At milestone 5 take a walk inland for about 8 minutes. Up to 20 travellers stay out there.

MALAY ARTS AND CRAFTS

Kelantan and Trengganu are the two Malaysian states which have most noticeably managed to maintain their own Malay culture. Culture and tradition both have deep roots here and haven't yet been buried by Chinese or western influences, as is pretty much the case on the west coast.

Much of the arts and crafts tradition has been kept alive in Kelantan and Trengganu. It really is true, as many people have written, that the eternal fruitfulness of the climate means people have time to participate in the arts without having to struggle for their material subsistence. This parallels Bali closely.

MALAY KITES

There are two different types of kite; one is the 'layang layang' and the other the 'wau'. Builders of the 'wau' are specialists, real designers, whose kites are works of art. 'Layang layang' are more children's toys made simply of paper and bamboo. 'Wau' can be up to 2 metres long and have an even larger wingspan. The most famous kite is the 'moon kite' (wau bulan) which, due to a unique method of construction, emits a high pitched note in the wind. Sometimes one will be left out all night in a strong breeze.

BATIK

Kelantan and Trengganu batik differ greatly from that made in Java. Not only are the patterns less detailed and the colours more glaring, but here you'll find mostly stamp batik. You can read about how batik is made in the Yogya section of this book. Warming/ Gaworski in their excellent book THE WORLD OF INDONESIAN TEXTILES voice the opinion that batik production only made inroads on the east coast in the 1950s. Besides the aforementioned batik workshops in Kg.Pulau Rusa, you'll find a batik workshop on Jl.Haji Busu in KT.

KAIN SONGKET

Songket is produced on traditional looms, usually as a cottage industry. Different patterns of gold and silver threads are woven in. 'Kain songket' is used in many kinds of garments, such as evening dresses, scarves, and blouses. Originally, however, the cloth was used as a sarong to be worn by both men and women on special occasions, such as weddings or state functions.

BETWEEN KL AND KUANTAN

Most of this route is located in the state of Pahang - covering 35,932 km², it's the largest state in West Malaysia. Even today more than 80% is covered with tropical rainforest. Jungle trips are possible, e.g. a visit to the Taman Negara National Park, which covers a huge area. Two inland lakes, Tasek Chini and Tasek Bera, are a bit difficult to reach.

TAMAN NEGARA

This national park is mostly located in Pahang, although parts also stretch into Kelantan and Trengganu. Gunung Tahan, in the northwesternmost corner, is the highest mountain in West Malaysia at 2187 m. People in good shape can hike to Tahan, but be sure to get one of the various "visitor's books" in the park headquarters and make sure you are really up to it. Nowhere in the Taman Negara are there any roads. The only way to get around is on the rivers and jungle trails. The jungle region of central Malaysia is about 130 million years old. This means that while other parts of the world were undergoing the destructive forces of the ice ages or changes in water level and climate, nothing much has changed here climate-wise. The tropical rain forest is a focal point of botanical and zoological evolution; it's one of the oldest forest areas in the world. At the moment the park headquarters in Kuala Tahan is only able to take in a maximum of 400 visitors at a time. Many of these tourists never take any hikes at all. We can remember one group of Hong Kong Chinese who were ambushed by blood-sucking leeches on their first ten minute expedition and never again left the well-tended lawns of Kuala Tahan! A trip to the Taman Negara is very rewarding. Be sure to come in good shape and bring the proper equipment, plus a desire for adventure. The costs are really minimal, despite what you might read in other travel guides. People without much time should try to set aside at least 3 or 4 days. With less than that there's not much point. Just for the trip in or back, you should plan a whole extra day.

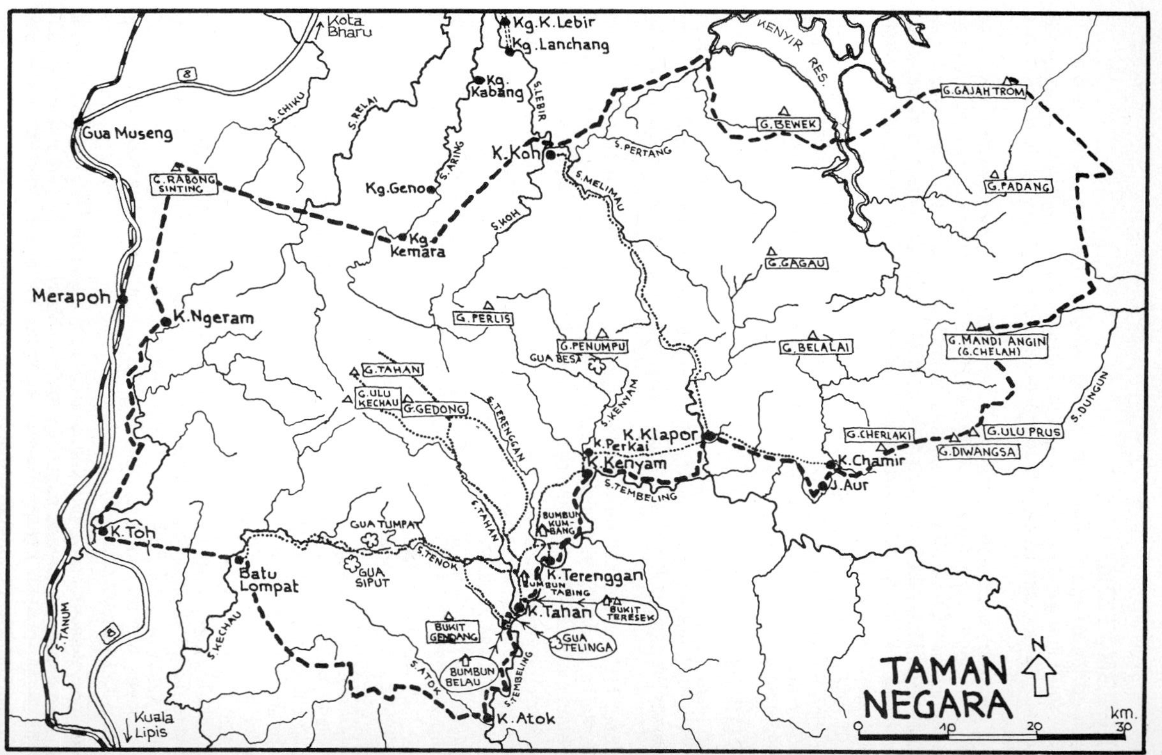
Kota Bharu
Kg. K. Lebir
Kg. Lanchang
Kg. Kabang
KENYIR RES.
8
S. CHIKU
S. RELAI
S. LEBIR
G. BEWEK
G. GAJAH TROM
Gua Museng
S. ARING
K. Koh
S. PERTANG
G. RABONG SINTING
Kg. Geno
S. MELIMAU
G. PADANG
S. KOH
Kg. Kemara
G. GAGAU
Merapoh
K. Ngeram
G. PERLIS
G. PENUMPU
G. BELALAI
G. MANDI ANGIN (G. CHELAH)
GUA BESA
G. TAHAN
G. ULU KECHAU
G. GEDONG
S. TERENGGAN
S. KENYAM
S. DUNGUN
K. Klapor
G. CHERLAKI
G. ULU PRUS
K. Perkai
K. Kenyam
K. Chamir
G. DIWANGSA
S. TEMBELING
J. Aur
BUMBUN KUMBANG
GUA TUMPAT
S. TAHAN
K. Toh
S. TENOK
Batu Lompat
GUA SIPUT
K. Terenggan
BUMBUN TABING
BUKIT TERESEK
K. Tahan
S. TANUM
S. KECHAU
BUKIT GEDONG
GUA TELINGA
S. ATOK
BUMBUN BELAU
S. TEMBELING
N
TAMAN NEGARA
km.
0 10 20 30
Kuala Lipis
K. Atok

INFORMATION

Pick up the 61-page information booklet when you book your reservations in KL. You'll find general info along with detailed trail descriptions. On the basis of this info, you should be able to make a general plan of your activities during your visit.
An excellent source of information is the *Guide To Taman Negara,* published in 1971 (no. 3 + 4) in the *MALAYAN NATURE JOURNAL.* It is now available as a reprint for M$1.50. We weren't able to find the guide in any bookstore in Singapore or Malaysia, only in the Penang Museum. Zoologists and botanists won't be able to do without reading an essay in it *(The Distribution of Large Animals in Taman Negara).*
The many guest books lying around in the park restaurant are another source of info. If they're not available ask for them! They offer great reading along with many practical tips. The park remains closed between mid-November and mid-January.

COSTS

Normally you'll have to make an advance payment of M$20 p.p., later credited to your bill, when booking in KL. The boat ride to Kuala Tahan costs M$15 per person. A night in the hostel costs M$7, in a bungalow for a double M$20 or M$40, camping M$3. Nights in one of the hides (lookouts in the jungle) run to about M$3. Boats can be rented for river trips - a typical trip might be from Kuala Tahan to Kuala Trenggan costing M$50 for the boat. A guide to Gunung Tahan costs M$400. A fishing permit costs M$10, a camera permit M$5.

A package deal inclusive of free welcome drink, breakfast, lunch, afternoon tea, and dinner costs M$30 p.p. A meal in the restaurant costs between M$3 and 7 but the food is nothing special, expensive, and consists of small portions. You can prepare your own food: in Kuala Tahan there's a shop where you can get food and other things. Everything's cheaper in Jerantut, though; be sure to bring lots of fruit since the prices in the park are influenced by scarcity.

JUNGLE TREKS

This is the high point of any Taman Negara Trip! You can choose between the short excursions around the headquarters and 7 to 10 day treks to Gunung Tahan. Worth recommending is the RENTIS TAHAN - TRENGGAN trek. You take a boat up the Sungei Tembeling past many rapids to the ranger post. Then there's half an hour's hike to BUMBUN KUMBANG HIDE where you spend the night in the middle of the jungle. The next morning you walk six hours back to Kuala Tahan. This is a trip of moderate difficulty. The only hard part is crossing the Sungei Trenggan. After rainfall, the water rises up above belt level. A good hike is to GUA TELINGA, a bat cave. There are some very steep and slippery parts.

For trips of several days duration, you can rent a tent for M$5 per day. Be sure to take enough to eat and especially to drink. Many of the rivers marked on the info sheets contain drinkable water; you'd be better off, however, using purification tablets. Such tours are great for two people.

EQUIPMENT

For jungle tours it' vital to wear the proper boots. There are many different opinions as to which boots are best. We found the locally produced jungle boots ideal. They are made of canvas and have a thick, well treaded rubber sole. In addition you need to wear a pair of thick woollen socks. Your long pants should be tied inside the boots. Wear a light cotton shirt or T-shirt. On your head wear a wide hat (really nice when it rains!). When it rains a bit harder (and when doesn't it rain in the jungle?), you should have a plastic tarp that you can also use as a poncho. When folded up, such tarps take up almost no space. For longer trips, you'll also need a small tent.

LEECHES

Those who have never run into (or stepped on) these creatures will be sure to make their acquaintance here. Generally, they are pretty harmless creatures which lie along jungle paths and wait for a warm-blooded animal to pass by. Usually they crawl into your boots or up your pant leg. They fasten themselves to your skin with their suckers and draw blood. At the same time they secrete an enzyme which keeps your blood from clotting for a while. When they're nice and fat, they fall off. If, however, they've crawled through your boots and socks down to your feet and tanked up there, they won't be able to get back out again due to their increased volume. So don't be surprised if your feet are coated with blood. Preventive measures: tie your pants into your boots, and spray your boots with one or more rounds of insect repellent (such as Johnson's OFF). The leeches are then dissuaded, at least for a while. Smokers seem to be better off than non-smokers (you might try rubbing your feet with tobacco!). In the evening or during a break, you can remove the leeches - but don't rip them off. It is much better to get them to loosen themselves with a glowing cigarette or a bit of salt. The bleeding wounds should then be washed and covered with plaster. In the Taman Negara we found these unpleasant creatures only on the ground. In other South East Asian tropical forests they fall out of the trees onto you. The only way to be completely safe is to remain on the headquarters lawn.

BOOKINGS / HOW TO GET THERE

Since accommodation is limited, be sure to book well in advance. The address in KL: River Park Sdn. Bhd., 260H 2nd Mile, Jl.Ipoh, 51200 Kuala Lumpur, tel 03 4415299, telex MA 28202 SUNGEI. You have to pay a deposit of M$20 p.p: 80% will be refunded on a cancellation two weeks before departure. After that the deposit will be forfeited.

Single travellers, possibly even a couple, might head for Kuala Tembeling without an advance booking and hope to get a place in an unfilled boat. You're better off, however, registering in KL.

From KL, take bus or taxi via TEMERLOH to JERANTUT M$12.-(16.-) - the local bus from Temerloh to Jerantut costs M$3. If you're coming from the north, get a bus (4 hours) or taxi (1 1/2 hours) from KUALA LIPIS. There are taxis from Jerantut charging terrible prices for a ride on the paved road to KUALA TEMBELING. At 10:30 and 12:40 h there's also a bus charging M$2. Around

14:00 h, sometimes a bit earlier, the boats depart for KUALA TAHAN. If you're coming from KUANTAN, take a bus (M$6.40) or taxi (14M$) to Jerantut. If you're coming from SINGAPORE or KOTA BHARU, take the train to TEMBELING HALT, but make sure you ask the conductor to stop there. From here, it's just half an hour on foot to where the boats dock. The trains always stop in Jerantut. River Park in KL also has minibuses charging M$14 one way to Kuala Tembeling. If there are not enough people, they even pay a taxi.

KUALA LIPIS

Until 1986 this was the end of the road. Now, heading north, you can either go by rail or take the new road via Gua Musang. Kuala Lipis is a nicely situated town with a few old houses. Johnny Tan Boon Tok (48 Jelai Street, tel 311173, 312282) organizes jungle trekking tours. A typical three-day trek costs about M$60.

HOTELS

Nice *RESTHOUSE*** (tel 311267). Two hotels on the main street: *PARIS*** (tel 311136), *TONG KOK***, *SANG SANG** or *CENTRAL**, 100 Jl. Besar, tel 3112107. In addition there's the very clean *SRI LIPIS***, on the other side of the railroad.

LEAVING KUALA LIPIS

Three trains per day leave for KUALA KRAI at 7:00, 8:30, and 14:00 h. Prices: 1st cl.25.50, 2nd cl.11.50, 3rd cl. 7.10 M$. Buses / taxis to KL cost 6.-(12.-), KUANTAN 10.40(24.-).M$. At 8:00 and 10:00 h buses leave for KOTA BHARU via GUA MUSANG.

TASEK BERA

A very special route runs south from Temerloh to TASEK BERA. This is also of interest to people who want to go directly from Kuantan to Malacca and not take the new road 12 that was cut right through one of the remaining forests.

Take the two hour bus ride from Jl.Ibrahim to BAHAU (M$2.50). From there, go to SEREMBAN (1.90, 2 1/2 hours) - you can get from Seremban to Malacca for M$2.85 (see section *Between KL and JB).* If you want to stop off in Tasek Bera, you first have to get a permit from the Department of Aboriginal Affairs in Temerloh (behind the Temerloh Hotel). Only then are you permitted to spend the night in FORT SKANDA. From Bahau you can get to LADANG GEDDES for 60 c. Then go on by motorbike taxi for M$15 to Fort Skanda. TASEK BERA means "lake of changing colours". It isn't really what we'd call a lake, rather a maze of canals connecting smaller lakes or ponds. The "lake" is about 5 km wide and 27 km long. FORT SKANDA is the only market in a wide area. This is Orang Asli country. They belong to the 900 strong Semai tribe. Fishing is their most important source of livelihood. At the moment, the invasion of progress is limited to transistor radios. Rent a boat from the Orang Asli and let yourself be paddled around. By the way, during your visit to Fort Skanda, be sure to bring your own food.

TASEK CHINI

This is a lake similar to Tasek Bera. During the summer months, it's a sea of lotus blossoms! According to ancient legends a Loch Ness type monster inhabits the lake. The Orang Asli swear to it! Others tell of a sunken city in the Tasek Chini. You can take a day trip from Kuantan to the lake, rent a boat (costs M$80 from KG.BELIMBING) or spend a night in a raft-house on the river or in bungalows. A new bungalow resort was being built in 1987 on Laut Gumum, one of the numerous side lakes.

HOW TO GET THERE

About 56 km down the Kuantan - Temerloh road (between PAYA BUNGOR and KG.NEW ZEALAND) there's a road heading off to the left to KG. RAMBAI and KG.BELIMBING. About 28 km along, you come to Belimbing on the Pahang River. There isn't much traffic on the road. As far as we know there isn't a bus right to Belimbing. So take a taxi or try to get a lift from the fork. A second possibility is the crossroads after the village of MARAN; off to the left is a 10 km long road leading to KG.LUBOK PAKU. Three buses daily from Maran for 65c. There are also direct buses from Kuantan at 8:30 and 11:00 h for M$4.50. Lubok Paku is home of a Government Halting Bungalow costing about M$7 per night. Get boats from here to Tasek Chini for about M$80.

EAST MALAYSIA

We have divided Malaysia into western and eastern parts since they differ greatly from each other. In official language, one calls West Malaysia (the old Malaya) Peninsular Malaysia. In terms of area, the states of East Malaysia, Sabah and Sarawak are twice as big as the mainland. Only 2.5 million people live here, however. One of the links between the two parts is their common British colonial heritage. When Great Britain gave up her colonies on Borneo in 1963, nobody was certain whether these two states could survive. Many believed that Indonesia under Sukarno would absorb the northern part of the island. This they wanted to prevent at all costs, so Sabah and Sarawak were made states in the Federation of Malaysia.

Here is some information about the points differentiating East Malaysia from the mainland. It's important to remember that any visa or residency permit issued in Peninsular Malaysia is not automatically valid for Sabah and Sarawak.

CLIMATE & TRAVEL SEASONS

Sabah and Sarawak get most of their rain during the northeast monsoon. Kuching, a typical town, receives an average of 546 mm of precipitation during the wettest month of January, and only 173 mm during the driest month of July. Similar figures can be found for Sandakan in Sabah.

Temperatures are pretty constant all year round. In Sandakan, for example, the average daily high and low temperatures only range between 29 and 31.7°C. The lowest temperature ever recorded was 21°C. The rest of the country follows suit. The only exceptions are higher altitude areas, where it can get much colder at night.

The best time to visit is during the European summer. Keep in mind, though, that from June until the beginning of the rainy season the water level in the rivers is greatly reduced, making access to many areas difficult. For example we couldn't go from Kapit to Belaga during August, because of low water. If you plan to visit the interior, the period from March to June is best.

FESTIVALS AND HOLIDAYS

Besides those celebrated throughout the country, Sarawak and Sabah have a number of their own local festivals enjoyed by the various nationalities. Exact dates can be procured from the tourist offices in Kuching and Kota Kinabalu. In the middle of May, all of Sabah goes wild - the Kadazan are celebrating thanksgiving. The ancient dance of the Kadazan - ***Sumazau*** - is one of the high points of the ceremonies. At the end of May, try to be in Kota Belud for the largest and most important ***tamu*** of the year. Bajau ride into town on their horses. Cockfights are held, and old folk dances are performed. A smaller 'tamu' is held every Sunday morning. At the beginning of June (usually the 1st), Sarawak celebrates ***Gawai Dayak.*** After the rice harvest has been

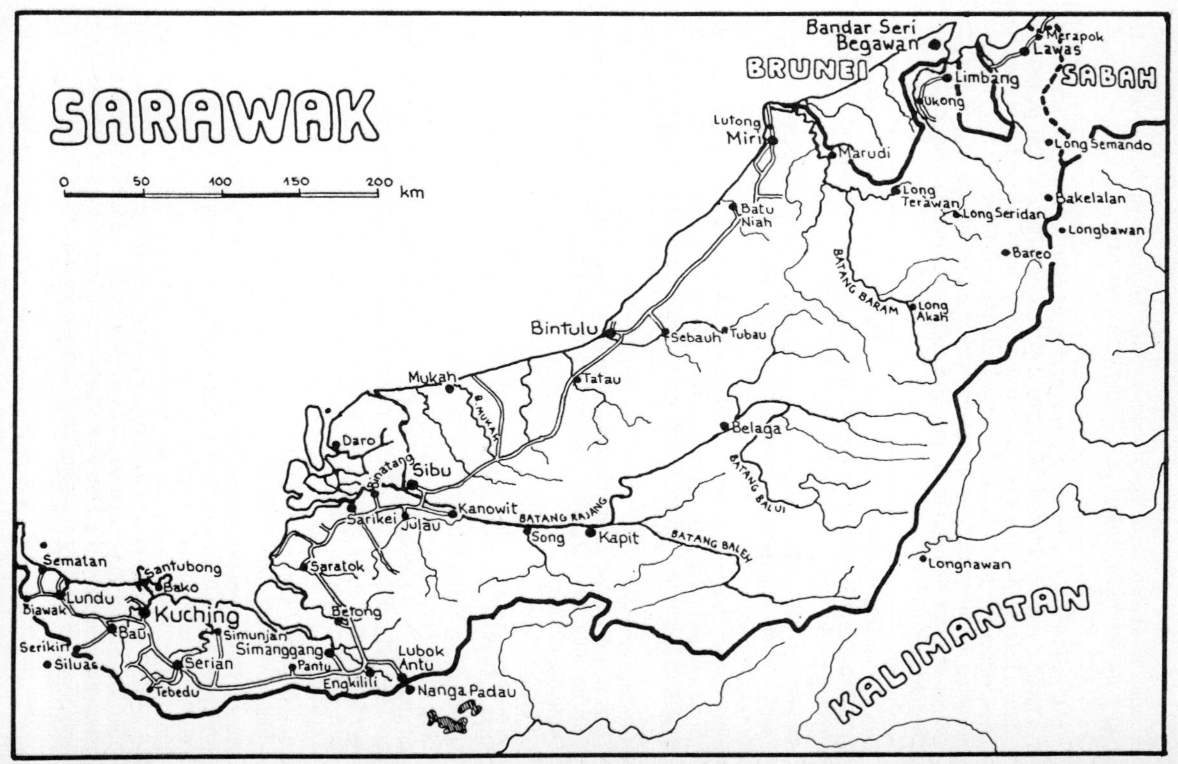
SARAWAK
0 50 100 150 200 km
BRUNEI
SABAH
KALIMANTAN
Bandar Seri Begawan
Merapok
Lawas
Limbang
Ukong
Lutong
Miri
Marudi
Long Semando
Long Terawan
Long Seridan
Bakelalan
Longbawan
Bareo
Batu Niah
BATANG BARAM
Long Akah
Bintulu
Sebauh
Tubau
Mukah
B. MUKAH
Tatau
Belaga
BATANG BALUI
Daro
Binatang
Sibu
Kanowit
Sarikei
Julau
BATANG RAJANG
Song
Kapit
BATANG BALEH
Longnawan
Sematan
Santubong
Bako
Lundu
Biawak
Kuching
Bau
Serikin
Siluas
Simunjan
Simanggang
Serian
Pantu
Tebedu
Saratok
Betong
Lubok Antu
Engkilili
Nanga Padau

brought in, several days of thanksgiving can begin. Longhouse visitors take part in the enthralling festivities. Tuak flows in streams!

***TUAK** is a kind of rice beer, yellowish to dirty white in colouring. When offered, it should never be refused. Normally a young girl will offer the guest a full glass. Those in the know will take only a very small sip and give back the glass. According to the ancient tradition, the girl must then drain it. The party becomes louder and louder, the gongs and drums sound, dancing begins. The guests, too, are required to dance. The noise and laughter last into the early morning hours.*

Blowpipe shooting contests take place during Gawai Dayak - probably the only time the old fashioned weapons are used. A rifle is preferred for hunting today. If you're lucky, you might even get to see the old war dance ***ngajat.***

Sarawak celebrates Malaysia's national holiday on August 31 (Hari Kebangsaan) in a different divisional capital each year. This is a tremendous occasion for the ulu-people, well worth a trip of several days. Iban and members of other tribes come down the rivers in their boats. They build small huts along the banks and wear their best clothes (mostly western) to show off a bit. The population of Bandar Sri Aman, where we partied, quadrupled during the fun. On July 1 in Keningau, Sabah, a famous tamu is held. Horse and buffalo races take place, and the most beautiful Murut and Kadazan girls are selected. There's also a large tamu in Kudat on the same day. Other important tamu are held on July 29 in Tuaran, end of August in Beaufort and the middle of September in Papar.

GETTING AROUND

Roads: The Trans-Sabah Highway between Kota Kinabalu and Tawau has been in service since 1982 - though not all parts are paved. Buses and trucks go more or less regularly. In 1984, the last section of the Sarawak Highway between Sibu and Bintulu was opened to traffic, although it can only be used by vehicles in the dry season. Some bridges are still missing. When the small part between Bandar Seri Begawan, Limbang and Lawas is finally finished, you'll be able to drive from Kuching all the way to Tawau - though only in a jeep or truck. Road building is really progressing in both states, so this information could soon be outdated.

Boats: Riverboats of various kinds and sizes are the most important means of transportation in Sarawak. All the major rivers are navigable, allowing you to reach the most isolated longhouse on the border to Indonesian Kalimantan. If there isn't a regular boat, you can either charter a boat (often very expensive), or you can wait by the jetty for a boat going in the right direction. This can require lots of time, but it's the best way to get into the interior. A prerequisite is a basic knowledge of the Malay language, the lingua franca in Borneo. Such boat trips into the blue are always the most interesting adventures.

Especially during the dry season, when the rivers don't have much water in the upper courses, you'll have to walk with the boat along the riverbank, pushing past rocks and shallows. At waterfalls you'll even have to portage through the jungle. During the rainy season, the rapids and the many uprooted trees carried downstream make river travel dangerous.

You can go by coastal steamer or other ships along the coast between Kuching and Tawau. There are a few speedboats. The regular connections are listed in the local sections.

Airplanes: MAS offers an excellent air network in both states. Domestic routes are usually flown by the reliable Fokker-Friendship F28 planes. Much smaller aircraft are used for the BN-flights. Reservations should be made as early as possible.

Trains: Only exist in Sabah between Tanjung Aru, Beaufort and Tenom. If you have a group of people, you can even charter a whole train car. Get more information at the Tanjong Aru train station.

ACCOMMODATION

Prices are generally a bit higher here than in the western part of the country. This is really noticeable in hotels. Expect to pay about M$20 for a double room. Places like Sandakan and Tawau are particularly expensive. What you pay in Iban or Kayan longhouses is up to you. Gifts are good, but leave the glass beads at home. Those days are long gone, even in the most isolated parts of Borneo. Hospitality is very important in many longhouses. Behave that way! Mass tourism has really destroyed a lot on the Skrang River in Sarawak. The tourist industry picked this river and has pumped countless groups of tourists through the longhouses along Sungai Skrang. The results present the strongest evidence against any kind of tourism.

We decided on the following price table for East Malaysia - all prices are for double rooms:

*	**up to 20 M$**
**	**up to 50 M$**
***	**up to 80 M$**
****	**over 80 M$**

NATIONALITIES & RELIGIONS

Dayak is the general term used for the proto-Malayan tribes of Kalimantan. Of the 1.3 million Sarawak population, about half are tribal members. Around 200 different tribes make their home on the island. The most important ethnic group in Sarawak is the Iban, making up about one third of the population.

Iban or Sea Dayak are mostly settled in the 2nd, 3rd, 4th and 7th divisions of Sarawak. Large numbers also live on the other side of the Indonesian border which was arbitrarily drawn by the colonial powers. Living in a longhouse is characteristic of their culture as with most other Borneo tribes. Up to 180 m long, 15-20 m wide and set on piles up to 5 m high, longhouses can provide shelter for up to 300 people. Each family has its own room *(bilek).* Most longhouses are on rivers with the kitchens *(dapor)* always looking inland. Some tribes also have an unroofed porch. A long, roofed porch *(ruai)* is toward the river side. It serves as a big living room, and all the *bilek* have doors opening onto it. Here people work, meet, grind rice, mend fishnets, and gather for festivities.

The chief of a longhouse is called *Tuai Rumah.* He settles disagreements, calls together the council of elders, declares divorces, and is the community representative with outsiders. The *bilek* of the *Tuai Rumah* is in the centre of the longhouse. Often his doorway is specially decorated and carved. Once in a while you'll see dusty old cannons in front. On arrival you'll have to present yourself to him for a talk and a cigarette.

The title of chief is not inherited - the most important men in the longhouse elect one of their own to be *Tuai Rumah.* The name of the longhouse changes with the new leader. There is only a superficial class system. Usually the *bilek* on the outer ends of the longhouses belong to less influential families.

Religious power among the Iban is in the hands of a medicine man *(manang).* In other tribes he is called *dayong* or *dajung* or sometimes *wadian.* The latter can also be a woman. He or she possesses magical powers, heals the sick, places people in trance, and is the longhouse legend and story-teller. If you've ever spent the night in the jungle among the sounds of cicadas, insects, frogs, birds, and monkeys - plus occasional thunder and lightning - you'll be able to understand why the religious conceptions of the Dayak are centred on the kaleidoscope of background noises. The inhabitants of the more isolated longhouses are still animists - although where missionaries have been busy, the spiritual beliefs have taken on a Christian variant.

The Iban, like other tribes, live from agriculture (rubber, mountain rice, corn, pepper) as well as hunting and fishing. Today many young Iban are leaving their traditional homes to seek work in the cities, in industry or on plantations.

HEADHUNTING

Dusty, smoked skulls of the longhouses' dead enemies can be seen hanging above the 'ruai'. The latest pieces probably date from WWII when the British pretty much legalized headhunting - at least for Japanese heads. In the past when a Dayak died, male members of his family would go out and seek to return with a captured enemy head. It was thought that the spirit or soul of a person was indestructible and remained in the skull. At weddings, too, the groom was required to present the bride's father with a head before marriage. The prized head would then be smoked and placed in a plaited rattan basket. The Iban were fond of hanging up nets with up to 30 skulls. According to Dayak beliefs, the captured heads bring new energy and life to the longhouse and the community.

Land Dayak (Bidayuh) are about 107,000 strong, and live mostly in Division 1 today. They are very peaceful people who have been pushed around in the past by the more aggressive Iban.

Kayan and Kenyah are mostly settled in Indonesian Kalimantan. In Sarawak you'll find them on the upper courses of the Baleh and Rajang Rivers. They are estimated to have about 20,000 members. There are some interesting differences between the Iban and Land Dayak on the one hand, and the Kayan and Kenyah on the other. The latter are aristocratic societies, meaning that some families have more privileges and authority than others. Slave holding used to be widespread. The lowest families on the social scale today are the descendants of slaves. Kayan and Kenyah are excellent metal workers and makers of parangs.

Their tattoos are especially interesting. They are real works of art, created by an extremely painful procedure. Often the design is cut into a kind of wooden stamp. This is then smeared with a mixture of soot, sugar cane juice, and water and then stamped onto the intended part of the body. Two utensils are necessary for tattooing: a sharply pointed steel nail with a long handle *(ulang)* and a metal rod. The nail is repeatedly driven into the skin with light taps from the rod.

Murut have a population of about 40,000 in the Tenom region of southern Sabah as well as in the 5th division (Lawas/Trusan) in Sarawak. Nowadays they largely live off their rice paddies, which have been supported by Sabah government projects. In addition they plant sweet potatoes, manioc, and sugar cane. Originally the Murut were semi-nomadic hunters who were pushed back into the less accessible jungle by the late-coming Kadazan. They have long since turned in their blowpipes for rifles.

Kadazan make up about 30% of the Sabah population. Sub-tribes are the Dusun (around Tuaran) and the Rungus (around Kudat). With slight dialect differences, all Kadazan speak the same language. Today they are mostly peasants who own their own land. The average farm size of 1-2 ha per farm is large by South East Asian standards. Many Kadazan no longer work on the farm but have gone into politics, administration, or teaching. For this reason, the importance of Christian missionaries and their school system in providing a high level of education shouldn't be underestimated.

Bajau make up about 15% of Sabah's inhabitants. They live on the west coast between Kudat and Papar. Another group can be found on the east coast, mostly around Lahad Datu. They only arrived in the 19th century; they were feared pirates between the Sulu Archipelago and Sulawesi. Today about half the Bajau live from fishing and the other half from agriculture. Especially in the Kota Belud area, cattle raising has become important, and the Bajau here have earned a name as the cowboys of Borneo.

Chinese make up a third of the Sarawak population, and about 20% in Sabah. The Chinese made their big push into the northwest coast areas of Borneo during the last century and the first thirty years of this one. As in other parts of South East Asia, they mostly come from southern China (Hokkien,

Hakka, Teochew, Canton and Hainan). They control the retail trade, industry, and transport, but in Sabah are also important in agriculture.

HISTORY

The history of the Malaysian states of Sarawak and Sabah is closely connected to that of Brunei. The language cripples in England managed to turn the Malay word ***Berunai*** (= Brunei) into Borneo (pronounced 'borneeoh'). This European name was given to the third largest island in the world. Today the whole island is called Kalimantan meaning 'island of the rivers'. Extensive trade relations have been maintained between the north coast of Kalimantan and the Chinese Empire since the 15th century. With the arrival of the European powers, first ***Portugal*** and then Spain, the traditional social and economic structure was greatly changed. In 1521, Brunei was attacked by the fleet of the world circumnavigator, Magellan. Brunei, which also controlled a large part of the southern Philippines, was conquered by superior Spanish weaponry. Century-long trading links were broken. A similar policy was also practised by the Dutch. Brunei was reduced to a mini-state. Pirates made the coasts unsafe.

In 1841 ***James Brooke,*** one of the typical representatives who helped create the British Empire, sailed on his ship 'The Royalist' along the coast of Sarawak. At that time the Iban and Malays were in rebellion against the Sultan of Brunei because he, or rather his proxy in Kuching, was forcing the people to work in the antimony mines. James Brooke knew right away which side to join. For the sultan's cause he used the firepower from his ship to 'restore law and order' as pacification measures of this kind are still being called. Out of gratitude, the Sultan of Brunei made James Brooke Raja of Sarawak, with a right to all state income in return for a pittance of $2500 a year from Brooke. This formed the basis of power for the White Rajas of Sarawak. From 1853 to 1904, the area was expanded to its present size. Until the 1930s, rebellions were common occurrences. The peacekeeping measures of the White Raja have gone down in history as great and heroic acts for the general good of Sarawak. It remains questionable if this really was the case. The Brookes gave the country an administration, it is true, and allowed the different nationalities some say. But they also conducted bloody campaigns against ethnic groups unwilling to submit completely to the White Raja rule.

The most important rebellions against the White Raja

1857: *A rebellion of Chinese coolies and settlers in Bau. They were able to capture Kuching. Later 3-4000 were killed by British troops.*

1858-61: *Uprising of the Iban under the leadership of the legendary Rentap on the Sungei Skrang.*

1863: *Large retaliation action against the Kayan on the Rajang.*

1896-1909: *Resistance of the Iban on the Batang Ai under the leadership of Bantin.*

1931-34: *Rebellion under Asun on the Sungei Kanowit*

The British empire forced the Sultan of Brunei to cede the island of Labuan in 1846. The weakened sultan had no other choice when faced with the threatening cannon of Her Majesty's fleet. Until 1888, Sabah was controlled and ruled by the privately owned ***British North Borneo Company.*** Two English merchants bought this part of Borneo from the Sultan of Brunei, but at the same time made payments to the Sultan of Sulu (Philippines) because the title was unsettled (the former President Marcos later staked a claim to Sabah). In 1888, Brunei and Sabah became British protectorates.

Between 1894 and 1905, the ***Mat Salleh Revolt*** broke out in Sabah. It began with the murder of two Dayak traders. Mat Salleh, headman of the village, was ordered to be brought to justice. First he refused to give himself up to a police unit; later he swore on the Koran to obey the laws of Sabah. In 1895 he showed up in Sandakan with a large number of armed followers to bring a complaint against the North Borneo Company. The governor of the day rejected it as unfounded. An arrest order for Mat Salleh was issued in 1896, but he seemed to have been swallowed up by the jungle. In 1897 he appeared again on the island of Gaya with a group of armed men and burned everything to the ground with the exception of his birthplace village. At that time the security forces of the Company were mostly Dayak from Sarawak. During the following military campaigns, head-hunting of the rebels was permitted. Villages were destroyed and the inhabitants killed. But not until 1900 was a large military force able to capture Mat Salleh and some of his supporters in Tambunan. Mat Salleh was killed, but 'peace' would not return for another five years.

During WWII the whole island was occupied by Japanese troops. In 1945, the major towns of Sabah were completely destroyed by American and Australian bomber attacks. After the Japanese capitulation, the third White Raja of Sarawak, Charles Vyner Brooke, handed over his private country to the British Crown after negotiating a royal compensation for himself.

Sabah and Sarawak achieved independence and became member states of the ***Federation of Malaysia*** at the same time in 1963. This was a time when the names of the two states were being bannered daily in the international press. Indonesia's president Sukarno saw the founding of Malaysia as an imperialist provocation and began a policy of open confrontation (konfrontasi). Communist guerillas received active support from Indonesia. Indonesian troops were even sent across the border into Sarawak and Sabah.

The guerilla problem along the border still hasn't been completely solved, even though the new Indonesian government under Suharto ended the 'konfrontasi' policy way back in 1965/66. In the past few years, the situation around Sarawak and Sabah has been greatly stabilized. The Philippines have given up their historic claim to Sabah, and have formed ASEAN (Association of South East Asian Nations) together with Indonesia, Singapore, Brunei, Thailand and Malaysia.

SUGGESTED READING

The Borneo Literature Bureau has published many interesting books about Sabah and Sarawak which were printed with local government support. They are hard to find overseas. You can find them in the libraries in Kuching and KK.

OLD SARAWAK - A PICTORIAL STUDY (Ed. by Lockard & Saunders; Kuching 1972). With text in four languages (English, Malay, Iban, and Chinese), there is a wide ranging picture section including old sketches, paintings and photos.

SARAWAK LONG AGO (Chater, W.J.; Kuching 1969). An amusing collection of anecdotes about the history of Sarawak.

LIFE IN A LONGHOUSE (Morrison, H.; Kuching 1962). A four language picture book with photos from the 1950s. It was put together by an active woman whose husband, an anthropologist, was the longtime curator of the Sarawak Museum.

VANISHING WORLD - THE IBANS OF BORNEO (Morrison, H.; New York, Tokyo 1978). The best book about the Iban available in Singapore or even in Europe.

THE PAGAN TRIBES OF BORNEO (Hose & McDougall, Reprint 1966). The standard work about the Borneo tribes, especially the Iban and Kayan of Sarawak. Both volumes were first published in 1912.

BORNEO PEOPLE (Macdonald, M.; London 1956). The author tells of his experiences on the island as a British colonial officer in the 1940s and 1950s.

NORTH BORNEO & ITS PEOPLE (Alliston, C.; London 1966). An informative and wide ranging book about Sabah.

BORNEO A Time/Life picture book.

NINE DAYAK NIGHTS (Geddes, W.; Oxford 1973). An anthropological research paper, though easy to read. Offers many insights into the life and myths of the Land Dayak.

A SARAWAK ANTHOLOGY (Ed. Dickson, M.G.; London 1965). A good introduction with wide ranging bits of information.

LIFE IN THE FORESTS OF THE FAR EAST (Spenser St. John, reprint, Kuala Lumpur 1974). The description of an adventurous trip through Borneo during the 1850s , especially the land areas which today belong to Sabah.

THE WHITE RAJAHS - A HISTORY OF SARAWAK FROM 1841 TO 1946 (Runciman, Steven; Cambridge 1960). The most comprehensive book about the history of Sarawak.

SARAWAK 1893 - 1968 (Rawlins, Joan; London 1972). Easy to read , though it praises the Brookes too uncritically.

SARAWAK

Malaysia's largest state is located on the third largest island in the world. 'Sarawak - the land of the head-hunters' is the promise to be found in the glossy ads hoping to entice civilization-weary tourists to seek adventure on the island. A river trip through the tremendous jungle to the longhouses of the various tribes is part of the standard programme for both group and individual tourists. According to taste, some people go in strictly organized tours up the Skrang River, an area set up to handle massive storms of visitors. Others spend several days on a boat trip to reach the most inaccessible village where, if possible, 'no tourist has ever been'. Conflicts are unavoidable where local people are being treated as tourist attractions. The Iban, Kayan, or Kenyah, who live in Sarawak as well as on the Indonesian side of the island, are traditionally open to guests - but not to European tourists with their high expectations. Tourists expect the longhouse to be open for examination into even the most intimate corners; meat is expected to be served and, come evening, the tuak should literally flow - OK, let's have things nice and primitive, please! No one stops to think that the people living here also have a need for privacy, that it's not easy to replenish their food stores, and that for them a good tin roof during the rainy season is the ultimate in comfort.

KUCHING

Sarawak's capital, on the southern bank of the Sungei Sarawak, is only about 20 km from the South China Sea. Even today, despite the Holiday Inn, it feels more like a Joseph Conrad novel than a modern metropolis. 'Kuching', by the way, is the Malay word for 'cat'; here's how it came about. When James Brooke landed here for the first time he pointed towards the village from the harbour and asked one of the natives the name. The native, however, thought that Brooke was pointing at a cat which chanced to be walking by and assumed he wanted to know the Malay word for 'cat'. So he told him 'kuching'.

The town's biggest attraction is the *SARAWAK MUSEUM* (open Mon-Thurs 9:15-17:15 h, Sat and Sun until 18:00 h). Admission is free. It holds the largest collection of archaeological and cultural pieces in all of Borneo. Since 1984 the old museum has housed the natural science collections and the new Dewan Tun Abdul Razak the ethnological and historical ones. In addition, you can study the flora and fauna of Sarawak. The museum was founded by the second Raja Brooke in 1888, probably with Alfred Russel Wallace, the discoverer of the dividing line of the same name, offering a few ideas. The Wallace line runs between Bali and Lombok and further to the north between Kalimantan and Sulawesi - to the west you find Asian flora and fauna, to the east the Australiao-Melanese varieties begin.

On the corner of Courthouse Rd. / Main Bazar is the *SUPREME COURT BUILDING* built in 1874. Its thick Victorian columns just don't seem to fit in on Borneo. In front is a *MEMORIAL* to the second Raja, Sir Charles Brooke. At each corner is a bronze relief representing the four main ethnic groups in Sarawak: Iban, Malay, Chinese, and Kayan.

The city is dominated by the *MASJID NEGARA,* the new national mosque with its golden dome.

The *ISTANA,* also built by the second Raja, is on the other side of the river (20 c by boat). Today it's the residence of the Sarawak governor. A bit further upstream is another structure giving strong testimony to the past greatness of the White Raja. *FORT MARGHERITA,* named for the Raja's second wife, is a police museum today. Between the istana and the old fort is a Brooke family cemetery. The super-modern Sarawak Parliament Building *(COUNCIL NEGERI KOMPLEKS)* is a new local landmark. A trip across the river is rewarding.

HOTELS

Good is the *KUCHING HOTEL***, 6 Temple Street, tel 413985. About the same, *KHIAW HIN*** at 52 India St. Other cheapies: *AH CHEW**,* 3 Java St. or *NG CHEW*,* 16-17 Courthouse Road. *SYN AH*,* 16 Market St. is loud and filthy. There aren't any middle class hotels under M$30. In the higher bracket you're best off at *KAPIT HOTEL****,* 59 Jl.Padungan. Or on the same street try the *SARAWAK HOTEL****,* no. 196. Cheap dorm in the *HOSTEL** behind the St.Joseph's Cathedral on Jl. Tun Haji Openg between GPO and Aurora Hotel.

FOOD

Indian-Malay food can be found on Jl. India. On Carpenter Street there's a big Chinese place squashed between two temples. Nobody speaks any English though! Between the Electra Building (great view from the roof!) and the bus station are lots of foodstalls. Nasi goreng or mee goreng are served for as little as M$1.50.

Good and cheap is *FOOK HOI* diagonally across from the GPO.

Get excellent Chinese food at *MANDARIN* in the Odeon Hotel on Jl.Padungan.

GENERAL INFORMATION

TOURIST INFORMATION - good information available from the Sarawak Tourist Association at 1-3 Temple Street, tel 240620. TDC Sarawak Regional Office at the AIA Building, Jl. Song Thian Chock, open Mon-Fri 9:00-16:30 h, Sat 9:00-12:00 h.

IMMIGRATION - Jl.Song Thian Chock, open Mon-Fri 9:00-16:30 h, Sat 9:00-12:00 h.

POST OFFICE - GPO on Jl.Tun Haji Openg.

BANKS - find the Chartered Bank near Holiday Inn. Overseas Union Bank and Hongkong & Shanghai Banking Corporation are on Jl.Tun Haji Openg near the market.

AMERICAN EXPRESS - Sarawak Travel Agencies, 4 Holiday Inn Arcade are the representatives.

BOOKS - a good bookstore is in the Holiday Inn, Jl.Tunku Abdul Rahman. Besides literature about Borneo, you might even get the two part Sarawak map with a scale of 1:500,000. It's the best Sarawak map you can buy. We weren't able to find this map anywhere else.

CONSULATES - Indonesia, 19 Jl. Deshon, tel 21734. Pontianak is a visa free entry / exit point.

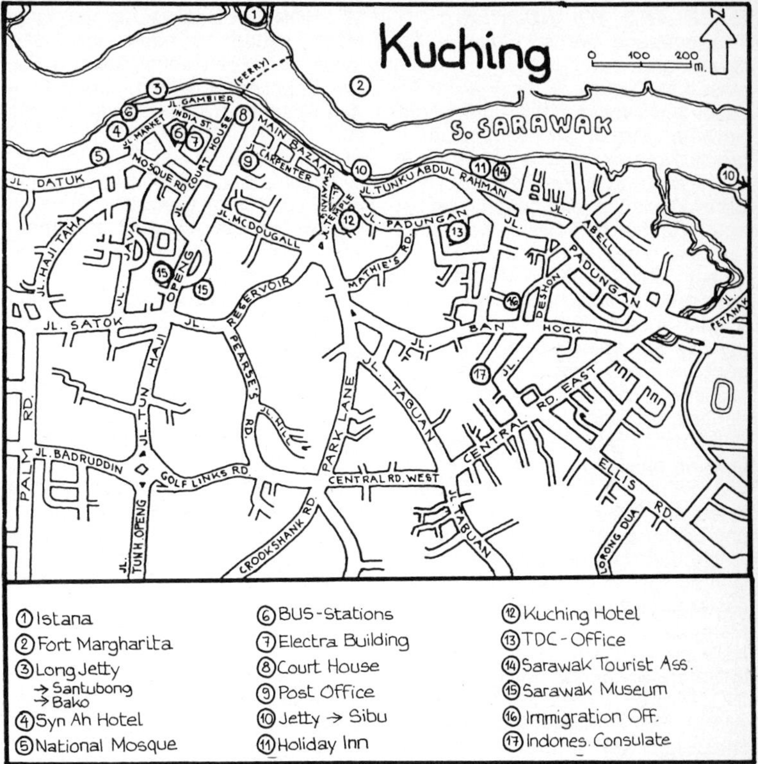

LEAVING KUCHING

BY AIR - DOMESTIC

Kuching Airport is about 10 km south of town, bus 12 or 12A leaves every 25 minutes for 80 c until midnight, a taxi costs M$18. MAS office in Leboh Power, Electra House, tel 454255. SAMPLE PRICES: BANDAR SERI BEGAWAN 192.-, BINTULU 97.-, KOTA KINABALU 198.-, LABUAN 173.-, MIRI 136.-, SIBU 60.-, JOHORE BHARU 147.-(night flight 125.-), KUALA LUMPUR 231.-(night flight 162.-), SINGAPORE 170.- M$. In addition there are the so-called BN-flights (Britton Norman Islander Flights), with which you can reach just about every tiny place in Sarawak, though sometimes only once a week.

BY AIR - INTERNATIONAL

The fastest way to Indonesian Kalimantan is by Merpati flights to Pontianak on Friday at 12:00 h for M$84. Agent in Kuching: Sin Hua Travel Service, 8 Temple Street, tel 23276.

OVERLAND TO INDONESIA

The overland border between Sarawak and Indonesia is generally closed to foreigners. This is not the case, however, for the land border between Sabah and Indonesia. In practice our experience is this: Travellers who travel from Kalimantan to Sarawak via the land border, and use an official border crossing point open for local border traffic, don't receive an entry stamp from the Malaysians in the passport. Instead they are issued a letter to be presented in Kuching to the Sarawak Immigration Office. What happens next, nobody knows. They probably won't send you back to Indonesia, at worst deport you. A lot depends on your tact and ability to talk. An official departure from Sarawak across this border to Kalimantan is not permitted. Since there aren't any border posts in the middle of the jungle, there's really only the Indonesian authorities to stop you. It's much easier to deal with them than with the Malaysians.

Here is a list of the immigration offices in Sarawak: Central office in KUCHING; Division Offices in BANDAR SRI AMAN, SIBU, MIRI, LIMBANG, SARIKEI and KAPIT; Branch offices in BAU, SERIAN, LUNDU, ENGKILILI, BINTULU, MARUDI, LAWAS and SUNDAR; Borderposts in SEMATAN, BIAWAK, SERIKIN, BUNAN GEGA PADAWAN, LUBOK ANTU, BATU LINTANG and SUNGEI TUJUH.

BY SHIP

Coastal ships regularly traverse all of Sarawak's coastline. Daily at 8:30 h either the M.V.MAS JAYA 1 or 2 or the M.V.CONCORD leave Kuching for SARIKEI. Change here for another boat to SIBU. Costs M$20 or M$17 to SARIKEI. The departure point is Marine Base (Jl.Pending, bus 17 or 1). Every Wed and Sat at 18:00 h the M.V.HONG LEE leaves on the same route, taking 18 hours for M$18 (deck) or M$29 (cabin). Agent is Ramin Shipping Sdn. Bhd., Chan Chin Ann Road, tel 57043. Sibu is also the port of call for the M.V.RAJAH MAS which leaves Mon and Thurs at 18:00 h. Agent is South East Asia Shipping Bhd., Lot 175, Jl.Chan Chin Ann, tel 22966. Irregular freight / passenger ships sail the entire coast making stops in Bintulu, Miri, Marudi, Limbang and up to Lawas. Get more info at the Siam Company, 28 Main Bazar, tel 22832.

Since 1986 a new car-passenger ferry, the CRUISE MUHIBAH, has run on the following route: Kuantan (Sat) - Kuching (Sun) - Kota Kinabalu (Tues) - Kuantan (Thurs) - Singapore (Fri) - Kuantan (Sat). Tariffs from Kuching are: KUANTAN 160.- (Standard cabin); 235.- (De luxe cabin); 350.-M$ (suite).

KOTA KINABALU 140.- (Standard cabin); 195.- (De luxe cabin); 300.-M$ (suite).

SINGAPORE 200.- (Standard cabin); 270.- (De luxe cabin); 355.- M$(suite).

Get your tickets at the Feri Malaysia Office, Menara Utama UMBC, Jl.Sultan Sulaiman, KL, tel 2388899, or right in Kuching at Malaysia Shipping Agencies Sdn. Bhd., Blok E, Lot 33, Taman Sri Sarawak Mall, Jl.Tunku Abdul Rahman, tel 418330. In Peninsular Malaysia, Feri Malaysia is also represented by Reliance Shipping & Travel Agencies Sdn. Bhd. They have offices in Penang, Malacca, Ipoh, and Johore Bharu.

BY BUS

The bus station is on Market Street. Buses 17 and 1 go to Pending. Long distance buses: BAU 1.85, LUNDU 6.20, SERIAN 4.-, BANDAR SRI AMAN 12.20, SARATOK 17.20 M$.

DAY TRIPS AROUND KUCHING

SANTUBONG

is set on the sea about 30 km from Kuching and is a popular place to bathe. Between 7:00 and 8:00 h in the morning, a boat will take you down the river for M$3. The boats tie up along Long Jetty (Jl.Gambier). Don't miss your ride back - leaves around 13:30 h; check! Beautiful countryside! In the background is the 800 m high Gunung Santubong. At one time this was an important trading centre. Nearby excavations show contacts with the Chinese empire as early as 700 to 1200 AD.

BAKO NATIONAL PARK

The 26 km^2 national park, situated on an ocean peninsula, is a place to relax, hike, and study the flora. There isn't an awful lot of fauna. But you can still see sambar deer, wild pigs, and once in a while proboscis monkeys which the Malays call 'orang belanda' or 'Dutchman' because they all have long noses. There are well marked paths throughout the park. You can spend the night quite cheaply in TELOK ASSAM in a kind of hostel for M$1.10. The two rest-houses only have two / three rooms each and cost about M$30. You'll have to organize your excursion before leaving Kuching. Address: Office of National Parks (in the forestry department), Jl.Gartek. Since 1987 a new road has been in use and an hourly bus (no. 6) runs to Bako for M$2.10.

KG.SEGU BENUK

If you don't have a lot of time and still want to visit a Land Dayak longhouse, then here's your chance. About 35 km away is Kg. Segu Benuk. Take a STC bus from the bus station - leaves around 11:00 h, for M$1.80. Don't forget the last bus back! It's not the best introduction - the longhouse is pretty touristy and whole busloads arrive regularly.

BAU

is a tiny nest west of Kuching. Gold prospectors were active here until 1890. Today the huge excavations have been flooded, and Tasek Biru (blue lake) is the town's main attraction. Only a few tourists make it here to swim in the fresh water and to enjoy the cheap lakeside food prices. For M$1.85, you can get a Bau Transport Co. bus at the bus terminal. From Bau you can get to the villages of LUNDU and SEMATAN and their beaches. From Bau, a bus for Lundu leaves every 1 1/2 hours until 15:00 h for M$3. Siar Beach is about 10 km from town. From Lundu, STC buses leave regularly for M$1.95 to Sematan. In Lundu stay at CHENG HAK BOARDING HOUSE**, in Sematan at THOMAS LAI SEASIDE RESORT**(*).

BETWEEN KUCHING AND BRUNEI

This huge region includes all the divisions with the exception of the fifth (Limbang). You'll find possibilities for river trips everywhere. With some knowledge of Malay and a sense of initiative, you can really get going. Don't take any difficult jungle treks alone and if a beginner, don't overestimate your abilities. There are too many imponderables. For one thing, you need the right touch when dealing with the Malaysian or Indonesian officials in the border regions. And secondly, health risks far away from civilization and the nearest hospital are much higher. On the other hand, a trip through Sarawak's jungle is a once in a lifetime experience.

TIPS FOR JUNGLE TREKS AND TRIPS

Don't go on a real jungle trip alone - find the right partners. Three to five people is about the right number. The general planning is very important: you should know as much as you can about the area you plan to visit. All kinds of information (literature, maps, discussions, addresses, interviews etc.) should be collected in advance. Resign yourself to doing without a lot of things which we are all pretty used to i.e. electricity, transportation, prepared meals, and super hygiene.

In most cases you'll be in a boat on long trips; on hikes over rough territory you'll hardly make 500 m per hour. If it's also swampy, you'll make even worse time. Those who aren't used to the endless green and dimness of a tropical rainforest can easily go into a rage.

OUTFIT

For day long hikes through the jungle, the right equipment is very important. Even a day's excursion to a longhouse can lead to your undoing if the country is rough and you have the wrong shoes. Here are just a few of the most obvious pieces of equipment you'll need (which, depending on the region, you'll have to add to):

- ❑ Jungle boots with thick soles, though not normal leather boots, which become too heavy when soaked with water. Besides they take too long to dry.
- ❑ Good cotton socks (and a second pair to change into).
- ❑ Sandals: rubber thongs are best, so your feet can have a rest from the boots.
- ❑ Pants with lots of pockets and a belt from which you can hang your canteen, parang and other things.
- ❑ Bathing suit or sarong, especially for women.
- ❑ Long sleeve shirts with button-down pockets, and T-shirts.
- ❑ A wide rimmed hat to protect you from the rain.
- ❑ A small plastic tarp which can also be used as a poncho.
- ❑ A small backpack - 12 kg could be the end of the world.
- ❑ Compass.
- ❑ Small tent - but it isn't always necessary since you'll mostly be going from longhouse to longhouse.
- ❑ First aid kit.
- ❑ Pocket knife with a can opener.
- ❑ Food - a bit of rice to offer your hosts and some canned goods.
- ❑ Wash kit including a small towel to wipe rain and sweat during the hike.
- ❑ Cooking utensils, including a good supply of matches and lighters which should be kept in a waterproof container.

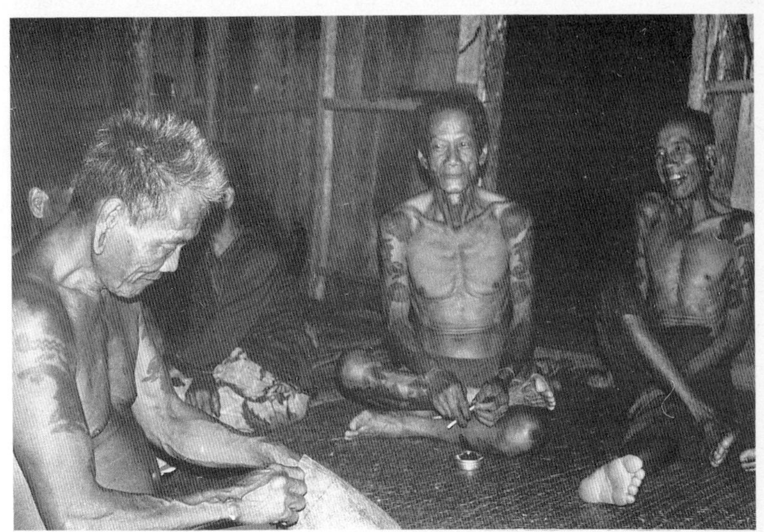

IBAN COUNCIL OF ELDERS, SARAWAK

UNPLEASANT ENCOUNTERS

There are dangers everywhere - on the road as well as in the jungle. But you don't have to worry about an orang utan á la King Kong; you probably won't even see one. Any animal hearing you tramp along the path will disappear. Much worse are the smaller members of the jungle population. You'll just have to accept the leeches (see the section on *Taman Negara* in the West Malaysia chapter).

And here's a word about the much maligned snakes. Very few are actually poisonous. It is important, however, to go through the jungle with your eyes open. If you should happen to step on a snake, it will feel threatened and bite. Even then the amount of poison you receive depends on when the snake bit last. In the worst case, the only thing which will help is treatment with serum, and this is only found in a hospital refrigerator. Paul's personal tip: it's important that the poison doesn't get into your bloodstream. Make cuts along the two teeth marks parallel to the arteries. Let them bleed as much as possible or squeeze the poison out. The bitten person should lie as still as possible. The shock and fear, both of the victim and the partners, require calm and proper behaviour. Remember that snake bites are seldom deadly - the danger to the victim depends on how long it's been since the snake last bit and the amount of poison remaining. Some people have even been bitten by a cobra and survived.

Insects such as wasps and hornets can be much more dangerous. Their nests are hung on trees or tree trunks and look like clumps of greyish brown clay. If you bump into a nest by accident, clear out of the area as fast as possible. The bites of scorpions and millepedes are also dangerous. Keeping your eyes open is the key!

These are just a few hints which our New Zealand friend Paul was able to come up with. The stories about the evil wilderness and headhunters with poisoned blow-pipe darts are white colonialist fantasies. We have decided not to mention any special village or region for you to see or any river to travel on. Organize such a trip yourself. Since all the tourists started going up and down the Sungei Skrang on completely organized trips, an awful lot has changed. We don't want to play a part in making that happen to other regions.

BANDAR SRI AMAN

Since 1978 the town is officially called BANDAR SRI AMAN, formerly SIMANGGANG. It takes about 4 hours by bus for the 135 km from Kuching. The way to the administrative capital of the 2nd Division leads through a number of pepper plantations as well as many so-called new villages. During the high point of the communist guerilla activity in the 1960s, whole villages were uprooted and placed in these fenced and guarded camps. Most of the people were Chinese.

HOTELS

In Sri Aman you can choose between three hotels. The best is *HOOVER* ****, 125 Club Road (tel 2173). Right around the corner are two other hotels: *ALISHAN**** and *TAIWAN****. In Alishan they serve very good, reasonably-priced Chinese food.

LEAVING BANDAR SRI AMAN

From Bandar Sri Aman, get a bus to SARIKEI (leaves daily at 7:30 and 13:30 h for M$12.20). Often the buses are booked up in advance. In that case take the STC bus to SARATOK (8:00 and 14:00 h, M$9.20) and from there the local bus to Sarikei for M$4.20. There are three hotels in Saratok (HOOVER, AMBASSADOR and GOLDEN CITY). Hourly from 7:00 to 16:00 h, a riverboat leaves Sarikei for SIBU (M$5), taking 2 1/2 hours. If you miss the last boat, you can spend the night in town. The cheapest accommodation is in RAJANG*, 1 Berjaya Road. A bit better is SARIKEI HOTEL**, 11 Wharf Road or SOUTHERN HOTEL***, 21 Repok Road.

DAY TRIPS AROUND BANDAR SRI AMAN

SELEPONG / GUA

Along the road back to Kuching, you come to SELEPONG, a longhouse right on the road. A bit further back is the longhouse GUA. It is an interesting example of a modern longhouse with glass windows, electricity, and gas stoves and it shows an attempt to keep the tradition of living together while still reaching out to the 20th century.

LUBOK ANTU

Another excursion might be to LUBOK ANTU (about 70 km, bus leaves five times daily for M$6). Lubok Antu is an important border crossing point to Indonesia. Indonesians come across the border to buy, or rather barter, pepper or latex for hard ringgit. You can stay in the Resthouse. At one time this was the departure point for a real adventure trip to Indonesia. It's only a two hour hike to NANGAPADAU. From there you can go by boat down to SEMITAU where you can get the regular Kapuas riverboat to PONTIANAK or PUTUSSIBAU. See the section in the Kalimantan chapter.

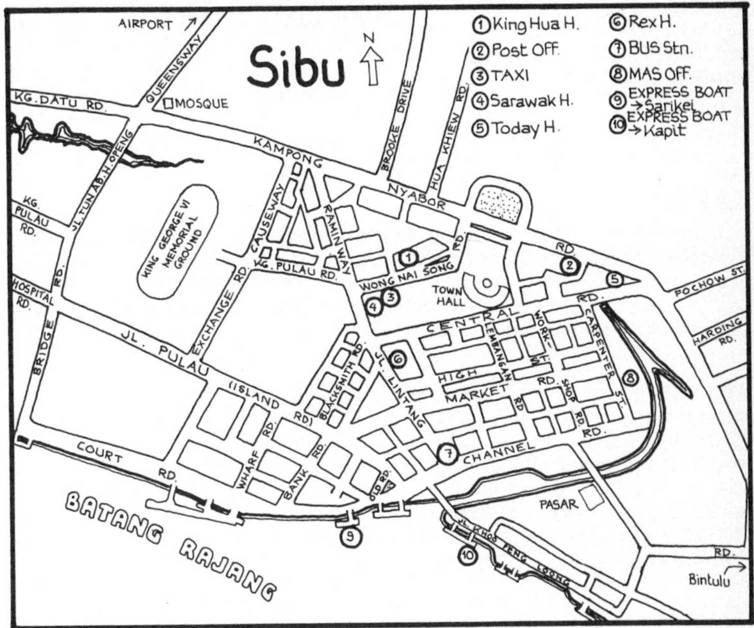

SIBU

is a bustling Chinese town. The Rajang River is still quite wide here allowing even good sized ships to steam up. The town is the centre of the timber industry in Sarawak as well as being important for the pepper and rubber trade. An Lively nightlife!

HOTELS

Some hotels, cheap in Sibu terms, can be found on Kg.Nyabor Road: *TODAY HOTEL****, no. 40 (tel 36499); *DIMAN HOTEL***, no. 27 (tel 337887) or *MALAYSIA****, no. 8 (tel 332299).

Or go to the *REX HOTEL****, 32 Cross Road. Also good is *METHODIST GUESTHOUSE*(*)*, 22 Island Road.

LEAVING SIBU

BY AIR

MAS office is on 19 Raminway, tel 26166. The airport is 6 km north of town. Bus 1 goes out there. SAMPLE PRICES:

BELAGA 76.-, BINTULU 53.-, KAPIT 48.-, MIRI 75.-, KUCHING 60.-, KOTA KINABALU 156.-M$.

BY SHIP

There are daily coastal ships to KUCHING (29.-M$) and express boats (33.-M$). Hourly up to 12:30 h express boats steam up the Rajang River for KAPIT, costs M$18. Two diesel engines get the boats really moving. The trip upriver takes 3 1/2 hours. You can disembark along the way in KANOWIT or SONG.

BY BUS

There are now daily buses to BINTULU. Takes about 12 hours depending on road and weather condition. Parts of the road are still not paved and rivers have to be crossed.

KAPIT

is a crazy place with an end of the world atmosphere! At the same time it's also the capital of Sarawak's 7th Division. More and more cars and taxis drive up and down the 15 or so miles of road - you'll see them again and again. They had to be brought up the Rajang from Sibu. Plans call for a connecting road to Kapit, but it's not in for this decade!

HOTELS

Several hotels in town: *HIAP CHONG* **, 33 New Bazaar (tel 96213), don't stay in the upstairs rooms when it's raining. *REJANG***, 28 New Bazaar (tel 96356) and *KAPIT LONGHOUSE* *** (tel 96415). The people in Rejang Hotel arrange trips to longhouses. Beware of strange guys offering you the same thing for tremendous prices! A new hotel is on Jl.Airport: *MELIGAI HOTEL***(*)*, tel 96611.Or stay in the *METHODIST GUESTHOUSE**, right near the church on the main square.

LEAVING KAPIT

River boats leave regularly for ENTAWAU (M$8) on the Baleh River and to BELAGA, costs M$17 and takes up to a day. During the dry season, meaning the months from July to September, there are usually no boats because there's too little water in the upper reaches of the Rajang. Just beyond Kapit the landscape becomes fascinating with the Pelagus Rapids, jungle, and the longhouses. Unfortunately a gigantic dam project will destroy all that.

BELAGA

In Belaga there's the HUAN KILAH LODGING HOUSE** and the BELAGA HOTEL** on the Main Basar, where you'll also find five places to eat. Electricity runs only from 6:00 to 22:00 h. If jungle hiking isn't one of your strong points, you'll have to turn back here. Either go by boat back to Kapit, or take the twice weekly MAS flight for M$47 to Kapit or M$76 to Sibu. The MAS agent is Lau Chun Kiat on the Main Basar.

Otherwise you'll have to organize your trip towards Bintulu. People will talk to you about it, since by now hundreds of people do this tour each year. There's already a travel agency. The price for the whole trip now runs to about M$50 p.p. for the easiest way i.e. 20 minutes by boat, one hour walk, and the rest by jeep. There are, however, other ways to reach Bintulu. There are other, less travelled paths over the mountains, though they're generally very strenuous and expensive.For a more difficult trip expect to pay between M$300-500. Important! Be sure to bargain, and don't pay until the end of the trip or at a change of guides.

BINTULU

The largest natural gas reserves in Malaysia were discovered off Bintulu at the end of the 1970s. A huge LNG (liquefied natural gas) plant has been in business since 1982. The LNG is transported by special tankers to Japan. Total costs for the project are estimated at M$3 billion. Shell holds a 17.5% share of the LNG project, Mitsubishi has 17.5% and the state owned company Petronas has 65%. This has turned the once sleepy little town of Bintulu into the "boomtown" of Sarawak.

You're back in civilization here with real hotels, movie theatres, and even a bar in the HOOVER HOTEL****, Keppel Road, or KEMENA LODGING HOUSE***(*) on the same road is a bit cheaper. Near the jetty (Lot 198) is AH NGA*(*). There are daily MAS flights to Sibu for M$64 or to Miri for M$57. Heading north (to Miri, 214 km or Niah) you can go by bus or taxi. Price: Bus Niah Junction M$12, taxi M$24; bus Miri M$19.

NIAH CAVES

spread over a total area of 100,000 m^2. The archaeological importance of the limestone caves wasn't discovered until the 1950s. Prehistoric wall paintings were found along with a 35,000 year old skull. Further graves have also been uncovered. Millions of swallows and bats live in the caves. From the many bamboo trestles which are everywhere, reaching sometimes up to the ceiling, the swallow nests are collected and used to prepare real bird's nest soup. Way back during the Ming dynasty, Sarawak was the most important exporter of this Chinese delicacy. A couple of years ago the caves were placed under the administration of the Sarawak Museum in Kuching. The forest area around the caves has become the Niah National Park. The swallow nest collectors have all been licenced to prevent too many from being taken.

HOTELS

Batu Niah has several not too expensive hotels such as *NIAH CAVES HOTEL***, *YUNG HUR LODGING** or *HOCK SEN HOTEL***. Another possibility is the *GOVERNMENT HOSTEL* in Pangkalan Lubang. In two large rooms, up to 15 people can sleep for

M$2.50. Cooking facilities are provided. You're best off booking in advance in Miri or Kuching at the Forestry Department.

HOW TO GET THERE
Take the bus from MIRI to BATU NIAH, leaving every morning at 7:00 and 12:00 h for M$8.50. Taxis over the same route cost M$15. Taxis from Bintulu cost M$24, buses to Niah Junction M$12. To BATU NIAH (13 km) either take a taxi or hitch-hike. Charter a boat to PANGKALAN LUBANG for M$25 or hike along the river shore (45 min.). Park boats only cost M$3 per person if they're available. From Pangkalan Lubang there is a 4 km long wooden walk-way, 1 m above the ground to the caves. After rain it becomes slippery. Under normal conditions, it takes about 45 minutes to reach the Great Cave (western entrance). A guide costs M$30.

MIRI

Uninteresting capital of the 4th Division. Oil was discovered here way back in 1910. Today the drilling has been intensified on off-shore oil rigs. A couple of kilometres north is the large refinery in Lutong connected by pipeline with Seria in Brunei.

HOTELS
There are several hotels on China Street such as *TAI TONG****, no. 26 - including a dormitory for M$5; *THAI FOH****, no. 18-19; *YEO LEE LODGING HOUSE****, no. 12, or try *MONICA LODGINGS****, 4 Kwang Tung Road. From the bus station you come to *SOUTH EAST ASIA LODGING HOUSE**** across High Street. More expensive is *NEW MIRI HOTEL*****, 47 Brooke Road, tel 34577.

LEAVING MIRI
BY AIR
MAS office, 239 Beautiful Jade Garden, tel 34407. SAMPLE PRICES: BARIO 70.-, BINTULU 57.-, KOTA KINABALU 90.-, KUCHING 150.-, LABUAN 57.-, LAWAS 59.-, LIMBANG 45.-, LONG SERIDAN 57.-, MARUDI 29.-, SIBU 75.-M$. To avoid the expensive Sultanate of Brunei with its cosmopolitan hotel prices, it's worth getting a flight to Labuan or Lawas.

BY BUS / TAXI
From Miri to BRUNEI (KUALA BELAIT) there are three daily direct buses at 7:00, 9:00 and 14:00 h for M$9.50. Bus to NIAH for M$8.50 and to BINTULU for M$19.

GUNUNG MULU NATIONAL PARK

The national park covers a 530 km² area in the 4th and 5th Divisions. At 2376 m, Gunung Mulu is the second highest mountain in Sarawak. To the north lie the massive chunks of limestone Gunung Api and Gunung Benerat. Be sure to check out the Melinau Gorge, where the river courses its way between the mountains - with steep 600 m high cliffs. Teams of scientists spent two years in the park studying the geological structure and cataloguing the flora and fauna. Here you'll find macaques along with gibbons and other kinds of monkeys, pangolins, the mouse deer, and many different types of birds including the hornbill. There isn't any big game, though - there aren't any tigers on Borneo, and the only elephants are in Sabah.

Many paths lead through the jungle; try the one to Melinau Gorge (19 km) or to Lubang Rusa (3 km). Gunung Mulu can be climbed from Melinau Gorge. Plan at least four days. The National Park contains the largest cave in the world. Eight 747s and 32 smaller planes would fit into DEER CAVE. CLEARWATER CAVE is 51 km long. So far only a few visitors make it to Gunung Mulu.

Since there are only a few beds in LONG MELINAU PAKU, you should book with the Forest Department in Kuching or Miri. Ask for the latest info. In the HOSTEL you pay M$5 per night, in the MULU HOT SPRING RESORT M$10. Two more expensive bungalows were being constructed in 1987.

HOW TO GET THERE

Get a bus (M$2.10) or taxi to KUALA BARAM at the mouth of the Baram. Express boats run from here at 7:30, 8:30, 9:00, 10:00 and 14:00 h on the three hour trip to MARUDI (M$12). In town is GRAND HOTEL** and MARYLAND HOTEL***, tel 55106. Daily at 12:00 h another express boat leaves for LONG PANAI / KUALA APOH for M$12. From here a longboat for M$7 will take you to LONG TERAWAN. After arrival a longboat will leave for MULU. Prices vary depending on number of people, between M$30-70.

SABAH

The easternmost state in Malaysia is about twice as big as Switzerland but contains only about 1,140,000 people. The coastal areas were once infamous pirate sanctuaries. Even today sea robbers ply their trade in the Sulu Archipelago between Sabah and the Philippines. Typhoons don't come this far south, which is how the land got its name, 'land below the wind'. Until 1963 when Sabah voted under UN auspices to join the Federation of Malaysia, the crown colony was known as 'British North Borneo'. In the mean time it has been rising industrially. Half the rare woods exported by Malaysia come from Sabah. The rape of the rain forests in recent years has led to irrevocable erosion damage. Reforesting programs and a reduction of exports are two methods being used to try and rectify the situation.

In Sabah there are several tribes besides Malays, who make up only 8% of the population - Kadazan on the west coast, Murut in the interior living off slash and burn agriculture, and the mostly Muslim Bajau who're settled around Mount Kinabalu. The port towns of Sandakan and Lahad Datu are trading centres for wood as well as smuggled goods. A large part of the military supplies for the Moro rebels on Mindanao (the Philippines) goes via Sabah.

For travellers, Sabah is an expensive place to visit. In the cities, the standard of living is fairly high. Kota Kinabalu is the departure point for climbing Mount Kinabalu, the highest mountain in South East Asia. Adventure trips can be made into the interior all the way to Indonesia. Or you can relax on the empty beaches of Kudat.

KOTA KINABALU

'Api Api' meaning 'fire' was the old Malay name for this town. Pirates burned down the town so many times no other name fit. During the British colonial period, the town was renamed Jesselton after a director of the North Borneo Company. When the break was made with the colonial past in 1968, the town was renamed after the nearby mountain Kinabalu - Kota (= town). Typically for Malaysia, it has been shortened to KK. Since it was completely destroyed in WWII, the modern reconstruction didn't leave any room for the romantic 'Raja Brooke' atmosphere still found in Kuching. A large part of the town is on land reclaimed from the ocean.

On the way to the airport south of town, you pass the *MASJID SABAH,* the second largest mosque in Malaysia, built in a modern style. You simply must visit the new *MUSEUM,* which boasts a collection of various objects from the Sabah tribes as well as old photos. It's located on Jl.Mat Salleh not far from the Telecoms building. It's open daily from 9:00 to 18:00 h, Fri closed. Take a walk up *SIGNAL HILL.* From here you have a good view of the town and the sea. If that doesn't satisfy you, 4 km northeast of town, a hundred meter high glass and concrete structure dominates the countryside. The *SABAH FOUNDATION COMPLEX* seems almost futuristic, and from the rotating restaurant at the top you can enjoy the view if you've brought along enough traveller's cheques.

HOTELS

'Cheapies' are in the area around Jl. Perpaduan, such as *ISLAMIC***,* 8 Jl. Perpaduan (tel 54325), a bit rundown. Partly furnished with ac rooms are *KIN FAH***,* 7 Jl.Haji Yaakub (tel 53833) and *NAM TAI***,* 7 Jl.Merdeka (tel 54803). Several middle priced hotels can be found in the new Segama Quarter: *BILAL****,* Block B, Lot 1 (tel 56709) or *ORIENTAL***,* Block B, 6-8 (tel 56712). International class prices can be found in the hotels downtown such as the Hyatt, Capitol and Shangrila. One reader suggested *LIKAS GUESTHOUSE*** incl. breakfast in Kampong Likas on 371 Jl.Likas. Take bus for 50 c from Pasar.

FOOD

Get good and cheap Indian food in *TAJ,* Jl.Tugu. It's not quite as good in the *ISLAMIC.* The foodstalls around the bus station and at the night market on Jl.Tugu are cheap, too. Try Chinese as well at *SUI SIEN,* 46 Jl. Pantai and at *JADE FOUNTAIN* behind the Cathay Cinema. Many restaurants are also found in Sinsuran quarter, i.e. *MEE WAH.*

GENERAL INFORMATION

TOURIST INFORMATION - good material at the Sabah Tourist Association (tel 211424) on Lorong Jesselton. TDC Sabah office in Block L, Lot 4, tel 211698. Just round the corner, on Jl.Tun Fuad Stephens, is the office of SABAH NATIONAL PARK HEADQUARTERS, POB 626, tel 211585. Open Mon to Thurs 8:00-12:45 h, 14:00-16:15 h, Fri 8:00-11:30 h, 14:00 -16:15 h, Sat 8:00-12:45 h.

IMMIGRATION - office on Jl.Haji Yaakub not far from Bandaran Berjaya.

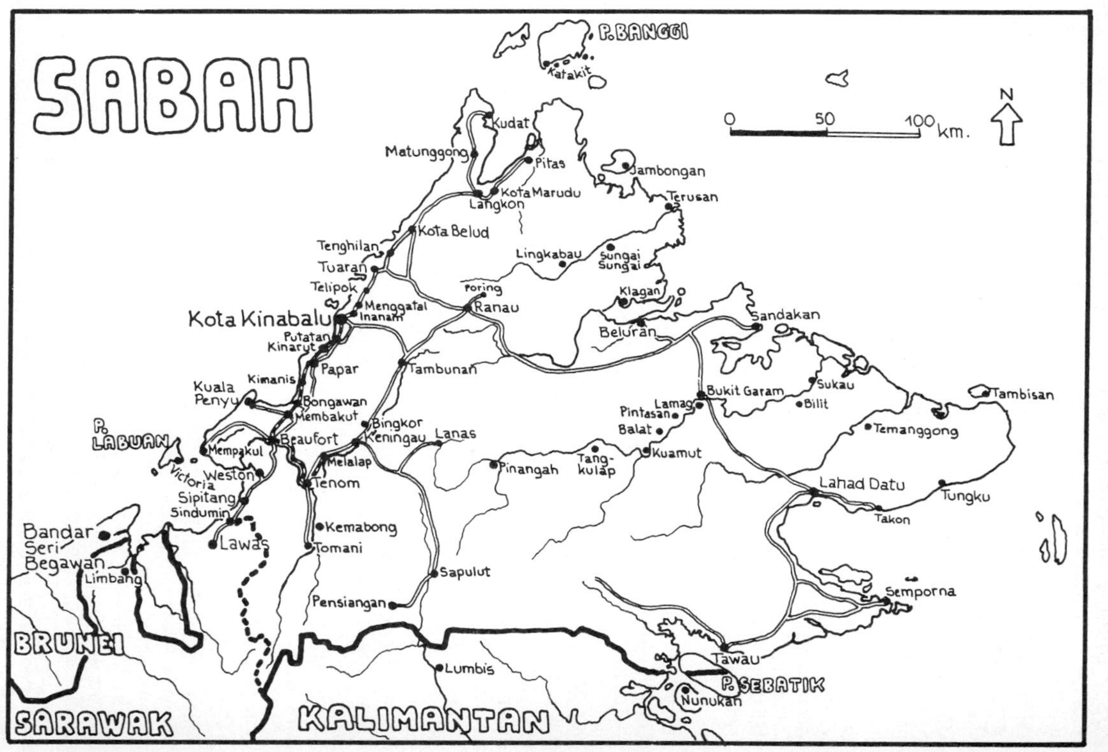
SABAH
P. BANGGI
Katakit
0
50
100 km.
N
Kudat
Matunggong
Pitas
Jambongan
Kota Marudu
Langkon
Terusan
Kota Belud
Tenghilan
Lingkabau
Sungai Sungai
Tuaran
Telipok
Poring
Klagan
Menggatal
Inanam
Ranau
Sandakan
Kota Kinabalu
Beluran
Putatan
Kinarut
Papar
Tambunan
Kimanis
Sukau
Kuala Penyu
Bongawan
Bukit Garam
Tambisan
Lamag
Bilit
Membakut
Pintasan
Bingkor
P. LABUAN
Beaufort
Keningau
Lanas
Balat
Temanggong
Mempakul
Kuamut
Melalap
Tang-kulap
Victoria
Weston
Pinangah
Tenom
Lahad Datu
Tungku
Sipitang
Takon
Sindumin
Kemabong
Bandar Seri Begawan
Lawas
Tomani
Limbang
Sapulut
Semporna
Pensiangan
BRUNEI
Tawau
Lumbis
P. SEBATIK
Nunukan
SARAWAK
KALIMANTAN

POST OFFICE - GPO with poste restante in Jl.Tun Razak (Segama Quarter).

AMERICAN EXPRESS - Discovery Tours Sdn. Bhd., 122 Wisma Sabah, tel 221714.

RENT-A-CAR - there are three rent-a-car companies in Sabah: AVIS, Hyatt Kinabalu Hotel, Jl.Datuk Salleh Sullong, tel 51577; SINTAT, Block L, Lots 4-6, Sinsuran Complex, tel 57729 (Hornbill Tours next to Tourist Office), and HERTZ, Block B, Sedco Complex, tel 221635. AVIS asks M$540 per week for a Toyota Corolla. Try and bargain for a lower price!

LEAVING KK

BY AIR - INTERNATIONAL

The airport, 6.5 km from town, is regularly served by the airport buses 12 and 13; a taxi costs M$8. Airport tax, like everywhere else in Malaysia, is M$3 for domestic flights, M$5 to Brunei and Singapore, and M$15 for international flights. MAS office is on Jl.Kemajuan (Complex Karamansing), tel 51455. In addition the following other airlines serve KK: Cathay Pacific (tel 54758), Singapore Airlines (tel 55444), Philippines Airlines (tel 218925) and Royal Brunei (tel 53211). SAMPLE PRICES: BANDAR SERI BEGAWAN 65.-, HONG KONG 658.-, MANILA 414.-, SINGAPORE 346.-M$.

BY AIR - DOMESTIC

There are daily flights to West Malaysia. The night flights to KL and Johore Bharu are especially good deals. However, they're usually booked up well in advance. Be sure to book any flight well ahead of time. The Fokker flights to Sarawak are much cheaper than the jets. SAMPLE PRICES: BINTULU 110.-, JOHORE BHARU 301.- (night flight 256.-), KENINGAU 38.-, KL 380.- (night flight 266.-), KUCHING 198.-, KUDAT 50.-, LABUAN 43.-, LAHAD DATU 88.-, LAWAS 47.-, MIRI 82.-, SANDAKAN 69.-, SIBU 56.-, TAWAU 80.-M$.

BY SHIP

Those who aren't afraid of the risks can travel with the barter-traders. These smugglers and small merchants sail from Sabah to the Philippines. The best places to hook up are in Labuan or Sandakan. The boats are often held up by pirates, and they sometimes have to shoot it out with the Philippine police. The officers at Sabah Immigration told us about two Dutchmen who had been shot shortly before on the Sulu Sea. One man, badly injured with an upper arm wound, made it back to Sabah. Sabah Immigration will give you an exit stamp for that kind of trip only when specially requested. On your arrival in the Philippines, you can probably expect real difficulties. They will surely not send you back since entry and exit by boat are strictly forbidden. For that reason don't expect an entry or exit stamp in Davao or Zamboanga. In Sabah you will, however, get the important entry stamp.

Since 1986 a new car-passenger ferry, the CRUISE MUHIBAH, runs on the following route: Kuantan (Sat) - Kuching (Sun) - Kota Kinabalu (Tues) - Kuantan (Thurs) - Singapore (Fri) - Kuantan (Sat). Tariffs from KK are: KUCHING 140.- (Standard cabin); 195.- (De luxe cabin); 300.-M$ (suite). KUANTAN 265.- (Standard cabin); 380.- (De luxe cabin); 550.-M$ (suite). SINGAPORE 310.- (Standard cabin); 445.- (De luxe cabin); 620.- M$(suite).

Get your tickets at the Feri Malaysia Office, Menara Utama UMBC, Jl.Sultan Sulaiman, KL, tel 2388899, or right in Kota Kinabalu at Harrisons & Crossfields Sdn. Bhd., tel 215011. In Peninsular Malaysia, Feri Malaysia is also represented by Reliance Shipping & Travel Agencies Sdn. Bhd. They have offices in Penang, Malacca, Ipoh, and Johore Bharu.

BY BUS / TAXI

Sabah's road system experienced a real boost with the completion of the stretch from KK to Sandakan, Lahad Datu and Tawau. However, the Trans Sabah Highway is only partially paved. Sample prices per person for Bus (B) and Taxi (T): KOTA BELUD 8.-(B), 16.-(T), MT.KINABALU 10.-(B), RANAU 15.-(B), 23.-(T), KENINGAU 19.-(B), 24.-(T), SANDAKAN 35.-(B), KUDAT 19.-(B), 23.-(T), BEAUFORT 7.-(B), 10.-(T) M$. Taxis and minibuses depart for Kota Belud, Beaufort, Sandakan and Kudat from the corner of Jl.Polis / Jl.Tunku Abdul Rahman. Everything else leaves from the bus station.

BY RAIL

Diesel trains run three times daily to BEAUFORT. Price: M$4.80. Railway station is in Tanjung Aru.

DAY TRIPS AROUND KK

PULAU GAYA - PULAU SAPI - PULAU MANUKAN

A number of mostly unpopulated islands just a few kilometres off-shore are in the bay of KK. Together they form the Tunku Abdul Rahman National Park created for their wonderful coral reefs and beautiful sandy beaches, The big drawback is that you have to rent a fishing boat to get there, and they charge incredible prices.

TANJUNG ARU BEACH

Nothing special, but still a nice place to visit; near the airport. Full on Sundays. Everyone picnics under the casuarina trees (foodstalls and a restaurant at

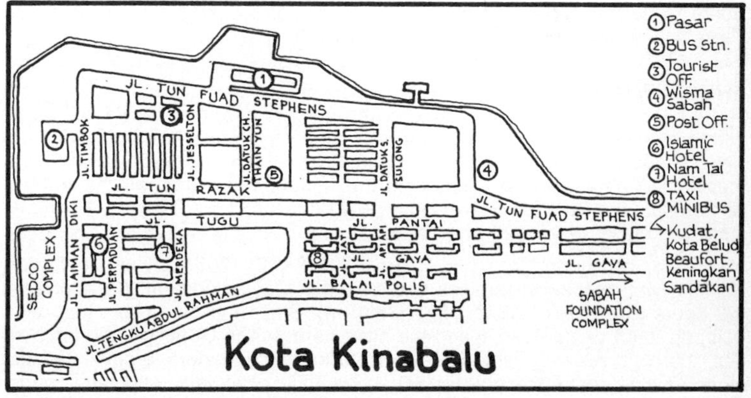

your service). After your meal you can join the promenade in Prince Philip Park. Those who can afford it keep their yacht here or play on the nearby golf course. Take the airport bus or come by taxi for M$3.

MOUNT KINABALU

If you're reasonably fit, you should make plans to climb the 4101 m Kinabalu. You'll need four days to make it up to its very cold heights. There isn't any snow, though. The mountain is a focal point for the whole national park that covers an area of 754 km^2 and includes vegetation types ranging from lowland rainforest through the montane oak, rhododendron, and conifer forests to the alpine meadow plants and stunted bushes of the summit zone. This is an area that probably has some of the richest flora in the world.

HOW TO GET THERE

Like all the other national parks, you have to book in advance. Address: Park Warden, Kinabalu National Park, POB 10626, Kota Kinabalu, tel 211585. You can take care of this by word of mouth at the office (BANDARAN SINSURAN), next to the Tourist Office on Jl.Tun Fuad Stephens. In the morning at 7:30 and 12:30 h, the minibuses from the Tuaran United Transport Company will take you for M$8.50 to the park headquarters and further on down the road to Ranau. It takes about 2 1/2 hours to do the 100 km to the park. Taxis charge M$15.

ACCOMMODATION

Register in the old headquarters. They also have a canteen. In the new main camp, there's a Steak & Coffee House serving good food, as well as a small museum which offers presentations about the flora and fauna. A possible place to stay is across the way in twin bed cabins with bath costing M$100. Otherwise there's a youth hostel with a 46 and 52 bed dormitory for M$15, offering student rates, and renting sleeping-bags for M$4. Last of all there are new duplex cabins for M$200, with two rooms and space for six people or 3 rooms for M$300.

THE CLIMB

For equipment you'll need a thick jacket, good shoes, and a sweater, along with a sleeping-bag (which you can rent after registering in KK). Guides are only necessary for the last bit of the climb. Cost M$50 per day for 1-3 people. A jeep for 12 people to take you from the headquarters through the tropical rainforest to the POWER STATION costs M$20; on foot you'd need 1 1/4 hours. Here you are already 1829 metres up.

In another two hours, you're in CARSON'S CAMP (2651 m) where there's drinking water, cooking facilities and sleeping accommodation. It's another 2 1/2 hours to PANAR LABAN HUT (3660 m). Since the new cabin has been built, up to 65 people can spend the night here. In the Gunting Lagadan New Hut, there's a two-way radio connection to the headquarters, a small kitchen, sleeping bag rental (reserve in advance), toilet, showers, and bunk beds. However, it isn't heated, meaning it gets quite cold at night.

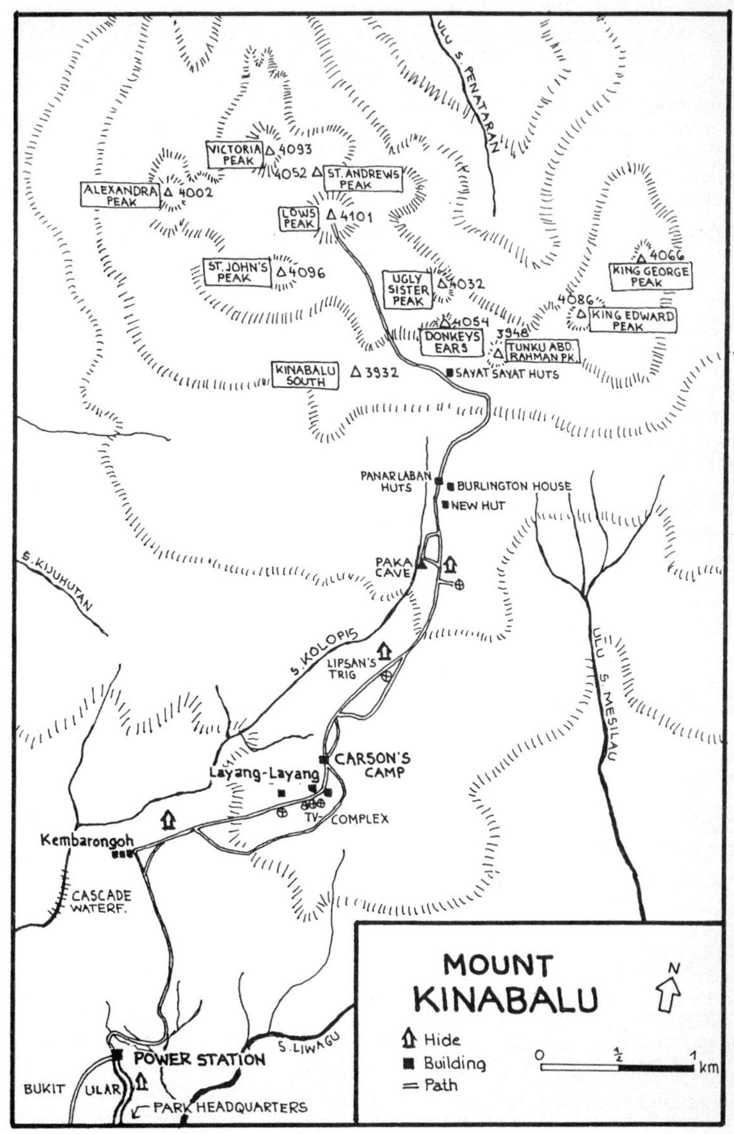
ULU S. PENATARAN
VICTORIA PEAK
4093
4052
ST. ANDREWS PEAK
ALEXANDRA PEAK
4002
LOWS PEAK
4101
4066
KING GEORGE PEAK
ST. JOHN'S PEAK
4096
UGLY SISTER PEAK
4032
4086
KING EDWARD PEAK
4054
DONKEYS EARS
3948
TUNKU ABD. RAHMAN PK.
KINABALU SOUTH
3932
SAYAT SAYAT HUTS
PANAR LABAN HUTS
BURLINGTON HOUSE
NEW HUT
PAKA CAVE
S. KIJUHUTAN
S. KOLOPIS
LIPSAN'S TRIG
ULU S. MESILAU
CARSON'S CAMP
Layang-Layang
TV-COMPLEX
Kembarongoh
CASCADE WATERF.
MOUNT KINABALU
N
Hide
Building
Path
0
½
1
km
S. LIWAGU
POWER STATION
BUKIT ULAR
PARK HEADQUARTERS

Those who still have the energy can go on up another hour to SAYAT SAYAT HUT (3810 m). On the smooth granite cliffs up here, hardly anything grows. The peak is clouded over, but on both sides you can see other lower peaks. A bit further along you come to the SACRIFICE POOL where they used to sacrifice seven roosters and seven eggs to the spirits of the mountains. At LOW'S PEAK you've reached the top of the highest mountain in South East Asia. At sunrise the view can't be beaten. The trek back down to the headquarters will take you a day.

DAY TRIPS IN KINABALU NATIONAL PARK

A number of people stay at headquarters to enjoy the many marked trails. PORING offers a good alternative. Take the first minibus for M$4 to RANAU, takes 50 minutes, HOTEL RANAU****, tel 75351, and the RESTHOUSE*, tel 75256. Here you'll have to organize your own wheels. The simplest is to take a shared taxi in the morning or on weekends to the Poring Hot Springs (18 km) for about M$4. Otherwise you'll have to rent a car for M$20-30. In Poring you can find accommodation in the OLD CABIN (6 persons, M$100) or in the NEW CABIN (4 persons, M$80). You pay M$8 in the HOSTEL DORM, or M$2 on the camping ground. Next door are some small shops offering drinks and processed foods. A bath in the hot springs is best of all. Several basins can be filled with hot or cold water. They were installed during the Japanese occupation. The hot sulphur baths were typical Japanese relaxation for the Tenno troops. Many paths lead through the jungle to waterfalls, caves, bamboo forests, and to the rafflesia - the largest flower in the world.

BETWEEN KOTA KINABALU AND BRUNEI

An overland trip is the most interesting way to reach Sarawak and Brunei. Your first stop should be ***PAPAR,*** a Kadazan village about 40 km south of KK. There's a RESTHOUSE* here, tel 088 73518. Check out the old Chinese temple or make an excursion into some of the surrounding villages. Get to Papar from KK by bus, train or taxi. Then go on to ***BEAUFORT*** which was named after a governor of the British North Borneo Company. In the village, the FOH LODGING HOUSE* is right opposite the station, PADAS HOTEL****, or ECONOMY INN**** right in town. Go by minibus to ***MENUMBOK*** (2 hours). From there you can go on by ferry for the 45 minute ride to Labuan, costs M$5.

LABUAN is still a duty free port. At one time it belonged, along with Penang, Singapore, and Malacca, to the British Straits Settlement. An Australian military cemetery is a reminder of the heavy fighting here just before the end of WWII. A stone memorial reminds visitors of the handing over of the island by the Sultan of Brunei to the English. There aren't any cheap places to stay. You can try on Jl.Okk Awang Besar in the KIM SOON LEE*** (no. 141) or in the AURORA*** (no. 112). There's a speedboat connection from Labuan to Bandar Seri Begawan for M$20 and flights to BINTULU 96.-, KK 43.-, KUCHING 173.-, LAWAS 31.-, MIRI 57.- and SIBU 130.-M$.

The second alternative is to go on from Beaufort to ***SIPITANG*** and then to ***MERAPOK.*** By taxi you'll need M$12.50 for the first bit and M$10 for the second. In ***SINDUMIN,*** just before Merapok, you'll have to get a Sabah exit stamp in your passport.

You can get the Sarawak entry stamp in ***LAWAS*** (if you come from Bandar Seri Begawan), reachable by bus on the new road for M$4.50. Just in case, be sure to go and find the immigration authorities, otherwise you'll have problems later on. You can spend the night in RASA SAYANG LODGING HOUSE*. From Lawas you can go on by a combination of bus/boat (M$12) to Bandar Seri Begawan. Another possibility is to go by plane inland to LONG SEMADO or BAKELALAN, near the Indonesian border, for M$36 or M$40 with a small Twin Otter.

People who prefer more unusual trips should go on from Beaufort to ***TENOM*** by train. It follows the river and passes through a ravine where a huge hydro-electric plant has been built. Cost from Beaufort is M$8.35 (Relcar.) or M$2.75 (Diesel Eco). Since the train goes very slowly, you have lots of time to enjoy the countryside. Tenom is Murut country. There are six hotels in town. The cheapest is KIM SAN**, dormitory for M$10, but not exactly clean. The owner is very business-like. The other hotel is TENOM***, on the road to Beaufort. Try the food across from the Shell station in KEDAI MAKAN YUN LEI.

From Tenom there are taxis to ***TOMANI*** and Keningau. In Tomani, there's no hotel, but a big open resthouse where you can spend the night for free. The nicest suspension bridge in Sabah is here! For M$5, you can get a taxi to ***ULU TOMANI (BEKUKU).*** Then go on foot into the villages. In the morning there are taxis from Tomani to Tenom (M$7) as well as from Tenom to ***KENINGAU*** for M$9. Stay the night in HOTEL RAI***, ALISHAN**** or HIAP SOON****. The village became one of the best fortified Japanese bases during WWII. If you want to go back to KK, get a Landrover for M$19 or a taxi for M$24 via ***TAMBUNAN*** (Resthouse*). Tambunan was the last hideout of the national hero Mat Salleh. In 1897 he reduced the first British settlement on the island of Gaya off KK to rubble. He then retreated to Tambunan where he built a fort. In 1900 the British, using Dayak troops, stormed the fort and murdered Mat Salleh.

There is also a second route back to KK right through the Crocker Range to ***PAPAR,*** but it isn't paved. From Keningau, take the new road down to ***PENSIANGAN.*** You can get to ***LUMBIS*** in Indonesia by way of the Sungei Sembakung. At the moment the exit stamp must be procured in Pensiangan (though this might change!). The people in Lumbis know full well that the only way to get through is by way of the river. This makes the prices the way they are. The trip takes you from longhouse to longhouse until you reach the coast.

BETWEEN KOTA KINABALU AND KUDAT

Tamu, the famous Sabah markets, can be found north of KK, and there you'll find an interesting mixture of the different nationalities making up Sabah. Besides the Kadazan, there are Bajau, Chinese, Indians, and Malays, all offering their wares. The markets don't take place daily, however, so check in advance with the tourist office in KK before you head out anywhere. The 'tamu' in Kota

Belud, Tuaran, and Tamparuli are the most famous. ***TUARAN*** and ***TAMPARULI*** (market on Wed) are on the road heading north, taxis cost about M$12.

KOTA BELUD is located about 80 km from KK. Minibuses make the trip in about 2 hours and charge M$5 per person; otherwise there are taxis. Stay the night in the RESTHOUSE** on Jl.Ranau. The largest and nicest tamu takes place here every Sun morning behind the mosque.

The road then goes on to ***KUDAT***. Minibuses charging M$10 for the 2 hour ride leave from the Shell station between 9:00 and 10:00 h. Kudat has four hotels: HASBA**, KING NAM TONG**, KUDAT*** and SUNRISE**** (seafood is to be recommended). Otherwise there's a RESTHOUSE** with a large terrace. Up here there are beautiful, white sandy beaches with off-shore coral reefs and islands. From Kudat itself, you can visit the beaches north of town. When passing the airport runway, stay on the road running along the coast. Even under the casuarina trees on the main beach of Bak-Bak, it's peaceful during the week. The whole Kudat peninsula is one big coconut forest. From Kudat you can get flights to SANDAKAN M$54 and KK M$50. Taxis to KK cost M$23, a minibus will take you for M$19.

BETWEEN KOTA KINABALU AND TAWAU

The new Trans-Sabah Highway goes right through Sabah from KK to Sandakan. The road goes around Mount Kinabalu and through Ranau and the timber region to the old capital of North Borneo.

SANDAKAN

can be reached from KK by Landrover in 8 -10 hours for M$35. MAS will fly you there for M$69. The city is the most important port for wood exports in the country. Like KK, it was almost completely destroyed during WWII. The new town consists of monotonous blocks of houses. Visit the *SANDAKAN ORCHID HOUSE* with its remarkable collection of rare orchids. There are other botanical exhibits, along with hunting weapons and art objects, in the Forestry Exhibition.

HOTELS

This is the most expensive town in all of Sabah, all hotels****. Expect to pay about M$50 for a cheap double in *MAYFAIR*, Jl.Prayer, *PARIS*, 45 Jl.Tiga, (really dirty), or in *KIN NAM SING*, 51 Jl.Empat.

DAY TRIPS AROUND SANDAKAN

GOMATONG CAVES

Located 32 km south of the Bay of Sandakan. Here, as in Niah, swallow nests are collected from the shaky scaffolding.

PULAU SELINGAN

This island is also known as Green Turtle Island due to the many turtles, some 100 years old, populating the island. Get a permit to visit from the National

Park Warden in Sandakan. Unless you can get a ride in a park administration speedboat (leaves several times a week), the trip could be very expensive. It takes about 2 hours. The island of Lihiman, just 2 km away, belongs to the Philippines.

SEPILOK ORANG UTAN SANCTUARY

You can cover the 25 km in 45 min.with bus Sepilok Batu 14 (M$1). Feeding time is 11:00 h and it takes about half an hour to walk to the feeding place through jungle. Good trails for hiking.

The 'forest people' (= orang utan in Malay) only live on Borneo and Sumatra. Some estimates suggest that only 5000 still live in the wild. People are constantly pushing back the territories of the individual animals into even smaller areas. Their freedom of movement has been greatly reduced, and no single part of Sabah contains more than 100 of the animals. The main reason for the reduction of the orang utan population is considered to be the deforesting of the great forest areas by the lumber industry. Also not to be underestimated is the capture of wild orang utans for zoos and as pets around the world. The mother is killed so that the baby animals can be captured and sold. An attempt is being made in Sepilok to prepare tame orang utans for the wild so that they can be released. They are having success, too.

LAHAD DATU

The new road from Sandakan to Lahad Datu is now complete. Buses cost M$14. Those who'd rather fly should check with the MAS office on Jl.Tiga in Sandakan, tel 42211. Flights cost M$40. The hotels in Lahad Datu are expensive, as you'd expect. In MIDO (home of the MAS office) rooms will set you back M$100. Try the KUNAK****, tel 85200, the PERDANA****, Jl.Bajau or VENUS****, Jl.Seroja, tel 81900.

TAWAU

The town, a centre for smugglers to the Philippines, is located in a farming region. Here you'll mostly find travellers on their way to or from Indonesia. Accommodation is relatively cheap for Sabah; try the NAM WAH LODGING HOUSE**, 893 Jl.Masjid, tel 72269. If it's full check FOO GUAN***, 152 Jl.Chester, tel 71700 or SOON YEE****, 1362 Jl.Stephen Tan, tel 72447. It's possible to take a trip up to SEMPORNA, about 110 km north of Tawau. Taxis cost about M$15. Two hotels: ISLAND VIEW*** and SEMPORNA****. Many islands and coral reefs.

LEAVING TAWAU

Taxis to LAHAD DATU charge M$30 per person. You can fly it for M$40. If you want to go on to Indonesia (NUNUKAN), check whether you are allowed to enter by boat. Otherwise you'll have to fly. For the 35 minutes of air-time with BOURAQ to TARAKAN, you have to shell out M$152. You can book at the Merdeka Travel Service, 41 Dunlop Street. There is an Indonesian consulate in Tawau.

SINGAPORE

This is a mostly Chinese city with a few sprinklings of Indian and Malay. The dynamic people have made Singapore into the most important finance, production, and trading centre between Hong Kong and the Persian Gulf. Ancient tradition has been thrown overboard in the name of progress. In the process, a lot of atmosphere has been lost, much to the detriment of nostalgia-seeking tourists. Bicycle rickshaws are out of place on the multi-lane highways. The old Chinatown has almost completely given way to high-rise office buildings. Multi-level shopping centres, offering an international selection of wares, have just about replaced the tiny Chinese shops. Only the splendid architecture of the British colonial past seems to be immune. Sir Stamford Raffles, the founder of the former crown colony, still has his place in front of the parliament building. About 2.6 million people live in this island country with a surface area of 619 km^2, about the size of West Berlin.

The country had no natural resources when it seceded from Malaysia in 1965. Since then, an authoritarian regime has pushed for capitalist development and the search for profits. The prevalent buy-and-sell mentality has brought a high standard of living within a short time.

For some the atmosphere is too sterile; others enjoy the comfort of a modern city, especially after a long trip through underdeveloped regions. Those who are pleased to see the clean streets should also keep in mind that even the thoughtless toss of a cigarette butt can lead to a heavy fine.

A duty free port, Singapore is still a shopping paradise for western tourists. Due to the present strength of European currencies, things can be really cheap. An incredible selection entices you to buy. Just don't forget the basic rule of the east - bargaining and price cutting (outside department stores) are part of the ritual.

VISAS

Citizens of most western countries may visit for up to three months without getting a visa in advance. Normally you'll receive a 14 day visitor's permit upon entry. In some cases you may have to show your money and departure ticket. If you want to extend for another 14 days, either spend a day in Johore Bharu and return or fill in an application at the *IMMIGRATION DEPARTMENT,* Empress Place, tel 3374031.

Upon arrival, a neat appearance is a big help. However, long hair on men is no longer a problem. Don't play around with the extremely strict drug laws here. Even a long-forgotten crumb from a Thai stick can land you in jail - so make sure you're clean before you reach the border. The possession of only half an ounce (15 g) of marijuana or hashish counts as trafficking. Anyone with more than 15 g of heroin can expect the death penalty. We emphatically advise against taking drugs across the border - any border for that matter.

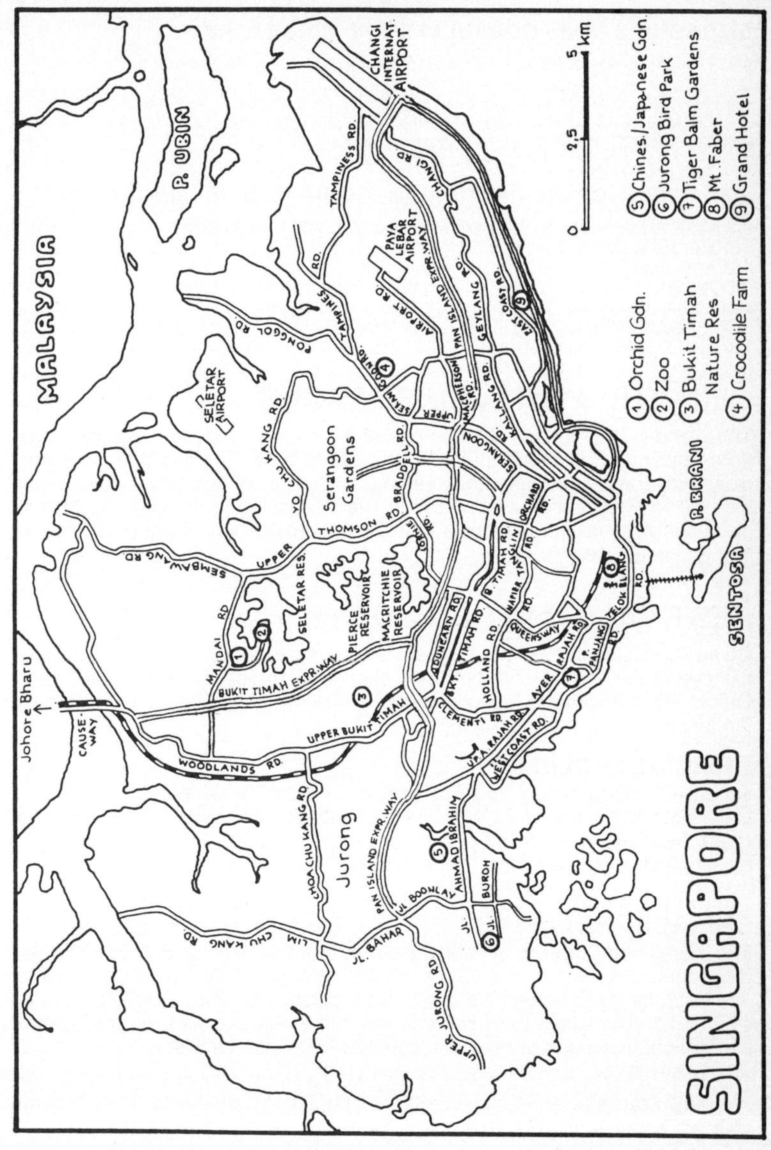
SINGAPORE
MALAYSIA
P. UBIN
SELETAR AIRPORT
CHANGI INTERNAT. AIRPORT
PAYA LEBAR AIRPORT
Serangoon Gardens
Jurong
Johore Bharu
CAUSE-WAY
SENTOSA
P. BRANI
PIERCE RESERVOIR
MACRITCHIE RESERVOIR
SELETAR RES.
0
2,5
5 km
① Orchid Gdn.
② Zoo
③ Bukit Timah Nature Res
④ Crocodile Farm
⑤ Chines./Japanese Gdn.
⑥ Jurong Bird Park
⑦ Tiger Balm Gardens
⑧ Mt. Faber
⑨ Grand Hotel

EMBASSIES AND CONSULATES IN SINGAPORE

AUSTRALIA, 25 Napier Road, tel 2354231; Mon-Fri 8:30-12:00, 14:00-16:00 h.
CANADA, Faber House, 230 Orchard Road, tel 7371322; Mon-Fri 8:00-12:30, 13:30-16:30 h.
UNITED KINGDOM, Tanglin Road, tel 4739333; Mon-Fri 9:00-12:00, 14:00-16:00 h.
NEW ZEALAND, 13 Nassim Road, tel 2359966; Mon-Fri 9:00-12:00, 14:00-16:00 h.
UNITED STATES, 30 Hill Street, tel 3380251, Mon-Fri 8:30-12:00 h.

EMBASSIES OF NEIGHBOURING COUNTRIES IN SINGAPORE

BRUNEI, 7A Tanglin Hill, tel 4743393; Mon-Fri 8:30-12:30, 13:30-16:30 h.
BURMA, 15 St. Martin Drive, tel 2358704; Mon-Fri 9:30-13:00, 14:00-17:00 h.
INDIA, 31 Grange Road, tel 7376809; Mon-Fri 9:00-17:00 h.
INDONESIA, 7 Chatsworth Road, tel 7377422; Mon-Fri 8:30-12:30, 14:00-16:30 h.
MALAYSIA, 301 Jervois Road, tel 2350111; Mon-Fri 8:30-15:15 h..
PHILIPPINES, 20B Nassim Road, tel 7373977; Mon-Fri 9:00-12:00, 14:00-16:30 h.
THAILAND, 370 Orchard Road, tel 7372644; Mon-Fri 9:00-12:30, 14:00-17:00 h.

CLIMATE & TRAVEL SEASONS

The island is located just 180 km north of the equator. As you'd expect, Singapore enjoys a year-round maritime, tropical climate. The average maximum daily temperature throughout the year is 30°C. The city has never been cooler than 19°C. Precipitation is also pretty evenly distributed all year round. A bit more rain does fall in the months from October to January. Even so, there isn't any real rainy season.

FESTIVALS AND HOLIDAYS

Chinese, Muslim, and Hindu festivals are set according to their own individual calendars. For this reason the dates change each year so ask in the Tourist Office! The dates of the Malay and Indian festivals have already been listed in the Malaysia and Indonesia sections.

OFFICIAL HOLIDAYS

January 1, Good Friday and Easter Sunday, and December 25 (Christmas Day). August 9 is the *NATIONAL DAY*. Especially impressive are the huge parades (with participation by the various nationalities), military parades, and dances, including the typical Chinese lion and dragon dances.

CHINESE HOLIDAYS

The stores start hopping several weeks before the *CHINESE NEW YEAR* in Singapore. One, two, or even three months extra pay is paid out by employers. The huge family get-togethers must be prepared and holiday clothes must be sought out. The whole town is on its feet until, with everyone on the point of exhaustion, they retire to relax and celebrate with their families.

The *BIRTHDAY OF THE MONKEY GOD* is celebrated twice yearly especially in the two temples on Cumming Street and Eng Hoon Street. They include both processions and Chinese opera. Men stick needles through their tongues and cheeks while in a trance. Parents pray to the powerful Monkey God to stand as godfather for their children so that they will have its strength.

Another splendid festival can be found in the White Cloud Temple on Ganges Ave. where the *BIRTHDAY OF THE SAINT OF THE POOR* (Kong Teck Choon Ong) is celebrated. In the Taoist Temple on the corner of Clarke St./North Boat Quay the *BIRTHDAY OF THE THIRD PRINCE* is celebrated.

In the seventh month of the year, the souls of the dead return to earth from purgatory. Through the *FESTIVAL OF THE HUNGRY GHOSTS,* an attempt is made to win their approval by putting tasty snacks everywhere.

In the middle of the eighth month, when the moon is especially round, the *MOONCAKE FESTIVAL* is held in honour of a victory over the Mongol dynasty. Tiny round cakes are baked. On the night itself, incense is burned, and the children carry lanterns through the streets. For four weeks in October and November, the Taoist faithful make a pilgrimage to the island of Kusu to pray to the *GOD OF PROSPERITY.* Ferries leave from the World Trade Centre.

GETTING AROUND

Singapore's role as the trading centre of South East Asia is well served by one of the biggest harbours and one of the most modern airports in the world. On landing, Changi Airport, in service since 1981, gives a good first impression of the city's dynamic character. Its huge duty free shop ensures that, even on the shortest stopovers, you still have time to spend money.

BUS: The cheapest way to get around is by SBS (Singapore Bus Service Ltd.) bus. Routes for all the buses are listed in the somewhat confusing SBS guide, available for 70 c at airport newspaper stands and stationery shops as well as in the city. For one ride you pay between 40 c and 80 c depending on how many fare stages you pass through. Besides buses with a conductor, there are also OMO lines (One Man Operation), where you just pay a standard rate. These include the CBD Ring Buses running within the Central Business District. It's a good idea to obtain a 1-Day or 3-Day *Singapore Explorer Bus Ticket.* Costs S$5 or S$12. You can buy it in any of the big hotels.

MRT: Since November 87 the city has had one of the most technologically advanced railway systems in the world. The MRT (Mass Rapid Transit) runs underground in the city. You have to use a vending machine; find your fare on the fare list, and put the correct amount of coins in the machine. At present fares range between 50 c and S$ 1.10.

TAXIS: On the island there are more than 10,000 taxis which are still relatively cheap . In the city centre area, they can only be found at certain taxi stops. Most are air-conditioned. Rates: The first 1500 m S$1.60, every subsequent 300 m 10 c for up to 10 km, and then 10 c for every 250 m thereafter; nights between 12:00 and 6:00 h add 50%, each additional person (beyond two) costs 50 c, and any piece of baggage costs S$1. Add a S$3 surcharge on any journey starting from Changi Airport., and a S$1 surcharge for all trips departing the CBD between 16:00 and 19:00 h on weekdays and between 12:00 and 15:00 h on Saturdays.

You can order a radio taxi by calling 4525555, 4747707 or 2500700. Any complaints should be made to the Registry of Vehicles, Sin Ming Drive, or at the Tourist Office, Raffles City Tower.

TRISHAWS: Every once in a while, you'll see a trishaw. Normal prices are paid by elderly Chinese women who use them to go to market in the morning. Tourists, however, have to pay for an expensive, nostalgic sightseeing tour.

Private and **RENT-A-CARS** are one of the most expensive ways to get around. The rates are higher than in Malaysia, and the heavy toll to enter the CBD during the rush hour and the high cost of parking downtown make a car uneconomic.

ACCOMMODATION

Singapore has a huge selection of hotels in all categories and price classes. Luxury hotels are going up all the time. If you arrive in the afternoon or late in the evening, you'll probably have a difficult time finding a room, especially if you don't want to spend a lot of money. To arrange your hotel telephone from the airport or the first phone booth you see. The price levels are generally higher than in Malaysia.

We decided on the following price table for Singapore - all prices are for double rooms:

*	**up to S$15**
**	**up to S$30**
***	**up to S$60**
****	**over S$60**

FOOD & DRINK

Singapore offers you one of the greatest food paradises in Asia if you are willing to lay out the cash. We confine our descriptions here to Chinese food, since Malay and Indian fare have already been discussed in the Malaysia section. A must, when eating Chinese food, is mastery of the chop sticks. You gain a lot of face if you show competence. In Singapore you have a chance to try the regional varieties of Chinese food:

CANTONESE FOOD is the most prevalent, since most Chinese in South East Asia originate from Guangdong Province. The dishes are only mildly spiced, using lots of ginger. Meat and vegetables are only lightly fried in peanut oil. One speciality is the tiny stuffed dough balls, *dim sum,* which can either be steamed or quickly fried. You can hunt for your favourite types in bamboo baskets. A dim sum meal can take hours; in the end you only pay for what you actually eat.

SZECHUAN cooks use lots of garlic and chilli; food in general is more heavily spiced. Try Szechuan duck or chili chicken.

PEKING FOOD is that of the imperial court, with lots of Mongolian and Muslim influence. Instead of rice, dumplings and noodles are often served in the north. The main speciality is *Peking duck.* The delicacy is not in the meat, rather in the crisp, spicy brown skin with an underlayer of fat. It is prepared by blowing air under the skin during the roasting.

SHANGHAI FOOD is a treat for stew lovers and people who appreciate fish dishes. The liberal use of soy sauce makes everything taste a bit sweet.

HAINAN FOOD from the large tropical island off Vietnam offers its own speciality: chicken rice - rice is boiled in chicken broth and served with chilli, ginger, soy sauce and chicken.

HUNAN presents the delicacy *chor chong tung.* It's made of small pieces of chicken served with big red chillies and various sauces. Hunan's native son, Mao Tsetung, once said that all the true revolutionaries come from places where spicy food is appreciated: Spain, Mexico, Bengal and, of course, Hunan.

A FEW SPECIALITIES TO LOOK FOR:

100 YEAR EGGS are actually only a couple of weeks old. Fresh duck eggs are laid in a mixture of dirt, rice husk and ash. After fermentation the egg white is darker and the yolk dark red. They aren't to everyone's taste.

BIRD'S NEST isn't exactly what it sounds like, just the edible threads out of which swallows build their nests. It's an expensive delicacy served with quail eggs and chicken broth.

SHARK'S FIN SOUP is made from well-cooked fins mixed with chicken and shrimp - excellent.

YAM POT is a hot puff-pastry pie which can be filled with fish, chicken, pork, shrimp or vegetables - wonderful.

STEAMBOAT - this is most fun if you have at least six people; the raw ingredients (fish, shrimp, meat, liver, vegetables, etc.) are boiled in a pot of simmering broth placed on your table. Before eating you should dip them in chilli or soy sauce. To top the meal off, you drink the rich broth into which egg has been beaten.

Those who want to eat cheaply at the foodstalls don't have to give up on the delicacies. Besides spring rolls, Hainan chicken rice, dim sum from Canton, soups (with meat, fish and vegetable bases), soybean curd, and shrimp balls, you might go out of your way for:

HOKKIEN MEE, fried noodles according to a Hokkien Province recipe. The noodle soup is also excellent.

CARROT CAKE, a mushy mixture of radish and carrots baked with eggs - filling and tasty.

OYSTER OMELETTE, a very reasonably priced omelette featuring - you guessed it!

CHAR SIEW, grilled pork painted with a spicy, hot but sweet sauce and served on rice with gravy.

Otherwise you'll find the typical Malay fried noodle dish **MEE GORENG** and of course **NASI GORENG** or the Indian filled pancakes **MURTABAH.** To wash it all down, try a freshly squeezed fruit juice. Especially refreshing is sugar-cane juice.

MONEY

EXCHANGE RATE	**1US$ = 2.04S$**
INFLATION RATE:	**1.1%**

The monetary unit is the Singapore dollar containing 100 cents. In circulation are the following denominations of bank notes: 10,000, 1000, 500, 100, 50, 10, 5, and 1S$. Coins are 50, 20, 10, 5, and 1 cent. The Singapore dollar is a very stable currency, widely accepted throughout South East Asia. Just a few years ago the Singapore, Brunei and Malaysian dollars were all exchanged 1:1:1.

Today the rates vary; only the Brunei Dollar is still on par. Currency and traveller's cheques can be imported and exported at will. Every currency in the world is available here. Especially cheap are the weaker Asian currencies such as Indian Rupees, Burmese Kyat, or Philippine Pesos. Beware of the import and export restrictions in the various countries. Before going to visit any money changers on Raffles Square or Collyer Quay (if you want to get the best rate), have a look in the latest issue of the *Far Eastern Economic Review* or *Asiaweek* to find out the going rates. Singapore is the perfect place to pick up money transferred from home. It's best to do it through a big international bank.

BANK OF AMERICA, Clifford Centre, 24 Raffles Place, tel 5353322.
CHASE MANHATTAN BANK, 50 Raffles Place, Shell Tower, tel 2242888.
FIRST NATIONAL BANK OF CHICAGO, 76 Shenton Way, Ong Building, tel 2239933.
CITIBANK, 5 Shenton Way, UIC Building, tel 2242611.

INCOME AND COST OF LIVING

In 1986 the average weekly incomes were: for all workers S$250, in administration and management S$600, in sales and services S$220, in industrial production, transportation, etc. about S$200. An average of 22% is lost from the workers' gross pay cheques for the Central Providence Fund. This is matched by equal payments by the employers.

The average traveller (if there's such a person!!) will have to budget S$12 to 16 per day for accommodation. Eating at the foodstalls is extremely cheap. For S$2-3 you can get a complete meal. Altogether you should plan to spend between S$25 and 30 per day. Public transportation is cheap.

ECONOMY

In the 1970s the gross national product grew at an amazing rate (1978-82 8.8%) but has now levelled off at about 3-5%. Since 1979, at the government's initiative, a program called the second industrial revolution is under way. The idea is to increase the amount of industrialization in the country. An attempt is being made to switch from labour intensive to capital intensive industries. Qualified workers are in surplus here. Jurong Industrial Estate is a result of the first big state-supported industrialization program in the 1960s and early '70s.

The workforce is structured as in no other South East Asian country. 36% are employed in industry, 41% in sales and services, 22% in public service and only 0.4% in fishing and agriculture. Compare this to Indonesia where you have 11% in industry, 25% in sales and services, 15% in public services, and 54% in fishing and agriculture. All together Singapore has (after Japan) the highest standard of living in Asia. The splendid economic advancement in the country's eighteen years has worked to the benefit of everyone. Not only has industry taken off, but Singapore has also become the accepted financial centre of South East Asia.

NATIONALITIES & RELIGIONS

Of the 2.6 million inhabitants, 76% are ethnic Chinese, 15% Malay and 7% Indian. The rest are of European or Eurasian origin. The official national languages are ***English, Malay, Tamil, and Mandarin.*** However, the formal Chinese dialect, Mandarin, is only spoken by a small number of people here. About 42% of the Chinese are Hokkien, 22% Teochew, 17% Cantonese, 7% Hainanese, and 7% Hakka, just to name the most important. The school system takes the four mother tongues into consideration. English is steadily becoming more popular. Even many Chinese families have begun speaking English at home. The effect which this will have on the historical and cultural identity of the different ethnic groups remains to be seen.

The majority of the Chinese are ***Buddhist*** (Mahayana), with a limited number following the Hinayana faith. The 300,000 ***Muslims*** are mostly Malay as well as a few Indians. The 100,000 ***Hindu*** are almost all from the Tamil community. There are about 150,000 members of the two main ***Christian*** faiths. As the government of Premier Lee Kuan Yew has maintained a fairly even-handed policy concerning the nationalities, there haven't been any major conflicts since independence despite the fact that the Chinese make up three-quarters of the population.

HISTORY

A city called ***Tumasik*** (sometimes also referred to as Temasik) is mentioned in the ancient Javanese chronicles. It was, in all probability, situated on the site of the present day Singapore. Chinese and Javanese merchants were aware of the city as far back as the 14th century. The city is said, according to legend, to have got its name in this way. A Malay prince was stranded during a heavy storm on the island and spied a mysterious animal which he took to be a lion. 'Singa' means lion and 'pura' means city. There are, however, other explanations: for example, all cities within the Majapahit sphere of influence were called *lion cities.*

At the end of the 14th century the city was captured and destroyed by the Thais. In the centuries following, there were only a few fishing villages on the island. It was left to the English, eager to find bases for the lucrative China trade, to recognize the island's strategic location. .

Stamford Raffles *joined up as an office clerk with the East India Company at the tender age of 14. He quickly made a name for himself at the main office in London, and so in 1805 was sent as assistant secretary to Penang. A trip by ship to the Far East in those days took several months, and Raffles took wise advantage of the time to bone up on the Malay language and culture. Soon he was an accepted expert. By 1808 he was already working for the High Court in Penang. In 1810, Stamford Raffles was in Calcutta where the British Governor General Lord Minto appointed him Governor of Java. Since Holland had been annexed by France, British troops occupied the Dutch colonies to keep them out of French hands. Raffles tried to institute liberal reforms on Java, but the colonies were returned to Dutch control in 1816.*

Raffles, a confirmed nationalist, warned the British government and the East India Company of the consequences for British trade. His attempt to get other bases in Sumatra besides Bencoolen received only half hearted support. Sometimes he operated on his own initiative.

On January 29, 1819, Stamford Raffles landed on the island of Singapore and signed a treaty with the rightful Sultan of Johore, Hussein. Hussein's brother had usurped the throne and was known for his friendship with the Dutch. The Union Jack was raised over the island on February 6, 1819. In 1824 the seizure of the island was confirmed in a treaty between England and Holland. In 1823 Raffles left Singapore for England where he died three years later. His two volume work, A HISTORY OF JAVA, was a great academic achievement, at the time offering the most wide ranging study of the history, culture, ethnology, zoology, and botany of the island of Java.

In 1820 Singapore already had 5000 inhabitants. Raffles' idea of a free port, in effect the exact opposite of the Dutch monopoly control of their colonies, quickly made Singapore into an important trading centre. In 1826 the colony was combined with Penang and Malacca to form the ***Straits Settlement.*** For the next 137 years, Singapore was the most important British base 'East of Suez'. An enormous stream of immigrants headed for Singapore even in its first 50 years. Most came from the provinces of southern China, giving the ethnic Chinese a majority by 1837. As the British began getting increasingly involved in the politics of the Malay sultanates, the sitting governor in Singapore became the high commissioner of Malaya. Tin and rubber were almost exclusively exported through the city.

In 1942 the allied forces capitulated to the ***Imperial Japanese Army.*** The city was occupied for three years. This was for Singapore, as for the rest of South East Asia, the beginning of a new epoch. Political parties were formed, and the independence of Malaya and Singapore was now only a matter of time. In 1959, the first legislative assembly was elected. The left leaning ***PAP*** (People's Action Party) won 43 of the 51 seats. The party chairman, Lee Kuan Yew, became premier. In 1963, Singapore was made a member of the Federation of Malaysia. The reasons for this were the British concern about an independent Singapore moving to the left, and the fact that nobody believed the tiny island could survive on its own. The left wing was soon forced out of the PAP by supporters of Lee Kuan Yew, and they formed their own party (Barisan Socialis). Economic and ethnic conflicts were the prime motives for the secession of Singapore from the Federation of Malaysia in 1965, after only two years of membership. Since then, the PAP has maintained its authoritarian rule over the city. Even so, the form of planned capitalism instituted here seems to be a success. In December 1984, two opposition politicians were able to get elected into Parliament.

LANGUAGE

There are four equal national languages in the republic: English, Mandarin, Malay, and Tamil. English is spoken and understood everywhere.

SUGGESTED READING

The Inside Photo Series has quite a good and informative volume out on Singapore. Also check the Malaysia section literature.

SINGAPORE - THEN AND NOW (Tyers, Ray; Singapore 1975). The two volumes describe and picture the old buildings which to a large extent have been sacrificed for progress. A fantastic pictorial view of history. Unfortunately out of print at the moment; try in the National Library.

THE FIRST 150 YEARS OF SINGAPORE (Moore, Donald / Moore, Joanna; Singapore 1969) A recommendable history of the city.

THE SINGAPORE GRIP (Farrell, J.G.; London 1978). A novel dealing with colonial Singapore of the 1930s before the Japanese invasion.

KING RAT (Clavell, James; London 1962). Personal experiences of the successful author in a Japanese prisoner of war camp in Changi.

TANAMERA (Barber, Noel; London 1981).The spellbinding story of two lovers and two great dynasties: one British, the other Chinese. The novel sweeps from British ruled Malaya of the 30s through the Japanese occupation to the birth of the new nation.

THE CITY

Strictly speaking, this is the part of Singapore along the river. A better description today would be what the city fathers have tenderly christened the CBD (Central Business District). Private cars can only enter this area from Mon through Sat from 7:30 to 10:15 h if they pay a S$5 toll (taxis S$2) or have at least four passengers. This is supposed to reduce the terrible rush hour madness. All traffic lights heading into the CBD are then permanently switched to red.

Begin your tour at *RAFFLES PLACE,* the city's old business centre. Highrise blocks, banks, airline offices, and shopping centres have shot up like mushrooms in the area. The old English colonial atmosphere is constantly being forced to make way for 21st century architecture. Today an underground garage has replaced the beautiful old corner house on Battery Road where once upon a time you could get terrific milkshakes. A profit-oriented jackhammer policy has led to the razing of just about everything of aesthetic value. Go through *CHANGE ALLEY* (quite small) to *RAFFLES QUAY.* Most of the people here are tourists. See how the clever shop and stand proprietors have signs written even in Russian, to lure in the odd Soviet sailor who might need a Japanese watch or a custom-tailored suit. Don't let yourself be talked into anything before you've been here a while - there are no 'one-time offers'!

QUEEN ELIZABETH WALK begins on the other side of the river. It's a small green park right on the sea. A new city highway runs in a big curve over the ocean (or newly reclaimed soil) making the new world visibly present even here.

From here you can see the *MERLION* (part lion part fish), which is the city landmark. On the Singapore River (North Boat Quay) there's one of the many *STAMFORD RAFFLES MONUMENTS.* Raffles is said to have landed here in 1819. Lots of Victorian buildings can be found near Raffles' landing place: *PARLIAMENT HOUSE, VICTORIA MEMORIAL HALL, SUPREME COURT,* and *TOWN HALL.* The *CRICKET CLUB* is still one of the more exclusive clubs in the city. *ST.ANDREW'S CATHEDRAL* is stylishly neogothic, dating from 1856. Cricket is played on the huge grass field, the *PADANG* . Something else from the British colonial period to check out is *RAFFLES HOTEL,* on the corner of Beach Road / Bras Basah Road. Time seems to have stood still. The hotel was built in 1886 and soon developed into the social rendezvous of the city's Europeans. Rudyard Kipling, Joseph Conrad, Somerset Maugham, and Noel Coward were among the select clientele, and so today there's the Writer's Bar. Those with a few extra dollars should try a Singapore Sling (S$6). There's a nice story about the billiard room and the cool Englishmen. Two gentlemen are playing billiards, and with typical English imperturbability one informs the other that a tiger is sitting under the billiard table. "Oh, this is the second one this week!" comes the not very surprised answer. Right next to the hotel is the futuristic *RAFFLES CITY.*

The old Chinese residential quarter with its traditional style of buildings is being chewed up more and more by highrise office and apartment buildings. Only a few parts are supposed to be kept for the benefit of the tourists. On the other hand, even hard-core nostalgia freaks would have to admit that the houses are very old, lack sanitary facilities, and just don't meet the expectations of people today. For all practical purposes, Chinatown is northwest of Raffles Place. In the evening it still gets going, proving it's Chinese. People play mahjong - a kind of dominoes - buy and sell, skin snakes for the next meal, sniff and select durian. Old people practise a kind of shadowboxing (tai chi) to keep in shape while at the same time achieving peace and harmony.

One of the oldest Chinese temples *(THIAN HOCK KENG TEMPLE)* can be found on Telok Ayer Street. The 'Temple of Heavenly Happiness' is mostly used by Taoists from Hokkien. In 1840 all the granite columns and woodcarv-

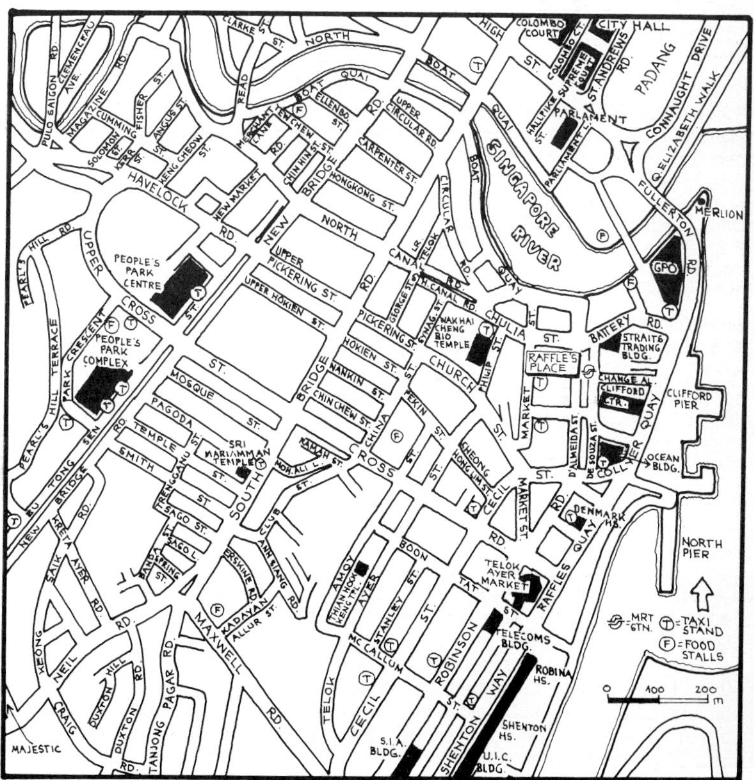

ings along with the deity statues were brought here from China. In Chinatown you can also see one of the city's most important Hindu temples. The *SRI MARIAMMAN TEMPLE* was built in 1843 and provides a vivid contrast to its Chinese surroundings.

Real India can be found in *SERANGOON ROAD.* This is where you can get the best saris as well as freshly mixed curry powder. The most important mosque is the *SULTAN MOSQUE* on North Bridge Road. Even here the 20th century has gained admittance in the form of a huge digital clock. There are about 500 other temples and mosques in the city. If this interests you, get more info from the STPB (Singapore Tourist Promotion Board) in Raffles City.

Another walk leads up to *FORT CANNING* (nothing of which remains) and through *CENTRAL PARK,* where you'll find the oldest cemetery in town, and then on to the *VAN KLEEF AQUARIUM* (open daily 10:00 to 18:00 h, admission S$1). The aquarium has a good collection of tropical fish - more than 4000 species. On the other side of the park on Stamford Rd. is the *NATIONAL MUSEUM* (open daily 9:00 to 17:30 h, admission S$1). It's a well equipped museum with historical, archaeological, and ethnological collections.

If you're on the upper end of Orchard Road, have a look in the *BOTANICAL GARDEN* (Cluny Rd., open daily 5:00 to 23:00 h, free admission). There are beautiful strains of orchids and paved paths through a little bit of virgin jungle!

DAY TRIPS AROUND SINGAPORE

If you plan to be here for a while, then of course you could visit Johore Bharu (Malaysia) or even the Riau Archipelago. But here are a few alternatives within the republic.

MOUNT FABER

At 130 m the name may be a joke, but it still offers a good view of the city and harbour. Take bus 143 to Mount Faber Road. A station for the Sentosa cable car is on the hill. One way from Mount Faber to Sentosa costs S$3.50. By the way, you can also get a good view of the city from the top of the many high-rises, such as the 28th floor of the Mandarin Hotel, Pan Pacific Hotel, Westin Plaza or Westin Stamford.

PULAU SENTOSA

The island is not a very impressive tourist attraction - except for visitors from neighbouring countries who might have never seen a real Swiss cable car except in the movies. The ride is pretty interesting though; from 60 m you do have a good view of the city and harbour. Note: a gondola fell and crashed in February '83. On the island you'll find an artificial swimming lagoon, Fort Silosa, Pioneers of Singapore, and a surrender chamber with wax figures representing the 1942 capitulation of the allies and the Japanese surrender in 1945. There is also a coralarium. Everything's pretty touristy! Prices: normal admission ticket is S$3.50 including the round trip boat ride. Admission for the above mentioned except Surrender Chamber is included. A composite ticket costs S$7 and includes all sights. Ferries leave the World Trade Centre every fifteen minutes from 7:30 h; the last ferry returns at 23:00 h.

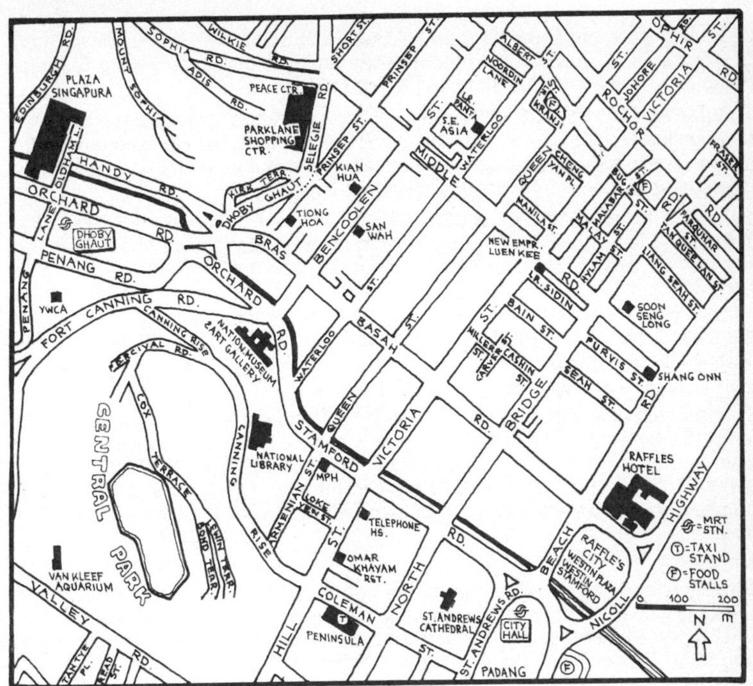

TIGER BALM GARDEN

The Chinese millionaire and businessman Aw Boon Haw had a park built on Pasir Panjang Road. Tiger Balm is by now well known everywhere; you can even find the little red jars in Europe or the States (by the way, it works wonders with headaches!) Many grotesque Buddha figures made of brightly painted cement are in the park. Scenes from Chinese mythology and history round off the Disneyland-like set-up. The various depictions of hell are quite good! Buses 10, 30, 97, 143, 145, 146, 184, 192, 200. Open daily 8:00-18:00 h.

JURONG

This is the oldest part of the modern industrial quarter. About 600 businesses have settled here since the 60s. Of interest is the huge JURONG BIRD PARK. About 2 ha of land on the slopes of Jurong Hill have been covered over by a net. Admission: S$3.50. Open daily from 9:00 to 18:30 h, Sat/Sun/Hol until 19:00 h. First take a bus to Jurong Interchange: 10, 30, 98, 154, 157, 165, 178, 183, 184, 192, 196, 197, 198, 199, 206. Then take bus 250 to Jl.Ahmad Ibrahim.

In Jurong there are two other parks. The CHINESE GARDEN (Yu Hwa Yuan) is 13 ha in size. Buildings and facilities are an imitation of the Peking Summer Palace. Open daily from 9:00 to 18:00 h, admission S$2.

The JAPANESE GARDEN (Seiwaen) is reportedly the largest Japanese garden outside Nippon. Admission S$1 or S$2.50 for both parks. Take any of the above mentioned buses to Jurong Interchange, and then bus 242. None of the three parks is too far from the interchange.

BUKIT TIMAH NATURE RESERVE

This is the last remaining piece of jungle area on the island. About 75 ha in size, it's located east of Upper Bukit Timah Rd., about 12 km from town. A hike here is especially worthwhile for people who otherwise won't get a chance to go on jungle treks. We even spotted a few flying lemurs and macaques. Good paths lead through the forest. Take buses 170-173, 177, 180-182, or 200 up to Jurong Road. Another road leads from Jl.Anak Bukit to the forest.

SELETAR RESERVOIR

The largest water reservoir on the island has been turned into a park. Nearby is the ZOO (Mandai Lake Road) which, unlike other such facilities in South East Asia, is well tended. Admission: S$3.50, open daily 8:30-18:00 h. Not far away is the largest ORCHID GARDEN in the city. Open daily 9:00-18:00 h, admission S$1, for which you can buy an orchid. You can get there by bus 171 from Queen Street.

ISLANDS TO THE NORTH

Several islands lie off Singapore to the northeast. The smallest is CONEY ISLAND (Pulau Serangoon). The two larger ones are PULAU TEKONG and PULAU UBIN. They are still pretty untouched. You can reach them all from Ponggol Jetty. Buses 82 or 83 will take you from the city to Ponggol. Chartered speedboats cost S$50 for 5 people.

ISLANDS TO THE SOUTH

There are a bunch of other southern islands besides the aforementioned Sentosa Island. A must for every visitor is a harbour tour given by the Port of Singapore Authority. HARBOUR CRUISE (2 hours), 10:00 and 13:30 h, Mon-Sat. Price: S$5, leaves from the World Trade Centre Ferry Terminal. The WORLD TRADE CENTRE is on Telok Blangah Rd. (Sentosa cable car), buses 10, 20, 30, 61, 84, 93, 97, 100, 125, 143, 145, 146, 163, 167, 176, 180, 186, CBD 1.

At CLIFFORD PIER the so-called JUNK CRUISES are offered. First of all, they are too expensive (S$20), and secondly, they're packed with 10-day package tourists who, while doing South East Asia, just want to get some quick photos of the harbour. Not to be recommended! If you want to visit the islands on your own, your departure point is also the World Trade Centre.

PULAU KUSU / ST.JOHN'S ISLAND, 10:00 and 13:30 h, last boat back at 16:00 h, price S$5 including return. On Sun/Holidays nine boats. The islands west of Sentosa are almost all plastered over with industry. You can see the oil refinery on Pulau Bukum from Sentosa's swimming lagoon.

As Indonesia's PULAU BATAM is a visa free point of entry and there are regular ferries from Singapore, it's worthwhile to visit the island of BINTAN. Check in the *Sumatra* chapter.

HOTELS

Singapore has a huge selection of hotel rooms in all categories. Cheapest are the various **DORMITORIES** on Bencoolen Street. Charging S$6 or 7 per bed are *GOH'S HOMESTAY* at no. 175. Other dormitories are at no. 173 *(PHILIP CHOO HOMESTAY,* tel 3366960) and at no. 49/50 *(PEONY MANSION,* tel 3385638). Double rooms** are also offered in all the places mentioned. On the 6th floor of the Asia Radio Building on Bencoolen Street is *TRAVELLERS' CLUB**. At the other end of the price scale is *SIM'S RESTHOUSE**, 114A Mackenzie Rd. (tel 3364957). Managed by Sim's brother is *FRIENDLY GUESTHOUSE**, 357A Serangoon Rd. (Perumal Road), tel 2940847. Many readers recommended *AIRMASTER ***, 36B Prinsep Street, tel 3383942. At 562A Serangoon Road is *TRAVELLERS' INN** right across from the gas station. Or try *SANDY'S PLACE**, 355 Balestier Road, Goodwill Mansion, 4th floor, tel 2526711. There's an overhead bridge from the supermarket right to Goodwill Mansion. More expensive is *SUSAN LIM***, 20 Upper Circular Road, tel 5325532, dorm costs S$5, double rooms S$40. Since these places are only half legal - they aren't zoned as hotels - the scene can change very quickly.

The **CHEAP HOTELS** can be found around the blocks between Bras Basah Rd./Beach Rd./Rochore Rd./Bencoolen St. Here you'll have to look around. Not bad is *KIAN HUA***, no. 81 (tel 3383492) or *SAN WAH***, no. 36 (tel 3362428). At 7 Waterloo St. next to the Chinese temple you will find the *SOUTH EAST ASIA**** (tel 3382394) or just round the corner at 161 Middle Road *TAI LOKE HOTEL***. At no. 55 *WATERLOO HOSTEL***, tel 3366555. At 26 Middle Rd. is *SOON SENG LONG***, tel 3376318. Also good is *TIONG HOA***, 4 Prinsep St. (tel 3384522). Recommendable and clean is *SHANG ONN***, corner of Beach Rd./Purvis St. (tel 3384153). Or try the *TAI HOE HOTEL***, 30 Verdun Road (tel 2984911). Two reasonable hotels are located on Jl.Besar (extension of Bencoolen Street.): *CENTRAL HOTEL***, tel 2984122 (Allenby Road) and at no. 407 the *PALACE HOTEL**. (tel 2983108), bus 65, 92, or 106 go to Jl.Besar.

MIDDLE CLASS HOTELS: Those who want to stay a bit out of town should check into the *GRAND**(*)*, 25 /26 Still Road South (formerly Karikal Road), tel 3455261, in Katong. In the city there are the *TANGLIN COURT HOTEL****, 2-4 Kim Yam Road corner of River Valley Road, tel 7373581 or try the *STATION HOTEL****, Keppel Road (tel 2221551). An alternative are the two YMCAs: *METROPOLITAN YMCA****, 60 Stevens Road (tel 737755), or the *YMCA**** at 70 Palmer Rd. (near Finger Pier), (tel 2224666). Both are a bit out of town. It might be worthwhile to check some of the more expensive hotels as most of them give discounts of 40% or more on their published room rates. If you want TV, swimming pool, room service, etc. try *HOTEL SUPREME****, Kramat Lane (right on Orchard Road), tel 7378333; *LADYHILL HOTEL*****,

Ladyhill Road, tel 7372111; *SLOANE COURT*****, 17 Balmoral Road, tel 2353311. All three establishments charge around S$50 for a double.

Should you really want to spend a night in *RAFFLES,* get ready to pay S$160 for a double. Similar atmosphere at *GOODWOOD PARK HOTEL*****, 22 Scotts Rd., tel 7343706.

FOOD

For people with a well-stuffed wallet, Singapore can be the greatest food trip in the world. From morning till night you can gorge on the culinary delights of exotic Asia (and more!). But even in the many foodstalls you can eat well and save. Here, first of all, is a list of the evening markets where the different foodstalls are set up. More and more the *street hawkers* are being grouped together. The original atmosphere is therefore a bit formal, perhaps more antiseptic, which shouldn't hurt the quality of the food. Some hawkers take in more than S$500 per day. An advantage of the new *food centres* is the improved hygiene. Health inspectors make regular rounds, and each foodstand proprietor is required to undergo a periodic medical check up. You can eat here without qualms.

We really like *NEWTON CIRCUS.* (MRT Newton). Start with a Hokkien Fried Mee (noodles with pork and shrimps), then have an oyster omelette and for desert fresh pineapple or fried bananas (pisang goreng). That should all cost about S$5. In the city itself is the *TELOK AYER MARKET,* set in a huge market hall that's been declared a historical monument (Shenton Way/Raffles Quay). It's especially nice for lunch. In Winter 87 /88 the whole building was reconstructed. Of similar quality are *EMPRESS PLACE* and *BOAT QUAY.* Less well known is *FOOD ALLEY* (Murray St., near Maxwell Rd.). Old fashioned atmosphere can still be found on *CHINA SQUARE* (Cross St. /Pekin St./China St./Amoy St.). Here you'll find the best turtle soup. Malay satay is best sampled in the *SATAY CLUB* (at the end of Queen Elizabeth Walk). Each skewer costs 30 c. In general the food centres mostly offer Chinese food. Indian and Malay food are mainly restricted to murtabah and satay.

Go really southern Indian style, meaning eating with your right hand off banana leaves, in *KOMALA VILAS,* 76/78 Serangoon Road. Even better is *NEW MADRAS WOODLANDS* on Upper Dickson Road right round the corner. Good, too, are the two Indian non-vegetarian places across from the Sultan Mosque (North Bridge Road): *JUBILEE* (no. 771/773) and *ISLAMIC* (no. 791/797). Cheap is *UJAGAR SINGH,* 7 St. Gregory's Place (across from the USA embassy on Hill Street). You can try north Indian cooking in *OMAR KHAYAM,* 55 Hill Street (tel 3361505) - reserve a table in advance! The menu is sheer poetry! Start with a Tandoori chicken - the chicken is seasoned in 13 different spices for 6 hours. Then move on to prawn curry a la Kashmiri. The art of mixing spices reaches the ultimate here. To top it all off, have a harem coffee - prepared at your table. It's worth it to let a few dollars fly. Less expensive, but as good, is *MOTI MAHAL,* 18 Murray Street (Food Alley), tel 2214338. The Far Eastern Economic Review praised it as "One of the best Indian restaurants any-where!" Here, too, the specialities are from Kashmir and Punjab.

Those who've lived off nasi Padang on Sumatra and have learned to prize hot food needn't miss it here. Check out *RENDEZVOUS,* 4/5 Bras Basah Rd. or another nasi padang place on the corner of Beach St./ Seah St. For the real thing, of course, you'll need plane tickets.

It's hard to write about the huge number of Chinese restaurants - there are just so many of them. And of all these, there are just too many excellent ones. Before trying Chinese cuisine, read the Food & Drink section of this chapter. What we are sold in the west as Chinese cooking has little in common (besides the name) with the high state of the culinary arts found in the Middle Kingdom (or Singapore for that matter). Here are just a few suggestions. You can get an excellent 'steamboat' with 'chicken rice' in *YET CON,* 25 Purvis Street. We paid about S$40 including beer for 6 people. Still, check the price in advance! The same goes for *dim sum* during the afternoon in *EASTERN PALACE,* 448 Lucky Plaza Shopping Centre, Orchard Road. Dim sum and other Cantonese dishes are also served in *PEKING MAYFLOWER RESTAURANT,* 4th floor, International Building, Orchard Road. You'll find lots of Cantonese restaurants in *PEOPLE'S PARK.* Try Hakka food in *MOI KONG,* 22 Murray Street. You might also order prawns fried in red wine. Hainanese chicken rice can be found in *SWEE KEE,* 53 Middle Road or in *VICTORIA,* 87 Victoria Street. Szechuan cooking is available in the expensive *OMEI,* Hotel Grand Central, 22 Cavenagh Road.

McDonalds and Kentucky Fried Chicken have broken into the Singapore market (Liat Towers, Orchard Rd.; Shenton Way; People's Park and Airport). Westward-looking Singaporeans seem to like such things!

SHOPPING

Many travellers only go to Singapore to shop, get film developed, send mail, or pick up a visa. Just to make it plain, the advertising hails this city as a shopping paradise. You can figure out for yourself the ulterior motives behind such ads. If you don't watch out, your financial resources can take a big dive. Whether this really is the time and place to get a new stereo is something you'll have to decide for yourself. Remember the customs authorities back home are sure to take a big interest in your purchases, raising the price even more. Never believe what salespeople say about custom duties back home - how should they know? Anyway they won't see their customers swearing at the cashier's window in London, LA, or Darwin. Since Singapore is a dutyfree port, most imported goods are tax free, meaning no import duty.

If you intend to buy something, get an idea what the thing would cost back home and then check the price in a big ***DEPARTMENT STORE*** where they have fixed prices. Then, in most cases, you can get it more cheaply after long bargaining with one of the small dealers. Addresses of the big department stores:

JOHN LITTLE, Specialist's Centre, Orchard Road / Somerset Road.
METRO GRAND SCOTTS, Scotts Shopping Centre, Scotts Road.
METRO GRAND LUCKY PLAZA, Lucky Plaza, Orchard Road.
METRO SUPREME, Supreme House, Penang Road.
C.K.TANG, Dynasty Hotel, Scotts Road / Orchard Road.

ISETAN, Wisma Atria Shopping Centre, Orchard Road.
YAOHAN STORES, Plaza Singapura, Orchard Road.

The ***CHINESE EMPORIUMS,*** featuring goods from the People's Republic of China, are also of interest. They offer a good selection of jewelery, silk, arts and crafts, as well as exotic odds and ends:

CHINESE, International Building, (upper) Orchard Road.
ORIENTAL, People's Park Centre, New Bridge Rd./Upper Cross Street.
OVERSEAS and TASHING, People's Park Complex, New Bridge Road.
KLASSE DEPARTMENT STORE, Lucky Plaza, Orchard Road.

The ***SHOPPING COMPLEXES***, such as People's Park, Plaza Singapura, or Lucky Plaza are shopping centres which at first glance seem to be huge warehouses, but actually consist of hundreds of small private shops. Since similar wares are offered by a large number of dealers they are a good place to do some bargaining. In general the shopping complexes surrounding Orchard Road have a higher price level than those in the less well-known streets. When purchasing cameras and other expensive items, be sure that an international guarantee card is included and that the date and serial number are noted on the receipt.

ADDITIONAL SHOPPING TIPS

FILM - is more expensive in Indonesia and Malaysia than in Singapore, so stock up here. You can have Ektachrome film developed directly from KODAK within 24 hours at 305 Alexandra Rd. The shops offer good prices for colour prints.

BOOKS - here you'll find the largest selection of English language literature, including books about Malaysia and Indonesia. Check out the large shop on the second floor of Plaza Singapura (Shizuoka Yajimaya). MPH has six branches: 71 Stamford Road (corner of Armenian St.), Centrepoint, and in the Afro-Asia Bldg. on Robinson Road. Times Bookshop is rapidly expanding (Lucky Plaza, Specialist's Centre, or Centrepoint). Books about South East Asia at Selecta Books, Tanglin Shopping Centre.

WESTERN FOOD - after weeks of eating Asian, a simple bottle of wine with cheese and 'real' bread can be worth a few dollars. These delicacies are available in any big supermarket, such as Cold Storage Supermarket (Centrepoint) or Jason's (Orchard Towers).

HANDICRAFT CENTRE - South East Asian arts and crafts can be found on Tanglin Road behind Tudor Court. The prices, however, might make you decide to do the travelling instead. There are also more reasonably priced handicraft shops all around town.

CHINATOWN - in the area between New Bridge Road, South Bridge Road and on to the south, there are only a few streets left, reminiscent of old fashion Chinatown. A walk through the side streets is still rewarding, with many interesting tiny shops offering temple accessories, jewelery, porcelain, traditional medicines, and specialities. Early in the morning on Smith Street there's a nice market specializing mostly in food. In the evening the same area transforms into a night market where textiles and foodstalls predominate. Before flying home you might stock up on orchids at the morning market (30 c a piece). Another tip: there are Chinese medicines based on natural ingredients for just about every ailment - some are said to be better than what's offered by modern chemistry.

GENERAL INFORMATION

TOURIST INFORMATION - the STPB (Singapore Tourist Promotion Board) has its main office at Raffles City Tower, 250 North Bridge Road, tel 3396622. Open daily except Sun and Fri from 8:00-17:00 h. Several magazines and brochures are available free of charge offering tips as to what's going on and where to buy. Look for: *The Singapore Visitor, Singapore Official Guide, Lion City,* or *Weekly Guide.* They are also available in all the big hotels. Try to buy a copy of *The Secret Map of Singapore* or *The Secret Food Map of Singapore.*

POST OFFICE - the General Post Office is on Fullerton Road, open except Sun 8:30-18:00 h, Sat until 14:00 h. Singapore has the cheapest and most reliable postal system in the region, so send your letters and parcels home from here. Parcels shouldn't weigh more than 10 kg. Costs to Europe S$21.

TELEPHONING- from the phone booths you pay 10 c for three minutes. Many international calls can be dialled direct (IDD calls). There are three time zones for IDD calls. Between 12:00 and 21:00 h, Western Europe costs S$3.60 a minute (or S$2.60 to the UK), between 21:00 h and 24:00 h it's only S$3 (S$2.30), and between midnight and 12:00 h it costs S$2.40 (S$2). Collect or reverse charge calls aren't permitted. Open round the clock are the GPO, Fullerton Building, the Telecom Bldg. at 35 Robinson Road, and the Commcentre Killiney Road / Exeter Road. The Telephone House at 15 Hill Street.is open until 21:00 h. In the airport's arrival hall it's possible to make calls free of charge - good for hotel booking.

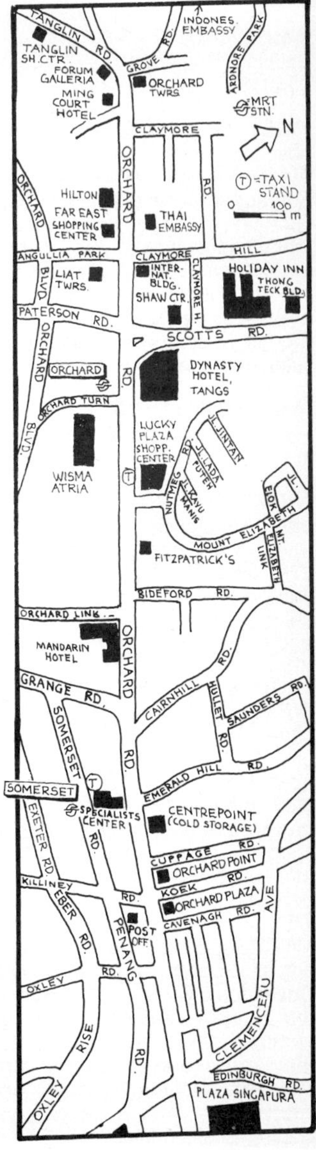

AMERICAN EXPRESS - UOL Building, Somerset Road, #02-02, tel 2358133.

FIRST AID - the two most important hospitals are the Alexandra Hospital, Alexandra Rd., tel 635222 and the Singapore General Hospital, Outram Rd., tel 2223322. You can call an ambulance on 999. Private medical practitioners and dental surgeons are usually outfitted with modern equipment, especially those located around Orchard Road. Addresses are listed in the yellow pages.

INSTANTASIA CULTURE SHOW - is held for tourists at 11:45 each day in the Raffles Hotel. Costs S$5.

NEWSPAPERS - besides the papers in Chinese, Tamil, and Malay, there is the English language daily, *THE STRAITS TIMES*. In the international hotels you can also find a wide selection of international newspapers and magazines.

NIGHTLIFE AND ENTERTAINMENT - can mostly be found on Orchard Road. Try ANYWHERE in Tanglin Shopping Centre (beer S$6; no admission) where two live groups play oldies. Nice atmosphere! A newer establishment in the same shopping centre is HAVEN LOUNGE. More expensive with cover charges between S$15 and S$25 are TOP TEN at Orchard Towers, or RUMOURS at Forum Galleria, diagonally across. Good music too at RAINBOW, Cuscadden Road, right across from the Boulevard Hotel. There are a number of movie theatres, though they are more expensive than in Malaysia. Western films are usually subtitled in several languages including English, Malay and Chinese.

LEAVING SINGAPORE

BY AIR

The modern Changi Airport is 20 km east of town. You reach the city via a multi-lane expressway by taxi (normal rate plus S$3 airport tariff), by the airport bus (SABS) for S$4, or cheapest of all with the regular city bus (SBS) for 80 c - try bus 390 to Queen Street. The airport tax is S$12 for international flights, and S$5 for flights to Malaysia or Brunei. Here is a list of the important international airlines which serve Singapore:

AEROFLOT, Meridien Shopping Centre, 100 Orchard Rd, tel 2355252.
AIR CANADA, Meridien Shopping Centre, 100 Orchard Rd, tel 7328555.
AIR FRANCE, Orchard Towers, 400 Orchard Road, tel 7377166.
AIR INDIA, 5 Shenton Way, tel 2259411.
AIR LANKA, # 2 PIL-Bldg., 140 Cecil Street, tel 5418888.
AIR NIUGINI, #17-05 Goldhill Square, 100 Thomson Rd., tel 2504868.
ALIA, 15 Beach Road, #03-11, Beach Centre, tel 3388188.
BRITISH AIRWAYS, #05-01 Far East Plaza, 14 Scotts Rd., tel2535922.
CATHAY PACIFIC, #17-01 Ocean Bldg.,Collyer Quay, tel.5331333.
CAAC, #01-53 Anson Centre, 51 Anson Rd. , tel 2252177.
CHINA AIRLINES, #04-01 Lucky Plaza, Orchard Rd. tel 7372144.
CZECHOSLOVAK AIRLINES, Holiday Inn, Scotts Rd., tel 7379844.
GARUDA, #13-03 Goldhill Square, 100 Thomson Rd. tel 2502888.
INTERFLUG, Far East Plaza, Scotts Road, tel 73371 88.
KLM, #01-02 Mandarin Hotel, 333 Orchard Rd., tel 7377622.
LUFTHANSA, #03-01 Tanglin Shopping Centre, Tanglin Road, tel 7379222.

MAS, #02 Singapore Shopping Centre, 190 Clemenceau Avenue, tel 3366777.
PAKISTAN INTERNATIONAL, Ming Court Hotel, Orchard Rd, tel 7373233.
PHILIPPINE AIRLINES, 10 Parklane Shopping Mall, Selegie Road, tel 3361611.
QANTAS AIRWAYS, Mandarin Hotel, Orchard Road, tel 7373744.
ROYAL JORDANIAN AIRLINES, Beach Centre, Beach Road, tel 3388188.
ROYAL NEPAL AIRLINES, SIA-Bldg., 77 Robinson Road, tel 2257575.
SABENA, International Plaza, Anson Road, tel 2217010.
SAS,#01 Finlayson House, 4 Raffles Quay, tel 2251333.
SINGAPORE AIRLINES, SIA Bldg, 77 Robinson Rd. tel 2238888.
SIA-TRADEWINDS (charter flights to Malaysia) tel 2254455.
TAROM ROMANIAN AIRLINES, #03 , 3 Coleman Street, tel 3381467.
THAI AIRWAYS #08-Keck Seng Tower, 133 Cecil Street, tel 2242011.
TURKISH AIRLINES, Far East Shopping Centre, Orchard Road, tel 7324556.
UTA, #14 Orchard Towers, 400 Orchard Road, tel 7377166.
YUGOSLAV AIRLINES, Liat Towers, 541 Orchard Rd., tel 2353017.

Here are sample prices for flights to neighbouring countries, one-way, in S$, ISIC prices in parenthesis: BANDAR SERI BEGAWAN 320.-, BANGKOK 483.-(258.-), COLOMBO 874.-, DENPASAR 579.-(423.-), HONG KONG 644.-(423.-), JAKARTA 345.-(182.-), KOTA KINABALU 346.-, KUALA LUMPUR 98.-, KUCHING 170.-, MADRAS 847.-, MANILA 699.-(489.-), MEDAN 297.-(177.-), PAKANBARU 203.-, PALEMBANG 265.-, PENANG

150.-(107.-), TAIPEI 1095.-(566.-), TOKYO 1375.-(731.-).

In most cases you won't have to pay the official IATA tariffs. Besides student rates, there are the excursion tariffs. Otherwise the cheap travel agencies often offer tickets at way under the official rates. Check the ads in the newspapers. Book your ISIC flights from Holiday Tour & Travels, Ming Court Hotel, 4th Floor, tel 7345681. German Asian Travels at 1503 Straits Trading Building, 9 Battery Road can give you info about cheap flights. They offer a return ticket to Jakarta for S$260.

If you're flying to Europe, Australia or the US, first check out the student rates. The cheapest are PERTH for

S$657, MELBOURNE and SYDNEY S$750. Flights to Western Europe with an ISIC cost around S$700 no matter where you fly into.

BY BUS

Cheapest is bus 170 from Queen Street for 80 c to JOHORE BHARU. For S$1 there's also the Johore-Singapore Express, non-stop. At the border, everyone has to get out and walk through Malaysian immigration before getting on another bus to the JB bus station. Bus 170 leaves every 10 minutes from 5:20 h to 0.10 h. In JB you can get local buses in all directions.

Right from Singapore, different companies' buses leave to all major Malaysian cities. *KUALA LUMPUR-SINGAPORE EXPRESS*, tel 2928254, leaves from the Queen Street terminal daily at 9:00 and 10:00 h for KL. Price: S$16.10. *MALACCA - SINGAPORE EXPRESS,* tel 2935915, from Lavender St., corner of Kallang Bharu, daily at 8:00, 9:00, 10:00, and 11:00 h for S$11 to Malacca. *HOSNI EXPRESS*, tel 2926757, has a night bus right to Penang that leaves at 18:00 h from Golden Mile Tower Terminal on Beach Rd. *AA-EXPRESS-COACH SERVICE,* tel 7341329, has buses to KL, Butterworth / Penang, Ipoh, and Hat Yai. *MASMARA-TRAVEL*, tel 7326555 2947034 leaves from Lavender St. terminal. Buses mainly to the east coast, e.g. Kuantan (departure 9:00, 10:00 and 22:00 h, S$16); Kuala Trengganu (departure 8:00 and 20:00 h, S$23); Kota Bharu (departure 7:30 h, S$30); KL (departure 9:00 and 21:00 h, S$17.

BY TRAIN

The train station is on Keppel Rd., bus 20 from Beach Rd. or buses 10, 145, 146, 186. Information tel 2225165. Seven trains leave daily to KL (6:45, 7:45, 8:30, 15:00, 15:45, 20:25, 22:00 h). The Ekspres Rakyat / Sinaran (6:45, 7:45 and 15:00 h)) arrives in KL at 13:15, 14:20, and 21:40 h. The train at 22:00 h goes right through to Bangkok. SAMPLE PRICES 3rd cl. (2nd, 1st):

SEGAMAT 6.80 (11.-,24.30), GEMAS 7.80 (12.60, 28.-), WAKAF BHARU 24.90 (40.50, 89.90), BANGKOK 80.40 (only 2nd cl., 175.60 1st cl.), KL 13.50 (21.90, 48.60), IPOH 20.50 (33.40, 74.10), BUTTERWORTH 26.60 (43.30, 96.-). Ekspres Rakyat / Sinaran: KL 17.- (ac 55.-), BUTTERWORTH 30.- (ac 50.-).S$.

BY SHIP

There are fewer and fewer regular ship connections every day, and Singapore is no exception to this trend.

Daily at 10:00 h, a small ship leaves Singapore and arrives 90 minutes later in PULAU BATAM. The trip costs S$20. Departure point is Finger Pier. You can get tickets right on the pier.

At 10:00 and 14:30 h, a boat leaves for TANJUNG PINANG, costs S$65. There are also three jet foils to BATAM (visa free entry-exit point). Costs S$40.

Several boats leave daily from there to Tanjung Pinang. From TANJUNG PINANG you have daily boat connections to PAKANBARU. This combination is the cheapest route to Sumatra. Compare with the corresponding part of the *Indonesia* section. Information at Inasco Enterprises, 63 Robinson Rd. (5th floor), tel 2216421. Or phone TSS, tel 2616240. Information also at German Asian Travels, 1403 Straits Trading Building, 9 Battery Road, tel 5335466.

THAILAND

Thailand - 'Land of the Free', is a proud name for the former Kingdom of Siam. It's obvious today that this was the only South East Asian country never to fall under western colonial domination. This Buddhist nation was able to carry on its culture with relatively little outside influence. Despite the great language difficulties, the exotic temples and picture-book world seen in holiday catalogues are enticing more and more tourists into the country. More than 3.5 million per year - has what used to be called colonialism now evolved into cultural chauvinism? Take a look around the tourist quarters in Bangkok or Pattaya. Those familiar with them know that not just the land, but also the Thai women, are being cruelly exploited. What thinking person could support this kind of Third World tourism? There are, however, some 'farang', as foreigners are called, who want to visit Thailand outside the tourist ghettos.

In the south, along over 2000 km of coastline, you can kick back on the palm dotted beaches. Besides Phuket or Krabi, the vacation paradises during the European winter, and Ko Samui, home to backpack tourists, you can check out less well known provincial towns and fishing villages along the coast. Go out to explore unpopulated islands or check out a traditional Thai bathing resorts at Hua Hin or Songkhla for a look at how the natives enjoy their holidays.

In the north, Chiang Mai is the candle attracting the buzzing tourists. Here you'll find travel agencies organizing treks out to the hilltribes. Those who want to set out on their own, will have to struggle with the communication problem or stick to the well beaten path. A trip through the 'Golden Triangle' is not an opium-smoker's dream, rather filled with the hard reality of minority and refugee problems, political power struggles and bandit holdups. In the central and northeastern parts of the country, outside of the metropolis of Bangkok, you'll see evidence of the many influences on the country's history and culture.

VISAS

Entering Thailand is usually no problem. You can enter the country any time without a visa. In this case a ***15-day visa*** will be stamped into your passport. Customs officials can refuse to let you enter if you don't have at least US$250 and a return ticket, though. Poorly dressed individuals are often turned down.

If you wish to stay longer than 15 days, however, you should definitely apply for a ***60-day visa*** at the nearest Thai Consulate well in advance. We have heard that the Penang Thai consulate has even issued 90-day visas to tourists. The visa costs US$5 for tourists and US$15 for visitors with non-immigration status. From the date of issue the visa has a validity of 90 days, meaning that you have to enter the country within this period. For the visa you'll need 2 passport pictures, a valid passport, and - in Europe - travel confirmation (= airline ticket or voucher) . On entering the country customs expects you to have at least US$500, but this is rarely checked.

Extending your tourist visa - (15-day visas can sometimes be extended, too) You can have your 60-day tourist visa extended twice for an additional 30 days each time. In Bangkok this will cost you 300 Baht. You can, alternatively, leave the country, pay a short visit to Burma or Malaysia, and then apply for a new visa from there. If you want to have it extended in Thailand, though - go to Immigration, dress well, and look your best. Address:

Immigration Department, Thai Police, Soi Suanplu, Sathon Tai Road, tel 2869176, 2869230. For the extension of your visa you will be expected to show a hefty US$1000.

THAI EMBASSIES OVERSEAS

AUSTRALIA: 111 Empire Circuit, Yarralumla, Canberra, ACT 2600. Consulates in Melbourne and Sydney.
CANADA: 85 Range Road, Suite 704, Ottawa, Ontario K1N 8J6, tel 2371517. Consulates in Toronto, Montreal, and Vancouver.
NEW ZEALAND: 2 Burnel Ave, PO Box 2530, Wellington 1, tel 735538.
UNITED KINGDOM: 29/30 Queen's Gate, London SW7 5JB, tel 5890173.
UNITED STATES: 2300 Kalorama Road, NW, Washington DC 20008, tel 6671446. Consulates in Boston, Chicago, Philadelphia, and Honolulu.

THAI EMBASSIES IN NEIGHBOURING COUNTRIES

BURMA, 81 Prome Road, Rangoon, tel 12471/16555.
INDONESIA, Jl.Imam Bonjol 74, Jakarta, tel 343762.
MALAYSIA, 206 Jl.Ampang, Kuala Lumpur, tel 488222.
SINGAPORE, 370 Orchard Road, tel 7372158.

FOREIGN EMBASSIES IN THAILAND

BURMA, 132 Sathon Nua Road, tel 2344698, open Mon-Fri 9:00-12:00 h.
INDIA, 46 Soi Prasarnmitr Sukhumvit 23, tel 2580300 open Mon-Fri 8:30-11:30 h.
INDONESIA, 600-602 Petchburi Road, tel 2523135, open Mon-Fri 8:30-12:30, 14:00-16:30 h.
MALAYSIA, 35 Sathon Tai Road, tel 2861390-2, open Mon-Fri 8:30-12:30 h.
PHILIPPINES, 760 Sukhumvit Rd:, tel 2590139, open Mon-Fri 8:00-12:00, 13:00-17:00 h.
AUSTRALIA, 37 Sathon Tai Road, tel 2860411, open Mon-Fri 8:00-12:30 h.
CANADA, Bommitr Bldg., 138 Silom Road, tel 2341561, open Mon-Fri 8:00-16:30 h.
NEW ZEALAND, 106 Wireless Road, tel 2518166, open Mon-Fri 7:30-16:30 h.
UNITED KINGDOM, 1031 Wireless Road, tel 2530191, open Mon-Fri 8:00-16:30 h.
UNITED STATES, 95 Wireless Road, tel 2525040, open Mon-Fri 8:00-12:00 h, 13:00-17:00 h.

CUSTOMS

200 cigarettes (or 250 g of tobacco), 1 litre of wine, 1 litre of spirits, 1 camera, and 5 rolls of film are ***duty free.*** All additional gifts have to go through customs. Bringing weapons, pornography, or drugs into the country is prohibited. Nor may Buddha-statues or antiques be taken out. Up to US$10,000 worth of foreign currency may be taken in or out of the country. Thai currency is limited to 2000 Baht when coming in and 500 going out.

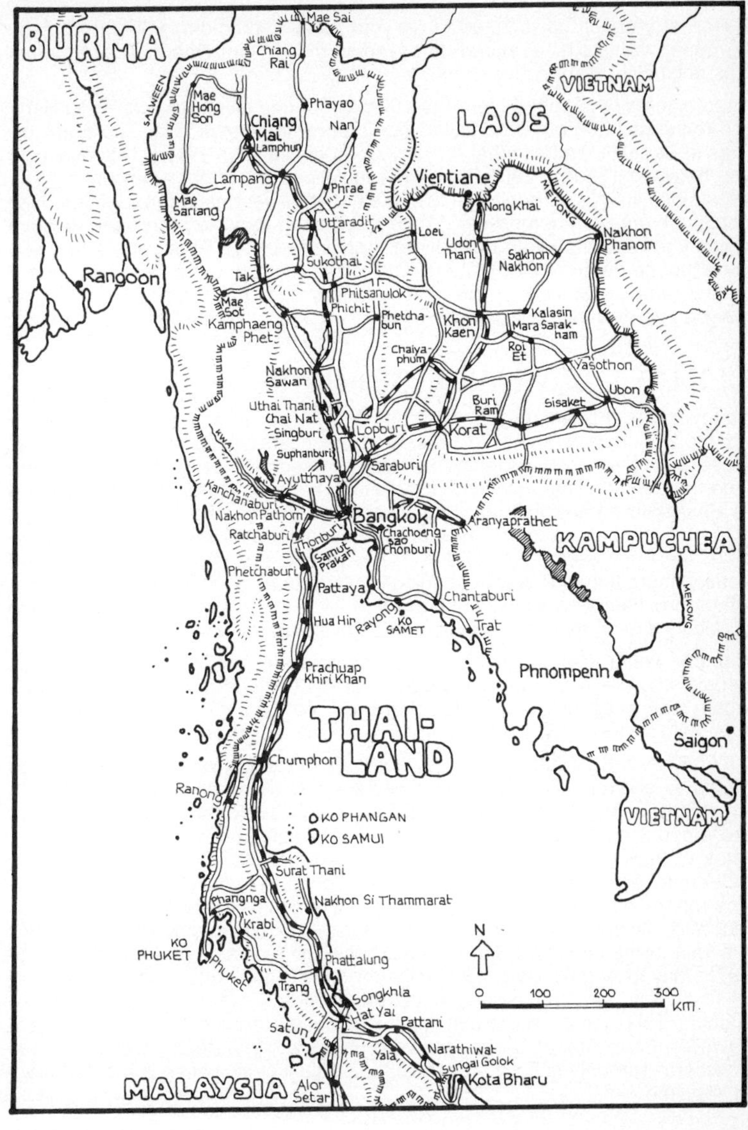
BURMA
LAOS
VIETNAM
KAMPUCHEA
THAI-LAND
MALAYSIA
Mae Sai
Chiang Rai
Phayao
Mae Hong Son
Chiang Mai
Lamphun
Nan
Lampang
Phrae
Mae Sariang
Uttaradit
Loei
Vientiane
Nong Khai
Udon Thani
Sakhon Nakhon
Nakhon Phanom
Sukothai
Tak
Rangoon
SALWEEN
MEKONG
Phitsanulok
Mae Sot
Phichit
Phetcha-bun
Khon Kaen
Kalasin
Mara Sarak-ham
Roi Et
Kamphaeng Phet
Chaiya-phum
Yasothon
Nakhon Sawan
Ubon
Uthai Thani
Chai Nat
Buri Ram
Sisaket
Singburi
Lopburi
Korat
KWAI
Suphanburi
Saraburi
Ayutthaya
Kanchanaburi
Nakhon Pathom
Bangkok
Aranyaprathet
Ratchaburi
Thonburi
Chachoeng-sao
Chonburi
Samut Prakan
Phetchaburi
Pattaya
Chantaburi
Hua Hin
Rayong
KO SAMET
Trat
Prachuap Khiri Khan
Phnompenh
Saigon
Chumphon
Ranong
KO PHANGAN
KO SAMUI
Surat Thani
Phangnga
Nakhon Si Thammarat
Krabi
KO PHUKET
Phuket
Phattalung
Trang
Songkhla
Hat Yai
Pattani
Satun
Narathiwat
Yala
Sungai Golok
Kota Bharu
Alor Setar
N
0
100
200
300
km

Never let yourself be tempted to try your hand at drug-smuggling; too many European tourists have ended up spending much more time in Thailand than was originally planned....

All foreigners who spend more than 90 days of one calendar year in Thailand are required to fill out a so-called ***tax clearance certificate.*** There are offices in Bangkok and all other towns with an Immigration Office. This may cost you between 175 and 1800 Baht; the regulations are rather ambiguous. You should definitely have dealt with this matter before your departure. If not, it may become even more expensive. There is no harm in saving the bank receipts which you received when officially exchanging money. These prove that you have had no need for employment. Officials in the countryside are much more lenient when it comes to this sort of thing, and their offices won't be as crowded as those in Bangkok.

CLIMATE & TRAVEL SEASONS

Sunny, tropical beaches, Buddhist temples whose golden stupas tower high up into the deep blue sky - pictures and brochures often hold the promise of these and other visual delights, but reality can sometimes look quite different. One frequently meets travellers complaining because their planned beach-trip to Phuket in mid-August was rained on, and others who found themselves slithering through northern Thailand's mudbanks from one Meo-village to the next, their shoulder bags still full of unexposed film because they dreaded nothing more than the idea of bringing home pictures of overcast skies. Others, who found themselves sweltering away at 41°C in the shade in Mandalay and suddenly had no desire to continue their travels are no rarity, either.

Nobody would plan a day-trip to Bournemouth in mid-December, and only people who are not aware of the fact that the summer months are the worst would plan to spend June in San Francisco. All the same, travellers in South East Asia frequently forget that there are rainy and dry periods here, too.

THE RAINY SEASON - May to October: the southwest monsoon brings humid air and rain from the Indian Ocean, especially to the west coast (Akyab, Irrawaddy-Delta, Rangoon, Phuket). There is less rain in the interior, though the amount continuously increases up until September/October. The yearly rates of the coast, however, (3000 mm upwards) are never reached (Korat: 1220 mm). All the same, there have been floods in Bangkok as early as May. The rate of precipitation in Burma is highest during July and August (Rangoon 582 mm; Mandalay 433 mm). There is always the chance, however, of hardly any rain falling in central Burma at all during the monsoon periods, as, say, in 1975. May to August are good months for travelling in north, northeast, central Thailand, and around the south coast on the side of the Gulf of Siam (e.g. Ko Samui). This period is not suitable for travelling around the Indian Ocean, however. From September to October there is a high rate of precipitation everywhere. The only half-way tolerable region during this phase is the northeast of Thailand.

THE COOL SEASON - November to February: relatively cool weather by Thai standards - but this still means temperatures varying between 20°C in the mornings and 30-33°C in the early afternoon. In Mandalay the temperature may fall as low as 16°C and it can get pretty cold at nights, especially in the mountains. There is always the possibility, however, of it still raining so heavily in mid-November (as we ourselves experienced in 1985) that many planned activities are simply not on. The dates we have given here are of course only the standard mean. Beginning and duration of the rainy periods vary from year to year.

THE HOT SEASON - March and April: starting February, the temperatures rise. People moan about the heat, and the ensuing water shortage constitutes a further inconvenience. This is especially noticeable in northeast Thailand and upper Burma, where clouds of dust gather above the dried-out fields. Temperatures of 40°C in the shade and more are not seldom here. The only pleasant place to be during this season is at the coast, where the bathing resorts are usually bustling with activity. The north, which lies higher, is in general cooler, but you should refrain from going trekking at this time of year nonetheless, as the clear cut mountains offer hardly any protection from the burning sun.

The best thing to do during this season is to hit the beaches - anything else would just end in a puddle of sweat.

FESTIVALS & HOLIDAYS

Many Thai holidays are of Buddhist origin and therefore tied to the religious calendar. As the Buddhist era (1987 is the year 2530 after Buddha, 1988 - 2531) is tied to the lunar cycle, the exact dates of the holidays vary by a few days each year. State holidays are set by the western calendar.

NEW YEAR - Actually, New Year is celebrated three times in Bangkok and many other parts of the country: ***Occidental New Year*** is celebrated on January 1st. The festivities are generally held at international hotels and on the square in front of Bangkok's Royal Palace. The festivities for the ***Chinese New Year*** (January/February) are for the most part held within the family. You can watch the preparations in busy Chinatown during the last couple of days beforehand. The exact date is fixed according to the first full moon of the year.

The ***Thai New Year,*** better known as *SONGKRAN,* is celebrated in mid-April, at a time when the whole country is suffering from the oppressive heat and waiting for the coming of the rains. For the farming population, this marks the beginning of the harvest. During this time you may find yourself being doused with cold water in the middle of the street, even days before the actual festivities begin. This can be a pleasant refreshment as long as one is prepared for it and not in Bangkok. Here, the water poured upon unsuspecting pedestrians is bound to be filthy Klong-water. A procession carries the Buddha-statue out of the National Museum through Thonburi the day before the feast. The population pours perfumed water over the statue on the Sanam Luang. At home, all Buddha statues are cleaned and bathed, too. Homes are cleaned and families pay their respect to their elders by carrying out ceremonial hand-washings and giving them small gifts. Many go on a pilgrimage to Chiang Mai, where the festivities are especially elaborate.

VISAKHA BUCHA - celebration of the birth and illumination of Buddha, as well as his final entry into nirvana. Lantern parades are held outside all temples in the evening. Believers circle the buildings three times with flowers and candles held between folded hands. Inside the temples, monks preach the teachings of Buddha. A central celebration is held in the Wat Phra Kaeo. The celebration takes place in mid-May.

THE ROYAL PLOUGHING CEREMONY - is held the following month. Astrologers set the exact date. A representative of the King, usually the Minister of Agriculture, carries out a symbolic sowing ceremony on Sanam Luang. Farmers from all over the country come to witness the ceremony, which for them marks the beginning of the sowing season. One grain of rice from the ceremony mixed with one's own seed is said to guarantee a good harvest.

ASANHA BUCHA - celebration in July, held in memory of Buddha's first sermon. Processions with flowers and candles around the Bot.

KHAO PHANSA - the long period of fasting starts the day after Asanha Bucha and lasts for three months, until the rainy season has passed. Monks are not allowed to leave the monasteries at night during this period, and rules generally become stricter. This is the time of year that young men enter into the monasteries, and ordination festivities are held everywhere.

THOT KATHIN - the fasting period ends October/November. It is now that people meet in their local temples to bring the monks new robes and offerings.

LOY KRATHONG - the great lantern parade is celebrated in November, after the rainy season has ended. Small boats made of banana peels and adorned with burning candles, incense, and flowers are set afloat on the lakes, klongs, and rivers, an offering to the goddess of water, Mae Khingkhe.

PHRA BUDDHABAHT - a footprint of Buddha is venerated in the Wat Phra Buddhabaht, between Saraburi and Lopburi. This large temple celebration with dancers and a market is held in February.

MAKHA BUCHA - lantern parade around the temples, held in honour of the speech Buddha made in front of 1250 people.

Further regional temple celebrations are held throughout the year. We would especially recommend the temple celebration in Nakhon Pathom, at Thailand's largest pagoda, and the one at the Golden Mount in Bangkok, both of which are held in November.

STATE HOLIDAYS

April 6th: CHAKRI DAY - enthronement of the first Chakri king and founder of the Royal City of Bangkok, festivities in the Wat Phra Kaeo.

May 5th: CORONATION DAY - Rama IX, the present king, was crowned on May 5th, 1946. Celebration at the Royal Court.

August 12th: THE QUEEN'S BIRTHDAY - Queen Sirikit has been Thailand's First Lady since 1950.

October 23rd: CHULALONGKORN DAY - death of King Chulalongkorn (Rama V statue in front of the Parliament), who is considered to be the sovereign who opened up the country to western influences.

December 5th: THE KING'S BIRTHDAY - national holiday. His 60th birthday was celebrated all year in 1987 (according to Buddhist tradition, 5 x 12 is a sacred number). Parades and celebrations in honour of the King are held all over the country.

GETTING AROUND

Thailand is a well-developed country as far as transportation goes. However, the entire road and rail system is tied into Bangkok as the hub. Work on connections bypassing the capital has only begun in the last couple years. Except for Malaysia, all the land frontiers (Burma, Laos, Kampuchea) are closed to foreigners.

TRAINS: All raillines feed into the Bangkok hub. The State Railway of Thailand is a safe and reliable means of transportation which is suffering under the competition from private bus companies. Take Chiang Mai as an example: Ac-buses charge 250 Baht and take about 9 hours. The express train costs 255 Baht second class plus 100 Baht or 70 Baht for a berth and takes 13 1/2 hours. The only consolation is that it's more comfortable. There are daily international train connections from Bangkok to Malaysia.

NORTHERN LINE: Ayutthaya (72 km), Lopburi (133 km), Phitsanulok (389 km) Lampang (642 km), Chiang Mai (751 km).

NORTHEASTERN LINE: Korat (264 km), Surin (420 km), Ubon (575 km), Khon Kaen (450 km), Udon (569 km), Nong Khai (624 km).

EASTERN LINE: Prachinburi (122 km), Aranyaprathet (255 km).

SOUTHERN LINE: Nakhon Pathom (64 km), Kanchanaburi (133 km), Hua Hin (229 km), Surat Thani (651 km), Hat Yai (945 km), Sungai Golok (1159 km).

BUSES: Road building really took off here in the 1960s. With heavy financial aid from the US, the big highways in the north and northeast were built. The Vietnam War was the strategic reason. Non-ac buses serve just about every village in Thailand. Airconditioned buses run between the major cities. Thai bus drivers like to play racedriver - going 120 km/h is nothing unusual. Accidents are seldom but when they happen, it can be very bad. An example from 1978: Three travellers were taking an ac bus from Chiang Mai to Chiang Rai. At a small village a totally drunk Thai got on and within a short time took over at the wheel. The travellers tried to get the driver to stop. Finally they reached a police station. The only reaction of the English speaking policeman: "Never mind, don't worry!" On one of many curves the bus broke through the barrier and tumbled down the embankment. 20 year old Bettina and six other passengers were killed. The only method for dealing with drunk or drowsy drivers is to GET OFF! Don't try to convince other passengers of the danger.

FLIGHTS: Thai Airways offers extensive domestic service in addition to flights to Vientiane and Penang. Those with little time and lots of cash should be good customers. There is an airport tax of 20 Baht on domestic flights. For foreign flights it's 120 Baht. By now, Thai Airways has a shuttle service at almost every airport in the country. The cost usually is between 30 and 40 Baht. This way you can save the expensive taxi fares.

CAR RENTALS: Those who choose to hop around Thailand in a rent-a-car should have at least some experience in Asian driving. There are traffic regulations, but few people act accordingly. The chaos in Bangkok is only the beginning. In the country large vehicles such as trucks and buses always have right of way, along with water buffalos, pigs, chickens and ducks. Try to get the smallest car for about 500 Baht a day. Addresses of several rent-a-car firms:

*AVIS,*10/1 North Sathon, tel 2330397. Also in Phuket and Chiang Mai.
HERTZ, 987 Ploenchit Road, tel 2524903 Also in Chiang Mai and Phuket.
*KLONG TOEY CAR RENT,*1921 Rama IV Road, tel 2519856.
*KING CAR RENT,*18/1 North Sathon, tel 2337907.
*ROYAL CAR RENT,*2-7 Soi 20,Sukhumvit Road, tel 2581411
BANGKOK CAR RENT, 57/13 Wireless Road, tel 2526428
INTER CAR RENT, 45 Sukhumvit Road, Soi 3, tel 2514910.

ACCOMMODATION

You won't have any trouble finding a hotel in the major cities. Everything's available from the cheapest dumps to international class. In the smaller towns, hotels aren't usually marked with Latin lettering. In the provinces you can expect cheap or middle class hotels to be red light staffed. Single male travellers will really pick up on this! Cheap places always spring up where the traveller scene gets together. Some of the huts on the beach at Ko Samui or the guesthouses in Chiang Mai are very frugally furnished and generally cheaper than the most reasonably priced Thai hotels. We decided on the following price table for Thailand; the prices are for double rooms - single travellers are usually charged the same price or only slightly cheaper.

*	**up to 100 Baht**
**	**up to 200 Baht**
***	**up to 400 Baht**
****	**over 400 Baht**

FOOD & DRINK

At a first glance Thai food just seems to be another of the many Chinese varieties. Upon getting to know it better, you'll notice the Malay influence - everything is cooked in coconut milk. The effects of the Indian curries should also be kept in mind. In general, Thai dishes are loaded with spice. The basic food ***rice,*** *KHAO,* is served with different side dishes and sauces. 'Kao' is also the general term for 'eat' - a good indication of rice's importance here. There are strong regional differences in the food. For example, only in the northeast you find *SOM TAM,* a kind of salad, made of honey, vinegar, ground peanuts, tomatoes, red chilies, and papaya. It comes with *KHAO NEO* (sticky rice) that you roll into tiny balls and dip in the salad.

Normally Thais eat with a ***fork and spoon.*** Meat and vegetables are sliced up before cooking. Sometimes you'll be offered chopsticks at foodstalls.

The cheapest meals are at the ***foodstalls.*** Just a few Baht gets you a clear soup with vegetable, meat or fish stock. Just as inexpensive is *KHAO PAT,* fried rice, often served simply as *KHAO MUU DAENG* with small strips of fried pork, onions, and egg. As a side dish you'll find cucumber and hot sauce with chilies. There are two different kinds of noodles: *GUE AE TIAO* , white rice noodles, and *BA MII,* yellowish wheat-flour noodles. They can be served in different ways, usually with meat or fish: *MUU* is pork, *GAI* chicken, *NUEA* beef, *PED* duck, *PLAH* fish, *GUNG* shrimp, *PUU* crab, and *GUNG* lobster.

Thai curries have several levels of hotness: *GAENG GHAREE* is a mild Indian curry known locally as *GAENG MASMAN. GAENG PET* is hotter, and call the fire department for *KHIAU WAAN.* These curries are prepared with various types of meat. Along with them you can expect white boiled rice *KHAO PLAO.*

Soups aren't served before meals, rather as the main meal. *KHAO TOM* is a rice soup containing meat, such as chicken *KHAO TOM GAI.* Especially spicy is *TOM YAM,* a hot sour soup. Try Tom Yam Gai.

KHAI (not to be confused with 'gai') is ***egg*** - *KHAI TORD* is fried eggs. *KHAI LUAK/TOM* are soft boiled or hard boiled eggs which in the end are pretty much the same here. *KHAI YAD SAI* is an omelette filled with meat or vegetables.

CHA is the term used everywhere in the orient for ***tea.*** *NAAM* (water) *CHA* (tea) *RAWN* (hot) is hot black tea. *CHA RAWN* is served with milk and sugar, *CHA DAM* just with sugar. Ice tea *(CHA YEN),* especially served with lemon, can be very nice. *GAFAE* - coffee is a favourite local drink with condensed milk, *GAFAE DAM RAWN* is the same without milk. Sweet black ice coffee *OH LIANG* is quite refreshing.

NAAM, water, is served as *NAAM YEN* cold water, *NAAM KAENG* ice water, *NAAM MANAU* lemonade or lemon juice, also served in combination with various fruit juices as a fruit drink. The cheap local favourite is Coke. Singha, Kloster and Amarit beers are found everywhere, though they're relatively expensive. The number one alcoholic drink is *MEKONG WHISKY* (tastes like cheap brandy). Thais will be constantly calling on you to join them in a nip. In such case you'd be smart to dilute the stuff with water.

Like all the tropical countries, Thailand offers an incredible variety of tropical ***fruit.*** Everyone should try *DURIAN,* queen of tropical fruits, at least once. This green thorny fruit is impossible to miss even for the uninitiated since it stinks like crazy. It's advisable to let an expert pick one out for you. Fruit is usually only available during certain seasons, durian from April to June. At that time you'll find *SAPAROT* pineapple and *MAMUANG* mango. A bit later you get *NGOH* rambutan, *LAMYAI* longan (especially good in Chiang Mai), *MUNG KUT* mangosteen, and *KANOON* jackfruit. All year round you'll find in the markets *GLUAI* - various kinds of banana. They are sold on the street and in bus stations as *GLUAI TORD* - baked bananas. Otherwise there are *SOM* mandarines, *SOM OH* huge oranges and *MALAKAW* papaya.

MONEY

EXCHANGE RATE:	**1US$ = 25.90 Baht**
INFLATION RATE:	**2.6%**

Thailand's monetary unit is the ***Baht*** with 100 ***Satang.*** The following banknotes are in circulation: 500, 100, 50, 20, and 10 Baht, as well as coins worth 5, 2, and 1 Baht and 50 and 25 Satang. The worth of the Thai Baht fluctuates little in comparison to the US$. There is no black market rate of exchange. The Baht is subject to fluctuation in comparison to the £, however, and this, in turn, depends on the £ - US$ rate of exchange.

Up to US$10,000 worth of Baht, foreign currency, and cheques may be imported into the country without having to be declared. This is hardly ever checked, though. If you have a great deal of money along and wish to play it safe, you should declare the complete sum of money upon entering the country.

When exchanging large sums of money, you should always check the rates offered by money-changers in the areas around Silom/Suriwong/New Road as well as those offered by the banks. You might be able to save a couple of Baht. If you plan to stay in the Bangkok and Chiang Mai areas, traveller's checks in many currencies are OK.

If you plan to spend most of your time in Bangkok and Chiang Mai, US$, £ or A$ traveller's cheques will do. Even taxi-drivers accept US$ by way of payment.

INCOME AND COST OF LIVING

The minimum wage in Bangkok is 73 Baht a day (April 1987) - this boggles the mind, especially if you consider the fact that officially one is meant to work 48 - 54 hours per week! The minimum wage is 67 Baht in the provinces of Chiang Mai, Korat, and Chonburi, 61 Baht in all other provinces. And these figures are not even binding - they only go for commercial workers, and industrial workers frequently receive even less. The same goes for women and children. Farmers, who usually only have a very limited area of land to cultivate, make less still. A realistic estimate of the yearly (!) income of an inhabitant of the north-east region would lie at around 2000 Baht. An average German tourist spends about 1357 Baht a day, a Swiss about 1968 Baht, and a US citizen almost 3500 Baht!

When planning your travel budget, remember that Bangkok is much more expensive than the provinces. Expect to spend about 150-250 Baht a day for accomodation and meals, then add the cost of transportation. One can easily get by on 150 Baht a day in Chiang Mai, Chiang Rai, Phuket, or Ko Samui if one's standards are not too high. This, however, does not include souvenirs, trekking-tours, rents for motorbikes, or trips to the most popular restaurants. All the same, there is no reason to spend 3500 Baht a day!

ECONOMY

Thailand has about 53.5 million inhabitants of whom 65% are engaged in agriculture. Only around 11% are employed by industry. Even so, industry pulls in 28% of the GDP. The most important areas are textiles and food processing, both of which exploit cheap labour. Over half the industrial capacity is concentrated in the Greater Bangkok area, a magnet drawing ever more people from the countryside. The problems caused by ever increasing urbanization can only hope to be solved through an improvement in rural life - an utopia?

The roots of Thailand's problems are rural. ***Agriculture*** only produces 22% of the GDP. Half the peasants in Thailand's fertile central region are tenant farmers and heavily in debt. In bad years, the land and everything they own must be mortgaged to middlemen, money lenders or large landowners for usurious interest charges. Sometimes they're even forced to put the entire next crop up as collateral just to survive. Not much was changed by the land reform program started in 1975. The average family survives on less than 2 1/2 ha of land. Thailand produces enough rice for herself and for export, though the yield per hectare is constantly decreasing, especially in the northeast where lack of rain is turning land into prairie. To counter this, the land area under production is being increased by logging in mountains and rainforests.

Besides rice and semi luxury foods which make up 50% of Thai ***exports,*** rare woods are a major export product. The export of raw materials is falling more and more as local production and processing increases. But the country still operates at a balance of payments deficit traceable to the high cost of imported technology and energy (oil). Thailand's natural gas fields meet only a small part of its own needs.

Over 2.6 million tourists visit the country per year. Only a small part of the approx. US$1 billion earned by way of tourism actually remains within the country as a foreign exchange cushion, though; most of the money goes to foreign organizers. Another considerable sum of money goes towards importing those goods that no tourist wants to have to do without.

NATIONALITIES & RELIGIONS

82% of the population are ethnic ***Thai,*** making this country, unlike its neighbours, relatively homogeneous. Ethnic minorities are mostly found in the northern and southern provinces. The four southern provinces on the border to Malaysia (Pattani, Yala, Narathiwat and Sadao) are 80% inhabited by ***Malay Muslims.*** Guerilla forces are fighting for the independence of the provinces. This is a delicate problem for the two ASEAN allies, Thailand and Malaysia.

Another ethnic minority, this time in the north, are the ***hilltribes.*** Their present population of 500,000 is constantly increasing due to the improving standard of living and the arrival of many people from across the borders in Laos and Burma (details in the *North Thailand* section).

A further, economically important minority are the 3.5 million ethnic ***Chinese.*** A Thammasat University study shows that 63 of the 100 largest companies in Thailand are controlled by ethnic Chinese. In addition, 23 of the 25 most influential men in the Thai economy are of Chinese origin. Though the economic ties between the two countries date back to the 13th and 14th centuries, the big wave of immigration came in the middle of the last century. After the founding of the People's Republic in 1949, the stream of immigrants dried up. A number of laws have been passed in an attempt to reduce Chinese influence, but the clever people from the Middle Kingdom seem just as adapt at circumventing these regulations as they are at increasing their market share.

Though freedom of ***religion*** is guaranteed in Thailand, Buddhism is pretty much a state religion. We can't go into the teachings of Buddha here, but we would like to give you some tips on behaviour as far as religion goes.

In principle you should respect the religion of your hosts, no matter what your personal opinion or preference might be. Buddha is always a holy person, and it's the ultimate in bad taste to treat a Buddha statue disrespectfully. Snapshots of you sitting on a Buddha are improper. Women should keep their distance from monks; try not to touch them or be photographed with them. A monk is supposed to withdraw himself from all earthly temptations. At one time they weren't even supposed to speak to women. For Buddhists, the head, as opposed to the foot, is a holy part of the body. For that reason you should never grab a Thai's head or stick out your foot to them.

HISTORY

Unlike other South East Asian countries, Thailand was spared the trauma of colonial rule. As a buffer state between Great Britain's sphere of influence to the west and south (British India, Burma, Malaya) and the French colonies to the east (Laos, Cambodia, Vietnam), Thailand was forced to perform a careful balancing act between the two great powers. In 1896 both powers agreed to honour the eternal neutrality of Siam without forgetting to allow for their own economic and strategic interests. But the country never was occupied militarily.

Archaeological discoveries of ceramics and weapons in ***Ban Chiang*** and near Kanchanaburi show that the country was inhabited 7000 years ago. Mon tradition also tells of an early civilization. In several waves of immigrants during the 7th and 8th centuries AD, the Thai people arrived from the present day southern Chinese province of Yunnan. The Lao and Shan also belong to this population group. Due to pressure from the Mongolians in the north, this trend was intensified.

The first Thai principalities were founded in ***Chiang Mai*** and ***Chiang Rai.*** In 1238 they were finally able to push back the once mighty Khmers to the south. In ***Sukhothai*** they founded the first capital of a greater Thai kingdom. In 1350 ***Ayutthaya*** became the new capital of Siam, as the kingdom was then known. The land developed into one of the important great powers of continental South East Asia. The geographical expansion stretched far beyond the present day borders. Angkor was conquered.

After the mortal enemy, Burma, burned and razed Ayutthaya in 1767, a new capital was founded in ***Bangkok.*** The successful General ***Taksin*** took on the title Rama I and was the first king of the still ruling Chakri dynasty. King ***Mongkut*** (1851-1868) is viewed today as the reformer and modernizer of the kingdom. His policy which partly consisted of brilliantly playing the British and French off against each other, was continued by his son ***Chulalongkorn*** (1868-1910). During his reign the country's infrastructure made great gains. The railroad from Malaya to Chiang Mai was built. The entire education system was reshaped and universities were founded. Chulalongkorn also took the major step towards ending slavery by issuing a decree prohibiting people from being born into slavery. He opened the country to several European nations and employed Britons, Belgians and Italians in his civil and military administration. Both kings changed the traditional social structure but also remained true to certain traditions. They are considered today to be the forefathers of modern Siam.

In 1932 Siam became a constitutional monarchy with ***Pibul Songgram*** as the strong man of a nation called Thailand. In 1940 it was allied with the axis powers of Japan, Italy and Nazi Germany. With Japanese support, parts of Laos, Cambodia and Malaya were annexed. In 1944 Pibul Songgram was deposed and Thailand allied herself with her former enemies. Pridi Phanomyong, leader of the anti-Japanese movement during the war, worked out a new constitution with his political friends. But he was deposed as soon as 1947 in a military coup under the leadership of Songgram. He went into exile and years later became spokesman for the Free Thailand Movement based in the People's Republic of China. Under Songgram's leadership the country became strictly anti-communist and a member of SEATO (South East Asia Treaty Organization), the Asian counterpart of NATO. With this move he broke with Thailand's tradition of neutrality. The military and Marshal ***Sarit*** ended this period of one-man rule with another coup in 1957. Sarit is one of the most controversial leaders in the nation's modern history. He was well liked by the people, while those in the know labelled him as the most corrupt dictator the country had ever known.

Field Marshal Thanom ***Kittikachorn*** became the new premier and led Thailand ever deeper into the pockets of the USA. During the Vietnam War the country was covered with a network of US military bases. US B-52 bombers flying out of Udon, Utapao and Ubon delivered their devastating payloads over Vietnam and Laos.

General elections were held in 1969 to form a Parliament whereby power again remained in the hands of Kittikachorn and his military sidekicks. The continuing differences between Parliament and the military led to the dissolution of Parliament, suspension of the constitution and the declaration of martial law. Kittikachorn promised it would be a short transition period of several months during which a new constitution could be worked out and a transition cabinet formed. It lasted almost two years.

We have here a typical example of Third World military dictatorship. In most cases not even the appearance of constitutional rule is sought. No meetings are permitted, political parties and free trade unions are forbidden; human rights are ignored. An independent judiciary is replaced by martial law and drumhead court-martials. Trips abroad are forbidden. In addition to these measures you'll usually find a stop on wage increases despite run-away inflation. Real power lies in the hands of the army and police. Corruption played an important role in Thailand. Field Marshal Prapas and Kittikachorn's son Colonel Narong acquired multi-million dollar fortunes during this period.

Many student leaders were arrested in October 1973 - for years they had been the regime's most active critics. On the 13th October, hundreds of thousands of people poured onto the streets to protest the arrests. The police and army began random firing from roofs and helicopters at the crowds with heavy machine-guns. 71 people were killed and hundreds injured. Bitter street fighting followed. The end of the ruling military clique was at hand when Kittikachorn, Prapas and Narong fled the country.

King Phumibol (Rama IX) announced over radio and television the resignation of the military regime and at the same time named the rector of Thammasat University, Sanya Dharmasakti, as the new premier. This university had always been the centre of the resistance, and this was seen as a victory for the student movement. But, Sanya was faced with the thankless task of managing a country left in tatters. There were huge waves of strikes, a rise in criminal activity, an inflation rate over 15%, critical conflicts with communist guerillas in the north and northeast and Muslim separatists in the south, just to name a few of the problems. One year after the bloody October massacre, the King announced the establishment of a new constitution. The first free elections were held in early 1975. No party was able to achieve a working majority. The slightly left-wing Democratic party under ***Seni Pramoi*** formed a minority government but resigned after defeat in the first parliamentary vote. Seni's half brother Kukrit, first secretary of the Social Action Party, formed a new somewhat more right-wing government. In the period following, the parties took turns in the driver's seat until the military decided to take the tiller again in October of 1976.

General ***Kriangsak*** became premier in 1977. He differentiated himself from his predecessors with a domestic policy of reform and an even-handed foreign policy, especially with Vietnam. Kriangsak was deposed in early 1980, and the Parliament named General ***Prem*** as his successor. A year later there was an unsuccessful coup attempt by young officers wanting to give the country long awaited reforms.

The only stable force in the course of all the political skirmishing has been the King, who still holds substantial powers. The problems facing Thailand have remained largely untouched in the wake of various democratic and military governments. Domestic political reform is just so much spilled milk as testified to by the pragmatical declaration of the young officers in April 1981. While the communist guerilla in the northeast and south has lost its fight and constitutes no danger any longer, the Muslim separatist movement in the south has remained active. Since Kriangsak Thailand has once again become strictly anti-communist. The conflicts along the border to Kampuchea have led to new arms shipments from, and joint field manoeuvres with the US Army.

LANGUAGE

Thai belongs to the Sino-Tibetan language family. The term ***Austro-Asian*** languages is frequently used to refer to the Mon-Khmer and the Sino-Tibetan groups. Like Chinese, Thai is a monosyllabic tone-language. This model, utterly different than that of most western languages, is what constitutes the biggest problem for foreigners.

In Thai the same word can theoretically have five different meanings, depending on the ***intonation*** of the speaker. In conventional Thai one speaks of five different pitches - rising, falling, high, low, and middle. In north Thailand there are even seven pitches. Pronunciation is not the only thing foreigners have difficulties with, though; ***script*** constitutes a further problem. The Thais adopted the Dewanagari transcription, taken from the Mon who, in turn, developed it out of the Pali-script of south India in the 13th century. Thai people write from the left to the right, leaving no space between individual words.

Even with a dictionary you will have many problems with the Thai pronunciation. In addition to the various pitches there are also 44 consonants and 32 vowels, most of which simply do not exist in western languages. The basic vocabulary offered here can only be seen as a small help. We would suggest having a Thai pronounce the words for you. Then try to imitate the sing-song way in which they speak.

SMALL DICTIONARY

Vowels: i - as in tip; **ii** - as in creep; **e** - as in pen; **ai** - as in buy; **aa** - as in father; **a** - as in Dad; **u** - as in loot; **uu** - as in pool; **ue** - as in prune; **eu** - as in French deux; **ee** - as in Paul Klee, or French Cartier; **ae** - as in where; **ao** - as in "how now, brown cow", better yet as in 'ciao'; **aw** - as in awe; **o** - as in knock
Consonants: p - as in put, but closer to a 'b'; **ng** - as in wrong, frequently used as an initial consonant; **t** - as in tea, but closer to a 'd'; **kh** - as in contact; **k** - closer to a g; **ph** - as in Peter; **th** - as in Thailand
All other vowels and consonants used below basically correspond to the English pronunciation.

NUMBERS:

NEUNG	1	CHAET	7	YII SIP	20
SAWNGH	2	BET	8	SAAM SIP	30
SAAM	3	KAU	9	NOING ROI	100
SII	4	SIP	10	NOING PHAN	1000
HAA	5	SIP ET	11		
HOK	6	SIP SAWNGH	12		

QUESTIONS:

KRAI	who, whom	THIINAI	where, where to
ARAI	what	THAORAI	how much/many
MEU ARAI	when	TAMMAI	why

PERSONS:

DIICHAN (f) PHOM (m)	I	KHAO	he, she, it
KHUUN	You (sing. + pl.)	RAO	we

TIME:

CHAO	morning	DAEO NII	now
TIANG	noon	TII LANG	later
YEN	evening	YANG	not yet
KHUEN	night	WAN	day
WAN NII	today	ATHIT	week
PRUNG NII	tomorrow	DUEAN	month
MUEA WAAN NII	yesterday	BII	year

ADDRESSING OTHERS:

When addressing others, you use only the Christian names, or with KHUUN

KHUUN	you (formal and informal), or Mr., Mrs, etc.
NUU/KHUUN NUU	young/unmarried woman
MAE NAI/KHUN NAI	elder/married woman.

SHOPPING:

SUEH	buy	PAENG	expensive
KHAI	sell	MAI PAENG	cheap
RAKA TAO RAI	how much is it?	MII	there are

ACCOMMODATION:

RONG RAEM TIINAI	where is the hotel?	HONG SUAM	toilet
RONG RAEM	hotel	GUN CHAE	key
HONG	room	YUNG	mosquito
HONG NAAM	bathroom	MUNG	mosquito net

TRAVELLING:

THANON NII ARAI?	which street is this?	ROT YON	car
MUEANG NII ARAI?	which town is this?	MAWTOESAI	motorbike
SAI	left	YUEM	rent
KHWA	right	BENSIIN	petrol
THRONG PAI	straight ahead	MUEANG	town
PAI...	I am going to...	NAKHON	city
ROT MEE	bus	BAAN	village
SATHAANI ROTMEE	bus station	DOY	mountain
ROT FAI	train	KAU	hill
SATHAANI ROT FAI	railway station	MAE NAAM	river
RUEHA	boat	KO	island
TAA	harbour	HAAT	beach
RUEHA BIN	aeroplane	AO	bay
SAANAM BIN	airport	NAAM TOK	waterfall
TEKSI	taxi	THANOM	road
YUUT	to stop	SOI	lane

FOOD & DRINK

GIN	eat	GAI	chicken
DUEM	drink	PED	duck
HIYU	hungry/thirsty	BAMII	yellow noodles
A-HAAN A-RO-I	the food is good!	GU-AE TIAO	white noodles
GAEP DANG	I would like to pay!	KHAO	rice
RAANAHAAN	restaurant	KAO PAT	fried rice
RAWN	hot	KHAI	egg
YEN	cold	KHAI JIAO	omelette
WAAN	sweet	SAPAROT	pineapple
PRIOWAAN	sweet & sour	GLUAI	banana
PET	sharp, spicy	MAPRAO	coconut
TAWT	roasted/baked	MAMUANG	mango
TOM	cooked	MALAKAW	papaya
YANG	grilled	SOM	orange
PING	toasted	NAM	water
PLAA	fish	NAM KAENG	ice
KUNG	lobster	CHA	tea
PUU	crab	GAFAE	coffee
PLAAMUEK	octopus	LAO	alcohol, brandy
MUU	pork	BURII	cigarette
NUEA	beef		

CONVERSATION:

Female speakers add the formal particle KHA to their sentences, male speakers KHRAP. These particles are also used in the sense of 'yes' and as linking particles between sentences.

SABADII	How are you?	PRAWT	please (as a request)
YUU RAEM TIINAI?	Where do you come from?	CHUUN	please (as an invitation)
		JUEARAI	What is your name?
MAI/MAI PEN RAI	no/that doesn't matter	DJUEA...	my name is...
THAI RUUPDAI MAI?	may I take a picture?	ARUN SAWAT	good morning
PHUUT THAI NITNOI	I speak a little Thai.	RADI SAWAT	good night
(MAI) KAOJAI	I (do not) understand.	FARANG	foreigner
KOP KHUN KHRAP/KHA	thank you (m/f)		

SUGGESTED READING

Many of the following books can be found in the large bookstores in Bangkok. You might also try the libraries of the foreign cultural institutes such as the British Council.

GENERAL READING:

THAILAND IN THE 80's (various authors; Bangkok 1984). An officially published handbook - wide ranging and informative on country, people, economy, administration etc.

CONFLICT OR COMMUNICATION (reprint of various articles out of the magazine 'Business in Thailand', Bangkok 1980). An excellent introduction to the social structure of the country and the mentality of the people.

CULTURE SHOCK! THAILAND (Cooper, R. & N.; Times Books, Singapore 1982). Amusing and relaxed, this is a good aid for a better understanding of the Thais and for knowing how to behave as a 'farang'. A good book to buy and read during your stay in Thailand.

THE POLITICS OF HEROIN IN SOUTH EAST ASIA (McCoy, Alfred; New York 1973). A scrupulously researched book about the opium business in the Golden Triangle area and its neighbouring countries.

THAILAND FROM THE AIR (Invernizzi, Luca / Cassio, Alberto; Bangkok 1984). Large format book with excellent photographs taken from a rather unusual visual angle.

THAILAND - SEVEN DAYS IN THE KINGDOM (Warren, William, and "50 of the World's Greatest Photographers", Singapore 1988). This beautiful, large format picture book full of stunning photography is the result of the joint efforts of 50 renowned international photographers who spent a week travelling around Thailand in 1987.

THAILAND - A SHORT HISTORY (Wyatt, David; New Haven 1984). Excellent introduction to the history of Thailand from the pre-Thai period to our times.

THAI-RAMAYANA (a translation by M.L.Manich Jumsai of the King Rama I version, Bangkok). There are several versions of this epic, beloved throughout South East Asia. The Thai version includes many of its own fairy tales and legends.

PEOPLE OF THE HILLS (Chaturabhand, Preecha; Bangkok 1980). Extremely readable descriptions of seven different hilltribes.

PEOPLES OF THE GOLDEN TRIANGLE (Lewis, Paul & Elaine; London 1984). Very comprehensive introduction to all hilltribes. Large format, many colour photographs.

UNDERSTANDING THAI BUDDHISM (Jumsai, M. L. Manich; Bangkok). Written in an out-of-date style, this book nevertheless contains all the necessary information.

INSIGHT GUIDE THAILAND (Apa, Singapore 1983). A travel guide with nice pictures and extensive route descriptions. Few practical tips.

THAILAND - A TRAVEL SURVIVAL KIT (Cummings, Joe; Melbourne 1987). A traveller book from the well known series.

THE SHELL GUIDE TO THE NATIONAL PARKS OF THAILAND (Dobias, Robert; Bangkok 1982). Description of all national parks with practical tips concerning climate and getting there. Many maps.

THAILAND - BURMA The Traveller's Guide (by us; Huddersfield 1988). A very comprehensive guide covering all regions of the country.

MAPS:

THE LATEST THAILAND HIGHWAY MAP (ed. by the Roads Association of Thailand; Bangkok 1986). The most comprehensive road atlas of the country at the present time. Many city maps. English and Thai.

APA MAP 1:1,500,000 (Singapore 1987). Sights are marked. Based on a topographical map. Not always reliable!

ESSO MAP 1:2,000,000 (Bangkok 1986). Thai and English, main roads with distances in km, city map of Bangkok, city and road index.

BANGKOK STREET DIRECTORY (Bangkok 1984). 265 pp. street atlas of the capital. Thai and English. Bus stops and government offices.

MAP OF BANGKOK & MAP OF CHIANG MAI (Nancy Chandler; Bangkok). Nicely drawn and illustrated maps with interesting markets, shops, restaurants, sights etc.

LATEST TOUR'S GUIDE TO BANGKOK & THAILAND (Bangkok). To be recommended as all bus routes are included.

BANGKOK

Welcome to Bangkok - just 200 years old, five million inhabitants, and problems wherever one looks. Travellers hurry through this town in a frantic rush - get some information, buy a ticket, go on a quick shopping-spree, and then it's off to enjoy the comfort of some tourist ghetto. Sweating and swearing, they stumble from one travel agency to the next, trying in vain to find the cheapest connecting flight. When they're in a hurry to get to the Immigration bureau they get stuck in traffic jams in the middle of rush-hour, and on top of everything else their travel funds have just about run out.

Many travellers have had this sort of experience in Bangkok. In addition, there's the city's negative image; anyone who has been there has some tale of robbery and deceit to tell. The traveller hotels do their part in contributing to this negative image, too. The city is huge. There is no actual centre of town. You have the tourist area here (Sukhumvit Road), the historical centre there (Sanam Luang), and the shopping centres and government offices somewhere completely different. The distances between the respective areas are too great to be covered on foot. As a result all of Bangkok seems to be mobile, driving through the intricate network of streets in taxis, tuk-tuks, on motorcycles and every other conceivable form of transportation. All this adds up to give the Bangkok air its special 'aroma'.

This is Thailand's metropolis, the city from which 90% of the country's foreign trade is controlled. Here one finds a dense concentration of industry, administration, and Thais hoping to find a better life. By now, every tenth Thai lives in the capital. While the city is heavily influenced by the western way of life, the countryside retains its ancient, rural traditions. Here, so-called progress develops slowly, if at all. But you can get to know the traditional way of life in Bangkok, too, for this is also a city of culture and religion. Nowhere will you find as many English-speaking Thais as in the capital, and nowhere will you receive as much information concerning the history and culture of the country. There are four hundred temples in the city, scores of market-places, and a National Museum in which you can easily spend an entire day. Those who spend a longer period of time in town will soon discover that it has much to offer in the way of night-life, too; restaurants in Bangkok are cosmopolitan, and there is enough entertainment for everyone, even those who are not in search of a hostess. Take your time when exploring Bangkok - it's worth it!

Begin your sightseeing tour by paying a visit to the

TOURIST OFFICE, where you will be able to purchase a good city-map with all bus routes (important!) for only 35 Baht. Ask about anything you might be particularly interested in as the employees have an amazing selection of hectographed leaflets. They will not volunteer any unless you ask detailed questions, though. You will also find the administration of bungalows in the Khao Yai National Park here. Address: TAT (Tourist Authority of Thailand), Ratchdamnoen Nok Road, tel 2821143-7, open from 8:30-16:00 h. Right next door you'll find the

RATCHDAMNOEN STADIUM. Thai-boxing competitions are held here. In this form of boxing the use of the entire body is allowed, including the feet. Much atmosphere and heavy gambling - typical Thai entertainment. Take the cheapest seats - they are the most fun. Opening hours: Mon, Wed, and Thurs 18:00 hours, Sundays from 17:00 and 20:00 h. The best fights don't start until about 21:00 h. Prices: 140-280 Baht, ringside seat 600 Baht. More Thai-boxing competitions can be seen at

LUMPINI STADIUM, Rama IV Road: Tues, Fri, Sat, starting at 18:00.h. Those with little time can take a bus directly to

SANAM LUANG, the large square in front of the Royal Palace. This is one of the cultural centres of town, and site of many festivals and ceremonies. There is so much to see around the square that you will barely be able to digest it all at once. On all accounts go to the

NATIONAL MUSEUM. Originally, the *second king,* a sort of vice-sovereign of days gone by, had his palace built here. Parts of it still stand today, as does the temple at the entrance of the museum. A thorough tour through this, the largest of all of Thailand's museums, will give you a good idea of the country's history, from prehistoric days all the way to the Bangkok period.

You'll find the prehistoric collection (which includes a neolithic grave found near Kanchanaburi) in the first large building on the left. The Buddhaisawan chapel on the right was built for one of the most venerated Buddha-statues of the country, Phra Buddha Singh. The statue is carried through Bangkok and Thonburi for the Songkran Festival annually.

The connecting central building of the museum is the former palace of the second king. You will find all sorts of fascinating objects from the Bangkok period here; the royal throne of Thailand's second king, elephant saddles, Khon-masks, marionettes, costumes, stamps, weapons, musical instruments, gifts to the royal family etc.

The newer museum halls surround this old building. Start your tour in the south wing, to the left of the entrance. On both floors you will find South East Asian and specifically Thai works of art, many of which stem from the period before the Thai people had even started populating their present-day national territory (Dvaravati / Mon, Lopburi / Khmer, Sri Vijaya and others). You will find objects of art from the more recent Bangkok period - sculptures, ceramics, textiles, coins etc. - on the ground-floor halls of the northern wing. In the upper floor you will first come across a hall of Hindu art-objects from Sukhothai, then a hall containing art from the north of the country (Chiang Saen and Chiang Mai). You will find sculptures and ceramics from the Sukhothai period in the adjoining room. Art of the Ayutthaya period and U-Thong (Mon) period can be found in the next two rooms. The last room contains furniture of the Bangkok period.

Open: Tues-Thur, Sat/Sun 9:00-16:00 h, admission 30 Baht. A free guided tour is held on Tuesdays (Thai art and culture), Wednesdays (Buddhism) and Thursdays (early or late art-tour alternates weekly).

The *NATIONAL THEATRE* is just around the corner. Demonstrations of classical dances are among the most frequent performances. For information call 2215861 Mon-Fri 8:00-16:30. The theatre organizes numerous musical performances from February to April , some of them held at the gallery. Traditional dances are performed on the last Friday of every month. Entrance fee 30 Baht.

The *THAMMASAT UNIVERSITY,* one of Thailand's largest universities, is right next door. Considered a centre of political resistance, this university was taken by force by armed police and militia in 1976. It is generally thought of as a barometer of young intellectuals' political ideas. A coup d'état or change of government, not exactly rare in Thailand's history, is often heralded by general student assemblies. The university is a good place to get to know English-speaking students. You will find

WAT MAHATHAT, the Buddhist college, in the narrow alley opposite the university. Pali-teachings and old religious traditions are studied here. Opening hours: 9:00-17:00 h daily. A big market within the temple-grounds is organized on Buddhist holidays, where, amongst other things, traditional Thai medicine is sold (import into foreign countries prohibited!). The wat itself is one the largest and oldest in Thailand, and between 300 and 400 monks live here. If you are interested in Buddhism this is a good place to meet monks, as many of them speak English. The meditation centre (section 5) is open to foreigners (even women!!) upon prior appointment. There is a library of English material on Buddhism, open to the public. Good-luck amulets as well as other religious trinkets are sold outside.

The buildings of the *ROYAL PALACE* occupy the entire area south of the square all the way to the river. An imposing white wall surrounds the palace and the Royal Wat Phra Keo.

When the Royal Palace was moved to Bangkok in 1782, Chinese merchants made up the population of the area. They had to move further south, to what is at present Bangkok's Chinatown. The highest elevation of the city, safe from floods and looking down upon the rest of the capital, was reserved for the Palace. New wings were added over the years, and even western elements of style were permitted under Rama IV, who is generally considered to be the sovereign who opened the country to western influences.

Admission to the palace is 100 Baht. Do not be scared off by this exhorbitant price - it's well worth it. A visit to the Vimanmek Teakwood Mansion and a rather confusing brochure containing a ground-plan of the premises and dealing with the interior of the palace and the temple are included in the price. The Royal Palace is open to the public 8:30-11:30 and 13:00-15:30 h. The ticket office is closed at lunchtime. You can still stay inside, though; it is agreeably quiet. People dressed too casually are often not let in by the guards. Shorts are absolutely unacceptable.

Also included in the price of admission is a visit to the temple museum and the royal collection of coins and decorations.

In the first building beyond the entrance you will find the

ROYAL COLLECTION OF COINS AND DECORATIONS - coins from the 11th century to the present day, jeweled medals, flags, coats of arms etc. are exhibited. Open 9:00-15:00 h daily except Sat. Behind this building you will find

WAT PHRA KEO. The gateway, guarded by gigantic demons called Yaks, leads to the temple-square. The square itself is surrounded by a covered arcade, the walls of which are adorned with beautiful murals depicting scenes out of the Ramayana. The heavily decorated Emerald Buddha stands facing the entrance. The 66 cm statue is probably made of jasper, though experts are not quite certain. The image was first found in 1443 in Chiang Rai, where it was hidden behind a fine coat of plaster. Under no circumstances should you point your feet at it. Photography within the chapel is also strictly prohibited. The beautiful monumental doors are guarded by bronze lions. Various buildings stand on an elevated marble platform opposite the main entrance of the bot. Here, you will see the world-famous royal pantheon, whose echelon roof is crowned by a gilded prang. The library with its pyramid-shaped mondhop roof is next to it, and the golden chedi is situated just beyond. On the north side of the library you will come across a stone model of the Angkor Wat temple. Beyond this, on a lower level, there is the prayer hall, adorned with colourful glass flowers, as well as many other buildings.

You can reach the Royal Palace by walking through the gate southwest of the bot. The first building you will come across is the Amarinda Palace. Originally, Rama I had wanted this to be a courthouse, but it was later used as the setting for coronation ceremonies. The central Chakri Maha Prasad Palace, situated south of the large square, was built no more than 100 years ago. The architectural design seems like an odd mixture of Victorian mansion and Thai temple. The small pavilion, not unlike the one in Bang Pa In, has been considered a typical example of Thai architecture ever since a replica of it was exhibited at the World Fair of 1958. Beyond it, you will find the Dusit Palace, originally intended by Rama I to be a coronation hall. Since the death of this king, however, it has only been used as a site for funerals.

The *TEMPLE MUSEUM* in the west section is well worth a visit. Should you feel like giving your, by now, surely rather sore feet a rest, there is a small restaurant right next door to it. You will find an interesting exhibition on the ground floor of the museum concerning the restoration programme which was started in the early 1980s. Buddha figures and the Manangasila throne are among the things of interest exhibited on the first floor.

The area opposite Wat Phra Keo and the Ministry of Defence (cannons in the front garden) bustles with activity. Birds, turtles and flowers are sold here. The population offers sacrificial gifts to the patron god of the city in the newly erected

LAK MUANG SHRINE. This reaches its climax on the day before the official lottery-draw. Gamblers come in the hope of receiving good luck. In return, they pay for performances of traditional dances, which you can witness for free in an adjoining, open room.

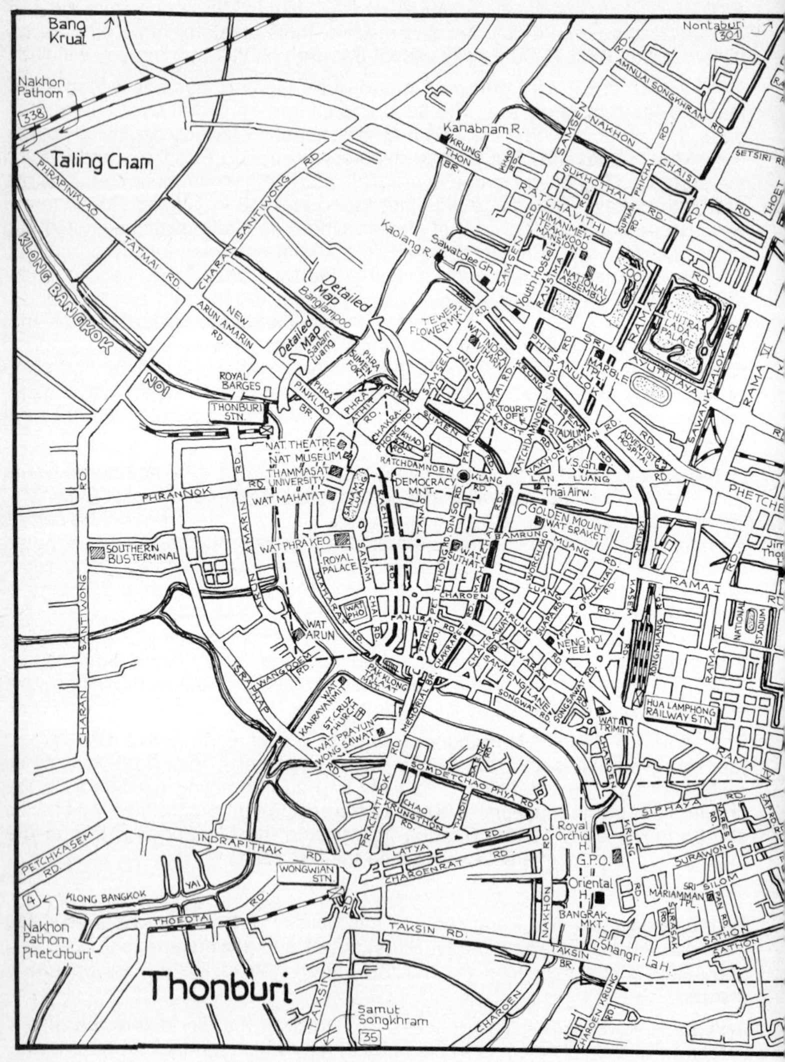
Bang Krual
Nakhon Pathom
338
Taling Cham
Nontaburi
301
Kanabnam R.
KRUNG THON BR.
PHRAPINKLAO
KLONG BANGKOK NOI
TATMAI RD.
CHARAN SANTIWONG RD.
NEW ARUN AMARIN RD.
Kaolang R.
Sawatdee Gh.
Detailed Map Banglampoo
Detailed Map Sanam Luang
ROYAL BARGES
THONBURI STN.
PHRA PINKLAO BR.
PHRA SUMEN FORT
PHRA ATHIT RD.
CHAKRAPHONG RD.
NAT. THEATRE
NAT. MUSEUM
THAMMASAT UNIVERSITY
WAT MAHATAT
SANAM LUANG
WAT PHRA KEO
ROYAL PALACE
WAT PHO
WAT ARUN
PHRANNOK
SOUTHERN BUS TERMINAL
ARUN AMARIN
MAHARAT RD.
SANAM CHAI
ISRAPHAP
WANGDOEM RD.
WAT KANRAYANMIT
ST. CRUZ CHURCH
WAT PRAYUN WONG SAWAT
PAK KLONG TALAAT MKT.
MEMORIAL BR.
PRACHATIPOK RD.
SOMDETCHAO PHYA RD.
KRUNGTHON RD.
INDRAPITHAK RD.
LATYA
CHAROENRAT
WONGWIAN STN.
PETCHKASEM RD.
4
KLONG BANGKOK YAI
THOEDTAI
Nakhon Pathom, Phetchburi
TAKSIN RD.
Thonburi
Samut Songkhram
35
SAMSEN RD.
AMNUAI SONGKHRAM RD.
NAKHON CHAISI RD.
SUKHOTHAI RD.
SETSIRI RD.
RATCHAVITHI
VIMANMEK TEAKWOOD MANSION
Youth Hostel
NATIONAL ASSEMBLY
ZOO
CHITRALADA PALACE
RAMA V
TEWES FLOWER MKT.
WAT INDRAVIHARN
WISUT
PHITSANULOK
SRI AYUTTHAYA
MARBLE TPL.
SAWANKHALOK RD.
RAMA VI
TOURIST OFF.
KASAT
STADIUM
NAKHON SAWAN RD.
ADVENTIST HOSPITAL
V.S.Gh.
RATCHDAMNOEN KLANG
DEMOCRACY MNT.
LAN LUANG
Thai Airw.
GOLDEN MOUNT WAT SRAKET
BAMRUNG MUANG RD.
WAT SUTHAT
TANAO
DINSO RD.
TITHONG
CHAROEN KRUNG
PAHURAT
CHAKRAWAT
CHAKRAPET
YAOWARAT
NENG NOI YEE
SAMPENG LANE
SONGWAT RD.
SONGSAWAT RD.
WAT TRIMITR
HUA LAMPHONG RAILWAY STN.
RAMA I
RAMA IV
RONGMUANG
KRUNG KASEM
NATIONAL STADIUM
PHETCHBURI
SIPHAYA RD.
Royal Orchid H.
G.P.O.
Oriental H.
BANGRAK MKT.
Shangri-La H.
SURAWONG
SRI MARIAMMAN TPL.
SILOM
SATHON
NARES RD.
TAKSIN BR.
NAKHON RD.
CHAROEN KRUNG RD.

WEEKEND MARKET
NORTHERN BUS TERMINAL
Lopburi, Ayutthaya
AIRPORT
PRADIPAT RD.
SUTTHISARN
INTRAMARA RD.
SOI INDRAMARA RD.
PHAHOLYOTHIN RD.
WIPHA WADEE RANGSIT RD.
PRACHASONGKROH RD.
Tumpnakthai R.
RATCHADAPHISEK
VICTORY MNT.
DINDAENG RD.
BANG NAM RD.
RATCHAPRAROP
SUARN PAKKARD PALACE
EXPRESSWAY
MAKKASAN STN.
PRATUNAM MKT.
N
0 500 1000 1500 2000 2500 3000 m.
Bangkok
NEW PHETCHBURI RD.
Bang Kapi, Minburi, Chachoengsao
3278
Hilton H.
BRITISH EMBASSY
PLOENCHIT RD.
ERAWAN SHRINE
Akamon R.
ASOKE
INDIA EMBASSY
SOI 3 (NANA NUA)
Atlanta H.
SUKHUMVIT RD.
Whole Earth R.
NETHERLD EMBASSY
NEW ZEALD.
U.S. EMBASSY
WIRELESS (WITHAYU)
RATCHADAMRI RD.
LUMPINI PARK
LUMPINI STADIUM
SOI 16
(SOI THONGLO)
SOI 55
SOI 63
SOI EKAMAI
(SOI 71)
PHRAKANONG - KHLONGTON RD.
RAMA IV RD.
Malaysia H.
SOI NGAM DU PHLI
SUANPLU
Detailed Map Silom Rd.
LINCHI RD.
KASEMRAT RD.
EAST. BUS TERMINAL
Sukhumvit Rd. Detailed Map
Chonburi
34
Samut Prakan
3

If you've had enough of culture and temples for the day, why not walk down Chakraphong Road, which will lead you to

BANGLAMPOO, Bangkok's traditional shopping district. This is also one of the main traveller hang-outs in town, and the shops have adapted accordingly; there were always many shops selling textiles in this area, but now one also sees western-type boutiques, travel agencies, and audio shops popping out of the ground almost overnight. Thais usually shop in Tani Road and the small side alleys. A walk through these small sois might be nice. Try the ones west of Chakraphong Road, where cars are a rarity. Here, the streets still belong to the people and animals - you will see street hawkers, children playing, and local women gathered together for a friendly evening gossip while men play music on traditional bamboo instruments. Tiny, weather-beaten houses, almost hidden by palms or mango-trees, lie behind the wooden fences. Banglampoo's most famous temple is

WAT BOVONIVES (Wat Bovorn). It's situated south of the city wall and Klong Banglampoo at the oval square, which is the terminus of many bus routes. The temple was erected under crown prince Mongkut in 1827, as a centre for the traditional sect of Dhammayuti, a sect he founded himself. The prince spent 14 years living here before he became king. The Wat soon became one of the most important temples of Thailand. The prince's successors, King Rama VI and Rama VII, spent some time living here as monks, too, as did the present king. There is a famous four-metre bronze statue of Buddha (Sukhothai period) in the bot. The murals here tell of the shortcomings of the people before Buddhist influences cleansed them, and of the gradual development of a 'good' Buddhist society. It is both interesting and surprising that those European influences depicted - western buildings, horse-races, ship-loads of missionaries, and even church-goers in western clothing - are drawn in a positive, even friendly manner. The two viharn behind the bot are only opened for special occasions. Remains of the former city wall can be seen at the meeting point of Klong Banglampoo and Menam Chao Phya.

South of the Royal Palace you will reach

WAT PHO (or Wat Phra Chetuphon) by way of Sanam Chai Road. It is open daily 8:00-17:00 h, entrances can be found on Chetuphon and Thiwong Road. Admission 10 Baht.

Construction of the Wat Pho began as early as 1789, under Rama I. It was erected on the site of an even older wat, said to have been built in the 16th century. Rama III had the wat restored and ordered the general knowledge of his time to be graphically inscribed on the temple walls for the illiterate population. Unfortunately, the murals have for the most part faded. Rama III was also the sovereign under whom the great viharn containing the famous 50 metre reclining Buddha was erected.

Coming through the Chetuphon Road entrance, you will find yourself in the western temple area. Walk north past the numerous souvenir-stands, fortune-tellers, and small buildings, and you will come to the temple of the huge reclining Buddha. The temple was re-gilded in honour of the king's 60th birthday in 1987. East of the temple, you will find four large chedis, each decorated with different-coloured tiles, one green, one orange, one yellow, one blue.

The medical building, founded under Rama III, lies behind the yellow chedi. The first students of medicine were taught here 150 years ago. Traditional eastern medicine is still taught here to this day, and patients are treated in the late afternoons. You can get a good medical massage (80 Baht for 30 minutes, 120 Baht for an hour) in the eastern section of the temple area. Roughly twenty stone statues give you an insight into the method of this form of massage, which was originally taught by Indian *rishis.* The central bot stands in the almost perfectly square eastern courtyard, separated from the rest of the courtyard by four viharns connected by an arcade. There are approximately 400 Buddha figures from different periods within the viharn and passageways. Scores of stone figures, brought to Thailand as ballast on Siam-bound ships from China, stand in the inner courtyard. The entrances to the central bot are guarded by bronze lions, the pedestal is decorated with a marble relief depicting scenes out of the Ramayana. Rice-paper reproductions of these scenes can be bought at the souvenir-stands. The doors, decorated with detailed inlays of more scenes out of the Thai-Ramayana, are beautiful, too, as are the carved and gilded window shutters. Scenes out of Buddha's life decorate the inside walls.

Giving shelter to over 300 monks, the monastery bordering onto the sacred buildings south of Chetuphon Road is the largest in the capital.

THONBURI, just west of the river, could actually be considered Bangkok's twin town. It was the first sanctuary for King Taksin's defeated army after the destruction of Ayutthaya. Ever since Rama I had the Royal Court moved to Bangkok in 1782, however, the political, industrial and business life moved with it. Although one could say that today the two huge cities have merged into

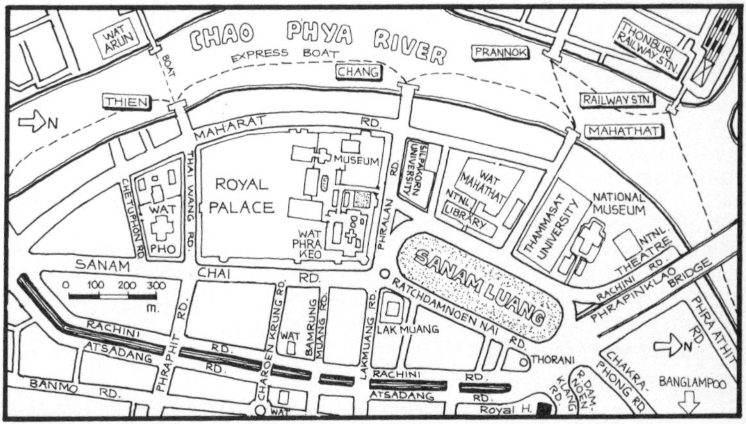

one densely populated area, there are still marked differences between them. While westernization is on the rise in Bangkok, Thonburi is still very much a traditional Thai town. Although there are plenty of streets and even expressways, the rivers and klongs are the most important connection in town. Speedboats chauffeur well-dressed businessmen and schoolchildren back home in the late afternoons, cement and charcoal are manoeuvred through even the most tricky of canals on wide barges, and the floating supermarket has an extensive stock of all essentials. Life is centred around the waterways; floating petrol-stations are as common as the floating shops that offer their wares at the riverbank. Each house has its own landing-place, which also functions as a bathing and washing-place for the whole family. Toilets, however, are on the mainland. Nevertheless, westerners are shocked again and again by the sight of small children merrily bathing in the murky waters. Sites for new buildings along the big canals near the Menam Chao Phya are just as rare as in any other large town, and as a result the wooden houses stand crowding each other, reaching into the actual rivers. If you drive out into the suburbs you will find that these are not quite as densely populated; trees grow on the riverbanks, and each house has an intensely cared-for garden at the back, giving this part of town an almost rural appearance.

You will only be able to experience this side of Thonburi from a boat (for information on klong-boats, see *Getting Around).* Start your tour shortly after sunrise, when it is still cool and you will be able to watch the families enjoying their morning bathe. If you do not feel like exploring the city on a public boat, we would recommend the informative klong-tour organized by STA Travel, Thai Hotel, 78 Prachathipatei Road. This tour will also take you to a small floating market. The former, large

FLOATING MARKET near Wat Lao has suffered so much from the thousands of tourists that come to look at it daily, that it has been reduced to a cheap tourist attraction. These days the alleged market-women only paddle their vegetable-laden boats up and down the river for the benefit of the tourists' cameras. We would recommend Damnoen Saduak. Thai Wang Road near Wat Pho will lead you to the *Chang landing-place,* and from here you can catch a ferry for 50 Satang to

WAT ARUN, the temple of dawn. Try to be there by sunrise, for then you will see the prangs (chedis built in the Khmer style, each covered with Chinese porcelain) reflect the early rays of sun in many beautiful colours. The various sized towers symbolize the Buddhist universe, with the holy mountain in the middle, surrounded by the world's oceans. You will see stone figures inside, one of them representing a European sea-captain, brought to Thailand from China. You will come across these figures in many other temples, too. A steep stairway leads to the top of the highest prang (86 m), from where you will have a good view of Bangkok. The wat is open daily 8:00-16:30 h. Admission 5 Baht.

You will be able to see the

ROYAL BARGES in a boat shed at the Klong Bangkok Noi. Take an express-boat from one of the landing places to the train station in Thonburi. From here, walk along the road left of the tracks for about 200 metres, then turn right and walk across the bridge to the other side of the klong. You will find a narrow wooden plank-way leading past a number of rather impoverished-looking houses to the boat shed on the northeast side of the bridge. It is easier to get there with one of the boats that travel up the Klong Bangkok Noi. Tickets for these boats cost 5 Baht. The shed is open daily from 8:30-16:30 h, admission 10 Baht.

Try to climb the *GOLDEN MOUNT* in the late afternoon or early morning, when it is still comparatively cool. This is where the golden chedi of Wat Sraket stands. The chedi contains a highly venerated Buddha-relic, and you will have a fine view from up here. A celebration with a fair and a pilgrimage is held here in November each year. You will find

WAT SUTHAT southwest of the Golden Mount. This temple was built approximately 150 years ago. Beautiful murals decorate the walls of the huge bot. Much money and effort was invested in having them restored a few years ago. In addition you will be able to admire a large Buddha statue from the Sukhothai period. The temple is open 9:00-17:00 h daily. You will see a gigantic swing in the middle of the busy road in front of the temple. Highly dangerous competitions were held here at a Hindu-Brahman festival of days gone by. These were prohibited under Rama VII.

From here, we would recommend a walk down the Bamrung Muang Road. The shops in this street sell a fascinating variety of temple-accessories. The eternally long road leading east from the Wat Pho,

the *NEW ROAD* or Charoen Krung, was the first road ever to be built in the city on the site of a former elephant-path under Rama IV (1851-1868). Previously, boats were the main form of transportation. European merchants who had their warehouses near the river demanded that the king build them a road to make the transportation of their goods easier. European influences are apparent around the entire area surrounding the Central Post Office.

You will find the

INDIAN MARKET on the west bank of the canal, on Pahurat Road. Here you can buy various textiles, saris, brocade materials for temple-dancers, jewelry etc. Stands selling Indian sweets can be found along Chakrapet Road, where there is also an Indian restaurant opposite the Chinese temple.

The narrow *SAMPENG LANE* can only be traversed on foot. We would recommend starting your walk at the corner of Pahurat Road and crossing the long in a southeasterly direction. An incredible variety of wares is sold here as well as in the side alleys (Itsaranuphap Lane etc.). The area is always relatively cool, even at noon, as the houses are tall and protected from the harsh sunlight by light-coloured sunblinds. The whole area, from here right up to the railway station, is called Bangkok's

CHINATOWN. Approximately 3 million Chinese live in Thailand. Many of them have been living here for generations. They have been able to establish a role for themselves within Thai society much more easily than in many other South East Asian countries, and this may be due to the common ethnicity shared by the Thai and Chinese people. One can not, however, speak of an unproblematic relationship between the two. Chinatown is especially fascinating when celebrations are held or during the period of preparation for the Chinese New Year.

The solid gold Buddha in *WAT TRIMITR* weighs almost 6 tons. The figure was made in the 14th century, but wasn't discovered until 1955, when what was thought to be a bronze Buddha was brought from an old ruin to a new wat. It fell to the ground and received a crack in its outer shell, thus revealing the true statue hidden within. The wat is open daily 9:00-17:00 h. Walk down New Road and you will come to one of the oldest banking and business districts in the south of town. You will see the

ORIENTAL HOTEL right next to the river. This old building has lost much of its original charm owing to modernization. Take a look at the old wing ('decent' clothing required), and you will see what it looked like in the days when Joseph Conrad and Somerset Maugham lived here as semi-permanent guests. From the terrace you will have an imposing view of the river and Bangkok's twin town Thonburi. The hotel offers a luxury tour to Ayutthaya and Ancient City. A cold buffet is included in the price. It's rather expensive, though, and we would recommend the much more reasonably priced boat-rental service at the landing-place south of the hotel, instead. From here, boats travel up and down the Chao Phya at regular intervals, a cheap tour, well worth it!

If you want to visit any of the following places you'll have to visit them one by one, seeing as they are rather far apart.

Go west down Rama IV Road and you will reach the famous

SNAKE FARM (Pasteur Institute). Poisonous snakes are milked here at 11:00 and 14:30 h Mon-Fri, only at 11:00 h on Sat, Sun, and holidays. The venom is used to produce antivenin serum. The institute was founded in 1922 in order to research and fight the rabies epidemic. A small exhibition about snakes can be looked at. It's open 8:30-16:30 h, Sat, Sun, and holidays till 12:00 h. Admission 40 Baht. This includes a booklet containing interesting facts. Call 2520161-4 for information.

The very popular *ERAWAN SHRINE,* a spirit house, stands in front of the large Erawan Hotel (Ratchadamri Road/Ploenchit Road). The four-faced god Brahma is venerated here. His statue is decorated with lotus wreaths and believers ask for blessings. Some even hire musicians and female dancers to circle the shrine clockwise and perform classical dances as a sign of their worthiness.

Walk to the end of Soi Kasemsam (goes off Rama I Road) and you will find the *JIM THOMPSON HOUSE.* Admission 100 Baht, students 30 Baht. It is well worth the price, seeing that the house is not only beautiful and built in the finest Thai tradition, but contains an extensive collection of South East Asian art objects to boot. These objects were collected by Jim Thompson, the man who managed to re-vitalize the Thai silk-industry after WWII. He disappeared without trace in the jungle of the Cameron Highlands, Malaysia, in 1967. It is open to the public 9:00-17:00 h Mon-Fri.

The *SUAN PAKKARD PALACE* (Sri Ayutthaya Road) is a small private museum in a traditional Thai setting. The only thing justifying the rather steep price, however (50 Baht, students 30 Baht), is the exotic garden, which is truly beautiful. Open 9:00-16:00 h except for Sundays.

The *ZOO,* situated near the National Assembly, is not especially exciting. Young Thais roam through the gardens and lovers go rowing on the lake in the late afternoons. This is one of the few quiet and relaxing spots in the hectic city. Admission 8 Baht, open daily 7:30-18:00 h. Opposite the eastern entrance of the zoo you will see the

CHITRALADA PALACE, private residence of the royal family. Nearby you will find

the *MARBLE TEMPLE,* also known as the Wat Benchamabopitr. It was built mainly out of white Italian marble during the reign of King Chulalongkorn. The palace has a pleasant garden with turtles in the moat. It is open daily 9:00-17:00 h, admission 10 Baht. It's particularly nice in the early mornings when the monks say their prayers. King Chulalongkorn (Rama V) and his father, King Mongkut, were the first Thai kings to be favourably disposed towards western influences. After a visit to Europe the king returned home deeply impressed, and had roads, bridges, and palaces designed and built for him by European architects. As early as 1904 the king had a car - one of the first automobiles in South East Asia - which he proudly drove daily up and down the road in front of the

HOTELS

You might have a difficult time finding a cheap hotel room if you don't arrive in Bangkok until evening. The first thing you should do in a case like this is start calling the hotels. They are reluctant to name their price on the telephone, however. The many guesthouses are a cheap alternative. You are almost certain to find a room in Khaosan Road, even late at night. If you wish to stay at a 'classy' hotel, there is a way to save money; have a large travel bureau in Bangkok reserve your rooms for you - you will receive a discount of up to 50% (maybe more!) owing to the excessive supply of hotels. Pay attention to the location of your hotel, as distances in Bangkok are great.

In the past few years many new guesthouses have been opened on Khaosan Road in Banglampoo. The area has established itself as a travellers' meeting-point, and accommodation is very cheap. Most guesthouses offer either simple double rooms (80-150 Baht) or dormitories (approx. 40 Baht per person). We would advise bringing your own linen or youth hostel sleeping bag, as well as a padlock for your backpack. The houses are often managed by young people who treat them as private pensions. They sell food and drinks and will help you with any problems you might have. As the walls are very thin, however, guesthouses are rather noisy. In addition, they are likely places to be robbed in. You will find one guesthouse next to the other on

KHAOSAN ROAD. You will also find plenty of restaurants, travel bureaus, a launderette (12 Baht per kilo or 25 Baht per machine - self service) and a branch of the Krung Thai Bank, which is open from 8:30-20:00 h.

You will find the *BALL BALL** next to the bus stop on Chakraphong Road; the *SIAM** a little further north. There are several guesthouses in the small soi, e.g. *LOTOS**, or *88 CHAKRAPHONG**. You will find the *CHUANPIS** (tel 2829948, cheap dormitory) and *J GUESTHOUSE** in no. 86. On Khaosan Road you will find the *V.C.** (with its own restaurant), *P.B.** (with a large billiards-room on the ground floor - 40 Baht an hour), opposite *HELLO**, *WALLY**, and *CHART**. In a small though rather noisy side-alley *SUNEEPORN** (tel 2819872) near the *LEK** (large with new rooms facing the road, older ones with worse showers behind them, and a restaurant). Further guesthouses can be found opposite the two hotels *NITH CHAROENSUK*** and *NEW SRI PRANATORN***. Rooms with ac: *TOP**, *BONY**, behind these *TUM** (tel 2829954), *V.I.P.** (tel 2825090 - with its own restaurant, popular), *PR 215**, *NUT**, opposite *DIOR**, *ICE**, and *C.H.** (tel 2823276, nice people, pleasant roof-garden, clean, 24-hour restaurant), and *CHADA** (with a pleasant restaurant). In another side alley *VS**, *HARN** and *ET**.

Further east, on Tanao Road, you will find the *NEW PRIVACY** (run by friendly people, quiet courtyard). In the alleys behind it *CENTRAL** (no. 10, tel 2820667 - the modern section is better than the old one). Just around the corner, *S.GH** and *SWEETY** (large rooms). South of Ratchdamnoen you will find *P** and *FRIEND GUESTHOUSE**. There are more guesthouses southwest of the Democracy Monument, e.g. the *T.I.C.** (105 Bunsiri Road - delicious ice-cream is made across the street from here). Another guesthouse, the *V.S.** (6/14 Soi Suphakon, Lan Luang Road) is further east. North of Khaosan Road *BANGLAMPHU** and *TV** (7 Samsen Road, tel 2827451).

On Phra Athit Road, opposite the UNICEF building: *PEACHY**, *BEER**, and *NEW HAWAII**. Mama manages *APPLE 1** (10 Phra Athit Road, tel 2810128), her daughter runs the rather noisy *APPLE 2** (tel. 2816838). In a small alley in between Apple and Khaosan Road you will find the *ROOFGARDEN**, *NGAMPIT**, and *CHUSRI** (100 metres behind the temple).

It is a little more quiet further north, in **TEVES.** The *BANGKOK YOUTH HOSTEL*** (with IYHF-card**, dormitory*) can be found at 25/2 Phitsanulok Rd., tel 2820950 (large, clean rooms with showers and wc). In a quiet side-street near the National Library, 71 Samsen Road, Tarat Tawarach Soi 3, you will find the *SAWATDEE GUESTHOUSE** (tel 2825349, family atmosphere, small garden, communal showers and lavatories). Right next door the *SHANTI LODGE**, run by the brother and quite similar (restaurant serving traveller-food). Also *YOON'S***, 241 Ratchavithi Road, near Chitralada Palace (tel 2432420, clean and pleasant but rather noisy).

If you are looking for a little more comfort in Banglampoo, try looking up one of the following hotels: *PHATHANA***, 233 Samsen Road, tel 2811455. Behind the Mercedes show-room in Ratchdamnoen Road

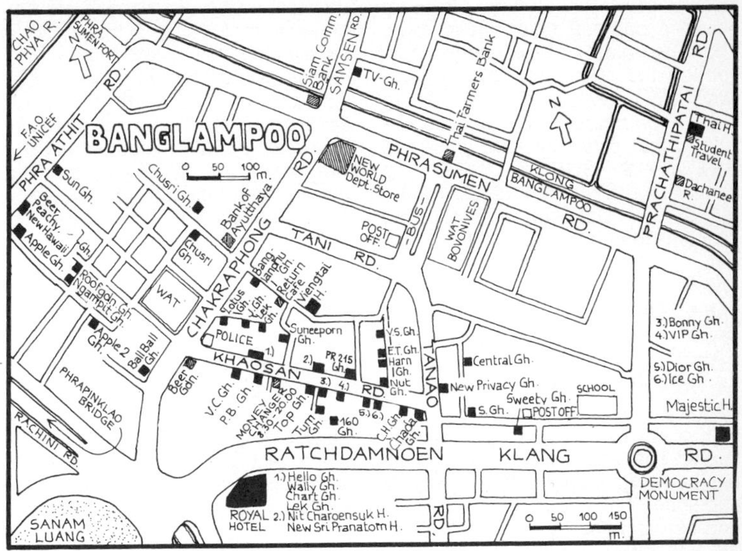

you will find the *RATCHDAMNOEN 90***, tel 2241843 (mainly Thai guests, good, clean rooms). The *ROYAL HOTEL***** is one of the more expensive hotels in the area, tel 2229111, at the corner of Sanam Luang (student discount). You will receive a discount when booking via a travel agency for the *VIENGTAI HOTEL*****, Tani Road, tel 2828672. The *MAJESTIC HOTEL***** can be found in 97 Ratchdamnoen Road, tel 2815000.

You can always try getting a better rate by bargaining, even in the more expensive hotels. There are several hotels in the centre of the tourist area in **SUKHUMVIT ROAD.** The *ATLANTA****, Sukhumvit Road Soi 2, tel 2526068, is reasonable (many travellers, simple restaurant, large rooms with private bathrooms, swimming-pool). Or try the *GOLDEN PALACE HOTEL**** in Soi 1 (swimming-pool). On Sukhumvit Road itself you will find the *REX HOTEL*****, no. 762, tel 3910100. In the side roads you'll come across the *CROWN HOTEL****, Soi 29, tel 3910511, *STARLIGHT**, Soi 22, tel 3913644 (said to be very sleazy), *FORTUNA*****, Soi 5, tel 2515121 (bargaining possible). The *HOLIDAY***, Soi 6, is new. Many Arabs stay at the rather run down *MIAMI****, Soi 13, tel 2525140 (private bathrooms, partially air-conditioned, pool). The *OPERA**** is pretty comfortable, Phetchburi Road, Soi Somprasong behind the First Hotel, tel 2524032.

There are more traveller hotels in the **EMBASSY AREA,** near Rama IV Road. The *MALAYSIA***-*****, 54 Soi

Ngamduplee, tel 2863582, has acquired a bad reputation these days. There are plenty of bad stories concerning the place, but is nearly always fully booked all the same. There is a notice board in the reception. A little further down the road you'll find *FREDDY'S GUESTHOUSE***, tel 2866722, and the new *LEE GUESTHOUSE***. Opposite the Malaysia (Soi Sri Bamphen), try the *BOSTON INN*** (up to four people can share one of the large double rooms, pool), or the *PRIVACY**** (Mahamek).

FOOD

As far as eating is concerned, Bangkok is a truly cosmopolitan town. In the old part of town you will be served Thai and Chinese food almost exclusively, though. You can get exquisite **THAI FOOD** at the posh and very expensive *BUSSARACUM,* 35 Soi Phiphat off Convent Road (Silom Road), the *D'JIT POCHANA ORIENTAL,* directly opposite the Oriental Hotel in Thonburi (regular boat service from the Oriental and Royal Orchid Hotels, free of charge), the *KAOLANG,* a floating restaurant on Menam Chao Phya at the very end of Ayutthaya Road, and the *KANABNAM* in Thonburi. From here, restaurant-boats leave their landing-places at 20:00 h daily. If you are prepared to pay a higher price for a good meal in a beautiful setting, try the *D'JIT POCHANA,* 60 Soi 20 Sukhumvit Road. Among the hundreds of Thai restaurants there are a few that offer entertainment in the form of music and classical dances. These are usually pretty touristy and expensive, though (over 200 Baht!). Try the *BAAN THAI,* Soi 32. One of the few exceptions: *RUEN THEP,* Silom Village in Silom Road, 30-60 Baht for a meal, good choice, large helpings. Classical music and dances are performed free of charge in the garden in the evenings. Thai and international food is served by waiters on roller skates in the *TUMPNAKTHAI,* 131 Ratchadaphisek Road, tel 2778833, the largest garden restaurant in town, with room for 3000 guests, Thai dancing, and fast service. If you wish to have a table near the stage, call and reserve in advance! A meal with several courses will cost you between 100 and 150 Baht and is quite an experience.

While a meal in any of the above mentioned restaurants will cost you at least 60 Baht, there is always the possibility of eating cheap at the many **FOODSTALLS**. A rice or noodle dish, often of surprising quality, will cost you 10-20 Baht. Cheap meals and snacks (e.g. grilled corn on the cob for 3 Baht) are available just about everywhere in the old part of town, as well as at all markets and in the markethalls, e.g. *BAMRUNG MUANG ROAD* on the north side of the road, west of the bridge. No one here speaks English, so do not be too timid to take a peek into the various pots. If you are, why not ask for the delicious-looking meal someone at the next table is eating. Fresh sweet cakes and spicy snacks are available all over the city's streets, e.g. in the streets north of Khaosan Road.

The *YONG LEE* on Sukhumvit/corner of Soi 15 is very popular. Good Tom Yam with giant shrimps and mushrooms is served. You will find a large Thai chicken restaurant near the Malaysia Hotel, on the corner of Rama IV and Soi Ngam Duphli. They have an English menu - try the special, *Chicken in a basket.*

Most restaurants in Khaosan Road serve **TRAVELLER-TYPE FOOD** and are pretty cheap. The Thai meals served are usually rather flavourless, though. The *VIP* and *HELLO RESTAURANT* are popular - saté is served. Good food is also served at the *CHUANPIS*. You can also eat well in the various department stores, especially if you have a craving for European food. The *NEW WORLD DEPARTMENT STORE* in Banglampoo has a food centre on the eighth floor. Here you can enjoy cheap Asian and European meals, as well as a fantastic view of the city.

You will find many **INDIAN RESTAURANTS** in the area around the GPO. Good curries are served at the *MOTI MAHAL*, 18-20 Old Chartered Bank Lane, opposite the Oriental Plaza. The late Lord Mountbatten's former cook is responsible for the best Indian food in town at the *HIMALA CHA CHA*, 1229 / 11 Charoen Krung Road (between Surawong and Silom Road). Equally high prices are charged at the *OMAR KHAYAM* and the *AKBAR*, Soi 3 Sukhumvit Road. Real Indian food is served at the *ROYAL INDIA*, 392/1 Chakraphet Road (restaurant in the back part of the house).

Friends of **JAPANESE COOKERY** will love Bangkok. Fresh ingredients from the nearby sea make sashimis and tempuras particularly tasty, and the prices are reasonable. The excellent *AKAMON* serves delicious food in a distinguished Japanese setting, 233 Sukhumvit Road Soi 21 (Asoke) towards New Phetchburi Road. Good Japanese food is also served at the *AMBASSADOR HOTEL*, 171 Sukhumvit Road, in between Soi 11 and 13. Try the excellent buffet for 90 Baht (+ tax and service) at lunchtime. There is also a food centre with many stalls beyond the large restaurant in the ground floor.

Something for hungry people: Many of the big hotels offer all-you-can-eat buffet lunches for 80-100 Baht. European, Chinese, and Japanese specialities are frequently served, too.

SHOPPING

If you plan to go shopping in Bangkok, get a copy of Nancy Chandler's *Market Map* (50 Baht) and the monthly *Official Shopping Guide*, which can be obtained free from the Tourist Office (TAT).

ALWAYS BARGAIN! Take your time. Try to learn the Thai numbers by heart and never pay more than a piece is worth, no matter how much you want it. Remember - the average inhabitant of Bangkok lives on 2000 Baht a month.

Do not buy ***BUDDHA STATUES!*** Ever since Thais travelling abroad discovered that Europeans use the holy figures as - amongst other things - lamp-stands, it has been forbidden to take them out of the country. Exceptions are only made if you are able to prove convincingly that you are a Buddhist yourself.

Not only merchandise is cheap in Thailand; ***SERVICES*** are, too. Have your own travelling-bag crafted by local artisans, have your personal shirts or dresses sewn by tailors (who will even copy European models from catalogue pictures), or have a set of letter-paper printed at one of the small printing shops. When in Chinatown or Banglampoo, keep an eye open for workshops. The tailors in Sukhumvit are more expensive, but they speak fluent English for the most part.

There seems to be an inexhaustible supply of ***ANTIQUES*** in Thailand. Many of them are fakes. A whole section of the working population lives off their production. If you want to take real antiques out of the country you will need the permission of the *Fine Arts Department* in Na Phrathat Road. This takes about three weeks.

Bangkok is the place to buy ***GEMS.*** Sapphires and rubies can be bought almost everywhere. Small stones with little flaws are sold for only a couple of Baht. If you do decide to buy, always insist on a certificate of authenticity and a receipt - you wouldn't believe how many foreigners have been swindled. Always remember that all gems can be produced synthetically. You can watch the gems being cut for free on the 5th floor of the Japan Airlines Building, Patpong 1, at *Associated Lapidaries Co. Ltd.* Ban Mo is considered the centre of the gem-business, Pahurat Road, north of Memorial Bridge.

SILK is available in different colours and degrees of purity all over town. You can buy pillows, ties, dresses etc. or simply silk by the yard (= 90 cm). The width is usually 1.20 m. Average quality costs between 100 and 200 Baht. Jim Thompson House quality costs more, of course (see *Jim Thompson House).*

HILLTRIBE ARTS & CRAFTS should be bought in northern Thailand, where the choice is bigger. If you are interested in objects from different regions, take a look around the *State Handicraft Centre* (Narayanaphand) on Lan Luang Road, near the R.S.Hotel, west of the klong - no bargaining! Silverware and niello work, dolls and masks, wood-carvings, rice paper, temple-rubbings, bronze objects, fans, sun umbrellas and much more is available cheap all over Bangkok.

Longing for wine, bread and cheese? ***WESTERN FOOD*** can be bought in *Foodland* (the Ploenchit and Patpong Road branches have a particularly central location) and in department stores.

Good ***DEPARTMENT STORES:*** *SOGO,* Amarin Plaza, near the Erawan Hotel in Ploenchit Road, *NEW WORLD* in Banglampoo, which has its own amusement-centre and a little zoo, Phrasumen Road/Chakraphong Road, and the *CENTRAL DEPARTMENT STORE,* Silom Road, near New Road, with an additional branch on Rama I Road.

FILMS were hardly more expensive than in Europe in 1987. One is officially only allowed to import five rolls, though this is rarely checked. There is a Kodak branch on Sap Road. They do a good job developing Ektachrome, but not, however, Kodachrome films. You will have to pay roughly 130 Baht for 36 prints (10x15 cm) at one of the many Photo-Service shops. This usually includes a voucher for an A4 enlargement.

BOOKS and ***MAPS*** can be bought at the Asia Bookshop, Sukhumvit Road near Soi 15 (the most extensive stock of books in Bangkok), as well as in the large bookshop on Patpong Road. Further bookshops: Chalermnit Bookshop, Erawan Arcade, Ploenchit Road; DD Books, Soi Asoke; Book Chest, Soi 2, Siam Square (small but with a large supply of good maps).

DESIGNER WARE replicas such as Lacoste shirts and socks, Rolex, Cartier, Gucci, Ebel, and Omega watches, as well as Jourdan leather accessories are among the most popular souvenirs tourists take back home. Before buying a watch, have it opened and make sure that the drive mechanism is made exclusively of high-grade steel. Should you find any blue or red plastic parts, do not buy it. Generally, the imitations are of a reasonably high quality and very cheap. Polo-shirts 40-50 Baht (try Patpong, or near the Indra Hotel, especially between 19:00 and 23:00 h). Textiles, shoes, tapes etc. are extremely cheap. Try Tanao Road (Khaosan Road).

You may find that the ***PRICE*** of identical objects varies from shop to shop. This is particularly the case with clothing. The shopping-arcades of the large hotels are most expensive; after these you get the air-conditioned shops on the main business roads, the shopping malls, and the department stores. Your best bet is to shop at the markets, where you can always bargain.

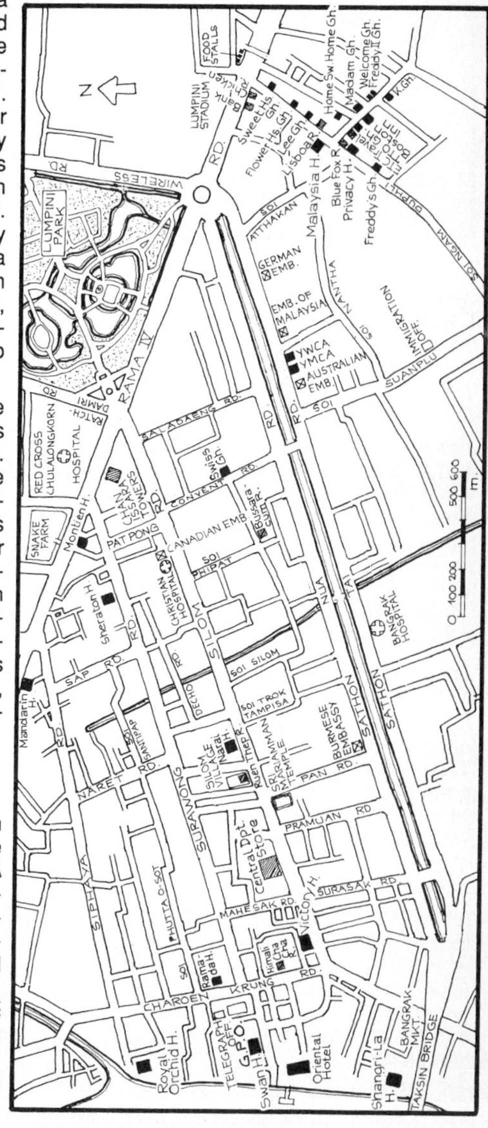

MARKETS

Weekend Market (Chuan Chatuchak, opposite the Northern Bus Terminal) A very big and colourful market is held here on Saturdays and Sundays 7:00-18:00 h. Clothes, household goods, food, live animals, tapes, souvenirs, electric appliances, and plants are among the things offered. Only plants are sold during the rest of the week.

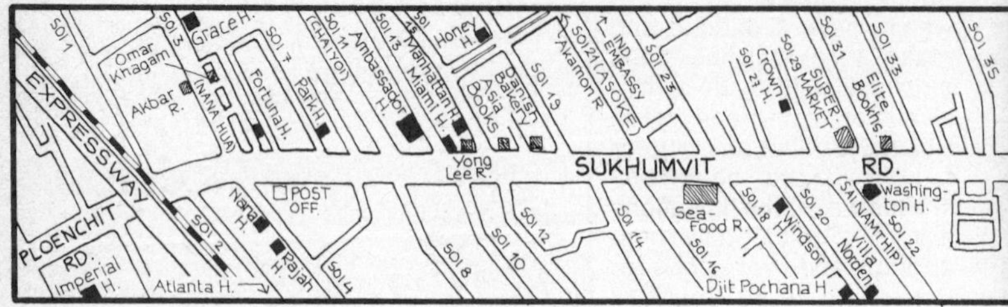

Bangrak Market (south of the GPO, near the river) Exotic fruits (early mornings are best), clothing, and flowers for the house-temples are sold here daily.

Teves (north end of Luk Luang Road) Daily flower market selling flowers, plants, orchids, and palm-trees in all shapes, colours, and sizes. On the other side of the klong you'll see a large vegetable and fruit market reaching all the way down Samsen Road. Clothing and food-stalls on the other side of the road.

GENERAL INFORMATION

TOURIST INFORMATION - the tourist office on Ratchdamnoen Road (TAT) is open from 8:30-16:00 h. This is the place to get your city map (35 Baht), informative literature (*Official Shopping Guide, Bangkok This Week, Pattaya,* and *Where),* as well as hectographed leaflets.

TOURIST POLICE - an English-speaking branch of the police has been opened at 509 Vorachak Road, behind the Golden Mount, because of the many 'tourist' problems (mainly robbery). Open daily 8:00-24:00 h, tel 2216206-9.

IMMIGRATION - go to Soi Suanphlu, Sathon Tai Road, tel 2869176 or 2869230. Officially, you can only have your 60-day visa extended (2x2 weeks, 300 Baht each). 14-day visas are sometimes extended for another 7 days, too (300 Baht). Dress well and look your best!

POST OFFICE - the GPO is on New Road, open Mo-Fri 8:00-20:00 h, till 13:00 h at the weekend. Picking up a letter at the poste restante counter will cost you 1 Baht. Telegrams can be picked up in the next room. An airmail letter to Europe costs 15 Baht, an aerogramme 8.50 Baht, and a post-card 8 Baht. Parcels cost approximately 470 Baht for 10 kg and take 8-16 weeks by seamail. Parcels can usually weigh up to 20 kg, sometimes only 10 kg - find out beforehand, the maximum weight can vary from country to country. 1 kg sent by airmail will cost you 250 Baht, 3 kilos 550 Baht. The packing service is open 8:30-16:30 h Mo-Fri, 8:30-12:00 h on Saturdays. You can get a big parcel, complete with plastic string and styrofoam pads, for 40-50 Baht .

TELEPHONES - reaching foreign countries is no problem from the Telecommunication Centre, which is on the right, behind the GPO. It is open around the clock. You can also try calling from any of the large hotels. Collect calls are only possible to

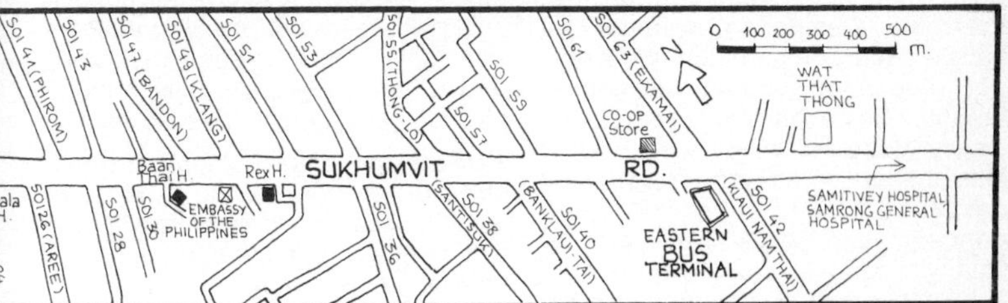

France, Italy, Spain, GB, and a couple of countries outside of Europe. A three minute call to the UK will cost you 240 Baht, a person-to-person call 320 Baht, 80 Baht for each additional minute.

BANKS - large branches of the *THAI FARMERS BANK* will change up to three Eurocheques per person in one month without asking questions. Central branch: 142 Silom Road. The *EUROPEAN ASIAN BANK,* 28 Surasak Road, tel 2338660 accepts international traveller's-cheques. The *BANGKOK BANK* is best suited for having international money orders transferred to. A transfer will take approx. 1 week. You will also receive a good exchange rate here, as at the airport and at the *THAI MILITARY BANK.* All banks are open Mon-Fri from 8:30-15:30 h, those that have branches in the tourist-centres are sometimes open 24 hours.

AMERICAN EXPRESS - S.E.A. Tours in the Siam Centre, Rama I Rd. represent the company in Bangkok. Because stolen cheques are allegedly often used for black-market dealings, you may find that your cheques will not be replaced until you are back home. Do not have letters sent to you poste restante at the office, as many letters have been lost and the employees are rather unfriendly. Should you buy traveller's cheques with your AMEX card here, be sure to count them upon receipt. You will also be able to get traveller's cheques at the Bangkok Bank with an AMEX card.

MEDICAL AID - the biggest hospitals in town are the *BANGKOK CHRISTIAN HOSPITAL,* 124 Silom Road, tel 2336981, the *RED CROSS HOSPITAL,* Rama IV Road, tel 2526930, and the *ADVENTIST HOSPITAL,* 430 Phitsanulok Road, tel 2811422. The *SAMRONG GENERAL HOSPITAL,* Sukhumvit Road Soi 78, tel 3932131-5, 3931050-4, is a good private clinic. Consultation hours are 8:00-16:30 h, Mon-Fri. The 45 bus stops right in front of the door. *Sex tourism* has left its mark, even in the medical field. The Grace Hotel, for instance, has its own VD clinic. You will receive better and cheaper treatment at the *BANGRAK HOSPITAL,* Sathon Tai Road, tel 2860431. This hospital specializes in the treatment of VD and works in cooperation with the WHO. Hundreds of patients are treated daily according to the newest medical methods. The atmosphere is correspondingly unpleasant.

NIGHTCLUBS - Bangkok's nightlife is notorious. It offers hundreds of ways of spending money. In spite of the male domination, women can have a good time here, too. We would not recommend going out alone, though. The expensive hotels have classy clubs featuring live music or discotheques, Patpong offers shady dance bars with or without gogo dancers, and there are loads of sleazy Thai nightclubs where men can choose one of the many girls sitting behind a large sheet of glass. There is something for everyone here -massage parlours, transvestite bars..

GETTING AROUND IN BANGKOK

Everybody knows that rush hour in Bangkok is hell on wheels. Avoid being caught in the traffic between 7:00 and 9:00 h, 16:00 and 17:30 h.

TAXIS - approximately 90% of the country's vehicles are registered in Bangkok; these include over 1 million cars. A great number of these are taxis, scores of which can be seen fighting their way through the chaotic traffic at any time of day. The fare always has to be agreed on before you actually set off. Some drivers will try to get an exceptionally high price from you, especially those at the airport or standing in front of the large hotels. Don't get taken for a ride! Send them away, there are plenty of empty cabs around. Always remember that most taxi-drivers have to pay for gas or petrol themselves, as well as the rent for the car (200 Baht daily). Here are some fair prices: short distances 30 Baht (sam sip), medium-length distances outside of rush hour 40 Baht (sih sip), longer distances 50 Baht (hah sip). Taxis with green registration-stickers are more expensive. These can usually be found standing outside of the big hotels. All new cars have air conditioning, but there are plenty of old cars - veritable rubbish-heaps - that don't. And if they have black plastic seats and you get caught in the rush hour....

BUSES - the cheapest form of transportation, though not the least problematic. Beware - pickpockets favour the routes predominantly used by tourists (especially city-airport buses). They have developed a special talent for slicing handbags and back pockets from behind. Ever since buses have been granted their own lane, rush hour has become much less of an ordeal, particularly because buses are allowed to drive in both directions on one-way streets. As the final destinations of the buses are only provided in Thai letters, you'll have to go by the numbers. Be careful not to get into the wrong buses or go in the wrong direction. This can easily happen; ac-buses (with a red sign) and non ac-buses (with a blue sign) have the same numbers but got to completely different destinations. The ac-buses are very comfortable.

A map of Bangkok with all bus routes *(The Latest Tour Guide to Bangkok and Thailand* - 35 Baht) can be bought at the Tourist Office in the airport, the Tourist Office in town, and at most hotels and bookshops. It is a reliable map that will help you get almost anywhere. Tickets for the non ac-buses cost 2 Baht. A ride in one of the ac-buses will cost you 5-15 Baht, depending on the distance.

TUK-TUKS - are small, converted scooters (Vespa), also known as Samlors. They are usually a little cheaper than taxis. If you have luggage or are more than two, you might find them a little tight. The drivers rarely go long distances (to the airport, for instance), and we suggest you don't ask them, as you always end up inhaling the exhaust fumes of every car in the radius of a hundred metres. Always make sure that the driver has understood where you want to go - most of them do not speak English.

BOATS

Ferries - You can cross the Menam Chao Phya from various landing-places for a fee of 0.5 Baht. The ferries are relatively tall and have a roof. Most passengers stand.

Klong Boats - these are long, narrow boats with an outboard motor. They can often be rented for about 100 Baht an hour. You will find their landing-places behind Wat Pho, near the Thammasat University, and at the Oriental Hotel (many tourists). Boats for rides down Saen Sae Klong can be rented at the Pratunam Market, boats for rides down the Phra Kanong Klong at the Rung-A-Roon Market behind Soi 71. Boats leave for Klong Mon every half hour from Tha Tien Pier behind Wat Pho between 6:30 and 18:00 h. The price is 4 Baht. Boats going up the Klong Bang Waek leave Samphan Phut Pier (Memorial Bridge every fifteen minutes, 4 Baht, from 6:00 to 17:00 h. Klong boats down the Klong Bang Khoo Wiang and the Klong Bang Yai leave from the Tha Chang Pier. The boats leaving Wat Dao Khanong (Krung Thep) go down the Klong Dao Khanong.

Express Boats - these travel regularly between Nonthaburi (North) and Krung Thep Bridge (South) 6:00-18:00 h daily. They leave every ten minutes 7:00-8:00 h, every quarter of an hour 6:00-7:00 h, 8:00-9:00 h, and 15:00-18:00 h, every 1/2 hour between 9:00 and 15:00 h. These long boats with their many seats are a pleasant, open-air alternative to the hot, crowded buses. Prices: 3 - 7 Baht.

LEAVING BANGKOK

BY AIR

Don Muang Airport lies 28 km south of town. The new National Airport is just 500 m away from the International Airport. A minibus commutes between the two regularly (20-40 Baht). Banks offering reasonable rates of exchange can be found in both airports, e.g. the Thai Military Bank (open 6:30-24:00 h, sometimes around the clock). There is also a post office (in both departure halls, open 24 hrs. daily), a left luggage office (in both, open 6:00-22:00 h, 20 Baht per day and per item of luggage), a hotel booking agency (international arrivals; for cheap as well as expensive hotels), a tourist office (international arrivals), and the Airport Transport Service. You have the following ways of getting into town:

A ***minibus service*** will take you to any major hotel for a fee of 100 Baht.

The ***shuttle service,*** which leaves for the Asia Hotel (Phya Thai Road near Petchburi Road) every 30 minutes, costs 60 Baht.

In front of the airport you'll see ***ac-taxis*** as well as private cars who will offer a ride into town for 300 Baht. The taxis just around the corner, on the main road, will only cost you 150 Baht if you bargain well. A ride to the airport from town will usually only cost you about 120 Baht.

The cheapest (and slowest) alternative are the ***local buses.*** Careful, though; pickpockets love these lines. A ride into town from the bus stop, 50 metres from the arrival hall, costs 2 Baht and takes approx. 1 1/2 hours.

Buses stop running at around 22:30 h. Bus 59 goes to Khaosan Road, bus 29 goes to the railway station via the Northern Bus Terminal. If you want to get to Rama IV Road (Malaysia Hotel etc.) stay on the bus until you reach Rama IV Road, then change to bus 4, 46, or 47. Ac-bus 10 will take you to Samsen Road for 15 Baht until 20:00 h. If you want to get to Silom Road take ac-bus 4, which runs until 19:00 h. If You want to get to Sukhumvit Road or the Eastern Bus Terminal, your best bet is taking ac-bus 13, which runs until 20:00 h. (see also *Getting around in Bangkok).*

A ***train*** will take you into town from the suburban station opposite the airport. We would only recommend doing this between 6:30 and 9:00 or 16:30 and 18:00 h, as it is only then that trains leave every 20 minutes.

Airport tax is 150 Baht for international flights, 40 Baht for domestic flights.

Examples of prices (in US$) offered for one-way flights to neighbouring countries at cheap travel bureaus:

CALCUTTA 141, COLOMBO 173, DHAKA 141, DELHI 197, DENPASAR 270, HONG KONG 135, JAKARTA 190, KATHMANDU 175, MANILA 160, RANGOON 101, SINGAPORE 119.

You will hardly ever have to pay the much higher IATA rates if you go to the right places. The following travel agencies offer flights at prices considerably below those of the IATA. This doesn't mean that you will always be able to get a cheap flight from Bangkok; flights to Burma, for instance, cost 4000 Baht return with Thai and 3600 Baht with UBA these days. A flight from Calcutta to Rangoon costs US$132.

Compare the prices of the following ***agencies:***

STA TRAVEL, Thai Hotel, 78 Prachathipatai Road, tel 2815314-5.
TRAD TOURS, Viengtai Hotel, 42 Tani Road, tel 2815788.
TTS TRAVEL SERVICE 2/9 Sri Bamphen Road, off Rama IV, tel 2826095.

These three travel bureaus sell tickets at reduced rates to students with a valid ISIC identification card.

TRU TRAVEL, Dusit Thani Bldg., Silom Road, in between the Indian temple and Pramuan Road, tel 2353813-7.
TAA TRAVEL, 84 Sukhumvit Road, opposite Fiat, tel 2518843.
K TRAVEL, 6 Sukhumvit Road, next to the railway station, tel 2523337.
TTS TRAVEL, Soi Nana Tai, Sukhumvit Road, near Rajah Hotel.
ETC, 2/12 Sri Bamphen Road, 100 metres from the Malaysia Hotel, tel 2871477 and 203 Khaosan Road, tel 2822958.

These travel agencies also sell tickets to Europe at reduced rates. You can get a plane to Athens, Amsterdam, Rome, Paris, or London via Dhaka with BANGLADESH BIMAN for US$ 400. AEROFLOT flights to Copenhagen and London cost a little more.

THAI AIRWAYS offers the following inland-flights: CHIANG MAI 1275 or 1020 (nightflight), CHIANG RAI 1575, HAT YAI 1760 or 1410 (nightflight), MAE HONG SON 1585, PHITSANULOK 730 PHRAE 860.-, NAN 900.-, SURAT THANI 1380, PHUKET 1545 or 1240 (nightflight), UBON 1080, UDON 1010 Baht.

Flights can be reserved weeks in advance in the Thai Airways office (by telephone if you like) and can be paid for later in any travel agency. If you have booked a flight with any airline be sure to check up on your reservation, as some agencies sell confirmed tickets for flights that are already fully booked.

ADDRESSES OF IMPORTANT AIRLINES

AEROFLOT, 7 Silom Road, tel 2336965-7
AIR INDIA, Amarin Tower, 500 Ploenchit Road, tel 2569614
AIR LANKA, 1 Patpong Road, tel 2369293
ALIA, 56 Silom Road, tel 2360030-9
BANGKOK AIRWAYS, Don Muang, National Airport, tel 5237116
BANGLADESH BIMAN, 56 Surawong Road, tel 2336178
BURMA AIRWAYS, 208/1 Surawong Road, tel 2349692
CAAC, 134/1-2 Silom Road, tel 2351880-2
CATHAY PACIFIC, 109 Surawong Road, tel 2331331
CHINA AIRLINES, Siam Centre, 965 Rama I Road, tel 2519656-9
EGYPT AIR, 120 Silom Road, tel 2337601-3
GARUDA, 944/19 Rama IV. Road, tel 2330981-2
KOREAN AIRLINES, 946 Rama IV. Rd., Dusit Thani Bldg., tel 2349283
LOT, 485 Silom Road, tel 2352223-7
LUFTHANSA, 331/1-3 Silom Road, tel 2341350
MALAYSIAN AIRLINE SYSTEM, 98-102 Surawong Road, tel 2349795
PAKISTAN INTERNATIONAL, 52 Surawong Road, tel 2342961-5
PHILIPPINE AIRLINES, 56 Surawong Road, tel 2332350-2
QANTAS AIRWAYS, Charn Issara Bldg., 942/51 Rama IV Road, tel 2360102
ROYAL NEPAL AIRLINES, 1/4 Convent Road, tel 2333921-4
SIA (Singapore Airlines), Silom Centre, 1 Silom Road corner of Rama IV. Road, tel 2360303
THAI AIRWAYS, 6 Larn Luang Road, tel 2800090
THAI INTERNATIONAL, 89 Vibhavadi Rangsit Road, tel 5130121,

BY BUS

Bangkok has three main bus stations. With the exception of a few ac-buses most buses leave town from one of these stations.

To the east coast: **Eastern Bus Terminal**, Sukhumvit Road, opposite Soi Ekamai, tel 3913301. You can reach the terminal by taking bus 38 from the airport (via Northern Bus Terminal), ac-bus 13 via Sukhumvit Road, or bus 40 from the Southern Bus Terminal via the train station. From the Eastern Bus Terminal you can catch buses to:

BAN PHE (Ko Samet) (70, return 120), ac-buses need approx. 3 hrs., CHANTHABURI (309 km) 56 (105), CHONBURI (80 km) 18 (35), PATTAYA (138 km) 29 (50), RAYONG (236 km) 38 (69), TRAT (387 km) 70 (128) Baht. The figures given in parenthesis are for ac-buses.

To the north and northeast: **Northern Bus Terminal,** Phaholyothin Road (road leading to the airport), tel 2794484. This terminal can be reached by taking bus 29 from the railway station, ac-bus 10 from the Southern Bus Terminal, ac-bus 13 from Sukhumvit Road. All three of these buses also run from and to the airport. From the Northern Bus Terminal you can catch buses to:

AYUTTHAYA (75 km)17, BANG PA IN (63 km) 13, CHIANG MAI (713 km; ac-buses need approx. 9 hrs.) 133 (242), CHIANG RAI (844 km) 157 (283), KORAT (Nakhon Rachasima, 256 km)

51 (92), LAMPANG (610 km) 115 (207), LAMPHUN (689 km) 131 (227), LOPBURI (153 km) 32 (60), LOEI (560 km) 106 (191), NAKHON PANOM (727 km) 136 (245), NONG KHAI (614 km) 115 (209), PHITSANULOK (498 km) 78 (171), SUKHOTHAI (544 km) 84 (153), SURIN (452 km) 86 (155), TAK (524 km) 80 (146), UBON (675 km) 126 (229), UDON (561 km) 106 (191) Baht. The figures given in parenthesis are for ac-buses.

To the south and west: **Southern Bus Terminal,** Charan Sanit Wong Road, Thonburi, tel 4113270. This terminal can be reached by taking bus 28 from the Northern Bus Terminal, bus 40 from the Eastern Bus Terminal via the train station, and ac-bus 10 from the airport. From the Southern Bus Terminal you can catch buses to:

CHUMPHON (499 km) 95 (160), DAMNOEN SADUAK (109 km) 35, HAT YAI (1022 km) 187 (339), HUA HIN (220 km) 47 (74), KANCHANABURI (129 km) 23 (53), KRABI (867 km) 161 (290), NAKHON PATHOM (56 km) 13 (24), NAKHON SI THAMMARAT (814 km) 150 (270), PHETCHBURI (150 km) 35 (54), PRACHUAP KHIRI KHAN (323 km) 63 (105), PHUKET (922 km) 165 (299), RANONG (614 km) 110 (198), SAMUT SONGKHRAM (78 km) 18 (33), SURAT THANI - ferry harbour to Ko Samui (668 km, 10-12 hrs. with ac / non ac-buses) 125 (225) TRANG (1133 km) 174 (314) Baht. The figures in parenthesis are for ac-buses.

Although they are almost twice as expensive as regular buses, we would nevertheless recommend taking ac-buses for long journeys, e.g. to Chiang Mai (9 hours), Surat Thani (10 hours), or Phuket (14 hours). In spite of the rather unnerving videos which are shown for the entire length of the ride, we consider them much more comfortable. Food and drink (though nothing exciting) is included in the price, and sometimes you will even be picked up from your hotel. Night-buses are cheaper. It is worth paying the extra fare just for the view, though. The drivers are often a bit over-eager, and racing against the buses of competing companies is frequently one of their favourite pastimes. Thieves are often along for the ride, too, so take care! Also do not forget to bring warm clothing; an air-conditioner turned on full blast all night long can get quite chilly. The non ac-buses get cold at nights, too.

The ac-buses either leave from their company offices or from the bus terminals.

Ac-buses to **Chiang Mai** (250-300 Baht):

Indra Tour, Ratchaprarop Road, tel 2516197; Transportation Co., Phanom Yothin Road, tel 2794484-7; Piman Tour, 60 Ratchprasong Road, tel 2516428; Grand Tour, 566 Ploenchit Road, tel 2520335-7.

Ac-buses to **Phuket** (250-300 Baht):

Transportation Co., (see above), departure Southern Bus Terminal; Grand Tour (see above); Prince Travel Service, 295 Bangkok Bazaar Road, tel 2516298; Thai Transport Co., Ratchdamnoen Klang Road, tel 2228147; Phuket Travel Service, 77 / 7 Visutkasat Road, tel 2829837.

Ac-buses to **Ko Samui** (225 Baht):

Thai Transport Co., (see above), Sophon Tour, Majestic Hotel Ratchdamnoen Klang Road, tel 2816172, Pak Thai Tour, Phra Sumane Road, tel 2812283, and Udomrat Tour,

Ratchdamnoen Klang Road, tel 2212617.

BY RAIL

Trains leave Bangkok in five directions - to the north, the northeast, east, south, and northwest. Generally, trains are slower and more expensive than buses. They are much more comfortable, though. You can sleep wonderfully in the second class. Air conditioned trains tend to get a bit chilly at nights. Tourists have been drugged and robbed - not frequently, but a couple of times - so be wary of strangers offering food.

We would suggest buying the tickets yourself up to 90 days in advance at the Advance Booking Office in the Main Railway Station, open Mon-Fri 8:30-18:00 h, Sat and Sun till 12:00 h noon. Reservations from abroad by bank draft are also possible. If you're planning to take the train to Butterworth, definitely book in advance (seats can only be reserved up to the Malaysian border). There is an information office at the railway station, tel 2237010 + 2237020. This is the place to get the newest schedule (if it's available).

Examples for prices in the 2nd class - figures in parenthesis for 3rd class - without extra charges (for detailed information concerning additional charges see *GETTING AROUND* in General Information):

Northbound

Departures: Den Chai (near Phrae) - 6:40, 7:05, 22:00 h; Phitsanulok - 8:30 and 20:00 h; Chiang Mai - 15:45, 18:00, and 19:40 h; trains to Phitsanulok need only 5 hrs. if you take one of the Railcar Specials, 11:05, 17:05, 23:05 h. AYUTTHAYA 31 (15), LOPBURI 57 (28), PHITSANULOK 143 (69), LAMPANG 221 (106), LAMPHUN 247 (118) CHIANG MAI 255 (121) Baht.

Northeastbound

Departures: 6:50, 7:15, 15:25, 18:45, 21:00, and 23:20 h to Ubon. 6:30, 19:00, and 20:30 h to Nong Khai. 9:05 h to Korat. Daily Railcar Specials to Khon Khaen at 8:20 and 22:30 h taking 7 hrs. and to Surin at 10:55 and 21:50 h, taking 6-7 hrs.

Eastbound

Departures: Aranyapraphet - 6:00 and 13:10 h; Chachoengsao - 7:00 h; Prachinburi - 9:40 and 17:25 h; Krabin Buri - 8:05, 11:25, and 14:55 h.

CHACHOENGSAO (13), ARANYAPRATHET (48), KRABIN BURI (33) Baht.

Northwestbound

Departures: Kanchanaburi / River Kwae - 8:00 and 13:55 h, from the Thonburi station. The Thai railway offers a special day-return ticket to this area at the weekends and on holidays (75 Baht). The train leaves from the main station at 6:35 h (!), stops at Nakhon Pathom (45 minutes), and at the bridge, which can be crossed on foot. The train stops at the final station, Nam Tok, for 2 1/2 hours. There is a further stop at Kanchanaburi on the ride back. Arrival in Bangkok 19:35 h.

NAKHON PATHOM (14), KANCHANABURI (28), NAM TOK (49) Baht.

Southbound

Departures: Hua Hin - 9:00 h; Sungai Golok (Malaysian border) - 12:30 and 14:00 h; Butterworth / Penang (Malaysia) - 15:15 h; Hat Yai - 16:00 h; Nakhon Si Thammarat - 17:30 h; Trang - 18:30 h.

RATCHBURI 54 (25), PHETCHBURI 73 (34), HUA HIN 94 (45), PRACHUAP KHIRI KHAN 125 (59), CHUMPHON 177 (83), SURAT THANI 229 (109), NAKHON SI THAMMARAT 285 (136), HAT YAI 319 (152), SUNGAI GOLOK (border) 385 (184), BUTTERWORTH 448, KUALA LUMPUR 689, SINGAPORE 952 Baht. You will need approximately 2 days for the 1927 km journey from Bangkok to Singapore.

Combined train-bus-ferry tickets to Ko Samui cost 229 Baht (2nd Class) or 180 Baht (3rd Class), departure 18:30 h, arrival in Ko Samui the next morning at 10:30 h. Beds cost an additional 70 or 100 Baht, ac 80 Baht.

DAY TRIPS AROUND BANGKOK

DAMNOEN SADUAK

This small town is best known for its floating markets, especially since the markets in Thonburi have become so commercial. We would recommend disembarking before the boat actually starts going through the market; the bridges and riverbanks are the best places from which to watch the tumultuous activity. This way one does not disturb those at work. Unfortunately, large and loud groups of tourists in motor-boats are becoming more and more common these days. Market women have to watch out for the waves caused by these boats, lest their wares get wet. On top of everything else the tourists are only - if at all - interested in buying gaudy souvenirs from the riverbank merchants, not the actual wares offered at the market itself. It is a tragic but safe assumption, therefore, that these markets will soon become thoroughly commercial, too, like those in Thonburi. Bridges and footpaths have been built to protect the market, but these are just a further contribution to the gradual loss of authenticity of these beautiful floating bazaars.

HOW TO GET THERE

Get up early and take the 78 bus from the Southern Bus Terminal in THONBURI to DAMNOEN SADUAK, 110 km west of Bangkok. The first busses leave at about 7:00 h, after that every 1/2 hour. The ride will cost you 30 Baht. Small motor boats leave for the TONKEM floating market every 15-20 minutes for 5 Baht directly from the bus-stop. If you want to see the other markets nearby, KHUN PITHAK and HERE KUE, you'll have to pay more (approx. 300 - 400 Baht for a 1 1/2 hour tour - bargain!). You will also find a minibus terminal next to the bus-stop. From here you can catch a ride to the market for 1 Baht, or you can walk along the canal - approx. 1.5 km.

NAKHON PATHOM

This is one of Thailand's oldest towns. You will find the country's largest pagoda here, which was the point from which Buddhism spread into this part of the country. A smaller chedi, probably built by the Mon, stood on the site of today's huge *PHRA PATHOM CHEDI* as early as the 4th century. Even in those days the chedi was said to have had a height of 39 metres. In the 11th century the Khmer added a prang. Today it is one of the highest chedis in the whole world (over 120 metres). Because of the imposing design and construction of the temple one speculates that this is where monks from Ceylon must have founded the first Theravada-Buddhism Centre in Thailand.

When he was still prince, King Mongkut set out for numerous pilgrimages to this temple ruin in the middle of the jungle. Once king, he decided to have a gigantic chedi built on top of the ruins. Construction began in 1853 and was completed in 1870. The small settlement Nakhon Chaisri, 20 km south of the chedi, was 'transplanted' to the temple. Four viharn pointing to the north, east, south, and west were erected on top of a platform surrounding the central chedi. In each you will find various works of art as well as a different Buddha statue (N: standing Buddha, S: Buddha being supported by a serpent E: Buddha beneath a Bodhi tree, W: resting Buddha).

A stairway leads up to the second platform from the main entrance in the north. Here you will find beautiful plants, benches, Chinese temple figures and a large, impressive Buddha statue.

During construction, King Mongkut lived in a small palace east of the chedi. The palace no longer stands today. His successor, King Rama VI, often stayed here, too, and also had a small palace built, this one in a thoroughly western style, just two km west of the pagoda. This palace - *SANAM CHAN* - lies in the middle of a beautiful park and is used as an administrative office today. After the Lay Krathong festivities in November, a ten-day temple-celebration is held outside the pagoda. Musical competitions are held each evening and open air films are shown. There is also a fair as well as a very nice market in front of the big chedi every evening.

HOW TO GET THERE

You can combine your trip to NAKHON PATHOM with your trip to the floating market. Catch a regular bus leaving the Bangkok Southern Bus Terminal for 13 Baht (ac 24 Baht) or catch a bus from DAMNOEN SADUAK for 15 Baht. The last Bangkok-bound busses leave town at about 16:00 h. If you're planning to go to Damnoen Saduak from Nakhon Pathom, get up early and catch bus 78, which leaves from the big chedi.

Diesel-railcars from Thonburi (Bangkok) and Kanchanaburi (only 3rd class, 14 Baht on both routes) will also bring you to the huge chedi. Trains coming from the south (Phetchburi, Hua Hin, Surat Thani) also stop at Nakhon Pathom. Nakhon Pathom is also the station to change at if you are coming from the south and heading for Kanchanaburi.

CROCODILE FARM

The local and imported beasts you can see here are actually bred for their leather. They are worth quite a bit live too, though, as you can tell from the masses of tourists. Apart from crocodiles, a number of other creatures are also held captive on the large farm grounds. There is a big self-service restaurant. You can also try a bowl of crocodile-soup at the foodstand opposite. This soup is especially popular among the Chinese, who claim that it has aphrodisiac qualities.

Open daily 8:00-18:00 h, tel 3950477, admission 80 Baht. The animals are fed in the late afternoons 16:30-17:30 h, show Mon-Fri on the hour between 9:00 and 11:00 h, also at 12:00 and 17:00 h at week-ends. Half an hour later there is also an elephant show.

HOW TO GET THERE

Continue due south from Samut Prakan. The road branching off to the right at kilometre-stone 28 leads to the 'Farm of 30,000 Reptiles'. Samut Prakan is the final destination of the ac-busses 11 and 8. You can also get there by regular busses 25, 45, 119, and 102.

A minibus shuttle-service runs regularly from the final stop to the farm (5 Baht). A taxi will cost you 10 Baht.

ANCIENT CITY

A huge open-air museum lies about 6 km further south. The first impression one gets of Ancient City is that of a miniature model of Thailand. The 80-acre park is even shaped like the country. Detailed miniature replicas of about 80 famous Thai buildings and temples can be seen here. This way you can walk to all the places you'll miss during the rest of your trip. There is much greenery here, lovely artificial lakes and waterfalls. Most visitors come by bus or their own car (prices for parking will vary according to the size of your car). A bicycle would be ideal for discovering this 'shrunken Thailand', but unfortunately these are not allowed. At the entrance, the 'Thai-Malay border', you will be given a detailed 'map' so as not to lose your way when in the 'mountains of northern Thailand' or at the 'south coast'. Open daily 8:30-18:00 h, admission 50 Baht.

GLOSSARY

ARCHITECTURAL AND RELIGIOUS TERMS

bot — temple building where religious services are performed; monks are ordained here.

chedi — a decorative bell-shaped pointed tower that stands on its own and often contains religious objects.

mondop — a square temple building build on a sacred relic.

prang — a Khmer-style spire; often with a rounded top.

viharn — temple building containing sacred objects (library).

CENTRAL THAILAND

AYUTTHAYA

Ayutthaya was the capital of the Siamese Empire for 417 years. 33 kings ruled the country from here, until the city was destroyed by Burmese troops in 1767. The huge area in which you can visit the ruins of former temples and palaces will give you an idea of how big this city must once have been. In the 17th century, the period marking the peak of Thailand's power, the city could easily have been compared with any large European town of the time. Europeans, Chinese and Japanese lived in some of the city's districts. The imposing temples symbolized the might of the Thai leaders, who paid for all this profusion by collecting taxes.

Rent some form of transport in Ayutthaya - this way you'll be able to see as much as possible. If you are good at bargaining you might be able to hire a tuk tuk for half a day for only 200 Baht. The drivers aren't too keen on acting as tourist guides, though. To really see all there is to see, you will need at least an entire day. Take a ride from the bus station to the centre of the ancient town (approx. 20 Baht). While the restoration scheme of the Thai government has certainly restored some of the buildings to their former appearance, it has also resulted in a sad loss of character. The central grounds, for instance ('English' lawn, paved parking lots), seem quite sterile.

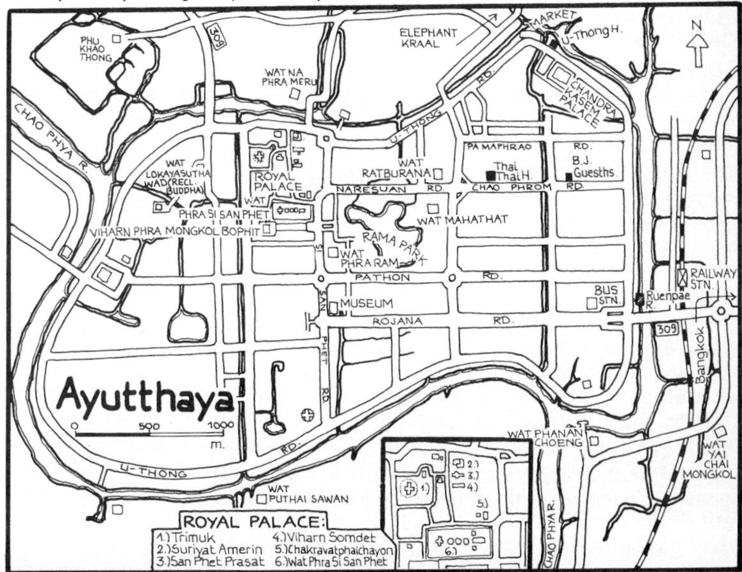

WAT YAI CHAI MONGKOL - can be found southeast of the railway tracks, outside the actual historical city. King Naresuan is responsible for the temple's present form; he had the 62-metre chedi and the reclining Buddha statue added in honour of his great victory over his Burmese adversary in 1592. Continue southwest down this road and you will reach

WAT PHANAN CHOENG - This temple may have stood here before the actual city was founded. Archeologists have found out that the 20-metre sitting Buddha is 26 years older than the town itself. King Mongkut had the statue completely restored. You can hire a boat for a sightseeing tour around the town for 200 Baht from the landing-place behind the monastery. If you have a car or a tuk tuk, start your tour on the island at the

NATIONAL MUSEUM (Chao Sam Phya, admission 20 Baht, open Wed-Sun 9:00-12:00 h and 13:00-16:00 h) - golden amulets, statues and other excavated objects of interest are exhibited here, among them bronze Buddha statues that are over 1000 years old. North of the museum you will find

RAMA PARK - a small park where you can stretch out and relax next to a pleasant little lake. East of the park you will be able to visit the ruins of

WAT MAHATHAT - (admission 20 Baht), the biggest of all of Ayutthaya's temples. It was founded in 1384. Many new parts were added over the centuries. Only the walls of the original building remain. The ruin of the formerly huge central prang will give you an idea of how large it must have once been. Opposite you will find the

WAT RATBURANA - (admission 20 Baht). The seventh king of Ayutthaya had this temple with its Khmer-style prang built in 1424 as a burial-place for his two elder brothers, who had lost the fight to succeed to the throne.

CHANDRA KASEM PALACE - There is a second museum in this reconstructed palace of the Crown Prince. King Mongkut later had a tower built here, from which he observed the stars. Return down Naresuan Road, past the statue of King U Thong, and you will reach

WAT PHRA SI SAN PHET - (admission 20 Baht) Construction on the impressive royal temple buildings began in 1448. Several modernizations and alterations were made before the temples were burnt to the ground by the Burmese conquerors in 1767. If you enter the enclosed grounds by way of the south entrance you will see three restored viharn containing the ashes of former kings. Continue west along the wall and you will reach

VIHARN PHRA MONGKOL BOPHIT - a restored temple with one of the biggest bronze Buddha statues in all of Thailand. It dates back to the 15th century. The viharn was reconstructed with minute attention to detail in 1956. There's a lot going on here, especially at the week-ends - fortune-tellers etc. Drinks and souvenirs can be bought just opposite - try the sticky rice cooked in a bamboo stick! Northwest of here you will find the remnants of the walls of the former

ROYAL PALACE, which was built in 1350 during the reign of the first king. The eighth king decided to have his palace moved a little further north, nearer the river, no more than 100 years later. Here you will find the ruins of the *SURYAT*

AMARIN HALL, King Narai's former residence. The neighbouring *SAN PHET PRASAT HALL* (to the south) was built in 1448 as a reception hall for foreign dignitaries. The ceremonial hall *VIHARN SOMDET* was erected during the reign of the 24th king of Ayutthaya at the beginning of the 17th century, as were the next building and the *CHAKRAVAT PHAICHAYON HALL* at the eastern side of the palace. The king used to salute parades and pageants from here. The open-air wooden *TRIMUK* pavilion west of the San Phet Prasat Hall wasn't built until 1907 under King Chulalongkorn. In the west of the town you will find the rather secluded

WAT LOKAYASUTHA. One of the biggest-ever reclining Buddhas, made of stucco, can be seen here. Now that the monastery has burnt to the ground, the statue lies beneath open skies.

HOTELS

If you plan on staying in Ayutthaya for a while, stay at the *B.J. GUESTHOUSE*,* Ng. 16/7 Naresuan Road, tel 251512 (small garden, nice people, bicycles for hire), or at *VAN'S GUESTHOUSE*,* 51 Horatanachai Road, tel 241187, near the minibus station (gets rather loud at night). *HOTEL U-THONG*** can be found near the Chandra Kasem Palace, tel 251136 (stuffy, dark, and expensive). *HOTEL THAI THAI*** is at 13 Naresuan Road, tel 251505, east of Wat Ratburana. If you have some surplus money for a good meal try *RUNPAE,* the floating restaurant near the bridge - excellent Thai food!

HOW TO GET THERE

The easiest way of getting to Ayutthaya is by catching a bus from the Northern Bus Terminal or from the Victory Monument (buses for AYUTTHAYA leave every 10 minutes, cost 17 Baht, and take 1-1 1/2 hours). The bus drivers will let you get off at the place from where songthaew can be hired for tours.

You can also catch a train for 31 Baht (15 Baht) in 2nd (3rd) class. It will cost you 11 Baht from Don Muang station. Two trains leave the historic city for Chiang Mai daily, one at 17:03 h, the other at 19:23 h. You can catch a songthaew to the ruins from the station, too.

BANG PA IN

This former summer palace of the Ayutthayan kings was built in the 17th century. It was forgotten when Bangkok became the new royal city. It was not extended or put to a new use until steam boats started travelling up the river at the end of the 19th century. This is when the curious mixture of Thai, Chinese and European styles came into being.

The actual palace, *AISAWAN THIPPA-AT,* lies surrounded by a small body of water in one of the river bends. The small Thai-style pavilion in the middle of the lake is particularly beautiful. The *WEHAT CHAMRUN* residence was established by wealthy Chinese and built in a thoroughly Chinese style - beautiful furniture with mother-of-pearl inlays and wood carvings. The *WAT NIVET THAMAPRAWAT* was built in the style of a Gothic church under King Chulalongkorn. It seems strangely out of place. You will have to cross over in a sampan (a small, non-motorized boat) to reach it, as it is on the other side of the river. Except on Mondays and Fridays, Bang Pa In is open to the public 8:00-15:00 h, admission 10 Baht.

HOW TO GET THERE

Buses for BANG PA IN leave Bangkok's Northern Bus Terminal every 30 minutes, cost 13 Baht, and take approx. 2 hours to get there. There is also a regular bus service between Ayutthaya and Bang Pa In, or you can charter a boat for 300 Baht. The 'Chao Phya Express Boat', tel 2225330, offers a boat ride to Bang Pa In and Wat Phai Lom on Sundays for 120 Baht. The boat leaves Wat Mahathat Pier at 8:30 h and returns at 17:30 h.

LOPBURI

As of the 10th century, large parts of the Menam area came under the influence of the eastern Khmer Empire. Their peculiar culture with its severe bronze Buddha statues and vaguely phallic prangs (a sort of stupa) was adopted by the Thais, who penetrated the area from the north in the 13th century. Lopburi was an important religious and political centre of the independent Mon Empire as early as the 7th century. During the Khmer-period it was the seat of the vice king. After that, the city lost much of its significance until King Narai of Ayutthaya had it declared second capital of Thailand in the 17th century. Today the city has about 40,000 inhabitants.

The historic town lies west of the railway tracks. A less impressive, new shrine, the *SARN PRA KARN SHRINE* which stands on the site of a former Hindu shrine, can be seen at the level crossing. The monkeys sitting in the Banyan trees demand food in a most aggressive manner. A little further north you will see the three laterite prangs of the *PRANG SAM YOD* (11th century), distinctive mark of the city. Southwest of the station you will find the partially restored and frequently extended *WAT MAHATHAT,* a large Buddhist temple with a typical Lopburi-style prang. King Narai had the *NARAI RAJA NIWET PALACE* built at the river, southwest of town. Inside you will find a National Museum. Here you will be able to look at Lopburi art objects, all heavily influenced by the Khmer style (opened Wed-Sun, 9:00-16:00 h). The buildings were constructed in the Thai as well as the European style. A Greek adventurer, Constans Phaulkon, influenced King Narai when it came to designing the palace.

North of the palace you will find the *WAT THONG -THONG,* built during the Ayutthaya period. It was built in the western style and was to be a church for foreign envoys who lived in the city. You cannot go into the Catholic church, the former residence of Phaulkon (to the left of the church), or the former residence of the first French envoy (to the right of the church), northeast of the wat. One of the first European descriptions of the town was given by the representative of Louis XIV. According to this description, Lopburi must have been an impressive city indeed. Today, this is difficult to imagine, as the ruins are

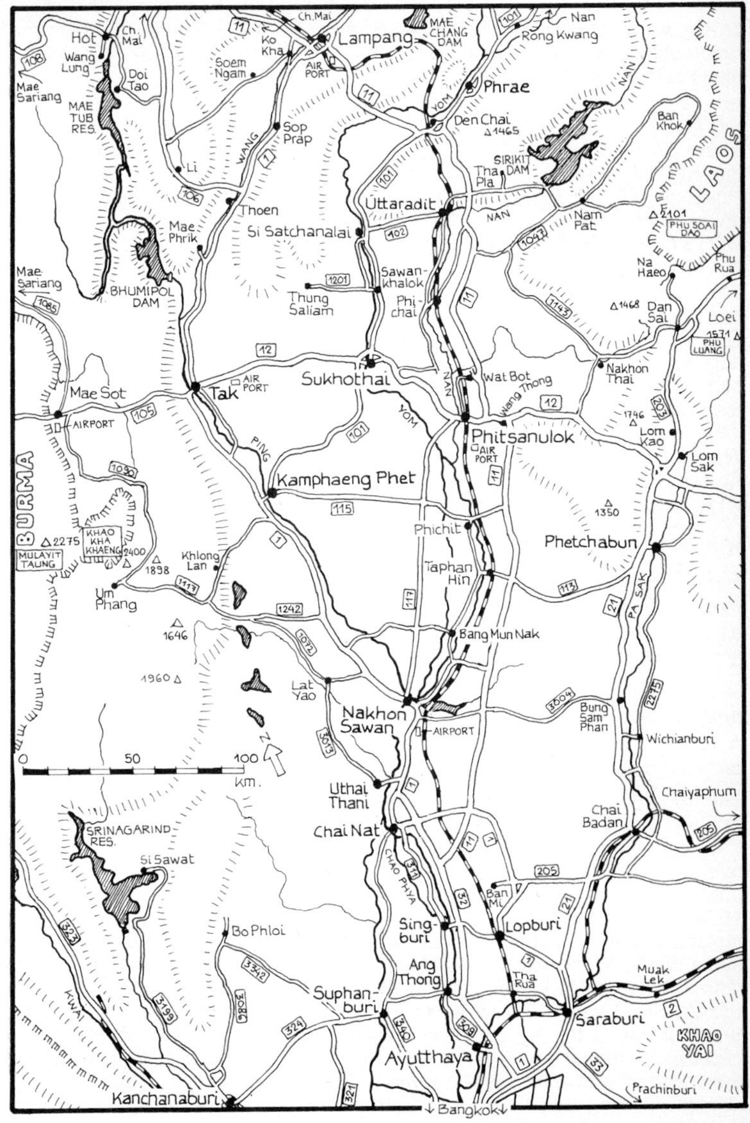
Lampang
MAE CHANG DAM
Nan
Rong Kwang
Phrae
Den Chai
Hot
Wang Lung
Mae Sariang
Doi Tao
MAE TUB RES.
Soem Ngam
Ko Kha
AIR PORT
Sop Prap
Li
Thoen
Uttaradit
SIRIKIT DAM
Tha Pla
Ban Khok
LAOS
Nam Pat
PHU SOAI DAO
Si Satchanalai
Mae Phrik
BHUMIPOL DAM
Sawan-khalok
Thung Saliam
Phi-chai
Na Haeo
Phu Rua
Dan Sai
Loei
PHU LUANG
Nakhon Thai
Sukhothai
Tak
Mae Sot
AIRPORT
Wat Bot
Wang Thong
Phitsanulok
Lom Kao
Lom Sak
BURMA
Kamphaeng Phet
Phichit
Phetchabun
KHAO KHA KHAENG
MULAYIT TAUNG
Khlong Lan
Um Phang
Taphan Hin
Bang Mun Nak
Lat Yao
Nakhon Sawan
Bung Sam Phan
Wichianburi
km.
Uthai Thani
Chaiyaphum
Chai Badan
Chai Nat
SRINAGARIND RES.
Si Sawat
Ban Mi
Sing-buri
Lopburi
Bo Phloi
Ang Thong
Tha Rua
Muak Lek
Suphan-buri
Saraburi
KHAO YAI
Ayutthaya
Prachinburi
Kanchanaburi
Bangkok
YOM
NAN
WANG
PING
PA SAK
CHAO PHYA
KWAI

barely visible in the typically provincial town. *PRANG KHAEK,* another small Hindu shrine built in Khmer style, can be seen standing north of the palace, in the middle of the chaotic traffic.

HOTELS

There are two large hotels in town, the *HOTEL ASIA***, 1/7-8 Surasak Road, tel 411892 (ugly new building opposite the palace), and the *TAIPEI HOTEL***, Surasongkram Road, tel 411524 (which is actually mainly a brothel for Thai men). If these two don't take your fancy, try the cheaper *GOLDEN TOWN**, opposite the three large stupas. It is rather loud and dirty here, but you'll have a good view of the Prang Sam Yod from the roof. The *TRAVELERS DROP IN CENTRE**, 34 Wichayen Road, Soi 3, run by New Zealanders, might be an alternative.

HOW TO GET THERE

Five trains stop in Lopburi daily, some from the north (PHITSANULOK), some from the south (BANGKOK - cost 28 / 57 Baht for 3rd / 2nd class). A bus from or to Bangkok's Northern Bus Terminal will take about 4 hrs. (50 Baht ac, 36 Baht non-ac). Buses from Lopburi to SINGBURI cost 8 Baht, to SARABURI, the place to change buses if you're heading for the Khao Yai National Park, 12 Baht. The Lopburi bus terminal is south of the second roundabout, approx. 1.5 km away from the town centre.

KANCHANABURI

If the only thing of interest here were the famous Bridge of the River Kwae (better known as the River Kwai), which inspired Pierre Boulles' novel as well as the subsequent motion picture, a trip to Kanchanaburi wouldn't really be worth it. But there is more, so plan to stay a couple of days if you have the time.

After arriving, go to the *TOURIST OFFICE,* tel 511200, open daily 8:30-16:30 h. A trishaw from the station costs 10 Baht, shorter distances only 5 Baht. You will receive good information here.

The town itself is sadly lacking in character - just one of many provincial towns. You will find a small *MUSEUM* with a partial reconstruction of the infamous P.O.W. camp that used to be here (admission fee 20 Baht) in the wat at the river. You can get a good idea of what life must have been like for the 60,000 prisoners of war who had to build the railway tracks to Burma during the war. 16,000 of them died due to accidents, malnutrition and diseases, mainly malaria. Many of the dead were buried in one of the two *CEMETERIES.* One of these can be found near the station (20 Baht with a chartered songthaew), the other lies at the Kwae Noi, 3 km south of town, surrounded by beautiful countryside. Small groups would do well to hire a songthaew, which will give you a 3-4 hour tour of the museum, the temples, and the bridge for 300 Baht. Bicycles can be rented opposite the Aree Bakery for 10 Baht a day - these can be taken aboard any of the ferries for free.

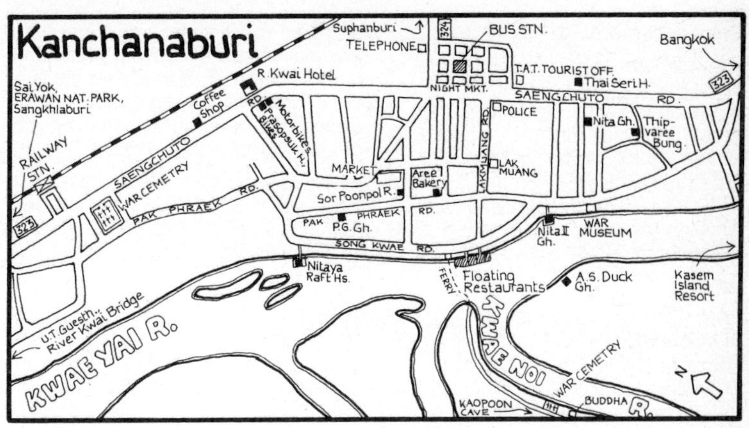

HOTELS

By now, there are several guest-houses in Kanchanaburi, e.g. *THIP VAREE**, 211 1-4 Saeng Chuto Road, tel 511063 (none too clean, but with private bathrooms and lavatories), *P.G.**, 297-303 Pak Phraek Road, tel 5115114, (new and clean with a nice terrace leading out into the garden), or *U.T.**, 25/5 Menam Kwae Road, towards the bridge. *NITA GUEST-HOUSE**, 03 Visudhirangsi Road, tel 511130, quiet, no private bathrooms, with a dormitory. Nitaya and Changkrit are friendly and able to give you good information (approx. 200 metres from the TAT office, towards the museum). If you feel like spending the night at the river in the *NITAYA RAFT HOUSE**, a simple floating bamboo house, bring your mosquito-net. There are a number of hotels along the main road (Saeng Chuto Road), e.g. the *THAI SERI HOTEL***, no. 142, tel 511128, the *PRASOPSUK HOTEL***, ac***, no. 277, tel 511777, and the two *RIVER KWAI HOTELS* (next door to each other), the first* (ac**), tel 511565, the second****, tel 511269, modern, luxurious, with a discotheque. You can rent one of the bungalows offered by *KASEM ISLAND RESORTS*****, tel 511603, south of town, near Chukadon Pier.

FOOD

Foodstalls are opened up in the evening on the road along the river leading to the bridge. You can get good food here (approx. 50 Baht per person) - the atmosphere is best just before the sun sets. The *SOR POONPOL*, opposite the old cinema, is a good restaurant. No menu or sign, though. You'll find the *AREE BAKERY* just around the corner. If you walk down the road from the River Kwai Hotels you'll come to the *SUNYA RESTAURANT*, where good, cheap food is served. Boat tours and floating overnight-accommodation (60 Baht per person) can be organized from here.

HOW TO GET THERE

A ride to NAM TOK (49 Baht) via NAKHON PATHOM (14 Baht) and KANCHANABURI (28 Baht) from the Thonburi station is an absolute must.

The diesel railcar leaves twice daily.

You will have to pay 17 Baht to get to Nam Tok from Kanchanaburi, 1 Baht to get to the bridge. If you take the 8 o' clock train you will be in Kanchanaburi at 10:34 h and in Nam Tok at 12:20 h. This train stops at the bridge at 10:38 h. The second train leaves Thonburi at 13:55 h, arrives in Kanchanaburi at 16:24 h, and in Nam Tok at 18:35 h. The first train from Nam Tok leaves at 6:05 h, from Kanchanaburi at 8:06 h. The train that stops at the bridge leaves Nam Tok at 12:35 h (reaches the bridge at 14:20 h), and arrives in Thonburi at 17:00 h.

Buses leaving from the Southern Bus Terminal in BANGKOK take 3 hours and cost 28 Baht / ac 53 Baht. NAKHON PATHOM 16 Baht.

DAY TRIPS AROUND KANCHANABURI

BOAT RIDES ON THE RIVER KWAE

Hire a boat (up to six people) at the merging point of the Kwae Yai and the Kwae Noi. It will cost you 600 Baht for half a day and is well worth it. There are various tours to choose from.

Go up the KWAE NOI and you will come to a cemetery. A little further up you will see a huge Buddha statue looking down upon the river and the mountains beyond. There are no roads in this area and tigers are said to live here. If you head down the MAEKLONG you will pass small islands that are surrounded by lotus blossoms. There is a Chinese cemetery at the riverbank. A grave here may cost up to 10 million Baht. You will also have access to the museum from here. If you go up the KWAE YAI you will pass a number of raft-houses with TV-antennas (!) before reaching the famous bridge.

THE BRIDGE AT THE RIVER KWAE

Another way of getting to the BRIDGE AT THE KWAE, which lies 4 km northwest of town, is to hire a songthaew for 40 Baht per vehicle. Railcars also go up the mountains to what is today the final train station twice daily.

During the war, the Japanese planned a 419-km connecting line between the Burmese and the Thai railway systems. This was to ensure the transportation of future supplies. In only one year, from October 1942 to October 1943, the 60,000 P.O.W.s had completed the line, which went straight through the jungle. It went along the River Kwae, over the Three Pagoda Pass (Chedi Sam Ong), all the way to Thanbyuzayat in Burma. The prisoners, Indians, Thais, Burmese, Chinese, Indonesians, Malays, and members of the Allied Forces, were forced to live a life in the jungle unfit for human beings. Part of the bridge was destroyed during the war. The British had segments of the line dismantled in Burma and at the border.

BAN KAO

Several roads branch off to the Kwae Noi (south) from the road leading to the Three Pagoda Pass. Few of these are paved, though. Traffic is sparse. You will find one road, however, that leads to BAN KAO, 15 km away. Continue southeast past the village and take the road branching off to the right.after 5 km. After a further 1 km you will have reached the RIVER KWAE FARM***. Rafts and

RAFTING ON THE RIVER KWAE YAI

simple bamboo huts, suitable only - if indeed at all - for large groups, are available. Very isolated, 32 km from Kanchanaburi. Most of the food served comes straight from the farm.

You will find a small archeological museum 2 km west of BAN KAO (continue for another km after having reached the sign saying *Welcome to Tao)* . A Dutch archeologist made some significant discoveries here while being held prisoner in the P.O.W. camp during WW II. He managed to keep them secret until the war had finished. Later excavations were rewarded with human skeletons, clay pieces, and other objects that are conclusive proof of there having been human life in this area over 10,000 years ago. Open Wed-Sun (not public holidays) 9:00-16:00 h, free of charge.

Continue northwest for another 8 km (bad road conditions) and you will reach the weather-beaten ruins of the former *City of Lions* (MUANG SING), which was built in the style of the Khmer (PRASAT). They built a rectangular fort on this bend of the river around the 12th and 13th centuries, hoping to be able to protect their border from here. The moat and the original outer walls can still easily be made out. Paths paved with huge laterite blocks will lead you through the main entrance to the central prang, also built out of laterite stone. Several works of art in the Lopburi style were discovered while the ruins were being restored. These can now be seen in the museums of U Thong and Bangkok.

There is a junction 5 km northwest of the ruins. Turn off to the right and you will reach the main road after a further 5 km. If you turn left instead, you will reach a dead end at the river after 7 km. You will be able to cross over on a ferry for 25 Baht. Go downstream and you will reach the YANG THONE RIVER KWAI bungalow village****, including three meals a day. If you feel like spending the night here you can also charter a songthaew from the Kanchanaburi tourist office or the River Kwai Hotel for 300 Baht.

You can also spend the night at the RIVER KWAE JUNGLE HOUSE**** (including meals), 5 km northwest of the above mentioned junction. It can be reached from the Lum Sum train station. Apart from these, there are other bungalows and rafts where you can also spend the night; information can be obtained at the Kanchanaburi tourist office.

NAM TOK

You can take an adventurous 77-km train-ride past mountains, cliffs, and rivers from Kanchanaburi. It will take 2 hours to reach NAM TOK, the final station on the line, and it will cost you 17 Baht. You can also take the 8203 bus, which costs 15 Baht and gets you there in an hour. The bus leaves every 1/2 hour. To get to the BUNGALOWS SAI YOK NOI**-****, cross the wooden bridge 300 metres north of the station. The bungalows are only 200 metres from the main road, from where the Kanchanaburi-Thong Pha Phum bus can be caught.

Make an excursion to the KHAO PHANG WATERFALL, 1 km north of the big junction (west of Nam Tok). Many picnickers come here at the week-ends - it is only worth it during the rainy season, though (June-August). Organized travel groups will also arrive by train. After the frantic ride with the *Death Railway* they will almost always immediately retire to the rather quiet RIVER KWAI VILLAGE HOTEL****, tel Bangkok 2517552.

Boats can be rented from the PAK SAENG PIER, 3 km west of the station, on the other side of the main road. Up to 12 people will fit into one of the boats leaving for the Sai Yok Nai National Park. The boats will cost at least 800 Baht. A 4-hour tour to the park and back will cost you 1000-1200 Baht.

You can also rent a boat that will take you to LAWA CAVES and back for 500 Baht (approx. 2 hours). The Lawa Caves are the largest stalactite caves in the area.

SAI YOK YAI NATIONAL PARK

You can get to the Sai Yok Yai National Park (108 km from Kanchanaburi) as well as any other place along road 323 by taking bus 8203 headed for Thong Pha Phum (35 Baht). The bus leaves Kanchanaburi every 1/2 hour. If you only want to go as far as the National Park you will have to pay 25 Baht. The road branching off to the park is signposted on the left side of the road. Sometimes motor-cyclists will offer to take you down the 3 remaining km of road for 10 Baht. If not, you will have to walk.

Archeological discoveries made in the park include a woman's skeleton from the neolithic period. A former Japanese military camp can be found in the totally overgrown area near the waterfall. WWII veterans often set out in search of it. With a little luck you may even come across some of the original train tracks. Cross the suspension bridge to the west side of the river. The National park reaches all the way to the Burmese border and most parts of it are almost inaccessible and totally uninhabited. Tigers and wild elephants still live in the Tenasserim mountain area, part of the park. The park's main attraction is the waterfall, which is most beautiful during the dry period, when the water level of the Kwae Noi is lowest.

You can spend the night at expensive bungalows*** run by the park administration (if you bargain, **), as well as at cheap raft houses** floating on the Kwae Noi.

THREE PAGODA PASS

You will reach the Three Pagoda Pass, the border to Burma, if you continue north on road 323. The countryside here has only just recently been opened up to tourism. You will see work-elephants and huge road-building machines. The fine wood of the visibly diminishing tropical rainforest is cut in sawmills at the sides of the road, and the gradual degeneration to Alang Alang-grass steppe seems inexorable.

THONG PHA PHUM, where the paved road ends, is the final stop of all buses coming from Kanchanaburi. There is not much to see here, apart from a huge and imposing Buddha set before the most bizarre cliff-formations at the end of the village. You can spend the night at the SOR BOONYONG BUNGALOWS**.

Trucks and songthaew go up to the border but you might have to change in SANGKLABURI. Expect to pay around 200 Baht.

ERAWAN NATIONAL PARK

The Erawan National Park is 70 km from Kanchanaburi, at the upper course of the Kwae Yai. It is situated in a narrow, wooded valley encompassing the river. There are a number of beautiful waterfalls along the river, and you can walk past most of these while exploring the valley. We would recommend getting an early start. Do not go at the weekend, as many people come here during their free time. Take the blue 8170 bus from Kanchanaburi (every 45 minutes) to the market-place for 20 Baht. The last Kanchanaburi-bound bus leaves between 15:30 and 16:00 h. You can spend the night on the wooden benches of the Boy Scout Camp near the bamboo bridge for 20-30 Baht (only with permission, though) or in one of the bungalows*.

SUKHOTHAI

When the Thais first came from the north, they managed to conquer this former Khmer-controlled area in 1238 A.D. They gained control over large parts of the country due to a strong army and clever politics. The king had Ceylonese monks come to the country in order to spread the pure teachings of Buddhism (Theravada Buddhism) and to displace the influence of the unpopular Khmer. Many of the former typically Khmer-style religious buildings were re-built according to the taste of the era. King Khamhaeng (1275-1317), the 'Father of

Thailand', derived the first Thai alphabet from the Mon script. He managed to unite the country in spite of the many different ethnic groups living there. Sukhothai lost much of its might during the reign of his successors, however, and in the 14th century it became part of the Ayutthayan Empire.

Don't miss the ruins of Sukhothai if you're interested in Thai history and have plenty of time. There are far less tourists here than in Ayutthaya, although these ruins are by no means less fascinating . You will find the ruins 11 km outside of present-day Sukhothai, at road no. 12 leading to Tak. Ancient Sukhothai, former Royal City of Thailand, lies west of its modern version. One kilometre before the old town, to the right, you will pass the

SUKHOTHAI CULTURE CENTRE, which consists of a hotel, a huge restaurant for bus-loads of tourists, and a few shops selling arts and crafts at 'tourist prices'. The hotel grounds (see *Hotels)* are separated from the ruins by a river. You will come across the first temple ruin outside the actual town fortification. Start your tour at the National Museum. The old

TOWN FORTIFICATION and its moat make up a 1810 x 1400 metre rectangle, which used to surround the former city area. The remains of 16 temples and 4 Hindu shrines stand within. In addition, there are 70 further ruins outside of the town fortification. The

RAMA KHAMHAENG NATIONAL MUSEUM (4) is closed on Mon, Tue, and on holidays. Otherwise it is open from 9:00-12:00 h and from 13:00-16:00 h. Admission 10 Baht. The exhibits are unfortunately not presented as well as they could be. All the same, the museum is worth a visit; the exhibits on the ground floor will give you a good idea of the art of the Sukhothai period.

WAT MAHATHAT (3), the Royal Temple, is in the centre. It was Siam's most significant religious gathering place during the Sukhothai period. Since 1953 the central chedi, the substructure of the ordination hall, the viharn, as well as 209 smaller chedis and several other buildings have been dug up on the 240 x 280 metre temple grounds. The rows of pillars to the east used to support the wooden roof of the large, adjoining bot. Various Buddha figures have been restored and returned to where they originally stood. The three laterite prasat of

WAT SI SAWAI (5), a formerly Brahman temple built in the Khmer style in the 13th century, are further south. The Hindu temple was later re-modelled to a Buddhist temple. Shiva statues as well as Buddha figures were discovered here. Unfortunately the recent restoration work on the stucco decorations has only been partially successful. The Ceylonese style stupa and the bot ruins of

WAT SRA SI (2), north of the Royal Temple, are on a small island in a lake. The Loy Krathong celebrations are held here every November. The nearby

MEMORIAL (1) depicts King Rama Khamhaeng.

We would suggest taking the northwestern exit if you want to go on to the ruins in the north. After 1 km you will reach the roof-less

WAT SI CHUM with its highly venerated, huge, 14th century sitting Buddha, *Phra Atchana*. The square mondhop (30 metres long and 15 metres high) used to be surrounded by a moat. The interior space is almost entirely filled with the huge Buddha statue. To the left there is a narrow passage-way lead

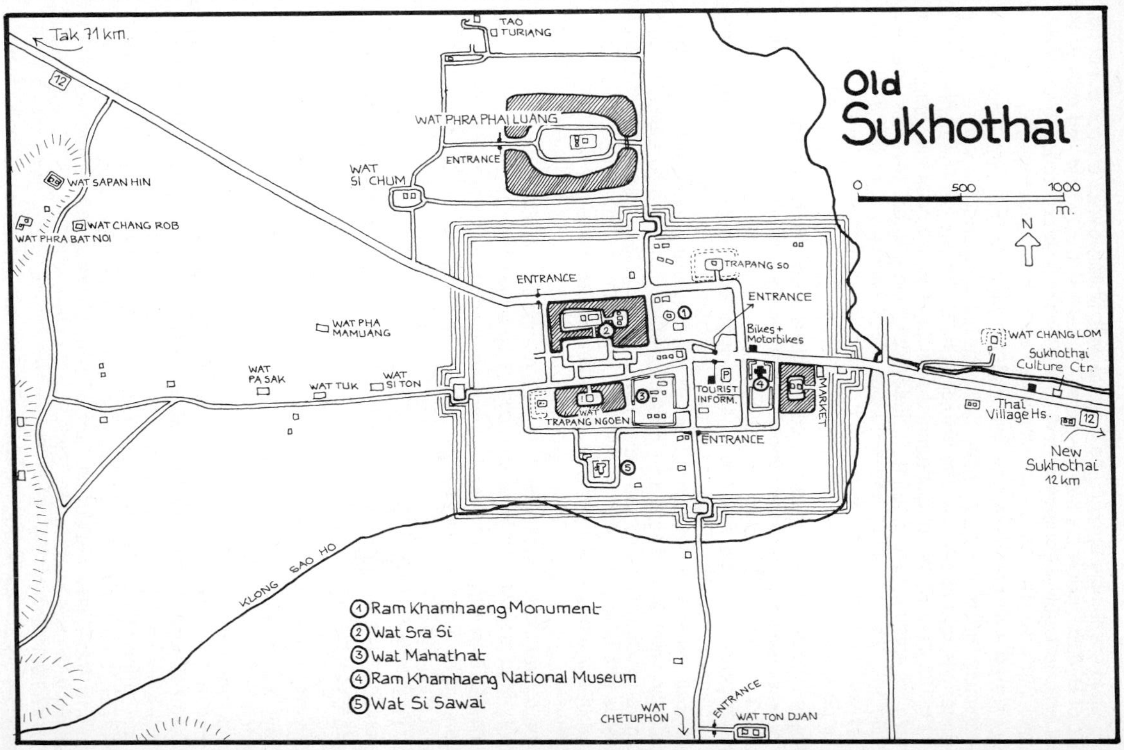
Old Sukhothai
0
500
1000
m.
N
Tak 71 km.
12
TAO TURIANG
WAT PHRA PHAI LUANG
ENTRANCE
WAT SI CHUM
WAT SAPAN HIN
WAT CHANG ROB
WAT PHRA BAT NOI
ENTRANCE
TRAPANG SO
ENTRANCE
Bikes + Motorbikes
WAT PHA MAMUANG
WAT PA SAK
WAT TUK
WAT SI TON
WAT TRAPANG NGOEN
P
TOURIST INFORM.
MARKET
ENTRANCE
WAT CHANG LOM
Sukhothai Culture Ctr.
Thai Village Hs.
12
New Sukhothai 12 km
KLONG SAO HO
1 Ram Khamhaeng Monument
2 Wat Sra Si
3 Wat Mahathat
4 Ram Khamhaeng National Museum
5 Wat Si Sawai
WAT CHETUPHON
ENTRANCE
WAT TON DJAN

ing up to the temple through the 3 metre wall. Murals depict scenes out of the life of Buddha inside the narrow, gloomy passage. Every now and then you'll be able to catch a glimpse of the huge Buddha statue through occasional, small windows. The impressive statue can also be seen from above.

WAT PHRA PHAI LUANG is 700 metres further to the right. This temple (originally Hindu) is said to have been the most important temple during the Khmer period, maybe even the actual centre of the capital. The northernmost of the the three Khmer prasat remains standing and has been fully restored, as have the entire temple grounds, including the square stupa, several monastery buildings, the mondhop, and a chapel which encloses a reclining Buddha. Several Buddha statues were found in bricked up niches in the walls during the period of restoration.

Many *KILNS,* some of them in ruins, some restored, lie scattered among the heaps of rubble north of the temple. These kilns are usually 6 metres in length and 3 metres in width and made of brick. The famous Sawankhalok ceramics (=celadon) were made in these. These fine ceramics were manufactured here by Chinese artisans as early as in the 13th century. They were exported to all parts of South East Asia from here. In the beginning, four different types of celadon were produced here - cream coloured, unpatterned ceramics, and similar ones with sun-, fish-, and flower motifs. Many fragments of broken plates and bowls lie about. They were usually broken before they even came out of the oven. Pretty pictures can often still be made out on many of the pieces.

There are further ruins in the wide area reaching from west of the town to the foot of the mountains. We would recommend climbing up to

WAT SAPAN HIN. A 12.5 metre, standing Buddha looks down upon the valley from up here. Good view! Go through the southern exit, continue for 2.5 km, and you'll reach

WAT CHETUPHON. There used to be a sitting, a walking, a reclining, and a standing Buddha at the respective four corners of the massive mondhop. Today only the sitting and the walking one remain.

HOTELS

New Sukhothai is a rather sad provincial town with 23,000 inhabitants and countless mosquitoes. Walk north up Tree Chot Road from the bus station and you'll reach the busy and loud Singhawat Road. This is where most of the hotels are. *SUKHOTHAI HOTEL***, no. 15, tel 611133, popular among travellers, restaurant, large rooms with shower / lavatory. *SWASDIPHONG*-***, no. 56, tel 611567, large single rooms, enough space for two people. *KITMONGKOL HOTEL***,* opposite in no. 43, tel 611193, large and clean rooms, modern building, peaceful upper floors. *CHINAWAT HOTEL*,* 1-3 Nakhon Kasem Road, tel 611385, not far from the bus station, friendly and relaxed atmosphere. *RIVER VIEW HOTEL***,* 92/6 Nakhon Kasem Road, tel 611652, south of the bus station, large rooms with showers and lavatories. *RAJTHANEE HOTEL***-*****,* 299 Charoen Vithi Road, tel 611031. This modern, five-storey building lies at the city limits towards the old town. It is the top hotel around and well worth its price. The *YUPA** is a guesthouse that was opened on the upper floors of a private home in 1987. Large, well lighted, and with a big terrace. The turn-off is signposted.

FOOD

If you're the kind of person who likes a cozy atmosphere and restaurants decorated with many precious small objects, go to the *DREAMCAFE* (ac) next to Swasdiphong Hotel, opened from 8:00-23:30 h. Good Thai food is served cheap here, as well as European breakfast and ice cream. You get to choose from several books and magazines and many cassette tapes. Most of the hotels have their own restaurant. Many travellers go to the *SUKHOTHAI RESTAURANT*. The *INDHIRA RESTAURANT* is downstairs in the Swasdiphong Hotel. Opposite the cinema you'll find the *NIGHT MARKET* beneath a large roof. Good, cheap food. Speciality of the market - sweet crab bread for 1 Baht.

GENERAL INFORMATION

BANKS

There are several banks on Singhawat Road, e.g. the *BANGKOK BANK* behind the Kitmongkol Hotel. The *THAI FARMERS BANK* is on Charoen Vithi Road, directly behind the bridge, and opens from 8:30-15:30 h.

ADMISSION FEES

The admission fee to the Old Sukhothai Historical Park is 20 Baht for foreigners, 5 Baht for Thais. You'll have to pay extra to visit the northern, western, eastern, and southern temples. Bicycles (20 Baht for foreigners, 5 Baht for Thais) and other vehicles cost extra, too. All this money goes towards paying for the restoration of the historical park, which sometimes seems to have not quite come off (flower-beds and paved roads, looking rather out of place among the many ancient ruins). Approx. £3.5 million were spent on the project, sponsored in part by Unesco and other international organizations.

TRANSPORTATION TO AND FROM OLD-SUKHOTHAI

A ***bus*** will take you to the ancient city for 5 Baht from the bus-stop at the road to Tak, 300 metres behind the bridge, on the right. Don't get talked into hiring a tuk-tuk for 100 Baht or a taxi for 200 Baht!

Bicycles are for rent for 20 Baht at the restaurants on the road opposite the museum. They're an ideal form of transportation as long as you're not travelling on an extremely hot day.

K. Vitoon also offers ***motorcycles*** for 45 Baht an hour. These are more suitable for trips to the temples outside the old town fortification.

Half-day ***tuk-tuk*** tours (150 Baht) are offered in New Sukhothai, e.g. at the Chinawat Hotel. The Swasdiphong Hotel offers tours with an ac minibus to Old Sukhothai (120 Baht) and Si Satchanalai (150 Baht). Food and drink is included in the price, but not the admission fees to the ruins. You can also rent bicycles from the hotel for 30 Baht. Cars can be rented for 2000 Baht / 4 hours, tuk-tuks for 150 Baht / 4 hours, motorcycles for 100 Baht / 4 hours, bicycles for 30 Baht / day, and bicycle rickshaws for 160 Baht / 6 hours across the road from the state-run bus company.

HOW TO GET THERE

Buses from BANGKOK (440 km, 6-7 hours) leave from the Northern Bus Terminal. Ac buses cost 154 Baht (departure from Sukhothai at 9:00, 11:00, and 22:00 h), non-ac buses are more frequent and cost 84 Baht.

You can catch a bus from CHIANG MAI (300 km, 5 hrs.) for 72 Baht and 100 Baht (ac buses), CHIANG RAI 83 Baht (ac buses cost 110 Baht), TAK (80 km) 19 Baht, SAWANKHALOK (37 km) 10 Baht, PHITSANULOK (58 km) 14 Baht, KAMPHAENG PHET (77 km) 19 Baht, KHON KHAEN (365 km, 6 1/2 hours), 155 Baht (ac), PHRAE (5 hours) 72 Baht, and UTTARADIT (95 km) 20 Baht. The overland buses stop directly in the city centre, local buses from Tak etc. stop north of Singhawat Road. Thanjit Tour buses stop close to the bus station, Win-Tours buses stop at the Chinawat Hotel, where Win-Tours tickets are also sold.

MAESOT

The town of Maesot lies in the frontier area of Thailand and Burma. The Menam Moei, 5 km from town, marks the border. The main source of income of this small, up-and-coming town seems to be smuggling to and from Burma - there are many shops in town that will buy gems. The few customs officials present will allow you to pass through the checkpoint. You can watch the wares being brought over to Burma by foot and boat from the river's bank. One can even walk across during the dry period. The Thai observers sitting at the riverbank (by the flag) will let you cross over without making a fuss. There are numerous stands on the Thai side of the river, selling simple arts and crafts (basket- and leather goods) and other Burmese goods (i.e. gems).

This small town sometimes makes international headlines when the Burmese Army drives guerilla troops of the *KAREN NATIONAL UNION* over the border. This is the point at which the *PAN ASIAN HIGHWAY* (Istanbul-Singapore) is meant to cross the border into Burma. Chances of this happening in the near future are rather slim. Moulmein is 100 km from here. The 86 km road from Mae Sot to Tak is the only thing that could really be called a highway up to now.

HOTELS

There are three reasonably priced hotels in town, the *FIRST HOTEL*** at the bus station, the *MAE MOEI**, and the Chinese hotel *SIAM***. The *MAE SOT HILL HOTEL***** is east of Mae Sot, on the road leading to Tak; pretty bungalows set in a large park behind a gateway resembling that of a castle.

HOW TO GET THERE

Mae Sot is in the mountains. A bus from TAK will cost you 20 Baht, a minibus 25 Baht, and a taxi 30 Baht per person. You will have to stop at several military check-points along the way. Catch a pick-up for the last 5 km to the border from the stop near Mae Sot's shopping centre (5 Baht). You will pass the airstrip 1 km out of town. There is a daily flight to CHIANG MAI (430 Baht), and to PHITSANULOK (370 Baht) via TAK (155 Baht). A road to MAE SARIANG has already been built. There is no public transportation along this route, however. Getting along by truck is quite wearisome. You can drive as far as UMPHANG in the south, from where you will be able to get to KAMPHAENG PHET.

NORTH THAILAND

The northern provinces are among the most fascinating regions in all of Thailand. The landscape here varies, the mountains are the highest in the entire country (Doi Inthanon, 2595 metres), and the valleys are wide and fertile. Most fascinating of all, however, are the many different peoples you will find here, some of whom have only been living in this region for a few decades.

Chiang Mai, Thailand's second-largest city, is the main tourist hang-out of the region and an important centre of traffic and trade. In recent years travellers have also discovered Chiang Rai in the 'high north' and Mae Hong Son in the 'wild west'. The first resort hotels and guesthouses have already been opened in the rural areas. Trekking-tourism has expanded considerably; more and more 'new' areas are discovered for organized trekking tours by the season.

The hilltribes are becoming increasingly commercialized, though this now takes a more subtle form than just a few years back. Always bear in mind that a trip to the Burmese border can be dangerous. Unaware trekkers are frequently robbed. Some tourists have even been killed. While it is true that armed bus robberies and assaults on boats travelling along the Kok river have become less common during the past few years, one should always remain aware of the fact that the increasing impoverishment of the hilltribes is making desperate; crime is on the rise in those areas particularly affected.

HILLTRIBES

Chao khao (literally mountain people) is the official term of the Thai government for the six minority groups living in northern Thailand at the present time, the *Meo, Yao, Lahu, Lisu, Akha,* and *Karen.* In the vernacular they are referred to as 'hilltribes'. This is a rather inadequate term, however, seeing as most of the hilltribes didn't live in the mountains originally, but in wide fertile valleys from which they were driven away by other, stronger peoples.

Linguistically, all of the hilltribes belong to the sino-tibetan group of languages, as do the Thai. Among the main characteristics of the languages of this group are the predominantly monosyllabic words, whose meanings are determined by the pitch and their location in the complete sentence. Although the languages of the hilltribes come from the same group, however, the languages of two tribes may be as different from one another as English is from Russian.

Most of the hilltribes employ so-called slash-and-burn agriculture, just as many Thai farmers do, too. A section of jungle - these days usually secondary forest - is roughly cut down, the remains are burnt to the ground. Whole regions are enshrouded by smoke between February and April. Many bare mountain slopes in northern Thailand are sad reminders of this rather wasteful form of agriculture. The new fields thus gained are cultivated only until they will yield no more, for the process of fertilizing fields is unknown to the hilltribes. Some of the hilltribes only leave a field uncultivated for a couple of years, in order to let it 'regenerate' for a while. These days, however, many of the fallow fields are being confiscated for the government's afforestation schemes.

Most of the hilltribes first came to Thailand as refugees. While 70-80% were actually born in Thailand, less than 20% have the Thai citizenship. The others are considered illegal immigrants. To this day whole village communities seeking refuge from the brutal, murderous, and violent Shan United Army (SUA) cross the border to northern Thailand from Shan State in Burma.

The Thai government has been striving to aid the hilltribes since 1953. The tribes are permitted to settle in the mountains, and the government is busy developing health-, agriculture-, and education programmes for them. The hilltribes are granted the right to their own languages and cultures. In practice, however, the government has to consider national and international interests first - there is simply no way the government can let the hilltribes burn down the last remains of the Thai mountain forests, regardless of the fact that slash-and-burn agriculture is a substantial part of their culture. The government has also had to prohibit the cultivation of poppy due to international pressure. The object of the aid programmes, therefore, is to get the hilltribes to give up their traditional forms of agriculture and replace them with other, more 'up-to-date' ones. Various foreign organizations, among them the Worldbank, as well as Dutch, German and Canadian groups, are more or less supporting the Thai government in its efforts. Their alleged goal, next to afforestation, is to offer the hilltribes an alternative to poppy cultivation. Coffee, rubber, nuts, fruits, and vegetables are among the *cash crops* that are being offered. None of these can compete with opium, however; poppy grows more or less on its own, even small amounts of raw opium go for a reasonably large sum of money, merchants come directly to the hilltribes, and transportation is free of charge. The hilltribes have experienced nothing but difficulties with all newly introduced cash crops. As soon as a project has been closed by the government, the hilltribes are left to their own devices; transportation no longer works out, the middle-men are only willing to pay ridiculously low prices, and on top of everything else the farmers of the lowlands start producing the same crop and selling it cheaper.

Meeting the hilltribes; if you are interested in the hilltribes, we would recommend that you first learn to tell the respective tribes apart from one another. The easiest way of doing this is by buying a couple of post-cards in Chiang Mai and trying to commit the different clothing, headgear, and jewelry of the hilltribe women to memory. Though the women do not walk around the villages wearing their most festive clothes - as on the pictures - you will find that even their everyday clothes are marked by the same characteristics. Telling the men of the various tribes apart from one another is much more difficult. Most of them wear spacious, black trousers and a western-type jacket or a shirt bought at the market.

The Meo (from the Chinese: "barbarians") call themselves Hmong ("free people"). One assumes that they originally came from Tibet and moved to China via Siberia and Mongolia several milleniums ago. Most Meo still live in southern China today, many have also settled in Vietnam, Laos, and Burma. Their first Thai settlements were not founded until the end of the 19th century. These days the approx. 65,000 tribe members make up the second-largest group of hilltribes in the country (second only to the Karen). Their villages are scattered far apart from one another in at least 13 provinces of northern and central Thailand. They are divided into sub-groups of Blue and White Meo according to the clothes worn by the women. They became infamous in the 60s and 70s, when they joined forces with the communists against the Thai Army (Red Meo). 50,000 White Meo also live in refugee camps along the border to Laos. They were on the 'wrong' side during the Vietnam war, when they lived in Laos but sympathized with the Americans.

The Yao call themselves Mien. Many of the words in their language come from Chinese. They probably originated in southern China. The first Yao came from Laos in the mid-19th century. Today, the Yao have settled in southern China, Vietnam, Laos, Burma, and northern Thailand (approx. 33,000). Here they have settled mainly in the provinces of Chiang Rai, Phayao, and Nan. A further 10,000 Yao live in refugee camps along the border with Laos.

The Yao are the only hilltribe that have an alphabet - they have adopted the Chinese one. With it, they have put their songs, legends, history, and the names of their ancestors down on paper. Sometimes fathers teach their sons how to read, sometimes a Chinese teacher is hired for the whole village. As well as the script, many Chinese customs have also been adopted by the Yao.

The Lahu: The Thais and the Shan call this tribal group Musur or Musoe. One believes that the Lahu originally came from southwestern China, possibly even Tibet, from where they gradually moved south to Burma, Laos, and Thailand over the centuries. The first Lahu settlements in Thailand were reported in 1891. Approx. 39,000 Lahu live in Thailand at the present time, most of them in the province of Chiang Rai as well as in the northern parts of the Chiang Mai and Mae Hong Son provinces.

The Lahu are divided into various groups, four of whom have settled in Thailand: Lahu Nyi (red), Lahu Na (black), as well as Lahu She Leh and Lahu Shi (yellow).

The Lisu: The Thais call the Lisu Lisaw. Linguistically, they belong to the tibeto-burmese branch of the sino-tibetan group of languages. Many words (up to 30%) have been adopted from Yunnanese.

It is thought that the Lisu originally came from southern China. The first Lisu to come to Thailand via Burma (which is the route all Lisu took) arrived in 1921. Approx. 21,000 Lisu live in Thailand at the present time. Their villages can be found in nine different provinces, most of them in the provinces of Chiang Rai and Chiang Mai as well as in the vicinity of Pai.

The Akha dislike the name the Thai people have given them, Kor or I-gor. It is thought that the Akha originally came from the highlands of Tibet, and that they entered northern Thailand via Yunnan (where most of them still live today), northern Burma, and Laos over the centuries. The first Akha are said to have settled in northern Thailand around 1900 (the Ulo-Akha). Many - predominantly Loimi-Akha - are still crossing the border from Burma on a regular basis today. Approx. 24,000 Akha live in Thailand at the present time, scattered in six provinces. Most of the villages are in the province of Chiang Rai as well as in the northern part of the Chiang Mai province.

The Karen are called Kariang or Yang by the Thai people. Their 240,000 tribe members make them the biggest hilltribe in Thailand (51% of all hilltribes). Their origin is unclear. They lived in Burma for many centuries, and they first came to Thailand during the 18th century. Mainly White Karen live in Thailand at the present time, most of them concentrated along the Burmese border from Mae Hong Son to Kanchanaburi, others scattered in several of the northern and central provinces. The Karen have been waging a bloody guerilla war against the central Burmese government for decades on the other side of the border. The conflict becomes particularly harsh during the dry season of every year. The white Karen are divided into Skaw Karen and Pwo Karen, the latter sometimes falsely labelled Red Karen.

The Lawa: Called Lua by the population of northern Thailand, the Lawa are not considered a hilltribe by the government. They were among the first inhabitants of Thailand and had settled in the river valley of the Ping river as early as in the 8th century, considerably earlier than the Thai people. They are of austro-asian origin and belong to the Mon-Khmer group. Most of them have been fully absorbed into Thai society. The approx. 13,500 who have retained their tribal identity have settled on the Bo Luang plateau between Hot and Mae Sariang as well as in the mountains southeast of Mae Hong Son. They are responsible for only very little of the destruction of the mountain forests. This is due to their intricate rotation system of cultivating rice-terraces. The rotation enables them to use the same fields over and over again.

The Lawa are animists and ancestral worshippers. They have combined their traditional belief with Buddhism, as have the Thais.

TREKKING TO THE HILLTRIBES

Most of the travellers who come to northern Thailand want to visit the hilltribe villages and experience the adventure that must surround them. Others simply want to get out of the cities and into nature.

WHEN TO GO TREKKING: November - February; the days are pleasantly warm during this period, the nights cool, the mountains cold, and there is virtually no rain at all - this is the best of all times to go trekking. March - April; this is when it gets hot (noontime temperatures 32°C - 35°C), the temperatures fall below 12°C at nights, though, and it is generally very dry and dusty - you won't have much fun trekking at this time. May - October; it may rain for 15 or even 25 days of a month during this, the rainy period. It often only rains in the evenings and at nights, though. Still, trekking tours during this period usually end up as mud fights.

HOW TO GO TREKKING: Trekking tourism has expanded considerably during the last couple of years. Dozens of travel agents and tour promoters are willing to furnish you with a tailor-made trekking experience. Increasing numbers of guesthouse are being opened in the very heart of the mountains. Indi-

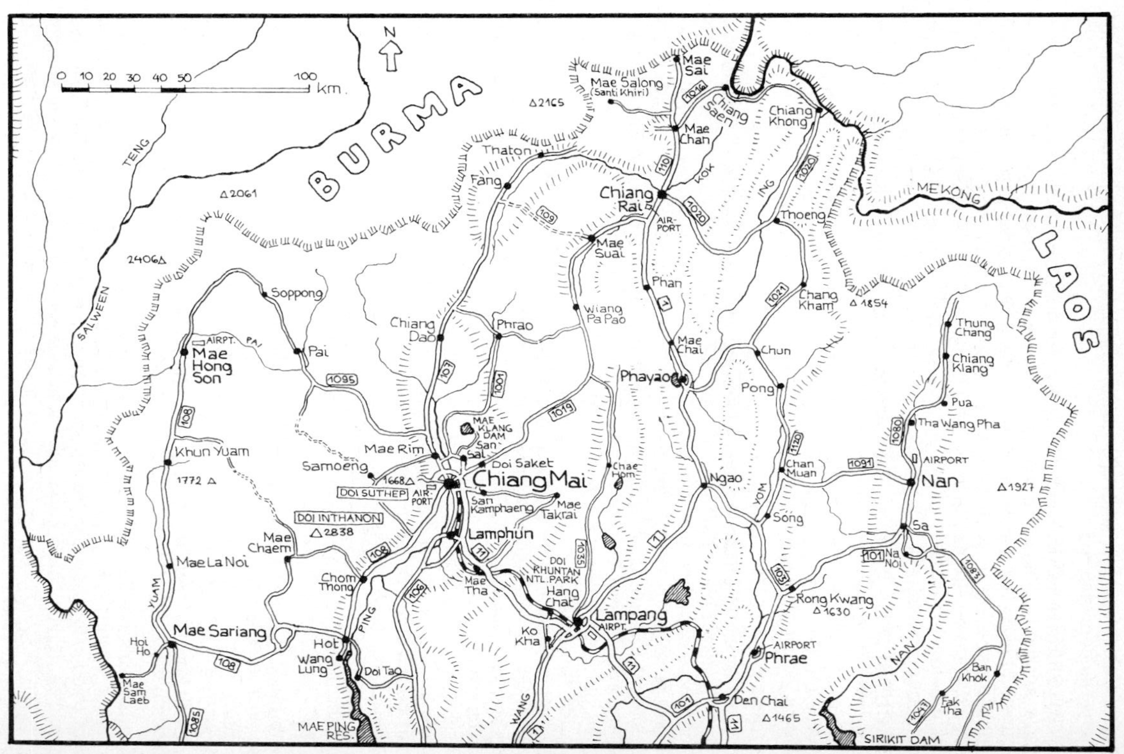
LAOS
BURMA
MEKONG
SALWEEN
TENG
YUAM
PING
WANG
YOM
NAN
ING
KOK
PAI
0 10 20 30 40 50 100 km.
N
Mae Sai
Chiang Saen
Mae Chan
Chiang Khong
Mae Salong (Santi Khiri)
Chiang Rai
AIR-PORT
Thoeng
Chang Kham
Chun
Pong
Phan
Mae Chai
Phayao
Mae Suai
Wiang Pa Pao
Thaton
Fang
Phrao
Chiang Dao
Mae Rim
Samoeng
Pai
Soppong
Mae Hong Son
AIRPT.
Khun Yuam
Mae La Noi
Mae Sariang
Mae Chaem
Chom Thong
Hot
Wang Lung
Doi Tao
MAE PING RES.
Hoi Ho
Mae Sam Laeb
Chiang Mai
AIR-PORT
Doi Saket
San Sai
MAE KLANG DAM
San Kamphaeng
Mae Takrai
Lamphun
DOI KHUNTAN NTL. PARK
Hang Chat
Ko Kha
Mae Tha
Lampang
AIRPT.
Chae Hom
Ngao
Song
Chan Muan
Phrae
AIRPORT
Den Chai
Rong Kwang
Na Noi
Sa
Nan
AIRPORT
Tha Wang Pha
Pua
Chiang Klang
Thung Chang
Ban Khok
Fak Tha
SIRIKIT DAM
DOI SUTHEP
DOI INTHANON
Δ 2838
1668 Δ
Δ 1927
Δ 1854
Δ 1630
Δ 1465
Δ 2165
Δ 2061
1772 Δ
2406 Δ
1
11
101
103
106
107
108
109
110
1001
1016
1019
1020
1021
1035
1041
1080
1083
1085
1091
1095
1120

vidual trekking (alone; without a guide) is also on the rise, regardless of the many dangers involved.

SIGHTSEEING TOUR - half or full day: Tourists are driven to villages which have adapted perfectly to sightseeing-tourism. In most cases this form of tourism is even the major source of the village's income. They have a perfect right to expect you to either buy something off them or give them money, should you wish to take their picture. If you're keen on portrait pictures take them here - the inhabitants of the more 'unspoilt' villages might feel too insecure to pose in front of a camera.

EXCURSIONS - 2-3 days: On these tours you will walk from one village to the next, along standard routes. This type of excursion is also included in most Thailand package deals. Usually one doesn't have to hike for more than a maximum of 2-3 hours daily. A boat-ride and an elephant-ride ("safari"!) are nearly always included in the price.

TREKKING TOUR - 4-5 days: Trekking tours for 4 - 10 travellers can be booked at over 40 trekking tour organizers and guesthouses in Chiang Mai. Most travellers enjoy their trip, but whether or not it turns out to be the mind-boggling experience that brochures promise depends largely on the guide. There is no point listing the organizations with the best guides at this point, seeing as the guides change frequently. Try to get information from other travellers, and if any of them had a particularly good trip, try to find out the name of their guide. It is always a bonus if your guide is a hilltribe member himself and/or speaks the languages of those hilltribes which you will be visiting. Try to estimate the amount of time you will spend hiking in advance, and bear in mind that the trip often goes steeply up and downhill, and that there is virtually no shade (seeing as the surrounding jungle has been burnt down). Have your guide explain the trip to you in detail before leaving; which villages you will be visiting, how you will be getting there, how long it will take, how long will you have to hike, what will the terrain and the weather be like, how many people can be accommodated, maximum number of people taking part in the tour, meals, how much of the necessary equipment is furnished, how much weight will one have to carry, etc. Attention: sometimes several groups are put together along the way, contrary to what your guides might have originally told you.

The trekking organizations usually furnish a small, often miserable backpack as well as one blanket per person (which will certainly not suffice during the winter). One hikes 2 - 8 hours per day and spends the night at a hilltribe village. The guide usually cooks meals from the supplies brought along. You will usually have to sleep on mats on the ground. Do not expect a toilet and don't be embarrassed to use the garden instead.

Equipment: good shoes as well as sandals, at least one change of clothing, sun-hat, water flask, argentic salt tablets to cleanse water, sun lotion and insect (mosquito) repellent, toilet paper, torch, matches, personal wash kit, and medicine. November to February: warm sleeping-bag and an insulation mat to sleep on. If you don't have one along, insist that the tour organizers furnish you with a second blanket. It can get extremely cold at nights (close to freezing point). May to mid-November: rain gear, high shoes.

Valuables: Deposit cheques, cash, travel documents in the safe of your hotel / guesthouse. Have them give you an exact receipt and take a photocopy of your passport along. (Be careful with cheque- and credit cards; they are frequently misused, and you won't notice that you've been taken advantage of until weeks later!!) The safest place to leave your valuables is in one of the safe deposit boxes of the Krung Thai Bank, Charoen Muang Road, Chiang Mai (cost: approx. 30 Baht per week).

Smoking opium: Hilltribe members know very well that many tourists come just to try opium, and they will frequently offer it. Take care; if you want to try some, start off carefully - you never know how a new drug will affect you. Remember that opium is a seriously addictive drug; heavy withdrawal symptoms have been known to occur after only one week of regular consumption. Never take opium when drunk, and above all do not mix it with any other drugs. Do not attempt to bring drugs back to Chiang Mai, let alone Europe, from the mountains - the risk is much too high. Smoking opium is illegal in Thailand. If caught, you may have to go to prison for 1 - 10 years!

Cost: 5-day/4-night tours with ten participants usually cost approx. 800 - 900 Baht per person. Add another couple of hundred Baht if a safari (elephant-ride) is included.

Trekking from different places: Good trekking tours are also organized from Chiang Rai and Mae Hong Son. Guesthouses here either organize tours themselves or will be able to tell you where to go. Tours are also organized by the guesthouses in Mae Sariang, Pai, Thaton, Mae Salong, and Mae Sai.

TREKKING WITH A PRIVATE GUIDE: You can hire a guide who speaks the hilltribe languages and will organize a tour according to your personal interests any time. This will mean paying a little more than for a group-tour, however, approx. 500 Baht per day from Chiang Mai. You will be able to hire a private guide for less than half of this sum in the smaller towns.

INDIVIDUAL TREKKING: The Thai Tourist Organization (TAT) does not recommend going trekking alone in the hilltribe territories. The region is large and quite rough, and there is no way one can guarantee tourists' safety. Be aware of the fact that you will not be able to communicate in Thai or English with the Akha or the Lisu. The standard routes are pretty safe; one can hardly lose ones way and will not run into many unexpected difficulties, especially if one brings ones own food along. It is easy to find accommodation, the hilltribes here are used to tourists and have adopted certain codes of behaviour. If you plan to hike to remote areas you should definitely be well equipped, informed, and - if possible - experienced. Most of the mountain-paths are not signposted. There are no trustworthy maps of the area. A few copies of the by now out-of-date topographical maps (with a scale of 1:250 000) as well as trekking-maps of the areas south of Fang and the Mae Kok river area are available in Chiang Mai. *WARNING: Individual trekkers have been shot in the past as well as during the 1987/88 season!*

MOTORCYCLE TREKKING: You will have the chance of covering a large area of beautiful landscape and visiting many hilltribe villages in a relatively short time when travelling by motorcycle. There are many paths suitable for motorcycles off the main roads, but only for those who are experienced in dirt-biking! The paths are frequently washed out or very narrow. They are often unfit for traffic during the rainy season. You can either rent a motorcycle with a driver, or drive yourself and take a guide along on the back. We would strongly recommend you take a good look at the map David has drawn onto his library wall, however (Ratchamanka Road Soi 2, next to the Saitum Guesthouse, Chiang Mai). This is probably the most precise existing map of the area. Avoid those regions marked as dangerous. Motorcycle-trekkers travelling on their own are still frequently shot down from their bikes in the frontier territories.

HOW TO BEHAVE IN A HILLTRIBE VILLAGE: When visiting the hill-tribes Western travellers find themselves confronted with a society and a culture almost incomprehensible to them. Thus a visit to the hilltribes is a challenge to anyone's tolerance and adaptability.

Always remember that you are a guest. Find out about customs and taboos beforehand. Once there, do not forcefully try to find out all there is to know; be satisfied with what the hilltribe members are prepared to show you of their own free will. Observe the people without making a nuisance out of yourself, and only take pictures after previously having asked for permission. You will frequently find that you will make better experiences by leaving your camera in its bag and simply listening and observing. If you do not act in an acceptable way the consequences will be particularly noticeable to those travellers visiting the village after you. The wrong kind of behaviour may even lead to a certain village no longer acting hospitably towards tourists.

CHIANG MAI

Also known as 'the rose of the north', Chiang Mai is slowly but surely developing into a modern city. The town lies in a wide, fertile valley, enclosed on the east and west by mountains 2000 metres in height.

Chiang Mai became the capital of the Lanna Thai kingdom in 1298. The city was founded by King Mengrai, a Thai-Lao prince from Chiang Saen who managed to unite several Thai tribes and extended his sphere of influence over the entire northern region of the country. He founded Chiang Rai in 1262 and made Chiang Mai the capital after having overthrown the Mon kingdom of Haripunchai (present-day Lamphun).

The Lanna Thai kingdom flourished during the 15th century. The 8th Buddhist World Council was held in Chiang Mai in 1478. Relationships which up-and-coming Ayutthaya remained strained, however, marked by competition and conflict. Lampang was conquered by the Ayutthayan forces in 1515. Lanna Thai became a vassal of Burma's mighty King Bayinnaung in 1556. With the exception of a few brief spells of independence, Chiang Mai remained under Burmese regency for the next 220 years. Not until 1775 did General Taksin manage to re-integrate the northern provinces into the new Thai kingdom. A half autonomous prince of the Lampang dynasty ruled the north until 1938, when Chiang Mai became the capital of the province.

There are many places to visit in the town's old quarter. The ground-plan of the actual old city is a perfect square, each side measuring 1500 metres in length. Parts of the former

TOWN FORTIFICATION and *MOAT* (19th century) are still preserved. The city gate on Tapae Road was not built until 1986, however, and it looks more like a cheap facade on a film set than anything else. The rather rural character of the old quarter is quite fascinating; the low, wooden buildings, set in gardens, can only be reached by way of narrow alleys. Of the many typical wats with northern-style architecture you should definitely visit

WAT PHRA SING, religious centre of the western part of the old quarter. There are beautiful murals and wood-carvings.

WAT CHIANG MAN, in the northeast of the old town, is even older. Legend has it that King Mengrai resided here while the city was being built. You will find two viharn on the temple grounds. The right hand one enshrines two of Chiang Mai's most famous Buddha statues. One is said to be over 1000 years old and to come from India, the other was made in the 7th century and belonged to a king of the Haripunchai kingdom. The power to bring rain is attributed to the two statues by the local population, and they are carried through town in a procession held annually for the Songkran festivities. The building is usually only opened to the public on Sundays and Buddhist holidays, from 9:00-17:00 h.

WAT CHEDI LUANG is said to have had a 90 metre chedi from 1454 to 1545, when it was destroyed by an earthquake. A 60 metre ruin remains. An all but disintegrated staircase leads up to a gilded Buddha statue. The shrine of the town's patron spirit, the lak muang, is to the left of the main entrance of the temple.

We would suggest taking a bicycle, a motorcycle, or a bicycle-ricksha to any of the following places, all of which are outside the old town.

WAT SUAN DOK is in the west of Suthep Road. The numerous, small, white chedis are burial sites of former rulers of Chiang Mai. The temple grounds are particularly beautiful at sunset. Continue west down the road for another 3,5 km, then turn left. After 1 km you will reach

WAT UMONG, a forest temple. The monastery, which was founded by King Mengrai, has been pretty much destroyed, however. Tablets sporting inscriptions such as *Today is better than two tomorrows* or *Do good tomorrow, says the fool - the wise man did good yesterday* are fastened to the trees.

WAT JED YOD is north of the old town, by the super-highway, in the middle of a pretty park. It was built in 1455 and modelled on the north Indian Mahabodhi temple in Bodh Gaya, the site of Buddha's Enlightenment. The

NATIONAL MUSEUM is to the west of the temple. Religious works of art from various cultural eras as well as more recent examples of Thai arts and crafts

Chiang Mai
ZOO
UNIVERSITY
DOI SUTHEP
"SUPERHIGHWAY"
HUAI KAEO
Rincome H.
RD.
Alt Heidelberg
Ch.Mai Orchid H.
YMCA Interntl. Hostel
CHOTANA RD.
CHOTANA
WAT KUTAO
STADIUM
RATTANKOSIN
BUS →Fang, Hot →Lamphun
CHANGPUAK GATE
Mithai
MANI NOPARAT
SI PHUM
SINGHARAT
WAT CHIANG MAN
RATCHAPHANIKAI
WANG KAEO RD.
PHRA POKKLAO
NIMMANHEMIN
KULAP
SUAN
MALARIA CENTER
Mabuhay R.
RATCHA-WITHI RD.
SUAN DOK GATE
INTHA-WAROROT RD.
SUTHEP RD.
WAT PHRA SING
PHRA SING RD.
RATCHDAMNOEN RD.
Mangsayirat R.
WAT SUAN DOK
WAT UMONG
JHABAN
WAT CHEDI LUANG
MUANG
CHAIYAPOOM
TAPAE GATE
MOON
RATCHAMANKA RD.
WAT MENGRAI
SAMLAN
PARK
KOTCHASAN
BUNRUANGRIT
BAMRUNGBURI RD.
CHANGLO RD.
CH.MAI GATE
BAN YEN RD.
SURIWONG
THIPANET RD.
WUALAI
NANTHARAM RD.
NTNL. THEATRE
MOUNTAIN PPL. CULTURE PROJECT
0 250 500 750 1000 m
AIRPORT
IMMIGRATION OFF.

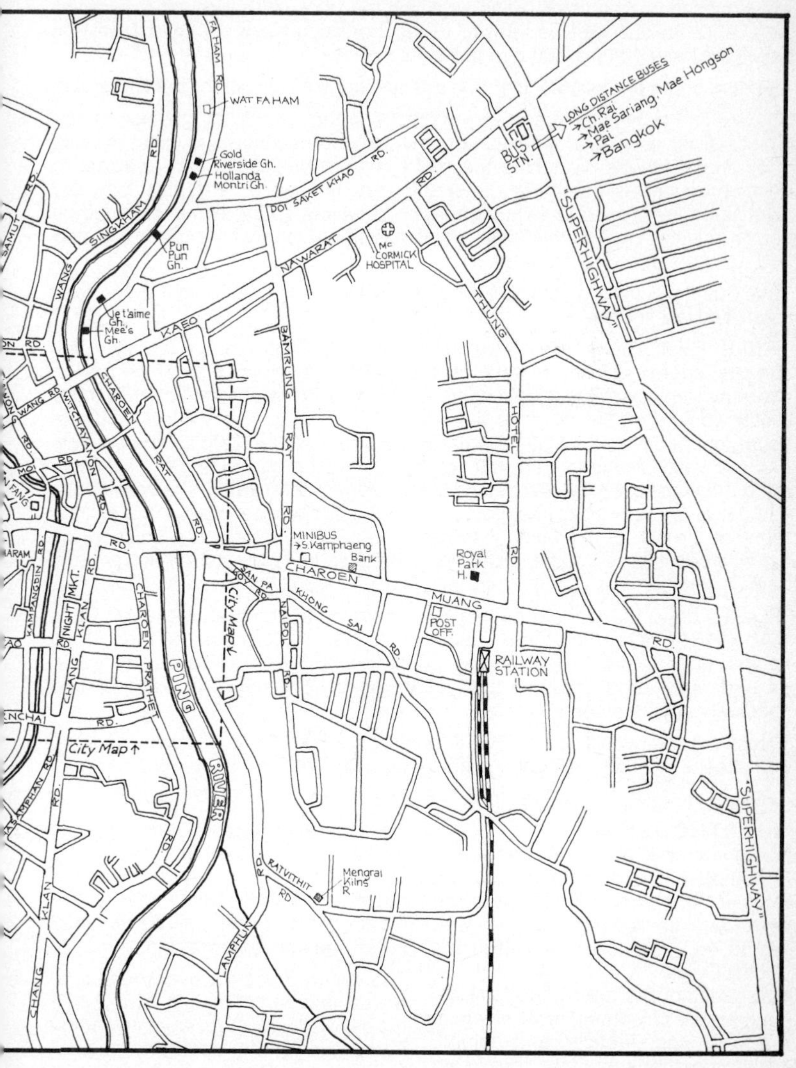
WAT FA HAM
FA HAM RD.
Gold Riverside Gh.
Hollanda Montri Gh.
DOI SAKET KHAO RD.
BUS STN.
LONG DISTANCE BUSES
→Ch. Rai
→Mae Sariang, Mae Hongson
→Pai
→Bangkok
"SUPERHIGHWAY"
Pun Pun Gh.
Je t'aime Gh.
Mee's Gh.
Mc CORMICK HOSPITAL
NAWARAT
KAEO
BAMRUNG RAT RD.
THUNG HOTEL RD.
WANG SINGKHAM RD.
WITCHAYANON RD.
CHAROEN RAT RD.
MINIBUS →S. Kamphaeng
Bank
Royal Park H.
CHAROEN MUANG RD.
SAN PA KOI RD.
KHONG SAI RD.
NAIPOL RD.
POST OFF.
RAILWAY STATION
City Map
NIGHT MKT.
CHANG KLAN RD.
CHAROEN PRATHET
PING RIVER
City Map
Mengrai Kilns R
RATVITHIT RD.
LAMPHUN RD.
"SUPERHIGHWAY"

are exhibited on two floors. Kilns, in which the famous Thai celadon ceramics were once baked, can be viewed in the front courtyard. Opened Mon-Sun 9:00-12:00 and 13:00-16:00 h, admission 2 Baht.

The area south of *CHIANG MAI GATE* is another nice district to walk around in.

You will find a number of artisan workshops in the vicinity, all of which manufacture silver jewelry, wood carvings, ceramics, or lacquerware using the old, traditional methods. Watching the black lacquer bottles, boxes, and tablets being produced is particularly interesting. A bamboo fibre netting to which layer upon layer of black lacquer is applied makes up the basis for all of the above objects. Each of the layers of lacquer is polished with a mixture of clay and ashes (see also *Shopping).*

Take bus no. 3 towards the zoo. The *UNIVERSITY* is 5 km from the centre of town. You will find the

TRIBAL RESEARCH CENTER in building no. 15, which is at the far end of the campus, approx. 1.5 km from the main entrance. (A ground plan of the university is available in the first building to the left, the *Office of the Rector*). A study group working on the hilltribes has opened a small and very interesting museum, opened Mon-Fri 8:30-16:30 h, closed from 12:00-13:00 h. The employees are often unable to give you proper information concerning the hilltribes; go to the small but very interesting library (Mon-Fri 9:00-16:00 h) if you wish to find out more. A number of good books on the subject are listed in the bibliography at the end of this book. A rather short but very informative brochure on the hilltribes can be bought for 35 Baht. Trekking tours are not organized from here.

Continue down the road for another 600 metres and you'll reach the *BOTANICAL GARDENS* (Arboretum), opened from 8:30-16:30 hours, and the *ZOO,* opened daily from 8:00-17:00 hours, admission 10 Baht. The zoo is located on an unusually large and very pretty area on a hill slope. The open-air bird sanctuary covers an entire valley.

Across the road you'll find a *THAI-GERMAN DAIRY FARM* stall. Milk, yoghurt, and cheese (100 g for 10 Baht) is sold from 8:00-17:00 h.

GUESTHOUSES

There are well over 100 hotels and guesthouses of all standards and rates in town. You will be given an up-to-date list of guesthouses (who pay to be entered on the list) in the Tourist Office.

The guesthouses are run by families, young men, or women, most of whom are very kind, friendly, and helpful. Most guesthouses have their own trekking service or will at least be able to tell you how to go about organizing a trekking tour. Some rent out bicycles, a few free of charge. The cheaper places usually do not have hot water. Season December to February, better prices can be obtained out of season by bargaining.

The centre of the traveller-scene is in the eastern part of the old town, within the city walls. Most restaurants can be found along the southern part of Moon Muang Road; guesthouses are in the alleys beyond.

For those arriving at Tapae Gate with a town bus (all four lines stop here), it is not far to the first guesthouse;

*GEMINI HOUSE**, 22 Ratchdamnoen Road, tel 236355. Thai-style house with a garden restaurant, very noisy.

*KAMOL GH**, 1 Ratchdamnoen Road Soi 2, in the opposite alley. Wooden Thai-style building and bungalows set in a pleasant garden.

Walk south down Moon Muang Road from Tapae Gate, and you will find the entrance to the

*NEW THAI GERMAN GH**, 33/1 Moon Muang Road, behind Oasis Bar. The place has a bad reputation. The new

*SAI TUM GH**, 21 Moon Muang Road = Ratchamanka Road, Soi 2, tel 211575, flat wooden buildings built upon stilts, dormitory. Quite peaceful. Right next door you'll find

*T. N. GUEST HOUSE**, 13 Ratchamanka Road Soi 2; quiet. The

*SOMWHUNG GH**, 2 Ratchamanka Road Soi 2 is opposite. Narrow, long, brick building. Cheaper rooms are available in wooden shack next door.

Cross Ratchamanka Road by the canal and go into the next alley. The

*TOY HOUSE**, 45/1 Moon Muang Road Soi 2, is a new building. No garden. Their rooms on the upper floors are well lit and pleasant.

K. WIN HOUSING, 25 Moon Muang Road Soi 2, is directly opposite. New, two-storey building with sparsely furnished rooms. To the left you'll find

*TOP NORTH GH**-****, 15 Moon Muang Road, Soi 2, tel 213900. Very popular, clean. Nice rooms with bathroom and hot water. Multi-storey, concrete building, pretty little garden, bamboo restaurant, peaceful location. Just beyond is

*DIOR HOUSE**, 48/4 Moon Muang Road, Soi 2, tel 236106, peacefully located brick building. Restaurant.

*KENT G.H.**, 5 Ratchamanka Road, Soi 1, tel 217578, new, peacefully located brick building, small garden and roof terrace, dormitory, run by English people. The

*CHIANG MAI YOUTH HOSTEL**, 31 Prapokklao Road Soi 3, tel 212863, is nearby. Rooms or dormitory available, good place for information, extremely peaceful, reduced rates for people with an International Youth Hostel Card. Nearby you will find

*MANIT GH**, 55 Ratchapakinai Road, tel 214352. Wooden house with an adjoining building, large garden.

Old quarter, northeastern district

There are a number of older guesthouses in this area, some of them with a rather negative image. Of the better ones, we would recommend:

*ORCHID GH**, 22 Moon Muang Road, Soi 6, tel 236357 - old wooden building with very nice, large rooms. The

*NUMBER ONE GH**, 27 Moon Muang Road, Soi 7, all rooms have a shower and toilet. The

*SRI PHUM**, 27 Moon Muang Road, Soi 8, small, quiet building, bathroom with hot water. You will find the

*BAN RAI**, Wiang Kaeo Road, next to Wat Chiang Man. The popular, Ban Rai Steakhouse is in the garden.

Outside the eastern city wall

Walk out of the old town through Tapae Gate, then head north for 300 metres. Turn right at the sign. After 100 metres you will reach

*LEK HOUSE**, 22 Chaiyapoom Road. Brick house with a large garden and a barracks-style adjoining building. Unstrained atmosphere, many French guests. The place is run by Yves.

*CHANG MOI GH**, 29 Chang Moi Kao Road, small, clean rooms, peaceful location. Nearby,

*RAMA HOUSE**, clean rooms, warm community showers. The place is run by a friendly couple.

*TIMES SQUARE GH***, 2/10 Tapae Road Soi 6, tel 232448, new, hotel-style building, rooftop restaurant, bathrooms with warm water, run by French people.

*LEK GUEST HOUSE**, 53 Kotchasan Road. No relation to the Lek House run by Yves.

*GARDEN HOUSE**, 2 Kotchasan Rd. Old Thai-style building, rural atmosphere, whole wheat bread.

On the west bank of the river

There are three well known guesthouses between Charoen Prathet Road - a large, noisy road with much traffic - and the river:

*GALARE GH****, 7-7/1 Charoen Prathet Road, tel 233885. New Thai-style building, very comfortable, some of the rooms ac

CHUMPOL GH-***, 89 Charoen Prathet Road, tel 234526. Rather noisy, boring looking building, reasonably cheap. The garden of the

*CHIENGMAI GH** (ac ***)*, 91 Charoen Prathet Road, tel 236501, is right next door. This is one of the first guesthouses ever to have been opened in the city. The new adjoining buildings make it look pretty silly.

On the east bank of the river

Start on the eastern side of Nawarat Bridge (buses 1 and 4). Head south for 500 metres, then turn left into a signposted alley. You will find the

*RACHA GH** 4/11 Lamphun Road Soi 2, tel 244103. Two-storey, brick building, burglar proof, hot showers; lounge and restaurant, pleasant, secluded atmosphere.

*RIVERSIDE GH**, 63 Charoenrat Road, tel 241896. Multi-storey, brick building, small terrace, snack-bar.

Charoenrat Road continues north from Nakhon Ping Bridge (buses 1 and 3). This narrow, twisty road can be quite dangerous for pedestrians and cyclists. There are a couple of guesthouses here, right by the river.

*MEE'S GH**, 193/1 Charoenrat Road, tel 243534 solid building, peaceful.

*JE T'AIME GH**, 247/9 Charoenrat Road, tel 241912. Do not be misled by the name. This is a prim and proper guesthouse, but the woman in charge sometimes has terrible temper tantrums.

*PUN PUN GH**, 321 Charoenrat Road, tel 243362; old, two-storey building, gloomy rooms, simple bungalows down by the river. Beds with mosquito nets, restaurant serving health food. Bicycles are free.

*HOLLANDA MONTRI GH***, 365 Charoenrat Road, tel 242450; clean rooms with bathroom and hot water. The place is run by Dutch people, You can use the pool of the Rincome Hotel for 20 Baht .

*GOLD RIVERSIDE**, 381 Charoenrat Road, tel 244550; brick bungalows with good beds in a large, wonderfully uncared-for garden with many trees. Friendly family, very peaceful.

Towards Doi Suthep

There are many hotels but hardly any guesthouses on Huay Kaeo Road (towards Doi Suthep).

*YMCA INTERNATIONAL HOSTEL** (ac***),* 24 Mengrai Rasmi Road, tel 221819; modern building in a quiet alley, a good place to get to know young Thais; cafeteria, small shop, and library.

HOTELS

Next to the guesthouses, there are also over 50 hotels in town charging various rates. You will definitely get your money's worth at the

*A&P HOTEL**,* (ac***), 41 Moon Muang Road, tel 212309; five-storey concrete building, well away from the main road, much greenery, nice rooms, and a good view from the top. Hot water available in the mornings and evenings.

*ANODARD HOTEL**** (ac****), 57 Ratchamanka Road, tel 211055; concrete block with nice rooms and a public pool (18 Baht admission, opened 9:00-21:00 h).

*PRINCE*****,* 3 Tai Wang Road, tel 236744; modern, clean, with a pub and pool.

*ROYAL PARK*****,* 471 Charoen Muang Road, tel 242755, opposite the railway station in a large park. New, five-storey building with modern interior architecture, bungalows, pool.

*MONTRI*** (ac***) corner of Ratchdamnoen / Moon Muang Road, tel 211070; clean, hot shower, good food (including Thai) is served downstairs at the Peacock Pizzeria.

*NEW CHIANG MAI*** (ac***), 22 Chaiyapoom Road, tel 236561; clean, large rooms, central location.

*RIVER VIEW LODGE*****,* 25 Soi 2, Charoen Prathet Road, tel 251110; antique-studded hotel, which also has a restored teak-house, garden, and restaurant.

Now for a couple of the luxury hotels that package deal tourists usually get sent to. (Double rooms cost between 1000 and 5000 Baht).

CHIANG MAI ORCHID, tel 222099, first class hotel of international standards, comfortable ac-rooms, pool.

The following four can be found on Chang Klan Road, near the night market:*SURIWONGSE,* tel 236789, *CHIANG INN,* tel 235655, and *DUSIT INN,* tel 251033.

FOOD

"Steak with baked potatoes and veggies" (about 50 Baht) has been the traveller-hit for the last couple of seasons. If this is your scene, go to the *BAN RAI STEAK HOUSE,* Wiang Kaeo Road, west of Phra Pokklao Road, or to the *LEK HOUSE,* 22 Chaiyapoom Rd. This is also a good place for a nice breakfast with whole wheat bread, as is the *GARDEN HOUSE,* Kotchasan Road, Soi 2.

The *PEACOCK,* Moon Muang Road by Tapae Gate, serves the best, indeed the only good pizza in town (35 Baht for a big helping).

The best fruit juices and shakes are served at *DARET'S,* Moon Muang Road, an ancient, ugly, and very noisy traveller hang-out. The food here is not too good, though, nor can we vouch for the food which is served at the new branch on Chaiyapoom Road.

If you wish to eat cheaply, go to the market or to the foodstalls on Chaiyapoom Road, north of Lek House (good noodles). There are also many foodstalls at the *ANUSARN MARKET,* in a side-alley southeast of the night market.

WANGKUNG RENA, an excellent, cheap seafood-restaurant, is nearby. The many restaurants on Chang Klan Road (southern end of the night market) are particularly well-visited in the evenings. Thai, Chinese, and seafood is served.

Indian and Pakistani food is served opposite, at the *AL SHIRAZ,* 123 Chang Klan Road.

The *THAI-DANISH DAIRY FARM* on the southern part of Moon Muang Road offers dairy products and homemade cakes.

Good northern Thai food is served at the *AROON RAI,* Kotchasan Road, approx. 500 m south of Tapae Gate.

Good northeastern Thai food and fine, cheap chicken (grilled chicken with honey - 34 Baht a piece) is served at the *HONEY BARBEQUE CHICKEN* next to the Porn Ping Hotel, Charoen Prathet Road.

Good Thai food is also served across the road at the *RUENTHAI,* as well as at the *RIVERSIDE,* Charoenrat Road, 200 metres north of Nawarat Bridge, above the river - live music is performed in the bar in the evening.

You can put together your very own Thai meal at any of the markets between 16:00 and 17:00 h (e.g. Chiang Mai Gate). Buy the different ingredients at the different stands. Beware of red dishes, though - they are usually very hot. Just ask: "Prik mai?", then wait for an answer. "Mai prik!" = "Not hot!"

You will find more restaurants and bars along the road leading to the university, e.g. *PIM,* where good, middle-sized steaks cost 35 Baht.

Excellent Indian and Thai vegetarian food is served at the *WHOLE EARTH RESTAURANT,* Sri Dornchai Road near Chang Klan Road, opened from 11:00 - 14:00 h and from 18:00 h. The restaurant is set in a nice garden and run by people who are into transcendental meditation - good atmosphere, classical Thai- and guitar music is performed live in the evenings, drinks are expensive. There is another vegetarian restaurant, the *MANGSAV IRAT,* approx. 800 metres outside of the Suan Dok Gate (the western gate). Good Lassi is served, about 8 Baht per meal.

SHOPPING

Chiang Mai is a veritable shopping paradise for those in love with northern Thai arts and crafts as well as antiques. (Watch out for the export-rules!) When buying opium pipes from the Meo, make sure that they haven't been used - you may have big trouble with the customs officials back home if they have.

A large ***NIGHT MARKET*** is held daily between 18:00 and 22:00 h (sometimes during the daytime, too) on several floors of a large building (as well as in the cellar and on the surrounding pavements of Chang Klan Road). The building was built just for this purpose. While there isn't much of an oriental atmosphere, the shopping is good, especially for clothing, jewelry, hilltribe arts and crafts, genuine as well as 'new' antiques, imitation designer ware (Lacoste etc.), and cassette tapes. Lacquerware, silk, and umbrellas are also pretty cheap. Next to the many hilltribe stands there are also stands run by business-people who have shops offering a larger variety of wares in town. Definitely try to bargain!!

Most of the shops selling ***ARTS & CRAFTS*** and ***ANTIQUES*** can be

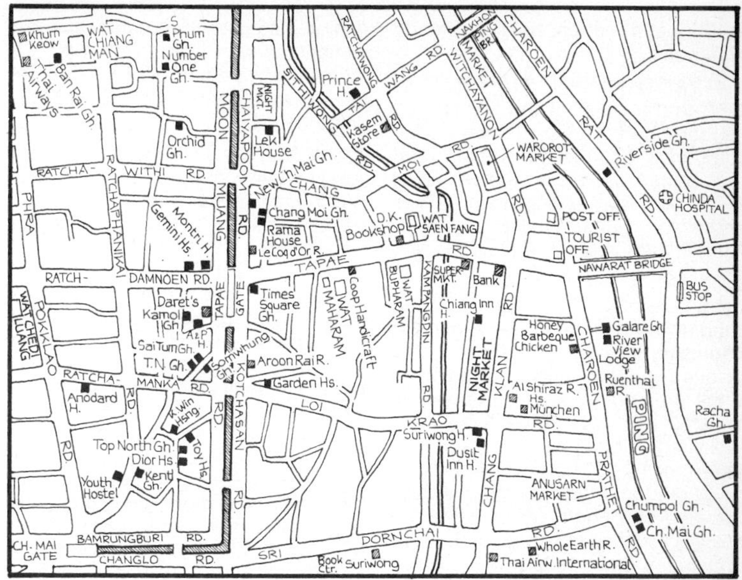

found on Tapae Road. As at the night market, bargaining is an absolute must. Seeing as the town isn't all that large, you can spend a couple of days trying to get a better price; simply drop in every now and then and see if it's gone down - you're almost certain to get what you want in the end.

Nice, cheap, genuine hilltribe wickerwork can be bought at COOP HANDICRAFT, two doors next to the Thai Farmers Bank on Tapae Road (shop-signs in Thai only). The hilltribes receive a share of the profits.

Many merchants sell silverware on Wulai Road. You can also buy nice silver in a couple of shops along the road leading to San Kamphaeng. Wood-carvings are manufactured, exhibited, and sold in the wooden building complex of Banyen, 500 metres south of the entrance of town.

MENGRAI KILNS, 31/1 Ratuthit Road, 2 km east of Nawarat Bridge, sells excellent ***THAI CELADON.*** The shop is run by a New Zealander and has a range of pieces superior to that of the SIAM CELADON in San Kamphaeng.

You will find the ***WAROROT MARKET*** north of Tapae Road, by Wichayanon Road. Clothing, food, and household goods are sold at this market, which is mainly patronized by the local population.

Fish, meat, fruit, and vegetables are sold at the ***SOMPHET MARKET*** along the northern end of Moon Muang Road. The market is also known as the 'civil servant's market', as it doesn't open until the early afternoon.

The TANTRAPHAN ***SUPERMARKET***, in the cellar of the building on the corner of Tapae / Chang Klan Road, sells good whole wheat bread and buns, as does the KASEM STORE on Ratchawong Road. This is where the guesthouses buy their 'home-made-bread' and their cheese.

Good ***MAPS AND BOOKS*** are sold at the D.K. BOOKSTORE, 234 Tapae Road. If you plan to go trekking in the mountains, this is the place to come for good trekking maps (so far maps of the area south of Fang as well as the Mae Kok River area have been published). Topographical maps with a scale of 1 : 250 000 (which are now out of print and becoming pretty rare) can also be bought. We would definitely recommend buying *Nancy Chandler's Chiang Mai Map,* which includes the entire city area as well as all bus routes and excursions out of town. All good maps are also available at the TRAVELLER LIBRARY (see below). If you can't find what you're looking for at D.K.'s , try the SURIWONG BOOK CENTRE, Si Dornchai Road (the employees speak very little English, though). There is another bookshop on Chang Klan Road.

Old army surplus ***JUNGLE BOOTS*** as well as backpacks etc. can be bought at MITHAI'S, Mani Noparat Road, east of Fang Road.

GENERAL INFORMATION

TOURIST INFORMATION - you will find the TAT Office on Praisani Road, corner of Tapae Road, tel 235334. Lists of the departure times of all public transportation as well as the prices of all the official tour companies, hotels, and guesthouses are sometimes available. You will also find the Tourist Police here, tel 232508 and 222977, daily from 6:00-24:00 hours.

TRAVELLER LIBRARY - David's library service can be found on 21/1 Ratchamanka Road Soi 2, 15 metres from Moon Muang Road, right next to the entrance of the Sai Tum Guest House. David has a gigantic map of northern Thailand drawn onto the wall, which he researched on his own. Maybe the map is even being published and sold by now. He will be able to explain even the most unusual routes to you with the aid of photographs - an absolute MUST for dirt bikers planning to go off the road. You can also read books about Thailand here, borrow novels, buy maps, and drink soft-drinks. Open Mon-Sat 8:00-17:00 h.

POST OFFICE - The General Post office is on Charoen Muang Road, just before the railway station. All poste restante mail addressed to here is entered in a book. You will find another post office on Praisani Road, 100 metres beyond the TAT Office. The post offices are open from 8:30-12:00 and 13:00-16:30 h Mon-Fri, from 9:00-12:00 h on Sat, Sun, and holidays. The telegram counter, tel 241056, is open 24.hours daily.

LONG DISTANCE CALLS - The counter at the GPO offers a 24 hour service. You can also call home from the INTERNATIONAL TELEPHONE SERVICE, 44 Sri Dornchai Road, between 9:00 and 22:30 h. The post office at the airport offers telegram and international telephone services between 8:30 and 16.30 h.

IMMIGRATION - on the road leading to the airport, tel 213510.

BANKS - There are several banks on Tapae Road. The Exchange Service of the Krung Thai Bank, north of the night market, is open from 8:00-20:00 h daily. The Charoen Muang Road branch now also offers safe deposit boxes for tourists for 30 Baht a week.

MEDICAL AID - McCORMICK HOSPITAL, Kaeo Nawarat Road, tel 241107, bus no. 3. The outpatient department's consultation hours are from 13:00-20:00 h, Mon-Fri. Call before going (241311). CHINDA HOSPITAL, Charoenrat Road, shortly behind Nawarat Bridge. LANNA HOSPITAL, by the super-highway, tel 211037-42 (private hospital).

Up-to-date information concerning MALARIA is available at the Malaria Center, 18 Boonruangrit, tel 221529 (beyond the western gate, 300 metres to the right, then turn left).

LAUNDRIES - You can do the 'dirty work' for just a few Baht at various laundries in town (10 pieces approx. 25 Baht). Simply ask for the nearest one at your guesthouse. A load will cost you 20 Baht at JIARANAI LAUNDRY, 178 Chang Moi Road, a dryer costs 15 Baht - open daily from 8:00-20:00 h.

SWIMMING - there is a clean, public swimming pool in the old section of town, at the ANODARD HOTEL, 57 Ratchamanka Road, tel 211055 (18 Baht, 9:00-21:00 h).

TRANSPORT IN CHIANG MAI

There are four different ***BUS LINES*** that run through town. A ride on any of the lines costs 2 Baht (some tourists get taken for a ride for 5 Baht). ***SONGTHAEW*** (motor-samlor) cost 5 Baht per person, ***TUK-TUKS*** are at least 10 Baht per vehicle. ***RICKSHA*** drivers usually ask for outrageous sums of money, the standard rate for a medium-length ride is 10 Baht.

MOTORCYCLES are a wonderful way of getting about in the north - good roads, safe forest and country lanes, little traffic outside of the towns, and a pleasant climate. You will be able to rent them at the shops on the southern end of Moon Muang Road, at the guesthouses, and in the vicinity of the night market (many Enduros for hire). The bikes are usually in pretty good condition, but give them a thorough check anyway, and make sure that the license plate is well fastened. The kilometre indicator should be in working condition, too. They usually cost between 100 and 200 Baht a day, if you want to rent one for a longer period of time you might get away with 80 Baht a day. One is usually not asked to show a driving license. Unfortunately, insurance is not even offered - you will always be the one responsible in case of an accident!

BICYCLES: The shops on the southern end of Moon Muang Road rent out bikes for approx. 20 Baht a day, as do some of the guesthouses. They are ideal for getting around the old section of town and the country roads that surround the city (little traffic here). Beware of the main roads in town, however, as well as the arterial roads leading south, east, and west, which are crowded and dangerous.

RENTING CARS - The standard rates are 450 to 550 Baht per day. Make sure that the car is in good, working condition before renting it - many of the smaller firms try to rent out absolute wrecks.

HERTZ, Chiang Inn Hotel, 100 Chang Klan Road, tel 235655. AVIS, Huay

Kaeo Road (opposite the Chiang Mai Orchid), tel 222013. CHIANG MAI MUL TOUR, 271 Moon Muang Road, tel 233809. JONG JAROEN TOUR, 52/2 Sri Dornchai Road, tel 236588. PHAYATEWAN TOUR, 175/12 Pra Pokklao Road, tel 222086.

LEAVING CHIANG MAI

BY PLANE

The airport is in the southwest of town and can be reached by songthaew for 30 - 40 Baht. THAI INTERNATIONAL: Chang Klan Road, tel 234150. THAI AIRWAYS: 240 Phra Pokklao Road, near Ban Rai, tel 211044-6, opened from 7:30-17:00 h daily, flies to the following places: BANGKOK daily 1275 Baht, CHIANG RAI daily 300 Baht, NAN and PHRAE 5 times weekly for 380 Baht and 280 Baht, PHITSANULOK daily 505 Baht, MAE HONGSON 2-3 times daily 310 Baht, MAE SOT and TAK 4 times weekly for 430 Baht and 415 Baht, KHON KAEN Fri and Sun 1780 Baht, SURAT THANI via Bangkok daily 2260 Baht, PHUKET 2400 Baht, and HAT YAI 2580 Baht.

BY TRAIN

The railway station is in the very east of town on Charoen Muang Road. Buses 1 and 4 stop here, bus 3 ends here.

There are three direct daily trains to BANGKOK. Two express trains at 16:50 h (arrival 6:25 h) and 18:30 h (arrival 7:35 h) and one Rapid Train at 15:20 h (only 2nd class), arrival 5:45 h.

Trains from Bangkok arrive in town at 6:35, 7:40, and 8:40 h.

SAMPLE PRICES: 537 Baht (1st class), 255 Baht (2nd class), 121 Baht (3rd class). Several extra charges are added to the price - express train 30 Baht, Rapid Train 20 Baht, 2nd class sleeper 70-100 Baht, ac 80 Baht.

BY BUS

The central bus station for all destinations outside of the province as well as CHIANG RAI, MAE HONG SON, MAE SARIANG, PAI, LAMPANG, and NAN is at the super highway by Kaeo Nawarat Road, tel 242664 (buses 3 and 4; tuk-tuk from the old quarter approx. 20 Baht).

If you want to go to THATON, FANG, LAMPHUN, or HOT, you need to go to the Chang Puak bus station on Chotana Road, 211586 (500 metres beyond the north gate). Buses to PA SANG, LAMPHUN, and some of the ones to CHIANG RAI and LAMPANG also stop at Nawarat Bridge (Charoen Muang Road / Lampoon Road). Buses to CHOM THONG and HOT stop at the Chiang Mai Gate (south gate).

To BANGKOK: ac bus no. 18 (orange) approx. every hour between 6:00 and 21:00 h for 133 Baht, 10 hours; Super ac bus no. 18 (blue) at 9:30 and 10:00 h as well as 7 times between 19:15 and 21:30 h for 242 Baht, 8 hrs.), the ac bus also stops in TAK (42 Baht, 4 hrs.) and in KAMPHAENG PHET (70 Baht, 5 hrs.). The large, private ac buses to BANGKOK leave from the respective company offices and from the Anusarn Shopping Centre near the night market (cost: 150-280 Baht). Some guesthouses sell tickets with no extra charge - sometimes the buses will even come and pick you up for free.

To CHIANG RAI: direct with bus no. 166 (green) every half hour between 6:00 and 17:30 h for 47 Baht, 3 1/2 hrs. (ac 66 Baht, 3 hrs., departures at 8:00, 12:00, and 16:45 h; super ac buses cost 85 Baht, 3 hrs.). To CHI-

ANG RAI via LAMPANG (25 Baht, 1 1/2 hrs.): bus no. 148 (green) every half hour between 5:30 and 16:00 h for 66 Baht, 5 hrs.

To MAE HONG SON via MAE SARIANG (50 Baht, 4 hrs.): bus no. 170 (orange) at 6:30, 8:00, and 11:00 h. There is also a night bus at 20:00 and 21:00 h for 97 Baht, 9 hrs. (the buses departing at 13:00 and 15:00 h only go as far as MAE SARIANG).

To PAI: 7:00, 8:30, 11:00, and 14:00 h for 50 Baht, 4 hrs. Once there catch a pick-up to MAE HONG SON at 14:00 h or at 7:30 or 10:30 h the next day (50 Baht, 4 hrs. - dusty!); ac buses to MAE HONG SON cost 148 Baht.

To SUKHOTHAI: bus no. 155 (orange) at 7:00 and 15:00 h for 72 Baht, 5 hrs. (ac buses at 10:00 and 12:00 h for 100 Baht, 5 hrs.). On to PHITSANULOK from SUKHOTHAI: 6 hrs., 82 Baht, ac buses 117 Baht. Buses to PHITSANULOK every 3 hours from 9:00 h, 67 Baht, 5 hrs.

To NAN: bus no. 169 (orange) every three hours from 8:00 h for 80 Baht, 6 hrs. (ac buses 100 Baht, 5 hrs.). The non-ac bus also stops in PHRAE, 49 Baht, 3 hrs.

To THATON: bus no. 1231 at 6:00, 7:20, 9:00, and 11:30 h for 37 Baht, 4 hrs. (you will reach the CHIANG RAI-bound boats on the Kok river in time with the first two buses).

To FANG: bus no. 1231 every half hour between 6:00 and 17:30 h for 32 Baht. From here you can catch a minibus to THATON for 7 Baht, 1 hour; to MAE SAI 60 Baht.

To LAMPHUN: bus no. 181 (blue) and 182 (white) every fifteen minutes between 6:00 and 18:00 h for 6 Baht, 30 minutes. From here its another 45 minutes to PA SANG, 10 Baht.

You have a choice if you're heading to the northeast; to KORAT (NAKHON RATCHASIMA): bus no. 635 (orange) at 4:30, 6:30, 10:00, and 14:30 h for 145 Baht, 11 hrs. (ac buses leave at 8:00, 17:00, 18:30, and 20:00 h for 262 Baht, 12 hrs.). To KHON KAEN: bus no. 175 (orange) 5 times between 5:00 and 11:00 h, 153 Baht, 12 hrs. (ac buses at 8:00 and 18:10 h for 214 Baht, Super ac buses at 19:00 and 20:00 h, 275 Baht). To LOEI: bus no. 636 (orange) at 7:30, 17:30, and 19:00 h for 109 Baht, 9 hrs. (ac bus at 20:30 h for 195 Baht). From here you can continue on to UDON THANI for 135 Baht, 11 hours (ac buses 242 Baht).

DAY TRIPS FROM CHIANG MAI

BOR SANG/ SAN KAMPHAENG

Minibuses to San Kamphaeng, 13 km southeast of town, leave regularly from the corner of Charoen Muang Road / Bamrung Rat Road. They cost 5 Baht. Buses to Bor Sang, 4 km in front of San Kamphaeng, cost 2 Baht. 4 hours in a tuk-tuk shouldn't cost you more than 80 Baht.

Many workshops that make and sell arts and crafts have been opened up along the road leading to BOR SANG during the last couple of years; lacquerware, silver, wood-carvings, silk, and semi-precious stones are for sale. Watching the men and women at their meticulous work can be quite fascinating. You will be able to count on a large discount if you're shopping without a commission-hungry 'helper', i.e. a taxi driver or a local guide. The smaller, non-ac shops are usually the cheapest of all. Find out about the standard prices at the Chiang Mai night market beforehand.

Hand-made paper and silk umbrellas are manufactured in the workshops of BOR SANG. You can choose the pattern and material you like best from a catalogue, and for a small additional charge your souvenir will be sent directly home (50 Baht additional charge on the standard postal rate - packages to Europe may weigh up to 20 kg).

Cotton and silk materials, in part still woven on the traditional looms, are produced in SAN KAMPHAENG. You can watch the traditional process of work at the touristy but nevertheless interesting Shinawatra workshop, the largest workshop in the area, 73/5 Mae-on Road. A weaver earns approx. 9 Baht per metre and usually manages to weave about 10 metres a day. The silk materials are characterized by typical geometrical designs and bright colours. Silk and cotton materials (over-expensive!) are offered for sale here as well as along the main road.

WAT DOI SUTHEP

This wat is 16 km northwest of town. You can get there by taking a minibus from Mani Noparat Road by the northern, White Elephant Gate, or by taking bus no. 3 to the final stop (the zoo) and then changing onto a minibus (departures every 15 minutes until 17:00 h - 30 Baht up, 20 Baht down). A taxi will cost you approx. 200 Baht there and back. The temple is closed to the general public after 16:30 h.

You can reach WAT DOI SUTHEP (at an altitude of 1080 metres) by climbing the 290 steps of the staircase. A cable car service allows even the weary and ill to visit the temple (5 Baht).

A winter residence of the King, the PHU PING PALACE with its beautiful gardens, is further up the road, 5 km above the wat (minibus from the wat 10-15 Baht). The palace is only opened to the general public from Fri-Sun, and even then only as long as no member of the Royal Family is staying there at the time. Both the wat and the palace are situated on the slopes of the 1690 metre DOI PUI. You can climb this mountain if you wish. You will reach the summit after an exhausting 3-hours hike from Wat Doi Suthep. Start early!

The unpaved forest path left of the palace leads to DOI PUI, a Meo village. Don't feel that going here is an absolute must, however; everything is very touristy, and the village is included in most of the sightseeing tours offered by the Chiang Mai trekking organizations. The clever Meo are mainly interested in your money.

LAMPHUN

Buses from Chiang Mai, 26 km further north, leave for Lamphun every 30 minutes from Lamphun Road near Nawarat Bridge (6 Baht). The first part of the trip from Chiang Mai will take you down a beautiful, rather narrow, tree-lined road. Lamphun is Thailand's oldest preserved town. The former capital of the Haripunchai Kingdom was founded in 660 A.D. Queen Chama Devi, who is still highly honoured to this very day, was the first ruler of the city. Lamphun wasn't

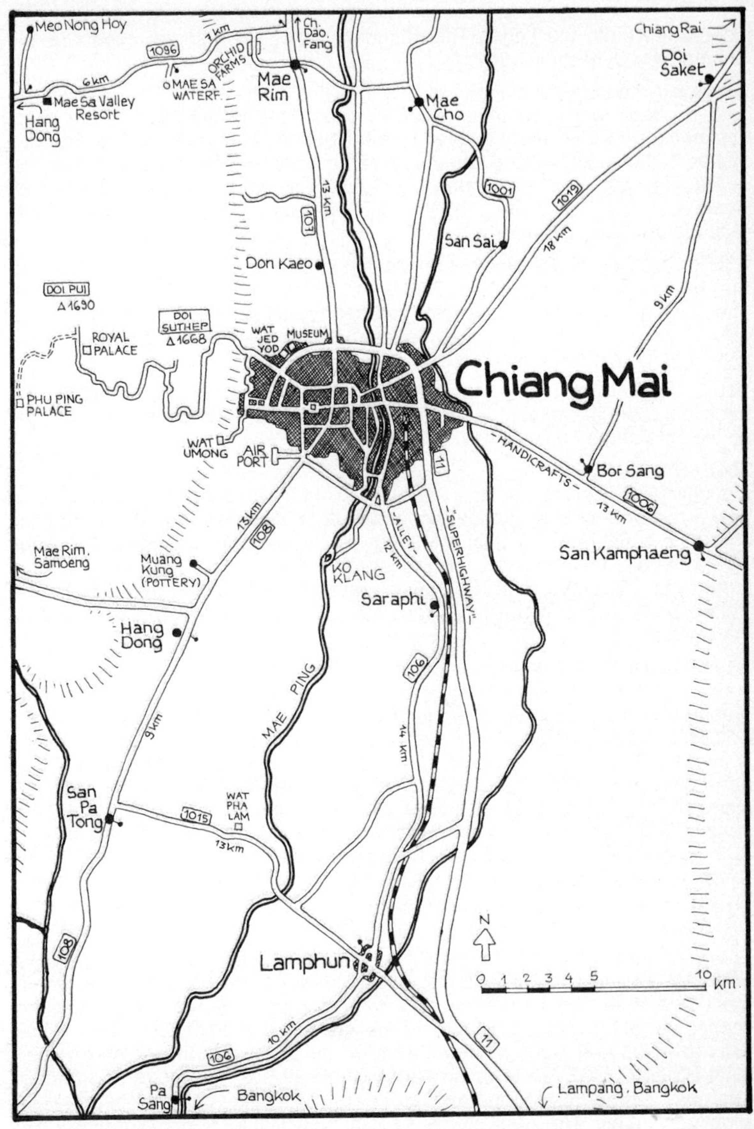
Meo Nong Hoy
7 km
1096
6 km
Mae Sa Valley Resort
Hang Dong
MAE SA WATERF.
ORCHID FARMS
Ch. Dao. Fang
Mae Rim
Mae Cho
Chiang Rai
Doi Saket
1001
1019
13 km
107
San Sai
18 km
Don Kaeo
DOI PUI
1690
9 km
DOI SUTHEP
1668
ROYAL PALACE
WAT JED YOD
MUSEUM
Chiang Mai
PHU PING PALACE
WAT UMONG
AIR PORT
11
HANDICRAFTS
Bor Sang
1006
13 km
13 km
108
"SUPERHIGHWAY"
ALLEY
12 km
San Kamphaeng
Mae Rim, Samoeng
Muang Kung (POTTERY)
KO KLANG
Saraphi
Hang Dong
106
MAE PING
9 km
14 km
San Pa Tong
WAT PHA LAM
1015
13 km
N
Lamphun
0 1 2 3 4 5 10 km
108
10 km
106
11
Pa Sang
Bangkok
Lampang, Bangkok

incorporated into the Lanna Thai Kingdom until King Mengrai overthrew the Chama Devi dynasty in 1281.

We would recommend going to the WAT PHRA THAT HARIPUNCHAI with its golden chedi, which contains a sacred relic. The construction of the chedi commenced in 897, the wat itself was built in 1157. Don't miss the amazing murals in the small building to the right of the entrance. They depict scenes out of Heaven and Hell. The gigantic bronze gong and the rather dilapidated Dvaravati-style SUWANA CHEDI in the northwestern corner of the temple grounds are also noteworthy.

A small MUSEUM definitely worth visiting is directly opposite, opened Wed-Sun (except for Fri) from 9:00-12:00 h and 13:00-16:00 h, admission 10 Baht. The WAT KU KUT, sometimes also referred to as the Wat Chama Devi, is approx. 1 km to the west of town. Several Buddha figures can be seen in the niches of its pyramid-shaped chedi.

You can spend the night in the centre of town at the GUEST HOUSE TU'S*. Excellent food is available at the market from 16:00 h - dozens of women set up big pots of their best dishes.

MAE SA VALLEY

It is difficult to explore the Mae Sa Valley with public transportation. You could take a bus or a minibus to Mae Rim and walk or hitch-hike from there. You can charter a songthaew in Chiang Mai for a half-day tour for around 150 Baht. The well-built, paved road is also ideally suited for a first venture on a hired motorcycle. The Mae Rim - Sameung Road (H1096) leading into the Mae Sa Valley turns off Highway 107 (Chiang Mai - Fang) after 12 km (watch out for the signpost!).

After a mere 1.4 km you will reach ADISARA FARM, where you can hunt for shrimps and fish in a tiny artificial lake for a small fee, and then have them prepared for you in the adjoining restaurant. 1 km further on you will pass two ORCHID FARMS (admission: 5 Baht). Specially treated, gilded orchid jewelry is available here; you can observe the delicate process at the Mountain Orchid Farm daily at 11:00 h. The road leading to the MAE SA WATERFALL, which is made up of several small cascades and pools connected by little footpaths, turns off to the left at km stone 7 (admission: 5 Baht). Foodstands have opened up on the parking lot - ideal conditions for a pleasant picnic. The ELEPHANT CAMP is just 3 km further on, on the left hand side (the signpost is quite difficult to find at first). Admission: 40 Baht. Performances are held daily from 9:00-11:00 h. A 2-3 hour elephant ride through the jungle will cost you 250 Baht.

The road branching off to the right at km stone 15 leads to the ERAWAN RESORT****, admission 20 Baht. Beautifully set bungalows and much entertainment available. An expensive and strikingly unauthentic performance of scenes out of the daily life of the hilltribes as well as traditional dances is held daily at 11:00 and 14:00 h. An rather new, but at least authentic Meo village, BAN HMONG MAE SA MAI, is nearby. Continue past the resort and turn left after just 200 metres. After 1 km you will reach a small bridge. Keep heading slightly to the left. The 7 km stretch is sometimes unfit for traffic after heavy rain. You can spend the night at the MAE SA MAI BUNGALOWS***, to the right of the village entrance. The CHIANG MAI RESORT, which lies at an altitude of 1050 metres, is the 'highest' of the entire valley's attractions. The nights up here are cool. There is a small zoo that can be visited in the resort.

DOI INTHANON

Lying southwest of Chiang Mai, the 2595 metre Doi Inthanon is Thailand's highest mountain. The entire, approx. 1000 km^2-sized area is a National Park. Many Meo and Karen live in the relatively open, sparsely wooded area. The road leading to Doi Inthanon branches off 1 km in front of Chom Thong. A road leading to the *MAE KLANG WATERFALLS* branches off to the left after 8 km. It's a mere 500 metres to the falls from the turn-off. Continue along the main road and you'll soon reach the park entrance (road toll: 20 Baht per car, 5 Baht per motorcycle, 30 Baht per pick-up). There are two waterfalls worth a visit along the 47-km uphill road - *WACHIRATHAN* (beyond km stone 20, 500 metres off the road) and *SIRIPHUM* (1/2 hour on a footpath from km stone 31). You will pass a Meo village and an experimental farm on your way to the latter. The farm is one of the King's pet projects; the hilltribes are being encouraged to cultivate flowers, vegetables, and strawberries instead of opium, and some at least are being taught how, at the farm. The relatively expensive *BUNGALOWS**** in the Meo village constitute the only accommodation the park has to offer. A huge, Air Force *RADAR STATION* was erected on the peak of the mountain, which can be reached by way of a paved road. Don't take any photographs; this is considered a restricted military zone. The *GRAVE* of Chiang Mai's last king, *Inthawichayanon,* is located right next to the parking lot. It was the king's last wish to be buried up here, and thousands come to visit the simple burial site each year. The lowest-ever temperature recorded up here was -8^{0}C. It gets extremely cool every evening and sometimes even at noon.

HOW TO GET THERE

First, get to CHOM THONG, 58 km southwest of Chiang Mai (bus 14 Baht, 1 1/2 hrs.). Once there, rent a pick-up for the day (500-600 Baht, pick-ups available next to the temple), and drive up to the peak - there is no regular public transportation on the mountain.

FROM CHIANG MAI TO MAE HONG SON

Head southwest down H108 (much traffic) from Chiang Mai. You will be travelling through a fertile plain. Stop by at the cattle market (only on Saturday mornings) after 24 km. Many people like coming to the *OB LUANG CANYON* (KM 17) at the weekend; a section of the Chaem river has managed to burrow a 50 metre canal into the cliffs - not exactly breathtaking. The road will gradually start climbing, until it reaches the level of a raised plateau. From here you will have a wonderful view of the mountains.

MAE SARIANG - a small market-town with several Burmese-style temples - *WAT UTTHAYAROM* and *WAT SRI BUNRUANG* are in the centre of town, *WAT CHOM CHAENG* is 1 km south of town, on a small hill commanding a fine view. There is a pretty good hotel in the centre of town, the *MITAREE***. The *MAE SARIANG GUEST HOUSE**, at the bus station, is not worth the price. There are several good restaurants along the busy Viang Mai Road - the *RENU* has an ac-room, the restaurant opposite even has an English-language menu. The *BLACK AND WHITE CAFE*, opposite the cinema, is said to be the only ac-bar between Chiang Mai and Mae Hong Son. 4 buses leave for CHIANG MAI daily between 10:30 and 18:00 h (50 Baht, 4 hrs.). Buses to MAE HONG SON leave at 10:30, 12:00, and 15:00 h (52 Baht, 4 1/2 hrs.).

MAE HONG SON

Approx. one half of the province's population is made up of various hilltribes, the other half of Shan. Only in Mae Hong Son itself are 2 % of the population Thai. The town was peaceful and secluded until well into the 50s. Elephant paths constituted the only connection to the outside world, and an elephant-ride to Chiang Mai could easily take several weeks in those days. Then the airstrip was finished, and in 1968 an all-weather-road was built to the town. These days the northern route (via Pai) is also open to traffic during the dry season. The area is particularly beautiful when the sunflowers bloom in November/December.

The daily *MARKET* in the centre of town (6:00-18:00 h) has little more to offer than any other market in northern Thailand. You may occasionally see Meo and Karen shopping in their traditional costumes. Two Burmese-style chedis, *WAT CHONG KAM* and *WAT CHONG KLANG* are reflected in the little lake in the centre of town. More than 30 interesting wooden statues are kept in a back room on the left side of the right hand temple. Wat Chong Kam is the final destination of the *POI SANG LONG* procession. 10-16-year old boys are inaugurated as novices all over Thailand at the beginning of March. A walk up to *WAT DOI KONG MU,* whose chedis tower over the entire town, is most pleasant. You will have a fine view of the town, the valley, and the green, jungle-overgrown mountains in the west from up here.

GUESTHOUSES & HOTELS

An increasing number of guesthouses are being built now that Mae Hong Son is becoming so popular.

*MAE HONG SON GUEST HOUSE**, 18 Khunlum Praphat Rd. Soi 2. This comfortable, wooden house is built upon stilts and has a pleasant family atmosphere - small rooms with two mattresses, big enough for four people. Great place for information, several guides available.

*GALARE GUEST HOUSE**, Thai house in rural surroundings, about 800 m out of town, to the north. The owners are very helpful and friendly.

*GUYSORN GUEST HOUSE**, Praeha Utis Rd., tel 611308 - new, simple bungalows and restaurant with a campfire site.

*PETER'S GUEST HOUSE**, an old wooden building in a shady, uncared-for garden. Two large private rooms, the rest of the building is used as a dormitory.

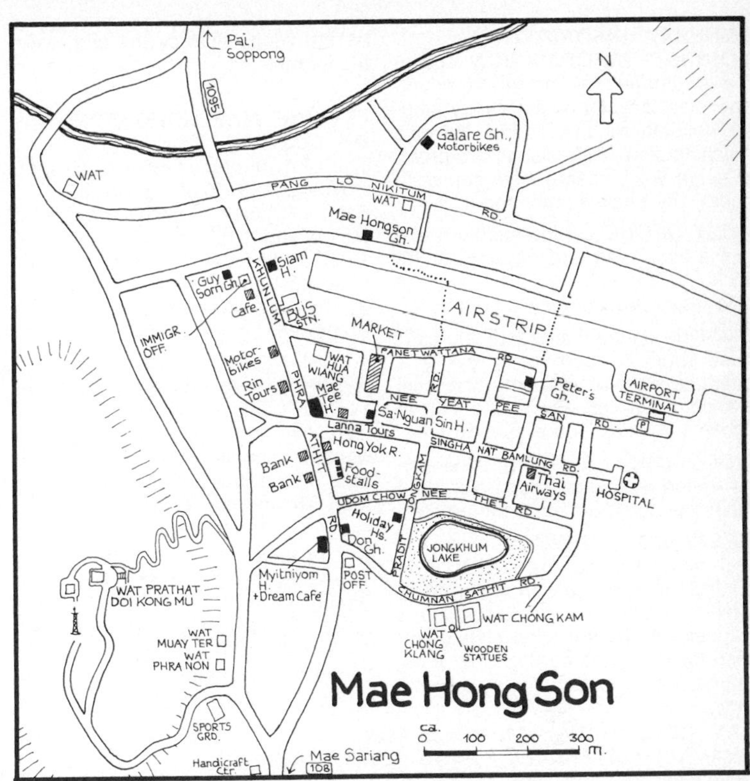

*HOLIDAY HOUSE**, also known as Chong Kham Guest House, is west of the small lake. It is a new, very clean terrace-house commanding a nice view of the lake.

*DON'S GUEST HOUSE**, opposite the Mitniyom Hotel - this is part of Don's Trekking Organization. New guesthouses will no doubt develop here soon.

You'll have to go to a hotel if you want more than just basic comfort.

SA-NGUAN SIN HOTEL-***, 35 Singhanat Road, tel 611241. Old Thai hotel, large rooms, some shower/lav, fan, mosquito net, but no lounge.

You will find the following hotels on the main road, Khunlum Praphat: *SIAM HOTEL**-****, no. 23, tel 611148; clean rooms, shower/lav, some ac; *MAE TEE HOTEL**-****, no. 55; clean hotel; *MITNIYOM HOTEL*-****, no. 90; new building, some rooms ac; you'll find the *DREAM CAFE* downstairs; music and dancing from 21:00-2:00 h. *SARM MORK VILLAS****, tel 611478; brand new - huts and rooms.

GENERAL INFORMATION

TOURIST INFORMATION - go to the guesthouses and the trekking agencies for information - very helpful. In spite of the Tourist Police's touching sign, "Tourists we are proud to serve you", nobody here seems to speak any English (main road).

POST OFFICE - at the southern end of the main road, open Mon-Fri 8:30-16:30 h, Sat 9:00-12:00 h. You can also make telephone calls from here.

BANKS - on the main road, you can't miss them - cash and traveller's cheques are also accepted; the local branch of the Thai Farmers Bank also accepts Visa, as it does everywhere.

MOTORCYCLES - 125 cc bikes can be rented at several shops along the main road for 120 - 200 Baht per day.

TREKKING AGENCIES - you will find many on the main road. The guides will make sure that you aren't blown to bits by a mine and don't wander into the crossfire, should you wish to trek to the border. Boat trips, rafting, and elephant rides can also be arranged, motorcycles and jeeps are for rent.

LEAVING MAE HONG SON

BY BUS

The PAI-bound 4-wheel pick-up leaves at 7:30, 10:30, and 14:00 h (50 Baht, 4 1/2 hrs.). Only the first pick-up will get you to PAI in time to catch the 13:30 bus to CHIANG MAI. You will need dust-proof goggles if you wish to see any of the marvelous landscape.

To CHIANG MAI via MAE SARIANG: take the bus at 6:00, 8:00, 10:30, or 14:00 h (97 Baht, 9 hrs.). There are also two night buses (which we wouldn't recommend). There is even said to be a BANGKOK-bound ac bus (358 Baht, approx. 16 hrs.).

BY PLANE

Thai Airways Office: 71 Singhanat Bamlung Road (tel 611297). There are 2 - 3 daily flights from and to CHIANG MAI (310 Baht, flights arrive and depart around noon).

DAY TRIPS FROM MAE HONG SON

PHA SUA WATERFALL / PANG TONG / NAPAPAK

Drive down the road leading to Pai until just before km stone 17, shortly before HUAI PHA (sometimes HEU PA). Turn off at km stone 10 or 17; both of the dusty roads branching off lead to HUAI KHAN (7 km). Continue down the road another 4 km from here, and you'll reach the PHA SUA WATERFALL - ideal for a bathe. Beyond the waterfall you will have to drive up extremely steep, unpaved roads. The road branching off to the left leads to the PANG TONG ROYAL PALACE (21 km). This is where the King stays when he visits the region; pleasant wood and bamboo garden with a horse husbandry. The passable road straight ahead will lead you to Meo, Kuomintang, Shan, and Karen villages, all situated in the unstable frontier area. Avoid this area if you're travelling on your own. You'll arrive in NAPAPAK after 24 km. We would recommend taking a guide plus pick-up (1000 Baht) for this trip.

NAM PHLANG DIN

Charter a pick-up to the village of HUAI DUA, by the Pai river in the southwest (6 km, 80 Baht per vehicle). After a one-hour boat-ride (charter approx. 700-800 Baht) you will arrive in NAM PHLANG DIN, inside the Burmese border.

You will have to pay the Karenni Guerilla Army 500 Baht per person (for which you will receive receipts) in order to be let over the border. Two Padaung women who artificially elongate their necks by wearing tight, metal rings were forced to live in a village on the Burmese side as a tourist attraction. Travel agencies in Chiang Mai offer the trip at a high price - it's not worth it! The two women are said to have fled during the heavy fighting in the spring of 1987. *WARNING: Crossing the border means leaving Thailand. To set an example, the government had several tourists arrested for "illegally crossing the border" in 1987. The culprits were later expelled from the country.*

FROM MAE HONG SON TO PAI

The 111 km H1095 from Mae Hong Son to Pai has been under construction for years. The road becomes unfit for motorcycles after heavy rain - we would suggest putting your bikes aboard a bus, should you get caught in a down-pour. The *THAM PLA* cave is in a little park on the left hand side of the road, shortly before KM 18. An underground brook flows into a small pool full of semi-tame fish, just waiting to be fed. Fish food can be bought at the parking lot. You will reach *HUAI PHA*, the last village for the next 50 km, just beyond. After this the road only remains paved for a few km - then it becomes extremely tricky. You will finally have a good, unobstructed view of Burma in the north after 48 km. After a fleeting glance into the deep valley on the right it's back into the jungle. You will reach *MAE LANA JUNCTION* after 56 km - once here, you're halfway to Pai! The road becomes very bad beyond Mae Lana - bridges constructed of trees and extremely steep sections of the road will make your nerves tingle. After having mastered them, you will reach *YAPANAE*, a rather uncomfortable Red Lahu village. A small foot-path leads up into the sparse forest shortly beyond KM 64 (rather difficult to find). If you do a little climbing on the cliff wall you may see strange looking, wooden beams in the various caves. These are ancient coffins, dating back 2000 years!

SOPPONG - This Shan village has developed into a centre of commerce for the surrounding hilltribe villages. There are at least three guesthouses here already, all of very simple standards - the *J GUEST HOUSE**, tiny bamboo huts with thin mattresses; *DUM GUEST HOUSE** with 3 rooms, and *SO CHEAP GUEST HOUSE**, with small bungalows behind the restaurant. None of these have a toilet yet, the use of the public lavatory costs 1 Baht! The 4-wheel drive bus to PAI leaves at 10:00, 13:00, and 16:30 h (20 Baht, 2 hrs.). Buses to MAE HONG SON depart at 9:00, 13:00, and 15:30 h (30 Baht, 2 1/2 hrs.).

THAM LOT - You will reach the STALACTITE CAVE by way of the "New Road", a bad forest road measuring approx. 8 km in length. You can either walk, ride a motorcycle, or rent a truck in Soppong. After 2 km you will pass through the Lahu village of VANALUANG. You will reach the Shan village of BAN TUM (also known as Tumlord) after 6 km. If you keep going straight ahead at the turn-off in the village you will reach the *CAVE LODGE* after another 300 metres. It is run by an Australian, John, and his wife Pio, who used to be a trekking guide. The lodge is a large house, with many mattresses for rent and several bamboo-huts. A mattress costs 30 Baht, breakfast 20, lunch 20, and dinner 30 Baht. The very efficient Pio (especially business-wise) also bakes wonderful cakes and buns. The place is always packed during the season. Helpful information concerning day-trips is available, as is a very precise map of the cave, information concerning the right behaviour in hilltribe villages, a guide for excursions, and news from the traveller scene. If you turn right in the village instead of going straight ahead, you will walk straight into the *FORESTRY NATIONAL PARK*. You can spend the night at the very simple *NATIONAL PARK BUNGALOWS** at the edge of the forest. Lav/showers are separate, 20 Baht per person. Cheap food is sold at the stalls along the path. A nice, 400 metre walk through the forest will bring you to the entrance of THAM LOT. The Nam Lang river flows through the cave in a northeast-southwesterly direction for 400 metres.

Continue along the new route of the H1095 from Soppong. You will be able to see the Lisu village of NAM RIN below, to the right, after 10 km (km stone 78). You will find the *LISU LODGE** beyond the school, at the edge of the village. It is large hut with several comfortable community rooms and a balcony. There is a lavatory in the house, bathing facilities at the brook. Everyone helps cook. The 4-wheel drive buses will stop in Nam Rin if you ask the drivers (15 Baht from Pai). From here, the H1095 winds its way up a 1261 metre pass, which you will reach after 8 km. Beautiful view! After another 5 km and several hairpin bends you will be back in the valley of the Pai river.

PAI

Surrounded by high mountains and narrow valleys, Pai was isolated from the rest of the country for a long time. The H1095 is responsible for bringing scores of travellers to the clean town, which has managed to retain much of its easygoing atmosphere nevertheless. There are no tourist attractions in Pai. Still, the chedis of *WAT KLANG* (in the centre of town) and the *WAT LUANG* are worth a visit. Pai is ideally located for setting off on hikes or longer excursions to hilltribe villages. It gets so cold up here between November and February that you will often see people wearing thick woollen caps and anoraks.

GUESTHOUSES

All of Pai's guesthouses offer double rooms for 30-80 Baht per person. They are very simple.

*DUANG GUESTHOUSE** is opposite the bus station. One wooden and one brick building offer a total of 7 double-rooms, as well as a dormitory.

*PAI GUESTHOUSE**; a two-storey, wooden building with double rooms and a lounge, 4 bungalows in the garden. There are only 2 lav/showers for a maximum of 20 guests; guides for jungle excursions available.

*PAI HOUSE CAFE** is directly opposite. There are small wooden bungalows behind the restaurant. Friendly owner, who is also able to give you some proper information. The

*PAI HOTEL** is 50 metres further on. Two large wooden houses and one brick building in the background (for those who want something more solid) offer a total of 17 rooms.

KIM GUESTHOUSE (=DUANG 2)* is approx. 400 metres out of town, to the west, just beyond the hospital. The rooms are separated from each other by plywood, warm showers are available. Continue along this road for another 3 km, and you'll reach the

*MUSLIM GUESTHOUSE**, Ban Nam Ho, just beyond the wat; large, two-storey country-house. If you want to live out here, contact the Muslim shop on the main road; the young woman, a teacher, speaks excellent English.

LEAVING PAI

Buses to CHIANG MAI depart at 6:30, 8:30, 10:30, and 13:30 h (50 Baht, 4 hrs.); 4-wheel drive pick-ups to MAE HONG SON via NAM RIN (Lisu Lodge 15 Baht) and SOPPONG (20 Baht) depart at 7:00, 11:00, and 13:30 h (50 Baht, 4 1/2 hrs.).

DAY TRIPS FROM PAI

It's fun hiking in the vicinity of Pai, although the places you can go to aren't too spectacular. You can visit Lisu, Shan, Red Lahu, and Kuomintang-Chinese villages in the west without getting lost. Stop by at the WAT NAM HU (3 km, at the fork in the road) and look at the Chiang Saen Buddha, whose hinged hair-bun contains sacred water. The waterfalls at the end of the paths are not too exciting.

WAT MAE YEN in the east (3 km) stands upon a hill from which you will have a fine view.

FROM CHIANG MAI TO THATON

Leave Chiang Mai through the northern Chang Puak gate. The H1096 leading to the *MAE SA VALLEY* (see there) branches off after 12 km. The road leaves the fertile plain and starts its twisty descent into the Ping river canyon after 49 km. The *YOUNG ELEPHANTS TRAINING CENTRE* is to the right of the river, at km stone 56 (bus from Chiang Mai 13 Baht, 1 1/2 hrs.). Young elephants are trained for jungle work here, except during the hot months (from March - May). Very touristy; whole busloads of tourists come to see the daily show from 9:30-11:00 h (admission 40 Baht). It is interesting and amusing nevertheless, especially if there are any particularly young elephant calves around. You can ride through the jungle on an elephant's back after the show (100 Baht per person if you drive a hard bargain).

FANG - Its closeness to Burma and its involvement with opium- and arms smuggling have characterized this town. These days things have quieted down; the Thai Border Police now have everything under control. At the entrance of town: *ROZA HOTEL***, modern concrete building, 200 metres from the road, next to the hospital. You'll find the new and huge *CHOK THANI*** (ac***) nearby, on the right hand side. *D.J.** (ac**) is also relatively new. For fans of hotels built in the old Thai style, there are three to choose from: *METTA WATTANA**, *SHRI CHUKIT**, and *WIANG FANG**, which is by the bend of the main road; all three organize trekking tours. *NAIFHUN HOTEL** is at the northern town exit, to the left; motel-style, clean rooms with large beds. A bus leaves from CHIANG MAI every half hour (32 Baht, 3 hrs.) A minibus leaves THATON every 10 minutes (7 Baht, 40 min.). A pick-up ride along the H109 from CHIANG RAI will cost you 50-60 Baht (only possible if it's dry).

THATON -The small settlement lies by the Mae Kok river. A monumental, sitting, white Buddha in Chiang Saen style towers over Thaton. *WAT THATON* on the hill slopes, with its pretty monks' houses, lies nestled at the statue's feet. You will have a wonderful view over the plain and the river all the way to the mountains from the white Buddha. Turn left just before the bridge and you'll reach *THIP'S TRAVELLERS HOUSE**. Rather mean little huts are for rent below the temple hill, some with lav/shower and even mosquito nets. The *BEER GARDEN RESTAURANT,* which also belongs to the complex, is nicely located, directly at the river. Beware - the patroness is very business-minded and the food none too good. If you turn right at the bridge you'll reach the *SIAM MAE-KOK GUESTHOUSE**; wooden building with small, simple rooms; a very cozy *COFFEE SHOP* downstairs. *CHANKASEM GUESTHOUSE**, is on the same road, directly at the landing place. Inter-connecting rooms, large restaurant directly by the river. The bus to CHIANG MAI costs 37 Baht and takes 4 hrs.; you can also take the minibus to FANG (7 Baht) and then one of the Chiang Mai-bound buses (32 Baht, 3 hrs.) that leave every 1/2 hour until 17:30h. The river-boat to CHIANG RAI departs at 12:30 h (160 Baht, 4-5 hrs.).

BOAT RIDES ON THE KOK RIVER - Longtail-boats (no seats!) leave the boathouse at 12:30 h. The trip to Chiang Rai along the *MAE KOK RIVER* costs 160 Baht and takes 4-5 hrs. Take a jacket or a blanket along for padding. These boats are unfortunately much too fast and loud for people to enjoy the magnificent river-landscape. If nobody wishes to disembark or get on along the way, the boat will only stop once, at *MAE SALAK*, for a quick registration (photocopy with visa-number necessary). There are also 12 other stops at which you can be let off, should you so desire. If you've got time to spare, why not do the trip in a total of three days, on a bamboo raft? All of the guesthouses in Thaton organize these kind of trips; there are always plenty of travellers willing to go along during the season, and the rafts are ready and waiting. A raft can hold up to 6 people. Two boat-guides and many mats, blankets, mattresses and portable cooking plates are included in the price of 2400 Baht per boat. Food will cost you extra. *WARNING: Two tourists are said to have been shot dead on the Kok river in the summer of 1987. This has been the first incident after a long and peaceful period. It's best to travel in larger groups!*

CHIANG RAI

Almost 1 million people live in this, the northernmost of Thailand's provinces. Chiang Rai produces most rice of all of the Thai provinces, although only 1/3 of its area is used for agricultural cultivation. The capital, Chiang Rai, was founded as early as 1262 by King Mengrai as the centre of his kingdom. Chiang Mai was not founded for another 48 years. The town has a peaceful and relaxed feeling to it, in spite of the many modern buildings that have been erected during the last couple of years. It is nowhere near as hectic as Chiang Mai.

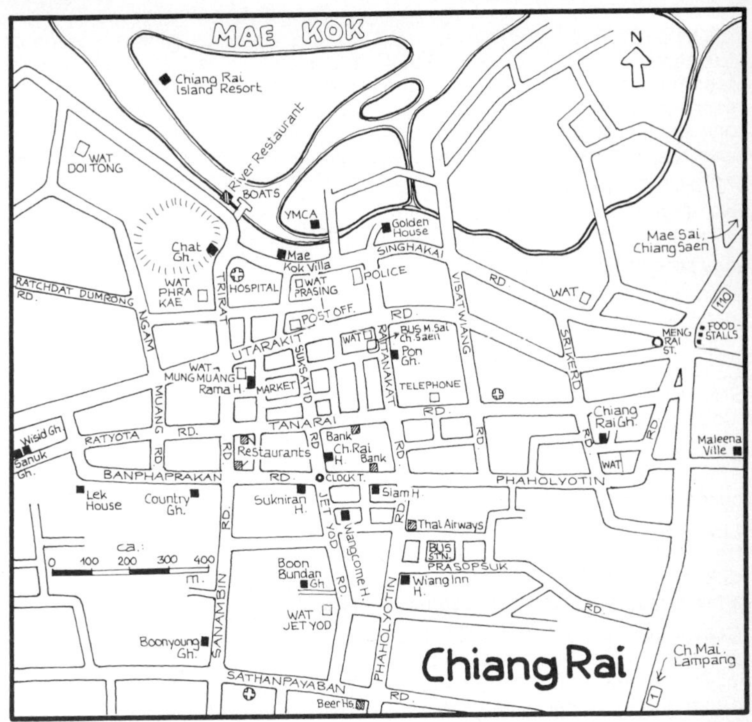

The famous Emerald Buddha was discovered in the chedi of *WAT PHRA KAEO* in 1436. Legend has it that the chedi was once partially destroyed by a flash of lightening, thus revealing the statue. Back then it still had an outer coat of plaster, however, and not until part of the plaster chipped off did one discover the actual, green Buddha beneath. The actual material, incidentally, was jasper. There are few sights in Chiang Rai. No cultural musts!

GUESTHOUSES & HOTELS

*CHAT GUESTHOUSE**, 1 Trairat Rd., tel 713459, wooden building, dormitory, rooms.

MAEKOK VILLA-*** (= CHIANG RAI YOUTH HOSTEL),* 445 Singhakai Rd., tel 311786; old mansion with gigantic dormitories, as well as bungalows.

GOLDEN HOUSE (=GOLDEN TOUR HOUSE),* 246 Soi Pitagrad, Singhakai Rd. is a peacefully located, new building; dormitory.

BOONBUNDAN GUESTHOUSE-**,* 1005/13 Jet Yod Rd., tel 712914; huts set in a large garden, restaurant with videos, new terraced house with ac, all very quiet and peaceful.

BOONYOUNG GUESTHOUSE *-** (formerly Ton's House), 1054 Sanambin Rd., tel 712893; large main building with rooms and dormitory, small huts; small garden with an open-air restaurant; very relaxing.

*PORN HOUSE**, 503 Rattanaket Rd, two large Thai buildings in a yard, dormitory.

*GOLDEN TRIANGLE****, 590 Phaholyotin Rd., tel 711339, very pretty, flat terraced houses; nicely furnished rooms, some ac.

*CHIANG RAI GUESTHOUSE**, 717/2 Sriked Rd., very simple, rather dark rooms in an old house, very friendly.

*MALEENA VILLE*** (ac***), 863 Wat Pranon Rd., tel 712931; new, solid bungalows on a narrow piece of land.

*LEK HOUSE**, 163/1 Banphaprakan Rd.; nice Thai style wooden building with large and small rooms as well as a few bungalows; family atmosphere.

*COUNTRY GUESTHOUSE**, Banphaprakan Rd.; newly renovated, lovely mansion with a small park and a garden restaurant; tiled bathrooms and marble sinks; the young owners speak English very well.

*WISID GUESTHOUSE**, 21/4 Ratyota Rd.; Thai building and airy bamboo huts on a small piece of land; restaurant serving exotic dishes - birds, lizards, and snakes.

*SANUK GUESTHOUSE**, 21/3 Ratyota Rd.; Thai building and bungalow; cozy atmosphere, meals are eaten with the family.

The cheaper hotels in town are not really worth the money. For those demanding quality, how about the *RAMA HOTEL***-***, 331/4 Trirat Rd., tel 311344; clean town hotel. *CHIANG RAI ISLAND RESORT**-****, tel 311865; spacious bungalow resort on the island in the Kok river. *WIANG INN HOTEL*****, 893 Phaholyotin Rd., tel 711543; average standard hotel. *WANGCOME HOTEL*****, 869 Pemawibhata Rd., tel 711800; luxurious hotel with very reasonable prices.

FOOD

You can eat good meals for a reasonable price at the various night markets in town. The DOH RUNG MARKET is opposite the Wiang Inn Hotel. You will find a further night market on Sanambin Road. Good, cheap Thai and Chinese food is available at the HOR NALIGA by the clock tower. You will find more good Chinese restaurants along the southern side of Tanarai Road, opposite the market. Rather expensive, but excellent Tom Yam is served at the RUEN THONG by the Super Highway, not far from Wat Sriked. Nobody here speaks a word of English.

GENERAL INFORMATION

TOURIST INFORMATION - go to the YMCA, easy to find from Singhakai Road (follow the signposts), on the island in the river, tel 311313, open Mon-Sat from 8:30-19:00 h.

TREKKING TOURS - all guesthouses organize trekking tours. Prices for typical tours: 2 days/1 night 350 Baht; 3 days/2 nights 500 Baht; 5 days/4 nights 750 Baht. Raft trips on the Kok river are offered for 1500 Baht. The trip takes 3 days / 2 nights and goes all the way to the Mekong. You will spend one night sleeping on the raft, the other in a hilltribe village.

MEDICAL AID - the Overbrook Hospital is opposite Chat House, tel 311366. There is a provincial hospital on Sanambin Rd.

LEAVING CHIANG RAI

BY PLANE

Thai Airways Office: 870 Phaholyotin Rd., tel 711179, right by the bus station. The small "shorts" fly to CHIANG MAI (300 Baht), BANGKOK (1575 Baht), and PHITSANULOK (805 Baht) daily.

BY BUS

The central bus station is on Phaholyotin Rd. All ac buses leave from here, as do most local buses. Buses to Mae Sai and Chiang Saen also stop at Rattanaket Road, in front of the police station. SAMPLE PRICES: BANGKOK (175 Baht, 14 hrs.), ac (283 Baht, 12 hrs.), CHIANG MAI (47 Baht, 3 1/2 hrs.), ac (66 Baht, 3 hrs.), super-ac (85 Baht, 3 hrs.), SUKHOTHAI (83 Baht, 6 hrs., ac 110 Baht), LAMPANG (50 Baht, 3 1/2 hrs.), CHIANG KHONG (15 Baht).

BY BOAT

River-boats depart for THATON daily at around 10:00 h, (160 Baht, 5-6 hrs.). There is always at least one stop in MAE SALAK for a registration of the passengers (passport or photocopy incl. visa number necessary). The rapids and whirlpools can get quite dangerous during the rainy season (July-October).

DAY TRIPS FROM CHIANG RAI

LAAN TONG LODGE

The small business town of MAE CHAN is the closest place to go shopping for the many hilltribes in the area, who make up the majority of this district's population. A minibus from Mae Chan to the lodge will cost you 10 Baht (regularly between 9:00 and 17:00 h). The H1089 turns off to the left towards HUAI MA HIN FON exactly 1 km beyond Mae Chan. Pass the HOT SPRINGS (8 km) and a pleasant green valley. You will see the LAAN TONG LODGE after 13 km, on the left hand side. Many pretty bamboo huts, all set on a large piece of land by the river; solar showers available in a separate house, large restaurant; the resort belongs to two women, one from Thailand, the other from Australia. There are several Yao-, Lahu-, Lisu-, and Akha villages in the vicinity, all of which can be easily reached (guides and information available at the lodge).

MAE SALONG (in Thai: SANTI KHIRI)

This settlement was founded on the slope of the Doi Mae Salong 27 years ago, by former Kuomintang soldiers, who had fled to Burma after Mao Tse Tung's victory in 1949 and were later driven away to Thailand in 1961. New roads and paths have been constructed in the entire area during the last few years with the express object of making the region easier to supervise and putting an end to the opium business. The *MAE SALONG GUESTHOUSE** is on the left hand side, after 100 metres; flat building with clean rooms, some with lav/shower for 40 Baht per person; Chinese food is served if ordered in advance, very friendly owner; treks can be organized, with mules if necessary. The *JIN SAE HOTEL** is around the corner, to the right; wooden building with 10 rooms, the top hotel in town. Continue along the steep road and turn left at the wat. You will reach the *MAE SALONG RESORT***** after 400 metres; well tended resort with bungalows (700 Baht) and terraced houses (500 Baht). You will reach the road branching off to BAN PHA SANG (2 km north of MAE CHAN) with the MAE SAI-bound bus from CHIANG RAI (8 Baht); once there, catch a pick-up (40 Baht). It's only 30 Baht for the trip back down.

DOI TUNG

The H1149 to the huge DOI TUNG (18 km) branches off to the left after 11 km, in the village of BAN HUI KRAI (19 km before reaching Mae Sai). A bus to this turn-off from Mae Sai will cost you 5 Baht, a minibus to the peak another 30 Baht. We would recommend going here just for the fantastic view. You will first pass through a Shan village. After 7 km you'll reach the Akha village of BAN PAKA. The *AKHA GUESTHOUSE** is at the village exit, to the left; very simple bamboo huts; bad reputation; a minibus to here will cost you 10 Baht. You will reach the mountain saddle and a military post shortly before KM 18. The next 300 metres are extremely steep, after that you've made it - the WAT PHRA THAT DOI TUNG lies at an altitude of over 1500 metres. You will have a glorious view of the wide valley and the hills all the way to Burma on a clear day. Relics of Buddha are said to have been put here by King Achutaraj of Chiang Saen in 911.

MAE SAI

This northernmost of all Thai settlements mainly thrives by doing business with Burma. You can watch the many people scurrying back and forth. You will have to buy Burmese souvenirs at the many shops in front of the bridge, seeing as only the Thai are allowed to enter Burma. There is a *JADE FACTORY* on the main road which can be visited (closed on Mon). Mainly kitsch-souvenirs are offered, however. You will have a good view of the area from the *WAT DOI WAO* on the hill to the left, in front of the river.

HOTELS

You will find one of Thailand's most beautiful guesthouses here. Turn left before the bridge and continue towards the river for almost 1 km.

The *MAE SAI GUESTHOUSE*-*** is directly on the river; good restaurant, friendly owners; motorcycles 150 Baht, bicycles 15 Baht.

The *CHAD GUESTHOUSE**, Soi Wiangpan, is at the entrance of town, in front of the bus station, down the alley leading to the wat; nice, traditional rooms, garden with tables; warm water; very friendly and helpful family; good motorcycles for rent.

Walk down the main road from the bus station. You will see the *MAE SAI HOTEL*** (not too clean) on the right hand side.

The *TOP NORTH*** is 50 metres further on, on the left hand side.

LEAVING MAE SAI

Regular buses leave for CHIANG RAI (15 Baht) via BAN HUI KRAI (turn-off to Doi Tung, 5 Baht), BAN PHA SANG (turn-off to Mae Salong, 8 Baht), and MAE CHAN (turn-off to Chiang Saen, 8 Baht).

Buses to CHIANG SAEN cost 15 Baht (you will probably have to get off before Mae Chan, at the turn-off, and then wait for the Chiang Saen bus). You will only be able to get to SOB RUAK (Golden Triangle) via Chiang Saen if you want to get there by bus. There are 3 daily ac buses to CHIANG MAI (83 Baht). There is a direct bus to BANGKOK at 16:30 h (169 Baht), as well as 5 ac buses between 8:00 and 17:30 h (305 Baht).

CHIANG SAEN

It is thought today that Chiang Saen must have been built around 1325, most probably on the site of an even earlier town, which must have been very significant during the period of Thai migration south. The city was destroyed between 1000 and 1100, either by the Khmer or by a particularly serious earthquake. Ancient chronicles dating back to 1328 tell of how Chiang Saen was re-founded in 1325. It was then put under the sovereignty of the Lanna Thai kings, who resided in Chiang Mai. Today it is a quiet, peaceful market town. Neighbouring Laos can be seen on the other side of the Mekong river.

Parts of the ancient town wall as well as ruins of former temples can be seen standing unobtrusively next to modern-day buildings and gardens. *WAT CHEDI LUANG* with its 58 metre, octagonal chedi is beautifully set in a tree-studded park. The pyramid-shaped *WAT PA SAK* (admission 20 Baht!!) is just outside the western town gate. It looks splendid when seen from the west, too. You will be able to climb the 300 steps to the *WAT PHRA THAT CHOM KITTI* and enjoy the splendid view of the town, the Mekong, and the plain, if you walk north up the path next to the town wall. You will also find the *MUSEUM* at the western town gate, open daily from 8:30-12:00 and 13:00-16:00 h, closed on Mon and Tues. You will be able to look at a most impressive collection of typically Chiang Saen style Buddha figures, as well as other cultural heirlooms.

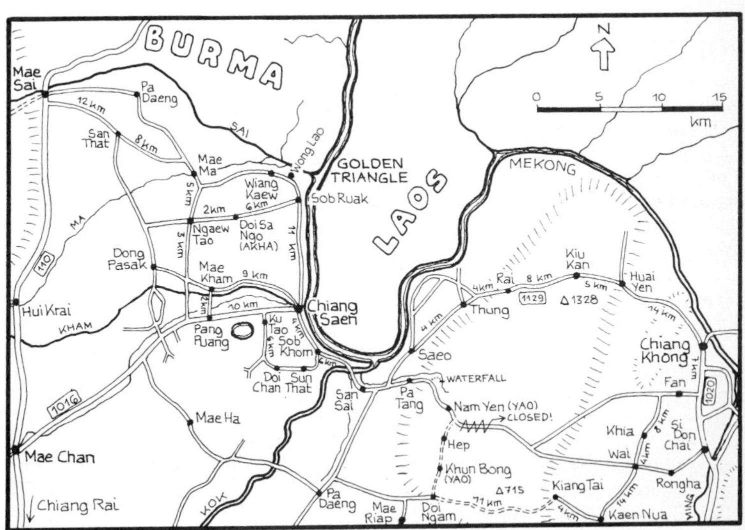

GUESTHOUSES

Walk straight on towards the river from the bus station, then turn right onto the embankment road. You will reach the *LANNA HOUSE**, 39 Rim Khong Road, on the right hand side after 300 metres; wooden bungalows and a dormitory; hot showers and a restaurant.

*LE MEKONG** is just a little further on, also separated from the river by the busy road. If you turn north from the embankment road, in contrast, you will reach the

*CHIANG SAEN GUESTHOUSE** behind the Wat Phra Khao Pan; simple rooms, nice restaurant. There have been a few complaints concerning the owners in recent times. The pretty

*KIM HOUSE** is at the riverbank, approx. 1 km further upstream; simple rooms, dormitory, bungalows, restaurant, information, and bicycles.

You will find the *SUREE GUESTHOUSE** in town, a modern building behind the post office, on the right. The friendly owner is a good cook, bicycles for tours into the surrounding areas are available. Just follow the signs from the bus station to reach *SIAM GUESTHOUSE**.

LEAVING CHIANG SAEN

Buses to CHIANG RAI or MAE SAI (you will usually have to change at the turn-off in front of Mae Chan) cost 15 Baht. It is said that the Mekong boat rides to CHIANG KHONG - which had stopped for a long time - are now running again. You can charter a boat of your own for 3000 Baht. Minibuses to Sob Ruak, the Golden Triangle, leave from next to the Sala Thai Restaurant at the Mekong (10 Baht, until 17:00 h). You can also get there by boat from here (30 Baht return).

GOLDEN TRIANGLE (SOB RUAK)

The prestige of the notorious Golden Triangle, an area covering several hundred square miles and in which roughly three quarters of the world's opium is produced, has been concentrated into one single point on the map for tourists: the triangle made up of Laos, Burma, and Thailand at the point at which the Mae Sai river (Ruak river) merges with the Mekong. This picturesque, formerly peaceful settlement has recently become almost absurdly popular. Don't come expecting to find poppy growing out of every nook and cranny - you'll find souvenir stands, guesthouses, and restaurants instead.

GUESTHOUSES

The guesthouses are all quite close to one another. New ones are being built all the time. We would suggest checking them out one by one and then making your selection. The *GOLDEN HUT**, the first guesthouse, stands alone at the river mouth of the Mae Sai river, just a stone's throw from Burma. You will find the *GOLDEN TRIANGLE GUESTHOUSE** right next to the memorial. We would recommend the *GOLDEN LODGE*** for people with higher standards. The *KN** is new.

HOW TO GET THERE

If you don't have a motorcycle you can get to Sob Ruak via Chiang Saen. You can also catch a minibus (10 Baht) or a boat (30 Baht return).

LAMPANG

Approx. 50,000 people inhabit this provincial capital, which is 100 km southeast of Chiang Mai. It used to be the centre of a Mon kingdom before the Khmer and Thai came to this region. Remains of Hindu stucco-works have been excavated here. All that remains of the former town wall is an octagonal brick tower. The white, earthen ceramics from Lampang, which are usually subsequently painted blue or brown, are well known.

The *WAT SI RONG MUANG,* Tha Krao Noi Road, and the *WAT SRI CHUM* in the road of the same name, are two beautiful temples adorned with Burmese style wood-carvings.

You will find one of the most beautiful temples of northern Thailand just a few km from Lampang. The *WAT PHRA KAEO DON TAO* is on the right hand bank of the Wang river, 1 km northeast of the central Rasada Phisek Bridge. The famous Emerald Buddha of the Royal Temple in Bangkok used to be kept here. You will be able to see a mighty chedi, a splendid Burmese style chapel, and a beautiful Thai style temple. There is also a small museum in the temple grounds. The 'temple of the 20 chedis', *WAT CHEDI SAO,* is 3 km further northeast from here, surrounded by paddies; it is particularly beautiful during the rainy season, when the rice glows a lush green.

HOTELS

There are several cheap hotels on Boonyawat Road, e.g. the *SRI SANGA*,* no. 213, tel 217070; cheap double rooms with lav/shower. You will find the *ASIA LAMPANG*** (ac***), no. 229, tel 217844, by the large roundabout with the clock tower; generally for people with higher standards; restaurant.

*THIP CHANG***,* 54/22 Thakrao Noi Road, tel 218222, beyond the clock tower, on the extension of Boonyawat Road; this is Lampang's no. 1 place, with ac, pool, coffee shop, and a restaurant. The *LAMPANG**,* 696 Suan Dok Road, tel 217311, is also in the centre of town, while the *SIAM**,* 260 /29 Chat Chai Rd., tel 217472 is a little further out of town, towards the railway station.

LEAVING LAMPANG

BY PLANE

Thai Airways Office: 314 Sanam Bin Road, tel 217078. Flights to PHITSANULOK (430 Baht) and PHRAE (140 Baht) depart on Tues and Thur.

BY TRAIN

Bicycle rickshas and horse-drawn carriages (rather unusual for Thailand) are the main forms of public transport in Lampang. Minibuses within the city limits cost 3 - 6 Baht. A train (the station is definitely worth visiting!) to CHIANG MAI costs 25 Baht (3rd class only runs early in the mornings, at 4:14 and 5:21 h, 2nd class directly to Chiang Mai at 6:34 h). A train to PHITSANULOK or directly to BANGKOK will cost 221 Baht 2nd class, 3 trains per evening.

BY BUS

The bus station is far in the southeast of town. Good connections to CHIANG MAI 25 Baht, TAK 40 Baht, CHIANG RAI 50 Baht, PHITSANULOK, and SUKHOTHAI. There are nine daily buses to BANGKOK (115 Baht, ac 207 Baht).

DAY TRIPS FROM LAMPANG

WAT PHRA THAT LAMPANG LUANG

This temple, one of the most beautiful in northern Thailand, is 18 km southwest of town, on the right hand side of the Wang river. Take a minibus from the centre of Lampang to KO KHA (10 Baht). Once there, walk 3 km (turn right beyond the bridge) to the monastery (motorcycle taxi 10 Baht, minibus 2-3 Baht, very rare, though). If you're coming on a motorcycle from Chiang Mai on the H11, you can turn right towards KO KHA at km stone 13. From here it's 12 km south on the H1034. If you're coming up the H1 from the south, turn left between km stones 587 and 588. It's another 5 km to the temple from here.

The WAT PHRA THAT LAMPANG LUANG is at least 1300 years old. It lies slightly elevated, surrounded by a strong wall - the temple used to be used as a fort. You will have to enter left of the main gate, between the two modern Chinese temples. Many posts donated by the faithful support the branches of the Bodhi tree, thus preventing them from breaking off. There is an emerald Buddha said to be of the same material as the much more famous emerald Buddha in Bangkok (i.e. jade) in the museum at the end of the first courtyard; numerous other Buddha statues are exhibited rather unattractively.

The inner courtyard is dominated by a 45 metre chedi. Six viharn and chapels, some with beautifully carved facades, contain Buddha statues and splendid relic-shrines. Most of them are between 500 and 700 years of age.

You will easily be able to spend a couple of hours here, should you be into temples. The brochure entitled "The history of..." (10 Baht) is unfortunately rather lacking. Admission (donation): 5 Baht.

ELEPHANT TRAINING CENTRE

The training centre for young elephants is 54 km northeast of Lampang. You will have to turn off the Chiang Rai-bound H1 to the west between km-stones 655 and 656; walk down the path for 1,5 km. Approx. a dozen young elephants are trained for their future forest-work in a beautiful valley basin, by a brook.

The elephant calves are between 3 and 5 years of age when they first come to this centre. What follows is a five-year period of education and training. There aren't nearly as many on-looking tourists here as there are in the training centres near Chiang Mai. The performances are very interesting and a lot of fun, especially when very young calves are among the elephants. The elephants are 'taught' between 9:00 and 11:00 h daily, except for Buddhist holidays, those days on which a half or a full moon will follow, and the dry season from March to May. Buses to the village of BAN PANG LA (we would suggest getting off at the signpost) leave Lampang from 6:15 h (17 Baht, 90 min.). A taxi from Lampang will cost you approx. 300 Baht. Market women sell bananas and sugar cane, with which you can feed the pupils, at the parking lot.

NORTHEAST THAILAND

Ever since the border to Laos has been closed, few tourists travel to the northeast of the country, which is also known as Isan. The rather monotonous landscape has few sights as such to offer. The people living in the densely populated area are poor. The land regularly dries out during the dry period, only to be flooded again during the rainy period. Many forests that formerly helped regulate the area's water supply have now been cut down. These days an effort is being made to prevent further damage by building dams and initiating other water-regulation projects.

Many inhabitants of Bangkok come from this, the poorest area of Thailand. Should you meet someone in the capital who speaks English and is prepared to take you home to the family, we would certainly recommend doing so; this may be a unique chance to gain some insight into the traditional, rural life of this region.

The US government helped pay for and construct the Friendship Highway No. 2, which leads to the northeast, and was built mainly for strategic reasons. The area bordering onto Laos was of great political significance during the Vietnam war . Up until 1973, numerous American bases in this region helped considerably to boost the economy of the surrounding provincial towns. Many bomb attacks on Laos and Vietnam were launched from here.

The best time to travel to the northeast is after the rainy period has ended, in November/December. In all, there is less precipitation here than in the lowlands. Midday temperatures have been known to rise to 40°C in the shade at the end of the dry period. Beware!

KHAO YAI NATIONAL PARK

This second largest of Thailand's National Parks (2000 km²) was the first ever to have been founded in the country (1962). It is situated in the hilly region of the Dongrak mountain range. The park is not at all difficult to reach, and about 500,000 people visit it yearly, especially at the weekends, when the Thai railway system offers special cheap package deals.

You can go on several short tours on 11 marked trails of varying degrees of difficulty on your own in the park. If you're interested in one of the longer tours, maybe even climbing a mountain, you will need a guide, a tent, and the necessary equipment. The different trails are marked with their different colours every 25 metres. Always take enough water and plenty of food along. Do not leave the marked trails if you are on your own; even an experienced trekker can break a leg.

A rather unreliable map of the park with all paths, waterfalls etc. included can be bought at the *TOURIST OFFICE* and the *VISITOR'S CENTRE* of Khao Yai.

These offices also organize guides. If you wish to hire one, you will have to pay 100 Baht daily to the Park Headquarters on top of the fee for the guide himself, which you have to agree on beforehand. Animal-observation tours for a minimum of eight, costing 15 Baht per person, are organized every evening. Do not expect to meet a herd of wild elephants, though.

Excursions to the different waterfalls are fun. A short walk from the Visitor's Centre (cross the bridge) will get you to the *KONG KAEO WATERFALL* - many tourists and very loud. You can continue up the river-bed from here if you want to get away from the crowd.

A 6-km path marked in red leads east to the *HAEW SUWAT* waterfall from the Kong Kaeo waterfall. You will need between 3 and 4 hours for the walk, which ends at the northwestern dead-end road. Getting back is rather wearisome - few vehicles drive along the road.

The following waterfalls can be reached from the northeastern dead-end road. The footpath that starts at the parking lot at the end of the northeastern road (where snacks and drinks can be bought) leads to two waterfalls. Only a couple of metres from the road you will also find the *HAEW SUWAT* path, clearly marked by the litter of many previous visitors. It gets a little better 1 km further on. The two waterfalls you will find here are a good place for a refreshing bathe and a fantastic shower. The last path leading to the *HAEW PRATHUN* is a little difficult to follow, as paths continuously branch off to the left and right.

A path marked in red leads 3 km from the back end of the parking lot along the stream to the *PHA KAEY MAI CAMP.* Halfway there you will reach the *PHA KAEY MAI WATERFALL,* also known as the orchid waterfall. The name is due to the beautiful, orchid-laden tree you will see next to the waterfall. The path leading here is very beautiful, but the waterfall itself is a bit of a disappointment.

There are other, more extensive jungle-tours you can go on, too. Find out about the condition of the paths beforehand. Various visitors have lost their way on the longer trails and have thus been forced to spend a night in the jungle. This is not much fun unless you come well prepared. Most jungle-paths are old elephant-paths, and fallen tree-trunks as well as animal paths may confuse your sense of direction. In addition, large animals are continually making new paths - do not go on long trails without a guide! The hundreds of leeches constitute a further problem, especially during the rainy season.

The rainy season in the park begins in March, and it's worst from July to October. November and December are the best times to visit the park. It is at this time that the elephants come out at night.

If you want to observe animals, go to the Visitor's Centre for information. You will also find a small exhibition here. With a little luck and a good eye you will be able to observe wild boars, porcupines, wild oxen, mongooses and civet cats, even during the day-time. The salt-spots at night are better, though. Normally, all noisy humans get to see during the day-time are birds, harmless small animals, and a large variety of creepy-crawlies. Tigers, bears and elephants are very rarely seen, although there are several herds of wild elephant that live around the headquarters, in all a total of 150 animals. Thus Khao Yai has the largest continuous population of wild elephants in Thailand. All big animals prefer the central part of the park because of the many big game poachers causing havoc on its outskirts. One will frequently even hear shots on the road between the TAT bungalows and the headquarters at night - the slain animals are quickly loaded into waiting vehicles and are gone before anyone knows what's happened. The landscape is a mixture of real jungle and grassy steppe, with small artificial lakes and even a golf course.

ACCOMMODATION

The Tourist Office runs the *KHAO YAI MOTOR LODGE***-****,* which is in the centre of the park. Bungalows of various sizes big enough to accommodate up to ten people (with bathroom and kitchen) cost between 600 and 2000 Baht. Contact TAT in Bangkok, tel 2825209, for information and advance booking.

The huge tents on the camping grounds are a cheaper place to spend the night; you will have to pay 10 Baht for a camp-bed, another 10 for a blanket. We would suggest bringing your own sleeping bag, as it can get pretty cool. Male travellers can (sometimes) also spend the night with the Rangers or near the foodstalls at the Visitor's Centre, where most people - including the Rangers - eat.

Here you will also find the *WUNG GONG GHEOW RESTAURANT,* where wild deer sometimes come to see if there's anything edible in the litter baskets. It's 3 km from the Visitor's Centre to the Motor Lodge.

HOW TO GET THERE

To get to the National Park from Bangkok, either take a bus or catch a train to PAK CHONG. Buses leave the Northern Bus Terminal at 7:00 and 9:00 h for 74 Baht (ac). It will take you about 3 hours to get to the park. Return buses to Bangkok leave at 15:00 h.

The minibus in PAK CHONG will take you the rest of the way (leaves 17:00 h Mon-Fri, 10:30 and 17:00 h Sat and Sun, cost 20 Baht, takes 4 hours for 40 km). The yellow TAT-buses drive directly to the bungalows. You could also hire one of the blue songthaew, which stop just about everywhere and will take you as far as the checkpoint. From here it is still another 10 km to the Tourist Office, though. You can catch one of the yellow buses back to Pak Chong for 15 Baht at 7:00 h Mon-Fri, 8:00 and 15:00 h on Saturday and Sunday. Admission for the park is 5 Baht per person, 10 Baht per motorcycle, 30 Baht per car.

KORAT

Korat, officially called Nakhon Ratchasima, is the northeastern region's second largest town with 205,000 inhabitants. It constitutes an important centre of trade and traffic, connecting the northeastern highlands to Bangkok. This is where many US airbases were stationed. The numerous nightclubs and bars in the town remind one of this era. It was from here that General Prem organized the resistance against the officers who tried to overthrow the Thai gov-

ernment in April of 1981. The town is the first settlement found on the highlands when travelling north from Bangkok, and a good point from which to set off on various excursions.

In the centre of the old town one can still see the remains of the former *TOWN FORTIFICATION.* The former, rectangular town wall (its long sides 1700 metres in length, the adjacent sides 1500 metres), the moat, and several ruins within the fortification are relics of a period in the 8th-10th centuries when this was an important and influential town.

In front of the town gate, in between Ratchdamnoen and Chumphon Road, you will be able to see the

KHUNYING MO MEMORIAL (Thao Suranari). This woman led the forces responsible for repelling the Laotian invaders when most of the men of the region were at war against Burma. The bronze monument, which was erected in 1934, contains her ashes. The local inhabitants constantly decorate the memorial with wreaths of flowers and other sacrificial gifts. Khunying Mo remains a regional heroine to this day. The

MAHA WIRAWONG MUSEUM in the courtyard of the Wat Suthachinda has an interesting collection of Khmer art and objects of former eras. Open Wed - Sun 9:00-12:00 h and 13:00-16:00 h, admission fee 5 Baht.

The *TOURIST OFFICE* can be found at the highway, shortly before the road leading to the centre of town branches off. Address: 53/1 - 4 Mukmontri Road, tel 243427 and 423751. A giant swimming pool is right next door.

HOTELS

There are some cheap hotels in the old town, e.g. *LUK MUENG***, 1925 Chumphon Rd., tel 242837, *CHUMPHON***, 701 Pho Klang Road, tel 242453, *SRI SUA***, 809 Suranari Road, tel 243321, or the *MUANG THONG**, 1302 Chumphon Road, tel 242090, a wooden building. The largest hotel in the area lies a little out of town, *SRI PATTANA****, 346 Suranari Road.; tel 242833, ac, restaurant, nightclub.

LEAVING KORAT

BY BUS

Local buses leave the bus terminal in the northwest of town. Buses to PAK CHONG (Khao Yai National Park - 2 hour ride) leave every 20 minutes, cost: 20 Baht. The last bus leaves at 16:00 h. Buses to CHOKCHAI every 20 minutes for 6 Baht, last bus: 19:30 h. Buses to PHIMAI (14 Baht) leave every half hour, as do buses to Surin (3 hrs.; 33 Baht) and several buses that travel along the Highway no. 2: to KHON KAEN (2 1/2 hours; 39 Baht), UDON THANI (3 1/2 hours; 43 Baht), NONG KHAI at the border to Laos (4 hours; 60 Baht), YASOTHON (54 Baht), and CHAIYAPHUM (27 Baht). Regular buses to Bangkok (256 km) cost 51 Baht, ac buses usually leave from the company offices (for the most part in Chumphon Road), cost: 92 Baht, 3 hours. There are also buses headed for the east coast, e.g. RAYONG (4 hours; 50 Baht).

BY TRAIN

The northeastern railway line from BANGKOK to NONG KHAI also passes Korat (104/50 Baht - 2nd/3rd cl.). The Thanom Chira station is more central than the Korat station. Long distance trains rarely stop here, however. Connections to KHON KAEN, UDON, and NONG KHAI, though buses are faster. The other train line running through Korat leads east.

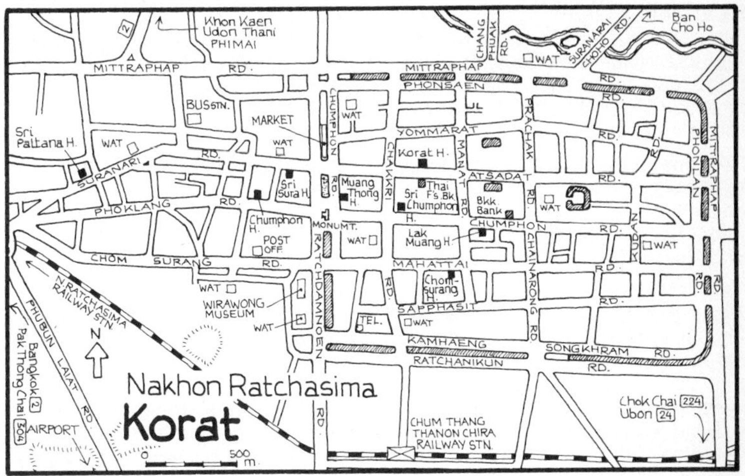

DAY TRIPS AROUND KORAT

PHIMAI

Several Khmer ruins dating back to the 11th - 13th centuries were discovered in and around this small town, among them the large *PRASAT HIN PHIMAI*, one of the most beautiful Khmer temple grounds in the country, which has been restored to its former splendour. At the time when it was built, the Khmer had extended their sphere of influence well into the west. The Buddhist-Hindu temple grounds are proof of the fact that Phimai must have once been an important Khmer centre. The monumental Angkor Wat in present-day Kampuchea was probably modelled on this temple. The central prang, which symbolizes the sacred mountain and the seat of gods, can be reached from all four cardinal points by way of four paths. These in turn can be reached by way of four entrances in the rectangular wall which surrounds the sacred grounds. The temple is open from 7:30-17:00 h, admission 20 Baht.

Some of the discoveries made here as well as some beautiful pieces of stone masonry are exhibited in the small *MUSEUM* opposite the temple grounds at the main road. It is open daily from 8:30-16:30 h, admission 20 Baht.

One of the country's most beautiful *BANYAN TREES* (ficus benjamini) can be found near the town. Its incredible amount of foliage, branches, and aerial roots make an impressive sight. Take the road towards Korat and turn right 400 metres after the bridge. After a further kilometre and a narrow bridge across a storage lake you will already be able to see the huge tree from afar. A small temple stands beneath its enormous roof of leaves. You will find several foodstalls under a corrugated iron roof opposite. Take a bus from KORAT for 14 Baht. Buses leave every half hour and need 60 - 90 minutes for the 55 km stretch.

BAN DAN KWIEN

Rust-coloured, red clay earth which is used for pottery can be found at the river near this village. The beautiful objects made from it are exhibited at the sides of the road and are for sale. You can hardly miss the village. You will find an exhibition of 100 Asian carts and a collection of wood turning to the right of the village entrance.

Take one of the buses that leave for CHOKCHAI every 15 minutes. You'll be able to watch the potters at work 15 km behind Korat, at Road no. 24. Beautiful vases, stools, tiles, and lamp shades are made here with the simplest of tools before being baked in kilns. Most of the objects are too heavy and large to be taken home as souvenirs, though.

PAK THONG CHAI

Buses headed to this silk-weaving village leave Korat every 30 minutes till 20:00 h, cost: 9 Baht. It takes about 1 hour to cover the 35 km stretch. You will find most of the silk weavers in the following street: take the second road left after the telephone station, then turn left again. Here you will find women weaving the hand-spun and -coloured silk to colourful materials on their old weaving looms. It takes them a long time to finish one metre of silk material patterned with the traditional rhombic design, and the price of 150 Baht per metre is definitely fair. In many cases you will find that the small family businesses only manufacture materials intended for special, festive clothing, which have to be ordered weeks in advance. If you want to buy some silk yourself, you'd be better off shopping at the larger businesses, to the right of the main road. Here modern weaving looms are used. There are also two hotels (*) in the village.

SURIN

The 40,000 inhabitants of this provincial town, 450 km from Bangkok, experience an annual tourist invasion during the third weekend of November for the splendid *ELEPHANT ROUND-UP.* About 200 elephants are organized for this spectacle. They show off their strength and agility in parades and competitions. Few of these creatures are still used for carrying tree trunks out of the jungle. Most of them still have to work in the Surin area, though.

You will be able to observe some of these trained creatures at work in THATUM, 48 km north of Surin on the road to Roi-et. Over the last few years machines have been taking over from the elephants, however, as the animals are unable to work during the dry period, when the heat becomes too intense. The best time to come here is between June and October.

HOTELS

Predictably, the entire town is booked up for the elephant round-up. You will have little hope of finding a room unless you're taking part in an organized tour. During the rest of the year accommodation poses no problem in Surin. There are two ac hotels on Thanasarn Road, the *NEW HOTEL*** (no. 22), tel 511341 and the *SAENG THONG*** (no. 155-161), tel 512099. Two further hotels can be found on Krung Sri Road, the *KRUNG SRI**, no. 15/14, tel 511037 and the *ERAWAN**, no. 37, tel 511328, both non-ac.

HOW TO GET THERE

Many travel agencies offer organized tours for those wishing to witness the elephant spectacle in late November. During the rest of the year trains from BANGKOK to KORAT are best. A one way, 2nd class (3rd class) ticket costs 153 Baht (73 Baht). Two special diesel-trains headed for Surin leave BANGKOK at 10:55 h and 21:50 h daily. The ride takes 6-7 hours. Buses from BANGKOK's Northern Bus Terminal drive directly to Surin (451 km) for 86 Baht (ac 155 Baht), from KORAT for 33 Baht.

UDON THANI

This town, lying close to the border to Laos, is an important centre of commerce in the northeast of the country. Many American soldiers were stationed here during the Vietnam war. Peace and quiet returned to the area when they were withdrawn by the US government in 1973 - many of the bars and nightclubs have since been closed down. Most of the night-club owners, by then rich, moved south to Bangkok, where, 15 years later, they are probably making even more.

HOTELS

There is a great supply of empty hotel rooms in Udon, a remnant of the American days gone by. The *KING***, 57 Pho Sri Road has nice rooms, as does the *VICTORY*** in no. 60, ac, tel 221462. The *CHAIYAPORN***, 209-211 Mak Khaeng Road and the *SRI UDON***, 79-91 Amphoe Road, tel 221816, are similar. You will find the cheap *PARADISE*** near the bus station, 44/29 Pho Sri Road,, tel 221956. The *CHAROEN****-*****, 549 Pho Sri Road, tel 211331, is the best hotel.

LEAVING UDON THANI

BY AIR

While planes are fastest, they are also most expensive - 820 Baht via Khon Kaen. The plane continues to Ubon from Udon, cost: 700 Baht. Thai Airways, 60 Mak Khaeng Road, tel 221004.

BY BUS

Buses from BANGKOK (561 km, 7 hrs.) cost 106 Baht, ac 191 Baht. From KORAT buses cost 43 Baht. There are also buses from NONG KHAI (12 Baht). There are two possibilities of getting to the north of Thailand from the northeast: Take a bus to LOEI (3 1/2 hours - 31 Baht). From here take a bus down the newly built road to LOM SAK (3 1/2 hours - 50 Baht), then catch one to PHITSANULOK (2 1/2 hours, 37 Baht). You can also take a bus directly to SUKHOTHAI.

BY RAIL

The three daily trains from BANGKOK take 10 hours. A ride via KORAT and KHON KAEN costs 198 / 95 Baht, 2nd/3rd class.

DAYTRIPS AROUND UDON THANI

BAN CHIANG

The discoveries dating back furthest of all were made in the village of BAN CHIANG, 47 km east of Udon. The human bones that were discovered here by the local inhabitants were considered magical until an American decided to take a closer look at them in 1966. It was then realized that these bones were almost 7000 years old. Further excavations, carried out on a grand scale in the 70s, revealed fragments of clay, weapons, and other items of daily use. Many of the discoveries are exhibited in a small museum near the excavation sites. Buses from Udon to Ban Chiang cost 25 Baht.

PHU KRADUNG

The mountains surrounding Loei are considered the coolest region in all of Thailand. Temperatures sometimes fall to below freezing point in the cool months (November - January). During the hot season (March - May) temperatures in the lowlands have been known to rise above 40^{0}C. An incredible variation of flora has developed in the 60 km^2 sized park - which stretches from the foot of a mountain to the very top of a raised plateau - due to this temperature fluctuation. The landscape often reminds one of Europe. While dry, deciduous monsoon forests dominate the lowlands, the plateau itself is characterized by pine, oak, and maple trees, whose leaves become a flaming red in March and April. At the same time the splendid foliage of rhododendron groves and azalea bushes (in the Suan Sawan), both of which thrive on the cliff walls, add a further note of colour to the beautiful park. Rare birds live here (hornbills, peacocks), as well as wild boars, sambar-deer, various monkeys, langurs, bears, and even a couple of wild elephants. The steppe-like landscape of the 1500 m plateau is ideally suited for hiking. One of the most popular treks leads to various waterfalls - the vegetation in the river valleys is particularly beautiful. Other paths lead along the precariously steep cliff walls. There are several vantage points offering a breathtaking view of the valley below.

Dial 5790529 for the National Park Division of the Forestry Department for the Phu Kradung National Park.

ACCOMMODATION

You can spend the night in a tent for 40 Baht per person. Unless you have your own sleeping bag along, you will probably have to rent a blanket for the night. The park also offers 16 expensive bungalows****.

HOW TO GET THERE

Minibuses leave from LOEI and KHON KAEN in the early morning. Coming from LOEI or CHUM PHAE, you can also get off the bus at the point where the road leading to the park branches off. From here catch a

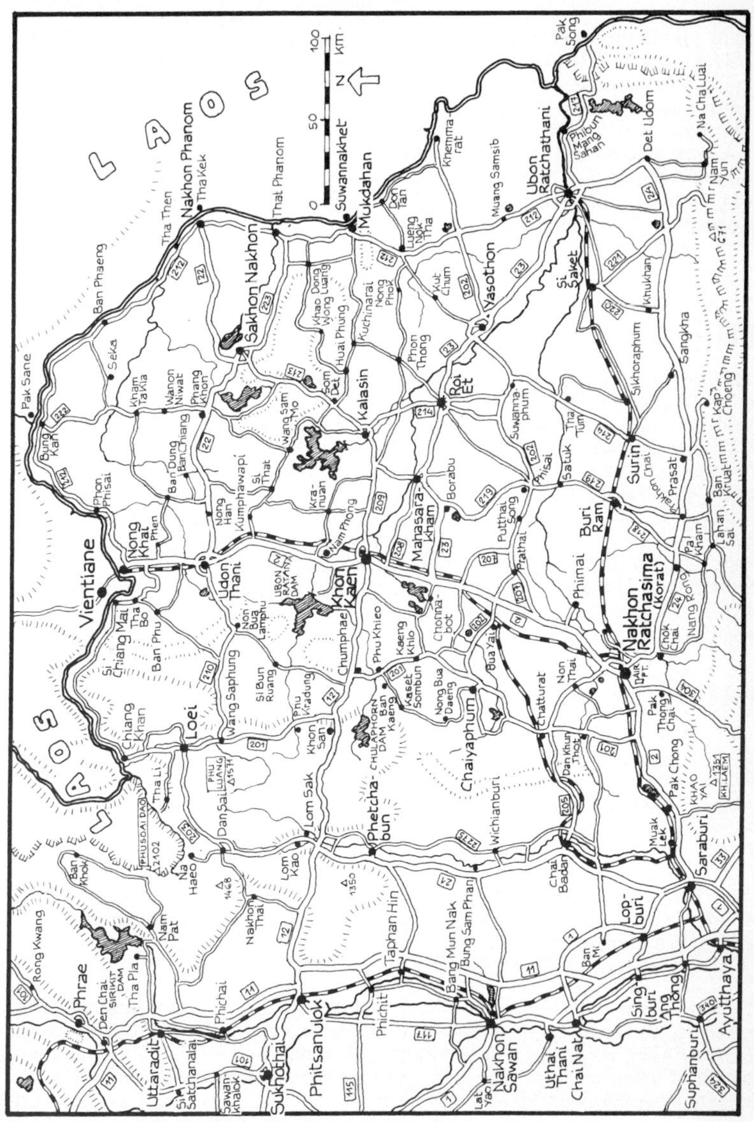
LAOS
Vientiane
Nong Khai
Udon Thani
Khon Kaen
Sakhon Nakhon
Nakhon Phanom
Tha Kek
That Phanom
Suwannakhet
Mukdahan
Kalasin
Roi Et
Yasothon
Ubon Ratchathani
Si Saket
Surin
Buri Ram
Nakhon Ratchasima (Korat)
Mahasarakham
Chaiyaphum
Phetchabun
Loei
Lom Sak
Lom Kao
Chiang Khan
Chiang Mai
Phitsanulok
Sukhothai
Uttaradit
Phrae
Nakhon Sawan
Uthai Thani
Chai Nat
Lopburi
Saraburi
Singburi
Ang Thong
Ayutthaya
Suphanburi
Phimai
Chatturat
Pak Chong
Khao Yai
Sirikit Dam
Ubon Ratana Dam
Chulaphorn Dam
Nong Han
Kumphawapi
Phon Phisai
Bung Kan
Pak Sane
Seka
Ban Phaeng
Tha Then
Don Tan
Khemmarat
Phibun Mang Sahan
Det Udom
Pak Song
Muang Samsib
Sikhoraphum
Sangkha
Prasat
Nang Rong
Chok Chai
Pak Thong Chai
Phu Khieo
Chumphae
Nam Phong
Dan Khun Thot
Wichianburi
Chai Badan
Taphan Hin
Phichit
Bang Mun Nak
Bung Sam Phan
Nakhon Thai
Dan Sai
Na Haeo
Tha Li
Wang Saphung
Non Thai
Bua Yai
Phu Luang
Phu Kradung
0 50 100 KM
N

share taxi to the park entrance, BAN SI THAN STATION (5 Baht - 8 km), where you will find an information centre offering maps showing all hiking treks in the park. The park is closed during the rainy period, from June to September. During the rest of the year it is well visited, though; even people from Bangkok (444 km away) often come up here for the weekend. Getting to the Park HQ is no piece of cake - you will have to hike uphill for three hours. Leave your superfluous luggage at the information centre or hire a carrier for 5 Baht per kilo. After a 5.5 km hike - much of it up ladders and staircases - you will finally have reached the edge of the plateau. From here it is another 3 km to the HQ.

THE EAST COAST

The coastal area east of Bangkok has always been an area put to intensive agricultural use - the people living at the ocean fish, those living further inland cultivate sugar cane, cassava, and rubber trees. The area has always been extremely popular among travellers, too; at the weekends many of Bangkok's inhabitants will come here to escape the heat and humidity of the city and to catch a refreshing breath of cool, sea air. The long periods of good weather and the beautiful beaches have now also enticed many tourists and travel firms to come here. Numerous large hotels and restaurants were opened in Pattaya, goal of many package tourists, and the little fishing village soon became one of the world's centres of international sex-tourism. There is still a lot of 'real' atmosphere in the area east of Pattaya, though, and this is a region well worth visiting.

PATTAYA

It's a man's world, and Pattaya might have been created just to prove this to all those still unconvinced. 800,000 tourists come here yearly, making Pattaya Thailand's largest tourist centre apart from Bangkok itself. Here on a cheap package deal, expecting exotic love beneath tropical palms (...in 'bachelor hotels', more likely), the average Pattaya visitor (young, male and single - though not for long) spends more than 4 days cooped up in one of Pattaya's 12,000 hotel rooms. (At least that's what the statistics say - but what they do there in all that time is never mentioned...) Thus Pattaya could be viewed as a wonderful (or rather miserable) example of the problems tourism can create in a Third World country.

If you feel like cultivating your suntan instead of taking part in the expensive activities, we would suggest moving to the hotels near the YMCA-beach, *JOMTIEN BEACH,* which lies south of Pattaya. The hotels in *NAKLUA,* the northern district of town, are also pleasant. Thai families sometimes stay here, the atmosphere in many of the sois seems more rural than anything else, and you will be woken by the sound of cockerels crowing, not disco-music.

HOTELS

Most of the cheap hotels can be found on Pattaya 2 Rd., a noisy connecting road. The rooms are usually pretty sleazy. You will find a list of Pattayan guesthouses in the Tourist Office. They are not exactly cheap, but you might have luck bargaining if there isn't too much business. Mosquitoes can be a real pest here at certain times of the year - watch out for simple bungalows or hotels surrounded by greenery and water.

The *PATTAYA YOUTH HOSTEL***, Summer Place, Central Pattaya Rd., corner of Pattaya 2 Road, tel 428139, offers rooms starting at 100 Baht, some of them with ac. We found *THE COUNTRY LODGE**-***** (northern Pattaya 2 Road, beyond the Alcazar, tel 418484) quite acceptable - simple and comfortable bungalows with or without ac, two pools, reasonably quiet. The *BEACH PLAZA****, Beach Road near Soi 4, tel 418916, offers ac rooms and a discotheque. There's always a lot of activity in the *PALM LODGE****, tel 418779. You will find *BOONPRASERT**, tel 419144 and *CAESAR**(*)* in Soi 10. The *B.R. INN***, tel 419449 and the *DROP INN***, tel 419803, are on Soi 12. The *THIP**(*), SUN & SAND****, tel 419829, *SAREENA****, tel 419526, and *YOUR PLACE***, tel 419917, are on Soi Chaiyasit (near the post office).

In Naklua, try the *GARDEN LODGE *****; tel 419109, pretty and peaceful, with a pool, a private beach, and a beautiful tropical garden. You'll find *J.M.**(*)*, Naklua Road, tel 419727, further out of town - quiet bungalows with large rooms.

In the south, try the *YMCA CAMP***** at the northern end of Jomtien Beach. After a further 2 km of beach you will reach the *SEA BREEZE*****, tel 418475, which has nice rooms and a small pool. All you have to do to reach the beach is step out of the hotel and cross onto the other side of the road.

FOOD

No other South East Asian bathing resort offers such a variety of food - you can eat Chinese, Indian or Japanese meals, enjoy German, French, Italian, Belgian (potato fritters & sausages), Lebanese and Mexican food. You have the choice of being served by well-dressed waiters in high-class restaurants or simply grabbing a quick bite to eat in one of the many fast-food chains. Stroll through the streets in the evenings and study the menus. Breakfast is usually served quite late - a good, English breakfast of bacon, eggs and sausages is available almost everywhere.

GENERAL INFORMATION

TOURIST INFORMATION - TAT office: Pattaya, 382/1 Beach Road, tel 418750, quite close to the bus stop. The amount of information available here is amazing. Another good source of information is the 'Village'. An evening spent staggering from one bar to the next is all it takes to find out what goes on where. All languages are spoken, and it usually doesn't take long for some 'permanent traveller' to latch onto you and bombard you with all the latest hot infos.

POSTAL SERVICES - you will find the post office in the Chaiyasit Shopping Centre, tel 419340, 183/18 - 20 Soi Chaiyasit. Send and receive telegrams from here. You can make telephone calls (inc. international) from the *TELEPHONE EXCHANGE SERVICE,* South Pattaya Road corner of Pattaya 2 Road, open 24 hours.

IMMIGRATION - you will pay 300 Baht for a 30-day visa extension at the Chonburi District Immigration Office, Soi 8, tel 419374.

POLICE - there is a police station on Beach Road, near Soi 7. The Tourist Police can be found next door to the TAT-office, tel 419371.

MEDICAL SERVICES - you can reach the *PATTAYA MEMORIAL HOSPITAL* by calling 419422 There are also several private clinics in town, all specializing in the treatment of venereal diseases.

BANKS - there are several banks that have a currency exchange service, usually open until the late evening. Try the Bangkok Bank, 545 Beach Road, Thai Farmers Bank, 22 South Pattaya Road, or Siam Commercial Bank, 277 Beach Road.

CAR RACES - car races are held at the weekends near Highway 36, 15 km east of town. Admission is 80-150 Baht.

CABARET - the staggering variety of entertainment may deceive; most of it is aimed at hooking up male tourists with prostitutes. Nevertheless, there are some shows that are really worth it, even in the eyes of traditional, conservative-minded Thais; whole families go and see the drag show put on at the *ALCAZAR,* 78/14 Pattaya 2 Road, tel 418746. The 200 Baht admission fee is pretty steep, but the show is of international standards. You can hardly expect to see a better one in Paris or Berlin. The *TIFFANY SHOW,* Pattaya Sport Bazaar Bldg., tel 429642, is of a similar high standard.

TRANSPORT IN PATTAYA - minibuses inside Pattaya cost 5 Baht. The set price to Jomtien Beach (south) is 20 Baht, to Naklua (north) 10 Baht.

Catch a minibus heading in your direction, state your destination, and pay when you get off - bargaining in advance signifies that you wish to charter the bus. If you wish to be taken to a remote place or even outside of the city limits, you should always definitely agree upon a price with the driver before you leave. Charter for 2 people - 30 Baht, 5 Baht for each additional person.

Motorcycles (100-200 Baht an hour or 150-500 Baht a day), jeeps (300-500 Baht), and cars (from 800 Baht) are for hire along Beach Road, as are sailing boats, surf-boards, water skis and parachutes (for prices see above). Bicycles can be rented, too, for 20 Baht an hour or 80-100 Baht a day. If you are planning to hire a vehicle for a longer period you will always be able to bargain.

HOW TO GET THERE

Buses to Pattaya leave Bangkok's Eastern Bus Terminal every half hour. The ride takes 2 1/2 hours, cost 29 Baht, ac 50 Baht, return ticket 90 Baht. Buses also leave the Northern Bus Terminal on the hour, cost 53 / 96 Baht. Ac buses costing 110 Baht leave from the major hotels. The weekend flight and limousine service from Don Muang Airport (1500 Baht) is only recommended for wealthy travellers. Thai Airways minibuses leave the airport three times daily for Pattaya, cost 190 Baht. There is also a large bus that leaves from the airport on the hour between 7:00 and 19:00 h, cost 100 Baht. Buses from RAYONG cost 20 Baht, from SATTAHIP 11 Baht.

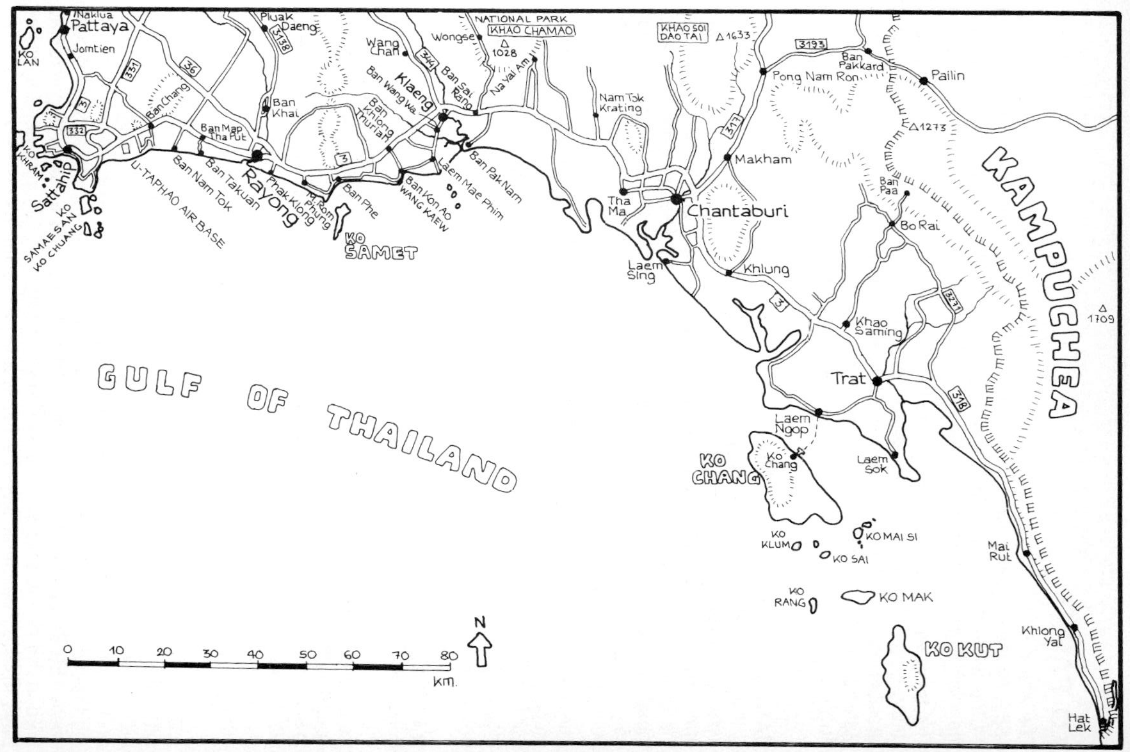
Naklua
Pattaya
Jomtien
KO LAN
Pluak Daeng
3138
Wang Chan
Wongse
NATIONAL PARK
KHAO CHAMAO
Δ 1028
KHAO SOI DAO TAI
Δ 1633
3193
Ban Pakkard
Pong Nam Ron
Pailin
Δ 1273
KAMPUCHEA
Δ 1709
331
36
Ban Chang
3
332
Ban Map Tha Put
Ban Khai
Klaeng
344
Ban Sai Rang
Na Yai Am
Ban Wang wa
Ban Khlong Thuriah
Nam Tok Krating
317
Makham
Ban Paa
Bo Rai
KO KHRAM
Sattahip
KO SAMAESAN
KO CHUANG
U-TAPHAO AIR BASE
Ban Nam Tok
Ban Takuan
Rayong
Phak Klong
H. Rom Phung
Ban Phe
KO SAMET
Ban Kon Ao
WANG KAEW
Laem Mae Phim
Ban Pak Nam
Tha Ma
Chantaburi
Laem Sing
Khlung
Khao Saming
3271
Trat
318
GULF OF THAILAND
Laem Ngop
KO CHANG
Ko Chang
Laem Sok
KO KLUM
KO MAI SI
KO SAI
Mai Rut
KO RANG
KO MAK
Khlong Yai
KO KUT
Hat Lek
0 10 20 30 40 50 60 70 80
km.
N

KO SAMET

The Khao Laem Ya Samet island group was declared a nature reserve in 1981. Numerous bungalow villages with cheap restaurants have been opened on the white, sandy beaches of Ko Samet since (5 Baht admission), making the island one of the most important traveller meeting-points on the east coast.

The fresh-water supply as well as the many malaria-carrying mosquitoes constitute quite a problem on the island. Should you notice early symptoms of a possible case of malaria, go to the Ko Samet Health Centre or the Ko Samet Malaria Clinic immediately. The latter can be found in the village, near the Buddhist temple. A free blood test will be administered here.

PARADISE BEACH (Ao Phao)

is the only beach on the west coast of the island. There are beautiful sunsets here. The beach lies in a rather flat bay, surrounded by rocks. The surf is generally low, and the beach can reached by boat or foot. Due to its being so flat the beach becomes very large indeed at low tide, but it is not quite as nice as those on the east coast of the island. There are many stones and corals. You can go fishing from here or do some coral diving. Excursions to the neighbouring islands of Kudee and Talu cost 120 Baht.

The tides on the east coast are much stronger, and the surf, in consequence, much rougher. Sometimes entire beaches are flooded when the tide rises. The northern beaches can be reached from a road starting at the large landing-place in the village. The bungalows here are usually supplied with fresh water regularly.

HAT SAI KAEO

is in the very north of the island. Thai groups like coming here, especially at the weekends or on holidays, when they enjoy seafood beneath the palm-trees of the restaurants at the northern end of the beach. While the grown-ups spend their time fooling around with surfboards, the children are usually allowed to venture into the shallow water with large car tires which are used as life preservers. Some of the bungalow villages here are very well built and quite expensive. Thai groups often pitch their tents beneath the palm trees during the holiday season.

AO PHAI

with its 3 kilometres of coconut palm studded bay has the finest sand of the entire island. Surfboards can be rented here (350 Baht a day; lessons 80 Baht an hour, also available at many other beaches on the island), as well as sailing boats (100 Baht per hour). A trip to the coral reef in the 'glass bottom boat' costs 150 Baht. You will mainly find farang tourists here, and the music and food in the restaurants is correspondingly 'western'. Cliffs start separating the bays from one another towards the south, where the caves become smaller and smaller.

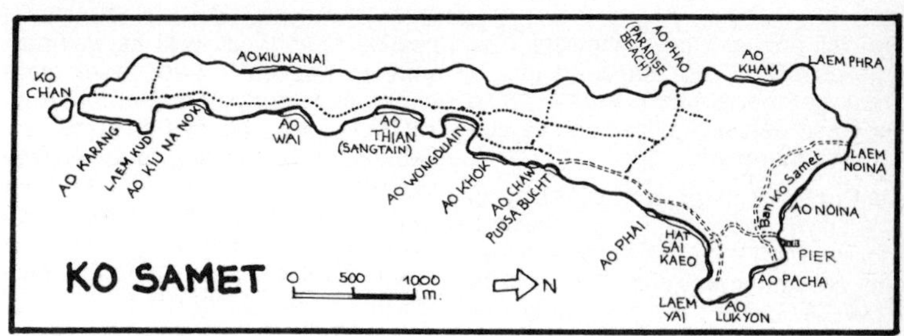

PUDSA

This beach can still be reached by walking. There are many palms on the sandy, white beach.

CHAW (also known as Nuan Beach)

is surrounded by the steep KHOK and TAWON cliffs. Predominantly simple huts have been built on the beautiful beaches. A footpath, which becomes worse and worse as it progresses, leads along the beach, over the cliffs, to the southernmost tip of the long island. Other paths lead through the island's woody thickets to the west coast. A dead end road leading through part of the island will take you to

WONGDUAIN

a large beach with a mixed group of visitors and several restaurants. Further south you will reach

THIAN (Sangtain, Candlelight-Beach)

which has small, rather rocky beaches. Here wells provide the water, i.e. the water - if available at all - will be brackish. You can also buy water in containers (20 Baht for 20 l), which are brought over from the mainland.

ACCOMMODATION

Outside of the main season you will be able to get a hut with a fan and shower for 40 Baht. The prices rise dramatically during the season (November - March), sometimes to 100 Baht. Many of the resorts have running water and electricity.

Paradise Beach: The bungalows of *S.K.HUT**, with a view of the peninsula, *DHOM**, and *RATANAS*** are all rather simple.

Ao Phai: *CHARLEE VILLA* offers huts with*** and without showers*. *TAP TONG BUNGALOWS* have their own restaurant and windsurfing school. The huts of *SEABREEZE** are behind the restaurant, not directly on the beach. Pleasant atmosphere. This is where the road to Paradise Beach branches off. *AO PHAI INN**, with its own restaurant, offers huts on cliffs with no protection from the sun whatsoever. Continue north up the blindingly white beach and you'll reach *NUI'S**, *NAGA** (with a traveller-library), both set on cliffs, *SEA SAND**, a large resort at the beach, and *WHITE SAND BUNGALOWS*-****, which has huts of varying standards. The huts of the *SAIKOEW VILLA****

are well built and have showers. The huts of *TOY*** are crowded into a pretty garden. *SAMET KOAW*****, a large and beautiful settlement, can be found further north.

Ao Pudsa: The large *TUBTIM BUNGALOWS** resort has its own restaurant with a TV and a fine view. The huts are rather crowded. The *PUDSA BUNGALOWS** can be found in a palm grove.

Ao Chaw: The *SEA GULL BUNGALOWS*** are comfortable. You can also pitch tent here.

Ao Khok: The cheap *SUNFLOWER BUNGALOWS** can be found north of the landing place. Double huts** are also available with shower and lavatory. Two cheap restaurants lie beyond the bungalow village.

Ao Tawon: The pretty huts of *THARN TAWON**-****, which lies in a charming area, have shower and fan. There is also a pretty good, though rather expensive restaurant commanding a fine view of the bay. People staying in the huts receive food-coupons.

Wongduain: Some of the large bamboo huts of the *SAMET RESORT*** have their own shower. Simple huts* are also available. The huts of the *SUWITT*** (with shower) are smaller. The two restaurants that stand next to each other on the beach are extremely popular among travellers. Here virtually transparent huts can be rented*, as well as well-built wooden houses**. Two rather more expensive bungalow settlements, *WONG DUEN RESORT**** (with an expensive restaurant) and WONG DUEN VILLA*** can be found further south. Although the bungalows have bathrooms and there is a disco, a ticket office, and much more, the huts are outrageously overpriced.

Sangtain: Pleasant atmosphere, good pancakes. The *CANDLELIGHT BEACH*-*** settlement offers tiny bungalows on cliffs as well as a restaurant. *DURNGTIEN VILLA** has a simple restaurant and a number of huts on a pretty little beach.

Ao Wai: The *SAMET VILLE***** offers luxurious and comfortable bungalows, three meals a day included in the price.

HOW TO GET THERE

The small fishing village of BAN PHE lies 18 km east of Rayong. A minibus from Rayong will cost you 10 Baht. Buses from BANGKOK's Eastern Bus Terminal cost 70 Baht (ac), 120 Baht return. Small boats will bring you to the off-shore island of KO SAMET from BAN PHE for 20 Baht.

There are several restaurants and hotels in BAN PHE, many shops selling shell and coral jewelry, fruit-stands at which to stock up for the trip over to the island, and an international pay-phone at the landing place for boats to Rayong.

CHANTABURI

Chantaburi, 342 km from Bangkok, has 38,000 inhabitants, many of them Vietnamese Christians who settled here after having suffered religious persecution in their own country. Their influence can be felt everywhere. Most of them live near the river. The typical, red Vietnamese plaitworks are sold in some of the shops.

The *CATHEDRAL,* built in the French style, was constructed in 1880. You will find it on the opposite river-bank. There are pedestrian bridges southeast of the market, concealed behind the wooden buildings. Change currency at the Thai Farmers Bank near the market-place. Some of the gems which are cut in town come from the nearby mines. Should you wish to visit these, drive to

KHAO PHLOI WAEN, a few kilometres north of town. A stupa built in Ceylonese style and a mondhop containing a reproduction of Buddha's footprint can be seen on the 150 metre hill. The earth is dug up out of deep shafts in the hill-side. Sometimes there is even a blue sapphire among the normally dark stones that are found here.

HOTELS

Spend the night at the *MUANG CHANT*** by the main road, 257-9 Sri Chan Road, tel 312909, or at the *KAEMSAN 1***, 98 Benjamarachuthid Rd. You'll find the best hotel in town, *MARK'S TRAVEL LODGE****, 14 Raksakchamoon Road, tel 311647, north of the bus station.

HOW TO GET THERE

Going down the shorter road from CHONBURI via BAN BUNG and KLAENG to CHANTABURI is much faster than taking the Sukhumvit Highway, which runs along the coast. Buses from Bangkok cost 56 Baht, ac 103 Baht. Buses to RAYONG leave town from 10:30 (40 Baht ac).

TRAT

This town, furthest east of all towns on the coast and closest to Kampuchea, is the place to set off from should you wish to discover the part of the eastern coast which has not yet been opened up to tourism. The narrow coastal strip, which still belongs to Thailand, is constantly being patrolled by the military. Spending the night is cheap here (bungalows 150 Baht). The road to KLONG YAI is sometimes closed when relations with Kampuchea become strained. Buses are rare, and the paths leading to the beaches from the main road are none too good. Most of the beaches can be found between kilometre stones 41 and 47 - there is no accommodation available here, though. If you want to get to the off-shore islands, leave Trat for LAEM NGOP in the early mornings. As the boats are rather expensive, we would recommend bargaining one day in advance in order to avoid unpleasant surprises. Visiting KO KUT and KO MAK, the islands furthest south, is particularly expensive. You might be able to spend the night on KO KRAAT or KO CHANG. Ask the fishermen.

HOTELS

Spend the night at the *MUANG TRAT HOTEL***, 4 Sukhumvit Road, or the *THAI ROON ROJANA****, 98 Benjamarachuthid Road.

HOW TO GET THERE

There are four ac buses that leave BANGKOK daily for Trat (128 Baht).

SOUTH THAILAND

If you're travelling south from Bangkok, down Highway no. 4 or by train, you'll be travelling along the main traffic connections of the region, which reach all the way through the Malaysian peninsula to Singapore. You will never be far from the ocean whilst travelling down this 1600 km stretch - wonderful beaches, coral reefs, and small, tropical islands perfect for relaxing and forgetting the hectic activity of the large cities, can be found in abundance. The distance between Bangkok and the Malaysian border is 1000 km. Don't let the many fast buses and trains tempt you to rush through this area - there is much to see. Excursions to the traditional bathing resorts and the mountains cost time and effort, true, but they offer an almost unique chance of gaining an insight into the life of the people of this area. The landscape becomes increasingly tropical as you travel south. You will come across more and more mosques in the towns - Malaysian influences cannot be denied.

HUA HIN

The smell of freshly-baked sweets hangs over the night market. People sit about enjoying the cool evening and the food sold at the various cook-houses. Imitation Lacoste shirts and Rolex lie neatly arranged next to the many fruits of the foodstands. Two rather forlorn looking backpack travellers stand in the midst of all this. Though they have only just arrived, they have already decided to go straight on to Ko Samui - 'cause there certainly doesn't seem to be much going on here! This was witnessed in 1987 in Hua Hin. And if you've come expecting to find secluded, palm-studded beaches, you really should move further south. You will have an equally hard and fruitless time trying to find a Pattayan-type night-life, exotic temples, or any other traditional sights. If you are content with a genuine Thai bathing resort atmosphere, family picnics at the beach, shops full of shell souvenirs, and truly delicious seafood, however, then you've come to the right place! You can also set off for various excursions into the beautiful surrounding area from here.

38,000 people live here, in the oldest of all of Thailand's bathing resorts, which lies only 188 km from Bangkok on the southern railway line. When construction on the line was completed in 1921, the royal head of the railway, Prince Purachtra, ordered the

RAILWAY HOTEL to be built. This European-style hotel with tennis courts and a golf course (the first in the country, incidentally) was intended for a rich, distinguished clientele. The high society would meet here during the hot season and enjoy the cool sea breeze. Rama VI was so enchanted by the place that he decided to have a

SUMMER RESIDENCE (Klai Kangwon=without troubles) built just 2 km north of the harbour. The Royal Family still visits frequently to this very day. Unfortunately, the residence is fenced in - no visitors are allowed. The bungalows of other members of the Royal Family can also be found in and around Hua Hin.

HOTELS

You'll find the *RAILWAY HOTEL*****, very stylish with rooms costing over 1000 Baht, directly at the beach, at the end of Damnoen Kasem Road, tel 511012. It has been restored entirely to its original style and is now called *THE CENTRAL HUA HIN RESORT*. It offers bungalows at the beach as well as huge, Victorian-style rooms commanding a fine view over the ocean. It may seem strangely familiar to those who have seen the film 'The Killing Fields'.

Private rooms costing between 50-100 Baht can be rented across the road, behind the tourist market. Good and cheap western breakfast is served here. We would recommend the new *JED PEE NONG HOTEL***-***, 17 Damnoen Kasem Road, tel 512381. All rooms are clean and have a bathroom and lavatory, a fan or ac. The *RAMUNG HOTEL***, tel 511940, Damnoen Kasem Road, towards the railway station, offers rooms with a fan, bathroom, and balcony. The following hotels all have similar prices:

*SUPHAMITRA HOTEL*** (ac***), 19 Amnuaey Sin Road, tel 511208, with showers and fans or ac, new and quite nice, near the market.

*HUA HIN GUESTHOUSE****-****, Poonsuk Road, tel 511653, small and pleasant.

*MEECHAI**, 57/2 Phetchkasem Road, tel 511035, with its own restaurant, simple and cheap, though rather loud because of the nearby through street.

FOOD

Fantastic Thai seafood with fresh fish, lobsters, and other sea creatures is served at several restaurants directly at the beach and on Phetchkasem Road. Fish are kept in large basins or on ice in front of the restaurants, and you can choose yourself the fish you wish to eat.

The *SEANG THAI SEAFOOD RESTAURANT* near the pier is our personal favourite. The extensive, illustrated menu offers expensive lobster meals as well as equally good, cheaper dishes. The *CHAROEN POCHANA*, another seafood restaurant, lies opposite. The atmosphere here is better than in the restaurants east of the market, most of which are on or near the rather loud Phetchkasem Road. The fish is just as good and fresh here, though. Try the *SUPHAROS RESTAURANT*, 69/2-3 Phetchkasem Road. The *KHOUNG SENG*, a Chinese seafood restaurant, is right next door.

The food served at the *NIGHT MARKET* is cheap, too. The market begins as soon as it gets dark, and chairs and tables are set up on the large, central square, so that you can sit comfortably and observe the bustling activity around you whilst eating.

The *KHAOKANG BAANTHAI*, Dechanuchit Road, only a few metres east of the night market, serves delicious coconut ice-cream.

The *CORNER BAR*, a pub which can be found in the same road, is the place to go late at night, opened from 16:00 hours until the early morning.

GENERAL INFORMATION

TOURIST INFORMATION - the last time we were there, the local tourist office (competent people, good information concerning everything, even connections) was in the Damnoen Kasem Road - by now they may have moved.

POST - the post office is across the road from the tourist office. International phone calls can be made.

TRANSPORTATION IN AND AROUND HUA HIN - bicycle rickshas are a popular form of transportation - 5-10 Baht for short distances, 15 Baht for longer ones, e.g. from the railway station to the beach. Minibuses for 3-4 Baht per person leave Chatchai Hotel for the area surrounding town. Bicycles (80 Baht a day) and motorcycles (150-200 Baht) can be rented opposite the tourist market. A day's sightseeing with a taxi will cost you approx. 300 Baht plus petrol - the set price for a ride to the Khao Sam Roi Yot Park is 600 Baht.

LEAVING HUA HIN

BY TRAIN

The railway station is approx. 1 km from the beach. Most of the trains to BANGKOK (87 / 44 Baht for the 2nd/3rd class) via NAKHON PATHOM (69 / 33 Baht) leave at night. We would recommend taking the train that leaves Hua Hin at 6:01 hours and arrives in Bangkok at 10:00 hours. Change to the diesel train in Nakhon Pathom (departure 9:09 hours), if you're headed towards Kanchanaburi. Southbound trains leave at 16:16 h and 17:43 h, the train to Malaysia and SINGAPORE (837 Baht - 2nd class) leaves at 18:53 hours. Trains to HAAD YAI (244 / 116 Baht) leave at 19:58, to NAKHON SI THAMMARAT (209 / 100 Baht) at 21:28 h. If you're headed towards SURAT THANI (154 / 74 Baht) we would recommend taking the last train at 22:14, which reaches the ferry-harbour for boats to Ko Samui the next morning at 5:59 hours.

BY BUS

Most buses stop at the downtown bus station, west of the night market. Ac buses to BANGKOK (74 Baht, 3 1/2 hours) leave every hour. The cheaper ones (47 Baht, 4 hours) leave every half hour. Buses to PHETCHBURI cost 15 Baht, 1 hour; PRACHUAP KHIRI KHAN 21 Baht, 1 1/2 hours; SURAT THANI 89 Baht, 8 1/2 hours; RANONG 74 Baht, 6 1/2 hours. Ac buses from Bangkok to SURAT THANI stop at the overland bus station, 3-4 km north of town at the Suphapchon Restaurant. They are frequently booked up, however. A minibus from Hua Hin to the restaurant will cost you 4 Baht.

PRACHUAP KHIRI KHAN

This provincial town lies at the southern end of a bay. Many fishing boats lie moored in its natural harbour, which has the additional protection of a number of offshore cliff islands. The 'mirror mountain', *KHAO CHONGKRACHOK*, home of many cheeky monkeys, is quite close to the beach. You will be rewarded with a fine view if you climb the 415 steps of the staircase leading to the small temple on the mountain's peak. Next to the offshore islands and the town, you'll be able to see a mountain range which is actually in Burma. At this point, Thailand is just a couple of kilometres in width.

The town isn't really worth an extended stay, though - it has too little to offer. The beaches close to town and along the bay are none too clean and the water is murky.

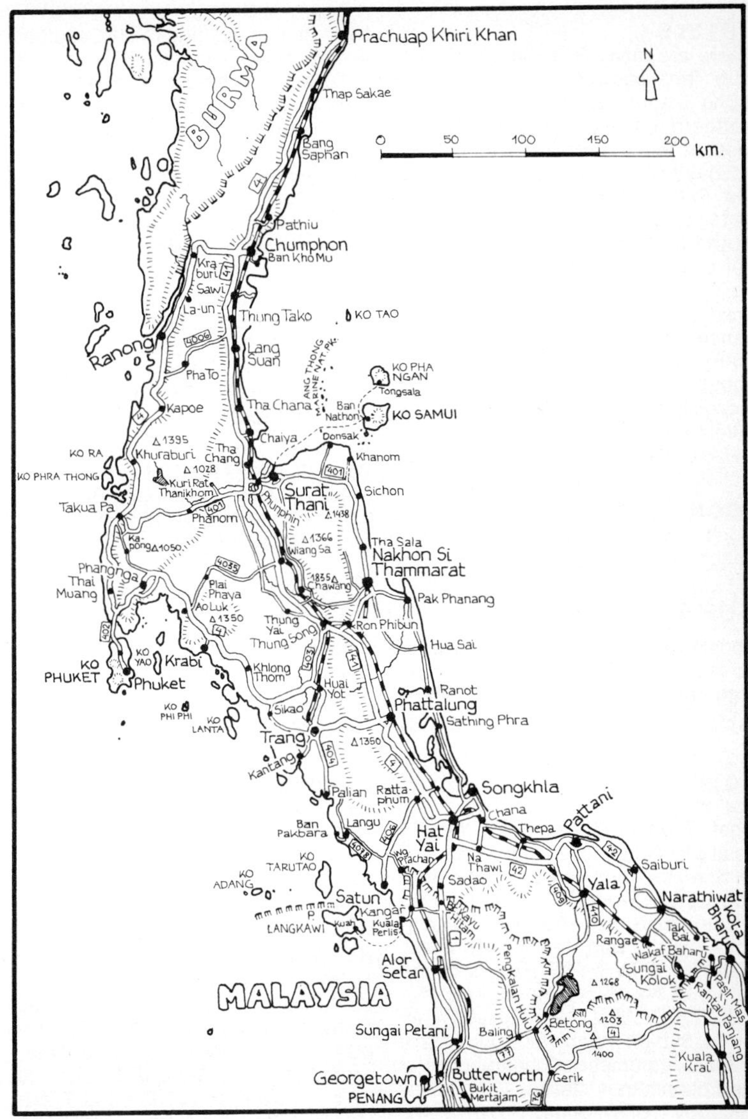
Prachuap Khiri Khan
BURMA
Thap Sakae
Bang Saphan
0 50 100 150 200 km.
N
Pathiu
Chumphon
Ban Kho Mu
Kraburi
Sawi
La-un
Thung Tako
KO TAO
Ranong
Lang Suan
ANG THONG MARINE NAT. PK.
KO PHA NGAN
Tongsala
Pha To
Kapoe
Tha Chana
Ban Nathon
KO SAMUI
Donsak
Chaiya
Khanom
KO RA
Khuraburi
Tha Chang
KO PHRA THONG
Kuri Rat Thanikhom
Surat Thani
Sichon
Takua Pa
Phanom
Phunphin
Ka-pong
Wiang Sa
Tha Sala
Nakhon Si Thammarat
Phangnga
Thai Muang
Plai Phaya
Ao Luk
Chawang
Pak Phanang
Thung Yai
Thung Song
Ron Phibun
Hua Sai
KO PHUKET
KO YAO
Krabi
Phuket
Khlong Thom
Huai Yot
Ranot
Phattalung
KO PHI PHI
KO LANTA
Sikao
Sathing Phra
Trang
Kantang
Palian
Rattaphum
Songkhla
Chana
Pattani
Ban Pakbara
Langu
Hat Yai
Thepa
Saiburi
KO TARUTAO
KO ADANG
Wg. Prachan
Na Thawi
Sadao
Yala
Satun
Narathiwat
P. LANGKAWI
Kuah
Kangar
Kuala Perlis
Bukit Kayu Hitam
Tak Bai
Kota Bharu
Rangae
Waka Baharu
Sungai Kolok
Alor Setar
Pengkalan Hulu
Pasir Mas
Rantau Panjang
MALAYSIA
Sungai Petani
Baling
Betong
Georgetown
PENANG
Butterworth
Bukit Mertajam
Gerik
Kuala Krai

HOTELS
There are many *BUNGALOWS**-**** with fan, showers, and lavatories along the embankment road at the northern bay, close to the beach. Most of these are patronized by Thai holiday-makers. The people running the *SUK SAN BUNGALOWS*, tel 6111145, are not particularly friendly. At the weekends it is very difficult to get a room here, but outside of the season the place is nearly always empty. Loud motorcycles are a nuisance in the evenings, as are the many hungry monkeys roaming about, and the mosquitoes. Bring a mosquito net or coils. There are more hotels around, e.g. *HOTEL YUTTIICHAI**, 200 metres from the railway station.

FOOD
Don't miss the foodstands at the beach promenade south of the harbour in the evenings. The seafood served here is fantastic! We would definitely recommend trying the Tom Yam prepared by the fat, jolly cook. The young, particularly spicy coconuts sold at the stands along the embankment road are a further culinary delight.

HOW TO GET THERE
BY TRAIN
Take the train from BANGKOK at 12:30 h for 142/78 Baht in the 2nd/3rd class (incl. Rapid extra charge), arrival 17:20; the other three trains do not arrive until much later (between 21:27 and 23:34 h).

BY BUS
Buses leave BANGKOK regularly between 4:30 and 17:20 h (63 Baht, 323 km), ac buses leave at 8:00, 12:00, and 16:30 h (105 Baht).

SURAT THANI
People usually only stop at this actually rather uninteresting town en route to Ko Samui. Most travellers see no reason to stay here longer than it takes to organize further transportation. The

TOURIST OFFICE is in the west of town, on Na Muang Road.

HOTELS
For those who have to spend the night: *THAI TANI HOTEL***, 306-308 Talat Mai Road, tel 272977, reception on the 3rd floor, clean rooms with shower. *TAPI HOTEL**** is on Chonkasem Road, no. 100, near the harbour and the Ban Don Bus Terminal. *MUANG TONG HOTEL*** is on the corner of Na-Muang Road. The *MUANG TAI HOTEL*** is of similar standards, 390-92 Talad Mai Road. There are also a number of cheap hotels at the Phunpin train station, 13 km away (*QUEEN*, SRI RAMIE*, THAI FAH** etc.).

LEAVING SURAT THANI
BY PLANE
Thai Airways Office, 3/27-28 Karun Rat Road, tel 272610 (1 km south of the Bus Terminal). Daily flights to BANGKOK, to PHUKET, and to NAKHON SI THAMMARAT.

BY TRAIN
There are daily trains to BANGKOK . Seats can only be reserved for the trains at 17:48, 18:20, and 20:42 h (224/107 Baht for the 2nd/3rd class, approx. 11 hrs.). Four daily trains to HAT YAI between 23:18 h and 3:25 h (144/57 Baht, 2nd/3rd class). Two

trains leave for SUNGAI GOLOK around midnight (216 Baht).

An international express leaves for BUTTERWORTH (Penang) at 1:55 h (279 Baht, 9 hrs.), from where it heads on to KUALA LUMPUR (507 Baht, 18 hrs.), and SINGAPORE (747 Baht, 28 hrs.)

BY BUS

All non-ac buses and local buses leave from the Bus Terminal east of Ban Don harbour.

If you want to get to Bangkok or Hat Yai we would recommend taking an respective company offices. You will find several offices on the road running parallel to the river. Ac buses to BANGKOK leave 11:15 and 20:00 h (225 Baht, 9 hrs.) many non-ac buses leave between 7:00 and 21:00 h (125 Baht, 10 hrs.). Ac buses to HAT YAI leave at 5:30 h and at 16:00 h (150 Baht, 5 hrs.), several non-ac buses leave for Hat Yai before noon (67 Baht).

The Surat Thani-PHUKET route leads through one of the most beautiful stretches of countryside in Thailand; many non-ac buses leave between 5:30 and 13:00 h (61 Baht, 6 hrs.).

BY BOAT

Speed boats, express boats, and night boats leave Ban Don, Don Sak, and Khanom for KO SAMUI and KO PHA NGAN all day and night, as do (car-) ferries (see *How to get there: Ko Samui* and *Ko Pha Ngan).*

KO SAMUI

Ko Samui, the country's third-largest island, lies in the southwestern part of the Gulf of Thailand. The island measures a total of 247 km^2 in size, 14 km in width, and 20 km in length. 25 % of the island consists of plains, mainly used for raising coconut-palms. An alleged 2 million coconuts are shipped to Bangkok monthly. The central, jungle-overgrown highlands of the island are only put to a very limited agricultural use; the local inhabitants plant durians, rambutans, langsats, and mangosteen on the outer slopes, in their gardens, which the unpractised tourist's eye will barely be able to distinguish from the jungle.

The days when Ko Samui was still a well-kept secret among travellers, when the island could only be reached by fishing boat and could only be travelled around on foot, have long since passed. Car ferries and speedboats now travel back and forth regularly, a 50 km, concrete road circles the island, and a few smaller roads branch off to the highlands within. An airstrip has even been built on the northeastern tip of the island. Scores of tourist bungalow resorts have been founded on the most beautiful of the beaches, and it didn't take long for large, modern hotels to be erected. Ko Samui, in other words, is on its way to becoming yet another international tourist ghetto. The only thing which has stopped this from happening yet is the fact that the water supply constitutes quite a problem which the owners of the large hotels have been trying to solve for years.

NATHON

The island's main town generates a laid back atmosphere of laissez-faire. It has adapted perfectly to the needs of western travellers, without, however, competing for their business. The speed boats and night boats arrive here. Obstinate Thais may try to talk you into renting a bungalow at their resort if you arrive outside of the main season, but this will be the last annoyance you will have to deal with once there. Nathon seems swept clean of tourists soon after the boats have left, especially in the evening; a mysterious magnetic force seems to immediately attract all travellers to the nearest beaches. Don't worry if you should arrive too late to find a bungalow on your first night there; there are plenty of places in town that can offer perfectly acceptable temporary accommodation.

HOTELS

There are a few hotels on Beach Rd., e.g. *CHOKHANA*** and *CHINTA***. *SAMUI BUNGALOWS***, next to the post office; with fan and bathroom. *CHAO KAO***-*****, tel 2528150, is a little further on; comfortable bungalows.

FOOD

There are many restaurants (mainly serving European food) along the pier and the northern intersecting road. If you've been longing for pizza, a hamburger, or a steak, you've come to the right place. Chinese restaurants and restaurants serving the typical Thai curries can be found on the side roads. Those wishing to cook for themselves can stock up at the supermarket in the first parallel road. The market (in the morning) is the best place to go for fruit, vegetables, and fish.

GENERAL INFORMATION

WHEN TO GO - Ko Samui has its own micro-climate; you can theoretically spend the entire year on the island if you are in the right districts at the right time. You had better stay in the north, west, or south of the island during the northeast monsoon from mid-December to mid-February. The wind seems to stop blowing between April and June, when it sometimes becomes unbearably hot. Chaweng and Lamai are both totally booked up in July/August as well as over Christmas/New Year. The height of the season is between mid-December and March.

TRAVEL AGENCIES - there are many small travel agencies along the pier offering bus, train, boat, and plane tickets. You can also have a flight confirmed from here (for a small fee), and book international flights. This will cost you approx. 1000 Baht more than it would in Bangkok. You will be able to buy train tickets without having to pay any extra charge at the Thai Airways Office. Generally, all travel agencies will give you friendly and helpful information concerning the various possible ways of leaving the island.

POST OFFICE - at the northern end of the pier, with an international telephone and poste restante service, very helpful employees. The packing service is in front of the post office. Seamail packages need 4 months to reach Europe from here. Open Mon-Fri 8:30-16:30 h, Sat till 12:00 h.

IMMIGRATION OFFICE - on the main road, right next to the police station. You can have your 2 month tourist visa extended by 30 days here;

bring 2 passport pictures and a photocopy of your passport.

TOURIST POLICE - 3 km south of town, tel 421245.

BANKS - You will find the Krung Thai Bank and the Thai Farmers Bank on the main road. The Krung Thai Bank is open daily from 8:30-20:00 h. Having a money order wired here is no problem. There are also safe deposit boxes and a poste restante service.

MOTORCYCLES / JEEPS - are cheaper in Nathon than they are at the beaches. Motorcycle 150-250 Baht, moped 120-200 Baht, jeep 400-500 Baht. You will be able to tell which places rent out vehicles by the signs in front of the shops. Petrol costs 9 Baht/litre at the petrol station on the main road, a hefty 11-12 Baht / litre at the mini-petrol stations along the circular road.

PUBLIC TRANSPORT ON THE ISLAND

Pick-ups with bench seats (songthaew) are the most common form of public transport on the island. They come to all of the island's beaches at least twice daily. Their final destinations are usually written on the front of the car. You can stop them (or have them let you out) anywhere along the line. A ride will cost you between 10 and 20 Baht, depending on the distance.

HOW TO GET THERE

BY TRAIN / BUS

From BANGKOK: A particularly pleasant trip for those who buy the combined train - bus - boat - ticket, which leaves Bangkok at 18:30 h (arrival Ko Samui 10:30 h), 180 Baht for 3rd class, 299 Baht for 2nd class (seat), 369 Baht (sleeper - upper bunk), 399 Baht (lower bunk), 449 Baht (ac-sleeper - upper bunk), 479 Baht (lower bunk); these are the prices for those buying their tickets at the train station. You will have to pay an extra 40 Baht at travel agents. 5 further trains arrive between 23:13 and 4:42 h; we would not recommend taking any of these as you'll have to hang around for ages upon arriving.

A direct ac bus leaves for Ko Samui at 20:00 h (288 Baht, incl. ferry, 15 hrs.). A non-ac bus leaves at 19:00 h (143 Baht, 16 hrs.).

From PHUKET: Several ac minibuses leave for Ko Samui before noon (150 Baht, 4 hrs. + ferry). 8 local buses to SURAT THANI leave before noon (61 Baht, 6 hrs.).

From KRABI: Direct ac minibuses leave every morning (100 Baht, approx. 7 hrs.). The local bus to SURAT THANI leaves every hour between 6:00 and 14:30 h (50 Baht, 3 hrs.).

From HAT YAI: Direct ac minibuses cost 150 Baht. Three local buses to SURAT THANI leave in the morning (67 Baht, 5 hrs.).

From PENANG: Daily ac minibuses at 4:30 h for M$40 (400 Baht, 12-14 hrs.). There is also a daily train at 13:35 h (arrival in SURAT THANI 22:09 h; you might just make it in time to catch the night boat) - 2nd class seats 279 Baht.

BY BOAT

New boats and companies are constantly offering their services to KO SAMUI from SURAT THANI or vice versa. A Nathon-bound speedboat leaves Ban Don daily at 9:30, 14:30, and 17:00 h (60 Baht, 2 hrs.).

Express boats leave Don Sak and Khanom 3 times daily (60 Baht, 1 h plus bus 1 h). The ferry to the Ko Samui ferry jetty leaves from Don Sak (from Khanom when the surf is particularly high) 5 times daily between 8:00 and 17:30 h (40 Baht, 1 1/2 hrs.). Motorcycles 30 Baht, cars 175 Baht (incl. driver), minibus 200 Baht. Ko Samui looks its best as you approach the ferry jetty from the sea; pretty bungalows beneath a long, palm-fringed beach. The night boat from Ban Don leaves at 23:00 h (50 Baht, 6 hrs.) - not recommended, seeing as the entire crew sometimes sleeps through the trip along with the passengers. There have been two collisions with the boat returning from the island during the last two years!

BEACHES AND BUNGALOWS

The word that Ko Samui is a traveller's paradise has spread rapidly in the last couple of years. The more travellers go, the more bungalow resorts are opened. But there is no cause for panic yet; you will nearly always find what you're looking for if you consider carefully before deciding which beach and which bungalow you wish to stay at.

We would recommend the following course of action. Choose a beach from the descriptions given and have yourself taken there by pick-up. Leave your luggage at a restaurant and then set out in search of a hut on foot. Take anything for the first night but try to reserve something better for the next couple of days. If you feel that the beach you've ended up on isn't really the one you had in mind, simply rent a motorcycle and continue your search on the island's other beaches the next day. You can always reserve your dream bungalow, should it be momentarily booked up. Heavy bargaining is possible outside of the season if there are only a few travellers around. Those with sensitive ears would be well advised to find a bungalow not too close to the generators and restaurants.

The most popular beaches (and the ones that are most frequently overcrowded) are in the east of the island. Those in the north are not visited quite as often, and those in the west and south even offer perfect solitude at times. The simple-type bungalows are slowly but surely vanishing off the face of the island. The new ones are much more comfortable. The price you will be expected to pay depends largely on the facilities offered (size, private bathroom, glass windows, good mattress, easy chair, terrace, fan, or even ac), as well as the general prices at the rest of the beach. Prices have little to do with the location or quality of the resort.

Simple bungalows can still be rented for approx. 30 Baht a night. Expect to have to pay between 50 and 100 Baht if you want to have a private lavatory or shower. Those bungalows with chairs, tables, a good mattress, and a fan will cost between 120 and 180 Baht. The better resorts raise their prices by 25-100% during the high season (June 16th-August 31st and December 20th-January 10th).

All bungalow resorts have their own restaurants. The food served at many of them is both cheap and good.

BO PHUT BEACH

This rather steep, coarse beach is in a 3 km, curved bay in the north. Suitable for swimming and windsurfing all year round. A couple of windsurfing schools have been opened here during the past few years. The beach is nicest at the northern end of the bay, it merges with the village of Ban Bo Phut in the south. Many French travellers come here. There are even a few French and Belgian restaurants. Prices are a little above average.

BUNGALOWS AND HOTELS

There're 11 bungalow 'villages', most of them*, some of them**-***, e.g. *WORLD BUNGALOW**-***, bungalows of various standards in a nice garden. Rowing and motor boats can be rented. Both the *PALM GARDEN** and the *CALM** offer tidy bungalows in a palm-tree plantation. The *PEACE* *-** offers larger bungalows, especially suited for families, as well as a nice beach. The *SAMUI PALM BEACH***** offers well-tended bungalows, ac, and large terraces, 9 of them directly on the sea. *HEME**** offers two terraced houses at the exit of the village.

BIG BUDDHA BEACH

This relatively small bay commands a view of two offshore islands and a colossal Buddha statue. Whether or not it is tasteful to expose oneself in front of Buddha's eyes is something everyone will have to decide for themselves.

The white sandy beach is quite beautiful in the summer, when the wind blows from the west. The water becomes rather choppy when the wind gets stronger. The sea retreats a little when the wind blows from the east (in the winter), and it is then that the beach suddenly becomes very wide and rather ugly (mud and slippery stones), especially at low tide. The beach is not suitable for swimming at all during this time of the year.

BUNGALOWS AND HOTELS

Big Buddha Beach has become increasingly popular in recent times, in spite (or maybe just because) of the nearby road. As a result, more and more bungalow villages are squeezing themselves in between those already existing. The newer resorts all offer bungalows of very high standards, some built of brick, with fans, and even tiled bathrooms. The prices are generally rather high. There are 13 bungalow resorts here at the present time, most of them *-**.

Try the *FAMILY VILLAGE BUNGALOW**-** (ac***), brick huts, clean and tidy; good restaurant, family atmosphere. The *SUNSET BUNGALOWS** are right next door; simple huts in the old style. *KINNAREE BUNGALOW**-** and *PIAK BUNGALOW**-** are among the more recent resorts, both with slightly superior, bungalows. *NARA LODGE****-****, a well-cared for hotel with terraced houses, hidden behind a high wall. The new road to the airport branches off from here.

CHOENG MON BEACH

This beautiful, small bay is at the northern tip of the island. The white, sandy beach is lined with coconut-palms and casuarina-trees. The middle section of the bay has a wonderful beach and is suitable for bathing all year round. It is most suitable for children, too. The small offshore island to the west is a challenge to any traveller. Exploring its rather rugged terrain can be quite exhausting, though. You can walk over to the island when the tide is low in the summer, you will have to swim across at high tide in the winter. The seclusion of this lovely bay came to a rather abrupt end in 1987, when the Imperial Group decided to have two hotels built here. Though they did not turn out quite as ugly as everyone feared, they are still a thorn in many a traveller's side.

BUNGALOWS AND HOTELS

There are 6 bungalow villages on the bay at the present time. The cheapest (and simplest) huts are still those closest to the sea, those further back are more comfortable and more expensive. You will find the *OASIS**-**** in the very east, on top of the hill; new bungalows situated in a palm grove. You will be able to reach the secluded and rocky Phung Bay from here. *ISLAND VIEW**, a spacious resort run by a nice family, offering simple bungalows. The beach in front of it is not suitable for bathing. *CHATKAEO RESORT** is run by a Chinese woman; new bungalows, all with a view of the restaurant. *CHOENGMON BUNGALOWS** offers simple as well as more comfortable huts. *T&T BUNGALOWS**** is owned by a German; the large, high, and well furnished huts stand in a circular arrangement, quite far from the actual beach. The exclusive restaurant furnished with chairs made from tree roots at the driveway also belongs to T&T. *P.S. VILLA** offers bungalows of varying standards and has a nice restaurant. The *TONGSAI BAY HOTEL***** is Ko Samui's most expensive hotel (over 2000 Baht). Its white bungalows on the slope and the 3-storey hotel complex give it a vaguely Mediterranean appearance. All of the bungalows are fully-ac suites with large terraces commanding a wonderful view of the bay. The hotel has a salt-water pool as well as a small stretch of private beach. Drinking water is obtained from a spring which is 5 km away from the hotel. For reservations from Bangkok, call 2540023. *BOAT HOTEL****;* the same hotel group has dreamed up a particularly expensive gag; 36 boats from Bangkok's klongs have been hauled ashore and converted into luxury suites. They now lie scattered among the beach's cheaper bungalows.

CHAWENG BAY

This 6 km, slightly curved bay opens up to the east. One bungalow resort stands next to the other, but one still gets the impression of a totally uninhabited, tropical beach when regarding it from the view point in the south. All resorts are between the rarely used laterite path and the wide and beautiful sandy beach. Prices here are higher than at the other beaches and the general atmosphere is much more touristy. There are differences between the respective sections of the beach, so we have given separate descriptions.

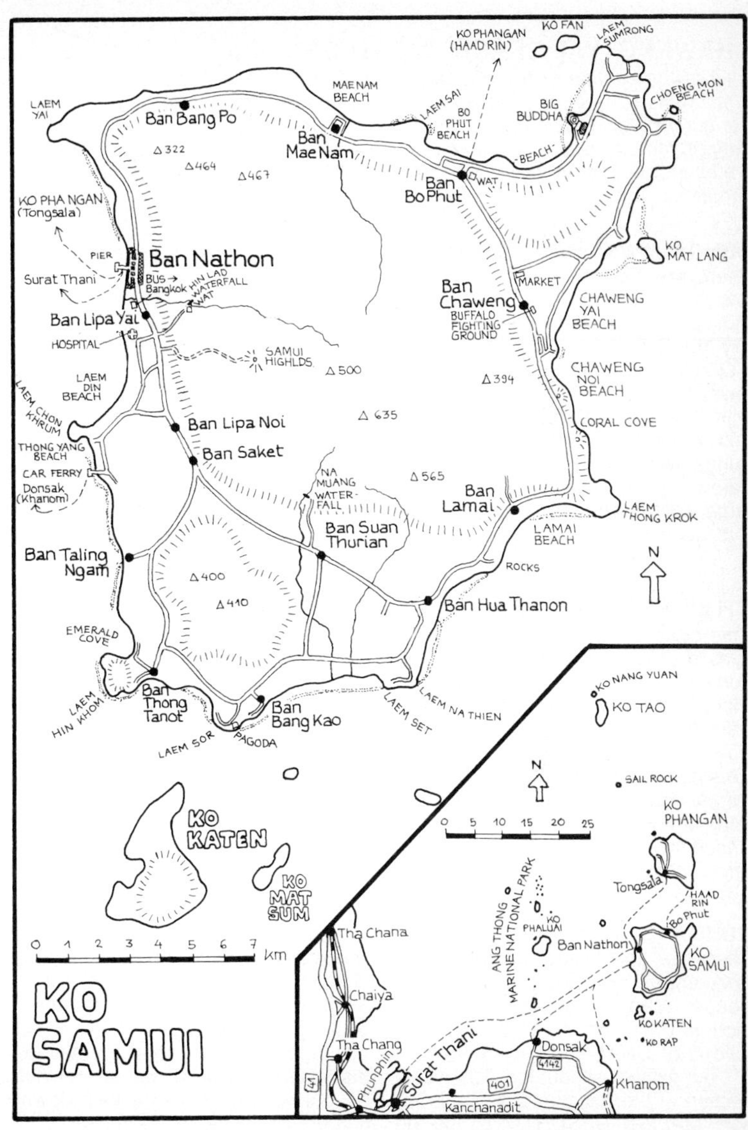
KO SAMUI
KO PHANGAN (HAAD RIN)
KO FAN
LAEM SUMRONG
CHOENG MON BEACH
BIG BUDDHA
MAE NAM BEACH
LAEM SAI
BO PHUT BEACH
BEACH
LAEM YAI
Ban Bang Po
Ban Mae Nam
Ban Bo Phut
WAT
KO PHA NGAN (Tongsala)
PIER
Ban Nathon
Surat Thani
BUS → Bangkok
HIN LAD WATERFALL
WAT
Ban Lipa Yai
HOSPITAL
SAMUI HIGHLDS.
KO MAT LANG
MARKET
Ban Chaweng
BUFFALO FIGHTING GROUND
CHAWENG YAI BEACH
CHAWENG NOI BEACH
CORAL COVE
LAEM DIN BEACH
LAEM CHON KHRUM
Ban Lipa Noi
Ban Saket
THONG YANG BEACH
CAR FERRY
Donsak (Khanom)
NA MUANG WATER-FALL
Ban Lamai
LAEM THONG KROK
LAMAI BEACH
Ban Suan Thurian
Ban Taling Ngam
ROCKS
Ban Hua Thanon
EMERALD COVE
Ban Thong Tanot
Ban Bang Kao
LAEM HIN KHOM
LAEM SOR
PAGODA
LAEM SET
LAEM NA THIEN
KO KATEN
KO MAT SUM
0 1 2 3 4 5 6 7 km
N
KO NANG YUAN
KO TAO
SAIL ROCK
KO PHANGAN
Tongsala
HAAD RIN
Bo Phut
ANG THONG MARINE NATIONAL PARK
KO PHALUAI
Ban Nathon
KO SAMUI
KO KATEN
KO RAP
0 5 10 15 20 25
Tha Chana
Chaiya
Tha Chang
Phunphin
Surat Thani
Donsak
4142
401
41
Khanom
Kanchanadit

CHAWENG YAI BEACH, NORTHERN END

This is the section of the bay favoured by real beach freaks; the sea is so shallow that the beach becomes several hundred metres long at low tide - perfect for jogging and frisbee. You will be able to reach the island of Ko Matlang on foot at these times. The reef to the south forms a small lagoon of warm water at low tide, in which you can safely bathe all year round, even in the winter.

BUNGALOWS AND HOTELS

There are around two dozen bungalow resorts on this part of the beach, most of them of rather high standards. Try the following: *MATLANG RESORT***, tidy, rather crowded bungalows in a nice, small, sandy garden with flowers. *THE BLUE LAGOON**, this resort has erected new, simple bungalows.*POPPY INN***, pretty bungalows (with fan) beneath palms; large restaurant with open terrace; this resort doesn't seem quite as crowded as many others. *O.P. BUNGALOW*-***, this resort is owned by a Chinese, the bungalows have been erected to the right and left of a nice garden. Chinese restaurant and a wonderful stretch of beach beneath shady trees. *SAMUI CABANA***-*****, tel 272222 ext. 205; this resort becomes increasingly crowded towards the back, very comfortable bungalows, room service, coffee shop, beach bar, and seafood terrace.

CHAWENG YAI BEACH, CENTRE

This beach looks like the tropical paradise everyone has always spent their lives dreaming of; fine, white sand, palm-trees and blue water, ideal bathing conditions at high as well as low tide. The surf can get quite high in the winter, though, when the beach becomes very narrow. And this beach has more to offer than just stunning natural splendour; there's lots happening here, too. There are beach restaurants featuring regular video performances, discos, a Thai restaurant with classical Thai dancing (the Manohra), windsurfing schools (at the Arabian Restaurant), a diving base (Ko Samui Divers in the Malibu Resort), a supermarket with a travel agency, and a branch of the tourist police. Those travellers who are willing to pay a little extra for entertainment, activities, and accommodation will feel at home here.

BUNGALOWS AND HOTELS

There are approx. two dozen bungalow resorts on this section of the beach. Many of them charge the highest prices on the island. Try the following: *CHAWENG GARDENS**-****, bungalows without fan. The nicest section of the beach starts at this resort. *MALIBU RESORT***, during the height of the season ***. Bungalows without a view of the sea; the only two-storey restaurant on the island is directly on the sea. *FIRST BUNGALOW*-****, the southernmost resort, bustling with activity. *THE VILLAGE *******, under the same management as the White House; 19 rather crowded bungalows with fan in a lush flower garden. *PANSEA*******, for reservations call Phuket 076/216137. The international chain of hotels has had 100 luxury bungalows with all extras erected here, all in a large, beautiful garden. The bungalows are very spacious, all have ac and a large terrace, and all are connected to each other by little paths. Very few have a view of the sea. Many activities are offered free of charge, e.g. catamaran-sailing, windsurfing, bicycles, and badminton. Motorboat outings will cost you 600 Baht per person per day. Cars are available. Those with enough money can hire a teak schooner, a junk, or a yacht. *WHITE HOUSE*****, tel 272222 ext. 208; tastefully decorated rooms are available in the terraced houses as well as in the white, three-storey building, all with full service and private terraces.

CHAWENG NOI BEACH

Separated from Chaweng Yai Beach by a small cape, this is a picturesque bay with smooth cliffs. The surf gets too high for bathing in the winter.

BUNGALOWS AND HOTELS

Few of the original bungalow resorts have survived; most of them had to make way for the new, large luxury hotel. Of the ones remaining we would recommend: *SUNSHINE*, RELAX RESORT**, or *CHAWENG NOI**, all with very cheap huts, all at the southern, rocky end of the beach. *IMPERIAL SAMUI*****, for reservations from Bangkok call 2540023. All rooms of the tastefully arranged buildings command a view of the sea. Terraces, a restaurant, and a salt water pool have been built on various levels of the slope. The pool with its natural cliffs is fascinating. It is unfortunately also rather difficult to keep clean.

LAMAI BAY

This sickle-shaped, 5 km bay attracts travellers from all over the world. Many come in search of an easy life for little money, and indeed, Lamai Bay does seem to offer everything the traveller's heart may desire, including a rich natural splendour and good connections to the rest of the island. As there are marked differences between the respective sections of beach, however, we will give you separate descriptions.

LAMAI BEACH, EASTERN BAY

The sea is very shallow here, only hip-deep at low tide. White, sandy beach alternates with smooth, flat boulders. The heavy breakers in the winter are for the most part held in check by the offshore cape. Thus bathing is possible all year round.

BUNGALOWS

The few resorts on this part of the beach are all situated on the slope, surrounded by coconut plantations which are great places for taking nice walks. This area is still quite peaceful and relatively far from the road. New resorts will no doubt be built here in the not-too-distant future. We'd recommend *SILVER CLIFF**, all bungalows on the slope, with a view of the sea. You will have a particularly nice view of your section of the bay as well as the whole of Lamai Beach from the restaurant.

LAMAI, NORTHERN BEACH

There is an offshore reef right up to the level of the village of BAN LAMAI in front of this section of the beach. Rocks peek out of the water at low tide; unsuitable for bathing.

BUNGALOWS

There are well over a dozen bungalow resorts here. While the first couple can still be reached by way of a side road, the others are all quite close to the main road or the village. Try the *WEEKENDER VILLA**, which is a very nice resort in spite of its closeness to the main road; 3 different types of bungalows, many activities: windsurfing, canoe rides to the reef, snorkelling, dirt biking, boat trips to the islands, and currency exchange.

CENTRAL LAMAI

This nice section of the beach with its intermittent boulders is suitable for bathing at high and low tide. The sand is rather coarse. The waves get very high in the winter, when the beach becomes rather short. This beach still generates an atmosphere of total freedom, in spite of the fact that new bungalow resorts are constantly being opened, some even behind those already existing, others along the driveways. This is one of the favourite haunts of permanent travellers, who float back and forth between Goa, Bali, Kathmandu, and Ko Samui. You will meet romantic hippies for whom time seems to have stood still here, as well as children who have never had to experience a bitter, European winter. Many travellers manufacture jewelry in their bungalows and then sell it; a flea market is held every Sunday. You will find the cheapest restaurants with the best traveller food here, as well as the cheapest huts. Spontaneous beach parties are an everyday occurrence.

There are two things you should know. People have been known to be robbed on this beach, one of the sad side-effects of this kind of 'alternative' tourism. In addition, several of the resorts smell simply terrible due to the fact that the soaking pits, which are used as junk heaps, are filled to the brim (e.g. Paradise Bungalow and Bungalow Bills).

BUNGALOWS

There are two dozen bungalow resorts on the beach at the present time, and more are being built by the season (mainly in the terraced house style and with corrugated-iron roofs). The *WHITE SAND** resort is still built in the old style. Many permanent travellers stay here, and this is where the flea market is held on Sundays. *PALM** offers bungalows at various prices, the cheapest ones directly on the sea. The *NICE RESORT** makes up a mind-boggling sight; A-frame-bungalows standing next to each other like rabbit hutches; only recommended for those travellers who like feeling crowded.

LAMAI, SOUTHERN COAST

The WONDERFUL ROCK makes up the end of Lamai Bay in the south. Those resorts even further south actually belong to BANG NAM CHUET BAY, but they still profit from the well-known name of Lamai. The Wonderful Rock is an oddly shaped cliff reaching far into the sea and commanding a fine view of the bay. The surf gets rather high and wild in the winter, while bathing in between the rocks in the summertime can be a lot of fun. Wonderful Rock is especially popular among Thai holiday-makers because of its many souvenir-stands and snack-bars.

BUNGALOWS

*WONDERFUL ROCK BUNGALOWS** offers very simple huts dotted between the boulders. There are several cheap resorts on the road along the flat beach (many pebbles), e.g. *NOI BUNGALOW**. The *SWISS CHALETS*** are situated at a raised altitude and command a spectacular view of the sea; spacious bungalows in a large resort with a very nice restaurant serving Thai and Swiss dishes. *ROCKY BUNGALOW**, the last resort on Lamai, has a private, sandy beach framed by round boulders. The offshore reef 100 m from the island keeps the surf in check in the winter, making this a pleasant time to stay here. The sea is too shallow for bathing in the summer, however.

SOUTH COAST

Though you won't find any endless beaches down here, you will find secluded bays with truly idyllic bungalow resorts. You should definitely have visited this part of the island before claiming that Ko Samui is totally spoilt and overcrowded. If you are more into peace and nature than perfect but crowded beaches, then you've come to the right place. No arterial road runs along this part of the coast up to now (though one is planned); you will only be able to reach the resorts by way of dead ends.

LAEM SET

Turn off H4170 towards the sea at the sign saying "Laem Set". You will reach the rocky bathing resort after 1.3 km.

BUNGALOWS AND HOTELS

*CHATALET***** (the name may have changed by now), immediately to the left, at an approx. 200 metre beach with coarse sand. Comfortable terraced houses. The beach is safe for swimming when the tide is high. A 200 metre driveway turning off to the right from the dead end road will lead you to *NATAIN BUNGALOW**, a small, beautiful resort on a slope, commanding a wonderful view of the coastline. Nice restaurant. You can also hire motorcycles here. Continue on down the dead end road for 400 metres to the *LAEM SET INN****, tel 077/273130 (wireless telephone), this resort is run by Mr. Parry, an Englishman. The restaurant is good but rather expensive.

EMERALD COVE

This secluded bay at the southwestern tip of the island can be reached by way of a 2 km, rather bad, dirt road. There is nothing but a sleepy fishing village down here, as well as two bungalow resorts, one to the left of the village and one to the right. There is quite a distance between the two resorts. You will be able to walk out towards the four strange looking cliffs in the sea for a whole kilometre when the tide is low. Even when the tide is high the water only ever gets chest-deep at the most.

BUNGALOWS

The *EMERALD COVE BUNGALOWS** are arranged in two lines, at right angles to the beach. They make a rather dismal impression. The restaurant is not at the beach, but on the other side of the bungalows. The huts of the *SEAGULL BUNGALOW**, about 500 metres further on, have been artfully integrated into the landscape, some on the jungle-overgrown slope, others directly on the beach, in between the mangroves; nice beach restaurant.

A TOUR OF THE ISLAND

The island has nothing spectacular to offer apart from its beaches. There are no cultural "musts". All the same, a tour of the island is well worth it. The easiest way to do such a tour is by motorcycle or jeep. The public pick-ups do not drive around the whole island. You can drive all the way to Chaweng Noi, then get out, walk 4 km, and catch another pick-up to the rest of the island at Lamai Beach. This 4 km stretch between Lamai and Chaweng Noi is one of the most beautiful roads of South East Asia. Don't miss it!

If you start your tour in Nathon and circle the island in a clockwise direction, turn around after you've climbed the first hill and enjoy the magnificent view. You will pass BIG BUDDHA BEACH before reaching the first attraction after 25 km; the 12 metre statue of the sitting *BIG BUDDHA* and the wat that goes with it are located on a small island connected to the mainland by two dams. The statue is not particularly old, nor is it particularly beautiful. Still, set against the blue,sky and the tropical ocean it does seem quite impressive.

A bumpy dirt road will lead you through palm-tree plantations to the northeastern tip of the island. Don't forget to enjoy the splendid sight of Choeng Mon Beach and Chaweng Beach along the way.

Turn right at the bend of the road in Ban Lamai and you'll reach the *CULTURAL HALL.* You will mainly find objects brought to the island by Chinese merchants during the last century exhibited here, i.e. weapons, tea services, instruments, clocks, and old, agricultural tools. The *WONDERFUL ROCK* (also known as *GRAND ROCK)* is at the end of Lamai Beach. Mainly Thais seem to be attracted to the large, strangely shaped Grand Ma and Grand Pa cliffs. Western travellers might be more interested in the wild surf, which seems particularly savage during the rainy season.

Continue along the main road to the Muslim fishing village of Ban Hua Thanon until you reach the road branching off to the *NA MUANG WATERFALL.* A brook forms many pretty cascades here. The pools are good for bathing. Continue back to the settlement of Suan Thurian from here. Once there, go down H4173 towards the sea. Turn right and then left again (at the sign), and you will reach the *PAGODA,* which makes an impressive sight directly by the sea. You will ultimately return to the main road at Ban Saket by continuing through the dense palm-trees along H4170. An unsignposted, most impressive road built for the Air Force branches off at this small settlement. It leads to a radar station on top of a hill, from where you will have a splendid view. Back on the main road, you will reach the road branching off to the *HIN LAT WATERFALL* after approx. 1 km. You will have to walk upstream for 30 minutes in order to reach the highest of the cascades. You can combine this outing with a proper little jungle-trek; just stick to the brook and keep going inland.

KO PHA NGAN

This island is only 20 km north of Ko Samui. It covers an area approx. 2/3 the size of that of its 'big sister'. The two islands can't really be compared, though; while Ko Samui is gentle and easy-going, Ko Pha Ngan seems rather wild and savage. Tourists for whom Ko Samui is simply too touristy come here, to Ko Pha Ngan. Quite a few seem to do this, so there are not enough bungalows to go round during the height of the season, when tents are offered by way of temporary accommodation. In the expectation that the island might turn into a gold mine one day, just as Ko Samui did, new bungalow resorts are being built by the season.

TONGSALA

The main settlement of the island is a tiny fishing village which has practically nothing to offer. There is a post office and a telegraph service (poste restante possible), a currency exchange booth (15% additional charge), a small travel agency, and a couple of shops.

GENERAL INFORMATION

TRANSPORTATION ON THE ISLAND Pick-ups that will take you to the island's beaches for 5-20 Baht await you as the boat comes into the harbour of Tongsala. Motorcycle-taxis are also available. You can hire a motorcycle for 200 Baht per day on the island.

HOW TO GET THERE

Catch the speedboat from SURAT THANI / BAN DON via Ko Samui at 12:30 h (75 Baht, arrival 16:15 h). The night boat at 21:00 h will cost you 60 Baht. Speedboats from NATHON (Ko Samui) leave at 10:00 and 15:00 h (30 Baht, 40 min.).

There are no landing-places at the pier, so you will have to change onto a smaller boat once there, which will then bring you to the beach for another 5 Baht. More boats offer their services as the season progresses.

A boat leaves BO PHUT (Ko Samui) for HAAD RIN BEACH at 15:30 h (50 Baht, 45 min.).

BEACHES AND BUNGALOWS

EAST OF TONGSALA

The first section of the beach is disappointing; we would not recommend to stay here.

There are several bungalow resorts on sandy bays and cliffs all the way to the Laem Haad Rin (cape). The road stops at Ban Kai; from here you will either have to walk or organize a boat. This is the right area for those travellers looking for peace and quiet. Try the following: *LAEM THONG**, simple huts in a beautiful area. *SUNSET BUNGALOW**, cheap huts set on cliffs. *PALM BEACH**, bungalows set in a palm-tree plantation.

HAAD RIN BEACH

This is the most beautiful and popular beach on the southwestern part of the island; fine sand, corals to the left and right, good swimming. More and more bungalow resorts are being built here. The surf gets extremely high (and the swimming a little dangerous) between October and February. You can reach this beach from Ban Tai by longtail boat (20 Baht) or on foot (2 hrs.). You can also catch a boat from BO PHUT on Ko Samui.

Try the following resorts: *SEAVIEW**, said to serve the best food on the beach. *HAAD RIN BUNGALOW**, directly by the sea. *SEA WIND*, SUN RISE*, PALITA LODGE*, PARADISE**, all at the southern end of the beach, and *LIGHTHOUSE**, on the cape. You will be able to exchange foreign currency at a very bad rate at the *PHUSIRI RESTAURANT*.

MAE HAAD BAY

This bay is in the northwestern part of the island. The beach here ends rather steeply and is made up of coarse sand. You can reach the bay by pick-up from TONGSALA (20 Baht, 1 hour). Try *MAE HAAD RESORT** or *ISLAND VIEW**, bungalows of various standards, good restaurant, directly by the sea. From here you can reach Wang Sai waterfall.

SEETANU BAY (also SRITHANU or SI THANOO)

Long, yellow, sandy beach in a curved bay with many palm-trees and mangroves in the western part of the island. *SRITHANU BUNGALOWS**, very simple huts with an even simpler restaurant.

WOK TUM BAY

This section of the island's coast is characterized by small coves and mini-beaches. Many travellers come here in spite of the fact that the swimming is not too good. The beaches can easily be reached by pick-up from Tongsala (10 Baht). More and more new bungalow resorts are being built here. *CHARN'S BUNGALOW**, with fantastic food, e.g. shark curry, crab soup with coconut milk, Irish Coffee. *SIRIPUN BUNGALOW*-*** serves even bigger helpings and offers even larger bungalows with lav/shower. *PHANGAN*-***, also with lav/shower. *COOKIES**, the name says it all (special cookies available). *SUNSET**, *DARIN**, and *OK** are all located on the small beaches, in between the boulders. Mr. Ban of *KIET** offers island tours with a boat as well as snorkelling expeditions. He will sometimes venture as far as Ko Samui and the Marine National Park.

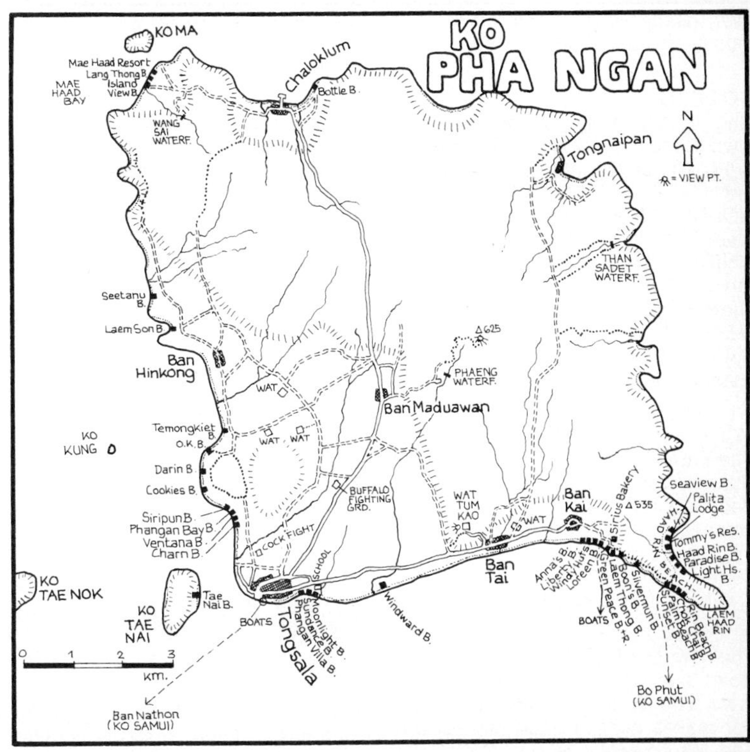

KRABI

This busy provincial capital on the west coast was still completely unknown to travellers in 1986. Nothing much has changed in the town since, but the surrounding countryside, particularly the beaches and offshore islands, has proved to be a tempting lure for travellers from all over the world. You will now even find the name of Krabi mentioned in the brochures of travel agencies who usually specialize in package deals. The (sad?) results are already clearly visible - Krabi was virtually flooded with tourists in January of 1988. You will find a particularly large number of German tourists fighting their way through the four streets of the small town. As there are only a limited number of rather short beaches, Krabi is not as suitable for accommodating hoards of tourists as, say, Phuket or Ko Samui. Those who have heard of Krabi, however, desperately want to go there - tourists looking for peace and quiet will thus be terribly disappointed.

HOTELS

One normally only spends a night in town if one is planning to continue on to Phi Phi or one of the other islands the next day. *MAD MAX GUESTHOUSE**, 36 Joafa Road, friendly and clean. *SU GUESTHOUSE**, central location, above Suzuki; rooms with fan and mosquito-nets, community shower. *BLUE BUILDING GUESTHOUSE** (no official name as yet), Soi Ruam Chat, on one of the upper floors of the blue building.

We'd suggest avoiding the *NEW HOTEL*** with its small, shabby rooms. The *VIENG THONG HOTEL***, 155 Uttarakit Road, tel 611288, very central, opposite the floating restaurant, has acquired a bad reputation due to the many professional girls that work there. Travel agencies selling bus and boat tickets can be found in the lounge.

The new *THAI HOTEL*** (ac***), Isara Road 3, tel 611122, is in the centre of town. The tastefully decorated interior makes quite a good impression. The *NAOWARAT HOTEL***-*****, tel 611581, is approx. 2 km out of town, on the arterial road; all rooms ac.

FOOD

There are many small restaurants and foodstands in town. Travellers like hanging out at the *AMATA COFFEE SHOP* and the *TIP HOUSE*, both of which serve pancakes, fruit shakes, and ice cream. The *REAN PARE* (the *FLOATING RESTAURANT)* is particularly beautifully located. A gangplank connects the restaurant to the riverbank. Good meals at prices a little above average.

GENERAL INFORMATION

INFORMATION - maps, informative brochures, and tips for excursions to Ko Phi Phi are available at the TIP HOUSE, which is run by friendly young men. Breakfast, snacks, and drinks are also served.

BANKS - There are several banks on Uttarakit Road, Mon-Fri 9:00-15:30 h. You will not be able to exchange money at the beaches or on the islands.

POST - the post office on Uttarakit Road has a Poste Restante counter and an international telephone, Mon-Fri 8:30-16:30 h, Sat 9:00-12:00 h, near the pier.

MOTORCYCLE RENTALS - you can hire a Honda TX (110 cc) for 150-200 Baht a day. Travel & Tours also rent out motorcycles.

LEAVING KRABI

BY BUS

To the beaches: pick-ups to AO NANG BAY (15 Baht) drive through town and stop at various places, e.g. Pattana Road, in front of Travel & Tour. Buses to AO LUK leave from two different places in town.

Direct ac buses to BANGKOK leave the Krabi Bus Office at 16:00 and 16:30 h (290 Baht, 14 hrs.). Non ac buses leave town at 16:00 and 17:00 h (161 Baht). Local buses to all destinations in the south leave from the bus station at Krabi Junction in Talad Kao, 5 km north of Krabi (minibuses for 3 Baht on Uttarakit Road).

Buses to PHUKET leave every hour between 6:00 and 15:00 h (35 Baht, 4 hrs.). Buses to KO SAMUI via SURAT THANI (50 Baht) leave at 9:00 and 11:00 h (100 Baht, approx. 7 hrs.-price includes the ferry to Ko Samui).

Buses to SURAT THANI leave every hour between 6:00 and 14:30 h (50 Baht, 3 hrs). There are 4 buses to HAT YAI via TRANG (30 Baht) and PHATTALUNG (40 Baht) between 10:25 and 13:55 h (60 Baht, 5 hrs.).

There are daily ac minibuses to KO SAMUI (190 Baht) and SURAT THANI (150 Baht) at 11:00 h. Ac minibuses to SINGAPORE (495 Baht), KUALA LUMPUR (440 Baht), PENANG (385 Baht), and HAT YAI (150 Baht) leave at 7:00 h - tickets and information available at Krabi Sea Tour, 256 Uttarakit Road, tel 611110, and others.

BOATS TO KO PHI PHI

PEE PEE MARINE TRAVEL, 201/3-4 Uttarakit Road, tel 611496, Mon-Fri 8:00-16:00 h. A 3-hour sightseeing and bathing trip around Phi Phi Le and all its natural beauties is included in the price of 200 Baht, as is the return trip on the following day. One way ticket: 150 Baht.

KRABI SEA TOUR, 256 Uttarakit Road, tel 611110; a boat leaves daily from the Rean Pare Restaurant at 9:00 and 13:00 h (100 Baht one way, 2 1/2 hrs.).

The SONGSERM express boat (tickets for sale at the desk of the Vieng Thong Hotel) only heads for Ko Phi Phi on Tuesdays and Thursdays at 13:00 h - 1 1/2 hrs., 200 Baht one way. The boat also leaves for PHUKET from Ko Phi Phi daily (200 Baht).

KRABI'S BEACHES

AO NANG BEACH

This beach measures approx. 800 metres in length, has fine sand with little pieces of coral, and is surrounded by wooded cliffs on three sides. Large stones peek through the sand at the northern end of the beach. The view of the picturesque cliffs and the offshore islands is wonderful. Minibuses from Krabi cost 15 Baht. The *KRABI RESORT***** (dormitory*) is at the northern, rocky end of the beach. Office in Krabi: 53-57 Pattana Road, tel 611389. This is the best resort on the beach. Good restaurant. Windsurfing, fishing, diving, and ping pong also possible. The *CORAL BEACH BUNGALOWS** are right next door; very simple huts. There are several very simple bungalow resorts in a palm grove beyond the dusty road. Prices start at 50 Baht.

PAI PONG BEACH

Hidden behind cliffs, beautiful, white Pai Pong Beach forms a pretty bay with clear, blue water. It is truly idyllic, with palm trees and even a little jungle. You can reach the beach by walking over the small hill (15 min.) or by boat. There is only one resort here, the *PAI PONG BEACH BUNGALOWS*-**;* nice huts scattered amongst the palm trees; good, rather expensive restaurant. Go to the Amata Coffee Shop for information and reservations.

RAI LEH BEACH/ PRANANG CAVE (PRINCESS CAVE)

This peninsula, surrounded by steep cliffs, can only be reached by boat from Ao Nang Beach for 20 Baht per person. The fantastic limestone formations tower above the beach and reach all the way into the sea. The water has formed several large caves in the cliff walls. The northern bay is flat and rocky. You will be able to reach the second large bay (Rai Leh) on foot from here, but only when the tide is low. Walk past the solidly built bungalows of the apparently privately-owned resort. The *PINE** resort, right next to it, has a good restaurant serving excellent seafood. Advance reservations at Pine Tour, 20 Isra Muang, Krabi. Walk inland along the footpath to the beach with the many cliffs and the Pranang Cave, which can be seen on the cover of many travel brochures these days. The *CLIFF** and the *GIFT** were the first resorts to open bungalows here, but many have since followed.

HAT NOPARAT THARA

Continue along road 4202 beyond the Krabi Resort. You will reach a very flat beach after 1 km. Single kasuarina-trees grow along the beach. There are many open air restaurants here, as well as the HQ of the MU KO PHI PHI National Park. You can spend the night at the *PARK BUNGALOWS**.*

EXCURSIONS FROM KRABI

SHELL CEMETERY (SUSAN HOI)

An entire ledge of rock is made of thousands of small, fossilized shells, said to be 75 million years old. Many Thais like coming here. Most travellers, however, remain pretty unmoved by the sight. You can either come here via H4204 or with a chartered boat.

WAT THAM SUEA

134 monks and 133 nuns live in this cave-monastery. Their master, PRA ARCHAN JUMNEAN SEELASETTHO, is venerated in a large, extended grotto containing Buddha statues, stands, and meditation pictures. He teaches a highly individual form of meditation which does not, however, contradict the Buddhist teachings; reflecting upon one's inner organs. Turn off onto H4 2 km east of Krabi Junction, shortly before km stone 107. You will find several pick-ups here, ready to drive you down the remaining 2 km of road to the wat.

PHANOM BENJA NATIONAL PARK

A passable, narrow road branching off 500 metres east of Krabi Junction will lead you to this wild, almost inaccessible National Park. You will pass a waterfall with many levels along the way. You will reach the HQ after 20 km. You can climb to the top of KHAO PHANOM on a five-day, guided tour through the dense jungle. Go to the Tip House for further information.

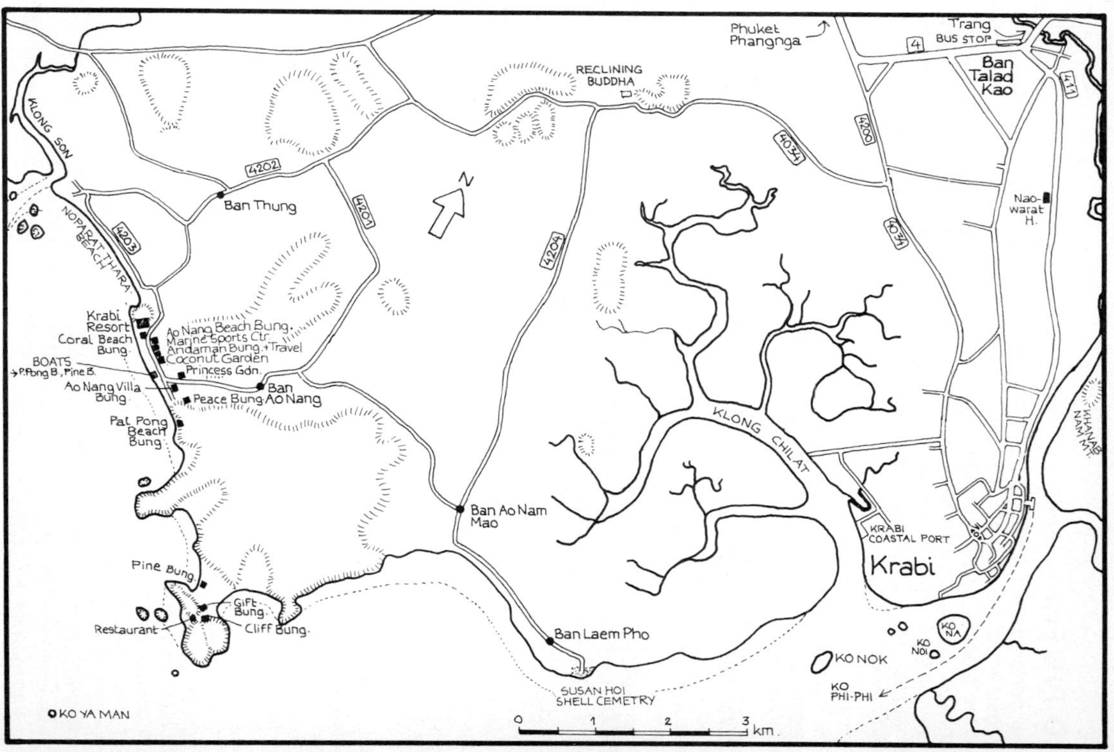
Phuket
Phangnga
Trang
BUS STOP
4
Ban Talad Kao
411
RECLINING BUDDHA
4200
4034
KLONG SON
4202
Ban Thung
4201
N
4204
Nao-warat H.
NOPARAT THARA BEACH
4203
Krabi Resort
Coral Beach Bung.
Ao Nang Beach Bung.
Marine Sports Ctr.
Andaman Bung.+Travel
Coconut Garden
BOATS
→ P.Pong B., Pine B.
Princess Gdn.
Ao Nang Villa Bung.
Ban Ao Nang
Peace Bung.
Pat Pong Beach Bung.
KLONG CHILAT
KHANAB NAM MT.
Ban Ao Nam Mao
KRABI COASTAL PORT
Krabi
Pine Bung.
Gift Bung.
Restaurant
Cliff Bung.
Ban Laem Pho
KO NA
KO NOI
KO NOK
KO PHI-PHI
SUSAN HOI SHELL CEMETRY
KO YA MAN
0 1 2 3 km.

KO PHI PHI

The perfect island for living one's tropical dreams - imagine two large and rugged limestone cliff formations, coconut-palms on the one side and jungle on the other. They are connected to each other by a flat land bridge, which forms semi-circular, blindingly white bays of sand on either side. The clear water of the bays shimmers in every conceivable shade of blue, and you will already be able to make out the corals from the boat - wonderful for snorkelling and diving.

Actually, Ko Phi Phi consists of two islands; all resorts can be found on KO PHI PHI DON, while the rather coarse, uninhabited KO PHI PHI LE is only suited for outings. Part of Ko Phi Phi has been declared a National Park. The HQ can be found at the Noparat Thara Beach near Krabi.

BEACHES AND BUNGALOWS

Most of the traveller bungalow resorts are east of the village, in TON SAI BAY. All resorts offer simple bungalows costing between 50 and 100 Baht. There are a few more comfortable ones with lav/shower for 160-200 Baht. The bungalows can only be reached on foot or by boat. *PHI PHI ANDAMAN*-**,* (with dormitory). There is often a water shortage during the height of the season. *LAEM INN*;* beneath palm-trees. *TON MA PLAO** has been built on a cape; almost no shade at all.

All other bungalows are located on the long LONG BEACH, which reaches all the way to the Laem Tong Cape: *HAD HIN*; BANG MAN*, LONG BEACH** and others.

The *PEE PEE ISLANDS CABANA**-**** are located west of the main village, at the lowest point of the bay. Contact Pee Pee Marine Travel, 201 Uttarakit Road, Krabi, tel 075/611496 for advance booking. All the posh day-visitors from Phuket are fed at the restaurant of this high class resort. Many boats drop anchor here.

To find peaceful bungalows, cross over to the other side of the narrow land bridge, to YONG GA LEM BAY (also known as BACK BEACH). *P. P. CHARLIE BEACH RESORT****, in the coconut-palm plantation; spacious bungalows with lav/showers. Reservations from Phuket at P.P Charlie Beach Resorts, Makham Bay. There is a daily boat from there to Ko Phi Phi. You will find the *GIFT BUNGALOW NO. 2** at the very edge of the bay; very simple huts, nice restaurant. *TON SAI VILLAGE***,* at the end of Ton Sai Bay.

LO BA KAO BEACH is located on the east coast of the island. You will only find the *PEE PEE ISLAND VILLAGE***** here up to now, tel Krabi 075/612064 (contact Pee Pee Island Resort, 158/20 Yaowaraj Road, Phuket, tel 076/215014 for advance booking).

FOOD

All bungalow resorts have their own restaurant. The prices are a little higher than they would be on the mainland. You will be able to dine most cheaply at the various *FISHERMEN PUBS* in the village. The *MUSLIM RESTAURANT* west of the village serves good grilled fish. You will be able to eat 'à la carte' at the *PEE PEE ISLANDS CABANA*.

LEAVING KO PHI PHI

To KRABI: Pee Pee Marine Travel, 13:00 h (150 Baht, 3 hrs.); Krabi Sea Tour, 8:30 and 13:00 h, (100 Baht, 2 1/2 hrs.); Songserm only Tues and Thur, 10:30 h (200 Baht 1 1/2 hrs.) To PHUKET: Songserm daily (except for Tues and Thur) at 10:30 as well as daily at 16:00 h (200 Baht, 1 1/2 hrs.). You will be able to get to JUM ISLAND and KO LANTA with the boats of the resorts on these islands.

EXCURSIONS

VIEW POINTS

A climb to one of the VIEW POINTS is an absolute must for those planning to spend a couple of days on Ko Phi Phi. You will only be able to fully appreciate the beauty of this island by looking down upon it. Photographers might enjoy climbing the eastern hill in the morning. The ascent begins behind the village. Ask for LANG HUA. You will be able to see all the way to the northern cape of the island from there. The hill beyond Ton Sai Village is best suited for the afternoon. You will need 15 minutes to climb it, part of the way along safety ropes.

ISLAND TOUR

You can organize a boat-trip around Phi Phi Don yourself. Hire a longtail-boat (1/2 day) at the village or with the aid of the people running your resort. There is enough room for about 8 people in one of these boats. Snorkelling is best in front of LONG BEACH and in front of LO BU DI, the southernmost beach on the island's west coast.

KO PHI PHI LE

Regular boat-trips are offered to the rugged, southern island of Phi Phi Le with its interesting cliff formations (100 Baht). A visit to the island is included in the price for those who have bought a return ticket from Pee Pee Marine in Krabi as well as those who have made an outing arrangement from Phuket.

The following places are visited: VIKING CAVE, with prehistoric cave-paintings and many swallows' nests; you can visit the cave for 20 Baht if the sea is relatively calm and the mating season has passed. The LO SA MAY BAY looks like a deep fjord. One usually drops anchor in the nice MAYA BAY in order to go snorkeling. Beware of the water serpents!

DIVING OUTINGS

1 - 3-day diving outings to Ko Phi Phi are organized from the diving bases of Phuket. The shallow bays and the colourful coral reefs are perfect for beginners and advanced divers alike. Semi-professionals may find it a little boring - at best you might see a couple of miniature leopard sharks.

PHANG NGA

The provincial capital Phang Nga is exactly 93 km from Krabi as well as Phuket. The town is famous for its beautiful bay with the steep limestone cliffs towering out of the sea. There is a Tourist Office in the government buildings opposite the striking cliff, 3.3 km out of town, towards Phuket.

HOTELS

There are a number of cheap hotels on the main road. The *RUK PHANG NGA** is in the centre, at the bus-stop, opposite the *RATANAPONG***. The nicer *LAK MUANG*** is a little further out of town; rooms with lav/sink.

There are no hotels of middling prices in town. The *PHANG NGA VALLEY RESORT*****, 4 km out of town towards Phuket, 400 m to the right of the H4, is an expensive Thai-hotel with bungalows and a guesthouse, restaurant, Thai Dance Show, and a fish-pond (admission 10 Baht).

The *PHANG NGA BAY RESORT HOTEL*****, 20 Tha Dan, Panyee, tel 076 /411067, is on the road leading to the bay, 8 km from the centre of town.

HOW TO GET THERE

A local bus from KRABI will cost approx. 25 Baht. The bus from PHUKET costs 22 Baht. A minibus ride to the harbour from town will cost 8 Baht. Package deals from PHUKET are offered for 250-500 Baht per person.

BOAT RIDE THROUGH THE PHANG NGA BAY

You can reach the landing-place from town by minibus for 8 Baht. A slow, roofed boat which holds up to 10 people can be hired for 300-400 Baht for a 4-hour trip (bargain!). You can start as early as 7:00 h, faster boats for larger groups do not leave the harbour until 10:00 h. You can gain a good general impression of the bay and the places you will stop at by taking a look at the large map in the hotel lobby. The water in the shallow bay is nearly always calm, thus the trip can be done at virtually any time of year. It is best between December and April, however, when the sky is blue and clear. Don't forget to bring your sun-hat, suntan lotion, and something to drink; in spite of the sun-roof it is not possible to be seated in the shade all of the time.

Your trip will start with a ride down the wide KHLONG KHAO THALU, past mangrove swamps and striking, overgrown cliff formations, e.g. the 'small dog', KHAO MA CHU. You will then reach the PHANG NGA BAY with its many steep and rugged limestone cliffs rising out of the sea. These seem to be held together only by the intricate root-systems of the tropical plants growing upon them. There are also many dark grottoes and stalactite caves in the area. The James Bond film "The Man with the Golden Gun" made these bizarre cliff formations famous back in the early 70s.

You will stop for a short break at the small island opposite the 'James Bond cliff', KHAO TAPU. The trip gets really exciting when the boat chugs towards a sheer, seemingly solid cliff wall, only to nose its way into a last-minute cave entrance just in time. A Muslim village in which all the houses are built upon stilts is right next to the island of KO PANYI. The village has developed into a veritable mecca of restaurants and souvenir-stands in recent times. All tour groups are spoilt with loads of fresh seafood upon arriving in the village. At the end of the trip you will chug through another mangrove swamp before visiting one last cave, THAM LOT (this cave is sometimes also visited at the beginning of the trip, depending on the tides).

PHUKET

Thailand's largest island lies at the edge of the Andaman Sea, in the Indian Ocean. The island is connected to the mainland by the Sarasin Bridge. Large and smaller bays as well as white, sandy beaches make this an ideal traveller hang-out. The island airport has now also made Phuket accessible for jet-set tourists. The beaches have accordingly been transformed into tourist traps. The island's wealth is based on extensive tin resources, which are found on the island itself as well as in the sea. Malaysian influences can be seen everywhere - 25 % of Phuket's population (from 'bukit' - Malaysian for 'hill') is Muslim. Buddhist Thais (55 %) and Chinese continue making up the bulk of the population, however.

PHUKET TOWN

The centre of the island, PHUKET TOWN, 50,000 inhabitants, is little more than a transit stop en route to the beaches for most travellers. There are a couple of very nice BUILDINGS in town, e.g. the Thai Airways building near the market and the Chinese building on Yaowaraj Road near Talang Road. A shopping spree might be a good idea for those planning to spend a longer time at the beaches; you can buy cheap fruit (at the market), souvenirs (shell necklaces and tin products), and cheap clothes.

HOTELS

You'd be better off spending the night at one of the beaches. For those who have to stay in town, however, we would suggest trying the following hotels: *THAVON HOTEL****, 74 Rasada Road, tel 211333; large ac hotel, not too expensive. *ON ON HOTEL*-***, 19 Phang-Nga Road (one parallel to the one above), tel 211154; impressive facade and interesting staircases. SINTAWEE*-***, no. 81, tel 212153, on the same road.

GENERAL INFORMATION

TOURIST INFORMATION - 73-75 Phuket Road, tel 212213, open daily until 16:30 h; information and maps available. You will also receive a brochure distributed by the local police here, warning against drug abuse and skinny dipping, both of which are heavily fined on the island. There are many plainclothes policemen out to nab tourists with drugs - beware!

TOURIST POLICE - the beaches on Phuket are not safe, in two respects. Tourists (particularly women) are often mugged on the beaches in the evening, while the surf gets dangerously high during the monsoon period (European summer). In case of an emergency call the Tourist Police, tel 212213, open till 16:30 h daily, or the police, tel 212046.

POST - General Post Office, Montri Road, open 8:30-12:00 and 13:00-16:30 h, from 9:00-12:00 h on holidays. The Telephone Centre on Phang-Nga Road, just around the corner, is open 24 hours. If you want to call for less than the minimum of three minutes, we would recommend going to the private telephone office opposite, instead; here you will be timed.

BANKS - there are several banks east of the roundabout, e.g. Bangkok Bank and Thai Farmers Bank on Phang Nga Road. You can also exchange money at the Thai Farmers Bank on Patong Beach, open Mon-Fri 8:00-15:00 h. Moneychangers will exchange money at the weekends, too.

ENTERTAINMENT - there is a boxing stadium south of town, at the end of Phuket Road. Competitions are held every Saturday evening at 19:30 h - seats 60-150 Baht. There is a little recreation park on the small peninsula in the south. The park can also be reached by continuing on down the extension of Phuket Road.

TRANSPORTATION ON PHUKET

BUSES, MINIBUSES, TUK-TUKS, PICK-UPS

Upon arriving on the island you will be greeted by pick-ups waiting to take you to the beach of your choice. Be aware of the fact that many drivers receive a commission from the resort owners. It can therefore happen that you end up being taken to a resort which pays a higher commission than the one you actually wanted to go to. In addition, the drivers at the bus station sometimes ask for outrageous prices. If you want to avoid this whole mess, just take a tuk-tuk to the market, where you can change onto a normal bus. Tuk-tuks and minibuses in town cost 5 Baht. Buses to RAWAI and NAI HARN leave from the roundabout (Bangkok Road / Ranong Road), all other local buses leave from Ranong Road (next to the market).

To PHA TU or WAT CHALONG 6 Baht, KO SIRAY or AO PO 8 Baht, LAEM KA, RAWAI, KATA, KARON, SURIN, or PATONG 10 Baht, NAI YANG or KAMALA 15 Baht, NAI HARN 20 Baht. All of the above rates are only valid during the daytime. You will have to drive a hard bargain in the evenings.

MOTORCYCLES / JEEPS

These constitute a popular form of transport. Motorcycles can be hired at all of the bungalow resorts for about 150-250 Baht, jeeps cost approx. 500 Baht. You will not be able to rent a car for under 900 Baht per day (in town).

LEAVING PHUKET

BY BUS

We would suggest taking a tuk-tuk (5 Baht) to the bus station, which is southwest of town. All regular buses as well as some of the ac buses leave from here. Other ac buses leave from the company offices, most of which can be found on Phuket Road. Ac buses to BANGKOK leave every 20 min. between 16:00 and 17:40 h (299 Baht, 14 hrs. - longer during the rainy season). 7 non ac buses leave for Bangkok between 6:00 and 18:30 h (165 Baht).

Numerous buses leave for RANONG (61 Baht, 4 hrs.). Ac buses only take 3 1/2 hrs. (180 Baht). Buses to HAT YAI leave at 6:20, 7:40, and 9:00 h (91 Baht, 8 hrs.). An ac bus leaves at 9:00 h (200 Baht). There are numerous buses to TRANG (62 Baht, 6 hrs.). Buses to KRABI leave at 12:50 and 14:30 h (38 Baht, 4 hrs.). Buses to PHANG NGA leave approx. every 100 min. (22 Baht, 2 hrs.). Non-stop ac minibuses for KO SAMUI cost 150 Baht. There are 6 daily buses to SURAT THANI (61 Baht, 6 hrs.).

BY SHARE TAXI

To SURAT THANI between 7:30 and 14:00 h (150 Baht, 4 hrs.). Taxis depart from the Pearl Cinema on Phang Nga Road. To HAT YAI and TRANG for 200 and 150 Baht respectively (6 and 4 hrs.). Taxis depart from the crossroads near the Pearl Cinema.

BY PLANE

Thai Airways Office, 78 Ranong Road, tel 211195, in a nice building right by the market. The Thai Airways bus to the airport 40 Baht, local buses leave between 9:00 and 11:00 h (10 Baht). The daily flights to BANGKOK cost 1545.-, HAT YAI 510.- and 595.- (jet), TRANG 315.-, SURAT THANI 315 Baht. 4 weekly flights to KUALA LUMPUR 1640 Baht, flights to PENANG on Friday and Sunday 990 Baht.

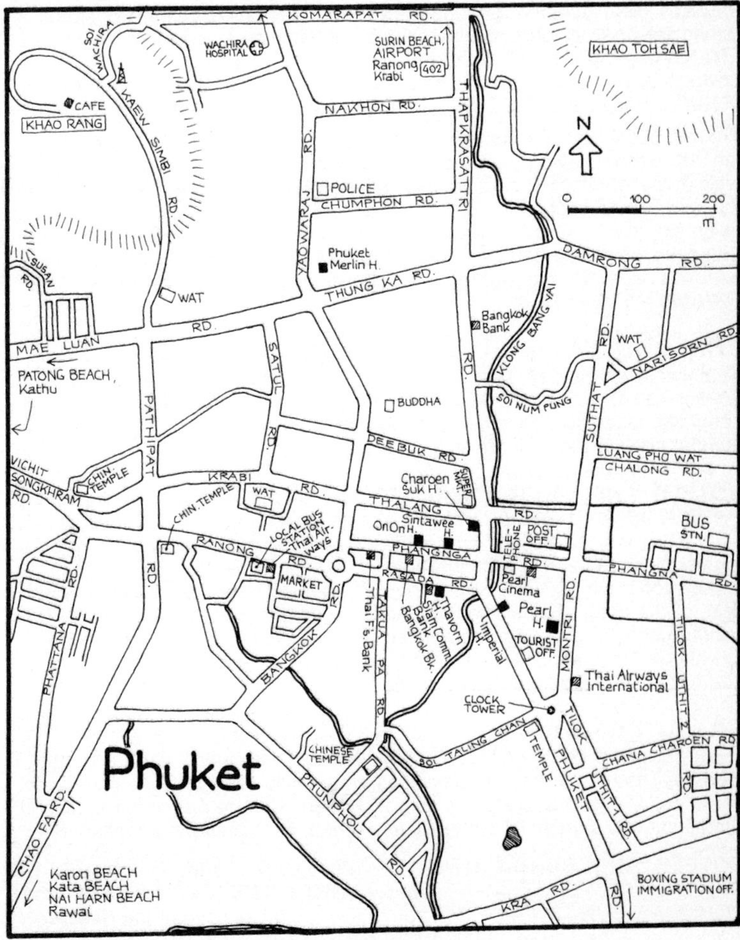

BY BOAT
To KO PHI PHI at 8:00 h (200 Baht, 2 hrs.), on to KRABI (Tue and Thur) at 10:30 h (200 Baht, 1 1/2 hrs.). You can also get to KO PHI PHI with one of the excursion boats and then stay for a couple of days before returning. Make sure your tour organizers know the exact date you wish to return, should you decide to do this.

BEACHES AND BUNGALOWS

Phuket's most beautiful beaches are in the west. The eastern beaches are rather flat and not particularly suitable for bathing. A road leading to LAEM PHAN WA branches off to the left from the road leading south from Phuket Town. It ends 10 km from town, at the new *AQUARIUM* and *MARINE BIOLOGICAL RESEARCH CENTRE*, both of which are worth visiting (10 Baht).

You will pass a small road branching off to the harbour and *MAKHAM BAY* on the left, before driving past the large tin refinery by the sea. The "Sang Jan" junk drops anchor at the above-mentioned harbour, daily island tours from 7:00 h for 600 Baht. An excursion boat to Ko Phi Phi also leaves from here daily; ask at P.P. Charlie Beach Resorts. 10 m in front of the aquarium a road branches off to the left to *CAPE PANWA*, a small peninsula with sandy beaches and an old lighthouse. There is a new luxury hotel, *CAPE PANWA*****, tel 213563.

CHALONG BAY - LAEM KA BEACH

Shallow Chalong Bay can be reached by way of the H4024 (11 km from Phuket Town). The bay terminates in the south at a small cliff formation called Laem Ka. Chalong Bay is not suitable for bathing. It is a good place to set off on boat rides to the offshore islands, though.

HOTELS AND BUNGALOWS
*PHUKET ISLAND RESORT*****, on a hill east of the main road, with some rooms costing over 1800 Baht. There is not even a single metre of beach in front of the hotel. For this reason the management offers a shuttle service to various beaches, usually Nai Harn and Kata. The resorts at the southern end of the bay are of Rawai-type standards, e.g. *ROONGROJ RESORT****, *AO CHALONG***, or *LAEM KA BEACH INN***.
Fresh fish and other sea creatures are prepared at the huge *KAN EANG 1* and *KAN EANG 2* restaurants, on the beach (a signpost will direct you there from the main road).

RAWAI BEACH

(17 km). In the south of the island. This area has been fully developed for tourism. The narrow beach sometimes gets a little dirty, though. You can hire boats to the offshore islands, which offer such effective protection against the winds that one can safely bathe all year round, even during the monsoon.

HOTELS AND BUNGALOWS
SALALOI BUNGALOW*-*** and PORNMAE BUNGALOW** are both reasonably cheap. The RAWAI RESORT HOTEL***-**** is more expensive. Good seafood at the *RIMLAY*.

LAEM PHROMTHEP

(19 km). There is no beach at the island's southernmost tip. Instead there is a beautiful, rather rocky landscape. A winding road from Rawai Beach leads through coconut-groves to the highest point of the area. Organize a pick-up or a motorcycle and go up in the evening; there are beautiful sunsets sometimes, but it is unfortunately always rather crowded.

BUNGALOWS

LINDA'S BUNGALOWS ** on a small beach. You can reach the resort by way of an unpaved road leading north. Once here, you are only one hill from Nai Harn Beach.

*PHROMTEP PALACE COUNTRY RESORT*****, tel 211599, 600 metres from the cape, very pretty bungalows on a hill. The observation restaurant serves exquisite dishes. Bathing at Nai Harn Beach (800 metres), shuttle service free of charge.

NAI HARN BEACH

(18 km). This wonderful beach is on the western side of the island's southern tip. Fine, white, sandy beach, a picturesque lagoon, rocky hills to the left and right,

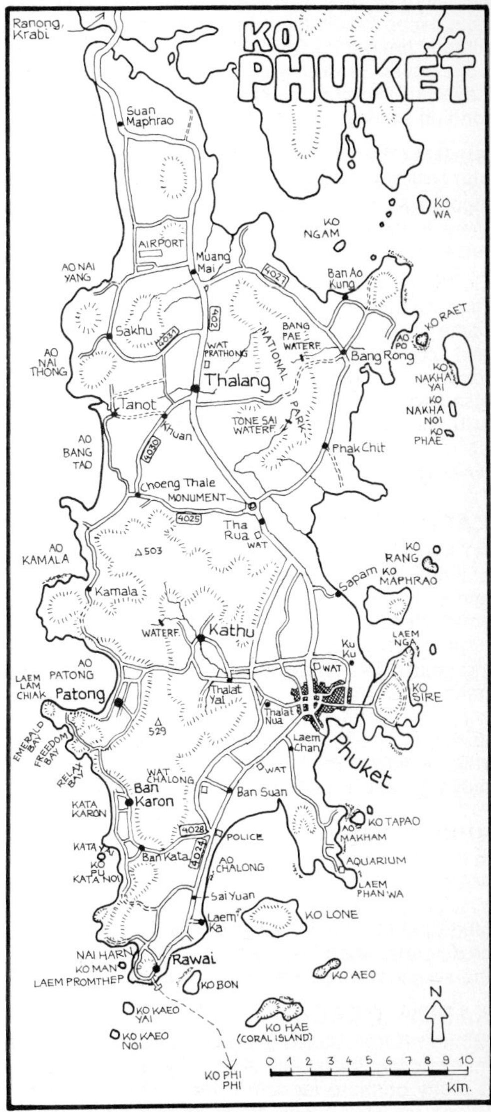

partially overgrown with coconut-palms, and breathtaking sunsets. The surf gets exceptionally high during the monsoon period, however, and there have already been a number of casualties. We would only recommend staying here from November to March. The beach used to be a veritable El Dorado for all travellers, but now the cheap resorts and restaurants have had to make room for high society.

BUNGALOWS AND HOTELS
*NAI HARN BUNGALOW***, behind the lagoon, 10 min. to the beach on foot, there is also a shuttle service, good restaurant (LUK NOI).

Go through the garage of the Yacht Club. Once on the other side, you will come upon *ON THE ROCKS**, no direct access to the beach, clean, good food, great tunes. *AO SANE*-*** is also nearby, on a small sandy beach with pieces of coral; nice bungalows on a slope and between trees. *PHUKET YACHT CLUB*****, tel Bangkok 2514707; ostentatious modern building which seems to eat its way up the slope in steps, rooms cost between 2000 and 6000 Baht!

*JUNGLE BEACH RESORT*****, far beyond the Yacht Club on a slope with ancient trees. Rooms and bungalows with fan or ac cost between 400 and 1000 Baht. There is a small beach good for snorkelling down below. Unsuitable for bathing, though; shuttle service to Nai Harn Beach free of charge. More hotels are being built at the present time.

KATA BEACH

(17 km). On the island's west coast. Beautiful beach, but it can get pretty windy at times. There are two bays here, KATA NOI and KATA YAI, separated from each other by a projecting cliff. There are many corals and fish all around the small island of KO PU; good snorkelling. CLUB MED occupies over half of the Kata Noi Bay area. Video bars with Thai girls have popped out of the remaining ground like magic mushrooms. The centre, with many discos, bars, pizza parlours, restaurants, motorcycle and jeep rentals as well as a couple of cheaper resorts, is in the north of the bay, which is sometimes also called Kata-Karon. The prices at the restaurants are outrageous. Only well versed private detectives might be able to find a cheap restaurant in the area, and even they will have a hard time.

BUNGALOWS
In Kata Noi: *KATA NOI RESORT**-****, *MABUHAY**, *WESTERN INN**. In Kata Yai: *WEST WIND BUNGALOW** behind Club Med, *FRIENDSHIP*** at the crossroads, and *CHAO KHUAN**** on the southern end of the bay, next to several seafood restaurants (*MIA'S* and *BOUNTY* are excellent).

On Kata-Karon Beach: *KATA GUESTHOUSE***, *KATA VILLA**, *TROPICANA**, *SHANGRI-LA**-**** (many complaints) and others.

KARON BEACH

(20 km) Karon Beach merges with Kata in the north. 3 km in length and with many dunes, this beach isn't really all that special. It is marked off by cliffs and a pretty offshore lagoon in the north. A motorcycle path leading to Patong Beach via Relax Bay starts at this point. Industrious people have started

building hotels on Karon beach like mad. All cheap resorts have had to make room for these new projects. The restaurants here overcharge their customers. Ask your fellow travellers which of them currently has the best reputation. More and more video-bars with Thai girls are opening up here, too, on this hitherto very proper beach.

HOTELS AND BUNGALOWS
At the southern end, crowded in between the hill, the road, and the nice beach: *MARINA COTTAGE*****, bungalows beneath palm-trees, popular restaurant; *KAKATA INN 85***** and *RUAN THEP INN*****, all with bungalows for approx. 600 Baht. Lying in an open field, separated from the beach by a road, you'll find (among others) *THAVORN PALM BEACH*****, a gigantic, newly-built hotel for package deal tourists. *KARON VILLA*****, large hotel with 2 pools. *KARON BUNGALOW****, *MY FRIEND**-***, and *DREAM HUT**-** are beyond. To the north, beyond the lagoon: *PHUKET OCEAN RESORT****, *KAMPONG KARON***** (beautiful wood carvings), *KARON ON SEA****-****, nice resort on a slope, beneath palm trees. There are several foodstands and bars around the large tree.

RELAX BAY
(18 km). This beautiful, white, sandy bay with its occasional kasuarina-trees lies in between Karon and Patong Beach. Relax Bay can only be reached on foot (20 min.) or by motorcycle right along the coast. You will also be able to reach the bay by jeep from Patong (3 km). Almost the entire beach is now occupied by the large *LE MERIDIEN PHUKET*****, a seven-storey luxury hotel.

FREEDOM BAY / EMERALD BAY
(19 km). Excursion boats often come to these two pretty, small bays southwest of Patpong. There is good diving and snorkelling here, and the beach is ideal for picnickers. The two bays can also be reached on foot, by motorcycle, or jeep by way of several very steep paths. Emerald Bay can also be reached by walking through the Coral Beach Hotel grounds.

PATONG BEACH
(15 km). This delightful beach with its fine, white sand has been fully developed for tourism. Western package deal tourists as well as individual travellers inhabit the scores of hotel and bungalow resorts (over 50!) along the 3 km beach. Dozens of bars, discos, massage parlours, nightclubs, shops, and restaurants stand crowded on the central sand road as well as on part of Bangla Road. Prices here are not much higher than at the resorts further south.

HOTELS and BUNGALOWS
You will find many different types of places offering accommodation here, from fully ac, first class hotels to simple bamboo huts. There is nothing for low budget travellers, though. Most of the resorts are very close to each other; it shouldn't take you all that long to check them out and make your choice. Prices for a room range from 150-3600 Baht, the average seems to lie somewhere between

300 and 600 Baht (cheaper still if you bargain!). The rates are reduced to half of this during the rainy period (May-October).

*PATONG BEACH BUNGALOWS***-*****, simple bungalows; *PATONG BAY GARDEN RESORT*****, terraced houses. The following places offer rooms with electricity and a shower for under 300 Baht: *SALA THAI***, *ALOHA***, and *ROYAL PALM**-**** at the southern end; *BANGLA*** and *HAPPY HEART **** on the central section of beach. *SUNSHINE GARDEN****, at the northern end of the beach. The *CLUB ANDAMAN***** resort with a hotel and bungalows at the northern end of the beach is particularly appealing. *BAAN SUKHOTHAI ***** offers an unusually extensive service; bungalows with fully furnished, modern kitchens (even washing machines!).

GENERAL INFORMATION

TOURIST POLICE - turn left at the southern end of the beach, behind Holiday Resort. You will find a local police station on the central sand road. Open 8:30-12:00 and 13:00-16:30 h, from 9:00-12:00 on holidays.

POST OFFICE - right in the centre of town diagonally across from the police station. Open daily 8.30-12.00 and 13.00-18.30 h.

CAR RENTALS - PHUKET RENT A CAR is on the sand road, tel 321292, SEAGULL COTTAGE TOUR is on the road leading to the beach, tel 321238. The petrol sold at the station by the beach is at least 10 % more expensive than it is elsewhere.

KAMALA BEACH

(26 km). A partially unpaved road leading north from Patong will take you past a restaurant (good view from here), past NACHA BEACH, up a very steep mountain, and through a beautiful landscape all the way to KAMALA BAY. Pick-ups rarely drive along this 5 km coastal road (10 Baht). You will reach Kamala more easily from Surin; a narrow road leads all the way to long and bare Kamala Beach - many pretty, small coves en route. Only very few rooms of the KRATHOMTHIP** in the fishing village on the southern end of the bay offer lav/fan. Fish will be prepared according to your specific requests at the simple restaurant.

SURIN BEACH

(24 km). The large parking lot and the many food and souvenir stands are a dead giveaway - this beach is mainly patronized by Thais. The village cattle can sometimes be seen grazing on the lawn of the golf course.

HOTELS

*NANGKUAN BUNGALOWS*** and its *RESTAURANT* are right next to it. Continue north and you will reach a private bay with what could be considered Phuket's most beautiful bungalow resort, *PANSEA*****, all bungalows on a slope with a view of the sea, comfortably furnished, ac. *BANG TAO HUTS***** are behind Pansea, on a cliff.

BANG THAO BAY

(24 km). A secluded section of beach north of Surin. The film "Killing Fields" was made here. Thai families used to enjoy coming here for picnics. Now most of the beach's area is occupied by the large *DUSIT LAGUNA RESORT HOTEL*****, bounded by lagoons on both sides, nice beach out front.

NAI YANG BEACH

(30 km). Located in the northwest of Phuket, this pretty beach is most suitable for bathing. The airport is nearby (but it is still reasonably quiet). Many shady kasuarina-trees directly on the beach. This bay has been declared a National Park, because giant turtles come here in order to lay their eggs in the sand. The friendly employees are able to tell you where hiking is best on this part of the island.

BUNGALOWS and HOTELS

*PARK BUNGALOWS****, pretty huts scattered among kasuarina-trees, 2 rooms, 4 beds, and a bathroom, 4 people can share a hut for 250 Baht. Tents* are also available. The restaurant closes at 20:00 h on the dot.

*PEARL VILLAGE*****, a new beach resort of slightly raised standards, hidden behind the kasuarina-trees, right next to the National Park. Many activities, including a mini golf course and a diving school.

EXCURSIONS ON THE ISLAND

KHAO RANG

Charter a pick-up or walk to KHAO RANG hill from Phuket town. You will have a wonderful view of the town and the entire island from the TUNG-KA CAFE and the small park nearby.

TIN MINES

You will find quite a few mines in the east, near Phang Nga Bay, as well as along the road leading to the airport, further north. Large areas are excavated in the open-cast mines. Dredgers are now also being used in the bays, seeing as the method of dredging saves quite a bit of money. The refinery was built 8 km south of Phuket Town, directly at the coast, on the road leading to Laem Phan Wa.

WAT CHALONG

This famous temple is 8 km southwest of Phuket Town. There are several venerated statues of monks who were considered particularly worthy under the reign of Rama V here (you may hear a different story concerning the significance of the statues - there are many versions).

KHAO PHRA TAEO WILDLIFE PARK

Go down H402 to Thalang, then turn off to the east and follow the signposts directing you to the TON SAI WATERFALL (turn right at the fork in the road). The administrative offices and BUNGALOWS**** (room for up to 20 visitors) are in the middle of one of Phuket's few remaining patches of unspoilt jungle. Several monkeys and birds live in this wildlife preserve. There are even said to be wild bears. Some of the animals live in large, fenced-in areas (macaques, birds, tortoises and others). There is also a small restaurant down by a lake and a very worthwhile exhibition dealing with the important ecological system 'rainforest'. You will be able to hike along several paths. One of the simple tours leads past the waterfall, which is only pretty during the rainy season.

KO SIRAY (ALSO CALLED SIRE)

An island off the east coast, connected to Phuket by a bridge. A large reclining Buddha was erected on the highest point of the island. The touristy village in the south of the island is home to a few sea gypsies, a group of people who must either have descended from the Andaman/Nikobar people or have originated in Melanesia. They are considered excellent navigators, are animists, and have quite a few customs and traditions. Apart from their very dark skin and slightly reddish hair, they can hardly be told apart from Thais.

On the east coast you find restaurants and picnic grounds along a shallow, sandy beach. *MADAM PUYE*, well known for her fantastic food from Nai Harn Beach, has opened her new restaurant right on the beach. She rents *BUNGALOWS*** with private shower and toilet, too. From here you can rent boats to *KO KHAI NAI*, an island with white beaches and coral reefs. You can reach the island by a 20 minutes boat ride.

EXCURSIONS BY BOAT

You will be able to set out on excursions to the offshore islands and coral reefs from all of Phuket's beaches. It is worth organizing these outings yourself. Try to get a couple of people organized, so that the boat will be at least half full. Expect to have to pay approx. 600 Baht for an outboard motorboat for the day. Outings to Ko Bon cost 150 Baht per boat from Chalong Beach, 300 Baht to Coral Islands. The latter outing is offered for less from Rawai.

CORAL ISLAND

KO HAE is approx. 6 km off the coast of Rawai, off Phuket's southern tip. Many snorkelling expeditions come here to see the beautiful reefs, and the island has been nicknamed CORAL ISLAND as a result. There are huts** for all those who want just beach, palms, and ocean. The food here is expensive, however.

KO LONE

There is a hotel, the LONE ISLAND RESORT***-****, on this island, which is 3 km off Chalong Beach. You will be brought over free of charge if you contact the town office in advance, 243/7 Ranong Road, Phuket Town, tel 211526.

KO MAI THON

Day outings are also organized to this island, 16 km off Chalong Beach. Many nice beaches and reefs make this a place well worth going to. The fishing is said to be pretty good here, too.

HAT YAI

Southern Thailand's centre of commerce and traffic (130 000 inhabitants), almost 1300 km south of Bangkok, is a modern town sadly lacking in character. Malaysians come here to buy the wares that are cheaper in Thailand than in their own country, and of course to indulge in night-time activities that are forbidden in puritanical, Muslim Malaysia. In contrast to Pattaya and Bangkok, most of Hat Yai's nightlife goes on in the hotels. The city has more to offer than just prostitution, however - there are numerous discos, some of them with live music and laser shows.

The viharn of *WAT HAT YAI NAI* contains a Buddha statue measuring 35 m in length and 15 m in height. The statue, 'Phra Ohut Mahathat Mongkol' is highly venerated by the population of the town as well as the Malaysian Chinese. The votive gifts brought to the statue are exhibited atits foot. The temple is 4 km southwest of town, towards the airport in Ban Hat Yai Nan.

HOTELS

If Hat Yai's entertainment and shops are not your cup of tea and you feel that you would rather be staying in a place with a typically Thai atmosphere, get on a bus and go to Songkhla.

For those who can handle it there are many hotels. The *LAEMTHONG HOTEL***, Thamnoon Vithi Road, tel 244959, ac rooms***, is clean and well worth its price. Central location, 400 metres from the railway station.

*KING'S***, tel 243966, ac-rooms*** and the *MANDARIN***, tel 243438, are both on the same road, Niphat-U-Thid 1 Road. The *HOK CHIN HIN**, tel 243258, is a cheap Chinese hotel.

There are further hotels on the parallel street, Niphat-U-Thid 2 Road, e.g. the *CATHAY***, tel 243815, the *METRO***, tel 244422, and the *PACIFIC***, tel 245202 - reckon on a 100-Baht extra charge for ac rooms in all hotels.

The cheapest hotels on Niphat-U-Thid 3 Road are the *KIM HAU***, tel 243532, the *SEANG FAH****, tel 243833, and the *YOUNG DEE****, tel 244499.

FOOD

You should have no problem with food in Hat Yai - there are many small restaurants and foodstalls. There is also a small night market near the Savoy Hotel in the evenings.

Cakes and pastries can be bought at the *ROYAL BAKERY*, 41 Thamnoon Vithi Road and 200/11 Niphat-U-Thid 1 Road. You'll find *THE BEST CAFE* (live music) right next door.

There's a large Muslim restaurant near King's Hotel, the *MUSLIM-O-CHA*. Good seafood restaurants can be found all over town. Food will frequently be served to you outside.

GENERAL INFORMATION

information concerning traffic connections and hotels in Hat Yai and Songkhla. Contact the Tourist Police in an emergency, same office, same number.

BANKS - THAI FARMERS BANK, 188 Petchkasem Road, BANGKOK BANK, 37 Niphat-U-Thid 2 Road. There are more banks in Road 1, some of them open until 19:00 or even 20:00 h. If you arrive late at night or at the weekend you'll have to go to the money changers or to one of the big hotels, e.g. King's Hotel. The rates you will receive at the money changers are none too good, however - they usually exchange M$, only sometimes will they exchange US$.

POST - The General Post Office is near the large bridge. You can make international phone calls at any time of the day or night from the Telephone Centre, Phang-nga Road.

TRANSPORT - tuk-tuks within the city limits cost 4-5 Baht. We would suggest taking a songthaew to the airport (12 km, 30 Baht - the cheapest deal in town). Thai Airways also offers a good transportation service. Taxis are expensive - bargain! Hotels and travel agencies will frequently add the driver's commission to their price if you let yourself be chauffeured about in a bicycle ricksha .

SHOPPING - An extensive variety of ware is offered in Hat Yai, a veritable shopping paradise, especially for Malaysians. Try the areas around Niphat-U-Thid 3 Road and the parallel Roads 1 and 2. Clothing, cassette tapes, leather ware, and arts & crafts are cheap. Fruits and nuts are particularly good - try the cashew nuts. You will find a large market at the Songkhla bus stop.

BULLFIGHTS - are held in Hat Yai's new arena near the Nora Hotel on the first of every month, also at the Hat Yai Nan Arena near the airport, where two bulls are made to fight against each other on the second weekend of every month. Admission: 30 Baht.

THAI BOXING - competitions are held every Saturday from 14:00-17:00 hours in the Television Stadium, admission 5 Baht.

LEAVING HAT YAI

BY PLANE

In order to get to the airport, 12 km west of town, take the Thai Airways airport bus or a songthaew for 30 Baht. If you're headed towards Malaysia or Singapore, you'll have to pay 150 Baht airport tax, otherwise it's 20 Baht. Prices for daily flights: BANGKOK 1760 Baht, night flight 1340 Baht; PHUKET 510 Baht (595 Baht with a jet); CHIANG MAI via Bangkok 2450 Baht; KUALA LUMPUR 1500 Baht (return fare), PENANG 730 Baht, if you return within 14 days 1110 Baht return, SINGAPORE 3500 Baht, if you return within 14 days 3760 Baht return.

Thai Airways office: 166/4 Niphat-U-Thid Road 2, tel 245851-2. You'll find the MAS office in the Nora Hotel, Thamnoon Vithi Road, tel 243729, 245443.

BY BUS

All non-ac buses leave from the Muncipal Market. The new bus station for all overland buses is out of town.

Buses to SONGKHLA cost 11 Baht and leave every 15 minutes between 6:00 and 19:00 h, 45 minute ride; PADANG BESAR 13 Baht, 1 hour; PATTANI 30 Baht, 2 1/2 hrs.; NARATHIWAT 50 Baht, 3 hrs., SURAT THANI 67 Baht, 5 hrs., departures at 5:30, 8:30 and 11:30 h; PHATTALUNG 22 Baht, 2 hrs.; TRANG 35 Baht, 3 hrs.; SATUN 22 Baht, 2 hrs.; KRABI 60 Baht, 5 hrs.; PHUKET 94 Baht, 8 hrs.; and NAKHON SI THAMMARAT 110 Baht.

Ac buses to SURAT THANI (160 Baht) leave at 14:00 and 17:00 h. There is a daily ac bus to PHUKET (169 Baht, approx. 6 hrs.) at 9:30 h. Direct buses to KO SAMUI including ferry for 150 Baht.

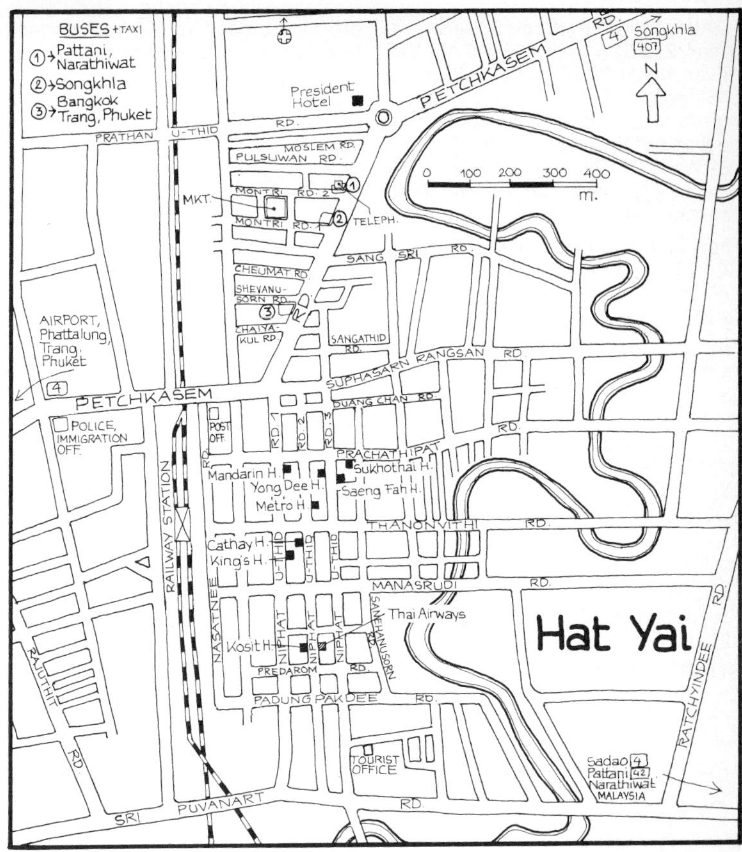

Should you seriously be planning to take a bus all the way to BANGKOK from here, there are several companies offering ac rides (300-339 Baht, approx. 15 hrs., departures between 13:30 and 18:00 h). Further buses to Malaysia: There is a daily bus to BUTTERWORTH (Penang) at 12:00 and 14:30 h for 200 Baht. There are also buses to KL for 380 Baht (12 hrs.) and SINGAPORE for 450 Baht (19 hrs.).

BY TRAIN

We would suggest buying the tickets for the rest of your journey as soon as you arrive in town. The railway station is in the centre of town.

An 'International Express' leaves daily from Hat Yai to Malaysia. The ride to Butterworth takes 4 hrs. including a one hour stop in Padang Besar. You will arrive at 12:10 h Malaysian time (= Thai time + 1 hour). You can catch the 14:45 express to

KUALA LUMPUR from Butterworth, arrival 21:15. A train to SINGAPORE leaves KL at 22:00 h. You will arrive in Singapore at 6:40 h on the following morning. 2nd class prices (not including possible extra charge): BUTTERWORTH (Penang) 118 Baht, from here to KUALA LUMPUR 240 Baht, from here to SINGAPORE 240 Baht.

There are also two trains to SUNGEI GOLOK at the eastern border via YALA, departures at 4:30 and 6:03 h, 42 Baht, 4 hrs.

Trains to the north leave at 14:23, 15:02, 16:55, 17:15 h and many other times. They drive via SURAT THANI (114 / 55 Baht 2nd / 3rd class) and HUA HIN (244 / 116 Baht), and reach BANGKOK (313 / 149 Baht) at 6:35, 7:05, 8:35, and 10:00 h.

Some prices for the 2nd / 3rd class: PADANG BESAR 30 / 11 Baht, SUNGEI GOLOK 87 / 42 Baht, PHATTALUNG 37 / 18 Baht, PRACHUAP KHIRI KHAN 217 / 103 Baht, YALA 48 / 23 Baht.

SHARE TAXIS

Share taxis leave town daily to various places in southern Thailand as well as Malaysia between 7:00 and 17:00 h. They will not leave until they are fully loaded with 6 passengers, however. Prices per person:

SONGKHLA 12 Baht, 30 minutes, 30 km; SATUN 35 Baht, 1 1/2 hrs., 96 km; PADANG BESAR 25 Baht, 1 hour, 67 km, point of departure: near the market and the President Hotel, Prathan-U-Thid Road. Taxis to Songkhla also leave from the railway station and Wat Cheu Chang (see below).

PHATTALUNG 35 Baht, 1 1/2 hrs., 96 km; NAKHON SI THAMMARAT 70 Baht, 2 1/2 hrs., 189 km; SUNGAI GOLOK 120 Baht, 3 hrs., 285 km, point of departure: near the Wat Cheu Chang, Suphasarnrangsan Road.

PHUKET 220 Baht, 6 hrs., 480 km; KRABI 120 Baht, 5 hrs., 311 km, point of departure: Sang Chan Road near the Hat Yai Inter Hotel.

SURAT THANI 150 Baht, 4 hrs., 330 km, point of departure: Niphat-U-Thid 2 Road, in front of the Cathay House.

PATTANI 50 Baht, 1 1/2 hrs., 132 km, point of departure: opposite the Cathay Hotel, Niphat-U-Thid 2 Road.

BETONG 110 Baht, 4 hrs., 276 km, point of departure: Chaiyakul Road. PENANG 200 Baht, 5 hrs., 220 km, point of departure: various hotels.

SONGKHLA

Mainly Thai holiday-makers come to visit this provincial capital on the Gulf of Thailand. The coastal town has 85 000 inhabitants. Boats and ships can reach the Thale Sap inland lake, which is separated from the sea by an 80 km strip of land, by way of a narrow canal north of town. Putting a harbour here was of course the natural thing to do, and the once important harbour city still has much of its former atmosphere. The harbour is not suitable for today's huge ships, though; the canal is too shallow for them. In consequence, only small fishing boats and Thai Navy ships drop anchor here these days. Songkhla has lost much of its business importance ever since Hat Yai blossomed to its present state. All the same, Songkhla has much more to offer to tourists.

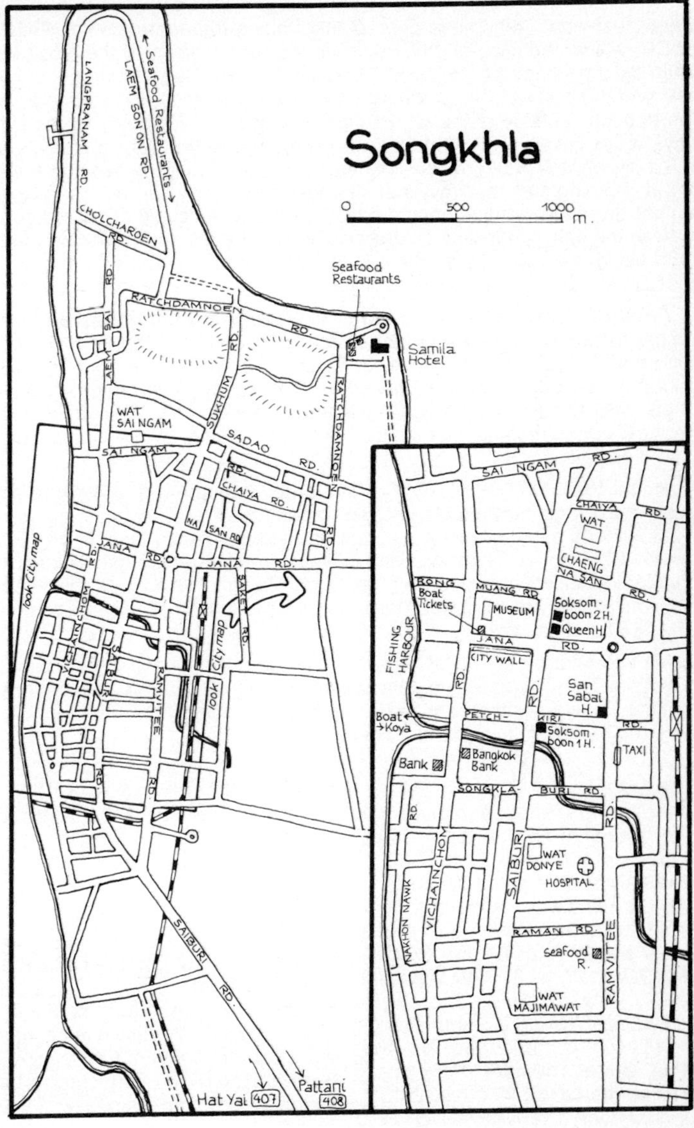
Songkhla
0 500 1000 m.
Seafood Restaurants
Samila Hotel
LANGPRANAM RD.
LAEM SON ON RD.
Seafood Restaurants
CHOLCHAROEN RD.
RATCHDAMNOEN RD.
LAEM SAI RD.
SUKHUM RD.
WAT SAI NGAM
SADAO RD.
SAI NGAM
CHAIYA RD.
NA SAN RD.
JANA RD.
SAKET RD.
look City map
VICHAINCHOM
SAIBURI
RAMVITEE RD.
SAIBURI RD.
Hat Yai 407
Pattani 408
SAI NGAM RD.
CHAIYA RD.
WAT CHAENG
NA SAN RD.
BONG MUANG RD.
Boat Tickets
MUSEUM
Soksomboon 2 H.
Queen H.
FISHING HARBOUR
JANA RD.
CITY WALL
San Sabai H.
PETCH-KIRI RD.
Boat ← Koya
Soksomboon 1 H.
TAXI
Bank
Bangkok Bank
SONGKLA-BURI RD.
WAT DONYE
HOSPITAL
NAKHON NAWK
RAMAN RD.
Seafood R.
WAT MAJIMAWAT
RAMVITEE

Several beef-wood trees have been planted along the approx. 5 km *SAMILA BEACH*, which stretches all the way from the road leading to the lake to the Muslim fishing village of *KAO SENG*, south of town. Do not come expecting some kind of Hawaiian athmosphere - the city is too close and the water isn't clean enough. Outside of the rainy period (October - December) the beach is always well-visited. In the northeast of town, next to the Samila Hotel, you'll see the *MERMAID STATUE*, the trademark of the city. Many seafood restaurants, a camping site, the Navy's anchorage, and a ferry can be found on the long, narrow, sandy tongue of land beyond. Up until a couple of years ago the ferry was the only connection to Road 4038, which runs north over the tongue of land along the coast. Today there is also a huge bridge further inland, which crosses over the lake via the island of Ya.

The *FISHING HARBOUR* is in town, at the western bank. Baskets full of shrimps, fish, and other sea creatures are unloaded onto the narrow planks behind the old houses in the evening. Boats leave for *KO YA* from here. The island can also be reached by way of a newly constructed bridge, however. You can visit two old temples on the island and watch the 'Pha Ko Yo' - the chequered cotton material that is also sold at the stands by the bridge - being woven in the village.

The central *WAT MATCHIMAWAT* (Wat Klang), Saiburi Road, is 400 years old and the most important temple in town. It has many nice sculptures and murals, as well as beautiful stone cuttings and stucco decorations, in part influenced by Chinese art. There is a little museum in the northern temple complex. Archeological discoveries made in southern Thailand as well as the population's votive gifts are exhibited here. It is closed on Mon and Tues, as are nearly all Thai museums.

You will find another *MUSEUM* between Jana and Roimuang Road, near the bus station. The Chinese-style palace was built as a private residence for the influential Phraya Sunthranuraksa family in 1878. Open from 9:00-12:00 and 13:00-16:00 h except for Mon and Tues.

HOTELS

For those with enough money we would recommend the bungalows and rooms of the *SAMILA HOTEL*****, tel 311310, directly at the beach. The rooms are not always in the best condition, however. There are some cheaper hotels in town - the *SOOKSOMBOON 1****, tel 311049, Petchkiri Road, new hotel. The old *SOOKSOMBOON 2***, Saiburi Road, tel 311149, is managed by the brother of the number 1's owner. You'll find the *QUEEN****, tel 311138, right next door. The *NARAI HOTEL**, 1212 Chai Khao Road, tel 311078, is cheap. The *SAN SABAI***, 1 Petchkiri Road corner of Ramviti Road, tel 311106, has new rooms with bathrooms and fans.

FOOD

There are many good, albeit expensive, seafood restaurants at the beach. Truly excellent seafood is served at the ROY HIM, a large, open-air restaurant south of the hospital on Ramviti Road. You may choose from the displays out on the street.

GENERAL INFORMATION

POST - opposite the market on Vichianchom Road. International calls can be made from the nearby Telephone Office.

BANKS - you will find branches of the BANGKOK BANK, THAI FARMERS BANK, and the BANK OF AYUTTHAYA on Vichianchom Road near the market.

TRANSPORTATION IN SONGKHLA - songthaew within the city limits cost 3 Baht per person.

BOAT TRIPS ON THE LAKE - are organized daily at 9:00 and 14:00 h for 50 Baht per person. A minimum of six passengers have to get together, otherwise the trip is off. Tickets can be bought on Jana Road, west of the museum. The boats leave from the end of the Jana Road extension.

HOW TO GET THERE

Buses and taxis from NAKHON SI THAMMARAT and SURAT THANI come here via the tongue of land and the new bridge. The fastest way of getting here is via Hat Yai, as the latter is better developed traffic-wise. A regular bus commutes between the two towns for 11 Baht. Buses depart from Rong Muang Road in Songkhla. If you're coming from Narathiwat, first take a bus to Pattani (24 Baht), then one to Nathawi (18 Baht), and finally one to Songkhla (13 Baht). Taxis to HAT YAI (12 Baht) and Pattani leave from the Ramviti Road near the former bus station and from the corner of-Jana Road and Saiburi Road. Taxis and buses bound for Nakhon Si Thammarat leave from the southern end of Ramviti Road.

FROM THAILAND TO MALAYSIA

SATUN

Satun, the capital of the southernmost province on Thailand's west coast, is mainly inhabited by Muslims and Chinese. This small, rather out of the way port has little to offer in way of attractions. Some travellers come here in order to catch a boat to KUALA PERLIS in Malaysia. From there, the Langkawi islands can be reached more easily.

HOTELS

*SALINDA HOTEL*** (ac***), 11 Wiset Mayura Road, tel 711115; information and rather shabby rooms available. *SATULTANEE*** (ac***) (also known as SATUN THANI), 90 Satun Thani Road, tel 711010, cheaper, in the centre of town. *RIAN THONG HOTEL** (also RAIN TONG), 124 Samunta Pradit Road, tel 711036, a Chinese hotel with large, clean rooms, opposite the landing-place. *WANGMAI HOTEL***-*****, 43 Satun Thani Road, tel 711607, modern, ac hotel at the edge of town, mainly accommodates business people and Malaysian tourists.

GENERAL INFORMATION

IMMIGRATION OFFICE - 500 metres from the landing-place, opposite the large mosque. Don't forget to have an entry stamp put into your passport - you will have great difficulties when leaving the country if you do.

LEAVING SATUN

Buses leave for TRANG every hour between 5:30 and 11:30 h (30 Baht). From there you can catch buses to KRABI or PHUKET.

A bus to HAT YAI will cost you 20 Baht, a share taxi 35 Baht - these leave from the Salinda Hotel, the ones driving to La-Ngu leave from the Satultanee Hotel. A share taxi to the border check-point WANGPRACHAN (40 km) will cost you 20 Baht. 7 long-tail boats leave for KUALA PERLIS in MALAYSIA between 6:30 and 14:00 h (30 Baht or 3 M$). Once there, you will find an Immigration Office directly at the landing-place for the Langkawi ferry. Attention: Banks in Kuala Perlis are closed on Thursday afternoon and Friday.

WANGPRACHAN

The westernmost land border check-point on the Thai-Malaysian border is 40 km northeast of Satun, in the Thale Ban National Park. A share taxi from Satun will cost you approx. 20 Baht. The closest Malaysian town, Kangar, can only be reached by taxi (20 M$).

Crossing the border between 11:00 and 13:00 h is unfortunately impossible, due to the lunch breaks of the officials in Thailand and Malaysia, which (predictably) are at 11:00 and 12:00 h respectively.

The Thai and Malay custom offices are right next to each other, so that you will be able to carry out the Double-Entry-Visa procedure (out-in-out-in) in approx. 1/2 an hour. With a little luck your share taxi might even still be around upon re-entering Thailand.

PADANG BESAR

Take a bus to PADANG BESAR from Hat Yai for 15 Baht. You will be let out right at the border. Ask for an exit-stamp to be put into your passport, then walk approx. 10 minutes until you reach the Malaysian check point. As a pedestrian you will be checked quite thoroughly, but as long as you are able to produce a reasonably large sum of money (or cheques etc...), you will be given the stamp and permission to enter. Exchange currency at the railway station or in the coffee-shop near the bus station (bad rates!). Buses bound for Butterworth leave from here, the last one at 20:00 h (5.70 M$). The border is closed at 17:30 h Thai time, which is 18:30 h Malaysian time.

SA DAO

This, the most frequently used border check-point, is used by most taxis and Penang-bound buses from Hat Yai and is just a few kilometres south of town. One usually drives through here after a short sojourn at the border.

BETONG

This frontier town is inhabited by 40,000 people and lies at an altitude of 580 metres. It is situated on a narrow strip of land reaching well into the national territory of Malaysia. The town is usually shrouded in fog. A bus ride from Yala (down a lovely 140 km road and through a beautiful limestone formation landscape) will cost you 31 Baht and take 4 1/2 hrs. The Pattani river has been dammed east of the road, approx. 50 km towards Betong, and has thus created the 50 km^2 BANGLANG LAKE. You will be able to visit a SAKAI settlement after having travelled towards Betong for 80 km. The Sakai are the Negroid, first inhabitants of the Malaysian peninsula, and their settlement is just 4 km off the road. There are many palm-oil, coffee, and rubber plantations in the wide valleys of the area. You will be stopped and thoroughly checked at several check points along the way. You will reach the southernmost tip of Thailand and the border to the Malaysian state of Perak shortly beyond Bentong.

SUNGAI GOLOK

There is a further border check-point on the east coast, especially interesting for those who plan to continue straight on to the east coast of Malaysia. Sungai Golok is already strongly influenced by the Malaysian way of life. Generally, it is a rather uninteresting town. The post office is next to the Plaza Hotel.

HOTELS

The rooms of the *ASIA HOTEL***, 44 Charoenket Road, tel 611101, some rooms ac***, are good and well worth the price.

The same can be said of all of the following: *MERRY***, tel 611214, and *THANI***, tel 611046, both on Chuenmaraka Road, *MERLIN****, tel 611003, and the *SAVOY***, tel 611093, both on Charoenket Road.

Cheap and simple rooms are available at the *ERAWAN GUEST HOUSE**, 21 Chuenmaraka Road.

There are many more hotels in town, some of them in the more expensive categories, with discos and massage parlours. The town's largest hotel, the *GRAND HOTEL*****, 104 Arifmarka Road, tel 611219, is the only hotel in town that has a pool.

HOW TO GET THERE

A normal train heads for Sungai Golok from Hat Yai at 4:30 h, arrival 8:15 h. The express leaves Hat Yai at 6:03 h, arrival at the border 9:35, 2nd class 87, 3rd class 42 Baht.

FROM SUNGAI GOLOK TO MALAYSIA

Either cross the border on foot, or catch a motorcycle for 5, a ricksha for 10 Baht. Once in Malaysia, take bus 29 to KOTA BHARU (2 M$, taxi 3.30 M$). The border is closed at 17:30 h Thai time (18:30 h Malaysian time).

TAK BAI

You will find this border check point 38 km further east, directly at the coast. A bus from Narathiwat will cost you 10 Baht. The ferry to Kampong Pengkupor (Malaysia) costs 5 Baht or 50 Malaysian cents. From here a bus to KOTA BHARU will cost you 1.40 M$, a taxi 2.30 M$.

INDEX

GENERAL INFORMATION 7

BRUNEI 32

BURMA 39

INDONESIA 67

MALAYSIA 347

MAPS